Invitation to
PSYCHOLOGY

THIRD EDITION

Invitation to
PSYCHOLOGY

THIRD EDITION

John P. Houston
University of California, Los Angeles

Constance Hammen
University of California, Los Angeles

Amado Padilla
Stanford University

Helen Bee

HBJ

Harcourt Brace Jovanovich, Publishers
San Diego   New York   Chicago   Austin   Washington, D.C.
London   Sydney   Tokyo   Toronto

ISBN: 0-15-546913-4
Library of Congress Catalog Card Number: 88-81035
Printed in the United States of America

Preface

The writing team for this, the Third Edition of *Invitation to Psychology*, has been greatly strengthened by the addition of Constance Hammen and Amado Padilla. Dr. Hammen brings breadth and depth to the areas of personality, assessment, and abnormal and clinical psychology, while Dr. Padilla solidifies the areas of cognitive, developmental, and social psychology. While our writing team has changed, our basic approach to the writing of a good text has not. As was true in the first two editions, this edition contains two types of chapters. And because this organizational structure is the key to the successful use of this text, we would like to take a moment to describe the two kinds of chapters and their functions.

The first type of chapter covers the basic data and research findings within each of the traditional areas of psychology. These "basic" chapters provide up-to-date and complete coverage of important developments in each area. The second type of chapter is more innovative. These "exploring" chapters examine some of the practical applications and implications of the findings discussed in the basic chapters. We describe how basic psychological data are being used to bring about improvements in everyday life, and we discuss continuing, often controversial explorations into some frontier areas of psychology. In other words, information about explorations and applications that is often scattered throughout the pages of other texts is brought together into systematic chapters in this text.

The exploring chapters do not follow every basic chapter, of course. They are included only when it seems reasonable and interesting to include them. The first exploring chapter follows an introductory, a physiological, and a perception chapter, and the second does not appear until after the basics of learning, memory, and cognition have been discussed. In short, exploring chapters have not been forced into the table of contents. They appear only when they can illuminate and illustrate some present-day applications of psychological theory and discovery.

Though we discuss many unique and challenging new topics in the revised and updated exploring chapters, we have not done this at the expense of our basic chapters. The basic chapters are written to hold a reader's interest through a balance of engaging writing, solid, timely examples, and clearly presented, essential information. The basic chapters, too, have been thoroughly revised to reflect the current state of the art in the various areas of psychology.

We believe that this dual-chapter approach does more than resolve the dilemma of differing expectations. It also protects the flow of the main text, allows maximum flexibility in topic coverage, and avoids choppiness. Instructors may choose what they want to cover in the way of applied information in that exploratory chapters may be selectively emphasized or even omitted. Students will never be confused about what is and what is not essential, established information.

In short, like the newest generation of computers, *Invitation to Psychology* is "user friendly." It is also as up to date as we can make it. We have reviewed every line of manuscript for this new edition to make sure that it will present our science as it stands today. Examples abound throughout the book, but the following samples will illustrate the variety and depth of the changes in this new edition, either in the body of the text or in carefully selected boxed inserts:

- The introductory chapter now includes coverage of recent medical advances involving Parkinson's disease, information about the effects of pollution on human behavior, and a new section on ethics.

- Chapter 2, on the physiological basis of behavior, contains new material on shock treatment, brain scanning techniques, recent discoveries concerning the link between violent behavior and head injuries, the relationship between behavior and the endocrine system, changes in the brain as we age, genes and personality, and chromosomal abnormalities and retardation in recent discoveries involving Down syndrome.

- Chapter 3, on sensation and perception, provides new material on psychophysics, on the extremes of boredom as examined in the investigation of sensory isolation or sensory deprivation experiments (REST), and on the effects of organizational tendencies in pattern recognition.

- Chapter 4, the first exploring chapter, contains a new section on brain research, endorphins, and the relationship between autism and endorphins. Another discussion of the use of applied physiological psychology examines such issues as brain-tissue transplants and the role of the autonomic nervous system in cases of "voodoo death." Revised information is included on sleep and dreams, how drugs alter and distort the perceptual processes (with up-to-date information on new "designer drugs"), hypnotism, and the latest research findings on ESP.

- The chapter on learning (Chapter 5) provides new information on punishment and learning and on ethology in the context of innate-versus-learned behaviors. Chapter 6 discusses mental rotation as a visual encoding device, semantic-network models, and spreading-activation models and lexical memory. Chapter 7 includes new material on epigraphy, the use of symbols, and mental manipulation, and it covers the ways in which language increases in linguistic complexity.

- The second exploring chapter (Chapter 8) provides up-to-date coverage of the applications of classical conditioning in the use of alcohol aversion therapy to treat our most serious drug problem, classical conditioning and the immune system, and cancer and conditioning.

- Chapter 9, on motivation, and Chapter 10, on emotion, provide new coverage of the complex relationship between these two topics. In Chapter 9, new material has been added on rates of infusion, biological motives involving innate and learned tastes, eating disorders, and hormones and neurons. In Chapter 10, the discussion of theories of emotion now covers new material on facial feedback and opponent-process theory.

- The exploring chapter for motives and emotions, Chapter 11, contains extensive revisions of sections on aggression, sex, stress, learned helplessness, sexual diseases (including AIDS), and contraception.

- Chapter 12, on development, includes new information on external influences during gestation and on separation anxiety, updated information on the neonatal period and the neonatal sensory system, and updates on motor development and social and emotional development during the first two years of life. This chapter now also covers early friendships and includes expanded treatment of moral development and identity formation.

- Chapter 13 once again explores five developmental issues, four of which have been extensively reworked and one of which—day care— is entirely new. The sections on child abuse, divorce, teenage parenthood, and sex differences and stereotypes contain expanded information. The new day-care section includes research findings on day care, caregivers, curriculum, and how to find a quality day-care program.

- Chapter 14, which deals with personality, contains expanded discussions of the unconscious and the dynamics of personality, an extensive revision of the section on personality types (especially the trait theory of personality), a reworked discussion of cognitive social-learning approaches to personality, and a revised discussion of recent developments in theories about the self and problems with phenomenological approaches.

- Chapter 15, on assessing personality and behavior, contains revised information on the Wechsler Intelligence Scale and new material on neuropsychological testing.

- Chapter 16, which explores the uses and misuses of testing, contains new material on polygraph testing, an expanded discussion of bias, and new information on test utility, baserates, the Barnum effect, fairness, computerized testing, and the fundamental attribution error, as well as a revision of the section on race differences and IQ testing.

- Chapter 17, on abnormal psychology, includes new case studies for many of the major mental disorders. The chapter has been expanded by the addition of much new information on schizophrenia, affective disorders, and suicide, and it includes a reordered discussion of the causes of abnormality and the prevalence rates of mental disorders. The discussion on anxiety disorders has been reformulated and the sections on substance abuse have been revised. Also new in this chapter is the coverage of psychosexual disorders, psychological disorders among children, and eating disorders.

- Chapter 18, which deals with the treatment of psychological problems, contains an expanded discussion of modeling procedures, new sections on seeking professional help, psychotherapist training, community mental health programs, and a section on psychotherapy in the media.

- Chapter 19, the first of two chapters dealing with social psychology, has been expanded to include new material on expectancies, interpersonal interaction, dispositional attribution, attractiveness, social-impact theory, and selective exposure.

- The last exploring chapter, Chapter 20, contains new and expanded coverage on the kinds of love, racial prejudice, the role of television in our lives, and helping behaviors. Also new is an entire section on health psychology, with discussions of attitudes toward health practices, nutrition, exercise, and social support and health.

As you can see, the structure of *Invitation to Psychology* is familiar, but much of the coverage is new, in order to reflect the fresh and ever-changing nature of the subject matter.

This edition of *Invitation to Psychology* also provides a variety of pedagogical aids, including new boxed inserts, full-color photo essays on biology, perception, development, and abnormal psychology, extensive chapter summaries, more than 350 photos and illustrations, a comprehensive glossary, and appendices that deal with statistics and with psychology as a profession. And, because we have produced this edition in paperback form, we are able to deliver extensive, quality coverage of the material into student hands at a reasonable cost. Finally, a complete ancillary package is also available. It includes an excellent study guide, a testbook, a computer-generated test bank, and an instructor's manual. A number of computer software packages are available for use with either IBM PC systems or with the Apple II series computer. Ten supporting films are available, as is a complete slide package and an alternative transparency package. In other words, the ancillary package is one of the most complete to be found in the field.

We hope that you will find our text engaging as well as instructive, and we welcome any comments and suggestions that will help us to make this an even more useful book in future years.

JOHN HOUSTON
CONSTANCE HAMMEN
AMADO PADILLA
HELEN BEE

ACKNOWLEDGMENTS

Bob Ahlering
Central Missouri State University

Paul M. Biner
Ball State University

Garvin Chastain
Boise State University

Lawrence H. Cohen
University of Delaware

Keith S. Dobson
University of British Columbia

Robert O. Engbretson
Southern Illinois University (Edwardsville)

Barry Gillen
Old Dominion University

Fred Grote
Western Washington University

Dorothy Mercer
Eastern Kentucky University

Mark Miller
Louisiana Tech University

Dennis Mitchell
University of Southern California

Al M. Prestrude
Virginia Polytechnic Institute and State University

Catherine A. Seiler
University of New Orleans

Robert M. Stern
Pennsylvania State University

Peter J. Urcuioli
Purdue University

Frank J. Vattano
Colorado State University

Contents

Invitation to

PSYCHOLOGY

THIRD EDITION

I   What Is Psychology?

Suppose an airline pilot and a psychologist arrive at a social gathering. When the pilot is introduced and his occupation is mentioned, no one is likely to be confused or apprehensive about what he does. Airline pilots fly airplanes. But when the psychologist is introduced and her profession is revealed, the reactions of the other guests may be quite varied. Psychologists hear things like, "Watch out, she'll analyze you," "Now I'll have to watch my step, because he will be able to figure out why I'm so crazy," "I'd better not make any Freudian slips," and so on. These kinds of comments may well embarrass the psychologist whose area of specialization may have very little to do with the direct assessment of people's problems.

People outside the field of psychology often believe that every psychologist is an expert at figuring out people's emotional difficulties and detecting hidden personality quirks, but this is usually not the case. In fact, most psychologists do *not* focus on these kinds of issues. Psychology is an extremely diverse field, involving many different types of people engaged in many different forms of study.

THE MANY FACES OF PSYCHOLOGY

It is the diversity of psychology that will be the underlying theme of this text, because we want to introduce you to the full range of activities that are included under the heading, "psychology." Like most sciences, psychology is divided into dozens of fairly distinct fields. Some psychologists devote their entire careers to the study of human memory. Another group studies emotional development. Others focus on the impact of groups on individuals. And, of course, still others work within a number of these different areas at the same time.

It is probably fair to say that most individuals no longer try to become general psychologists. They train to become specialized types of psychologists and as such are classified as social psychologists, clinical psychologists, developmental psychologists, and so on. One reason for these divisions within psychology involves the enormous amount of psychological knowledge that is now available. No one individual can master all of the information that has resulted from the vast amount of research undertaken in the last century. There is just too much to know. Hence, even though they may work in more than one area, psychologists specialize and become experts within a relatively narrow group of interests. Fifty or a hundred years ago, it was possible to be a general psychologist and comprehend most of psychology, but not any longer.

In short, if you are thinking of becoming a psychologist, it is good to realize from the beginning that you will need to concentrate on a certain type of psychology. As you read through this text, which covers most of the major fields of specialization, you should be able to discover which areas of psychology appeal to you the most. And if you enjoy a particular chapter in this text more than other chapters, you might do well to look for an advanced course in that area of specialization.

At the same time, you should not get the idea that psychology is a collection of totally unrelated areas. People can, and do, work in more than one area at a time, and many of the areas of specialization are closely intertwined. For example, a human memory psychologist will appreciate the fact that memory can be understood, or at least pursued, on a biological or chemical level. Similarly, a psychologist who specializes in abnormal psychology knows that information obtained in developmental psychology, personality, and motivation may affect her own area of concentration. As we shall see, the diverse areas of psychology all feed into one another.

In this chapter, we want to bring the overall field of psychology into focus for you as rapidly as possible, so in the first section we will briefly introduce the major divisions of psychology. Next we will consider a definition of psychology, and then we will explore some of the methods that psychologists use in gathering information. Finally, we will consider the different approaches or points of view that have developed within psychology.

AREAS OF SPECIALIZATION

One of the quickest ways to describe the field of psychology is to say a few words about each of the areas of specialization. In a sense, we can define psychology by indicating what sorts of things psychologists do. Then, as we consider each division of psychology in greater detail in later chapters, you will already have some idea of the overall structure of the field.

The areas of specialization discussed in this section generally parallel the topics covered in the text. In other words, this section serves to introduce the plan of the book as well as the major branches of psychology.

Physiological

Physiological psychologists are interested in the physical basis of behavior. They want to know, on a basic physiological level, how the machine we call our body works, and how that functioning relates to behavior. At present, the main areas of concern within this field are the functions of (1) the brain, (2) the nervous system, (3) the endocrine glands, and (4) the genetic mechanisms. Each of these four overlapping areas of concern is discussed in detail in Chapter 2. For now, let us look briefly at some examples of how researchers explore the workings of these systems.

The human brain is of major interest to physiological psychologists. At present, the challenge is to learn how brain activity is related to behavior. One classic line of research was conducted by James Olds (Olds, 1973; Olds & Milner, 1954). It is possible to implant tiny wire microelectrodes in the brain of a living animal without impairing the health of the animal. When a small electrical current is sent down the wire implanted in a specific part of the brain, that part can be stimulated. Working with rats, Olds found some amazing effects when electrodes were implanted in a brain structure called the hypothalamus. He structured his experiments so that each time a rat pressed a bar its brain was stimulated briefly. What happened under these conditions? The rats began to press the bar . . . , and press the bar . . . , and press the bar. They would not stop. Olds assumed a "pleasure center" was being stimulated. Some rats will press the bar 20 to 40 *thousand* times without stopping. They will drop from exhaustion before they quit. They will ignore food, water, and sex in order to press the bar. Since Olds's early work, investigators have become a little skeptical about the existence of specific, definable brain centers or structures associated with pleasure. The old concept of specific centers is presently seen as an oversimplification of a very complex situation. Researchers now tend to associate reward and pleasure with complex pathways and systems, rather than one specific part of the brain.

Brain stimulation researchers usually carry out their studies on nonhumans. But other approaches to physiological psychology involve humans. For example, the whole area of psychosurgery, which is based on the notion that surgical treatment of the brain can be used to lessen abnormal human behavior, is extremely controversial. Basically, the idea is to remove, destroy, or alter certain areas of the brain of a living human in an effort to eliminate the disordered behavior displayed by that individual (see the box titled "Parkinson's Patient with Brain Graft Termed 'Visibly Improved.' "

Physiological psychology is growing rapidly. Part of this growth involves reaching out to other areas of knowledge about the neural underpinnings of behavior. Many physiological psychologists now receive virtually the same training that is given to people working in the fields of neurochemistry, neuroanatomy, neurophysiology, and

---

◆ *PARKINSON'S PATIENT WITH BRAIN GRAFT TERMED "VISIBLY IMPROVED"*

Dickye Baggett, who made history by becoming the first Parkinson's disease patient to undergo a brain-graft procedure in the United States, is "visibly improved," her doctors said.

Vanderbilt University physicians transplanted cells from the 42-year-old clerical worker's adrenal glands into her brain in an attempt to reverse the symptoms of her disease. That attempt is beginning to show success, neurosurgeon George S. Allen said.

Parkinson's disease affects as many as 1.5 million Americans, most of them over the age of 50. It is caused by the death of brain cells that secrete dopamine, a hormone that is important in transferring information from cell to cell in the brain. Victims develop severe tremors and rigidity of the limbs and frequently also develop dementia, a deterioration of mental functioning.

The adrenal glands, which are above the kidneys, also secrete dopamine, but the hormone is of no value to Parkinson's victims because it cannot reach the brain. By transplanting the adrenal cells into the brain, surgeons hope to circumvent this problem.

Physicians in Mexico City, who pioneered the technique used at the Nashville, Tennessee, university, said their first patient, Jose Luis Meza, who received the operation more than a year ago, seems to have reached a plateau: his condition is not improving any more, but it is not deteriorating either. Meza is raising vegetables in his backyard and selling them from a small store in front of his house. Their second patient, an engineer from Toluca who was forced to quit working because of his illness, has now returned to his job.

From T. H. Maugh, April 23, 1987, *Los Angeles Times*, p. 33. Copyright, 1987, *Los Angeles Times*. Reprinted by permission.

neuropharmacology. All of these specialists study the nervous system and their concerns overlap. Even though they may focus on different aspects of the nervous system, they are all tied together by their interest in the nervous system as a whole.

While the brain and the nervous system fascinate physiological psychologists, they are not the only foci of the work of these researchers. As we mentioned earlier, physiological psychologists are also interested in the relationships between glandular activity and behavior. For example, they know that if the thyroid gland must be removed, the flow of thyroid hormones stops and dramatic behavioral changes occur. The hypothyroid individual experiences a lowered metabolism and becomes physically and mentally sluggish. But if this same individual is given regular and correct doses of thyroid hormones, these unwanted effects can be eliminated (Carlson, 1986).

Physiological psychologists are also interested in genetic mechanisms and the relationships between heredity and behavior. They may study such diverse topics as the role of heredity in the development of intelligence or its role in alcoholism. Dominey's research on sunfish (1984) represents another example of this interest in heredity versus environment. He has discovered that there are two types of male sunfish. One builds nests, courts females, and drives off intruders. The other type is a sneaky creature. It is smaller, defends no territory, and mimics the female in color and behavior. By imitating the female, this type of male avoids aggression and actually slips between the larger males and the females and is thus able to fertilize the eggs as the female spawns. Dominey's discovery has perplexed psychologists and biologists alike. What can account for this disparity in male-sunfish behavior? Is it learned behavior, or is it inherited? At present no one knows.

The field of *physiological psychology* is extremely broad. Among the many topics currently under study in this field are the nervous system, vision, hearing, smell, muscular activity, emotion, hunger, pain, thirst, sexual behavior, sleep, abnormal behavior, learning, memory, language, and development. We will learn more about many of these topics and the research of physiological psychologists in these areas in later chapters.

Sensation and Perception

Some psychologists focus on the sense organs and how they operate. These psychologists are primarily interested in the physiological structure and functioning of the eye, the ear, the nose, and other sensory systems. But other psychologists want to know what we do with the information we receive through our senses. In short, they try to discover how we organize and interpret this information.

Suppose you and a friend have just talked with an acquaintance who has been fired. During the conversation the fired person said, "I don't care. It's probably for the best anyway." You and your friend heard the same statement. Pretty much the same sound waves entered your ears. In other words, you both experienced the same sensation. But your perceptions of the situation may differ. Your friend may say, "I'm glad she doesn't care and is handling it so well." You,

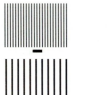

FIGURE 1–1   Our Senses Aren't Perfect: Selective Adaptation   *Hold your book about 1½ feet in front of you. Cover the two right-hand patterns. Stare at the bar between the two grills on the left for twenty seconds. Then look at the dot between the two grates on the right side. The bars in the upper grate will appear more widely spaced than those in the lower grate. This perception occurs even though the bars in the two right-hand grids are equally spaced. (After Coren, Porac, & Ward, 1984)*

on the other hand, might say, "I don't think she really means that. I think she is covering up her disappointment." Your perception of the situation differs from your friend's, even though you both experienced the same sensation.

From this example we can see that perceptions are hypotheses, or guesses, about what is "out there." These guesses are usually based on limited or potentially confusing sensory information, such as an ambiguous remark or tone of voice. They are also governed by past experience. In this case, your perception is influenced by your experience with other friends who have been fired, as well as your limited knowledge of your acquaintance's earlier feelings about her job. We tend to perceive, or give meaning to sensory information, on the bases of what we expect to perceive and on what we have perceived in the past.

There are many interesting demonstrations of the fact that our perceptions of the world around us can be inaccurate. Figure 1–1 demonstrates a phenomenon called *selective adaptation.* This effect shows that what is "out there" is not always what we perceive.

The crucial importance of sensation and perception can be grasped if you try to imagine what it would be like not to have any sensory systems—no vision, hearing, smell, taste, touch, or feeling. Things would be frightening and monotonous, to say the least. You would have no sense of contact with the external world. Indeed, you would have no contact with your own body. You wouldn't hear your own voice, or feel pain, or feel your muscles move. You would exist in a black, silent, odorless, tasteless, unfeeling world. More than likely, you wouldn't survive very long.

In Chapter 3 we talk about *sensation* and *perception* in some detail. For now, let us consider only one example of the kind of experiment done by psychologists in this field. In a perceptual conflict (or visual capture) experiment, the subject is seated facing a window. A square piece of plastic hangs behind the window, while a black cloth covers the subject's hand. The subject is asked to reach behind the window to feel the piece of plastic and to look at it through the window. But the "window" actually is a distorting lens, so the square is projected onto the subject's retina as a rectangle. (The black cloth keeps the subject from seeing a distorted image of the hand.) The subject is then asked to identify the object. The subject is seeing a rectangle but feeling a square. What will the subject report? If the distortion is not too great, many subjects report that the object is a rectangle, even though it is a square. This kind of experiment demonstrates the dominance of vision in humans (Radeau & Bertelson, 1976). In other words, if our senses give us conflicting information, we trust our eyes more than our other senses.

This dominance of vision does not appear in all species. Sharks depend on their sense of smell, as they do not have a well-developed visual system. Bats rely on their hearing when tracking their prey in the dark. Clearly, such dominance of one sense over the others will have a major influence on behavior. We will examine many more experiments and concepts involving sensation and perception in our Chapter 3 discussion.

Learning and Conditioning

Learning psychologists investigate learning in all of its manifestations, from the very simple to the very complex. They examine learning as it is displayed by lower animals and they study the complicated learning processes exhibited by humans. They are also concerned with the relationship between learned and instinctive behavior (Gould & Marler, 1987). In general, psychologists define *learning* as a relatively permanent change in behavior that is the result of practice. We will deal with this definition in detail in Chapter 5. For the present, let us consider one learning situation, known as *avoidance conditioning,* that illustrates the type of learning experiment performed by psychologists.

In a typical avoidance conditioning situation, a rat is placed in one end of an oblong box. There is a barrier between the rat and the other end of the box. The end of the box that contains the rat is painted white; the other end is painted black. If the rat does not jump over the barrier to the black side within a specified time period (say, 15 seconds), the learning psychologist administers a mild electric shock. In other words, the rat has 15 seconds to make a particular response or it will be punished. When shocked, the animal quickly jumps the barrier. What happens as the rat has more and more experience in this situation? It learns to jump over the barrier as soon as it is placed in the white end. It never waits long enough to be shocked, for it has learned an avoidance response. The white end of the box becomes associated with the shock, so the rat jumps out every time it is put there. After the avoidance response has been well learned, experimenters can unplug the apparatus so that no more shocks will be delivered. What happens then? The rat keeps right on jumping; it never waits long enough to discover that the situation is no longer dangerous.

Now, you may say, "Well, I know a lot about rats and boxes, but does this have any relevance to human life?" The answer is yes. We all undergo avoidance conditioning without even knowing it. Remember, the essence of avoidance conditioning is that the animal is punished if it fails to make a response within a specified time period. School children, too, must complete their school assignments on time or they will suffer some unpleasant consequences. Most children respond the way the rat does. They learn to complete their assignments within the allotted time to avoid the negative consequences.

As another example of the value of avoidance conditioning in human life, consider Ivar Lovaas and his attempts to teach language to autistic children (Lovaas, Schaeffer, & Simmons, 1965; Lovaas, 1977, 1978). Autistic children display the following characteristics: (1) they are withdrawn and very unresponsive to other people; (2) they demonstrate serious deficiencies in language development and use; and (3) they exhibit odd, repetitive movements such as arm flapping and body rocking. Prior to the efforts made by Lovaas, few people had had much success at all in helping these children. Lovaas observed that the children were extremely withdrawn from other people, so it was not surprising that they had failed to learn language. It was as if there were a wall between them and the rest of the world.

Conditioning procedures can sometimes help autistic children become more sociable.

Principles discovered in the laboratory can be used to treat compulsive behaviors such as smoking.

Lovaas concluded that these children could never learn to talk until their wall of social isolation was broken down. He decided that the first necessary step had to be the building of social behavior, and that the learning of language could then follow. He also concluded that avoidance conditioning procedures, patterned after the rat in the box, could be useful.

The floor of a small room was covered with metallic tape through which a mild electrical current could be sent. The barefoot child was placed on one side of the room, and the experimenter on the other. If the child did not show a social response, such as approaching, smiling at, touching, or hugging the experimenter within a certain amount of time, he received a mild shock. Although such treatment appears somewhat cruel, it led to a rapid increase in social activity. Lovaas reports that the children became more social and responsive to other people, not just in the room used for the conditioning, but elsewhere as well. The children also seemed happier, and they became more responsive to later efforts to teach them language. It would appear that the simple experimental procedure developed with white rats in the laboratory helped reduce human suffering.

Over the long run, Lovaas's efforts to develop normal language usage in these children were not entirely successful. Although they became much more sociable, the children remained deficient in their use of language even after long periods of treatment. Nevertheless, Lovaas's efforts represented a good example of the way that laboratory-based principles of learning can be applied outside the laboratory. As we shall see in Chapter 8, principles of learning developed in the laboratory, often with rats as subjects, have been applied to a wide range of human problems. Such principles have been used to treat fear, headaches, poor scholastic performance, marital discord, drug and alcohol abuse, obesity, grief, compulsive behavior, and a wide spectrum of mental disorders (see Houston, 1986).

Memory

The field of memory is closely related to that of learning. When we study *memory* we focus on what happens to learned responses after we stop practicing them. Do they simply fade away as time passes, in a decaylike process? Is our ability to remember one set of materials affected by our learning of other materials? Are things that we learn somehow stored within us forever and merely unavailable at any given moment, rather than permanently lost? Do we usually remember things for short periods of time in the same way that we remember things for long periods of time, or is there a difference between short-term memory and long-term memory? Researchers are seeking the answers to these and other questions, as we will see in Chapter 6.

Several different theories of memory also are discussed in Chapter 6. One approach (Postman & Underwood, 1973), called the interference theory, argues that if we learn one set of materials, our ability to remember those materials will be disrupted by other learning that we engage in. Consider this example. If you are given the phone number 983-2167, and asked to remember it, you will not have too much trouble. But if, after you have learned 983-2167, you are also asked to learn 987-6126, 827-1672, 679-3812, and 283-9176 and *then* asked to recall the first phone number, you will probably have some trouble remembering it.

Another approach to memory conceives of the human organism as an information processing system. The overall memory event is considered to begin with the coding of incoming information, followed by storage of that coded information, and ending with retrieval and utilization of that information.

Still another approach to memory emphasizes the importance of our wishes, needs, and desires in determining what we will and will not remember. We all know that if something is important to us, or we are very interested in it, we have little trouble remembering it. On the other hand, we are all capable of forgetting information that is boring to us.

As you can see from these examples, the field of memory is very active at present, with a number of theories seeking to explain both the overall process and its various aspects.

Cognition

The field of *cognitive psychology* covers such complex mental activities as language use, thinking, problem solving, reasoning, sensing, perceiving, and imagining. In short, cognitive psychologists are interested in higher-order mental activities. They want to understand the complex, unseen mental events that we normally call "thinking."

Obviously, these psychologists have set a difficult task for themselves. It is one thing to study something like avoidance conditioning, which can be done without reference to what goes on "inside the head," but what if you want to study something like a "mental image"? For example, think of a horse three inches tall. Whatever you are envisioning as you think of this tiny equine creature is a mental image. It is a real experience, but extremely difficult to measure and define. Can we be sure two people ever experience the same image? We cannot. If we ask 400 people to think of tiny horses we will have 400 different images of horses with which to contend. And yet, cognitive psychologists believe these internal, relatively unmeasurable events are important, and they want to understand them.

Progress is being made in spite of the obvious difficulties. For instance, researchers have shown that certain kinds of learning can be improved if we invent visual images for the elements we are trying to learn (Best, 1986). If we want to remember that *horse* is to be paired with *orange*, it helps to think up some visual image involving the two, such as a horse eating an orange, or a person painting a horse orange. Our ability to remember the pair *horse–orange* will be better if we have a visual image than if we have no image at all. Other researchers have observed that it is easier to develop visual images for concrete words, such as *horse, table,* and *sun,* than for abstract words, such as *justice, appealing,* and *obtuse,* and that both our thinking and our behavior are affected by this fact.

As we will see in Chapter 7, imagery is not the only topic that interests cognitive psychologists, but it is an example of their concern for internal, unseen mental events that occur "within our minds."

Cognitive psychology is obviously closely aligned with the fields of perception, learning, and memory. Like these other fields, it has grown increasingly popular in recent years (see Anderson, 1985; Neimark, 1987). In fact, some have used the term "cognitive revolution" to characterize the renewed interest in how and what people think, and in how cognitions affect feelings and behaviors. Some of these applications will appear throughout this textbook in the sections dealing with child development, social behavior, personality assessment, abnormal psychology, and the treatment of psychological problems.

Motivation and Emotion

When psychologists speak of *motivation* they are referring to whatever it is that energizes, directs, activates, and arouses us. They are interested in drives, motives, needs, wants, and wishes. An example will help here. Suppose two children complete a spelling test. One child scores 80 percent correct, while the other scores 40 percent correct. Can we conclude that the first child knew more words? No. We must consider the children's *motives* before we come to any conclusion. It might turn out that the second child knew all the words but was not motivated to write them down during the examination. The child may not have cared, may have been rebelling, or may have been too sleepy. The first child, on the other hand, may have known only 80 percent of the words, but may have been so motivated to do well that all of the known words were recorded. Thus our conclusions about how much the children knew must take into account their motives as well as their knowledge.

Some motivation psychologists focus on basic biological drives such as hunger, thirst, and sexuality. Others focus on complex, perhaps acquired human motives such as the need to achieve, the need to be with other people, and the need for power. Thus, motivation

These runners and this man may not look like they are engaged in similar activities, but all of these individuals may be driven by the need to achieve.

Emotions are intense, relatively uncontrollable feelings—as this angry basketball coach illustrates.

psychologists address a wide range of concerns—and they certainly end up asking themselves some difficult questions. For example, there is a rare and poorly understood disorder called *anorexia nervosa* that tends to strike young, intelligent women from well-to-do families. These women virtually stop eating. They refuse all efforts to get them to eat; they lose weight, become weak, and, if not force fed, they may die of starvation. The motivation psychologist wants to know why this occurs. No one is yet sure of the answer, but several possibilities have been offered. Some argue that the disorder has some physiological or chemical basis. Others have concluded that the disorder is psychological in origin. Psychologists in the latter group feel that the reaction may be brought on by intensely disturbing events in the girl's life, such as the loss of a loved one, or extreme isolation. Other researchers note that a history of overconcern with obesity often precedes this reaction. Whatever the final explanation of this disorder may be, it shows that motivation psychologists address complex problems that can be of considerable practical concern. Chapters 9 and 11 examine several of these problems in some detail (see also Houston, 1986).

The field of **emotion** is closely related to that of motivation. Emotions are characterized as intense, relatively uncontrollable feelings that affect our behavior. They tend to be either positive (joy, bliss, love) or negative (anger, hate, disgust). Either kind of emotion can affect our behavior significantly—in other words, emotions can act as motives. If we are extremely angry, for example, and attack someone either physically or verbally, then we say we are motivated by anger. Because of this considerable overlap between emotion and motivation, the two topics are often treated together. We will consider emotions in some detail in Chapter 10 and then discuss some practical matters concerning the control of everyday motives and emotions in Chapter 11.

Developmental

Developmental psychologists are concerned with human growth and the factors that affect that growth. Therefore, they also study the interaction of physical growth and experience. We are what we are partly because of our genetic makeup, but our experiences also affect what we are. Developmental psychologists want to understand how these two factors influence our development, both separately and together.

Until recently, developmental psychologists focused on the development of the child, but now they look at the entire life span from prenatal events to death (see Turner & Reese, 1980). They are concerned with all aspects of development. For example, they study the development of language, thinking, emotion, social behavior, and physical capacities. They also consider, in their study of aging, factors such as memory loss, menopause, "identity crises," despair versus hope, and physical decline.

Like psychologists in other areas, developmental psychologists ask some very intriguing questions. For example, are love and affection necessary for normal *physical* growth? In other words, can physical growth be retarded if the child does not receive his or her share of love? The surprising answer appears to be yes. Lytt Gardner (1972) has described cases of what is called *deprivation dwarfism*. Children raised without love and affection can become stunted physically. They tend to be small and underweight. The growth of their bones is actually retarded and resembles that of younger children. Deprivation dwarfism, in short, is a dramatic example of the interaction of physical growth and emotional experience. Developmental psychology studies many crucial interactions of this sort, as Chapters 12 and 13 show.

Personality

Personality psychologists study how we differ from one another. They look for the individual patterns of behavior that make each of us unique. They would not be interested in the fact that you are sitting or lying down as you read this text. That is the way most people read. But if you read each page five times and memorize every key word, or if you remember concepts by associating them with musical tones, that unique behavior would be of interest to personality psychologists because it sets you apart from other people. Generally speaking, personality psychologists explore the development of personality, the functioning of personality, personality assessment, and the abnormal personality.

There are many different approaches to understanding personality. Some researchers feel that personality is best viewed as learned behavior—an individual may have an aggressive personality because being aggressive has paid off in the past. Freudian psychologists believe that personality is best understood in terms of the conflicts that arise among our desires, our reason, and our conscience. Still others feel that the best way to think about personality is to locate an individual on a scale made up of a series of personality dimensions. For instance, each of us falls somewhere between being completely friendly and completely unfriendly. In a similar manner, each of us can be assessed along dimensions of honesty, fearfulness, aggressiveness, and so on. If they can determine which of the many thousands of possible personality traits are the most important, and can locate an individual with reference to those dimensions, then personality psychologists feel that they can develop a clear picture, or *profile,* of the individual's personality. As we will see in Chapter 14, no single approach to personality has formulated a definitive way to develop a personality profile, but each approach has helped to clarify some part of the puzzle of human uniqueness and diversity.

Assessment

The field of *assessment* is closely related to that of personality. In this area psychologists are interested in assessing personality, achievement, and ability differences. Psychologists have developed tests and measures for almost every conceivable ability, and for many different forms of achievement. There are tests to gauge intelligence, anxiety, creativity, musical ability, clerical aptitude, scholastic achievement,

TABLE 1–1 Sample Items from the Remote Associates Test of Creativity Developed by Mednick and Halpern

The subject's task is to find a fourth word that is related to all three words in an item.

1) cookies   sixteen   heart   _____ *

2) poke   go   molasses   _____ *

3) surprise   line   birthday   _____ *

4) base   snow   dance   _____ *

*Answers

1) sweet, 2) slow, 3) party, 4) ball

fearfulness, dominance, shyness, internal versus external control, prejudice, and sexuality. But not all of these tests and measures are valid. Many of them remain experimental and of dubious value.

In Chapters 15 and 16, we shall explore the ins and outs of such measurements. For now, let us look at a sample test. The Remote Associates Test, developed by Sarnoff Mednick and Sharon Halpern (1959), is designed to assess creativity. Mednick has defined creativity as the ability to bring remote elements into new and useful combinations. The test he and Halpern developed, sometimes referred to as the RAT, is supposed to measure this ability. Table 1–1 contains some of the items from this test. Try them. They are fairly difficult. After seeing these items, many people complain that they do not seem to have anything to do with what *they* think of as creativity. Such complaints illustrate an important point concerning testing. The test items do not necessarily have to have what is called *face validity.* That is, they do not necessarily have to seem appropriate, as long as they have *predictive validity.* Predictive validity refers to the ability of the test to predict behavior. Thus, if people who score high on the RAT also do creative things, such as write music, novels, or scientific papers, then we can say that the test is valid. If it predicts behavior, we can use it, even if the items do not seem appropriate.

In our chapters on assessment we shall consider a number of different personality, aptitude, and achievement measures, particularly intelligence tests. We shall also consider some of the legitimate uses, and some of the abuses, of these tests in the world outside the laboratory.

Clinical and Abnormal

Clinical and *abnormal* psychologists are by far the most numerous type. They are interested in the diagnosis, treatment, and understanding of a wide range of emotional and behavioral problems. They address themselves to the problems of mental illness in all its forms as well as to criminal activity, mental retardation, drug addiction, and less serious problems of adjustment.

Clinical psychologists may work in a university or hospital position, or in some sort of mental health clinic. They may be in private practice or work in prisons and private or public mental institutions. We will explore their therapeutic methods and their concerns in Chapters 17 and 18.

Over the years, mental illness has proven very difficult to define and categorize. However, most psychologists now accept the taxonomy of mental disorders developed by the American Psychiatric Association and contained in Table 1–2. Some of these categories will also be examined in greater depth in Chapters 17 and 18.

Counseling, School, and Community

Psychologists in several areas are working to help people beyond the confines of mental hospitals, clinics, and doctors' offices. These psychologists want to take psychology to the people rather than waiting for troubled people to come to them. For example, the concerns of *counseling* psychologists are similar to those of clinical psychologists, except that counseling psychologists deal with the problems of high school and university students. *School* psychologists are like counseling psychologists, but they focus on the social and educational development of elementary school children and work closely with both parents and teachers to stimulate and guide successful development.

Finally, community psychologists are working to move mental health care out of the hospitals and into the community. *Community psychology* is based on the idea that many troubled people can be treated in community mental-health centers, where they can maintain their contact with family and friends rather than being shut up in an unfamiliar hospital. Community psychologists are also concerned with the prevention of mental illness. They know that many human difficulties stem from such problems as poverty, crime, family violence, unemployment, and prejudice. Hence they are concerned with defining and eliminating these contributory factors; they want to deal with the social and environmental roots of mental problems.

Social

The area of *social psychology* is closely linked to those of personality and development. Social psychologists focus on the effects that people have on one another. Because we develop, for the most part, among other people, and because our personalities are heavily affected by those around us it is often difficult to maintain a clear distinction between social psychology and the other areas. Social psychologists focus on *people* as stimuli and deemphasize other aspects of the environment (see Baron & Byrne, 1984).

The topics that have been of greatest importance within the field of social psychology have shifted somewhat over time. Popular topics have included attitude formation and change, conformity, persuasion, liking, racial prejudice, aggression, desegregation, inter-group conflict, and the measurement of public opinion. More and more often, social psychologists are being asked to help solve the problems of society at large.

TABLE 1–2   Major Diagnostic Categories

Disorders usually first evident in infancy, childhood, or adolescence   A variety of intellectual, emotional, physical and developmental disorders, including attention deficit, hyperactivity, eating disorders (such as anorexia nervosa and bulimia), autistic disorder, childhood anxieties, and gender identity disorders.

Organic mental disorders   Disorders in which the psychological symptoms are directly related to injury to the brain or abnormality of its biochemical environment; may be the result of aging or the ingestion of toxic substances (for example, lead poisoning or extreme alcoholism).

Psychoactive substance-use disorders   Includes excessive use of alcohol, barbiturates, amphetamines, opiates, cocaine, and other drugs that alter behavior. Marijuana and tobacco are also included in this category.

Schizophrenia   A group of disorders characterized by loss of contact with reality, marked disturbances of thought and perception, especially hallucinations and delusions, blunted or inappropriate emotions, and bizarre behavior.

Delusional (paranoid) disorders   Disorders characterized by such delusions as those that involve feelings of being persecuted; reality contact in other areas is satisfactory.

Mood disorders   Disturbances of normal mood; involving extreme depression, abnormal elation and excitement, or alternating periods of elation and depression.

Anxiety disorders   Includes disorders in which anxiety is the main symptom (generalized anxiety or panic disorders) or anxiety is experienced unless the individual avoids certain feared situations (phobic disorders), performs certain rituals or thinks persistent thoughts (obsessive-compulsive disorders).

Somatoform disorders   The symptoms of these disorders are physical, but have no known organic basis. Psychological factors appear to play the major role. Included are hypochondriasis and conversion disorders.

Dissociative disorders   Temporary alterations in the functions of consciousness, memory, or identity due to emotional problems. Included are psychogenic amnesia, fugue, depersonalization, and multiple personality.

Sexual disorders   Includes problems of sexual aim (for example, sexual interest in children) and sexual performance (for example, impotence, premature ejaculation, and frigidity). Homosexuality is considered a disorder only when the individual is unhappy with his or her sexual orientation and wishes to change it.

Developmental disorders and personality disorders   Long-standing patterns of inflexible and maladaptive behavior that constitute immature and inappropriate ways of coping with stress, solving problems, and dealing with others and such developmental disorders as mental retardation, autism, and learning disorders.

Source: Adapted from *Diagnostic and statistical manual of mental disorders* (3rd ed., revised), American Psychiatric Association, 1987. Adapted by permission.

As an example of research in this area, we may note that social psychologists have long been interested in conformity to group pressure. In a classic demonstration of the power of group pressure, Solomon Asch (1956) ran many experiments based on the following pro-

If you encountered this group of people standing on a street corner in a large European city, your tendency to stereotype people into categories might lead you to believe that the individual on the left is a member of a punk rock band.

totype. Eight subjects are seated in a semicircle before a screen. The subjects are informed that the experiment involves a test of their ability to judge the length of lines. Three lines, labeled A, B, and C, are projected on the screen. B is the shortest line. Unknown to the true subject, seated in the last seat, the other seven "subjects" are in league with the experimenter and have been instructed to answer incorrectly. The experimenter then asks each "subject" which line is the shortest, with the true subject responding last. Each confederate, in turn, says "C," rather than "B." Asch and other researchers conducting similar experiments have found that the unfortunate individual at the end of the line will often succumb to social pressure and answer "C," too. When asked why they said "C," most people responded that they could not stand the pressure and embarrassment of being "different" and "standing out" in the group. In the chapters on social psychology at the end of this textbook we will discuss even more dramatic examples of conformity.

Another area of social research has to do with *attribution*, or our tendency to make assumptions about why people behave the way they do. Many different kinds of results have been obtained in the course of attribution research. For example, stereotypes, or the tendency to attribute certain characteristics to whole groups of people, have been found to be influential. Thus we all feel we "know" what fraternity members, professional wrestlers, used-car salesmen, and Irish poets are like. We attribute certain motives and characteristics to individuals in these categories without ever considering what that particular individual is like.

Another interesting effect is called *attribution error* (Ross, Bierbrauer, & Polly, 1974). This refers to our tendency to underestimate the impact a situation can have on our behavior. Upon hearing of a case of child abuse, or stealing, or murder, we often say, "I would never do that." But if we actually found ourselves in desperate circumstances, we might well resort to behavior of which we never thought ourselves capable. We overestimate our ability to control our own behavior, and we likewise underestimate the impact a situation may have on us.

Environmental

Our early ancestors had little impact on their environment. Though they learned to light fires, build dwellings, and use tools, those ancient efforts hardly touched the land. Now our ability to alter our physical environment is almost limitless. We can turn deserts into gardens even as we turn forests into deserts. We can create life-support systems that allow us to survive on the bottom of the sea or in space.

Because we are all heavily affected by our environment, and because we are moving into an era of greater and greater environmental control, it is not surprising that a discipline called *environmental psychology* has evolved. Environmental psychologists are concerned with how our physical environment, which we often create, affects our behavior (see the box titled "Bad Air Makes Bad Things Happen"). We alter the environment and the environment, in turn,

◆ BAD AIR MAKES BAD THINGS HAPPEN

Most policemen would agree that the hotter it gets, the more incidents there are of family violence, muggings, and assault. And lest you think that this sounds too much like the once-popular "lunar theory," . . . there is scientific proof that bad air makes bad things happen.

Evidence that chemicals in the air we breathe affect our brains is growing. Scientists suspect that the airborne toxins turn some people to violence. In Los Angeles, for example, and other cities, hot weather can worsen the effects of pollution. That's when some people, goaded by bad air, come out swinging.

Researchers like psychologist James Rotton of Florida International University in North Miami have linked higher crime rates to air fouled with chemicals. The worst pollutant, according to Rotton, is ozone. He estimates that, every year, ozone provokes hundreds of cases of family violence in big cities with bad air.

Potentially, this could be a huge problem. Consider, for example, that of the 300 largest cities in this country, one-third have broken the federal clean-air laws on ozone in the last three years.

"If we reduce the ozone by 50 percent, we can reduce the incidence of violence by a thousand cases," says Rotton.

Ozone has some beneficial properties, however. When it appears in the stratosphere, twelve miles above the earth, ozone protects us from the harmful rays of the sun. But when ozone forms closer to the earth's surface—the sunlight helps to make ozone when it hits chemicals from car exhaust and industrial sources—it threatens our health.

Rotton and his colleagues studied two years' worth of police and pollution data in Dayton, Ohio. They found that on warm, dry days—high pollution days—there were more assaults and cases of family violence. Rotton concludes that, without wind, rain, or humidity to wash away air poisons, bad air moves people to mischief. To corroborate his theory that warm, pollution-racked air causes aggressive behavior, Rotton ran additional tests, using mathematical techniques to rule out factors other than pollution. His findings did not waver. He said, "If you already have some trouble in your life, irritating pollutants can push you over the edge."

Rotton is now studying how people react to low, subtoxic levels of ozone. That is the kind of pollution—usually more than what is allowed by federal clean-air laws—found in large amounts in cities with a population of more than 100,000 people.

Even the scientists advancing these theories agree that blaming antisocial behavior solely on hot, dirty air is risky business. "Behavior is complex and can be altered by so many things," says Lawrence Reiter of the Environmental Protection Agency (EPA). "So you have to make sure that behavioral changes are due to a chemical [in the air] and not some other factor."

Reiter studies how chemicals and pollutants affect our brains, nervous systems, and behavior. He is in an emerging field called neurotoxicology.

"One of the problems of this research," he says, "is that we are trying to evaluate an abnormal state of the brain when we still don't know enough about how the brain works normally."

But the findings that link high levels of both pollution and crime do fit into the growing knowledge that, in the long run, many chemicals can cause nerve damage and behavioral changes.

For example, scientists have known for years that mercury causes brain damage: The nineteenth-century "mad hatters" stammered, twitched, and trembled from inhaling mercury vapors in

London hat factories. Today, many factories use masks and protective hoods to shield workers from the worst effects of chemicals.

In recent years, scientists have demonstrated that lead lowers children's intelligence. As a result, the EPA has slashed the amount of lead allowed in gasoline. In time, the agency may ban leaded gas altogether.

"The problem," say Reiter, "is how do you interpret behavioral change—and prove it is based directly on a chemical?"

This is the question that researchers like Gary Evans of the University of California at Irvine and Steve Jacobs, formerly at Harvard, are trying to answer. They searched for the subtle "other factors" that Reiter refers to. They studied people living in the chemical soup of Los Angeles.

The psychologists talked to 6,000 people from all walks of life by telephone. They asked about stress on the job and at home, and about physical and mental health symptoms. Then they matched the levels of dirty air to the neighborhoods of a random group.

According to Jacobs, people showed an uncanny knack for knowing when the air was bad. Even without knowing the official measurements, they could tell that the invisible ozone was high. Jacobs said that Los Angeles residents felt depressed when they thought the air was dirty "*and* they had a major stress such as divorce or losing a job."

Interestingly, lower income people felt more smog, says Jacobs. He thinks this may be because they tend to live in more polluted areas.

If pollution makes people limp with depression, how can it also make them angry and aggressive?

"One explanation," says Jacobs, "is that we are seeing one problem with two stages. First you get irritable and aggressive. And then, due to chronic pollution and stress, the next stage is depression. This is a problem that's not going away."

Environmental watchdogs have fought hard to reduce the levels of smog choking our cities. Since 1970, when Congress passed the Clean Air Act, there has been a reduction in the six worst air pollutants: carbon monoxide from vehicle exhaust; nitrogen dioxide from industry and automobiles; sulfur dioxide from power plants; ozone from chemicals mixing with sunlight; lead from gasoline; and particulates such as dirt, dust, and soot from industry. Yet, considerable levels of these poisons still wash over our cities, threatening our physical and, apparently, our mental health.

"The Clean Air Act sets very strict health standards," says Lee M. Thomas, head of the EPA. "In many cities, it is impossible to reach those standards. To do it, we will call on state and local governments and individuals to make some tough choices. Ultimately, people may need to make basic lifestyle changes, such as limiting how often and where they drive their cars."

"All federal laws on pollution have focused on death and disease," adds Rotton. "But crimes and mental illness cost us too. When planning our cities, we need to take that into account."

The bottom line, some researchers maintain, is that if we don't clean up our air even faster, we can expect more mental depression and more crime.

From "Can bad air make bad things happen?" by R. Londer, (1987, August 9), *Parade*, pp. 7–8. Reprinted with permission from *Parade*, copyright © 1987.

affects what we can do and how we feel. Environmental psychologists study humans in the "real world" in order to understand the complex relationships between our behavior and our ability to control and change our environment. Thus, environmental psychologists study such things as crowding, privacy, territoriality, noise, air and water pollution, and environmental design.

Let us look at some examples of the kinds of questions that interest environmental psychologists. High and Sundstrom (1977) established two kinds of college dormitory rooms—flexible and fixed-pattern. In the flexible variety, the students were allowed to rearrange the furniture any way they preferred. In the rigid or fixed type, the furniture could not be moved. Students living in the flexible-condition rooms had more visitors and more interpersonal activity than did the students living in the rigid-condition rooms. The flexible condition allowed the students to set up their rooms so that they were better able to enjoy warm, friendly social relations. The fixed pattern, while perhaps good for studying, did not appear to be very inviting in terms of social activity.

This experiment gives some idea of the impact of the physical environment on our activities and on our happiness. It is one example of what psychologists call environmental design. Environmental design, or the effort to arrange the environment so that productivity and a sense of well-being are maximized, is not limited to dorm rooms. Buildings, housing projects, communities, and, in fact, entire cities can be enhanced by environmental design.

Industrial, Organizational, and Human Factors

Industrial psychologists look at human problems within the industrial setting. They are concerned with such things as employer-employee relationships, morale, productivity, testing and selection of employees, and the development of more efficient machinery. Thus one industrial psychologist may try to discover why a certain airplane is unsafe. Another may try to determine why auto workers are having trouble operating a new piece of equipment efficiently. Still another may be studying how the layout and location of lunch rooms and rest areas relate to worker well-being and productivity. A *personnel* psychologist (one type of industrial psychologist) will be concerned with fitting particular people into particular jobs, while a *management* psychologist (another variety of industrial psychologist) will advise a corporation's executives on problems such as how to resolve conflicts among employees. *Organizational* psychologists try to help businesses reorganize in an efficient manner. *Engineering* psychologists try to ensure that equipment and hardware are designed with the limits and capabilities of those using them in mind. In short, industrial psychologists attempt to improve the safety, efficiency, and well-being of workers in a broad range of occupations.

The Psychologist as an Onion

Many psychologists are like onions; beneath the outer layer is another layer, beneath that another, and so on. A psychologist may appear to be working exclusively in one area of specialization, but when you peel away the first layer you find the individual has an intense interest in a closely related field. And under that layer you may find a strong concern for still another related area of psychology.

An industrial psychologist might be concerned with the internal comforts and design of this farmer's "home away from home."

The reason for these multiple interests is that most of the areas of psychology are closely intertwined with one another. From the way we have been describing the different areas, you might conclude that psychology is divided into neat, nonoverlapping areas of specialization. But in fact, many of the areas blend into one another. Hence the psychologist who calls herself an environmental psychologist may well have multiple interests ranging over such fields as social, community, clinical, abnormal, and personality psychology.

Suppose you are a developmental psychologist. Isn't it clear that you might also be interested in just about any other area of psychology? The developmental field includes concern for the development of learning, memory, and cognitive abilities. Motivation, emotions, and personalities must also undergo developmental processes, and social as well as abnormal behaviors also develop and change over time. Keep in mind as you read through the chapters of this book that although the material is organized around specific topics, psychologists are all primarily interested in human behavior, and human behavior is many-sided.

Psychologists practice their specialties in many different settings. Some specialties are much more popular than others. Readers interested in learning more about who does what, and where they do it, are referred to Appendix A—Psychologists: Here, There, and Everywhere.

DEFINING PSYCHOLOGY AND ITS GOALS

A Definition

In a sense, we have already taken a stab at defining psychology. We have done it, not with a single sentence, but by describing what different types of psychologists do. And yet, it would be satisfying if we could come up with a sentence that encompassed most of what we mean by psychology. Many have tried. None have succeeded to everyone's satisfaction. Most definitions emphasize that psychology is a *science*. They also point out that it is the *study of behavior*. In using the term behavior they wish to include not only observable behavior, such as movement, gestures, and words, but also physiological changes, such as events within the nervous and glandular systems, and unseen mental processes such as thoughts and dreams. In other words, **psychology** may be defined as the science of behavior, as long as it is understood that behavior includes a wide range of activities.

Goals

People have varying conceptions of the goals of psychology. The broadest view of psychology holds that its aim is the understanding, the prediction, and the helpful alteration of behavior. An additional aim is the eventual improvement of human life.

A distinction that deserves mention here is the one between *basic* and *applied* research. Basic research psychologists explore problems that often seem to have little immediate relevance to the world outside the laboratory. For example, a psychologist may be very interested in whether spoken words are more easily learned than written words. Many people wonder about the importance of such research, but basic researchers point out that research with no immediate, obvious use may someday prove quite useful. In addition, it may lead to information that will have an important practical use. In other words, *basic research* is conducted with an eye toward understanding behavior regardless of its immediate usefulness. *Applied research*, on the other hand, is more concerned with the immediate benefits that may be derived from the practical application of research findings. But the two fields are by no means separate. Applied research often uses data and principles that were discovered in a basic research program, and basic research is often inspired by applied efforts.

METHODS OF PSYCHOLOGY

Now that you know what general kinds of problems intrigue psychologists, and what their overall goals are, you may be asking how they go about gathering the information that interests them. In short, what techniques do psychologists use in their research efforts? There are several basic methods of data gathering that deserve special attention in this regard.

Experiments

The *experiment* is by far the most popular and most influential of the data-gathering techniques used by psychologists. Since psychological experiments often differ from those you may encounter in other areas of science, we should spend a little time looking at them. We will begin by presenting a sample experiment.

The Question   All psychological experiments start with a question. The question in our sample experiment is this: Can we improve memory by using a *mnemonic technique?* Mnemonics (pronounced nemonics) are discussed more fully in Chapter 8. They are designed to improve memory by relating new material to material we already know. For example, suppose you were asked to remember HOUSE, GABLE, ELEVATOR, FLOOR, UPSTAIRS, DOOR, EAVE, WINDOW, ATTIC, INSULATION, and CARPET, in that order. At the same time you also had to remember CHIMNEY, SIDEWALK, BASEMENT, FIREPLACE, CEILING, BEDROOM, TILE, SEWER, BARN, TERRACE, and TREES, in the correct order. The task might be easier if you make up sentences whose words begin with the first letters of the words in the list you are trying to remember. For example, if you can remember, "**H**uge **g**reen **e**lephants **f**ly **u**pside **d**own **e**very **W**ednesday **a**fternoon **i**n Chicago," you might be well on your way to remembering the first list. When asked to recall the list you would "decode" your sentence. You would know that the first word began with **H,** the second with **G,** and so on. Similarly, your recall of the second list of words might be aided if you remember the sentence, "**C**an **s**illy **b**lue **f**iremen **c**atch **b**ig **t**angled **s**nakes **b**y **t**ickling **t**hem?"

This mnemonic technique might work, but we need to run an experiment to be sure. Accordingly, we bring in a large group of subjects, instruct them in how to use this particular mnemonic device, and then test their ability to remember the two lists. The average experimental subject recalls about 75 percent of the words on the two lists. It seems as though this mnemonic technique really works. But

Although much of our text discussion on experiments focuses on verbal learning, experiments take hundreds of different forms. This child is being tested for skills that affect her motor learning.

does it? Can we conclude, from the obtained results, that memory can be improved through the use of these devices? Or is there an alternative explanation for the results obtained? Maybe *everyone*, whether they use a mnemonic or not, can recall 75 percent of the lists.

Control Groups   In order to determine whether the use of the mnemonic technique is a critical factor in our experiment, we need a **control group**—a group of subjects that does not use the mnemonic technique, but does try to recall the words. The control and the experimental groups are treated identically except that the experimental group receives the experimental manipulation (instruction in how to use mnemonics), while the control group does not. If the only difference between the experimental and control groups is the experimental manipulation, then any differences in final outcome must be due to that experimental manipulation. In short, if the experimental group recalls many more words than the control group, then the instruction in how to use the mnemonic technique must have helped the experimental subjects.

A control condition eliminates an alternative interpretation of the data. In our example, the inclusion of a control condition eliminates the possibility that all subjects, whether they receive the mnemonic instruction or not, can recall almost all the words. The number of control groups an experimenter uses in an experiment depends on how many alternative explanations of the data are possible. In some situations many control groups are necessary, while in others one or two will suffice. But in all cases, a control group eliminates an alternative explanation.

Subjects as Their Own Control   Sometimes we do not actually use a new group of subjects as our control, because subjects can serve as their own control in certain experiments. Suppose we are interested in the effects of coffee drinking on memory. We might have a single group of subjects try to recall a list of words after they have not had coffee for 24 hours and then test them again right after they each drink a cup of coffee. We can then compare our subjects' ability to recall without the aid of coffee (control condition) to their recall performance following a cup of coffee (experimental condition). The subjects serve as their own control.

Although it is not always possible to use subjects as their own control, doing so ensures that the experimental and control conditions will be identical except for the experimental manipulation. As we will see when we discuss random assignment, getting two equivalent groups of people to use as experimental and control subjects can frequently be a problem. Using subjects as their own control avoids this difficulty.

Dependent and Independent Variables   One good way to understand any psychological experiment is to identify the dependent and independent variables in that experiment. A variable is any condition or event that changes. The **independent variable** is the condition or event that the experimenter varies. In our experiment, the independent variable is the use of mnemonics. In one condition mnemonics are used, while in the other they are not. The experimenter wants to observe the effect of this independent variable on the subject's behavior. The subject's behavior that is affected by variations in the independent variable is called the *dependent variable.* In our experiment, retention of the words is the dependent variable. We want to see if variations in the independent variable (use of mnemonics) will result in variations in the dependent variable (retention). It is the ability to have tight control over independent variables that makes the experiment such a useful and appealing data-gathering technique.

Random Assignment   Suppose we use a large class of students as subjects in our mnemonic experiment. Suppose further that, for the sake of convenience, we assign all the students sitting in the front of the room to the experimental condition and all the students in the back half of the room to the control condition. Then, assume that we observe that the experimental group recalls many more words than the control group. Can we conclude from this that mnemonic methods facilitate recall, or is there something definitely wrong with the way we assigned subjects to conditions? Is it not possible that students choosing to sit in the front of a class might differ from those preferring to sit in the back of the room? They might be more eager, more motivated, or perhaps better learners. If they differ from the control subjects before the experiment is conducted, then we do not know whether the observed difference in recall is due to the use of a mnemonic method or to prior differences between the two groups. In other words, we need to eliminate an alternative explanation.

One way to do this is, as we have seen, to use subjects as their own control. Another way is to use *random assignment* when picking subjects and controls. We can do this by mixing up all the students' names in a hat, blindly pulling them out one at a time, and assigning them alternately to the experimental and control groups. This means that no characteristic of the subjects, such as seating preference, can affect which group the individual will be put into. Subjects from all over the room will be randomly assigned to the two groups. Furthermore, by assigning subjects in this random manner, we assume that the two groups will be equal to one another in all respects. Characteristics that might affect the ability to recall words, such as motivation, intelligence, age, sex, and health, should be equally represented in each group.

When we use random assignment we assume the groups are equal before the experiment begins. Then we introduce the independent variable—the use or nonuse of a mnemonic method. Finally, we test for recall. If the experimental and control groups differ in recall, we can now assume that this difference is due to manipulation of the independent variable and not to any prior differences between the groups.

When Is a Difference Significant?   When we conduct an experiment, we almost always find some difference between the performances of the experimental and the control groups. Suppose our control group recalls, on the average, 11 words, while our experimental group recalls 12. What do we make of this difference? It could mean that mnemonics helped the experimental group. On the other hand, a small difference like this might be due to chance. If we ran the experiment over again the results might be reversed, or there might be no difference at all.

Statisticians have developed many statistical tests that help us decide whether or not a given difference in performance should be considered significant or trustworthy. (Some of these tests are described in Appendix B, the Statistical Appendix. The fact that statistics is put in the appendix does not mean that the topic is unimportant. On the contrary, a knowledge of statistical techniques is crucial for almost any professional researcher. If you go on in psychology, you will undoubtedly be exposed to these important concepts and tools.) Basically, these tests determine how likely it is that a given difference will appear by chance. If it is unlikely that a given difference would occur due just to chance alone, then we can accept it as an important difference. If the difference is very likely to occur by chance, then we can conclude little or nothing from our experiment. In psychology, if a given difference is likely to occur by chance less than 5 in 100 times, we normally consider it a significant difference.

Multiple Variables   Suppose our experiment did show that mnemonic-using subjects recalled more words than nonusers. Would we then want to proclaim to the world that mnemonics always work? No. We would probably want to qualify our conclusion, and argue that mnemonics may work under some conditions but not necessarily under all conditions. For example, the age of the subject might make a difference, or the length of the list, the type of words in the list, the sex of the subjects, and so on. Most psychological experimenters recognize that many factors may contribute to a result. Accordingly, most psychological experiments involve more than one independent variable. In an experiment such as the one we have just been discussing, the experimenter might suspect that the ability to profit from mnemonics depends on the level of education achieved by the participants. Therefore, she might set up her experiment so that subjects of both high and low levels of education either used or did not use mnemonics. In this way she could determine if the benefits derived from mnemonics were limited to highly educated people, people of lower levels of education, or both.

"Blind" Experiments   Sometimes it is important to consider whether or not the subjects know which condition they belong to. Suppose we are interested in the effects of caffeine on driving an automobile. We have some subjects drink coffee and others drink nothing at all. Imagine that all the subjects then take a driving test and the subjects who drank coffee do better than the subjects who did not drink anything. What's wrong with this procedure? The problem is that the coffee drinkers know they have been treated in a special way—they know that they had coffee while other subjects did not. As a result, their driving performance may have been affected by this knowledge

rather than by caffeine. Many of the coffee drinkers may have tried harder or may have been motivated to contribute to the success of the experiment.

The solution to this problem is to use the **single-blind technique.** This means that we try to make sure the subjects do not know which condition they belong to. In the caffeine experiment this might be accomplished by having all subjects, both experimental and control, drink coffee. But the coffee given to the controls would have the caffeine removed. In this way, unless they are very sensitive to the effects of caffeine, the subjects would not know which condition they belong to, and any observed difference in driving could be attributed to caffeine alone.

The experimenter should not know which condition the subject belongs to either. There is just as much danger of error coming from the experimenter as from the subject. Suppose the experimenter administering the driving test knows whether or not a particular subject had caffeine. This knowledge might subtly influence the experimenter's assessment of the subject's driving. Without necessarily meaning to do it, the experimenter might judge the driving of a caffeine subject to be better than the driving of a noncaffeine subject, even though the performance of the two subjects was identical. The obvious solution to this problem is to have two or more experimenters. One experimenter administers the coffee and then sends the subjects out to an uninformed, or "blind" experimenter for the driving test.

In summary, the best experiment is the one in which *neither* the subject *nor* the experimenter knows which condition the subject belongs to. This is called the **double-blind technique.** Unfortunately, it is not always possible to run experiments in a fully blind fashion. For example, suppose we want to observe the effects on driving of covering one eye. There is no way we can conceal from the subject the fact that one of his eyes is covered.

The experiment is preferred by psychologists for gathering data because it allows precise control over both independent and dependent variables. But for a number of reasons, we cannot always cast our questions about behavior in an experimental mold. There are times when we must rely on other means of gathering information. We will now look at some of those alternative techniques.

Naturalistic Observation

Suppose we want to know about the effects of starvation on learning. We cannot starve half of our group of college sophomores down to 80 percent of their normal body weight, while the control subjects are allowed to eat. Or, suppose we are interested in the effect that being mugged has on personality. We cannot mug half our subjects and then compare their personalities with unmugged subjects. But the effects of starvation and mugging are still of great concern. What do we do? We may turn to an alternative method of gathering data, called **naturalistic observation**, in which we seek out naturally occurring instances of what we want to study. We might contact the police and hospital officials in an effort to find people who have been mugged. Once located, these people could be studied. Similarly, we might seek

Using naturalistic observation techniques, psychologists can interview anorectics and their families to acquire information about anorexia and its effects.

out prisoners of war who have suffered starvation, or go to a country that is in the grip of famine. Naturalistic observation is not as controlled a technique as the experiment, but when experimental manipulation of a particular variable is unethical, immoral, or impractical, we must turn to observation techniques.

One recent application of the observational approach involves families that are having difficulty getting along together. The researcher wants to know what kinds of problems they have, but he cannot just bring them into the laboratory and say, "OK. Now fight among yourselves." They will be self-conscious and will not behave normally in this artificial situation. So some researchers hit upon the idea of leaving a tape recorder running in the home of the family during the week. Presumably, over this long period of time, family members will be more likely to interact the way they usually do. In this manner the researcher hopes to obtain a more realistic picture of what goes on in the family than could be obtained in the laboratory. Of course, there remains the serious question as to whether or not the members of a family can act normally when they know that a tape recorder is recording their conversations.

Tests

Psychologists gather an enormous amount of information through the use of tests. As mentioned, they have tests of just about every conceivable aptitude, emotion, achievement, attitude, and feeling. Tests are particularly useful when psychologists are attempting to compare one subject with another. The business of developing and validating tests is a complicated one. We will spend some time looking at tests, their uses, and their abuses in Chapters 15 and 16.

Interviews and Questionnaires

If we want to know how people feel, and what they do, why not just ask them? This proposition forms the basis for two related and widely used methods of gathering data. In an interview, the subject is asked to respond verbally to a series of questions posed by the interviewer. On a questionnaire, the subject gives written responses. There are many different types of interviews and questionnaires. They range from in-depth interviews of single individuals to nationwide surveys, such as the Gallup Poll and the Roper Poll. Interviews and questionnaires have been useful in investigating many different problems, but they all function on the basic assumption that subjects can provide useful information if we just ask them for it.

Obviously, the great danger with these two techniques is that subjects may misrepresent themselves. Most people probably want to present themselves in the best light possible. Suppose someone asks, "Are you nervous and anxious?" The impulse is to reply quickly, "Who me? No, of course not." It can work the other way around, too. In the days of the draft, many men being screened for compulsory military service felt tempted to present themselves as unreliable, unhealthy, irresponsible, or just plain crazy.

Psychologists are aware of these tendencies to present false information, of course. Through experience, and by checking information against independent sources, it is possible for them to balance out many of these biasing effects.

Case Histories

Case histories are often useful when an individual is seeing a psychologist in connection with some type of therapeutic effort. Many psychologists believe that a patient's present difficulties can best be understood in the light of that individual's past experiences. Accordingly, the psychologist will try to develop a history, or biography, of the individual. Information is obtained from the patient and from any other appropriate source available, such as parents, friends, and hospital records. Once the history is completed the psychologist may attempt to interpret the patient's present difficulties in terms of earlier, perhaps causal events. Case histories, including the course of therapy as well as background material, can also be useful in that large numbers of histories can serve as data banks for researchers. Investigators can sometimes find valuable information buried within large groups of case histories and may thereby avoid running a lengthy or costly experiment to gather pertinent data.

Correlation

There is another important method of dealing with data when an experiment is impossible, and this is the method of correlation. Suppose, for example, that an investigator is interested in the relationship between child abuse and school performance. Obviously the experimenter cannot manipulate the independent variable, or establish varied and controlled amounts of child abuse. But when many cases of child abuse are already on record, the experimenter can study how abuse is related to school performance. The experimenter can *correlate* the two factors by examining the extent to which they vary together. Does school performance go down as the degree of abuse goes up? Or is the opposite true? Or are they independent of one another?

The Correlation Coefficient (r) Psychologists use a statistical method that produces a **correlation coefficient (r)** when they study relationships between variables. The relationship expressed by r is best seen in a **scatter plot** (see Figure 1–2). Suppose fifty subjects are tested for their ability to recall a long list of words after having practiced them for several days, *and* then they are tested for their ability to recognize a long series of pictures after having studied them for several days. The question is whether the ability to recall words correlates with the ability to recognize pictures.

Each dot in Figure 1–2 represents one subject's performance on both tasks. This figure indicates that there is a strong relationship between performance on the two tasks. That is, quite a few people who did well on one task did well on the other. Similarly, people who did poorly on one task tended to do poorly on the other. Very few people who did well on one task did poorly on the other.

The value of r can vary from +1.00 to −1.00. When r is +1.00, the correlation is perfect and positive. If each subject remembers

FIGURE 1–2 A Scatter Plot Representing a Substantial Positive Correlation *Each dot represents the scores of a given individual on two different memory tests. The dashed diagonal line is the line upon which all entries would fall if the correlation were a perfect positive one (r = +1.00).*

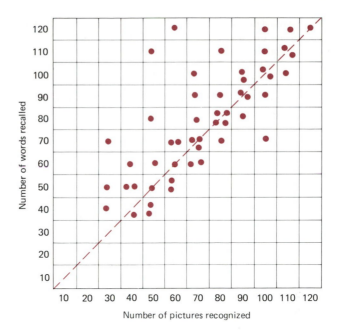

words and pictures equally well, so if you know how many words they recalled you would automatically know how many pictures they remembered, then *r* would be +1.00. In the case of a perfect and positive correlation, all the dots would fall on the diagonal line as shown in Figure 1–3a.

If *r* equals −1.00, the correlation is again perfect, but in this case it is negative. This means that as one variable goes up, the other goes down. The longer you use a ballpoint pen the less ink it contains; the correlation between the amount of time spent writing and the amount of ink remaining would be −1.00 (see Figure 1–3b).

A correlation of 0.00 means there is no relationship between the variables. If you correlate height with scores on an intelligence test the correlation will be 0.00. Knowing a person's height will not help you predict his intelligence, and vice versa (see Figure 1–3c).

Correlations between +1.00 and −1.00 represent the degree to which two variables are correlated. Thus +.86 represents a fairly strong positive relationship while −.10 represents a weak negative relationship. The scatter plot in Figure 1–2 represents a fairly strong positive correlation. Remember, we are talking about two aspects of a correlation: *degree* (how much of a correlation) and *direction* (positive or negative). A positive and a negative correlation of the same size represent the same degree of relationship, but in the opposite direction. The Statistics Appendix discusses correlation in greater detail.

Correlation and Causality When two variables correlate, this does not necessarily mean that one *causes* the other. For example, geese fly south in the fall and children go back to school. In the spring, geese fly north and children leave school. There is a strong correlation here, but we would not want to assume that geese cause children to go to school, or that the activities of children influence the migration of geese. As the world rotates on its axis, we grow older. But we would

FIGURE 1–3 Some Hypo-
thetical Correlations (a) A
*perfect positive correlation
(r = +1.00). Although it is most
unlikely to occur in any form of
human behavior, this is what a
correlation of +1.00 between two
tests of memory would look like.
(b) A perfect negative correlation
between time spent writing and
amount of ink left in pen
(r = −1.00). As time spent writing
increases, the amount of ink
decreases. (c) A correlation of 0.00
between intelligence test scores and
height would look like this.
Knowing a person's height will not
help us to predict that person's
intelligence.*

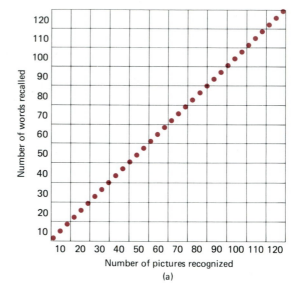

(a)

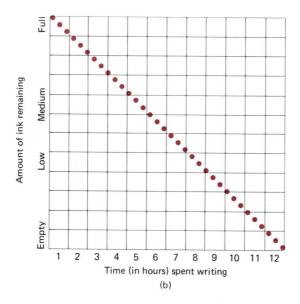

(b)

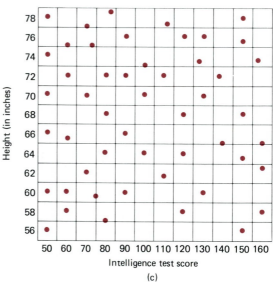

(c)

not want to insist that the earth's rotation should be stopped so that
we will stop growing older. We know the two factors correlate, but
we also know that it would be wrong to assume a causal relationship
between the two.

Psychologists have to be careful about how they interpret correlations. They can easily fall into the trap of assuming that a correlation implies causality. Many correlations seem logically related, and
sometimes correlations really do represent causal relationships. The
amount of ink left in your pen is determined by how long you use
that pen. But a significant correlation does not always imply causation. Hence, in the absence of any other evidence for the existence of
a causal relationship, we cannot accept a correlation as proof of causality. In an experiment, we are much more likely to assume a causal
relationship than we are in the case of a correlation.

Ethics and Experimentation

Having examined some of the methods psychologists use to study behavior, we now turn to the crucial ethical issues that face investigators when they engage in research. In the past, human subjects in psychology experiments were often treated quite poorly. They were shocked, deceived, and made to feel uncomfortable. We have already noted Lovaas's use of shock in working with autistic children and we have mentioned Asch's acutely embarrassing conformity experiments. But the last twenty years have witnessed a dramatic shift away from this cavalier kind of subject treatment. Now, the basic rights of the subjects are of great concern to the academic research community. Experiments that were once done routinely are no longer conducted.

Levels of Review   Today, most psychological research is conducted at universities, using students as subjects. The rights of these subjects are protected at several levels. Many psychology departments have their own review boards, whose members require that experiments conform to the standards established by the American Psychological Association (1982). Research that is funded by an outside agency, such as the National Science Foundation or the National Institute of Mental Health, must also conform to the strict standards imposed by those agencies.

The ethics of experimentation have changed drastically since the Nazis conducted outlaw medical experiments during World War II.

Animals as well as humans need to be treated ethically and humanely during experimentation.

The Problem of Risk   Most guidelines require that subjects in psychology experiments not be put at either physical or psychological risk unless the potential benefits of the study being conducted far outweigh the risks involved. Most experiments involve little or no risk, but occasionally an important study involving risk will force the review board to struggle with the "risk-benefit" ratio.

Informed Consent   Nearly all studies are conducted only after informed consent has been obtained from the subjects. Informed consent means that each subject has been told about the procedures involved in the study and about any risk involved. All such subjects are free to end their participation at any time without penalty, and they are also informed of how their privacy will be protected. Sometimes studies involve deception—that is, the subject is not told the whole truth about the study. Sometimes, if the deception is mild and little risk is perceived, a review board will approve such a study. At other times review boards will simply refuse to approve, stating that deception and informed consent are incompatible.

Debriefing   Debriefing is an important part of any experiment. It entails telling subjects about the purpose and results of the experiment, and especially about any deception involved.

Animal Experimentation   The use of animals in experimentation is incredibly controversial at the present time. It is easy to understand why animals are utilized for laboratory research; their use is convenient and practical. They may be treated in ways that would be clearly inappropriate for humans. Researchers using animals are subject to stringent health, comfort, space, feeding, and care requirements. They are required to seek ways of minimizing pain and to seek alternative methods of experimentation, if possible.

Nevertheless, segments of our society are outraged by the treatment experimental animals receive. It is their position that animal research is often unbearably painful and simply should not be conducted. Each of us must wrestle with our conscience and try to weigh the risk-benefit issue as it applies to animal experimentation (Cohen, 1986; Miller, 1986).

VARIED PERSPECTIVES

Historical Roots

There are at least four important approaches to the study of psychology that are dominant in the field today. But before we describe these current perspectives, which are the main focus of this section, we need to know a little bit about the roots of these modern ways of looking at psychology. Every science has a long and complex history; psychology is no exception. It did not spring into existence full blown and without a past. In fact, many scholars suggest that we must go back to Greek philosophy to find the deepest roots of psychology. These scholars point out that Aristotle was interested in memory, sex differences, aging, physiology, and reasoning—all still vital concerns of today's psychology—and that he influenced later thinking about these topics. Psychology may be young as a science, but the questions it encompasses are ancient and enduring.

While the thinking of the ancient Greeks is still reflected in modern psychological investigation, more recent philosophical traditions have had a profound influence on today's major psychological perspectives. In the 1620s, the French philosopher René Descartes argued that some of our ideas are the results of experience, while others, such as the ideas of God, self, perfection, and infinity, are innate or present from birth. This line of reasoning came to be known as *nativism*. An opposing school, called *empiricism*, was developed by a group of British philosophers in the seventeenth and eighteenth centuries. According to empiricists John Locke, David Hume, and James Mill, *all* ideas are acquired through experience and none are innate. As we shall see, these opposing views still echo in many modern debates about perception, learning, and development, and have yet to be resolved.

A giant step toward the psychological perspectives currently adhered to by most psychologists was taken during the mid-nineteenth century, primarily by a group of Germans that included Hermann von Helmholtz, Ernst Weber, Gustav Fechner, and Wilhelm Wundt. These scholars shifted their focus, and ours, away from philosophical thought toward systematic experimentation. They proposed that the only way we can truly learn about human behavior is to experiment in a precise fashion; merely thinking about behavior will not enlighten us. Today, thanks to these pioneers, experimentation is the backbone of most approaches to psychology.

Finally, we must note Charles Darwin's contributions to psychology. His conception of the continuity of the heritage of humans and animals allowed later scholars to study animals in the hope of learning something about humans. Animal experimentation is essential in many modern fields of psychology. In addition, Darwin's theory of evolution led many psychologists to explore the adaptation of the organism to its environment and the interactions of individual differences with genetic influences.

Thus the thoughts and actions of scholars ranging all the way from the ancient Greeks, through the French and English philosophers, to Darwin and the German experimentalists, set the stage for the dominant modern perspectives that we will consider now.

Four Leading Approaches

Think about being a passenger on the next space shuttle launched by the United States. How do we go about understanding this event? The answer is that we can understand it from a number of different perspectives. We can look at the historical, scientific, political, financial, or military aspects of the situation. We can look at it in terms of psychological elements. Or, if we wish, we can focus on the biology of the flight in space. We may even reduce the chain of events to a series of complex chemical reactions. At still another level, we could try to trace and comprehend the vast numbers of electrical events occurring within the nervous systems of the participants. While we are at it, we could try to describe and understand the occasion in terms of the laws of physics and mathematics.

Knowing about an event from one viewpoint does not rule out looking at the same event from a different point of view. Just because we might be able to trace the neurological patterns that underlie space travel does not mean that a political or a psychological analysis of the same occasion would be useless.

Any psychological event may also be viewed from a number of different perspectives. Within the field of psychology there are several different ways of studying behavior. We will take a brief look at four leading approaches.

The Physiological Approach   From the physiological perspective, behavior is to be understood in terms of the complex neural, glandular, genetic, and muscular events that underlie observable behavior. Any given behavior, such as an individual learning a list of words, can be reduced to the neural events that occur within the brain and nervous system. Obviously, this is a valid point of view. According to this view, psychology is something of a misnomer. A ''psychological'' event is really nothing more than a physiological event that we have not yet traced to a physiological level. Someday researchers may be able to create blueprints of the entire nervous system. If that day ever comes, scientists will be able to follow the underlying neural patterns that accompany all behavior. Probably none of us will be around to see this happen. We are just beginning to scratch the surface of the physiology of behavior. Our research methods are still somewhat primitive, and our knowledge of the nervous system is spotty and incomplete. Nevertheless, all behavior logically can be understood on a physiological level.

The ***physiological approach*** is a relatively old one. By the early nineteenth century, physiology had become a scientific discipline. Some physiologists were attempting to link various parts of the brain or spinal cord with specific behavioral responses. Later, Gustav Fritsch and Eduard Hitzig developed the method of electrical stimulation of the brain, so that they could study the body's responses to stimulation of specific brain areas. All of this early work set the pattern for psychology as a systematic, experimental method of studying behavior. But physiological research lagged until the advent of such space-age wonders as large computers and microsurgery. Now, researchers can observe a specific nerve cell at work in a living subject, or monitor the physiological reactions of an astronaut in space. With the development and use of vastly improved experimental techniques like these, the physiological approach is attracting more and more adherents, and the years to come are certain to see great advances in this area.

The Behaviorist Approach   The classical behaviorist's point of view is very different from the physiological approach. The ***behaviorist approach*** focuses on observable behavior, such as moving, gesturing, and talking. What goes on in the nervous system is of little interest to behaviorists. Furthermore, the strict behaviorist does not care

B. F. Skinner

about subjective elements such as thoughts, ideas, and images. These are considered impossible to measure and are thus excluded from consideration.

According to this strict approach, if psychology is to be a science, it must deal only with elements that can be directly observed and measured by an independent observer. You can experience your own mind working, but no one else can. Therefore, strict behaviorists ignore this type of inner experience. But today, more and more behaviorists are leaning toward a less rigid definition of behaviorism and they are finding ways to include such basically human "internal behaviors" as thinking and feeling within the scope of the behaviorist approach.

The psychologists most often associated with the development of the behaviorist approach are John B. Watson (1879–1958) and B. F. Skinner (1904–). Watson, who is often labeled as the founder of behaviorism, criticized the use of introspection, the method of trying to understand human behavior by examining and reporting our own experiences and feelings. He objected strongly to the idea that these vague self-reports of internal mental states could contribute anything to the science of psychology.

B. F. Skinner, probably the best-known and most influential contemporary American psychologist, expanded and refined the behaviorist approach. His scientific writings, as well as his popular books, *Walden Two* (1948) and *Beyond Freedom and Dignity* (1971), have had an incalculable impact on modern thinking. Essentially, Skinner agrees with Watson that observable behavior, rather than internal mental states, should be the prime concern of psychologists. He argues that our behavior is modified by environmental pressures, and he insists that the principles of learning and conditioning developed in the laboratory with animals can be used to alter human behavior.

The Cognitive Approach   Cognitive psychologists focus their studies on the workings of the mind. They too wish psychology to be a precise science, but they believe that mental events can also be studied in a rigorous manner. In contrast to the strict behaviorists, adherents to the **cognitive approach** believe that it is possible to understand subjective experiences like perceiving, sensing, knowing, thinking, problem solving, daydreaming, and imagining.

The cognitive point of view is not a new one. Internal mental states have long been of interest to scholars. In fact, it was a cognitive trend (which included introspection, as we have seen) that Watson originally attacked when he launched behaviorism in the 1920s. Introspection was nothing more than an early, doomed tool of the cognitive approach. But after several decades during which behaviorism reigned supreme, the cognitive approach has surged back with new and more refined research methods that deflate many of the behaviorist's objections to the study of the "mind." As new experimental techniques are developed, cognitive psychologists use them to explore unanswered questions in such fields as developmental and abnormal psychology, learning, and perception. The cognitive point of view is one of the fastest growing approaches in psychology today.

The behaviorist approach to behavior would concern itself with observable action. The cognitive approach would consider what these people are thinking.

The Psychodynamic Approach Sigmund Freud (1856–1939), founder of psychoanalysis, may be the best-known name in the field of psychology. Even though his **psychodynamic approach** (outlined in Chapter 14) is not as popular as it once was, it has had an enormous influence on psychology. Freud's approach is based on the idea that our behavior reflects the interplay of dynamic, conflicting, unconscious drives within us. Specifically, he believed that the human personality has three basic components. First, there are the strong, primitive, biologically determined urges that, if left unchecked, may destroy us and those around us. This aspect of personality is called the *id*. Freud singled out the sexual and aggressive drives as being crucial in our lives. A second part of each personality, the *ego*, tries to satisfy these basic urges in such a way that we are not harmed. Each individual's ego is concerned about his own safety but has no regard for society's needs. Fortunately, each of us also has a conscience, a sense of right and wrong, called the *superego* by Freud. This third aspect of the human personality is imposed on us by our interactions within society, and it serves to monitor and control the actions of the other two components. For example, if we want to hit someone and we think we can get away with it, our conscience tells us the action is unethical and we should not do it. To put it simply, the id says, "Gimme, gimme, gimme," the ego says, "I'll get it for you if I can," and the superego says, "Don't! It's wrong." But according to Freud, these conflicting impulses are so threatening that we suppress our conscious awareness of them, which makes life more difficult.

Freud believed our troubles in life are due to the conflicting and incompatible demands of these three components, and our ineffective, unconscious attempts to reconcile these demands. For forty years he tried to refine and spell out the conditions under which these components develop and interact. He devised the therapeutic method he called psychoanalysis and invented such techniques as

A seemingly simple situation, such as a man asking a woman for a date, can be viewed from all four perspectives—physiological, behavioristic, cognitive, and psychodynamic.

free association and dream analysis to resolve the conflicts. Although the psychodynamic perspective has fallen from favor in recent years, psychoanalysis is still a widely used form of therapy, and many of Freud's concepts, such as the idea of unconscious conflicts, have become part of our culture.

These four approaches—physiological, behaviorist, cognitive, and psychodynamic—cut across many areas of psychology. In general, Chapter 2 typifies the physiological approach, Chapter 5 represents a behaviorist approach, Chapter 7 contains the cognitive approach, and psychodynamic theory and therapy are outlined in Chapters 14 and 18, respectively. We should note that these four approaches do not begin to exhaust the "schools" of psychology. For example, humanistic psychology, outlined in Chapter 14, is also often included in lists of major approaches.

Fields versus Approaches

Many fields of psychology, such as motivation, learning, social, and developmental, may be viewed from any or all of the four perspectives just described. For example, suppose we are interested in motivation and have just observed a man asking a woman for a date in a very cheerful, confident manner. How do we go about understanding the man's behavior? We can use a physiological approach if we wish, by looking at the tissue needs and neural functioning of the participants. We can adopt a behaviorist point of view and talk about how the man has tried a similar approach in the past and been rewarded for his efforts. We can adopt a cognitive approach and consider what the participants are thinking and deciding as they act. And finally, we can think about the situation in terms of the psychodynamic interplay of desire, reason, and conscience (see Figure 1–4).

Each of these approaches is valid. Although proponents of the various approaches sometimes act as though their point of view is the

FIGURE 1–4 The "Layer Cake" of Knowledge *Many of the fields of psychology can be understood from several different approaches.*

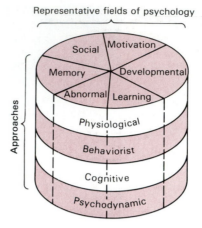

only correct one, we can see that this is not the case. The same event may be understood in many different ways. In the chapters to come we will be covering a wide range of topics, and we will have occasion to view these topics from a number of different points of view. Only through an understanding of the complexity and the uncertainty of psychology can a student grasp the status of this infant science.

TWO KINDS OF CHAPTERS

We have written the chapters of this text so that some of them reflect basic, experimentally derived principles and generalizations, while others illustrate the uses of these principles in the everyday world outside the laboratory. Each "Exploring . . ." chapter describes some practical applications and some new or controversial topics within a given area. Each of the other chapters focuses on the fundamentals and the current state of knowledge within a specific area.

By separating basic and exploratory chapters in this way, we hope to bring you both a firm idea of what is fundamental information within an area and a vivid impression of the current controversies, applications, and explorations within that same field.

SUMMARY

1. Psychology is a large, complex field of study that may be broken down into various distinct areas of specialization.

2. Physiological psychology is the study of the physical events that underlie behavior, such as the functioning of the brain and nervous system, the glandular systems, and the genetic systems.

3. Perception psychologists study the structure and function of the sensory systems. They are interested in how we organize, interpret, and relate to our past experiences incoming sensory information that is often incomplete and potentially confusing.

4. Learning psychologists are concerned with a wide range of learning tasks, all of which involve relatively permanent changes in behavior that are the result of practice.

5. Memory psychologists are interested in what happens to learned responses after we stop practicing them. They want to know how and why we forget certain information and retain other material.

6. Cognitive psychologists are interested in complex inner mental activities such as language, thinking, problem solving, reasoning, remembering, imagining, and perceiving.

7. Motivation and emotion psychologists are concerned with what energizes, directs, activates, and arouses us. Motivation psychology focuses on drives, motives, needs, wants, and wishes. People studying emotion focus on the strong, relatively uncontrollable feelings that affect our behavior.

8. Developmental psychologists are concerned with human growth and the factors that affect change across the life span.

9. Personality psychologists are interested in how we differ from one another and how we act in unique, consistent ways.

10. People in the field of assessment are concerned with measuring personality, achievement, and ability.

11. People in the fields of abnormal, clinical, counseling, school, and community psychology are involved with the understanding, diagnosis, and treatment of a wide range of problems including mental illness, criminal behavior, drug abuse, academic difficulties, and conflict, both within hospital settings and in the community.

12. Social psychologists are concerned with the ways people affect one another. They are interested in such things as attitudes, conformity, liking, prejudice, aggression, and attribution.

13. Environmental psychologists study the relationships between human behavior and the environment, which is increasingly subject to human control.

14. Industrial and organizational psychologists focus on human problems in industrial settings and look for ways to make machines easier and safer to use.

15. Any given psychologist may be involved in and interested in a number of these intertwined areas.

16. Psychology as a whole may be defined as the science that studies behavior, where behavior includes observable behavior, unseen inner mental events, and physiological events.

17. The goals of psychology are to understand, predict, and change behavior, and to improve the quality of human life.

18. The experiment is one of the most powerful data-gathering methods in psychology.

19. Experiments involve independent variables, which are variables that the experimenter manipulates, and dependent variables, which refer to the subject's behavior. An experiment is designed to see if changes in the independent variable will result in systematic changes in the dependent variable.

20. Many experiments involve multiple dependent and independent variables.

21. A control group is a group introduced into an experiment to eliminate an alternative explanation of the results. Assignment to groups is done on a random basis. Tests of statistical significance are used to evaluate experimental findings.

22. The best experiment is one in which neither the subject nor the experimenter knows which condition the subject belongs to. This is called a double-blind experiment.

23. Observation of naturally occurring events is often used when an experiment would be impractical, illegal, or immoral.

24. Tests are widely used as information-gathering instruments.

25. Psychologists use interviews and questionnaires to ask subjects what they think and do rather than observe them do it. Subjects may give false responses to these types of instruments.

26. Case histories, or biographies of specific individuals, are often useful in therapy situations.

27. The correlation coefficient (r) expresses the degree to which two variables vary together. A significant r does not necessarily imply a causal relationship.

28. Ethical issues that concern psychologists include the rights of the subject, risk, informed consent, debriefing, and animal experimentation.

29. Any given event can be viewed from a number of different perspectives. In psychology, any given topic or event can legitimately be studied from (among others) a physiological, a behaviorist, a cognitive, or a psychodynamic approach.

KEY TERMS

abnormal psychology	basic research	control group
applied research	behaviorist approach	correlation coefficient (r)
assessment	clinical psychology	counseling psychology
attribution	cognitive approach	dependent variable
attribution error	cognitive psychology	developmental psychology
avoidance conditioning	community psychology	double-blind technique

emotion

environmental psychology

experiment

face validity

independent variable

industrial psychology

learning

memory

mnemonic technique

motivation

naturalistic observation

perception

personality

physiological approach

physiological psychology

predictive validity

psychodynamic approach

psychology

random assignment

scatter plot

school psychology

selective adaptation

sensation

single-blind technique

social psychology

ADDITIONAL READING

Bausell, R. B. (1986) *A practical guide to conducting empirical research.* New York: Harper & Row.
This is a good presentation of the basics of psychological research methods.

Hergenhahn, B. R. (1986) *An introduction to the history of psychology.* Belmont, CA: Wadsworth.
This text presents a brief, very readable survey of the history of psychology.

Hilgard, E. R. (1987) *Psychology in America: A historical survey.* San Diego: Harcourt Brace Jovanovich.
This resource is probably the best and most complete history of psychology in our country.

Holland, M. K. (1985) *Using psychology.* Boston: Little, Brown.
This text offers some helpful hints about how psychology can be used by the individual in dealing with life.

Schultz, D. P. (1987) *A history of modern psychology.* San Diego: Harcourt Brace Jovanovich.
This is a clear, precise presentation of the basics of American psychology.

2

The Physiological Basis of Behavior

M uch of psychology has to do with the observable behavior of organisms. Quite often we ignore the underlying physiological events within the nervous, glandular, and genetic systems that account for, or are associated with, such behavior. Thus we look at how people walk, talk, sleep, think, learn, eat, and drink without really attending to the physiological aspects of these activities. There is nothing wrong with restricting our attention to observable behaviors. We can, after all, learn a great deal about behavior without ever considering events within the nervous system. But behavior is the result of incredibly complex nervous, glandular, and genetic events within the body. The study of these physiological underpinnings of behavior is a major and expanding area of psychology. *Physiological psychology* is the branch of psychology that seeks to understand the physiological mechanisms that underlie behavior.

Think of it this way. Suppose we own a powerful new computer. Some people will be interested primarily in what the machine can do, while others will want to know how it does what it does. In other words, some people will want to know how to feed information into the machine, how to instruct it, and how to use it. Others will be fascinated by the electronic events within the machine that account for its capabilities. In much the same way, some psychologists are fascinated by the physiology of the human body and wish to understand the complex internal events that account for overt behavior.

This chapter introduces what physiological psychologists have discovered about the machine that we call the human body. We shall discuss the nervous system, the brain as the central organ of the nervous system, the glands, and genetic influences on behavior.

THE NERVOUS SYSTEM: AN OVERVIEW

The term *nervous system* refers to the network of all of the nerve cells in the human body. It forms the primary communication system that enables us to receive, process, and react to information originating both within and outside of the body. The nervous system is subdivided into two major components: the *central nervous system* and the *peripheral nervous system.* The central nervous system is composed of the neural material in the brain and in the spinal cord. Complex decisions, evaluations, and command signals originate in the central nervous system. All other neural material is part of the peripheral system.

As we shall see later, the peripheral nervous system is broken down into further subdivisions (see Figure 2–9). For the present, think of the peripheral system as having two functions. First, it sends information into the central nervous system from the external environment, the muscles, and the organs. Second, the peripheral system sends messages out from the central nervous system to all the muscles and glands of the body. In other words, one portion of the peripheral system is involved in carrying information into the central nervous system, where that information is processed; the other portion of the peripheral system carries the command signals generated within the central nervous system back out to glands and muscles located throughout the body.

LEVEL ONE: THE NEURON

The nervous system of the human body is a vast, intertwined network of electrical and chemical events. To understand it, we must break it down into its components. In our discussion, we will begin with the neuron, a cell that is the basic building block of the entire nervous system. Both the central and the peripheral systems are composed of neurons. As we will see, the neuron is a cell that is specialized for communication within the body. We will then consider functional groups of neurons, the overall nervous system, and, finally, the brain itself.

The Neuron: The Basic Unit

The nervous system, like the rest of the body, is composed of billions of cells. The human brain alone contains about 130 billion cells, although it weighs no more than three pounds. The nervous system contains only two types of cells, however. One type, the **neuron**, is involved in all behavior of the organism, from the detection of the external environment to the functioning of the internal organs of the body, and from locomotion of the body to complex cognitive activities such as learning, thinking, and imagining. The neuron is the basic unit of the nervous system, and it is this specialized cell that is the focus of this section. The other type of cell, which we will not consider in detail, is called the **glial cell.** Although glial cells have long been thought of as functioning solely to provide support services for the neurons, some physiological psychologists now suggest that glial cells may be involved in such neural activities as memory storage (Diamond, Scheibel, Murphy, & Harvey, 1985). We will have to wait for more research before we can draw firm conclusions.

What Does a Neuron Look Like?

We are born with all the neurons we will ever have, and neurons do not regenerate when they die. The brain does increase in weight and mass as we grow, but this increase is due to the further development of neurons already present, and to the growth of glial cells. Neurons die all the time; it has been estimated that each of us loses as many as ten thousand every day of our lives. Fortunately, these losses do not seem to affect us, probably because we start life with millions of neurons to spare.

As cells with the specialized function of communication, neurons have some physical properties that set them apart from other body cells. In addition, depending on their location and particular function, there are even differences *among* neurons. Figure 2–1 illustrates a type of neuron that is found at various sites in the nervous system. Figure 2–2 shows some specialized neurons that are found only at particular locations.

Though they come in a variety of shapes and sizes, all neurons have three main parts: the cell body, the dendrites, and the axon.

The **cell body** of the neuron is composed of jellylike **cytoplasm**, a nucleus, and a cell membrane (see Figure 2–1). The **nucleus** contains the chromosomes and genes that originally determined that the cell

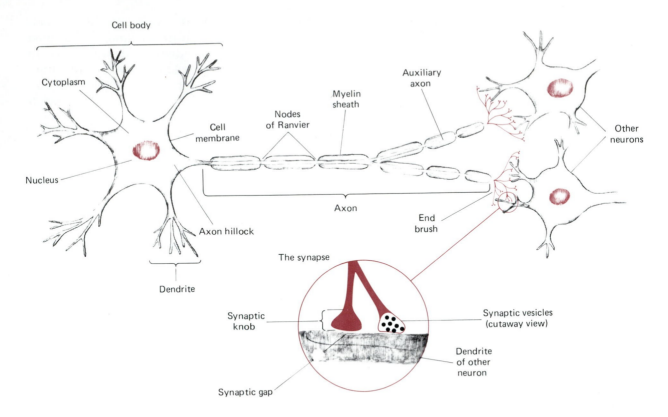

FIGURE 2–1 The Neuron and Its Component Parts *The enlarged insert shows the synapse.*

would grow into a neuron, rather than some other type of cell. The *cell membrane* encloses the nucleus and the cytoplasm and serves as the ''skin'' of the cell.

The surface of the cell body of most neurons is covered with branching, fingerlike projections. These are called *dendrites.* As Figure 2–2 shows, dendrites may be long, spindly, and few in number, or they may form a thick, bushy network.

The third important part of the neuron is the *axon*, a long tail that projects from the cell body. The axon varies in length from a fraction of an inch to several feet, depending on its location in the nervous system.

Figure 2–1 shows that the axons of some neurons are covered with a *myelin sheath.* Wrapped tightly around the axon, this white sheath apparently insulates the axon and may serve to increase the speed of neural transmission. Myelination may take different forms at different locations in the nervous system. For example, in the peripheral nervous system *Schwann cells* wrap themselves around an axon many times (Figure 2–3). As Carlson (1986) puts it, it is something like a fried egg being wrapped around a rope.

Notice also that where the Schwann cells end, the sheath appears pinched. These constricted areas are called *nodes of Ranvier.* At the nodes, the myelin sheath is interrupted and the axon is exposed. The myelin sheath is a recent development in evolution. More recently evolved animals have more myelinated axons than do phylogenetically older animals.

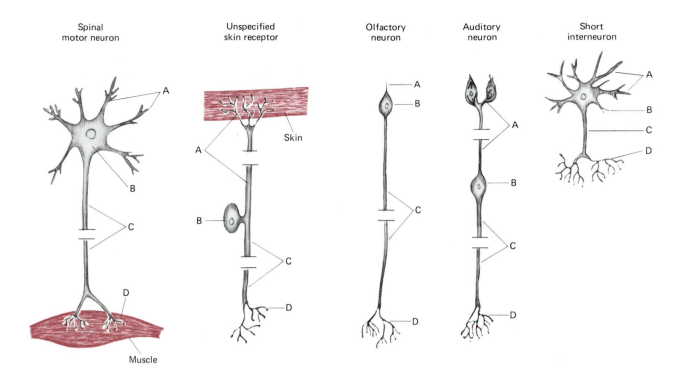

Spinal
motor neuron

Unspecified
skin receptor

Olfactory
neuron

Auditory
neuron

Short
interneuron

Skin

Muscle

FIGURE 2–2   Various Types of
Neurons Found in the Nervous
System   *A: dendrite; B: cell
body; C: axon; D: axon end brush.*

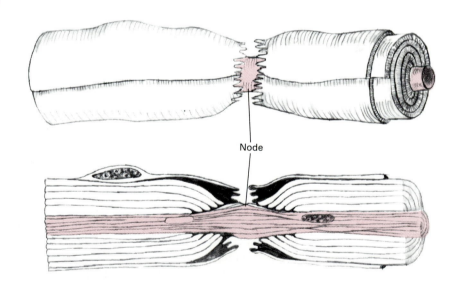

Node

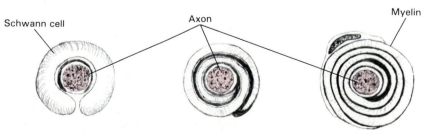

Schwann cell

Axon

Myelin

FIGURE 2–3   Peripheral
Nervous System Myelination
*During development, Schwann
cells tightly wrap themselves many
times around an individual axon to
form one segment of the myelin
sheath.* (After Carlson, 1986)

The myelin sheath is turning out to be very important. There are at least 40 human disorders (multiple sclerosis, for one) that have been tied to problems with the myelin sheath. Researchers have already achieved some success in alleviating animal disorders involving sheath problems by means of genetic manipulation techniques (Maugh, 1987).

As you can see in Figure 2–1, the axon may branch and form an *auxiliary axon.* At the end of the axon or the auxiliary axon, there is another bushy part, aptly called the *end brush.* The enlarged insert in this figure shows how each strand of the end brush terminates in a bulbous structure known as the *synaptic knob.* Inside each synaptic knob there are small structures called *synaptic vesicles*, which function as storage containers for chemicals called *neurotransmitters.* These chemicals are involved in the transmission of a nerve impulse from one neuron to another, as we will see later. The structures shown in the enlarged insert are collectively called the synapse. The *synapse* is the junction point where a nerve impulse passes from the axon of one cell to the dendrite of the next cell.

Although Figure 2–1 depicts the neuron as forming synapses with only two other neurons, most neurons transmit their messages to many others. Similarly, most neurons receive messages from many other neurons. Because of this, there is an astronomical number of different paths by way of which a neural message may be transmitted. Billions of cells are all interconnected; no wonder we seem so complicated to one another!

How a Neuron Works: Three Types of Information Processing

Now that we know a little bit about how a neuron is built, let us focus on how it functions. The messages sent and received by neurons are electrochemical in nature. In general, the dendrites of the neuron are stimulated by the activity of other neurons that communicate with it. This stimulation results in an electrical potential. When this electrical potential builds up to a certain level it causes the firing of an electrical impulse, which travels from the cell body down the axon to the synaptic knobs. This impulse involves energy equal to about one-billionth of a watt and lasts approximately one millisecond at any given point on the neuron. When the electrical impulse reaches the synaptic knobs, it does not jump across to the next neuron. Instead, it causes the chemical neurotransmitters in the synaptic vesicles to be released. These neurotransmitters then travel by diffusion across the *synaptic gap.* The synaptic gap is the tiny space (approximately five-millionths of an inch wide) between the synaptic knob of one neuron and the dendrite of the next neuron (see the insert, Figure 2–1). Once across the synaptic gap these neurotransmitters stimulate the next neuron, and the process begins again.

In short, each neuron serves as a link in the overall neural communication system; it picks up information, carries it along its own length, and passes it on to other neurons. This is a complex task, involving three distinct types of information processing. First, the message must be carried from the dendritic receiving end along the axon to the synaptic knobs, where it can be passed on to other neurons. This type of information processing can be called *axonal con-duction.* Second, the information must be passed on to other neurons across the synaptic gaps. This form of information processing is usually called *synaptic transmission* (Brown & Wallace, 1980). Third, because any given neuron is stimulated by many other neurons, it must have some way of summarizing all this incoming information. This form of information processing is called *integration.* If the incoming information is strong enough, the neuron will fire. We will discuss these three types of information processing in detail in the next three sections.

Type I: Axonal Conduction

Since we have already discussed the parts of a neuron, we will look at axonal conduction first and then move on to the other types of information processing. Although it seems logical, the flow of electricity through a wire is not a good analogy for the way in which the neural impulse moves down the axon. For one thing, the neural impulse travels nowhere near as fast as electricity. While electricity travels near the speed of light, the fastest neural impulse moves at little more than two hundred miles per hour, and some travel only a few feet every second.

Lighting a fuse is a better analogy. Remember what it is like to light a firecracker? If you do not hold the flame close enough, the fuse will not ignite, even though it may become hot. But when the flame is close enough, the fuse ignites—to its full capacity. The size of the flame makes no difference in terms of the amount of ignition. If it ignites at all, it burns just as strongly in response to a small as to a large flame. Once the fuse ignites, you can stand back and watch the burning band move down the fuse, with each burning part igniting the next. The behavior of the neural impulse is similar, except, instead of combustion, an electrical impulse moves down the axon. In addition, the neuron is not used up like a fuse. It can fire over and over again.

The Electrochemical Impulse or Action Potential   What is the nature of this tiny electrical impulse that moves along the axon? As Figure 2–4 shows, the impulse, called an *action potential*, is a two-stage

FIGURE 2–4   The Action Potential   *As the electrochemical impulse travels down the axon toward the end brush, the membrane changes its permeability. Sodium (Na^+) ions rush inside the membrane, depolarizing the cell and creating the action potential. Then potassium (K^+) ions rush out and the resting state is restored.*

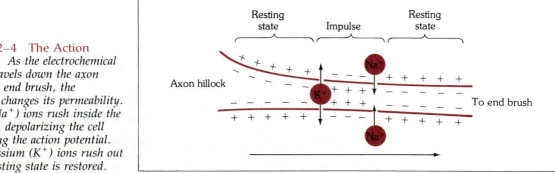

process. The fluid outside the cell and the cytoplasm within the cell are both filled with tiny, electrically charged particles called *ions.* The membrane, or "skin" of the cell, is *differentially permeable* to these different kinds of electrically charged particles. In other words, some kinds of particles can go through the membrane more easily than others. In its resting state, the cell membrane allows potassium ions in and keeps sodium ions out; sodium ions are too large to pass through the pores of the membrane. Because the particles inside and outside the cell are differentially concentrated, there is a small electrical difference across the membrane at the resting state: the inside is slightly more negative than the outside, and the cell is said to be *polarized.*

When the cell body is stimulated by the preceding neurons, the membrane at the point where the axon emerges from the cell body suddenly changes its permeability. This event initiates the actual appearance of the action potential. Sodium ions come rushing inside the membrane. Through this process the inside of the cell becomes positively charged relative to the outside. When this happens, the cell is said to be *depolarized.* This reversal of electrical charge induces the next section of the membrane to become permeable, and so on, all the way to the end of the axon. Immediately after sodium ions come rushing in, positively charged potassium ions go rushing out through the membrane, and the resting state is restored. Thus the action potential is created by the rapid exchange of charged particles through the "skin" of the axon.

The impulse does not diminish in strength as it travels. It is the same size when it reaches the end brush as it was when it began, even though it may have traveled as far as two or three feet. Furthermore, the impulse travels in one direction only—from the beginning of the axon, or *axon hillock*, to the end brush. It does not travel back into the cell body from the axon.

What Determines Impulse Speed? The speed of the impulse depends on such things as the diameter of the axon and the presence or absence of myelin. Impulses travel faster down thick axons than down thin axons, and impulses in myelinated neurons move faster than impulses in neurons without myelin.

The All-or-None Principle Like a firecracker fuse, neurons fire at their full capacity, or not at all, depending on whether they are stimulated sufficiently to cause them to reach their firing threshold. This is known as the *all-or-none principle.* A given neuron will fire more often if it is stimulated by more neurons, but the size and speed of the impulse will not increase as the number of stimulating neurons is increased. Firing always occurs in an all-or-none fashion.

The Refractory Period The refractory period is a short period of time (a few thousandths of a second) following the firing of an impulse when the cell becomes insensitive to stimulation and is temporarily incapable of firing again. The point of least excitability, called the *absolute refractory period*, occurs immediately after the cell's initial firing. During this period, the cell is incapable of firing again, no matter how strong the stimulation. Gradually, sensitivity returns to the neu-

FIGURE 2–5 Absolute and
Relative Refractory Periods
*For the first 2 msec following the
firing of the neuron, the neuron is
incapable of firing again, no
matter how strong the stimulation.
This is the absolute refractory
period. For the next 4 msec, the
neuron can fire if it receives
greater than normal stimulation.
This is the relative refractory
period. About 6 msec after firing,
this hypothetical neuron will fire
again if given normal stimulation.*

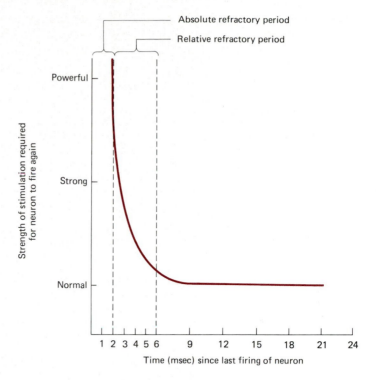

ron. If the cell is stimulated during the latter part of its refractory
period (which is called the ***relative refractory period***), it may fire, but
only if the stimulus is strong. Some neurons recover rapidly and are
capable of firing as many as 1,000 times per second. Others may be
able to fire only a few times per second (see Figure 2–5).

Type II: Synaptic Transmission and Neurotransmitters

We have looked at the structure of the neuron and at the movement
of an impulse along the axon. Now let us focus on what happens in
the synaptic gap when a message is sent from one neuron to the next.
This is the second type of information processing that each neuron
performs (Bear, Cooper, & Ebner, 1987).

   When an electrical impulse travels down the axon and reaches
the synaptic knob, it stimulates the synaptic vesicles to release the
chemical neurotransmitter they contain (see Figure 2–6). (There is
some controversy concerning the source of neurotransmitters. While
some authors state that the neurotransmitters come from the synaptic
vesicles, others feel that the substances originate in the background
cytoplasm of the synaptic knob and not in the vesicles [see Dunant &
Israel, 1985].) This neurotransmitter then crosses the synaptic gap and
is taken up by specialized receptor sites on the receiving dendrite or
cell body of the next neuron. This is a complex process, but a quick
one. The entire synaptic event can occur in a few thousandths of a
second.

   The chemical neurotransmitters that are discharged from one
neuron and deposited on the next neuron have one of two effects. In
one type of synapse, the transmitter substance increases the permeability of the next neuron and thus depolarizes that cell, contributing

FIGURE 2–6 The Synapse

When an action potential travels along the axon to the synaptic knob, it stimulates release of the neurotransmitter from the synaptic vesicles into the synaptic gap. The neurotransmitter crosses the gap and is taken up by the receptor sites on the receiving neuron. In one type of synapse the neurotransmitter increases the probability of the next neuron's firing, while in another type of synapse, the neurotransmitter reduces the chance of firing.

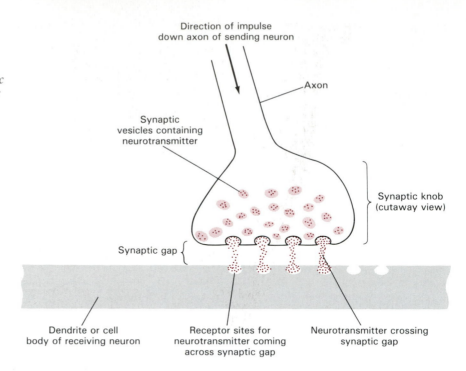

to the initiation of a new impulse. In the second type of synapse, the chemical neurotransmitter causes the next neuron to become even more polarized, and thus even less likely to fire.

Some neuroscientists have compared this situation to the existence of both a gas pedal and a brake pedal in a car. If we had only excitatory synapses a runaway condition could result, comparable to driving without brakes. Without both excitatory and inhibitory synapses we might not be able to integrate the variety of messages received from the surface receptors, make the fine adjustments necessary for the performance of complex behaviors or control our vital body functions.

Although we do not yet know exactly how many different transmitter substances there are, many have been identified. Some synapses employ *acetylcholine (ACh)*, while others use a chemical known as *norepinephrine.* Still others use *serotonin.* (See Table 2–1.) The evidence suggests that a given neuron can produce more than one kind of transmitter; during communication with other cells, one or more of these chemicals may be released (Chan-Palay et al., 1982). Release of multiple transmitters can occur simultaneously in certain instances (Black et al., 1987).

Certain chemical substances interfere with synapses. We are speaking here of chemicals found in the external environment, not substances normally appearing within the body. If these substances invade the body, they may interfere with neural transmission in a number of ways. For example, botulism is caused by botulinus toxin, found in some spoiled canned foods. The toxin prevents the release of acetylcholine and so may cause fatal respiratory paralysis. Curare,

TABLE 2–1   Probable Transmitter Substances

Probable Transmitter Substance	Location	Hypothesized Effect
Acetylcholine (ACh)	Brain, spinal cord, autonomic ganglia, target organs of the parasympathetic nervous system	Excitation in brain and autonomic ganglia, excitation or inhibition in target organs
Norepinephrine (NE)	Brain, spinal cord, target organs of sympathetic nervous system	Inhibition in brain, excitation or inhibition in target organs
Dopamine (DA)	Brain	Inhibition
Serotonin (5-hydroxy-tryptamine, or 5-HT)	Brain, spinal cord	Inhibition
Gamma-aminobutyric acid (GABA)	Brain (especially cerebral and cerebellar cortex), spinal cord	Inhibition
Glycine	Spinal cord interneurons	Inhibition
Glutamic acid	Brain, spinal sensory neurons	Excitation
Aspartic acid	Spinal cord interneurons, brain (?)	Excitation
Substance P	Brain, spinal sensory neurons (pain)	Excitation (and inhibition?)
Histamine, taurine, other amino acids; peptides such as oxytocin and endogenous opiates; many others	Various regions of brain, spinal cord, and peripheral nervous system	(?)

Source: After Carlson, 1986.

a poison used by South American Indians to tip arrows, occupies the postsynaptic receptor sites of victims and thus prevents ACh from stimulating the postsynaptic membrane. This poison (now used by certain Indian groups only to hunt monkeys and other small animals) kills by paralyzing the muscles involved in breathing. Certain types of nerve gases developed for military purposes destroy the enzyme *acetylcholinesterase (AChE)*, which ordinarily deactivates ACh. This leads to a buildup of acetylcholine and prevents further synaptic transmissions. Transmitters other than acetylcholine may also be affected by foreign substances that invade the body. For example, the tranquilizer chlorpromazine inhibits the synaptic release of norepinephrine so that neural transmission is decreased.

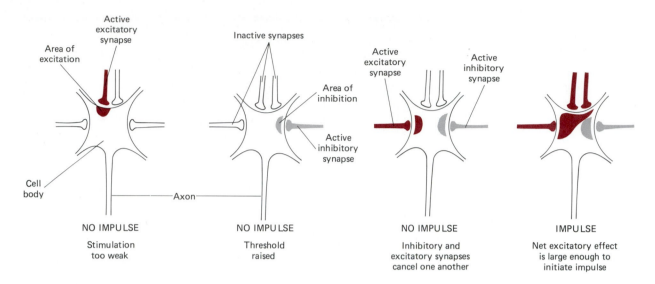

FIGURE 2–7 A Schematic
Representation of Integration
*The algebraic sum of excitatory
and inhibitory synapses at a cell
body determines whether a neuron
will fire.*

Type III: Integration

Integration is the third type of information processing performed by
the neuron. Each neuron is stimulated by many other neurons, so the
situation is not simple. Some of this stimulation is excitatory, while
some of it is inhibitory. Stimulations from other neurons can come in
rapid sequence or they can be spaced out in time. Multiple stimulations can occur in small localized areas or they can be spread out over
the dendrites and cell body of the receiving neuron. Some of the stimulation comes in waves and patterns. The neuron must process all of
this information and either fire or not fire. In short, integration is a
very complex process and it is not yet well understood.

Figure 2–7 shows a simplified version of a single neuron being
stimulated in different ways. Apparently, all neurons have sites
where excitation occurs and sites where inhibition occurs. The cell
body and dendrites of most neurons are surrounded by synaptic
knobs from other neurons. At any given moment, some of these synaptic knobs are active and some are not. The algebraic sum of the excitatory and inhibitory synapses determines whether a particular neuron
will fire. If there are either too few excitatory synapses or too many
inhibitory synapses, the neuron will not fire. If the firing threshold is
reached, a step that usually involves many excitatory synapses, then
the cell fires an impulse.

LEVEL TWO: FUNCTIONAL GROUPS OF NEURONS

In the preceding discussion, we focused solely on single neurons and
their relationships with their immediate neighbors. Obviously there
is more to the nervous system than these elements and relationships.
We now turn to the next higher level of organization, which consists
of functional groups of neurons.

Types of Groups

Neurons are arranged in several distinct kinds of groupings within
the body. First, the cell bodies of certain neurons group together at

various places in the nervous system. When one of these cell body clusters is located inside the brain or spinal cord, it is called a *nucleus.* A single nucleus is too small to form an important structure of the nervous system, but groups of nuclei may form larger structures, such as the hypothalamus in the brain. When a cell body cluster is found outside the brain and spinal cord it is called a *ganglion.* There are chains of ganglia that run parallel to the spinal cord on each side of the backbone. A second distinct grouping of neurons is formed of axons and dendrites, which also tend to cluster together. A bundle of axons, and sometimes dendrites, is called a *tract* when it is found running from one place to another in the brain or in the spinal cord. When these fiber bundles are found outside the brain and spinal cord, they are called *nerves.* The optic nerve, for example, is a bundle of axons that have their cell bodies in the retina of the eye.

The axons that compose the nerves are myelinated. Myelin is white in color, so nerves are white. Cell bodies, on the other hand, are gray in color. Since most of the cell body clusters are found in the brain, they lend their color to brain tissue. This is why the brain is referred to as "gray matter."

Afferent, Efferent, and Interneuron Groups

We can identify neuron groupings according to the direction of the messages they carry. *Afferent* groups, having their dendrites in the eyes, ears, skin, and other sense organs, carry messages inward to the spinal cord and brain. *Efferent* groups carry messages from the brain and spinal cord outward by synapsing on the muscles and glands. Impulses from efferent groups make it possible for us to move about in the environment. A simple way to remember these relationships is to use the SAME acronym, or **S**ensory = **A**fferent, **M**otor = **E**fferent.

Connecting neurons, called *interneurons*, receive stimulation from afferent groups, and they synapse on efferent groups. As their name implies, these connecting groups integrate incoming messages from afferent groups and coordinate the outgoing messages of the efferent groups. Most of the neurons in the brain are interneurons.

Activity involving the brain requires afferent neurons, efferent neurons, and interneurons, but there is some neural action involving these three groups that does not involve the brain, as the simple reflex arc in Figure 2–8 shows. Reflex arcs like this help you keep your balance without having to clear each message through your brain. Other reflex arcs serve to pull your hand away from a hot object before you are consciously aware of the heat. In short, acting before you think is not always a bad idea.

LEVEL THREE: THE NERVOUS SYSTEM

We can now consider the nervous system as a whole. We will look first at the overall structure of the nervous system and then, in the next section, focus on the brain as the central element in our nervous apparatus.

Although all the various parts of the nervous system work together in an interdependent manner, it is easier to understand the

FIGURE 2–8   A Simple Reflex
Arc   *In this example, free nerve
endings in the skin, when
appropriately stimulated, transmit
signals along the sensory neuron to
an interneuron in the spinal cord.
The interneuron transmits the
impulse to a motor neuron. As a
result of the stimulation of the
motor neuron, muscle fibers
contract.* (After Curtis, 1985)

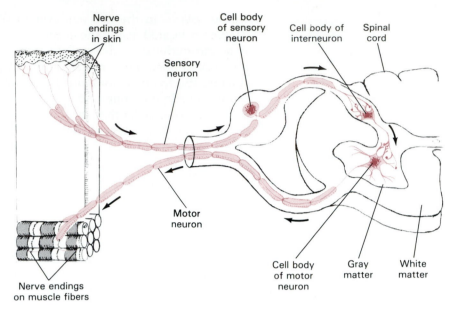

structure and functions of the system if we divide it into a number of
parts and consider each separately. As we have seen, the first important distinction is between the peripheral and central nervous systems. Each of these can be subdivided further (Figure 2–9), according
to the nervous tissue structures that they include.

The *peripheral nervous system* includes the nerves and ganglia
that connect the sense organs, muscles, glands, and internal organs
with the spinal cord and brain. The *central nervous system* includes
the brain and the spinal cord. Thus, the central nervous system in-

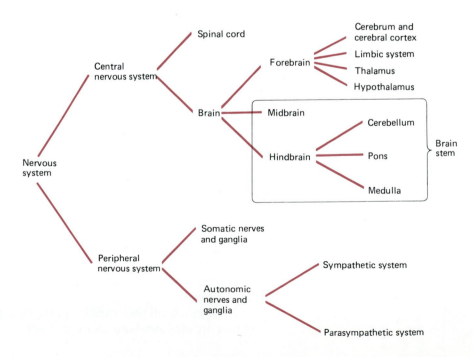

FIGURE 2–9   Organization of
the Nervous System

cludes most of the neurons in the body. The central nervous system may be thought of as the integrating and coordinating center for all body functions and behavior. The peripheral nervous system brings information into and out of the central nervous system. Some neurons begin in one system and end in the other.

The Peripheral Nervous System

The peripheral system forms a nerve network between the brain and spinal cord and all parts of the body. Without the peripheral nervous system we would be unable to move about or to know anything about the external environment. The peripheral system brings information into the central nervous system and carries commands back out to the muscles.

In addition, our internal organs would not function without the peripheral nervous system. Thus the peripheral system seems to have two basic functions, one relating to the external environment and one relating to the internal environment. The division of the peripheral system relating to the external world is called the **somatic** division, while the portion relating to the internal world is called the **autonomic** division (see Figure 2–10). We will consider each of these divisions, beginning with the somatic.

The Somatic Division   The somatic division of the peripheral system is composed of the afferent neurons that bring sensory information in from the outer parts of the body and the efferent neurons that send

FIGURE 2–10   The Peripheral Nerves and Their Locations
This drawing includes the nerves serving the somatic system and those serving the sympathetic and the parasympathetic divisions of the autonomic system.

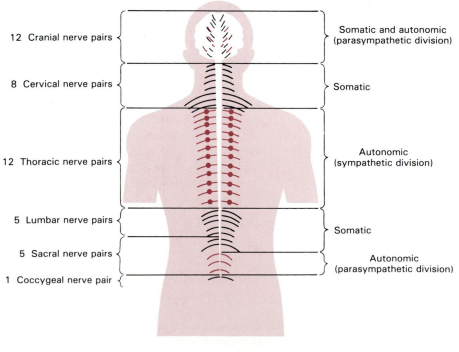

12 Cranial nerve pairs

8 Cervical nerve pairs

12 Thoracic nerve pairs

5 Lumbar nerve pairs

5 Sacral nerve pairs

1 Coccygeal nerve pair

Somatic and autonomic (parasympathetic division)

Somatic

Autonomic (sympathetic division)

Somatic

Autonomic (parasympathetic division)

——— Somatic system   ——— Autonomic system

This Special Olympics participant has suffered efferent neuron damage and thus experiences paralysis of the muscles served by those neurons.

information from the brain and spinal cord out to the skeletal muscles. (Remember the SAME acronym: **S**ensory = **A**fferent, **M**otor = **E**fferent.) Although they send impulses in opposite directions, many of these afferent and efferent neurons are bound together in the same nerves for most of their length. The afferent neurons tell the brain what is "out there," the brain decides what to do about it, and the efferent neurons carry the brain's commands to the skeletal muscles.

Damage to afferent somatic neurons can result in a loss of sensation in the body part serviced by those neurons. Destruction of efferent somatic neurons can result in paralysis of the muscles in the part of the body served by those neurons. Since destroyed neurons are not replaced, these conditions may be permanent.

The Autonomic Division   The autonomic division of the peripheral nervous system consists of the nerve network that extends to various internal parts of the body and exercises control over the glands, the smooth muscles, and the heart. Smooth muscles are located in the blood vessels, the stomach and intestinal walls, and in some other internal organs. They get their name from the fact that they are not striped in appearance as are the skeletal muscles.

The autonomic nervous system derives its name from the fact that it appears to operate as an independent system of control. It controls many of our body processes without requiring any conscious effort from us. We do learn to control some autonomic functions, such as urination and defecation, but these functions would be carried out even if we did not learn such control. The autonomic system controls such things as constriction of our blood vessels, the action of our sweat glands, and the activity of our adrenal glands. In general, it controls involuntary actions.

The autonomic division is further divided into two parts, the sympathetic and the parasympathetic systems. Although many organs receive input from both systems, these systems are different from one another in structure and in the manner in which they operate. As Figure 2–11 shows, the ganglia, or clumps of neurons that form the *sympathetic system*, are interconnected so that they form a long vertical chain on each side of the spinal cord. It is because of these interconnections that the sympathetic system acts as a unit. When one organ is affected, all organs under the control of this system are affected. It was this interconnected quality that led to the name of the system. It was called "sympathetic" because early scientists believed it was responsible for making internal organs work "in sympathy."

The *parasympathetic* ganglia, on the other hand, are more scattered than are those of the sympathetic system. In general, they are located near the organs they affect. Since they are less interconnected than those of the sympathetic system, they tend to act less as a unit, and in a more piecemeal fashion.

As you can see in Figure 2–11, these two systems affect the same organs, but they act in an opposing manner. For example, while the sympathetic neurons cause the pupil in the eye to dilate, neurons in the parasympathetic system cause it to constrict. While digestive ac-

FIGURE 2–11   The Sympathetic
and Parasympathetic Systems of
the Autonomic Nervous System
*Effects on various body structures
are listed for each subsystem.*

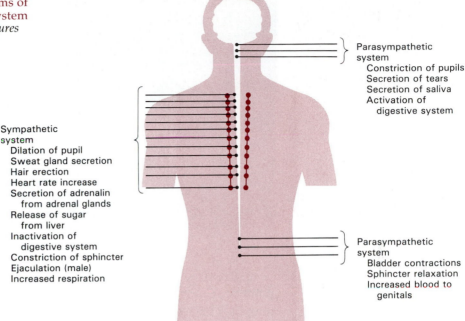

Parasympathetic
system
    Constriction of pupils
    Secretion of tears
    Secretion of saliva
    Activation of
        digestive system

Sympathetic
system
    Dilation of pupil
    Sweat gland secretion
    Hair erection
    Heart rate increase
    Secretion of adrenalin
        from adrenal glands
    Release of sugar
        from liver
    Inactivation of
        digestive system
    Constriction of sphincter
    Ejaculation (male)
    Increased respiration

Parasympathetic
system
    Bladder contractions
    Sphincter relaxation
    Increased blood to
        genitals

tivity is increased by the parasympathetic system, it is decreased by
the sympathetic. Because the autonomic nervous system has influence or control in both directions, the internal environment can be
kept in a balanced state.

The sympathetic system prepares our bodies to deal with emergency situations. It readies us for "fight or flight." When animals are
given chemicals that deactivate the neurotransmitters of the sympathetic system, they have trouble learning to escape from electric shock
(Lord, King, & Pfister, 1976). The activation of this system accounts
for the surge of energy you feel when you are angered or badly frightened. When we see the hair rise on the back of an angry animal or
feel "goose bumps" while we watch a scary movie, we know the sympathetic system is operating. This system can speed up the heart,
send blood to the muscles, and release sugar from the liver for quick
energy.

The parasympathetic system predominates when we are relaxed
or inactive, or when an emergency has passed. This system also carries out the body's maintenance needs. It promotes digestion, provides for the elimination of wastes, directs tissue repair, and restores
the supply of body energy.

The two parts of the autonomic nervous system are not totally
independent, however. There are occasions when they work together, rather than antagonistically. The sexual response in the male
is an example of a behavior in which the two systems cooperate. The
parasympathetic system is necessary for the erection of the penis,
while the sympathetic system is engaged for ejaculation. As an additional example, imagine a young child rounding a corner and finding
an enormous, snarling dog. The child would be terrified (action of the

Activation of this buck's sympathetic system permits it to flee danger. A hunter witnessing the animal's flight probably would experience a surge of energy also.

sympathetic system) and might also urinate involuntarily (a parasympathetic response). The point to be made here is that the nervous system is very complex, and our neat, convenient distinctions sometimes oversimplify what actually occurs.

The Central Nervous System

We are now ready to explore the great integrating network known as the central nervous system. First we will look briefly at the general system, and then we will focus in detail on the brain.

The *spinal cord* (see Figure 2–12) is a thick cable of nerve fibers that runs up the interior of the bony spinal column to the brain and carries electrical impulses in both directions. Although some of the messages entering the spinal cord stimulate motor neurons that extend beyond the cord in a reflex circuit, most messages are relayed up the spinal cord to various parts of the brain. Because of this function, the spinal cord can be considered a trunkline by which the periphery of the body communicates with the brain.

Neural Development

If we look at the human organism in the fetal stage of life, we can see that the structure of the nervous system emerges from a single tube of neural tissue (Figure 2–13). The lower part of this tube will become the spinal cord. As development progresses, the lower part of the tube puts out streaks of neural tissue along its length; this tissue will become the peripheral nervous system. The top of the tube swells into an enlargement that will become the brain. This upper enlargement grows rapidly, and separate sections can soon be distinguished. The *hindbrain* is the lowest section of the upper end of the neural tube. The next section is called the *midbrain.* Finally, the *forebrain* is the section that develops at the very top of the neural tube.

All brain structures are present in the newborn child. However, these structures require time to develop fully. This is one reason that

FIGURE 2–12 A Segment of the Human Spinal Cord *Each spinal nerve divides into two fiber bundles at the vertebral column— the sensory root and the motor root. The sympathetic ganglia, which form a chain, are part of the autonomic nervous system. The butterfly-shaped gray matter within the spinal cord is composed mostly of interneurons, cell bodies of motor neurons, and glial cells. The surrounding white matter consists of ascending and descending fiber tracts. (After Curtis & Barnes, 1985)*

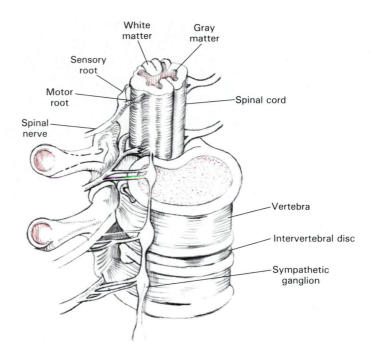

FIGURE 2–13 The Human Brain at Four Stages of Development *(After Kalat, 1984)*

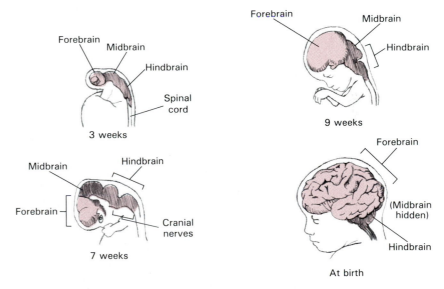

newborn children cannot walk, while many animals, such as horses, can walk at birth. As noted, neurons do continue to grow after birth. They multiply, not in number, but in size and complexity. Not only do they become larger, but the complexity of their dendritic networks increases. Thus the adult human brain is considerably more complex than the fetal brain in both its structure and its function.

THE BRAIN

The brain is the culmination of neural development. It is this structure that truly sets us apart from the rest of the animal kingdom. No other species possesses a brain as highly developed as ours. The

 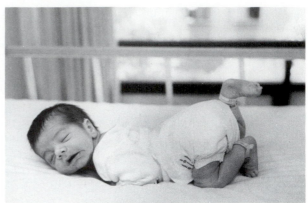

The brain of a newborn foal is more developed that the brain of a two-day-old human infant, enabling the foal to walk at birth. But before long the superiority of the human brain will begin to assert itself.

enormous importance of the brain in our lives more than justifies the time we will spend discussing its development, structure, and function in the pages that follow.

Some people compare the human brain to our best computers and think of it as a data processing system. But the brain probably has far greater capacity and versatility than any machine we have ever developed. Consider, for example, its immense storage capacities. We all have memories of events that occurred early in our childhood. Some memories are very old. Have you ever listened to your grandmother reminisce about events that occurred fifty or sixty years ago? The events may not have been particularly significant, and yet they can be retrieved with great clarity. We sometimes play trivia games, trying to answer such questions as "Who won the World Series in 1970?" The fact that we *can* answer these questions is a testimonial to our memory capacity.

The brain has the ability to contemplate and examine itself. Questions such as "Who am I?" and "Why am I here?" have occurred to all of us. Furthermore, the brain has the ability to change itself (and even to destroy itself). There is evidence that physical changes occur in the brain as learning takes place. In addition, when a portion of the brain is missing at birth, or is later damaged, other sections of the brain can often take over the functions of the missing or destroyed tissue. Clearly, most machines do not possess these capacities.

The brain is extremely versatile. Parts of it act like sensory organs. For example, some brain cells sense changes in the composition of the blood and cause other cells to make appropriate adjustments. Other brain cells act as if they were glands; they produce hormonal substances. Still other cells act like executive secretaries; they evaluate signals and decide if they should be brought to the attention of other parts of the brain.

Techniques for Brain Study

Before we discuss the structure and functions of the brain, it would be helpful to consider the methods physiological psychologists use in studying this great neural structure. Typically, study of the brain is carried out by some combination of four basic techniques: *lesions* or surgical ablation, electrical or chemical *stimulation, recordings* of the electrical activity produced in the brain, and *scanning techniques.*

Lesions and Surgical Ablation   Having noted that injury to the brain results in behavioral disorders, early scientists began experimenting with procedures that destroy the tissue at particular brain sites in animals. Basically, there are two ways this destruction can be accomplished. One involves surgically cutting or removing neural tissue, a process called ablation. The other procedure uses a wire electrode inserted into a particular brain site to cause a lesion, or small injury. In the latter procedure, an electrical impulse of greater voltage than those occurring naturally in the brain is delivered to the site. This "burns out" a small area surrounding the electrode.

Following the ablation or lesion, the animal's behavior is observed carefully to see if there are immediate or delayed changes, and to see if the changes disappear with time, retraining, or therapy. For example, a lesion made at a particular site in a rat's hypothalamus stimulates extreme overeating. The rat eventually becomes grossly overweight (Teitelbaum, 1975). A lesion made at a nearby site in the hypothalamus results in just the opposite effect. The rat stops eating and will starve to death unless it is force fed. However, some investigators (Freed, de Medinaceli, & Wyatt, 1985) have found that the effects of damage to some parts of the brain can be overcome with certain drugs or specialized training procedures.

Electrical and Chemical Stimulation   The electrical stimulation technique also uses an electrode that is inserted into the brain of a living animal, but the electrical current used is too weak to cause damage. If we adjust the current carefully, the brain tissue seems to accept the stimulation almost as if it had been self-generated. A brain site can be gently stimulated in this manner, and the resulting behavior can be accepted as behavior that would also have been the result of natural brain activity. In a sense, we "fool" the brain. In the classic study mentioned in Chapter 1 (Olds & Milner, 1954), an electrode was implanted in the brain of a living rat and tied into a control mechanism that the rat could operate. Stimulation of this particular brain site apparently results in an extremely pleasurable sensation. The rat would forego food, water, and sex in order to stimulate its own brain. The animal would even tolerate pain in order to operate the control lever that stimulated its brain.

The electrical stimulation method has been used during human brain surgery to map out areas of defective tissue that need to be removed. In this procedure, the patient is given a local anesthetic for the opening of the skull, but remains awake during the mapping of defective tissue. (The brain itself contains no cells that act as pain receptors, so it does not hurt to touch the exposed brain. This also means that headaches are not due to pain in the brain.) To map the brain the surgeon uses an electrode that resembles a pencil. Various spots on the brain are touched lightly, and the patient reports the sensations that accompany these stimulations. Vivid memories, sensory experiences, and a wide variety of thoughts have been reported. These mapping operations have added to our growing store of knowledge concerning the functions of various parts of the brain.

Electrical techniques have been used in treatment efforts as well as in research projects. *Electroconvulsive shock treatment* has led a checkered career as outlined in the box titled "Shocking the Brains of Depressed People."

The chemical stimulation technique, used primarily with animals, involves the insertion of a thin tube, so that the open end touches the area of the brain being studied. A smaller tube is filled with a few crystals of a chemical substance and inserted into the implanted tube. The chemical is then released at the stimulation site. The type of chemical used depends on the nature of the study. However, it is generally a substance that is believed to affect synaptic transmission. The introduction of these chemicals stimulates behavior in a manner similar to that produced by electrical stimulation. The advantage of chemical stimulation is that the effects last longer than those induced by electrical stimulation, and thus provide a longer observation period. Like electrical stimulation, chemical stimulation has the advantage of not permanently affecting the animal's body.

Recording of Neural Activity Just as it is possible to put electrical impulses into the brain, it is also possible to record them as they appear naturally in the brain of the living organism. There are two basic ways to make such recordings. First, electrodes may be pasted to the individual's scalp and connected to a recording device called an electroencephalograph that translates the gross electrical activity of the brain into a line of pen tracings on a roll of paper. This method produces what is called an *electroencephalogram*, or *EEG.* It is this method that led to the coining of the term *brain wave*. Although this recording method may appear fairly primitive and generalized, it can be used easily with humans, and a great deal of important knowledge about different mental states has been accumulated from its use. The greatest advances in our understanding of epilepsy have occurred since the development of the EEG. The wave pattern of the brain during an epileptic seizure is quite different from any pattern produced by the normal brain.

Second, it is possible to record the activity of a single neuron in the brain of a living animal. The development of the microelectrode, which is about one ten-thousandth of a millimeter in diameter, permitted this breakthrough. Implantation of such an electrode in the brain allows the scientist to observe the behavior of a specific neuron, without having to contend with the "noise" that is picked up from neighboring neurons by larger electrodes. Many intriguing results have been obtained using the microelectrode technique. For example, if certain sounds are presented to an animal, electrodes planted deep within the animal's brain can detect the activity of certain individual cells. However, if other sounds are presented, then other individual cells will react within the brain.

◆ *SHOCKING THE BRAINS OF DEPRESSED PEOPLE*

Electroconvulsive shock-therapy (ECT) has had a stormy, up-and-down history. The origin of this therapy was in a belief, never firmly established or refuted, that epileptics have a partial immunity to schizophrenia. Based on this belief, attempts were made to treat schizophrenia by large doses of insulin to cause seizures. Insulin shock, however, had numerous drawbacks. Ugo Cerletti, after years of experimentation with animals, developed a method of inducing seizures by an electric shock across the head (Cerletti & Bini, 1938). Electroconvulsive shock (ECT) was quicker than insulin and less medically dangerous; patients awakened calmly and usually did not remember the shock.

ECT had some apparently beneficial effects for some schizophrenics but proved to be more helpful in depression. It developed a bad reputation during a period of excessive use. Some patients were given ECT a hundred times or more, without their consent. When antidepressive drugs became available, ECT passed out of favor.

In more recent years, ECT has returned to use with some major modifications. It is now used almost exclusively for treating a small minority of people with endogenous depression, with even rarer use for schizophrenia. It can be used only with the patient's permission, and even then it is usually limited to six to eight applications, on alternate days. To reduce the intensity of side effects, the intensity of the shock has been greatly reduced from earlier practice, and it is now often applied to one side of the brain only. Muscle relaxants or mild anesthetics are given to minimize discomfort and the possibility of injury.

ECT is now used mostly for three kinds of endogenously depressed patients (Scovern & Kilmann, 1980; Weiner, 1979). First, it is used for patients who have not responded to any of the antidepressant drugs; ECT produces good results in most of these patients (Paul, Extein, Calil, Potter, Chodoff, & Goodwin, 1981). Second, it is used for patients with suicidal tendencies. ECT decreases the risk of suicide simply because it acts faster, usually having antidepressant effects in a week or less, as compared to two or three weeks with drugs. Third, ECT has proved particularly effective for those depressed patients who also suffer from delusions. The effects of ECT are long-lasting (usually at least a period of months, in many cases years) but not permanent; a relapse can be prevented in most cases by antidepressant drugs.

There is still much uncertainty about how ECT exerts its effects. One possibility is that it decreases receptor sensitivity at presynaptic inhibitory receptors (Chiodo & Antelman, 1980). It also increases brain concentrations of tyrosine hydroxylase, an enzyme that is critical for the synthesis of catecholamines (Masserano, Takimoto, & Weiner, 1981). In addition, ECT increases hormone release from the hypothalamus and pituitary (Fink, 1980).

ECT remains a controversial therapy. In 1982, the citizens of Berkeley, California, voted to make it illegal in their city. One major reason for the opposition to ECT is that it causes a state of confusion and both retrograde and anterograde amnesia in many patients (Summers, Robins, & Reich, 1979). The cognitive and memory losses can be reduced, without interfering with the antidepressant effects, by using lower intensity shock and by applying the ECT to just one side of the brain (Miller, Small, Milstein, Malloy, & Stout, 1981). Squire, Wetzel, and Slater (1979), using a variety of laboratory tests of memory, found that people's demonstrable memory deficits dissipated steadily during the first one to six months after ECT; the complaints about memory loss lasted several months longer. It is possible that subtle but real deficits last longer than the laboratory tests reveal. It is also possible that the memory deficits that patients experienced early after ECT cause them to be more aware of the normal forgetfulness that all of us have.

From *Biological Psychology*, Second Edition, by James W. Kalat © 1984, 1981 by Wadsworth, Inc. Reprinted by permission of the publisher.

CATs, PETs, and NMRs: The Scanning Techniques

The last twenty years have witnessed the development of dramatic new techniques that allow us to see what is going on inside the human brain without actually opening up the skull. We will briefly mention three such techniques, all of them based on sophisticated computer technology.

CAT Scan In **computerized axial tomography** (CAT) the subject's head is placed in a large doughnut-shaped apparatus. An X-ray source is located on one side of the doughnut and an X-ray detector on the other. The X-ray beam is passed through the subject's head and the amount of it that penetrates the brain is detected on the other side. The brain is scanned in successive slices, like a package of luncheon meat. Numerous measurements are taken and the data is then fed into a computer. The result of all of this is a series of two-dimensional pictures of what is going on inside the brain. Clearly, CAT scans are extremely helpful because they can assist surgeons to decide when, where, and how to operate. Tumors, blood clots, injuries, and degenerative diseases can be identified "from the outside." CAT scans are useful to psychologists because they can help eliminate or confirm physical bases for behavioral problems.

PET Scan **Positron emission tomography** (PET) permits the surgeon to determine the amount of metabolic activity going on inside the brain. First, the patient is injected with radioactive glucose. This substance tends to accumulate in areas of the brain that are especially active metabolically. Using a machine similar to the CAT scanner, pictures of slices of the brain are produced that clearly indicate different levels of activity (see Color Plates 4 and 5).

NMR Scan **Nuclear magnetic resonance** (NMR) is another recently developed method for looking inside the head. The NMR scanner resembles the CAT scanner, but NMR uses a magnetic field instead of X-rays to make measurements of the variations in levels of activity in the brain. The patient's head is passed through a powerful magnetic field. Using sophisticated equipment, this procedure also leads to valuable picture-slices of the living human brain.

The Hindbrain

Now that we know something about experimental techniques, we can begin our discussion of the three major portions of the brain: the

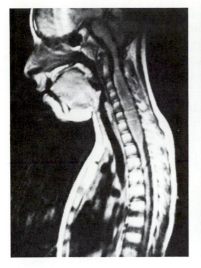

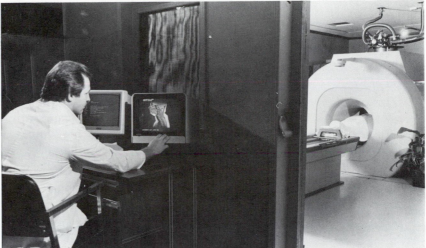

This lateral profile (above) made using NMR enables researchers to view the soft tissues of the brain and spinal cord. The NMR scanner (right) resembles the CAT scanner, but the NMR uses a magnetic field and sophisticated computer technology to measure internal activity levels in the body.

hindbrain, **midbrain**, and **forebrain.** We will start by considering the elements that comprise the hindbrain, or lowest portion of the brain.

The Medulla   The **medulla** can be identified in Figure 2–14 as a swelling on the lower brain stem. The medulla contains a number of important nuclei. Some of these nuclei belong to the autonomic nervous system and help to control breathing, heart rate, and blood pressure. Other nuclei serve as relay and routing stations for nerve fibers coming in from the cranial nerves. Still others serve a similar function for sensory and motor tracts carried by the spinal cord.

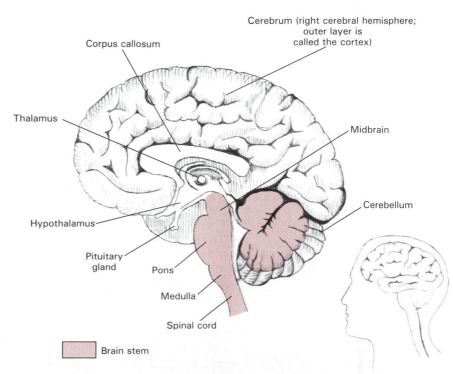

FIGURE 2–14   The Human Brain and Some of Its Components   *This view shows the inner face of the right cerebral hemisphere. The brain stem is shown in color. The reticular activating system is not shown but may be thought of as the "core" of the brain stem.*

The Cerebellum By looking at Figure 2–14 and the photographs on page 69, you can locate the *cerebellum,* which is composed of two creased or convoluted lobes that fit snugly under the cap of the brain. The main function of the cerebellum is to smooth out and coordinate muscular activities. Electrical stimulation of certain points in the cerebellum of an experimental animal produces postural changes, agitation, circling, and muscle spasms (Buchholz, 1976). It is the cerebellum that enables us to stand upright and to keep our balance. Without the cerebellum we would lack the coordination needed to thread a needle, perform surgery, or play a piano, and we would be a disaster on ice skates or a bicycle.

The Pons The *pons* (see Figure 2–14), named after the Latin word meaning "bridge," actually acts as a bridge between the two lobes of the cerebellum. The pons also contains nuclei related to respiration.

The Midbrain

Connecting the hindbrain and the forebrain is the relatively small brain division known as the midbrain (see Figure 2–14). The midbrain contains nuclei that are important for visual and auditory functioning. These visual and auditory centers perform a fairly primitive orientation function, such as turning the head toward the source of a sound.

The Brain Stem The division known as the **brain stem** does not fit easily into our scheme of hind, middle, and forebrain for a simple reason—it includes all of the hindbrain and midbrain and also makes contact with the forebrain (see Figures 2–9 and 2–14). Even though we discuss the brain stem here under the heading of midbrain, keep in mind that the brain stem is not a simple structure.

As the spinal cord emerges from the bony spinal column and enters the skull, it enlarges into the brain stem. In terms of evolution, the brain stem is the oldest part of the brain. This division is found within the brains of *all* vertebrates. Most of the neural activities occurring in the brain stem are automatic, or reflexive in nature. In higher animals the brain stem also connects the spinal cord with the new, or upper, parts of the brain, in order to relay incoming sensory messages to the upper brain.

The Reticular Activating System (RAS) The **reticular activating system** is another one that is difficult to grasp. Some have described it as the "core" of the brain stem. This system begins in the hindbrain, extends through the midbrain, and sends its fibers up into the forebrain. The RAS is a tangled mass of neuronal fibers that looks crisscrossed (or reticulated) when viewed under a microscope. The primary function of the RAS is to regulate levels of arousal and attention, ranging from sleep through states of high alertness. In a sense, we may think of the RAS as being responsible for "turning down" incoming stimuli so that we can sleep at night and then "turning up" the stimuli in the morning so we will wake up. Electrical stimulation of the RAS causes a sleeping animal to awaken, and an animal that is awake to become more alert. Destruction of certain parts of the RAS causes permanent unconsciousness.

The Forebrain

The forebrain consists of a number of vital structures, including the *thalamus*, the *hypothalamus*, the *limbic system*, and the *cerebrum* and its outer layer, the *cerebral cortex* (see Figures 2–9 and 2–14). The forebrain is bilaterally symmetrical (as are the entire brain and spinal cord). That is, there are two cerebral hemispheres, two thalami, and so on. We will deal with each structure in order, but first it should be pointed out that we see the most differentiation between species at the level of the cerebrum. The cerebrum is virtually non-existent in the lower vertebrates. Fish have no tissue that can be recognized as a cerebrum. As we move from the lower vertebrates up to the human species, it is primarily cerebral growth that accounts for the change in brain weight compared to body weight. The human has more brain per pound of total body weight than any other animal, and in the human brain, three of every four neurons are located in the cerebrum.

The Thalamus   In the human brain the thalamus, which looks like a couple of joined eggs, functions as a relay station between incoming sensory messages and the outer layer of the cerebrum, the cerebral cortex (see Figure 2–14). One part of the thalamus receives input from the eyes and projects this information to the visual areas of the cortex. Another area relays information from the ear to the auditory area of the cortex. And finally, a third area receives messages coming up from the spinal cord and projects them into the area of the cortex that deals with the sense of touch and body position.

The Hypothalamus   The hypothalamus is located between the thalamus and the pituitary gland (see Figure 2–14). In recent years the hypothalamus has received a great deal of research attention. Though it is only about the size of a lump of sugar, it has proved to be vital in regulating a wide variety of body functions and behaviors. The hypothalamus appears to be a motivational and emotional control center governing sexual behavior, eating, and drinking. As we saw earlier, stimulation of certain areas of the hypothalamus can induce a satiated animal to continue eating, and stimulation of other nearby areas can cause a hungry animal to fast. Comparable effects have been found for drinking behavior (Stricker, 1976). Cells that sense changes in body temperature and make the appropriate balancing changes are located in the hypothalamus too, as are groups of cells that regulate reproductive cycles and the expression of aggression. Hypothalamic stimulation can cause resting cats to leap into predatory attacks (Berntson, Hughes, & Beattie, 1976). This tiny structure also is implicated in the control of sleeping and waking. Additionally, because of its intimate neural and circulatory connections with the pituitary gland, the hypothalamus is the ultimate controller of the vital endocrine system. By influencing the pituitary, it regulates the secretions of the other endocrine glands as well.

The Limbic System   The limbic system forms a border of neural tissue around the upper end of the brain stem (see Figure 2–15). It is an

FIGURE 2–15 The Limbic System *Shown here in color, the limbic system is an interconnected system consisting of several structures.*

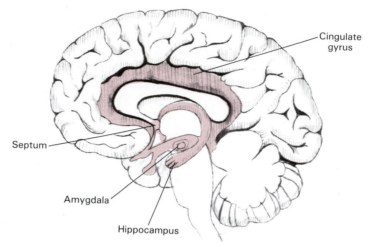

interconnected system composed of several structures. The limbic system is important in emotional behavior and in the ability of the organism to carry out basic survival activities, such as fleeing from danger. Apparently some areas of the limbic system produce calmness and others involve emotional hypersensitivity. Electrical stimulation of some limbic areas generates a rage response, whereas stimulation of other nearby areas elicits fearful behavior. (See the box titled "Murder on Your Mind?" for a discussion of recent discoveries that imply a link between violence and severe head injuries.) Although it is not yet clear how the limbic system controls these emotional effects, the *cingulate gyrus, hippocampus,* and *amygdala* (see Figure 2–15) have all been implicated. For example, lesions of the amygdala have been found to block a wide variety of predatory behaviors in many species.

The limbic structures are also involved in attention, learning, and memory. Stimulation of the amygdala or the hippocampus, if given immediately after a training trial, causes the organism to forget the content of the training trial (Murray & Mishkin, 1985). The limbic structures of human patients have been implanted with stimulating electrodes for therapeutic purposes. When stimulated in this way, these patients report pleasant, positive sensations. Electrical stimulation of the *septum* also has brought relief from the physical pain of advanced cancer. Other patients, in addition to experiencing positive emotions, have become more alert, quicker, and more accurate in mental calculations during limbic stimulation. Lesions in the limbic system result in loss of the ability to carry out planned activities. Humans who have suffered limbic damage have been observed to forget what they intended to do if they are distracted even slightly.

The Cerebrum and the Cerebral Cortex The **cerebrum** is the most prominent brain structure in the human organism. Located on top of the brain stem, it looks like a giant flower in the process of blossoming. It almost completely envelops the structures below it (compare Figures 2–14 and 2–16).

The surface layer of the cerebrum is called the **cerebral cortex** (cortex means thick skin or rind). The cortex is the most important

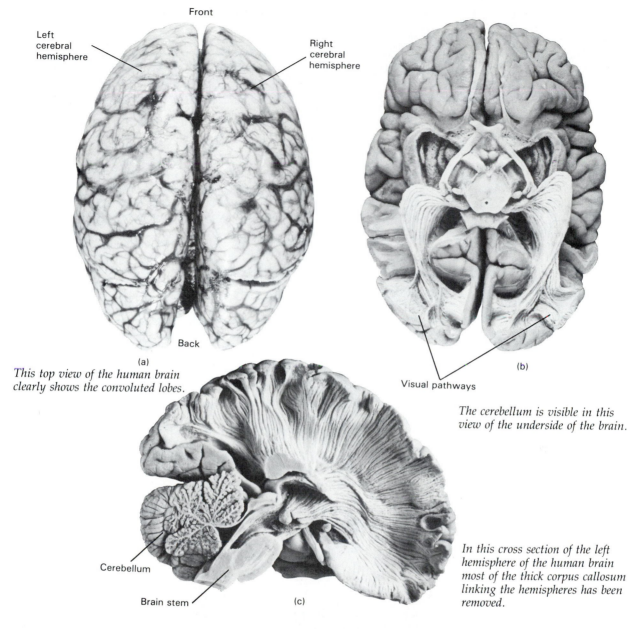

Front

Left
cerebral
hemisphere

Right
cerebral
hemisphere

Back

(a)

*This top view of the human brain
clearly shows the convoluted lobes.*

(b)

Visual pathways

*The cerebellum is visible in this
view of the underside of the brain.*

Cerebellum

Brain stem

(c)

*In this cross section of the left
hemisphere of the human brain
most of the thick corpus callosum
linking the hemispheres has been
removed.*

part of the cerebrum. In fact, the rest of the cerebrum is often described as the support system for the cortex. The cortex is wrinkled or folded into a convoluted pattern of ridges and valleys. The deeper valleys are called *fissures.* The most important fissure is the one that runs down the middle of the cerebrum from front to back and divides the cerebrum into two halves. These halves, a left and a right, are called *cerebral hemispheres.* The hemispheres are symmetrical in structure and are joined together by a thick band or cable of neural material called the *corpus callosum* (see Figure 2–14 and cross section above). It is this band that carries information back and forth between the hemispheres and allows one half of the cortex to know what the other half is up to.

◆ *MURDER ON YOUR MIND?*

What drives a person to murder? Researchers who have sought to explain the kind of random violence that explodes within some troubled individuals usually come up short. Psychiatrist Dorothy Otnow Lewis believes that she has discovered part of the answer—a hitherto undescribed and unreported constellation of mental and physical problems that she calls "limbic psychotic aggressive syndrome."

Lewis and her colleagues examined two groups of men and women: 15 convicted murderers on death row in five different states and 22 others in various stages of incarceration or hospitalization. The first striking finding was that severe head injury, from childhood onward, was very common in both groups. In all, more than 80 percent of the murderers had had some form of head trauma—which the researchers recognized by scars, neurological symptoms, CAT scans, and hospital reports.

One possible effect of the head injuries was to damage the thinking and emotional systems of the murderers, Lewis says. As well, the majority of the murderers had long-standing, but previously undiagnosed, psychiatric problems and lower than average cognitive abilities. "Injuries such as these may make already susceptible people more impulsive," she says.

Much, but not all, of the head trauma suffered by the murderers came at the hands of parents or other relatives. Two-thirds of the murderers, for example, had been physically abused as children. Lewis points out that child abuse was not the only cause of head injury, however. One criminal was run over by a horsecart at the age of 12; another was hit on the head at the age of 6 by a glass bottle dropped from a tree. "These types of injuries tend to be ignored by those who examine murderers," Lewis says.

Lewis documented many cases in which the future murderer, in addition to suffering actual physical abuse, was a witness to extreme family violence. "In terms of this syndrome, it may be just as important that the child witnessed the violence as to have suffered it," she says. "The effects seem to be just as devastating."

Perhaps because of the head injuries, or perhaps for other causes, many of the murderers also suffered seizure-like symptoms. Lewis emphasizes, however, that none could be diagnosed as epileptic. Still, of those measured, almost half showed abnormal EEG's and experienced blackouts and lapses of consciousness. More than half of the murderers had had periods of amnesia, and virtually all showed other mental and physical symptoms such as frequent memory lapses and episodes of déjà vu.

Finally, the researchers documented evidence of brief psychotic behavior in virtually all of the murderers. This ranged from intermittent suicidal tendencies and loose, illogical thinking to visual and auditory hallucinations, bizarre ideas, and extreme mood swings. This was despite the fact that almost all of the murderers were able to maintain an appearance of normality and most had not been diagnosed previously as mentally ill.

"The great majority of people out there with head injuries, epileptic symptoms, and psychotic behavior are not violent," Lewis says, "but when you put all of these together with a history of family violence or abuse, you can create an extremely violent person." Although she admits that no model, including hers, will be likely to describe all recurrent violent crime, she believes that hers does better than previous attempts.

Lewis thinks that a clearer understanding of the genesis of recurrent violent behavior may lead to better ways of treating those who commit it. Breaking the limbic psychotic aggressive syndrome down

As we go up the evolutionary scale, we observe an increase in the number and size of the ridges and valleys, or convolutions of the cerebral cortex, as well as an increase in the overall size of the cerebrum itself. The rat brain has a cerebrum, but it is only in animals as advanced as the rabbit that the hemispheres form a major proportion of the brain. Even in rabbits the cortex is rather small, and it is smooth rather than convoluted. As we move up the scale to the dog, the cortex increases in size and begins to fold into a convoluted pattern. Moving on to the ape, we find the cortex continues to enlarge and fold. Finally, in the human we find the largest cortex and the greatest number of convolutions.

THE CORTEX AND BEHAVIOR

Because the cortex represents the most advanced aspect of brain development and because it has been shown to be incredibly important in controlling and integrating behavior, we shall devote this section to what is known and what has yet to be discovered about the functioning of this mushroomlike structure that lies just beneath our skulls.

Each of the cortical hemispheres is divided into four sections, or lobes, as shown in Figure 2–16. The *central fissure* separates the *frontal lobe* from the *parietal lobe.* The *lateral* (side) *fissure* separates the

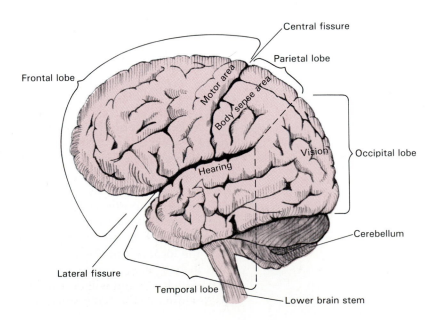

FIGURE 2–16   The Exterior of the Left Cerebral Hemisphere
This view shows the major fissures and lobes of the cerebrum.

temporal lobe from the frontal and parietal lobes. The fourth, or *occipital lobe*, lacks a major fissure, but it forms the rear end of the hemisphere. These physical divisions are, to some extent, also functional divisions. That is, each of these areas seems to govern certain aspects of our behavior. Therefore we will look at several types of behavior in order to get an idea of how these cortical lobes function.

Sensory Areas of the Cortex

Vision   The occipital lobes of each hemisphere are concerned with vision. When light strikes the retina in the back of each eye, neural activity is initiated. The message is carried along the optic nerve, through the optic chiasm, and into the visual cortex. The *optic chiasm* is a point where the optic nerves meet and then divide in a special way. Fibers from receptors on the nose side of each eye end up in the brain hemisphere opposite that eye. Fibers from the temple side of each eye do not cross over; they lead to the hemisphere on the same side as the eye. (Figure 2–19 illustrates these visual pathways.)

Accidents and experiments have demonstrated clearly that the occipital lobe is involved with vision. If you were undergoing brain surgery and the surgeons electrically stimulated your occipital cortex, you would experience, or "see," flashes of light. Similarly, if this portion of your brain were destroyed, you would suffer an extreme loss of vision.

Research with cats suggests that cells within the occipital lobe are very specialized. By recording from single neurons in this area, researchers found that some neurons fire only when the cat is shown a vertical slit of light. Others fire only when the slit is horizontal. Still others respond only when two edges at a specific angle are presented. And some neurons are stimulated only by movement in the visual field (Hubel & Wiesel, 1965).

Hearing   Sound receptors inside the ear send messages to hearing centers lying along the lateral fissure in the temporal lobe (see Figure 2–16). Like the cells in the visual cortex, cells in this portion of the brain are highly specialized. Recordings from individual neurons in this area reveal that some cells respond only to low-pitched sounds. Both vision and hearing will be considered in more detail in Chapter 3.

Body Senses   Along the central fissure in the parietal lobe lies a section of sensory cortex that we will call the body sense area. When this area receives messages from the skin receptors, we experience the sensations of touch, heat, cold, pain, and body movement. Each area of skin on our bodies is connected to a specific, identifiable area of this body sense portion of the cortex. In other words, when someone touches our nose or our wrist, the neurons in a very specific area of the brain begin to fire. Part (a) of Figure 2–17 will help you understand the locations of these areas. Imagine that we have cut a human brain in half at the central fissure in order to look at the surface of the back half. As you will note in Figure 2–17a, the body is represented upside-down in the body sense area. That is, most of the lower por-

FIGURE 2–17   Primary Motor and Sensory Areas of the Human Brain   *The labels indicate projections of various body parts on the cortex.*

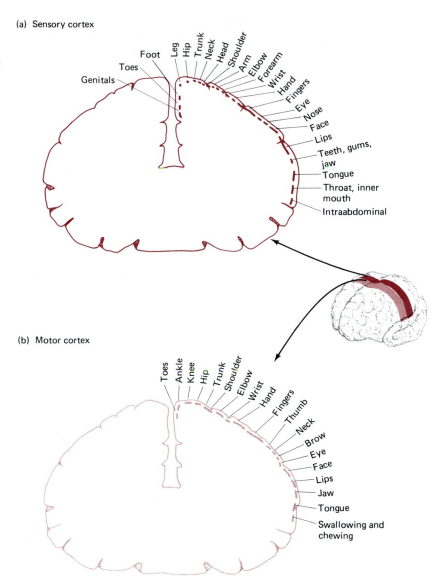

(a) Sensory cortex

Genitals, Toes, Foot, Leg, Hip, Trunk, Neck, Head, Shoulder, Arm, Elbow, Forearm, Wrist, Hand, Fingers, Eye, Nose, Face, Lips, Teeth, gums, jaw, Tongue, Throat, inner mouth, Intraabdominal

(b) Motor cortex

Toes, Ankle, Knee, Hip, Trunk, Shoulder, Elbow, Wrist, Hand, Fingers, Thumb, Neck, Brow, Eye, Face, Lips, Jaw, Tongue, Swallowing and chewing

tions of the body (toes, feet, and legs) send messages to the top of the brain section, while most of the upper portions of the body (hands, arms, and face) send messages to the lower portion.

The amount of cortex devoted to a particular area of the body is directly related to the sensitivity of that body part. Humans have a lot of cortex representing the face and hands, and these areas are very sensitive to touch. Dogs have very little cortical representation of the forepaws. However, raccoons, which use their forepaws to explore their environment, show a much greater cortical representation of this body part (Welker, Johnson, & Pubols, 1964).

Stimulation of the body sense cortex causes sensations of touch, movement, or pressure in various parts of the body. Injury to this area disturbs sensation but does not usually result in its complete loss. For example, a person with such an injury may not be able to make fine distinctions between the temperatures of objects, but he will be able to tell the difference between hot and cold.

Movement and the Cortex

The motor cortex is an area of the cortex that governs motor activity, or actual movement. It is located toward the back of the frontal lobe and lies along the central fissure (see Figures 2–16 and 2–17).

As part (b) of Figure 2–17 shows, the body is also represented upside down in the motor cortex, and more cortex is devoted to those body parts where fine muscular control is exercised. Stimulation of the motor area results in movement of a specific body part. Touching the "toe area" with a pencil electrode, for example, will bring about toe movement.

Learning, Thinking, and the Association Areas

We have discussed the sensory and motor areas of the cortex, but these sections actually only represent small portions of the whole. What about the rest? The other cortical areas, lying between and around the sensory and motor areas, are called *association areas.* They were given this name because it was thought that learning took place here as new associations were formed.

Although our understanding of the association cortex is still limited, we do know that it is involved in the more complex functions of perception, learning, thinking, and language (Mishkin & Appenzeller, 1987). Several kinds of evidence lead us to this conclusion. For example, lesions in association cortex near the occipital lobe lead to problems in depth perception. Some association areas in the lower temporal lobe also appear to be related to visual ability. Though destruction of these areas does not cause blindness, it has been shown to hamper the organism's ability to recognize visual forms and to distinguish among different forms. Damage to some association areas results in loss of the ability to recognize objects by touch. A blindfolded person with such damage may handle a familiar object, such as a pencil, but be unable to identify it.

Certain association areas in the frontal lobes seem to involve the kind of thought necessary for problem solving. Animals with lesions in certain association areas seem unable to remember the solution to a simple problem (such as where food is) for more than a few seconds (Rosenkilde & Divac, 1976). Humans with damage in frontal areas also have trouble remembering the solutions to problems. Problems that require switching back and forth from one solution method to another are especially difficult (Milner, 1964; Passingham, 1985).

Electrical stimulation of certain areas of association cortex has elicited very vivid memories. In brain-mapping operations preceding the removal of brain tumors (see pages 61–62), surgeons discovered that stimulation of certain association areas caused the patients to relive childhood events, even to the point of reexperiencing the emotions associated with those events (Penfield, 1969). Thus, we are fairly certain that memory functions are tied into these association areas.

FIGURE 2–18 Cortical Comparisons *Drawings of the cortex of three species show the widely varying percentages of tissues given over to motor, sensory, and associative activities. Notice that the human associative cortex is extensive compared to the other species.*

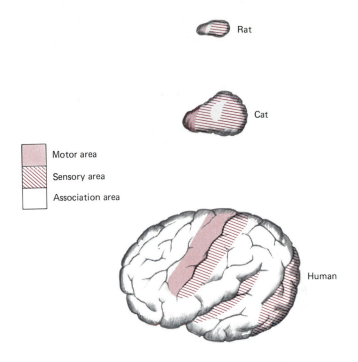

Species differ considerably in the amount of their cortex that is devoted to sensory, motor, and associative functions (Figure 2–18). Humans have a much higher percentage of associative cortex than any other species (Hill, 1985).

Language and the Cortex

Some association areas of the cortex are involved in the complex processes of producing and understanding language. Let us look at these particular association areas in some detail.

It has been observed that damage to certain temporal lobe association areas may result in a type of language disability called aphasia. Patients with aphasia may be unable to understand what is said to them. They may have trouble giving the name of an object, even though they recognize it. These are not problems in the motor cortex governing the muscles used in speech, since there is not a total loss of speaking ability. Apparently, these disabilities are due to the loss of the integration between sensory and motor functions that is normally performed by the association area.

In the mid-1800s, a patient who had lost the ability to speak was shown to have suffered damage to the left hemisphere of the frontal lobe just above the lateral fissure. This early finding opened up an area of research that has proved to be one of the most intriguing in all of psychology. It began a chain of studies that have finally demonstrated that active language ability—the ability to speak and write—is generally located in the left hemisphere. The right hemisphere is much less verbal. In other words, although our brain appears symmetrical, it does not always function in a symmetrical manner. The left side tends to do things the right side does not, and vice versa. This general conclusion has been bolstered by recent split-brain research, which is discussed in the next section.

Two Brains?

Some time ago, a surgical technique was developed to relieve severe epilepsy. The operation involves cutting the corpus callosum, the thick band of neural material that connects the two hemispheres of the brain. The idea is to prevent a seizure that begins in one hemisphere from spreading to the other hemisphere. The operation is often successful; epileptic effects can be greatly reduced (Gazzaniga, 1970, 1983, 1985).

Although developed to relieve epilepsy, these operations have also revealed some incredible information about the functioning of the brain. Specifically, they have led to dramatic demonstrations of the differences between the two halves of our brain. To understand these experiments we must look more closely at the nature of the split-brain condition.

The experimental situation is diagrammed in Figure 2–19. The corpus callosum has been cut, disconnecting the two halves of the cortex. They cannot communicate with one another. The subject is seated in front of a screen and instructed to stare at a point in the center of the screen. A visual stimulus, such as a word, is then flashed for one-tenth of a second either to the right or the left of this center point. If the experimenter presents a word in the left side of the visual field, or to the left of the center point, this information goes

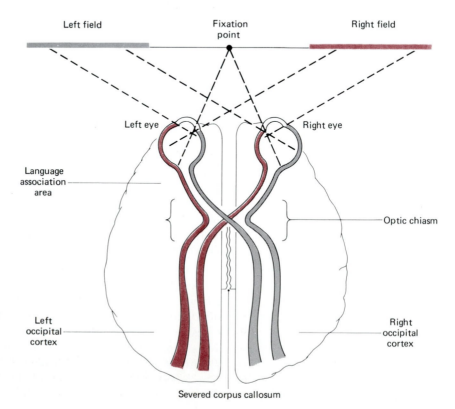

FIGURE 2–19 Preparation of the Split-Brain Experiment
This drawing shows the paths of conduction from the left and right visual fields to the right and left cerebral hemispheres. When a visual stimulus is presented in the left field only, all neural messages are conducted to the right hemisphere. When a visual stimulus is presented to the right field only, all neural messages go to the left hemisphere.

only to the right side of the brain. If the experimenter presents a visual stimulus in the right visual field, this information goes only to the left side of the brain. Thus, by presenting visual stimuli either to the subject's left or right, researchers can "talk" to one half of the brain alone, without the other half's knowing what is going on. Normally, the corpus callosum relays information between the two halves, but in the split-brain situation, we are in the unique position of being able to address one half of the brain at a time, so we can explore the capacities and abilities of each half separately (see Gardner, 1984; Rohn, 1984; Smith & Ellsworth, 1985; Sperry, 1985).

Some split-brain experiments have revealed surprising differences between the two hemispheres. The left side of the brain tends to specialize in active speech events such as talking and writing. If we present a word to the left side of the brain by placing it in the right visual field, the split-brain subject can read it and say it aloud. If the same word is presented to the right side of the brain (placed in the left visual field), the patient cannot say it out loud.

Although this type of demonstration suggests that the right side of the brain is severely limited in terms of language ability, it is not totally incompetent with respect to language. If the right side of the brain is asked to recognize a word rather than to say it, it performs very well. Nevertheless, the left side does seem to be more actively involved in language.

Other split-brain studies have found several behaviors that seem to be controlled by only one hemisphere. In general, the left hemisphere controls not only speech, but also a number of related activities, such as reading, writing, and mathematical calculations. The right hemisphere helps us orient ourselves in space, recognize structural shapes and textures, and identify and remember musical forms. Although the two hemispheres are normally in constant communication across the corpus callosum, they each have their own specialized functions.

Many observers believe that the left hemisphere produces our intellectual, analytical, and critical behaviors, while the right hemisphere is responsible for making us more spatially aware, intuitive, and artistic. But we must guard against making a complex situation seem simple. Though several studies suggest that musical ability resides in the right hemisphere, some evidence (Shanon, 1980) suggests that the left side is also involved in the arranging and composing of music. Specifically, as musical decision tasks become increasingly complex, the left hemisphere seems to become more and more involved. Thus it would be inaccurate to claim that *all* musical ability, or any other ability for that matter, lies within one hemisphere (see also Hink, Kagan, & Suzuki, 1980; Naeser, 1980).

Other split-brain studies have revealed three additional aspects of brain functioning that we might not have expected to find. First, split-brain patients can sometimes perform *better* than individuals who have not undergone severing of the corpus callosum. Ellenbery and Sperry (1980) sent one simple decision task to one hemisphere of split-brain individuals and simultaneously sent a second task to the other hemisphere. These split-brain subjects were much better able to do both tasks at the same time than were normal subjects. Presumably, the intact corpus callosum in the normal subjects forced the two halves of the brain to work together on one task or the other and did not allow the two hemispheres to work independently as they appear to have done in the split-brain individuals.

Second, there may be important sex differences in hemispheric specialization. For example, a group of women recognized the emotion expressed by a face in a photograph faster if that photograph was shown to the right hemisphere rather than the left. In contrast, a group of men did about equally well with their left and right hemispheres in this emotion-judging task (Ladavas, Umilta, & Ricci-Bitti, 1980; Hines & Shipley, 1984).

Third, the asymmetry of your brain functioning may depend on whether you are right- or left-handed. All but about 5 percent of us are right-handed and right-handed individuals generally show the pattern of specialization we have been discussing. But the situation is less clear when left-handers are examined. Some left-handed individuals show no asymmetry, with both hemispheres handling many tasks. Other left-handed subjects show a pattern of specialization that is just the opposite of that observed in right-handed people (Piazza, 1980; Rubin & Rubin, 1980; Witelson, 1985).

Some research evidence suggests that, at any given moment, one side of the brain is in control, while the other side "is loafing" (Shannahoff-Khalsa, 1984). EEG brain wave recordings also show that the left hemisphere may be more active than the right when the subject engages in speech. When the subject switches to spatial tasks, the right side of the brain may become more active, while the activity of the left side subsides (Galin & Ornstein, 1972). All of this evidence has tempted some researchers to conclude that we have two brains. Other researchers insist that the experiments simply show that the hemispheres have developed some specialized functions. Further research should clarify this question.

How Your Brain Changes

Although each of us is born with all of the neurons we will ever have, our brain does develop and change. It is responsive to events in the environment, to the passage of time, and to chemical conditions.

Let us look a little more closely at the impact of experience on the brain. It has long been known that the electrical activity of the brain changes during learning. EEG recordings made while cats are learning a new response and while they are not learning anything show a marked difference in the electrical activity of the brain during such periods (Figure 2–20). During nontraining periods, the emitted brain waves are rapid and of low amplitude, but during learning, the waves show a distinct shift to what is called *theta activity;* the waves become much slower and of larger amplitude (see Bennett, 1977).

While these changes are interesting, they are, after all, only temporary. But even more dramatic permanent changes have also been noted. Spinelli, Jensen, and DiPrisco (1980) trained animals to avoid a shock by pulling back their legs. The dendrites of neurons in their brains were then compared with the cortical neurons of untrained

1 sec.
├──┤

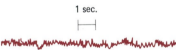

Nonlearning activity of the brain

Theta activity occurring during learning

FIGURE 2–20   Theta Activity of a Cat's Brain as Revealed by EEG Recordings   *During learning, the cat's brain waves become much slower and of a greater amplitude as compared to the rapid, low-amplitude waves recorded during nonlearning periods.*

FIGURE 2–21 Permanent Changes in the Brain as the Result of Experience *Dendrites of neurons from the somatosensory cortex of a trained animal (left) are clearly more complex than those of an untrained animal (right).* (After Spinelli, Jensen, & DiPrisco, 1980)

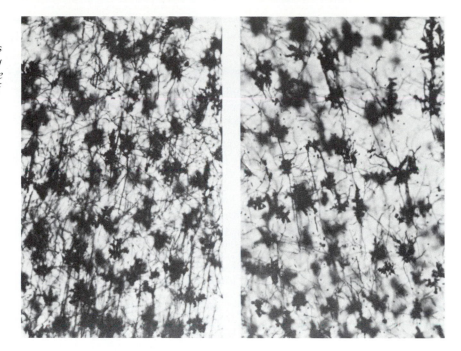

animals. As may be seen in Figure 2–21, the number and complexity of the dendritic branches in certain areas of the brain were significantly increased as a result of training.

Dramatic studies (see Rosenzweig, 1984; Held et al., 1985) have shown that by stimulating animals in various ways (handling them, for example) and by giving them stimuli to feel, touch, and smell, it is possible to increase brain weight, blood supply, and cell size. Truly our brains are the product of our experience. They also change as we grow older, as is illustrated in the box titled "Do Our Brains Grow Old in the Way That Food Becomes Stale?"

Systems and Loops

Before we leave the nervous system to focus on glands and genes, the complexity of the brain needs to be emphasized once again. As you read this chapter, you might easily conclude that specific structures within the brain handle specific functions all by themselves, without any contact with other parts of the brain. Modern neuroscientists know that we must guard against this false assumption. They know that the brain is a complex entity composed of many interrelated and intertwined systems. A single, apparently simple function may involve complicated systems and communication loops within large portions of the brain. These systems and loops are just beginning to be traced and understood, but one thing is already clear: there is no such thing as a simple brain function.

THE ENDOCRINE SYSTEM

Physiological research into neurons, nervous systems, and brains is booming, and we can anticipate major advances in our understanding of the neural machinery underlying behavior. But other physiological elements besides the nervous systems are important determinants of

◆ *DO OUR BRAINS GROW OLD IN THE WAY THAT FOOD BECOMES STALE?*

Clearly, disease and accidents can lead to dramatic alterations in the human brain. But this wonderful organ also changes with the mere passage of time, even in healthy adults. As we grow older our brains change in a variety of ways. First, neurons may be lost from a number of different areas. The brain of a perfectly healthy senior citizen may thus be slightly smaller than the brain of a person in his or her twenties (de Leon et al., 1982). Second, although a specific neuron may continue to function, its capacity to act may be decreased, often through the deterioration of the cell's dendrites. Loss of dendritic function leads to a lessened capacity of the neuron to communicate with other neurons (Scheibel, 1985).

The exact causes of these changes are unknown, but Cerami, Vlassara, and Brownlee (1987) have made the startling suggestion that such age-related cell changes may be similar to what happens to food as it toughens and grows brown with age. We all know what happens to food when we leave it in the refrigerator for two weeks; it becomes tough and unappetizing. Food chemists have understood this so-called "browning" process for many years. It is the result of glucose becoming attached to proteins without the aid of enzymes. But until Cerami and his colleagues published their findings, no one suspected that our own body's decline and death might be due to a similar "browning" process. In addition to describing the complex chemical reactions involved in human cell "browning," these researchers also suggest that one day we may have drugs that lessen this aging process. The loss of cells and cell function that comes with age may or may not lead to an overall loss of general intelligence. On the one hand, older people do sometimes show slowed reaction times and even memory losses. On the other hand, they continue to profit from experience; they continue to learn, and it may be that their capacity for certain kinds of experience-related judgments is actually better later in life.

behavior. It is to one of these, the network of glands called the *endocrine system*, that we now turn.

There are two types of glands in the body. The first type, which is of relatively little interest to psychologists, is called the *duct* or *exocrine gland.* Duct glands produce saliva, tears, and sweat. The other type of gland, which directly affects behavior and thus attracts the attention of psychologists, is the *ductless* or *endocrine gland.* They are called "ductless" because they secrete their products directly into the blood.

The activity of the endocrine glands is as essential to the integration of behavior as is the nervous system. In fact, the endocrine and nervous systems interact in various complex ways. For example, the action of some endocrine glands is controlled by the nervous system, while secretions from some glands affect the excitability of certain neurons.

The secretions of the endocrine glands are called *hormones.* Hormones are very powerful chemical substances that affect the individual's physical state and behavior in particular ways. Their potency is tremendous. The adrenaline present in your body is the equivalent of one teaspoon in a lake 100 meters in diameter and two meters deep.

FIGURE 2–22   The Endocrine
Glands and the Hormones
They Secrete

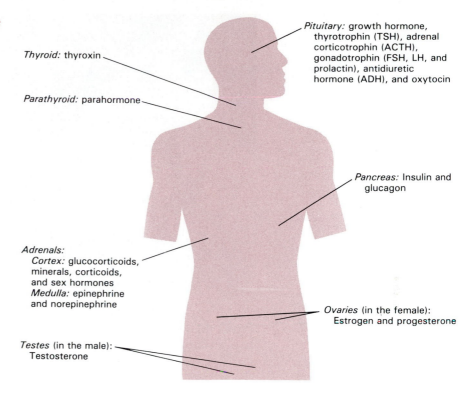

Thyroid: thyroxin

Parathyroid: parahormone

Pituitary: growth hormone,
   thyrotrophin (TSH), adrenal
   corticotrophin (ACTH),
   gonadotrophin (FSH, LH, and
   prolactin), antidiuretic
   hormone (ADH), and oxytocin

Pancreas: Insulin and
   glucagon

Adrenals:
   Cortex: glucocorticoids,
   minerals, corticoids,
   and sex hormones
   Medulla: epinephrine
   and norepinephrine

Ovaries (in the female):
   Estrogen and progesterone

Testes (in the male):
   Testosterone

Figure 2–22 identifies the major endocrine glands and lists some
of the hormones they secrete. Since the hormones are discharged into
the blood, the endocrine system influences behavior in a broader but
slower way than the nervous system, which operates in a more localized manner. Hormones are carried in the blood to a variety of body
sites, such as internal organs, other glands, and certain parts of the
central nervous system. We will look at three vital endocrine
glands—the *pituitary*, the *thyroid*, and the *adrenals*—and the hormones that they secrete.

The Pituitary Gland

The pituitary gland was once referred to as the "master gland" (because it produces many hormones and controls the hormone secretion of other glands), but it is now known that this gland is tightly
controlled by the hypothalamus. Substances secreted by the hypothalamus both stimulate and inhibit pituitary hormone production.
The pituitary, which is located very close to the hypothalamus, is
about the size of a kidney bean. It secretes several important hormones, some of which influence nonglandular tissue, and some that
control the activities of other endocrine glands.
    The pituitary releases at least eight hormones, but we will men-
tion only a few of them. One of the most important is the *antidiuretic*
hormone (ADH). Antidiuretic hormone is manufactured in the hypothalamus, but stored in the posterior lobe of the pituitary. This hormone acts on the kidneys, causing them to decrease the amount of
water that is drawn from body tissues and passed to the bladder.

We can be sure that once this dehydrated man receives enough fluid, the high level of ADH in his body will be reduced.

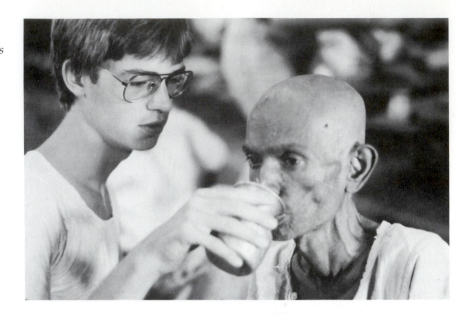

When the body is dehydrated, more ADH is released. Ordinarily the hypothalamus stimulates the pituitary to release ADH at a relatively low rate. When the body is hydrated (when water intake is excessive) the release of ADH stops completely. In such cases the amount of urine excreted is vastly increased. *Oxytocin* is another important pituitary hormone. It acts on smooth muscles. Uterine contractions during childbirth and the release of milk from the mammary glands are induced by the release of oxytocin. The *growth hormone*, as the name suggests, affects a number of metabolic functions that determine the growth of the body, including both bone and soft-tissue development. Underproduction of this hormone results in arrested development, and the affected child becomes a midget. Overproduction of the hormone during youth produces a giant.

The Thyroid Gland

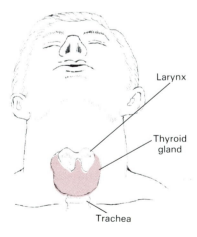

FIGURE 2–23 The Thyroid Gland *(After Curtis & Barnes, 1985)*

The thyroid gland, located at the base of the neck (Figure 2–23), plays an important role in controlling the rate at which the body burns food to provide energy. The primary effect of the thyroid hormone, *thyroxin,* is to raise the body's metabolism. That is, it causes an increase in the body's use of oxygen, and it raises the level of heat production. When thyroxin is secreted in abnormally large amounts, it leads to a condition known as *hyperthyroidism.* A person with this condition becomes excitable, "keyed up," and may have trouble sleeping. This condition also involves weight loss, increased sweating, intense thirst, and an increase in heart rate.

When thyroxin is secreted in smaller amounts than normal, *hypothyroidism* results. Because it affects metabolism, thyroxin affects growth. Untreated hypothyroidism in infants leads to *cretinism,* a condition characterized by stunted growth and mental retardation. Adults with hypothyroidism gain weight, feel sluggish, and are often tired. Because they sweat less than normal they may have trouble adjusting to high temperatures and may show puffiness of the skin.

The Adrenal Glands

Lying on top of the kidneys, the adrenal glands secrete a number of different hormones. Only some of the more important adrenal hormones will be considered here.

Cortisol   The hormone cortisol affects the release of sugar from the liver and thus influences the body's ability to produce quick energy. **Cortisone** is a synthetic form of cortisol that is used in treating shock, allergic reactions, and inflammatory disorders such as arthritis and bursitis. Because cortisone treatment sometimes produces emotional symptoms such as depression, it is possible that cortisol and related hormones play a role in the development of mental disturbances.

The Sex Hormones   The sex hormones include **androgens**, a group of male hormones, and **estrogens**, a group of female hormones. Both androgen and estrogen are secreted by the adrenal glands of both sexes. More androgen and less estrogen are secreted by the adrenals of males, while more estrogen and less androgen are secreted by the adrenals of females.

When these sex hormones are out of balance, changes in the physical appearance and behavior of the individual may appear. As you might expect, oversecretion of androgen in the female and oversecretion of estrogen in the male promote the development of secondary sex characteristics of the opposite sex. Females develop deeper voices and grow facial hair. Their breasts shrink. In males, the voice becomes higher pitched and breasts begin to grow. These men lose their facial hair. Persons who wish to undergo a sex change are usually given estrogen or androgen treatments prior to surgery so that their secondary sex characteristics will change.

In a condition known as the *adrenogenital syndrome,* or *AGS,* the adrenal glands produce a hormone that begins, at the fetal stage, to masculinize the individual regardless of genetically determined sex. In other words, both AGS boys and AGS girls become more masculine. At birth, although the internal reproductive organs are female, the external genitals of AGS girls appear somewhat masculine. The degree of masculinity depends on the amount of the masculinizing hormone secreted. Studies indicate that such girls engage in considerably more rough outdoor play than unaffected females. They prefer playing with boys and are less interested in playing with dolls. They are also less interested in personal grooming. The AGS boys differ from unaffected males by being significantly more active in rough, outdoor activities.

Epinephrine   The hormone **epinephrine**, also called **adrenalin**, acts in a number of ways to prepare the individual for emergency action. It makes the heart beat faster and increases blood pressure. It directs blood away from the digestive system and toward the vessels of the skeletal muscles. It increases sweating. The mother who lifts a car to free her pinned child demonstrates the kind of action this hormone can provoke.

Norepinephrine The hormone *norepinephrine*, also known as *noradrenalin*, is one of the chemicals stored in the synaptic vesicles of neurons, as we noted earlier. It functions as a transmitter of neural messages in the brain and in certain neurons of the sympathetic nervous system. Thus this hormone, secreted by the adrenal glands, must be important in the overall functioning of our nervous system.

In summary, as they travel through the bloodstream and affect a wide range of structures and functions throughout the body, the hormones of the various endocrine glands exert powerful influences on our lives.

The Heart as an Endocrine Gland

While the endocrine glands pictured in Figure 2–22 have traditionally been thought of as all there is to the endocrine system, the whole story is not yet clear. The heart itself, usually thought of as a sophisticated and finely tuned pump, may also be a major endocrine gland as well. As Cantin and Genest (1986) put it:

> The heart is a pump: a muscular organ that contracts in rhythm, impelling the blood first to the lungs for oxygenation and then out into the vascular system to supply oxygen and nutrients to every cell in the body. That has been known since the publication in 1628 of William Harvey's *Essay on the Motion of the Heart and the Blood in Animals*.
>
> Within the past few years it has been discovered that the heart is something more than a pump. It is also an endocrine gland. It secretes a powerful peptide hormone called atrial natriuretic factor (ANF). The hormone has an important role in the regulation of blood pressure and blood volume and in the excretion of water, sodium, and potassium. It exerts its effects widely: on the blood vessels themselves, on the kidneys and the adrenal glands, and on a large number of regulatory regions in the brain. (p. 76)

Pheromones

We have mentioned hormones that are secreted into ducts (the exocrine hormones) and discussed hormones that are secreted into the bloodstream (the endocrine hormones). There remains another fascinating form of glandular secretion—one that is ejected into the external environment. The box titled "Another Kind of Hormone" will introduce you to the world of *pheromones.*

BEHAVIORAL GENETICS

Our discussion of the biological foundations of behavior would be incomplete if we did not consider hereditary influences. The study of heredity, called *genetics*, is concerned with how physical characteristics are passed from parents to offspring. Psychologists have become increasingly interested in one particular aspect of heredity, namely the inheritance of behavioral traits. This interest has led to the field of psychological inquiry called *behavioral genetics.* Behavioral geneticists are interested in discovering the extent to which such character-

The antennae of male moths, such as the cecropia moth shown here, can detect minute amounts of the pheromones emitted by females. When a male moth detects the pheromone of a female of the same species, he will fly toward the source.

◆ ANOTHER KIND OF HORMONE

Pheromones (from *pher*, meaning "to carry," plus hormone) are chemical signals exchanged between organisms, generally members of the same species. They are usually produced in special glands and discharged into the environment.

Communication by pheromones seems to be most prevalent among the insects. Pheromones, for example, serve as sex attractants, drawing males to females. Among the best studied are the mating substances of moths. One female gypsy moth, by the emission of minute amounts of a pheromone commonly known as disparlure, can attract male moths that are several kilometers downwind. Since the male can detect as little as a few hundred molecules of the attractant per milliliter of air, disparlure is still potent even when it has become widely diffused.

Pheromones play a variety of other roles in insect communication. Ants lay down pheromones as trail markers, signposts to a food source. When a honey bee stings, it leaves not only the stinger in the victim's skin but also a chemical substance that recruits other honey bees to the attack. Similarly, worker ants of many species release pheromones as alarm substances when they are threatened by an invader; the pheromone spreads through the air to alarm and recruit other workers. If these ants, too, encounter the invader, they will release the pheromone, so the signal will either die out or build up, depending on the magnitude of the threat.

Pheromones have also been found among mammals. The most familiar are the scent-marking substances in the urine of male dogs and cats, which serve as a warning signal to other males. Male mice, it has been found, release substances in their urine that alter the reproductive cycles of the females. The smell of urine from a strange male, for example, can alter hormone balance and interrupt the pregnancy of a female, leaving her free to mate with the newcomer.

Sex attractant pheromones have also been found among the primates. It is suspected that sex attractants are exchanged among members of the human species, but no human substance has yet been isolated and definitely identified as a pheromone. However, the fact that the apocrine sweat glands, the sources of "body odor," begin to function at puberty strongly suggests that the chemicals they produce originally played such a role. Similarly, striking differences in the capacity of men and women to detect certain odors may be a clue to the existence of human pheromones.

From *Invitation to Biology* (4th ed., p. 470) by H. Curtis and N. S. Barnes, 1985, New York: Worth. Reprinted by permission.

istics as intellectual ability, emotional disturbance, and personality are influenced by heredity. In other words, psychologists are interested in inherited behavioral characteristics rather than inherited physical attributes such as hair color, eye color, height, or patterns of baldness.

The roots of this new field of study extend back to the observations of Sir Francis Galton (1869). Noting that a relatively small number of English families produced most of England's scientists, Galton suggested that genius is inherited. Early studies of his theory were poorly controlled and failed to separate the influences of heredity from those of environment. But today's behavioral geneticists have combined the methods of genetics and psychology and have taken great strides toward good, solid experimental control.

For years psychologists have been debating the issue of heredity versus environment. Some have argued that behavior is determined by heredity alone. Others believe that heredity can be discounted and that environment is the major determinant. The latter view was held by the famous early psychologist John B. Watson (1919) who argued that if the environment could be fully controlled, children could be made into scientists, criminals, or whatever was desired. But the new behavioral geneticists recognize that both heredity and environment are important. The current view among psychologists is that while heredity sets the limits for what a person's behavior can be, environment determines where within those limits the person's behavior actually will be. For example, your genetic makeup may determine that you can score anywhere from 85 to 130 on an IQ test. But your environment—basically, your experience—will determine where within that genetically determined range you actually fall. If your experience has been a rich one, full of talk, encouragement, learning, books, and people, you may score close to 130. If, on the other hand, your experiences with learning have been meager, you may score closer to 85. We will explore the question of heredity and IQ at length in Chapter 16, because it is a controversial social issue as well as a scientific puzzle.

Chromosomes and Genes

Microscopic examination of the nucleus of a single cell taken from the human body reveals a number of particles, known as *chromosomes*, which exist in specific pairs. In each cell there are 46 individual chromosomes, or 23 pairs. Chromosomes are identified as X and Y chromosomes on the basis of their physical structures. The larger ones look something like Xs, and the smaller ones look a little like Ys (see Figure 2–24).

Chromosomes that make up the first 22 pairs are similar (although not identical) in structure, being either both Xs or both Ys. But pair 23 may or may not be similar in structure, and it is here that a basic distinction between humans is determined. If pair 23 contains two X chromosomes, the individual is female. If this pair contains an X and a Y, the individual is male.

The chromosome contains the basic units of heredity. If you place a chromosome under a powerful microscope, you will see that it is composed of elements known as *genes*. Although the exact number is

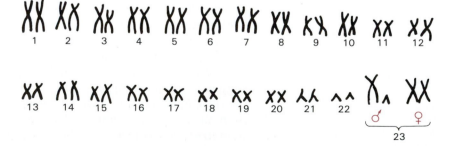

FIGURE 2–24   Representation of Paired Human Chromosomes   *Note that the twenty-third pair differs in males and females.*

FIGURE 2–25   A Schematic Representation of DNA Structure   *P = phosphate, S = sugar, A = adenine, T = thymine, G = guanine, C = cytosine. During cell division, DNA structure splits (see bottom portion of figure) and re-forms as two new, identical structures by picking up appropriate P, S, A, T, G, and C elements from the surrounding cell cytoplasm.*

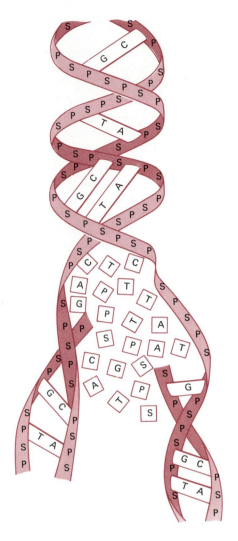

not known, there probably are thousands of genes in each chromosome. Genes are actually large, complex molecules of a chemical substance called **DNA** (deoxyribonucleic acid). The physical structure of the molecule resembles a ladder that has been twisted to form a spiraling shape. James Watson and Francis Crick called the structure a double helix (see Figure 2–25). The sides of the "twisted ladder" are chains of alternating sugar and phosphate (Ss and Ps in Figure 2–25). The "rungs" are attached to the sugars and are composed of matched pairs of bases (adenine with thymine and guanine with cytosine). It is the specific sequences of these matched base pairs in the rungs of the ladder that establish and define the hereditary instructions for each individual organism as it develops.

When the cell divides and forms a new cell, the DNA structure begins to uncoil, splitting down the middle as the matched bases break apart. As each base pair separates, appropriate bases, as well as new sugars and phosphates, are picked up from the surrounding cytoplasm of the cell, and a completely new strand is formed that is identical to the original (see the lower portion of Figure 2–25). In this way, each cell in a person's body has *exactly* the same genetic structure as every other cell in the body. An exception to this rule occurs when genes are mutated, or changed, by environmental forces such as radiation. When mutated genes are contained in cells other than the reproductive ovum or sperm cells, the mutation affects only one individual. When the mutation occurs in the reproductive cells, the mutation may be passed to offspring.

Another exception to this rule of exact duplication has to do with reproduction. Ova and sperm cells are formed by a process of division in which the 23 chromosomal pairs split, with one pair-member going to one cell and the other member going to another cell. Thus, each ovum and each sperm cell contains only half the 46 chromosomes found in all other cells. At conception, each of the 23 chromosomes in the sperm cell unites with a corresponding chromosome in the ovum to form the full 23 pairs. These single unmatched pair-members of the ovum and sperm are in an unstable state. In fact, if fertilization does not occur within a few days, these cells become incapable of uniting and die.

Since all cells in the female body contain only X chromosomes in the twenty-third position, each ovum will receive an X chromosome in the twenty-third position. This means that the fertilized ovum will have at least one X chromosome, that brought by the ovum. Cells in the male body contain both an X and a Y chromosome in the twenty-third position, and sperm cells thus contain *either* an X or a Y chromosome. Chance, and perhaps the internal condition of the womb, decide whether an X or a Y sperm will reach the ovum. If the X-containing sperm fertilizes the ovum, both chromosomes will be Xs, and a female child will develop. If the Y-containing sperm fertilizes the ovum, an XY pair results, and a male child will develop (see Kolata, 1986).

Although human genes have not been isolated and counted, there may be from 20,000 to 120,000 in each cell of the human body. Each gene is believed responsible, either by itself or in concert with other genes, for some particular aspect or stage in the development of the organism. Thus, the genes provide the instructions for the development of cells into the masses that we recognize as our various body parts. The genes determine the nature of our physical features—the color of our eyes, hair, and skin, the length of our bones, the shape of our noses.

Genes determine behavior as well as physical structure and appearance. In fact, although behavior is often determined by more than one gene, there have been some demonstrations of complex behavior being determined by single genes. For example, some colonies of bees control disease by uncapping the hive cells of diseased larvae and throwing the sick and dangerous larvae out of the hive. Genetic analysis has shown that just two genes are involved here. One gene controls the opening of the cell; a bee must possess this particular gene or it will not open cells containing sick larvae. Another individual gene controls the removal and disposal of the diseased larvae.

Depending on their genetic makeup, some bees will only uncap, some will only remove, some will do both, and some will do neither (Rothenbuhler, 1964).

Finally, genes are not only responsible for controlling growth and development; they also control many of the ongoing daily activities of the cell, such as metabolism, excretion, and membrane permeability.

Dominant and Recessive Genes

Like chromosomes, the genes also pair. Each individual receives a gene for hair color from the mother and a gene for hair color from the father. These genes pair up and, according to their nature, determine the individual's hair color.

An important characteristic of some genes is their state of being **dominant** or **recessive.** When the genes of a gene pair (received from the father and the mother) are alike, either both dominant or both recessive, the individual will show the trait that is determined by that gene pair. When the genes of a gene pair are not alike (when one is dominant and the other is recessive), the individual will show the trait determined by the dominant gene but will carry the recessive gene and may transmit it to an offspring (see Figure 2–26). It is for this reason that children sometimes look more like their grandparents than their parents.

This pattern is well demonstrated by the behavior of the genes determining eye color. Genes transmitting the trait of brown eyes are dominant, while those transmitting blue eyes are recessive. When both parents carry only genes for brown eyes, the offspring will be brown-eyed, since both parents can contribute only a dominant gene. Similarly, when both parents carry only genes for blue eyes, the offspring will be blue-eyed, since only the recessive genes are available

FIGURE 2–26 The Transmission and Expression of Dominant and Recessive Genes *In each of the six cases illustrated here, a child will receive one of the four possible gene pairings shown. Case 1: All offspring carry only dominant genes; Case 2: All offspring carry only recessive genes; Case 3: All offspring express the dominant gene trait but they all carry the recessive gene; Case 4: All offspring express the dominant gene trait. Half of them carry the recessive gene and half do not; Case 5: Half of the offspring express the recessive gene. Half express the dominant trait but carry the recessive gene; Case 6: Three quarters of the offspring express the dominant trait. Two thirds of these carry the recessive gene. One quarter of the offspring express the recessive gene.*

	First parent	Second parent	Offspring			
Case 1	D — D	D — D	D — D	D — D	D — D	D — D
Case 2	R — R	R — R	R — R	R — R	R — R	R — R
Case 3	D — D	R — R	D — R	D — R	D — R	D — R
Case 4	D — D	D — R	D — D	D — D	D — R	D — R
Case 5	R — R	D — R	D — R	D — R	R — R	R — R
Case 6	D — R	D — R	D — D	D — R	D — R	R — R

D = Dominant gene   R = Recessive gene

for transmission. However, when one parent carries only dominant, and the other carries only recessive genes, the child will show the dominant brown-eyed trait, but will carry, unexpressed, the recessive blue-eyed gene. It is not possible for two brown-eyed people to produce a blue-eyed child unless they both carry a recessive gene for blue eyes. A blue-eyed person cannot possess a gene for brown eyes.

Which of each parent's genes a child will inherit is determined by chance. When a cell divides to form the ovum or the sperm, it is a matter of chance as to which of the 23 pair-members will go to a particular reproductive cell. A random splitting of 23 pairs can result in more than eight million different possible reproductive cells. One lucky sperm cell among millions of swimming sperm cells unites with one ovum out of the hundreds of ova produced by the female during her reproductive life to produce a fertilized ovum. For these reasons, it is extremely unlikely that any two individuals will have exactly the same genetic makeup.

There is one exception to this rule of uniqueness in heredity. This is the case of identical, or *monozygotic*, twins. Such twins develop from a single fertilized ovum that divides and grows into two separate individuals. Since the twins come from one fertilized ovum, they have exactly the same genetic identity. That is why identical twins are so much alike in every respect. Fraternal, or *dizygotic*, twins, on the other hand, are no more likely to have the same heredity than ordinary siblings, since they develop from two separate fertilized ova. It is often difficult to determine if twins are truly identical. As we all have noticed, ordinary siblings often look very much alike. If they are close in age they may even be able to pass as twins. "Looking alike" is not a good gauge as to whether twins are monozygotic or not. Dizygotic twins may look alike, and if they are of the same sex, they may be mistaken for monozygotic twins. Only an examination of their genes will tell.

It is helpful here to distinguish *phenotypes* from *genotypes.* The phenotype of an individual is his or her observable behavior and appearance. The same individual's genotype is his or her genetic makeup. Thus, two brown-eyed brothers may look phenotypically similar and yet be genotypically distinct if one brother carries two dominant eye-color genes and the other brother carries one recessive and one dominant gene (see Figure 2–26, Cases 4 and 6).

Chromosomal Abnormalities

Although it is not yet known exactly how the genetic material, DNA, directs the individual's development and behavior, recent research is beginning to provide clues to this process. Much of this research has focused on the effects of chromosomal abnormalities, particularly abnormalities in pair 23 (the sex determiner).

While loss of an entire chromosome during cell division usually results in the death of the developing organism, some individuals are born with a missing pair member. Occasionally, a female is born with only one X chromosome in pair 23, instead of the usual two. This condition, known as *Turner's syndrome*, results in a child who is short, has a webbed neck, and fails to develop sexually at puberty. In

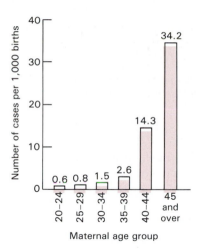

FIGURE 2–27 **Frequency of Births of Down Syndrome Infants in Relation to Age of the Mother** *The number of cases shown for each age group represents the occurrence of Down syndrome in every 1,000 births by mothers in that group. The risk of having a child with Down syndrome increases rapidly after the mother's age exceeds 40. An increased risk is also thought to occur after the father's age exceeds 55. (After Curtis & Barnes, 1985)*

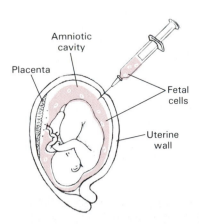

FIGURE 2–28 **Amniocentesis** *To avoid endangering the fetus and to ensure that the amniotic fluid contains enough fetal cells to make disorder detection possible, this procedure is usually not performed until the sixteenth week of pregnancy. (After Curtis & Barnes, 1985)*

addition, such persons show specific intellectual disabilities in mathematical reasoning and spatial organization of the visual field.

Sometimes the pair 23 chromosomal position contains an extra chromosome, in addition to the normal pair. For example, in a condition known as ***Klinefelter's syndrome***, there are two X chromosomes and a Y. Although they develop male characteristics, persons suffering this condition have retarded sexual development and physical abnormalities and are occasionally mentally deficient. On the other hand, some persons having an XXY configuration in pair 23 are sexually classified as female and do not experience these difficulties. A Polish track star was disqualified from competing with other female athletes in a 1967 international competition because she possessed an extra Y chromosome.

Chromosomal abnormalities in other than the twenty-third pair have been observed. For example, the presence of three copies of chromosome pair 21 results in a form of mental retardation known as ***Down syndrome.*** This disorder was originally called mongolism because of characteristic facial features which cause such individuals to look oriental or "mongoloid." Specifically, the eye has an upward slant, and the eyelid is considerably thickened. Down syndrome individuals have short thick bodies and a high probability of organ abnormality, as described in the box titled "Down Syndrome."

As Figure 2–27 indicates, Down syndrome is much more likely to occur among the offspring of older women, especially those over 45. The reason for this fact is not yet known.

Other conditions that have been linked to genetic structure involve particular types of dominant and recessive genes rather than extra or missing members of chromosome pairs. Particular dominant genes are known to be responsible for baldness in men and for cataracts of the eye. Certain recessive genes are responsible for color blindness.

A comparatively rare metabolic disorder, known as ***phenylketonuria (PKU)***, is carried by a recessive gene and may result in mental retardation. In this disorder, the individual lacks an enzyme that is necessary to break down a particular amino acid found in certain protein foods, such as milk. If the disorder is uncontrolled, nervous tissue in the body is adversely affected. Fortunately, PKU is easily diagnosed by a urine test, and the infant can be put on a special diet that is free of the amino acid, thus preventing potential damage to the nervous system.

In fact, it is now no longer necessary to wait for the birth of a child before detecting PKU. Using a technique called ***amniocentesis***, it has been possible, since the early 1970s, to detect PKU before birth. Figure 2–28 illustrates this procedure. First, the position of the fetus is determined using ultrasound. Then a needle is inserted into the amniotic fluid surrounding the fetus and fluid containing fetal cells is withdrawn. The cells are grown in tissue culture and analysis for PKU can then be conducted. Amniocentesis is helpful in connection with more than just the detection of PKU. It is also invaluable in prenatal detection of a number of other genetic disorders, including Down syndrome and sickle-cell anemia.

◆   *DOWN SYNDROME*

Down syndrome is a genetic condition that can have devastating consequences. The disease is the commonest cause of mental retardation in the U.S., with a frequency of one in 700 live births; children born with the disorder suffer from a spectrum of physical and mental problems, many of them severe. In addition, it is believed that the genes implicated in some of the symptoms of Down syndrome are the same ones that can, when altered or improperly controlled, lead to a variety of clinical disorders, including leukemia and Alzheimer's disease, in otherwise healthy individuals. For these reasons Down syndrome is currently the focus of an intensive investigation that promises to yield a wealth of information on gene expression and the molecular basis of disease.

Down syndrome is hardly a new disease. Evidence of its antiquity can be found in the form of a ninth-century Saxon skull that has the same dimensions as the skull of a typical modern patient with Down syndrome; a variety of artistic renditions dating from the 15th century depict infants whose facial features are characteristic of the syndrome.

The syndrome was not formally recognized, however, until 1866. In that year John Langdon Down, physician at the Earlswood Asylum in Surrey, England, published the first comprehensive description of the disorder. His account was based on the observation that certain mentally retarded patients have a distinctive constellation of physical symptoms: notably epicanthic folds of the eyes, flattened facial features, unusual palm creases, muscular flaccidity, and short stature.

It is now known that individuals with Down syndrome are affected by a wide variety of abnormalities, both anatomical and biochemical. Forty percent of them are born with congenital heart defects, most have small brains, and many are at increased risk for developing cataracts or other vision impairments because of defects in the lenses of their eyes. Biochemically they suffer from elevated levels of purines (two of the nitrogenous bases that form DNA and RNA)—a condition that by itself can lead to neurological impairment, mental retardation, and immune-system deficiencies. Additional complications include susceptibility to infection and a twenty- to fiftyfold increase in the risk of developing leukemia.

It is not surprising, therefore, that individuals with Down syndrome typically have shortened life spans. In 1929 their estimated life expectancy was only nine years. By 1980 improved medical care had increased that average to more than 30 years, and now 25 percent of individuals with Down syndrome live to the age of 50.

As the average age of individuals with Down syndrome increases, another aspect of the disease has come to light. In the past few decades it has become clear from the study of autopsy material that all individuals with Down syndrome over the age of 35 develop the same kind of abnormal microscopic senile plaques and neurofibrillary tangles in the brain as people who die from Alzheimer's disease, the major cause of presenile dementia. Individuals with Down syndrome also appear to be at a significantly increased risk of developing the cognitive symptoms of Alzheimer's disease.

From ''The Causes of Down Syndrome'' by D. Patterson, 1987, *Scientific American*, *257*, pp. 52–53. Copyright © 1987 by Scientific American, Inc. All rights reserved.

Twin Studies

Although many different experimental techniques are used in studying behavioral genetics, the *twin study* has been a particularly influential way of investigating the impact of heredity on human behavior. This technique involves the comparison of monozygotic and dizygotic twins. Remember that identical, or monozygotic, twins develop from a single fertilized ovum, and so they have exactly the same heredity. Dizygotic, or fraternal, twins do not. They are no more alike genetically than ordinary siblings. Researchers have assumed that both kinds of twins are equally likely to have experienced the same environment. If this assumption is true, then studies comparing these two types of twins should distinguish between genetic and environmental influences. For example, it has been found that fraternal twins are slightly more similar with respect to IQ scores than are ordinary siblings. Assuming that fraternal twins share more common experiences than do siblings of different ages, this finding suggests that environment has an effect on IQ scores. Other twin studies show that the IQ scores of identical twins are more similar than those of either ordinary siblings or fraternal twins, suggesting that heredity may also have an influence on IQ scores (Erlenmeyer-Kimling & Jarvik, 1963; Scarr & Carter-Saltzman, 1979).

Some research suggests that heredity influences the development of a particular kind of mental disturbance called schizophrenia. Studies have found that schizophrenia is more common among people who have a close relative, such as a parent or sibling, who is schizophrenic. Studies of twins have found that the number of times both members of a pair are schizophrenic is considerably higher when the twins are identical (monozygotic) and thus have the same heredity, than when they are fraternal (dizygotic) (Crowe, 1982; Gottesman & Shields, 1966).

Recent work at the Minnesota Center for Twin and Adoption Research has led to the conclusion that many of our ordinary personality traits, such as worry, aggressiveness, and optimism, are all, to one degree or another, influenced by heredity (Wellborn, 1987). Investigators tested hundreds of identical twins and representatives of the population at large to obtain percentages that indicate how much personality traits are determined by heredity (Figure 2–29). However, the ability to separate environmental from hereditary influences on behavior by using twin studies is not as clear-cut as it may seem. Some of the basic assumptions of such twin studies have been challenged during the debate on IQ and heredity, as we will see later in Chapter 16.

Selective Breeding and Inbred Strains

Other methods used by behavioral geneticists to examine inherited behavioral characteristics include selective breeding and the development of inbred strains. Although these methods are used with lower animals, much can be learned about humans because the process of genetic transmission, if not identical, is at least very similar across species.

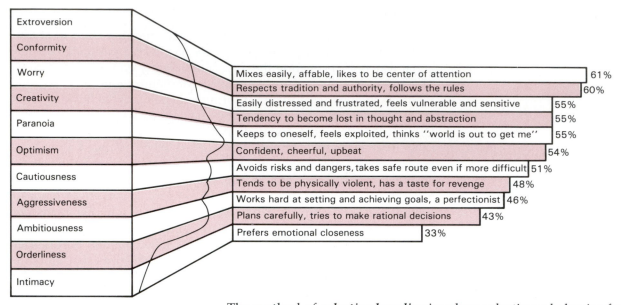

Mixes easily, affable, likes to be center of attention	61%
Respects tradition and authority, follows the rules	60%
Easily distressed and frustrated, feels vulnerable and sensitive	55%
Tendency to become lost in thought and abstraction	55%
Keeps to oneself, feels exploited, thinks "world is out to get me"	55%
Confident, cheerful, upbeat	54%
Avoids risks and dangers, takes safe route even if more difficult	51%
Tends to be physically violent, has a taste for revenge	48%
Works hard at setting and achieving goals, a perfectionist	46%
Plans carefully, tries to make rational decisions	43%
Prefers emotional closeness	33%

Traits (left side): Extroversion, Conformity, Worry, Creativity, Paranoia, Optimism, Cautiousness, Aggressiveness, Ambitiousness, Orderliness, Intimacy

FIGURE 2–29   Extroverts Are Born, Not Made   *The percentages show how much these personality traits are determined by heredity rather than culture. The figures are based on new findings from the Minnesota Center for Twin and Adoption Research. For the 11 traits listed researchers are confident they can make very close estimates of how much genes influence behavior in the general population—but what the percentages will be in one individual is impossible to say.* (After Wellborn, 1987)

The method of **selective breeding** involves selecting a behavior for study and then breeding animals according to how much of that behavior they show. The reasoning behind these studies is that if a trait is determined by heredity, then it will be possible to change it by selective breeding. If the trait is not determined by heredity, then it will not be influenced by this technique. Selective animal breeding has been going on for centuries, of course. But breeding for traits that are relevant to psychological concerns, such as intelligence, is quite new. In one study, designed to investigate hereditary influences on learning ability, rats were selected and bred according to how well they did on a maze-running task. Females that did well in learning to run the maze were bred with males that did well. Females that did poorly were bred with males that did poorly. By mating several generations of the offspring of these original runners according to the same criterion, two strains eventually were developed: a maze-bright, and a maze-dull strain. When the descendants were tested a year later, rats from the maze-bright strain were found to be markedly superior to those from the maze-dull strain in learning several different kinds of mazes (Rosenzweig, 1969). In fact, animals can be bred for a wide variety of traits including aggressiveness, maternal instinct, sex drive, desire for alcohol, and curiosity.

The technique of **inbred strains** involves interbreeding animals that are related to each other. By interbreeding over many generations, we may decrease genetic variability. In fact, in a fully developed inbred strain, the members may be considered genetically identical. Often, if one member is observed to differ in behavior from the others in the strain, we can conclude that this difference is most likely environmental, as all members are genetically the same.

Heredity, Environment, and Evolution

At the beginning of this section we pointed out that both environment and heredity play important roles in determining who we are and what we can do. This fact requires further comment. There are many ways that heredity and environment interact. Recall the selective breeding research that produced maze-bright and maze-dull strains of rats. Additional research has discovered that when rats are reared in an "enriched" environment—a cage with a variety of toys that young rats like, such as ladders, platforms, and swings—their learning ability becomes much greater than that of rats raised without such stimulation. In fact, if maze-dull rats are provided such stimulation in their youth, they can become as capable as maze-bright rats. This indicates that while it may not be possible to make a genius out of a mentally dull person, it is possible to design an environment that will help the person make the most of his or her genetic endowment.

Another example of the heredity–environment interaction is found in connection with schizophrenia. As noted earlier, twin studies have demonstrated a strong genetic component in the development of schizophrenia. As the relationship to a schizophrenic becomes closer, the chances of an individual's developing schizophrenia increase. Early research indicated that when the schizophrenic relative is a parent, sibling, or fraternal twin, the chances that the individual also will become schizophrenic are about 15 out of 100. But when the afflicted relative is an identical twin, the chances increase to about 86 out of 100 (Kallmann, 1953, 1958). This research suggests that individuals inherit a predisposition to become schizophrenic. However, if heredity were the only determinant, we would expect that if one identical twin became schizophrenic, the other one would always become schizophrenic. Such is not the case. The difference between this expectation and the 86-percent figure reported by researchers probably represents the contribution of environment. While heredity may set the stage, environment determines whether or not the show will go on. Exactly what kind of environment stimulates schizophrenia in a predisposed person is not yet known; however, studies of family relationships of schizophrenics suggest that their families tend to be characterized by stress and discord (Lidz, 1967).

Another way that environment and heredity interact relates to survival. When an environment is altered in some way, we often observe changes in the species living in that environment. We say that the species "adapts" to the environment. What happens is that individuals possessing the particular genetic structure needed to cope with the new environment are able to survive. They reproduce and pass the genetic configuration necessary for survival on to their offspring. Those without the needed genetic structure perish, and thus their inappropriate genetic configuration is withdrawn from the population's gene pool.

In general, we observe the following genetic–environmental interaction cycle. Environment makes a demand. Through "survival of the fittest," the species responds genetically to the environmental demand. The environment makes a new demand. The species responds again. There may well be a day when we see this same kind of species response to the environmental demands brought about by pollution. Those individuals possessing a genetic makeup that allows them to survive in a polluted environment may continue living and reproduce. No doubt, this represents one way to overcome the problem of environmental pollution. But it is a drastic solution, requiring the

Individuals capable of thriving in this kind of polluted world someday may evolve, but we hope that more direct efforts at control will be made before such a drastic change in genetic makeup is required for survival.

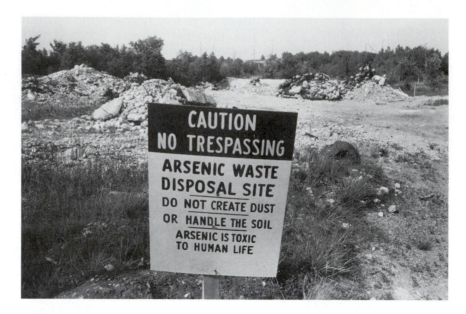

death of many genetically unprepared individuals. One would hope the more reasonable solution, reduction of pollution, will be accomplished before the species alters its genetic makeup in response to an unnecessary environmental demand.

Sociobiology

Sociobiology (Ligon & Ligon, 1982; Montagu, 1980; Wilson, 1975) is a controversial way of thinking about behavior and genetics. Sociobiologists argue that *social* behaviors, as well as individual characteristics and tendencies, are inherited and are shaped by the mechanisms of natural selection. Thus they argue that sheep have inherited the tendency to stay in groups because flocking together helps the species' chances of survival. Sheep with a "flocking gene" are more likely to survive and pass on that gene than are sheep without it, who tend to wander off and be eaten by predators. Living in a group has certain advantages such as early warnings of danger by other members and efficient defense systems coordinated by the strongest members of the group. A similar argument would apply to the human tendency to live in groups. Genes that determine cooperation and communal living are likely to be selected, or passed on to future generations, because individuals possessing them are more likely to survive and reproduce. When life is reduced to the survival of the fittest, humans who live in supportive groups will have a better chance to survive and perpetuate the species through reproduction.

The sociobiological hypothesis of inherited social behavior seems very reasonable in the straightforward examples that we have been considering, but it becomes controversial when it is applied to more complex forms of social behavior. Consider altruism (Zahn-Waxler & Cummings, 1986), the tendency to help others at one's own expense, such as giving one's life to save children. Critics say this behavior should not be maintained in the population because it results in the loss of reproductive capacity and tends to sacrifice the braver members of the group as well. Sociobiologists reply that if parents can rescue their offspring, even though doing so may cause their own death, then that action will save the lives of individuals who also possess the gene for altruism. Thus, more genes for altruism will probably be preserved in the group by the death of the parent than are lost.

Many social behaviors that at first seem difficult to explain in terms of natural selection have been interpreted by sociobiologists. For example, infanticide, or the killing of the young in one's own group, might seem contrary to Darwinian theory. But sociobiologists argue that infanticide may be adaptive and naturally selected. A new dominant male monkey sometimes will kill offspring of other, lesser males. By killing these offspring the dominant male is increasing the survival chances for his own offspring, who presumably carry the adaptive genes that vaulted their father to the dominant position (see also Alford, 1980). In other words, just about any human or animal social behavior can be seen as adaptive if the interests of the species rather than the individual are considered (see Buss, 1985; Trivers, 1985).

One major objection to the sociobiological approach is that socio-biology can explain almost any social behavior *after the fact*, but it is incapable of predicting what adaptive social behaviors will evolve. For example, it is all well and good to say that humor is a naturally se-lected trait because humor enhances communication. But who could have predicted the evolution of laughter?

SUMMARY

1. The nervous system is composed of the central and peripheral subdivisions which, together, receive, process, and react to information.

2. The neuron, the basic unit of neural communica-tion, is composed of a cell body, dendrites, an axon, and axonal end brushes.

3. When stimulation of a neuron by other neurons is intense enough, an electrical impulse is initiated that travels down the axon to the synaptic knobs.

4. The impulse causes chemical neurotransmitters to be released from synaptic vesicles. These chemicals travel across the synaptic gap where they, in turn, stimulate or inhibit the next neuron.

5. The electrochemical impulse is generated by a rapid exchange of tiny, electrically charged particles across the cell membrane. Neurons fire according to an all-or-none principle.

6. The absolute refractory period is a short period of time following an impulse when the cell is insensitive to further stimulation.

7. In one type of synapse the neurotransmitters stim-ulate the next neuron, while in another, the neuro-transmitters inhibit the next neuron. It is the algebraic sum of the excitatory and inhibitory events that deter-mines if the cell will fire.

8. Cell bodies often cluster into nuclei and ganglia. Axons and dendrites form nerves and tracts.

9. Afferent neurons bring information in from the senses. Efferent neurons send commands to the mus-cles and glands.

10. The central nervous system includes the spinal cord and the brain.

11. The somatic division of the peripheral system brings information in to the central nervous system and sends commands out to the muscles.

12. The autonomic division of the peripheral system automatically controls the functions of our internal or-gans and structures.

13. The sympathetic division of the autonomic system prepares us for emergency action. The parasympathe-tic division dominates when we are quiet and relaxed.

14. The brain is studied with lesions, recordings of electrical activity, stimulation, and scanning methods. Stimulation is also used in electroconvulsive shock therapy.

15. The hindbrain includes the medulla, the cerebellum, and the pons.

16. The midbrain is a relatively small brain division connecting the hindbrain and forebrain.

17. The brain stem, the oldest part of the brain in evolutionary terms, includes the hindbrain and midbrain and also makes contact with the forebrain.

18. The reticular activating system (RAS) is found in the core of the brain stem. The RAS regulates levels of arousal.

19. The forebrain includes the thalamus, the hypothalamus, the limbic system, and the cerebrum.

20. The thalamus relays incoming sensory information to the cortex. The hypothalamus is an emotional and motivational control center.

21. The limbic system is involved in emotional behavior, attention, learning, and memory.

22. Each cerebral hemisphere is divided into four lobes: the frontal (movement), the parietal (body senses), the temporal (hearing), and the occipital (vision) lobes.

23. The association areas of the cortex are involved in higher mental functions, such as learning, thinking, and language.

24. Our brains change with age and experience.

25. Split-brain studies suggest that the language ability is generally located in the left hemisphere of the brain while the right hemisphere deals mainly with nonverbal activity such as spatial reasoning.

26. Brain functioning involves poorly understood communication loops and systems rather than single structures devoted to specific functions.

27. The pituitary gland secretes at least eight hormones that affect the operation of the body. Thyroid hormones govern the body's metabolism, while the adrenal glands secrete sex hormones, cortisol, adrenalin, and various other hormones.

28. The heart may be an endocrine gland, too.

29. Pheromones are biological molecules ejected into the environment.

30. Recent thinking suggests that heredity sets the limits on behavior while experience determines where within those limits behavior will actually fall.

31. Each cell contains 46 chromosomes, grouped into 23 pairs. The larger chromosomes look like Xs, while the smaller ones look like Ys.

32. Each chromosome contains thousands of genes, or complex molecules of DNA. It is these molecules that contain the genetic instructions.

33. Each ovum and sperm cell contains only half the 46 chromosomes. When the ovum and sperm unite, the new set of 46 chromosomes determines the genetic makeup of the new individual.

34. Recessive genes are displayed only if the individual possesses two of them. Otherwise, the dominant gene is expressed.

35. Chromosomal abnormalities can lead to retardation, abnormal behavior, physical deformities, and abnormal sexual development.

36. Genetic abnormalities of the fetus can be detected by means of amniocentesis.

37. Personality, IQ, and a predisposition toward schizophrenia may be affected by genetic makeup.

38. Selective breeding and the use of inbred strains are two techniques that may help us understand the genetic determinants of behavior.

39. Sociobiology is the school of thought which holds that social behavior has a genetic component.

KEY TERMS

absolute refractory period
acetylcholine (ACh)
acetylcholinesterase (AChE)
adrenalin
adrenals
afferent
all-or-none principle
amniocentesis
androgen
antidiuretic hormone (ADH)
association areas

autonomic
auxiliary axon
axon
axon hillock
axonal conduction
behavioral genetics
brain stem
cell body
cell membrane
central fissure
central nervous system

cerebellum
cerebral cortex
cerebral hemispheres
cerebrum
chromosomes
computerized axial
   tomography (CAT)
corpus callosum
cortisol (cortisone)
cretinism
cytoplasm

dendrites
depolarized
differentially permeable
dizygotic
DNA
dominant
Down syndrome
efferent
electroconvulsive shock
  treatment
electroencephalogram (EEG)
end brush
endocrine (ductless) gland
endocrine system
epinephrine
estrogen
exocrine (duct) gland
fissures
forebrain
frontal lobe
ganglion
genes
genetics
genotypes
glial cell
growth hormone
hindbrain
hormones
hyperthyroidism
hypothalamus
hypothyroidism

inbred strains
integration
interneurons
ions
Klinefelter's syndrome
lateral fissure
lesions
limbic system
medulla
midbrain
monozygotic
myelin sheath
nerves
nervous system
neuron
neurotransmitters
nodes of Ranvier
noradrenalin
norepinephrine
nuclear magnetic
  resonance (NMR)
nucleus
occipital lobe
optic chiasm
oxytocin
parasympathetic system
parietal lobe
peripheral nervous system
phenotypes
phenylketonuria (PKU)
pheromones

physiological psychology
pituitary
polarized
pons
positron emission tomography
  (PET)
recessive
recordings
relative refractory period
reticular activating system (RAS)
scanning techniques
Schwann cells
selective breeding
serotonin
somatic
spinal cord
stimulation
sympathetic system
synapse
synaptic gap
synaptic knob
synaptic transmission
synaptic vesicles
temporal lobe
thalamus
theta activity
thyroid
thyroxin
tract
Turner's syndrome
twin study

ADDITIONAL READING

Carlson, N. R. (1986) *Physiology of behavior.* Boston: Allyn and Bacon.
This text presents a good, solid survey of the physiological bases of behavior.

Cotman, C. W. & McGaugh, J. L. (1980) *Behavioral neuroscience.* New York: Academic Press.
This text offers broad, somewhat high-level coverage of the field of behavioral neuroscience.

Curtis, H. & Barnes, N. S. (1985) *Invitation to biology.* New York: Worth.
This is a biology text, but one that is especially helpful to the student of physiological psychology.

Kalat, J. W. (1984) *Biological psychology.* Belmont, CA: Wadsworth.
This resource presents basic coverage of the entire field of physiological psychology.

3 Sensation and Perception

You are out driving with a friend when you both see a brown object on the road some distance ahead. If your eyesight and your friend's eyesight are roughly comparable, you both experience the same sensation; you both possess a visual image of a small brown object. But you do not let it go at that. You try to make sense out of the visual image. You begin to interpret the sensation. You might say, "There's a paper bag blowing across the road." At the same time your friend might say, "There's an animal crossing the road."

Why do two people interpret the same visual image differently? This is the kind of question we try to answer when we study perception. *Perception* refers to the ways that we understand our environment by interpreting incoming sensory information.

The field of perceptual psychology is loosely defined and covers a multitude of interests. Thus it is helpful to draw a distinction between sensation and perception. When psychologists speak of *sensation* they are referring to the way the sensory systems operate on a physiological level. Psychologists interested in sensation want to know how raw sensory information is brought into the organism through the senses. If they are interested in how a sensation of "blueness" is established, for example, they will look to the eye and its functions to provide them with the answers. They would be more concerned with the image of the brown object on the road than with people's evaluations of that image.

Psychologists focusing on perception will be more interested in how the individual organizes and makes sense of the raw incoming sensory information. These psychologists would focus on the ways that individuals interpret the brown object on the road. Of course, most psychologists in this field are interested in *both* sensation and perception, and the two topics are closely interwoven.

The study of sensation traditionally has considered the physiology and functions of the sense receptors, and the nature of the physical stimulus that is associated with each sensory system. Perception, on the other hand, is studied by considering the higher-order cognitive processes that make sensations meaningful. Perceptions are guesses about what is out there. Given sensory information that is often limited and ambiguous, we can only theorize about the external world.

In this chapter we will examine both sensation and perception. We will discuss each sensory system and consider the character of its function. Then, we will explore the higher-order perceptual processes.

PSYCHOPHYSICS

Psychophysics is the branch of psychology that is concerned with sensory processes; specifically, it deals with the relationships between physical stimuli and resulting sensations. A psychophysicist might be interested in what happens to your impression of a light when the intensity of that light is tripled. Would you report that the light had tripled? Perhaps you would, but then again, perhaps you would not. It is to this kind of intriguing problem that the psychophysicist addresses himself and his research.

Specialized Receptors and Transduction

We cannot hear with our eyes. We cannot taste with our ears. We cannot see with our skin. We are bathed in sound and light, and yet only the eye responds to light, while the ear alone responds to sound. These obvious facts lead to one conclusion: there must be specialized sensory nerve endings that respond only to certain types of energy. These specialized nerve endings are called *receptors.* Some of the specialized nerve endings, or sensory receptors, have been studied more closely than others. When we discuss the various sensory systems, we will note some of the differences between receptors that perform different functions.

These receptors do something in addition to detecting stimulus energy. They *transduce* or convert that energy into electrochemical signals that the brain can utilize. When sound waves impinge on our ears, they do not "go into our brain" in an unmodified form. Our brains are not vibrating when we hear sound. Instead, the auditory sensory system converts vibration into the language of the brain through a process called *neural coding.*

Absolute Threshold

Clearly, not all levels of stimulus energy will cause our receptors to respond. Therefore, we will want to learn *how much* of a particular energy is required to trigger one of these specialized receptors. There are levels of light that are so low we cannot detect them. There are sounds we cannot hear and pressures so slight that our touch receptors cannot detect them. Before we can begin to understand the sensory systems, we need to know the minimum amount of stimulus energy to which an individual will respond.

The minimal size of the stimulus that is required for the individual to respond is referred to as the *absolute threshold.* The absolute threshold for any sensory system is established by presenting increasing amounts of stimulus until the subject is able to detect the presence of the stimulus 50 percent of the time. The rule of "50 percent detection" has been established primarily because psychophysicists agree that it is a logical standard. Thus if we wish to establish an absolute visual threshold, we might expose subjects to a series of dots of light at varying levels of brightness. The level of brightness at which the subjects could detect the stimulus 50 percent of the time would be called the absolute threshold. Some approximate absolute threshold levels are given in Table 3–1. They are only approximations, because the absolute threshold is absolute in name only. In any actual situation, there is a range of stimulation at which a subject can detect a given input some of the time, but not all of the time.

Difference Threshold and Weber's Fraction

As you might expect, threshold values are not fixed. They depend on the nature of the stimulus, the conditions under which the test is made, and even on the motivation of the person being tested. For

TABLE 3–1   Some Approximate Absolute Threshold Values

Vision	A candle flame 30 miles away on a dark clear night
Hearing	The tick of a watch under quiet conditions at 20 feet
Taste	One teaspoon of sugar in two gallons of water
Smell	One drop of perfume diffused in a six-room apartment
Touch	An insect wing falling on your cheek from a distance of one centimeter

Source: After Galanter, 1962.

example, your room may be so quiet at 3 A.M. that you can really hear a pin drop, but when you are having a party in that same room, you might not even notice that someone is talking to you. On the other hand, if you suspect that someone is talking about you, then your threshold will drop—low threshold means high sensitivity. Striking a match may help tremendously in locating a keyhole in the dark, but striking a match in a well-lit room will make little difference. These examples suggest another question we may ask about the stimuli for activating the sense experiences. How much of an increase in the level of stimulus energy does it take before we notice a difference? The concept to which we are referring is the *difference threshold,* and it is defined as the minimum amount of stimulus change that is necessary for a difference to be detected. This threshold is defined as the level of difference that is detectable 50 percent of the time. The term *just-noticeable difference (jnd)* is often used in referring to the difference threshold.

Around 1834, a German physiologist, E. H. Weber, studied the ability of humans to discriminate between stimulus intensities. He found that a detectable change in a stimulus is proportional to the intensity of the stimulus. In other words, if a stimulus is very intense, then a big change in that stimulus must occur before the change can be detected. If the stimulus is less intense, then less change will be necessary for the subject to notice a difference. For example, if a subject judging weight differences is given a 100-g (gram) weight, then he will need 102 g before he can detect a difference between the two. If he is given a 200-g weight, he will need a 204-g weight to detect a difference. If given 400 g, he needs 408 g to be able to notice a difference, and so on. The proportion, called *Weber's fraction,* is defined as $\Delta I/I = k$, where I (Greek iota) is the size of the stimulus taken as a referent, ΔI is the size of the difference necessary to be noticed, and k is the resulting constant of proportionality. Table 3–2 lists some values of Weber's fraction for different senses. The constant of proportionality varies among the different senses, as Table 3–2 shows. Over the course of much research, the constants have been shown not to hold at very weak and very strong levels of stimulus intensity, but they are reliable at the levels of stimulus intensity we encounter in everyday life.

TABLE 3–2   Weber's Fraction Values for Different Senses

Vision (brightness)	1/60
Kinesthesis (weights)	1/50
Pain (thermally aroused)	1/30
Hearing (middle frequency)	1/10
Pressure (skin)	1/7
Smell (India rubber)	1/4
Taste (salt)	1/3

SENSORY ADAPTATION

At this very moment you are probably not aware of the fact that your hands and the tip of your nose are cooler than your armpits. It is likely that you feel about the same degree of warmth all over your body. You also probably have not noticed the pressure of your clothes against your skin. Think about your left foot for a moment. Feel anything you had not been noticing? Similarly, you probably have not been hearing all the sounds around you. Stop for a moment and listen. Have you ever put on cologne and noticed that after a few moments you could not smell it anymore, only to have a friend later in the day tell you that you smell good (or bad)?

What we are talking about here is called *sensory adaptation.* After a period of continued stimulation, with no change in the intensity or character of the stimulus, the threshold increases. That is, the receptor adjusts to, or "gets used to," the stimulus and stops responding to it. If the stimulus changes in some way, the receptor is likely to begin responding again. Changes in the organism can also affect the receptor's response to the constant stimulus. For example, you probably are much more conscious of the sounds around you right now because you have just been motivated to notice them.

There is an experiment you can do at home that will help you experience sensory adaptation. Fill one pan with very cold water, one with very hot water, and one with lukewarm water. Put one hand in the hot water and one in the cold water. Leave them there for two minutes. Then take them both out and plunge them into the lukewarm water. What will you feel? The hand that has been in the hot water will tell you the lukewarm water is very cold, while the hand that has been in the cold water will tell you that that same pan of lukewarm water is very hot. This is because each hand has "gotten used to" the temperature in its first pan. The temperature in the second pan therefore seems intense.

The tendency toward adaptation varies among the senses. Olfactory adaptation in humans occurs fairly rapidly. Not long after you enter the fish market, you can no longer detect the fishy odor. Pain, on the other hand, appears not to adapt. People who have experienced prolonged pain, such as a toothache, usually report that it does not decrease over time.

You might think that the visual system does not adapt either. After all, no matter how long we stare at something, it does not disappear. In fact, the visual system does adapt to a constant stimulus, but objects do not disappear from view, because our eyes make continuous tiny movements, even when they stare at something. Because of these eye movements, the stimulation is not constant. However, it is possible to present unchanging stimulation to the eye, as shown in Figure 3–1 (Ornstein, 1977). When this is done, the visual system adapts and the projected letter fades from view.

Sensory Adaptation Can Be Helpful

If you think about it, you will realize how helpful sensory adaptation is to us in our daily lives. Imagine being constantly aware of your cold nose, the pressure of your clothes, and the rumble of distant

FIGURE 3–1 The Apparatus Used in Demonstrating Visual Adaptation *A tiny projector is mounted on a contact lens worn by a subject. The projector casts an image onto a screen and thus into the eye. Since the contact lens and projector move with every movement of the eye, the image upon the eye is completely steady. Under these conditions, the projected image tends to disappear completely.*

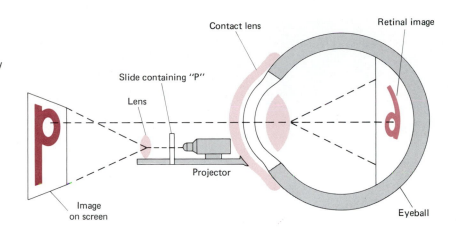

traffic as you try to take an exam. With all those unimportant messages coming in, you might not be able to concentrate at all. And if we could not adapt to bad odors, our lives would be far less pleasant. On the other hand, *not* adapting can be helpful, too. For example, it would be dangerous if pain adapted, because we would be unaware of injuries and ailments that require treatment. And if the tiny movements of our eyes did not prevent visual adaptation, we would also be in danger.

Boredom: Good or Bad?

What happens when we adapt to the majority of incoming sensory stimuli? What happens when "nothing is happening"? In early ***sensory deprivation*** experiments (Heron, Doane, & Scott, 1956), volunteer subjects wore goggles and gloves and lay for long periods of time in small, dim, soundproof rooms. In spite of very good pay most subjects could stand this sensory deprivation for a few days at the most. These early studies report that subjects began to hallucinate, think unclearly, and become confused. They also frequently felt anger and frustration.

More recent studies, however, seem to suggest that sensory deprivation, or the ***Restricted Environmental Stimulation Technique (REST)***, as it is now called, can actually be beneficial (Suedfeld, Ballard, & Murphy, 1983; Suedfeld & Kristeller, 1982). Hallucinations are less common than thought and some mental processes may actually improve. In one technique, involving floating in an isolated tank filled with salt water, subjects report pleasant and relaxing sensations. So at least part of the time, sensory isolation seems to be good for us. We will discuss sensory deprivation again in Chapter 9.

THE MINOR SENSES

Cells scattered over the exterior and interior of the body have gradually developed the specialized function of sensing the state of the environment, both external and internal. Sensory cells in the body are organized according to one of three patterns: clustered, somewhat localized, or widely scattered. Cells in the first category are clustered together in one location to form specialized sensory organs. Hence,

FIGURE 3–2   Dominant and Minor Senses   *A dog wearing a lighted collar follows the scent trail of a pheasant carcass that has been dragged across a field. Obviously, the sense of smell is more important to some animals than it is to humans.*

we have eyes and ears. Cells in the second category, while somewhat localized, do not form special organs. Taste buds embedded in the tongue, back of the mouth, and the nose belong to this group. Other cells in this group include those clustered together inside the skull near the auditory apparatus and in the joints of the body that sense body position and movement. Cells in the third category are widely scattered throughout the body. Thus, the sensations of touch, temperature, and pain come from receptors that lie under the skin or near internal organs. These cells are less clustered than either of the first two types.

We can think of all sensory cells as specialized neurons that differ from other neurons in that they are stimulated, not by synaptic transmission from other neurons, but rather by some form of external stimulus. Some receptor cells are stimulated by light, some by sound, some by chemical substances, and still others by mechanical energy in the form of pressure or heat. But each is sensitive to a particular form of external energy.

Dominant and Minor Senses

Senses for which specialized sensory organs have evolved — vision and hearing — are called our dominant senses because we depend on them much more heavily than we depend on the minor senses such as smell and taste. Think about which sensory system you would give up if forced to part with one. Which would it be? Although the loss of *any* sense is traumatic, most people, without hesitation, choose sight as the *last* sense they would elect to lose. Hearing is another sense most people would not want to sacrifice. The sense of smell is not crucial in our lives (at least not as crucial as it seems to be to the dog in Figure 3–2). It is not very important to birds either but plays a crucial role in the existence of many species. Our minor senses are necessary for efficient functioning, and sometimes even survival, but they have less impact on our behavior than our major senses do. Thus we will deal with the minor senses swiftly and then consider the eye and the ear in much greater detail.

The Skin Sensors

There are four basic skin sensations — pressure, pain, warmth, and cold. Microscopic examination of the skin has revealed several different cell structures that function as sense receptors. Some specialized fibers end in branches called free nerve endings. The ends of others are encapsulated in various globular bulbs or corpuscles, and still others end by wrapping around the base of a hair. (Figure 3–3 illustrates these different types of sense receptors.) Some years ago, it was believed that each of the four basic skin sensations must come from the activation of a different type of cell. However, more recent research has found that this explanation is too simple. First, while some of these receptor cells respond more readily to one kind of stimulation, they can also respond to the other types of stimulation. It has been discovered that touch receptors will respond to certain sound waves. The sensitivity of the touch receptor to sound is lessened if the skin

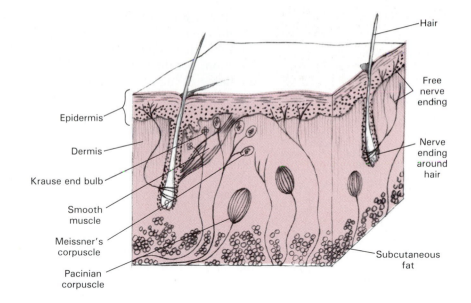

FIGURE 3–3 The Cell Structures of the Skin Sensors *Pressure, pain, warmth, and cold are sensed by receptor cells that respond to various types of stimulation and interact in producing the various sensations.*

Hair

Free nerve ending

Nerve ending around hair

Epidermis

Dermis

Krause end bulb

Smooth muscle

Meissner's corpuscle

Pacinian corpuscle

Subcutaneous fat

is either cooled or warmed (Green, 1977). Second, it now seems that the different types of receptor cells interact in producing the various sensations. That is, a given stimulus, such as a hot one, may stimulate several different types of cells. The brain then interprets this pattern of stimulation.

The interaction of the skin receptors is most clearly demonstrated by some rather complex skin sensations. For example, an itch is produced by light and repeated stimulation of the pain receptors of adjacent areas. A tickle is produced by lightly stimulating adjacent pressure receptors. And the sensation of "hot" can be produced by the simultaneous stimulation of receptors sensitive to warmth and receptors sensitive to cold. That is, some of our sensations are the result of more than one type of receptor being stimulated in complex ways.

Position Sensors

Two groups of receptors provide information about the position of our body. Receptors in the first group, the *kinesthetic receptors,* are located around the muscles, tendons, and joints. When we move, these receptors provide feedback. They tell us which muscles are contracted and which are relaxed. They tell us how our body weight is distributed and where our feet are in relation to the rest of our body. Without these sensors it would be difficult to walk. We would literally have to watch every step. But even if visual feedback were substituted for kinesthetic feedback, it is unlikely that we could accomplish complex movement sequences such as dancing or bowling.

Receptors in the second group, the *equilibratory receptors,* provide us with our sense of balance and our position relative to gravity. These receptors are more localized than the kinesthetic receptors. They are located in a skull cavity near each inner ear and housed in structures called the *semicircular canals* and the *vestibular sacs.* The semicircular canals and vestibular sacs are shown in Figure 3–4.

These youngsters on a park ride are pushing their kinesthetic and equilibratory receptors to the limit as the sensor cells labor to provide information about balance and weight distribution to the brain.

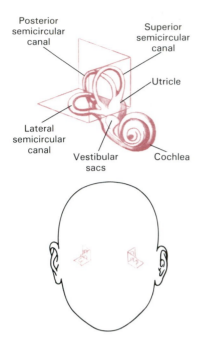

Posterior
semicircular
canal

Superior
semicircular
canal

Utricle

Lateral
semicircular
canal

Vestibular
sacs

Cochlea

FIGURE 3–4 The Equilibratory Receptors *Located near the inner ear, these receptors are housed in the semicircular canals and the vestibular sacs. (After Carlson, 1986)*

The semicircular canal structures consist of three curved tubes roughly perpendicular to one another. The canals are filled with a fluid that moves as the head moves. When the body is rotated in any direction, the fluid moves and presses against hair cells embedded in the lining of the canals. This movement of hair cells by fluid initiates neural messages that are carried to the brain. In this way, these sensors provide information that the body is moving.

The vestibular sacs are located between the semicircular canals and the hearing apparatus of the ear. Movement of a gelatinous substance in these sacs also moves hair cells that are in contact with free nerve endings. The vestibular sensors are sensitive to the tilting of the head at an angle.

Smell

For many vertebrates, smell or olfaction is a primary source of information about the external environment (see Figure 3–5). But for humans, as well as other vertebrates, such as birds and marine mammals, it is considerably less important. The importance of smell to the animal is reflected in the amount of brain tissue that is devoted to olfaction. In the shark, for example, almost the entire brain is devoted to olfaction. Porpoises and humans, by contrast, have very little brain tissue relating to the sense of smell.

The olfactory receptors are located high in the roof of the nasal cavities in a section of tissue called the **olfactory epithelium.** Gases that enter the nose are deflected upward, where they stimulate the olfactory cells (see Figure 3–6). Activated olfactory cells send their messages directly, without intermediate synapse, to the olfactory area of the brain.

Curiously, the olfactory cells undergo a continuous turnover every few days throughout our entire life (Graziadei & Graziadei,

FIGURE 3–5 The Importance of Scent *The white-tailed doe sniffing her newborn fawn is forming a permanent olfactory bond with her offspring. The scent releases a chemical in the mother's brain that sends a strong signal to her memory system indicating that this is an important odor to remember.*

FIGURE 3–6   The Olfactory
Epithelium   *The olfactory
receptors send their messages
directly to the olfactory area of the
brain.*

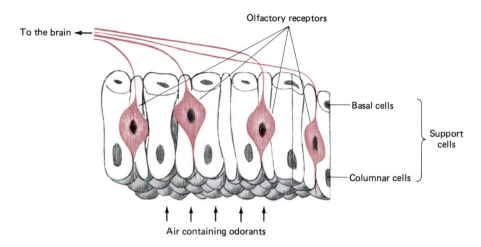

1978). Precursor cells, not yet capable of detecting odors, are constantly maturing into sensitive olfactory receptors (see Figure 3–7). When they reach maturity, they function for a few days and then degenerate, as their function is taken over by newly matured cells. There is always a fresh crop of cells that is doing the work.

How many basic odors are there? The answer is not clear, despite several attempts to classify them. Early in this century it was suggested that there are six basic odors: flavory, fruity, foul, burnt, spicy, and resinous. But more recent work (see Table 3–3) suggests that there are seven primary odors, and perhaps many more, each of which may be detected by a different kind of receptor cell. Note that the two systems of classifying odors do not overlap very well. Such disagreements are typical of attempts to identify basic odors, because people find it difficult to describe what they experience when they sniff (see Frijters, 1980).

FIGURE 3–7   The Maturation
and Degeneration of Olfactory
Neurons   *Precursory cells (a),
not yet able to detect odor, mature
into functioning neurons (b). These
mature cells operate for a few days
and then degenerate (c) as they are
replaced by newly matured cells.*

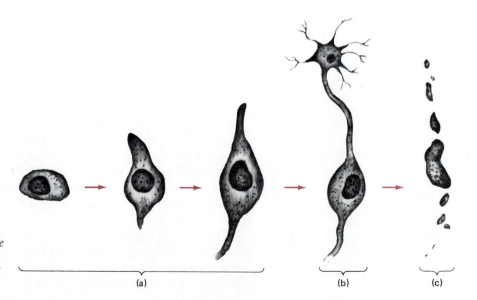

TABLE 3–3 Seven Odors That May Be Primary

Each of these basic odors may be detected by a different receptor cell. Other odors are assumed to be the result of our experiencing several of these basic odors simultaneously.

Primary Odor	Chemical Example	Familiar Substance
Camphoraceous	Camphor	Moth repellent
Musky	Pentadecanolactone	Angelica root oil
Floral	Phenylethylmethyl ethyl carbinol	Roses
Pepperminty	Menthone	Mint candy
Ethereal	Ethylene dichloride	Dry-cleaning fluid
Pungent	Formic acid	Vinegar
Putrid	Butyl mercaptan	Bad egg

Source: Adapted from Amoore, Johnston, & Rubin, 1964.

Taste

The receptors for the sense of taste are sensitive to fluid substances. Located along the sides and back of the tongue, as well as in the throat, these receptor cells are clustered together in groups called *taste buds.* The bumps you see on your tongue contain several hundred taste buds, and each taste bud contains about 20 taste receptor cells. The tongue and mouth also contain touch, pain, and temperature receptors similar to those found scattered over other parts of the body. In the mouth, these also serve in the total experience of taste, as we shall see.

The taste receptors are somewhat nonspecific. That is, although each responds most readily to certain substances, they all can be stimulated by any of the four basic tastes. The four basic tastes are sweet, salty, sour, and bitter. As Figure 3–8 shows, cells located toward the tip of the tongue are most responsive to sweet substances. Others, located farther back, are more responsive to salty substances, and so on. Some of these specific areas overlap.

The pleasure we obtain from eating is due to a lot more than stimulation of the taste receptors alone. All the widely varied flavors we experience are made up of various combinations of the four basic flavors, but other sensations that are not tastes contribute to the overall enjoyment. For example, the olfactory cells are stimulated by the food's aromas. Thus, when your nose is congested from a cold, food "tastes" decidedly flat. Sometimes olfaction actually provides the flavor experience. (If you doubt this, close your eyes, hold your nose, and then try to distinguish between a bit of potato and a bit of apple.) The stimulation of pressure receptors in the mouth adds to the enjoyment of different food textures, and stimulation of temperature receptors may also be a contributory factor. A stalk of celery is not very good if it is not crisp. Puddings are better without lumps, and, for

Which of the four basic tastes are these people experiencing?

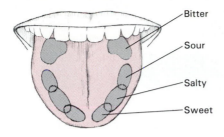

FIGURE 3–8 **Areas of Taste Sensitivity on the Tongue** *Notice that some of the areas overlap.*

most Americans, beer is better cold than warm. Mild stimulation of pain receptors by certain spices, such as pepper and ginger, can add to the enjoyment of food. Visual sensation, too, may affect the experience of eating. Cooks the world over know that the manner in which food is presented adds to its enjoyment. A little garnish can make the difference for a dish that did not turn out "just right." On the other hand, imagine eating your dinner under a blue light, or being served gray meat and green eggs (see color plates; see also Christensen, 1980).

Some animals have taste cells that respond to substances that other animals are not able to taste. Dogs and monkeys apparently can taste water. Humans cannot taste water, but they can taste minerals in the water. On the other hand, cats apparently cannot taste sweets; they are uninterested in our desserts. Rats, dogs, and horses, however, like sweets as much as people do.

THE MAJOR SENSES I: HEARING

Before we can discuss hearing, we must consider the mechanics of sound. We will look at the physical stimulus that causes the ear to react. What is it, after all, that we are hearing? After answering this question we will explore the workings of the ear itself.

Sound Waves

The ear responds to changes among the molecules of the air. Think of the ripples that are created by dropping a pebble into a pool of still water. At the point where the pebble enters the water, it takes the place of water molecules occupying that spot, causing them to move away. They push adjacent water molecules away, which, in turn, displace other molecules. On the surface, the water forms ridges and valleys, and the waves move outward in concentric circles. These surface ripples become flatter and farther apart the farther they are from the point of impact. Finally, they dissipate or flatten out entirely.

Sound waves are similar, except that air instead of water is moved. When an object such as a drum or a tuning fork is struck, causing it to vibrate in the air, a similar process occurs. As the object moves in one direction, it pushes the air molecules together; this is called *compression.* When it moves back in the opposite direction, it leaves an area where there are fewer molecules; this is called *rarefaction.* As the tuning fork continues to move back and forth, these alternating areas of densely packed and loosely packed air molecules create waves in the air like those on the surface of the water. At sea level, sound moves through the air at 1,100 feet per second.

Figure 3–9 shows a segment of the wave of compression and rarefaction that radiates out in all directions from the vibrating object. It is this kind of physical event that activates the sound receptors in the ear. The lower portion of Figure 3–9 shows how the nature of this wave can be symbolized by a continuous curving line, called a *sine wave* in the case of a simple tone. Notice that the highest peaks of the sine wave correspond to the areas of highest air compression, while the lowest valleys on the sine wave correspond to the areas of

FIGURE 3–9 The Creation
and Form of a Sound Wave

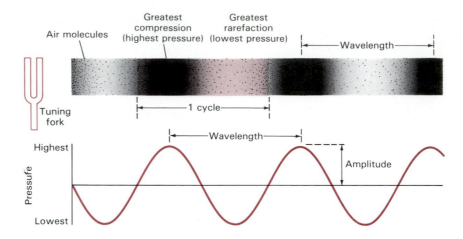

lowest compression. There are three characteristics of a sound wave that should be understood: its frequency, its amplitude, and its complexity.

Frequency   The *frequency* of the sound wave is a measure of how rapidly the pressure changes occur in time. Think of frequency as the number of complete waves that pass a fixed point in a second. A complete wave means both a high-pressure and a low-pressure area — one complete cycle of the motion. Frequency is measured in cycles per second (cps) or hertz (Hz), which means the same thing. A single cycle is shown in color on the sine wave in Figure 3–9.

A *wavelength* is the distance between two corresponding points on the sine wave — the distance from one peak to the next, as shown in Figure 3–9. Wavelength increases as frequency decreases. A sound wave with a high frequency completes more cycles per second and thus has a shorter wavelength. A low-frequency sound has a longer wavelength, since it goes through fewer cycles per second. What we experience when we hear different frequencies is called *pitch* (Siegel & Siegel, 1977). High-pitched sounds come from high-frequency sound waves. Low-pitched sounds result from sound waves having fewer cycles per second, or low frequencies and longer wavelengths. In short, the faster the tuning fork vibrates, the greater the frequency and the higher the pitch. Humans are able to hear sounds with frequencies anywhere from 20 to 20,000 cycles per second. Vibrating piano wires produce sounds with frequencies ranging from about 30 to about 3000 Hz. A tuba produces a sound frequency range of about 45 to 320 Hz. A baritone voice ranges from 96 to about 320 Hz. The violin ranges from 190 to 3000 Hz.

Amplitude   *Amplitude* refers to how far the air molecules have been moved from their original position — in other words, to the amount of compression and expansion they have undergone. The height of the peaks of the sine wave represents amplitude. Amplitude corresponds to the intensity of the vibration and to the sensory experience of loudness as well. When the source of a sound wave undergoes intense vibration, the amplitude of the wave is high, and we experi-

FIGURE 3–10   Decibel Scaling of Familiar Sounds   *This scale also shows the thresholds of hearing, hearing damage, discomfort, and pain. Note that hearing damage can occur at intensities below the discomfort level.*

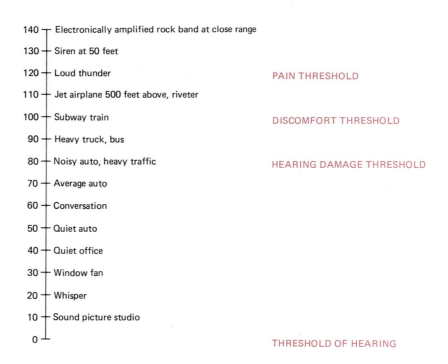

db	Sound	Threshold
140	Electronically amplified rock band at close range	
130	Siren at 50 feet	
120	Loud thunder	PAIN THRESHOLD
110	Jet airplane 500 feet above, riveter	
100	Subway train	DISCOMFORT THRESHOLD
90	Heavy truck, bus	
80	Noisy auto, heavy traffic	HEARING DAMAGE THRESHOLD
70	Average auto	
60	Conversation	
50	Quiet auto	
40	Quiet office	
30	Window fan	
20	Whisper	
10	Sound picture studio	
0		THRESHOLD OF HEARING

ence a loud sound. When the source vibrates less intensely, the wave's amplitude is lower, and the sound is fainter.

A unit of measure called the *decibel (db)* has been devised for use in gauging the intensity of a sound. Figure 3–10 lists some familiar sounds that have been scaled in decibels. Sounds of 120 db will be experienced as painful, but prolonged exposure to sounds with intensities no higher than 90 db can result in hearing damage.

An increase of 10 db in a sound's intensity is very roughly equal to a doubling of perceived loudness. Perceived loudness of a sound is not entirely a function of amplitude, however. Loudness is also influenced by the frequency of the sound wave. The range of frequencies to which the human ear is most sensitive runs from about 800 to 6000 Hz. We can hear sounds with lower and higher frequencies, but they must be more intense for us to detect them. This means that a sound with a frequency in the middle range, say 1000 Hz, will sound much louder than a sound having a very low or very high frequency, even though their physical intensities are the same.

Complexity   The sound represented by the sine wave in Figure 3–9 is a pure tone. That is, the wave has a single frequency. However, the sounds we hear in everyday life possess complex waveforms. A complex wave consists of a fundamental wave, or pure tone, plus additional waves, or *overtones,* whose frequencies are multiples of the fundamental wave. The peaks and valleys of the fundamental wave are retained in a complex wave form, but the overtones combine to produce additional smaller waves at the high and low points so that the wave has a more jagged appearance than the smooth sine wave shown in Figure 3–9. For example, when middle C is struck on

Our hearing requires careful protection against excessive noise if we are to avoid hearing loss.

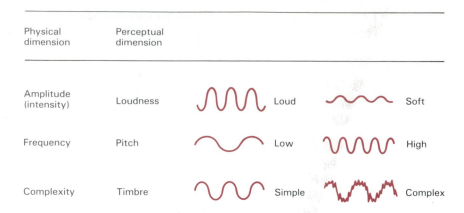

Physical dimension	Perceptual dimension				
Amplitude (intensity)	Loudness		Loud		Soft
Frequency	Pitch		Low		High
Complexity	Timbre		Simple		Complex

a piano, the wire vibrates in a fundamental wave of 256 Hz. However, overtones of 512, 768, and 1024 Hz are also created. These overtones are, respectively, twice, three times, and four times the frequency of the fundamental wave. The overtones have less amplitude than the fundamental wave, but they add to the *complexity* of the wave and to the quality of the perceived sound.

The complexity of a sound is experienced psychologically as *timbre* or tone quality. Because of timbre, or wave complexity, we are able to distinguish the same musical note when it is played on different instruments. Although the same fundamental sound wave is perceived, each instrument amplifies certain overtones and deadens others and thus gives the characteristic sound of that instrument. The screech of brakes or a jet's roar may not be musical, but they too are characteristic sounds that result from complex waves. The relationships among frequency, amplitude, and complexity are summarized in Figure 3–11. We now will discover how the structure of our ear enables us to perceive sound waves and to distinguish among them.

The Components of the Ear

Several structures in the human ear are involved in hearing. The outer, the middle, and the inner ear (see Figure 3–12) each play an important role. The *outer ear*—the visible part—serves to channel sounds toward the eardrum. The *eardrum* is a thin, flexible membrane covering the opening into the middle ear. The *middle ear* is a bony cavity housing three connected bones called the *hammer,* the *anvil,* and the *stirrup.* The eardrum is connected to the hammer, the hammer to the anvil, the anvil to the stirrup, and the stirrup to the *oval window.* The oval window is another membrane, which covers the opening into the *inner ear.*

For now, think about what happens when a sound wave enters the ear. It hits the eardrum and causes it to vibrate. This vibration is transferred along the hammer to the anvil, to the stirrup, and finally to the oval window. Because the eardrum is much larger than the oval window, small movements of the eardrum are magnified and intensified into a condensed pressure on the oval window.

Now what happens? The vibration of the oval window sets into motion a fluid contained inside the *cochlea.* This cochlea is the bony,

The physiological bases of behavior are centered in the neural, glandular, and genetic systems of the human body. Abnormalities in the structures and functioning of the components of these systems are often reflected in dramatic behavior changes. Technological advances in recent decades have enabled neuroscientists and physiological psychologists to discover important information about the links between behavior and physiology and to find ways to help individuals whose systems have malfunctioned.

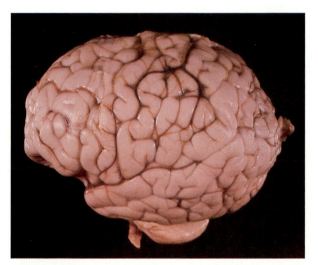

COLOR PLATE 1

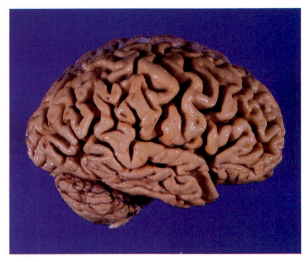

COLOR PLATE 2

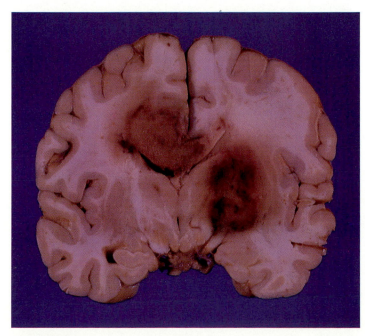

COLOR PLATE 3

As a major component of the central nervous system, the brain plays a vital role in controlling and integrating behavior. Brain-study techniques that have been utilized for many years and that enable us to compare a normal brain (Color Plate 1) with the atrophied brain of a victim of Alzheimer's disease (Color Plate 2) or the diseased brain of an AIDS patient (Color Plate 3) have recently been supplemented with revelations made possible to researchers through modern scanning techniques.

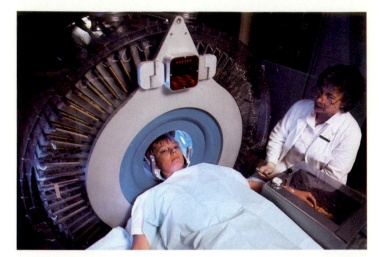

COLOR PLATE 4

PET scans (Color Plate 4) permit a comparison of the amounts of metabolic activity occurring in the brains of normal individuals and Alzheimer patients. The lighter colors in Color Plate 5 represent greater metabolic activity.

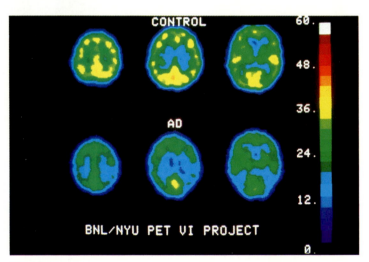

COLOR PLATE 5

COLOR PLATE 6

The blood-sugar imbalance characteristic of diabetes led to the discovery that the systematic injection of insulin offsets many of the damaging effects of this insidious disease (Color Plate 6). Major complications of diabetes include cardiovascular problems, damage to the retina's blood vessels, loss of vision, and severe kidney problems.

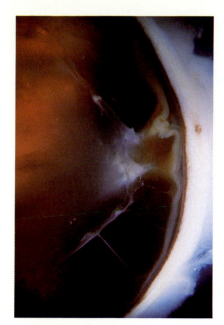

COLOR PLATE 7

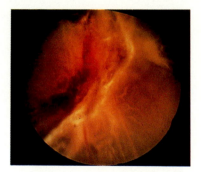

COLOR PLATE 8

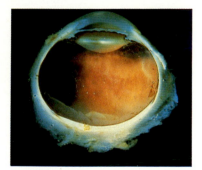

COLOR PLATE 9

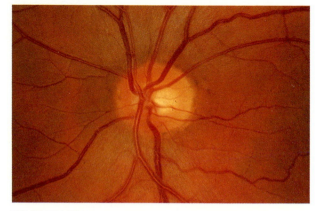

COLOR PLATE 10

Untreated diabetes may result in deformed retinas and retinal hemorrhaging, visible in Color Plates 7 and 8. Contrast these photos with the normal retina, optic nerve, and distinct, undamaged retinal blood vessels shown in Color Plates 9 and 10.

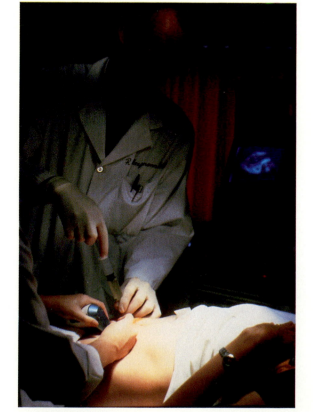

COLOR PLATE 11

Many behavioral problems have been linked to genetic factors. Detection of genetic disorders has been vastly improved by the development of amniocentesis (Color Plate 11), a technique in which a sample of the amniotic fluid is withdrawn and analyzed for chromosomal abnormalities.

The identification of the specific gene responsible for the sickle-shaped red blood cells in Color Plate 12 makes it possible to identify the carriers of sickle-cell anemia, a treatable but not curable disease that almost exclusively afflicts blacks.

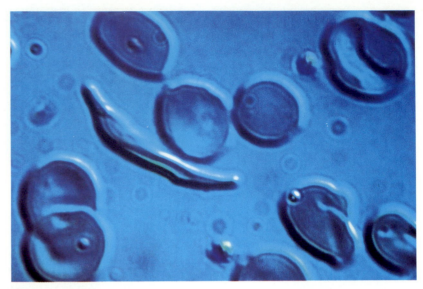

COLOR PLATE 12

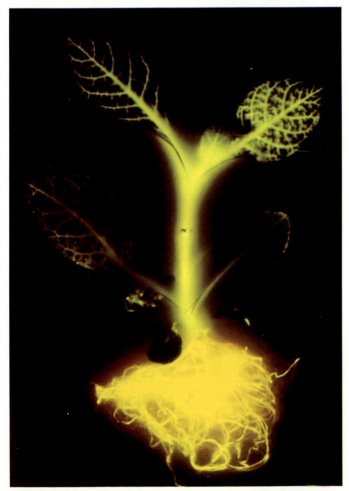

COLOR PLATE 13

Even more striking advances in the field of genetics are on the way. A group of researchers at the University of California in San Diego inserted a gene from a firefly into the DNA of a tobacco plant. The result—a tobacco plant that glows like a firefly (Color Plate 13).

FIGURE 3–12   The Structure of the Human Ear

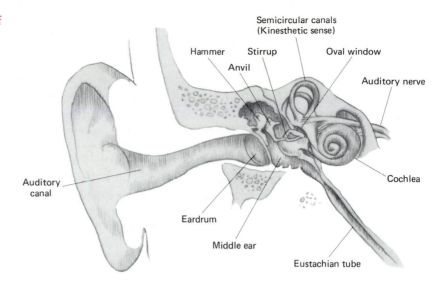

coiled tube depicted in Figure 3–12. Inside this tube the sound waves, now converted to the movement of a fluid, are detected by auditory nerve cells, converted to neural impulses, and sent to the brain. Specifically, as fluid inside the cochlea moves, it presses against a structure called the **basilar membrane,** causing it to move. This, in turn, bends and displaces tiny hairs in a structure called the **organ of Corti.** The bending of these hairs is what finally stimulates nerve endings situated near the hairs and sends volleys of neural impulses to the brain along the auditory nerve.

Theories of Hearing

How does a structure as small as the organ of Corti (the size of a small pea) enable us to discriminate among thousands of tones? There are two main theories of pitch discrimination. First, **place theory** argues that the pitch of a tone is determined by the area of the basilar membrane that is displaced by that sound wave. High-frequency tones tend to displace the narrow end of the basilar membrane, intermediate tones displace the other end of the membrane, and low-frequency tones tend to displace the entire membrane equally. Second, **frequency theory** argues that pitch is determined by the frequency of impulses traveling up the auditory nerve. The higher the frequency, the higher the tone. Probably neither theory can account for all pitch discrimination, but both have something to offer.

Detecting Position and Distance

Position of a Sound   Suppose you were blindfolded and asked where a ringing bell was located. More than likely you would be very accurate in pinpointing the location of the bell, or at least the direction from which the sound came. How can we accomplish this feat? At low frequencies, we locate the sound by detecting the difference between the times the sound wave arrives at our two ears. The wave hits the near ear first and then washes over to the far ear. Our ears are very sensitive to such minor differences. Under the best of conditions we can detect differences as small as 0.00003 of a second.

As the frequency of the sound is increased, we have trouble detecting time differences and shift to another cue: intensity differences. The sound reaching the near ear is more intense than that reaching the far ear, and we can detect this difference. Fortunately, most sounds are mixed, or composed of many frequencies, so we can usually use both time and intensity differences to detect position.

Sounds coming from directly in front, above, behind, or below give us problems because the sounds reach both ears at the same time and with the same intensity. We sometimes make errors in trying to locate sounds in these positions. One way we improve our chances is by turning our heads. In this way, a sound that was coming from directly in front is now approaching from the side and can be located using the time and intensity cues.

Surprisingly, we can also locate a sound using only one ear (Butler & Flannery, 1980). If one ear is blocked, the other, somehow, can still determine location, although not as easily. Clearly, we have a good deal more to learn about the ways in which we locate sounds.

Distance of a Sound   We are also able to determine how far away a sound source is. Apparently we do this by considering the *reverberant* quality of incoming sounds. If an incoming sound has bounced off various objects on its way to our ear, we judge the source to be farther away than if it has not echoed and reechoed across some distance. If we hear the same sound in an echoic chamber (one that allows the sound to bounce and echo) and in an anechoic chamber (one where the sound does not echo), we will judge the echoing sound to be farther away.

The Doppler Effect   The next time you are standing by a highway, listen carefully to an approaching car. Although the engine sound does not really rise as the car approaches and fall after it passes you, it will sound that way to you. What happens is that the motion of the car compresses the sound waves as the car approaches and then expands the waves as the car pulls away from you. This is called the **Doppler effect.** It helps us to determine the movements of sound sources toward and away from us. Most of us make use of it, whether we are consciously aware of it or not.

Hearing Your Body   The human ear is responsive to an enormously wide range of pressures. Yet there are certain frequencies to which the ear is fairly insensitive—and with good reason. If our ears were sensitive to very low frequencies, we would constantly be hearing the vibrations, movements, and rustlings of our own bodies—even our own heartbeats. These body sounds would compete with our attempts to hear more important external sounds. Thus, strangely enough, to be sensitive in one way our ears must be insensitive in another.

Put your fingers in your ears and listen. You have stopped most external sound. What you are hearing is your body—your muscles contracting in your arms and face, and perhaps even your heart.

Grind your teeth about. There is a lot of sound within us which, if we were sensitive to it, could detract from our ability to hear survival-related external sound.

The Sound of Noise: Auditory Pollution

Many sounds are clearly pleasant. And some, like the sound of a power mower in an elevator, are just as clearly unpleasant. We call the undesirable sounds noise, but what is music to one person may be noise to another. Teenagers may scoff at their parents' classical tastes in music, while the parents, in turn, cannot comprehend their offsprings' love of rock. In spite of this ambiguity in the meaning of noise, many sounds can be damaging, both physically and psychologically, and it is to some evidence for this conclusion that we now turn.

On a purely physical level, studies of noise pollution show that permanent damage may occur when one is repeatedly exposed to sounds no greater than 80 or 90 db (see Figure 3–10). The problem is that our lives are permeated with sounds of greater intensities than these limits. Raloff (1982) concludes that over 50 percent of production workers regularly come into contact with sounds loud enough to damage their hearing, especially their ability to hear high-pitched sounds. Unfortunately, damage is not limited to the workplace. Many of our modern entertainments, such as highly amplified music, easily exceed the damage limit.

Increasingly, our neighborhoods are so permeated with varied and loud noises that we suffer, if not actual physical damage, at least an unfortunate degree of psychological distress. Meecham and Shaw (1983) and others have shown that murder, suicide, and auto accident rates are higher in noisy neighborhoods than in quiet ones. Excessive noise can impair cognitive performance in children as well (Wachs, 1982). Excessive noise levels may also lead to high blood pressure, ulcers, and heart disease (Cohen & Weinstein, 1981).

While it seems that our lives are getting noisier all the time, some progress is being made against noise pollution. Jet planes are becoming quieter, just as citizen groups are becoming more adamant about noise abatement. The federal government has imposed limits on the levels of noise to which workers may be exposed. Still, we have a long way to go before we achieve auditory serenity.

THE MAJOR SENSES II: VISION

Vision is a dominant sense in the human, and so it has been widely studied by psychologists. Humans depend heavily on vision and often trust it more than any other sense (Rock & Harris, 1967; Radeau & Bertelson, 1977). The expression, "I'll believe it when I see it," reflects this special dependence on vision.

Light

Just as our discussion of hearing dealt first with sound waves and then with the ear, our discussion here will first examine light and then the eye. The stimulus to which the visual cells of the eye respond is a band of electromagnetic energy known as light. Visible light is actually a very narrow section of the overall electromagnetic spectrum that includes many different types of rays, such as radio waves, radar, microwaves, and X rays.

Light rays are *not* like sound waves that produce pressure changes in air. Light needs no medium. It can travel through empty spaces, while sound cannot. (If you strike two pieces of metal together in a vacuum, there will be no sound. There is no sound on the moon, because it has no atmosphere.) However, we can still talk about a light wave in terms of its wavelength, its amplitude, and its complexity. Wavelength is used to distinguish between the different *types* of radiation. As Color Plate 16 shows, wavelengths vary tremendously, from a few trillionths of a meter to many kilometers. Radio waves have very long wavelengths, while X rays have very short wavelengths. Visible light has wavelengths that vary from about 380 to 760 nanometers (nm, billionths of a meter).

We experience the wavelength of visible light as **color,** or **hue.** The amplitude of the wave is proportional to the **intensity** or **brightness** of the color we see. Complexity refers to the combination of light rays of different wavelengths. We experience complexity in terms of **saturation,** or the degree to which a particular color is pure. For instance, pure emerald green is a saturated color, but the grayish-green color of sea water is not saturated. Color Plate 17 illustrates these dimensions of color.

The Eye

The eye is a wonderful mechanism. Its sensitivity and flexibility are amazing. We have little trouble functioning in dazzling, midday desert sunlight, and yet we can detect a candle flame 30 miles away on a dark night. We can see objects a few inches in front of our faces and also detect stars that are many light years away in the heavens. Such an important and capable system certainly deserves attention.

The eye is composed of a number of different structures (Figure 3–13). Light enters the eye through a transparent covering known as the *cornea.* The amount of light entering the eye is controlled by the *iris* (the colored part of the eye). The iris is a muscular structure which, by tensing or relaxing, can make the black opening in our eye, the *pupil,* either smaller or larger. Once past the iris, the light passes through the lens. The lens, along with the cornea, focuses the light on the *retina.* The retina is the light-sensitive surface of the inside of the eye.

The parasympathetic division of the autonomic nervous system protects the retina from too much light by causing the iris to regulate the size of the pupil, but the sympathetic division may also affect pupil size. When we are aroused emotionally, or even interested, our pupils dilate. One study, using a technique called pupillometry, found that when heterosexual men looked at pictures of nude women the pupils of their eyes increased in size. Homosexual men showed the same reaction while looking at pictures of nude men (Hess, Seltzer, & Shlien, 1965).

The lens focuses light reflected from objects, so that we can see both near and far objects clearly. If you are looking into the distance,

FIGURE 3–13 Cross Section of the Right Eye as Seen from Above

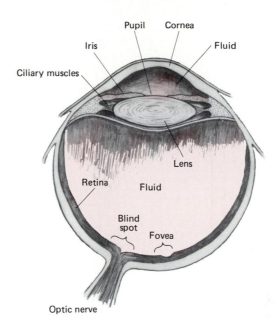

the ciliary muscles make the lens thinner. If you are looking at a close object, such as the print on this page, the muscles make the lens thicker. This system does not always work perfectly, however. ***Near-sighted*** people cannot focus on distant objects because the eye is too long or the cornea is too curved. ***Astigmatism*** is a corneal defect that makes images fuzzy or distorted. ***Farsighted*** people have trouble seeing close objects, because the eye is too short or the lens has hardened with age and lost some of its flexibility. Fortunately, eyeglasses can correct all three of these common visual defects.

The Retina: Rods and Cones

Let us consider the retina and its structure and function. There are two types of visual receptors in the retina. Because of the way they look, these receptors are called ***rods*** and ***cones*** (see Figure 3–14). The rods respond to a wide range of stimuli. They are sensitive to light of any wavelength and function at very low intensities. Because of this sensitivity, the rods enable us to see at night and in very dim light. The cones, on the other hand, are discriminating receptors. Different cones respond to different wavelengths. Because of this specificity, the cones allow us to experience the sensation of color, which will be discussed shortly. The cones are relatively insensitive to low levels of light, so they do not function when we take moonlight walks. That is why the landscape at night appears to have lost its color.

Though the rods do not allow us to see color, they are more sensitive to some wavelengths than to others. The rods respond at fairly low levels of intensity to wavelengths around 500 nm (Figure 3–15). The cones, too, are more sensitive to wavelengths about this size. In the color spectrum, wavelengths this size correspond to green. At other wavelengths, both the cones and rods require much greater intensities before they respond. Compare the threshold for wavelengths around 750 nm with that for wavelengths around 500 nm.

FIGURE 3–14 Magnified
Section of the Retina

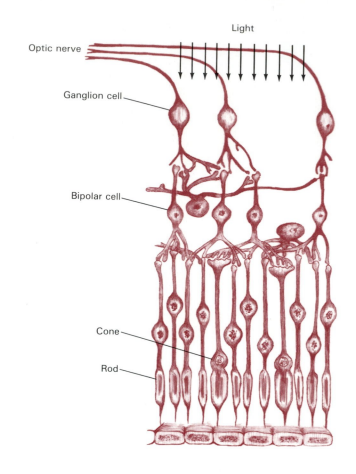

FIGURE 3–15 The Threshold
for Cone and Rod Vision
According to the Wavelength of
Light

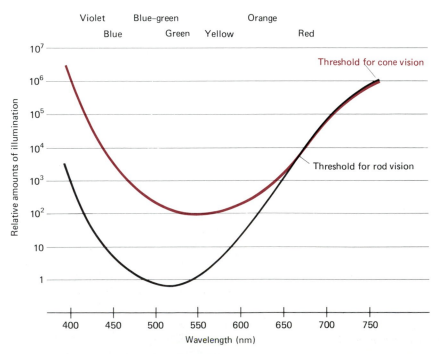

The retina is composed of three layers of cells (Figure 3–14). Contrary to what you might expect, the light-sensitive rods and cones are found *behind*, rather than in front of, the two other layers of cells. ***Bipolar cells*** make up the layer of cells lying just in front of the rods and cones. These cells are not sensitive to light, but they are stimulated by the rods and cones. The bipolar cells, in turn, stimulate the cells in the third layer, which lies in front of the bipolar cells. These third-layer cells are called ***ganglion cells.*** It is the long axons of these cells that form the optic nerve to the brain. To stimulate the rods and cones, light must pass through the cornea, the lens, the fluid in the eyeball, and by the ganglion cells and the bipolar cells.

The ganglion cell axons leave the eye where the optic nerve joins the eyeball. At this junction, there are no visual receptors. For this reason, we have a small ***blind spot*** in each eye. Ordinarily we do not notice the blind spot because our eyes make tiny movements that compensate for this deficiency. But the blind spot can be demonstrated when we make an effort to control these movements, as you can see if you try the test illustrated in Figure 3–16.

The retina contains many more rods and cones than it does bipolar and ganglion cells. Each eye has about 120 million rods and 5 or 6 million cones but only about 1 million ganglion cell axons in its optic nerve. Rods are found in all areas of the retina except the *fovea,* a small indentation just to the right of the optic nerve in Figure 3–13. The cones are found primarily in and around the fovea, where they are densely packed together. Light entering the eye from the side is thus more likely to stimulate rods than cones. You may have noticed that it is difficult to identify the color of objects that are seen from the "corner" of your eye. This is because light from this part of the visual field is directed by the lens to the rods in the peripheral retina, and rods do not provide color sensations.

Since there are fewer bipolar cells than there are rods, each bipolar cell is likely to receive impulses from many rods. And since there are still fewer ganglion cells, they receive impulses from many bipolar cells. But *at the fovea,* where the cones are concentrated, individual bipolar cells and ganglion cells may serve only one cone. Because of this direct one-to-one relationship, vision at the fovea is much sharper than at other areas of the retina. In a sense, the foveal cones have their own private lines of communication with the brain, so the brain is better able to interpret their signals. Thus, cone vision provides better acuity, or sharpness, than rod vision.

On the other hand, rod vision allows the detection of fainter light than does cone vision. This is because many rods synapse on each bipolar cell, making it more likely that the bipolar cell will fire. There is a simple demonstration of the ability of the rods to detect faint light. On a dark, clear night, focus your eyes on a point next to a faint star. You will find that you can see the star more easily this way than if you looked directly at it, but though you will be able to detect

FIGURE 3–16 Locating the Blind Spot *Hold the book out in front of you. Cover your left eye and focus on the dot. Notice that you can see the X with your peripheral vision. Now move the book toward you. At one point the X will disappear, indicating that the light reflected from the X is striking your blind spot. You can find your other blind spot by covering your right eye and focusing on the X.*

●

the star more easily, it will be "fuzzy." This is because you are using bipolar and ganglion cells that must serve many rods.

When we "focus" on something, such as the print on this page, we do more than focus the lens for the correct distance. We also keep moving our eye so that the fovea aligns directly with light from the words we want to read. In other words, to "focus" also means to use foveal, or cone, vision. To demonstrate how much sharper and clearer cone or foveal vision is than rod or peripheral vision, focus on a point about a quarter of an inch into the left margin of this page. Then try to read the words with your peripheral vision. You will be able to see the words, but not well enough to read them.

Dark and Light Adaptation

Everyone has had the experience of walking into a dark movie theater and being unable to see well enough to find a seat. This stumbling blindness is temporary and begins to recede within a few moments. In less than half an hour, your eyes have adapted so that you can see the seats and people quite clearly. This process of adjusting to low levels of illumination is called *dark adaptation.* The reverse process, which occurs when you go from the theater into the afternoon sun, is called *light adaptation.* Light adaptation occurs more rapidly than dark adaptation.

The human eye is capable of responding to a very wide range of light intensities (see Figure 3–17), but at any one moment, it is able to respond only to a fairly limited range of intensities. When we go

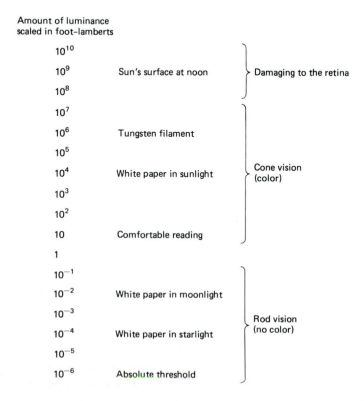

FIGURE 3–17 Scale of Luminance Levels to Which the Eye Is Sensitive *One foot-lambert is defined as the amount of light from a surface one foot square located one foot from a standard candle. (After Riggs, 1975)*

Amount of luminance scaled in foot-lamberts

Luminance	Example	Vision range
10^{10}		
10^{9}	Sun's surface at noon	Damaging to the retina
10^{8}		
10^{7}		
10^{6}	Tungsten filament	
10^{5}		
10^{4}	White paper in sunlight	Cone vision (color)
10^{3}		
10^{2}		
10	Comfortable reading	
1		
10^{-1}		
10^{-2}	White paper in moonlight	
10^{-3}		Rod vision (no color)
10^{-4}	White paper in starlight	
10^{-5}		
10^{-6}	Absolute threshold	

FIGURE 3–18 Dark Adaptation Curves *The curves show the smallest amount of light that can be detected by the cones or rods as the minutes pass.*

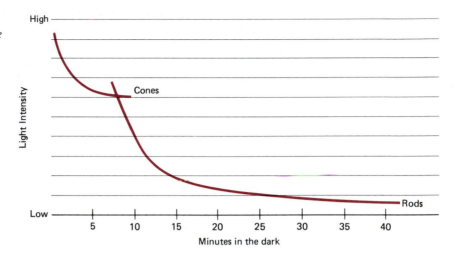

into a dark place after having been in the light, it takes time for our rods and cones to begin responding to the lowered level of light. Figure 3–18 shows the process of dark adaptation graphically. The curves show the minimum light intensity that can be detected at any given minute. As time passes, both the rods and the cones become more and more sensitive to fainter and fainter light levels. As you will notice, the cones adapt much more quickly than the rods, but they have adapted about as much as they can after 10 minutes. The rods, on the other hand, continue to adapt for almost an hour and eventually become sensitive to very low levels of light (Wist, 1976).

Color Vision

Young-Helmholtz: Trichromatic Theory Two major theories of color vision have been proposed. Neither of them has been completely proved or disproved, but research suggests that they both have something to offer (DeValois & Jacobs, 1968; MacNichol, 1964). The first explanation, often called **trichromatic theory,** was proposed by Thomas Young in 1802 and was modified some 50 years later by Hermann von Helmholtz. This theory notes that we have three types of broadly tuned cones, and that each type contains a different kind of light-sensitive substance. The theory hypothesizes that each type of cone is most sensitive to one particular wavelength but will also respond, although less vigorously, to light with shorter or longer wavelengths. All colors are produced by the stimulation of various combinations of these three kinds of receptors. For example, when the "red" and "green" cones are simultaneously stimulated, the sensation of "yellow" is produced.

The Opponent-process Theory In 1870, Ewald Hering proposed another way of understanding color vision. According to his theory, known as **opponent-process theory,** color cells are organized into pairs as follows: red-green, blue-yellow, black-white. The two members of each pair are opponents in the sense that when one is excited the other will be inhibited. For example, if the cells that process red are activated, cells processing green will be inhibited. If cells processing blue are excited, cells processing yellow will be inhibited, and so on. Since only one type of cell in each pair can be activated at a given moment, the paired colors cannot be experienced simultaneously. That is why we do not see a reddish-green color or a yellowish-blue color. However, since red or green may be active at the same time as yellow or blue, we do have sensations of yellow-red, blue-green, blue-red, and yellow-green.

This theory also explains *after images.* If you stare at the blue patch in Color Plate 20 for a short time and then look at the gray square, you will see a yellow patch on the gray. In the same manner, if you stare at the blue patch and then look at the yellow square, you will see a brighter yellow patch. The same effects can be demonstrated with red and green. These after images occur, according to Hering's theory, because staring at the blue patch forces a great many of the yellow-blue receptors into the blue phase. When you shift your gaze to a neutral or yellow surface, the process momentarily reverses, and yellow is experienced.

The most recent thinking about color vision maintains that components of both the Young-Helmholtz theory and the opponent-process theory may be necessary to fully explain color vision (see Brou, Sciascia, Linden, & Lettuin, 1986).

Color Blindness Normal vision is called **trichromatic,** because experiments show that it uses three systems of color vision: light-dark, red-green, and yellow-blue. If a color-blind person is missing one of the color systems, his vision is termed **dichromatic.** If he is missing the red-green and blue-yellow color systems, his vision is called **monochromatic.** Monochromats see only black, white, and shades of gray. This is comparable to having only rod vision.

Many kinds of animals, including rats, dogs, cats, cows, and bulls, are monochromatic, but few people are. All the fancy food coloring in dog and cat food is for the benefit of the human purchaser, as the animals cannot detect color. One type of dichromatism is yellow-blue color blindness, but this form is extremely rare. The most common form of partial color blindness is red-green blindness. This type of dichromat cannot distinguish between red and green but can see yellow and blue. These variations of color blindness are illustrated in Color Plate 18.

PERCEPTION AND EXPERIENCE

Now that we have traced some of the pathways of sensation, we can begin to explore the set of processes known as perception. If you will recall, sensation refers to the raw information we receive through our senses, while perception refers to how we organize and interpret that evidence. Perception is a process of building on sensation. Incomplete or ambiguous sensory information is filled in and smoothed over. It is changed by the addition of information drawn from memory. Parts of the sensation are amplified; others are pushed into the background. Some aspects are noted; others are ignored. Meaning is assigned, and judgments and interpretations are made.

In short, the perceptual process is complicated. One thing we can say with certainty is that past experience has a great deal to do with perception. We relate what we sense to what we have already experienced. We make guesses about what incomplete sensory information means on the basis of what we already know. As we progress through our discussion, we will see many examples of how experience affects perception, and at the end of this chapter, we will take a closer look at the role of experience in perceptual development.

PERCEPTION IS NOT PERFECT: ILLUSIONS

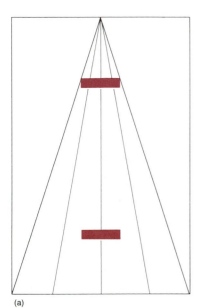

(a)

(b)

FIGURE 3–19 The Ponzo Illusion *Which bar in each illustration appears longer?*

Even though we think of our perceptual processes as mechanisms that allow us to become aware of our environment, these perceptual processes are not perfect. Sometimes we misperceive, or come to the wrong conclusion about "what is out there." Sometimes our eyes or ears are fooled. We call certain characteristic distortions in perception ***illusions.*** Illusions are interesting in and of themselves, and they also can help us understand the functioning of our perceptual processes. Scores of illusions have been studied in the laboratory. Many of them vividly demonstrate that perception involves the processing of incoming sensory information and that our processing can be misleading. For these reasons, we will begin our exploration of perception in the fun house of illusions.

The Ponzo Illusion Figure 3–19a demonstrates the Ponzo illusion. Although the horizontal bars are exactly the same length, the one at the top of the picture looks much longer than the one at the bottom. The Ponzo illusion is explained by the fact that lines converging at the top of a picture are ordinarily associated with distance. Thus the area where the top bar is located is perceived as farther away. Because the top bar is also seen as much farther away, we conclude that it must be much longer than the bottom bar.

You might think that this illusion occurs only because a special kind of geometric drawing is being used. However, this is not the case. In one perception study, three different photographs were examined. One photograph was of a line drawing similar to that in Figure 3–19a. Another was a picture of railroad tracks (see Figure 3–19b). A third was of an open field, with a few sketchy furrow marks. Researchers in this study found that the Ponzo illusion actually appeared more often in the realistic scenes than in the geometric drawing (Leibowitz, Brislin, Perlmuth, & Hennessy, 1969).

The Gamma Phenomenon If a subject is placed in a darkened room and asked to view a pinpoint of light some 10 feet away, an interesting illusion called the Gamma phenomenon can be created by alternately dimming and brightening the stationary point of light. Many subjects will report that the light appears to be moving closer to them, and then farther away.

Additional Illusions Figure 3–20 shows several additional illusions. The Poggendorff illusion, (b) in Figure 3–20, has been shown by researchers to be exaggerated when the diagonal line is more steeply slanted and when the parallel bars are more separated (MacKay & Newbigging, 1977).

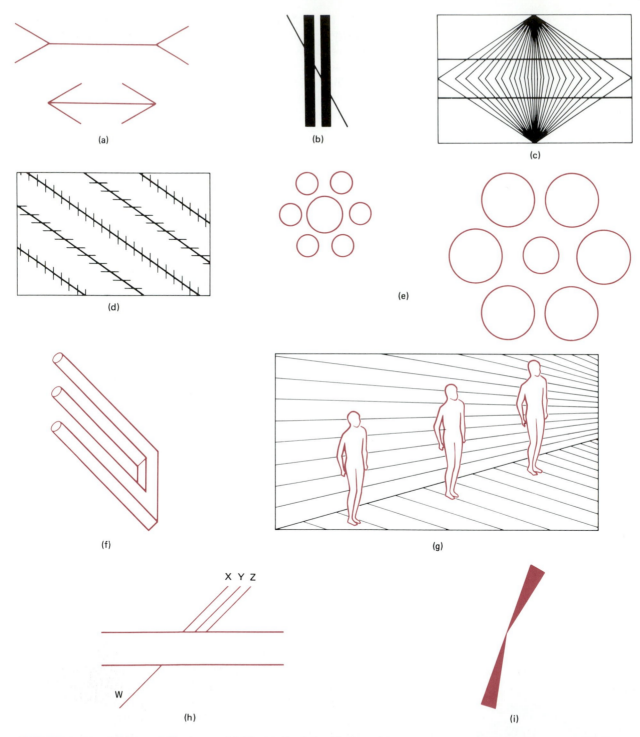

FIGURE 3–20 Additional Illusions *(a) The Müller-Lyler illusion: although the upper line appears longer than the lower line, they are exactly the same length. (b) The Poggendorff illusion: the segments of the diagonal line appear offset, even though the line is straight. As the line is brought closer to the horizontal, the illusion disappears. (c) Wundt's illusion: the horizontal lines appear to bend in the middle though they actually are parallel. (d) Zollner's illusion: the short lines cause the diagonal lines to appear to diverge and converge, although they are parallel. (e) Which center circle is bigger, the one to the left or to the right? (f) There is something missing, isn't there? (g) Which figure is the tallest? Measure them. (h) Which line connects with W? Hold a ruler against W and find out. (i) The Bourdon illusion: the left edge of the figure is straight but appears bent.*

ELEMENTS OF THE PERCEPTUAL PROCESS

Given that perception is a complex process whereby we make sense of incoming sensory information, what are the elements of the process? Psychologists have identified selective attention and organization as two important components of the overall perceptual process. *Selective attention* refers to the fact that we cannot attend to all of the many sensory stimuli that bombard us every moment. *Organization* refers to the processes whereby we interpret or make sense of the stimuli that we do attend to. Thus, in the process of perceiving, we select and we organize.

Attention of the Selective Kind

Let us deal with selective attention first. Selective attention may be defined as the "concentration and focusing of mental effort on specific stimuli while excluding other stimuli from consideration" (Best, 1986, p. 36). At any given moment, our sensory apparatus is being stimulated by many varieties of stimuli. For example, as you read this sentence, your hands are within your visual field, and yet, until now, you were probably not aware of them. Similarly, there are sounds in your environment that you have been ignoring. Thus, the first step in the overall perceptual event is one of selection. What we select can be of great importance to us. If we fail to attend to crucial elements in the environment, we may suffer. For example, while in a lecture we may select elements with little payoff, such as the relaxing hum of an air conditioner, while ignoring more important elements, such as the words of the lecturer.

Obviously, many personal qualities, such as our own interests, needs, wants, and wishes, will affect what we attend to. But before

If this student can study effectively in a parking lot, he must certainly be engaging in selective attention.

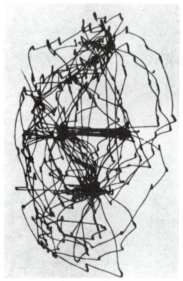

FIGURE 3–21 Attention and Selectivity *Let's face it, attention is selective (see explanation in text). (After Yarbus, 1967)*

we consider those elements, let us focus on the external stimuli and their power to draw our attention.

Several characteristics of a stimulus have been identified as attracting our perceptual attention. Because of the effect of these features, advertisers often employ them in designing signs and messages they want us to notice. *Change* in the stimulus is the most compelling attention-getter. Any sudden change in the sensory environment is immediately noticed. This effect may be partly a function of sensory adaptation. You may have adapted to the low-level noise of the library where you are studying, but you will notice immediately if it suddenly becomes very quiet or loud. On the other hand, part of the impact of change may be because our brains are geared to detect change. Having an evolutionary history of being prey to some animals and predator to others, we may notice change in our environment because it has been adaptive in keeping us alive.

A very compelling form of change is *movement*. It is hard to resist tracking a moving object with your eyes. Advertising signs that use lights to create a moving pattern are much more noticeable than stationary lights. Studies of the visual centers in the frog have shown that some of this animal's neurons respond only when dark spots move across its visual field. The researchers named these specific neurons "bug-detectors" (Lettvin, Maturana, McCulloch, & Pitts, 1959).

There are other stimulus features that draw our attention. The *size* of an object is one of these features. Generally, the larger the object, the more noticeable it is. In a similar manner, *intensity* captures attention. Bright lights, loud noises, strong flavors, and intense pain demand our attention, and get it. *Color,* too, causes us to take notice of our surroundings. As you might expect, pure colors tend to be more noticeable than "muddy" colors. It has also been found that certain wavelengths are more attractive, and are more easily recognized, than other wavelengths (Heider, 1971). Apparently, red and blue are more captivating than green and yellow.

Finally, we should mention again that we seem to be individually tuned to notice certain stimulus features in the environment. Our own *needs* and *interests* appear to amplify certain stimuli and cause us to pay attention to them. If we are hungry, we are more likely to notice food items than nonfood items — even the ones printed on the pages of a magazine. If we are interested in fashion, we are more likely to pay attention to other people's clothes.

It is not difficult to demonstrate the selective nature of our attention in a rather dramatic way. Yarbus (1967) had a subject look at a photo of the face of a young girl for several minutes. At the same time, he recorded the subject's eye movements. As you can see in Figure 3–21, the subject attended most often to the "high information" areas of the photo (for example, more time was spent looking at the eyes than at the chin).

Organization

Very early in the study of sensation and perception, psychologists became aware that perception is a building process. We do not see the world as a random, chaotic display of shapes, colors, and sizes.

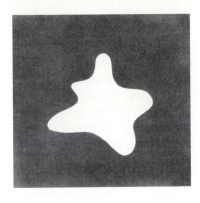

FIGURE 3–22 Figure and Ground *The smaller enclosed portion tends to be perceived as an amoeba-like figure, while the surrounding field tends to be perceived as background. Try to see the surrounding field as the object.*

We organize it and give it meaning. To indicate that the perception of the whole is different from the sum of its sensory elements, early psychologists developed the term *gestalt* (Heider, 1970). The term refers to our tendency to perceive certain kinds of patterns and configurations in our environment (see Coren & Girgus, 1980).

Figure-ground Probably our best known perceptual inclination is that we usually see things as objects against a distinct background. We form a figure from part of an incoming sensory message and relegate the rest of the message to the role of background. This is called the *figure-ground tendency.*

Let us look at some examples of the figure-ground tendency. If a visual field contains two homogeneous portions, and one encloses the other, the enclosed portion will be seen as the figure and the surrounding portion will be perceived as background. Figure 3–22 demonstrates this fundamental rule. Even though both portions are printed on the same surface, the figure appears to stand out and the background appears to recede to a position slightly farther back.

Certain statements can be made about the character of the figure and the ground in any visual perception (Rubin, 1958). The figure seems to be an intact "thing." The ground, on the other hand, appears more like "substance," and it is relatively shapeless. The figure appears closer, and in front of the ground. The figure sometimes appears brighter, even though its actual intensity may not be different from the ground's (Coren, 1969). The figure seems more impressive, and it is better remembered.

Another interesting quality is that any given element cannot be seen as both figure and ground at the same time. Figures 3–23, 3–24, and 3–25 show some additional figure-ground examples. Look at Figure 3–23. Can you see the vase as *both* a vase and a background for

FIGURE 3–23 Reversible Figure *Both the vase and the faces can be seen as figures, but not simultaneously.*

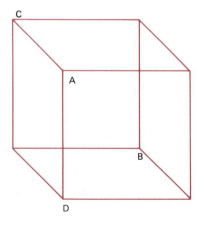

FIGURE 3–24 A Necker Cube *Which corner is closer to you, A or B? Is A or C closer to you? Is B or D closer to you?*

FIGURE 3–25 The "Winson Figure" *Can you see this as a face and an eskimo at the same time? (After Gregory & Gombrich, 1973)*

the faces at the same time? It switches back and forth very quickly, but never quite seems to be both at once. This tendency to see the elements as one or the other, as figure or ground but not both, is a fundamental characteristic of our perceptual process. Apparently this tendency to perceive figures against backgrounds is innate. Evidence for this conclusion has been collected from research involving people who have been blind from birth and have then been given sight through surgery. Although these individuals do not see well in general, they see things as objects against backgrounds as soon as they can see.

We have emphasized figure-ground relationships of a visual sort in our discussion, but the reader should keep in mind that figure-ground tendencies affect perception through other senses as well. The concept of figure-ground applies to *all* our perceptual processes, not just entertaining, visual ones. For example, an auditory message may also be divided into a type of sound figure and background. The song of a bird is heard as the "figure" against a background of traffic noises. As Grasha (1983) puts it:

> You and I are able to identify and describe a particular taste, texture, sound, smell, object, or bodily sensation because it is somehow different from other things in the background. Salt, for example, has a taste different from a steak, and a foul odor is noticeably different from the fresh air you normally breathe. It is also important to remember that figure-ground relationships are not only related to identifying and describing physical stimuli. . . . *Figure and ground do not always represent physical stimuli. They may also be ideas.* The judgment that a particular president or ball player is better than others is made with regard to a background or frame of reference of thoughts and feelings regarding other presidents and ball players. The background has a great deal to do with the interpretation that events are given. A french fry will not taste as salty if the steak is also salty. A foul odor will not seem quite as bad if the air we breathe is normally foul. A particular ball player or president may not look as good if compared to the best ball players or presidents in history. (p. 49, emphasis in original)

Grouping Tendencies   In addition to possessing figure-ground tendencies, we are also inclined to perceive stimuli according to the ways in which they are grouped.

FIGURE 3–26 Closure
Although the pictures are constructed of a number of irregular black shapes, distinct figures are perceived.

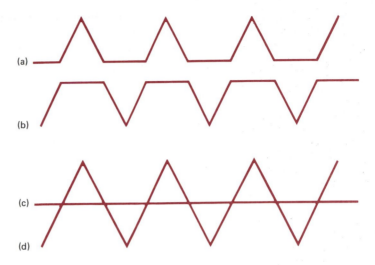

FIGURE 3–27 Continuity *In the top figure, (a) and (b) are clearly perceived as separate lines. But when they are combined, as they are at the bottom, they disappear and two new lines, (c) and (d), appear.*

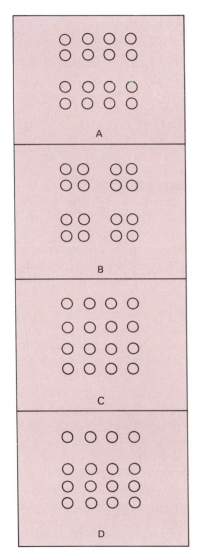

FIGURE 3–28 Proximity *We perceive things that are close together as groups. We tend not to see A, B, C, and D as merely groups of 16 circles. To experience the strength of proximity, try to see A as 4 groups of 4, B as 1 group of 12 and 1 group of 4, or D as 1 group of 2 and 1 group of 14.*

To perceive an object, it is not necessary that the visual image contain a complete representation of that object. In fact, we ordinarily receive visual information that is full of gaps. In the process of *closure,* we fill in the gaps and connect the disconnected elements. As you will find when you look at Figure 3–26, we tend to fill in and connect dark areas so that a completely enclosed figure appears. The fact that we can recognize the dog, horse, and rider in the figure is evidence of closure. Closure is not limited to visual stimuli, of course. Most of us can recognize a favorite song or even a symphony if we hear a few notes of the main theme, and poets can evoke a whole landscape with a few well-chosen words.

Closely related to closure is the tendency referred to as continuity. The idea of *continuity* is that elements that go in the same direction are perceived as "hanging together," or forming a unity. Continuity is demonstrated in Figure 3–27. The upper two lines are perceived as separate. But when they are put together, as they are in the lower drawing, they disappear, and two new lines are perceived.

Proximity refers to the fact that we often make patterns of things that are close together. Perceptual grouping occurs when elements are near each other (see Figure 3–28). When we see several people standing on a street corner, we perceive them as a "group," and as separate from the individuals who are crossing the street or getting on a bus. Sounds as well as sights are organized according to this tendency. When we hear two short buzzing sounds, then a pause, then two buzzes, then a pause, and then two more buzzes, we perceive three groups of buzzes. We do not think of them as six separate buzzes, or two groups of three buzzes. Because they are located close together in time, they are perceived as groups. As a final example, consider the following: N owi sth etim ef o ral lgoo dme ntoc om etot heaid. We must fight against the influence of proximity to make sense of the phrase.

Just as we organize according to proximity, we also group together elements that are similar to one another. If, among the people on the street corner, there are some that are young and carrying books, we are likely to see them as school children. We perceive them as forming a group separate from the others. This tendency to group according to *similarity* is illustrated by Figure 3–29.

To sum up, our perceptual processes are guided by strong inclinations to perceive things according to certain rules. Among the more important are the tendencies to see things as objects against a background, to fill in gaps, to perceive continuity in elements that go in the same direction, and to form groups of adjacent and similar elements.

COMPLEX PERCEPTUAL ABILITIES

Now that we have observed how our organizational tendencies affect our perceptions, we can focus more sharply on some of our perceptual abilities. Specifically, we shall discuss what is known about our ability to recognize patterns, to perceive movement, to judge distances, and to perceive language.

Pattern Recognition

We begin with *pattern recognition.* Humans and animals have a finely tuned ability to recognize one object as being "basically" the same as another. A triangle is a triangle, whether it is part of the roof of a house, a drawing on paper, or one side of a pyramid. We recognize a given word as being the same whether it is printed on paper, spoken, or handwritten on the back of an envelope. We know a melody, whether it is sung by a four-year-old, played on a piano, or whistled. How, or by what perceptual process, do we recognize these patterns? Pattern recognition is so ingrained in our experience that we rarely even notice that we do it.

Psychologists have given close attention to the processes involved in pattern recognition. Much of this research is guided by one of several information-processing theories. These theories seek to explain how we organize and process incoming stimuli. For example, the *template-matching*, or *prototype-matching*, hypothesis proposes that patterns are recognized because stimuli are matched in the brain with a standard, idealized form called a template or prototype. According to this view, the gable of a house is compared with an abstract, idealized triangle stored in memory. "Held up against" this stored, ideal triangle, the house's gable is recognized as a triangle.

Another hypothesis, referred to as *feature analysis*, also has guided a great deal of research. This hypothesis states that the stimulus is broken down into its elements and analyzed by feature detectors located in the brain and retina. Studies using microelectrodes to record from specific visual neurons in the brains of cats have provided considerable research evidence in support of this view. As we saw in Chapter 2, Hubel and Weisel (1965) found that some cells respond only when lines of light, or a straight edge of light against dark, are presented to the cat's eye. Other neurons respond only to lines of a specific orientation and location in the visual field. Some neurons are active only when the line is moving, while still others are responsive only to corners, to specific angles, or to lines of a certain

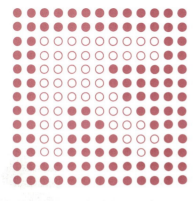

FIGURE 3–29   Similarity   *Note how the similarity of circles determines figure and ground.*

width and length. In other words, it may well be that the elements of a stimulus, such as the angles and the sides of a triangle, are analyzed separately. We may not, after all, hold the entire triangle up to an abstract triangle, or template.

Best (1986) characterizes feature analysis as follows:

> Consider the letter *H*. It has two approximately vertical lines that are about the same length. Both of these vertical lines begin and end more or less in the same place, relative to the border of the page. An *H* has a horizontal line that intersects the two vertical lines, more or less at their midpoints. I have just provided a sort of checklist of things that an *H* must have. This list is not an exhaustive list; the relative lengths of the horizontal and vertical lines probably have additional stipulations. Nevertheless, a system endowed with the checklist just mentioned could scan a particular character, noting which items on the checklist the character had and which it did not. If a given character had all the items on the checklist, the system would conclude the character was an *H*. Thus, characters like these:
>
> ⊢ ⊣ ⋈ would not be called *H's*.
>
> . . . The basic assumption is that all complex stimuli are composed of distinctive and separable parts known as *features*. Pattern recognition is accomplished by counting the presence or absence of the features, and comparing the count with a tabulation of the features associated with different labels. (p. 59)

Perception of Movement

Sometimes *movement perception* appears to be brought about by the successive stimulation of adjacent sense receptors. If you pull a shirt over your head, the movement of the shirt is felt as successive touch receptors are stimulated. An airplane approaches, and most of the sound reaches one ear. When it is directly overhead, stimulation of both ears is about equal. Then, as the plane passes on, more of the sound reaches the other ear.

However, this explanation is oversimplified. When we watch a tennis match we move our heads back and forth so that the light reflected by the ball is always directed at the same retinal area. Yet we know the ball has moved. Conversely, as we turn our head and look around a room, the light reflected from objects stimulates successive regions of the retina. And yet we perceive that the objects are stationary. Thus the perception of movement is very complex. There are a number of different cues that we use some of the time, but not all of the time, in deciding whether something is moving. Sometimes the movement of our head or eyes helps us determine movement, as at the tennis match. If an object blocks and unblocks successive portions of the background, we conclude that the object must be moving. Or if we see one side of an object appear while the other side disappears, we may assume that it is crossing in front of us. In short, there is no simple, single way that we perceive movement (see Poggio & Koch, 1987). We use many cues in the environment, and our conclusions about movement depend on how we interpret those cues (Rock, Auster, Shiffman, & Wheeler, 1980).

Apparent Movement

Sometimes we perceive movement when there really is not any (Ramachandron & Anstis, 1986). For example, if a large, movable background is pulled past a smaller stationary object, the object appears to move, and the background appears steady. This trick of perception, called *apparent movement,* has been used in many western movies. The actor sits on a rocking saddle while the scenery is dragged by behind him, giving the impression that he is riding.

Another type of apparent movement, called *stroboscopic movement,* is common in everyday life. Stroboscopic movement appears when stationary stimuli are presented sequentially (Beck, Elsner, & Silverstein, 1977). For example, two lights separated by a small space are flashed alternately. As one goes on, the other goes off. The result is that the light seems to jump from one position to the other. Stroboscopic movement, which is also called the phi phenomenon, is often used by designers of lighted advertising signs. Neon arrows, "moving" toward the place of business, are created by synchronized blinking lights.

Movies represent another example of stroboscopic movement. There really is not any movement in a movie. It is merely an illusion that is created when a series of still photographs are recorded on a strip of film and run through a projector in rapid succession.

Still another form of apparent movement is the *autokinetic effect,* an illusion similar to the Gamma phenomenon described earlier. If you sit in a completely dark room and stare at a stationary pinpoint of light, the light will soon appear to move. Although this effect has been studied a great deal, it is not well understood. Some researchers have concluded that the apparent movement of the light is produced by small, uncontrollable eye movements (Gregory, 1973), but it is most likely that it occurs because of the absence of a stimulating background. A background functions as a frame of reference by which we gauge movement. The autokinetic effect is easily destroyed by presenting the point of light against a dimly lighted background, or by presenting it with other points of light.

Depth Perception

How is it that we perceive a three-dimensional world when the image cast on the retina is only two dimensional? How do we add depth to our perception of objects? What cues do we use to determine that the objects we see are some distance from us? As it turns out, we use many different cues in perceiving depth (Gogel & Tietz, 1980). Let us consider some of them.

Binocular Vision   In this world, some animals are predators and some are prey. Most of those that are preyed upon, such as rabbits and deer, have their eyes on the sides of the head so they can see danger approaching over a wide area. Most predators, such as lions and foxes, have their eyes set close together on the front of the head. This arrangement allows them to have *binocular vision,* which helps

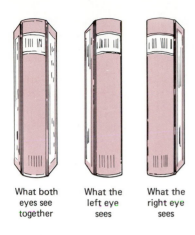

What both   What the   What the
eyes see   left eye   right eye
together   sees   sees

FIGURE 3–30   Binocular
Disparity   *Each eye sees
something different.*

them in hunting. Humans also have this predatory vision and it has a great influence on the way we see the world.

Binocular vision is helpful in perceiving depth. Since the eyes are set two or three inches apart, each receives a slightly different view of the visual field. When we focus on a three-dimensional object, both eyes receive light reflected from the front of the object. But, in addition, each eye can receive light from one side of the object as well, as Figure 3–30 shows. To demonstrate this, place your finger on the tip of your nose and alternately close each eye. You will see one side of your finger with one eye and the other side with the other eye. Ordinarily we do not see double images, however. Instead, the two images are combined by the brain in a process called **stereopsis.** Somehow, the brain puts the two different images together, and we experience one three-dimensional sensation rather than two different images.

Binocular Convergence   Binocular vision provides another cue to depth in the form of binocular convergence. **Binocular convergence** refers to the fact that our eyes turn toward each other, or converge, when we fixate on close objects. When an object is far away, the eyes turn so that the lines of sight are parallel. It is not yet known for certain how convergence contributes to distance perception, but the eye muscles responsible for the inward and outward turning probably provide us with depth information as well (Hochberg, 1971). Convergence gives depth information over relatively short distances (that is, six to 20 feet from the observer).

Interposition   Many depth cues do not depend on binocular vision. When one object stands in front of another, the front object partially conceals the one in back. This is an extremely effective depth cue called **interposition.** In Figure 3–31, the figures perceived as being farther away are partially hidden by the figures in front.

Aerial Perspective   Objects that are clear and distinct appear closer than objects that are hazy and indistinct. This perceptual effect, known as **aerial perspective,** can be observed in broad landscapes and city scenes. Distant mountains or buildings seem to fade in comparison to nearby objects.

A dependence on aerial perspective can be dangerous. Suppose a person lives in Los Angeles, a very smoggy city. Living under these conditions, it is easy to establish standards of aerial perspective that do not apply in other situations. Specifically, something that is seen clearly in Los Angeles *must* be close, for if it were far away it would be obscured by pollution. Suppose a Los Angeles resident drives out to the desert for the first time and runs out of gas. Looking down the road she sees a town ahead. Because she can see the town so clearly, it must (according to her Los Angeles standards) be close. Luckily, she does not try to hike the short distance in 100° weather, for when help arrives, it turns out that the town is 20 miles away.

FIGURE 3–31   Interposition as a Depth Cue   *Objects that partially block out other objects are seen as closer.*

Texture Gradient   Another depth cue, **texture gradient,** refers to the fact that textured surfaces nearby appear rougher than distant surfaces. As the distance increases between the surface and the viewer,

FIGURE 3–32 Texture Gradient
*Textured surfaces look rougher
close up.*

the details of the surface blend together and the texture appears increasingly smooth, as Figure 3–32 shows. If you look across a field of grass or down a brick walk, the texture gradient will be apparent. The texture formed by the blades of grass near you appears rough. Farther away the grass looks more like a green carpet, because the fine detail is not visible.

Linear Perspective   If you look down a railroad track you will notice that the parallel tracks appear to come together in the distance. This effect is referred to as *linear perspective,* and it is another cue we use in depth perception. Figure 3–33 shows the effect of converging lines on a two-dimensional surface. Although you know the drawing is flat, the lines appear to recede into the distance.

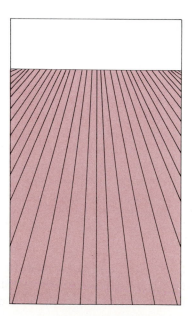 

FIGURE 3–33 Linear Perspective
*Parallel lines appear to come together
in the distance.*

FIGURE 3–34 Relative Size
Smaller objects appear to be farther away than larger objects.

Relative Size   The **relative sizes** of objects often serve as depth cues. If we see two similar objects and the image of one is smaller than the image of the other, we judge the smaller image to be farther away, as illustrated in Figure 3–34.

Motion Parallax   Another depth cue is called motion parallax. **Motion parallax** refers to the fact that if we move, objects near us appear to move more than objects far away from us. If we are moving past a number of objects located at different distances from us, the objects will appear to move across our visual field at different speeds. Those located nearest to us move most rapidly. Those that are far away appear to move more slowly. These differences in speed aid in our perception of depth and distance. Try it. Look out the side window of a moving automobile and notice how trees growing alongside the highway appear to speed past in a blur, while distant trees move very slowly.

Here is another simple demonstration of motion parallax. Hold your two forefingers out in front of you, but at different distances. Now wag your head from side to side. You will notice that the close finger seems to move more than the far finger. In addition, notice that it moves in the opposite direction from your head (Gogel, 1980).

Depth Perception: Innate or Learned?   Some interesting experiments concerning depth perception have been performed with the aid of an apparatus known as the "visual cliff." As shown in Color Plate 26, the visual cliff is created by covering two surfaces, one shallow and one deep, with a patterned material, and then laying a thick sheet of glass over both sides. Infants, both animal and human, have been tested in this apparatus to determine if depth perception is an innate ability or if it is learned from the experience of falling (Gibson & Walk, 1960). Very young infants are able to perceive the "drop-off." They avoid the deep side of the apparatus without ever having fallen. Babies will crawl across the shallow side to their mothers, but they will not cross the glass covering the deep side. Even though the child may pat the glass on the deep side with its hand, and thus receive information that the surface is solid, it will refrain from moving onto it. Infant animals behave similarly. When placed on the glass covering the deep side, a one-day-old goat stood on the narrow board ledge and then jumped across the cliff to the shallow side.

Although these studies suggest that there is a strong innate component to depth perception, depth perception can be altered by experience (Bradley & Shea, 1977). Experiments were conducted in which monkeys, kittens, and chimpanzees were fitted with translucent goggles at birth. These goggles, worn continuously for the first several months of life, permitted diffuse light to enter, but the animals could not see distinct patterns. When the goggles were finally removed, the animals showed, among other problems, impaired depth perception (Riesen, 1965).

Which of the many depth cues we have discussed are used by babies in perceiving the visual cliff? A number of studies indicate that the texture gradient created by the difference between the patterned material on the deep and shallow sides, binocular convergence, and motion parallax from head movements are all effective cues. In a further refinement, monocular infants were tested in a special visual cliff apparatus that equalized the texture difference between the surfaces. Thus, in this experiment, both binocular cues and texture gradient were ruled out. And yet these babies also perceived and avoided the drop-off, indicating that motion parallax by itself is an effective depth cue (Walk, 1968). Just by wagging their heads, the babies were able to detect the cliff.

Language Perception

Recent years have seen an upsurge in studies of the perception of both written and spoken language. We will examine language in Chapter 7, but let us look now at some examples of work on language perception.

First, consider the skill you are practicing at this moment — reading. Highly skilled readers do not fix their gaze on every single word as they read (Mason, 1980). If we can read with fewer eye fixations, we will absorb information more effectively than slow readers can. It appears that reading goes more smoothly if we are able to absorb written material in chunks or units of information (such as phrases or words) instead of breaking the material down into syllables or letters. Research on reading indicates that we do read words as units, rather than as collections of letters or syllables. If subjects are asked to proofread materials that contain spelling errors, the subjects are much more likely to pick up errors in uncommon words than in common words such as "the" (Healy, 1980). This is because common words are more often perceived as whole units and are not normally broken down into, and perceived as, isolated letters. Uncommon words, however, are more likely to be perceived as collections of letters.

What about spoken rather than written language? In one study (Ganong, 1980), words were presented against a noisy background, making them difficult to understand. It was found that words were much more easily understood if they were contained in sentences, and if they were words that occur very often in normal speech. Spoken language is also much more likely to be understood if it is expected (Mills, 1980). If you expect to hear words having to do with education, you will be more likely to recognize and understand those words than if you had not been expecting education-related words.

Adaptation effects have been observed in spoken language perception. If a particular sound is repeatedly presented, the tendency to perceive that sound will be reduced, much as we cease to smell fish after we stand in a fishmarket for a few minutes (Diehl, Lang, & Parker, 1980).

PERCEPTUAL CONSTANCY

Let us turn to some other concepts that have been particularly influential in the field of perception. The first of these, *perceptual constancy*, refers to the fact that we perceive a consistent world in spite of incomplete, ambiguous, and potentially confusing sensory information (Wallach, 1985). For example, when we see a person some three blocks away, we do not say, "Here comes one of those tiny people." Look about you right now. Do you see any doors? What shape are they? Rectangular? Look again. More than likely, the retinal image is not a rectangle, and yet we all perceive doors as rectangular. As we walk toward a building, the retinal image of it becomes larger, but we do not perceive it as growing. These are all examples of perceptual constancy. We perceive a stable world in which objects do not change haphazardly but retain their characteristics across any number of viewing conditions.

A number of different constancies have been identified. *Size constancy,* as suggested above, refers to the fact that objects are perceived as retaining their actual size regardless of the distance from which they are viewed (see Norman, 1980).

Shape constancy is the principle involved in our example of doors viewed from different angles. Notice, in Figure 3–35 that the shape of the door changes from rectangular to trapezoidal as it swings open. Such shape changes in the retinal image, however, are not considered as a property of the door itself but rather as evidence of the door's having moved from a closed to an open state.

Brightness or *color constancy* refers to the fact that objects are perceived as having a specific color even though they are viewed in a number of different illumination levels. Snow in dark shadow is perceived as white, and coal in bright sunlight is seen as black, even though the amounts of light they reflect are similar under these conditions. Although a piece of white paper in moonlight reflects far less light than a piece of gray paper in daylight, it is perceived as brighter or whiter than the gray paper, at any time.

Location constancy can be demonstrated under experimental conditions, though it has few correlates in everyday experience. In an early experiment, Stratton (1897) made a special pair of goggles with lenses that inverted and reversed the visual field. When he first put on these glasses, he had difficulty moving around in his upside-down and backward world. Over a period of weeks, however, his perceptual processes adjusted so that the objects in his visual field returned

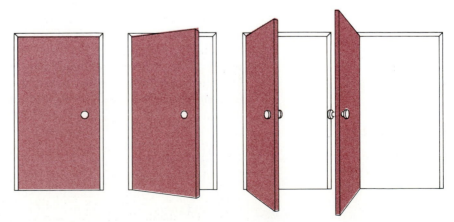

FIGURE 3–35 Shape Constancy *A door is a door, no matter what angle we view it from.*

to their proper places. He no longer felt he was looking up at the ground and down at the sky, to the left to locate his right hand and to the right for his left hand. Once he adjusted to the abnormal condition, a change back to the "normal" was as disruptive as the initial change.

Experimentally, Professor Kohler of Innsbruck, Austria, wore the same type of glasses for a number of weeks (Kohler, 1962). Although he reports that the world never "looked right," no matter how long he wore the glasses, he was able to move about with considerable dexterity. He could even pilot his bicycle about narrow, twisting streets after a few weeks of practice.

PERCEPTUAL EXPECTATIONS

Much of what we perceive is due to our *expectations* about what we are likely to perceive. In other words, we perceive what we expect to perceive. We have learned from past experience that our world is constructed of stable and constant elements, so we believe it is predictable. We have grown accustomed to the shapes and sizes of things, we have learned when they are likely to be encountered, and we have constructed a set of expectations that we call reality. In a sense, we are "set" to perceive in a certain way. ***Perceptual expectancy*** can affect many aspects of perception. If you were shown the ambiguous picture in part (a) of Figure 3–36 after you listened to a discussion about young women, you might see the younger woman first. If shown the picture after a discussion about aging, you might see the older woman first. In other words, the identity of the figure will vary according to your perceptual set. The identity of one symbol in part (b) of Figure 3–37 will also vary according to your set. Subjects shown the symbol as one member of a group of letters saw it as a "B," while subjects shown the same symbol as one member of a group of numbers saw it as a "13" (Bruner & Minturn, 1955).

Depth perception also can be influenced by perceptual expectancies. If a person is watching the sky through a window and expecting to spot a plane, a gnat on the window may be perceived momentarily as a distant plane. The BaMbuti Pygmies, living in dense tropical forests, experience a world without vast open spaces. The greatest open distance these people are likely to perceive is a clearing a few yards wide. An anthropologist reported an interesting depth effect resulting from this limited view. One of the Pygmies accompanied him out of the forest and onto an open plain. In the distance, a herd of buffalo was grazing. When he saw the animals, the Pygmy did not interpret his sensory information as a distant buffalo herd, even though he was familiar with forest buffalo. Rather, he believed them to be nearby insects (Turnbull, 1961). In other words, the Pygmy interpreted the visual image according to his perceptual expectations. Since his ordinary environment did not include much depth, he did not have a set to perceive the visual image of buffalo.

The perceiver's needs and values also affect the character of perceptions. A person who needs to see something may be "ready" to see it and more likely to notice it if it does appear. In one experiment, subjects were asked to identify words that were briefly flashed before them. They were quicker to recognize words that were related to their

A B C D E

10 11 12 13 14

(b)

(a)

FIGURE 3–36 Ambiguous Figures *Is (a) a young or an old woman? In (b) the symbol for 13 is identical to the symbol for B.*

own interests. For example, the word "sacred" was more quickly recognized by subjects interested in religion (Postman, Bruner, & McGinnies, 1948; see also Mills, 1980).

Our needs not only cause us to notice certain stimuli, but they also cause us to distort the true character of the stimuli. A classic study demonstrated how needs and values affect the perceived nature of the stimulus. Children from low-income homes and from high-income homes were asked to gauge the size of coins relative to a standard circle. The children from poorer homes were found to overestimate the size of the coins (Bruner & Goodman, 1947). Later research showed that it was indeed the value of the coins that produced the overestimation of their size, and not merely the greater or lesser familiarity that certain children might have had with coins (Bruner & Postman, 1948).

In short, we perceive what we expect to perceive, and our perceptions can be influenced by our interests and values. These effects are not limited to controlled laboratory experiments. Without doubt, our perceptions of other people are heavily affected by what we expect them to be. Politician, professor, student, librarian, and chemist are all labels that can easily create certain expectancies if applied to an individual.

PERCEPTUAL DEVELOPMENT AND LEARNING

Having made a case for the idea that perception is much more than the bare sensations we receive from the environment, we now will look more closely at the role of experience in perception. To what extent is experience involved in perception? We do not have a final answer to this question, even though philosophers and scientists have been studying it for hundreds of years.

The philosophers of the seventeenth and eighteenth centuries could not agree about this issue. The Nativists, including Descartes and Kant, believed that perception is innate. They argued that we are born with perceptual ability and do not have to learn it. The Empiricists, including Berkeley and Locke, insisted that we learn to perceive through our experiences with the environment. Modern psychologists believe that an integration of these views is likely to be correct.

At least three techniques have been used to study the question of innate versus learned perception. First, researchers have worked with people who were born blind and acquired vision through surgery after they became adults. Observation of the initial visual experiences of these people has provided information about innate and learned perceptual abilities. Von Senden (1960) reported studies of persons, blind from birth, who acquired vision in adulthood through the removal of cataracts. He found that the ability to distinguish between figure and ground was present immediately upon removal of the bandages. The patients also had the ability to fixate on the figure, to scan it, and to visually track it when it moved. However, other perceptual abilities had to be learned through experience. The patients were unable to visually identify objects they had known by touch, such as the faces of family and friends. They could not identify common shapes, such as triangles, without counting the corners. These abilities were gradually acquired, but the learning was slow and never matched that of normally sighted adults. The acquired recognition of an object did not transfer well when the object was found in a different context.

For another person with restored sight, the dominance of vision over the other senses, which normally sighted persons experience, never developed. This patient was unable to learn to trust his vision. When he was blind, he was able to cross streets alone, but after the operation, he was frightened by traffic and refused to cross by himself. He never experienced completely normal vision. He would not bother to turn on lights at night, but would sit in the dark all evening (Gregory, 1966).

The second technique used to study innate versus learned perception involves experimental animals raised in conditions of restricted light stimulation, without the normal forms of visual experience. For instance, newborn kittens were fitted with translucent goggles that let in diffuse light but prevented the detection of any visual form. At three months the goggles were removed. Although some simple ability to perceive was intact, complex visual ability was severely curtailed. The kittens could make distinctions on the basis of size, color, and brightness, but they were unable to track a moving object, perceive depth, or discriminate shapes (Riesen, 1965). Apparently, the last three abilities must be learned at an early age.

The third technique involves testing the perceptual capacity of normal infants. Such experiments require much ingenuity because infant humans have limited means of expressing themselves. If they could talk, or had better control of their motor response, many of our questions could be answered. Because many studies of normal infant responses must wait until the child is old enough to produce a particular motor response that can be measured, we cannot be sure that the detected abilities are truly innate. The child learns a great deal, and perhaps most of its perceptual skills, before it is able to crawl. For this reason, these studies must be viewed with caution.

In summary, most psychologists believe that some perceptual abilities are inborn, but that experience plays an important role in the unfolding and proper development of these abilities. A great many studies currently are seeking to clarify the border between abilities that are innate and those that are acquired.

SUMMARY

1. Sensation refers to the raw information we receive through our senses, while perception refers to the way we organize and interpret that information.

2. Sensation involves specialized receptors and transduction.

3. The absolute threshold refers to the minimum amount of stimulus energy required to make an individual respond. The difference threshold is the minimum amount of stimulus change that can be detected.

4. Weber's fraction states that a detectable change in a stimulus is proportional to the intensity of the stimulus ($\Delta I/I = k$).

5. Sensory adaptation refers to the fact that sensory receptors stop responding to constant, unchanging stimulation.

6. Recent REST studies suggest that sensory deprivation can be good for us.

7. Pressure, pain, warmth, and cold represent the major skin sensations. Skin sensations can be produced through the stimulation of different types of skin receptors.

8. Kinesthetic receptors, located in muscles, tendons, and joints, provide feedback concerning the position of our body. Equilibratory receptors, located in the semi-

circular canals and vestibular sacs, provide us with our sense of balance.

9. Gases entering the nose are deflected up to the olfactory epithelium, where they stimulate olfactory receptors.

10. Olfactory receptors undergo a continuous change-over every few days. Some researchers assume that there are six or seven basic odors that are detected by specific receptors.

11. Although each taste receptor responds most readily to one of the four basic tastes (sweet, salty, sour, or bitter), they are all somewhat responsive to all tastes. Cells responsive to the four tastes are located in relatively distinct areas of the tongue.

12. Sound waves are created by air molecules being alternately pushed together (compression) and spread apart (rarefaction). The frequency of the sound wave, heard as pitch, refers to how rapidly the pressure changes occur.

13. Amplitude refers to loudness and increases as intensity of the vibration increases.

14. A complex sound consists of a fundamental wave plus certain overtones. Complexity is experienced as timbre.

15. The hammer, anvil, and stirrup conduct sound vibrations from the eardrum, through the middle ear, to the oval window, which covers an opening into the fluid-filled inner ear.

16. Sound vibrations enter the cochlea where the basilar membrane is stimulated. This membrane, in turn, bends and displaces tiny hairs in the organ of Corti. It is the bending of these hairs that stimulates nerve endings to fire neural impulses to the brain.

17. Location and distance of a sound source are judged by using time, intensity, and echoic cues.

18. Visible light wavelengths vary from about 380 to 760 nm and are experienced as hue, or color.

19. The amplitude of a light wave is experienced as brightness. Saturation refers to the purity of a color; a pure, saturated color reflects light of a single wavelength.

20. Light passes through the cornea, past the iris, through the lens, and across to the back of the eyeball, where it strikes the light-sensitive retina.

21. Nearsightedness, farsightedness, and astigmatism can be corrected with lenses that focus the image properly on the retina.

22. Cones are cells that allow us to perceive color. They are insensitive to low intensities. Rods do not provide color vision and are sensitive to many different wavelengths and intensities.

23. The rods and cones are located in the retina behind a layer of bipolar cells and a layer of ganglion cells.

24. The blind spot is the spot where the ganglion cell axons leave the eye on the way to the brain.

25. Cones are concentrated in the fovea, a small indentation next to the optic nerve. Rods are located all over the rest of the retina.

26. Dark adaptation refers to the process whereby rods and cones become more sensitive to low intensities.

27. The Young-Helmholtz theory of color vision proposes three types of cones — one type for red, one type for blue, and one type for green.

28. The opponent-process theory maintains that colors are organized in pairs. Excitation of one member of each pair inhibits excitation of the other member.

29. Perception involves prior learning and experience. Illusions demonstrate that perception is far from perfect.

30. Stimulus qualities that draw our attention include change, movement, repetition, size, intensity, and color. Needs and values can affect perception as well.

31. We tend to organize according to figure-ground, closure, continuity, proximity, and similarity tendencies.

32. Pattern recognition may occur according to a template-matching process or through feature analysis.

33. Perception of movement can be brought about by the stimulation of adjacent sensory receptors, although more than this must be involved.

34. Apparent movement effects include stroboscopic movement and autokinetic effects.

35. Depth perception is aided by many cues, including binocular vision, binocular convergence, interposition, aerial perspective, texture/gradient, linear perspective, relative size, and motion parallax.

36. Much of our ability to perceive depth may be innate.

37. The perception of written and spoken language is currently under heavy investigation.

38. Perceptual constancy of shape, size, location, and color refers to our ability to perceive a stable world in spite of confusing sensory input. Perceptual expectation refers to the fact that we perceive what we expect to perceive.

39. The context in which a stimulus occurs will often affect how that stimulus is perceived.

40. Some perceptual abilities may be innate, but learning and experience play an important role in the development of these abilities.

KEY TERMS

absolute threshold
aerial perspective
after images
amplitude
anvil
apparent movement
astigmatism
autokinetic effect
basilar membrane
binocular convergence
binocular vision
bipolar cell
blind spot
brightness (color constancy)
closure
cochlea
color/hue
complexity
compression
cone
continuity
cornea
dark adaptation
decibel (db)
dichromatic
difference threshold
Doppler effect
eardrum
equilibratory receptors
farsightedness
feature analysis
figure-ground tendency
fovea
frequency

frequency theory
ganglion cell
gestalt
hammer
illusions
inner ear
intensity/brightness
interposition
iris
just-noticeable difference (jnd)
kinesthetic receptors
light adaptation
linear perspective
location constancy
middle ear
monochromatic
motion parallax
movement perception
nearsightedness
neural coding
olfactory epithelium
opponent-process theory
organ of Corti
organization
outer ear
oval windows
overtone
pattern recognition
perception
perceptual constancy
perceptual expectancy
pitch
place theory
prototype-matching
    hypothesis

proximity
psychophysics
pupil
rarefaction
receptors
relative sizes
Restricted Environmental
    Stimulation Technique
    (REST)
retina
rod
saturation
selective attention
semicircular canals
sensation
sensory adaptation
sensory deprivation
shape constancy
similarity
sine wave
size constancy
stereopsis
stirrup
stroboscopic movement
taste buds
template-matching hypothesis
texture gradient
timbre
transduce
trichromatic
trichromatic theory
vestibular sacs
wavelength
Weber's fraction

ADDITIONAL READING

Anderson, J. R. (1985) *Cognitive psychology*. New York: W. H. Freeman.
Anderson is one of the best-known researchers in the field of cognition and his book is a good source of advanced information.

Best, J. B. (1986) *Cognitive psychology*. St. Paul: West.
This text is another excellent source of information about perception and attention.

Curtis, H., & Barnes, N. S. (1985) *Invitation to biology*. New York: Worth.
This biology text contains excellent coverage of the physical basis of sensation.

Glass, A. L., & Holyoak, K. J. (1986) *Cognition*. New York: Random House.
This book offers an advanced look at perception and its relationship to the overall field of cognition.

Wolfe, J. M. (1986) *Readings from Scientific American*. New York: W. H. Freeman.
This is an interesting collection of twelve articles having to do with current research in the field of vision.

4

Exploring Physiology and Perception

GENETIC MANAGEMENT

Cloning
Genetic Engineering
Genetic Counseling

USES AND MISUSES OF HORMONES

Uses of Hormones
Misuses of Hormones

EMPLOYING BRAIN RESEARCH

Endorphins: Pain, War, Jogging, and Trances
Autism and Endorphins
Parkinson's Disease
Brain-tissue Transplants

SLEEP AND DREAMS

Sleep as an Active Process
Sleep Deprivation and the Purpose of Sleeping
Eye Movements and Brain Waves
Patterns of Sleeping and Dreaming
The Need to Dream
Dream Theories and the Purpose of Dreaming
Hypnopaedia
How Long Does a Dream Take?
Sleep Disorders

DRUG ABUSE

Types of Drugs
"Designer" Drugs
The Variability of Drug Reactions
Drugs and Death

HYPNOSIS

Entering the Hypnotic Trance
The Hypnotic Trance
Hypnotic Effects
Hypnotized Eyewitnesses
Role Playing
Who Can Be Hypnotized?
The Uses of Hypnosis

MEDITATION

What Is Meditation?
How Do We Meditate?
What Are the Effects of Meditation?

EXTRASENSORY PERCEPTION

Personal versus Scientific Observations
Types of ESP
Reasons for Caution

What do we know about human behavior up to this point? We learned a good deal about the physiological aspects of behavior in Chapter 2. We followed the interwoven pathways of sensation and perception in Chapter 3 and observed the ingenious experiments that have confirmed these basic facts about human functioning. Professionals in the field of psychology would like to be able to say that all of this varied knowledge has resulted in advances beneficial to the human condition, but much of the basic research we have examined still awaits an application. Progress is being made toward the fruitful use of much of this information, however, and so in this, our first "exploring" chapter, we will pursue some of these applications. In addition, we will discuss new, challenging, and controversial areas of investigation. Thus, while the basic chapters cover fundamental issues, we now move into the arena of innovative work at the frontiers of psychology.

GENETIC MANAGEMENT

As our knowledge of genetic mechanisms advances we begin to see more and more ways to use this information. Some of these applications are straightforward while others are entangled with disturbing moral and ethical questions.

Cloning

Cloning is an extreme instance of what can be done with modern genetic techniques. We have all seen or heard of sci-fi movies and stories about clones, or duplicate human beings. While no humans have been cloned yet, cloned toads are hopping about right now, and many observers speculate that it is only a matter of a few years before humans can be cloned (Stine, 1977). Whether we will ever *want* to clone human beings, or make duplicates of ourselves, is another matter entirely (one that we will discuss in the next section), but advances in genetic research have clearly made the cloning of humans a scientific possibility.

Cloning means growing identical animals from cells taken from a single parent. Since the clone is grown from the cell of a single parent, it has the genetic material from only that one parent; it is genetically identical to that single parent. As you will recall, normally reproduced individuals have genetic material from two parents and are thus not identical to either parent.

John Gurdon (1969) of Oxford University has cloned a whole colony of identical South African toads. His cloning technique, called the *nuclear transplant method,* is shown in Figure 4–1. The nucleus of an epithelial cell taken from the intestine of a tadpole is extracted from the cell surgically. This extracted nucleus, which contains *all* of the genetic information from the tadpole, is then inserted into a toad egg that has had its own nucleus, and therefore its genetic identity, destroyed by ultraviolet radiation. The recipient egg cell now has the complete genetic code from a single parent, the tadpole, and is ready to develop according to those genetic instructions. The end result is a toad identical to the one that the parent tadpole grows to be. Many clones, or identical individuals, can be grown from cells from the same tadpole.

FIGURE 4–1 Cloning by the Nuclear Transplant Method
The nucleus of an unfertilized egg is destroyed. Then the nucleus from a donor animal is put into this egg cell. The resultant animal is genetically identical to the original donor animal. The clone has but a single genetic parent (the tadpole).

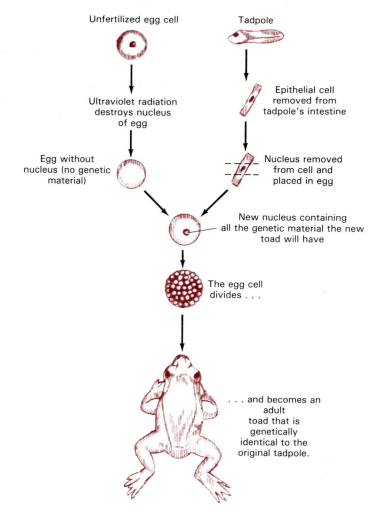

Unfertilized egg cell

Tadpole

Ultraviolet radiation destroys nucleus of egg

Epithelial cell removed from tadpole's intestine

Egg without nucleus (no genetic material)

Nucleus removed from cell and placed in egg

New nucleus containing all the genetic material the new toad will have

The egg cell divides . . .

. . . and becomes an adult toad that is genetically identical to the original tadpole.

Although these early cloning efforts with amphibians began nearly two decades ago, cloning of warm-blooded mammals has proved to be much more difficult. The first instance of mammal cloning was reported by Karl Illmensee and Peter Hoppe at the University of Geneva. They were able to grow three mice from single cells of parent mice by using a technique similar to the one employed by Gurdon (see Hackett, Fuchs, & Messing, 1984; Marx, 1981; Singer & Wells, 1985). If mice can be cloned, will the ability to clone humans be far behind?

Genetic Engineering

Genetic engineering includes all efforts to change or exchange undesirable genes for more desirable ones. If a person suffers from a disorder that has been linked to a particular gene, then the genetic engineer will, someday, seek to replace that gene with a gene that would cure the disease. In a sense, cloning is an extreme example of genetic engineering where *all* of the genetic material that an organism possesses is controlled by the experimenter.

At present, genetic engineering is in its infancy. We are still learning how to splice, replace, and manipulate single genes. Still, some astounding discoveries are being made. Genetic researchers have been able to make synthetic genes, to combine human cells with mouse cells to produce human-animal cells, to perform genetic surgery on bacteria, to place mouse embryos that have been frozen and thawed into foster-mother mice and produce normal offspring, to grow complete carrots from single carrot cells, and to clone amphibians. In addition, a group of researchers at the University of California at San Diego recently inserted a gene from a firefly into the DNA of a tobacco plant (Ow et al., 1986). The result was a tobacco plant that glowed like a firefly (see Color Plate 13). In other words, some pretty amazing things have been going on.

Genetic engineering holds both promise and peril for humanity. On the positive side, we might expect superior genetic health if we could control and manipulate the many genetic factors that cause human suffering. Table 4–1 lists some conditions that are often genetically determined. Many of these forms of suffering might be reduced if we could perfect genetic engineering techniques. But the dangers in genetic engineering are also great. Prominent among these is the possibility that our moral judgment will be distorted and we will begin to think that we can determine "what is best" for humanity. Who will decide what kind of people will be engineered? What kinds of people should be "made"? Do we want only geniuses? Should we grow our own ball teams rather than scout them? People are understandably uneasy with the thought of human beings planned and genetically constructed by other humans. But if genetic knowledge continues to increase, we soon will be forced to face questions like these. The genetic engineering approach also raises the danger that, by selecting only a narrow band of "desirable" traits, our species will suffer a loss of genetic variability — variability that some feel is vital to the evolutionary process.

The danger and promise inherent in genetic engineering are immense. Who will decide what kinds of people should be "made"?

TABLE 4–1   Some Types of Human Suffering That Are Often Determined by Genetic Factors

1. Some forms of dwarfism
2. Degeneration of the nerve cells
3. Frizzy, breakable hair
4. Breast development in men
5. No breast development in women
6. Blindness
7. Weakness in facial muscles
8. Cyst development in the kidneys
9. Heart problems combined with narrow shoulders
10. Absence of the iris
11. Combination of pigmented stools, nausea, and violent behavior
12. Allergies
13. Webbed fingers and toes
14. Short arms and legs; normal head and body
15. Short fingers
16. The "white" of the eye is blue
17. Deafness
18. Soft bones
19. Drooping eyelids
20. Degeneration of the muscles
21. Jaundice
22. Red blood cells oval instead of round
23. Bone growths and tumors
24. Gout
25. Skin disorders
26. Growths in intestines
27. Spots of white hair in dark-haired people
28. Overly woolly hair
29. High levels of blood cholesterol
30. Tiny eyes
31. Epilepsy
32. Flipper-like limbs
33. Mental retardation
34. Missing fingers
35. Extra fingers
36. Eye cancer
37. Nearsightedness
38. Tumors in endocrine system
39. Diabetes
40. Malformed jaw

Genetic Counseling

When a woman conceives and bears children, those children receive whatever combination of genes happen to come together from the sperm and the ovum of their parents. If the parents are carriers of a recessive gene for some disease, such as PKU, sickle-cell anemia (a blood disease, more common among blacks than whites), or Tay-Sachs disease (a degenerative disease of the nervous system, more common among Jews than others), their children run a one-in-four risk of receiving that recessive gene from both parents and thus inheriting the disease (Clark, 1981).

Until recent years, parent carriers could do little to predict this possibility and avoid having afflicted children. Similarly, there was no way to predict chromosomal abnormalities, such as Down syndrome (Mongolism), Turner's syndrome, or Klinefelter's syndrome, and thus avoid having children with those disorders. However, two new techniques have made both prediction and avoidance of recessive-gene diseases and chromosomal abnormalities possible.

First, geneticists have discovered precisely which gene on which chromosome carries the signal for certain diseases. This has been discovered for Tay-Sachs disease and for sickle-cell anemia, but not for PKU or for other serious diseases such as cystic fibrosis — a fatal disease affecting the lungs and intestinal tract.

This new information means that it is possible to analyze the cells of a prospective mother and father to see whether either or both of them is carrying a recessive gene for some detectable disease. The genetic testing is accompanied by the collection of a detailed family medical history for both parents. This procedure, usually described as *genetic counseling*, is done before conception, so that the parents can make an informed decision about whether to bear children or not (see Takashima, Ohkura, Arima, Osawa, & Suzuki, 1980).

The second development affecting the decision process for parents is a technique called *amniocentesis* (see Figure 2–28, page 91), which is used during pregnancy. About 15 weeks after conception, a sample of the amniotic fluid (the fluid in which the developing fetus floats) is taken from the mother for laboratory analysis. This fluid, which has the same genetic makeup as the cells in the fetus's body, is analyzed for the presence of detectable recessive gene defects and chromosomal abnormalities, such as Down syndrome. The physician can then tell the parents whether the fetus has any of these disorders. If the fetus is not normal, the parents can consider the option of abortion — if such a decision is consistent with their moral views.

For some types of diseases, such as Tay-Sachs disease, these two new strategies can be used in combination. A couple — particularly a Jewish couple — may want to have blood tests done initially to detect the presence of the recessive gene that carries Tay-Sachs. If they are both carriers, they may wish to have amniocentesis performed after conception to see if the child has inherited the disease.

For other disorders, the decision process is more complex. The recessive genes for sickle-cell anemia can be detected in the parents before conception, but the presence of the disease cannot be reliably determined by amniocentesis. Thus, parents who know they are both carriers of a recessive gene for this disease must decide whether to bear children, knowing they run a one-in-four risk of having an affected child.

Cystic fibrosis presents still more difficulties. Carriers cannot be detected ahead of time, and the disease cannot be diagnosed with amniocentesis. Only parents who have already borne one CF child know that they carry the recessive genes. Their decision is whether to risk further pregnancies.

Obviously, the moral and ethical issues are difficult ones and must be faced by each couple individually, but the development of new techniques holds the promise that such decisions can be based on better information about the risks involved (Lewin, 1981).

USES AND MISUSES OF HORMONES

Uses of Hormones

Another area of research where practical applications are being found for basic research concerning physiological development involves the uses of hormones. As our knowledge of hormonal action increases, we are more and more likely to try to reduce human suffering through *hormonal manipulation.* Sometimes these efforts succeed but, in other cases, hormonal treatment is questionable. As Cotman and McGaugh (1980) point out, our knowledge is not extensive enough for us to go about dosing people with hormones as though we knew all of the consequences of such actions.

On the positive side, there do seem to be some circumstances where hormonal treatment is effective. We have seen that hypothyroid individuals (people without sufficient thyroid hormones) may suffer stunted growth, mental retardation, weight gain, and sluggishness. Properly adjusted doses of thyroid hormones relieve these symptoms without causing any bad side effects. Similarly, Addison's disease, caused by an adrenal cortical insufficiency, can be rendered less debilitating by the administration of appropriate hormones. The symptoms of Addison's disease are very unusual. Afflicted persons have lowered sensory thresholds. They can detect far weaker taste stimuli than normal people can. Their sense of smell can be as much as 100,000 times more sensitive than that of normal individuals. Their sense of hearing is also disturbed. While stricken individuals can detect pure tones at very low levels, they have trouble discriminating among language components. All of these symptoms can be relieved by means of hormonal treatment. One final area in which hormonal treatment has been useful involves human sexuality. Reduced testicular action in men can lead to a reduction of interest in sexual activity. When testosterone is administered to these men, it can restore their sexual drive to normal levels.

Misuses of Hormones

Cotman and McGaugh (1980), while noting the constructive uses of hormones we have just mentioned, also describe some misuses of these substances. They state, "Therapeutic manipulation of the neuroendocrine system has far outdistanced a scientific understanding of the neuroendocrine integrative system" (p. 548). One major problem with hormonal treatment is that we do not yet know the long-range consequences of administering these substances. Sometimes they are tragic. Years ago some pregnant women were given a synthetic female hormone called diethylstilbestrol (DES) in an effort to prevent miscarriages. It is now becoming clear that the daughters of these women run a high risk of developing vaginal cancer at about the age of puberty due to their mothers' use of this synthetic compound as a form of estrogen.

Therapists have treated many male sex offenders by giving them antiandrogen to reduce their level of testosterone, the male hormone. This has the effect of lowering the man's sex drive while he undergoes psychotherapy. As the man learns to direct his sex drive into socially acceptable channels, the antiandrogen dose is gradually reduced. This therapy apparently has helped men to eliminate their antisocial behavior (Kalat, 1984). The problem is that we know nothing at all about the long-range consequences of this treatment. Even though the short-term social effects have been positive, the danger remains that physical problems will develop later.

The point is that caution should be exercised in administering hormones. They are powerful substances, known to have negative long-range consequences, and their liberal use is dangerously premature.

EMPLOYING BRAIN RESEARCH

Endorphins: Pain, War, Jogging, and Trances

In this section we discuss ways in which our growing knowledge of brain functioning has led to the relief of human suffering. Our story of the control of pain begins in the middle 1970s when startling reports began to appear, claiming that the human brain produces opium-like substances. Opium, a powerful painkiller, is made from the milky-white juice of unripe poppy seed pods, but we now know that the brain produces its own substances, called *endorphins*, which resemble opium in their ability to reduce pain.

Because the discovery of endorphins is a fairly recent one, the full functioning of these amazing chemical substances is not yet understood. It is known that endorphins are directly involved in the control of pain. This fact is demonstrated vividly by the implantation of electrodes in the brain stems of human patients at points where endorphins are localized. Electrical stimulation of the patient's brain releases the brain's endorphins which, in turn, inhibit pain. When these patients experience an attack of pain, they stimulate their own brain by using a hand-held device that activates the electrode. They experience almost immediate relief when stimulation triggers the release of endorphins. The electrode is not visible; it is implanted under the skin. Obviously, this form of treatment is not used in mild cases of pain. The pain must clearly be severe and intractable before these extreme measures are utilized (Lewis & Leibeskind, 1983).

Unfortunately, prolonged administration of endorphins for pain relief results in progressively weaker analgesic effects and signs of withdrawal when medication is discontinued. That is, endorphin treatment produces tolerance and dependence (addiction), just as does morphine.

Since their discovery, the endorphins have been implicated in a number of physiological and psychological states. Stress appears to contribute to production of endorphins. For example, soldiers may become euphoric during combat and frequently report an absence of pain, even from severe wounds. Analgesia and varying degrees of euphoria seem to be the most common factors in these states.

Dedicated joggers have been tested and shown to have an increased pain tolerance. Many individuals also experience a "runner's high." Researchers have found endorphin levels to be four times higher in athletes during maximum exertion than before exercise. Endorphin levels increase in direct proportion to the effort exerted by runners. Thus, the irritability, restlessness, and mild depression reported by joggers when they cannot run appear to result from mild endorphin withdrawal.

Of a more speculative nature is the hypothesized link between endorphins and trance states or near-death experiences. James Henry (1982) of McGill University in Canada has pointed out that the anal-

Endorphins can help reduce pain—but clearly not entirely.

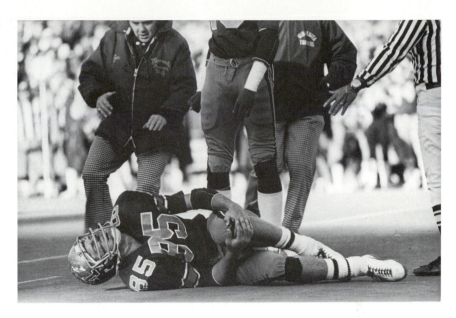

gesia and euphoria common to other opiate-mediated behaviors occur during the spiritual trance state. The trance state typically follows several hours of strenuous ritualistic dancing. The dance is usually accompanied by music that is monotonous, rather than melodious, which may itself contribute to the euphoric state. It has been speculated that disco or rock music—with its repetitive beat—may produce a similar effect. The trance state is also pain free. During the trance individuals often pierce their skin or walk on coals without apparent discomfort. At the end of the trance there is usually a profound physical collapse, an experience that has been reported for strenuously active participants at rock concerts.

The near-death experience has a similar "spiritual" component. There are marked elevations of endorphins before death, which may account for the flash of memories, loss of pain perception, euphoria, and out-of-body experience reported by those who have had near-death experiences.

Much of the research reported here is in the preliminary stages of development. In the near future scientists may be able to apply the results of this research to the treatment of, for example, mental illness, memory impairment in the aged, learning disabilities, and chronic intractable pain.

Autism and Endorphins

As we learned in Chapter 1, autistic children are severely disturbed individuals who display unusual behavior that has been of great interest to psychologists. Table 4–2 contains some of the most characteristic behaviors of these children.

The causes of autism are not well understood. One intriguing hypothesis has been suggested by a number of investigators (Kalat, 1984; Panksepp, Herman, & Vilberg, 1978). Specifically, on the basis of observations that autistic children often seem to ignore extremely

TABLE 4–2 Characteristic Autistic Behavior

1. *Social isolation.* The autistic child largely ignores other people, shows little attachment even to parents, and retreats into a private world.

2. *Stereotyped behaviors.* The autistic child rocks back and forth, bites the hands, stares at something, rotates an object with the hands, or engages in other repetitive behaviors for long, uninterrupted time periods. Each autistic child has an individualized repertoire of preferred stereotyped behaviors.

3. *Resistance to any change in routine.* The child establishes strong habits.

4. *Abnormal responses to sensory stimuli.* The autistic child may ignore visual stimuli and sounds, especially speech sounds, sometimes to such an extent that others assume the child is deaf. At other times the child may show an excessive "startle reaction" to very mild stimuli.

5. *Insensitivity to pain.* Autistic children are amazingly insensitive to cuts, burns, extreme hot or cold, and other pain, at least some of the time.

6. *Inappropriate emotional expressions.* Autistic children have sudden bouts of fear and crying for no obvious reason; at other times they display utter fearlessness and unprovoked laughter. Their emotions seem to spring from spontaneous internal sources rather than from any event in the environment.

7. *Disturbances of movement.* Varying among individual autistic children, and from one time to another, there may be hyperactivity or prolonged inactivity.

8. *Poor development of speech.* Some autistic children never develop any spoken language. Others begin to develop speech and then lose it. Some autistic children learn the names of many common objects and develop good pronunciation, but never use language to ask for anything or to interact socially.

9. *Specific, limited intellectual problems.* Many autistic children do well, even unusually well, on some intellectual tasks but very poorly on others. The exact pattern of impairment varies from one case to another. It is difficult to estimate their overall intelligence because they generally do not follow directions well for standard IQ tests.

Source: After Kalat, 1984.

painful stimuli, it has been suggested that these children suffer from *too much* endorphin production; they act as though they have been given an injection of morphine or another powerful painkiller. For some unknown reason, the brains of autistic children may be producing excessive quantities of endorphins. Animal studies seem to support this view. Increasing or decreasing the amounts of painkillers given to animals seems to produce behavior that mimics that of autistic children.

Only very recently, and only on an experimental level, have drugs that reduce endorphin production been given to autistic children. Barbara Herman and Kathryn Hammock at Children's Hospital National Medical Center in Washington, D.C., have given an endorphin blocker to several autistic children. The results have been encouraging. While none of the children exhibited improved speech patterns, abnormal behavior was reduced and the treated children seemed to be more responsive to their social environment. Self-destructive behavior, such as cutting, bruising, and hitting oneself, was also reduced by the administration of endorphin blockers (McAuliffe, 1987).

Parkinson's Disease

Parkinson's disease (PD) is an unfortunate but common brain disorder. It involves progressive damage to the part of the brain that controls movement, posture, and balance. Its causes are unknown. The major primary and secondary symptoms are listed in Table 4–3. Figure 4–2 illustrates one of the practical problems victims of PD face.

PD victims are usually 40 years old or older before they are stricken. PD is not usually fatal but can be extremely debilitating and may confine the patient to bed in extreme cases. Sufferers do not all experience the same constellation of symptoms; it has been said that no two PD patients are the same.

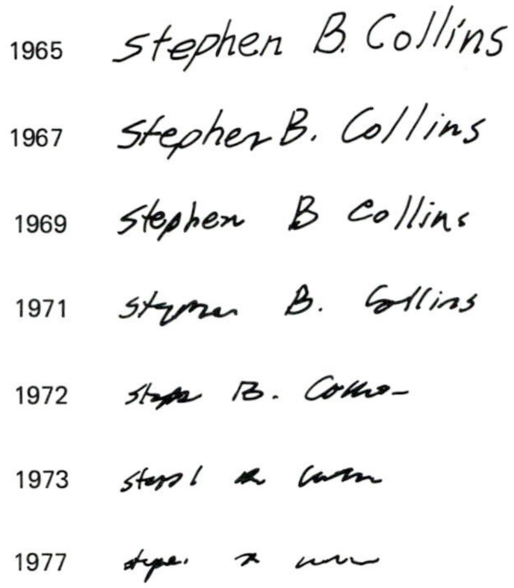

Treatment of the disease eluded researchers until they discovered that the brains of patients suffering from Parkinson's disease showed very low levels of *dopamine,* an important neurotransmitter found in the central nervous system. This discovery led to the finding that if L-dopa (a synthetic substance that is converted to dopamine by the body) is administered, many patients will show marked improvement. Bedridden patients are able to sit up. Patients who could stand but not walk before L-dopa begin walking. Some can even run. Speech difficulties clear up. The effect does not last forever, however. After a number of years the patient no longer responds well to the drug; the so-called "L-dopa honeymoon" is over and subjects again display the tragic symptoms of PD. It is not known whether this lessening of the effect of the drug is due to growing tolerance or to progressive development of the underlying disorder. In addition to its declining efficacy, L-dopa also has some negative side effects, such as nausea.

FIGURE 4–2   One Effect of Parkinson's Disease   *PD leads to progressively smaller and smaller writing until it becomes illegible.*

TABLE 4–3   Primary and Secondary Symptoms of Parkinson's Disease

Primary Symptoms	Secondary Symptoms	
1. Stiffness	1. Depression	10. Breathing problems
2. Tremor	2. Sleep disorders	11. Difficulty in voiding
3. Slowness	3. Senility	12. Dizziness
4. Poverty of movement	4. Forced eye closure	13. Stooped posture
5. Difficulty with balance	5. Speech problems	14. Foot swelling
6. Difficulty walking	6. Drooling	15. Sexual problems
7. Delay in starting to move	7. Difficulty in swallowing	16. Oily skin
8. Arrest of ongoing movement	8. Weight loss	17. Mask-like expression
9. Difficulty in writing	9. Constipation	
10. Decrease in normal arm swing		
11. Shuffling steps		

While L-dopa is presently the single most effective drug for PD, many other drugs are being tested, and there is hope that major breakthroughs will be made in the near future. Recently several young people took an illegal "designer" drug related to the narcotic Demerol and developed PD symptoms. The illegal drug damaged the area of the brain associated with PD. It is hoped that information about how this illegal drug produced the symptoms of Parkinson's disease will eventually lead to a better understanding of PD itself.

Brain-tissue Transplants

We are all aware that human heart, kidney, and liver transplants have been accomplished with considerable success in recent years. But transplantation of entire brains is another matter. Brain transplants are still the stuff of fiction, although the transplanting of animal brain *tissue* has actually been accomplished. Many of these tissue transplants have involved research in the ongoing fight against Parkinson's disease.

The animal brain-tissue transplant story begins with rat research. First, researchers destroyed that part of the rat's brain that produces dopamine. The rats in the experiments then displayed behavior that resembled PD behavior in humans. The next step was for experimenters to transplant into the destroyed brain areas cells that had been taken from the same brain area of unborn rat fetuses. The recipient rats showed a marked improvement in behavior as the transplanted tissue established itself (Freed, Cannon-Spoor, Krauthamer, Hoffer, & Wyatt, 1983). Perhaps someday human transplants of this type will be done routinely. However, at present, the concept of human fetal brain-tissue transplanting is extremely controversial on moral and legal grounds.

The most dramatic transplant work done with humans began in the early 1980s in Sweden. Doctors there were influenced by earlier work that showed that if a portion of a rat's own adrenal gland was transplanted into the appropriate brain sites, the brain would begin to produce dopamine. A pronounced improvement in the rat's behavior would follow. The Swedish doctors tried this same technique with two middle-aged patients afflicted with severe cases of PD. At first, as widely reported by the American media, it seemed the patients might benefit. But such was not the case over the long run; little or no improvement was noted. However, doctors in other countries, including Mexico and the United States, have pressed on and conducted many similar operations. The results of many of these efforts appear to be much more hopeful and promising than the original Swedish studies. Positive results, at least of the short-term variety, have been reported in many cases.

We will discuss additional examples of applied physiological psychology in Chapter 18 (for one related area of investigation, see the box titled "Voodoo Death?"). Specifically, we will consider psychosurgery, the very controversial practice of destroying parts of the brain in order to reduce unwanted emotions and behavior such as depression, aggression, and epilepsy. We will also discuss the chemical and physical treatment of mental illnesses such as schizophrenia

◆ *VOODOO DEATH?*

Almost everyone knows of cases in which someone with a strong "will to live" survived well beyond others' expectations, or in which other people "gave up" and died of relatively minor ailments. The extreme case of the latter is "voodoo death," in which a normal, healthy person dies apparently just because he or she believes that some curse has destined death.

These phenomena were generally ignored as unworthy of scientific attention until Walter Cannon (1942), a scientist of the highest prestige, published a collection of reasonably well-documented reports of voodoo death. A typical example was a woman who ate a fruit, then was told that it had come from a taboo place. Within hours she was dead. The common pattern was that the "magic spells" were effective only when the intended victim knew about them and believed in them. In each case the hexed victim believed that he or she was sure to die soon. The friends and relatives believed the same thing and began to treat the victim as a dying person. The victim was overwhelmed with a feeling of hopelessness, refused food and water, and died usually within 24 or 48 hours. Obviously death by starvation or thirst would take much longer. In some manner the terror and feeling of hopelessness led to the death. (For further examples, see Cannon, 1942.)

It is tempting to look with disdain on these ignorant victims and to say that this sort of thing could never happen in our society. True, you and I would not die if a witch doctor pointed a bone at us — but presumably only because we do not believe in witch doctors. There are many people in civilized societies who have died of trivial medical problems mainly because they expected to die. For instance, a bomb exploded near one person but failed to injure him; he died anyway a day later. Many people attempting suicide have taken some pills and died, even though they did *not* in fact take an overdose.

A story is told — I have heard this story several times, but no one seems to know when or where it happened, so I do not know how much of it is factual and how much is embellishment — of a fraternity that decided to initiate a new pledge in what they considered a particularly imaginative way. They bound his arms and legs, blindfolded him, and tied him to a railroad track. Unbeknown to the poor pledge, they tied him to a track that was never used, but which was adjacent to one that was used. Along came a train. Although the young man was in no physical danger, he had every reason to believe he was, and he died.

Anecdotes of this sort are fascinating, but they tell us nothing about the mechanisms of what is happening. An interesting clue to what may be happening in some of these cases comes from an animal study. Curt Richter was conducting experiments on the swimming abilities of rats under various circumstances (Richter, 1957). Ordinarily, rats can swim in turbulent warm water nonstop for 48 hours or more. However, very different results occurred when Richter cut off the rat's whiskers just before throwing it into the tank. (A rat's whiskers are very important to it in finding its way around.) The rat swam frantically for a minute or so, then suddenly sank to the bottom, dead. Richter repeated this procedure with other laboratory rats and found the same results with some, though not all. He then tried some wild rats, which are known to be more nervous and emotional than the laboratory strain. *All* the wild rats died quickly. Autopsies showed that the rats had not drowned; their hearts had simply stopped beating.

It is not impossible for a rat to swim without whiskers. If the whiskers are trimmed hours or days in advance, the rat can swim for hours. Evidently the sudden deaths resulted from combining the de-whiskering operation with immersion into the water.

As in the case of human voodoo death, the question arises: why did the rats' hearts stop beating? The apparent explanation pertains, again, to the autonomic nervous system. The rat is exposed successively to three very frightening experiences: being held in a human hand, having its whiskers removed, and then being thrown into the water. This combination of events first stimulates the rats' sympathetic nervous systems to the maximum extent possible, raising their heart rates greatly. But after they swim frantically for a minute or so, finding no escape route, their parasympathetic systems become highly activated, both as a rebound from the strong sympathetic activation and as the natural response to a terrifying, apparently inescapable situation. The combined effect is such an extreme parasympathetic response that the rats' hearts stopped beating altogether.

Richter further demonstrated the importance of the apparent escapability or inescapability of a danger in one more experiment. As before, he cut a rat's whiskers before putting it into the water. However, just when the rat stopped swimming and started to sink, he rescued it and allowed it to revive on a safe, dry platform. Thereafter, whenever he threw it into the water, it swam successfully for many hours. Having once been rescued, the rat was apparently "immunized" against feeling extreme terror in this situation.

Richter's results suggest the hypothesis that "voodoo death" and perhaps many other cases of sudden death in a frightening situation may be due to excessive activity by the parasympathetic nervous system, either as a rebound effect or as a response to a frightening but hopeless situation. Although this is not the mechanism responsible for the majority of heart attacks, it may be a significant factor in some cases.

From *Biological psychology*, Second Edition, (pp. 23–25) by J. W. Kalat. © 1984, 1981 by Wadsworth, Inc. Reprinted by permission of the publisher. Some text citations have been deleted from the original.

and mood disorders. But now we will explore a variety of altered states of awareness including sleep, dreams, drug states, hypnosis, and meditation. The study of each of these represents an exploration of a unique set of perceptual data.

SLEEP AND DREAMS

Sleep as an Active Process

When asked to describe the state of sleep many people characterize it as "a blank state," "like being unconscious," or "like being dead." But we now know that sleep is not a passive, blank state. It is an active, rather dynamic process (Webb, 1973). First, we are not always unconscious when we are asleep. The act of dreaming, which we all experience every night, is a kind of conscious state. We go through all sorts of mental activities during dreams, and we can remember many of them the next day. Second, we can carry out simple plans while we are asleep. Many people can instruct themselves in the evening to wake up at a certain time in the morning. If this surprises you, ask a few of your friends if they can do it, and you will see that it is not an uncommon ability. Other people cannot quite manage to wake themselves up according to their instructions, but if they set an alarm clock for a certain time, they are able to wake up just before that awful sound penetrates their sweet slumber. Third, we are not comple-

Although it may not look like it, these two sleeping women may be mentally active. They may be dreaming, they may be keeping track of time, and they may be sensitive to certain external stimuli, such as the announcement of their flight.

ly indiscriminating while we are asleep; we can discriminate among different stimuli. If a truck goes by while you are asleep you will not awaken. But what happens if, in the dead of the night, someone jiggles your doorknob or tampers with your window? Instant alertness. The more intense but harmless stimulus (the truck) does not disturb you, while the less intense but potentially dangerous stimulus arouses you immediately. Similarly, most parents hearing the smallest sound from their newborn child's room will awaken immediately.

Sleep Deprivation and the Purpose of Sleeping

Sleep Deprivation   At one time or another we have all been warned about the importance of getting a good night's sleep. Early experiments suggested that going without sleep could lead to impaired performance, anxiety, and even hallucinations, but later work (see Webb & Cartwright, 1976) suggests that *sleep deprivation* (depriving people of sleep), even for several nights and days, is not really all that harmful. In fact, Webb and Cartwright conclude that the major effect of going without sleep is good old sleepiness! Apparently we can go for long periods without sleep and not suffer much at all beyond the discomfort of being sleepy.

Making Up for Lost Sleep   Another interesting aspect of sleep deprivation is that its unpleasant effects do not go on accumulating endlessly as deprivation continues. If a person has been deprived of sleep for 10 days and is then allowed to sleep as much as he wants, he will not sleep 80 hours. In fact, it seems 10 to 15 hours of sleep in such a situation is adequate. It is not necessary to "make up" all the lost sleep.

Sleep as Repair   Intuitively, we think of sleep as a time when we restore our energies and "rest up" after having worn ourselves out during the day. This restoration, or repair, theory is, in fact, one of the two major theories of sleep. Some investigators have suggested that sleep allows our systems to replenish various neurotransmitters that have become depleted during the day. But the experimental evidence for the repair theory is very thin; the theory is appealing but cannot, without better experimental support, be accepted completely.

Sleep as Conservation   The second major theory of sleep proposes that sleep enables us to conserve energy when there is no need for action, or when action would probably do more harm than good (Webb, 1974, 1982). This interpretation is like the idea that bears hibernate during the winter months because there is little food available, and winter activity would be more harmful than helpful to them. Through the process of natural selection, bears that tend to sleep during the cold months do better and reproduce more often. In a similar manner, humans that sleep at night, rather than stumble around in the dark, may be more likely to survive and reproduce. This interpretation argues that sleep is tied to the energy needs of the species and to the capacity of the environment to satisfy those needs at particular times. Investigators are currently exploring this theory and others, but more research will be required before the need to sleep is fully understood (see Dement & Mitler, 1973).

Eye Movements and Brain Waves

How do we know when an individual is dreaming? One simple way is to awaken the person and ask, "Well, how about it? Were you dreaming?" This works, of course, but can we tell when an individual is dreaming without waking him? The answer is yes, we can. There are two physiological correlates of dreaming that have become especially important in this area of study.

REM Sleep   While investigating sleep, Aserinsky and Kleitman (1953) noticed an unusual occurrence. Several times during the night their subjects' eyelids moved in rapid, rather irregular patterns, indicating that the eyeballs beneath the closed eyelids were moving. At

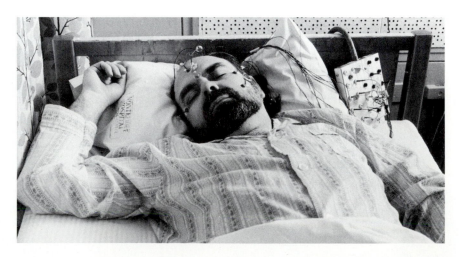

As this subject sleeps, the sensors affixed to his head record his REM and brain-wave patterns.

the same time the subjects' heart and breathing rates increased, as though the subjects were experiencing emotions. Wondering what these changes indicated, these investigators woke the subjects and asked them what, if anything, they had been experiencing. Almost every time subjects were awakened during periods of ***REM***, or ***rapid eye movement***, they indicated that they had been dreaming. When awakened during periods of ***NREM***, or ***no rapid eye movement***, they usually reported that they had not been dreaming. Thus was born one of the simplest and most effective means of detecting dream events. The distinction between REM sleep and NREM sleep has become one of the most basic and important distinctions in the field.

This is not to say that REM is a perfect predictor of dream events. To the contrary, there are times when subjects awakened during REM sleep report no dream, and times when dreams are reported during NREM sleep. But REM is a good predictor. It is probably fair to say that during REM sleep, dreaming will be reported 75 to 85 percent of the time, while dreaming will be reported during NREM sleep no more than 15 percent of the time.

EEG Records   As we saw in Chapter 2, the electroencephalogram (EEG) is a record of the electrical activity of the brain obtained by attaching electrodes to the scalp. The electroencephalograph (the device that produces electroencephalograms) is sensitive enough to pick up the electrical activity of those portions of the brain lying under the electrodes and translate this activity into tracings of a pen on paper.

When a person relaxes with closed eyes but remains awake, the brain waves detected by the EEG device assume a characteristic form called ***alpha waves*** (see Figure 4–3). Alpha waves are of low amplitude, or size, and occur at a rate of about 10 per second. But as the person drifts off to sleep, the form of the brain waves begins to change. The waves become slower and larger until they finally assume the second form shown in Figure 4–3. These large, slow waves are called ***delta waves***, and they are characteristic of NREM sleep without dreaming. During NREM sleep, delta waves occur at a frequency of 1 or 2 per second.

After the person has been asleep for an hour or so, the brain waves again begin to look like those of the waking state. They become faster and smaller — but the individual is still asleep. It is at this point that REMs begin to appear. In fact, the person is probably dreaming at this stage, labeled REM sleep in Figure 4–3. In other

FIGURE 4–3 Brain Waves and Muscular Activity During Periods of Wakefulness, Dream-free NREM Sleep, and REM Sleep   *During REM sleep, when dreaming most often occurs, muscular activity is at a minimum, while brain-wave activity resembles the waking state.*

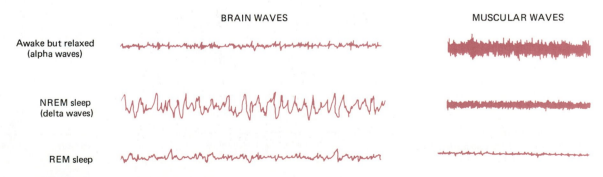

	BRAIN WAVES	MUSCULAR WAVES
Awake but relaxed (alpha waves)		
NREM sleep (delta waves)		
REM sleep		

words, dreaming most often happens when rapid eye movements are occurring and brain waves are approximating those of the waking state.

Though most people change positions several times during a night's sleep, voluntary muscular activity of the body is at its *lowest* level during REM sleep, as Figure 4–3 shows. Evidently during REM sleep, the brain is in its most active state, while the body is in its least active state.

This is only a simplified version of the relationship between brain waves and sleeping. Actually, as a person falls asleep the brain waves pass through several different stages. A detailed account of the brain waves would describe the waking state, four stages of dream-free NREM sleep where delta waves gradually replace the faster, smaller alpha waves of the waking state, and finally REM sleep, where the brain waves approximate the waking state. But the basic distinction between NREM sleep and REM sleep has proven to be the most important one.

Patterns of Sleeping and Dreaming

Sleep Patterns and Age A number of different temporal patterns have been observed in studies of sleeping and dreaming. The first of these is the development of a daily sleeping pattern as the individual grows older. As Figure 4–4 shows, babies alternate periods of waking and sleeping very often during a 24-hour period. Anyone who has raised children is painfully aware of the implications of this pattern. Fortunately, as the child grows older there are fewer alternations. Naps are reduced in number and finally eliminated. The child eventually begins to sleep through the night and adopts the normal pattern shown by adults.

Sleep, Dreams, and Age The total amount of time a person sleeps and dreams also changes as a function of age. According to Kendler (1977), the total amount of sleep required by an individual drops from approximately 16 hours a day at birth to 5 or 6 hours in old age (see

FIGURE 4–4 Approximate Periods of Sleep as a Function of Age *Note that the total amount of time spent asleep during a 24-hour day decreases with age, and the time spent sleeping is consolidated into fewer and fewer periods.*

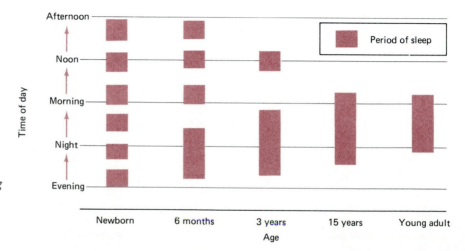

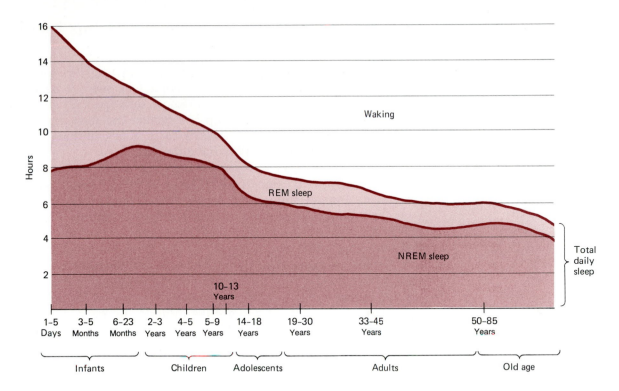

FIGURE 4–5 Changes in the Total Amount of Daily Sleep, REM Sleep, and NREM Sleep as a Function of Age *The total amounts of time spent sleeping, time spent in REM sleep, and time spent in NREM sleep all drop as humans age. (After Kendler, 1977)*

Figure 4–5). At the same time, the total amount of REM sleep per day drops from approximately 8 hours to 1 hour, while NREM sleep drops from about 8 hours to 4 or 5 hours.

Nightly Sleeping and Dreaming There are also patterns in the depth of sleep and the amount of dreaming that tend to occur during any given night. As Figure 4–6 shows, a person falling asleep quickly passes through the four stages of NREM sleep and for an hour or so experiences heavy, dream-free sleep. Then, as the night progresses, we see an alternating cycle of REM and NREM sleep. The periods of REM sleep become longer and the depth of NREM sleep becomes less and less as the night goes on. The REM periods tend to recur every hour and a half (Dement, 1972). In other words, it appears that we do most of our dreaming in the later hours of the night and that we alternate dreaming and nondreaming throughout the night. The pattern depicted in Figure 4–6 is for an average young adult. Obviously,

FIGURE 4–6 Typical Periods of REM and NREM Sleep During an Eight-hour Night *The data graphed here depict the pattern for an average young adult. (After Van De Castle, 1971)*

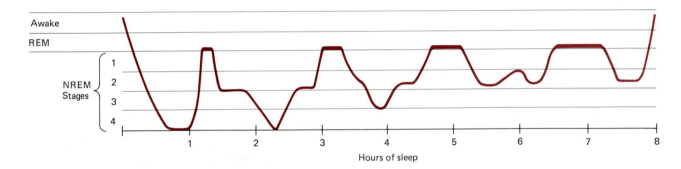

the pattern will change with age, and in addition, large individual differences do exist.

The Long and the Short of It   Not everyone seems to have the same degree of need for sleep. We all know people who seem to be able to get along on almost no sleep. We also know some people who seem to need many more hours of sleep to function the next day. Some need 4 to 6 hours, while others need 9 to 10 hours, although 7 or 8 hours seems about average. Why the differences?

Hartmann (1973, 1978) reports research in which short sleepers (6 hours or less) were compared with long sleepers (9 hours or more). The short sleepers turned out to be active, hard-working people who were relatively satisfied with themselves. Though ambitious, they did not worry a lot. They were extroverted, conventional, and "all-American." The long sleepers, on the other hand, were a little more difficult to categorize. They were more unconventional and critical, and they held a wide variety of opinions. Some were mildly neurotic and unsure of themselves. Interestingly, it was in the amount of dreaming time that these two groups differed the most. Both short sleepers and long sleepers spent about the same amount of time each night in nondream sleep, but long sleepers spent almost twice as much time in dream-related sleep.

The Need to Dream

There appears to be a need to dream. Dement (1960) awakened a group of subjects each time they displayed REM. In this manner he effectively eliminated REM sleep, and presumably dreaming, for five nights. A group of control subjects was awakened with equal frequency, but during NREM sleep. Compared to the control subjects, the REM-deprived subjects became grouchy, nervous, irritable, and unable to concentrate. When finally allowed to sleep, the REM-deprived subjects dreamed approximately 60 percent more than normal until they made up their lost REM time. Thus there is little doubt that we need to dream, but why we need to dream remains a mystery, and it is to that mystery that we now turn.

Dream Theories and the Purpose of Dreaming

What are the functions of dreaming? Why do we dream? What do our dreams mean? Do they mean anything at all? These questions about dreams have led to a variety of theories about dreaming and countless interpretations of dreams. Even though many people believe that dreams do reveal something about the dreamer, there is little agreement about what dreaming represents. What your dreams mean will depend on the theory of dreams to which you subscribe. Several prominent figures in psychology have proposed theories about dreaming.

Freudian Dream Theory   Freud's theory is perhaps the best-known explanation of dreams and dreaming. According to *Freudian dream theory,* dreams are designed to fulfill unconscious, unacceptable impulses. There are within each of us impulses, needs, and desires that we cannot express or gratify openly. To act on these impulses would bring criticism and punishment from society, as well as self-condemnation. Suppose a person feels extremely hostile. To express this hostility openly would create serious problems and real dangers. However, if direct hostile action is out of the question, what can the person do to satisfy this impulse? He can dream about it. But if he dreams openly about direct hostile acts, he will feel guilty and anxious about that too. Freud proposed that when we dream, we camouflage or disguise the true meaning of the dream in order to avoid this guilt and anxiety. In this way we can have the best of two worlds; we can satisfy our nasty impulses and still avoid having to think of ourselves as having those impulses.

Symbols in Freud's Theory Freud described a number of different ways we disguise the true meaning of a dream. For example, we use *displacement* to shift our attention from the true meaning of the dream to some more acceptable but actually minor element. If we have a dream about an adorable kitten whose paw has been hurt, it may be that the true, hostile meaning of the dream is expressed by the claws on the little hurt paw.

According to Freud, we also use *symbols* to camouflage the true meaning of a dream (Altman, 1975). A symbol is one thing that stands for another. Because Freud emphasized the role of repressed sexual impulses in the development of dreams, he interpreted many objects found in dreams as symbols standing for sexual organs or activities (see Table 4–4). Thus if you have a dream about an enormous locomotive plunging down a narrow mountain ravine and into a tunnel, you know what Freud would say.

Freud (1933) distinguishes between the manifest content and the latent content of a dream. The **manifest content** is what we can recall.

TABLE 4–4 Examples of Sexual Dream Symbols in Freudian Dream Interpretation

Female Organs	Male Organs	Sexual Intercourse
Enclosed spaces	Elongated objects	Climbing steps
Boxes	Tree trunks	Climbing a ladder
Ovens	Umbrellas	Going up a staircase
Hollow objects	Knives	Driving a car
Ships	Neckties	Elevator rides
Closets	Airplanes	Riding a horse
Wagons	Trains	Crossing a bridge
Caves	Snakes	Riding a roller coaster
Hats	Hoses	Flying in an airplane
Pockets	Flames	Movement or combination of male
Drawers	Bullets	and female symbols

It is often jumbled, illogical, seemingly meaningless, and bewildering. The *latent content* is the true meaning of the dream that will be revealed when the disguises are stripped away from the manifest content. We will have more to say about Freud's theories in Chapter 14, but we must note here that Freud's theory of dreams is by no means universally accepted. In fact, it has been heavily criticized. There is very little experimental data to support it (Cohen, 1974). Indeed, it is hard to think of experiments that could prove or disprove it. The very idea that dreams have any meaning at all is still being heavily debated—so do not believe anyone who claims to know for certain what dreams mean.

Hall's Dream Theory   Calvin Hall (1953) argues that, rather than hiding the meaning of a dream, symbols may express the meaning in a literary, metaphorical fashion. Hall agrees with Freud that symbols are used, but Hall's position can lead to some very different interpretations of a given dream. For example, suppose we dream of a robin's nest. According to Freud, the nest might be a symbol for some strong feelings about "home" that we are trying to conceal. Hall, on the other hand, would argue that we are trying to experience the concept of home in an expressive, rather than concealing, manner.

Dreams as Crude Thinking   Other investigators argue that the confused, incomprehensible nature of dreams has little to do with an expression of concealed wishes. They argue that dreams represent nothing more than crude thinking, much like the disjointed thinking expressed by senile people or by people under the influence of alcohol. According to this view, dreams involve the same kinds of faulty analysis, distorted memories, and misjudged situations as these other examples of imperfect thinking.

External Events and Dreams   Most dream theories assume that the contents of our dreams are influenced by events in our lives. That is, dreams are not pure fantasy. There is some experimental evidence to support this idea that our lives, past and present, affect our dreams. Breger, Hunter, and Lane (1971) examined the dream content of patients scheduled for surgery and found that both direct and symbolic expressions of this stressful state appeared in their dreams. Others have shown that names spoken to sleeping people during REM sleep will sometimes be incorporated into their dreams, but not all immediate and recent events find their way into dreams, and the contents of dreams often seem to be unrelated to external stimuli or recent experiences.

Consolidation   Some investigators suggest that dreaming may help memory consolidation. Tilley and Empson (1978) had subjects memorize stories and then go to sleep. Half of the subjects were repeatedly awakened during periods of dreaming, while the other subjects were awakened during nondream periods. In the morning it was found that the dream-deprived subjects had more trouble recalling the story than did the subjects deprived of nondream sleep.

"House Cleaning"   One modern theory of dreaming, proposed by Crick and Mitchison, argues that dreams represent a needed process of unlearning to erase false or nonsensical memories. Dreaming is seen as a kind of mental "house cleaning" whereby we forget false or distorted memories (see Melnechuk, 1983). Interestingly, this theory suggests that we might be better off *not* trying to remember our dreams because to try to remember them might be the same thing as rehearsing false information.

Dreams and Sensory and Motor Practice   Another idea about the function of dreams is that dreams give us a chance to exercise sensory and motor aspects of the nervous system. All that moving about of the eyeballs, for example, may just serve to keep them in shape. Lewis, Sloan, and Jones (1978), in fact, found that depth perception was better following dreaming than just before dreaming.

In spite of these intriguing theories and experimental results, we still have no clear understanding of the function of dreaming. We do not really know whether we should even bother to try to interpret dreams. They remain a mystery, in spite of all the work that has been done with them and the emphasis placed on them by many investigators and clinicians.

Hypnopaedia

Can we learn while we are asleep? It would be nice if we could, but the available evidence suggests that *hypnopaedia,* or learning while asleep, probably is a myth (Rubin, 1968). Most laboratory studies of hypnopaedia have been poorly designed and poorly controlled. In a typical experiment, a tape of 15 one-syllable words will be played 30 times while one group of subjects is asleep and not played while a control group sleeps. Both groups then attempt to learn the lists. The experimenters usually report that the experimental subjects, having heard the words while asleep, will learn them faster than the controls will.

But many of these studies fail to take into account the fact that we "come in and out" of sleep, and that it often takes a while to fall asleep. It may be during these periods that the learning occurs, and not during periods of true sleep (Aarons, 1976).

How Long Does a Dream Take?

One common assumption is that dreams last only a few moments and that hours or days of dream events are compressed into these short periods. The available evidence suggests that this is not the case. Dement (1972) has shown that if subjects are awakened from a dream and asked how long the dream took, their estimate of the time is quite comparable to the length of REM sleep just experienced. This experiment and others indicate that events in a dream progress at a realistic pace, taking about as much time as the same events would take if they actually occurred.

This is not to say that we cannot ever dream of a week's worth of events during a ten-minute dream. We probably do, sometimes. But perhaps we merely have the feeling that a week's worth of events has occurred. Like movie directors, dreamers have ways of suggesting to their "audience" that some time has passed between one scene and the next.

Sleep Disorders

Sleep Apnea Beyond the rather common complaint of insomnia, there are several other unfortunate types of sleep disorders. In **sleep apnea,** the sufferer repeatedly awakens, gasping and feeling out of breath. Only upon awakening can he breathe again. Apparently, sleep apnea is caused by a failure of the diaphragm to contract while the individual is asleep. Some people suffer from hundreds of these breathing failures each night. There is no good treatment for the condition. Sleeping pills can be very dangerous because they act as respiratory depressants which, combined with sleep apnea, could lead to death (Dement & Zarcone, 1977).

Narcolepsy In a sense, narcolepsy is the opposite of insomnia. People with **narcolepsy** fall into REM sleep uncontrollably and repeatedly no matter what they are doing. They may be talking, working, or driving a car. Their days can be filled with these little REM-sleep episodes (Montplaisir et al., 1978), which can be extremely incapacitating. Sometimes people with narcolepsy suffer from "blackouts." They function effectively during these periods but are unable to remember what they have done. Sometimes they suffer from sudden attacks of muscle weakness and collapse, even though they remain awake. Amphetamines have been prescribed for this condition but these drugs are dangerous because the individual can develop a tolerance to them very quickly.

Sleepwalking As children, many of us were sleepwalkers, or **somnambulists.** We would sit up, get out of bed, and walk about with a rather blank look on our face. We had our eyes open and often engaged in innocuous behavior such as carrying a pillow about with us, bundling up a blanket, or rearranging books on a shelf. Getting our attention would be difficult and we would seldom speak more than a few words. If left to our own devices, we would eventually wander back to bed and remember little of our walk in the morning. If awakened by our parents, we would often feel foolish and embarrassed. We usually outgrew our sleepwalking escapades by the time we became adults.

Because of its mild nature, many would prefer not to call sleepwalking a disorder at all. For years it was generally assumed that when people walked in their sleep they were acting out an ongoing dream, but such does not appear to be the case. Sleepwalking does not occur during REM sleep; it would actually be impossible to walk about during the toned-down REM state. Sleepwalking also occurs during the early part of the night and not later when REM sleep and dreaming are more prevalent.

DRUG ABUSE

Types of Drugs

The Wide Array For thousands of years humans have been smoking, sniffing, swallowing, and (at least for the last century) injecting an enormous range of chemical substances into the bloodstream in their efforts to relax, sleep, relieve pain, produce alertness, encourage calmness, reduce anxiety, stimulate insight, and increase a sense of well-being (Weil & Rosen, 1983). And for thousands of years, human societies have been trying to limit this kind of drug use by placing restrictions on the types of drugs, the hours and places of use, and the age, sex, and social position of users.

The legal sanctions a culture establishes against the use of certain drugs often seem arbitrary. In this country, alcohol and tobacco are legal while marijuana is not. And yet many authorities agree that alcohol and tobacco are the most dangerous of these three substances. Because many drugs alter and distort perceptual processes, a consideration of their effects is included in this chapter.

Table 4–5 lists some of the major drugs and their effects. As this table indicates, humans have been interested in altering their internal state in just about every imaginable way. Clearly, individuals vary enormously in terms of what drugs they prefer and how much of each drug they require to achieve the effects they are seeking. Moreover, users of many drugs develop a *tolerance* to the drug, which means they require increasing amounts of it to achieve the same effects. Steady use of many drugs can lead to physical *dependence,* or addiction. Once dependence is established, the user needs the drug just to feel normal and will suffer a painful process of *withdrawal* if deprived of the drug.

Amphetamines The drugs chemically labeled *amphetamines* are strong stimulants. Before the risks were known, amphetamines were sold without prescription under such trade names as Methedrine, Dexedrine, and Benzedrine. Many people used them to stay awake; dieters used them as appetite suppressants. Users today commonly refer to them as "speed," "uppers," "meth," and "crystal."

The effects of amphetamines are strong and dramatic. They increase wakefulness, alertness, and arousal. Users experience a sense of confidence and energy. Many report that while they are under the influence of amphetamines, they feel they can solve any problem and accomplish any task. Typically, users have a great sense of well-being and do not feel tired despite lack of sleep.

Unfortunately, the effect is illusory. The drug merely gives a feeling of being competent and on top of things. The drug hides fatigue from users, but they perform like the tired people they really are. Often, users will work hours on a problem they just "know" they can solve, but the problem actually will not be any easier to solve than it would be without the drug.

Excessive use of amphetamines can be extremely dangerous because users build up a tolerance to such substances. They require more and more of the chemical to achieve the same effect. Prolonged and excessive use can lead to depression, suicidal tendencies, disrupted and psychotic thinking, and perhaps brain damage (Julien, 1981).

TABLE 4–5 Drugs and Their Characteristics

Category	Name	Source	How Taken	Medical Use	Effect (Last Hours)	Typical Dose
Narcotics	**Morphine**	Opium from opium poppy	Injected	Relieves pain	5–7	10–20 mg
	Heroin	Extracted from morphine	Injected; sniffed	None in U.S.	3–6	Variable
	Codeine	Extracted from opium and morphine	Swallowed; injected	Relieves pain	3–5	10–30 mg
	Methadone	Synthetic	Injected; swallowed	Relieves pain	4–6	10 mg
Hallucinogens	**LSD** (lysergic acid diethylamide)	Ergot alkaloids	Swallowed	Experimental	5–15	100–500 μg
	Mescaline	*Peyote* cactus	Swallowed	None	5–15	200–400 μg
	Psilocybin	*Psilocybe* mushroom	Swallowed	None	4–10	25 mg
	Marijuana	*Cannabis sativa* plant	Smoked; swallowed	Experimental	2–5	1–2 cigarettes
Stimulants	**Cocaine**	From coca plant	Sniffed; injected; swallowed	Deadens pain	10–60 minutes	Varies
	Amphetamines ⎰Benzedrine ⎱Dexedrine Methedrine	Synthetic	Swallowed; injected	Relief of depression	3–5	2–10 mg
Depressants	**Barbiturates** ⎰Phenobarbital Nembutal Seconal Amytal	Synthetic	Swallowed; injected	Sedation	3–5	20–100 mg
	PCP (phencyclidine)	Synthetic	Smoked; swallowed; injected	Sedation of large animals	Varies	Varies
	Methaqualone	Synthetic	Swallowed	Sedation	4–8	Varies
	Alcohol	Fermented or distilled grains, potatoes, etc.	Swallowed	Antiseptic	1–5	Varies

TABLE 4–5   (continued)

Category	Name	Desired Effects	Long-term Effects	Physical Dependence	Mental Dependence	Physical Damage
Narcotics	**Morphine**	Sense of well-being; prevention of withdrawal symptoms	Addiction; constipation; loss of appetite	Yes	Yes	No
	Heroin	Same as above	Same as above	Yes	Yes	No
	Codeine	Same as above	Same as above	Yes	Yes	No
	Methadone	Prevention of withdrawal symptoms	Same as above	Yes	Yes	No
Hallucinogens	**LSD** (lysergic acid diethylamide)	Distortion of senses; insight; euphoria	Can precipitate psychosis	No	Perhaps	Unknown
	Mescaline	Same as above	None known	No	Perhaps	Unknown
	Psilocybin	Same as above	None known	No	Perhaps	Unknown
	Marijuana	Increases perceptions and sense of well-being	None known	No	Perhaps	Unknown
Stimulants	**Cocaine**	Exhilaration; excitement; sociability	Psychosis; convulsions; depression	No	Yes	Yes
	Amphetamines Benzedrine Dexedrine Methedrine	Alertness; activeness; confidence	Loss of appetite; depression; psychosis	No (?)	Yes	Yes (?)
Depressants	**Barbiturates** Phenobarbital Nembutal Seconal Amytal	Tension reduction; sense of well-being	Addiction; convulsions; psychosis	Yes	Yes	Yes
	PCP (phencyclidine)	Same as above	Addiction; psychosis; depression	(?)	Yes	Probably
	Methaqualone	Same as above	Addiction; liver damage	Yes	Yes	Yes
	Alcohol	Tension reduction; sociability; sense of well-being	Neurological damage; cirrhosis of liver; psychosis	Yes	Yes	Yes

In addition to the expensive and fleeting high of cocaine, its users may also encounter paranoia and psychological dependence.

Cocaine **Cocaine,** or "coke," has become extremely popular in recent years. Because it is expensive and fashionable this stimulant is often described as the champagne of illegal drugs. Cocaine, like amphetamines, gives feelings of exhilaration, sociability, confidence, energy, and well-being. Because amphetamines and cocaine have similar effects, much street cocaine is diluted with the cheaper stimulants.

Typically, cocaine is sniffed or injected, although it is occasionally swallowed, rubbed on the gums, or blown into the throat. The euphoric effects of a small dose are usually short-lived, leading to a desire for another dose, and then another. The effect is often described as tantalizing because it makes users want to intensify or prolong the effect, and so they take more if it is available. Large doses can lead to acute paranoia and virtually all dosages tend to reduce appetite (Resnick, Kestenbaum, & Schwartz, 1977).

Recent years have seen the appearance of "crack," an inexpensive, and often impure, solid form of cocaine. The widespread availability of "crack" and its relatively inexpensive price-tag make it a real danger to the potential user.

LSD **Lysergic acid diethylamide (LSD),** or acid, is an unpredictable drug. Users can never be sure whether they will have a good or a bad experience with this substance. The possibility of a bad "trip" is compounded by the fact that LSD's effects are usually very strong. Thus, if one has a positive experience, it may be highly positive. But if the experience is negative, it is likely to be strongly negative. Most users feel the chances of having a good experience can be improved if they are among friends, in a good mood, feeling confident, and using unadulterated LSD. But even these safeguards cannot guarantee a positive experience. Once embarked upon what turns out to be a bad trip, a user cannot stop the undesirable effects. There is no choice but to "ride it out" for hours.

LSD produces heightened and distorted sensory experiences. Both sights and sounds may be intensified or magnified and may appear more beautiful and significant. Simple, stationary, familiar objects may appear to move, shift, grow, flow, and change into other objects. Depending on whether one is in a good or a bad mood, these changes can appear interesting or terrifying.

One user reports that a woman walking down the street "turned into an ostrich." Another individual states, "As I watched the hillside, covered with vegetation, the entire scene turned into a munchkin-type city, filled with undulating towers and minarets. The busy sounds of the city became clear to me, and the buildings took on grinning faces that swirled and laughed with me."

Users sometimes report that LSD enhances their ability to think and perceive. They say they can understand more about life while under the influence of the drug, and they claim to have insights that are well beyond anything they can achieve without the drug. Such mystical experiences are often hard to put into words, and LSD has not made users better able to describe their discoveries. As a result, there is very little objective evidence for the new insights and perceptions that LSD users proclaim.

Use of LSD does not lead to tolerance or physical dependence. Whether it leads to psychological dependence is not yet known (McWilliams & Tuttle, 1973). LSD does appear to have triggered psychotic reactions in some users, which is not too surprising; it is an extremely powerful drug.

LSD is not the only drug used to produce hallucinations. Mescaline, drawn from cactus, psilocybin, extracted from "magic" mushrooms, DMT (dimethyltriptamine), and DOM (dimethoxy-methylamphetamine) all produce psychedelic effects.

PCP   **Phencyclidine (PCP),** known as "angel dust" or simply "dust," is a difficult drug to classify. Some feel it most clearly resembles the hallucinogens because it does occasionally produce visions and visual distortions similar to those associated with LSD. But PCP can have other effects as well. In very low doses it can induce a becalmed, pleasant state. Higher doses can lead to disrupted motor activity, violence, panic, psychotic behavior that may last for weeks, chronic depression, and even death (Smith, 1978). PCP is sold legally as an animal tranquilizer and may work well for calming down a rhinoceros, but for humans it appears to be a very dangerous drug.

Marijuana   The physical effects of smoking **marijuana** *(cannabis)* are relatively simple to describe. This drug, whose active ingredient is tetrahydrocannabinol (THC), usually elevates the pulse rate, causes dryness of the mouth, and reddens the eyes. Beyond these simple effects, few marked physical changes have been observed.

The psychological effects of marijuana are not so easily catalogued (Paton & Pertwee, 1973). Many readers of this text will have used the drug and will have formed their own ideas as to what its effects are. Some enjoy the drug more than others. Some have smoked more or stronger marijuana than others. Hence, reports of the marijuana experience are bound to vary widely.

Many users of marijuana say that the drug produces a sense of excitement, relaxation, and happiness. Others report either no reaction or such negative feelings as anxiety and depression. Sensory experiences may be enhanced. Food may taste better, music may take on added dimensions, and visual stimulation may be intensified. Time sometimes seems to pass more slowly. The user, if she or he has smoked enough, may become drowsy and less attentive, and find it difficult to read or to carry on a conversation. There is some evidence that marijuana can adversely affect reaction time, accuracy, and concentration. Because of this, driving or operating machinery can be dangerous when an individual is under the influence of marijuana. A report sponsored by the National Academy of Sciences (1982) concludes that serious national concern over the use of marijuana is warranted.

Sometimes marijuana can lead to frightening experiences. Many people report feelings of anxiety and paranoia upon using this drug. Others report that they feel more creative and insightful while under the influence. As with LSD, it is hard to find evidence to support this contention. Perhaps most marijuana smokers would agree with the user who said, "Smoking dope enhances whatever mood you happen to be in. If you are feeling pretty good it will make you feel terrific. If you are worried or fearful, it can make you paranoid. It is an intensifier of what you are."

What about the long-range effects of marijuana? Will smoking it now lead to trouble in the years to come? While marijuana is by far the mildest of the hallucinogens and does not lead to physical dependence and murderous impulses as early studies claimed, the drug is not without problems. While researchers have not conclusively proved that marijuana leads to physical damage, they have not shown it to be harmless either. Marijuana has been suspected of (1) affecting the immune reactions; (2) affecting the throat and lungs and leading to cancer and emphysema faster than cigarettes; (3) reducing sexuality; and (4) reducing motivation (see National Institute on Drug Abuse, 1976; Zinberg, 1976).

Possible side effects like these seem to have given many users some second thoughts. Marijuana use may actually have peaked in the late 1970s and even some long-term users have given it up. There seems to have been a lessening of marijuana use among high-school students (Collins, 1983). Among their reasons for quitting are concern for health, lack of approval from friends and family, bad personal experiences with the drug, fear of legal consequences, and the use of substitutes (Raffoul, 1980).

Heroin **Codeine, morphine,** and **heroin** are all derived from the opium poppy. They are called narcotics because they dull the senses and because they are addictive. All can be used as pain-killers, even though heroin is not used for this purpose in the United States. Heroin is by far the most potent of the three, while codeine is the mildest.

In contrast to other "mind-altering" drugs, heroin does little to the thought processes or to the sensory processes. It is primarily a mood- or emotion-changer. It makes one feel good rather than inducing altered forms of thought.

Users of heroin describe two main effects. First, there is the brief "rush" or thrill that is experienced immediately after intravenous injection. The second, longer-lasting effect is variously described as "a great sense of well-being," or a sensation "like a warm blanket." One user has said, "It reduces all your drives to zero. You are in a state of 100 percent gratification."

But there is a steep price to pay for the pleasure. Heroin is a very addictive drug. Dependence may develop easily and is extremely difficult to break, even though a few people appear to be able to use it for long periods without becoming dependent. As dependence increases, the pleasure disappears. The user begins to feel bad when not on the drug and normal when on it. As physical dependence develops, the user must have the drug to avoid the aches and pains, cold sweats, nausea, and "the shakes" that accompany withdrawal. At this stage, there is little joy left in the use of the drug beyond the "rush" (Sideroff & Jarvik, 1980).

There is evidence that heroin use can lead to physical damage, too. Heavy use can affect the normal pituitary-thyroid function in humans. Furthermore, heroin addicts, while using the drug, dis-

Members of organizations such as Mothers Against Drunk Driving (MAAD) and Students Against Drunk Driving (SAAD) obviously realize the dangers inherent in alcohol use—and are trying to do something about it.

play increases in chromosome damage. When they quit, the damage decreases (Falek & Hollingsworth, 1980).

Heroin addiction can lead to disease or death from such causes as dirty needles, impure drugs, and malnutrition. Clearly, sharing needles has contributed to the current upsurge in AIDS and AIDS-related conditions. Heroin use also leads to crime, because of the need to buy an ever-increasing daily supply of an expensive substance. Some people argue that these problems are caused by the legal prohibitions against the drug, rather than the drug itself. These people point to the English system of medically controlled, legal prescriptions of heroin for registered addicts and say that the United States should adopt the same system. Others reply that even in England, many addicts do not register for controlled doses of heroin, and in any case, the government should not encourage heroin addiction. The arguments continue, but heroin usage remains illegal in this country because the drug is so addictive.

Alcohol   Of all the known drugs, *alcohol* is the most widely used— and abused. It has been with us since the earliest civilizations flourished thousands of years ago. Cultural attitudes toward alcohol have varied enormously. Sometimes the drug has been reviled. At other times, and in other places, it has been revered. Today it is widely accepted as a part of sociable recreation, but regardless of the prevailing attitude and the pleasure the drug brings, alcohol has always been a potentially dangerous substance because it is both addictive and physically damaging if abused (Liska, 1981).

Alcohol is a depressant like the barbiturates (see Table 4–5) and Quaaludes (methaqualone), and as such, it poses certain problems. Because it depresses our inhibitions first, most drinkers feel it is a stimulant, even though it is actually impairing their capacities. In short, alcohol tends to increase one's sense of competence while actually reducing it. Thus the drunken individual leaving a party feels that driving a car will be simple when, in fact, serious sensory impairment, double vision, slowed reactions, nausea, and dizziness may make that individual unable to drive safely (Bacon, 1973). Our culture pays a heavy price for alcohol. Table 4–6 lists just some of the consequences we must bear for its use.

Small amounts of alcohol can bring a sense of well-being and sociability. Many people say that a drink or two helps them relax and feel more comfortable in their lives. But three or four cocktails will blunt the average person's sensory and motor abilities noticeably (see Table 4–7). Very heavy drinking may also lead to aggressiveness, anger, and violence (Tinklenberg, 1973), and eventually to the drug dependence called alcoholism. In short, alcohol creates problems as well as moments of relaxation.

Prolonged and heavy use of alcohol can damage the brain and the liver. Chronic alcoholics often end up in mental institutions; in fact, one of every four male patients admitted to a mental hospital is an alcoholic (Segal, Huba, & Singer, 1980). Chronic alcohol abuse is also believed to shorten life expectancy. Table 4–8 compares the longevity of many prominent American writers on the basis of known alcohol abuse.

TABLE 4–6   Some Social and Personal Consequences of Alcohol Use

1. Over 25,000 alcohol-related traffic fatalities occur annually.
2. The alcoholic's life span is shortened on the average by over 10 years.
3. Suicide is over 50 times more common among alcoholics than among non-alcoholics.
4. Excessive use of alcohol increases by over 20 times the probability of cirrhosis of the liver.
5. Alcoholics have significantly higher rates of hypertension, ulcers, and cerebrovascular disease than nonalcoholics.
6. Almost half of all arrests are alcohol-related.
7. Alcoholism is a major element in divorce rates and broken homes.
8. For men over 25, alcohol-related disorders are the most common diagnoses among those in mental hospitals; for women over 25, they are among the most common.
9. Two million arrests for public drunkenness occur annually.
10. The lives of nearly 40 million Americans are directly affected by alcohol problems.

Source: After Sarason, 1976.

TABLE 4–7 Blood Alcohol Levels and Behavioral Effects for People with Moderate Drinking Experience

Level of Alcohol in the Blood	Behavioral Effects
0.05%	Lowered alertness; person usually "feels good"
0.10%	Reaction time is slowed; less caution is exercised
0.15%	Reaction time is greatly slowed
0.20%	Marked suppression of sensory-motor abilities
0.25%	Severe motor disturbances, such as staggering; perceptions greatly impaired
0.30%	Semistupor
0.35%	Level for surgical anesthesia; death is possible
0.40%	Death is likely (usually because of respiratory failure)

Source: After Ray, 1983.

TABLE 4–8 Life Span Data on Selected Nineteenth- and Twentieth-century American Writers

Authors noted for alcohol abuse		Authors not noted for alcohol abuse	
Years of birth and death	Life span, years	Years of birth and death	Life span, years
1809–1849 Edgar Allan Poe	40	1807–1882 Henry W. Longfellow	75
		1807–1892 John G. Whittier	85
1869–1935 Edw. A. Robinson	66	1869–1950 Edgar Lee Masters	81
		1869–1949 Booth Tarkington	80
1876–1916 Jack London	40	1876–1941 Sherwood Anderson	65
		1878–1967 Carl Sandburg	89
1879–1955 Wallace Stevens	76	1878–1968 Upton Sinclair	90
		1879–1931 Vachel Lindsay	53
1885–1933 Ring Lardner	48	1885–1928 Elinore Wylie	43
		1885–1950 Carl Van Doren	65
1885–1951 Sinclair Lewis	66	1885–1972 Ezra Pound	87
		1886–1961 Hilda Doolittle	75
1888–1959 Raymond Chandler	71	1886–1918 Randolph Bourne	32
		1886–1963 Van Wyck Brooks	77
1888–1953 Eugene O'Neill	65	1887–1972 Marianne Moore	85
		1887–1976 Samuel Eliot Morrison	89
1889–1945 Robert Benchley	56	1887–1962 Robinson Jeffers	75
		1888–1965 T. S. Eliot	77

TABLE 4–8   (continued)

Authors noted for alcohol abuse		*Authors not noted for alcohol abuse*	
Years of birth and death	Life span, years	Years of birth and death	Life span, years
1892–1950 Edna St. V. Millay	58	1888–1974 John Crowe Ransom	86
		1889–1973 Conrad Aiken	84
1893–1960 J. P. Marquand	67	1889–1953 Ben Ames Williams	64
		1890–1980 Katherine Anne Porter	90
1893–1967 Dorothy Parker	74	1891–1980 Henry Miller	88
		1892–1971 Reinhold Niebuhr	79
1894–1961 Dashiell Hammett	67	1892–1973 Pearl S. Buck	81
		1892–1982 Archibald MacLeish	90
1894–1962 E. E. Cummings	70	1894–1961 James Thurber	67
		1895–1981 Caroline Gordon	86
1895–1972 Edmund Wilson	77	1895– Lewis Mumford	(93)
		1896–1970 John R. Dos Passos	74
1896–1940 F. Scott Fitzgerald	44	1897–1975 Thornton Wilder	78
		1897– Kenneth Burke	(91)
1897–1962 William Faulkner	65	1897–1955 Bernard DeVoto	58
		1898– Malcolm Cowley	(90)
1899–1932 Hart Crane	33	1899–1979 Allen Tate	80
		1899–1977 Vladimir Nabokov	78
1899–1961 Ernest Hemingway	62	1899–1985 E. B. White	86
		1900–1968 Yvor Winters	68
1900–1938 Thomas Wolfe	38	1902–1967 Langston Hughes	65
		1903–1987 Erskine Caldwell	(84)
1902–1968 John Steinbeck	66	1903–1978 James Gould Cozzens	75
		1904–1965 R. P. Blackmur	61
1905–1970 John O'Hara	65	1904–1979 James T. Farrell	75
		1905– Robert Penn Warren	(83)
1908–1963 Theodore Roethke	55	1907–1964 Rachel Carson	57
		1907–1973 W. H. Auden	66
1911–1983 Tennessee Williams	72	1912– Mary McCarthy	(76)
		1912–1982 John Cheever	70
1914–1972 John Berryman	60	1914– Ralph W. Ellison	(74)
		1914–1982 Randall Jarrell	51
1917–1977 Robert Lowell	60	1915– Arthur Miller	(73)
		1919– J. D. Salinger	(69)
1922–1969 Jack Kerouac	47	1920– Howard Nemerov	(68)
		1923– Norman Mailer	(65)

Source: After Davis, 1987.

"Designer" Drugs

So-called *"designer" drugs* are chemical variations of controlled synthetic drugs and have effects similar to those of narcotics, stimulants, and hallucinogens. If a particular drug is illegal, the criminal producer can slightly alter the chemical composition of that drug and create a new drug. This accomplishes two things. First, it often produces a drug that still has the desired effects. Second, it produces a drug that is not (at least temporarily) illegal (Kirsch, 1986).

Ecstasy   *Ecstasy (MDMA)* has often been called the "drug of the '80s." At low doses it is mildly intoxicating and not particularly dangerous, but at doses of 100 milligrams and up the drug becomes toxic. The desired effects include heightened alertness, positive mood, increased sense of emotional warmth and love, and increased ability to work effectively. Negative reactions include muscle tightness, teeth-clenching, nausea, pain, restlessness, blurred vision, rapid eye movement, decreased sensitivity to pain, altered blood sugar levels, and sometimes, hallucinations.

China White   "Designer" heroins, sometimes referred to as **China White,** are quite numerous. Kirsch (1986) lists at least nine varieties. These drugs mimic the effects of heroin, but unfortunately, they also lead to a great number of deaths. Chemical analysis reveals that some of these designer drugs are actually thousands of times stronger than morphine.

MPTP   This Demerol "look-alike" is the substance that has led to the Parkinson's disease-like symptoms we discussed earlier in this chapter. Apparently, clandestine chemists attempted to produce MPPP, which is a derivative of the painkiller Demerol. Through faulty methods they produced MPPP that was contaminated with MPTP. *MPTP* attacks the part of the brain that controls movement and destroys the cells there.

The overriding problem with designer drugs is that the user is never sure what she or he is getting. There are so many ways to alter the chemical structure of a drug, and so many ways that the criminal chemist can make deadly mistakes, that to ingest one of the look-alikes is to take a serious chance.

The Variability of Drug Reactions

Table 4–5 and the above examples give some typical reactions to the listed drugs, but it is really a hopeless task to try to describe drug effects with any accuracy. Because so many factors can influence an individual's response to a drug, it is impossible to list all of that drug's potential effects. The amount of a given drug that one takes will often affect the nature of the reaction. The quality of the drug affects the reaction as well. One of the problems associated with the use of illegal drugs is that there is no guaranteed way of obtaining a pure drug. More than likely, illicit drug purchases result in the individual's taking impure, cut drugs that may be dangerous, or at least short-change the user in terms of the expected effects.

Experience with a drug also will influence the effect. A person taking LSD for the first time may find the result quite unpleasant or even terrifying, but a person who has experimented with LSD over a period of time under friendly, supportive conditions may well enjoy the experience. Humans can learn to cope with the effects of many drugs.

A user's physical condition can influence a drug experience, too. So can one's mood. As mentioned, users of marijuana often claim that the drug exaggerates whatever mood they happen to be in. Personality is still another factor in drug reactions. If a person is healthy and stable, then a more pleasant drug experience is likely to occur than if one is neurotic or psychotic. Finally, the social setting can affect the type of reaction. If the setting is friendly, accepting, instructive, and warm, a person is most likely to have a good time. In short, no one can count on having a particular kind of drug reaction, because he is affected by too many variables.

Drugs and Death

The person who is dying of cancer experiences fear and pain. Drugs such as morphine are used to reduce this burden. What about more powerful but illegal drugs, such as heroin? Should they be used to lessen suffering? Some say there is no reason in the world to worry about harmful effects when the patient is dying anyway. But others, on moral and ethical grounds, object to the use of these substances under any circumstances, even those as extreme as terminal cancer. What about the patient who is not dying but is in horrible pain? Should some kind of effective but illegal drug be used on a temporary basis, in spite of the risk of dependence, to lessen this suffering? There are no agreed-upon answers to these questions yet. But society will have to come to grips with the fact that these dangerous and normally illegal substances may have reasonable applications within the medical field.

HYPNOSIS

Entering the Hypnotic Trance

The first thing that should be said about hypnosis is that we do not know exactly what it is yet. We do know some things about it, but a full understanding of its causes and consequences still eludes us. *Hypnosis* has had a checkered career within psychology. Because hypnosis has long been used as a form of entertainment, psychologists have often looked down on the entire topic. But in recent years, some psychologists have made concerted efforts toward a fuller understanding of this mysterious process (McConkey, 1983).

There are any number of ways to induce a hypnotic trance (Council, Kirsch, Vickery, & Carlson, 1983). A hypnotist may ask subjects to fix their gaze on a swinging pendulum, the second hand of a watch, or a point of light. But the hypnotist always invites the subject to enter a trance. Speaking in a soft, modulated tone, the hypnotist encourages the subject to relax, to become calm and drowsy, and to listen only to the sound of the hypnotist's voice. The subject is

Despite the use of hypnosis as a form of entertainment, some psychologists have begun to accept its depth and complexity.

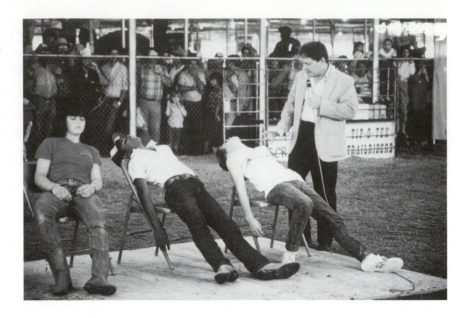

encouraged to give up control and not worry about anything. The element of invitation is essential to the induction of hypnosis. No hypnotist can force someone into a trance. The subject must be willing to give up control, to be receptive to the hypnotist's suggestions, and to tolerate distortions in time, space, and causality.

The Hypnotic Trance

The hypnotist's long, softly murmured invitation often leads to the *hypnotic trance.* People who have experienced it describe it as a state of calmness, mental relaxation, and detachment. The subject is definitely not asleep; there is little similarity between sleep and the hypnotic trance. Hypnotized subjects are content to be passive. They do not feel like making plans or doing things, and they often describe their minds as ''blank.''

At the same time, the hypnotized subject is extremely receptive to the suggestions of the hypnotist. If the hypnotist asks the subject to do something, the subject usually seems happy to oblige. If asked to be a traffic officer, the subject may start directing invisible cars. If the hypnotist suggests that there is a roast chicken on the table, the deeply hypnotized subject will happily go through the motions of carving and eating it. In general, a relaxed willingness to go along with the hypnotist is characteristic of the trance.

Hypnotic Effects

Perception   Many kinds of hypnotic effects can be demonstrated, including a variety of perceptual distortions. Subjects may be told their vision is blurring, and they will act accordingly. Or they may be told their vision is becoming extremely keen. In this case, they report feeling as though this were true, even though there is little evidence that their vision has actually improved. It is also easy to get subjects to report visual and auditory hallucinations—seeing and hearing things that are not there.

Emotional and Antisocial Behavior   Emotional behavior is extremely susceptible to hypnotic manipulation. Subjects can be induced to show the full range of emotions, from extreme happiness, through boredom, to pain and distress. The hypnotist can tell the subject that a funny joke will follow and then say, "The sky is blue." The subject will laugh. Similarly, subjects can be led to "see" funny, frightening, or boring situations and will act accordingly.

A word of caution is in order here. Before you submit to hypnosis, check the credentials of the hypnotist. Do not let just anyone hypnotize you, because it is possible to feel extreme distress under hypnosis. It is the emotional susceptibility that we have just been discussing that makes hypnosis dangerous. In the hands of an unskilled hypnotist you can be induced to feel things you would rather not feel, such as reexperiencing some extremely unpleasant event from your past, or experiencing some frightening hallucinated event.

A related question is whether or not a person under hypnosis can be made to engage in immoral or illegal acts. Can a hypnotist "control" people to the point where they will engage in activities that they would not participate in if they were not hypnotized? Generally speaking, it is very difficult to force a hypnotized person to do something that goes against their moral or ethical code. Remember, we have to be willing to be hypnotized, and if the hypnotist asks us to do something that goes against our will, we will refuse. But there is a danger here. If the hypnotist can convince the subject that the act is appropriate and necessary, then the subject may do it. For example, if a man is convinced by the hypnotist that a friend of his is really a threatening enemy, then the hypnotized subject may attack. If he is persuaded that someone's clothes are on fire, he may try to remove them.

Posthypnotic Amnesia   If told that they will remember nothing about their trance experiences when brought out of a hypnotic trance, many subjects will act as though nothing has happened since they first went into the trance (Cooper, 1979). The last thing they remember is the voice of the hypnotist inviting them into the trance. With appropriate instruction during the trance (such as, "You will remember everything when I snap my fingers"), this **posthypnotic amnesia** can be removed after the subject has been brought out of the trance. At the snap of the hypnotist's fingers, full memory of trance events floods back into the subject's surprised mind.

In another example, Orne (1966) has shown that subjects can be told the number 3 will disappear from their minds until told it will reappear again. Under the influence of this suggestion subjects cannot count properly. They will say, "1, 2, 4, 5," and "21, 22, 24, 25." They count six fingers on their hand—1, 2, 4, 5, 6. The experience is a frustrating one; the subject suffers from a sense of incompetence.

Hypnotic Age Regression   Heavily hypnotized subjects can be told they are going back in time and becoming younger and younger. This is known as *hypnotic age regression.* Such subjects appear to regress to childhood—to think, act, and speak as though they were children. Some researchers claim that long-buried memories of childhood events can be brought out in this fashion. But this idea is controversial. It is true that many memories do appear under these conditions, but some of them may be distortions. Other hypnotic memories of early childhood events turn out to have been described to the subject at a later date. In addition, subjects often seem to "role play" or act as though they were, say, five years old in order to respond to the hypnotist's suggestions. Experimental evidence suggests that no more accurate memories are recalled by hypnotically regressed subjects than by nonhypnotized subjects (Wood, 1983).

But a belief in hypnotic age regression persists. Quite a few therapists consider it a useful technique in therapy. Long-buried painful or disturbing events are presumably recallable in this state, even though the patient cannot normally recall them. Thus, through hypnotic regression, these therapists feel they can get at the roots of the patient's problems.

Posthypnotic Suggestion   **Posthypnotic suggestion** refers to the ability of some subjects to carry out instructions given to them under hypnosis after they have been taken out of the trance. For example, during the trance subjects may be told that when they come out of the trance they will not remember anything (posthypnotic amnesia), but if they hear the hypnotist cough, they will open a window. And indeed, research indicates that some subjects will carry out this sort of sequence. When asked why they opened the window, they will often say something like, "Oh, I don't know. It was stuffy in here."

Hypnotized Eyewitnesses

Many law enforcement agencies use hypnosis in an effort to recover the details of a crime. For example, Mary Smith may have witnessed a robbery on the street but seems unable to provide much detailed information about the crime. Under hypnosis, she appears to be able to recall a great deal of detail, such as a description of the suspect's face and clothing and the presence of a weapon.

Police officials have been extremely enthusiastic about hypnosis, but the hard scientific data are much less encouraging. Sometimes what the witness "remembers" is inaccurate or even fictitious. Dywan and Bowers (1983) showed subjects a set of pictures and asked them to describe each one. A week later, half the subjects were hypnotized and half were not. All of the subjects then attempted to recall the pictures again. While hypnotized subjects recalled more new information, what they did recall tended to be inaccurate and invented. Other studies (see Smith, 1983) conclude that, if anything, the memory of hypnotized subjects is actually *poorer* than that of nonhypnotized people. It is as though hypnotized people are so suggestible that they will even make up memories in order to be a "good subject." The most reasonable conclusion is that hypnosis should be used with great care. Some states, such as California, have banned the use of testimony from hypnotized subjects entirely. The true and proper use of eyewitness hypnosis has yet to be determined.

Role Playing

Hypnosis, as a true phenomenon, has been under heavy attack. Barber (1970) argues that hypnosis is highly overrated. He claims that many of the things that hypnotized subjects do can also be done by nonhypnotized subjects. For instance, the classic hypnotic demonstration shown in Figure 4–7 can also be accomplished by a reasonably strong, nonhypnotized subject. Barber argues that hypnosis is not a mysterious altered state of consciousness, but merely a reflection of things that we can all do if we are really motivated to do them.

Similarly, Orne (1970) says that *role playing* accounts for many so-called hypnotic phenomena. He argues that many of these effects are the result of the subjects' attempts to please the hypnotist. The subjects act the way they think a truly hypnotized person would act. They "fake it" to some degree, in order to be cooperative and helpful. When Orne's subjects were regressed back to their sixth birthday and asked to describe it, the flood of details they provided proved to be quite inaccurate. Many of the described events were out of place, wrong, or even invented. Orne also obtained psychological tests taken by some of his subjects when they were young children. He regressed these subjects back to the appropriate ages and gave them the tests again. Their new answers did not correspond to the answers they had given as children, in spite of their childish behavior under hypnosis.

Finally, Orne paid one group of subjects to pretend they were hypnotized while another group was truly hypnotized. He then invited an experienced, accomplished hypnotist to try to tell the hypnotized subjects from the faking subjects. The visiting hypnotist could not distinguish which group was which, although he stuck the subjects with pins and asked them to engage in all sorts of unusual acts. Well-motivated normal subjects can act exactly like hypnotized subjects, suggesting that at least some so-called hypnotic events represent role playing.

Who Can Be Hypnotized?

Percentages　We cannot all be hypnotized. Individuals differ considerably in terms of their susceptibility to hypnosis. Perhaps 10 percent of us do not respond at all, and only 5 or 10 percent of us can enter into the deepest sort of trances (Hilgard, 1965). The rest of us fall somewhere in between.

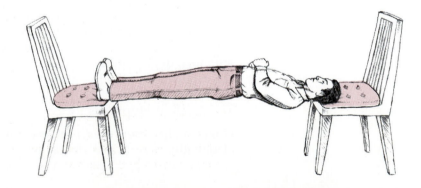

FIGURE 4–7　The Power of Hypnosis?　*When instructed to lie between two chairs, suspended only by the head and feet, a hypnotized subject will do so. But so can many healthy, strong, nonhypnotized individuals. Audiences tend to view this event as astounding simply because they do not question it.*

FIGURE 4–8   Illusions Used in Detecting Hypnotically Susceptible Subjects   *Susceptible persons report more frequent reversals than less susceptible persons.* (After Wallace, Knight, & Garrett, 1976)

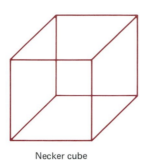

Necker cube

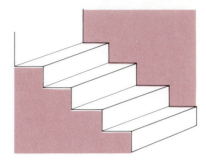

Schroeder staircase

Personalities   What kinds of people are susceptible to hypnotic suggestion? Perhaps the fairest answer is that many different types of people may be susceptible. Hilgard (1970) reports that individuals who are confident, normal, interested in subjective experiences, outgoing, and capable of becoming wrapped up in imaginative experiences are susceptible. This view of the susceptible personality is supported by work that suggests that sensation seekers tend to be interested in hypnosis (Stanton, 1976). But Hilgard (1970) also reports that strict punishment during childhood may lead to hypnotizability, too. The notion is that persons subjected to strict childhood punishment may be more responsive to following orders and may also be more prone to escaping into fantasy. Thus the available evidence suggests that very different kinds of people may be susceptible, and there is no one personality that is most readily hypnotized.

A related issue is the search for a simple means of detecting who will make a good hypnotic subject and who will not. Many investigators have tried to develop a simple test, but few have succeeded (Diamond, 1974). One encouraging effort is reported by Wallace, Knight, and Garrett (1976). They used the figures depicted in Figure 4–8. If you stare at these figures for a moment you will notice that they reverse themselves. The Schroeder staircase, for example, can be seen as a normal set of stairs leading upward, or as an upside-down staircase. As you stare at the figures you will notice that they flip back and forth. Wallace, Knight, and Garrett found that this tendency to see first one version and then the other can help to distinguish hypnotizable from nonhypnotizable individuals. Susceptible persons report more frequent reversals than nonsusceptible persons. There is also some evidence to suggest that susceptibility to hypnosis may be inherited.

Finally, McConkey and Sheehan (1976) point out that the hypnotist is just as important as the subject, and perhaps more important, in determining whether or not hypnosis will occur. These researchers report enormous variations in the success of hypnotic attempts, depending on the status, the sensitivity, the familiarity, and the experience of the hypnotist.

The Uses of Hypnosis

Hypnosis has been used in many branches of medicine. Pain associated with surgery and dental work can sometimes be reduced by means of hypnosis. Terminal cancer patients have also been made more comfortable by hypnosis. Presumably, pain and fear constitute a major portion of the experience the terminal patient undergoes, and both pain and fear have been shown to be quite responsive to hypnotic suggestion.

Psychotherapists have also found hypnosis to be useful. Unpleasant emotional responses such as anxiety and depression can sometimes be reduced through hypnosis. This technique may not cure anything, but if troublesome symptoms can be reduced, then the person may be better able to deal with his or her difficulties.

MEDITATION

What Is Meditation?

Although an interest in meditation has recently swept through this country, meditation has been practiced in other cultures for centuries. Basically, all *meditation* techniques represent attempts to alter consciousness through the systematic exercise of concentration. Techniques vary enormously; there is no one basic method. Zen meditation involves sitting quietly. Some techniques involve chanting. Still others, such as the whirling dances of the Sufi dervishes, involve energetic physical activity. In spite of these differences, all types of meditation appear to have a similar goal. They are all ways of achieving an inner quiet and a heightened or changed experience of conscious awareness.

One way to think about meditation is to think of it as the art of being in the "here and now." Ordinarily, our minds are filled with an ongoing stream of chatter: "When am I going, what have I done, what should I do, how do I feel?" Many meditation techniques try to eliminate this nervous activity. Tranquility is the goal. Stop the noise, focus on the experience of being alive, and know a sense of inner quiet and calmness.

How Do We Meditate?

There are many different ways to achieve this state of inner quiet. Some of them are quite simple. Try the following:

1. Sit quietly and count your breaths.
2. Repeat a simple phrase, or *mantra*, such as the word "calm" or "quiet," over and over again, under your breath.
3. Focus your attention on some part of your body. Many people use the "mystical third eye," or the point midway between the eyebrows. There is also the so-called "concentration on the navel." What this really does is to direct your attention to your breathing by focusing on the rise and fall of the abdominal area.
4. Some meditators simply sit back and observe the flow of their thoughts. What this method seeks is a sense of detachment, a way to stand back and be a quiet observer of our own chattering mind. It is as if we attempt to stand by the roadside and watch the traffic go by.

Although this woman may not be experiencing an extreme state of altered consciousness, she is at least relaxing as she meditates.

In using these methods, we do not attempt to force our mind to work purposefully or even logically. Rather, we gently guide and direct our attention toward a calm and tranquil position.

What Are the Effects of Meditation?

When meditating, many people report nothing more than a temporary sense of calmness. They feel relaxed and temporarily relieved of the tensions and worries of everyday life. Although limited, this effect is a good one. One researcher (Benson, 1975; Benson, Kotch, Crassweller, & Greenwood, 1977) argues that meditation techniques are simply fancy ways of inducing perfectly normal "relaxation responses." According to this view, there is nothing mysterious or unusual about meditation. Meditation techniques do nothing more than help us become tranquil and relaxed.

But some individuals report much more striking meditation effects. When meditation exercises are practiced regularly for some length of time, alterations in consciousness and perception sometimes occur. Subjects who meditated on a blue vase for 15-minute intervals, several times a week for 3 weeks, reported seeing the vase as more vivid or luminous, seeing changes in the apparent size and shape of the vase, and experiencing a sense of merging with the vase.

> The outlines of the vase shift. At that point they seem almost literally to dissolve entirely . . . for it to be a kind of fluid blue . . . a very fluid kind of thing . . . kind of moving . . . I began to feel, you know, almost as though the blue and I were perhaps merging, or that the vase and I were . . . it was as though everything was sort of merging and I was somehow losing my sense of consciousness almost . . . when the vase changes shape, I feel this is my body. (Deikman, 1963, p. 335)

Some of these subjects reported that the vase seemed to acquire a life of its own. Unusual body sensations were also common, such as a feeling of radiant heat throughout the body and tingling sensations (Deikman, 1963).

Additional qualities of the meditative experience, rather more dramatic than most accounts, are described by Gopi Khrishna in his book about Kundalini yoga (1967).

> Suddenly, with a roar like that of a waterfall, I felt a stream of liquid light entering my brain through the spinal cord. The illumination grew brighter and brighter, the roaring louder. I experienced a rocking sensation and then felt myself slipping out of my body, entirely enveloped in a halo of light . . . I felt the point of consciousness that was myself growing wider, surrounded by waves of light. (p. 210)

Obviously, we cannot all hope for (nor for that matter, would we all want) such an extreme experience, but, with a little practice, it is possible to gain some insight into what is meant by the calmness and tranquility of the meditative state.

EXTRASENSORY PERCEPTION

How often have you experienced something like this? Out of the blue someone says, "I wonder what old George is doing." At just that moment, George walks in the door. Half seriously, somebody remarks, "It must be ESP!" How often have you and someone else thought of exactly the same thing at exactly the same moment, as though there had been some type of mysterious mental communication between the two of you? How often have you heard people claim that someone has been able to predict a future event? "Just the day before it happened, she said she had a *feeling* something terrible was going to happen to him." These and similar experiences are quite common in our everyday lives. Do they represent new and unknown forms of perception and cognition, or are they merely coincidences? This is the question that lies at the heart of the ESP controversy. Some feel these unusual events can be explained in terms of the laws of chance and known physical principles while others believe relatively unknown forms of energy, perception, and cognition are responsible.

Extrasensory perception, or ESP, has become a household expression. And yet there is a good deal of confusion surrounding its meaning and its variations. In general, ***extrasensory perception (ESP)*** refers to perceptual, cognitive, or physical events that are independent of known physical principles and are independent of the activity of the known senses (smell, taste, touch, hearing, seeing).

Personal versus Scientific Observations

Before we examine the different types of ESP phenomena and the controversy surrounding them, let us spend a moment considering what we should and should not make of our own personal, subjective feelings about ESP events in our lives.

Suppose a woman on a skiing holiday breaks her leg in a fall. Twenty minutes after the accident her distraught mother calls and says, "I just *knew* something was wrong!" ESP? Perhaps not. Think of all the people who go skiing and all the concerned parents who make similar phone calls. And think how many skiing accidents occur. Is it so surprising that occasionally a phone call and an accident happen to coincide? No, it is not—in fact, if these coincidences did *not* happen occasionally we would really have something to wonder about. But to the people involved, such a coincidence appears extraordinary. They do not think about the thousands of accidents and concerned calls that do not occur at the same time. The one time that the call does follow the accident is remembered, and told over and over again, while the thousands of noncorresponding events are ignored. After all, when was the last time you heard someone exclaim, "I broke my leg and twenty minutes later my mother didn't call!"

We are not saying ESP does not exist, but we are saying the few personal experiences each of us has had cannot be used as proof of ESP. They may be coincidence. Scientific study, rather than anecdotes and personal observations, must be the field upon which ESP is proved or disproved.

Types of ESP

Telepathy **Telepathy** ("mind reading") refers to thought transference from one individual to another. A typical telepathy experiment uses a deck of 25 cards imprinted with five different symbols, five cards of each design (Soal & Bateman, 1954). The "sender" shuffles the deck and turns the cards over one at a time so that the sender can see which of the five symbols is present while the "receiver" cannot. The receiver indicates or guesses a symbol for each card as it is turned over. According to chance, the receiver should be correct 20 percent of the time—one out of every five guesses. If the receiver is correct more often than chance, a claim of telepathy can be made.

Clairvoyance *Clairvoyance* means the perception of objects or events that are out of the normal range of the senses. For example, Brand (1975) taped envelopes to regular school examinations. Unknown to the students, answers to half the questions were placed inside the envelopes. The envelopes were sealed, opaque, and never opened. Brand reports that the students did significantly better on the items whose answers were in the envelope than on those whose answers were not, even though both sets of questions were equally difficult.

In another study, Anderson and McConnell (1961) asked fourth-grade children to tell them what was inside sealed envelopes. Some of the time the envelopes contained numbers, sometimes arithmetical symbols such as $+$, $-$, $\times$, $\div$, sometimes colors, and sometimes letters. These investigators report that the children were able to predict the contents of the envelopes at a better than chance level, over some 5,560 total guesses. While not much better than chance, the difference between the number of correct guesses expected by chance (1,112) was significantly smaller than the number of actual correct guesses (1,192) according to appropriate statistical tests.

Telepathy may be thought of as one subclass of clairvoyance. Telepathy may be clairvoyance where the objects or events beyond the range of the known senses are the thoughts of another person.

Precognition The phenomenon of *precognition* is the supposed ability to foretell future events. Precognition also can be studied using the deck of cards described earlier. For example, a subject may be asked to guess the order in which cards will turn up before the deck is shuffled. Precognition has also been heavily investigated in connection with dreaming the future (Rogo, 1975).

Psychokinesis The label *psychokinesis* covers any mental operations that affect a material body—often called "mind over matter." Here a subject might be asked to influence the order in which a mechanical card shuffler shuffles a deck of cards. Some investigators prefer to have subjects wish for certain number combinations to appear on a throw of dice (McConnell, Snowden, & Powell, 1955).

Uri Geller, one of the world's best known and most controversial psychics, has mystified and amused nightclub audiences and scientists alike with his so-called psychokinetic powers (see Zeibell, 1976). Geller has often repaired watches, bent keys, and cracked gold rings, apparently using nothing more than the "power of his mind," but he is often suspected of being a skilled magician rather than a true psychic, especially since a magician named James Randi has publicly duplicated each of Geller's feats.

Others have claimed the ability to stop moving objects, to move stationary objects, to tilt scales, and to deflect a needle hanging from a thread inside a closed glass bottle. Kanthamani and Kelly (1975) report that some individuals are able to shuffle a deck of cards to match the order in which another, unseen deck had been shuffled earlier.

In fact, many hundreds of reports of telepathy, clairvoyance, precognition, and psychokinesis are available to the scientific community. Many of the studies seem to be tightly controlled, and yet most psychologists do not accept the validity of psychic phenomena.

Reasons for Caution

Despite all the claims and evidence in favor of psychic phenomena, psychologists remain skeptical. Why? Though some psychic researchers argue that stricter criteria are applied to their research than to more traditional forms of research, there are several reasons for being cautious about psychic claims. It is to these reasons that we now turn.

No Profit from ESP Phenomena   Psychic investigators themselves note that psychic abilities do not seem to be particularly helpful or useful in the world outside the laboratory. For example, a true clairvoyant should have a distinct advantage in gambling situations. And yet the available evidence suggests that ESP has not led to success in gambling (Brier & Tyminski, 1971; Greenhouse, 1975). Psychics have not helped police work very often either (Guarino, 1975).

Failure to Replicate   If a scientific principle is true, then its consequences can be replicated, or demonstrated over and over again. We are fairly certain that the force we call gravity is something we can accept, because every time we let go of an object, it moves toward earth. But ESP phenomena have proven difficult to replicate. A result obtained by one investigator seldom can be reproduced by another investigator. A psychic may be able to demonstrate a phenomenon at one time, or in front of one group, but not at another time, or in front of another group. In general, there will be resistance to accepting these phenomena as scientific facts until we are sure they are reproducible.

The Curious Use of Statistics   McConnell et al. (1955) had 393 college students try to influence the way thrown dice would fall by wishing for certain numbers. After approximately 170,000 dice throws, the results showed no effects from all that wishing. The subjects were correct on one out of six throws, which is just what is expected by chance.

But the investigators did not leave it at that. They began to play with the data in an effort to find an effect. They looked at the subjects' ability to guess at the beginning of each session as compared to their ability to guess toward the end of the session and found that the subjects apparently performed above chance early in the session and below chance later in the session. In other words, they reanalyzed the data until they found an effect. There are other instances of this tendency to use more and more statistical analyses following an initial failure (see Rhine, 1942). As you might guess, this kind of procedure increases most psychologists' skepticism.

New Methods—Poorer Results   Girden (1962) has pointed out that as new and better experimental procedures are developed, the number of positive ESP results goes down, rather than up. In most scientific fields the number of positive results goes up as the tools and procedures are improved. In days gone by, when experimental conditions were inadequate, hundreds of positive psychic results appeared. But the number of positives has been decreasing, leading to further skepticism.

Poor Controls   ESP experiments are not perfect. Although they are becoming better, many still suffer from inadequate control. The following experiment represents a type that has been run many times. A young man claiming to be telepathic was taken into one room in a large hospital complex. The sender, his female friend, was in another room several floors away. The sender then talked as she was shown various stimuli, such as slides of people, places, and things, while the young man attempted to receive her thoughts. What was said by both people, and when it was said, was carefully recorded over eight one-hour sessions. The results indicated that what the man said at a particular time sometimes corresponded quite closely to what the woman was saying at exactly the same time. ESP? Perhaps not. A crucial control is missing in this design. Another individual, unknown to either subject and unaware of the subjects, should have been asked to talk for the same amount of time in response to the same stimuli. It may well be that this control subject might have said similar things at the same time as the subjects, not through ESP but through chance. Any two people, drawn from the same population and asked to talk for eight hours, would probably speak of the same subjects at the same time, at least occasionally. Current events would be common topics. And if two people know one another, as in the described experiment, and share many common experiences, the chances of corresponding moments of common speech would seem to be even greater.

In short, the lack of adequate control has often hampered the acceptance of ESP research and has contributed to professional skepticism about it.

Unusual Events Through History   Many psychologists are skeptical about ESP because ESP effects seem to fall into a class of extraordinary phenomena that have come and gone throughout history. At one time, the existence of ghosts was taken for granted. The Loch Ness monster has been sought unsuccessfully for decades. Unidentified flying objects (UFOs) have been appearing for many years, but none have proved to be from other worlds. Witches, goblins, devils, and monsters have all withered under the light of careful scrutiny. The ESP phenomena are looked upon by many as similarly unsubstantiated and unlikely happenings. Although this rejecting attitude is not particularly scientific, it does reflect the present skepticism.

Interestingly, this heavy skepticism seems to be characteristic of the scientific community, but not of the population as a whole.

We have now reached the end of our first "exploring" chapter. While Chapters 2 and 3 were concerned with the basic facts of physiology and perception, this chapter has focused on some of the more controversial extensions of these areas as well as some practical applications of the basic data outlined earlier.

Our next "exploring" chapter is Chapter 8, which expands on and explores the basic data to be covered in Chapter 5 (learning), Chapter 6 (memory), and Chapter 7 (cognition).

SUMMARY

1. Cloning is the process of growing identical animals from cells taken from a single parent. It has been done with lower animals but not yet with humans. Cloning raises serious ethical questions.

2. Genetic engineering is the effort to exchange undesirable genes for more desirable ones in living animals. The movement is in its infancy, but controversial effects have already been obtained.

3. Genetic counseling informs people about the probabilities of genetic birth defects appearing in their offspring.

4. Hormones can be used to reduce human suffering, as in the cases of hypothyroidism and Addison's disease.

5. Our knowledge of hormonal effects is severely limited and there is always the danger of risking long-range negative effects when treating current problems with hormones.

6. The brain produces its own opium-like substances called endorphins. Stimulation of their production can reduce pain.

7. Endorphins have been implicated in the condition known as autism.

8. Parkinson's disease can be partially controlled through the use of L-dopa.

9. Brain-tissue transplants represent some of the most dramatic and promising forms of medical research.

10. When asleep, we are often conscious, can carry out a simple plan, and can distinguish among external stimuli.

11. Losing sleep is not particularly harmful.

12. It is not necessary to make up all lost sleep.

13. Some investigators feel sleep provides a restorative interlude during which our energies are restored.

14. The need to sleep may be related to the energy needs of the species and the capacity of the environment to satisfy those needs at particular times.

15. Dreaming can be detected with electroencephalograph (EEG) records and by rapid eye movements (REM).

16. The total amount of sleep needed drops with age. REM sleep drops with age, too.

17. REM and NREM sleep periods alternate during the night. Most REM sleep occurs later in the night.

18. It has been difficult to describe accurately differences between long and short sleepers.

19. If we are deprived of REM sleep, we will "catch up" when given the chance.

20. Freudian dream theory argues that dreams represent disguised fulfillment of unacceptable impulses.

21. Alternative dream theories argue that the symbols are expressive rather than concealing and that dreams are nothing more than low-grade thinking.

22. External events sometimes intrude on dream content.

23. Dreams may help memory consolidation.

24. Dreams may exercise sensory and motor aspects of the nervous system.

25. We probably cannot learn while we are asleep.

26. Dream time is not compressed.

27. Sleep disorders include sleep apnea, narcolepsy, and sleepwalking.

28. Drug use throughout history has involved a wide range of narcotics, hallucinogens, stimulants, and depressants.

29. The following drugs are discussed in detail: amphetamines, cocaine, LSD, PCP, marijuana, heroin, alcohol, and designer drugs.

30. Drug reactions are variable, depending upon amount, quality, experience, physical condition, mood, personality, and social conditions.

31. The use of illegal drugs to reduce pain in cases such as terminal cancer is being hotly debated.

32. One is hypnotized by being invited to enter into a trance by the hypnotist. The hypnotic trance is a state of calmness, relaxation, and suggestibility.

33. Emotions can be varied by the hypnotist. Unethical behavior can be created only if the hypnotist can convince the subject that it is actually ethical.

34. Hypnotic phenomena include posthypnotic amnesia, hypnotic age regression, and posthypnotic suggestion.

35. Some are skeptical of hypnosis, claiming that much of it is role playing on the part of the subject wishing to be cooperative.

36. Hypnotized eyewitnesses may be no more accurate in their reporting than nonhypnotized people.

37. Many different personality types can be hypnotized.

38. Hypnosis has been used in medical, dental, and psychotherapy situations to reduce pain, anxiety, and fear.

39. Many different meditation techniques attempt to alter consciousness through the systematic exercise of concentration.

40. ESP refers to perceptual, cognitive, or physical events that are independent of the operation of the known senses.

41. Scientific rather than personal observations must be the basis for judging psychic phenomena.

42. ESP includes telepathy, clairvoyance, precognition, and psychokinesis.

43. Skepticism concerning ESP is extremely strong in the scientific community.

KEY TERMS

alcohol
alpha waves
amniocentesis
amphetamines
China White
clairvoyance
cloning
cocaine
codeine
delta waves
dependence
"designer" drugs
displacement
dopamine
Ecstasy (MDMA)
endorphins
extrasensory perception (ESP)

Freudian dream theory
genetic counseling
genetic engineering
heroin
hormonal manipulation
hypnopaedia
hypnosis
hypnotic age regression
hypnotic trance
latent content
lysergic acid diethylamide
   (LSD)
manifest content
marijuana
meditation
morphine
MPTP

narcolepsy
no rapid eye movement (NREM)
nuclear transplant method
phencyclidine (PCP)
posthypnotic amnesia
posthypnotic suggestion
precognition
psychokinesis
rapid eye movement (REM)
role playing
sleep apnea
sleep deprivation
somnambulists
symbols
telepathy
tolerance
withdrawal

ADDITIONAL READING

Beers, R. F., & Bassett, E. G. (eds.). (1979) *Mechanisms of pain and analgesic compounds.* New York: Raven.
This is a first-class collection of papers concerned with pain and its neural mechanisms.

Ellinwood, E. H., & Kilbey, M. N. (eds.). (1978) *Cocaine and other stimulants.* New York: Plenum.
This text offers a useful discussion of the nature and effects of stimulants.

Fromm, E., & Shor, R. E. (eds.). (1979) *Hypnosis: Developments in research and new perspectives.* Hawthorne, New York: Aldine.
Many developments in the field of hypnosis are summarized in this edited volume.

Jones-Witters, P., & Witters, W. L. (1983) *Drugs and society: A biological perspective.* Monterey, CA: Wadsworth Health Sciences.
This text offers a discussion of psychoactive drugs, their history, and their effects.

Julien, R. M. (1981) *A primer of drug action* (3rd ed.). San Francisco: W. H. Freeman.
This book provides a detailed description of drugs and their effects on the body.

Kirsch, M. M. (1986) *Designer drugs.* Minneapolis, MN: CompCare Publications.
Up-to-date coverage of the so-called designer or look-alike drugs is presented in this volume.

5 Learning and Conditioning

Learning is vital to all higher forms of animal life. Without the capacity to learn, or to modify our behavior in accordance with our experiences, we would not survive. We would not be able to speak or to communicate through the use of language, as those skills appear to be learned and not innate. You would not be reading this text, as you would not have learned to read (and *we* would not have learned to write). No one would drive automobiles, live in houses, catch planes, or go to college. Our emotional, social, sexual, intellectual, and physical worlds would be entirely different from what they are now. Without the capacity to learn, our lives would be incredibly limited (and short, too). Spend a moment imagining what life would be like without the ability to profit from experience. Would we wear clothes? How would we eat? What would we do with members of the opposite sex? What would we do when it began to snow? Our behavior would be limited to so-called "innate" reactions, such as recoiling from pain, eating, and breathing. In fact, no one knows what life would be like if we did not possess the capacity to learn. Because learning has been so inextricably bound to our existence from our earliest days, we have trouble stepping away from it and thinking of life without it. But, without question, life as we know it would be altered enormously without the capacity to learn.

It is no wonder, then, that many psychologists study the processes by which we learn. In one way or another, concern for learning processes is inherent in the efforts of most, if not all, psychologists. Table 5–1 lists some of the types of questions asked by psychologists working in different areas. Clearly, all of these questions revolve around the concept of learning.

A DEFINITION OF LEARNING

Now that we have emphasized the importance of learning, let us spend a moment considering the meaning of the word. What do we mean by learning? Try to define it. It is difficult, not only for you but for psychologists as well. Through the years there have been many attempts to characterize learning in a few sentences (Domjan & Burkhard, 1986; Donahoe & Wessells, 1980; Hulse, Egeth, & Deese, 1980). None of these characterizations are completely satisfactory, but they do offer a rough framework within which to think about learning.

The definition we prefer was developed by Kimble (1967). It states that *learning* refers to a relatively permanent change in behavior potentiality that occurs as a result of reinforced practice. This definition excludes a large number of behavior changes that are not learned changes. For example, by including the phrase *relatively permanent*, Kimble excludes temporary behavior changes due to fluctuations in motivational states such as fear, thirst, hunger, and fatigue. If we are tired, we go to sleep. If we are hungry, we eat. These certainly represent dramatic changes in behavior, but they are only temporary. They do not represent new learning.

Kimble also uses the term *practice* to exclude other types of behavior changes from the category of learned changes. Extreme changes in behavior may be brought about through maturation, aging, disease, and physiological damage, but it is clear that changes of these sorts do not represent learned changes.

TABLE 5-1 The Involvement of Learning in Psychology

Area of Psychology	*Sample Concerns Involving Learning*
1. Physiological	What chemical changes in the brain account for learning and memory? What drugs will affect memory?
2. Perception	Do we learn to perceive depth, or is our depth perception innate? How does inaccurate perception affect learning?
3. Developmental	How do children learn sex roles? Are there certain times, or stages, when a child is ready to learn certain things such as reading?
4. Measurement and testing	Can we teach children to do better on intelligence tests? Do intelligence tests measure how much one has learned, how bright one is, or both?
5. Motivation	Will the urge to satisfy our curiosity help us learn? How do we acquire the need to achieve?
6. Emotion	Are emotions learned? Will strong emotions, such as fear and anger, help us learn or hinder our learning?
7. Personality	Can our personality traits be modified by learning? Is personality learned?
8. Abnormal and clinical	Is an abnormal fear of horses explainable in terms of learning? Is schizophrenia a learned reaction? How can the principles of learning help reduce suffering due to mental illness?
9. Social	Are attitudes learned? Can we learn to be independent of group pressure? Will an audience help or hinder learning?
10. Community	How do we teach families and friends to be more supportive of people in trouble? Can people having difficulties learn to seek support from the community?
11. Environmental	Can learning be improved by varying the environment? What is the relationship between crowding and learning?
12. Industrial	Can employees and employers learn to get along with one another? How do we best teach people to operate machinery in an efficient manner?

Note further that Kimble specifies changes in *behavior potentiality*. This phrase refers to the fact that learning is invisible. It lies within us as a potentiality, but it is not always expressed. We can only infer its existence through observation of behavior. For example, each of us has the capacity to recite the alphabet, even though we are not reciting it now. Still, the potentiality is there. If motivated to do so, we can all reveal the existence of learning by translating the potentiality into overt behavior. Keep in mind, however, that overt behavior does not always reflect learning in an accurate manner. If you are tired, or panicky, or disinterested, your performance on an examination may not reflect how much you really know. Individuals who have learned less than you may obtain a better score on the exam because they were more ready and able to take it.

Finally, Kimble argues that for a response to be learned it must be *reinforced*, or rewarded. Kimble's insistence on the necessity of reward is the most controversial aspect of his definition. Many people disagree with him. He argues that learning will not occur unless a response is followed by a reward. Dogs will not learn to roll over unless they are rewarded with something like food, praise, or a pat on the head. Grades and recognition reinforce students' studying behavior, and so on. Try to think of a situation where learning occurs in the absence of reward. Remember, rewards can be very subtle. We can reward ourselves by praising ourselves. The chance to satisfy our curiosity also appears to be rewarding, and so is the removal of unpleasant stimuli such as shock and irritating noises. Some psychologists argue that learning itself is a rewarding experience. In short, it may be impossible to come up with a learning situation that is free of rewards. Even though some psychologists maintain that reinforcement is not absolutely essential for learning to occur (Guthrie, 1952), most of them would, at the very least, agree that rewards affect behavior strongly. A more detailed discussion of reinforcement appears later in this chapter. Although Kimble's definition of learning is a good one, it is important to remember that all definitions of learning are probably inadequate. Use Kimble's definition as a rough index of what is and what is not learned behavior, but do not accept it as the last word on the subject.

The rest of this chapter will help to bring the field of learning into focus by describing basic learning procedures and commenting on their relationships to one another. We will begin by considering two very basic forms of conditioning, and then we will discuss human verbal learning. We will explore the major learning phenomena and principles as they apply to each of these situations. Then we will consider how prior learning can help or hinder us, how we sometimes learn by observing others, and how biological factors set limits on our ability to learn.

CLASSICAL CONDITIONING

Pavlov's Experiments

The first basic form of conditioning is called *classical conditioning*. Ivan Pavlov's studies with dogs, musical tones, and saliva are among the best-known experiments in the field of psychology and have had an enormous impact on modern psychology. Interestingly, Pavlov was not a psychologist at all but had been trained at the University of St. Petersburg in chemistry and animal physiology. Later education in physiology was followed by years of research on the nerves of the heart and various aspects of digestive physiology. In 1890 Pavlov was appointed professor of pharmacology at the St. Petersburg Military Medical Academy and he later became professor of physiology at the same institution. In 1904 he received the Nobel Prize in physiology for a series of experiments involving the nervous system and the

FIGURE 5–1 Pavlov's Salivary Conditioning Apparatus *Food is delivered to the dog's dish by remote control. Pavlov wanted to discover whether or not the reflex response that causes dogs to salivate when presented with food could be modified by learning. (After Yerkes & Morgulis, 1909)*

Pavlov and his assistants posed with one of his dogs at the time he was conducting his experiments in conditioning.

digestive secretions of the pancreas. He was very active conducting research in his laboratory until the time of his death in 1936.

Pavlov's basic procedures (1927) were established using a dog and the simple apparatus illustrated in Figure 5–1. Before a conditioning session, the dog's cheek was surgically treated so that saliva could be collected and measured accurately. After the restraining harness was in place, a tuning fork was sounded. Although the dog might move a bit in response to this tone, it would not salivate. A moment later, while the tuning fork was still sounding, dry meat powder was presented to the dog. As it ate the meat powder, saliva naturally began to flow. These procedures were repeated over and over again.

After pairing the tone and the meat powder repeatedly, Pavlov observed that the dog would salivate when the tone was presented alone. Before conditioning, the salivary response could be elicited only by the meat powder. Now it had become *classically conditioned* to the tone. Classical conditioning is often called *Pavlovian conditioning* and sometimes *respondent conditioning.* These labels may be used interchangeably.

Quiz Panic, Christmas Bells, and Autumn Leaves

It must be emphasized immediately that classical conditioning is important in human life; it is not just something limited to dogs, saliva, and laboratories. Suppose, for example, that you fail three math quizzes in a row. Each time, you sit there feeling depressed and nervous. So you study harder for the fourth quiz and go into the test situation feeling confident. But as soon as you sit down and face the teacher, the room, your classmates, and that test paper, you panic all over again; you cannot seem to help yourself. This unfortunate emotional reaction may well be classically conditioned. You have associated unpleasant emotions with the test situation so that when you reexperience the test situation, you also reexperience all of the associated negative feelings.

Not all classically conditioned reactions are negative. Many people experience warm feelings when they hear Christmas bells, or smell autumn leaves burning, or hear a certain person's name. All of these are examples of classically conditioned reactions.

The Four Elements of Classical Conditioning

The four crucial, defining elements in any classical conditioning situation are the following:

1. The *unconditioned stimulus (UCS)* The unconditioned stimulus is a stimulus that uniformly and consistently elicits an identifiable response prior to the experiment. In the Pavlovian situation the

This young student may already be experiencing negative feelings that have been classically conditioned to test situations.

UCS is the meat powder, for this stimulus consistently and uniformly elicits the salivary response.

2. The *unconditioned response (UCR)*   This is the response always elicited by the UCS. Salivation in response to presentation of the meat powder is the UCR in Pavlov's experiment. The UCR is generally a reflex or autonomic response.

3. The *conditioned stimulus (CS)*   The CS is the new, neutral stimulus introduced by the experimenter. The tone is the CS in Pavlov's experiment. Prior to the conditioning procedures, the tone does not elicit the salivary response.

4. The *conditioned response (CR)*   When the dog learns to salivate in response to the CS (tone), that salivary response is called a conditioned response (CR). The CR is a learned response to the CS, while the UCR is a response to the UCS.

You may well ask if there is any difference between the CR and the UCR. After all, in this example they are both salivary responses. But though they appear to be similar, they may be significantly different. They may differ in terms of amplitude (size), duration (length of time), and latency (the time between the presentation of a stimulus and the occurrence of the response). Figure 5–2 illustrates the stages of classical conditioning.

Temporal Arrangements of the CS and UCS

We have been speaking as though we always present the UCS just after we present the CS. This is a very common temporal arrangement, but we need not restrict ourselves to this pattern. We are free

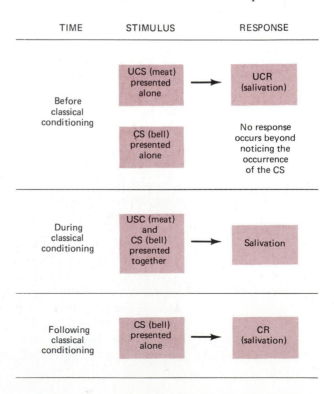

FIGURE 5–2   The Stages of Classical Conditioning   *A UCS will elicit a UCR before conditioning, while a CS will not elicit the to-be-conditioned response. During conditioning the CS and UCS are presented together, and the CS acquires the capacity to elicit a CR that is similar to the UCR.*

FIGURE 5–3 Temporal Arrangements of the CS and the UCS in Four Common Conditioning Procedures *The upward movement of a line represents the onset of a stimulus, while the downward movement of a line represents the offset of a stimulus.*

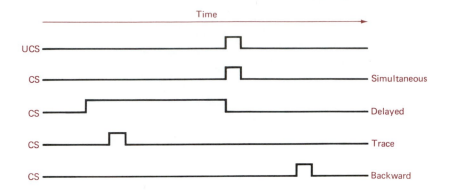

to vary the temporal relationship between the two stimuli. We can, if we wish, present the two at exactly the same time, or we can present the CS after the UCS. Figure 5–3 shows the temporal arrangements commonly employed by psychologists.

In *simultaneous* classical conditioning, the CS and UCS are presented at the same time and usually are terminated at the same time. In *delayed* classical conditioning, CS onset occurs before UCS onset, and the CS remains on at least until UCS onset. In *trace* classical conditioning, the CS is turned on and turned off before the UCS onset. In *backward* classical conditioning, CS onset and offset both follow UCS offset. Delayed conditioning is the most effective classical conditioning form.

If we wish to observe a CR in a simultaneous classical conditioning situation we must occasionally leave out the UCS, and observe whether or not the CS alone will elicit a response. If we do not do this we will not know whether the response is a conditioned response or an unconditioned response. However, these tests where the CS is presented alone need not be included in the delayed and trace procedures. This is because there is time for the CR to occur after presentation of the CS but before UCS onset. For instance, when Pavlov sounded a tone and waited a moment before presenting the meat powder, the dog would salivate in anticipation of the meat powder. The fact that the CR (salivation) will occur before UCS (meat) presentation makes it easy to observe a strengthening CR.

Additional Laboratory Examples

Classical conditioning is by no means limited to salivating dogs. It is a widespread phenomenon, as the following examples of laboratory studies make clear.

Eyelid Conditioning Many investigators have studied the eye blink and its susceptibility to conditioning. Various unconditioned stimuli have been used. For example, a small electric shock delivered to the orbital region of the eye will elicit an unconditioned blink (Gormezano & Fernald, 1971). A puff of compressed nitrogen on the cornea will do the same thing (Hall, 1976), as will the tap of a padded hammer on the cheek (Switzer, 1930). It is a simple matter to pair a CS, such as a tone, light, bell, or buzzer, with these sorts of uncondi-

FIGURE 5–4 Rabbit Eyeblink Conditioning Experiment *A puff of air directed at the eye or a mild shock to the skin below the eye serves as the UCS. Eye blinks are detected by a potentiometer.* (After Domjan & Burkhard, 1982)

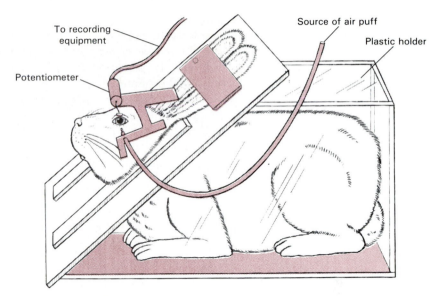

tioned stimuli. Following a number of pairings, the chosen CS will elicit a blink by itself.

Large rabbits are often used as subjects in eyeblink experiments (see Figure 5–4). This choice is made because, in contrast to humans, who do a lot of blinking, rabbits seldom blink in the absence of special training. Hence, when a rabbit does blink, we can be quite certain that that blink is in response to the stimuli presented.

Conditioning of Planaria Planaria (small freshwater flatworms) may also be classically conditioned. Thompson and McConnell (1955) placed a planarian in a container of water and paired the onset of a light (CS) with the introduction of electric current (UCS) into the water surrounding the flatworm. The electric current causes the worm to constrict or "scrunch up" (UCR). Classical conditioning is demonstrated when, after repeated pairings of the light and shock, the animal "scrunches up" in response to the light alone, before the shock is delivered.

Cardiac Conditioning A person's heart rate may also be classically conditioned. Using shock as a UCS, and something like a tone or light as a CS, it is possible to classically condition both increases and decreases in heart rate (Cohen & Johnson, 1971; Hall, 1976; Laird & Fenz, 1971).

Other laboratory studies have demonstrated that pupillary responses (Goldwater, 1972), chick embryos (Hunt, 1949), and human fetuses (Spelt, 1948) also may be classically conditioned. This type of conditioning occurs across a wide range of species, responses, and stimuli.

Classical Conditioning of Human Emotions

More closely related to our own lives is the fact that many of our emotional reactions, such as fear, joy, anger, and sadness, appear to be subject to classical conditioning. Imagine that you are enrolled in a seminar for psychology majors. The instructor is describing an intelligence test. She states that, on the average, nine-year-old children know the answers to a list of questions that she is going to read aloud. As an example, the instructor asks the person to your left, "What is the name of a color that rhymes with head?" The student promptly supplies the correct answer. She then turns to you and says, "In an old graveyard in Spain they have discovered a small skull which they believe to be that of Christopher Columbus when he was about ten years old. What is foolish about that?" You blink, momentarily distracted. Everyone is looking at you, waiting for the obvious answer, but you are having trouble coming up with it. You feel a warm flush creep into your face. Finally, after what seems an interminably long period of time, you provide the answer. Unfortunately, it is too late; classical conditioning has already occurred. When you see these students or the instructor on campus later on, or when you think of the seminar situation, you feel the sense of embarrassment you felt when you were unable to answer a simple question quickly in front of the group. Call it "conditioned embarrassment," if you wish. The point is that we are all subject to these sorts of conditioning events in our everyday emotional lives.

Classical Conditioning and Language

The very words we use in our languages may acquire some of their emotional impact through classical conditioning. If fond parents often hug their small child while saying, "I love you," then the positive feelings the child experiences can become classically conditioned to the word "love." When the child hears the word "love" in the future, these conditioned emotions probably will be evoked. We are not saying this is all there is to the meaning of words, but classical conditioning certainly adds to their emotional power.

Phobias

Phobias are strong, irrational fears such as a fear of heights, germs, snakes, darkness, indoors, outdoors, or death. We are not speaking of the uneasiness we might all feel if we stood with our toes hanging over a 400-foot cliff. That would be a normal anxiety. We are referring to extreme fears, such as a terror of being at the top of a flight of stairs.

Many of these fears may involve classical conditioning. If a young child saw his mother killed in a fall from a horse, he might develop an intense and lasting fear of horses through classical conditioning. The UCS would be the death of the parent. The UCR would be the horror produced by the death. The CS would be the horse, and the CR would be the conditioned fear of horses. In Chapters 8 and 18 we will see that many phobias can be successfully treated using our understanding of classical conditioning.

INSTRUMENTAL CONDITIONING

There is another major type of conditioning, called *instrumental conditioning.* Imagine you have volunteered to participate in a psychology experiment. You are asked to wait in a room that is empty except for an unfamiliar piece of equipment in one corner. The experimenter has given you no instructions at all. What would you do? More than likely you would examine the mechanical apparatus. Noticing several levers, you might move some of them. What if, to your surprise, a 25¢ piece rolls into a little cup at the bottom of the machine? Momentarily puzzled, you might move the levers again. Another quarter is delivered. By trial and error you discover that moving one particular lever in a certain manner always pays off in delivery of a quarter—so you settle down and move that lever in the required manner at a steady, rapid rate, piling up the rewards.

In fact, you have been undergoing a type of instrumental conditioning. The probability of a particular response on your part (the lever press) has been increased through the delivery of a reward or reinforcement (the money) immediately following your response. We could generalize to say that we will do again what has led to rewards in the past.

Our lives are filled with this type of conditioning. Students master course materials for rewards such as grades, recognition, job opportunities, and self-satisfaction. People go to work because they are regularly reinforced with paychecks and may be rewarded with raises, promotions, and the pleasure of a job well done. There is no question about the importance of this type of conditioning. However, there are serious questions about the relationship between instrumental conditioning and classical conditioning. Some psychologists feel the two types are quite distinct, while others see great similarities between them. We will discuss this dispute later in this chapter.

The prominence of instrumental conditioning within the field of learning has been influenced heavily by the thinking, experimentation, and writings of ex-Harvard professor B. F. Skinner. Skinner is responsible for one of the most celebrated pieces of equipment to be found in the field of psychological research. In its simplest form, shown in Figure 5–5, the Skinner box is nothing more than a container with a lever and a food tray. More exotic varieties have buzzers, bells, lights, and so on, as Figure 5–6 shows. The experimenter sets up the apparatus so that if the lever is pressed, a small food pellet will be delivered in the tray. A hungry rat, mouse, or hamster will learn to press the lever regularly in order to obtain the rewards. This learning situation, although very simple, appears to possess many of the characteristics of more complicated human learning situations. As a result, many psychologists believe we can learn a good deal about human behavior using this simple apparatus.

Skinner and his followers have labeled the instrumental conditioning situation *operant conditioning.* Although some psychologists would like to maintain a distinction between instrumental and operant conditioning (Ellis, 1972), the two are used interchangeably in this textbook.

Three Types of Instrumental Conditioning

Reward Training Psychologists have defined three closely related types of instrumental conditioning (see Houston, 1986). The first of these is *reward training*, in which the subject is rewarded for making

FIGURE 5–5 Simple Skinner
Boxes—Inhabited and
Uninhabited

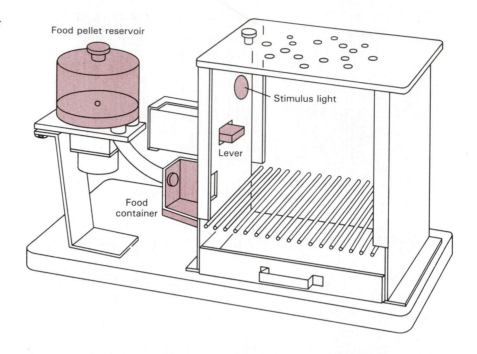

a particular response. We have already discussed several examples of
this common variety of instrumental conditioning, including rats
pressing levers for food and people going to work for paychecks. Another example of reward training has been labeled *verbal conditioning*
(Greenspoon, 1955). In a typical experiment, the subject is invited to
say words aloud as they come to mind. The experimenter murmurs
"um-hum" or "good" or some other subtle form of reward each time
the subject produces a certain type of word, such as a plural noun. If
the experimenter carefully rewards only plural nouns, subjects will

FIGURE 5–6 Skinner Boxes Are Big Business *Expensive pieces of equipment provide high-tech flexibility.*

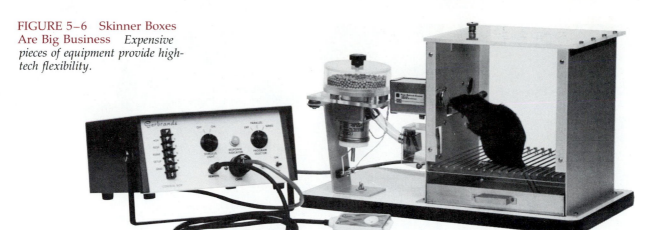

produce more and more of them in their supposedly spontaneous responses. Some psychologists feel this reward effect will appear only when the subject realizes that the experimenter is rewarding certain types of words (Spielberger, 1965). Other researchers have presented data that suggest that verbal conditioning can occur even when the subject is totally unaware of what the experimenter is doing (Kennedy, 1971). You might want to try this procedure with a friend, to see whether awareness plays a role. But either way, verbal conditioning is another example of reward training in which a particular response is rewarded if it occurs.

Avoidance Training   In *avoidance training*, an animal is noxiously stimulated if it fails to make a particular response. The apparatus used in avoidance conditioning often involves a two-sided box. One side is painted white and the other side is painted black. A low barrier or hurdle separates the two sides. A rat is placed on the white side of the barrier. If the animal is still on the white side after some designated period of time set by the experimenter (such as 15 seconds), it will be shocked. When the shock begins, the rat quickly scrambles over the barrier to the safe black side. If the rat is repeatedly placed on the white side and allowed 15 seconds before the administration of shock, it will soon learn to leap the barrier before the shock ever arrives. The rat apparently comes to associate the white side with shock and escapes from that fear-producing situation before the shock is introduced (Mowrer & Lamoreaux, 1946).

If the experimenter disconnects the electricity after the rat has learned to jump the barrier, the rat will continue to jump out of the white side of the box even though there is no longer any danger there. It has learned to be afraid of the white side of the box, and so it escapes from it. Many humans probably suffer from the same sorts of seemingly unfounded fears. For example, if a child is bitten by the first dog he encounters, he may shy away from all dogs thereafter, and so he will never learn that some dogs are friendly.

One way to break this unfortunate cycle is to confine the subject in the presence of the fear-producing stimulus. Hence, we might restrain the rat on the white side until it discovers that there is no

The power of reinforcement: would these people dress and behave as they do if they were not rewarded?

longer any danger. This confinement or restraint procedure is called *flooding.*

An instructive phenomenon that is related to the avoidance conditioning situation is **learned helplessness** (Alloy & Bersh, 1979; Maier, 1970). In the first phase of a learned helplessness experiment, a dog is restrained in a harness and shocked repeatedly without any chance of escape. The harness is then removed and normal avoidance conditioning procedures are established. Now the dog can avoid the impending shock by moving over to the other side of the enclosure. But the dog does not move, even though safety is close and accessible. It remains motionless while being shocked and makes no effort to escape. It is as though the animal is without hope. Strassman, Thaler, and Schein (1956) report similar sorts of reactions among prisoners of war. Prisoners who believe they have a chance of escaping will attempt to do so. Others, believing they cannot escape, become listless and apathetic and lose the will to resist their captors. Think about your own experiences in terms of this effect. Do you suffer from a mild sense of hopelessness in certain situations? Is there really nothing you can do to improve these situations or get out of them? More will be said about learned helplessness in Chapter 11.

Punishment Training   In **punishment training**, the animal or human subject is punished for making a particular response. Punishment training is designed to suppress a response, whereas both reward and avoidance conditioning are designed to build up or strengthen a response. If we wish to train our dog to stay off the furniture, we can smack it with a folded newspaper every time it jumps up. If we wish someone would stop talking so much, we can administer a mild punishment by saying, "I wish you would let someone else talk once in a while." It is important to keep in mind that although punishment is a powerful tool, its effects are tricky and sometimes unpredictable (Davidoff, 1976).

A great deal of controversy surrounds the use of punishment outside the laboratory. Some feel it is useful and some do not. The argument rages in the courts, in the schools, and in the home. Some of the practical problems associated with the use of punishment are as follows:

1. It has been argued that punishment does not work. For example, there is deep disagreement about whether imprisonment (a form of punishment) eliminates, or even reduces, future criminal behavior. Others argue that punishment fails only when it is used inappropriately; effective use of punishment requires strict application of laboratory-based principles involving timing, amount, and type of punishment.

2. Punishment has also been criticized for suppressing all behavior, and not just undesirable actions. Some critics argue that if you punish a child, you will get an overall suppression of the child's normal wide-ranging behavior instead of suppression of a specific unwanted behavior. But recent research suggests that this claim is false and that punishment can be focused accurately on specific behaviors (see Domjan & Burkhard, 1986).

3. Other investigators point out that punishment can lead to aggression and hostility on the part of the punished individual. This criticism does seem to have some validity (see Hutchinson, 1977). If a parent punishes a child, the probability of that child's becoming hostile in return increases.

4. A final problem with punishment is that it can lead to escape behavior. For example, if we punish a child for smoking at school, the child may quit school entirely.

The point here is that, moral issues aside, punishment is not easy to use effectively, and it can lead to unwanted side effects.

Positive Reinforcement, Negative Reinforcement, and Punishment

Because they are often confused, it is important to distinguish among positive reinforcement, negative reinforcement, and punishment. A *positive reinforcer* is anything we *present* to a subject following a response, in order to *strengthen* that response. Food pellets are effective positive reinforcers for rats, and praise is an equally effective positive reinforcer for human subjects. In short, positive reinforcers are things the subject likes, given as a reward for making a particular response.

A *negative reinforcer* is something unpleasant that we *remove* in order to *strengthen* a response. If we follow a given response with the removal of shock, then that response will be strengthened. The removal of something unpleasant can be as rewarding as the presentation of something positive. If a rat that is being shocked escapes from that shock by jumping a barrier, then that jumping response will be strengthened. Avoidance training involves negative reinforcers because shock is terminated or prevented when the rat jumps the barrier. If a child's toes feel less cramped and pinched when he takes off his new shoes, we may well find those shoes left at various locations all over the neighborhood.

Both positive and negative reinforcers strengthen responses. A *punisher*, on the other hand, is an unpleasant stimulus that we *present* to *eliminate* a response. Clearly, punishers are used in punishment training. If we follow a given response with a noxious stimulus, such as an electric shock, then that stimulus will act as a punisher and will suppress the response. Both punishers and negative reinforcers involve unpleasant stimuli. But punishers are designed to eliminate a response by presenting an unpleasant stimulus, while negative reinforcers are designed to strengthen a response by removing a negative stimulus.

Shaping

One of the interesting techniques developed within the context of instrumental conditioning is called *shaping.* Shaping is most often discussed in connection with reward training. Suppose we wish to teach a young child to put on a hat. We could stand about with an eager look on our faces, waiting for the hat to be put on correctly and spontaneously so we can reward the behavior. But the response will probably not occur spontaneously, so we evoke the response by using shaping procedures. That is, we must reward closer and closer approximations to the response we desire. We first reward (with praise, or some other appropriate reinforcement) any response that seems at all related to putting on a hat. If the child merely lifts the hat or holds it over her head, we reward her. Once a rough approximation is established, we require the child to make a closer approximation before we reward her. That is, we now reward the child only if she manages to pull the hat down onto her head a bit. By requiring closer and closer approximations to the desired response, we can shape responses that might otherwise never be acquired.

Shaping is something most parents do without being aware of it. As the child becomes able to dress herself, the parents selectively reward movements that approximate dressing behavior. As the child progresses, more stringent demands are made. The first time a child puts a foot in a shoe, she may experience warm praise and affection—even if it is the wrong shoe. But further refinements in her behavior soon will be required to maintain the same level of reward. That is, she will have to put both feet in the correct shoes before she is rewarded.

Responses as simple as a rat pressing a lever in a Skinner box must often be shaped. If left to its own devices, a rat might never learn to press the lever. This response must be shaped. The experimenter first rewards the rat each time it faces the lever, then rewards it only if it approaches the bar, and finally rewards it only if it actually presses the lever. In this manner, a rat can master the lever-pressing response in several minutes.

Professional animal trainers have used these techniques for years. The next time you turn on your television and see something like a bunny putting a big wooden dime into a model labeled "First National Bank," you can be sure it has been shaped to this response. The trainer did not wait around until the rabbit spontaneously banked the coin by itself. Breland and Breland (1966) have been successful in training animals to perform complex response sequences for many television programs and commercials. They also have trained whales and porpoises to perform elaborate routines at tourist attractions. As we shall see in Chapter 8, instrumental training procedures also are used in such human learning situations as educational programs, energy conservation, and the modification of abnormal behavior.

CLASSICAL VERSUS INSTRUMENTAL CONDITIONING: BIOFEEDBACK AND REINFORCEMENT

Voluntary versus Involuntary

We have been speaking as though instrumental and classical conditioning were distinct, clearly different types of learning. Traditionally, classical conditioning has been thought of as a "lower" form of learning involving involuntary visceral and glandular responses. Instrumental conditioning has been thought of as a "higher" form of conditioning involving voluntarily controlled skeletal muscles. Many psychologists have proposed that involuntary responses could only be conditioned through classical procedures, while voluntary responses could only be modified through the application of instrumental procedures.

This distinction has been challenged sharply by Neal Miller and his co-workers. Miller (1972, 1978) has conducted a number of studies that suggest that so-called involuntary responses can be conditioned through instrumental procedures. His reports are still very controversial (Dworkin & Miller, 1986; Miller & Dworkin, 1973). If they should prove to be correct, the traditional belief that the two types of conditioning represent distinct learning mechanisms operating within different levels of the nervous system will have to be modified.

The first step in Miller's research procedure is to inject a rat with curare. Curare is a drug that paralyzes the voluntarily controlled skeletal muscles, thereby removing them as a factor in the experiment. The drug leaves the involuntary system unaffected. Next, the animal's heart rate is monitored very carefully. Heart rates are not constant; they all vary a little. Each time the heart rate shows a small, spontaneous increase, Miller reinforces the animal. When the heart rate remains constant or decreases, reinforcement is withheld. The result is that the rate will increase, or will be instrumentally conditioned. How do you reinforce a paralyzed rat? One way Miller did it was to remove shock each time the heart rate increased. Presumably the relief was rewarding.

Miller has demonstrated that rats also will learn to decrease their heart rates when rewarded for spontaneous decreases rather than increases (see Figure 5–7). Thus he has shown that so-called involuntary responses can be modified by instrumental reward procedures, and that the traditional voluntary-involuntary distinction between instrumental and classical conditioning may not be valid. Miller has also

FIGURE 5–7   Heart Rate
Changes in Rats Rewarded for
Increases and Decreases in
Heart Rate *(After Miller & Banuazizi, 1968)*

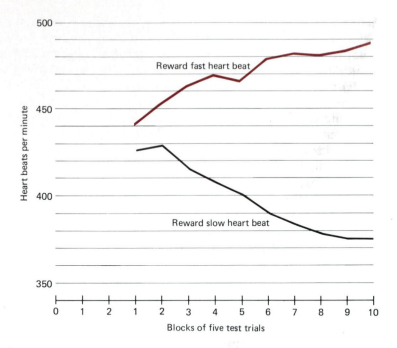

been able to instrumentally condition urine formation and intestinal contraction and has trained a rat to blush in one ear but not the other. These procedures have come to be called *biofeedback*, because the subject responds to its own internal biological cues and then modifies them (see Plotkin, 1979; Tarler-Benlolo, 1978).

The medical implications of these procedures are profound. Experimental studies have shown that high blood pressure, tension headaches, some types of vomiting, and secretion of stomach acid, which may cause ulcers, all can be modified by these biofeedback techniques (Blanchard & Young, 1974; Shapiro & Schwartz, 1972). If such findings can be applied in a practical way, much human suffering could be ended. In the basic biofeedback technique, the subject is rewarded with praise, money, or self-congratulation each time an improvement appears in the so-called involuntary condition. For instance, a subject might watch a TV screen which shows a "blip" each time there is a change in some internal condition such as heart rate. Reward can be delivered by an experimenter, or be self-delivered, each time a change is observed. Whether people can control such reactions beyond the confines of carefully monitored experimental laboratory conditions remains to be seen (Engel, 1972; Roberts, 1985).

Reinforcement versus Lack of Reinforcement

Many investigators have argued that instrumental conditioning involves reinforcement while classical conditioning does not. But if you examine classical conditioning carefully, you can detect components that do appear to be reinforcing. For example, in the eyeblink situation described earlier, the reinforcement may be the avoidance of the unpleasant air puff on the cornea. When the CS is presented, it serves as a signal that the air puff is about to be delivered. If the subject can blink quickly enough the puff can be at least partially avoided. Sounds rewarding, doesn't it? This interpretation suggests that reinforcement may operate in some classical conditioning situations just as it does in instrumental conditioning situations.

In summary, although they appear to be quite different and have traditionally been thought to differ, the two types of conditioning may not represent two distinct kinds of learning after all. They may yet turn out to be different expressions of some single, underlying learning mechanism.

COMPLEX HUMAN LEARNING

Types of Complex Tasks

Because humans are such complex verbal creatures and rely so heavily on language, it is not surprising that psychologists have developed quite a few techniques for studying verbal learning. We will look at some of these learning tasks and then consider whether they reflect conditioning procedures or some different kind of learning.

In a *free recall* task, subjects are given a list of verbal items and are then asked to recall the items in any order. Items are typically presented on a computer monitor. Since the subjects are free to recall the items in any order, this task enables us to learn about what they do with, or how they organize, the materials that they are trying to learn. From a long list of randomly presented nouns, for example, a subject might first recall all the nouns that had something to do with people, then move on to the nouns pertaining to animals, and so on. The subjects *cluster* responses according to categories. It seems that recalling the nouns by category makes the job easier. Not surprisingly, this suggests that some complicated organizational processes are going on in the subjects' minds. The materials are not retrieved in the same order as that in which they were presented to the subjects. The subjects actively process the materials, seeking ways to make the recall task easier. We will see more of these fascinating mental gymnastics in Chapter 8.

Serial learning tasks enable us to study sequential learning, or the learning of verbal materials in a given order. When we learn phone numbers, directions, the alphabet, or the spelling of new words, we are required to learn not only the individual items, but the order of the items as well. Whenever we try to memorize sequential materials, we are apt to discover that we can more easily remember the beginning and end items than the middle items. Such information can have practical implications. For instance, if you are studying for an examination or trying to memorize a list of guests to be greeted at a party, you might try putting the most important items toward the beginning or the end of the list.

In *paired-associate* learning tasks, subjects are asked to learn pairs of items. Which item goes with which? A typical paired-associate task may involve ten or twelve more or less meaningful pairs of words, such as wing-insulin, nurse-vapor, pepper-apparel, and so on, which are presented to the subject. The typical procedure is then to present one member of a pair (for example, wing) and have the subject try to recall the other member (for example, insulin). Paired-associate learning studies are useful because they approximate, in a controlled way, many everyday learning tasks such as learning a second language and labeling objects and events in the world. In fact, the whole developmental process of giving verbal meaning to our environment seems to involve paired-associate learning.

Relationship of Complex Human Learning to Conditioning

Do these verbal learning tasks represent distinct types of learning, or are they just variations on the basic classical and instrumental procedures? Though the answer is not yet clear, verbal tasks can easily be thought of as examples of classical or instrumental conditioning. Look at paired-associate learning as an example of instrumental conditioning. When we hear one word of a pair (a stimulus) we respond with the matching word of the pair (a response). We are then rewarded by the experimenter, who tells us we were correct. Then we congratulate ourselves on how bright we are. The situation resembles what happens when a rat presses a lever and receives a food pellet. Like the rat, we are rewarded for making a particular response. There are many other similarities between the verbal learning tasks and the more basic conditioning processes (Houston, 1986). In the next section we will examine some phenomena that appear to be common to classical conditioning, instrumental conditioning, and complex human learning. The fact that all three types of learning display these same phenomena suggests that they are quite closely related to one another.

BASIC CONDITIONING AND LEARNING PHENOMENA

Acquisition

Acquisition is the term used to refer to an increase in response strength with repeated reinforcements. It is the first of the effects that appear to be common to classical, instrumental, and verbal learning. We will begin by considering the acquisition of a response in classical conditioning. Each paired presentation of a CS and a UCS in classical conditioning is called a trial. As trials progress, the CR appears with increasing strength and regularity. As can be seen in Figure 5–8a, the amount of saliva elicited by the CS in salivary conditioning increases rapidly and then levels off as trials progress. This curve is called a *negatively accelerated performance curve,* which just means that performance increases rapidly at first and then levels off. Although this is not the only known kind of performance curve, it is the most common one.

Figure 5–8b shows the type of performance curve most often obtained in paired-associate learning. A trial in paired-associate learning is defined as one run through the complete list with the subject trying to recall the correct response word as each stimulus word is presented. As you can see, this curve has the same general shape as the salivary conditioning curve, so it is also negatively accelerated. Figure 5–8c graphs instrumental conditioning data that might be obtained when measuring the speed at which a rat will run down a four-foot runway in order to obtain food located at the end. A trial in this case is defined as one chance to run down the runway to obtain

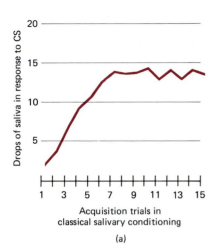

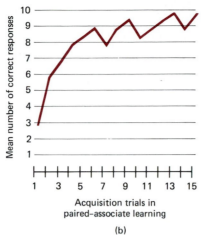

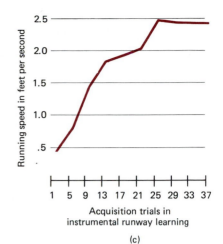

Acquisition trials in
classical salivary conditioning

(a)

Acquisition trials in
paired-associate learning

(b)

Acquisition trials in
instrumental runway learning

(c)

FIGURE 5–8   Acquisition Data Obtained in Classical Conditioning, Paired-associate Learning, and Instrumental Conditioning   *Note that all three performance curves have the negatively accelerated form.*

the food. Here again we note the characteristic shape of the curve. Increases in running speed are large during the early trials, and smaller during later trials. Remember that these are performance curves and not learning curves. As you will recall, performance is affected by motivation as well as by learning.

Extinction

We have just seen that similar acquisition curves can be graphed for classical, instrumental, and verbal conditioning situations. It is also possible to graph similar extinction curves. *Extinction* means a decrease in response strength with repeated nonreinforcements. If food is no longer given to a rat that has learned to press a lever, the animal will gradually cease its lever-pressing behavior. Similarly, if the UCS (such as an air puff) is removed from a classical eyeblink conditioning situation, then presentation of the CS (bell) alone will elicit a CR (blink) for a while, but not forever. The CR will slowly extinguish, or cease to occur, as the CS is presented repeatedly by itself. Although they are beyond the scope of this text, extinction-like effects also have been demonstrated in verbal learning situations (Postman, 1971; Postman & Underwood, 1973).

The extinction effect implies that any learned behavior may be eliminated by the withdrawal of reinforcement. For instance, Williams (1959) argues that temper tantrums are learned behaviors, maintained by the rewarding properties of the attention a parent gives a child when it throws a tantrum. Williams reasons that if social rewards, such as attention and concern are removed, then the behavior should subside, just as a rat will stop lever pressing when the behavior no longer brings food pellets.

Williams's idea was tested on a 21-month-old boy who threw a tantrum every night when his parents attempted to leave his bedroom. In order to avoid the tantrum behavior, the parents had responded by staying with the child until he fell asleep. To curb the tantrums, the child was put on an extinction schedule. That is, the parents gently but firmly left the child's room at bedtime, allowing

FIGURE 5–9 Extinction of
Tantrum Behavior *(After Williams, 1959)*

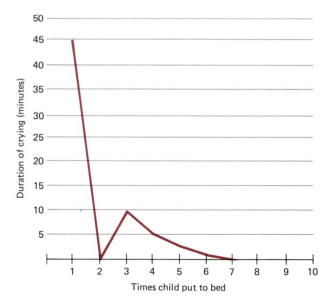

the tantrum to occur without reinforcement. As Figure 5–9 illustrates, the child stormed and raged for 45 minutes the first night before he fell asleep. By the seventh night without reinforcement, the length of the tantrum had dropped to zero. The unwanted behavior had been extinguished through the removal of reinforcement.

Spontaneous Recovery

Spontaneous recovery refers to the fact that an extinguished response will, with rest, recover some of its strength. Pavlov (1927) extinguished a classically conditioned salivary response by repeatedly presenting the CS alone, until no saliva flowed in response to the tone. The dog was then allowed to rest for several hours. During this period no stimuli were presented. At the end of the rest interval, the CS was again presented, and the dog's saliva began to flow again. The extinguished salivary response had recovered some of its strength during the rest interval, as plotted in Figure 5–10. This effect suggests that learning is resilient, and that repeated extinction and

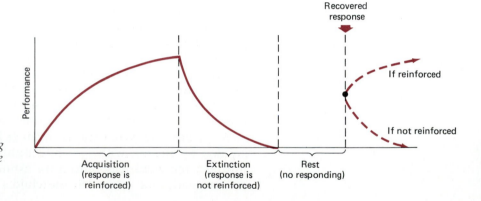

FIGURE 5–10 The Course of Acquisition, Extinction, and Spontaneous Recovery *During a period of rest, the strength of the extinguished response recovers spontaneously.*

FIGURE 5–11 The Resiliency of Learning *Many extinction sessions will be required to completely eliminate a conditioned response. (After Mazur, 1986)*

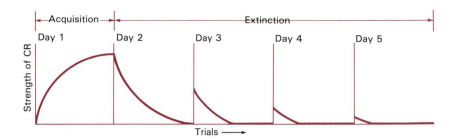

recovery cycles are needed to eliminate a conditioned response completely. In other words, if a response is acquired on Day 1 and extinguished on Day 2, the response, although weakened, will show some recovery by Day 3. If we then extinguish what is left of the response on Day 3, we will still be faced with some recovery on Day 4 and after, as Figure 5–11 shows. Spontaneous recovery has been demonstrated in instrumental conditioning (Lewis,1956) and verbal learning situations (Postman, Stark, & Frazer, 1968), as well as in classical conditioning.

Stimulus Generalization

Stimulus generalization means that if a particular response is conditioned to one stimulus, then similar stimuli will tend to elicit that same response. If an eye blink is classically conditioned to a particular tone, then similar tones will also elicit an eye blink. But if the new tone is too different from the original training stimulus, it will not elicit an eye blink. We have all been trained to stop for red lights while driving. In a foreign country, the red lights may look slightly different, but they will be familiar enough to make us stop. But if we are faced with lights that are too different, such as flashing violet ones three feet off the ground, then we will be less likely to stop. As the similarity between the original training stimulus and the new test stimulus decreases, the probability of the new test stimulus eliciting the response also decreases. This relationship between response probability and stimulus similarity is graphically illustrated by what we call a *stimulus generalization gradient* (Figure 5–12).

Stimulus generalization is an important, widespread effect that can have both positive and negative influences. If a child has learned to be polite at home, then he or she probably will be polite in similar situations, such as a grandparent's home, a friend's home, or a classroom. If the environment is very different from the home-training setting, then the polite behavior is less likely to occur—for instance, when the child is running about the neighborhood with a group of friends. On the negative side, if a child has learned that demanding, tearful behavior is an effective means of getting attention at home, then the same behavior is likely to appear in similar settings elsewhere.

As these examples indicate, stimulus generalization appears in classical and instrumental conditioning situations. It also appears in a variety of verbal conditioning situations. Lang, Geer, and Hnatiow (1963) presented a series of hostile words (*annihilation*) and some

FIGURE 5–12 A Stimulus
Generalization Gradient

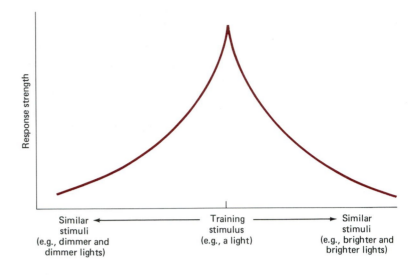

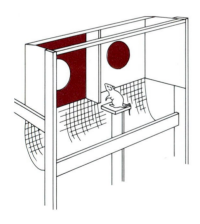

FIGURE 5–13 The Lashley
Jumping Stand *If the rat leaps
against the correct door, it opens
easily, and the rat lands safely on
the table. If the rat leaps against
the incorrect, locked door, it falls
to the net below. The two
differently marked doors are
randomly alternated from one side
to the other to ensure that the rat
does not merely learn a position
discrimination. The rat must
jump, as there is no other way to
escape the mild shock that is
applied.*

neutral ones (*abstract*) to a group of subjects. Each time a hostile word appeared, the subject received a mild shock, which caused a change in the **galvanic skin response (GSR).** The GSR is an index of how easily electricity will travel across the surface of the skin. When we are shocked, we perspire a bit, which allows the electricity to move across the skin more easily. To test stimulus generalization, these investigators then presented other words of varying degrees of hostility. They found that the more hostile the new test words were, the more likely the GSR would be to change. Neutral words caused no change in the GSR. This effect is called **semantic generalization.** When a response is connected to certain words, similar words will then evoke the same response (Maltzman, 1977). The more similar the new words are, the more likely they are to trigger the response.

Discrimination

Discrimination is essentially the opposite process from stimulus generalization. Suppose we place a rat in a Lashley jumping stand, as shown in Figure 5–13. The rat is faced with two distinctly marked doors. One of the two is always unlocked while the other is always locked. The rat is forced to jump by being mildly shocked. If it jumps to the correct door, the door swings open and the rat lands safely on the platform behind. If it jumps at the incorrect door it bumps its nose and falls unhappily into the net. When training begins, the rat is equally likely to jump at either door, falling half the time and landing safely half the time. But as training progresses, the rat begins to discriminate between the safe and unsafe doors. It comes to restrict its response to the stimulus that leads to safety and will no longer respond to the locked door. The rat has formed a discrimination. This is the opposite of stimulus generalization, which is the tendency to respond to similar stimuli in the same manner. The process of discrimination learning can break down, or counteract, the tendency to generalize. Discrimination is accomplished by rewarding a response to one stimulus, and by withholding reinforcement when the animal responds to the alternative stimulus. It is obvious that, without the ability to discriminate among stimuli, our lives would be difficult and dangerous. Imagine what would happen to a young child who had just learned some terrific swear words but had not yet determined when and where they could be used successfully. Imagine what would occur if you did not discriminate between red and green lights, or between brake and gas pedals.

REINFORCEMENT

Delay of Reinforcement

Because the principles of reinforcement have had such a strong impact on the entire field of psychology, it is important to deal with them in some detail. In this section we will discuss four major aspects of reinforcement. The first of these is *delay of reinforcement.* When we reinforce animals or humans for some particular behavior, we need not reinforce them immediately after the response. We can require the subject to wait for the reward. In fact, many of the reinforcements we receive in our everyday lives are delayed. We do not receive a grade in class until the end of the semester, and we do not receive a paycheck until the end of the week or even the month. The question we wish to address is this: what effect will delaying a reinforcement have on performance?

Numerous studies have demonstrated that in many situations, delaying reinforcements will reduce performance substantially but will not eliminate it completely. Figure 5–14a illustrates this basic pattern. If a child picks up his toys in the morning we can reward him immediately or wait until the evening. Apparently he will be more likely to pick up his things in the future if we reward him immediately. Similarly, if we want to train a dog to roll over, it should be praised and petted immediately after rolling over. Praising the animal four hours later will not help it learn at all. But if many responses seem to be most strongly affected by immediate reinforcement, there are situations in which humans can perform very well under conditions of extreme delay. As you know, students will work for years to

FIGURE 5–14 The Relationship Between Performance and Delay of Reinforcement and Between Performance and Amount of Reinforcement

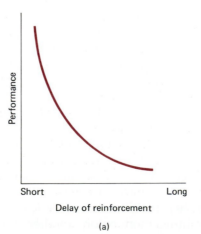

(a)

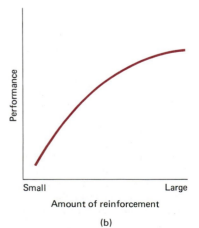

(b)

obtain a college degree. Thus, although immediate rewards often work best, they are not always essential for good performance.

Amount of Reinforcement

As you might imagine, the *amount of reinforcement* we deliver to an animal following its response also affects the way the animal responds. Although the issues are clouded here (see Kling & Schrier, 1971; Young, 1981), it appears that performance will increase as the amount of reinforcement increases, up to a point. Figure 5–14b illustrates this relationship. If you are training your dog, increasing the amount of food or praise you give it will increase its performance level. But as Figure 5–14b reflects, once the amount of reinforcement is quite large, further increases in reinforcement will not result in additional performance gains. Humans as well as animals will increase their performance levels as the amount of reward is increased. The longer and harder you laugh at an eight-year-old's joke, the more likely the child will be to tell you another.

Schedules of Reinforcement

We do not have to reinforce every single response our subject makes. If we are studying a rat's lever-pressing behavior we can reinforce every other response, one response every two minutes, every tenth response, or any other sequence of reinforcements we wish to try. Psychologists have been extremely interested in the effects of these partial reinforcement schedules because *partial reinforcement* is the rule rather than the exception in our everyday lives. Most natural learning occurs under some partial reinforcement pattern; we seldom find that our every response is being reinforced. When a grade-school student sits at her desk practicing handwriting, her teacher does not reinforce every single effort. The teacher may offer praise and encouragement occasionally, but the demands of the class as a whole limit the attention the teacher can give to any one student.

Psychologists know that 100 percent reinforcement is not necessary for learning to occur. The student will learn to write with only occasional encouragement. Much of our everyday activity is maintained by less than 100 percent reinforcement. But how do different patterns of reinforcement affect the rate at which we perform? As it turns out, different patterns of reinforcement have very different effects on performance. Though the number of patterns of reinforcement we can imagine is almost unlimited (Ferster & Skinner, 1957; Williams, 1973), four basic patterns have received the most attention.

Fixed-interval Schedules (FI) In a *fixed-interval schedule,* the subject is reinforced for the first response made after some fixed time interval has elapsed. We might set up our Skinner box to deliver a food pellet only after two minutes have elapsed. The rat can press the bar as often as it wants, but no matter how many times it responds, it will not receive any food until the two minutes have passed and it then makes one more response. The animal then has to wait two minutes more before another response is reinforced, and so on. How would you act in this situation? Would you bang away at the

FIGURE 5–15 Cumulative
Response Records Obtained
under Four Common Schedules
of Reinforcement *In a
cumulative response record we keep
track of the total number of
responses the subject has made
since the beginning of the
experiment. Each time a response
is made, the curve goes up a bit. If
the subject does not respond at all,
the curve becomes a straight,
horizontal line. A cumulative
response record can never go
down. The more vertical it is, the
faster the subject is responding.*
(After Williams, 1973)

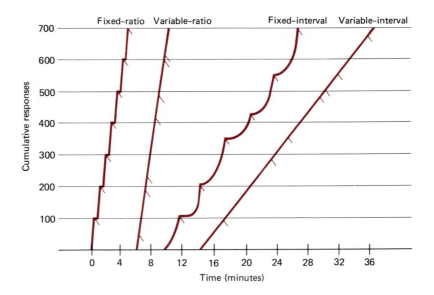

lever furiously? Probably not. More than likely you would soon discover the arrangement and refrain from responding until you estimated that the interval was about to end. There would be little reason
to respond before this time. As the end of the interval approached,
you would probably begin to respond more and more often, until you
actually received the reward. Then you would pause again. This is
just the strategy adopted by the typical white rat. As you can see in
Figure 5–15, the response pattern of an animal under a fixed-interval
schedule will display a **scalloping effect.** What this means is that the
animal will pause after a reinforcement and will begin to speed up its
response rate only as the end of the interval approaches.

If you are expecting an important letter but know that the mail
carrier delivers only at 10:30 A.M. and 3:30 P.M., your mail-checking
behavior may approximate the scalloping effect. You will not check
the mail often at 10:45, just after a delivery, but as 3:30 approaches
you might begin to check more and more frequently. Once the 3:30
delivery has arrived, you are not likely to do much checking until the
next day. Students studying for examinations may also fit this pattern. They will study just prior to an examination (a potentially reinforcing event) and then quit for awhile after the test and resume their
study behavior again before the next test (see also Figure 5–16).

Variable-interval Schedules (VI)   In a *variable-interval schedule,* the
subject is reinforced after variable, or changing, intervals. The subject
might first have to wait 15 seconds before a reinforcement can be
obtained, then 30 seconds for the next reinforcement, then 12 seconds, then 55 seconds, and so on. How would you respond in this
case? Probably you would engage in steady responding (see Figure
5–15). Not knowing how long you will have to wait, you will "check
in" regularly, responding in a steady manner. This schedule does not
produce scalloping, as the subject cannot judge the length of the waiting period. The shorter the average interval, the more responding we
will observe (Leslie, 1981).

FIGURE 5–16 Hypothetical Studying Patterns *Although examination patterns often resemble a fixed-interval schedule and scalloping frequently appears in students' studying behavior, exceptions do occur. Some people study only just before the exam, some keep up a steady rate throughout the semester, and some never study at all. In these cases the individual is probably responding to some alternative set of reinforcers and some other, more powerful, schedule.* (After Houston, 1986)

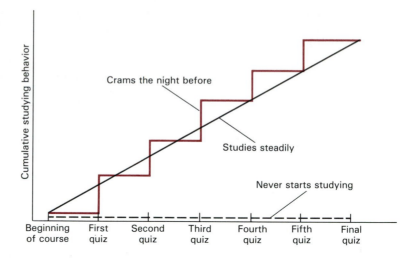

This is the type of behavior you would display if your mail carrier delivered twice a day, but you never knew when the next delivery might be. You would be mail-checking all day long.

Fixed-ratio Schedules (FR)   In a **fixed-ratio schedule,** the subject must make a certain number of responses before reinforcement is delivered (see Figure 5–15). In an FR-8 schedule a rat must press the lever eight times to receive a single pellet. If you know waiting will not help, and you know that you must make a certain number of responses before any reinforcement will be received, how would you respond? Clearly you would respond at a high rate, which is just what a rat or a pigeon will do. When factory workers were required to process a certain number of units (for instance, sew a given number of shirts or assemble a certain number of toasters) for a certain amount of pay, they were in the grip of an FR schedule. The more units they processed, the bigger their paycheck. This is an extremely efficient, if perhaps unfair, way to pull the maximum amount of work from a person. It is not surprising that labor unions have fought against this "piecework" method of paying employees, especially when the pay rates were so low that the worker had to perform at an extremely high rate to earn a living wage.

Variable-ratio Schedules (VR)   In a **variable-ratio schedule,** the ratio varies as the number of responses the subject must make changes from reinforcement to reinforcement. The subject may be required to make ten responses for the first reward, then five for the next, then four, and so on. This schedule also produces high response rates (see Figure 5–15). Slot machines are programmed according to VR schedules. They pay off after variable numbers of coins have been put into them. The tourist pumping endless quarters into a Las Vegas slot machine is innocently responding in accordance with a VR schedule.

Partial Reinforcement and the Extinction Effect

One of the most interesting effects of partial reinforcement (including FI, VI, FR, and VR schedules) has to do with extinction. Extinction following partial reinforcement schedules occurs more slowly than extinction following 100 percent or continuous reinforcement. In other words, if a subject has been reinforced every time it has made a response, then when the reinforcement is no longer delivered, the subject will stop responding (extinguish) relatively quickly. But if the subject has been partially reinforced and reinforcement is then removed completely, extinction will occur relatively slowly. The subject will continue to respond for quite a long time, even though it no longer receives any reinforcement at all. It seems that partial reinforcement accustoms subjects to the absence of reward, and so they are not so easily frustrated or discouraged by its total absence during extinction.

The Reinforcement Contrast Effects

Suppose you had a summer job selling soap door to door. Your employer said that for every ten boxes of soap you sold you would receive $1.00. So you set about the task of selling soap, and as time passes you become better and better at it. Then one day your employer tells you that you will no longer receive $1.00 for every ten boxes you sell; the rate has now been reduced to $.50 per ten boxes. What will happen to your performance? You might be tempted to quit. At any rate, you are not too happy and your performance suffers. The *negative reinforcement contrast effect* refers to the fact that your performance may temporarily drop *below* the level at which you would have performed if you had been receiving $.50 per ten boxes right from the start of the job (Peters & McHose, 1974). Temporarily you are so depressed that you do not even work as hard as you would have if $.50 had been the beginning rate (see Figure 5–17).

A *positive reinforcement contrast effect* would be demonstrated if the rate was suddenly shifted from $.50 to $1.00 and your performance temporarily jumped *above* the level at which it would have been had you received $1.00 from the beginning (see Figure 5–17).

FIGURE 5–17 Idealized Positive and Negative Reinforcement Contrast Effects *During the preshift phase, one group receives a large amount of reinforcement ($1.00), whereas the other receives a small amount ($.50). The amounts given to the two groups are then reversed during the postshift phase, yielding the contrast effects.*

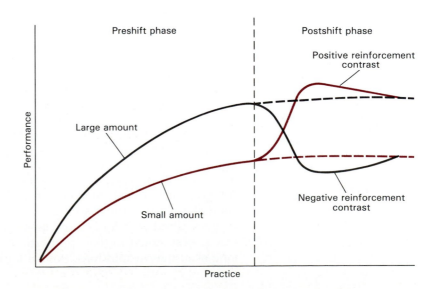

Secondary Reinforcement

Consider the following experiment. A rat is trained to press a lever. Each time the food pellet is delivered a distinct tone is sounded. After 150 trials the rat is removed from the Skinner box and placed in a new apparatus. In this situation, each time the rat climbs up a little block of wood the same tone used in the earlier situation is sounded. No food is ever delivered, but over a series of trials, the rat begins to climb the block of wood more and more frequently. It is being reinforced by the tone. The tone is what we call a *secondary reinforcer* or a *conditioned reinforcer.* A secondary reinforcer is a neutral stimulus that, through repeated pairings with a primary reinforcer, such as food, acquires the capacity to reinforce. Before the initial pairing of the tone and the food the tone had no reinforcing properties at all. After repeated pairings it did.

This simple demonstration is extremely important, for much of our own learning is reinforced with secondary rather than primary reinforcers. When we learn to do a new job, we are rewarded with rectangular pieces of green paper. Certainly there is nothing innately reinforcing about these pieces of paper. But money has become a powerful secondary reinforcer in our lives through repeated pairings with more basic reinforcers such as food, shelter, comfort, excitement, avoidance of pain, and so on. Money is one of the most obvious examples of secondary reinforcement in our everyday lives. See if you can think of some others before you read on. Diplomas, trophies, fancy clothes, gold, and social compliments such as "Nice going!" and "Good job!" may all represent secondary reinforcers. It seems that our behavior may be as strongly influenced by secondary reinforcers as it is by primary reinforcers.

Many psychologists believe secondary reinforcers are established through a process of classical conditioning. If a neutral stimulus such as light (CS) is repeatedly paired with a primary reinforcer such as food (UCS), then our positive reactions to the food become classically conditioned to the light. In the future, the previously neutral light will elicit all sorts of positively conditioned reactions (Bersh, 1951). Think about money as a CS and the many UCSs it is paired with in your life. Every time you buy something you are, according to this interpretation, undergoing a classical conditioning trial where the CS (money) is being paired with a UCS (the object or service purchased). With all this conditioning, no wonder money is a powerful secondary reinforcer.

TRANSFER OF TRAINING

When we learn something we do not learn it in a vacuum. We learn it in the context of our prior learning, which may either help us or hinder us with the new task. When our previous learning assists us in a new task we call it *positive transfer.* Ski instruction often involves the graduated length method, or GLM. New skiers begin with very short skis because these are the easiest to use. As their skills improve, they are fitted with longer and longer skis until they reach the length that is best suited to their proportions. Had they started learning on long skis, they would have done a lot more crashing than is customary in the GLM. Similarly, children learn math in a manner that best fosters positive transfer. Grade schoolers do not hear things like, "Today we will learn long division and then next week I will show you how to subtract." Instead, teachers begin with the simplest concepts that will help their students master the next level of difficulty.

Negative transfer occurs whenever prior learning interferes with our attempts to master a new task. When Americans go to England they have trouble learning to drive on the left side of the road, because their driving experience in the United States transfers negatively to the new task.

LEARNING BY OBSERVING MODELS

Our discussion to this point has assumed that some of what we learn occurs because of the consequences of our actions. We do not touch fire because we have touched it in the past and been burned. We do eat oranges because we have eaten them in the past and been reinforced by the sweet taste. But if the only way we could learn was to act and then wait for the consequences, we would not survive very long. We would jump off cliffs, eat poisonous plants, and take baby lions away from their mothers. Yet somehow we survive, and we often do it by observing and imitating the behavior of other people—the behavior of *models*. In this way, we can acquire the skills and knowledge of others without actually having to go through all the complex learning steps ourselves. Modeling is a shortcut to knowledge. We do not have to read a book to learn how to peel a banana before eating it; we can learn to do it by watching others.

Many different kinds of behaviors are learned by watching models. Bandura (1969, 1977), one of the leading researchers in this area, describes three classes of behavior that can be modeled.

1. *Observationally learned behavior.* In the case of an observationally learned behavior, the observer does something that he or she

"Hello, Singapore!" When the phone bill comes, this youngster's parents will be quite impressed with the power of observational learning.

has never done before after watching a model do it and be rewarded for doing it. For example, a child might eat a strange new food after watching her mother eat it and smile.

2. *Inhibited behavior.* Sometimes an already learned behavior is inhibited, or made less likely to occur, if the observer sees a model engaging in that behavior and being punished for it. A child usually will stop being disorderly in the classroom if a classmate is punished for the same behavior.

3. *Disinhibited behavior.* The observer sees a model getting away with some behavior that the observer has known how to do but has been afraid to do. For example, Bandura has shown that if a model gets away with aggressive behavior, then the observer probably will also aggress in a similar situation.

Bandura (1977) argues that there are four distinct processes necessary for the occurrence of modeled behavior. First, the observer must *attend* to the model. If you are not watching the model you cannot learn anything from him. Obviously, your ability to learn from models will depend on what kinds of models are available in your environment. If most of the friends of a 12-year-old boy use drugs, then he is more likely to model his behavior after them than after nonusers. Second, the observer must *remember* what the model does. If he does not remember it, then he cannot reproduce the act. Even if the 12-year-old has seen his friends roll a marijuana cigarette, he cannot duplicate that behavior unless he remembers how to do it. Third, the observer must be *physically able* to enact the modeled behavior. If the boy has seen his friends roll a cigarette, and remembers how to do it, he must also be able to perform the coordinated hand movements necessary to complete the act. Fourth, for a truly modeled behavior to emerge, the observer must be *motivated* to engage in that behavior. The boy must want to roll a cigarette before the act will occur. If he sees the consequences of the act as undesirable (as we hope he will), then he will not model his behavior after the behavior of his friends, even though he has paid attention to their behavior, remembers it, and is able to do it.

LATENT LEARNING

In a typical *latent learning* study, rats are given plenty of free time to wander about in a maze. They are not rewarded for making correct responses; they are not rewarded at all during this phase of the experiment (Seward, 1949). Control animals are not given any of this free time to wander through the maze. Then both control and experimental animals are rewarded for making correct responses in the maze. The question is this: will the experimental animals have learned anything from their "free time" in the maze even though they received no reward for making responses? The answer appears to be yes. Experimental animals learned the maze faster under conditions of reward than did the control animals.

Although this effect is stable enough, the interpretation of latent learning is controversial. Some have argued that latent learning proves that learning can occur in the absence of reward. Others have argued that movements in the maze may have been reinforced by subtle rewards beyond the control of the experimenter, such as the satisfaction of curiosity, the satisfaction of a need to exercise, or a need to explore. Thus, although latent learning does suggest that learning can occur without the reinforcement of specific responses, not all psychologists are convinced that this is true.

BIOLOGICAL LIMITS ON LEARNING

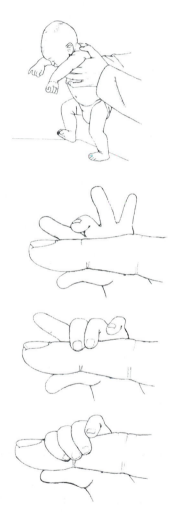

FIGURE 5–18 Prepared Human Behaviors *Newborn infants, when held erect, will engage in many of the movements associated with walking. The infant's hand-grasping behavior is extremely prepared, perhaps requiring no learning at all. The middle fingers are closed first and the thumb last.*

Taste Aversion

Not all animals are equally ready to learn all things. Biology sets limits on what we, and other species, can learn. Garcia and Rusiniak (1979) found that if a rat ingests a distinctive flavor, such as saccharin, at the same time it is X-irradiated, then the rat will associate that flavor with the illness caused by the radiation. The rat will avoid that flavor in the future. This effect is called conditioned *taste aversion*. But if an odor rather than a flavor is paired with X-irradiation, the rat will *not* learn to avoid that odor. For some reason, rats can associate flavors with illness but not odors. Similarly, the same rat will have trouble associating noises or lights with illness but will always associate flavors. It makes sense in terms of natural selection: animals that associate flavors with illness are more likely to survive because most illnesses are caused by flavored foods, not bright lights. Through natural selection, rats that are neurally wired to associate flavors with illness are the kinds that have survived.

Preparedness

Preparedness refers to the fact that many species seem quite ready to learn certain things but not at all ready to learn others (Seligman, 1975). You can teach a rat to press a bar or leap a barrier in order to obtain food, but if you try to teach that same rat to scratch itself for that same food you will be in the lab all night. Cats will learn to escape by pulling or pushing, but if you require them to lick in order to escape they will not do well at all. Humans seem extremely eager to do things like walk, talk, and grip with their hands (see Figure 5–18). We are able to learn these highly complex behaviors without special training. But if you have ever tried to teach small children to share, you will understand that some human behaviors are difficult to establish (McCarthy & Houston, 1980).

Species Specific Defense Reactions

Species specific defense reactions (SSDRs) are innate, automatic behaviors, such as running, flying, or abruptly remaining motionless, that occur when a sudden or novel stimulus appears. If you flash a piece of colored cloth at a pigeon, it will fly. If you show a gazelle a cardboard cow, it will flee. Bolles (Bolles, 1975; Bolles, Hayward, & Crandall, 1981) argues that SSDRs are very easily learned in new situations because they are already built into the animal's response repertoire. If an animal sees something novel or startling it will go into its SSDR immediately, and such innate responses are readily associated with a new frightening stimulus. But responses such as licking are not innate ways of responding to frightening stimuli and are thus much less likely to be associated with the frightening stimulus. SSDRs may account for some apparent limits on learning, particularly those on escape and avoidance learning observed in laboratory tests with various species.

Instinctive Drift

The biological limits on learning are further illuminated by the concept of *instinctive drift* (Breland & Breland, 1966). The Brelands trained a raccoon to put coins in a small box. Each time the raccoon put a coin in the box it was given food, and the response was quickly learned. But then the Brelands noticed that the raccoon was spending more and more time rubbing the coins together and dipping them into the empty box before releasing them. Apparently the raccoon's natural food washing behavior was creeping into the situation, even though the delay caused by "washing" actually meant the animal had to wait longer for its food. In time, the raccoon drifted away from its learned behavior and toward its instinctive behavior. Thus biological limits on learning are twofold: not only are we limited in what we can learn easily, but what we do learn can be diluted by instinctive or innate urges as well.

Ethology

That some behaviors are completely innate, some totally learned, and some a mixture of learned and innate factors seems to be a reasonable assumption. The precise manner in which innate and learned elements interact, however, remains a mystery.

Ethology, championed by such famous European researchers as Konrad Lorenz and Nikolaas Tinbergen, is a subdivision of biology that is centrally concerned with the relationship between behavior and the environment. Strictly speaking, ethology is the scientific and objective study of animal behavior and it is within this discipline that a belief in the interaction of learned and innate factors is most heavily investigated and defended. Six important ethological concepts are outlined below that provide an indication of the way that these specialized biologists think about the intertwining of learned and innate factors.

Reaction-specific Energy   One of the main concepts used by ethologists to account for innate behavior involves the term *reaction-specific energy*. Tinbergen (1952) has observed that the male stickleback fish will attack and drive off other males intruding into its territory but will not attack females. The term *reaction-specific energy* refers to the idea that there is a pool, or source, of energy that exists only for the occurrence of a particular behavior (the stickleback's attack behavior, for example).

Innate Releasing Mechanism   Using the stickleback as an example once again, we observe that this fish does not attack constantly but attacks only under certain conditions. To account for this fact ethologists speak of an innate releasing mechanism. One way to think of this factor is as a plug in a basin. The *innate releasing mechanism* stops up and contains energy that would otherwise be expressed as attack behavior.

Sign Stimulus　A ***sign stimulus*** is the stimulus that releases the re-action-specific energy. When an organism perceives the sign stimulus, the plug is pulled and the energy that exists only for a particular behavior is released. Sign stimuli tend to be fairly simple, but they have an enormous impact on the animal. The sign stimulus that releases stickleback attack behavior is the red belly of the intruding male. No other stimulus will trigger the same behavior. In the case of the stickleback, perfect replicas of male intruders without red bellies are ignored, but very unrealistic replicas *with* red bellies are attacked fiercely. Sign stimuli are assumed to innately open the flood gates without being dependent on learning.

Fixed Action Pattern　The stereotyped attack behavior released by the sign stimulus is called a ***fixed action pattern.*** When the stickleback sees a red belly, it attacks and drives the intruder away irregardless of anything else that may be occurring in its environment.

Vacuum Reactions　If a male stickleback fish has not aggressed for a long period of time (because it has not seen a red belly), it will some-times attack anyway. It may attack a stimulus that bears only a minor resemblance to the normal sign stimulus. In fact, if enough time has passed without the appearance of the normal sign stimulus, the fish may attack just about anything. This behavior, called a ***vacuum reaction,*** is interpreted as the result of the fact that the reaction-specific energy has built to the point at which it can no longer be contained and it blows out the cork without there having been a sign stimulus.

Supernormal Stimuli　Given a choice between its own egg and a larger egg, some birds, such as the oyster catcher, will incubate the larger egg (see Figure 5–19). Given a choice between its own brown-spotted egg and a black-spotted egg, some birds, such as plovers, will choose the ***supernormal stimulus.*** In other words, these behaviors seem to be strictly controlled by the nature of the sign stimulus.

With these ethological concepts we end our discussion of biological limits on learning. It should be understood that all of the types of learning considered earlier in this chapter are subject to biological constraints, even if these constraints have not yet been worked out in detail.

In the next chapter, we shift our attention to the study of memory. Specifically, we will focus on the investigation of what happens to learned information after we stop rehearsing it; we will consider what psychologists have discovered about the processes of forgetting.

FIGURE 5–19　Supernormal Stimuli　*An oyster catcher attempts to incubate a supernormal egg. (After Mazur, 1986)*

SUMMARY

1. Learning may be defined as a relatively permanent change in behavior potentiality that occurs as a result of reinforced practice. This definition excludes behavior changes due to motivational fluctuations, maturation, aging, disease, and physiological damage. Al-

though controversial, it suggests that reinforcement is necessary for learning to occur.

2. Pavlov, a Russian physiologist, made classical conditioning famous.

3. In classical conditioning, an unconditioned stimulus (UCS), which elicits an unconditioned response (UCR), is paired with a neutral conditioned stimulus (CS). Through repeated pairings the CS acquires the ability to elicit a conditioned response (CR) that is similar to the UCR.

4. The temporal arrangement of the CS and UCS may be varied. Simultaneous, delayed, backward, and trace conditioning procedures are among the common arrangements.

5. A wide variety of classical conditioning situations are known including, among others, eyelid, planaria, human emotional conditioning, and language learning.

6. In instrumental reward training the subject is rewarded if it makes a particular response. In avoidance training the subject is punished if it fails to make a particular response.

7. Flooding is a technique used to eliminate avoidance behavior.

8. Learned helplessness refers to the fact that, following repeated, unavoidable shock, an animal may fail to learn a simple avoidance response. In punishment training the subject is punished if it makes a particular response.

9. Punishment is an extremely controversial technique.

10. Shaping is a technique in which closer and closer approximations to a desired response are reinforced.

11. The traditional concept is that classical conditioning involves only involuntary responses, while instrumental conditioning involves only voluntary responses. This idea has been challenged by Neal Miller, who has demonstrated that so-called involuntary responses, such as heart rate and blood pressure, can be instrumentally conditioned.

12. The notion that classical conditioning does not involve reinforcement, while instrumental conditioning does, has also been challenged.

13. In free recall, the subject is presented a list of words and asked to recall them in any order. This task allows us to examine organizational activities. In serial learning, which is designed to study sequential learning, the subject must learn the order of the items as well as the items themselves. In paired-associate learning, the subject is required to associate pairs of items.

14. Although classical, instrumental, and verbal conditioning procedures appear to be quite different, they do possess many common characteristics.

15. Acquisition, or the increase in response strength with repeated reinforcements, most often progresses in a negatively accelerated fashion.

16. Extinction refers to a decrease in response strength with repeated nonreinforcements.

17. Spontaneous recovery means that an extinguished response will, with rest, recover some of its strength.

18. Stimulus generalization means that if a particular response is connected to a given stimulus, then similar stimuli will tend to elicit that same response. The greater the similarity, the greater the generalization.

19. In discrimination learning, the subject comes to restrict his response to one stimulus because a response to that stimulus has been reinforced, while responses to other stimuli have not.

20. If reinforcements are delayed following a response, then performance will decrease. If the amount of reinforcement delivered following a response is increased, then performance will increase, up to a point.

21. In a fixed-interval schedule of reinforcement, the subject is reinforced for the first response after a given time interval has elapsed. This produces the scalloping effect. In a variable-interval schedule, the time interval changes from reinforcement to reinforcement, producing a steady response rate. In fixed-ratio schedules, the subject must make a fixed number of responses before a reinforcement is delivered. In a variable-ratio schedule, the number of required responses varies. Both ratio schedules produce high response rates.

22. Extinction following partial reinforcement occurs more slowly than extinction following continuous reinforcement.

23. The reinforcement contrast effect illustrates the complexity of reinforcement.

24. A secondary reinforcer (such as money) is a neutral stimulus that, through repeated pairings with a primary reinforcer, such as food, acquires reinforcing properties of its own.

25. Secondary reinforcers may be acquired through a process of classical conditioning.

26. Positive transfer occurs when prior learning helps to make present learning quicker or easier. Negative transfer is said to occur when prior learning hinders present learning.

27. Sometimes we learn by observing and imitating the behavior of models without actually going through all the complex learning steps ourselves. We can learn new behaviors this way, or inhibit or disinhibit old ones.

28. For modeled behavior to occur, the person must attend, remember, be able to act, and be motivated to act.

29. Latent learning is sometimes interpreted as evidence for learning in the absence of reinforcement.

30. Biology sets limits on what we can and cannot learn. Taste aversion serves as an example of this variation in preparedness.

31. Species specific defense reactions (SSDRs) are innate, automatic responses to sudden or novel stimuli that can easily be associated with new frightening stimuli.

32. Instinctive drift refers to the fact that behavior tends to drift away from learned behavior and toward instinctual behavior.

33. Ethologists study behavior in relationship to the environment and consider innate behavior to be crucial and widespread.

34. Ethologists have developed concepts such as reaction-specific energy, innate releasing mechanisms, sign stimuli, fixed action patterns, vacuum reactions, and supernormal stimuli.

KEY TERMS

acquisition

amount of reinforcement

avoidance training

backward classical conditioning

biofeedback

classical conditioning

cluster

conditioned reinforcer

conditioned response (CR)

conditioned stimulus (CS)

delay of reinforcement

delayed classical conditioning

discrimination

disinhibited behavior

ethology

extinction

fixed action pattern

fixed-interval schedule

fixed-ratio schedule

flooding

free recall task

galvanic skin response (GSR)

inhibited behavior

innate releasing mechanism

instinctive drift

instrumental conditioning

latent learning

learned helplessness

learning

models

negative contrast effect

negative reinforcer

negative transfer

negatively accelerated performance curve

observationally learned behavior

operant conditioning

paired-associate learning tasks

partial reinforcement

Pavlovian conditioning

positive contrast effect

positive reinforcer

positive transfer

preparedness

punisher

punishment training

reaction-specific energy

respondent conditioning

reward training

scalloping effect

secondary reinforcer

semantic generalization

serial learning tasks

shaping

sign stimulus

simultaneous classical conditioning

species specific defense reaction (SSDR)

spontaneous recovery

stimulus generalization

stimulus generalization gradient

supernormal stimuli

taste aversion

trace classical conditioning

unconditioned response (UCR)

unconditioned stimulus (UCS)

vacuum reaction

variable-interval schedule

variable-ratio schedule

verbal conditioning

ADDITIONAL READING

Domjan, M., & Burkhard, B. (1986) *The principles of learning and behavior* (2nd ed.). Monterey, CA: Brooks/Cole.
This resource offers an in-depth survey of conditioning literature with an emphasis on animal research.

Grasha, A. F. (1983) *Practical applications of psychology* (2nd ed.). Boston: Little Brown.
This text contains good sections on the application of the principles of learning in everyday life.

Houston, J. P. (1986) *Fundamentals of learning and memory* (3rd ed.). New York: Harcourt Brace Jovanovich.
This volume includes a good discussion of many of the principles that are common to both animal and human learning.

Mazur, J. E. (1986) *Learning and behavior.* Englewood Cliffs, NJ: Prentice-Hall.
This text offers a survey of the basic principles of conditioning.

6 Memory

What do we know about memory and forgetting? Intuitively, we are all aware that learning is a relatively difficult task, while forgetting is painfully easy. As you study for the examinations in this course, you will probably spend many hours attempting to commit all the required information to memory. Unfortunately, you may find that your efforts will be somewhat frustrated. You are likely to forget much of the information quickly, particularly after the examination. Learning requires work, while forgetting seems effortless.

The fact is that normal forgetting is more drastic than many people suppose, as you can see for yourself by considering the following experiment. Suppose you memorize a list of "nonsense syllables," such as WUZ, JAT, CIS, BIL, LEM, RAK, TUR, NOP, FEX, ZEP, and GOW. You practice until you can recite them on demand. Then you cease practice, and we test your ability to recall the items over several minutes, hours, and days. What do you think will happen? Figure 6–1 shows the kind of recall results we can expect. The amount you remember drops dramatically at first and then begins to level off after two or three days. This rapid drop represents a lot of forgetting for the creature that is supposed to be tops in the animal kingdom. Of course, this *forgetting curve* may be higher or lower, depending on the difficulty of the list, but for nonsense syllables, forgetting is quite dramatic. Many kinds of forgetting curves drop rapidly at first and then level off, as Ebbinghaus demonstrated a century ago (1885/1913).

THE MEANING OF MEMORY

When psychologists study memory, they focus on what happens to learned associations, or stored information, *after* practice ceases. If we examine college students' studying behavior and the rate at which they learn and store information, we are primarily concerned with learning, or acquisition. But if we concentrate on what happens to that stored information *after* the students have finished studying, then we are primarily concerned with memory, or retention. After

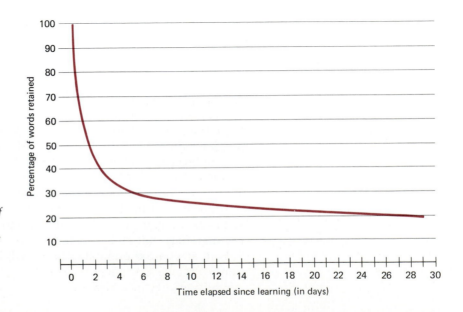

FIGURE 6–1 A Typical Forgetting Curve *After a list of nonsense syllables is learned, the percentage of the items that can be recalled drops rapidly and then levels off as the time between learning and test of memory increases.*

information is stored through practice, and practice has ceased, what happens to that stored information? Does it remain within us for the rest of our lives? Does it fade away? What factors will affect the rate at which it is lost? If we ask these kinds of questions, we are studying memory.

THREE MEASURES OF MEMORY

Recall

Given that we know that a substantial amount of forgetting occurs in a regular manner, what can be said about the available methods of *measuring* retention? Psychologists usually identify three methods. The first of these is the *recall* method. In a recall task the subject is required to reproduce the entire stored item. In effect, the subject is asked, "What is the item?" If you were asked the name of this textbook and were required to provide the exact title, without looking, you would be engaging in a recall test. If you were asked the name of the river that runs between Albany, New York, and New York City, you would be engaging in a recall test.

Recall tests are prominent in the field of verbal learning. They are often used in paired-associate situations where the subject, after some time interval ranging from seconds to weeks, is asked to recall one member when shown the other member of each pair (Kausler, 1974). When people talk about remembering something, they usually mean recalling something from memory. But retention also involves recognition and relearning.

Recognition

In a *recognition* test the subject is asked, "Is this the item?" (Underwood, 1972). If you were given EAST RIVER, ERIE CANAL, and HUDSON RIVER and asked to identify the body of water that runs between Albany and New York City, you would be engaging in a recognition test. Multiple-choice examinations are recognition tests. Responding to a red light is a recognition test. There are many kinds of recognition tests, both in and out of the laboratory, but all of them involve the ability to recognize a presented item as being correct, rather than having to recall it.

Relearning

A third means of measuring retention is called the *relearning* technique. First, a subject is required to learn a set of materials. The number of trials needed to master the task is carefully noted. Then, at some later time, the subject is required to relearn the same materials. If the subject has retained anything at all, relearning should be accomplished in fewer trials than were required for original learning. The greater the savings in relearning trials, the greater the retention has been. If your final examination covers materials already tested on the midterm, you probably will have to go back and relearn those early materials. But you probably will not have to spend as much time on them as you did originally; there will be a savings.

A teacher may estimate retention—measuring recall, recognition, or relearning—using a simple set of flashcards.

Recognition versus Recall

Because recall and recognition are by far the most widely used of the three measures of retention, we will spend a little time considering the differences between them. The first important fact to note is that recognition is almost always easier than recall. This is not surprising, is it? Our everyday experiences suggest that our ability to recognize far exceeds our ability to recall. Try a simple example. Name the seven dwarfs. Can you recall all seven? Perhaps not. But even though you might miss one or two in your recall efforts, you would never fail to recognize them all.[1] Try another example. Can you name the fifty states? Probably not, but you would surely recognize them all.

Nickerson and Adams (1979) revealed another gap between recognition and recall when they asked people to draw pennies in empty circles (see Figure 6–2). While none of us would fail to recognize a penny, almost none of us can recall one with much accuracy either. Ninety-five percent of Nickerson and Adams's subjects failed to recall the word "liberty" or to place it correctly. Half of the subjects even located Lincoln's head incorrectly. In other words, recall of the components of a common, always-recognized object was less than impressive.

Given that recognition is usually easier than recall (although not always—see Watkins & Tulving, 1975), an important question has occurred to psychologists. Does the difference between the two measures reflect some important aspect of the overall memory system, or is one measure simply easier or more sensitive than the other?

There have been two answers to this question. The traditional answer is that the recognition measure is simply more sensitive than

---

[1] Dopey, Sleepy, Happy, Grumpy, Doc, Sneezy, and Bashful.

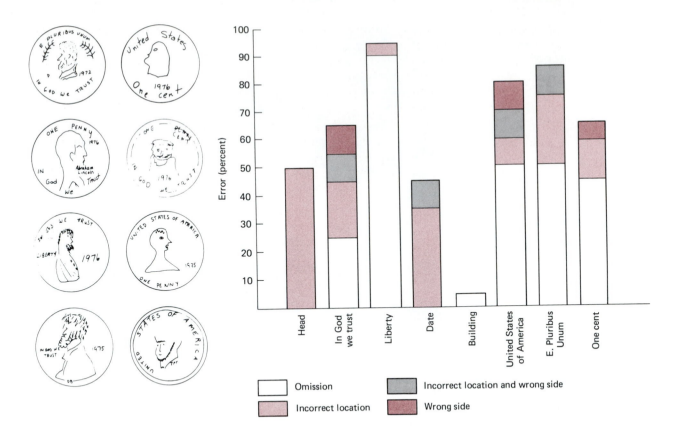

FIGURE 6–2 Types of Errors Produced During Recall of a Penny (After Nickerson & Adams, 1979)

the recall technique. Memorized items are assumed to differ in strength; that is, some items are more strongly memorized than others. Strong memories are recalled with little trouble. Other, weaker items are assumed to be strong enough to be recognized but not strong enough to be recalled. For instance, you might have trouble recalling the name of an Indian group that begins with A, but you will probably recognize Arapaho. According to this view, the difference between recognition and recall is just a matter of degree; it does not reflect anything important about the overall memory process (Tulving & Thomson, 1971).

The opposing view states that the recall and recognition processes are fundamentally different and that this difference tells us something important about the overall memory system. No one is convinced that he knows exactly what the difference is (Murdock, 1974), but some psychologists suggest that recall involves *more* processes than recognition. In recall, we must do two things: we must search for stored information and then reproduce it correctly. In recognition, all we have to do is identify stored information when it is presented to us. In short, psychologists are still trying to identify and spell out the importance of the difference between recall and recognition. They are convinced there is a difference, but they do not yet know just what that difference means (Anderson & Bower, 1974; Begg, 1979; Rubin & Kontis, 1983; Schmidt, 1983).

THREE COMPONENTS OF THE MEMORY SYSTEM

Most psychologists, regardless of their theoretical stance, divide the overall memory system into three basic components or processes. The three are usually referred to as *encoding*, *storage*, and *retrieval.* These three components are always used, whether you are trying to remember one item or a long list. You use each component whether you are trying to remember the important points in a chapter for your next history exam or whether you are merely trying to remember a phone number long enough to dial it. A great deal of research is being conducted to analyze how each component of memory works (or fails to work). Let us deal with them one at a time.

ENCODING

Encoding is the process by which we put information into storage, or commit it to memory. All of our efforts to establish some kind of internal representation, or memory, for some external stimuli—such as a list of words—are referred to as encoding. As it turns out, the encoding process may involve many diverse and complicated procedures. Let us look at several examples.

Encoding Demands

Suppose you are studying for a multiple-choice examination in a course on the history of the South Pacific. You are quite certain that you will be required to recognize such names as WICKLIFFE BAY, LAKE SENTANI, RAROTONGA, and MILINGIMBI. How would you go about studying these materials so that you would be able to recognize them on a multiple-choice exam? Would you memorize them completely? Not necessarily. It would be sufficient to commit them to memory just enough to enable you to recognize them. For instance, you might encode them as a bay beginning with WICK, a lake beginning with SENT, something ending in TONGA, and a place beginning with MILIN. With this amount of information you would be able to recognize the items. But what would you do if you knew you would be required to recall these same items in a short-answer test? In this type of examination the encoding just described would not suffice. You would need to encode entire items somehow. If you had encoded for recognition, your performance on a recall test might be very poor. The point is that the way we encode information often depends on the nature of the task at hand. If we know what will be expected of us, we may encode information in ways that will maximize our performance.

Chunking

Suppose we are presented the letters R-B-O-G-S-M-N-A-E-O, one at a time, and are then asked to recall them immediately. We may have trouble with this task. But if we rearrange these ten letters to spell BOOMERANGS, we will have no trouble at all remembering them. In fact, we will have "room left over" to store additional information. The encoding process of making one response (BOOMERANGS) out of many responses (the letters R-B-O-G-S-M-N-A-E-O) has been called *chunking* by George Miller (1956). Miller argues that our ability to recall a series of items presented once (such as a series of letters, words, or numbers) is limited to a relatively small number of chunks, but the amount of information contained in each chunk may vary. According to Miller, memory is limited to seven chunks plus or minus two (7 ± 2). R-B-O-G-S-M-N-A-E-O represents ten chunks of information. If left in this form this is about all we can be expected to store at one time. BOOMERANGS represents these ten individual elements recombined or encoded as a single chunk. When the ten letters are encoded as a single chunk, we have not exhausted our immediate memory capacity and can remember additional information.

By encoding many bits of information into a single chunk we can greatly expand the capacity of our immediate memory. Try to read through the following sequence once and then attempt to recall all the letters: TZEATRLNIOEGIBRENHALPE. Pretty tough, isn't it? But if we rearrange these letters into LION, TIGER, ELEPHANT, and ZEBRA, we can remember all 22 letters and have plenty of room left to remember additional items. It is as easy to remember these four animals (four chunks) as it is to remember GHPC (also four chunks), but the sequence of animals contains far more information (22 letters versus 4 letters). Memory is limited by the number of chunks and not by the amount of information contained in those chunks.

Visual versus Verbal Encoding

Information can be encoded verbally, visually, or both verbally and visually. If you are trying to remember ''ice-cream cone'' you can do it by remembering the three words ICE-CREAM CONE, or by developing a visual image of an ice-cream cone. Think of a triple decker: vanilla, chocolate, and jamoca almond fudge ripple; sugar cone; chocolate sprinkles on top. When someone asks you to remember this item, you can search for the stored words, or the visual image, or both. We can use both verbal and visual techniques for remembering

Children may encode television messages verbally, visually, or both verbally and visually.

the same item because encoding is flexible. Information may be committed to memory in many different forms (see Best, 1986).

Mental Rotation

It is all well and good to acknowledge that we experience these visual images on some subjective level, but is there any good, solid experimental evidence for their existence? One source of experimental support comes from the study of *mental rotation.* Suppose you must decide if the pairs of objects in Figure 6–3 are the same. How would you do it? Experimental evidence suggests that you might rotate one object mentally until it matched or failed to match the image of the other object. Shepard and Metzler (1971) asked subjects to pull one lever if they judged the objects to be the same and a different lever if they believed the objects were different. Measurements were made of how long it took the subjects to make these decisions.

The critical aspect of the situation was that the members of the pairs differed in orientation from zero to 180 degrees (see a, b, and c in Figure 6–3). Shepard and Metzler found that the more two figures

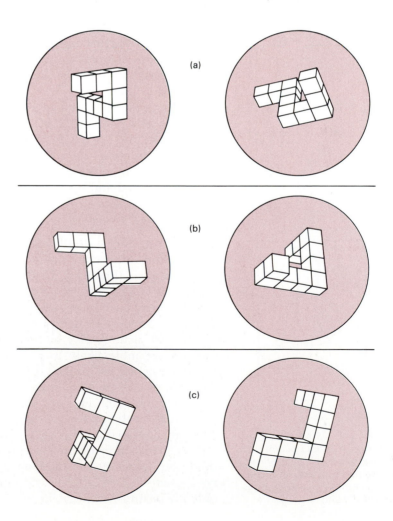

FIGURE 6–3 Mental Rotation—
Patterns Differing in Orientation
Are the members of each pair the
same or different? (After Shepard &
Metzler, 1971)

differed in orientation, the longer it took subjects to make a judgement. It was as though each subject were mentally rotating the figures. This interpretation was bolstered by the fact that that is exactly what subjects reported doing when they were questioned after the experiment. Mental rotation studies, along with other types of data, have convinced many psychologists that mental images do exist.

What Is an Image? "Pictures" versus Propositions

What exactly are these visual images that we all know, but which are so difficult to pin down? There are two major interpretations of images (Kosslyn, 1981; Pylyshyn, 1981). The *perceptual experience hypothesis* holds that, while we may not actually have "pictures in our head," our experience of an image resembles what happens when we look at a real object. There is some kind of sensation, no matter how fleeting, that approximates what we experience when we see something. In support of their position, proponents of this hypothesis note how people recall and describe one part of an object. For instance, people who are asked to describe a hawk's beak often report that they first evoke an image of an entire hawk and then search that image for the beak, which they then describe.

Advocates of the *propositional hypothesis* argue that all this business about perceptual experiences is too vague and that the best way to talk about images is in terms of propositions. A proposition is the abstract meaning behind an expression. A proposition can be expressed in many ways, but the meaning is always the same. For example, a proposition about a circle positioned over a square can be expressed as a picture of a circle over a square, by the words "circle over square," by the words "square under circle," and so on. In each of these expressions the underlying meaning, or proposition, is the same. According to these researchers, it is these kinds of propositions that are encoded and not some perception-like experience.

Memory for Pictures

Complicating the issue of visual versus verbal encoding is the fact that memory for pictures may be better than memory for names of those pictures (Brainerd, Desrochers, & Howe, 1981). If you are shown the words *tree, box, elephant, tape, car, child, sand, money,* and *card,* you may have more trouble remembering these words than you would if you were shown pictures of these objects. It has been suggested that pictures may be better remembered than words because pictures are more likely to be encoded both verbally *and* visually, while words are more likely to be encoded only verbally. This idea has been labeled the *dual-trace hypothesis* by Paivio (1971).

Of course, even memory for pictures can be improved if we supply verbal labels for the pictures. Bower, Karlin, and Dueck (1975) showed subjects drawings such as those in Figure 6–4 with or without an explanation of their meaning. They then asked subjects to draw the figures in the drawings from memory. Subjects who had been given the verbal labels did much better than did subjects given only the pictures.

(a)

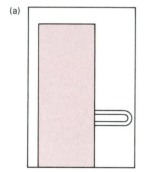

(b)

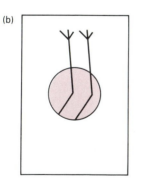

FIGURE 6–4 Memory for Pictures *(a) A child playing a trombone in a telephone booth. (b) An early bird who caught a very strong worm. (After Bower, Karlin, & Dueck, 1975)*

Acoustic and Semantic Encoding

In addition to this verbal-visual distinction, psychologists have also noted that information may be encoded in terms of acoustic qualities (the sound of it), semantic qualities (the meaning of it), or both (Horton & Turnage, 1976; Shulman, 1972). If you were asked to memorize the unique verse in Table 6–1 you might choose to do it in terms of the sounds of the items, rather than in terms of their meanings. But, if you were familiar with the meanings of the words as explained to Alice by Humpty Dumpty in Lewis Carroll's fantasy, you might use the meanings of the verse to help you commit it to memory.

TABLE 6–1   The "Jabberwocky" Poem

"You seem very clever at explaining words, Sir," said Alice. "Would you kindly tell me the meaning of the poem called 'Jabberwocky'?"

"Let's hear it," said Humpty Dumpty. "I can explain all the poems that ever were invented—and a good many that haven't been invented just yet."

This sounded very hopeful, so Alice repeated the first verse:—

> " 'Twas brillig, and the slithy toves
> Did gyre and gimble in the wabe:
> All mimsy were the borogoves.
> And the mome raths outgrabe."

"That's enough to begin with," Humpty Dumpty interrupted: "there are plenty of hard words there. 'Brillig' means four o'clock in the afternoon—the time when you begin broiling things for dinner."

"That'll do very well," said Alice: "and 'slithy'?"

"Well, 'slithy' means 'lithe and slimy.' 'Lithe' is the same as 'active.' You see it's like a portmanteau—there are two meanings packed up into one word."

"I see it now," Alice remarked thoughtfully: "and what are 'toves'?"

"Well, 'toves' are something like badgers—they're something like lizards—and they're something like corkscrews."

"They must be very curious-looking creatures."

"They are that," said Humpty Dumpty: "also they make their nests under sun-dials—also they live on cheese."

"And what's to 'gyre' and to 'gimble'?"

"To 'gyre' is to go round and round like a gyroscope. To 'gimble' is to make holes like a gimlet."

"And 'the wabe' is the grass-plot round a sun-dial, I suppose?" said Alice, surprised at her own ingenuity.

"Of course it is. It's called 'wabe' you know, because it goes a long way before it, and a long way behind it—"

"And a long way beyond it on each side," Alice added.

"Exactly so. Well then, 'mimsy' is 'flimsy and miserable' (there's another portmanteau for you). And a 'borogove' is a thin shabby-looking bird with its feathers sticking out all round—something like a live mop."

"And then 'mome raths'?" said Alice. "I'm afraid I'm giving you a great deal of trouble."

"Well, a 'rath' is a sort of green pig: but 'mome' I'm not certain about. I think it's short for 'from home'—meaning that they'd lost their way, you know."

"And what does 'outgrabe' mean?"

"Well, 'outgrabe' is something between bellowing and whistling, with a kind of sneeze in the middle: however, you'll hear it done, maybe—down in the wood yonder—and, when you've once heard it, you'll be quite content."

In summary, information may be put into memory store, or encoded, in many different forms. We may expand our memory capacity and ready it for selected tasks by varying the methods of encoding.

STORAGE

The second of the three components of memory is referred to as storage (Murdock, 1974). *Storage* refers to what happens to information over time, regardless of how it was encoded, and regardless of how it is eventually utilized. As an analogy, imagine that you place some bananas in a cupboard and close the door. Once they are in the cupboard, what happens to them? Do they remain intact, or do they change over time? How do they change? These are the same kinds of questions people ask when they study memory storage. Do our memories decay, or change, or do they remain intact throughout our lives? We will discuss some researchers' answers to these questions in later sections.

RETRIEVAL

The third and final component of the overall memory process is retrieval. *Retrieval* refers to the processes we use to pull information out of storage. At any given moment we may or may not be able to retrieve stored information. Try to recall the nine planets of our solar system. Can you remember all of them? If not, your retrieval function probably is at fault. The names of all the planets are most likely stored, but for the moment you may not be able to retrieve them all.

Be careful, by the way, to note that retrieval and recall are not the same thing. Retrieval is the overall process of pulling information out of storage, while recall is just one of several specific testing tasks used to measure the retrieval process.

Tip-of-the-tongue Phenomenon

We often find that at specific moments, stored information cannot quite be retrieved. Brown and McNeill (1966) have named this the *tip-of-the-tongue phenomenon (TOT)*, in honor of that frustrating moment when we *know* that we know a word, but we cannot quite recall it. For instance, what was your fifth-grade teacher's name? Who was the second president of the United States? Whose picture is on a five-dollar bill? Who wrote the *Iliad?* What was the date of the Magna Carta? *Continuum* is one English word with a double *u*. Can you think of another? One or more of these questions may give you the feeling you know the answer (it is stored), but you cannot quite recall it at this moment (retrieval is momentarily blocked for some reason). Table 6–2 should help you experience TOT.

Clustering and Organization in Retrieval

Retrieval does not occur in a haphazard fashion. When we are asked to recall a list of words, we do not just recall them in random order. We apply strategies in order to recall the most items we can in an organized way. Clustering in recall demonstrates this tendency to be

TABLE 6–2   The Tip-of-the-tongue Phenomenon

Look at each of the definitions below. Supply the appropriate word for the definitions, if you know it. Indicate "Don't know" for those that you are certain you don't know. Mark TOT next to those for which you are reasonably certain you know the word, though you can't recall it now. For these words, supply at least one word that sounds similar to the target word. The answers appear later in the text.

1. An absolute ruler, a tyrant.
2. A stone having a cavity lined with crystals.
3. A great circle of the earth passing through the geographic poles and any given point on the earth's surface.
4. Worthy of respect or reverence by reason of age and dignity.
5. Shedding leaves each year, as opposed to evergreen.
6. A person appointed to act as a substitute for another.
7. Five offspring born at a single birth.
8. A special quality of leadership that captures the popular imagination and inspires unswerving allegiance.
9. The red coloring matter of the red blood corpuscles.
10. Flying reptiles that were extinct at the end of the Mesozoic Era.
11. A spring from which hot water, steam, or mud gushes out at intervals, found in Yellowstone National Park.
12. The second stomach of a bird, which has thick, muscular walls.
13. The green coloring matter found in plants.
14. The long-haired wild ox of central Asia, often domesticated as a beast of burden.
15. The art of speaking in such a way that the voice seems to come from another place.

Source: After Matlin, 1983.

organized in retrieval. If asked to recall animals, and given ten or fifteen minutes to do so, people will produce results like those in Figure 6–5. Notice that the subject recalled animals in spurts of related creatures. Apparently he recalled a category, such as farm animals, cows, birds, or large sea mammals, and then recalled all the members of that category he could think of before moving on to another category. This tendency to do things in an organized way is not limited to retrieval. As we shall see, our tendency to organize, relate, categorize, and otherwise systematize information occurs in all phases of the memory process.

Storage versus Retrieval

In attempting to separate retrieval from storage processes, psychologists have looked to the distinction between recognition and recall tasks (Mandler, 1977). They reason that if something cannot be recalled, but can be recognized, then it is stored but cannot be retrieved. A recall task requires that an item be both stored and retrieved, but a recognition task bypasses the retrieval process. Retrieval is not necessary in a recognition task because the item is provided by the experimenter. (By the way, *vacuum* is the other stored double *u* word you were trying to retrieve.)

FIGURE 6–5 Clustering in Retrieval *Animals named over time in a portion of the 30-minute animal-recall task are clustered in categories.* (After Gruenewald & Lockhead, 1980)

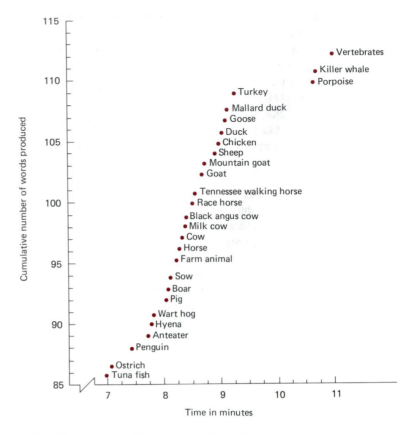

These movie critics often see the same film but come to very different conclusions about what it contains. These variations may be of the constructive type, the reconstructive type, or both.

Constructive versus Reconstructive Memory

Bartlett (1932) did some famous experiments that demonstrate the degree to which our previous knowledge distorts our efforts to remember new material. He had subjects read an Indian folktale called "The War of the Ghosts." He then asked them to try to recall the story and found that enormous distortions appeared. Subjects left out unfamiliar parts and added new elements, such as dark forests and totems. They shortened the story and made it more coherent. They substituted more familiar elements, such as fishing, for less familiar elements, such as seal hunting. In other words, their knowledge distorted memory.

The question we want to consider is, When do these distortions occur? Do they develop at the time of encoding when subjects are first exposed to unfamiliar material, at the time of retrieval, or both? The answer seems to be both. Changes seem to occur during encoding; such changes are termed *constructive changes.* Changes that occur at the time of the memory test are termed *reconstructive changes.*

Demonstrations of constructive and reconstructive changes have taken many forms, but an interesting experiment demonstrating reconstructive memory was conducted by Carmichael, Hogan, and Walter (1932). Subjects were first shown the figures in the center column of Figure 6–6. Then, at the time of recall, they were given one of the two descriptions shown on either side of the figures in the center column and asked to draw the figures from memory. As you can see

FIGURE 6–6   Reconstructive Memory Changes   *The effects of verbal labels on the retention of visually presented figures are apparent in the results of an experiment demonstrating reconstructive changes. Subjects received either one or the other of the alternative descriptions and then attempted to reproduce the figures in the middle column. Sample reproductions in the extreme left and right columns illustrate the impact of verbal labels on retention. (After Carmichael, Hogan, & Walter, 1932)*

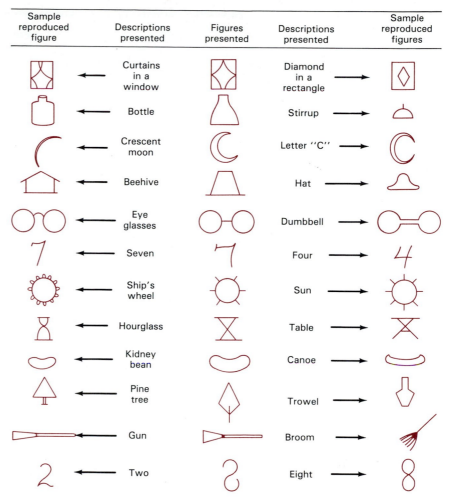

in the outer columns, the drawings were heavily affected by the verbal descriptions. The distortions must be of the reconstructive type because the subjects had not seen the verbal descriptions at the time of original encoding. Some of the practical implications of the constructive-reconstructive distinction will be discussed in Chapter 8.

Now that we have defined three different measures of retention (recall, recognition, and relearning) and three components of the overall memory system (encoding, storage, and retrieval), let us see what kinds of explanations of forgetting have been developed. In the next sections we will sketch important approaches to the understanding of memory. None of them is perfect. None of them has been accepted by a majority of psychologists. But each theory has some valuable perspectives to offer, and a final understanding of memory will probably draw on each of these diverse views.

INTERFERENCE THEORY

Retroactive Inhibition

The first approach to the understanding of memory that we will consider is called *interference theory.* According to this theory, forgetting is determined by what we do between learning and recall. If we learn

TABLE 6–3 Retroactive Inhibition Experimental Design

Group	First Task	Second Task	Third Task
Experimental	Learns A	Learns B	Remembers A
Control	Learns A	_____	Remembers A

new or additional material in the interval between original learning and recall, then recall of the original material may be impaired. The new learning *interferes* with our ability to remember the old learning. To demonstrate this theory for yourself, try to remember the telephone number 625-3971. That is not too difficult, is it? But now suppose you also had to remember 256-4576, 567-8954, 356-7653, and 456-8766. After learning these four intervening numbers it would be very difficult to go back and remember 625-3971. This powerful effect is called **retroactive inhibition.**

The basic experimental design for demonstrating this interference effect is depicted in Table 6–3. An Experimental Group first learns A, then learns B, and then attempts to recall A. The Control Group learns A, but not B, and then attempts to recall A. If the Experimental Group has more trouble recalling A than the Control Group does, we say retroactive inhibition has been demonstrated. The later learning of B interferes with the recall of A.

Retroactive inhibition effects are large and have been demonstrated many times (McGovern, 1964; Melton & Irwin, 1940; Postman & Underwood, 1973; Postman, Stark, & Burns, 1974). Although most studies of retroactive inhibition have been done in the laboratory, there is little doubt that our daily lives are strongly affected by this sort of interference effect. If you are required to memorize large amounts of organic chemistry, you may find that your ability to recall material you learned earlier will be disrupted by the materials you learned later. Gunter, Clifford, and Berry (1980) found that if subjects viewed successive TV news broadcasts, they suffered from retroactive inhibition, indicating that interference effects do occur in everyday life.

Proactive Inhibition

Another important type of interference, called proactive inhibition, can be demonstrated by the following experiment. Suppose that you are asked to learn a given list of words. After mastering the list you are asked to come back the next day. On returning, you attempt to recall the list you learned the previous day. Then you are required to learn a second list of the same type, involving different words. Once again, you are asked to return the next day, when you attempt to recall the second list. You progress in this way through a series of twenty lists. Each day, you recall the list from the preceding day and learn the list that will be recalled the next day. The question is this:

FIGURE 6–7   Proactive Inhibition as a Function of the Number of Previously Learned Lists   *Each point represents the results of a different experimental study.* (After Underwood, 1957)

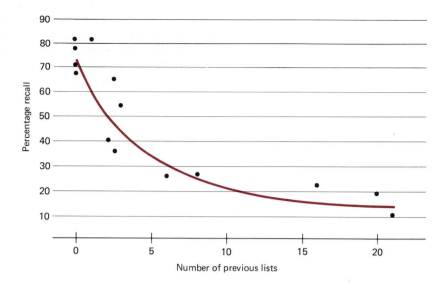

what will happen to your ability to recall as you progress through the lists? As compared to your ability to recall the first list, will your recall of later lists improve, stay about the same, or worsen?

Some people think that, because of practice in learning how to learn and recall these types of lists, recall of later lists will be better than recall of early lists. But such is not the case. Recall of the later lists will be extremely poor. The more lists you have learned previously, the poorer your recall of a newly learned list will be. It is as though all those previously learned items intrude on and confuse your attempts to recall the newest list. *Proactive inhibition* means that previous learning impairs our ability to remember new learning. It suggests that everything we have previously learned is a potential source of interference (Postman & Gray, 1977).

As Figure 6–7 shows, proactive inhibition effects are also large. Recall of the first list will be about 80 percent after 24 hours. Recall of the last list, after a similar 24-hour retention interval, will be reduced to about 20 percent. You will be able to recall no more than two out of ten items you learned just the previous day. That is a great deal of forgetting.

Table 6–4 shows the experimental design normally used to demonstrate proactive inhibition. If the Experimental Group has more trouble remembering B than the Control Group does, we say we have demonstrated proactive inhibition.

TABLE 6–4   Proactive Inhibition Experimental Design

Group	First Task	Second Task	Third Task
Experimental	Learns A	Learns B	Remembers B
Control	_____	Learns B	Remembers B

Both proactive and retroactive inhibition are powerful effects. Whether or not they can account for all forgetting remains to be seen. Still, few would deny that a good deal of forgetting occurs in accordance with them. The details of interference theory, which are well worked out, are beyond the scope of this text. It is sufficient to say that the interference approach is one of the most influential and best detailed interpretations of forgetting.

DECAY THEORY

It often seems as though our memories just fade away with the passage of time. It is as though some physical or chemical trace of an experience decays or degenerates as time progresses. The *decay theory* or interpretation of memory is an old one, and it is perhaps the one most widely believed by the general public. But surprisingly, there is no direct evidence to support the decay interpretation. Although the idea is a simple one, it must, at present, be treated as only an interesting possibility (Roediger, Knight, & Kantowitz, 1977).

Why hasn't anyone come up with an experiment that will conclusively demonstrate memory decay? To demonstrate decay we would have to have a subject learn A, then allow the passage of time during which decay would presumably occur, and then test for retention of A. The problem with this design is that, during the retention interval, the subject may be learning new material that will interfere with the ability to recall A. In other words, any memory loss we observe in this situation might be a retroactive inhibition effect, and not decay. Even normal, everyday activities can interfere. Thus, to improve our experiment, we would have to "turn off" our subject between the learning and the recall of A. But this cannot be done effectively. If, in attempting to "turn off" a subject, we put her to sleep after she has learned A (see Ekstrand, 1967), new, interfering learning may occur while the subject is dropping off to sleep, while she dreams, when she momentarily wakes up, or when she awakens just prior to recall. Thus experiments purporting to demonstrate decay may be demonstrating subtle retroactive inhibition effects instead.

And even if we could "turn off" our subject effectively during the retention interval, we still could not attribute a given retention loss to decay alone. Why not? The answer is, because of proactive inhibition. We must remember that every subject comes to our experiment with a long history of learning and a vast amount of previously stored information that can interfere proactively with any new learning. Thus, to establish a conclusive test of decay and to eliminate all potential interference effects, we would have to establish two impossible conditions. We would have to ensure that our subject had never learned anything at all before the experiment, and we would have to ensure that the subject engaged in no new learning during the retention interval.

Even though decay has not played a central part in memory research, it is a notion that persists and finds its way into other, broader interpretations of memory. Specifically, we will now turn to some information-processing approaches to memory, which build on the assumption that decay accounts for some types of forgetting.

SEPARATE-STORE MODELS

Prior to the 1960s, the interference approach to the understanding of memory dominated the field. But the advent of digital computers, and the development of information-processing concepts and languages, brought a new approach to the field of memory. This approach conceives of the human being as an ***information-processing system.*** According to this way of thinking, memory involves the flow of information through the organism, beginning with encoding and storage and ending with the retrieval of stored information.

The number of specific models of memory that have developed within this tradition is quite astounding (see Anderson, 1985; Atkinson & Shiffrin, 1971; Best, 1986; Wickelgren, 1978). We will consider a model of memory that represents a distillation of several different models, because many of the available models agree with one another in important ways. These areas of agreement are summarized by the flow diagram in Figure 6–8. Notice that the model in Figure 6–8 contains three distinct types of memory—***sensory memory***, ***short-term memory***, and ***long-term memory.*** Most recent information-processing models define three types of memory, while the older interference theory specifies only one memory process. In Figure 6–8 information is presumed to move through these three memory systems from left to right. Perceived information first enters sensory memory; it may then be transferred to short-term memory, and finally to long-term memory.

In essence, the argument for having three memories, or stores, is that the ways in which we remember items for very short periods of time differ from the ways in which we remember the same items for long periods of time. For example, if you wanted to remember 193-2040 for a very short time (say, 30 seconds), you might do it by remembering the sounds of the numbers and by arranging these sounds into some easily remembered pattern or rhythm, such as "one-nine-three-twenty-forty." If you wanted to remember the same number for two months, you might do it by remembering that you have a brother who is 19 years old, that you are three years older than he is, and that 20 is half of 40.

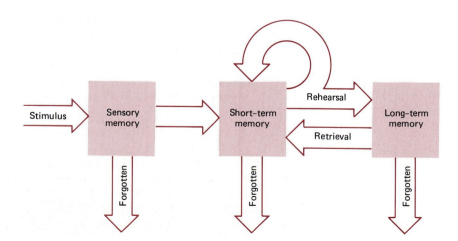

FIGURE 6–8 A Summary Separate-store Model of Memory

Of course, there are many other ways you might remember this item. This example reflects the information-processing theory that the rules, principles, and mechanisms that govern short-term memory differ from those that govern long-term memory. However, it is the task of the information-processing theorists to describe these differences in a clear and valid manner. The distinctions among sensory memory, short-term memory, and long-term memory are highly controversial. Many psychologists feel that the distinctions are invalid or, at best, poorly substantiated (Wickelgren, 1973). If you continue to study psychology you will soon find that the debate about whether memory is a unitary process or a series of stores is lively, widespread, and ongoing.

Sensory Memory

Whether or not the distinctions among the various memory systems are valid, let us examine each of the three memories as described by their proponents. What about the first of the three, the sensory memory? When we perceive something, such as a group of letters or numbers, the information is presumed to enter sensory memory. Information stored within the sensory memory decays, or fades, in a very short period of time—about half a second. If the information in sensory memory is not transferred to short-term memory, where it can be maintained, it will be forgotten.

What evidence is there for the existence of this sensory memory, where information is presumed to decay within half a second? Experiments by Sperling (1960) and others used displays like the one shown in Table 6–5. Such displays of letters were exposed to subjects for very brief intervals (1/20 of a second). The subjects were then asked to recall as many of the letters as possible. On the average they could recall about four. Then Sperling changed the rules. Instead of asking for recall of any and all of the letters he asked for a specific row. The subjects did not know which row would be tested until after the stimuli were removed. With this change in the rules, Sperling found that the subjects could recall that specific row with complete accuracy. It

TABLE 6–5   Sperling's Demonstration of Visual Sensory Memory

Step 1	Step 2	Step 3
Experimenter presents array for 1/20 second.	Tone signals which row subject is to recall.	Subject tries to recall correct row.
X G O B T M L R V A O F	High tone means recall top row. Medium tone means recall middle row. Low tone means recall bottom row.	For example, high tone signals subject to recall X G O B.

TABLE 6–6 Examples of Sensory Memory

Visual sensory memory. Take a flashlight into a dark room and turn it on. Swing your wrist around in a circular motion, shining the flashlight onto a distant wall. If your motion is quick enough, you will see a complete circle. Your visual sensory memory stores the beginning of the circle while you examine the end of the circle.

Auditory sensory memory. Take your hands and beat a quick rhythm on the desk. Can you still hear the echo after the beating is finished?

Tactile (touch) sensory memory. Take the palms of your hands and quickly rub them along a horizontal edge of your desk, moving your hands so that the heel touches first and the fingertips touch last. Can you still feel the sharp edge, even after your hand is off the desk?

Source: After Matlin, 1983

did not matter which row he asked for—the responses were always correct. But after the subjects had recited the specified row, they were unable to recall any items from the remaining rows. It was as though, for a very brief time, all items were available to the subject as some sort of after image or visual image. As the subject "read off" the row requested by Sperling, the other rows faded or decayed completely.

The processes involved in the sensory memory are not yet well understood. But Sperling's experiments dramatically demonstrate that we may store information in its entirety for a very brief moment after presentation (see also Massaro, 1972). If we do not attend to this briefly stored information, it will vanish quickly.

Iconic and Echoic Memory Sperling's experiments demonstrate the existence of a visual sensory memory, often called **iconic memory**. What about the other sense modalities? Sensory memories for taste, smell, and touch have yet to be documented experimentally, but an auditory sensory memory, wherein sounds are maintained perfectly for very brief periods of time, has been demonstrated (Crowder, 1978; Watkins & Todres, 1979). This form of auditory sensory memory has often been called **echoic memory**. Table 6–6 will give you some idea of what psychologists are talking about when they refer to sensory memory.

Short-term Memory

Let us return to the box labeled short-term memory in Figure 6–8. If we attend to the information stored in the sensory memory it will be transferred to short-term memory. If, after a brief presentation of the materials in Table 6–5, we recall or "read off" one row of items, then we say that these items have been transferred from sensory memory to short-term memory (the remaining items merely fade from sensory memory, or are forgotten). Once in short-term memory, an item will decay or be lost within approximately one minute unless it is rehearsed, or repeated (see Figure 6–9).

FIGURE 6–9 A Typical Short-term Memory Curve *The subject attempts to recall a nonsense syllable (e.g., FEX) after varying numbers of seconds. Immediately after the nonsense syllable is spoken out loud, a three-digit number is presented and the subject counts backwards by threes from that number until signaled to stop counting and recall the syllable. Counting backwards prevents the subject from rehearsing the syllable during the retention interval. Note how much forgetting occurs during the first seconds if rehearsal is prevented.* (After Peterson & Peterson, 1959)

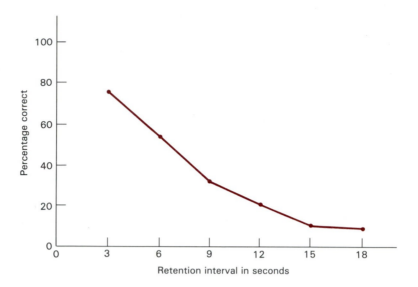

Thus, items decay from sensory memory in about half a second, while decay from short-term memory occurs after approximately one minute. If an item is rehearsed—if you say it over and over, either aloud or to yourself—it can be maintained in short-term memory and will not be lost. If an item is rehearsed often enough, it can be transferred from short-term memory to long-term memory. Information that makes it all the way to long-term memory is presumed to be stored quite permanently. Once in long-term memory, information does not have to be rehearsed to be maintained, but if information located in short-term memory is not rehearsed, it will be forgotten quickly. If you read off 87321657 and then somehow prevent

These gentlemen do not have time to rehearse each other's names often enough to transfer them from short-term memory into permanent long-term memory, so they solve the problem by exchanging business cards.

We can keep on learning new skills and ideas all of our lives, because our long-term memory has a storage capacity that is practically limitless.

yourself from repeating this sequence over and over to yourself, it will be forgotten within seconds. Figure 6–9 shows a typical short-term memory curve.

When an item is in short-term memory we are conscious of it. It is "in mind." When an item is in long-term memory it is not "in mind." What you are thinking of right now is in your short-term memory. Everything you know but are not now thinking of is in your long-term memory.

Storage Capacity of Short-term Memory   The capacity of short-term memory is quite limited. There are just so many items we can hold in short-term memory at a given moment. If someone reads words to you at a rate of about one every second, you will be able to hold perhaps 6, 7, 8, or 9 of them "in mind," but you cannot keep on adding new items without losing some of the old items. If your short-term memory is full and you try to add a new item, it will "bump out" one of the older items. Remember, however, as we saw in the section on chunking, that the capacity of short-term memory can be increased by increasing the amount of information contained in each chunk.

Long-term Memory

Information-processing researchers think of long-term memory as a storehouse where information is stored fairly permanently when we are not recalling it. The capacity of long-term memory is relatively unlimited, and we can continue to add information to this storehouse throughout our lives. Information is often lost from long-term memory through a combination of decay and interference, but the loss from long-term memory occurs far more slowly than losses from sensory memory and short-term memory.

We bring information back from long-term memory to short-term memory when we recall something. An appropriate probe, such as a question, makes us search through our permanent store and return the appropriate information to short-term memory, or consciousness. Think of a country to the north of the United States. What you just did was bring information back out of long-term memory into short-term memory. Thus, information can be in both long-term memory and short-term memory at the same time. An item also can be in long-term memory but not short-term memory—that is where "Canada" was before you thought of it. An item can be in short-term memory but not in long-term memory. Information you have just received, but have not yet rehearsed enough to permit its transfer to long-term memory, is in this state.

SEMANTIC-NETWORK
MODELS

Organization in Long-term Memory

Twenty years ago the professional journals were filled with studies of short-term memory, while little attention was given to long-term memory. But now more and more researchers are focusing on the complex and fascinating nature of long-term memory. These researchers share the conviction that when we put information into long-term memory, we do it in an organized manner. We do not store information passively, just as it is delivered to us. We structure, relate, and interconnect it automatically. Like librarians, we try to categorize our knowledge so that storage and retrieval are most efficient. And, ironically, we do most of this complex organizing without even being aware of it.

Back in the early 1960s, Tulving (1962) developed a technique that gave us some idea of the complexity of organization in long-term memory. In Tulving's study, a list of words is read to subjects in random order, and the subjects are then asked to recall them in any order they wish. Then they hear the same words again, but in a *new* random order, and are asked to recall them again in any order. This process is repeated over and over again. Even though the words are always presented in a new random order, the subjects begin to recall them in a fixed order. Trial after trial they recall the same words together, even though they were not located together in the lists read to them. It seems as though the subjects are building some internal structure out of the words. Perhaps they make up sentences or stories using the words or develop some kind of visual image. This effect, called *subjective organization*, shows that ordered output follows random input. It demonstrates, in a preliminary way, the existence of organizational efforts on the part of the subject. But subjective organization studies do not tell us exactly what *kind* of organization is developing. Nevertheless, the early work on subjective organization helped stimulate the investigation of semantic-network models, which we will examine next.

Common Characteristics

Having discussed interference theory, decay theory, and separate-store models, we now turn to semantic-network models, which are among some of the newest efforts in the study of memory. The phrase semantic-network model refers to quite a broad range of model building, but most of these models have at least two attributes in common. First, all *semantic-network models* deal with memory for *semantic* (meaningful) material. In some of the preceding sections we have discussed the retention of relatively meaningless material such as nonsense syllables. But now we focus strictly on the retention of semantic material such as words. Second, all of these models assume that the best way to think about semantic storage is in terms of multiple, interconnected associations, relationships, or pathways. Information is assumed to be embedded in an organized, structured network composed of semantic units and their functional relationships to one another.

We will discuss four semantic-network models, each of which deals with organized semantic memory. Our discussion will be limited to the study of *lexical memory*. A lexicon is an ordered set of words such as a dictionary or your vocabulary. When we speak of lexical memory then, we are concerned with memory for words as distinct from memory for grammar, sentences, experiences, or general knowledge.

Hierarchies

The first of the four network models we will look at is known as the *hierarchy model*. Obviously, we cannot possibly describe all of the

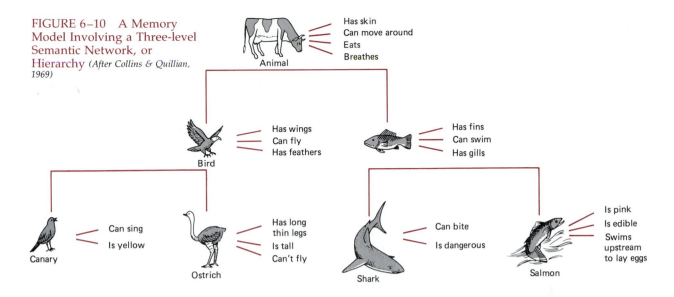

FIGURE 6–10   A Memory Model Involving a Three-level Semantic Network, or Hierarchy *(After Collins & Quillian, 1969)*

interrelationships among all of the words in a complete lexicon, but we can try to characterize the nature of the overall lexical structure. We will begin with the hierarchical approach, because several investigators hold that this is the best way to envision the structure of lexicons. Collins and Quillian (1972) have proposed an interesting hierarchical model (see Figure 6–10) in which the concept of "animal" is broken down into "bird" and "fish." "Bird" and "fish" are then broken down further into specific examples of each. At each word, certain characteristics of that word or concept are stored. Fish have fins, can swim, and have gills. Similarly, the canary can sing and is yellow. Think how effective this storage system is. If we locate "canary," we immediately know quite a bit about canaries. We not only know that they can sing and are yellow, but we also know, by moving upward in the hierarchy, that they have wings, can fly, have feathers, breathe, eat, move, and have skin. In short, the system is efficient because all of the attributes of each animal need not be stored with that animal.

Lindsay and Norman (1977) have also proposed a hierarchical model (see Figure 6–11). Bower and Hilgard (1981) describe the semantic network involved as follows:

> A realistic memory, of course, contains thousands of . . . concepts, each with very many connections, so that the actual topographical representation would look like a huge "wiring diagram." But a fantastic amount of information is inherently encoded in such graph structures. To see just a hint of this, consider the fragment of a semantic network surrounding the concept of a tavern [as shown in Figure 6–11]. This graph implicitly encodes the information that a tavern is a kind of business establishment (as is a drugstore), which has beer and wine, and Luigi's is an example of a tavern. It also gives some properties of beer, wine, and Luigi's. This is only a fragment, of course, and much more information could and would be in a realistic memory. But notice how very many questions one is enabled to answer with just this fragment. For example, it can answer questions that require chains of subset relations, such as that "Luigi's is an establishment" or that "A drugstore is a place." It can also read out the properties or classes that any two concepts have in common. Thus,

FIGURE 6–11 Fragment of a Hierarchical Semantic Network Surrounding the Concept of a Tavern *(After Lindsay & Norman, 1977)*

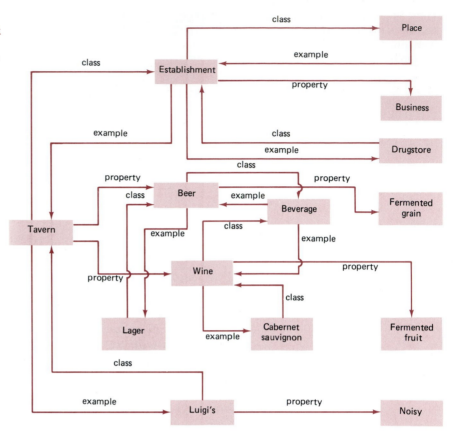

if we ask the system to compare the similarities and differences of beer and wine, it would quickly find that the similarities are that they are both beverages sold at taverns, but one is made from fermented grain while the other is made from fermented fruit. The number of factual relationships derivable and possible questions that can be answered increases exponentially as the number of encoded predicates or "bits of knowledge" increases. (pp. 450–51)

Theories about lexicons are in their infancy. To be complete, it seems that these blueprints or wiring diagrams would have to be incredibly complex.

Matrices

While many psychologists think of lexical organization in terms of hierarchies, others suggest that when we store information in long-term memory, we organize it into *matrices.* Figure 6–12 shows a sample matrix that organizes 16 animal words. (For comparison, 16 words are presented in hierarchical form.)

If you were given words to remember, how would you do it? Would you try to organize them into a hierarchy, a matrix, neither, or both? Broadbent, Cooper, and Broadbent (1978) tried to answer this question by giving words to one group of subjects in the form of a hierarchy, to another group as a matrix, and to a control group in random order. They then asked the subjects to recall the words. They

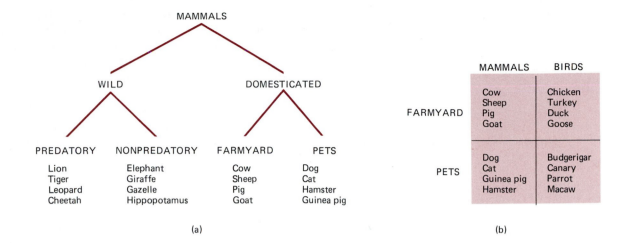

FIGURE 6–12 Two Ways of Thinking about Lexical Memory
Sixteen different animal words are organized in accordance with two semantic-network models: (a) hierarchy and (b) matrix. (After Broadbent, Cooper, & Broadbent, 1978)

reasoned that if humans used matrices naturally when storing information in long-term memory, then presenting the items in a matrix should help recall. What they found was that *both* forms of organization, hierarchy and matrix, helped recall relative to the control group. The two forms of organization seemed to be equally helpful. In other words, organization helps but we cannot be certain about the relative merits of these two alternative forms of organization.

Feature Models

Our third approach to the understanding of lexical memory is called the feature approach (Smith, Shoben, & Rips, 1974). The *feature approach* is concerned with our ability to decide whether certain nouns belong to certain categories. For instance, what will determine how long it takes us to decide that the noun *dog* belongs to the category *animal?* In the feature approach no mention is made of any spatial relationships. Instead, the crucial factor is the number of *features* or *attributes* that *dog* and *animal* have in common. *Dog* and *animal* have a great number of common features (both have skin, can move, eat and breathe, and so on). Thus we are quickly able to decide that a dog belongs in the animal category. Similarly, if two items have very little in common (for example, *dog* and *sand*) we are also able to come to a quick decision. In this case we would rapidly conclude that *dog* does not belong to the category *sand.*

Thus, we are able to make decisions quickly when there are either a great many common features between items or very few common features. When the number of common attributes is *intermediate,* however, we begin to have trouble. For example, is a *mold* a *plant?* We know they are both alive and that they both cannot move, but we cannot think of enough common attributes to let us make a quick and easy decision. Hampton (1979) argues that when we are confused in this manner we turn to a distinction between defining features and characteristic features. *Defining features* provide necessary and sufficient criteria for making a decision. For example, if an animal has feathers, it is a bird. There are no featherless birds and no non-birds have feathers. *Characteristic features*, on the other hand, are typical attributes of the items belonging to the category, but they are not in and of themselves sufficient for determining category membership. It is characteristic of birds to fly, but not all birds fly and some creatures that are not birds also have the ability to fly (consider insects, for example).

Hampton concludes that we turn to the identification of defining features when we are having trouble making a decision. With an intermediate number of common attributes we will consider *only* defining features. This takes a little more time and slows down our decision process.

Spreading-activation Models

The fourth and final type of semantic-network model is called the *spreading-activation model.* One of the early spreading-activation models developed by Collins and Loftus is contained in Figure 6–13. Several aspects of this model should be emphasized. First, notice that the model is not limited to hierarchical relationships. The relationships among the items are much more complex. Second, notice that the lines among the words vary in length. The longer the line between two words, the weaker the relationship between those two words. For example, the line between "red" and "sunrises" is longer

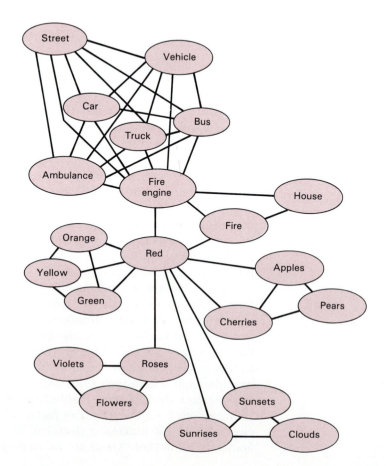

FIGURE 6–13   A Spreading-activation Model   *In this example the length of each line (link) represents the degree of association between two concepts.* (After Collins & Loftus, 1975)

than the line between "red" and "roses"; this indicates that red and roses are more meaningfully related than are red and sunrises.

The third assumption made in this model is that when an item such as "rose" is processed (for example, when a subject reads or hears the word *rose*), then activation spreads out along the pathways in all directions. This activation, although not precisely defined, refers to the idea that an activated item can be more easily processed than an unactivated one. For example, an activated item can be more easily retrieved, judged, recognized, or evaluated than an unactivated item.

Experimentation and theorizing about spreading-activation models is now widespread (Anderson, 1983; Stanovich & West, 1983; Reder & Ross, 1983). The model has had its most talked-about success in accounting for **priming effects** in **lexical-decision experiments**. In these experiments the subject is first shown a *prime*, such as the word *bird*. Then the subject is shown a *target* item for a very brief period of time. The target may be a word related to the prime, such as *canary*; an unrelated word, such as *box*; or even a "nonsense word" such as *pielf*. The subject's task is to make some decision about the target as quickly as possible, such as whether or not it is a word, or whether or not it belongs to a certain category. Experimental results have, in general, shown that the speed with which a decision can be made about the target is increased as the relationship between target and prime becomes closer. You can see how this result fits in with the spreading-activation model. The prime is assumed to activate material in the network; the closer the prime is to the target, the more activated, and thus the more easily processed, that target is.

LEVELS OF PROCESSING

The final approach to the understanding of memory that we will examine is called the **levels-of-processing approach** (Craik & Lockhart, 1972). According to this way of thinking durability of learning depends on how "deeply" we rehearse material. We can rehearse a list of words on a very shallow level by merely noting what they look like. This shallow form of processing is expected to lead to a weak memory. On a somewhat deeper level we can rehearse words in terms of how they sound. This intermediate level of processing should lead to better encoding and storage. Finally, we can rehearse words on a semantic level—that is, in terms of what they mean. This is seen as the deepest level of processing and should lead to strong, durable memories.

Here is a typical levels-of-processing experiment (Craik & Tulving, 1975). A long series of words was flashed on a screen, one at a time, for about a second each. In some cases the subjects had to judge whether the flashed words were typed in capitals. This is shallow processing. In other cases the subjects had to judge whether the flashed word rhymed with another designated word. This is intermediate processing. In still other instances, the subjects had to judge whether the flashed word belonged in a blank space in a sentence. This is deep processing involving semantics or meaning. Then, in a surprise move, the experimenters asked the subjects to recall all of the words that had been presented to them. It was found that the words that required deep processing were recalled best and the words that required only shallow processing were the most difficult to recall. Though there are exceptions (see Nelson, 1977), the literature generally suggests that the deeper the processing, the better the retention.

The levels-of-processing approach differs sharply from the separate-store concept in that it denies that there are distinct, crisp breaks between short-term memory and long-term memory. According to levels of processing there is a continuum of memory strengths, ranging from very weak, shallow-processed levels to strong, deep-processed levels. The deeper we rehearse, the more durable the memory, and the stronger the memory the longer the item can be remembered (Chatala, 1981; Maki & Schuler, 1980).

As you might suspect, there is disagreement about the proper ranking of various rehearsal tasks. For example, does rating the pleasantness of a word represent deeper or shallower processing than deciding whether the word fits into a blank space in a sentence? But there has been fair agreement, and Table 6–7 contains some of the tasks that are seen as involving shallow, intermediate, and deep processing.

In an effort to help clarify the processing notion, Craik and Lockhart (1972) distinguished between two types of rehearsal. *Type I*, or *maintenance rehearsal,* involves the shallow repetition of material in an effort to keep it in mind without necessarily putting it into any kind of permanent memory store. As Houston (1976) points out, this is the kind of rehearsal you would be engaged in as you repeated a phone number over and over again while searching for a pencil. *Type II*, or *elaborative rehearsal,* refers to our efforts to put information into more permanent storage through deeper processing and the use of the semantic rather than the acoustical aspects of the material.

Having discussed several different approaches to the understanding of memory, we must emphasize again that these approaches are not mutually exclusive or antagonistic. Proof of one does not necessarily deny the validity of the others. Each may well contain something of value, and a final understanding of memory will probably draw on, and depend on, each of these diverse approaches.

TABLE 6–7   Levels-of-processing Tasks

Level of Processing		
Shallow (Visual)	Intermediate (Acoustic)	Deep (Semantic)
Does this word begin with a capital?	Does this word have an "r" sound in it?	Can you hold this in your hand?
Do these two words begin with the same letter?	Does this word rhyme with this other word?	How familiar is this?
How many syllables does this word have?	Where does the accent fall in this word?	Is this a word?
Is this word typed in lowercase letters?	Does this word end in an "est" sound?	How pleasant is this?

ISSUES IN MEMORY

In this section we want to discuss some of the current issues within the field of memory. We begin with the fact that psychologists disagree about how many memory systems we really possess. Next we discuss how memory is influenced by our wants, needs, wishes, and desires. Then we consider the fact that what we remember is strongly influenced by the *context* in which the information was stored. Next, we address the theory of consolidation and the associated phenomenon of retrograde amnesia. And finally, we take a look at what is known about animal memory.

How Many Memories?

Having previously reviewed the three components of the separate-store model (sensory, short-term, and long-term memory), we should point out that this conception of memory poses many intriguing questions. For instance, how much rehearsal is required to move information into long-term memory? Can information sometimes go directly from sensory memory to long-term memory? What determines which of the items in short-term memory will be "bumped out" when new items are introduced? How can the fixed capacities of our memory systems be used in different ways to suit our purposes?

While we do not have the space to address all of these questions, there is one that deserves particular attention. Specifically, is there really a difference between long-term memory and short-term memory? Quite a few psychologists already have tried to find solid evidence for the distinctions among the various memory systems, while others have argued against these same distinctions. Some researchers attempted to distinguish between long-term and short-term memory on the basis of differing decay and interference effects within the two proposed stores. They argued that only decay operates in short-term memory and that interference effects do not appear there (Peterson & Peterson, 1959). But several studies have demonstrated that both retroactive and proactive inhibition occur in short-term memory, thus proving that short-term memory is not free from interference effects (Mendell, 1977; Posner & Konick, 1966).

Other researchers have proposed that short- and long-term memory may be distinguished in terms of acoustic versus semantic encoding. Baddeley and Patterson (1971) argue that we store information in short-term memory on the basis of the sounds of the items (acoustic encoding), while we store information in long-term memory on the basis of the meaning of the material (semantic encoding). But this distinction has also fallen on hard times. There is growing evidence that both semantic and acoustic encoding are employed for both long and short retention intervals (see Nelson & Rothbart, 1972; Shulman, 1972).

Researchers have found some clinical support for the distinction between long- and short-term memory. Human patients who have suffered bilateral damage to the hippocampus sometimes display a marked change in memory patterns (Baddeley & Warrington, 1970; Milner, 1966). Many of these patients had undergone surgery designed to relieve epilepsy. They were able to retain new information for short periods of time, indicating that their short-term memory was intact. They also were able to remember all events that had occurred before surgery, indicating that old long-term memory was intact. However, they were *unable* to retain any new information for long periods of time. It appeared as though nothing new could be stored in their long-term memory, despite an intact short-term memory.

These changed patterns imply that the patients' ability to transfer information from short- to long-term memory had been destroyed. These patients were able to carry on conversations because their short-term memory was intact, but they could not remember conversations or events that had occurred a few minutes earlier—presumably because they could not store new long-term memories. They knew what had happened before the trauma, but not what happened after it. For them, no matter how long they had been in the hospital, they had just arrived "yesterday."

These and other lines of evidence suggest that we cannot yet be entirely sure of the distinction between long- and short-term memory (Wickelgren, 1973). Whatever the final outcome, the three-stage models are currently useful and represent a meaningful way of looking at memory.

Episodic versus Semantic Memory   Breaking memory down into short- and long-term components is not the only game in town, of course. Psychologists have thought of several other ways to divide up the memory system. Some have argued that we need different models and theories to account for the retention of different *types* of information. For example, some make a distinction between episodic and semantic memory (Tulving, 1972; McCloskey & Santee, 1981). *Episodic memory* refers to the storage of information about temporally arranged or dated events such as personal experiences. *Semantic memory* refers to the storage of facts, words, concepts, and meanings that are *not* temporally ordered. Items in episodic memory might include:

I have an appointment with the dentist tomorrow at noon.

Joan graduated from the third grade two years before I did.

Yesterday I missed two buses in a row.

Items in semantic memory might include:

Ink tastes funny.

Geese have feathers.

4 + 4 = 9. (No one says the information has to be correct.)

Motivated Forgetting

The decay theory of forgetting suggests that retention losses are due to some type of physical deterioration that occurs over time. The interference interpretation emphasizes the fact that both new and old learning can interfere with our attempts to remember a given set of materials. And the information-processing approaches argue that forgetting is probably due to some combination of interference and decay. But none of these interpretations takes into account the needs, wants, wishes, and desires of the individual. In other words, they do not consider that we may be more or less motivated to remember certain information.

Some information may be very important to us and may thus be quite likely to be remembered—for instance, the name of an attractive person met briefly in a crowded social situation. Other memories may cause us pain or anxiety and thus be less likely to be remembered, such as the knowledge that we have shown weakness, been dishonest, or hurt another person. Although motivational factors are probably very important in determining what will and what will not be remembered, we have little direct experimental evidence concerning their impact (see Bjork, 1972; Clemes, 1964; Weiner, 1966).

Repression   Sigmund Freud (1933) developed a theory about motivated forgetting that was based on his observations of his patients. This ***theory of repression***, as Freud called it, is still widely used in clinical work. Freud discovered that when hypnotized, many people seem able to report in great detail about events from their early lives that they cannot normally remember. For example, one hypnotized man might be able to describe his fourth birthday in minute detail. When he is not hypnotized, these same memories would not be available to him. Freud theorized that many memories are somehow blocked, or repressed, because to remember them would be to experience pain, discomfort, or anxiety. If a child has stolen money from her mother and has felt extremely guilty about the act, then, later in life, the memory of this particular act might be repressed from conscious awareness. To remember it would be to feel guilty all over again. Freud suggested that many of the problems adults experience may be due to unpleasant or traumatic experiences in childhood. He assumed that many of these early, unpleasant experiences were repressed. Through hypnosis and other techniques, Freud believed,

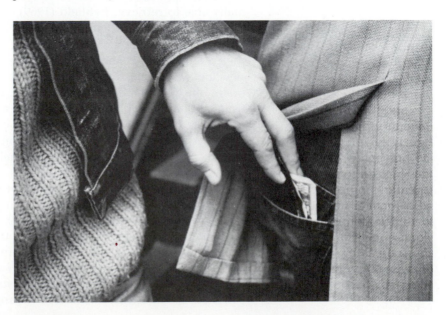

According to Freud, a thief may later repress the memory of his crime, especially if he feels guilty and anxious about it.

these repressed memories could be revealed. Then the patient, with the aid of the therapist, would learn to deal with them in healthier ways. Repression is a defense mechanism by which one avoids unpleasant memories by blocking them out of consciousness. Most interpretations of repression state that the individual is not consciously aware that unpleasant memories are being repressed.

Motivated forgetting—specifically repression—has not been heavily documented in an experimental sense. Most of what we know or guess about repression comes from clinical practice, where a therapist works with a patient in attempting to alleviate the patient's problems. The concept of repression is still controversial. Its widespread use indicates how strongly psychologists believe that memory can be affected by the individual's needs, fears, anxieties, and desires. The role of motivation in forgetting has not been worked out as well as, say, interference effects. But the possible impact of motivation on retention certainly deserves continued attention and further research.

Are Memories Forever?   One question often asked about the role of motivation in memory has to do with the permanence of memories (Loftus & Loftus, 1980). When we commit information to memory, does it remain stored within us for the rest of our lives, even though we may not always be able to retrieve it? If we cannot remember something, does it mean the information is no longer stored, or does it mean the information is still stored but cannot, for some reason, be pulled out of storage? There have been a number of different reactions to this question (Hull, 1952; Tulving & Madigan, 1970). Although the final answer still escapes us, several lines of investigation have shed some light on this issue.

Electrical Stimulation of the Brain   We can say with some certainty that many more memories remain in storage than one might imagine. There are apparently all sorts of stored memories that we are not normally able to retrieve. Penfield (1969) has demonstrated this fact. He has reported instances in which patients undergoing brain surgery had their brains electrically stimulated. While under local anesthesia, the patients were conscious and able to report what they were experiencing. As an electrode was touched to the surface of the exposed brain, the patients experienced vivid, detailed memories of events from the past. People, places, events, and sensations were reported in minute detail. Although we are not certain how accurate those reports were, they apparently corresponded to events that had occurred. As long as the electrode was held in place, the experience of memories from the past continued. As soon as the electrode was removed, such memories ceased abruptly. Sometimes the memories were of events that the patients had completely "forgotten." The electricity somehow activated memories that were stored but were beyond the normal retrieval capacities of the individual.

Of course, being able to reveal many old memories in this manner does not necessarily mean that *all* memories are stored permanently. But this type of research does suggest that the brain is a vast storehouse, filled with memories we cannot retrieve.

Hypnotic Age Regression   As we noted earlier, quite a few psychologists have investigated hypnotic age regression. This phenomenon also pertains to the question of the permanence of memories. Subjects are hypnotized and then told to return to childhood. Some begin to act as though they were children and drop all or most of their adult behavior.

As you might imagine, the discovery of this phenomenon created quite a stir. Some psychologists claimed that age regression provided evidence for the idea that all memories are permanent, because detailed, "long forgotten" information could be retrieved from regressed subjects. But again, we must keep in mind that being able to retrieve some apparently lost information does not necessarily mean that *all* memories are permanently stored and awaiting activation.

In addition, as we mentioned in Chapter 4, subjects undergoing hypnotic age regression often "role play" (McConnell, 1974); that is, they try to follow the hypnotist's suggestions. They act as if they were five or six, but they do not return to that age in any real sense. They often report events inaccurately (as determined through questioning of parents) and do things no child would do. If asked what time it is they may look at their wristwatch, something they did not have as a child. Their responses are attempts to act like a child, rather than the true acts of a child. Moreover, the things they "remember" from their early childhood are often things they have been told at later times by friends and parents. For all of these reasons, age regression should be viewed with caution.

State-dependent Memory: Context Effects

The context in which we learn something can strongly affect our efforts to recall that material. Specifically, if we learn something in a particular situation or environment, we will be more likely to remember that material later if we are tested for recall in exactly the same

State-dependent memory experiments suggest that this young woman might better be able to recall the material she is reading if she listens to the same music at the time of recall.

situation or environment. If there is a change in the context from learning to recall, we will not do as well on the recall test. In one experiment, Smith (1979) had subjects learn some material in Room 1 and then tested them for recall of that material either in Room 1 or in Room 2. The people who learned and recalled in Room 1 did better on the recall test than did the people who learned in Room 1 and recalled in Room 2. Smith then asked subjects switched to Room 2 to imagine Room 1 when they were being tested in Room 2. This simple reminder of the learning context enabled the subjects to cut some of their losses. This is called a *state-dependent memory effect*, because memory seems to be dependent on the state or context in which original learning occurred.

Drug States   Various drug states can serve as important contexts in memory, too (Eich, Weingartner, Stillman, & Gillin, 1975). If you learn something under the influence of a drug, whether it is caffeine, amphetamines, or alcohol, then you may be more likely to perform well on a retention test if you are tested under the same condition. Retention may be better under unchanged conditions, even if the drug state in question does not ordinarily enhance learning.

Verbal and Visual Contexts   Words learned in the context of other words, as in a sentence or a list, are better recalled if these other context words are present during recall (Smith, Glenberg, & Bjork, 1978). Pictures of objects, learned in the context of other pictures, also are better recalled if those context pictures are present during recall (Winograd & Lynn, 1979).

Wet or Dry?   Godden and Baddeley (1975) provide a dramatic example of the power of the context to affect recall. They had divers learn several lists of unrelated words either on dry land or under 20 feet of water. Then the divers were asked to recall the materials either in the same state they had learned them in or in the alternative state. As Figure 6–14 shows, recall was better under unchanged conditions than under altered conditions.

Courtroom Testimony   Our understanding of the impact of contexts on learning and understanding can have important practical implications. Loftus and Palmer (1974) showed subjects a film of a car accident. Half the subjects were then asked, "How fast were the cars going when they *bumped?*" The other half was asked, "How fast were the cars going when they *crashed?*" One week later, subjects who had been asked about how the cars *smashed* were more likely to remember that the film contained broken glass than were the subjects asked the *bumped* question, even though the film contained no glass.

Clearly this kind of effect is important in connection with courtroom eyewitness testimony. It suggests that a clever attorney, by asking the right questions, could alter our conception of the truth (see Reed, 1982).

A clever attorney, by asking the right questions, can lead us to accept her version of the truth.

Consolidation and Retrograde Amnesia

Some psychologists have argued that, for a memory to become permanent, it must undergo a *period of consolidation.* Once information

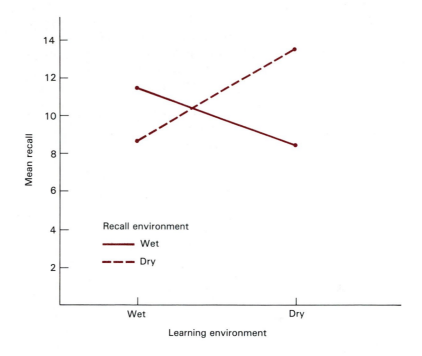

FIGURE 6–14 State-dependent Memory Context Effects
Divers learned word lists either under water or on dry land and then attempted recall either under the same conditions or under the opposite conditions. Recall was better when it was attempted in the same state as that in which learning initially occurred. (After Godden & Baddeley, 1975)

has been stored it must be left undisturbed for a while. During this undisturbed period the memory trace is presumed to become durable and permanent. If the newly formed memory trace is disturbed or disrupted, it will not solidify—it will be wiped out instead. The memory trace, like cement, takes time to harden. Before consolidation, the memory trace is vulnerable and may be destroyed by disruptive events.

What evidence is there for this theory? Many have argued that *retrograde amnesia*, or backward forgetting, supports the consolidation theory (Gold & King, 1974; McGaugh & Dawson, 1971). In a retrograde amnesia study, an animal, such as a rat, learns a particular response. Then the animal is subjected to some "amnesic agent," such as electroconvulsive shock. Electroconvulsive shock is produced when electric current is passed through the brain of the subject for a very brief period. The animal is then tested to see if it still remembers the learned response. Quite often, some of the learned behavior has been forgotten. The more time allowed between the learning and shock, the less the amnesic effect. It is as though the memory becomes more resistant to the disruptive effects of the shock as time passes. If the shock is delivered immediately after learning, before consolidation has had a chance to occur, then the learning may be almost totally lost.

Humans who have suffered brain injuries sometimes display retrograde amnesia. Accident victims often cannot remember what happened just before the accident, even though their memory of the more distant past is normal. The accident seems to disrupt immediate memories before they have a chance to consolidate, while older, "hardened" memories are unaffected by the traumatic accident.

Consolidation theory is often viewed as part of the information-processing approach, rather than a distinct theoretical approach.

Consolidation theory certainly is compatible with the information-processing approach. In fact, consolidation may be viewed as part of the process that transfers information from short-term memory to long-term memory.

At present, consolidation theory is extremely controversial. Evidence for the theory centers on retrograde amnesia, but some research suggests that there are alternative interpretations of the amnesia effect (Miller, Ott, Berk, & Springer, 1974; Quartermain & Botwinick, 1975).

Animal versus Human Memory

Do animals remember things the same way humans do, or are their memory systems different from ours? While some disagree (Winograd, 1971), it appears that there is a good deal of correspondence between our memory systems and those of the lower animals. This should not be too surprising. We have already seen that classical and instrumental conditioning and learning effects appear in both animals and humans. More surprising is the fact that animal memory was pretty much ignored until recently. In fact, a curious reversal has appeared in the research literature. Years ago, when the emphasis was on classical and instrumental conditioning, animal data were used to try to explain human behavior. Now, the opposite often happens; principles of memory discovered with human subjects are being used to explain animal memory. Demonstrations of retroactive and proactive inhibition, developed largely with human subjects, are now being run with animals (Wickens, Tuber, Nield, & Wickens, 1977).

Short-term memory is now investigated in animals, too (Reynolds & Medin, 1979). Many investigators of animal short-term memory use the *delayed-matching-to-sample procedure* (DMTS). Figure 6–15 shows some stimuli typically used in the DMTS technique. An animal, such as a pigeon, is shown the stimulus in the left side of the figure. Then follows a short retention interval, such as 18 seconds, after which the animal is shown the two stimuli on the right side of the figure. If it pecks at the "correct" stimulus, the one it has seen before, it is rewarded.

Another area of investigation that leads us to suspect that animal memory is similar to human memory has to do with *spatial memory.* Obviously humans can remember information about spatial relationships. When you lose your car keys you tend not to look in the same place over and over again. You remember where you have already looked and concentrate on looking in new locations. But can animals utilize spatial information in a similar manner? It would be useful to them if they could. If a bear empties the honey from one beehive, it would be worthwhile to remember *not* to check that hive for some time in order to allow the bees to replenish the supply.

That animals do have useful spatial memory is demonstrated in the apparatus depicted in Figure 6–16. Olton and Samuelson (1976) put a piece of food in the end of each of the eight radiating arms of the test apparatus. A rat was then placed in the center and allowed to choose and enter any arm it wished. After the rat ate a piece of food, no new food was introduced, but the rat could go back into any

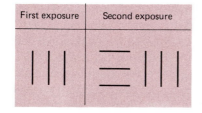

First exposure	Second exposure

FIGURE 6–15   Animal Memory and the Delayed-matching-to-sample Procedure   *In the DMTS procedure, the animal is first exposed to a particular stimulus configuration, such as the vertical lines. Then, after a delay, the animal is exposed to the old stimulus paired with a new stimulus, and its choice of stimulus is recorded. (After Houston, 1986)*

FIGURE 6–16   A Radial
Maze   *Rats placed in the maze
with food at the end of each arm
almost never reentered an arm
from which they had already taken
the food.* (*After Olton & Samuelson,
1976*)

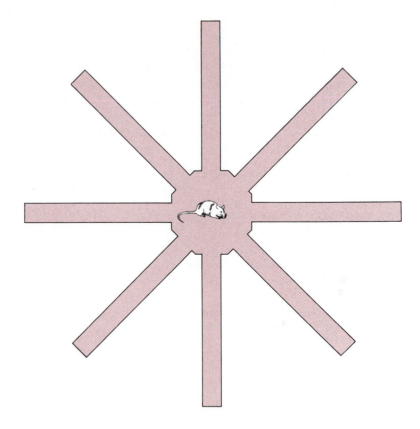

arm at any time. The investigators found that the rats almost never
entered a previously visited arm. Thus by utilizing their spatial memory, they became very efficient food gatherers. The implication is
that, like humans, they have good spatial memory.

In summary, while it is hard to compare data obtained from different species engaged in different tasks, the literature does suggest
that there are broad areas of agreement among animal and human
data. Memory differences among animals and humans seem to be
more a matter of degree rather than of kind. We shall pursue the
similarities among animals and humans in the next chapter when we
look at language in apes.

Answers to Definitions in Table 6–2		
1. despot	6. surrogate	11. geyser
2. geode	7. quintuplets	12. gizzard
3. meridian	8. charisma	13. chlorophyll
4. venerable	9. hemoglobin	14. yak
5. deciduous	10. pterodactyl	15. ventriloquism

SUMMARY

1. Retention curves indicate that forgetting is considerable at first and then levels off as time passes.

2. When we focus on memory and retention, we are interested in what happens to learned associations or stored information after practice ceases.

3. In a recall test of retention, the subject is required to reproduce the entire stored item. In a recognition test, the subject is asked if a given item is the correct item. In a relearning test, the subject relearns previously learned materials. If relearning is faster than original learning, we say a savings has appeared. Recognition produces the highest amount of retention, while recall produces the lowest.

4. A controversy exists as to whether recall and recognition represent fundamentally different aspects of the overall memory system or are merely differentially sensitive measures.

5. The three components of the overall memory system are encoding, storage, and retrieval. Encoding refers to the processes we use to store information efficiently. Storage refers to the maintenance of information over time. Retrieval refers to the processes we use to pull information out of storage.

6. Chunking is the encoding process we use to make a single response out of many responses.

7. We may encode information in visual and/or verbal form, and in terms of its sound and/or its meaning.

8. Mental rotation studies are taken as evidence for the existence of mental images.

9. Visual images have been thought of as perceptual experiences and as propositions.

10. Pictures tend to be remembered better than words. The dual-trace hypothesis accounts for this fact.

11. Encoding may be acoustical or semantic.

12. The tip-of-the-tongue and clustering phenomena are retrieval effects.

13. Memory distortions may be either constructive or reconstructive.

14. In interference theory, retroactive inhibition refers to the disruption of memory by subsequent learning. Proactive inhibition refers to interference due to prior learning.

15. Decay theory argues that memory traces decay or degenerate as time passes. This old and intuitively appealing idea has not received experimental support.

16. Separate-store models of memory propose that the ways we remember items for short periods of time differ from the ways in which we remember information for long periods of time.

17. The sensory memory is a store in which information will decay within a very brief period of time (perhaps half a second).

18. Iconic and echoic memories refer to visual and auditory sensory memories, respectively.

19. Short-term memory is seen as a store from which information will be lost within approximately one minute unless it is maintained by rehearsal. If rehearsed enough, information in short-term memory is thought to be transferred to long-term, or relatively permanent, memory. Items in short-term memory are "in mind." The capacity of short-term memory is limited. If it is full, old items will be "bumped out" by new, incoming items.

20. Long-term memory stores information with relative permanence. Everything we have learned, but are not now thinking of, is thought to be stored in long-term memory. Information can be lost from long-term memory, but at a very slow rate.

21. Information can be located in short-term memory alone, in long-term memory alone, or in both stores at the same time.

22. Semantic-network models all deal with semantic material and multiple interconnected relationships.

23. Four types of semantic-network models are currently popular: hierarchies, matrices, features, and spreading-activation concepts.

24. Lexical memory, or memory for words, represents organization in long-term memory.

25. Subjective organization and priming in lexical-decision studies are tools used in studying lexicons.

26. The levels-of-processing approach holds that "deeply" processed items are more durably stored. The levels approach argues against separate stores.

27. The existence of separate stores has not yet been proved.

28. Forgetting may sometimes be motivated. The concept of repression argues that we push fearful or unpleasant memories out of consciousness, in order to protect ourselves from them.

29. Memories may or may not be permanent. Neither electrical brain stimulation studies nor hypnotic age regression studies offer firm support for the permanence of memories.

30. State-dependent memory studies show that our ability to remember something is affected by the context in which we learn it.

31. Consolidation theory argues that for a memory to become permanent, or to "harden," it must be allowed an undisturbed period during which it can consolidate.

32. Retrograde amnesia studies with both rats and humans seem to provide evidence for consolidation theory, but these interpretations have been challenged.

33. Animal memory systems seem to be basically similar to human memory systems.

KEY TERMS

characteristic features
chunking
constructive changes
decay theory
defining features
delayed-matching-to-sample procedure (DMTS)
dual-trace hypothesis
echoic memory
encoding
episodic memory
feature approach
forgetting curve
hierarchy model (hierarchies)
iconic memory
information-processing system
interference theory

levels-of-processing approach
lexical-decision experiments
lexical memory
long-term memory
matrix model (matrices)
mental rotation
perceptual experience hypothesis
period of consolidation
priming effects
proactive inhibition
propositional hypothesis
recall
recognition
reconstructive changes
relearning
retrieval

retroactive inhibition
retrograde amnesia
semantic memory
semantic-network models
sensory memory
short-term memory
spatial memory
spreading-activation model
state-dependent memory effect
storage
subjective organization
theory of repression
tip-of-the-tongue phenomenon
Type I (maintenance) rehearsal
Type II (elaborative) rehearsal

ADDITIONAL READING

Anderson, J. R. (1985) *Cognitive psychology and its implications.* New York: W. H. Freeman.
This is an excellent summary of the field by one of the recognized leaders.

Best, J. B. (1986) *Cognitive psychology.* St. Paul: West.
This is a very readable discussion of the cognitive aspects of memory.

Carlson, N. R. (1986) *Physiology of behavior.* Boston: Allyn and Bacon.
This advanced-level text contains some excellent chapters on the biological correlates of both learning and memory.

Houston, J. P. (1986) *Fundamentals of learning and memory.* New York: Harcourt Brace Jovanovich.
This text is one of few that integrates animal and human data.

7

Cognition: Language, Concepts, and Problems

Cognitive psychology is one of the most active and complex areas within the general discipline of psychology today. In a history of the cognitive sciences, Gardner (1985) shows that the study of cognitive processes, such as thinking, reasoning, imagining, and problem solving, is complicated because so many other disciplines are involved in trying to understand how humans are capable of acquiring and using so much of the information to which they are exposed. Cognitive psychologists, for example, often need to interact with scientists in linguistics, computer science, neurosciences, anthropology, and other fields in order to make sense of human cognition. Because cognitive psychology is so broad and is interrelated with so many other disciplines, beginning students are often confused by the complexity of the field. And yet, the topics encompassed by cognitive psychology are of immense concern and are certainly gaining importance. Therefore, we will define this fast-changing field as clearly as possible. We will start with a general view of cognitive psychology and then take a more detailed look at specific topics within cognition.

Each of the five approaches that follow has something to offer, but none should be thought of as "the correct approach." In fact, most of these approaches are closely related to one another. Cognitive psychology has not progressed to the point where everyone has settled on a single vocabulary and a unified conception of the area. So, as you read these approaches, or points of view, do not try to form more than a rough, preliminary idea of what cognitive psychology is all about.

THE FIELD OF COGNITIVE PSYCHOLOGY

Herbert Simon, a pioneer in the field of artificial intelligence and an influential force in cognitive psychology, is one of few psychologists to have won the Nobel prize.

Five Approaches to Cognition

1. *Cognition as Information Processing* As we saw in Chapter 6, many cognitive psychologists conceive of the human as an information-processing mechanism and of cognition as the processing of this information. Viewed from this perspective, **cognition** refers to the knowledge that an individual has about the world around him. As such, cognition and its associated processes explain how sensory input is received by the person, how this input is stored in memory, how the person retrieves stored information, makes comparisons and decisions to solve problems, and produces outputs in the form of actions (Anderson, 1985). In this chapter, we will discuss how this abstract information-processing concept works, as we cover the topics of language acquisition and language use, concept formation, and problem solving.

Related to this information-processing approach are developments in computer science, especially artificial intelligence, which tries to get computers to behave intelligently. Such approaches have included computers that can play chess (Zobrist & Carlson, 1973) and programs that can solve problems (Newell & Simon, 1972). Programs simulating human memory are common (Cofer, 1975). Some investigators have tried to build emotional components into their programs to make them function more like humans. For example, Herbert Simon (1967) has attempted to build impatience and discouragement into a computer program. Building realistic information-processing models and computer-based "artificial intelligence" systems

Developments in computer science have resulted in computers that can play chess and checkers.

is a real challenge to cognitive researchers—which is one reason why efforts in these directions are certain to expand.

2. *Cognition as Mental Manipulation of Symbols*   Some definitions of cognition point out that much of what we call cognitive activity involves the mental manipulation of symbols. A ***symbol*** is anything that stands for something other than itself. Words are symbols. The word "goat" stands for a particular barnyard animal. The word "pencil" refers to a wooden writing instrument. Obviously, language is a symbolic endeavor. The box titled "Epigraphy, the Ancient Maya, and Cognition" discusses a practical application of the importance of the use of symbols.

But symbols are not limited to those found in language systems. Physical objects may function as symbols: a flashing red light signifies danger. Similarly, music and mathematics use their own symbolic systems of notation. Visual images may be thought of as symbols. Think of the face of a good friend. That image is a symbol; it stands for the person you are thinking of. Physical gestures, pictures, and diagrams also may be symbols. The crucial aspect of these symbols is that they all stand for, or signify, something other than themselves.

The beauty of a symbol is that it frees us from the present. It allows us to think of, or to experience, imagined or remembered objects or events. If you think of a pink frog wearing green socks, you are experiencing something you would not be able to experience without symbols. If you think of your fourteenth birthday, you are reexperiencing something you could not experience without symbols. Symbols allow us to take excursions into the past, into the future, and into the realm of fantasy. According to some cognitive psychologists, the mental manipulation of symbols constitutes the heart of cognition.

Maya hierogyphic writing utilizes a system of symbols to represent events, places, and actions.

◆ EPIGRAPHY, THE ANCIENT MAYA, AND COGNITION

The ancient Maya were New World Indians who inhabited what is today the Yucatan Peninsula of Mexico and the countries of Belize, Guatemala, and Honduras. These people built spectacular temple-pyramids and palaces throughout Mesoamerica from the time of the pre-Christian era until the Spanish conquest. They also developed a form of hieroglyphic writing that they used to record their historical, mythological, astronomical, and mathematical knowledge (see accompanying example of Maya script).

There is much enthusiasm among archaeologists today to better understand the Maya. However, the key to understanding the Maya has proven elusive until recently. The key that we are referring to has to do with how to read Maya hieroglyphics. Unlike the Egyptians, the Maya did not leave a Rosetta stone to help in the translation of the script they left carved on stone and painted in folded books.

One break in translating the hieroglyphics, however, has come from an unlikely source. In early 1981, David Stuart, a high-school sophomore, recognized a key morpheme —*pa*—, which helped him make sense of a hieroglyph that he was working on in Guatemala (for a definition of morphemes, see page 278). With this discovery, David Stuart has been able to translate numerous other Maya hieroglyphs and today he is an active Maya researcher. How did David Stuart get his start in the field of epigraphy (the study of inscriptions)? Also, of what relevance are the Maya and epigraphy to us in this chapter on language and cognition?

Let us begin with the latter question first. The Maya, like other cultures before and after them, invented a system for using symbols to represent objects, events, places, and actions. By the use of these symbols, the Maya were able to preserve important information for others to read if they knew the meanings of the various symbols. This chapter is about cognitive representation and the use of symbols.

David Stuart got his start as a Mayanist when he was 9 years old and accompanied his father, an archaeologist, to the Yucatan to study Maya civilization. David was fascinated by hieroglyphs, whose translation requires enormous skill in pattern recognition, problem solving, and the manipulation of symbols, all of which are critical topics in cognitive psychology. We hope that the issues discussed in this chapter will give you an appreciation of some of the skills that enabled David Stuart to become an epigrapher of Maya text.

3. *Cognition as Problem Solving* Still others prefer to think of cognition as problem-solving activity. According to this approach, cognitive activity includes the ability to identify problems, define and represent them with precision, explore possible solution strategies, act on these strategies, and examine the effects of these strategies (Bransford & Stein, 1984). This approach holds that much of our thinking is directed toward the solution of problems. For example, when you begin to study for an examination, you decide how to go about learning the material, and you set up some procedures to test your memory before you actually take the test.

There are other types of cognitive activity, however, that are not as easily recognized as having anything to do with problem solving. Daydreaming is one such activity. Can this activity be thought of as problem solving? Some psychologists argue that although it may be inefficient, daydreaming is actually a problem-solving activity. It may represent a kind of solution if it keeps your mind off something else that is bothering you. If you are having a hard time finding a solution to a particular problem, you might be better off for a while forgetting about the problem and doing something else—perhaps daydreaming. Many famous scientists and inventors have reported that they arrived at the correct solution to a problem after a period of rest from trying to solve the problem. This is known as the *incubation effect.* We will discuss incubation again later in this chapter.

Some cognitive psychologists think of problem solving as one specific type of cognitive activity rather than the only type of cognition. It is important to note that this kind of uncertainty is characteristic of this fast-growing field.

4. *Cognition as Thinking* Most of what has been said so far suggests that cognition may be equated with thinking. And, in fact, most cognitive psychologists do consider the nature of thinking to be their prime concern. People who study thinking must deal with an extremely wide range of activities, for thinking represents the highest, most complex form of human behavior. Thinking covers an enormous range of complex events. We are thinking when we try to solve a math problem, but we are also thinking when we remember someone's name, study for an exam, or solve a crossword puzzle. We are thinking when a long-forgotten memory pops into our minds for no apparent reason. We are thinking when we create great literary masterpieces, and we are also thinking when we notice an occasional pain in our stomachs.

As we have noted, some thinking is verbal or involves language (think of your name), but some does not (think of the shape of the Eiffel Tower). Some thinking seems to involve problem solving, while some does not. Some thinking involves concepts—for instance, symbols that classify objects with common qualities such as *dog, square,* and *blue*—and some does not. Sometimes thinking involves logic and reasoning and sometimes it does not. In other words, cognitive psychologists have carved out quite an area of study for themselves. By calling themselves cognitive psychologists they indicate that they are interested in one or more of these highly complex, interrelated forms of thinking.

5. *Cognition as a Collection of Related Activities* Finally, some psychologists prefer to hedge a little when it comes to defining cognition. Because cognition is so difficult to pin down, these psychologists simply list a number of factors that usually concern cognitive psychologists. They suggest that cognition involves knowing, perceiving, remembering, judging, thinking, reasoning, problem solving, learning, imagining, conceptualizing, and using language.

Some Conclusions As all of the preceding approaches make clear, the field of cognitive psychology does not restrict its attention to a few isolated phenomena. In a sense, cognitive psychology represents

COLOR PLATE 14

Color is so much a part of our world that we often take it for granted, forgetting how powerfully it can affect us. Bright blue skies and green fields (Color Plate 14) conjure up a summer's day, serene and cheerful, but if these same colors follow us home to breakfast (Color Plate 15), they can ruin almost anybody's appetite.

COLOR PLATE 15

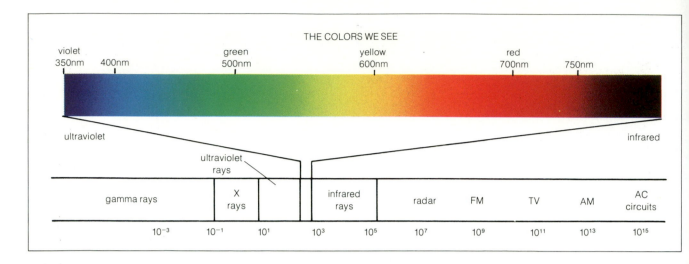

THE COLORS WE SEE

| violet | | green | | yellow | | red | |
| 350nm | 400nm | 500nm | | 600nm | | 700nm | 750nm |

ultraviolet   infrared

	ultraviolet rays							
gamma rays	X rays		infrared rays	radar	FM	TV	AM	AC circuits
	10^{-3}	10^{-1}	10^{1}	10^{3}	10^{5}	10^{7}	10^{9}	10^{11}	10^{13}	10^{15}

COLOR PLATE 16

When receptor cells in our eyes respond to waves of electromagnetic energy, we perceive light. Visible light waves make up only a tiny portion of the vast spectrum of electromagnetic radiation, as Color Plate 16 shows.

Color has three psychological dimensions. We experience the wavelength of a visible light as its *color*, or hue. Color Plate 17 shows that light with a wavelength of 480 nm appears blue to us, and 520 nm appears green. We perceive the amplitude of a light wave as the *brightness* or intensity of the color. The greater the amplitude, the brighter the color appears to us. The apples below reflect 520 nm waves of high amplitude, so we see them as bright green. The third psychological dimension is called *saturation*. Light of a single wavelength appears very saturated or pure to us, while light that mixes many wavelengths seems low in saturation. The apples here are a highly saturated green while the olives are low in saturation. Even pure colors seem less saturated if they are very pale, like the melon, or very dark, like the cucumbers. In effect, the saturation is watered down by white or black at these extremes.

COLOR PLATE 17

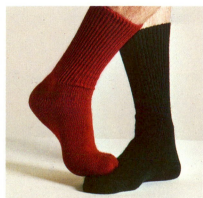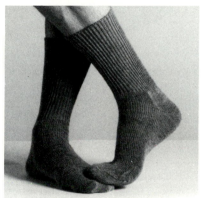

COLOR PLATE 18

Most of us can pick a matched pair of socks from this clothesline, but for color-blind people, the choice may be difficult or even impossible. There are three forms of color blindness. The person on the left evidently has red-green color blindness, which is the most common form. The person in the middle has yellow-blue color blindness, which is very rare. A person with monochromatic vision sees the world in shades of gray, as shown on the right. Many animals are monochromats, including dogs and cats, but few humans are completely color blind. The Dvorine Pseudo-Isochromatic Plates, shown below, are commonly used to test for color blindness. A color-blind person cannot distinguish the colored numbers from the background colors.

COLOR PLATE 19

COLOR PLATE 20

Color afterimages led Ewald Hering to develop his theory of color vision in 1870 (see pp. 123–24). Stare at the center of the blue patch for 30 seconds, then focus on the gray or yellow square. You will see a yellow patch on each, but the patch on the yellow square will appear brighter than the surrounding yellow. Similarly, if you stare at the red patch for 30 seconds, you will see a green patch when you look at the gray, and a brighter green when you look at the green square.

Hering believed that color vision depends on receptors that function in two different phases. For instance, our yellow-blue receptors transmit sensations of yellow in one phase and sensations of blue in the other phase, but they cannot transmit both colors at once. When we stare at the blue patch, the receptors go into the blue phase. When we switch to gray or yellow, we remove the blue stimulus, the receptor goes into the yellow phase, and we see a yellow after-image. Our red-green receptors behave the same way. Though Hering's theory does not fully explain color vision, this "on-or-off" process has been recorded in recent experiments using microelectrodes.

a reaction against earlier studies that focused on isolated, overt, observable responses (as classical conditioning studies do, for instance). Cognitive psychologists want to know what goes on in the mind, and they are not afraid to use "mentalistic" concepts such as ideas, thoughts, and images.

As you doubtless have noted, we have already covered some of the topics involved in cognitive psychology. Specifically, our chapters on sensation and perception (Chapter 3) and memory (Chapter 6) deal with key issues in the study of cognition. Sensation, perception, and memory are dealt with individually, rather than being included in this chapter, because of their traditional status in the field of psychology and because of their great size and scope. But you should realize that, in those chapters, we have already begun our study of cognitive psychology.

To sum up, it is clear that cognitive activities may be thought of in several different ways. We may merely identify the elements typically thought of as cognitive activities (for example, attention, perception, memory, judgment, language use, thinking, reasoning, problem solving, conceptualizing, imagining, and so on). Alternatively, we may think of cognition as the entire range of information-processing activities, as the mental manipulation of symbols, as problem solving, or as thinking. For our purposes, these various conceptions or definitions of cognition will be used interchangeably.

Topics in the Field of Cognition

In the rest of this chapter, we will consider specific topics in cognition that represent currently popular, active areas of study. The topics we will discuss fall under the general areas of (1) language, (2) concept formation, and (3) problem solving. Obviously, these areas are intertwined. Moreover, they make use of concepts from the areas of sensation and perception and memory as well. It is difficult, and sometimes impossible, to speak of one topic without referring to the others, but psychologists focus their attention on certain aspects of the overall flow of cognitive activities, and so will we.

Our strategy will be to break down the overall cognitive process and then focus on certain aspects of that process. However, influential thinkers within the field are attempting to build unified models or theories that will detail and encompass all of the elements of cognition. For example, Donald Norman and Daniel Bobrow state:

> Our goal is to understand human cognitive processes. The phenomena of attention, perception, memory, and cognition are interrelated—intertwined might be a better word—and the explanation for one set of phenomena helps to elucidate the others. Because of their interdependence, we believe it possible to uncover a single, unified story of processing structure for human cognitive processes (1975, p. 114).

These continuing attempts to build inclusive models of cognitive activity are far too complex for us to explore in this text, but as we examine certain parts of cognition, it is good to remember that some researchers are trying to see it as a whole.

LANGUAGE

Our ability to use language certainly sets us apart from other members of the animal kingdom. Of course, many other life forms have some fairly elaborate forms of communication. Birds often use one call to attract a mate, another call to sound a general alarm, and still another to ward off competing members of the same species. Similarly, everyone who has owned a cat has come to understand the various sounds a cat will use to communicate its needs and desires. It would be difficult to confuse the rising, spine-tingling cry of confronting rival males with the chirruping, trilling sound of a male courting a desirable female. You may have heard of von Frisch's (1974) work with the communication system employed by bees. Workers, returning to the hive, will "tell" where food is located by varying the speed and direction of their "dance." However, in spite of these examples (and there are many others), communications within the animal kingdom seem limited to a few basic types of response.

Humans, on the other hand, talk and write incessantly, expressing everything from their most basic needs to the most abstract intellectual concepts through a vast array of complicated language systems. Humans seem born to talk, and this distinctive quality does much to separate humanity from the rest of the animal kingdom.

If we are to understand cognitive processes we must understand language, for it is clearly vital to our thinking. Much of our thinking is aided by our language and perhaps is shaped by it as well. At the same time, we should remember that not all cognitive activity involves language. We have already noted how we can think in terms of visual images without having to put the thought into words.

We use language for many different purposes; Table 7-1 lists just some of the more common ways that we can use it effectively. Clearly, this flexible, adaptable tool called language gives us an enormous advantage over other members of the animal kingdom. The accomplishments contained in Table 7-1 would not be possible without language and are all far beyond anything the so-called lower animals can attain.

TABLE 7–1 Some Common Ways in Which Spoken and Written Language Are Used

Spoken Language	Written Language
Description of events/thoughts	Description of events, places, and objects
Information seeking/questions	Communicating current events
Teaching	Instructional materials
Expressing emotion	Storytelling, poetry
Greeting and thanking people	
Storytelling	Record keeping
Singing	

Written language enables humanity to "stockpile" information. If you think about it for a moment, you may well know more than the greatest minds of the past. Aristotle, Galileo, and Newton all seem relatively ignorant compared to you once you steep yourself in the contents of your local library. Writing ensures that knowledge is cumulative and readily available. We need not rediscover everything for ourselves or repeat the mistakes of the past. In short, writing makes language far more useful and flexible.

Even before the creation of writing and printing, our ancestors held a distinct advantage over the lower animals. However, they were quite limited in their ability to accumulate information and to pass it on from generation to generation. They had to transfer accumulated wisdom by word of mouth. This method was both time-consuming and, at times, inaccurate. It was also limited by the capacity of the memory systems of the individuals involved.

Spoken and written language do three things for us: (1) they allow us to communicate; (2) they allow us to store information beyond the capacity of our memory stores; and (3) they facilitate thinking by providing a system of symbols and rules relating those symbols to one another. Because these functions are so important in our lives, we will look more closely at humanity's marvelous gift of language.

Phonemes

All spoken languages are based on a limited number of different sounds. The entire English language, in all its apparent complexity, is based on about 45 basic sounds. Some languages involve no more than 15 basic sounds, and no known language uses more than 85. *Phonemes* are defined as sounds that function to signal differences in the words in a language. For example, in English the following words

An elder of Kenya's Masai tribe passes on a cultural legacy of tribal wisdom to the younger men. Societies with no written language often preserve remarkably detailed histories and legends in this way.

differ in meaning because of a single sound at the beginning of the word—*pin, bin, din, sin, kin, fin, win, tin, chin, thin.* Thus the sounds /p/, /b/, /d/, /s/, /k/, /f/, /w/, /t/, /ch/, and /th/ all function as different phonemes in English. Most phonemes, like most letters, have no meaning by themselves; they must be combined with one another to form meaningful units.

In our analysis of language, the phoneme is considered to be the basic unit. Linguists and psycholinguists have described in detail the physical events involved in the production of each of these basic sounds or phonemes. We will take just a quick look at this sort of analysis. For example, consider the *t* sound in *tap*, the *v* sound in *vat*, and the *b* sound in *bat*. As you say *t*, notice that your tongue touches the roof of your mouth and your lips are open. But when you say *v*, something very different happens. Your top teeth now touch your bottom lip. The tip of your tongue no longer touches the roof of your mouth. And when you say *b*, your top and bottom lips touch. Try some other basic sounds, such as the *g* in *gun* and the *th* in *the*. Each sound requires some distinctly different physical responses on your part.

The phonemes that we learn as English speakers often do not include the same sounds that are common to speakers of other languages. For instance, compare the English and Spanish word *pan*. The initial *p* in the English word *pan* (utensil) is aspirated (the *p* is produced with a puff of air), whereas in the Spanish word *pan* (bread), the *p* is unaspirated. In addition, the *a* in the Spanish word *pan* is pronounced like the *a* in the English word *pawn*. In fact, the Spanish word *pan* sounds much like the word *pawn* in English. Accordingly, the English speaker who attempts to learn a second language must frequently learn a new system of phonemes. Otherwise numerous errors will be made in the pronunciation of the new language.

Morphemes

A *morpheme* is the smallest meaningful unit in a language. A morpheme is usually composed of two or more phonemes—but not always. Some words, such as *A* and *I* are morphemes, or meaningful, even though they are composed of single phonemes. Many, but not all morphemes are words. Some are prefixes and some are suffixes. Thus, *fun, help,* and *fox* are all morphemes because they are meaningful units composed of two or more phonemes. They also happen to be words. But *-ly* and *-ness* are morphemes too. They have meaning when they are suffixes (as in *quickly* and *quickness*), and they are composed of two or more phonemes. Similarly, *un-* is a morpheme when used as a prefix (as in *unhappy*), even though it is not a word.

Words may be composed of single morphemes (*fun, help, fox*) or they may be composed of more than one morpheme. *Help* (a morpheme) and *less* (a morpheme) may be combined to form *helpless*, a word composed of two morphemes.

Every language has restrictions on the ways in which phonemes can be combined and ordered. The rules of our language do not allow us to put together just any phonemes to form a meaningful unit. Certain phoneme combinations are not allowed. For example, when was the last time you ran across an English word beginning with *ws*?

Never. *Ws* is not allowed, even though something like *wr* is allowed (*wrote, wry*). Similarly, English words do not begin with *pz*, while *py* is acceptable (*python, pylon*).

What does all this tell us? Our familiarity with acceptable and unacceptable combinations allows us to judge whether or not unfamiliar combinations are true words. For example, consider the following:

hkmurgy

zymurgy

pjmurgy

Which of these is a true word? If you chose *zymurgy*, you are correct. *Zymurgy* is a branch of chemistry dealing with fermentation. Perhaps you already knew the word *zymurgy;* more than likely you did not. Still, you were able to identify it as the true word. You probably chose it because you know that English words do not begin with *hk* or *pj*, while some do begin with *zy* (*zygote*). The *zy* combination is acceptable, and it allowed you to correctly identify a true word when there were no other clues to help.

Phrase Structure Grammar

Obviously, language is not limited to morphemes. We do not go about communicating in terms of isolated morphemes alone, although an occasional morpheme such as "Stop!" or "Yes!" can be extremely effective. We combine morphemes into words and words into sentences. Just as there are rules governing the combination of phonemes into morphemes and morphemes into words, there are complex rules governing the ways that we put morphemes and words together to make meaningful sentences. The rules that govern the ordering and positioning of sounds, morphemes, and words in sentences are called ***rules of grammar.***

The ordering of words makes all the difference when we want to understand an English sentence. For example, "An artichoke is a green, leafy vegetable" makes perfectly good sense, but only because the words are arranged according to the rules of grammar. If we scramble the words, ignoring the rules of grammar, we scramble the meaning as well. If someone said to you, "Green is leafy an vegetable artichoke a," you might head for the nearest exit.

Linguists have described the structure of the sentence, as prescribed by the rules of grammar, in terms of the various phrases the sentence contains. For example, consider the sentences in Figure 7–1. As you can see, each sentence is composed of a ***noun phrase*** followed by a ***verb phrase.*** Each of these phrases is then broken down into its own elements. These diagrams represent what is known as the ***phrase structure*** of the sentences.

Describing sentences in terms of phrase structure helps us understand what is and what is not an acceptable English sentence. At the simplest level, the diagrams in Figure 7–1 suggest that a verb phrase follows a noun phrase. We can see the importance of this particular rule by switching the positions of the noun and verb phrases. When we do this, we have "Ate the corn the big turkey" and "Flew over the city the green thing." We can still figure out what they

FIGURE 7–1 Examples of the
Phrase Structure of Sentences

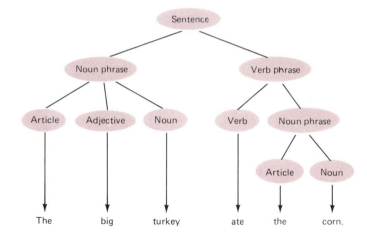

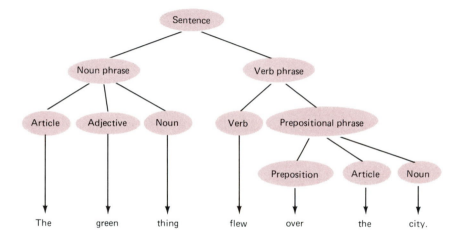

mean, but neither of these is an acceptable English sentence. In fact, they do not even sound like English sentences.

The rules of grammar are complicated and not always agreed upon even by natural users of a given language. But the fact that there are rules that govern the positioning of words within sentences cannot be denied. It is these rules of grammar, generally accepted within a given population, that enable humans to communicate with one another.

Problems with Phrase Structure Grammar Describing language in terms of phrase structure grammar certainly has value, but there are two limitations to this approach that need to be addressed (Houston, 1981). First, some sentences can have two different meanings. For example, "They are growing trees" could be intended to mean that certain people are in the business of raising trees or that certain trees are in the process of growing. Figure 7–2 shows the different phrase structures for this **ambiguous sentence.** Such ambiguous sentences suggest that the rules of phrase structure grammar are not perfect, because they let us generate "acceptable" sentences whose meanings

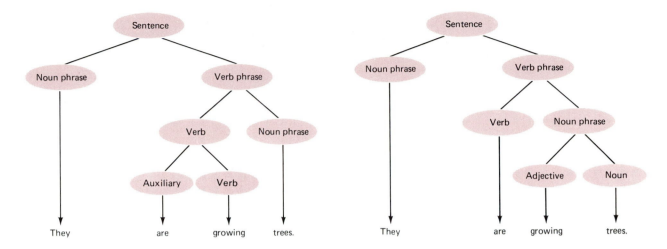

FIGURE 7–2 Phrase Structures of a Sample Ambiguous Sentence

are unclear. The correct phrasing of these sentences depends on which meaning is intended. These sentences are not handled adequately by phrase structure grammar because this form of grammar only deals with the actual words in the sentence. It does not take into account what the speaker *meant* by these sentences. Before we can completely understand language, we must know more about what the speaker means to communicate.

The second problem with phrase structure grammars is that they do not clearly identify the fact that different sentences can mean the same thing. For example, "Billy caught Joe" means the same thing as "Joe was caught by Billy," even though the phrase structures differ. Phrase structure grammar would imply that the two sentences are different because their structures are different. But we know they mean the same thing.

Deep Structure and Surface Structure

In addressing the problems associated with phrase structure grammar, Chomsky (1965) introduced the distinction between deep structure and surface structure. He felt that if we are to understand sentences we must consider not only the words used in the sentence but the speaker's *intent* as well. The wording of a given sentence is its **surface structure**, while the meaning or idea behind those words is the sentence's **deep structure** (Anderson, 1985). As we have noted, there is not always a one-to-one correspondence between deep and surface structure. Several different sets of words, or different surface structures, can express the same underlying deep structure.

Transformational Grammar

Chomsky then took his analysis a step further and introduced the idea of **transformational grammar.** According to this approach, deep-structure ideas can be expressed in different ways by applying various transformations to the underlying deep-structure content. Thus, if we have an idea about a dog chasing a cat we can transform this deep-structure material into various equivalent surface structures (the

John Anderson (cited frequently in this chapter) is a cognitive psychologist who has written extensively on the organization of the mind. He believes that we can understand the architecture of the mind by studying the cognitive processes involved in language acquisition and use.

FIGURE 7–3   Chomsky's Transformational Rules and Sentence Structures   *This figure shows how Chomsky views the relationship between deep structure and surface structure and the rules (transformational and phonological) that connect them.*

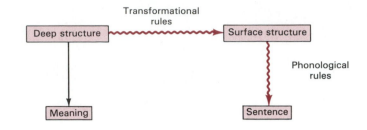

dog chased the cat or the cat was chased by the dog). Different transformations of the deep structure can generate many different surface structures that express the same idea. It is the task of transformational grammarians to describe the many different transformational rules that are acceptable in any given grammar.

Figure 7–3 shows the relationship between the deep-structure meaning and the surface-structure sentence. ***Transformational rules*** are used to change deep-structure meaning into the surface-structure features of a sentence, while ***phonological rules*** are used by the speaker to convert the rules into spoken speech. For example, actives and passives share the same deep structure; they describe the same event. Their deep-structure subjects and objects are the same, though their surface arrangement of noun phrases is different (see Figure 7–4). In the passive voice, a rule called the passive transformation rule acts to change the order of NP_1 and NP_2 to result in the surface-structure arrangement of the passive sentence seen in Figure 7–4. In addition, the morphemes *be* and *by* are introduced and ordered to form the full passive sentence. The transformational rules for the passive then are: interchange the deep-structure subject and the deep-structure object, add *was* before the verb and *by* on the other side of the verb.

Schemata

A ***schema*** is the organized body of information a person has about a particular object, concept, or event. For instance, we all have a schema, or body of knowledge, pertaining to basketball. Basketball involves a ball and a hoop, basketball teams have five players, the players tend to be tall, screaming is allowed during close games. We each have a schema representing what we know about tape, milk, politics, Mars, air, oats, Flash Gordon, and so on.

The point here is that distortions in our memory occur because we interpret incoming information in terms of our existing schemata

FIGURE 7–4   Phrase Structures of an Active and a Passive Sentence   *These two sentences share the same deep structure, but the transformational rules for the passive voice have been applied to the active surface structure.*

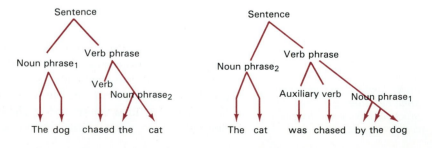

The schema you would apply to this room from the point of view of a burglar ready to burglarize the house would differ radically from the schema you would formulate of the room as a potential house buyer.

(plural for schema). We leave out parts of the prose that do not fit into our schemata and we add elements to the story that we draw from our schemata.

Schemata can aid recall as well as disrupt it. Anderson and Pickert (1978) had subjects read a neutral description of a house while pretending they were either a house buyer or a burglar. Then they were asked to recall the details of the house. When they had recalled all they could, the experimenter asked them to change their point of view and try to recall more material. The home buyer became a burglar and the burglar became a home buyer. Recall went up. The newly appointed burglar suddenly remembered that the front door was partially hidden by bushes. The newly appointed home buyer suddenly remembered that the living room was spacious. In other words, applying schemata associated with two different points of view permitted greater access to stored information.

In addition, schemata serve very useful purposes for us since they represent our knowledge about how features tend to go together to define objects or how events tend to go together to define episodes. This knowledge about what tends to occur with what is crucial to our ability to predict what we will encounter in our environment.

The Acquisition of Language

Having taken a look at the structure of language, let us briefly consider how humans acquire language in the first place. In this section we will *not* theorize about the mechanisms that might account for language development. We will merely consider the order in which the elements of language are acquired, saving theories for the next section.

Babbling   During the first few months of life, humans engage in little verbal activity other than crying, cooing, and gurgling. But at about 6 months babies begin to engage in an enormous amount of what appears to be spontaneous *babbling.* Much of this babbling resembles phonemes and syllables used by the adult population. An infant's babbling can be dichotomized into two types (Sachs, 1985). In the first, *reduplicated babbling*, the sounds consist of consonant-vowel combinations repeated in a stereotyped fashion (for example, "ba-baba" or "nanana"). This type of babbling makes its appearance at about 26 weeks of age and continues through to the end of the first year. The second type of vocalization is called *jargon babbling* and consists of strings of sounds uttered with a variety of stress and intonation patterns. From a distance, this jargon babbling sounds much like speech and infants sometimes use it in monologues in much the way they hear adults around them speaking over the telephone. This form of babbling demonstrates that infants are good mimics of intonation. Jargon babbling usually appears by the end of the first year and continues until the appearance of true speech at about 18 months.

All babies, regardless of nationality or living conditions, apparently begin to babble at about the same age and in the same manner. The recorded babblings of infants living in different countries cannot be distinguished (Atkinson, MacWhinney, & Stoel, 1970). Neither the amount nor the sound of the babbling appears to be much affected by the environment. Lenneberg (1967) reports a case in which a deaf child, born to deaf-mute parents, produced babbling that was quite comparable to the babbling of children with normal hearing.

In short, babbling appears to be innate, or predetermined. However, babies soon begin to concentrate on the phonemes and syllables that are part of the language they will be acquiring. Sounds more appropriate to other languages begin to drop out. This suggests that, as babies, we can make most of the sounds required to master *any* language. As we grow older, we lose this ability. By the time we are adults, we may find it impossible to make the phonemes required in some other languages. Anyone who has tried to learn a second language as an adult will know how hard it is to recapture sounds that all of us could once produce with ease.

Single Words and Holophrastic Speech   After about one year of life, babies start to acquire a limited vocabulary of true words. These first words mark the beginning of true language use. At first these words will not be spoken with complete accuracy. Through time, and with added experience, they approximate more and more closely the speech of adults.

The acquisition of language is a remarkable cognitive feat not only because the child must learn the basic sound system (phonemes and morphemes) of the language, a working vocabulary, grammar, and the ability to communicate competently in social interaction, but also because all of this occurs simultaneously. If we consider the fact that it has been estimated that the 6-year-old child has a vocabulary of from 8,000 to 14,000 words (Carey, 1977), we see that infants have a tremendous task ahead of them in just learning words. If a child begins by acquiring one word at 12 months, this means that he must acquire 4 to 8 new words (on the average) every day during the preschool years. Even though we now know a great deal about how early referential words are taught to children by their caretakers, we really know very little about the mechanisms by which children achieve such an impressive vocabulary in such a relatively short period of time.

Language begins through the use of single words in a way that is called *holophrastic speech* (Cairns, 1986). What this means is that babies and young children often use a single word to stand for an entire idea, thought, event, or sentence. When a young child uses a single word such as "Mama!" he or she may mean quite a bit more than that single word normally conveys. By saying "Mama!" the child may mean, "At last! Here comes Mama with my food!" A young child who says "Juice!" may be asking for a drink of a particular liquid, delivered in a particular container, at a particular temperature. Holophrastic speech underlines the fact that the child's comprehension far exceeds his or her ability to speak.

Two-word Utterances   At about 18 months (the time varies from child to child), infants begin the process of acquiring grammar. Once they have a modest vocabulary, they start to put together two words to express an idea. "Baby walk." "Daddy go." "More milk." These *two-word utterances* are minimal but true sentences. Once infants learn the process of putting two words together, they progress at a rapid rate, producing many two-word combinations daily. During this period, children also learn to use many different types (see Table 7–2) of two-word utterances (Braine, 1963; Miller & Ervin, 1964).

The important thing about this stage of language development is that these two-word utterances have been shown to be vital in terms of the semantic relationships that the child is communicating. Table 7–2 lists the eight most frequent semantic relationships documented by Brown (1973) in his study of language acquisition. The examples

TABLE 7–2   The Eight Most Common Semantic Relationships Found During the Two-word Stage of Language Development

Semantic Relationships	Examples
agent + action	mommy give, daddy sit
action + object	give money, open door
agent + object	mommy car, Angel bone
action + location	sit there, fall floor
entity + location	plane rug, phone table
possessor + possession	my mommy, baby bed
entity + attribute	truck red, house pretty
demonstrative + entity	dat tree, dis mop

in the table are taken from the two-word utterances found in the speech of a co-author's 20-month-old son. As can be seen from these examples, children talk a great deal about objects. They point them out and name them (Brown's demonstrative element) and they talk about where the objects are (location element), what they are like (attributive element), who owns them (possessor element), and who is doing things to them (agent + object elements). Objects, people, and actions and their interrelationships are the things that preoccupy the two-year-old infant and these are precisely the concepts that the child has just completed differentiating during the sensorimotor stage of cognitive development (to be explained in Chapter 12).

Telegraphic Speech Another characteristic of early language development is telegraphic speech. In **telegraphic speech**, children preserve the order of the words they hear in a sentence but leave out unimportant words. For example, if a mother says, "Here comes Daddy up the stairs," the child might say, "Daddy up stairs." The essential, stressed words are maintained in the proper order, while less important words, such as prepositions, articles, suffixes, and prefixes, may be omitted.

Telegraphic speech appears not only when the child is copying or imitating an adult's speech, but in the child's own spontaneous speech as well. "Want bed" will do very well to express the idea that the child wishes to go to bed now. Telegraphic speech may be thought of as an advanced version of holophrastic speech. In both cases, complex ideas are expressed in abbreviated fashion.

Longer Sentences Between the ages of two and three, children begin to produce longer sentences. They start to use more complex forms of grammar and string morphemes together in longer and longer sequences. According to Brown (1973), sentence length increases by what he calls the "law of cumulative complexity," so that utterances represent combinations of the basic structures and semantic units present in the two-word stage of development. For example, agent + action and action + object may be combined to give agent + action + object, as in "Daddy hit ball." In this way sentences become progressively more complex. Table 7–3 lists several processes Brown uses to describe how a child's speech advances in complexity.

Another feature of this stage of language development is the gradual appearance of a few inflections, such as the suffix -ing (making, going, seeing), the addition of s to pluralize nouns (cars, boats) and 's to indicate possession (daddy's boat, mommy's truck). Interestingly, these inflections are learned in a specific order with -ing being acquired first, followed by the plural s and then the possessive form 's. Brown (1973) characterizes the addition of grammatical morphemes by children to their language in very descriptive terms when he states that they (grammatical morphemes), "like an intricate sort of ivy, begin to grow up between and upon the major construction blocks, the nouns and verbs" (p. 249). Remember that at this initial stage of language development children are confined largely to nouns and verbs.

The process of acquiring the major grammatical morphemes and the full range of semantic relationships is gradual and lengthy. Some

TABLE 7–3 Processes to Explain How Children's Language Increases in Linguistic Complexity

1. *Conjoining.* In this process, overlapping expressions, such as action + verb and verb + object, are combined. Thus, the child who has previously said "Boy hit" and "Hit ball" now says "Boy hit ball."

2. *Expansion.* In this process, elements of simple grammatical relationships are replaced by noun phrases expressing other grammatical relationships. Thus, in an agent + action expression, the agent may be represented by a possessive noun phrase, yielding, for example, "My cookie all gone," or, for an action + location, "Sit Adam chair."

3. *Elaboration.* The basic declarative sentence incorporates the elements agent, action, object, and location. As utterances expand beyond two words, three or more of these expressions are included, but they always appear in the order prescribed by English. Examples are the following: "Adam ride horsie" (agent + action + object); "Tractor go floor" (agent + action + location); "Adam put truck window" (agent + action + object + location).

Source: After Cairns, 1986.

of these morphemes and relationships are still not fully controlled even when children enter school, but what is evident is that by the age of two years, the children have joined the community of speakers around them.

Theories of Language Acquisition

Now we are ready to consider the mechanisms that might account for language development. There are three major theoretical approaches that have been used to explain the acquisition of language by children. We will briefly summarize each theory.

Classical Conditioning There have been a number of different attempts to explain the process of language acquisition. One early theory suggested that much of our language is acquired through classical conditioning. For example, the meaning of the word "Mama" may be established in this way. The sound "Mama" (the CS) is repeatedly paired with the mother and her actions (the UCS). Thus, the baby's responses to the mother's comforting actions become classically conditioned to the sound "Mama." Similarly, "hot" (a CS) may acquire its meaning through repeated pairings with a certain class of unconditioned stimuli (soup, stoves, fires, and so on).

Instrumental Conditioning Many psychologists have suggested that language is acquired through a process of instrumental conditioning (Rachlin, 1976; Skinner, 1957). Their theory is that language is acquired because it is reinforced by parents and others in the child's environment. Each time the young child says "Dada," she is applauded and rewarded with a show of physical and social affection. Incorrect or undesirable sounds are either left unreinforced or they are punished. According to Skinner and his followers, language is acquired just like any other set of responses. *All* responses, language responses as well, are assumed to be acquired according to the principles of reinforcement, extinction, punishment, and generalization.

Many psychologists disagree with the conditioning approach to language acquisition. Their objections focus on the three points outlined below.

1. Language acquisition is much too complicated a process to be explained adequately in terms of simple conditioning. For example, recall the discussion earlier about the amazing growth of vocabulary by the time a child is six years old. Critics maintain that there is no basis for holding that so many individual words could be learned each and every day through a situation of simple conditioning. They feel that some other process must be at work to stimulate the rapid growth of vocabulary observed in young children.

2. The use of language has a creative aspect that is difficult to explain in conditioning terms. Specifically, young children use original arrangements of verbal units that they have never before heard or used. Therefore, the argument goes, these new combinations could not have been established through a process of reinforcement. The fact that children generate their own unique language patterns is indeed hard to explain in terms of reinforcement principles.

3. Finally, if language is established through reinforcement, then it would seem reasonable to expect that children living under widely varying social conditions would acquire language in different ways. But Slobin (1986) has presented evidence that, despite widely varying opportunities for social reinforcement, children in all cultures seem to acquire language in a relatively constant pattern. Even children born to and raised by parents who are deaf appear to acquire language in this pattern.

Psycholinguistic Theory The objections listed above to conditioning theory as a mechanism to account for language development have inspired some new approaches to the question of language acquisition and have stimulated the development of the ***psycholinguistic theory*** of language acquisition (Bohannon & Warren-Leubecker, 1985).

Work such as that done by Lenneberg (1969), Molfese (1977), and others has emphasized the biological, innate aspects of language acquisition. These researchers believe that humans are "prewired" or prepared in a biological sense to acquire language. We are born to speak, no matter what our living conditions, because there is an innate, predetermined quality to our acquisition of language.

A second part of modern psycholinguistic theory holds that children learn complex rules of grammar rather than mere strings of words (Chomsky, 1968). These acquired rules of grammar can account for the creative, generative quality of our language use, which causes difficulty for the conditioning approach. By applying a rule, rather than repeating a string of reinforced words, we can generate new and unique utterances.

Modern psycholinguistic theory argues that the child forms hypotheses about what is and what is not correct language usage and then proceeds to test these hypotheses. When one hypothesis proves to be incorrect, the child will revise or replace it, and continue testing until the correct rule is discovered.

In summary, the psycholinguistic approach offers a promising alternative to the conditioning approach, but both approaches may have something to contribute. Reinforcement, as well as innate mechanisms and hypothesis testing, may also contribute to the overall language acquisition process.

Chimpanzees and Language

Can animals learn language? Until recently, it seemed unlikely. In early studies, chimpanzees raised as human children could never learn to speak more than three or four simple words like "cup" and "up," and these only with great difficulty (Hayes & Hayes, 1952).

However, more recent investigations have revealed that the chimpanzee can do fairly well with language after all. The breakthrough came when Beatrice and Allen Gardner (1978) hit on a new idea: chimps may be able to learn language, but may not be able to *express* this learning verbally because they cannot use their vocal cords the way humans do. Accordingly, the Gardners taught the animals sign language rather than verbal language. Washoe, one of their best pupils, was able to learn close to 200 signs in a few years of training. In addition, Washoe was able to master simple sentences such as "hurry gimme toothbrush" and "you me go out hurry."

Another investigator has demonstrated these same learning abilities in chimpanzees using an entirely different approach. Premack (1976) taught a chimp named Sarah to communicate by using a technique that required Sarah to substitute variously shaped pieces of plastic for objects and actions. Then, using a magnetic writing board, Sarah communicated by placing appropriate plastic shapes on the board (see Figure 7–5). In a production task, Sarah might be shown some item, such as honey, and required to select appropriate plastic

FIGURE 7–5 Teaching Chimpanzees to Communicate
Sarah, after reading the message "Sarah insert apple pail banana dish" on the magnetic board, performed the appropriate actions. To be able to make the correct interpretation that she should put the apple in the pail and the banana in the dish (not the apple, pail, and banana in the dish), the chimpanzee had to understand sentence structure rather than just word order. In actual tests most symbols were colored. (After Premack & Premack, 1972)

symbols and place them on the board in an appropriate order from top to bottom, resulting in a word sequence such as "Sarah honey take."

Thus, through imaginative experimentation, Premack has been able to test his central hypothesis, which is that language can be acquired only by an animal with certain qualities of intelligence. These qualities include the recognition of similarity between two items, the ability to associate a name with an object, the ability to abstract attributes from an object, and the ability to infer causation. At the same time, it is clear that apes will never match adult humans in terms of human language usage. At best, it seems apes may be able to communicate with a language of symbols on a level with the least experienced human (Terrace, 1985). As one example of the amazing yet limited capacity of apes to learn language in the way that even children are capable of, Terrace states,

> Unlike children, who are able readily to add new items to their vocabularies in response to casual instruction (or without any instruction at all), apes are able to do so only in narrowly structured situations and with extensive drill. What appears to be lacking in the case of the apes is an understanding of the fact that one can refer to an object by its name. (p. 1021)

CONCEPT FORMATION

Definition of a Concept

A *concept* is a symbol that stands for a class or group of objects or events that possess common properties. Thus, *tree* is a concept. It stands for a vast number of different objects, all of which are relatively large, perennial plants with woody stems. Similarly, *girl, house,* and *book* are concepts because they stand for large classes of objects that possess certain common properties.

Some concepts, such as plant, animal, conflict, spicy, and illness, refer to large numbers of objects and events that possess a few common properties. Other concepts, such as *petunia, sparrow hawk, prize fight, peppery,* and *diphtheria,* refer to fewer objects and events and are based on greater numbers of common properties.

Concepts provide us with stability in interacting with our environment. They allow us to rise above the specific details of the environment and to treat objects or events that have common properties as members of a class. In other words, they greatly simplify our thinking processes. Imagine what life would be like if we had to label and categorize each new object or event we encountered. Fortunately, we can usually fit new objects and events into existing categories.

In learning language, children are confronted with the huge task of learning both concepts and language simultaneously. In forming the concept of *dog,* young children learn to classify a variety of specific instances as members of a set. They learn that the label *dog* may be applied to specific instances, but more importantly, they learn that *dog* refers to a *class of instances* that have certain properties or features in common. If children apply the word *dog* only to a specific dog—their own, for example—they have not really developed the concept of *dog.* It is only when they can apply the term to a number of specific

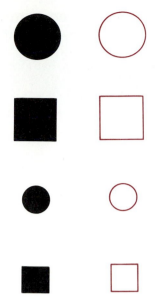

FIGURE 7–6 Typical Stimuli Used in a Concept-formation Experiment *There are three features involved in this study: size, color, and shape. The experimenter chooses the concept to be learned.*

instances in a reasonably accurate fashion that we can say that they have acquired the concept. It is equally important in concept mastery that the child be able to apply the term appropriately in the presence of various instances of the concept, and also that the child recognize other events or objects that are properly not part of the concept. Thus, instances of *cats*, *horses*, and *goats* must be rejected as inappropriate exemplars of *dogs*.

A Laboratory Example We know that concepts are widespread in our lives and important in our thought processes, but how do we go about studying them? Figure 7–6 shows the kind of stimuli that are used in a typical concept-formation experiment. As you will note, there are three features involved in this study: size, color, and shape. Each feature has two states, giving a total of eight different stimuli. Suppose the experimenter chooses *small–black* as the concept to be learned. That is, all objects that are small and black are correct instances of the concept while all other stimuli are not. Shape is irrelevant. It is the subject's task to discover the concept, or to become aware that any stimulus that is small and black, regardless of shape, is correct. Of course, the experimenter could choose a number of different concepts, such as all stimuli that are black, or square, or both.

Generally, psychologists use two major procedures in concept-formation experiments like that in Figure 7–6. In the **method of reception**, the experimenter shows one stimulus at a time and the subject indicates whether she thinks it is an instance of the concept. After the subject makes her response, she is told whether she is correct or not. She is then shown another stimulus, makes another judgment, and again receives feedback. This procedure progresses until the subject can correctly identify all instances of the concept. In the **method of selection**, the subject is free to test any stimulus in any order. The method of selection can lead to faster concept attainment because the subject is not forced to wait until a particular stimulus she wants to test is finally presented by the experimenter. She can test any stimulus at any time, and this method appears to be more efficient.

Concepts and Language

Almost all words are concepts, because they stand for more than one object or event possessing common properties. Proper nouns—names, such as Kermit the frog and Chicago—seem to be about the only words that are not concepts.

On the other hand, even though most words are concepts, not all concepts are words. Babies form concepts, such as *mother*, before any language has developed. The experiment depicted in Figure 7–7 demonstrates clearly that animals without language can form basic concepts.

A great deal of time is spent by adults in instructing children about concepts because concepts are essential for more complex behaviors such as learning of principles, problem solving, and symbolic activities (such as thinking). As a matter of fact, one of the principal objectives of formal education is the teaching of basic concepts that enable individuals to function in society with minimal difficulty.

FIGURE 7–7 Nonverbal Concept Formation *In this experiment, food is always placed under a triangle and never under a rectangle. Even though the size and shape of the triangle are varied from trial to trial, the duck can master the task, suggesting that a language-free concept has been formed.*

Schooling also instructs children that concepts can be revised, altered, and amended on the basis of new knowledge and experience.

Concepts and Perception

In what is now a classic study, Labov (1973) showed that the way in which objects are perceived and stored in memory is important in how they are categorized. For his experiment, Labov used cuplike objects such as those shown in Figure 7–8. The objects in the figure all resemble cups, although some are a bit unusual. The cups along the left side of the figure (cups 5 through 9) show increasing elongation. The cups across the top (1 through 4) show an increase in the ratio of width to depth; as they become wider they begin to look more like bowls. Other differences are obvious. Cups 10 through 12 are cylindrical, cups 13 through 15 are conical, and cups 16 and 17 have stems. In Labov's study, these drawings were presented one at a time, and subjects were simply asked to name them. This defined a neutral instructional condition. In other instructional conditions, subjects were asked to name the objects under different instructional sets. For example, subjects were asked to imagine the object sitting on a dinner table, or filled with potatoes, or filled with coffee that someone was drinking. After these differing instructions, subjects were asked to identify the objects, one at a time, using a label or phrase.

The results of Labov's experiments are graphed in Figure 7–9, which shows the percentage of subjects giving a particular name as a function of the width of the object and the instructional set. This figure indicates two important things about concepts. First, the frequency of *cup* responses decreases while the frequency of *bowl* responses increases as the width of the objects increases. The change is

FIGURE 7–8 An Experiment to Study Concepts and Perception *These various cuplike objects were used in the experiment by Labov studying the boundaries of the cup category.* (After Labov, 1973)

gradual, indicating that the boundary between the cup and bowl is not clearly demarcated. This should not be surprising if you look at the various drawings again. Second, the frequency distribution of the *cup* and *bowl* label is influenced heavily by the verbal instructions or context given the subjects. An object is more likely to be called a *bowl* if it is thought of as filled with mashed potatoes than if it is presented to subjects in the neutral context. These results show clearly that a category is defined both by the ***perceptual features*** of the object (width, for example) and by the verbal context under which the judgments are made.

FIGURE 7–9 The Results of Labov's Perception and Categorization Studies *This graph shows the percentage of subjects who used the terms* cup *or* bowl *to describe the objects shown in Figure 7–8 as a function of the ratio of cup width to cup depth imagined. The solid lines are for the neutral-context condition; the dotted lines are for the food-context condition. (After Labov, 1973)*

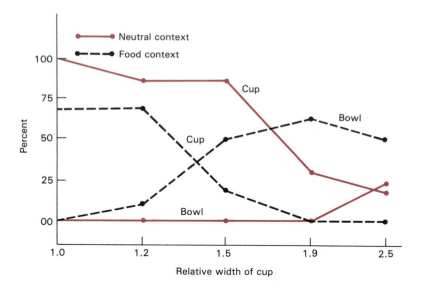

Theories of Concept Formation

Because concepts are immensely important in our thinking, many people have studied the question of how concepts are learned. We will look at one classical theory and one modern viewpoint in connection with this question.

Association Theory Many early investigators interpreted concept learning in terms of simple associations. That is, they tried to explain concept formation in terms of the principles of reinforced responding. Their approach was called **association theory** and they assumed that if an instance of the concept is correctly identified, the subject is reinforced when he is informed he is correct. If a stimulus is incorrectly identified, the subject undergoes extinction when he is told he is wrong. Through a long series of trials, the correct responses are associated with the appropriate stimuli. However, Horton and Turnage (1976) note that this view says very little about what goes on inside the learner's head. It does not explain the subject's active testing of theories about what is and what is not the correct solution. Largely for this reason, association theory is no longer widely accepted.

Hypothesis Testing The more modern and popular approach, which is known as the **hypothesis-testing theory**, assumes that the learner is an active processor of information, busily testing a series of guesses about what the concept is (Bruner, Goodnow, & Austin, 1956). According to this approach, the learner is constantly making *hypotheses* about the correct solution and testing them. For example, using the stimuli in Figure 7–6, you might first receive a *black-round-small* stimulus and guess that *black* is the concept. So you would say, "Yes, that is an example of the concept." If you were told you were wrong, you would have to change your hypothesis right away. If you were told you were correct in identifying *black-round-small* as an instance of the concept, you still would not know if your *black* hypothesis was correct. You would need to do some more testing. Suppose the next stimulus was *black-round-large;* you said, "Yes," and were told you

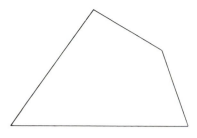

FIGURE 7–10   An Ambiguous Figure Concept   *Is this figure more like a triangle or a rectangle?*

were wrong. So much for the simple *black* hypothesis. But if you were correct again, you would continue testing your *black* hypothesis until you were proven correct or incorrect.

In other words, the general approach of hypothesis-testing theory is to develop a theory with a set of explicit assumptions about how human beings discover concepts. The basic idea is that a person formulates a hypothesis, remembers it, tests it, and revises it on the basis of new information. Overall, by thinking about the situation for a moment, you can see the complex kinds of guesses people might make and test on successive trials. It is just these sorts of complicated strategies that have intrigued investigators in this area. In short, hypothesis testing appears to give a better explanation of what goes on in concept formation than does the simple reinforcement-association view. We are not passive learners. We pursue the concept actively and discover it by testing a series of hypotheses.

Rules versus Prototypes

Many psychologists (see Rosch, 1978) think about concept formation in terms of *rule learning.* Consider the concept *pen.* The rules for membership in this category might be "it holds ink, is used for writing, and is shaped like a pencil." If you know these rules you can identify instances of the concept accurately. Obviously, the rules defining any given concept can vary enormously. "Anything black" might define one concept while another concept might be defined by the rule, "black and not square or square and not black." Difficult concepts usually involve more complex rules than simple concepts.

There is another way to think about concepts. Consider Figure 7–10. Is this figure more like a rectangle or a triangle? As you try to reach a decision, think carefully about what you are doing. Do you run over a list of rules defining these alternative concepts, reminding yourself that triangles have three sides and three angles, rectangles have four right angles and four sides? Or do you somehow try to compare this figure with some idealized models or mental images of rectangles and triangles that you have stored in your memory? These internal patterns or mental images are called **prototypes**, and a good way to think about a prototype is to imagine it as the best example of a category. Once we have developed a prototype, we take any presented stimulus and mentally "hold it up against" this prototype to see if the two match.

Clearly, both rules and prototypes can be used in concept formation. But many concepts are defined better by prototypes than by logical rules. Consider the concept *chicken.* If someone showed you a bird you had never seen before and asked you if it was a chicken, how would you go about making a decision? Would you start thinking about logical rules that define "chickenness"? Or would you somehow compare the overall appearance of the creature in question with your internal picture of an ideal chicken? You would probably use the prototype approach. Most of us cannot even *think* of a logical rule that defines "chickenness," much less use such a rule to make a decision about category membership. But we all have some internal prototype of "chicken" that we can use to categorize any strange new birds that come squawking into our lives (Houston, 1981).

Photos in magazines have probably provided this young girl with a prototype of feminine beauty.

PROBLEM SOLVING

Definition of a Problem

We are all faced with problems in our everyday lives. Sometimes it seems life is just an exercise in problem solving. Because problems are so important to us, it is not surprising that many psychologists have attempted to understand how we go about solving problems.

A *problem* may be thought of as a situation in which an organism is motivated to reach a goal but is blocked by some obstacle or obstacles. The organism emits various responses in its attempts to overcome the obstacle and reach the goal. Some problems are long-term, complicated issues. For example, if you want to become an attorney, you must overcome a whole series of obstacles before you attain your goal. Other problems are quite simple. If you wish to stop reading this book, just close your eyes. Problems may involve verbal, physical, emotional, or perceptual events, or combinations of these. The obstacles may be physical, social, emotional, multiple, imagined, or variable. In short, there are many different types of problems.

Examples of Problems

One of the best ways to gain a feeling for the complexity of problem-solving processes is to try to solve a few problems yourself. As you work your way through the problems in Table 7–4, try to be aware of the mental steps you are following. You should soon realize that the process is not a simple one.

You might also notice the diversity of the problems contained in Table 7–4. Some involve verbal processes while others are essentially perceptual. Some require logic and reasoning while others appear to involve a search of your memory stores. Some are more difficult than others. However, all of them represent situations where you are blocked from a goal (the solution) by one or more obstacles.

Four Stages of Problem Solving

For many years investigators have held that problem solving progresses through a series of stages (see Johnson, 1944). The most commonly identified stages are *familiarization, production, incubation,* and *evaluation.* When faced with a problem, we tend to prepare ourselves by becoming familiar with the problem, the obstacles, and the materials at hand. Next, we begin to produce alternative solutions to the problem. Finally, we evaluate the effectiveness of these alternative solutions. Occasionally, when we seem unable to find a solution, we will enter what has been called a period of incubation, during which we do *not* attempt to solve the problem. We rest and attend to other matters. Then, on returning to the problem, we sometimes find a solution that eluded us earlier.

Some psychologists challenge these definitions. They agree that we sometimes turn away from a problem. But what we actually do during the so-called incubation period is not known. Some people feel that a solution to the problem may somehow be worked out during this period. Others feel that the incubation period merely allows us to rest and clear our minds of "wrong starts" that had been hampering our efforts. Moreover, these four stages do not necessarily occur in a set order. Some problems seem to require us to move back

TABLE 7–4 Sample Problems*

1. By moving only two matches make four boxes out of these five boxes (using all matches in the solution).

2. Complete this meaningful sequence.

   O T T F F S S _ N

3. You are on the way to the city and you meet a man at a fork in the road. You do not know which fork to take. You know that the man is one of two brothers who live in the area. One of these brothers always tells the truth while the other never tells the truth. You do not know which one you are facing. You can ask him one question, which he can answer with a yes or no, which will assure you of taking the correct fork. What is that question?

4. Nine steel balls all look alike. Eight of the balls weigh the same amount, while one is heavier than the rest. You are given a pan balance and allowed only two weighings of any combination or number of these balls to discover which one is the heavy one. How would you find the heavy ball?

5. Without lifting your pencil from the paper or retracing a line, draw four straight lines through all nine points.

6. What is the longest word you can think of that spells the same thing forward and backward?

7. Using only six matches, arrange them to form four congruent triangles.

8. *Syllogism* 1
       All As are Bs.
       All Bs are Cs.
       Therefore, all As are Cs. (true or false?)
   Syllogism 2
       All As are Bs.
       All Cs are Bs.
       Therefore, all As are Cs. (true or false?)
   Syllogism 3
       Some As are Bs.
       Some Bs are Cs.
       Therefore, some As are Cs. (true or false?)

*Answers appear in Table 7–8 on page 303.

and forth among the stages, sometimes going all the way back to the familiarization phase.

Subgoals and Planning

There are certain strategies that can make our efforts to solve problems easier. First, complex problems should be broken down into subgoals, each more easily solved than the entire problem. Suppose your problem is that you have been skiing instead of studying and your final exam is in three days. The problem seems overwhelming. "I'll never be able to learn all that, all those notes, all that reading, aaarrrgh!'' Here is where subgoals can help. Do not think about the overall problem in all its sinister splendor. Break it down into smaller, more manageable chunks. Tell yourself, ''First, I'll do the reading. I won't even think about all those confused, incomplete lecture notes.'' Then break it down even further. ''Tonight I'll read the first chapter. I can do that. No problem.'' By taking things a little bit at a time, the overall task does not seem so immense and confusing. And you will be solving a part of the problem instead of worrying about it in its entirety.

By thinking of the steps you will take ahead of time, you can save wear and tear; it pays to plan ahead. For example, in preparing for your examination you might want to do all of the reading first, then concentrate on your notes, and finally go over both notes and reading the night before the exam. If you do not plan ahead and do not stick to your plan, you may suffer. ''I spent all of my time on the book. I know it perfectly. But I ran out of time. I never got to the lecture notes, and I bombed out on the exam.''

Hayes-Roth and Hayes-Roth (1979) point out that planning can be important in something as simple as running a series of errands during an average day. If you do not plan, you may end up back-tracking and wasting your time. Complex problems need to be broken down into subproblems and we need to plan our actions carefully, if we want to keep life relatively simple. Of course, some people prefer a life of hectic drama, and for them, planning is a waste of time.

Trial and Error versus Insight

One long-standing issue in the study of problem solving has been whether we solve problems through a gradual process of *trial and error*, or through an insight or ''Aha!'' experience where the complete solution suddenly occurs to us.

Early evidence for the insight conception was presented by Wolfgang Köhler (1925). He hung a banana from the ceiling of a chimpanzee's cage and placed several boxes in the cage as well. Wanting the banana, the chimpanzee engaged in some unsuccessful trial-and-error behavior, vainly reaching and jumping. Then, characteristically, the chimp seemed to withdraw from the problem for a time. During this period the solution seemed to come to the animal in a moment of insight. The chimp would jump up, stack the boxes under the banana, climb up on them, and reach the fruit.

These dramatic results have been reinterpreted by recent research on thinking. Most psychologists now agree that the solution probably is attained through some complex combination of trial and error on insight. In fact, insight can be looked at as a form of mental trial and error. The animal, through the mental manipulation of symbols, engages in a series of symbolic trial responses before discovering the correct one and translating it into overt, observable behavior.

Problems in Problem Solving

There are some obstacles we often encounter in our attempts to solve problems. Normally, we think of our past experience with the ele-

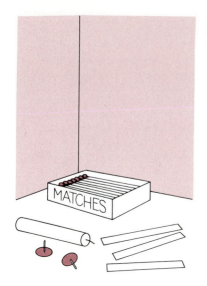

FIGURE 7–11   Functional Fixedness   *Using the materials shown, how would you go about attaching the lighted candle to the wall?*

ments of a problem as an advantage in our attempts to reach a solution. The concept of stimulus generalization discussed in Chapter 5 supports this notion. But, under some circumstances, our past experiences can hamper our efforts to solve problems.

Functional Fixedness   We sometimes suffer from **functional fixedness,** which results from being accustomed to using objects in certain prescribed ways. We have trouble freeing up our thinking enough to find novel uses for these objects. The function of the object is fixed by our past experience with it. Consider the materials in Figure 7–11. Using only these materials, how would you attach the lighted candle to the wall? See if you can work out a good solution to the problem before you continue reading. The most practical solution is shown in Figure 7–12 on page 300. Many people do not think of using the matchbox in their solution, because it is shown in Figure 7–11 performing its ordinary function of holding matches. When people are shown an empty matchbox with matches beside it, they are much more likely to use the box in their solution (Weissberg, DiCamillo, & Phillips, 1978). See the box titled " 'Breaking Out' of Functional Fixedness" for another example of resourcefulness in problem solving.

Mental Set   Sometimes, as we solve a series of related problems, we fall into the habit of using a certain procedure that has worked well on the first few problems (Atwood, Masson, & Polson, 1980). This habit is defined as a **mental set**. However, because we are so set on using this particular procedure, we may fail to notice that easier, simpler procedures may solve some of the problems. Consider the jar capacity problems in Table 7–5. In problem 1 you are given 3 jars (A, B, and C) that hold exactly 21, 127, and 3 cc of water, respectively. Your task is to obtain exactly 100 cc of water using these three jars and a water tap. You may want to try solving this problem and the others before reading further.

TABLE 7–5   Jar Problems*

Problem	Jar Capacities (in cc)			Amount of Water to Be Obtained
	Jar A	Jar B	Jar C	
1	21	127	3	100
2	14	163	25	99
3	18	43	10	5
4	9	42	6	21
5	20	59	4	31
6	23	49	3	20
7	10	27	7	3

*In each case, use a water tap and the jars to obtain the amount of water in the right-hand column.

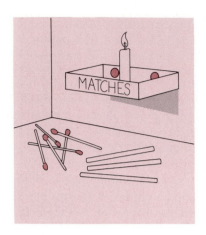

FIGURE 7–12 Functional Fixedness *The solution to the problem in Figure 7–11.*

◆ *"BREAKING OUT" OF FUNCTIONAL FIXEDNESS*

DEAR ABBY: With all the publicity you gave panty hose, I have a true story for you.

When Mt. St. Helens erupted in May of 1980, blowing the top 2,500 feet into the air, the volcanic ash was so heavy that in Spokane at 3 o'clock in the afternoon, it looked like midnight! In Yakima, Wash., breathing was difficult.

Automobiles sucked the ash into their air filters and the abrasion ruined the engines. When one family was stranded when their air filter became plugged, the husband removed the plugged filter, borrowed his wife's panty hose, wrapped them around the air intake as a filter, and they continued their trip in safety.

They were stopped by a highway patrolman near Moses Lake, Wash., where there was up to 7 inches of the volcanic stuff on the ground. (You can still see it.) The patrolman asked how they could keep going. They explained that they shook the ashes from the panty hose each time the engine quit.

The Highway Patrol then purchased panty hose for their cars and continued to help stranded motorists in that area. Panty hose saved many engines until proper filters could be installed.

KEN THELANDER, Seattle
DEAR KEN: Thank you for sharing your unusual story.

After a little experimenting, you will see that you can fill B from the tap, then fill A from B, leaving 106 cc, and then fill C twice from B to obtain 100 cc. Now move on to problem 2. Here you will find jars of different sizes and a different amount to be obtained. But again you can follow the sequence B minus A minus 2C to obtain the desired amount. As you work your way through the problems, notice that the B − A − 2C formula works for all of them. However, if you focus on problems 6 and 7, you can discover a much simpler solution. A minus C will do the trick for these two problems, but interestingly, subjects tend to solve problems 6 and 7 using the B − A − 2C formula, because they become *set* to using this method and fail to notice the easier solution.

Here is another example. Read down from the top of Table 7–6 to the bottom. Now look at the next-to-last word again. You may well have fallen into another mental set and failed to pronounce *machines* correctly.

Creativity in Problem Solving

Some individuals are much more gifted than others in solving problems. Albert Einstein was an especially creative scientist who could solve abstract problems that most of us would not understand even after the problem and the solution have been explained to us in the simplest of terms.

Creativity involves the production of original ideas, which, when applied to a problem, lead to its solution. Interestingly, original ideas are uncommon; it is more usual to find the juxtaposition of old

TABLE 7–6
Another Kind of Mental Set

MACARTHUR
MACINTOSH
MACCARTHY
MACBETH
MACDOWELL
MACKENZIE
MACDONALD
MACHINES
MACDILLON

ideas in new ways resulting in creative solutions. An example would be the invention of the Apple Computer by Steve Job. He did not invent the computer, but he used the computer technology then available to assemble a computer that would be more useful to a larger number of people due to its size, convenience, and simplicity.

What kinds of people are truly creative? Generally, persons characterized as creative tend to be highly individualistic and independent, low in conformity, persistent, curious, intuitive, and self-assured. Their behavior often is seen as self-centered and they are frequently not popular in the social sense.

When creative problem-solving strategies are studied, we find that the creative person spends more time trying to understand the problem at hand (familiarization). This individual also offers more hypotheses and arranges them from the most simple to the most complex to facilitate systematic testing. In addition, the creative problem solver copes with the frustration of failure better by being more flexible. In other words, the creative person is willing to spend more time exploring possible solutions to the problem and also knows when to step away from the problem for a time (incubation).

Teaching Thinking Skills

You might be wondering by this time whether it is possible to learn better thinking skills. Although there is now much experimental research on thinking skills such as those we have described in this chapter, there is relatively little applied research that actually attempts to teach thinking skills and then evaluates scientifically whether the student is better able to solve problems. One recent attempt to do this is worth mentioning. In this study, a group of psychologists at Harvard University were asked by the Venezuelan government if they could design some instructional materials to assist economically and educationally deprived children to do better on a wide range of classroom-related cognitive tasks (Herrnstein, Nickerson, de Sanchez, & Swets, 1986).

The course that Herrnstein and his colleagues designed consisted of six lesson series, each of which addresses a topic believed to be important to intellectual competence. Table 7–7 gives a complete list of the lessons and their units. The table also describes some of the main objectives of each unit. An important feature of the course is that the basic concepts and skills developed in one lesson are generalized and exercised in new contexts throughout the other lessons.

The course, which was tested with 400 seventh-grade students in Venezuela, was assessed for effectiveness. The results showed that the program had very beneficial effects on the sample of children studied when these children were compared to a control group of students on a wide range of intellectual tests and problem-solving tasks. It is not clear how long lasting the effects of course participation will be on the thinking skills of the children involved in the program, but clearly of interest is the finding that cognitive skills can be enhanced by direct instruction. This program of lessons is now available in English and is being tested with children in this country. We will have to wait for the results of these newer studies.

TABLE 7-7 Contents of a Course Designed to Improve Intellectual Competence

Series title, unit title, and description	*Series title, unit title, and description*

Lesson Series I: Foundations of Reasoning
  Unit 1: Observation and classification
    Using dimensions and characteristics to analyze and organize similarities and differences; discovering the basics of classification and hypothesis testing
  Unit 2: Ordering
    Recognizing and extrapolating different types of sequences; discovering special properties of orderable dimensions
  Unit 3: Hierarchical classification
    Exploring the structure and utility of classification hierarchies
  Unit 4: Analogies: Discovering relationships
    Analyzing the dimensional structure of simple and complex analogies
  Unit 5: Spatial reasoning and strategies
    Developing strategies to solve problems of resource allocation via tangrams
 	
Lesson Series II: Understanding Language
  Unit 1: Word relations
    Appreciating the multidimensional nature of word meanings
  Unit 2: The structure of language
    Discovering the logic and utility of rhetorical conventions
  Unit 3: Reading for meaning
    Analyzing text for explicit information, implicit information, and point of view
 	
Lesson Series III: Verbal Reasoning
  Unit 1: Assertions
    Exploring the structure and interpretation of simple propositions
  Unit 2: Arguments
    Analyzing logical arguments; evaluating and constructing complex arguments
 	
Lesson Series IV: Problem Solving
  Unit 1: Linear representations
    Constructing linear representations to interpret n-term series problems
	Unit 2: Tabular representations
	    Constructing tabular representations to solve multivariate word problems
	  Unit 3: Representations by simulation and enactment
	    Representing and interpreting dynamic problem spaces through simulation and enactment
	  Unit 4: Systematic trial and error
	    Developing systematic methods for enumerating all possible solutions; developing efficient methods for selecting among such solutions
	  Unit 5: Thinking out the implications
	    Examining the constraints of givens and solutions for problem-solving clues
	
	Lesson Series V: Decision Making
	  Unit 1: Introduction to decision making
	    Identifying and representing alternatives; trading off outcome desirability and likelihood in selecting between alternatives
	  Unit 2: Gathering and evaluating information to reduce uncertainty
	    Appreciating the importance of being thorough in gathering information; evaluating consistency, credibility, and relevance of data
	  Unit 3: Analyzing complex decision situations
	    Evaluating complex alternatives in terms of the dimensions on which they differ and the relative desirability of their characteristics on each of those dimensions
	
	Lesson Series VI: Inventive Thinking
	  Unit 1: Design
	    Analyzing the designs of common objects in terms of functional dimensions; inventing designs from functional criteria
	  Unit 2: Procedures as designs
	    Analyzing and inventing procedures in terms of the functional significance of their steps

Source: After Herrnstein et al., 1986.

In this and in the preceding two chapters, we have discussed a number of basic principles of learning and memory that are now fairly well understood. Many of these principles are common to the functioning of humans and animals, although of course, there are differences in the degree to which these principles apply to varying species, as we have seen. In the next chapter, we will show how many of these different learning principles can be applied to a variety of common problems to change maladaptive behaviors to more suitable behaviors and how we can improve our memory through the use of cognitive strategies.

TABLE 7–8 Answers to Problems in Table 7–4

1.
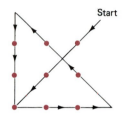

2. O T T F F S S <u>E</u> N

These are the first letters of the numbers one through nine.

3. Point to either fork and ask the man if his brother would say this was the correct fork. If he says "No," then it is the correct fork. If he says "Yes," it is the wrong fork.

4. Weigh any three against any other three. If one group of three is heavier than the other then it contains the heavy ball. If not then the remaining unweighed group of three contains the heavy ball. To determine which of three balls is the heavy one, weigh any one against any other one.

5.
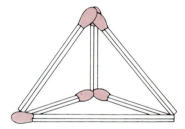

6. pop   (so so)
   otto   (not bad)
   madam   (very good)
   radar   (also very good)
   redivider   (excellent)
   step on   (good, but in-
   no pets   volves more
                than one word)

7.

8. Syllogism 1 is true in every case:

Syllogism 2 is false:

Syllogism 3 is false:

SUMMARY

1. Cognition includes such complex mental activities as using language, thinking, solving problems, reasoning, remembering, conceptualizing, imagining, learning, information processing, and the mental manipulation of symbols.

2. Language allows us to communicate, to store information, and to think efficiently.

3. Spoken languages are based on limited numbers of basic sounds called phonemes. English phonemes correspond roughly to the way we pronounce the letters of the alphabet.

4. A morpheme is the smallest meaningful unit in a language. Many morphemes are words but others are suffixes and prefixes.

5. Grammar or syntax refers to the rules that govern the ordering and positioning of sounds, morphemes, and words in sentences.

6. Linguists analyze sentences in terms of the phrases they contain. In English the phrase structure of a sentence normally involves a verb phrase following a noun phrase.

7. The major problem with phrase structure grammar is that it does not account for the speaker's intent, nor for the fact that some structures, such as the active and passive, have the same meaning.

8. The surface structure of a sentence refers to the actual words used while the deep structure refers to the meaning behind the sentence.

9. Transformational grammar considers the ways that deep structures are transformed into various surface structures.

10. The link between deep-structure meaning and the surface-structure sentence consists of transformational rules.

11. Schemata are bodies of knowledge we have about certain concepts, events, and objects. They affect how we store information.

12. Language acquisition begins with babbling at about 6 months. Two stages of babbling have been identified: reduplicated and jargon babbling. It has been documented that all babies babble at about the same time and in roughly the same manner, regardless of living condition.

13. Single, meaningful words begin to appear at about 1 year.

14. In holophrastic speech, the child uses a single word to stand for an entire idea, thought, or event.

15. Two-word utterances begin to appear at about 18 months. These minimal sentences can be studied by their clear semantic intent (for example, action + agent).

16. In telegraphic speech, the child leaves out unimportant words.

17. Longer sentences are acquired rapidly by a process that Brown refers to as the "law of cumulative complexity."

18. Some psychologists have felt that language is acquired according to the principles of classical and instrumental conditioning.

19. Modern psycholinguistic theory emphasizes biological, innate aspects of language acquisition, the learning of complex rules of grammar, the creative aspects of language use, and the testing of hypotheses by the child.

20. Chimpanzees can learn the basics of language when they are taught sign language or the use of plastic symbols in place of words.

21. Chimpanzees, however, do not have the capacity to use language at a level that is different from the least experienced human speaker.

22. A concept is a symbol that stands for a class of objects or events that possess common properties. Concepts facilitate thinking and related complex behaviors such as problem solving. In fact, much of formal schooling involves the teaching of concepts.

23. Almost all words except proper nouns are concepts, but not all concepts are verbal.

24. In the method of reception, the experimenter determines which stimuli will be presented to the subject during a concept-formation task. In the method of selection, the subject is free to test any stimulus at any time.

25. How we interpret certain concepts in our environment is known to be influenced by our perception of an object (for example, cup versus bowl) and our experience with the object.

26. Some psychologists feel concept formation can be understood in terms of simple reinforced associations, while others argue that hypothesis testing is critical to the process.

27. Concepts may be acquired through the use of rules, or prototypes, or both.

28. An organism faces a problem if it is motivated to reach a goal but is blocked by some type of obstacle. Some psychologists believe *all* cognitive activity may be of a problem-solving variety.

29. Problem solving follows four phases: familiarization, production, incubation, and evaluation.

30. Subgoals and planning are important in problem solving. A controversy exists as to whether problem solving occurs through trial and error or insight.

31. Functional fixedness means that we sometimes suffer in our problem-solving efforts because we cannot overcome our tendencies to use objects only in certain prescribed ways.

32. Mental set refers to situations where we fail to notice simpler procedures for solving problems because we have fallen into the habit of using certain more complex procedures.

33. The creative problem solver can be identified by traits of independence, persistence, curiosity, and so forth. The creative problem solver also approaches problems with greater flexibility and greater tolerance for frustration.

34. It is possible to teach thinking skills to children and to see the effects of such instruction on a wide variety of intellectual tasks.

KEY TERMS

ambiguous sentence	jargon babbling	prototypes
association theory	mental set	psycholinguistic theory
babbling	method of reception	reduplicated babbling
cognition	method of selection	rules of grammar
concept	morpheme	schema (schemata)
deep structure	noun phrase	surface structure
evaluation	perceptual features	symbol
familiarization	phoneme	telegraphic speech
functional fixedness	phonological rules	transformational grammar
holophrastic speech	phrase structure	transformational rules
hypothesis-testing theory	problems	trial and error
incubation	problem solving	two-word utterances
incubation effect	production	verb phrase

ADDITIONAL READING

Anderson, J. R. (1985) *Cognitive psychology and its implications*. San Francisco: W. H. Freeman.
This is an introductory textbook that covers the major topics in cognitive psychology.

Berger, D., Pezdek, K., & Banks, W. P. (Eds.). (1987) *Applications of cognitive psychology: Problem solving, education, and computing.* Hillsdale, NJ: Lawrence Erlbaum Associates.
This interesting collection of chapters shows how principles of cognitive psychology can be applied to such problems as television comprehension, computer programming, reasoning, and algebra word problems.

Cognitive Psychology.
Any current issue of this journal will contain several examples of contemporary cognitive research.

Gardner, H. (1985) *The mind's new science.* New York: Basic Books.
The author presents a readable history of cognitive science up through the present. The relationship between the different disciplines making up cognitive science is discussed, as well as main problems of interest to cognitive scientists in the past several decades.

Pinker, S. (1984) *Language learnability and language development.* Cambridge: Harvard University Press.
This is a good account of how language is learned and used. The author covers many critical topics involving the relationship between language and thought.

Rieber, R. W. (1983) *Dialogues on the psychology of language and thought: Conversations with Noam Chomsky, Charles Osgood, Jean Piaget, Ulric Neisser, and Marcel Kinsbourne.* New York: Plenum Press.
These conversations with some of the founders of cognitive psychology make for interesting reading. Learning how these scholars view some of the complex problems surrounding language and thought will prove insightful to students.

8

Exploring Learning, Memory, and Cognition

W e have just spent three chapters discussing learning, memory, and cognition research. Most of what we have talked about has been experimental and theoretical. By now, you may be wondering why psychologists have gone to all that trouble. Have those studies helped us improve people's lives, or are all those experiments and theories just isolated laboratory exercises that keep psychologists busy but have little to do with the outside world?

It would be wonderful if we could say, "Yes, all of our laboratory discoveries have led to immediate and important practical applications." But in fact, most of what we have discovered in the laboratory has not yet been of practical value. Most basic research is still just that: basic information that may someday suggest practical solutions to important problems outside the laboratory.

At the same time, some theories, methods, and data have been put to practical use, and several applications have been quite successful. Psychology is still a very young science, and psychologists are struggling with a vast, new, complicated area of study. But dividends are already appearing.

We want to describe some dividends—successful, practical applications of the principles of learning and memory. We will look first at applications of the principles of classical conditioning. Then we will explore some uses of instrumental conditioning, and finally we will see some useful applications of memory techniques.

APPLICATIONS OF CLASSICAL CONDITIONING

The Control of Enuresis

Bed-wetting, or **enuresis**, has been analyzed in terms of classical conditioning. Normally, a wet bed (the UCS) evokes a waking response (the UCR). In time, the wet bed is paired with bladder tension (the CS). Through repeated pairings, the bladder tension (CS) normally acquires the capacity to elicit the waking response (the CR). But some children do not learn this CS → CR connection, probably because wetting the bed does not awaken them. Therefore, these children sleep through the bladder tension and wet the bed.

As far back as 1938 psychologists were attempting to control enuresis through classical conditioning. They reasoned that since the CS (bladder tension) → CR (waking) connection has not been learned, it may be established by pairing the CS (bladder tension) with an alternative UCS that will elicit the desired waking response. If, each time the child's bladder is full, a bell rings loud enough to waken the child, then the waking response should become classically conditioned to the bladder tension.

How can the situation be arranged so that a bell rings only when the bladder is full? The answer is actually rather simple. Develop a special sheet containing fine electrical wires. As soon as the child begins to wet the bed, the urine (which fortunately is a fine conductor of electricity) closes an electrical circuit and causes a bell located near the child's head to ring. The bell wakes the child, thereby completing a "learning trial." Such an apparatus has, in fact, been developed and successfully marketed. After a period of learning, the child begins to wake up in anticipation of the bell. The CS (bladder tension) → CR (waking response) connection has been established. Of course the apparatus uses low-voltage batteries so there is no danger of shock. While controversial, this apparatus has been successful in many cases. It is a clear example of how basic research can provide a solution to a practical problem.

The Polygraph or "Lie Detector"

Another way in which the principles of classical conditioning have been put to work outside the laboratory involves *polygraph machines* or "lie detectors." These devices are supposed to be able to detect when a person is lying by recording changes in blood pressure, pulse rate, breathing, and the amount of perspiration produced by the skin. But strictly speaking, they are not lie detectors at all. They are emotion detectors. By recording changes in the four variables mentioned, we can detect strong, classically conditioned emotional reactions. As you know from experience, strong emotions, such as fear or anxiety, can cause an increase in sweating and heart rate, as well as a change in breathing.

Suppose as a young child you managed to crawl under your house and stumbled into a nest of large, fat, brown spiders. You suffered a number of bites, to say nothing of the scrapes and bumps acquired during your spectacular exit. In later years the mere mention of spiders, particularly fat, brown ones, might be enough to trigger a strong sense of disgust and fear. This reaction could be detected by the polygraph machine, even if you tried to conceal it. The situation involves classical conditioning. The UCS is the experience with the spiders in childhood, the CS is the verbal label "spider," and the CR is the fear and revulsion triggered by the mention of spiders.

The most familiar use of polygraph machines has been in police work. The notion is that criminals will lie to conceal their guilt, but they cannot control their emotional reactions, and so the lie detector will pick up these "signs of guilt" (see Figure 8–1). However, serious questions have been raised about this use of the polygraph (Lykken, 1975, 1979). For example, suppose four big police officers escorted you to a police station, attached you to a strange machine with wires, looked at each other significantly, and asked, "Did you murder Elizabeth K. Stone?" Even an innocent person might have a strong emo-

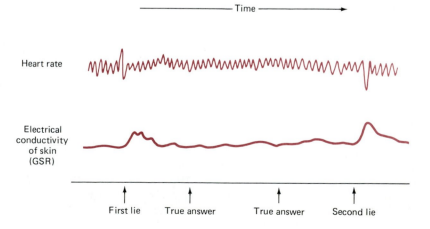

FIGURE 8–1 A Typical Record of Two Indices Used in "Lie Detection" *Here, the subject answers two of four questions truthfully. The galvanic skin response (GSR) refers to a change in the electrical conductivity of the skin. Both heart rate and GSR are affected by a lie but unaffected by a truthful answer.*

tional reaction to such a question asked under these circumstances. The polygraph cannot distinguish between *types* of reactions, such as guilt or alarm. It can measure only the *amount* of reaction. Therefore, direct questions such as "Did you murder Elizabeth K. Stone?" are unsuitable for detecting lies—or truth either.

One way to avoid emotional responses from innocent people in answer to such direct, general questions is to consider minute details of the crime or to focus on elements of the crime that could be known only by the guilty party. Suppose a victim has been murdered with the leg of a chair. The police might show all suspects a series of pictures of common objects, including the actual murder weapon. In this case, the murderer might reveal his guilt by reacting strongly to the murder weapon but not to the remaining objects. Innocent parties, on the other hand, would be unlikely to react strongly to the leg of a chair.

Even with these refinements, the use of polygraph records has been extremely controversial and their reliability often has been questioned. Some types of psychopathic individuals appear to be able to "beat the lie detector" because they have no strong feelings about their crimes. Similarly, drugs of various sorts will affect polygraph records.

In addition to police work, the polygraph has been used in psychotherapy situations. Suppose that a therapist is attempting to determine what is bothering a new patient. She asks the patient if he is in any way disturbed by, or concerned about, his sex life. He responds with a knowing look and a little chuckle. "No. No. Everything is just fine there. Just fine." But if, at the same time that the patient is speaking with such outward calm, the recording needles of the polygraph machine are jumping wildly, the therapist might suspect that the controlled verbal report is concealing strong inner reactions to the topic of sex. The word "sex" might be a CS for all sorts of emotional reactions, and the polygraph could be useful in detecting this area of concern.

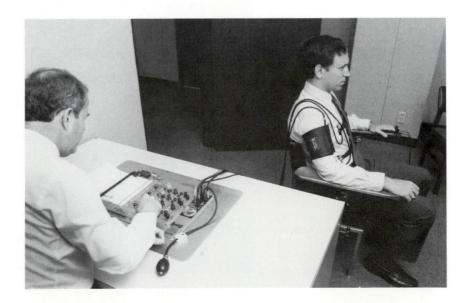

This man undergoing an FBI polygraph examination might be able to control what he says, but his emotional reactions will be detected in spite of his efforts to control them.

Fears, Phobias, and Systematic Desensitization

As we have seen, both positive and negative emotional reactions may be classically conditioned. If we consistently experience pleasure in someone's company, then the mere mention of that person's name (a CS) will set off pleasant feelings. In the same way, fear, anxiety, and guilt may also be classically conditioned to stimuli and situations.

Some people find themselves caught in the grip of extremely strong, apparently irrational fears. Cases have been reported in which individuals were terrified of such stimuli as illness, social contacts, death, being alone, injections, blood, going insane, pregnancy, medicines, and fainting, among other things. We are not speaking here about the mild uneasiness that we may all feel in connection with some of the stimuli and situations just mentioned. We are discussing overwhelming, specific fears called *phobias* that incapacitate the individual. For example, many people are so fearful of social situations that they can never bring themselves to leave the protection of their homes. Clearly, this extreme type of fear, or phobic reaction, should be treated if possible (Kidd & Chayet, 1984; Levine & Sandeen, 1985).

One technique used successfully to treat phobic reactions has been labeled *systematic desensitization* (Wolpe, 1958, 1969). Therapists using this treatment generally assume that phobic reactions are classically conditioned responses. A person who experiences strong fear in response to social situations, for instance, is assumed to have suffered some extremely frightening social experiences. As a result, social situations have become conditioned stimuli that elicit fear.

Systematic desensitization usually involves two phases. During the first phase, the subject is taught to relax deeply. He is asked to lean back in a chair in a darkened room. The therapist helps the subject learn to relax by asking him first to tighten and then to relax specific sets of muscles such as those in the hands, feet, legs, and

Peering out from behind the screen door, this agoraphobic is afraid to leave her house. Systematic desensitization therapy could probably help her.

TABLE 8–1   Anxiety Hierarchies

A. CLAUSTROPHOBIC SERIES

1. Being stuck in an elevator (the longer the time, the more disturbing).
2. Being locked in a room (the smaller the room and the longer the time, the more disturbing).
3. Passing through a tunnel in a railway train (the longer the tunnel, the more disturbing).
4. Traveling in an elevator alone (the greater the distance, the more disturbing).
5. Traveling in an elevator with an operator (the longer the distance, the more disturbing).
6. On a journey by train (the longer the journey, the more disturbing).
7. Caught in a dress with a stuck zipper.
8. Having a tight ring on a finger.
9. Visiting and being unable to leave at will (for example, if engaged in a card game).
10. Being told of somebody in jail.
11. Having polish on one's fingernails and no access to remover.
12. Reading of miners trapped underground.

B. DEATH SERIES

1. Being at a burial.
2. Being at a house of mourning.
3. The word death.
4. Seeing a funeral procession (the nearer, the more disturbing).
5. The sight of a dead animal (for example, a cat).
6. Driving past a cemetery (the nearer, the more disturbing).

Source: After Wolpe, 1961.

neck. By perceiving the difference between tightened and relaxed muscles, the subject learns to relax.

Before the second phase of therapy begins, the therapist asks the subject to make a list of fear-producing stimuli and situations and to rank them in terms of the degree of fear they produce. This list is called a *hierarchy* of fear-producing stimuli. Table 8–1 shows two typical hierarchies. The therapist begins the second phase of treatment by asking the patient to relax and then presenting the weakest of these fear-producing stimuli. The presentation may be accomplished in several ways. The therapist may ask the patient to make up a sentence containing the stimulus, such as, "A young man drove by the *cemetery* on his way to work." Or the therapist may merely ask the patient to think about, or dwell on, the stimulus under consideration until it no longer produces any fear at all.

This process involves *extinction* in that the CS (image of a cemetery, in this case) is presented without the original UCS that initially caused the fear to be conditioned. Hence, through extinction, or repeated presentations of the CS alone without the UCS, the CR (irrational phobic reaction) might be expected to subside. In addition, a *new* CR (relaxation) is also occurring at the mention of the CS (cemetery). Through this process, called *counterconditioning*, the new CR (relaxation) may become conditioned to the old CS (cemetery), replacing the old CR (fear).

Once the weakest of the hierarchical stimuli has been desensitized and no longer elicits fear, the therapist can move up the hierarchy, presenting more and more disturbing stimuli, one at a time. In each case, the patient is asked to relax in the presence of the disturbing stimulus. In this manner, a patient may overcome the fear-producing qualities of even the most frightening stimuli. This desensitizing method has been successful with many different phobias (Rachlin, 1976) and sexual dysfunctions (Masters & Johnson, 1966). It represents another example of the ways in which classical conditioning principles have already benefited mankind.

"Bad Habits": Coyotes and People

Classical conditioning techniques are used with both animals and humans to establish aversive reactions. In this procedure, classical conditioning breaks "bad habits" by associating their occurrence with unpleasant stimuli. This form of treatment is called *aversion therapy.*

Our first example involves the fact that coyotes like to kill and eat lambs. Conservationists and stockmen have feuded for years over what should be done about the coyote's expensive appetite. Typically, coyotes have been hunted and poisoned in great numbers, but Gustavson, Garcia, Hankins, and Rusiniak (1974) and Garcia and Rusiniak (1979) have proposed a more humane means of controlling the coyote. Their technique involves aversion therapy. They feed the coyote lamb flesh laced with lithium chloride, a chemical that makes the coyote ill. The lamb flesh is the CS, the lithium chloride the UCS, and illness the UCR and CR. After several pairings of the lamb flesh and lithium chloride, the coyotes are given a chance to attack live lambs. The big, hungry coyotes actually run away from the helpless, tasty lambs. The destructive predatory habit has been effectively eliminated without having to eliminate the predator itself. Additional tests indicated that the coyotes do not hesitate to attack and kill rabbits, their natural prey. The aversion is specific to lamb's flesh. The psychologists suggest that widespread programs of humane predation control can be established by scattering treated bait over the coyote's range. The predators will eat the bait, experience the illness, and stop attacking lambs. They will revert to their natural prey and thus help to preserve the balance of the ecosystem.

Similar sorts of classically conditioned aversive reactions also are employed with humans to control "bad habits." Typically, humans are stimulated with shock or noxious drugs while engaging in the behavior to be curbed—smoking, drinking, overeating, and so on. Lazarus (1960) reports a case in which a 10-year-old boy had developed the habit of waking and going in to his mother's bed during the middle of the night. The parents seemed unable to break the boy's habit. Finally, under the direction of a psychologist, electrodes were attached to the child's arm and he was asked to *imagine* that he was in his mother's bed. The child was asked to say "Mother's bed" when a vivid image was established. When the image was set, shock was administered.

The aversive treatment was successful. After a series of shocks paired with mental images, the habit was eliminated and the child remained in his own bed throughout the night. Note that an image of the behavior in question was sufficient in this case. The success of the treatment did not require that the actual behavior be associated with shock. It is conceivable that this form of aversion therapy, wherein the *thought* of a bad habit is associated with an unpleasant stimulus, may eventually be helpful in eliminating the following kinds of garden-variety bad habits listed by Holland (1980):

Drinking	Swearing
Smoking cigarettes	Procrastinating
Overeating	Being untidy
Biting fingernails	Arguing
Joint cracking	Avoiding exercise
Taking pills	Always arriving late
Smoking marijuana	Spending freely
Gambling	Grinding teeth
Shoplifting	Pulling hair
Not studying	(and whatever your specialty is)

Aversion therapy may not "cure" anything in a direct sense. It may just alter the symptoms of some disturbances. If a woman is eating herself into the 300-pound class because she is restless, bored, and frustrated by her life, eliminating the compulsive eating habit will not deal with the underlying problems. Although the woman might be better able to deal with her problems if she weighed less, the causes of her compulsive eating are likely to be unaffected by this type of treatment.

Alcohol and Aversion

Because the abuse of alcohol is our most serious drug problem, special mention of alcohol-aversion therapy is merited here. The basic method used to treat alcohol abuse with aversion therapy pairs the taste and smell of alcohol (the CS) with nausea (the CR). Nausea is caused by the injection of a chemical such as emetine. The chemical serves as the UCS. Just before the patients are about to feel the nauseating effects of the drug, they are asked to smell and taste various alcoholic beverages. Several trials a day for several days are followed by additional trials over longer spans of time.

While this form of therapy has been remarkably successful, it is not a foolproof method; it does not work in all cases. Wiens and Menustik (1983), for example, reported that 63 percent of their patients were still not drinking one year after therapy, but by the end of three years only about a third remained abstinent.

Cancer and Ice Cream

One of the terrible side effects of certain types of cancer treatment is nausea. Some patients are so revolted and nauseated by food during chemotherapy that they are unable to eat and lose dangerous amounts of weight. Bernstein (1985) and others have proposed that some of this revulsion may represent classical conditioning and, as such, should be controllable through the manipulation of conditioning principles.

People with cancer often eat before they receive their medication. Unfortunately, this common pattern can lead to aversive conditioning. The UCS is the drug. The UCR is the nausea caused by the drug. The CS is the taste of food, and the CR is the nausea conditioned to the taste of the food. As a result of this conditioning, cancer patients often become repulsed by their normal diet.

Bernstein was successful in dealing with this unfortunate instance of classical conditioning by having patients eat a *novel* food (such as unusually flavored ice cream) before they received their medication. The nausea thus became associated with this novel flavor and somehow blocked the development of feelings of repugnance for the normal diet. The patients, while revolted by the thought of the novel ice cream, experienced less distaste for their normal diet and were able to eat more and retain more healthful weight levels.

Conditioning and the Immune System

The human immune system is involved in the protection of the body against disease-causing germs and other foreign matter. As our first line of defense against disease, one would not think that this system would be subject to alteration through classical conditioning, but apparently it is. Ader (1985) and his colleagues first fed rats a novel flavor and then injected them with cyclophosphamide, a substance that suppresses the immune system. Later the rats were treated in one of two ways. Half of the rats were injected with germs. Their immune systems responded normally, suppressing the germs. The remaining rats were exposed to germs and were also reexposed to the novel flavor. In these cases, the immune system response to the germs was suppressed. The novel flavor served as the CS, the cyclophosphamide was the UCS, suppression in response to the drug was the UCR, and suppression in response to the novel flavor was the CR.

APPLICATIONS OF INSTRUMENTAL CONDITIONING

Instrumental conditioning procedures are widely used outside the laboratory. The procedures described in this section represent only a small sample of the total range of applications.

Train That Dog

The best way to gain a solid grasp of the principles of instrumental conditioning is to apply them yourself. If you can see them working and realize that you are actually creating a behavior change in your subject, then you will possess an understanding of instrumental conditioning that cannot be acquired by reading a book. For this reason, we present B. F. Skinner's classic method of training a dog. We urge you, if it is at all possible, to follow through with Skinner's techniques. Borrow a dog if you must. The experience will convince you

Pets can learn many behaviors if the teacher is familiar with the principles of instrumental conditioning.

of the power of conditioning. In addition, your animal and its newly acquired responses will become a conversation piece. The following description parallels Skinner (1975) very closely. (It should be noted that what we call instrumental conditioning Skinner calls *operant conditioning.* He does not use the label instrumental conditioning at all.)

In order for learning to be most effective, the reinforcement must be presented almost simultaneously with the desired response. If there is a delay of even a second between the occurrence of the response and the delivery of the reinforcement, conditioning will be slowed. Because throwing food to a dog may not be fast and accurate enough, Skinner suggests that we use a "conditioned" reinforcer. A conditioned reinforcer is a sign or signal that the dog has learned to associate with food. If the dog has been given food immediately after this signal a number of times, the signal will take on reinforcing properties of its own. It will become a **conditioned** or **secondary reinforcer.** Skinner points out that we need a clear, precise sound or visual element, such as the sound of a "cricket," a sharp tap on a table, or a flash of light to serve as our signal. He notes that waving an arm may not work because the animal may not always see you wave.

Suppose that you select a rap on a table with a heavy spoon as your signal. You begin training by turning this signal into a conditioned reinforcer. This is done by tossing 30 or 40 very small pieces of food to the dog in a quiet location. Rap the table sharply just before you toss each piece of food. Wait about 30 seconds between pieces.

If your dog begs or jumps on you at first, ignore this behavior. Do not rap the table or give food when this behavior occurs. Always wait until the dog is turned away from you and then rap the table. Throw the food to the same spot each time. After a while you can test the power of your conditioned reinforcer by waiting until the dog is in a fairly unusual position. If it dashes to the spot where you have been throwing the food when it hears the table rap, then you know your training is working. Skinner points out that time spent in this initial training will help a great deal in the later phases—so make sure, before you move on, that the dog goes quickly to the food location when you rap the table.

Skinner suggests that you begin the next phase by choosing some simple response, such as getting the dog to touch its nose to the handle of a door. Begin by reinforcing any movement on the part of the dog. If it is sitting, reinforce it when it begins to walk in any direction. When you have the dog moving around pretty well, begin to reinforce any turn toward the door. Watch the animal closely and try to rap the table each time it turns in the correct direction. Do not touch or talk to the dog. Make the table rap, the food, and the dog do all the work.

Once the dog has learned to face the door, begin to reinforce it only when it actually moves toward the door. Gradually the dog will learn to approach the door if that is the only way a rap and a reinforcement can be obtained. Then, once the animal spends most of its time near the door, begin to concentrate on its head. Reinforce any head movement that brings the nose closer to the handle. Be sure your table rap occurs at the right moment, right after the movement toward the handle. Once the dog touches the handle with its nose and is reinforced with a table rap and food, it will continue to repeat touching its nose to the handle until you have satisfied its hunger. As we learned in Chapter 5, this process wherein we reinforce closer and closer approximations to the final response we are after is called shaping.

Skinner states that a dog can be taught this behavior in perhaps five minutes, assuming a good amount of initial time has been spent in building up the strength of the conditioned reinforcer. Before you teach the animal another response, extinguish the nose-to-handle response. That is, stop reinforcing the animal when it touches its nose to the handle until it gives up this behavior entirely. If you feel, at any time, that your conditioned reinforcer is losing its effectiveness, go back and pair food with the table rap a few more times. Using these same general procedures, a dog can be taught many different responses. Whatever response you use, remember that you begin by reinforcing a very rough approximation of what you want. You then require closer and closer approximations to the final response before you reinforce.

These same simple techniques may be applied with other kinds of subjects and responses. Skinner suggests that the beginner try using a pigeon.

Behavior Modification

Another application of instrumental conditioning involves *behavior modification.* Behavior modification is a very general term referring to a large number of techniques currently used to change human behavior. Basic to all of these techniques is the assumption that the behavior in question is *learned.* Sometimes the learning involved in behavior modification, or *behavior therapy* as it is sometimes called, is classical rather than instrumental. Systematic desensitiza-

Research suggests that if this anorexic woman could be reinforced for weight gains, she might put back on some needed pounds.

tion, which we have already discussed, is an example of behavior modification involving classical conditioning. But there are also thousands of examples of behavior modification involving instrumental conditioning, and it is to these that we now turn. All of these behavior-modification studies assume that the target behavior is maintained by reinforcement. It is also assumed that the target behavior may be extinguished through the removal of the maintaining reinforcement. In other words, it is assumed that many human behaviors are subject to the principles that govern rats when they press levers for food pellets in Skinner boxes—the principles of instrumental conditioning.

We have already seen in Chapter 5 how temper tantrums can be extinguished through the use of behavior-modification techniques. In this section we will explore some of the ways that behavior modification has been used to alter other human behaviors. Later, in Chapter 18 we will discuss the uses of behavior modification in therapy situations.

Self-starvation   A dangerous condition of self-imposed starvation, called **anorexia nervosa**, has been successfully treated with behavior-modification techniques. As we noted in Chapter 1, this disorder usually affects intelligent young women, and patients have been known to die from it. Medical doctors generally have assumed that anorexia nervosa is a physiological condition, and they have sometimes prescribed tube feeding to prevent the death of the patient. Garfinkel, Kline, and Stancer (1973), among others, boldly assumed that the disorder is primarily psychological or behavioral, rather than physiological. Accordingly, they treated five women who had been hospitalized for the condition by rewarding them for weight gains. The rewards included weekend passes and the opportunity to socialize with friends. Figure 8–2 displays the dramatic results of their procedures. By the end of the treatment almost all of the patients' original weight had been regained.

FIGURE 8–2   Behavior Therapy Used to Modify Self-starvation   *This graph shows the effects of rewarding weight gains in five patients suffering from anorexia nervosa. (After Garfinkel, Kline, & Stancer, 1973)*

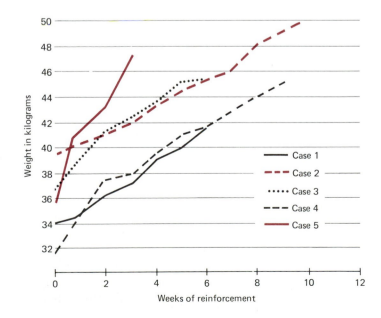

FIGURE 8–3   Behavior Modification and Energy Consumption   *This decal was used as reinforcement in an energy-conservation experiment.* (After Seaver & Patterson, 1976)

Energy Conservation   Some studies suggest that even the consumption of energy may be controlled by behavior-modification techniques. Seaver and Patterson (1976) monitored fuel-oil consumption in a neighborhood. Then they rewarded those families that managed to decrease their oil consumption by giving them a small press-on decal (see Figure 8–3). The delivery of these simple reinforcements proved to be effective in generating additional savings.

Kohlenberg, Phillips, and Proctor (1976) succeeded in reducing electricity consumption in a given neighborhood by means of behavior modification. They reduced "peaking" in electricity use (the tendency of families to concentrate their electricity use during specific times of the day) by giving small monetary rewards to families that reduced their peaking. Such peaking is inefficient and might well be cured through the use of simple reward systems administered by the power companies. In fact, there is no need to send decals, money, or other concrete rewards. A simple letter, such as that shown in Figure 8–4, has proved to be effective in curtailing energy consumption.

Token Economies   Many institutions, such as prisons and mental hospitals, use the behavior-modification technique known as a token economy. In a ***token economy***, desirable behaviors are immediately reinforced with tokens that may later be exchanged for primary rewards such as food, cigarettes, games, beverages, privileges, and so on. For example, staff members in some institutions for mentally retarded individuals give poker chips to the patients each time the patients display some desirable behavior such as being friendly, coop-

FIGURE 8–4   Behavior Modification and the Consumption of Electricity   *This form letter was sent to nonvolunteer consumer households in a monthly feedback condition. (Depending on whether the consumer was using more or less electricity than previously, various irrelevant parts of the letter were crossed out.) Electrical consumption was reduced when these letters were sent to consumers.* (After Hayes & Cone, 1981)

THIS IS NOT A BILL

Dear Consumer:

With all the concern over energy conservation, we thought you might like to know whether you are consuming more or less electricity now than in previous years. Based on our records for this address over the last three years, your consumption of electricity this last month was.

_____% below previous years. Congratulations! You are saving energy.

_____% above previous years.

(For those of you who would like more detail, this last month you consumed_____kWh of electricity, compared to the previous average of_____kWh. At today's prices, this means you saved/spent about an extra $_____.)

```
┌─────────────────────────────┐
│  DRIVERS NOT                │
│  SPEEDING                   │
│  YESTERDAY      9 4 %       │
│ ─────────────────────────── │
│  BEST RECORD    9 4 %       │
└─────────────────────────────┘
```

FIGURE 8–5   Behavior Modification and Speeding
Posting the percentage of yesterday's drivers not speeding and the best record to date significantly reduced speeding in experiments conducted on urban highways. (After Van Houten, Nau, & Marini, 1980)

erative, neat, helpful, outgoing, or enthusiastic. The poker chips are collected by patients and later are exchanged for desired objects and activities such as clothing, personal items, snacks, and the opportunity to engage in extra social and athletic events. Token economies are efficient because they allow for immediate, convenient delivery of reinforcement. Tokens have been used with some success in many settings, including mental hospitals, schools, and home settings (see Atthowe & Krasner, 1968; Lutzker & Sherman, 1974; Pommer & Streedbeck, 1974).

Stealing and Speeding   Those of us who live in large cities become accustomed (well, almost accustomed) to the sound of police helicopters patrolling our neighborhoods. We often wonder if these patrols actually frighten off any would-be burglars. Apparently they do, at least in high-density neighborhoods (Kirchner et al., 1980). In one test, helicopters patrolled 10-square-mile urban areas with about 50,000 residents. The patrols did not catch any burglars, but they did reduce the number of attempted burglaries significantly. When the same helicopters patrolled much larger areas (about 100 square miles) containing the same number of people, they were not effective in reducing crime.

Speeding can be controlled with behavior-modification techniques, too. Van Houten, Nau, and Marini (1980) erected the sign pictured in Figure 8–5. Then they monitored the speed of cars passing the sign daily and posted the percentage of drivers who did not speed on the previous day, as well as the best record to date. Speeding was reduced significantly over the six months that the experiment ran, and the fastest drivers slowed down more than drivers who were barely speeding. Posting the figures once a week worked as well as daily posting, but when no new figures were posted for long periods, speeding crept back up again.

Time-out, Stomach Pains, and Stuttering   People engaging in unwanted behavior often can give it up with the help of the ***time-out technique.*** Essentially, time-out temporarily stops the person from engaging in the behavior. It is assumed that the behavior is somehow rewarding to the person, so keeping the person from doing it will be mildly punishing. Miller and Kratochwill (1979) treated a 10-year-old girl who had been complaining of stomach pains for a year. Medically, there was nothing wrong with her, so each time she complained of pain, the investigators placed her in her room with a few books, but without television or toys. Using this time-out procedure, they were able to eliminate the complaints within a few weeks.

Stuttering has been reduced with the time-out technique, too (James, 1981). Since talking is seen as rewarding (we all love to gab), not talking will be mildly punishing. In this study the subject, a lifelong stutterer, was told to stop talking for at least two seconds each time he began to stutter. He was able to reduce his stuttering dramatically in various situations, including talking to himself, to the experimenter, to his family, over the phone, and in shops. But his improvement continued only if he was firm with himself and refused to let himself speak for a few seconds each time he began to stutter.

Money for Fat We have already seen in the discussion of anorexia that behavior therapy can help people gain weight. It may also help people lose weight, however. Kramer, Jeffery, Snell, and Forster (1986) point out that it is a fairly simple matter to get people to lose weight if they are given money to do so. These researchers also note that maintaining those weight losses over long periods of time is not so easy to accomplish. They feel that continued payment periods ranging up to a number of years are promising but that people do tend to backslide over the long run.

The Good-behavior Game Do you remember library period in grade school? That was when everyone tried to look studious while fooling around as much as possible. Well, apparently the librarians were on to us all the time, for they have tried to reduce disruptive behavior through the use of behavior modification. In an experiment reported by Fishbein and Wasik (1981), librarians used a good-behavior game with fourth graders. In this game the class is divided up into two or three teams. Then the librarian counts good and bad (wanted and unwanted) behaviors. The team that scores the highest is rewarded in some appropriate manner. It works; disruptive behavior can be reduced.

Shape Your Teacher In an amusing but instructive study, Gray, Graubard, and Rosenberg (1974) demonstrated that psychologists are not the only members of society who can effectively employ behavior-modification techniques. School children ages 12–15 were taught to use various reinforcements to reward, and thereby increase, the occurrence of positive responses from their teachers. The students were taught to smile, make eye contact, and sit up straight in their efforts

The teacher-pupil relationship is a two-way street. A positive attitude on the part of the teacher reinforces positive student attitudes which, in turn, reward the teacher.

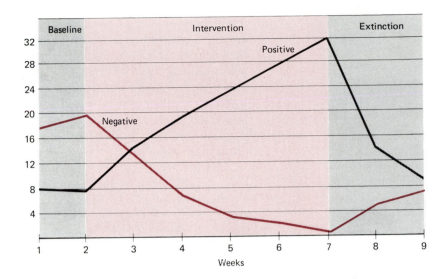

FIGURE 8–6   Behavior Modification and Teaching
Average numbers of positive and negative teacher responses made during the baseline, intervention, and extinction phases indicate the effectiveness of students' rewarding teachers. (After Gray, Graubard, & Rosenberg, 1974)

to shape their teachers' behaviors. They also practiced praising their teachers by saying such things as, "I like to work in a room where the teacher is nice to the kids," or "It makes me feel good when you praise me." Of course, saying such things sincerely required a good bit of practice, but the children did learn to use such rewards and to deliver them convincingly in class.

During the first two weeks of the study the students did not reinforce their teachers for positive acts. They merely acted as they had always acted. During this baseline period more of the teachers' responses to the students were negative than positive. Then, during the next five weeks, the students diligently applied their reinforcers to their teachers, praising them when they were friendly and positive and saying such things as, "It's hard for me to do good work when you are cross with me," when the teachers were negative. As Figure 8–6 shows, the number of positive teacher reactions rose dramatically during this time, while negative teacher responses declined in number. (Independent observers sitting in the classroom made all judgments about the nature of the teachers' responses.) Finally, during a two-week extinction session, the students withdrew their reinforcements. The teachers' positive responses quickly degenerated, suggesting that we all backslide and that continuing reinforcement is needed to maintain our desirable behaviors.

Cognitive Behavior Modification

Traditionally, behavior modification has been used to change people's observable behavior through the manipulation of conditioning principles. Psychologists using behavior modification tend to ignore "what goes on in the mind." Thus, people have been reinforced or punished for particular physical behaviors regardless of what they were thinking or feeling. But this seems to be somewhat shortsighted. It is obvious that what we think affects how we behave. Margraf, Ehlers, and Roth (1987) present a dramatic example of how thought affects behavior. Their study dealt with a female patient who routinely experienced powerful panic attacks at least once a day. The researchers presented her with false information concerning her heart rate; she was led to believe that she was experiencing a sudden increase in heart rate while her heart rate, in fact, was normal. In response to this false information, the patient panicked. As Figure 8–7 indicates, her heart rate shot up and her skin conductance level (perspiration level) increased rapidly. When the presentation of false information ceased, her panic reaction began to subside. In other words, there is no question whatsoever about the powerful impact of thought on behavior.

As researchers gradually recognized the effect of thought on behavior, they began to develop a new approach called *cognitive behavior modification (CBM).* The idea behind CBM is simple: we may be able to change the way people behave if we can change the way they think.

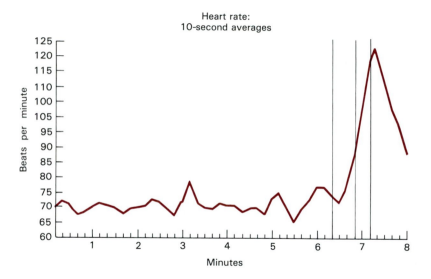

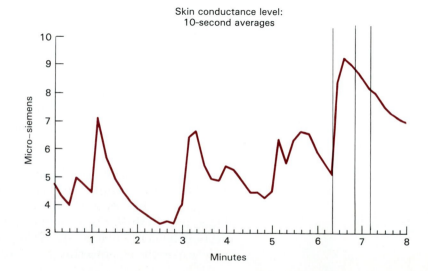

FIGURE 8–7 Thought Can Affect Behavior *These graphs show ten-second averages for heart rate and skin conductance levels during accurate and false heart rate feedback. The first vertical line indicates the beginning of false feedback of a 50 bpm increase, the second line, the end of the increase, and the third line, the beginning of the decrease back to baseline.* (After Margraf, Ehlers, & Roth, 1987)

One of the many different CBM techniques is *self-instruction training.* In this method, people are reinforced for rehearsing new ways of thinking that will affect how they act. Consider the case of a person who is constantly getting into trouble because she is too impulsive and always acts before she thinks. She could be reinforced for rehearsing the following strategies in the hope that if her thinking is changed, her actions will change too:

1. Do not jump in blindly when a problem arises. Define the problem in a measured manner.

2. Do not just try the first solution that pops into your mind. Mentally evaluate several alternative solutions before choosing one.

3. After acting, check the results of your actions carefully. Were they effective? If not, reconsider the remaining alternative solutions.

4. Always congratulate yourself when you solve a problem effectively; remind yourself to think before you act in the future.

Self-instruction training involves *self-talk*, which is the trick of mentally conversing with yourself about alternative courses of action before you leap blindly ahead. From this example, we can see that CBM attempts to alter thought in order to alter behavior.

Self-treatment

Another interesting development in the general field of behavior modification has been the increasing emphasis on *self-treatment.* It is expensive and time-consuming to have a therapist administer therapeutic procedures, especially when it appears that patients can conduct much of the treatment themselves. Ghosh and Marks (1987) tried a different approach in their treatment of agoraphobics, people who have phobic reactions to wide-open spaces (the opposite of claustrophobics). Psychologists have known for a long time that graded, systematic exposure to the specific situations or elements that cause a person's fear can lessen phobic reactions. Traditionally, the therapist has been the one to direct this exposure process. Ghosh and Marks divided their patients into three groups that received instruction from a psychiatrist, a written manual, or an appropriately programmed computer. All three groups improved over a six-month period, but no one method was any better than the other two. In other words, with a book or a computer we may be able to help ourselves without having to rely on a therapist (see also Hoelscher, Lichstein, Fischer, & Hegarty, 1987).

Biofeedback Training

As we saw in Chapter 5, biofeedback techniques give subjects information about changes within their own bodies that are normally beyond their awareness. Changes in heart rate may be monitored mechanically and electrically. The subject can be made aware of such changes by a clicking sound that occurs each time the heart beats. Each time the heart rate, or clicking, is slowed, the subject is rewarded. Reinforcements may be of several different types. Money,

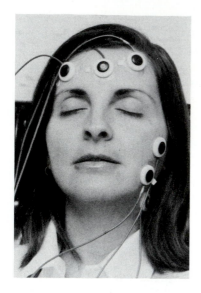

Electrical activity of the brain, according to some experts, can be altered through the use of reinforcement principles.

praise, self-congratulations, and the avoidance of shock have proved to be effective reinforcers in these types of situations. If the click rate speeds up or remains constant, reinforcement is withheld. In this way, the subject's heart rate may be lowered. A number of investigators have reported successful reward training in connection with such supposedly involuntary responses.

Biofeedback training has not been limited to the conditioning of heart rate. Blood pressure, electrical activity of the brain, skin temperature, salivation, vomiting, and tension headaches also may be affected by biofeedback techniques (Plotkin, 1979). Rare conditions, such as Raynaud's disease, can be controlled through biofeedback, too (Keefe, Surwit, & Pilon, 1980). People suffering from this disease experience painful spasms that cut off the blood flow in the toes and fingers. When the spasm ends, blood rushes back into the digits, causing additional pain. Patients inflicted with Raynaud's disease can be taught, through biofeedback procedures, to raise their skin temperature, which helps lessen the frequency and intensity of their attacks.

Biofeedback training may turn out to be an important application of instrumental reward conditioning outside the laboratory, but at present, the whole topic is extremely controversial and subject to heavy criticism. Even some important investigators within the field are skeptical of their own results (Miller, 1972). The only thing that seems certain now is that we can expect a flood of biofeedback studies in the near future. If we can learn to control and alter our internal responses, biofeedback training could become a major medical tool.

Computer-assisted Instruction (CAI)

As a final example of the ways in which instrumental conditioning has influenced life outside the laboratory, we will consider *teaching machines* and *computer-assisted instruction (CAI)*. If we can teach rats and pigeons complex responses in the laboratory by manipulating patterns of stimuli, responses, and reinforcements, why is it that we cannot do the same sorts of things in our classrooms? B. F. Skinner has long believed that we can (Skinner, 1968). It was Skinner's opinion that many of the teaching procedures used in classrooms were inadequate.

To overcome these difficulties Skinner developed what became known as the teaching machine. A teaching machine is an instrument that presents a series of *frames* to the student. Each frame contains an item of information and a question related to that information. The student answers the question by writing or typing the answer in a space provided for this purpose and then turns a knob or pushes a button that reveals the correct answer and the next frame. A typical frame looks like this:

> The important parts of a flashlight are the battery and the bulb. When we "turn on" a flashlight, we close a switch that connects the battery with the _____. (Skinner, 1968, p. 45)

In this way, the student can progress through a program of instruction one step at a time. The steps are small enough to avoid confusion and misunderstanding, and the immediate answers to questions reward attentive students.

Proponents of teaching machines claim that this method of instruction is markedly superior to the typical classroom situation. The advantages of the machine are that it (1) operates on the basis of reward rather than punishment, (2) reinforces the student immediately and every time a correct response is made, (3) allows the student to progress at her or his own speed, and (4) rigorously structures the material in an ordered fashion so that each bit of information builds on the previous piece of information. In other words, the teaching machine provides control over stimuli, responses, and reinforcement in a manner similar to that obtained in a laboratory Skinner box.

Mechanical teaching machines were replaced rapidly by computer-assisted instruction systems (CAI). Modern computers provide enormous flexibility in terms of storage, control, and presentation of information. Unlike mechanical teaching machines, CAI systems permit extremely complex and flexible programs of instruction. Students using CAI systems generally receive synchronized auditory and visual information and respond by operating a typewriter keyboard. Their responses are received and evaluated by the computer. If the student responds correctly, the computer moves to the next item. If the student answers incorrectly, the computer may present some remedial material to ensure that the student does not move on to the next item until he or she has mastered the current item. Many students can be taught simultaneously by a large computer.

CAI systems have been designed for many age levels and virtually all subjects. Kulik, Bangert, and Williams (1983) carefully reviewed a large number of CAI systems used in grades 6 through 12. They found that CAI systems significantly improved not only the students' performance, but their attitude toward learning as well.

IMPROVING MEMORY AND COGNITION

Chapter 6 described many experiments and theories involving memory processes. Have these efforts led to any useful information? Although attempts to apply what we have learned in the laboratory are just beginning, some practical suggestions have emerged. We will explore these suggestions in this section.

Don't Wait for "Memory Pills"

We are all painfully aware of the fact that our memory systems are less than perfect. We are often irritated and frustrated by our inability to remember necessary information at critical times. Everyone has experienced the frustration of trying to memorize complicated academic materials and the frustration of "knowing we know" the answer to a test item even though we are unable to retrieve it during the examination. Many of us have also found ourselves having to introduce a number of people to one another. More often than not, this task is difficult and can be embarrassing.

Can any of these frustrations be overcome, or at least reduced? Perhaps someday we will have drugs and chemicals that will help us. Even now, an injection of arginine vasopressin (AVP), a peptide normally made within the central nervous system, seems to improve learning and memory in some people (Weingarter et al., 1981). But these results are experimental and chemical solutions to our problems may never be practical.

First, Pay Attention

While we hope for the magical memory pill, can we *learn* techniques that will enable us to perform more efficiently? The answer is a qualified yes. We cannot make vast improvements in our general memory functions, but there are some techniques that will sharpen the abilities we have. The first of these has to do with **attention.** We must train ourselves to pay attention if we want to maximize our ability to retain.

What has attention to do with memory? Consider the fact that each and every minute of our lives we are being bombarded by an enormous jumble of sensory stimuli. We are awash in a bath of visual, auditory, olfactory, and other signals. And yet we do not, cannot, attend to all of these stimuli at any given moment. Most of them go unnoticed. For example, think about your right foot for a moment. Do you feel anything down there? More than likely you will feel slight tingling sensations or perhaps the pressure of clothing. All of these sensory events were unnoticed until you directed your attention to them.

This process of focusing our attention plays an extremely important role in memory. To put it simply, if we can train ourselves to attend to important stimuli, then we can improve our chances of remembering those stimuli. If we can train ourselves not to be distracted by unimportant stimuli, then memory will improve. If you are introduced to a stranger at a party, you may find that you are unable to remember that person's name later in the evening. More than likely, this is because you did not pay attention to the name when you were first introduced. You were too busy talking, looking, smiling, shaking hands, wondering what to say, and worrying about impressions. But you can train yourself to attend to names in such situations. With a little practice, the embarrassment of not knowing someone's name can be avoided. Your retention of other types of material, such as course work, also can be maximized through focused attention.

Repeat That, Please

Merely paying attention will not guarantee that you will remember someone's name. Attention is necessary, but not necessarily sufficient. Suppose, for example, that the name you are trying to recall is Farzad Kazeminezhad. You might easily attend to this name when you are introduced and still fail to remember it later in the evening. Memory research suggests that *repetition* or *rehearsal* will help in this situation. Saying the name over and over again, either aloud or to yourself, will improve your learning and retention of it. The more you rehearse the name, the more likely you will be to remember it later. You should also test yourself occasionally. For example, an hour after being introduced to Mr. Kazeminezhad you might try to recall his

Whether you are trying to remember concepts or dance steps, it is vital to focus your attention on the problem and repeat your learned response over and over again.

name. By doing this several times during the evening, you will improve your chances of remembering the name at a later time.

The more meaningful the material we are required to learn, the more easily it will be learned and remembered. If you are introduced to someone named Richard Shakespeare you will be more likely to remember him than you would Irdrach Prakeshaese. In a sense, we are all at the mercy of the materials we are trying to remember. The more meaningful the material is, the less you will need to rehearse it in order to remember it, as Figure 8–8 demonstrates.

Easy list	Medium list	Difficult list
RAN	COM	JOQ
TOP	BEF	QEZ
FIB	TEB	KUY
LET	GOZ	ZYT
TOW	RUF	XUY
SOP	DOZ	ZOJ
BAT	RAV	JYQ
CAP	KAM	QDK
POT	LIB	VOJ
HAT	HOL	VYK

FIGURE 8–8   Meaning and Memory   *Three lists of different levels of meaningfulness and typical recall data for each of the lists illustrate that it is easier to recall meaningful material.*

Average number of items recalled after 2-min. study time

Organize, If You Can

We must pay attention, and we must rehearse. Is there anything else we can do to improve our ability to remember? Research indicates that our attempts to retain information will be more successful if we can *organize* the material in some logical, consistent manner. As we saw in Chapter 6, organized material is easier to remember than unorganized material.

For instance, suppose you were introduced to all of the people listed on the left side of Figure 8–9 in the order shown. How many of them do you think you would be able to recall following the introductions? Now look at the arrangement of the same names on the right side of Figure 8–9. Here, the relationships among the people are expressed. The materials are organized. Not surprisingly, if materials are presented in an organized manner, they are much more readily remembered than if they are not organized. In fact, we often find ourselves attempting to discover the relationships among guests at parties. We ask the other guests where they met the host, for instance. Knowing the relationship reduces the burden on our memory systems.

Mnemonic Techniques

We have seen that organizing information, as well as attending to it and rehearsing it, can assist us in our efforts to remember. But what should we do when we cannot think of a way to organize the information? Imagine that we wish to remember HEX, IOT, DAV, ETE, ORT, UPO, and TIX. The letters just seem to sit there, requiring us to rehearse them over and over until we can remember them. An easy way to organize them does not seem available. What do we do in a case such as this? One option is to try to use what are known as *mnemonic techniques.* When we use mnemonics (pronounced nemon-

FIGURE 8–9 Organization and Memory *Organizing information about the people whose names appear in the list below makes them easier to identify and remember.*

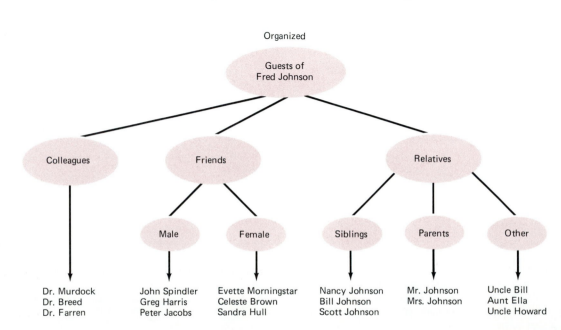

ics), we try to relate the unorganized information to information we already know. We may help ourselves remember the items listed above by observing that the first letters of the seven nonsense syllables spell HIDEOUT. By referring to HIDEOUT, an item we already know, we are on our way to remembering all of the nonsense items. There are many different mnemonic techniques available, but they all involve trying to remember unorganized materials by relating them to materials we have already organized and stored.

Let us take a closer look at some of the more useful mnemonic techniques.

Coined Phrases

We are all faced, sooner or later, with remembering items in a certain order. For example, the 12 cranial nerves listed in Table 8–2 must be learned by biology students in the order shown. One way to remember the order is to make up a sentence, or *coin a phrase*, that uses the first letter of each of the nerves. Table 8–2 shows two sample coined phrases that allow us to remember the order of the nerves. The first letter of each of the words is also the first letter of the appropriate nerve. Try making up a coined phrase yourself. The more bizarre and unusual it is, the better it will work. If you can remember the coined phrase, it will help you remember the nerves.

As Bower (1974) points out, the problem with this method, even though it is helpful, is that the names of the nerves themselves are not stored in memory. All we store are the first letters. Often we will be able to remember the coined phrase long after the names of the nerves have been lost. Bower suggests that a better mnemonic device would be one that contains the items themselves, or at least hints for remembering the items. Thus he suggests the 12 major cranial nerves may be remembered by storing the following:

> At the oil factory (olfactory nerve) the optician (optic) looked for the occupant (oculomotor) of the truck (trochlear). He was searching because three gems (trigeminal) had been abducted (abducents) by a man who was hiding his face (facial) and ears (acoustic). A glossy photograph

---

TABLE 8–2   The Major Cranial Nerves and Sample Coined Phrases Useful in Remembering the Nerves and Their Order

Nerves

Olfactory, Optic, Oculomotor, Trochlear, Trigenimal, Abducents, Facial, Acoustic, Glossopharyngeal, Vagus, Spinal Accessory, Hypoglossal

Sample Coined Phrase

On October one, three tiny ants fought against giant, vibrating super humans.

Sample Coined Phrase

On old, oscillating tree tops, agile, flying, army generals voiced silly humorisms.

(glossopharyngeal) had been taken of him, but it was too vague (vagus) to use. He appeared to be spineless (spinal accessory) and hypocritical (hypoglossal). (Bower, 1974, p. 140)

Interacting Images

One method for tying together two elements, such as foreign language vocabulary items, names and faces, and the meanings of concepts, involves the use of *interacting mental images.* Suppose we wish to remember the following pairs: horse-orange, pencil-bottle, nose-giraffe, auto-lawyer, and elf-chlorine. One way to learn these pairs is to rehearse them over and over again. Another, more efficient way is to form a "mental image" or "mental picture" of the two items as we try to learn them—for instance, an image of an auto and an image of a lawyer. The best way to remember these pairs is to imagine them *interacting* in some way. For example, form a mental picture of an elf making popsicles from chlorine, a lawyer running his auto into a lamp post, a horse eating an orange, a giraffe with a nose as long as his neck, and a bottle filled with pencils. A number of studies have demonstrated that interacting images often work better than noninteracting images (Begg, 1978; Robbins, Bray, Irvin, & Wise, 1974). Noninteracting images appear to be better than no images at all, but interacting images work best. There is also some evidence that unique, unusual images result in better retention (Lesgold & Goldman, 1973).

Invent a Story

A similar method for remembering lists of words is to develop *stories* that include the actual words to be remembered (Bower & Clark, 1969). Table 8–3 contains two lists of words. You could remember these lists by saying them over and over again to yourself, but a much more efficient technique is to make up stories such as those on the right side of Table 8–3. By remembering the story, you automatically remember the words, and a meaningful story is more readily remembered than a list of unrelated words. In fact, people learning lists by the story method typically remember between 80 percent and 100 percent of the words, while people trying to remember the words without making up stories have trouble remembering over 30 percent of the words (Bower & Clark, 1969). That is a significant difference. If we can train ourselves to use the story-telling method whenever it applies, we can improve our retention scores enormously.

The Method of Loci

The *method of loci* works by placing mental images of what we are trying to remember in ordered mental locations. This method was invented by the ancient Greeks, who used it to help them remember topics and issues during long public speeches. The first step in using the method of loci is to establish an ordered series of known locations. You might take a "mental walk" through a very familiar building, such as your home. A walk outside will do just as well, as long as it involves a series of known locations. At distinct points along

TABLE 8–3   Invent a Story

A list of words will be easier to remember if you make up a story that includes all of the to-be-remembered words.

Word Lists	Stories
Bird Costume Mailbox Head River Nurse Theater Wax Eyelid Furnace	A man dressed in a Bird Costume and wearing a Mailbox on his Head was seen leaping into the River. A Nurse ran out of a nearby Theater and applied Wax to his Eyelids, but her efforts were in vain. He died and was tossed into the Furnace.
Rustler Penthouse Mountain Sloth Tavern Fuzz Gland Antler Pencil Vitamin	A Rustler lived in a Penthouse on top of a Mountain. His specialty was the three-toed Sloth. He would take his captive animals to a Tavern where he would remove Fuzz from their Glands. Unfortunately, all this exposure to sloth fuzz caused him to grow Antlers. So he gave up his profession and went to work in a Pencil factory. As a precaution he also took a lot of Vitamin E.

your mental walk, you should "place" vivid images of what you are trying to remember—the first item in the first location, the second in the second, and so on.

Consider an example. Suppose you are trying to remember a list of items to be purchased at a hardware store. The items include nails, a hammer, a pair of pliers, a chisel, and a measuring tape. Now, suppose you have chosen a "mental walk" through your house as a means of supplying convenient, well-known "locations," or "hooks" on which to place the images of the objects to be remembered. It has been found that this system works best if the images are vivid and bizarre. Thus, if your walk begins at the front door, you might visualize the front door nailed shut with hundreds of green and maroon nails. Approaching the stairway, you might imagine a huge hammer with legs sliding down the bannister. In the kitchen you might have an enormous pair of pink pliers pinching the refrigerator in half. In the dining room you could visualize hundreds of little blue chisels buzzing about the food like flies. In the backyard, you might imagine a snakelike measuring tape devouring apples.

Try this method for yourself using the words in Table 8–4. First, establish your mental walk. Then fill the locations with vivid, unusual images of the items in the table. Test the system by "taking a walk" through your locations and seeing how simple it is to recall not only the items but their correct order as well.

TABLE 8–4 Common Words to Be Used in the Method of Loci

Establish an ordered sequence of known locations and "place" vivid images of the items in this list at distinct points along your "mental walk." The more bizarre and vivid the images, the better. Then see if you can recall the items in the list (in order) by "taking a walk" through your locations.

Forest	Gymnast
Mayor	Infant
Pillar	Shack
Rooster	Textbook
Tablespoon	Warplane

Rhymes

Our last example of mnemonic techniques is related to the method of loci. In this case, however, the pegs or hooks for the items to be remembered are not locations but common objects that are tied to numbers with **rhyme.**

We begin with a game for remembering lists of unrelated words (Miller, Galanter, & Pribram, 1960). First, we must remind ourselves of the old children's rhyme:

One is a bun.	Six is a stick.
Two is a shoe.	Seven is heaven.
Three is a tree.	Eight is a gate.
Four is a door.	Nine is wine.
Five is a hive.	Ten is a hen.

Rehearse the rhyme a couple of times. Once you have this rhyme firmly in mind, you are ready to move to the next step, which is to learn a list of ten unrelated words. You will associate the first word in the list with "One is a bun" by creating some vivid, unusual image containing both a bun and the first word. If the first word is "house," you might imagine a house made of steaming hot-cross buns, or a row of tiny red houses tucked neatly into a sliced bun. Each of the words in the list is tied to the appropriate rhyme element through the creation of some bizarre, vivid image.

Try this plan with the list of words below. Run through the list, one at a time. Give yourself enough time to establish a firm image for each word.

Car	Shirt
Flag	Drum
Clock	Scissors
Book	Pen
Knife	Ski

Now, assuming you have completed the task, we will test the effectiveness of the plan by asking a series of questions. Cover the list of words. What is the seventh word? What item in the list could be matched with the word "door"? What is the third word? What is the fifth word? You can probably sense what is occurring. The test words are so bound into your visual images that it is a simple matter to recall them. This plan for remembering has been tested experimentally. Bugelski (1968) had an experimental group learn lists of words using this plan and had control subjects learn the same lists without the plan. The experimental subjects recalled significantly more items than did the controls. In all likelihood, if you had not first learned the rhyme and been instructed in how to create images, your recall of the list would have been much less complete.

Keyword Method

The *keyword method* is a technique for remembering the English meaning of foreign words (Atkinson, 1975; Pressley & Levin, 1981). Suppose you want to remember that the Spanish word *carta* means "letter." The first step is to think of an English word that sounds like *carta*, such as "cart." This is the keyword. Next, form a visual image of the keyword and the English translation, such as a mail carrier pulling a kiddy-cart full of letters. Later, when you are given *carta* and asked for the English meaning, *carta* will remind you of "cart" which will, in turn, key off the visual image containing the "letter" you are after.

When Memory Fails: Context Effects

Sometimes we know we have information stored but we just cannot seem to get it out. There are at least two strategies for overcoming this sort of retrieval failure.

Re-creation of Context   Sometimes we can dig out the elusive memory by re-creating the *context* surrounding that information. If you cannot find your car keys, try to remember when and where you last had them. Then try to recall what you did and where you went after that. Following this mental trail may well lead you to the misplaced keys. If someone asks you what you were doing on the third Friday in August three years ago, you might laugh, assuming that the task of remembering so far back is impossible. But if you try to reconstruct the context, in a step-by-step fashion, you sometimes can come up with the answer (Norman, 1973). You might first recall that you were in high school three years ago. This would lead to the recollection that you were still on vacation in August. Then you might remember visiting your brother in Nebraska for ten days during the latter part of the month. Finally, you might be able to pin down the answer by recalling what you did on Friday nights while visiting with your brother and his family.

The First-letter System   If you are trying to recall names or words, you can run through the alphabet hoping that the letters will key off the desired items. Try recalling the presidents of our country. After you have gotten as many as you can, go through the alphabet, one letter at a time, and see if you can recall any more. You will probably surprise yourself.

How to Study

The SQ3R Method A number of different methods for absorbing information from textbooks and reading assignments have been developed. Perhaps the best known of these is the *SQ3R method*—Survey, Question, Read, Recite, Review.

The first step is to survey the assignment. Do not read the material at this point. Just skim over the chapter titles and headings to get an overall view of what is going to be discussed. Develop a good, basic idea of the content of the assignment. Second, transform these titles and headings into questions. Ask yourself what you will be seeking in each section. Third, read the material with the idea of answering the questions you have posed. It is easier to become actively involved in the assignment if you have a purpose, such as answering the questions. Fourth, without referring to the text, write out brief answers to the questions. Keep them simple. Fifth, review all material. Recite the answers to all of the questions you have developed.

The essence of the SQ3R method is active participation. You do not just passively plod through the material; you look it over, form questions about it, try to answer those questions, and review your efforts. In effect, this method invites you to make up your own tests and take them. You frame questions and pursue answers. We know, as a result of laboratory research, that being tested on material can help you remember it (Whitten & Leonard, 1980). So anything you can do to develop and take self-tests will probably help.

Where to Study

As we saw in Chapter 6, the physical context (including walls, chairs, instructors, and lighting) in which you learn material can give you effective cues to help you recall learned material later on. This is called a *state-dependent memory effect* because your ability to remember is dependent on whether or not the conditions of recall are the same as the conditions of learning.

Clearly, this finding has implications for students. Whenever possible, try to learn materials in the setting that will be used for testing. Perhaps you could study at off-hours in the classroom, rather than in the library. Try to sit in the same general area during lectures and exams. If you cannot study in the classroom, study in a similar classroom rather than out on the lawn.

Of course, most of your studying will be done away from the classroom. But there is still something you can do. When you are taking the test and cannot remember an item, try to recall the conditions under which you learned that item. Say to yourself, "Now I was in the library when I read that chapter. Let's see. . . ." Try to imagine the library room. There are some indications that simply imagining the learning situation can help recall.

SUMMARY

1. Important applications of the principles of classical and instrumental conditioning, as well as memory techniques, are beginning to appear outside the laboratory.

2. Enuresis (bed-wetting) has been controlled through classical conditioning procedures.

3. The polygraph machine, or "lie detector," can detect classically conditioned emotional states by recording changes in blood pressure, pulse rate, breathing, and perspiration. Its controversial use in police work and therapy is based on the assumption that the individual cannot conceal his or her inner emotional reactions.

4. Phobias are strong, irrational fears that can be eliminated through systematic desensitization, a process involving the extinction of classically conditioned fear.

5. A form of aversion therapy will keep coyotes from killing lambs. The coyotes are fed lamb's flesh laced with lithium chloride, a chemical that makes the animal ill. The coyotes then will shy away from live lambs even though they will still attack rabbits, their natural prey.

6. Smoking, overeating, and drinking, as well as other "bad habits," can be eliminated through aversion therapy by pairing the behavior, or the thought of the behavior, with shock, noxious drugs, or other unpleasant stimuli.

7. Classical conditioning may be helpful in treating cancer-related nausea and in causing immune-system alterations.

8. In Skinner's method of training a dog, responses are reinforced immediately by a conditioned reinforcer, such as the sound of a "cricket" that has been paired repeatedly with the delivery of food.

9. Behavior modification is a general term applied to numerous methods of behavior control. All of these methods assume that the behavior is learned through reinforcement and that it will extinguish if reinforcement is removed.

10. Temper tantrums may be extinguished by withdrawing social reinforcement. Self-starvation (anorexia nervosa) may be eliminated by rewarding weight gains. Energy conservation (fuel consumption and peaking in electrical use) may be reduced through the application of reward systems as well.

11. In token economies, desirable behaviors in institutional settings are reinforced immediately with tokens that later may be exchanged for more primary rewards such as food, cigarettes, games, and privileges.

12. Stealing and speeding have been reduced with behavior-modification techniques.

13. Time-out methods have been used to eliminate stomach pain and stuttering.

14. People may lose weight if offered money to do so.

15. The good-behavior game can reduce disruptive classroom behavior.

16. Teachers, as well as students, can be influenced by behavior-modification techniques.

17. Cognitive behavior modification (CBM), including self-instruction training, attempts to alter behavior by first altering thought.

18. Self-treatment methods appear to be gaining acceptance.

19. Biofeedback training refers to the instrumental conditioning of involuntary responses. If humans are made aware of, and reinforced for, changes in such responses as heart rate, electrical brain activity, skin temperature, salivation, vomiting, and tension headaches, changes in these conditions may be obtained.

20. Teaching machines present a series of frames to the learner. Each frame contains a bit of information and a question related to that information.

21. Simple mechanical teaching machines have been replaced rapidly by computer-assisted instruction systems (CAI). Computers allow far more flexibility in terms of storage, control, and presentation of information.

22. So-called memory drugs are a thing of the future.

23. We must train ourselves to pay attention and to avoid distraction if we are to improve our memory performance.

24. Repetition, or rehearsal, improves retention by improving learning.

25. Organized information is more easily remembered than unorganized material.

26. Mnemonic techniques work because we relate unorganized information to organized information that we already know.

27. Coined phrases are often useful. We can make up and remember a phrase using the first letters of the items to be remembered as the first letters of the words in our invented phrase. Coined phrases do not contain the items themselves and are thus of limited value. A better mnemonic uses words that remind us more closely of the items to be remembered.

28. A good method for tying together pairs of items is to invent interacting images.

29. Strings of items may be remembered by inventing a story that contains the actual items in their correct order.

30. The method of loci works by placing vivid, bizarre images of what we are trying to remember in ordered mental locations, such as places in a familiar building. Then, by taking a "mental walk" through the building, the items may be retrieved.

31. By remembering a simple rhyme such as, "One is a bun, two is a shoe, three is a tree," and so on, and by imagining a vivid interaction between these pegs and the items to be remembered, we can increase our capacity to remember.

32. The keyword method is a technique for remembering foreign language equivalents.

33. When retrieval fails, we can try to reconstruct context or use the first-letter system.

34. The SQ3R method of studying suggests that we survey, question, read, recite, and review.

35. State-dependent memory studies show that we can recall material better if the test situation is the same as the learning situation.

KEY TERMS

anorexia nervosa

attention

aversion therapy

behavior modification

behavior therapy

cognitive behavior
   modification (CBM)

coin a phrase

computer-assisted instuction

conditioned or secondary
   reinforcer

context

counterconditioning

enuresis

extinction

frames

hierarchy

interacting mental images

keyword method

method of loci

mnemonic techniques

organize

phobias

polygraph machine

repetition/rehearsal

rhyme

self-instruction training

self-talk

self-treatment

SQ3R method

state-dependent memory
   effect

stories

systematic desensitization

teaching machines

time-out technique

token economy

ADDITIONAL READING

Best, J. B. (1986) *Cognitive psychology*. New York: West.
This text offers comprehensive coverage of cognitive psychology with many excellent "focus on application" sections.

Grasha, A. F. (1983) *Practical applications of psychology*. Boston: Little, Brown.
Note this text's many intriguing examples of the use of learning principles in complex coping methods.

Houston, J. P. (1986) *Fundamentals of learning and memory*. San Diego: Harcourt Brace Jovanovich.
This resource provides complete coverage of basic phenomena with an emphasis on application.

Klein, S. B. (1987) *Learning: Principles and applications*. New York: McGraw-Hill.
This is a new text, with, as the title suggests, extensive coverage of the practical use of learning principles.

Mazur, J. E. (1986) *Learning and behavior*. Englewood Cliffs: Prentice-Hall.
This excellent new text provides good coverage of both basic and applied material.

9 Motivation

A s you are studying, you realize you are becoming distracted by a familiar impulse. You are getting hungry—and not just for any old food. It is time for the search for the perfect taco to begin again. You call your friend Fred, who has been looking with you for months now, and together you ride off into the night, ever hopeful.

THE DEFINITION OF MOTIVATION

As the scenario above shows, humans have many complex urges and impulses. A basic biological drive like hunger can stir up other interests—such as the desire for good company and the supreme taco. Psychologists describe all such wants, wishes, needs, desires, drives, and interests as motives. In the viewpoint of psychologists, *motives* (1) activate and arouse the organism, (2) direct the organism's behavior toward the attainment of some goal, and (3) determine the intensity or strength of the organism's behavior. In our scenario, the hunger motive not only arouses you and "gets you going," it also directs you toward a particular goal as well. An organism responding to such a motive is said to be motivated. The stronger our motivation, the more likely we are to act. The hungrier we are, the more likely we are to open a can of soup. If we are just barely hungry, we may forget the whole idea if the can opener is not in its customary drawer. But if we are starving, we will use a screwdriver to open that can, if that is all we can find.

In Chapter 5, we saw that learning resides within us and is invisible until it is converted into observable behavior by motives. For example, we have all learned how to open a can of soup, but we do not go about opening soup cans constantly. We have to be motivated before this learning will be utilized. *Motivation* is what translates learning into observable behavior.

Although it is a relatively new concept (it appeared after the beginning of this century), motivation has already been broadly interpreted and has seeped into many areas of psychology. For this reason, we will begin by describing some of the more important *theories* of motivation.

In the second half of the chapter, we will discuss the various *types* of motives that have been identified. First, we will discuss three basic biological needs and drives—hunger, thirst, and sex. Second, we will consider sensory-seeking drives, such as the need to explore and the desire to satisfy our curiosity. Finally, we will outline what is known about more complex, higher level human motives, such as the need to achieve.

APPROACHES TO MOTIVATION

Drive Theory

For many years, the most important concept in the field of motivation was that of drive. If an animal is deprived of certain essentials, such as food, water, or air, then we say it is in a state of *need.* This need leads to a state of arousal known as a *drive state.* This energized drive condition, in turn, will push the animal into behaviors that will reduce the need. Once the need has been satisfied, the drive will subside. Once a thirsty animal drinks its fill, it will cease that behavior as that state of tension and arousal recedes.

The concept of *drive* dominated the field of motivation for several decades, beginning in the 1920s. Organisms were thought of as being *pushed* into behavior by internal drives that arise in connection with physiological tissue needs (Houston, 1986; Hull, 1951; Logan & Gordon, 1981).

You may be wondering why we try to distinguish between needs and drives if they increase together. The answer is that they increase together only *up to a point*. If the need becomes too great, then drive cannot continue to increase. As Figure 9–1 shows, if we are too hungry we may reach the point where our drive begins to decrease. We become too weak to eat. When we are starving, our need is very high (the body desperately needs fuel), but our drive level is low (we become listless and exhausted rather than active and aroused). In other words, the need can continue to increase but the drive does not.

Drive theory has faced severe criticism over the years. Psychologists soon realized that they would have to invent a whole catalog of drives to account for all of the motivated behaviors they were observing. It is easy to think of a hunger drive and a thirst drive because these are necessary for survival, but what about such varied human interests as success, being with others, exploring, reading, wandering about department stores, chewing pencils, and cracking the backs of new books? To invent a drive for each and every motivated human behavior would be ridiculous and impossible. How could anyone hope to identify the tissue need corresponding to a space-exploration drive or a stamp-collecting drive?

As a result of this flaw in drive theory, many alternative conceptions of motivation have arisen. There is no doubt that some behaviors are motivated by drives associated with physiological need states, but many other behaviors do not come about in this way.

Incentive Theory: Push versus Pull

An individual who is not hungry will often eat if particular foods are made available. A box of fancy dark chocolates passed around after a full meal will not be neglected. We have all stuffed in "one more bite" long after any tissue need existed. Pretty, novel, complex, or interesting objects in the environment will draw our attention in the absence

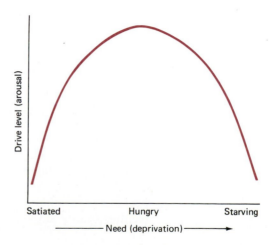

FIGURE 9–1 The Theoretical Relationship Between Need, as Determined by Deprivation, and Drive Level, or State of Arousal

of any deprivation. Because of these kinds of behaviors, psychologists have begun to focus on incentives. *Incentives* are objects or events in the environment, outside the organism, that pull the organism and motivate it in the absence of any known physiological need state.

Researchers have explored the effectiveness of incentives in a variety of experiments. Pfaffmann (1969), Sheffield (1966), and others have demonstrated that organisms will work for a sip of saccharin solution even though saccharin has no nutritional value and cannot reduce any tissue need. The organism simply likes the flavor and so it is motivated to experience it.

The best conception of motivation probably includes both drives (push) and incentives (pull). Drives and incentives are not independent; they clearly affect one another. The pull quality or attractiveness of a stimulus, such as a cheeseburger, increases as we become more and more hungry. Similarly, our drive state often seems to be increased by stimuli in the environment. If we are mildly hungry, the sight or smell of a broiled steak may seem to increase our hunger. Both internal drive states and external stimuli appear to be capable of energizing and directing our behavior.

Optimal-level-of-arousal Theory

Drive theory may cover the basic needs, but it is not a comprehensive theory of motivation. Incentive theory takes care of one additional aspect of motivated behavior: the pulling quality of external stimuli. But still another aspect of motivated behavior requires explanation. Animals sometimes act as though they want to *increase* rather than *decrease* the amount of arousal they are experiencing. Butler (1953) has shown that monkeys will solve discrimination problems for nothing more than the chance to look about a typical laboratory for a few moments. It seems they are motivated to increase the amount of stimulation they are receiving. In fact, both monkeys and humans sometimes want to increase stimulation and sometimes want to decrease it. Apparently, there is some preferred level of arousal that they seek to maintain. For instance, if you are at a noisy party and can no longer tolerate the noise, then escape from that party will be a reinforcing event. But if you have been sitting around for days with nothing to do, you will probably engage in behavior that will increase your level of arousal. You might even have some friends over for a nice, noisy party.

Many theoreticians have come to the same conclusion: animals have a preferred level of arousal (Berlyne, 1969; Lockhard, 1966; Routtenberg, 1968; Walker, 1980; Walters, Apter, & Svebok, 1982). Proponents of this position, which is usually called *optimal-level-of-arousal theory*, argue that if arousal falls too low, the animal will seek to increase it. This theory conflicts with drive theory, which maintains that all motivated behavior is directed toward reducing tension and arousal. Drive theory adherents conceive of the "happy" animal as one that is in a state of rest. Supporters of the optimal-arousal-level position argue that a satisfied animal is a moderately stimulated one. Neither theory alone can account for all motivated behavior.

Instincts, Ethology, and Imprinting

Instinctive behaviors, sometimes termed species-specific behaviors, are innate, predetermined patterns of behavior that are released when certain stimuli are perceived. For example, a male bird will attack when a rival male enters his territory. This instinctive attack behavior may be triggered by the bird's perception of particular markings and colors on the rival's wings and body. It is not a learned response acquired through experience. It is an automatic response to the triggering stimuli. All members of a given species display the same instinctive pattern of behavior in the same situations. Unlike drive-related behaviors, instinctive behaviors do not appear to be related to deprivation. Territoriality, maternal behavior, nest building, and nut burying are among the behaviors that have been described as instinctive in various species.

No one challenges the evidence that birds and insects follow instinctive patterns of behavior, but the concept of instinct becomes controversial when the question of instinctive human behaviors is raised. Some researchers argue that impulses such as aggression, jealousy, and territoriality are all instinctive, predetermined aspects of our behavior (see Bowlby, 1969). But many others insist that truly instinctive behavior is limited to "lower" organisms, while human behavior is much more flexible and responsive to variations in the environment.

Explaining human behavior in terms of instincts reached its peak at about the turn of the century. William James (1890) proposed that the instincts listed in Table 9–1 account for much of human behavior. The general process of proposing instincts in this fashion was heavily criticized, however. First, there was very little agreement about how many instincts actually existed and what they were (others had their own lists). Second, it was difficult to separate clearly learned behaviors from innate ones. And third, many so-called innate behaviors finally proved to be heavily influenced by experience.

This debate over instinct theory, after simmering for decades, has reemerged recently as a result of the work of a group of European ethologists. Ethology, as you will recall from the discussion at the end of Chapter 5, is a special branch of biology concerned with the evolution, development, and occurrence of behavior in relation to the environment. Konrad Lorenz, Karl von Frisch, and Nikolaas Tinbergen, all Nobel prize winners, are the most famous researchers in this area of investigation. Though they have used other species in their research on instincts, they suggest that humans are driven by the same basic impulses to defend territory, nurture their young, and so on. This is an important debate, for an understanding of what motivates human aggression might help to put an end to war and violent crime. We will return to the topic of aggression in Chapter 11.

One phenomenon that has drawn attention to the work of the ethologists is known as imprinting. Although some researchers feel that imprinting is just another form of ordinary learning, others have declared it to be a prime example of instinctive behavior. In its simplest form, ***imprinting*** refers to the fact that a newly hatched bird will

TABLE 9–1 Human Instincts Proposed by William James (1890)

Cleanliness

Constructiveness

Curiosity

Fearfulness

Hunting

Jealousy

Modesty

Parental love

Playfulness

Pugnacity

Rivalry

Secretiveness

Shyness

Sociability

Sympathy

Konrad Lorenz's observations of the behavior of graylag geese provided dramatic evidence of the instinctive response known as imprinting.

approach, follow, and form a social attachment to the first moving object it perceives. Lorenz noticed that if a gosling first encounters a human it will approach and follow that human in the future, even in preference to its real mother. Lorenz's observations have stimulated many experiments in which birds have been imprinted on peculiar objects such as footballs, moving lines, animals of other species, and colored boxes (Hoffman & Ratner, 1973).

Hess (1972) studied imprinting using the apparatus shown in Figure 9–2. This device consists of a circular walkway enclosed in clear plastic. A decoy model of a large duck emits a "gock, gock, gock" sound as it moves around the walkway. A newly hatched duckling is placed in the apparatus behind the model. As the model moves, the duckling follows, becoming imprinted on its new "mother." After imprinting, the duckling is given a choice between the mechanical model and its real mother. Imprinting is demonstrated by the fact that

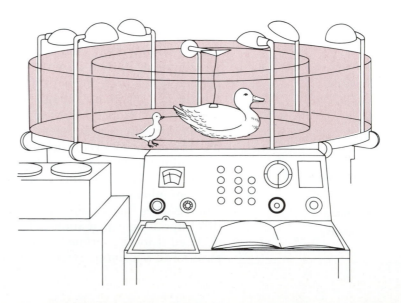

FIGURE 9–2   Hess's Apparatus for Studying the Imprinting Process *(After Hess, 1959)*

the duckling approaches and follows the model rather than the real duck. It will even climb over rather high barriers to be with its new "mother." The duckling's following behavior seems to be triggered by the moving model—but in fact, any moving object will release the behavior in a newly hatched duckling.

Hess has discovered some interesting effects while using this apparatus. He has shown that imprinting grows stronger as he increases the total distance that the duckling covers while following the model. He also has observed that there may be a *critical period* during which imprinting can occur (see Figure 9–3). Hess found that if the bird is too young or too old, imprinting will not take place. But if a duckling between 13 and 16 hours old follows a moving object, then maximum imprinting will occur.

The concept of a critical period is often cited as an important difference between imprinting and ordinary learning, but other researchers reject this idea (Hoffman & Ratner, 1973). They argue that the increase in imprinting up to 13 hours of age is due to the bird's growing ability to walk. When first hatched, the bird is so wobbly that it could not follow the model even if it wanted to. Thus, it may have the capacity to imprint at an earlier age but not the mobility to do so. These researchers also argue that the decrease in imprinting after 13 hours is due to the duckling's innately increasing fear of novel objects. When first hatched, the duckling shows no fear of anything, but it very quickly begins to flee from novel stimuli.

In short, the argument is that the bird has the *capacity* to imprint both before and after the so-called critical period but does not do so because it is too weak or too fearful. In support of this interpretation, Gaioni, Hoffman, DePaulo, and Stratton (1978) were able to imprint ducklings that were ten days old. They did it by exposing the ducklings to the model for long periods of time. Once the birds finally overcame their fear, they waddled after the model, imprinting on it.

Some researchers think that humans also imprint (Bateson, 1979). An infant's attachment to its mother or other caretaker often seems to have many of the characteristics of imprinting. Other investigators

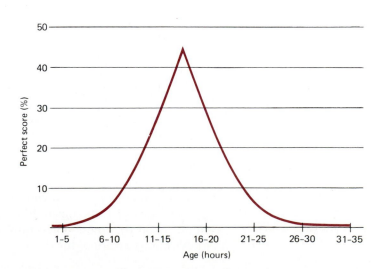

FIGURE 9–3 Imprinting as a Function of a Duckling's Age (hypothetical data)

disagree with this interpretation, however, and as yet there is not enough evidence to make a convincing case for it.

In summary, many types of animals show various behaviors that we think of as instinctive. These behaviors follow invariant patterns that are released by certain specific stimuli. They do not correspond to the types of behavior we ordinarily associate with drives. Given the current evidence, we must consider the possibility that some motivated human behavior is also of an instinctive sort. However, no experiments have yet shown instinctive responses, such as imprinting, in humans.

Thus far, we have considered drive theory, incentive theory, optimal-arousal theory, and instinct theory. We will look next at still another theory of motivation, one that has something in common with the preceding views but also has something new to contribute.

Unconscious Motivation

The possibility that our behavior may be controlled by *unconscious motives* has long intrigued psychologists. According to this theory, we are often unaware of the real reasons for our behavior; what we do is driven by motives inaccessible to our consciousness.

For example, we may "forget" important but unpleasant elements in our lives. If a student, already failing in a class, "forgets" to go to his final examination, or "forgets" to arrange transportation to that examination, we suspect some unconscious desire to avoid the situation. If another student fails an examination and says, "Oh well, I don't really think that course is worthy of my attention anyway," we suspect that without being aware of it, she is trying to reduce her disappointment. A young child who throws up every night and receives a lot of attention for doing so may not be aware that the vomiting is nothing more than an attention-getting mechanism. People who spend much of their free time cleaning their apartments may not realize that they are protecting themselves from depressing thoughts about their loneliness.

There are enough situations like these, where people seem unaware of the "real" reasons for their actions, to suggest that the concept of unconscious motivation may be useful.

Strong and Moderate Views   Sigmund Freud, the first great theorist of unconscious motivation, believed that hidden motives determine many of our actions. According to Freud, hidden sexual and aggressive impulses determine our actions even though society has forbidden their open expression. Thus, although society will not let us assault someone we dislike, we can do so symbolically in a dream or with a slip of the tongue. Freud also proposed that neurotic symptoms express the unconscious needs of an individual. We will consider Freudian theory in detail in a later chapter. For now, it is enough to know that Freud placed great emphasis on unconscious motivation, and his views were widely accepted for decades.

Recently, psychologists have preferred to temper the strong position taken by Freud. They now talk about the degree to which the individual is aware of his or her own motives. Sometimes we are perfectly aware of why we are doing something. We may be mean to another person because they have been mean to us and we want revenge. At other times, we may be only partially aware of our true motives. At still other times we may be completely unaware of what we are doing, and why we are doing it. For instance, an individual may have a need to be submissive and may go along with just about anything he is told to do. And yet, if he is asked how submissive he feels he is, he may say, "I'm not submissive at all." In other words, he may be totally unaware of this strong need or personality trait.

When we cannot understand why people act the way they do toward us, we may find it is because we have been unaware of the way we have been acting toward them. A person who complains that no one likes him may find that his jokes sound more like insults to his classmates. If we can become aware of how we are expressing our needs and how those expressions affect others, then we can change our own behavior so as to encourage more positive reactions from those around us.

This newer approach agrees that we do things without always being aware of why we do them, but it takes a much more moderate view of unconscious motivation than Freud did. Such moderation seems justified in the face of one important fact: we have not yet found ways to measure unconscious motivation. We know from experience that unconscious motives seem to exist and apparently affect behavior, but we have no good, clear proof of their existence. As we mentioned earlier, it is always difficult to measure mental activities—and unconscious ones are even more challenging.

Maslow's Need Hierarchy

Abraham Maslow (1971) has proposed an alternative way of classifying motives and viewing the interactions among these motives. Figure 9–4 shows Maslow's *pyramid of motives.* According to Maslow, motives are arranged in a *hierarchy.* Basic biological needs are found at the bottom of this hierarchy, while more complicated psychological motives are toward the top. The motives at one level must be relatively satisfied before the motives at the next level can direct and control behavior.

Suppose you found yourself stark naked, desperately thirsty, and ravenously hungry, on an apparently deserted island. What would you do first? Write the great American novel? No, of course not. You would attempt to satisfy the most basic needs first—find water and food. Once these concerns were taken care of you might seek or build shelter of some type and make yourself some kind of clothing or a blanket. Next you might begin to think about whether anyone else were living on the island. You might try to make contact with them, and so on.

Each time a level in Maslow's pyramid is satisfied, the individual moves on to the next higher level. Once some sense of love and belongingness is established, we are free to strive for self-esteem, respect, and success. The final phase, that of *self-actualization*, is apparently reached by very few of us. Most of us are stalled along the way. According to Maslow, the self-actualized individual can accept

FIGURE 9–4 Maslow's Pyramid of Human Motives
We must satisfy the needs at one level before we can move up to the next.

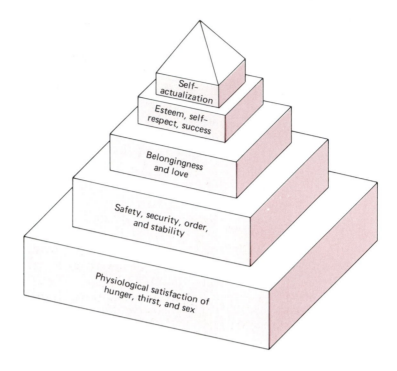

himself or herself, can accept others as they are, and can accept reality. That is not easy to do. How many of us, for example, can truly say we never wish we were someone other than who we are? The self-actualizing person rejoices in the experience of living. She or he is spontaneous, creative, and has a sense of humor. Such a person is in tune with the meaning and mystery of life.

The self-actualized life may be beyond our grasp, but fortunately we can reach this final level for brief periods. According to Maslow, *peak experiences*, where a sense of self-actualization is attained momentarily, are within reach of many of us (after we pay the rent, and call mother, and buy books, and deal with Bob, and so on).

The order of the needs in Figure 9–4 is somewhat arbitrary. For instance, it may make more sense to you to put *belongingness* above *esteem*. Fine. Do it. The point is that Maslow's general notion of a need hierarchy has some appeal. The exact nature and order of the steps is not overly important.

Of course, we do not move inexorably upward, never to return to the lower levels. The vagaries of life as well as recurring needs may force us back down the pyramid. If you are hard at work on Opus No. 1 and suddenly your piano is repossessed, you will undoubtedly turn to more practical concerns, at least momentarily.

Although we have emphasized the idea that lower needs must be satisfied before higher ones can be addressed, there is some flexibility here. Lower needs do not have to be totally fulfilled before we move upward. We can still work on our novel when we are hungry. We can pursue self-esteem when we are thirsty. In other words, lower needs must be *relatively* satisfied; they must not be so strong and pressing that they block our higher efforts.

Where do you think this participant in a Boston City Hospital nurses' strike is located on Maslow's pyramid of motives? She may be near the top, struggling for esteem, self-respect, and success.

We have discussed general approaches to the understanding of motivation. We have considered drive, incentive, optimal-arousal level, instinct, unconscious motives, and need-hierarchy theories. But we have not, as yet, said much about specific motives. Therefore, we will look next at what is and what is not known about several important motives. These motives are split into three rough categories: basic biological motives, sensory-seeking motives, and complicated human needs. This is a popular way to classify motives because it provides a convenient framework for thinking about motivation.

BIOLOGICAL MOTIVES I: HUNGER

Homeostasis

Our bodies must have certain essentials if we are to survive. Without appropriate amounts of food, water, air, sleep, and heat, life cannot be sustained. Our bodies contain complex *homeostatic mechanisms* that maintain proper levels of these essentials. These homeostatic mechanisms must keep *steady states* of each of these vital requirements, because the body cannot handle too much or too little of them.

A homeostatic mechanism is like a thermostat. If your refrigerator rises above a certain temperature, the thermostat detects this fact and turns on the cooling unit. If the temperature falls too low, the thermostat turns the cooler off. Basic biological motives, such as hunger and thirst, appear to operate according to homeostatic principles. If we need food, our internal systems "turn on" food-seeking behavior. When enough nourishment has been obtained, the system "turns off" food-seeking behavior. Different homeostatic systems probably regulate the other biological motives. We will now look at several of these basic motives in some detail.

Multiple Internal Stimuli for Hunger

If we assume that hunger and eating behaviors are at least partially controlled by some internal, homeostatic mechanism, then we are faced with a search for two parts of that mechanism. First, we must identify the means by which the body's need for food is relayed to the brain. What are the changes within our bodies that let the brain know that food is needed? Before the brain can initiate food-seeking behavior it must be "told" that such a need exists. Second, we must locate the part of the brain that receives the message and sends neural signs to the body to act. Let us look first at the internal cues that "tell" the brain about the needs of the body. As it turns out, there are many of them.

Glucostatic Theory: Blood Sugar and Short-term Control   For years, researchers have assumed that the level of sugar in our blood is the stimulus that triggers a hunger reaction in the brain, at least on a short-term basis. When our blood-sugar level is low, we feel hungry. Some studies have shown that when glucose (a kind of sugar) is injected into the system, eating is usually inhibited. Other studies have shown that insulin injections, which lower blood-sugar levels, will stimulate eating. According to this theory, which is known as *glucostatic theory*, as the level of sugar flowing through the brain is altered, the brain detects the change and instructs the body to either increase or decrease eating. But several other complex studies have suggested alternative interpretations. These researchers argue that we have yet to show that blood-sugar level is the main stimulus for hunger (Booth & Pain, 1970; Brown & Wallace, 1980).

Rate of Infusion   Geiselman (1983) has conducted some research that is particularly troublesome for proponents of glucostatic theory. She infused all of her rabbits with the same *amount* of glucose but varied the *rate* at which the glucose was delivered. The food intake of animals that were infused slowly decreased, as would be expected. But the food intake of animals that were infused quickly in the first half-hour nearly doubled after infusion. Classical glucostatic theory simply cannot account for this effect. Geiselman's research has clearly demonstrated that there is a great deal we do not know about hunger.

Lipostatic Theory: Fat and Long-term Control   Most animals regulate and maintain their weight over long periods of time with great accuracy. Animals in the wild do not go through extreme swings in their weight levels as the months and years go by. The human animal seems a bit of an oddity here, being capable of all sorts of faddish weight changes. But, in general, animals do seem to possess some precise internal mechanism for controlling body weight. Apparently this long-term mechanism involves a different stimulus from that involved in the control of how much one eats at any one sitting.

Some researchers say the stimulus involved in long-term weight control is probably a chemical in the blood that reflects the amount of fat (lipids) in the body. The higher the lipid level, the lower the overall eating pattern. Conversely, the lower the lipid level, the higher the eating level. **Lipostatic theory**, too, is controversial; not enough evidence is available at this time to convince the skeptics (Cotman & McGaugh, 1980).

Hormones (CCK) and Eating Behavior   Another theory that has been proposed to explain the mechanisms of hunger suggests that some type of hormone released into the bloodstream may circulate to the brain where it influences eating behavior. The most recent candidate is *cholecystokinin* (CCK), a hormone produced by the walls of the intestine (Dockray, Gregory, & Hutchison, 1978). Injections of this hormone can cause satiety, suggesting that it may be one agent that "tells" the brain about food levels in the intestines.

The Stomach as a Stimulus   When we are hungry, the walls of the stomach start to contract, and we feel hunger pangs. When we have eaten our stomach is distended, and we feel full. These stimuli obviously can play a part in the control of eating, sending messages to the brain which, in turn, relays instructions to the body. But stomach cues alone cannot account for eating behavior. People who have had their stomachs removed because of disease continue to feel the normal hunger drive (Wangsteen & Carlson, 1931).

Other Internal Agents   The picture that emerges seems to indicate clearly that eating behavior is determined by several factors. Sugar, fat, hormones, and stomach activity may all be involved in the regulation of eating, but the list of possibly important internal factors does not end there. Body weight, body temperature, and the activity of the liver have also been studied as regulatory factors (Brown & Wallace, 1980). The urge to eat, it seems, is wonderfully complex and multiply determined—no wonder dieting is so difficult!

Dual Hypothalamic Control

The second part of our search concerns that section of the brain that registers changes in the hunger stimuli and translates this information into action. The area of the brain that has been most often associated with hunger is the *hypothalamus*, a relatively small structure located at the base of the brain (see Figure 2–14 on page 65). For some time this structure has been thought to be the control center for hunger and eating.

This view of the role of the hypothalamus has been encouraged by electrical stimulation studies. By implanting an extremely fine electrode in the brain of a living animal and electrically stimulating specific areas of the hypothalamus, investigators have been able to increase and decrease eating behavior (Hoebel & Teitelbaum, 1962). Specifically, stimulation of the *lateral hypothalamus (LH)* sometimes increases eating behavior. Stimulating the *ventromedial hypothalamus (VMH)* inhibits eating.

Further support for the involvement of the hypothalamus in hunger comes from lesion studies, where certain areas of the brains of living rats and mice are destroyed. When the lateral hypothalamus is destroyed, the rat eats little or nothing. If the animal is not force-fed, it will develop the condition known as *aphagia*, and eventually it will starve to death. When the ventromedial hypothalamus is destroyed, the rat eats excessively and becomes enormously fat. This condition of obesity is known as *hyperphagia* (see Figure 9–5). In short, the

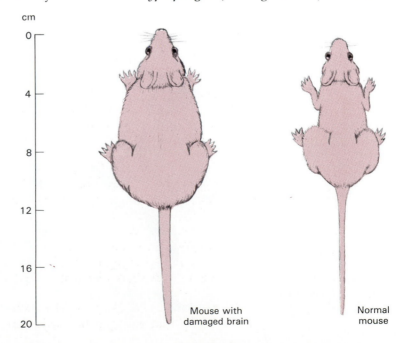

FIGURE 9–5 **Hypothalamic Control of Hunger** *The obesity of this mouse is caused by a lesion of the ventromedial hypothalamus.* (After Kalat, 1984)

Surgically caused lesions in the ventromedial hypothalamus resulted in enormous weight gains for this rat and experimental animals of other species.

lateral hypothalamus seems to be a "start" center, while the ventro-medial portion appears to be a "stop" center (Marshall, Turner, & Teitelbaum, 1971; Panksepp, 1971).

Beyond Homeostasis: External Stimuli

External as well as internal stimuli can affect eating behavior. As we noted earlier, most people have had the experience of seeing and smelling delicious foods, and eating them even though they did not feel at all hungry. The following experiment also demonstrates the power of external stimuli. Feed a solitary chicken until it stops eating. Then introduce a second, hungry chicken and allow it to eat. The first chicken, observing the second, will begin to eat again. In other words, complicated sensory and social stimuli can determine eating behavior, above and beyond the needs of the body.

However, external stimuli are not essential for eating behavior. Experiments have been conducted in which a rat, by pressing a lever or bar in the apparatus used for the experiment, can introduce food directly into its stomach without ever seeing, smelling, tasting, or chewing that food. Epstein and Teitelbaum (1962) found that rats will regulate their food intake in such a situation. They will maintain a stable body weight even if the experimenter varies the amount of food delivered by each bar press. If the bar press delivers more food, the rate of bar pressing will be reduced. If less food is delivered, the rat increases its response rate to obtain the same total amount of food. Thus, although external and sensory events can affect eating, the internal homeostatic systems can do the job without these cues.

Taste: Innate and Learned

It is obvious that humans intensely dislike some tastes or flavors and greatly enjoy others. The interesting thing about these strong taste

One of these children has most definitely encountered a taste that is unpleasant. Some strong taste preferences are innate while others are learned.

preferences is that some are innate and some are learned. Some species, such as the rat and the human, seem to enjoy sweetness without having to go through a process of learning to like sweetness; this preference is "built into" the organism. Similarly, some dislikes are also innate. If you give a human baby something bitter, the infant's facial expression will leave no doubt about the innately unpleasant nature of this flavor.

But other preferences definitely are learned. It has been shown, in what is called the **medicine-preference effect**, that a sick rat that tastes a novel food and then recovers will display an acquired preference for that flavor. Dislikes can also be learned. In a typical **taste-aversion study**, animals that are made ill after experiencing a novel flavor will show a distinct dislike for that flavor in the future.

Eating Disorders

Obesity Fat is fat, right? Wrong. The trouble with defining obesity is that the meaning of the term is affected by prevailing cultural attitudes about what is, and what is not, an overweight condition. Physical attractiveness is defined differently in different cultures. In addition, a given culture can shift its conception of obesity. Our culture currently places a premium on slenderness, but if you look at photographic images from around the turn of the century, you will discover that at that time a plumper figure was admired.

Nevertheless, obesity is a real societal problem. Being overweight can clearly be dangerous to one's health. It is probably fair to say that at present an *obese* individual exceeds by 25 or 30 percent the average weight of people with similar age, height, sex, and bone structure.

Hypothalamic malfunctioning may be at the root of some obesity. As we have already seen, lesions in the VMH of rats can lead to gross overeating. While not conclusive, such results suggest that the human hypothalamus may be critically involved in obesity.

Table 9–2 contains some interesting differences between the eating habits of obese and nonobese individuals. The findings in the table are the result of experimental studies (see Schachter, 1971). The interesting thing about these differences is that it is not yet known whether they involve learned behaviors or are the result of some

TABLE 9–2 Differences in the Eating Habits of Obese and Nonobese Individuals

1. Obese people are stimulated into eating by external cues, such as the presence of food or other food-related cues, whereas people of normal weight are controlled more often by internal cues such as internal hunger sensations.

2. Obese individuals seem to be less motivated to work for their food than are normal-weighted people.

3. Obese people are more particular about what they eat than are nonobese individuals.

4. Obese individuals often seem to have more trouble inhibiting their eating once it starts than do normal-weighted people.

Source: After Schachter, 1971.

underlying physiological disorder. It would not be too surprising to learn that both learning and physiological disorders contribute to obesity.

Anorexia Nervosa Being overweight is not the only eating disorder. *Anorexia nervosa* is a form of self-imposed starvation that can be extremely dangerous. It tends to afflict intelligent young women from middle- and upper-class backgrounds. These women, for very poorly understood reasons, become tremendously concerned with being overweight. They simply stop eating. Force feeding is sometimes necessary to prevent the death of the patient. Table 9–3 contains a list of anorexic symptoms.

As is the case with obesity, the causes of anorexia are sometimes thought to be physiological and sometimes social and psychological. Those who subscribe to the physiological interpretation (see Templer, 1971) suggest that anorexia may involve malfunctioning of the lateral hypothalamus (LH). In this sense, anorexia is seen as the opposite of obesity, which is presumed to involve problems with the ventromedial hypothalamus (VMH). Other researchers feel that anorexia is best thought of as an extreme psychological reaction to our culture's overemphasis on slimness and attractiveness. Still other experimenters (Bruch, 1973) believe that the roots of this disorder lie in disturbed family relationships.

TABLE 9–3   Criteria for Diagnosis of Anorexia Nervosa

1. Age of onset before 25.

2. Anorexia with accompanying weight loss of at least 25% of original body weight.

3. A distorted, implacable attitude toward eating, food, or weight that overrides hunger, admonitions, reassurance, and threats—for example:
   a. Denial of illness with a failure to recognize nutritional needs.
   b. Apparent enjoyment in losing weight with overt manifestations that food refusal is a pleasurable indulgence.
   c. A desired body image of extreme thinness with overt evidence that it is rewarding to the patient to achieve and maintain this state.
   d. Unusual hoarding or handling of food.

4. No known medical illness that could account for the anorexia and weight loss.

5. No other known psychiatric disorder, with particular reference to primary affective disorders, schizophrenia, and obsessive-compulsive and phobic neurosis. (The assumption is made that, even though it may appear phobic or obsessional, food refusal alone is not sufficient to qualify for obsessive-compulsive or phobic disease.)

6. At least two of the following manifestations:
   a. amenorrhea (absence of menstruation)
   b. lanugo (a thick, soft, downy growth of hair)
   c. bradycardia (persistent resting pulse of 60 or less)
   d. periods of overactivity
   e. episodes of bulimia (uncontrolled or excessive eating)
   f. vomiting (may be self-induced)

Source: After Feighner et al., 1972.

Sometimes anorectics seem to "lose control" and gorge themselves on food. This effect is called *bulimia*, and it tends to be followed by the use of laxatives or self-induced vomiting. Guilt about eating is also characteristic of bulimia (Halmi, 1978).

BIOLOGICAL MOTIVES II: THIRST

As we turn to a consideration of thirst, we find that the hypothalamus again is involved in this basic biological motive. In this case it appears that two types of stimuli trigger drinking behavior.

Cellular Dehydration: Osmotic Thirst

The concentration of certain chemicals, such as sodium, in the fluid around the cells increases as the amount of water in the body is reduced. When the concentration reaches a certain level, water passes out of the cells by osmosis, leaving them *dehydrated.* Certain cells within the hypothalamus are very sensitive to this *cellular dehydration.* When these cells are dehydrated, they trigger neural activity that results in drinking behavior. Thirst caused by cellular dehydration is called *osmotic thirst.*

Reduced Blood Volume: Volumetric Thirst

In addition to cellular dehydration, a lowered water level reduces the volume of the blood in the body. This *reduced blood volume* apparently causes the kidneys to secrete certain chemicals that circulate to the hypothalamus and stimulate it to initiate drinking behavior (Epstein, Fitzsimons, & Simons, 1969). Thirst caused by reduced blood volume is called *volumetric thirst*, and it may occur as a result of the following: bleeding, vomiting, lack of drinking water, diarrhea, or sweating.

What about Dry Mouth?

Apparently a *dry mouth* has only a secondary effect on drinking behavior. According to Cofer (1972), research suggests that a person can feel thirsty even when the mouth is completely anesthetized. Adolph (1941) prepared dogs so that when they drank, the water passed out through a tube inserted into the esophagus. The animals could drink but the water never reached their stomachs. When given free access to water, these dogs would soon stop drinking, but after a few minutes, they would return and drink the same amount all over again. It was as though the drinking behavior measured the amount of water that should have been sufficient, but when the body discovered it had been "fooled," the dog returned to drink again. Internal signals, rather than the amount swallowed, appear to govern the amount that is drunk. One more bit of evidence for the internal control of drinking can be demonstrated using the apparatus described earlier in which rats pressed a lever to deliver food directly to the stomach. If the equipment is altered to deliver water rather than food, the rat will quickly learn to regulate its water intake without seeing, smelling, or drinking the liquid.

Primary and Secondary Drinking

Primary drinking occurs after we lose some body fluid through sweating, bleeding, or simply breathing. But sometimes we drink when our body does not need any more liquid or even when it has more than enough. This is called *secondary drinking.* We may drink because we like the taste of a particular liquid, or because it contains alcohol, or because it helps us wash down food, or simply out of habit.

While primary drinking has been linked to cellular dehydration and loss of blood volume, secondary drinking is not so well understood. Presumably, learning and reinforcement contribute to secondary drinking. We have learned to drink when we eat because it makes swallowing easier. We drink beer because it makes us feel good. We drink a cup of coffee at the morning break because it is the sociable thing to do, even if we are awash in liquid already. Just as we sometimes eat when our body does not need the fuel, we sometimes drink when our body does not need the fluid.

BIOLOGICAL MOTIVES III: SEX

Sexual motivation differs from hunger and thirst in that it is not easily interpreted in terms of a drive conception of motivation. As Bolles (1975) puts it, "As soon as we leave hunger and thirst and look at other types of motivation, we encounter considerable difficulty applying a homeostatic type of drive concept." Sex seems to differ from the hunger and thirst drives in several ways:

1. Unlike food and water, sex is not essential for the survival of the individual. No one will die without sex. (You may think you are going to die, but you won't.) It is necessary for the survival of the species, of course, but not for the individual.
2. People seek increases as well as decreases in arousal. Most people enjoy the feeling of being sexually aroused, but almost no one likes to feel too thirsty or too hungry.
3. Humans can be sexually aroused by an extremely wide range of stimuli—a much wider range, in fact, than will arouse hunger or thirst.
4. The arousal of the human sex motive appears to be less affected by deprivation than are the other drives. Except for a short period immediately following sexual orgasm, the sex motive seems to be arousable at almost any time and does not show the regular increase over time that is displayed by the hunger and thirst drives.
5. Sexual behavior uses energy rather than replaces it.

The Neglected Study of Sex

Our culture is permeated with sex. It calls to us from advertisements, it threads through our conversations, it motivates crimes as well as numberless romances, it draws us into movie theaters and even sells books. But despite all this attention, surprisingly few substantial scientific investigations of sexual behavior have been conducted.

One reason for this neglect has been the generally repressive nature of our culture during past years. Restrictive Victorian attitudes and a general conception that sex is evil or wrong have pervaded our culture. This denial and hesitancy spilled over into the academic community. It is only recently that textbooks have begun to discuss sex in anything but the most cautious terms. For years, textbook discussions of sexual intercourse were strictly limited to the biological aspects of reproduction.

As a result, we do not know a great deal about human sexuality because we have not been gathering very much data. Some early investigators suffered for their efforts. John B. Watson, famous for his work in other areas, was heavily condemned for his work in the field of sexual behavior during the first part of this century. He connected his body and the body of his partner (a graduate student) to various recording instruments in order to measure their physiological reactions while they made love. Although his data are among the earliest reliable findings of this sort, Watson was driven from his academic position with his career in ruins.

Aside from Watson's efforts, most early studies and theories about sex relied on interviews. Freud based his early observations concerning the importance of sex on interviews with neurotic patients.

Alfred Kinsey's (1948, 1953) survey of American sexuality represented the next milestone in sexual research. Kinsey invited thousands of men and women to talk openly about their sexual activities. Most of them were willing to do so—something that many other Americans found hard to believe. The fact that the interviewees remained anonymous probably contributed to this willingness. One of the most reassuring bits of information to come out of Kinsey's work involved the remarkable number of individual differences regarding sexual behavior that exist among people. Millions of people were reassured about their own sexuality when they learned that the "normal" range seems to cover almost anything.

Prior to Kinsey's report, no one knew what anyone else was doing. We did not talk about how much we masturbated, or how often we had sexual intercourse. As a result of this lack of communication, many people were afraid they were abnormal, and they had no way to correct this impression. Then Kinsey reported such staggering facts as these: among men in their twenties and early thirties, the number of ejaculations ranges from none ever to four or more a day; among women, the number of orgasms ranges from none ever to dozens and dozens every week. Suddenly, *everyone* was normal. You could almost hear the nation heave a sigh of relief.

Another major step in exploring human sexuality was taken by Masters and Johnson (1970). Unlike most earlier researchers, these investigators attempted to discover what people do, and how they react, by watching them do it rather than by asking them about it. Following Watson's early lead, Masters and Johnson began their work by recording the reactions of the body during such simple forms of sexual activity as masturbation. Later they studied and recorded the reactions of males alone and of males and females while they were making love. The work of Masters and Johnson remains controversial. Nevertheless, it represents a pioneering effort in the realm of sexual research. Their investigations and Kinsey's sex surveys opened

William Masters and Virginia Johnson (photographed here in 1988) opened the doors to rational research in the realm of human sexuality nearly two decades ago.

the doors to rational research in the area of human sexuality. Many large-scale, well-conducted surveys have since contributed greatly to our understanding of this complex subject (see Hyde, 1979).

Parenthetically, it should be noted that the so-called "sexual revolution," which began in the early 1960s, has now slowed. Attitudes about sex, and sexual practices, seem to have become more conservative in the 1980s. The details of this return to traditional values will be discussed in Chapter 11.

Interacting Hormones and Neurons

Sexual activity depends heavily on hormones. As you will recall from Chapter 2, a *hormone* is a chemical that is released by an *endocrine* organ. These hormones circulate in the bloodstream and affect other organs of the body.

In the female, a group of hormones collectively called *estrogens* are released by the ovaries. In the male, *androgens* (including *testosterone*) are released by the testes. Males and females both produce androgens and estrogens; the principal difference between the two sexes is that males produce more androgens than estrogens while females produce more estrogens than androgens.

Hormones interact with neural factors to produce sexual behavior. The process is quite complex, but it appears that the hypothalamus is involved. It seems that the hypothalamus affects the pituitary gland (the "master gland") which, in turn, releases several different hormones that travel through the blood system to the ovaries and testes, where they stimulate the release of estrogens and androgens.

Animals and Humans: The Role of Learning

In the lower animals, sexual activity is much more stereotyped than it is in the higher forms of life. Among all of the lower mammals, the

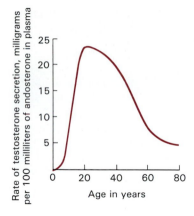

FIGURE 9–6 Levels of Testosterone Production in Men across the Life Span *(After Hyde, 1979)*

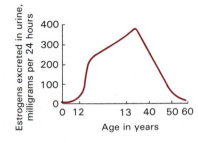

FIGURE 9–7 Levels of Estrogen Production in Women across the Life Span *(After Hyde, 1979)*

female sexual motive is inactive most of the time, and females ignore male sexual overtures. But at regular intervals, changes in circulating hormone levels in the female are associated with periods of estrus or "heat." During these intervals, the female actively seeks and accepts sexual contact with males of the species. The males, aroused by a variety of cues, such as odor, mating calls, and changes in the appearance of the sexual skin, approach the female, who chooses one or more mating partners.

Obviously, humans are a good deal more flexible than this. The human female may choose to engage in sexual activity at any time, regardless of her hormonal condition. Humans are not restricted in their sexual activity by a hormone-controlled cycle. In short, human sexuality is far more psychologically determined than is sexual behavior in lower animals. Figures 9–6 and 9–7 illustrate this point. Note that sex hormone production peaks very early in life and then declines dramatically. But we know that interest in sex extends well beyond this early peak, indicating that interest in sex is probably controlled by learning as well as by hormone level.

Sexual behavior among many lower organisms is less affected by learning. Mature birds and rats will engage in normal sexual activity even if they have been raised in total isolation. Such is not the case with the higher mammals, such as primates. Harlow (1971) demonstrated that monkeys raised in isolation do not engage in normal sexual behavior, suggesting that learning plays a necessary part in primate sexual development. Presumably, humans are even more dependent on learning in this area. Of course it is impossible to conduct an experiment in which humans are raised in isolation. However, Harlow's (1971) work suggests that our ability to perform normal sexual activities depends on both the learned ability to engage in specific sexual movements, such as thrusting the pelvis, and the influence of hormones.

The degree to which hormones control sexual behavior seems to decline as we move up the phylogenetic scale. If an adult male rat is castrated, the animal quickly stops its sexual activities. Castrated dogs show a more gradual decline, and castrated human males often continue to engage in sexual activity as though nothing had happened. In fact, the human male's expectations concerning his sexual ability following castration appear to be a major influence on what he actually does.

Females of all species except the human show a marked decrease in sexual activity after removal of the ovaries. Human females, on the other hand, generally continue to be interested in sex even though their ovaries have been removed.

It becomes evident that humans are much more susceptible to the impact of environment and experience on sexual activity than are the lower forms of life. Our adult sexual behavior, in contrast to the automatic, preset activities of the lower animals, seems determined by some complex combination of hormones and learning. We will return to sex and some practical problems associated with human sexuality in Chapters 11, 12, and 13.

The interest this young boy is evidencing in the photo he is looking at represents an impact of experience regarding sexual behavior and understanding that far exceeds the influence of experience on lower-organism sexuality.

SENSORY-SEEKING MOTIVES

This woman epitomizes a prime example of our desire for sensory stimulation. She is not driven to climb rocks by hunger or thirst. Rather, she is motivated by an impulse to explore, to manipulate, and to increase stimulation.

Many of the motivational systems that we have talked about so far have some identifiable physiological correlates. Hunger and thirst, for example, are associated with specific tissue needs within the body. Each of these fits a drive-reduction concept of motivation, because as a tissue need increases, arousal and drive also increase. Drive motivates the animal to engage in behaviors that will reduce tissue need.

But a good deal of our behavior does not seem to fit into this simple conception. We have already seen that sex, although it is usually categorized as one of the biological motives, cannot easily be thought of in terms of a drive model. Sex, especially among humans, has as much in common with the motives discussed in this section as it does with the drives considered previously. One of the things that sets sexual and other behaviors apart from clearly driven behavior is that we often seek to increase rather than decrease tension and arousal. We go to plays, movies, and sporting events, looking for excitement. We play games and attend parties. We seek sexual tension. We seek out other people, and we travel to unfamiliar places. Clearly, there is more to life than quiet contentment. We want some action, too. We need stimulus change, and we want to be able to satisfy our curiosity. These kinds of *sensory-seeking behaviors* fit the optimal-arousal-level theories described earlier better than they fit a simple drive concept.

Demonstrations of sensory-seeking behaviors are easily found. As we have seen, Butler (1953) discovered that monkeys will learn discrimination problems when the reward is nothing more than a brief look around a laboratory. Kish (1955) found that mice confined in darkness will learn to press a bar when the bar pressing does nothing more than turn a light on for a moment. If confined in light, mice will learn to press a bar to turn the light off momentarily. The mice do not seem to care if they spend the majority of their time in darkness or in light, as long as a stimulus change is provided.

FIGURE 9–8   The Lure of Complexity   *Berlyne's arrangements of visual materials were designed to produce stimulus complexity.*

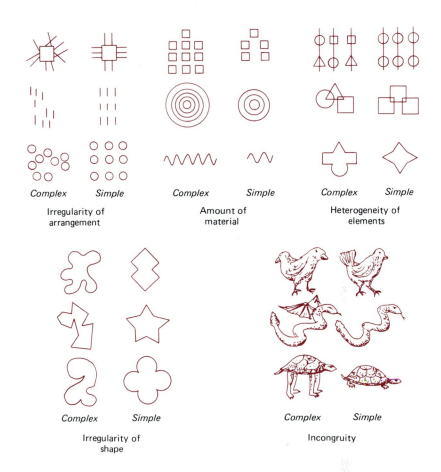

Defining complexity in terms of irregularity of arrangement, amount of material, irregularity of shape, incongruity, and heterogeneity of elements, Berlyne (1958) found that adult humans will pay more attention and look longer at complex stimuli than at simple stimuli (see Figure 9–8). In a similar vein, Cancelli (1979) found that subjects would more often ask to see photos of animals that were exposed for a split second if those photos were blurred and uncertain.

Harlow, Harlow, and Meyer (1950) found that monkeys will learn to open latches, becoming better and better at the task, when there is no reward beyond the pleasure of working with the latches. These monkeys were satiated in terms of all known physiological needs, yet they still learned complex behaviors (see Figure 9–9).

In *sensory-deprivation* experiments (Heron, Doane, & Scott, 1956), human volunteers are deprived of normal stimulation for long periods of time. Wearing goggles and gloves, they lie on a bed in a small, dimly lit, soundproof room, as Figure 9–10 shows. After several days, in spite of very good pay, most subjects refuse to stay any longer. Their need for stimulation apparently makes the deprivation situation intolerable. Many subjects begin to experience visual hallucinations, seeing things that are not there. After two or three days, all have difficulty thinking clearly and do poorly on problems they are asked to solve. They begin to be confused about what day it is

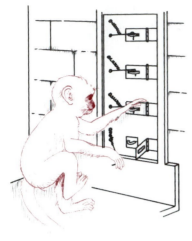

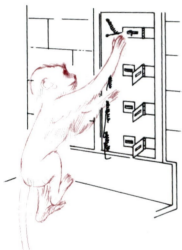

and where they are. Such confinement also leads to boredom, anger, and frustration. All these findings support the idea that we need moderate amounts of stimulus change and arousal just to keep us functioning well.

Deprivation dwarfism represents perhaps the most dramatic example of the impact of sensory deprivation on human life. Studies (see Gardner, 1972; Money, 1977) indicate that a lack of stimulating home conditions can actually lead to retarded physical growth. It has been demonstrated that children raised in hostile, unfriendly, neglectful, and uncaring situations can display stunted growth in spite of a normal diet. In addition, they appear sad and withdrawn.

Of course, we must be careful when suggesting that a lack of stimulation causes this retardation; these children often faced hostility and experienced emotional rejection as well. But a lack of stimulation seems to be one crucial aspect of situations that lead to deprivation dwarfism.

To return to the main thread of the chapter, recall that we first discussed the drive conception of motivation. We then pointed out that many behaviors, including sensory-seeking behaviors, do not seem explainable in terms of this theory. Faced with trying to defend their theory, many drive theorists responded by thinking up new drives to account for sensory-seeking behaviors. Some suggested an exploratory drive, others a boredom drive. Still others mention a manipulation drive, and several authors spoke of an activity drive (see also Eisenberger, 1972). But many psychologists objected to this flood of new drives. Naming new drives does not seem to add to our understanding of the behavior. In addition, no one has yet identified

FIGURE 9–9 Pleasure in Manipulation *Monkeys will open latches in the absence of any known physiological motive.*

FIGURE 9–10 A Sensory-deprivation Room *The subject is lying on a bed and wearing padded cuffs, translucent goggles, and a cap that is wired to record the electrical activity of the brain.*

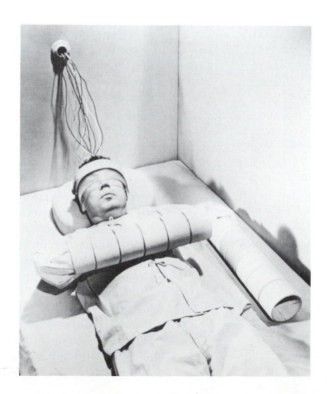

any tissue needs that could be said to cause these behaviors. For these reasons, it appears that the optimal-arousal-level approach is the one that explains these behaviors best.

Intrinsic versus Extrinsic Reward

Recently, investigators have talked about the relationship between intrinsic and extrinsic reward (Rosenfield, Folger, & Adelman, 1980; Williams, 1980). *Intrinsic reward* refers to the pleasure and satisfaction we get out of performing a task; for whatever reason, the task itself is rewarding to us. This is the kind of reward we have been talking about in this section dealing with sensory-seeking behavior. Harlow's monkeys manipulated latches for intrinsic rewards, and some people chop wood for the fun of it. *Extrinsic reward*, on the other hand, refers to rewards beyond the intrinsic pleasures of the task itself. Give those monkeys food for manipulating latches or pay a person to chop wood and you are giving extrinsic rewards.

There is a curious relationship between intrinsic and extrinsic reward. If you do a task for the fun of it (intrinsic reward) and are then rewarded extrinsically for doing the same task (someone pays you for doing it), you will lose interest in performing the task for intrinsic reward alone. For example, many a two-year-old paints a picture for the sheer pleasure of slopping paint about and is then rewarded extrinsically for painting when adults lavishly praise the result. Typically the child will be less interested in painting for painting's sake in the future. This is called the *overjustification effect*, and it suggests that extrinsic reward can undermine intrinsic reward. When we receive extrinsic reward for doing something we were quite content to do for intrinsic reward, we are robbed of a simple pleasure; we will no longer be satisfied with doing the task merely for its own sake (Williams, 1980).

In short, if someone is happily performing a desirable behavior for intrinsic rewards, leave them alone. Do not try to enhance their behavior by introducing extrinsic rewards.

COGNITIVE AND SOCIAL MOTIVES

A Variety of Needs

The last class of motives we will discuss seems quite removed from physiological need states. When we speak of *complex human motives*, we mean such motives as the need to achieve, the need to conform, and the need to dominate others. These motives, although perhaps derived from the more basic physiological drives, are much more heavily determined by learning and experience and are aroused and satisfied more in terms of cognitive and social events than are the physical drives. Failure to satisfy these needs does not lead to death, but frustration and failure in these areas can lead to severe disturbances.

Table 9–4 lists just some of the complex, perhaps acquired, human motives that psychologists have studied closely. Rather than discussing each of these complex motives in brief, we have chosen to consider several of them in some detail.

TABLE 9–4   Some Complex Cognitive and Social Motives

Achievement	The need to meet or exceed standards of excellence.
Affiliation	The need to be with other people.
Dependency	The urge to depend on others to organize our lives, help us, comfort us, and support us in work and play.
Greed	The urge to acquire and hold tangible and intangible goods, often at the expense of others.
Power	The need to acquire and hold the capacity to control other people and objects, while being free of constraints oneself.
Conformity	The urge to change one's ways of thinking, acting, feeling, and appearing so that they fit the norms of the group.
Certainty	The need to be able to predict what will happen next and to be able to understand surprising events.
Cognitive Consistency	The need to maintain consistency between our beliefs and actions.
Social Approval	The desire to have others approve of us and our behavior.
Nurturance	The urge to satisfy the needs of less capable people; to feed, help, support, protect, and comfort.
Order	The need to establish and maintain order within one's mental and physical life.
Play	The need to act for enjoyment without any further purpose.
Deference	The need to admire and support a superior through praise and action.

The Need to Achieve

A ***need to achieve*** may be defined as the need to meet or exceed standards of excellence. It almost goes without saying that this type of motivation is extremely common and powerful in our society. Why, for example, are you reading this text? You may be reading because you are interested in the subject, but more than likely you are primarily concerned with receiving a grade that will help you achieve your goals. In other words, your present behavior is motivated by a need to achieve (see Atkinson, 1983).

Measuring the Need to Achieve   Achievement motivation is most often measured using a projective test called the ***Thematic Apperception Test (TAT).*** Subjects are shown a series of ambiguous pictures, such as a man in a gown standing next to a table upon which another person is lying, and asked to make up a story about each scene. Who are these people? Why are they there? What are they doing? What will happen? The idea is that the person taking the test will project some of her or his needs and desires into the story. A person high in achievement motivation might construct a story about a struggling young medical student who succeeds brilliantly in an emergency, while a person low in achievement motivation might make up a story about two people taking a nap. Standard methods for scoring achievement imagery have been developed, and the TAT stands as the primary tool for measuring achievement motivation (see Chapter 15).

The Need Determines Behavior   People high in achievement motivation tend to exert more effort and to do better than people low in achievement motivation. For example, high achievers have been shown to do better on speed tests involving verbal and numerical tasks. They usually get better grades in school and are more upwardly mobile in society.

The Origin of Achievement Motivation   Clearly, this type of motivation is powerful. But how does it arise? Where does it come from? Although some people feel that achievement motivation may have some biological or genetic basis, the best guess is that it reflects early independence training. Children displaying high need for achievement were often required to be independent at an early age. As children, the high achievers were required to dress themselves, to earn their own money, to entertain themselves, and to put themselves to bed at an earlier age than low-motivation achievers.

In addition, achievement is warmly praised and rewarded in homes that produce high achievers. In brief, we are arguing that the need to achieve is learned or acquired through training, encouragement, and reward.

Fear of Failure and Hope of Success   Careful observers of achievement experiments note that some people are primarily motivated

Youngsters such as this one who undergo early independence training will probably grow up to be achievement-oriented individuals.

to avoid failure, while other people are primarily motivated to achieve success. Both types of motivation can lead to effort and success, but practitioners of the two types differ in terms of the kinds of risks they prefer to take. Those who seek success choose moderately difficult tasks where the payoff is also moderate. Those who wish to avoid failure choose either easy, low-payoff tasks where failure is unlikely, or very difficult, high-payoff tasks where failure is so probable that no one will blame them if it happens.

The Need to Affiliate

Another social-motive system that has received close attention is the *need to affiliate*, or to be with other people. Clearly, some of us prefer to work and play with other people. We have a need for human company; we like being part of a team. Others, with less need to affiliate, would rather work and relax alone.

Affiliation and Performance   There is evidence that the need to affiliate can affect performance significantly. McKeachie et al. (1966) compared the performance of high- and low-affiliation subjects in two classrooms. One class radiated a warm social atmosphere. There were many personal contacts involving both the teacher and the students and the general mood of the class was friendly, personal, and supportive. In the second classroom, much less social contact was made and the overall atmosphere was much more reserved. Students scoring high on affiliation received better grades in the friendly, supportive classroom than in the more reserved atmosphere of the second classroom, while the reverse was true for students scoring low on affiliation.

The Origin of the Need to Affiliate   Some theorists believe that the need to affiliate has a genetic or biological basis; we may be born to be the way we are. Others suggest that the affiliative tendency is learned. If a young child sees that all good things are brought by other people, and every time something good happens a person is present, then other people may take on a very positive quality (classical conditioning might be involved here). After all, if other people brought wonderful things in the past, perhaps they will also bring good things with them in the future.

Of course, many good things can happen in the absence of others. If a person enjoys fishing, reading, or model-building as a child, then solitude may acquire a positive value and may be sought during adult years. And even the most outgoing people like a little peace and quiet now and then.

The Need for Cognitive Consistency

The need to experience a consistent world seems to be a strong human motive. Leon Festinger (1957) developed the term *cognitive dissonance* to refer to our strong sense of uneasiness when we see inconsistencies among our attitudes, beliefs, and behaviors. For example, if we cheat on an exam but believe cheating is wrong, then we will feel uncomfortable. The uneasiness acts like a drive. It motivates us to change something—either our behavior or our belief—so that consistency is restored. We may stop cheating, we may convince ourselves that everyone cheats so it is not so bad, or we may deny that we cheat very much at all. But one way or another, we will try to reduce dissonance by making our behavior consistent with our beliefs. It is through the reduction of cognitive dissonance that we satisfy our need for *cognitive consistency.*

A person who smokes heavily and knows that smoking causes lung cancer must surely be in a state of cognitive dissonance; smoking and believing that smoking is dangerous are inconsistent. This dissonance impels the person to do something. Ideally, the person will stop smoking. But sometimes dissonance is reduced through less adaptive responses. The person may point to family members who have smoked and lived to a ripe old age, or minimize the number of cigarettes smoked, or scoff at the research showing a link between cancer and smoking. In other words, we are driven to reduce dissonance, although we do not always choose the best method of attaining that goal.

We will look at some of the social aspects of cognitive dissonance in Chapter 19, as the concept has stirred a good deal of research among social psychologists.

Attribution Theory

Imagine that you are trying to hire a new employee and that you have two applicants. On reviewing their records, you discover that each has lost a job in the past six months. How do you react to this situation? Do you say, "Well, I'll just flip a coin"? Probably not. Instead you will be motivated to find out more about why the applicants lost their jobs. If one was fired because of incompetence, while the other had the misfortune of working for a company that went bankrupt, then all other factors being equal, you will probably hire the second individual.

This example shows how we are motivated to infer or determine the causes of events. Furthermore, it demonstrates how our future behavior can be affected by these inferences about causes. This process of first assigning causes and then basing our future behavior on those causes is the essence of *attribution theory* (see Weiner, 1980).

We make inferences about the causes of our own behavior as well as about the behavior of others. Suppose you fail an important exam. You will probably ask yourself why. Your future behavior can be heavily affected by your answer to this question. If you attribute your failure to the negative impact of a flu bug you were fighting, then you might redouble your efforts on the next exam. On the other hand, if you attribute the failure to a total and permanent lack of ability, you may become depressed, stop studying, and even consider dropping out of school.

Attribution theory proposes (1) that we are motivated to determine causes of events going on around us and (2) that we base our future behavior on these inferences. Of course, we are not always entirely accurate. Sometimes we misjudge others and, just as often, we misjudge ourselves. In these cases of misjudgment, our behavior can be inappropriate. For instance, we may falsely accuse someone when their intentions were completely innocent, simply because we "misread" their behavior.

Clearly, we do not always try to find causes of events. We do not constantly wonder why the sun comes up or why whales weigh a lot. Psychologists have suggested a number of factors that seem to determine whether or not we are motivated to find causes. These factors include the following:

1. We tend to seek the causes of highly unusual events. We do not spend time wondering why there are no green dogs because we are accustomed to that fact, but if a green beagle showed up in your yard, you would very likely be motivated to find out just where it came from and why.

2. Negative and unpleasant events tend to arouse the motive to infer causes. If you have a terrific headache, you may wonder why, but if you *do not* have a headache, you are not very likely to spend much time wondering why you feel fine.

3. Uncertainty about the future also seems to lead us to seek causes. If you have to appear in court because you have 27 outstanding traffic tickets, you may spend quite a bit of time wondering how the court works, why you let things slide so far, and what will happen to you.

In summary, the motive to determine causes of events taking place around us is a powerful determinant of our behavior. Attribution is discussed in greater detail in Chapter 19.

The Need for Control

There may very well be a strong need to control one's environment, too. This **need for control** is stronger in some people than in others. Some of us are very concerned about determining the direction that our lives take, while others are more comfortable with a "wait and see" approach. Table 9–5 lists some of the items used in a recently developed control scale. By looking over these items you can see what psychologists are interested in when they discuss the need to control one's environment. If we experience a sense of control, then we tend to be happy, healthy, and content. But if we feel our control is threatened, or if we suffer repeated instances of a lack of control, we may slip into depression and a sense of helplessness, as we shall see in Chapter 11.

A striking example of the impact of control on our overall sense of well-being is found in the work of Rodin and Langer (1977). Half of the residents of an old-age home, whose ages were between 65 and 90, were given control over some aspects of their lives while the other half were not. The people given control were told that they would decide when movies would be shown. Each person in this group was also given a plant and the responsibility to care for that plant. The rest of the residents were not given the same kinds of control. They were told when the movies would be shown and they were informed that the nurses would care for their plants. Over time,

TABLE 9–5   A Measure of the Need to Control

A subject's agreement or disagreement with these items reflects the degree of the subject's desire for control.

1. I prefer a job where I have a lot of control over what I do and when I do it.
2. I enjoy political participation because I want to have as much of a say in running government as possible.
3. I try to avoid situations where someone else tells me what to do.
4. I would prefer to be a leader rather than a follower.
5. I enjoy being able to influence the actions of others.
6. I am careful to check everything on an automobile before I leave for a long trip.
7. Others usually know what is best for me.
8. I enjoy making my own decisions.
9. I enjoy having control over my own destiny.
10. I would rather someone else took over the leadership role when I am involved in a group project.
11. I consider myself to be generally more capable of handling situations than others are.
12. I would rather run my own business and make my own mistakes than listen to someone else's orders.
13. I like to get a good idea of what a job is all about before I begin.
14. When I see a problem, I prefer to do something about it, rather than sit by and let it continue.
15. When it comes to orders, I would rather give them than receive them.
16. I wish I could push many of life's daily decisions off on someone else.
17. When driving, I try to avoid putting myself in a situation where I could be hurt by someone else's mistake.
18. I prefer to avoid situations where someone else has to tell me what it is I should be doing.
19. There are many situations in which I would prefer only one choice rather than having to make a decision.
20. I like to wait and see if someone else is going to solve a problem so that I do not have to be bothered by it.

Source: After Burger & Cooper, 1979.

Research with senior citizens suggests that people will feel better and live longer if they have control over even simple aspects of their lives, such as being allowed to select or schedule recreational activities.

residents given these minor controls over their lives showed greater activity and higher morale than the residents not given these controls. The most startling result of the study was that patients given control actually tended to live longer than the no-control residents.

Changing Needs

One line of evidence reinforces the idea that these complex forms of human motivation are acquired rather than predetermined. This evidence shows that the complex needs of members of our culture are continuing to change over time. Veroff, Depner, Kulka, and Douvan (1980) administered measures of motivation to a group of Americans in 1957 and to a different group in 1976. The motives measured included the need to achieve, the need to affiliate, the need to control others, and the need to avoid being controlled by others. Over the span of years, men's achievement motivation stayed the same. Their need to affiliate subsided, and the needs to control and not be controlled both increased. Women, over the same time span, showed an increase in achievement motivation and in the need to avoid being controlled, while their needs to affiliate and to control others stayed the same.

The authors of the article are distressed by these results, which suggest a nationwide shift away from needing to be friendly and cooperative and toward greed, power, and selfishness. But if such complex human motives can change so markedly in 20 years, then there is always the possibility of further change. "Human nature" is not an innate, inflexible set of motives after all, and our more complex motives seem to evolve and shift with the changing times.

Having examined the field of motivation in this chapter, we now move on to the very closely related area of emotion. As you will learn, emotions can act as motives, as they propel us through the ups and downs of everyday life.

SUMMARY

1. Motivation energizes, directs, and intensifies behavior. It is often equated with wants, wishes, needs, desires, drives, and interests, and it translates invisible learning into overt behavior.

2. Drive theory argues that tissue needs create aroused drive states which in turn *push* the animal into behaviors that will reduce the need.

3. Incentive theory emphasizes the fact that external stimuli in the environment can motivate or *pull* organisms into certain behaviors.

4. Optimal-level-of-arousal theory argues that organisms seek a preferred level of arousal and are not always seeking to reduce arousal.

5. Some behaviors appear to be instinctively motivated. Instinctive behaviors are innate, predetermined, species-specific behaviors that are automatically released when certain critical stimuli are perceived.

6. In imprinting, newly hatched birds will approach, follow, and form a social attachment to the first moving object that is perceived. Imprinting increases as distance followed increases and may occur during a brief critical period.

7. A strong view of unconscious motivation argues that sexual and aggressive impulses, forbidden by society, remain active even though they are unconscious. A moderate view emphasizes the degree to which we are aware of our motives.

8. In his need hierarchy Maslow argues that basic biological needs must be relatively satisfied before more elevated psychological motives can direct our behavior. Self-actualization represents the final step upward in the hierarchy.

9. Homeostatic mechanisms within our body maintain steady states with respect to essential elements such as food, water, air, and heat.

10. Blood sugar, fats, hormones, and movements of the stomach, among other things, have been suggested as the stimuli that inform the brain that the body needs food.

11. The lateral hypothalamus may be a "start" center for feeding behavior and the ventromedial hypothalamus may be a "stop" center, but some researchers disagree with these findings.

12. External stimuli can affect feeding behavior, but internal homeostatic factors appear to be in final control of food-seeking activity.

13. The medicine-preference effect and taste-aversion studies indicate that some tastes are learned and some are innate.

14. Obesity and anorexia nervosa are two troubling eating disorders.

15. Drinking behavior is initiated by cellular dehydration within the hypothalamus itself and by reduced blood volume, stimulating the kidneys to release chemicals that, in turn, stimulate the hypothalamus.

16. Dry mouth appears to be only a secondary determinant of drinking behavior.

17. Primary drinking occurs after the loss of body fluid. Secondary drinking occurs in the absence of a need and may be due to habit, taste, or a need to wash down food.

18. Sex differs from hunger and thirst in that it is not essential for the survival of the individual; its arousal is sought, it is aroused by many different stimuli, it is less affected by deprivation, and it uses rather than replaces energy.

19. Kinsey's report and the work of Masters and Johnson have done much to reduce fears about what is and what is not normal and to indicate that individual differences in sexual behaviors are enormous.

20. Hormones interact with neural factors to produce sexual behavior.

21. Sexual activity among lower animals is more predetermined than it is among humans. Human females may engage in sexual activity at any time, while lower animals are in the grip of a rigid, recurring hormonal cycle.

22. Human sexuality is quite strongly influenced by learning.

23. Sensory-seeking behavior, for which no physiological correlates have yet been identified, is best understood in terms of an optimal-arousal-level conception of motivation.

24. Exploration, manipulation, and curiosity are powerful motivating factors in both animals and humans.

25. Sensory deprivation leads to confusion, hallucinations, frustration, and irritability.

26. Actual dwarfism may result from deprivation of sensory stimuli.

27. Extrinsic reward can undermine intrinsic reward as indicated by the overjustification effect.

28. Complex human motives are heavily determined by learning and are aroused and satisfied in terms of social and psychological events.

29. Frustration in such areas as the needs to achieve and affiliate will not cause death but can produce emotional disturbances.

30. People with a need to achieve seem to try harder and to do better. They also come from families where early independence was demanded and achievement was warmly received.

31. Achievement motivation is measured with the Thematic Apperception Test (TAT).

32. Some high achievers focus on avoiding failure while others focus on attaining success.

33. People with a high need to affiliate perform better in warm, friendly situations than they do in more reserved situations, while the reverse is true for people low in the need to affiliate.

34. Cognitive dissonance is an uneasiness resulting from inconsistencies among our actions and thoughts. We are driven to reduce dissonance by changing either our behavior or our beliefs.

35. Attribution theory holds that we are motivated to find out causes and that these attributions affect our behavior.

36. The need to control our environment is a powerful motive. Satisfaction of this motive leads to a sense of well-being.

37. The complex motives of Americans have shifted during the past 25 years, reinforcing the belief that such motives are acquired, not innate.

KEY TERMS

androgens

anorexia nervosa

aphagia

attribution theory

bulimia

cellular dehydration

cognitive consistency

cognitive dissonance

complex human motives

critical period

deprivation dwarfism

drive

drive state

dry mouth

endocrine organ

estrogens

extrinsic reward

glucostatic theory

homeostatic mechanisms

hormone

hyperphagia

hypothalamus

imprinting

incentive

instinctive behavior

intrinsic reward

lateral hypothalamus (LH)

lipostatic theory

Maslow's hierarchy

medicine-preference effect

motivation

motives

need

need for control

need to achieve

need to affiliate

obesity

optimal-level-of-arousal theory

osmotic thirst

overjustification effect

peak experiences

primary drinking

pyramid of motives

secondary drinking

self-actualization

sensory deprivation

sensory-seeking behaviors

steady states

taste-aversion study

testosterone

Thematic Apperception Test (TAT)

unconscious motives

ventromedial hypothalamus (VMH)

volumetric thirst

ADDITIONAL READING

Barron, R. A., & Byrne, D. (1984) *Social psychology*. Boston: Allyn and Bacon.
This book is an excellent source for those interested in cognitive and social motivation.

Carlson, N. R. (1986) *Physiology of behavior*. Boston: Allyn and Bacon.
This text presents good, precise information about the physiological underpinnings of motivation.

Franken, R. E. (1986) *Human motivation*. Monterey: Brooks/Cole.
This text offers a fine survey of the entire field of motivation.

Houston, J. P. (1985) *Motivation*. New York: Macmillan.
This is an eclectic look at the field.

Nebraska Symposium on Motivation. Lincoln: University of Nebraska, 1953– .
This ongoing series presents much of the crucial work in the area of motivation.

10 Emotion

Imagine that the Emotionless Man from Venus is riding in an automobile with an ordinary mortal. The two individuals are similar except that the extraterrestrial visitor has no emotions. They are driving 40 mph in a 25 mph zone. Suddenly, a 5-year-old girl darts out in front of the car. The automobile swerves and comes to a shrieking halt just inches away from the cowering child. The Emotionless Man says flatly, ''We missed her. Let's go.'' The reaction of the ordinary mortal at the wheel, however, is quite different. Sweat breaks out on his brow, his breathing is irregular, he feels weak, and his heart is pounding. In a strangled voice he says, ''That was close!'' The little girl bursts into tears. A crowd gathers, hovers about the girl, and glowers at the driver.

That night the same two individuals go to a rock concert. The band blasts away, and by the end of the first number, the Earthling has forgotten his near-accident. By the end of the first set, he is totally caught up in the music. His eyes shine; his heart pounds; he claps his hands and shouts with pleasure. Turning to his guest, he hollers over the roar of the crowd, ''Wasn't that great?'' ''Interesting,'' says the Emotionless Man, blank-faced as always, ''but it's over. Let's go.''

These imaginary situations reflect the impact of our emotions in our everyday lives. **Emotions** are uncontrollable feelings that are accompanied by physiological changes and often affect our behavior. They influence our lives in many important ways. Without them, the very experience of living would be profoundly altered.

We have all experienced, to one degree or another, such feelings as anxiety, jealousy, anger, joy, fear, grief, excitement, wonder, embarrassment, lust, and apathy. We all know firsthand the power of these emotions in our day-to-day lives. But emotions can also determine *extraordinary* events within our lives. For example, emotions evidently can bring on **psychosomatic** illnesses, or illnesses for which there are no known physical causes. Peptic ulcers, asthma, and hy-

We have all experienced and witnessed such emotions as anger, joy, fear, and embarrassment. What emotion is being displayed here?

pertension have all been related to stress. Many neuroses, and some psychotic behavior as well, can be traced to unresolved emotional conflicts. Of course, not all of our emotional experiences are negative or conflicting. Most of our finest moments in life fill us with positive emotions. The pleasure we feel when we master a difficult new skill, or share an adventure with friends, or explore the world around us, constitutes a good portion of what we feel is important in life. In other words, emotions heighten and color the entire range of human experience—from high pleasure through normal everyday reactions to truly psychotic behavior (Mandler, 1980).

THE STUDY OF EMOTION

Emotional events are complex and difficult to study because they can be understood on at least three different levels:

1. We can think of emotions as *subjective experiences*. Because we have all felt such sensations as envy, guilt, and anger, it is logical to focus on this subjective aspect of the overall emotional event.

2. We can look at emotional *behavior* rather than the internal, subjective experience. We can study and observe what appear to be overt behavioral manifestations of internal emotional experiences. Rather than being confused about what the subject is feeling, we can attend to the striking behaviors that accompany emotional events, such as laughter or crying.

3. We can focus on the *internal physiological events* that accompany emotions. Many investigators have based their studies on the fact that emotions are accompanied by changes in heart rate, perspiration, muscle movement, and so on.

Different psychologists have studied these three different aspects of the overall emotional event—a fact that has led to all sorts of confusion within the field. For example, changes in these three aspects of the emotional event do not always correspond exactly. A "poker face" can conceal strong emotional reactions. Similarly, behavior that appears to be expressing a certain emotion may, in fact, be hiding some other emotion. At some point, many of us have pretended interest when we really felt bored and have acted submissive when we really felt angry. The fact that we can, and do, "fake" emotional reactions to ease our way through life can definitely complicate the psychologist's task.

Classifying and Identifying Emotions

The task of classifying emotions, once a popular academic diversion, has fallen on hard times. There are just too many shades and variations among emotions to allow clear-cut, satisfactory definitions of them all. For example, Davitz (1970) had students write brief descriptions of their emotional states. From their responses, Davitz drew up a list of 556 different words and phrases describing emotional states. Modern psychology therefore limits itself to identifying a few major emotions. Plutchik (1980) proposes that there are eight basic emotions: fear, anger, joy, sadness, acceptance, disgust, anticipation, and surprise. Although he maintains that all of the other sensations we experience are complex combinations of these eight, explaining all of our emotional sensations in terms of these eight, or of any other short list of primary emotions, is a difficult task.

Although experts argue about exactly how many emotions there are, everyone does seem to agree that all emotions can be classified as either pleasant or unpleasant. (If you think about it, there just do not seem to be any neutral emotions.) In addition to the pleasant-unpleasant distinction, modern psychology also tends to classify emotions along a dimension from weak to strong.

Identifying the specific emotion that an individual is experiencing at any given moment is also a difficult task. We can ask people to report their emotional state, we can observe their behavior, or we can measure internal physiological changes. We can even use all three methods at once, but each of these methods has its faults, and none of them is entirely satisfactory. If we ask subjects what they are feeling, they may be unable to provide an accurate description, or they may be unwilling to do so. We have already seen that overt behavior sometimes conceals true emotions. And finally, even though we can detect internal physiological changes, we cannot be sure which emotion they reflect. The physiological changes accompanying one intense emotion can resemble those accompanying another, quite different emotion (for example, love as opposed to hate).

Cognition versus Emotion

Another distinction that causes some problems is the one between reason, or cognitive activity, and emotion, or feeling. This distinction is a familiar and widely used one. We hear people saying, "Intellectually, I know it would be in my best interests to be nice to him, but I just don't feel like it," or, "My head says one thing, but my heart says another."

Although this distinction is often useful, and suggests that emotion is nonrational, it is not as clear-cut a distinction as we sometimes think. Our thoughts can affect our emotions and our emotions can influence our thoughts. If you are enraged at someone, your intellectual interpretation of the situation will doubtless be colored by your anger. Similarly, if you come to understand, intellectually, that you have been cheated, then strong emotions certainly will arise. Cognition and emotions interact.

Definitions of Emotion

As we have noted, psychologists have not settled on one definition of emotion. We have already presented one definition in this chapter, but there are many others in use. Young (1973) defines emotion as "a strongly visceralized, affective disturbance originating within the psychological situation, and revealing itself in bodily changes, in behavior, and in conscious experience" (Young, 1973, p. 440). Strongman (1973) states that "emotion is feeling, it is a bodily state involving various physical structures, it is gross or fine-grained behavior, and it occurs in particular situations" (Strongman, 1973, p. 1).

TABLE 10–1   The Complex, Probabilistic Sequence of Events Involved in the Development of an Emotion

Stimulus Event	Inferred Cognition	Feeling	Behavior	Effect
Threat	"Danger"	Fear, terror	Running, or flying away	Protection
Obstacle	"Enemy"	Anger, rage	Biting, hitting	Destruction
Potential mate	"Possess"	Joy, ecstasy	Courting, mating	Reproduction
Loss of valued person	"Isolation"	Sadness, grief	Crying for help	Reintegration
Group member	"Friend"	Acceptance, trust	Grooming, sharing	Affiliation
Gruesome object	"Poison"	Disgust, loathing	Vomiting, pushing away	Rejection
New territory	"What's out there?"	Anticipation	Examining, mapping	Exploration
Sudden novel object	"What is it?"	Surprise	Stopping, alerting	Orientation

Source: After Plutchik, 1980.

Then there are some psychologists who would rather not try to sum up emotion in a single sentence. Plutchik (1980), for example, thinks of emotion as a complex sequence of events. As can be seen in Table 10–1, his view of emotion begins with an external stimulus event such as some "threat." This external event leads to some internal cognition, or thought, such as the idea of "danger" which, in turn, is associated with the feeling of "fear" that we normally identify as that emotion. Fear, in turn, leads to overt behavior such as "running or flying." This behavior has the effect of "protecting" the animal. Each of Plutchik's eight primary emotions involves this same sequence of five steps.

All of these definitions, whether they involve single sentences or sequences of events, are helpful in characterizing the overall concept of emotion. To refine this concept further, we will describe some of the more important aspects of emotional events and their consequences.

Emotion and Motivation

Emotions are clearly related to motives. In fact, many textbooks combine the two topics within a single chapter. The most obvious way that the two are related lies in the fact that emotions sometimes act like motives. They energize, direct, and sustain behavior. If you are experiencing emotional hostility, you may well display hostile behavior. Quite simply, your aggressive behavior is motivated by your emotional anger.

But it is probably fair to say that emotions and motives are related in even more complicated ways. It seems that motives can affect emotional states, too. If you are driven by a high need to achieve and fail an important examination, you may well feel strong depression or anger. Emotions and motives feed off one another and affect each other in a spiraling, reciprocal fashion. Although we have chosen to deal with the two in separate chapters, keep in mind that emotions can act like motives and that motives can influence emotional states.

THE PHYSIOLOGY OF EMOTION

When we experience strong emotions we feel "stirred up." We are aware that physiological changes are occurring within us, even though we may not be able to identify them accurately.

The Autonomic Nervous System

As we shall see, the brain and the central nervous system have a great deal to do with emotion (Pribram, 1980). In addition, the autonomic nervous system is heavily involved in the changes in our bodies that we detect during emotional states. We have already seen that the autonomic nervous system is divided into the sympathetic and parasympathetic systems. The sympathetic system governs changes that occur when the body is preparing for emergency action. Thus, during a strong emotional experience, such as terror, the sympathetic nervous system prepares the body for drastic action. Among other things, it increases the heart rate, which increases the flow of fuel to the cells, and raises the blood-sugar level for more quick energy. The parasympathetic system closes down these emergency measures once the need for them has passed. As our terror subsides, this system returns us to the normal state.

Many of the "symptoms" of strong emotion that we can feel and report are directly traceable to changes in these subsystems of the autonomic nervous system. Look at the changes listed in Table 10–2 that often accompany strong emotion. Then look at the components of the autonomic nervous system depicted in Figure 10–1. You will notice that the changes in Table 10–2 involve the structures that are served by the autonomic nervous system in Figure 10–1.

Viewed in this way, emotion appears to be adaptive, because it helps the body prepare itself to deal with emergencies. But intense emotional states can be disruptive as well as adaptive, as we shall see in the next chapter.

The Limbic System

The *limbic system* of the brain has long been known to be involved in emotion. In Chapter 2 we described the limbic system as a border, or edging, of neural tissue that lies around the upper end of the brain stem (refer to Figure 2–15). This system is composed of a number of different structures that are all interconnected. The involvement of

TABLE 10–2 Some Physiological Changes Associated with Emotion

1. The pupils of the eyes dilate.
2. Perspiration increases.
3. Breathing becomes more rapid.
4. Heart rate increases.
5. Blood pressure increases.
6. The level of sugar in the blood increases.
7. The gastrointestinal tract slows its actions.
8. Blood flows from the stomach to the brain and muscles.
9. The hairs on the skin become erect.

FIGURE 10–1 The Autonomic Nervous System and the Structures That It Affects
Notice how many of these structures seem to be involved in the emotional changes listed in Table 10–2.

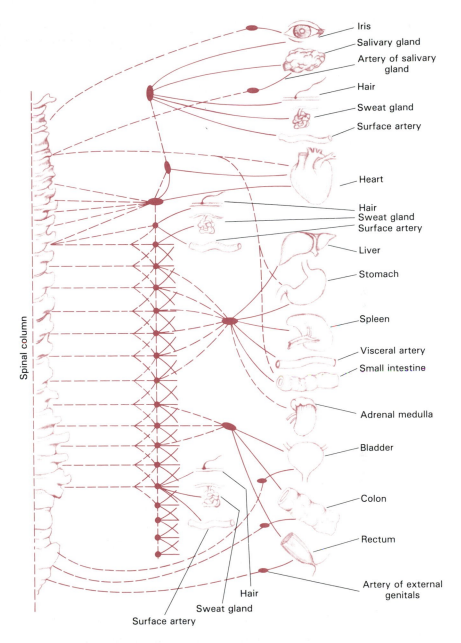

the limbic system in emotion has been supported by electrical stimulation and lesion studies. Stimulation of certain limbic areas produces rage and aggression, while stimulation of other areas yields fearful behavior.

One interesting aspect of the limbic system is that it varies less across mammalian species than do other brain structures, such as the cerebral cortex. Notice in Figure 10–2 that the size of the limbic system does not differ much from rabbit to cat to monkey, while the cerebral cortex shows a dramatic increase across these three species. This finding suggests that most mammalian species have similar emotional systems, despite the fact that they vary dramatically in terms of higher-order cortical functioning.

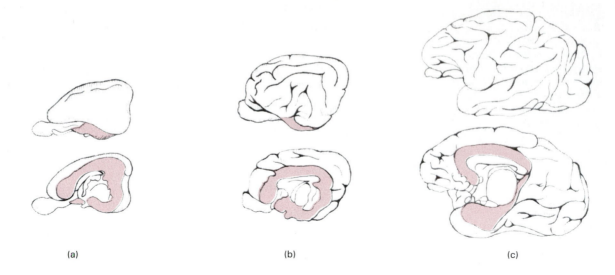

(a)   (b)   (c)

FIGURE 10–2   A Comparative Perspective on the Limbic Systems of Mammals   *Brains of (a) rabbit, (b) cat, and (c) monkey showing both the lateral surface* (above) *and the medial surface* (below). *The limbic system* (dark areas) *shows less variation across mammalian species than does the cerebral cortex.* (After MacLean, 1954)

THEORIES OF EMOTION

Having looked at the general nature of emotion and at some of the physiological correlates of emotion, we now consider the major theories proposed to explain emotional behavior and experience.

The James-Lange Theory and Facial Feedback

The Cart before the Horse   The **James-Lange hypothesis** is one of the earliest, most famous, and most controversial of the theories of emotion (James, 1890/1950; Lange, 1922). The theory is labeled James-Lange because William James and Carl Lange both came up with the same basic idea in 1884. According to their theory, the emotions we feel are the result of messages we receive from our bodies when they react to emotion-producing aspects of the environment. If you encounter a snarling dog, your body reacts first—you tremble, you sweat, your heart pounds. These physical changes, in turn, stimulate the *feeling* of fear.

This view makes things seem a bit backwards. We feel afraid because we are sweating, rather than sweating because we are afraid. We feel sad because we are crying, rather than crying because we are sad. Adherents to the James-Lange theory say that the physiological changes come first and that we then experience the emotion, but most of us tend to think that physiological changes such as trembling and sweating *follow* the emotion rather than precede it.

Evidence for the Theory   To be sure, the James-Lange theory seems to fit some situations. We have all had close calls where fear seems to follow physiological changes. Remember the last time you narrowly avoided a traffic accident? While you were slamming on the brakes, you probably felt very little emotion at all. It was only after you stopped the car and noticed your trembling hands and rapid breathing that you experienced the sensation of fear.

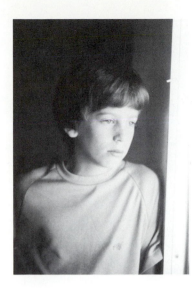

According to the facial feedback hypothesis, our awareness of our own facial expression determines how we feel. This sad young man may feel depressed because of the feedback he is receiving from the glum set of his facial features.

The best modern evidence for the James-Lange position comes from tests of the *facial feedback hypothesis*. According to this hypothesis, our awareness of our own facial expression determines how we feel (Ekman, Levenson, & Friesen, 1983; Riskind & Gotay, 1982). According to facial feedback theory, if a subject is given instructions that cause her to frown (asked to drop the corners of her mouth and to bring her eyebrows together), without being told that she is frowning, she will be likely to experience negative emotion. This facial configuration is apt to stimulate displeasure. According to the facial feedback hypothesis, if a subject is asked to raise and pull together the eyebrows, to raise the eyelids, and to draw back the lips horizontally, then fear is apt to be experienced. Try it and see if your experience confirms or contradicts the hypothesis.

Evidence against the Theory   Unfortunately, not all experiments support the James-Lange theory. If the James-Lange hypothesis is correct, a unique pattern of physiological changes should accompany each and every emotion. Joy's pattern of physiological changes should differ from the pattern associated with any other emotion, such as despair. If the changes were always the same, then how could we experience different emotions? This deduction has led to a great many studies of the physiological changes associated with various emotions.

With the exception of anger and fear (Ax, 1953), few investigators have been able to find different physiological patterns in association with different emotions. Many emotions seem to be accompanied by the same diffuse, general pattern of physiological change (Mandler, 1962). Clearly, no one has come close to identifying distinct physiological patterns for all of the many emotions we seem capable of experiencing.

Furthermore, the same person may show different patterns of physiological change when experiencing the same emotion at two different times. You might sweat when afraid on one occasion but not sweat the next time you experience fear. In addition, people differ in the patterns they display. One person might always sweat, while another might never sweat in response to fear stimuli. In short, the James-Lange hypothesis has not been consistently supported by experimentation.

The Cannon-Bard Theory

Walter Cannon, very much aware of the shortcomings of the James-Lange hypothesis, proposed an alternative view of the emotional mechanism (Bard, 1928; Cannon, 1927). He felt that external stimuli arouse the thalamus, which sends neural messages that trigger the physiological changes associated with emotion, and at the same time, sends neural messages to the cerebral cortex. It is these latter messages that result in the sensation of emotion.

Note that Cannon's theory, also referred to as the *Cannon-Bard theory*, says nothing at all about any supposed stimulation by the physiological changes. The Cannon-Bard theory completely avoids the troublesome James-Lange mechanism. Figure 10–3 diagrams the two theories.

FIGURE 10–3   Two Famous Theories of Emotion   *According to the James-Lange theory, perception of external stimuli triggers physiological changes that stimulate the brain to produce the sensation of emotion. According to the Cannon-Bard theory, perception of external stimuli arouses the thalamus, which simultaneously triggers physiological changes and stimulates the cortex to produce the feeling of emotion.*

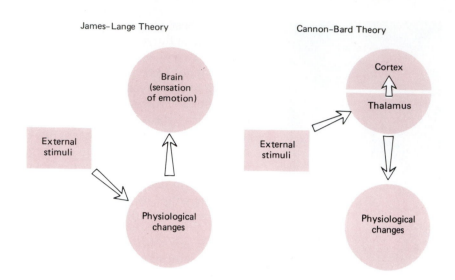

The Cognitive Theory

Many theories of emotion miss one very important aspect of the emotional experience, as the following example illustrates. Imagine that you are excited about seeing a new comedy film. On impulse, you go to the movie at three in the afternoon. There are nine other people in the theater. As the film progresses, you begin to feel slightly embarrassed, because you are not hearing enough laughter for this to be a truly funny movie. You leave the theater feeling slightly disappointed. Contrast that experience with what might happen if you attended the same film on a Friday or Saturday evening when the theater was full. In this case your excitement about seeing the film would be matched by the gales of laughter from the capacity crowd. You might enjoy the film enormously in this situation.

In both cases you entered the theater feeling excited, but in one situation you ended up feeling disappointed and in the other elated. Why? Some psychologists argue that we use our perception of what is going on around us to interpret our feelings. According to this view, emotion is the result of an interaction between internal arousal and our cognitive processes. If everyone around us in the theater is having a good time, we interpret our internal state of excitement or arousal as pleasure. If those around us do not seem to be having a good time, we interpret our state of arousal in a different manner. In other words, our emotions are not just the result of internal states of arousal. Our emotions are determined by our thoughts about what is going on as well (see Plutchik, 1980).

Stanley Schachter (1971) is one of the psychologists who believes that we interpret a given state of internal arousal in terms of what is going on around us. He conducted an experiment (Schachter & Singer, 1962) to demonstrate the effect. All of the subjects were told that the experiment was designed to study the effects of a "new chemical compound" on vision. They were all given an injection of this "compound" and asked to fill out a questionnaire in a waiting room. The experimental half of the subjects actually received an injection of epinephrine (adrenalin). One third of this experimental group was told nothing about the effects of the drug. One third was told, correctly, that the drug would produce increased heart and breathing rates and a jumpy feeling. The final third was told, incorrectly, that the drug would produce itching, numbness, and a headache. The control half of the group was injected with a saline solution that had no physiological effects. Then each member of the entire group was exposed to one of two experimental conditions. In the "angry" condition, a subject waited with a confederate of the experimenter who displayed more and more annoyance with the questionnaire, finally ripping it up and stomping out of the room. In the "happy" condition, subjects waited with a confederate who laughed, giggled, and threw paper airplanes.

Schachter's guesses about the outcome of the experiment proved to be correct. The uninformed experimental subjects and the misinformed experimental subjects, both experiencing unexplained internal arousal, interpreted this internal arousal in terms of what was going on around them. When the confederate acted happy, so did they. When the confederate was grouchy, so were they. Subjects in the control condition had no internal arousal to account for, and the correctly informed experimental subjects attributed their feelings to the drug. Subjects in these two groups were not affected by the behavior of the confederates.

This cognitive interpretation of emotion has generated a good deal of interest. However, other psychologists have failed to replicate the results, so we must be careful about accepting it uncritically (Rogers & Deckner, 1975).

Opponent-process Theory

Solomon and Corbit (1974) developed what they call the ***opponent-process theory*** of emotion. This theory depends heavily on the fact that most emotional states, whether positive or negative, tend to be followed by the opposite state. Negative feelings of dread or fear tend to be followed by positive feelings of pleasure or satisfaction. Negative states tend to follow positive states. The second, or opposite, state is what Solomon and Corbit call the opponent process. As Houston (1985) puts it,

> If your shoes hurt and you take them off, the opponent feeling of relief and pleasure is more than just a return to a neutral state. And if you are having a wonderful time at a party, and then the party ends, the opponent "letdown" will be more than just a return to a neutral state. No matter what the experience, positive or negative, our bodies are wired to produce the opposite feeling when the first feeling is terminated. Soldiers feel cheerful after combat. Students feel great once their exam is over. "It feels good when it stops." Politicians feel depressed after a winning election night. Victory is often followed by the blues. (p. 119)

Let us consider the theory a little more closely. Focus on the upper half of Figure 10–4. Imagine you have just arrived on a battlefield and are terrified. Your fear zooms up to a peak and then declines to a steady state. Then the battle ends. What happens to your emotional

FIGURE 10–4 Opponent-process Theory

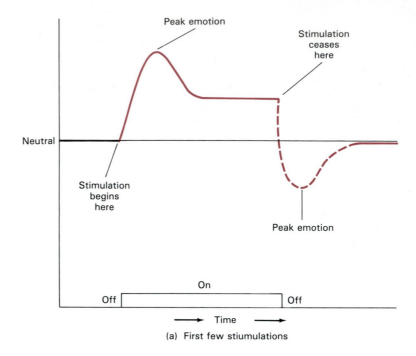

(a) First few stiumulations

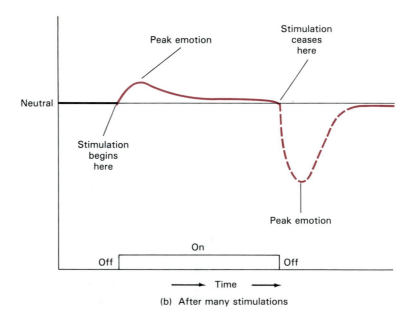

(b) After many stimulations

state? It swings wildly until it reaches a peak in the opposite direction. You are relieved and jubilant. Next, this opponent positive state gradually lessens too, so that you finally end up in a neutral state.

Remember, the initial emotional state can be either positive or negative. In the party example the shift was from positive to negative, but in other cases (such as removing tight shoes) the shift will be from negative to positive.

Opponent-process theory may explain why this young executive is caught in the trap of having to use more and more of a drug to maintain the original level of euphoria.

The next important aspect of the theory has to do with what happens when we *repeatedly* experience the initial state. According to opponent-process theory, the situation changes from the top half of Figure 10–4 to the bottom half. The strength of the initial process decreases while the strength of the opponent process increases. Suppose, for example, that an individual begins taking a drug. At first, the initial positive reaction is large, while the opponent negative reaction is small. But over time, as use of the drug continues, two things happen. First, the initial positive reaction lessens, and second, the opponent negative reaction increases. The individual is now threatened by addiction. At first this individual took the drug to experience the positive state. As the positive state diminishes with continued use, the person takes more and more of the drug to regain the pleasurable effects. But continued use does not help. In fact, it increases the negative opponent process. So the individual is caught; he increases his use of the drug to increase the positive state and reduce the negative state, but the opposite situation occurs: pleasure lessens while discomfort increases and the individual takes an ever increasing amount of the drug in a vain effort to recapture the original euphoria.

Sociobiological Theory

In Chapter 2 we discussed sociobiology, which holds that human social behavior is determined by natural selection. The same reasoning has been applied to emotional behavior (Chance, 1980; Weinrich, 1980). The idea is that emotions, like any other behavior, have adaptive value from an evolutionary point of view. Certain emotions have survived because they have helped the species survive. For instance, if an animal encounters a dangerous predator and does not feel fear, then it may not flee—and it may be eaten as a result. Animals that possess the fear emotion are more likely to escape, survive, and reproduce.

Although the details are not well worked out, sociobiologists suggest that every emotion has some kind of survival value. Anger protects us from aggression, joy facilitates courtship and reproduction, grief is associated with an adaptive cry for help, and so on.

Sociobiologists support their argument by noting that animals seem to have emotions, too. Some dogs appear to display jealousy and sulk when they are not given their regular treats. Chimpanzees seem to experience many familiar emotions; they laugh, get angry, sulk, and throw temper tantrums. These displays suggest that emotions are widespread in the animal kingdom. To a sociobiologist, this is further evidence that emotions are adaptive mechanisms that have evolved according to the principles of natural selection.

EXPRESSION OF EMOTION

When we are happy, we laugh. When we are angry or frustrated, we cry, scream, or yell. Are these methods of expressing emotion innate and biologically determined, or are they learned as we grow up? The answer seems to be that they are a little of both (Eibl-Eibesfeldt, 1980).

Children all over the world laugh when happy and cry when sad. This child's tears are an innate expression of unhappiness.

Innate Expression

Let us look first at the evidence that many of our modes of emotional expression are innate (see Buck, 1983; Rinn, 1984). One of the most obvious observations that we might make involves the fact that children all over the world laugh when they are happy and cry when they are unhappy. Deaf and blind children develop these same forms of emotional expression, even though they never have the chance to observe and copy the sounds and movements of others. Moreover, it is not just laughter and tears that mean the same thing in different cultures. Several facial expressions also apparently express the same emotions in many different cultures. When facial photographs of individuals experiencing such emotions as anger, sadness, surprise, disgust, and happiness were shown to subjects from many different countries, most subjects identified most of the emotions correctly (Ekman, 1971). This is not to say that everyone can identify all emotions perfectly, but some facial expressions do seem to mean the same thing in many different cultures.

Learned Expression

On the other hand, not all forms of emotional expression are purely innate. Clearly, we learn very complicated methods of communicating our emotions. If a young woman feels angry about something her date has just said, she may drive off in a huff, treat him with icy disdain, or slam a door. None of these ways of expressing anger is innate; they must all be learned. Conveying emotion through language may be the most obvious example of learned emotional expression. When surprised, W. C. Fields would fumble his hat up into the air and exclaim, "Godfrey Daniel!" Clearly, this is a learned expression. When someone calls you a no-good, low-down, thieving skunk, they are not expressing an innately determined pattern. They are utilizing learned methods of expressing emotion.

In short, when people express emotions they use both innate modes of expression, such as facial expressions, crying, and laughing, and learned modes, such as the expression of emotion through language.

NONVERBAL EXPRESSION OF EMOTION

The "Other" Language of Emotion

Ours is a language-oriented culture. We talk to one another and write to one another almost incessantly. We go on and on as though it were absolutely essential to tell *someone* about every last little event in our lives. Because we have this enormous enthusiasm for language, it is not surprising that we normally think of communication in terms of language.

But recent research has uncovered another language that we use constantly, even though we are not always aware that we are using it. We communicate a great deal through movements, gestures, facial expressions, and tone of voice. Much of this **nonverbal communication** has to do with the expression of emotion. Suppose you walk up to an attractive person at a party and in your own confident manner say, "Here I am at last." The person you are trying to charm gives you a brief, flat stare and turns away without a word—but with plenty of emotional communication. A little later, as you are nursing your pride by the punch bowl, you notice another attractive person smiling at you from across the room. You smile in return and look away, still smarting from your earlier fiasco. Then you glance up again and find this new person is *still* looking at you. The message seems unmistakable. All sorts of intensely pleasurable possibilities begin to dance in your head—and all before one word is spoken. Nonverbal communication is very effective in conveying emotion.

People can communicate very effectively in a nonverbal way. The student with his hand up is pleading, "Call on me!" The spectator is declaring "Kill the umpire!" without uttering a word.

Eye Contact

We have just seen that, in the right circumstances, prolonged *eye contact* can communicate positive emotion. But staring at someone for a long time does not always communicate positive feelings. Suppose you are waiting for a bus on a deserted street late at night and a man in a doorway stares at you. You receive quite a different message in this situation.

In general, extended eye contact seems to intensify an interaction. Whether the intensified feeling is positive or negative depends on the context in which the eye contact occurs and on the psychological state of the person receiving the stare.

Ellsworth, Carlsmith, and Henson (1972) ran an experiment that demonstrates the power of a stare. The experimenter stood at a busy street corner and stared calmly at drivers as they pulled up to the stoplight. She did not stare at drivers in a control group. The drivers that were stared at took off faster and crossed the intersection in less time than the controls. In this case, a stare seemed to convey a negative feeling and motivated avoidance behavior.

Extended eye contact usually indicates that the person doing the looking wants something. Our interpretation of what the person wants seems to depend on how we are feeling and on the context in which the eye contact occurs.

Movements, Gestures, and Posture

A person who likes you can communicate this feeling through subtle movements and gestures. Isn't it nice to have someone face you, lean toward you, and perhaps touch you gently on the arm? All of these small movements indicate liking.

If someone is boring you with endless stories of his latest non-adventures, how can you subtly let him know that you want him to stop talking without having to say, "Go away, I never want to see you again"? You can break eye contact, you can turn slightly and face away, you can glance about the room, and, if necessary, you can look at your watch. Most people will pick up these cues and realize they are losing their audience.

Waving, signaling with a crooked finger, falling asleep at the dinner table, gesturing rudely, and touching are all forms of communicating without words. In an additional example of this sort of communication, Mehrabian (1971) has outlined some of the ways that status may be revealed nonverbally. Low-status individuals usually act with deference toward people of higher status. Your boss can slap you on the back, walk through doors first, and barge into your office, but you cannot do the same things to him. If you invite your boss to dinner, he can cancel at the last minute, but you cannot cancel out on his invitation. He tends to be more relaxed physically than you are. He talks in an easier, more confident manner than you do.

Even our posture can convey much of what we are feeling. Weisfeld and Beresford (1982) found that aggressive, determined, and successful young people tend to hold themselves in an erect stance, as depicted in the left side of Figure 10–5. People who are less confident

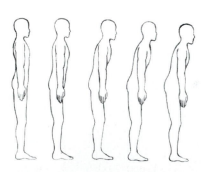

FIGURE 10–5 Scale Used for Rating Erectness of Posture as a Reflection of Dominance or Submissiveness *(After Weisfeld & Beresford, 1982)*

and more submissive tend to have more stooped posture. In other words, we have a fairly complicated physical language that we use to express dominance and submissiveness.

Personal Space

Did someone ever come up to you, stand with his or her face about four inches away from yours, and start talking? What did you do in this situation? Most people in our culture will back up. It makes us uncomfortable to have people invade our *personal space* in this way (Sanders, 1976). It is as though we move around in a bubble. We prefer to have people speak to us from outside that bubble, and if they come too close we feel uncomfortable. (Of course, there are a few people we wish *would* invade our space!)

Apparently the size of an individual's personal space may differ from culture to culture (Hall, 1966). If the spaces of two communicating people differ, then the two may end up with negative feelings about one another as a result of an invasion of personal space. The individual with a smaller space may think that the individual with a larger space is cold and aloof. The individual with a large space may feel that the person with a small personal space is intrusive.

Double-edged Messages

We have been talking about how we communicate feelings and emotions through nonverbal means, but we often use *both* verbal and nonverbal elements to communicate emotions. *Double-edged messages*, which simultaneously convey conflicting positive and negative feelings, often involve both verbal and nonverbal communication.

Suppose someone says, in a very bored tone of voice, "I *love* the way we *always* go out at night." The person receiving this message is likely to become defensive and say, "What do you mean? We just went to the movies." Or an employee may say, in a sneering tone, "Boy, the boss sure is one wonderful guy." Both of these examples involve a positive message delivered in a negative tone. What do we

Although we generally have a personal space that we prefer to maintain, the facial expressions of the people in this crowded scene suggest that there are times when we enjoy having our space invaded. As the photo on the right shows, however, even young children usually dislike having others impinge upon their personal space.

call this form of communication? Sarcasm. Sarcasm is a double-edged message. It is a safe, effective means of delivering a negative message, because one can always deny its negative quality. "But all I said was . . ." Note that when positive words are combined with a negative tone, the tone wins out. It seems it does not make too much difference what you say; it is how you say it that counts in conveying emotion.

Now let us look at the opposite of sarcasm: a negative message delivered in a positive tone. Suppose a child stomps across a newly washed kitchen floor with muddy feet. The child's mother may say, in a relatively affectionate tone, "You little monster! I'm going to break your neck!" Again the tone is predominant; the overall message is a relatively affectionate one. In this case the function of the message seems to be to convey some disapproval without being totally negative.

These examples suggest that there is a lot more to our communications than what we actually say. In fact, Mehrabian and Weiner (1967) have isolated *three* aspects of a face-to-face communication: facial expression, tone of voice, and verbal content of the message. Think about it for a moment. How would you rank the three in terms of importance? When someone speaks to you, what is most important in conveying feeling? The facial expression? The tone of voice? The content of the message? Mehrabian and Weiner concluded that verbal content accounts for less than 10 percent of the conveyed feeling. The tone of voice was a more important element, and they found that the facial expression was the most important element of all, accounting for over half of the conveyed feeling.

More recent work suggests that these early studies may have oversimplified things a bit. Although expression, tone, and content convey differential amounts of information, the weight given to these three elements will depend on such things as exactly what message is being communicated and the context in which the communication occurs (Ekman, Friesen, O'Sullivan, & Scherer, 1980; Hall, 1980).

EVERYDAY ANXIETY

We have now discussed the importance of emotion, the physiology of emotion, definitions of emotion, theories of emotion, and the expression of emotion. But we have not said much about any *specific* emotions. We do know that there are a great many specific emotions and combinations of emotions, including jealousy, fear, grief, excitement, disgust, joy, embarrassment, lust, and apathy, to name but a few. Rather than saying a few words about each emotion, we have opted to discuss two of them in some detail. We will begin with anxiety, and then we will consider frustration. We chose these two emotions because a great deal of research has been done on them, while some of the other emotions have hardly been explored.

Definitions of Anxiety

Do you remember how you felt the last time you waited for an examination at school to begin, knowing in your heart that you were not prepared? That sensation was what psychologists call *anxiety.* Do you remember the last time you anticipated taking part in an important athletic event, or applied for a job you really wanted, or knew you were going to be punished? Do you remember the last time you woke up feeling uneasy for no apparent reason? Each of these situations can elicit the important emotion known as anxiety.

Anxiety deserves special attention because it is so widespread in our everyday lives. In this section, we will discuss only *normal, nonpathological* anxiety, but you should know that extreme states of anxiety are common in many forms of mental illness. These extreme, pathological degrees of anxiety will be considered in Chapter 17. For now, we will attend to the definition and causes of ordinary, garden-variety anxiety.

Anxiety is difficult to define, but there does seem to be some agreement about its nature. Kagan and Havemann (1976) define it as "a vague, unpleasant feeling accompanied by a premonition that something undesirable is about to happen." Lundin (1979) defines it as a "feeling of dread, impending doom, or disaster." Young (1973) defines it as "a persistent foreboding or presentiment of harm."

Thus it seems that psychologists are talking about worry, fear, apprehension, dread, and misgiving when they speak of anxiety. Some psychologists distinguish between fear, as a reaction to specific objects or events, and anxiety, as a reaction to unknown or unidentified threats. For instance, you fear an unleashed pit bull, but you are anxious about all the unpredictable, awful mistakes you might make when you get into the big game. Other psychologists use fear and anxiety interchangeably, because the physiological symptoms are the same for both. In fact, anxiety is sometimes measured in terms of physiological reactions such as increased heart rate and breathing, sweaty palms, and so on. At other times, it is measured with paper-and-pencil tests that ask subjects to estimate how anxious they are or to estimate how many symptoms of anxiety they possess.

The Causes of Anxiety

What makes us anxious? Why do we have these vague, unpleasant feelings that something bad is about to happen? Psychologists have identified several conditions that apparently lead to anxiety. These conditions are not totally distinct from one another; in fact, they are interrelated.

Separation from Support   Suppose a child is suddenly taken away from its parents. All accustomed support is withdrawn. The child will feel tremendous anxiety. Freud and Burlingham (1943) described the anxiety of children taken from their parents and evacuated to safe rural areas in Great Britain during World War II. The children refused to eat, clung to some reminder of their parents such as a scarf or gift, and occasionally repeated their parents' names over and over again. We have all, in one way or another, felt anxious when separated from some support system.

Anticipation of Punishment   As children, we felt anxious when wondering how our parents might punish us for some infraction. Now we feel a similar anxiety while taking an exam we are not prepared for or while entering traffic court to face the judge. In these examples it seems to be the threat of impending punishment that stimulates anxiety.

An Inner Conflict   If we find that our actions are in conflict with our beliefs, we may experience anxiety. For instance, suppose a parent believes in busing as a means of achieving racial integration. This person's belief in the cause of racial equality is strong enough to prompt her to enroll her child in a volunteer busing program. But then someone says, "If you are so committed, why don't you move into a minority area, or at least work there? It's easy to send your child to an integrated school, but what are *you* doing?" The parent may well experience anxiety in this situation, because her actions do not seem to be consistent with her beliefs.

Uncertainty and Anxiety   Uncertainty about the future seems to be a major source of anxiety. If you are anxious about an examination, it may be because you are uncertain about your ability to perform. If you are certain of success—or for that matter, certain of failure—you will be less anxious. It is when we really do not know what is going to happen that we feel most anxious. In a typical experiment, three groups of subjects might be asked to count to 15 and told that they will receive a shock at the count of 15. One group would be given a sample shock that is described as strong. One group would be given a weak sample shock. The third group would be given no sample shock. Which group do you think would show the greatest increase in anxiety as the count of 15 approaches? More than likely the most uncertain group, the one given no sample shock, would be most anxious (see Figure 10–6).

Waiting is the hardest part. Much of this basketball player's anxiety may be caused by his uncertainty about how he will perform when he reenters the game.

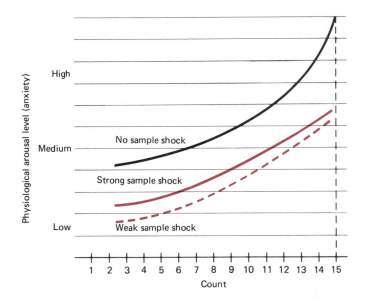

FIGURE 10–6   Anxiety and Uncertainty   *Typical data relating anxiety, as indexed by physiological arousal, to uncertainty about the strength of an impending shock indicate that the group that received no sample shock was the most anxious.*

Treating Anxiety

Obviously, we all suffer anxiety from time to time. But it is only when anxiety interferes with our life's activities that treatment seems necessary. When anxiety becomes disruptive, an individual can be treated psychologically through some form of counseling or psychotherapy, or through some type of chemical therapy. Both of these forms of treatment are considered in detail later. For our purposes here, it is sufficient to note that Americans consume enormous quantities of *tranquilizers*, drugs that reduce anxiety. The following information from Kalat (1984) indicates the extent of tranquilizer consumption in this country.

> At one time barbiturates were the most common class of tranquilizers, but they have been displaced by benzodiazepines. The benzodiazepines have a variety of useful effects; they act as anxiety-reducers, sleep-inducers, anticonvulsants, and muscle relaxants. They also have some undesirable effects, of which the most troublesome is their potential to be habit-forming. They also become very dangerous if taken in conjunction with alcohol.
>
> In 1977, people in the United States consumed 8,000 tons of benzodiazepine tranquilizers. Diazepam (Valium®), one of the benzodiazepines, was the most commonly prescribed drug in the country, and a similar drug, chlordiazepoxide (Librium®), placed third (Frazer & Winokur, 1977; Tallman, Paul, Skolnick, & Gallager, 1980). Tranquilizers are, in short, a highly profitable business. (p. 308)

Anxiety Is Not All Bad

By now you may have the impression that anxiety is just a lot of trouble for us, but depending on the task that we are trying to perform, anxiety can be a help or a hindrance. If the task is complex, such as trying to learn physics, anxiety will probably hinder our efforts. On the other hand, if the task is a simple one, such as sorting cards into piles, we may find that a little anxiety helps us to get going and keep going.

In the next chapter, we will discuss the effects of anxiety on such things as our ability to learn. We will also explore a number of mechanisms that we all use to cope with anxiety, but for now, we will look at another unpleasant emotional experience that is extremely important in our everyday lives.

FRUSTRATION

A Definition and Some Examples

Consider the common experiences listed in Table 10–3. We have all had days that parallel the one described in the table. By ten in the morning we are ready to exclaim, "What a *frustrating* day this has been!" All of the events in Table 10–3 have one thing in common: in each of them, some desired goal is not obtained or some existing motive is thwarted. Thus, we may define *frustration* as the unpleasant feelings that result when motive satisfaction is blocked or delayed (see Figure 10–7). We should note here that many psychologists define frustration as the blockage of a motive, rather than the feelings that follow such blockage. Because we are focusing on feelings, it seems appropriate to define frustration as an emotion rather than a blocking event.

Frustration and anxiety, although both very common and important, are not the same thing. While anxiety carries overtones of foreboding, fear, and apprehension, frustration carries a sense of disappointment, anger, and bafflement. Both can lead to serious psychological stress, but they are different emotions.

A sense of frustration can trigger many other emotional and behavioral reactions. If frustrated, we may become aggressive, apathetic, depressed, or assertive. We will consider these consequences

---

TABLE 10–3 Some Typical Daily Events That Lead to a Sense of Frustration

1. You get up without having had enough sleep.
2. Your coffee is cold and you are out of toothpaste.
3. You are late for your first class.
4. Someone fails to return your class notes.
5. Your conversations are interrupted.
6. As usual, your professor is not in his office during his office hours.
7. Your car will not start, and the necessary part is no longer manufactured.
8. The restaurant is crowded and your coffee is cold again.
9. Your date cancels out on you.
10. Alternative dates do not answer the phone.
11. You do not have enough time to get everything done.
12. The television goes out, the stores are closed, and your magazines are two years old.
13. The dog next door barks all night, and you cannot kill that mosquito.
14. You get up without having had enough sleep *again*.

FIGURE 10–7 The Elements
of Frustration   *A few of the most
common sources of frustration that
confront an adolescent looking for
an early sexual encounter.*

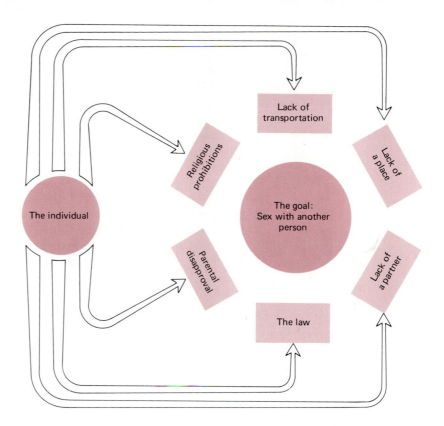

of frustration and our methods of coping with frustration in the next chapter. For now, as with anxiety, we will explore only causes. To do this, we have broken down the sources of frustration into three categories: delay, obstacles, and conflict.

Frustration by Delay

We become frustrated when we expect a goal to be obtained at a certain time but discover that achievement of that goal will be delayed. Suppose, for instance, that a group of friends plans a picnic and agrees to meet at a certain time and place. One member of the group does not show up on time. "Where the heck is Charlie?" The grumbling increases as the minutes pass. Charlie finally calls to say that he overslept but is on the way. The moans and groans of the group express the frustration caused by this delay. There is a chance that, for some, the entire picnic will take on a negative quality as a result of Charlie's failure to set his alarm clock.

If you are working on a project, such as repairing a radio, and you discover that you are missing one tiny part, you will feel frustrated. There is nothing to do but drop everything, go to the radio store, and then return and pick up where you left off before you discovered the missing part. Such a delay can certainly make you frustrated and irritable.

Frustration caused by delay seems inevitable in everyday life. We cannot avoid it completely. Some of our common reactions to it will be discussed in the next chapter.

Frustration by Obstacles

Physical Obstacles and Events   Physical objects or events can obviously prevent the attainment of goals. If your new house burns down before you can move in, you will (to say the least) experience a degree of frustration. Two people in love who are separated by an ocean will also feel frustrated. A locked door can cause frustration. Predation by coyotes causes great frustration among sheep ranchers. Storms and insects can block farmers in their attempts to reap a full harvest.

Social and Legal Obstacles   Frustration also can be caused by the actions of other people and by the laws and customs of society. If two people fall in love and want to get married, that goal may be blocked by parental attitudes, religious laws, or the customs of society. Without doubt, other people comprise one of the greatest sources of frustration in our everyday lives. The hermit living in an abandoned mine shaft in the desert claims, "People are just too durn much trouble." One thing he is objecting to is the frustrating quality of many human relationships.

Personal Obstacles   We cannot blame all of our frustrations on other people and external events and objects. Much of our frustration springs from our own personal limitations and our unrealistic expectations about what we can and cannot accomplish. Our mental and physical equipment may not be sufficient to attain the goals we desire. Students encouraged by their parents to attend college may be frustrated by their inability to earn the necessary grades in high school. The goal of being a professional basketball player can be thwarted by a five-foot physique. If a woman wants to be a concert pianist but is tone deaf, she will experience frustration.

In short, there are plenty of obstacles ready and waiting. The condition of frustration is bound to be a common one in our lives. To emphasize this point, we will look at another major source of frustration, that of conflict. Because conflict is such an important source of frustration and one that has received considerable attention in the literature, we will deal with it in some detail. Conflicts can result in many unpleasant emotions such as anxiety, guilt, fear, and shame, but because they tend to involve motive blockage, and because they frequently lead to a sense of frustration, the inclusion of conflicts in the discussion at this point seems appropriate.

CONFLICT

A Definition and Some Examples

Suppose you have to study for an examination. The need is desperate after all of the procrastinating you have done during the semester. The exam is tomorrow! You clear the decks, unplug the phone, and open the books. Then there is a knock at the door. You open it to discover some friends who want you to go to a great movie, right now. What do you experience? Conflict. Conflict refers to situations where two or more incompatible motives are aroused. The satisfaction of one motive leads to the denial of the other. You cannot study and go to a movie too. Conflict leads to, among other things, frustration. No matter what you do—go to the movie or study—you are going to feel somewhat frustrated. Conflicts are distressing. When we are caught in one, we feel torn by the pull of the opposing motive systems.

Conflicts come in all shapes and sizes. A child may want to pet a strange animal but is afraid of it. A young man may want to be independent but feels uneasy about breaking away from home. A young woman may want to excel in sports and make the dean's list but discovers that she cannot do both at once. Candy tastes good but is bad for your teeth. Menus create conflicts. Pizza or lasagna? Steak or shrimp? There is no way you can have them all, and having one ensures that you will not have the others.

Conflicts can be minor or major. Many of the lesser ones, such as choosing food in a restaurant, are handled with relative ease. But major conflicts can cause severe psychological stress. For example, Powell and Reznikoff (1976) point out that young, college-educated women in this country show signs of distress over the conflict between traditional, family-oriented roles and their own personal needs. Tradition says that they should take care of the children, drive a station wagon, and keep the dresser drawers neat. But the women's-rights movement has awakened them to the possibility of having a different kind of life, of finding a career, and of throwing off the sometimes-limiting cloak of tradition. The conflict is not an easy one to resolve, and it has resulted in measurable degrees of stress among these women. Interestingly enough, older women, more firmly entrenched in the traditional role, are not as conflicted over this issue.

The next time you feel distressed, try thinking about the situation as one involving a conflict. More than likely, if you enjoy this sort of self-analysis, you will see that incompatible motives are at work.

Types of Conflict

Approach-Approach Conflict For many years, psychologists have distinguished several different types of conflict situations. The first of these is called an approach-approach conflict. In **approach-approach conflicts** we want to reach two goals, but obtaining one means we cannot attain the other. We want to go to the mountains and to the shore for our vacation. We want to get a good night's sleep but we want to watch the late show on television.

"Poor baby!" one is tempted to say. All those good alternatives and unable to make a decision. It is true that this type of conflict is not all that bad. Life would certainly be pleasant if the only kind of conflict we ever had to face was the approach-approach variety. But even this mild conflict can cause some problems. Our pleasure in satisfying one of the two motives is always reduced by our regret over losing the other option.

Avoidance-Avoidance Conflict "Eat your spinach or go to bed!" Remember that one? "You money or your life!" "Study for the examination or fail it." These are all **avoidance-avoidance conflicts**, where we are caught between two unpleasant alternatives. The only way we can avoid one alternative is to do the other, and we do not want to do that either. These are nasty conflict situations. Try to avoid them if you can.

Approach-Avoidance Conflict Suppose you go to the beach with a group of friends one spring day. The sun is warm but the water is cold. Suddenly, someone shouts, "Let's go swimming." Friends all around you begin running into the near-freezing surf, laughing and splashing. You kind of shuffle about, nodding your head and faking a laugh. All you can think of is that icy water, but you do not want to be left out of the fun. You are in an **approach-avoidance conflict**. Very often a single goal will have both desirable and undesirable attributes. Cigarette may be enjoyable to some but they are a threat to health. Drinking beer may be fun but it makes driving dangerous. French fries taste good but they make you fat.

If you think about it for a few minutes, you will realize that approach-avoidance conflicts are very common. There just are not that many alternatives that are totally positive or totally negative.

Behavior in Conflict

How do we tend to react in these various conflict situations? Do we resolve them easily, or do they give us a great deal of trouble? A partial answer to these questions has been provided by Judson Brown in a now classic analysis of conflict behavior (Brown, 1948).

In Brown's experiment a rat is trained to run down an alley to a goal box where it is fed. Next, the same rat is given mild shock as it eats in the goal box. Finally, the rat is tested for its tendency to go to the goal box where it has been both fed and shocked. Obviously, this is an approach-avoidance situation. What would you do in a similar situation? The rat approaches part way down the alley, then hesitates and wavers. It cannot bring itself to go all the way to the goal box because of fear of the shock, but it cannot leave either, because of the pull of the food.

Brown analyzed this situation by breaking it down into the opposing approach and avoidance tendencies. First, he attached a small harness to a rat that had been trained to go to the goal box for food. This rat was never shocked. By measuring the strength with which the rat pulled on the harness, Brown discovered that the strength with which the rat pulled or the tendency to approach increased slightly as the distance between the rat and goal box decreased (see approach tendency in Figure 10–8). The closer the rat was to the food, the harder it pulled on the harness. (Think how often people run the last few yards to get into the water after having strolled across the beach on a hot day.)

Next, Brown put a harness on a rat that had been shocked in the goal box but had never been fed there. He measured the strength with which this rat pulled away from the goal box (see avoidance tendency in Figure 10–8). This rat tended to pull very hard near the goal box but not very hard at all once it was farther away. Notice that the **avoidance gradient** in Figure 10–8 is *steeper* than the **approach**

FIGURE 10–8   The Resolution of Opposing Approach and Avoidance Tendencies   *If the rat is closer than 120 cm to the goal box, it will move away because the avoidance tendency is stronger than the approach tendency. At all points farther than 120 cm from the goal box, the rat will approach. If left alone, the rat will vacillate around the 120-cm point.*

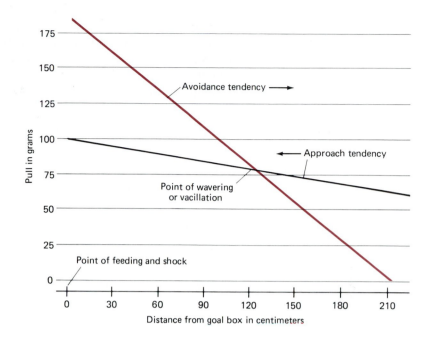

gradient. This difference in the steepness of the two gradients has important implications.

Think about the rat that has experienced both food reward and shock. Presumably, it has *both* the approach tendency and the avoidance tendency registered within its brain. As you can see in Figure 10–8, the tendency to avoid is greater than the tendency to approach at all points within 120 cm of the goal box. However, the tendency to approach is greater than the tendency to avoid at all points farther than 120 cm from the goal box. This suggests that the rat that experienced both food and shock will approach to about 120 cm but will stop there because at that point the tendency to avoid becomes stronger. This is just what happens in the laboratory. In other words, Brown's analysis predicts the hesitant, vacillating behavior that is actually observed. In an approach-avoidance situation we tend to waver, without resolving the conflict.

How can you change the point at which the rat stops and hesitates? There are two ways. First, you can increase its hunger. This will raise the approach gradient and move the point of hesitation closer to the goal box. Second, you can reduce the shock level. This will lower the avoidance gradient and move the point of hesitation closer to the goal box.

All well and good, you say. Now you know a lot about rats in harnesses, but what about people in conflict? It seems that Brown's analysis applies to our problems, too. For example, one pattern that is often observed among people living together is that they fight, break up, make up, fight, break up, make up, and so on. Their behavior resembles an approach-avoidance conflict. When they are living together (they are in the goal box), the avoidance tendency is stronger than the approach tendency. The only things they can see and think about are the negative aspects of the relationship. So they break up. But once they are apart, all they can see are the good aspects of the relationship (the approach gradient now is stronger than the avoidance gradient). So they get back together, only to be swung back the other way again, and so on. They are caught in an approach-avoidance conflict. People that manage to stay together despite conflicts presumably possess approach tendencies that outweigh their avoidance tendencies.

If vacillation is characteristic of the approach-avoidance conflict, what kinds of behavior would Brown predict in the other conflicts? The approach-approach situation is easily resolved. Once a step is made in either direction, toward either goal, the subject should continue to move in that direction as that tendency increases and the opposing approach tendency weakens. Once you decide to go out to the movie rather than study, movie-going should become more positive and studying less positive as you approach the movie.

According to Brown, the avoidance-avoidance situation is very difficult to resolve. The closer you move toward one unpleasant alternative, the worse it seems and the less obnoxious the alternative seems. So you turn and move toward the other alternative, only to have it become more obnoxious. You could sit at the dinner table staring at your spinach and thinking about going to bed all night long if your parents did not raise or lower a gradient somewhere.

Conflict is an important source of frustration as well as other unpleasant emotions—and conflicts are plentiful in life. In the next chapter, we will see what psychologists know about coping with unpleasant emotions, unruly motives, and maladaptive conflicts. We will also consider the highly important concept of emotion from a social psychological point of view in Chapters 19 and 20.

SUMMARY

1. Emotions are relatively uncontrollable feelings that affect our behavior.

2. Psychologists have focused on three aspects of the overall emotional event: the subjective experience, the observable behavior, and the physiological changes. Changes in these three aspects do not always correlate exactly.

3. Emotions are classified as pleasant or unpleasant and range from weak to strong. Some psychologists have attempted to identify a few basic emotions from which all others are derived.

4. Emotion can affect thought and vice versa.

5. Emotion can be defined as a complex sequence involving stimulus event, cognition, feeling, behavior, and effect.

6. Emotions and motives are closely related.

7. The autonomic nervous system is involved in many of the physiological changes that accompany an emotional event.

8. The sympathetic system of the autonomic system prepares the body for emergency action by increasing the body's energy resources. The parasympathetic system returns the body to normal when the need for emergency measures has passed.

9. The limbic system is also involved in emotion.

10. The James-Lange theory states that external stimuli create physical changes within us. These physiological changes then stimulate the sensations of emotion. According to this view we are sad because we cry and afraid because we tremble.

11. The facial feedback hypothesis supports the James-Lange theory.

12. The Cannon-Bard theory states that external stimuli arouse the thalamus which, in turn, simultaneously triggers the physiological changes associated with emotion and stimulates the experience of emotion by sending messages to the cerebral cortex.

13. Cognitive theory states that our interpretation of internal arousal will be affected by what we observe

going on around us, especially if we have no good explanation for why we feel the way we do.

14. Opponent-process theory holds that emotional states, both positive and negative, tend to be followed by the opposite state.

15. Sociobiological theory states that all emotions have an evolutionary history and that each has survived because it is adaptive.

16. We probably express emotions through both innate and learned mechanisms.

17. Nonverbal communication is one form of "language" that is very important in the expression of emotion. Positive and negative emotions may be expressed by a wide variety of movements, postures, and gestures.

18. Eye contact is an important form of nonverbal communication.

19. Personal space refers to the "bubble" of space surrounding each of us that we do not like to have invaded.

20. Double-edged messages simultaneously convey conflicting positive and negative emotions. Often, words convey one feeling while actions convey another, conflicting feeling.

21. Sarcasm refers to a positive message delivered in a negative tone. Negative messages may also be conveyed in a positive tone.

22. In a face-to-face communication, differential amounts of emotion may be conveyed by facial expression, tone of voice, and content of speech.

23. Anxiety, a vague feeling of dread and apprehension, may be caused by separation from support, antici-

pation of punishment, inner conflicts, uncertainty, or some combination of these influences.

24. Treating anxiety with drugs is big business.

25. Anxiety can hinder the performance of complex tasks and help in the performance of simple tasks.

26. Frustration, the unpleasant feeling that results when motives are blocked, may be caused by delay of reward, physical obstacles, social and legal obstacles, and personal limitations.

27. Conflict refers to situations where two or more incompatible motives are aroused.

28. In an approach-approach conflict, we want to reach two goals at once but cannot because reaching one denies the other.

29. In an avoidance-avoidance conflict, the only way we can avoid one unpleasant alternative is to choose the other unpleasant alternative.

30. In an approach-avoidance conflict, a single goal has both positive and negative attributes.

31. The tendency to approach an attractive situation increases as the distance to the goal is decreased. The tendency to avoid a punishing situation increases as the distance from that situation is decreased. The avoidance gradient is steeper than the approach gradient.

32. Animals will often vacillate some distance from the reward-punishment situation in approach-avoidance conditions. The avoidance-avoidance situation also leads to much wavering. The approach-approach conflict usually is resolved once movement toward one goal begins.

KEY TERMS

anxiety
approach-approach conflict
approach-avoidance conflict
approach gradient
avoidance-avoidance conflict
avoidance gradient
Cannon-Bard theory

double-edged messages
emotion
eye contact
facial feedback hypothesis
frustration
James-Lange hypothesis

limbic system
nonverbal communication
opponent-process theory
personal space
psychosomatic
tranquilizers

ADDITIONAL READING

Carlson, N. R. (1986) *Physiology of behavior.* Boston: Allyn and Bacon.
This text contains excellent sections on the physiology of mental illness.

Plutchik, R., & Kellerman, H. (1980) *Emotion: Theory, research, and experience.* New York: Academic Press.

This text offers a thoughtful exploration of the sociobiological, physiological, and dynamic approaches to emotion.

Tavris, C. (1983) *Anger: The misunderstood emotion.* New York: Simon & Schuster.
This book is another superior treatment of aggression, especially in its coverage of the myths surrounding anger.

II Exploring Everyday Emotions and Motives

Motives and emotions aid us in the struggle to survive. Without a hunger drive, we would never get around to eating. Without fear, our lives might well end at an early age. Without frustration, we might never be motivated to overcome any obstacles at all. Without sexual urges, the species would not survive.

THE UPS AND DOWNS OF MOTIVATION

Our motives and emotions can obviously give us a lot of trouble, too. In fact, much of what is commonly called unhappiness can be traced to difficulties we are having in coping with our emotions and drives. Obviously, there are many different ways our emotions and motives can cause unhappiness. Normal needs and urges may be frustrated. For example, sexual frustration leads to considerable distress. We may also be unhappy if we perceive our emotions and drives as being too weak. If we cannot seem to stay interested in our studies, we may feel inadequate and insecure. Or our needs may be too strong. Obesity, a common source of distress, can result from an uncontrollable degree of hunger. Our emotions may be strongly negative. If too many things go wrong all at once, severe depression can affect us all. If the depression becomes too strong, it can even lead to suicide. In other words, while emotions and motives help us survive, they can also make us unhappy in many different ways.

We will look first at two specific ways in which motives and emotions may cause problems in our lives. Then we will discuss some of the things psychologists have learned about dealing with these negative, unwanted aspects of our emotional and motivational makeup.

Can We Be Too Motivated?

One of the clearest demonstrations of how motivation can cause difficulties in our lives involves the *Yerkes-Dodson principle*. Yerkes and Dodson (1908) and others conducted a long series of experiments that showed that the most effective level of arousal will depend on the difficulty of the task. Arousal is often viewed as one facet of the complex concept of motivation. If a task is simple, a high level of arousal will lead to the best performance. But if the task is difficult, high levels of arousal will be disruptive, while lower levels of arousal will lead to maximum performance (see Figure 11–1).

This principle has important implications for everyday life. For instance, if you are highly aroused and motivated to beat your roommate at a game of chess, your performance may suffer because of your high level of motivation. It would be better if you were a bit calmer and less aroused. The Yerkes-Dodson principle suggests that there is such a thing as being too motivated, particularly when the task at hand is a difficult one.

As the task becomes easier, higher levels of motivation become more effective. If you have a job stuffing envelopes, you will need a higher level of motivation to perform at your most efficient level. Finishing this boring job quickly so that you can do something interesting may be the best motivation in this case.

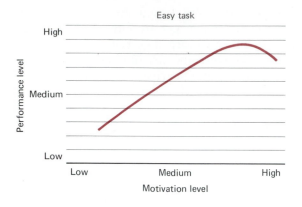

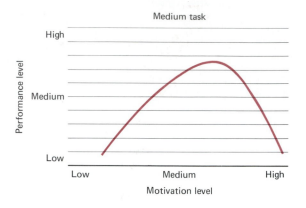

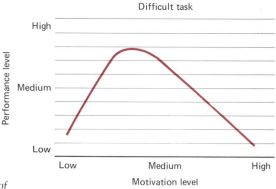

FIGURE 11–1 The Yerkes-Dodson Principle   *High levels of motivation yield the highest performance with easy tasks, but with difficult tasks, low levels of motivation yield the highest levels of performance.*

What Does Anxiety Do to Learning?

As a second concrete example of the way emotions can create difficulties for us, let us look at the relationship between anxiety and learning. If you are anxious, how will that anxiety affect your ability to learn in your classes? In other words, does anxiety help you by driving you on, or does it hurt you by disrupting your efforts to learn?

Again, as was the case with the general level of motivation, the answer involves the level of task difficulty. When the task is difficult, low-anxiety subjects tend to do better than high-anxiety subjects. When the task is very simple, high-anxiety subjects may do better than low-anxiety subjects (O'Neil, Spielberger, & Hansen, 1969).

Anxiety level is usually assessed by means of a carefully constructed questionnaire that asks about subjective feelings of worry and tenseness as well as by estimates of perspiration and heartbeat.

Anxiety and College Performance

What does all of this have to do with you? Very bluntly, it could mean a great deal in terms of your success or failure in college. Our best guess is that if you are highly anxious, you will be achieving at a lower level than an equally intelligent but nonanxious fellow student. The tasks required of you at college are probably hard enough so that high anxiety will interfere with learning. In other words, your anxiety may be limiting your ability to perform.

FIGURE 11–2   Levels of
Scholastic Aptitude and
Anxiety Levels   *At medium
levels of scholastic aptitude, low-
anxiety students do better than
high-anxiety students in college.
At extremely high and low levels of
aptitude, anxiety makes no
difference.* (After Spielberger, 1962)

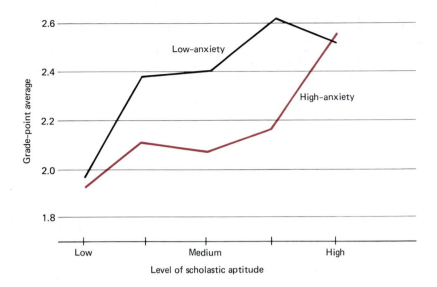

Spielberger (1962) has presented evidence that supports this idea.
He compared the average grades of high- and low-anxiety subjects
across several levels of scholastic ability (see Figure 11–2). He found
that at high and low levels of scholastic ability (as indicated by College Board scores) anxiety level did not make much difference. But at
intermediate levels of scholastic ability, where most students fall, the
low-anxiety subjects did significantly better than high-anxiety subjects. The average grades of low-anxiety students were higher than
those of high-anxiety students in the middle range.

Motivations and emotions can make a lot of trouble for us. We
know this by observing and experiencing the sometimes crippling effects of motivation and emotion in our lives. We have also been able
to demonstrate their adverse effects in tightly controlled laboratory
experiments. Given this knowledge, it would be wise to consider
what is known about controlling and alleviating these unwanted effects. Therefore, we will look at what psychologists have learned
about how we can cope with undesirable emotional and motivational
effects and their impact on our lives.

Please remember that we are dealing here with normal, everyday
emotional and motivational problems. Obviously, emotional disturbances can be very severe and may in some cases even lead to what
is generally known as mental illness. But such extreme difficulties will
not be considered in the present chapter. They will be taken up in
detail in Chapter 17.

COPING WITH ANXIETY

Since it appears to be such a pervasive and undesirable emotional
effect, we will deal first with anxiety. We have already seen in Chapter 10 that anxiety can be defined as a vague, unpleasant feeling accompanied by a sense of foreboding and dread. We know that factors
such as uncertainty about the future and internal conflicts can stimulate the feeling, and of course we know that anxiety is unpleasant
and disruptive. But what do we know about reducing, eliminating, or
at least dealing with this unpleasant sensation?

TABLE 11–1   Some Symptoms of Anxiety

Shortness of breath

Stomach problems

Sweating

Diarrhea or constipation

Irregular breathing

Jumpiness

Shallow breath

Muscle twitching

Muscle tension

Cold fingers and toes

Rapid heartbeat

Tiredness

Irritability

Headache

In Chapter 8 we discussed systematic desensitization as a means of ridding ourselves of phobias or irrational fears and in Chapters 5 and 8 we discussed biofeedback as a technique for controlling our so-called involuntary behaviors. In this section we want to discuss some additional techniques that are better suited to normal, everyday, unspecified anxiety and tension.

The Symptoms

Before we take up specific techniques for reducing anxiety, some of them planned and some unconscious, let us look at the symptoms that might lead us to try one or more of these methods. Table 11–1 lists the most common symptoms of tension and anxiety. If you find yourself trying to cope with several of these symptoms regularly, you are probably anxious and tense and might want to consider the following methods for reducing these unpleasant symptoms. (These same symptoms sometimes reflect underlying physical ailments, so if you suspect something is wrong with you, see your doctor.)

Autohypnosis

If you feel you are tense and anxious, consider the tension-relieving technique called *autohypnosis*, as outlined by Holland and Tarlow (1980):

Autohypnosis, or hypnotizing yourself, is not something magical. You do not become a robot, lose your consciousness, or feel weird. In fact, you may have hypnotized yourself before and not have been aware of it. You recover from the hypnotic effect naturally, in the course of a few minutes, feeling refreshed. You do not have to worry about how you will "come out of it"—this is automatic. If you put yourself "under," you will wake in a few moments without help. Try these simple steps:

Step 1. Find a soft, comfortable chair in a very quiet room. Arrange the chair so that it is facing a blank wall at a distance of five to ten feet. Place a thumbtack in the wall about a foot above your eye level when you are seated in the chair.

Step 2. Sit in the chair, staring fixedly at the tack while keeping your head level. Breathe regularly, slowly, and deeply, counting backwards with each breath from ten to one. Do not permit your eyes to move from the tack.

Step 3. When you reach *one*, continue staring at the tack. As you do so, imagine that your arms and legs are becoming increasingly heavy; do not move your arms and legs—imagine what it would feel like if they were too heavy to move.

Step 4. Continue staring fixedly at the tack. Now imagine that your eyelids are becoming increasingly heavy. Imagine that they are heavier and heavier. Imagine that they have lead weights attached to them. Think to yourself that it is hard to keep your eyes open, that they want desperately to close. At this point, let your eyes close (you may find that they will "close by themselves").

Step 5. Begin counting backwards from ten as you breathe deeply and slowly with your eyes closed. Focus your attention on your breath—imagine that your breath is visible, that it is purple clouds of mist or smoke, and that you are watching it go slowly in and out. Try to ignore all sensations except those associated with breathing. Do not move or attend to any part of your body.

Step 6. As you reach *one* in your counting, imagine yourself lying back in a tub of hot water; your head is relaxing comfortably and your body is floating gently in the warm water. Try to feel the warmth of the water on your skin. Tell yourself to go limp, to float, to relax completely. Continue to breathe deeply and slowly. Continue this stage for as long as you can focus on floating; if your mind begins to wander, to worry, to plan, or remember—stop, open your eyes, and get up. (pp. 79–80)

Hypnosis was discussed in detail in Chapter 4, so autohypnosis should not seem entirely new to you. The present analysis of autohypnosis involves an extension of the basic principles of hypnosis presented earlier.

Relax, Relax

Often our anxiety and tension are magnified by our inability to relax our bodies. We are physically tense without even knowing it. The following steps for *progressive relaxation training*, outlined by Holland and Tarlow (1980), can sometimes relieve physical tension:

Allow yourself at least one-half hour for the session. Select a quiet room with a couch or bed in which you will not be disturbed. Loosen any tight-fitting clothing. Until you learn the procedure, you will want to sit up with the book in your lap so that you can read each step as you proceed. After you learn the method you may wish to go through the entire session lying down on the bed or couch with your eyes closed. The method is called "progressive" relaxation because it progressively relaxes the body in a step-by-step procedure, beginning with the hands, then moving up the arms to the head, then moving down the body to the feet.

Step 1. Clench your right fist and feel the tension sensations in your arm. Clench your fist even tighter, noticing the tightness and the tension in your arm muscles. Now, completely relax your arm, letting your fingers partially straighten out. Observe the difference in the way your arm muscles feel.

Step 2. Repeat Step 1, only clench your fist slowly and release it slowly until it is completely relaxed. Pay attention to the difference in the way your arm muscles feel when tensed or relaxed.

Step 3. Clench your left fist while keeping the rest of your body as relaxed as possible. Feel the tension sensations in your left arm. Clench your fist tighter, and then completely relax. Notice the difference in the way your arm muscles feel.

Step 4. Repeat Step 3 more slowly; then completely relax.

Step 5. Bend both arms at the elbows and tense your biceps—the muscles in the front part of your upper arms. Imagine that you are lifting a heavy weight toward your chin. Notice the tension in your biceps. Tense them tighter, and then relax them completely, letting your arms straighten out. Feel the difference between being tense and relaxed.

Step 6. Repeat Step 5 more slowly.

Step 7. Straighten both of your arms, pressing the backs of your hands down against your legs until you feel the tension in the backs of your arms. Now relax and notice the difference.

Step 8. Let your arms completely relax. Lay them at your sides. Search for any tension sensations in your arms and relax them for about a minute. Just let your arms go completely limp. Imagine that the tension is flowing down your arms and out your fingers, leaving your arms completely inactive, limp, and heavy.

Step 9. Wrinkle your forehead by raising up your eyebrows as high as you can. Feel the tension throughout your forehead. Then relax your forehead; notice how it smoothes out.

Step 10. Frown hard, feeling the tension between your eyes. Now, relax and feel the difference.

Step 11. Close your eyelids tightly. Notice the tension all over your eyelids and around your eyes. Relax, but keep your eyes closed.

Step 12. Firmly clench your teeth, closing your jaws tightly. Feel the tension sensations in your lower jaw and temples. Now, relax and let your lips part; let your jaw hang loose.

Step 13. Press your head back, feeling the tension in your neck. Turn your head left, then right, noticing the different tensions in the sides of your neck. Bend your chin toward your chest. Now let your neck completely relax.

Step 14. Shrug your shoulders. Feel the tension in the tops of your shoulders and the sides of your neck. Relax and notice the difference in the way the muscles feel.

Step 15. Let your shoulders go completely relaxed, and then your arms, neck, jaw, eyelids, and forehead. Imagine the tension from these areas flowing out, down your arms and out your fingers. Be limp and loose. Notice the absence of tension sensations in these areas.

Step 16. Inhale deeply, and notice the tension in your chest. Hold your breath and observe the sensations of tightness in your muscles. Now relax completely by exhaling.

Step 17. Breathe slowly and regularly, letting the air go out of your lungs when you relax. Do this while relaxing the rest of your body.

Step 18. Tighten your stomach muscles and keep them tight. Notice the tension in your abdomen. Relax and notice the difference.

Step 19. Arch your back, feeling the tension sensations on both sides of your spine. Relax everywhere except in this part of your spine. Now relax your back as well.

Step 20. Breathe regularly while relaxing your arms, head, neck, upper and lower torso. Relax any area in which you feel tension sensations. Let these areas be loose and inactive.

Step 21. Straighten your legs and press your heels down hard against the floor or bed. Feel the tension in your thighs and buttocks. Now relax and feel the difference.

Step 22. Keep your legs straight and point your toes by moving your feet away from your face. Notice the tension in the calves of your legs. Relax, letting your feet move back to a normal position.

Step 23. Move your feet in the opposite direction, back toward your face. Notice the tension in your shins at the front of your lower legs. Relax the muscles in your shins and calves, letting your feet be limp and loose.

Step 24. Relax your feet, legs, lower torso, upper torso, arms and hands, neck, jaw, and face. Relax everywhere, feeling no tension. Breathe slowly and deeply, imagining all tensions to flow down your body and out your toes, leaving your body inactive, limp, and heavy. Remain totally inactive for a few minutes.

Any of the steps in this sequence can be isolated and more fully explored and repeated in further sessions. Doing this will enable you to detect very small tensions in your muscles. The more aware you become of your muscle sensations, the easier it will be for you to relax. Your training might be helped by putting the steps of the procedure on tape so that you can follow them without interruption. You can also extend the training by following the steps while sitting or standing. This will help you gain further control over your ability to relax while in public.

Deep muscle relaxation is something you learn to do by practicing. The progressive relaxation procedure outlined here, with practice, will increase your awareness of and your ability to control nervous tension. But even the first time you try it, you will feel more relaxed. (pp. 81–83)

Learning to relax is also something that we have considered previously. In Chapter 4 we discussed meditation techniques and pointed out that some psychologists (for example, Benson, 1975) think of meditation as nothing more than a means to attain a state of relaxation. The field is filled with guides to the reduction of anxiety through relaxation. Two helpful references are Egan (1986) and Watson and Tharp (1985).

Getting at the Sources of Your Anxiety

Autohypnosis and progressive relaxation training can be helpful, but they treat the symptoms of anxiety rather than the causes. Ellis and Harper (1975) describe some positive, direct steps we can take to alleviate not just the symptoms of anxiety but the sources as well. Our interpretation of their steps goes as follows:

Step 1. Try to trace your feeling of anxiety to its source. What is it, exactly, that is making you anxious? Define what is bothering you. This is not an easy task. As we have noted, anxiety is a diffuse, unfocused kind of feeling and is difficult to trace, but if you focus on the feeling and spend some time mulling over the possible causes of it, you can sometimes track them down. You can at least narrow the possibilities to, say, your feelings about your course work, or your social life, or your sense of athletic inadequacy. Ellis and Harper feel that the closer we can come to identifying the underlying determinants of the feeling, the better our chances of reducing it will be. Many of us spend so much time worrying and feeling anxious that we do not take time to think about *why* we are anxious.

Step 2. Having partially or completely defined the problem area, quickly deal with actual, concrete problems. Leave the more difficult problems for later. You can deal with the real problems in two ways. First, if there is something that can be done about them, get up and *do* it. If you have been worrying about an examination, simply stop worrying and start studying. In short, take direct action to deal with the anxiety-producing problem. Second, if the problem is a real one, but it does not appear that you can do anything about it, try to stop worrying about it. Worrying is a complete waste of time if nothing can be done anyway. Suppose a relative is in the hospital, or suppose you have applied for an important job. Now, no one is saying you can stop worrying completely in situations such as these, but, more than likely, you can cut down on the worrying if you try.

Step 3. Now let us deal with our other anxieties, those associated with less concrete dangers. Ellis and Harper suggest that we *do the thing we fear.* If you are anxious about getting up in front of groups, they feel you should take definite steps to do just that. Take a course in public speaking, for instance. If you are anxious about meeting new people, go out and meet a lot of new people. By doing the things that you fear, you may well discover they are not nearly as frightening as you supposed.

Step 4. Tell yourself worrying will only make things worse. Worry feeds on itself. When you get worked up about it, you can really feel anxious. Worrying wastes your time. It denies you the energy and time to deal effectively with tangible problems. Once people are in the habit of worrying, they often think of new things to worry about. In short, you must convince yourself that worrying does not help, it just makes things worse.

Step 5. Do not exaggerate. We often tend to magnify our anxieties. When we tell others of our concerns, we fall into the trap of exaggerating so the listener will really appreciate the depth of our problems. When our minds are set and locked in on anxiety, we make things seem worse than they really are. We become incapable of listening to the rational words of others and unable to judge the true scope of our difficulties.

Step 6. Use a little distraction every now and then. If you find that you are sitting around worrying instead of studying, take a short break. Go to a movie. Unlock your mind from the anxiety channel and tune in to a television channel. We are not saying you should become an escapist, but if you find you are wearing yourself out with anxiety, do not be afraid to distract yourself temporarily.

Step 7. Do not be surprised if your anxieties return. They usually do. Do not be disappointed to discover, after feeling that you have finally beaten your anxieties, that they are creeping back in. Just get after them again.

Step 8. Do not be ashamed to admit that you are anxious. Almost everyone is, sooner or later, in one situation or another. (Try to name one person who has never been anxious about anything, ever.)

Unconscious Coping: The Defense Mechanisms

Sometimes we try to deal with anxiety without really being aware that we are doing so. We *unconsciously* try to dispel anxiety. The types of unconscious coping methods we will now discuss have often been called *defense mechanisms*. The term was developed by Sigmund Freud, who used it to describe our unconscious attempts to defend against anxiety. Since Freud's time the concept of defense mechanisms has come into popular use, and it now is used in many different contexts. Before we describe specific defense mechanisms we will outline the four basic characteristics of *all* defense mechanisms.

1. Defense mechanisms are *unconscious* in the sense that we are not aware of what we are doing to reduce anxiety.

2. Defense mechanisms all involve *self-deception;* we distort reality in order to feel less anxious.

3. Although defense mechanisms involve self-deception, they can give us time to get over difficult spots in our lives.

4. Even though they involve distortion of reality, defense mechanisms are very common methods of coping with anxiety. Everyone uses them to some extent, and in moderation they are relatively harmless ways of making our lives more pleasant. So do not worry excessively if you suddenly realize that you have been using many of the following defense mechanisms. Many people do so. It is when a person uses defense mechanisms as his *primary* means of dealing with the environment that we begin to wonder if he may be losing touch with reality.

Keeping these four points in mind as we go, let us look at some of the more common defense mechanisms.

Rationalization   Suppose you fail an important examination. Your failure makes you feel anxious. What can you do? You can say, "I didn't care about that examination anyway. Nobody can do well in that course!" Or you can say, "Thank goodness I failed that. Now I'm sure I belong in another field. It was a blessing in disguise." Either way, your anxiety level has probably been reduced because you have explained away your failure. By *rationalizing* the experience in this manner, you reduce the symptom (anxiety) without dealing with the cause (the failure). A student who cheats on an examination and feels anxious about it may rationalize by saying, "Everyone does it; if you don't cheat you will fall behind." A person who is not invited to a party and feels hurt by the snub can claim, "I wouldn't have gone anyway." After spending more money than we should have spent,

This student appears to be getting ready to cheat on an examination. She may rationalize her behavior by telling herself that everyone cheats.

we often say, "Well, if I had waited, the price would have gone up." When we rationalize, we reduce anxiety by saying we have not really been frustrated, or we have not really acted wrongly or foolishly. Clearly, it would be better if we never rationalized, but apparently we cannot stop this behavior; without even being aware that we are doing so, we make excuses for our actions.

Reaction Formation   Suppose, at last, that you have your own apartment. An elderly aunt who took care of you for years when you were a child calls and says she needs a home. You invite her to move in with you, because you love her and feel grateful for all she has done for you. But as the weeks pass, you find her presence more and more irritating. Without meaning to, she cramps your style. You begin to dislike her, secretly. Disliking her makes you feel guilty and anxious. What can you do?

In a **reaction formation**, we act in a manner that is just the *opposite* of what we are truly feeling. We defend against anxiety by acting as though there is no need to feel anxious. You may be overly kind to your aunt, showering her with attention and consideration, even though you are secretly irritated by her. Without being aware of it, we can reduce our anxiety by acting as though everything is just the opposite of what it really is. Once again, it would be healthier if we could face our problems rationally and accurately, but our defense mechanisms shift into action without our awareness.

Repression   Sometimes we merely block unpleasant or anxiety-producing thoughts from consciousness. Without knowing it, we banish the thoughts from our minds. At this very moment you may be **repressing** some very unpleasant thought, such as the desire to hurt someone, or the memory of some extremely embarrassing event in your past. If these thoughts became conscious, they would make you anxious.

Repression is an extremely controversial concept. How can we ever be sure something is being repressed? There is little hard experimental evidence for this mechanism, but the term is used widely in clinical work and often appears in case histories. **Suppression**, as distinct from repression, occurs when we *consciously* avoid thinking about something unpleasant. "I'm just not going to think about it, it's too disturbing." This is not a true defense mechanism because it involves conscious rather than unconscious attempts to defend against anxiety.

Projection   **Projection** is the tendency to see in others the undesirable traits and qualities that we possess. A person who is stingy may attribute the trait to others. "I'm not cheap! Everyone I know is pinching pennies these days!" Projection can reduce anxiety in several ways:

1. By assigning to others the qualities that make us anxious, we may not seem so bad to ourselves. If we see everyone else as extremely aggressive or dishonest, then by contrast, our own hos-

tility or dishonesty does not seem so bad; perhaps it even seems normal.

2. By projecting, we can justify some of our own actions. If we see the world as mean, then when we are mean to people we can always justify our own hostility by saying, "They'd do it to me if I gave them the chance."

Identification   Suppose a scrawny little boy lives in a neighborhood filled with tough kids organized into groups. The boy is quite anxious about his physical limitations and the possibility of getting beaten up. What can he do? He can *identify* with the tougher members of his neighborhood group by taking on some of their qualities. He may walk, talk, and act like them, and so delude himself into believing he shares some of their power. He can reduce his anxiety by pretending he is more powerful.

Bettelheim (1943) reports an extreme case of identification. During World War II, prisoners in German concentration camps began to identify with their captors. They imitated the cruel and brutal behavior of the guards who were inflicting inhuman treatment on them. Of course, identification need not be so extreme. A teenager who adopts some of the mannerisms of his or her favorite movie star is sharing in the success and power of the chosen idol by identifying with that individual.

Displacement   **Displacement** is the tendency to unleash pent-up impulses on alternative objects. If you are very angry with your boss or your spouse but feel direct aggression toward them would make you anxious, you may find alternative objects to attack. You may yell at other drivers in heavy traffic. You may "take it out on the kids." You may kick the dog or mow the lawn down to a stubble.

Sublimation   In displacement, we try to find a new object on which to vent our frustrated desires. In the related mechanism of **sublimation**, we try to transform the actual motive or urge into some more socially acceptable form. For example, aggressive impulses may be handled by becoming a football player, a prosecuting attorney, or a police officer.

Fine Lines

These are not the only available defense mechanisms. Table 11–2 lists some additional forms. As you may have noticed, many defense mechanisms are interrelated. For example, reaction formation may be viewed as one type of rationalization; the line between sublimation and displacement is also a fine one. Thus you should not be too impressed by these lists of defense mechanisms. What is important is that we do cope with anxiety, and we often do it without being aware of what we are doing.

Having reviewed anxiety, and both conscious coping and unconscious coping, we now will see what is known about coping with frustration.

TABLE 11–2   Additional Defense Mechanisms

Intellectualization   The tendency to deal with extremely emotional events in intellectual, abstract terms. If a close relative dies, we can avoid much of the pain by thinking about the fact that everyone's time must come, that death is natural and to be expected, and that the deceased is not suffering.

Fantasy escape   Avoiding anxiety by escaping into fantasy or by satisfying frustrated desires in fantasy is commonplace. If we are anxious about school, we can daydream. If we are frustrated sexually, we can arrange quite satisfactory romances in our minds.

Undoing   We can reduce anxiety by atoning for unethical acts or impulses. We can confess our sins in a repetitive, ritualistic manner, and thereby "undo" the offensive act.

Compensation   If we are anxious about failure in one area, we can pursue success in another area. If we feel anxious about failing in school, we can seek relief by excelling in sports, business, or some other endeavor.

Denial   Defending against anxiety-producing realities by failing to perceive or recognize them. We can deny being unfair to someone by claiming that we do not care what they say and that we have never been anything but polite to them.

COPING WITH FRUSTRATION

By now, the concept of *frustration* should be a familiar one. It refers to the unpleasant emotions we experience when we undergo motive blockage. As mentioned in Chapter 5, we all experience some frustration almost every day. How do we deal with this unpleasant experience? What can we do, and what do we do, to prevent or reduce frustration?

As was true of anxiety, there are some modes of dealing with frustration that are relatively unplanned and unconscious. There are also methods of coping with frustration that are conscious, assertive, and planned. In other words, when faced with frustration we sometimes act in an unplanned fashion, responding in a manner that may or may not be adaptive. But we also learn methods of coping with frustration that involve conscious effort on our part. In daily life, we often use both planned and unplanned methods at the same time.

Some Guidelines

What's the Problem? If we feel frustrated, we can take steps to relieve that unpleasant sensation. Many of them focus on identifying and reducing the frustrating situation.

1. The first step is to identify and define the motive (or motives) that is being frustrated. Why do you feel frustrated? What is it that you want but are not getting? Let us say you decide that you are not seeing enough of someone you are attracted to.

2. The next step is to determine what is causing the blockage. What is stopping you from being with your friend? Here you have to consider all types of possible obstacles. Is it because your friend works too late? Is it because your diverse interests keep the two of you apart? Or is it because your friend does not want to be with you that much? It could be a combination of several factors.

3. Once the obstacles are identified, you must determine what will remove them. Perhaps it is a matter of removing practical barriers—for instance, changing working hours. Perhaps it is a matter of changing your own responses—if you stop nagging about working late, your friend will want to be with you more. Perhaps it is a little bit of both.

Action Is Necessary   The important point to remember is that action is usually necessary to alleviate frustration. Just sitting there feeling grouchy does not help. Even though it may seem difficult, take action. The best way to determine which actions you should take is to outline carefully, step by step, what it is that you want but are not getting, what it is that is causing the blockage, and what actions may reduce the blockage. Then you can try out alternative actions. If one does not work, do not give up. Try another solution.

Blocking Yourself   People themselves are often the source of their own frustrations, without knowing it. We all tend to blame our frustrations on other people or external events. "He just won't listen to me." "People here are so unfriendly." "Lord knows I've tried, but they just don't seem to understand." Such statements imply that the blame lies not with the speaker, but with others. And yet the speaker may be causing the frustration without knowing it. People may not listen to us or may not be friendly toward us, because *we* are uninteresting, unfriendly, boring, or hostile without knowing it. We have to become sensitive to the effects we are having on other people. For example, suppose a woman spends much of her time frowning. We already know that this kind of nonverbal cue can communicate negative feeling. If this woman becomes aware of her frowning and practices smiling (a simple behavior change), she may find that people will react to her in a more positive fashion. Simple changes in our behavior, based on a growing awareness of how our actions affect others, can reduce our frustration noticeably. If we can become more aware of the defense mechanisms we have been unconsciously using, we can alter our behavior accordingly.

Anticipating Frustration   A little foresight can often save us from frustration. Do not walk into situations that you *know* are going to be frustrating. Try to arrange your future so that blocked motives will be minimized. Suppose you have been seeing someone fairly regularly and, although the evenings usually start out smoothly, they often end in an argument. Do not go the next time unless something is changed. Analyze the situation and take corrective action beforehand.

Assertiveness Training

People often feel frustrated because they sense that they are being used or pushed around by others. Psychologists have conducted a good deal of research that suggests that people can reduce this kind of frustration by becoming more assertive (Beidleman, 1981; Halama, 1976; Kirkland & Caughlin-Carver, 1982). This research has prompted

Being assertive involves maintaining good eye contact and a firm manner. Through assertiveness training we can learn to ask for what we deserve and to say no in appropriate situations.

a large number of *assertiveness-training* studies. Through various practice procedures and role-playing techniques, people can learn to say no where they formerly said yes. When someone asks you for your help, your time, or your money, what do you do? You often say yes, even though you want to say no. At times we all feel obligated or forced into agreeing to do something we do not want to do. Then we experience frustration. "I wish I could just stay here and watch the ball game, but I promised Arthur I would have dinner with him." Assertiveness training suggests that we can learn to say no politely but firmly. Try it. The next time someone asks you to do something you do not want to do, just say no in a pleasant, firm way. You will probably discover you feel better.

Of course, people make many legitimate demands on us. But sometimes their demands are unreasonable, and then we have every right to say no. If we have not developed the technique of saying no, we often end up doing a lot of things we do not want to do and should not have to do.

Essentially, assertiveness training is designed to help us protect our rights as an interpersonal communicator. Table 11–3 contains the interpersonal rights to which Grasha (1983) believes each of us is entitled.

Assertiveness training suggests that we can learn to be more assertive in asking for what we deserve, as well as in refusing to do what we should not be expected to do. Frustration can be avoided with either technique, as Table 11–4 explains. We will see some therapeutic uses of assertiveness training in Chapter 18.

Coping with Unsolvable Problems

We have been speaking about problems that we can solve. In many cases, frustration can be reduced or eliminated by direct, assertive problem-solving methods. But sometimes it cannot. Sometimes there is nothing we can do to improve or change the situation. No matter

TABLE 11–3   A List of Interpersonal Rights

In interpersonal interactions each of us has the following rights:

1. The right to say no to a request
2. The right not to give other people reasons for every action we take
3. The right to stop others from making excessive demands on us
4. The right to ask other people to listen to our point of view when we speak to them
5. The right to ask other people to correct errors they made that affect us
6. The right to change our minds
7. The right to ask other people to compromise rather than get only what they want
8. The right to ask other individuals to do things for us
9. The right to persist in making a request if people do not listen the first time
10. The right to be alone if we wish
11. The right to maintain our dignity in relationships
12. The right to evaluate our own behaviors and not just listen to evaluations that others offer
13. The right to make mistakes and accept responsibility for them
14. The right to avoid manipulation by other people
15. The right to pick our own friends without consulting our parents, peers, or anyone else
16. The right to let other people know how we are feeling
17. The right to ask that others treat us with respect
18. The right to request that someone do us a favor
19. The right to take actions that protect us from racial, sexual, or ethnic discrimination
20. The right to choose with whom and when we will have sexual relations
21. The right to follow our conscience in making decisions, even though the decisions may be unpopular with other people
22. The right to resist demands that we think and act in a certain way

Source: After Grasha, 1983.

how hard we study, we cannot get into graduate school. No matter how hard we try, we cannot win over the person we find most attractive. No matter how hard we campaign, we lose every election. What can we do in these situations? How do we handle this sort of frustration? The first thing to do is to realize that this type of frustration is inevitable. No one gets through life without some of it. Just realizing that frustration is an integral part of life can sometimes go a long way toward reducing its bite. But what else can we do?

Increasing Frustration Tolerance   Apparently we can increase our tolerance of frustration through special training procedures. Keister and Updegraff (1937) found that school-age children could be taught

TABLE 11–4 Steps in Assertiveness Training

1. Examine your interactions. Are there situations that you need to handle more assertively? Do you at times hold opinions and feelings within you for fear of what would happen if you expressed them? Do you occasionally blow your cool and lash out angrily at others? Studying your interactions is easier if you keep a diary for a week or longer, recording the situations where you acted timidly, those where you were aggressive, and those that you handled assertively.

2. Select those interactions where it would be to your benefit to be more assertive. They may include situations in which you were overly polite, overly apologetic, or too timid, allowing others to take advantage of you, and at the same time you harbored feelings of resentment, anger, embarrassment, fear, or self-criticism for not having the courage to express yourself. Overly aggressive interactions in which you exploded in anger or walked over others also need to be handled differently. For *each* set of nonassertive or aggressive interactions, you can become more assertive, as shown in the next steps.

3. Concentrate on a specific incident in the past. Close your eyes for a few minutes and vividly imagine the details, including what you and the other person said, and how you felt at the time and afterward.

4. Write down and review your responses. Ask yourself the following questions to determine how you presented yourself:
   a. *Eye contact.* Did you look directly at the other person, in a relaxed, steady gaze? Looking down or away suggests a lack of self-confidence. Glaring is an aggressive response.
   b. *Gestures.* Were your gestures appropriate, free flowing, relaxed, and used effectively to emphasize your messages? Awkward stiffness suggests nervousness; other gestures (such as an angry fist) signal an aggressive reaction.
   c. *Body posture.* Did you show the importance of your message by directly facing the other person, by leaning toward that person, by holding your head erect, and by sitting or standing appropriately close?
   d. *Facial expression.* Did your facial expression show a stern, firm pose consistent with an assertive response?
   e. *Voice tone and volume.* Was your response stated in a firm, conversational tone? Shouting may suggest anger. Speaking softly suggests shyness, and a cracking voice suggests nervousness. Tape recording and listening to one's voice is a way to practice increasing or decreasing the volume.
   f. *Speech fluency.* Did your speech flow smoothly, clearly, and slowly? Rapid speech or hesitation in speaking suggests nervousness. Tape assertive responses before you try them out in problem situations, so you can practice and improve your fluency.
   g. *Timing.* Were your verbal reactions to a problem situation stated at a time closest to the incident that would appropriately permit you and the other person time to review the incident? Generally, spontaneous expressions are the best, but certain situations should be handled at a later time—for example, challenging some of your boss's erroneous statements in private rather than in front of a group he or she is making a presentation to.
   h. *Message content.* For a problem situation, which of your responses were nonassertive or aggressive, and which were assertive? Study the content and consider why you responded in a nonassertive or aggressive style.

5. Observe one or more effective models. Watch the verbal and nonverbal approaches that are assertively used to handle the types of interactions

with which you have been having problems. Compare the consequences between their approach and yours. If possible, discuss their approach and their feelings about using it.

6. Make a list of various alternative approaches for being more assertive.

7. Close your eyes and visualize yourself using each of the above alternative approaches. For each approach, think through what the full set of interactions would be, along with the consequences. Select an approach, or combination of approaches, that you believe will be most effective for you to use. Through imagery, practice this approach until you feel comfortable that it will work for you.

8. Role-play the approach with someone else, perhaps a friend or counselor. If certain segments of your approach appear clumsy, awkward, timid, or aggressive, practice modifications until you become comfortable with the approach. Obtain feedback from the other person as to the strengths and shortcomings of your approach. Compare your interactions to the guidelines for verbal and nonverbal assertive behavior in Step 4. It may be useful for the other person to role-play one or more assertive strategies, which you would then practice by reversing roles.

9. Repeat Steps 7 and 8 until you develop an assertive approach that you are comfortable with and believe will work best for you.

10. Use your approach in a real-life situation. The previous steps are designed to prepare you for the real event. Expect to be somewhat anxious when you first try to be assertive. If you are still too fearful of attempting to be assertive, repeat Steps 5 through 8. For those few individuals who fail to develop the needed confidence to try out being assertive, professional counseling is advised—expressing yourself and effective interactions with others are essential for personal happiness.

11. Reflect on the effectiveness of your effort. Did you "keep your cool"? Consider the nonverbal and verbal guidelines for assertive behavior discussed in Step 4; what components of your responses were assertive, aggressive, and nonassertive? What were the consequences of your effort? How did you feel after trying out this new set of interactions?

12. Expect some success with your early efforts, but not complete personal satisfaction. Personal growth and interacting more effectively with others are components of a continual learning process.

Source: After Zastrow & Chang, 1977.

---

to be more tolerant of frustration. When faced with difficult situations, the children were encouraged to deal with problems in a step-by-step manner. They were trained to engage in constructive problem solving rather than dissolving in tears of frustration the minute difficulties showed up. Adults, too, can learn to handle frustration by approaching problems in a calmer, more constructive manner and by dealing with them one step at a time rather than trying to solve the whole problem at once.

Lowering the Level of Aspiration   One major source of frustration in this culture has to do with our level of aspiration. We expect to accomplish so much and acquire so much that we are asking for frustration (Houston, 1981). If we can learn to expect a little less and learn that life can be quite pleasant with a little less, all sorts of frustration can be avoided. It is almost heresy, in this success-oriented culture, to suggest that we might all settle for a little less, but, without doubt, such an attitude can reduce frustration.

Lowering the level of aspiration is particularly relevant when you consider that the ladder of success is endless. Chafetz (1974) argues that most people in our society are doomed to failure because there is always one more step to be taken toward success. Sooner or later we reach the end of our abilities and feel frustration because we want to make additional progress toward success, but we cannot. Business executives, teachers, entertainers, athletes, and people in just about every other imaginable field experience this same sense of frustration. Those near the top may be just as frustrated as those near the bottom. One sure way to avoid this dilemma is to set a limit on what you want to achieve. Another is to pace yourself as you achieve. Enough is enough; there is more to life than scrambling endlessly up one more step on the ladder to success.

We do not mean to imply that you should now slam this book shut and forget about your studies because it is all hopeless anyway. Clearly, there are many levels of achievement we can attain and enjoy through good old hard work. It is all a matter of degree; what most of us thrive on is a level of aspiration that challenges us to do our best but does not defeat us.

AGGRESSION

One of the most common consequences of frustration is a sense of anger and aggressiveness. We have all experienced it. Late for an appointment, trapped in traffic, we will often rant and rage at the other drivers, at the stupidity of the traffic department, at ourselves, and at life in general. If one child takes a toy away from another, the victim may attack the thief. *Aggression* is not necessarily the only reaction we have to frustration, but it is a strong and very common one.

Adaptive versus Maladaptive Aggression

Obviously, aggression in response to frustration can occasionally be adaptive, but at other times it can also be extremely unprofitable. If a child is constantly bullied by the members of his neighborhood group, an aggressive reaction may be helpful. The child may gain respect among his peers and lessen the chances of intolerable treatment in the future. But if an employee of a large corporation has been turned down repeatedly for a raise, an aggressive response may not help at all. Screaming and shouting threats outside the boss's door may get the employee fired or arrested, but it will never get him a raise.

Displaced Aggression

Although aggressive behavior can sometimes lead to success, most of us do not charge around being aggressive whenever we feel frustrated. We have developed various indirect ways of expressing our pent-up feelings when directing those impulses toward the frustrating obstacle would be dangerous. We often pick a weaker, less dangerous substitute object and vent our anger on it. For example, the frustrated employee snaps at his family rather than the frustrating boss. Hitler and the Nazis blamed the Jews for all of their frustrations, using them as scapegoats. A young child will be cruel to her kitten rather than express her anger toward her mother. (We have already discussed this technique as displacement, a defense mechanism.)

Miller and Bugelski (1948) conducted an experiment that shows *displacement* in action. Some of the boys attending a summer camp were required to finish a very boring examination. The test took so long that the boys missed their weekly movie. An attitude survey, administered both before and after the test, indicated greater unfriendliness toward Japanese and toward Mexicans following the frustrating test. But none of the children directed their hostility toward the testers, who were the true source of their frustration. They displaced the aggression and directed it toward distant, general groups of people who had done them no harm.

Types of Aggression

One of the fascinating things about the study of aggression is that there are many different forms of this behavior. Moyer (1968) has pointed out that to fully understand aggression we must pay attention to the following forms, as outlined by Houston (1985):

1. *Predation.*   Predation refers to the attack made by a predator upon its prey.

2. *Intermale Aggression.*   Rivalry or intermale aggression is aggression triggered by a strange male of the same species. It may be genetically determined.

3. *Fear-induced Aggression.*   Fear-induced aggression is aggression that occurs when an animal experiences fear upon being surprised or trapped.

4. *Territorial Aggression.*   Territorial aggression refers to the tendency for animals to drive intruders out of their area. The

Bighorn rams are one of many animal species that engage in aggressive behaviors. This particular encounter may be characterized as either intermale or territorial aggression.

Fear-induced aggression occurs when an animal is surprised or trapped.

"owner" of the territory is more likely to stand and fight than the intruder.

5. *Irritable Aggression.* Aggression that is not preceded by attempts to escape is referred to as irritable aggression. Thus you may find that if you do nothing more than approach a strange dog in a friendly manner, the animal may snap at you. Or someone in the office may be grouchy and critical when you are trying to be friendly. Moyer thinks that stress, in any form, may increase this kind of aggression. When the trip to the beach begins, the whole family is cheerful, but by 5 P.M., when the family is tired, sunburned, and caught in traffic, tempers may flare.

6. *Instrumental Aggression.* Instrumental aggression is aggression that has been learned because it has paid off or has been reinforced in the past. It is not based on feelings, but on reinforcement. A person may beat his dog, not because he wants to hurt the animal, but because he has learned that he can control its behavior by hurting it. Hired killers may kill, not always for the thrill of it, but because the pay is good.

7. *Sex-related Aggression.* Moyer identifies sex-related aggression as aggression characterized by beatings, rape, and other assorted nasty acts. Although he acknowledges that little is known about this form of aggression, in spite of its social significance, he feels that it may well be a distinct form of hostility.

Innate Aggression?

Many investigators have proposed that aggression is innately determined. Freud, for example, felt that aggressive impulses build up within us and must be expressed in one way or another. Modern ethologists argue that animals are innately aggressive and that aggression is a survival-related pattern of behavior that is built into the organism (Eibl-Eibesfeldt, 1970; Lorenz, 1968). According to the ethologists, aggressive behavior is adaptive because it ensures that the strongest males will reproduce, it provides a food supply, and it protects the species against external dangers.

It seems clear that genetics is at least somewhat involved in aggression. For example, it has been shown many times that certain species, such as rats, chickens, and dogs, can be bred for violence and fighting ability (McLearn, 1969). To produce a violent strain, the breeder merely mates the most aggressive members of a given population. Genetics seems to play a role in human aggression, too, although the specific mechanisms are not yet well understood (Mednick, 1985; Mednick, Pollack, Volavka, & Gabrielli, 1982).

It is also clear that hormones play an important part in animal aggression, as the following quote from Kalat (1984) reveals:

> Much evidence points to an important role of the sex hormones in animal aggression (Goldstein, 1974; Moyer, 1974). Many species do little or no serious fighting before puberty. Fighting occurs mostly during the reproductive season when hormone levels are at their peak. As with sexual behavior . . . , androgen has both organizing and activating effects on aggressive behavior. A male rodent castrated in adulthood engages in little fighting; either androgen or estrogen injections can restore aggressive behavior (Brain, 1979). However, a male castrated during an early critical period engages in little fighting as an adult, even if it is given hormone injections in adulthood. If a female is given androgen injections during the critical period, her later aggressiveness is increased, particularly if she is given androgen injections again in adulthood (Moyer, 1974). (p. 312)

Learned Aggression?

While it is clear that genetic and hormonal factors play an important role in aggressive behavior, the role of learning and experience in the production of aggression also must be considered. Is aggressiveness innate, learned, or both? Scientists have been debating this issue for years. The upshot of the argument seems to be that experience is also an important determinant of aggressiveness. The accumulating evidence is just too strong to deny that learning and experience can affect aggression.

Bandura (1973, 1977) reports studies in which some nursery-school children saw films of children making aggressive attacks on a large inflated doll. Other children saw adults attack the doll in the classroom. Control children watched either nonaggressive films and models, or no films and models at all. All the children were then observed as they interacted with the same doll. As Figure 11–3 shows, the children viewing the different aggressive acts toward the doll all aggressed toward the doll more than the control children did. It seems that children will imitate aggressive behavior, whether they witness it being enacted by an actual person or on film.

In short, the available data suggest that if we are reinforced or rewarded for being aggressive, we will use aggression as a means of coping with the world. In addition, aggressive behavior may be established through a process of modeling or imitation, which we discussed in Chapter 5.

FIGURE 11–3   Modeled
Aggression   *Observing either
live or filmed models of aggressive
behavior increases the amount of
aggressive behavior displayed by
children.* (After Bandura, 1973)

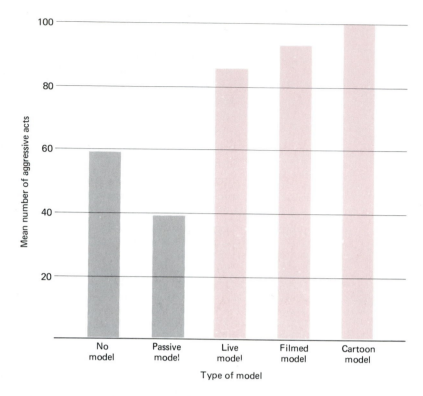

What do such studies tell us about violence in movies and on television? Does it have anything to do with violence in everyday life? People in the entertainment industry have tried to persuade us that television violence is beneficial. They claim that we can work off our aggressive impulses in a harmless manner by watching all kinds of violence on the tube. But some of the accumulating experimental evidence supports a different conclusion.

Steuer, Applefield, and Smith (1971) report that if children watch aggressive cartoons, they will be more aggressive in their daily lives than will children who have watched nonaggressive cartoons. A growing number of studies are showing that there may well be a relationship between violence and television fare, especially among young children (Freedman, 1984; Huesmann, Lagerspetz, & Eron, 1984; Singer, 1984). But even adults can be affected by watching television and movie violence. On several occasions, adults have copied criminal methods and actual violent crimes after seeing them depicted in movies and on television (Mankiewicz & Swerdlow, 1977). We will explore this topic in more detail in Chapter 20.

Despite this evidence, we should keep in mind that this issue is far from resolved. After a detailed review of the literature, Freedman, Sears, and Carlsmith (1981) conclude that "there is no good evidence yet that media violence contributes to violence and crime in our society" (p. 280).

The Control of Aggression

The control of aggression would certainly seem to be an important goal of society. Obviously, when one considers the prevalence of war and crime in the world, we must confess that we have not been very successful in attaining this goal. Nevertheless, some efforts to solve this problem have been made. Because there are so many types of aggression, it is not surprising to find that the problem of the control of aggression has been attacked from several angles. Baron and Byrne (1984) have outlined the following four techniques:

1. *Punishment*   Common sense suggests that either punishing aggressors for their violent behavior or simply threatening to do so may be an effective means of deterring such actions. On the basis of this belief, most societies have established severe penalties for aggressive crimes such as murder, rape, and assault. . . . In order for it to operate successfully, however, several conditions must be met. First, ***punishment*** must follow the objectionable behavior immediately, or at least very quickly. Second, it must be of sufficient magnitude to be aversive to the recipient. And third, there must be a clear contingency between the individual's behavior and punishment.

2. *Catharsis*   Suppose that one day you are strongly angered by your boss: she criticizes you harshly for something that was not your fault. After she leaves, you pick up the morning newspaper and tear it into small irregular shreds. Would this behavior make you feel better? And would it reduce your desire to "get even" with your boss in some manner? According to the famous ***catharsis hypothesis***, the answer to both questions is "yes." Briefly, this view suggests that providing angry individuals with the opportunity to "blow off steam" through vigorous but nonharmful actions will (1) reduce their level of arousal and (2) lower their tendencies to engage in overt acts of aggression. Both of these suggestions have enjoyed widespread acceptance for a number of years. At present, though, neither is strongly supported by available research evidence (Tavris, 1982).

3. *Exposure to nonaggressive models*   If exposure to aggressive models in films or on TV can induce heightened aggression among viewers, it seems only reasonable to expect that parallel exposure to nonaggressive models might produce opposite effects. That is, witnessing the actions of persons who demonstrate or urge restraint even in the face of strong provocation might serve to reduce the level of aggression shown by observers. That this is indeed the case is suggested by the findings of several experiments (Baron, 1972; Donnerstein & Donnerstein, 1976). In these studies, individuals exposed to the actions of nonaggressive models later demonstrated lower levels of aggression than persons not exposed to such models.

4. *Incompatible responses*   A final approach to the control of aggression rests upon the following basic principle. All organisms (including human beings) are incapable of engaging in two ***incompatible responses*** at once. For example, it is impossible both to daydream and balance your checkbook. Similarly, it is difficult (if not impossible) to feel depressed and elated at once. Extending this principle to the control of aggression, it seems possible that such harmful behavior can be reduced through the induction (among potential aggressors) of responses incompatible either with overt aggression itself or with the emotion of anger. And in fact, a growing body of research evidence suggests that this is the case. When angry individuals are induced to experience emotional states incompatible with anger or overt aggression, such as *empathy, mild sexual arousal,* or *humor,* they do show reduced levels of aggression. (pp. 352–59)

HELPLESSNESS AND DEPRESSION

We have been speaking of relatively successful modes of dealing with frustration. Even aggression can be adaptive. But sometimes our reactions to frustration may become problems in and of themselves.

Then we are faced with the problem not only of dealing with frustration itself, but also of trying to cope with our reactions to frustration as well. We will look next at two of these less desirable reactions, helplessness and depression.

Learned Helplessness

If frustrated repeatedly, and without any chance of avoiding unpleasant circumstances, both animals and humans will become helpless, hopeless, and often depressed. For example, Maier and Seligman (1976) and Peterson and Seligman (1984) have summarized a good deal of research that suggests that when animals are subjected to a series of inescapable shocks some hours before attempting to learn an avoidance response, these animals will perform very poorly when finally given the opportunity to learn to escape the shock. They appear without "hope" and do not even try to escape.

Learned helplessness has also been demonstrated with humans in the laboratory. Hiroto (1974) showed that if humans are subjected to an unavoidable loud noise, when they are given a chance to learn to stop that noise, they will fail to acquire the simple solution. They had learned to believe that anything they did would be unsuccessful. In an early study, Strassman, Thaler, and Schein (1956) reported that prisoners of war often became listless, apathetic, and detached in the face of continuous, unavoidable pain and punishment if they felt that no action on their part would change their state of helplessness.

A sense of helplessness, leading to an inability to respond effectively, is certainly part of everyday life. Many people who suffer a series of defeats will give up or quit trying even though continued effort might lead to success. Students become discouraged in school and graduates become discouraged in the job market. Many people feel they are in a rut but seem incapable of doing anything about it. In short, continuing frustration can lead people to believe that things are hopeless and that any responses they make will not do any good anyway.

Reversing Depression

Seligman (1977) has proposed that *depression* has a lot in common with learned helplessness. According to Seligman, we feel depressed when we feel our responses will not help us. We lose hope and do not feel like effective people. Table 11–5 contains a list of the similarities that Seligman perceives between depression and learned helplessness.

For the sake of argument, let us assume that Seligman is correct and that depression is a condition similar to learned helplessness. How do we go about reversing it? Learned helplessness in the laboratory is not easily reversed. However, Seligman (1977) feels that there are some techniques that can be used to alleviate depression and they are discussed in the following paragraphs. (Remember, we are talking about normal, everyday depression and not the extreme varieties associated with psychoses.)

TABLE 11–5 Similarities Between Learned Helplessness and Depression

	Learned Helplessness	*Depression*
Symptoms	Passivity	Passivity
	Difficulty learning that responses produce relief	Negative cognitive set
	Dissipates in time	Time course
	Lack of aggression	Introjected hostility
	Weight loss, appetite loss, social and sexual deficits	Weight loss, appetite loss, social and sexual deficits
	Norepinephrine depletion and cholinergic activity	Norepinephrine depletion and cholinergic activity
	Ulcers and stress	Ulcers (?) and stress
		Feelings of helplessness
Cause	Learning that responding and reinforcement are independent	Belief that responding is useless
Cure	Directive therapy: forced exposure to responses that produce reinforcement	Recovery of belief that responding produces reinforcement
	Electroconvulsive shock	Electroconvulsive shock
	Time	Time
	Anticholinergics; norepinephrine stimulants (?)	Norepinephrine stimulants; anticholinergics (?)
Prevention	Immunization by mastery over reinforcement	(?)

Source: After Seligman, 1975.

Aggression Training In the first method, **aggression training**, the subjects are goaded into anger and assertive action. They are prodded out of their hopelessness. A subject is told to sand a block of wood and is then criticized. The subject may then be told to count seashells scattered on the floor and will be criticized during this task as well. Eventually, most subjects blow up and yell something like, "I've counted my last seashell!" At this point the therapist apologizes and allows the subject to leave. The shift from apathy to anger and the reward for the anger (apology from the therapist) can do much to improve the person's perception of himself as a capable, strong, effective individual. Obviously, this technique can be easily abused; we do not want people to feel that they can aggress whenever they feel depressed.

Assertiveness Training We have already seen this technique. Here the subjects are encouraged to refuse requests and to practice asking for what they want. Both actions are rewarded.

Graded-step Reinforcement   Many of the techniques described by Seligman emphasize taking things by little steps. Do not overwhelm the subject. First tell the subject to do something *very* simple, where success is inevitable. Then reward that response. Gradually move on to more complex responses, rewarding the completion of each response. With this **graded-step reinforcement**, the subject can regain confidence gradually through a series of small successes, without being asked to do too much at once. If faced with a difficult task too soon, the subject may collapse and say, "See? It's hopeless! I can't do it."

Making a TTD List   If a depressed individual can make a **TTD list** of "things to do," and then *follow* that list, a sense of accomplishment and pleasure can be achieved. The tasks on the list must not be too difficult, and they must not be ignored or put off. Checking off each activity as it is completed can be a source of self reinforcement.

The Limit on Depression   Fortunately, depression seems to have a way of limiting itself. Most depressions go away by themselves. Some last a few hours, some a few days, and some may actually persist for years. But most of them disappear of their own accord. This is not to say depression is trivial. It is not; if severe enough it can lead to suicide (Cantor, 1976; MacKinnon & Farberow, 1976). Just telling a depressed person that he will probably feel a lot better soon, however, can be of great help. This is because depression often makes people feel as though they will *never* feel better.

Objections and Reformulations

Seligman's interpretation of depression as a form of learned helplessness has not gone unchallenged. Many felt that it was an oversimplification to draw a parallel between complex human depression and what a dog experienced in a shock box. Accordingly, Seligman (Abramson, Seligman, & Teasdale, 1978; Peterson & Seligman, 1984) developed a revised theory that emphasized much more heavily the mental and cognitive aspects of human depression than did the original formulation. Still, people have not been entirely satisfied by these revisions and some investigators have developed alternative theories of what goes on in a so-called helplessness situation without referring either to learned helplessness or to depression (Anderson, Crowell, Cunningham, & Lupo, 1979). For example, Anisman (1978) argues that shock depletes brain norepinephrine which, in turn, produces motor deficits that could account for the lack of escape learning.

REGRESSION, FANTASY, AND SELF-DEFEAT

We have discussed aggression, helplessness, and depression as unplanned modes of reacting to frustration. But there are others. In *regression*, the individual resorts to an earlier mode of behavior when current modes of behavior fail to overcome frustration. Suppose a 9-year-old boy wants to go to the movies. His father refuses. The boy slips into baby talk, although he has not used it in years, perhaps unconsciously attempting to cajole his father into agreement. He has regressed to a former mode of behavior. If baby talk does not work, he may try a temper tantrum or some other form of behavior that was successful at an earlier age.

Aggression, helplessness, and depression are three unplanned modes of reacting to frustration. Regression is another. Although this boy probably knows that a temper tantrum is inappropriate, he will resort to it if other means of getting what he wants fail.

Hiding from our problems rather than facing them may represent a form of regression. Certainly many of us will give in to regressive forms of behavior, but in the long run, this technique is a poor substitute for more adaptive methods of dealing with frustration.

When frustrated we can and do escape into *fantasy*. We can daydream of more pleasant things or gain imagined revenge. Our fantasy life can take us away from unpleasant realities, if only for a few moments. If used in moderation, fantasy is harmless enough. But if it becomes our dominant mode of dealing with frustration, it can become extremely limiting and self-defeating.

There are still other ways that we react to frustration. Most of them are unplanned and *self-defeating*. For example, we may eat too much, drink too much, or turn to drugs. We may overborrow or overspend. Some people turn to compulsive gambling. Others become "workaholics." Still others seek comfort in occult activities and, finally, some turn to suicide. Several techniques for avoiding these self-defeating reactions are described by Holland (1980) and Houston (1981).

COPING WITH STRESS

Stress, or the general response that the body makes to any demand made on it, has become a popular topic in psychology. In general, the greater the demands the environment makes on us, the greater the stress we experience. Stress is caused by many factors. It can be psychologically induced by such shocks as failing an examination or losing a loved one. It can be physically induced when we suffer an injury or are subjected to extreme heat or cold.

Stress versus Stressors

Sometimes the meaning of stress becomes confused because of a failure to distinguish between *stress* and *stressors*. Stressors are the stimuli that cause the stress reaction. Such things as separation, boredom, overstimulation, failure, injury, loss of employment, heat, drugs, conflict, threat, cold, and so forth are the stressors that lead to the stress response. The stress response is the complex physical and psychological reaction we have to these stressors.

Emotions and the Umbrella Concept

Stress is very definitely an emotional experience. When we are stressed, we are often in emotional turmoil. We have been considering various specific emotions including anxiety, frustration, anger, depression, and helplessness, all of which may be part of a stress reaction. In other words, the concept of stress can involve any or all of these negative emotions; it is the umbrella under which these specific emotions are found.

Exactly which of these negative emotions will constitute a particular stress response is very difficult to say. Part of this is due to the fact that different people react to the same stressors in different ways. One person might react to failure with anger or even indifference, while another might feel depressed and anxious. Whether these individual differences are innate, learned, or both remains an intriguing mystery. Nevertheless, it can be said with certainty that emotions such as those we have been discussing are strong components of the overall stress response.

The General Adaptation Syndrome

According to Seyle (1976), the body's reaction to stressful events occurs in a standard pattern of three distinct stages. The overall sequence of stages is called the *general adaptation syndrome (GAS)*. When first exposed to a stressful event, or stressor, the body displays the *alarm reaction* (see Figure 11–4). The adrenals release large amounts of hormones and the sympathetic nervous system becomes very active as the body makes complicated biochemical changes that can be described as emergency reactions. Then, if exposure to the stressor continues, the alarm reaction is replaced by the *resistance*

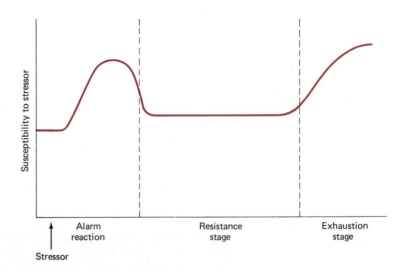

FIGURE 11–4 Seyle's Model of the Three Stages of the General Adaptation Syndrome

If stress is related to illness, as medical research seems to indicate, the high-pressure atmosphere of the stock market must be the source of many heart attacks.

stage. Here the body seems to "get ahold of itself" and begins to resist the impact of the continuing stressor. The physiological reactions of the alarm stage disappear, but if the stressor continues indefinitely, the body eventually will lose its ability to continue resisting. In the final stage, called the *exhaustion stage*, the body can no longer fight the stressor, some of the symptoms of the alarm stage return, and sickness or even death can occur if the stressor is not removed.

Stress and Life Changes

One of the more controversial ideas to come out of studies of stress is the theory that important life changes can be ranked in terms of the stress they produce. Thomas Holmes and his associates (Holmes & Holmes, 1970; Holmes & Masuda, 1974) have developed the scale of stressful events shown in Table 11–6. After studying thousands of interviews and medical records, these researchers have concluded that the more stress one experiences, the more likely one is to suffer a major *physical* illness. Specifically, they argue that we run a risk of developing one or more major illnesses within the following year if we acquire a total of more than 300 points on the stress scale during a one-year period.

To be more accurate in connection with college students, the stress scale would need to include additional stressors that students must face such as insufficient financial resources, poor or failing grades, and the breakup of a romantic relationship.

Type A Behavior and Type B Behavior

That is something to think about. It emphasizes one of the major conclusions developed in this field: psychological stress can cause physical disorder as well as mental illness. The number of studies that report direct relationships between physical problems and mental stress

TABLE 11–6 Stress Ratings of Various Life Events

Events	Scale of Impact	Events	Scale of Impact
Death of spouse	100	Change in responsibilities at work	29
Divorce	73	Son or daughter leaving home	29
Marital separation	65	Trouble with in-laws	29
Jail term	63	Outstanding personal achievement	28
Death of close family member	63	Wife begins or stops work	26
Personal injury or illness	53	Begin or end school	26
Marriage	50	Change in living conditions	25
Fired at work	47	Revision of personal habits	24
Marital reconciliation	45	Trouble with boss	23
Retirement	45	Change in work hours or conditions	20
Change in health of family member	44	Change in residence	20
Pregnancy	40	Change in schools	20
Sex difficulties	39	Change in recreation	19
Gain of new family member	39	Change in church activities	19
Business readjustment	39	Change in social activities	18
Change in financial state	38	Mortgage or loan less than $10,000	17
Death of close friend	37	Change in sleeping habits	16
Change to different line of work	36	Change in number of family get-togethers	15
Change in number of arguments with spouse	35	Change in eating habits	15
Mortgage over $10,000	31	Vacation	13
Foreclosure of mortgage or loan	30	Christmas	12
		Minor violations of the law	11

Source: After Holmes & Holmes, 1970.

is growing every day. Ambitious businessmen who work under considerable pressure are much more likely to suffer heart attacks than are males in the general population. Friedman and Rosenman (1974) report that men prone to heart attacks are (1) always conscious of and worried about time, (2) constantly engaging in compulsive behaviors designed to ward off harm, and (3) constantly feeling as though external pressures are bearing down on them. This pattern of behavior typifies what has come to be known as the *Type A* person (see Table 11–7). Those who do not display this driven pattern of behavior are known as *Type B* people (Goldband, 1980). Type B people tend to outlive Type A's by a noticeable margin. Many other studies support this evidence that psychological pressure seems able to kill us, or at least to make us seriously ill (Lovallo & Pishkin, 1980).

Techniques to Use

What can we do? Obviously, the most direct solution is to avoid stressful situations—take it easy. But we cannot always arrange our

TABLE 11–7   Type A Behavior Characteristics

The following is a list of some behaviors that characterize people prone to coronary heart disease.

Thinking or doing two things at once

Scheduling more and more activities into less and less time

Failing to notice or be interested in the environment or things of beauty

Hurrying the speech of others

Becoming unduly irritated when forced to wait in line or when driving behind a car you think is moving too slowly

Believing that if you want something done well, you have to do it yourself

Gesticulating when you talk

Frequent knee jiggling or rapid tapping of your fingers

Explosive speech patterns or frequent use of obscenities

Making a fetish of always being on time

Having difficulty sitting and doing nothing

Playing nearly every game to win, even when playing with children

Measuring your own and others' success in terms of numbers (number of patients seen, articles written, and so forth)

Lip clicking, head nodding, fist clenching, table pounding, or sucking in of air when speaking

Becoming impatient while watching others do things you think you can do better or faster

Rapid eye blinking or ticlike eyebrow lifting

Source: After Friedman & Rosenman, 1974.

lives to be free of stress. A stress-free life is impossible and probably unhealthy. There is evidence that moderate stress is necessary for good health. Too much *or* too little is what we need to avoid.

We have already discussed many techniques that can be useful in reducing stress and tension, as well as anxiety and frustration. These techniques include the following:

In a final technique, called *cognitive appraisal*, the individual is asked to imagine, or rehearse, the stressful event *before* it happens. For example, if you feel you are going to fail an examination, then try to imagine the failure event in great detail ahead of time. Your reaction to an actual failure may be lessened because of this prior cognitive appraisal. In addition, your cognitive appraisal of the situation may actually improve your chances of passing the examination by reducing your fear and worry.

Auerback, Kendall, Cuttler, and Levitt (1976) put the cognitive control of stress to a practical test. Two groups of patients about to undergo dental surgery were shown informative videotapes. One group received general information about the hospital's programs, the amounts of money spent on different programs, the numbers of patients served, and so on. The other group received specific information. They were told exactly what they would go through before, during, and after the surgery. As predicted, the distress felt by the group given specific, relevant information was less than that experienced by the general-information group. In other words, if you are going to undergo stress, find out as much about it as you can. Do not stick your head in the sand and say, "I don't want to know!"

SEX

We have discussed methods of coping with negative emotional experiences such as anxiety and frustration. We now will consider what we hope is a positive motivational system for most individuals, that of sex.

Sexual urges and gratifications obviously can be extremely pleasant, but sexual frustrations and insecurities lead to a great deal of psychological distress. Thus we find articles dealing with maintaining an erection (Sinclair, 1977), controlling premature ejaculation (Timmers, 1977), and reaching orgasm (James, 1977). Each of these problems seems to be of considerable concern to many people, and the helping professions are responding to these concerns.

Such problems are compounded by the fact that our culture is moving through a period of changing sexual practices and standards. In addition to our personal confusions and uncertainties, we now have to deal with social changes that are not yet well defined. What has psychology learned about these recent developments and our attempts to cope with them? We have chosen a number of topics that appear to be of particular concern in our everyday lives. This set of concerns does not cover the field by any means, but it is a representative sample (see also Zastrow & Chang, 1977).

Violence and Pornography

Now that pornography is commonplace, it is not surprising to learn that investigators have explored the effects of viewing pornography on sexual arousal. Folklore has it that men are more aroused by pornographic materials than women are. What do you think? It is pretty obvious that the pornography business has catered to male interests, but that does not mean that women do not like pornography. As it turns out, the few studies available suggest that women are at least as aroused by viewing and reading pornographic materials as males are (Kutschinsky, 1971; Mann, Sidman, & Starr, 1971). Some of these studies suggest that females may be even more aroused than males.

Pornography is now common in our culture. However, its effects on our behavior remain clouded and controversial.

As recently as 1970 a Presidential Commission on Obscenity and Pornography concluded that the viewing of pornography is harmless; the report found no evidence of adverse effects. However, the 1980s have seen an intensification of the debate, with a growing number of studies suggesting that pornography in general, and *violent* pornography in particular, may not be as benign as once thought. It now appears that viewing pornographic violence against women can have negative effects. Donnerstein (1980) reports that male subjects will deliver more shock to females after they have viewed violent pornography than before. Similarly, Malamuth and Donnerstein (1983) found that repeatedly exposing males to violent pornography increased rape fantasies in those males. More and more studies are suggesting that exposure to violent pornography leads to a tolerance of violence toward women (Malamuth & Check, 1980).

Changing Cultural Norms

Human sexual activity is affected, not only by personal experiences, but by the changing norms of a culture as well. Every society places some restrictions on sexual activity. Incest (intercourse between closely related individuals) is universally condemned, but adultery and homosexuality are forbidden in some cultures and comfortably accepted in others. Some cultures encourage masturbation and erotic play by children while others condemn such activities.

Until very recently our own culture had been moving toward a more permissive stance. Many activities thought to be harmful, degrading, or evil only 30 years ago were beginning to be accepted with a certain amount of calmness. Many Americans in the 1940s and 1950s were shocked by such topics as oral and anal sex, pornography, masturbation, group sex, extramarital sex and premarital sex. With the advent of practical birth-control methods, sex for pleasure rather than sex for babies became a common attitude during the 1960s and

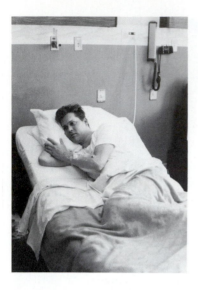

The costs of AIDS in terms of financial burden and human suffering have yet to be calculated.

1970s. More diverse and numerous sexual practices appeared to be on the increase. But the 1980s have seen a dramatic reversal of this trend. America's "honeymoon" with casual sex appears to be over. Two decades of uninhibited sex have given way to more cautious and more committed sexual activity.

Sexually Transmitted Disease

The reasons for this shift back to more traditional sex are probably many and varied. Some people found that uninhibited sex did not make them happy. Others merely became bored and turned back toward traditional activities. But very definitely, sexually transmitted diseases have become one of the primary deterrents to unrestrained sex. Clearly AIDS (acquired immune deficiency syndrome) has been the most frightening of these diseases, but as Table 11–8 shows, many other sexually transmitted diseases are intruding on our lives.

The great fear of AIDS is not unwarranted because, at the time of this writing, it is an incurable illness. Table 11–9 contains some of the questions that are frequently asked about this disease and their answers.

TABLE 11–8   America's Most Troublesome Sex Diseases

Until recent years, public-health experts counted barely five types of sexually transmitted diseases. Now, they know that more than a score exist. Causing the most concern—

AIDS

Acquired-immune-deficiency syndrome, since first reported in the U.S. in 1981, has each year doubled its number of new victims. AIDS damages the body's immunity against infection, leaving its victims without a defense against a host of serious diseases.

Cause: A virus called HTLV-III/LAV. However, not everyone exposed develops AIDS. Many of the estimated 1 million people infected by the virus so far have no AIDS symptoms.

Symptoms: Tiredness, fever, loss of appetite, diarrhea, night sweats and swollen glands.

When do they occur? From about six months after infection to five years and possibly longer.

How is it diagnosed? Doctors look for certain kinds of infections, do tests to reveal AIDS antibodies and show damage to white blood cells.

Who gets it? Three largest groups are sexually active gay men, 73 percent of cases; intravenous drug users, 17 percent; blood-transfusion recipients, 2 percent.

Treatment or cure: Nothing yet.

CHLAMYDIA

The "disease of the '80s," chlamydia hits between 3 million and 10 million Americans a year.

Cause: The bacterium *Chlamydia trachomatis*, spread to adults by sexual contact and to babies of infected mothers during birth.

Symptoms: For men, discharge from penis or burning sensation during urination. For women, vaginal itching, chronic abdominal pain, bleeding between menstrual periods.

When do they occur? Sometimes two to four weeks after infection. But many men have no symptoms. Four of 5 women won't notice one until complications set in.

Complications: In both sexes, possible infertility. In women, pregnancy problems that can kill a fetus and, occasionally, the mother. In babies, infections of the eyes, ears and lungs, possible death.
Diagnosis: For men and women, a painless test at a doctor's office. Symptoms need not be evident.
Cure: Usually with the drug tetracycline or doxycycline.

GONORRHEA

The number of cases of this ancient disease rose last year for the first time since 1978.
Cause: The bacterium *Neisseria gonorrhoeae.*
Symptoms: For males, a puslike discharge. Most infected women show no symptoms.
Complications: Many, from back pains and urination problems to arthritis and sterility. Babies of infected mothers may be born blind.
Diagnosis: Cell-culture tests.
Cure: Penicillin works in most cases. A sharp increase, however, is occurring in a strain of gonorrhea, called PPNG, that resists penicillin.

GENITAL HERPES

Twenty million Americans have genital herpes. Recurrences are frequent in some, rare in others. Some persons have only one outbreak in a lifetime.
Cause: Herpes-simplex viruses in skin-to-skin contact with infected area.
Symptoms: Blisters in genital area form and become open sores. Initial outbreak sometimes is accompanied by swollen glands, headache or fever, and its lesions may last weeks. Later outbreaks are shorter and less severe.
Diagnosis: A physician can make a test while sores still exist.
Cure: None is known. Acyclovir reduces severity of flare-ups.

TRICHOMONIASIS

Some 3 million men and women get this disease each year.
Cause: The parasite *Trichomonas vaginalis.*
Symptoms: For women, a frothy discharge, itching, redness of genitals. Men usually have no symptoms.
Diagnosis: Pap smear or microscopic examination.
Complications: None in men, gland infections in women.
Cure: Drug metronidazoile.

VENEREAL WARTS

Although often painless, these growths on and around the genitals can be dangerous and need medical attention.
Cause: HPV's, the human papilloma viruses.
How are they found? Some look flat. Some look like tiny cauliflowers. Some only a doctor can see. It takes a Pap smear to detect warts on the cervix.
What harm do they do? Babies exposed during childbirth may get warts in the throat. Some researchers believe that venereal warts caused by some types of HPV's increase risk of cancer of cervix, vulva, penis and anus.
Cure: Doctors can remove with the drug podophyllin. Some require surgery. Over-the-counter drugs for other skin warts should be avoided.

SYPHILIS

This once rampant disease is now on the decline, but it still can be life threatening.
Cause: The bacterium *Treponema pallidum,* an organism that can be killed with soap and water.
Symptoms: In two stages and usually in three weeks. First, a painless pimple, blister or sore where the germs entered the body. Then, a rash, hair loss, swollen glands.
Diagnosis: Blood test, microscopic examination.
Complications: Brain damage, heart disease, paralysis, insanity, death.

(Continued on page 436)

Babies born to untreated women may be blind, deaf, crippled by bone disease.
Cure: Penicillin.

PID

Pelvic-inflammatory disease is described by the Centers for Disease Control as the "most common serious complication" of STD's.

Causes: Infections from any of several diseases, including chlamydia and gonorrhea, that result in inflammation and abscesses of a woman's Fallopian tubes, ovaries and pelvis.

Possible harm: One in 7 women with a PID attack becomes infertile. After three attacks, up to 75 percent cannot conceive.

Diagnosis: Examinations of abdomen and pelvis, laboratory tests.

Cure: Antibiotics for some cases. Severe cases often require surgery that results in infertility.

Source: After *U.S. News & World Report*, June 2, 1986, pp. 54–55.

Individual Differences

Another area of anxiety and frustration within the realm of sexuality concerns comparisons with mythical "norms." One question that worries many people is whether or not they are normal, or measure up in terms of their sexual prowess. Recent years have seen a flood of books, systems, and aids that claim to do such things as "Increase Your Sexual Prowess In Three Easy Steps." Many of these manuals and materials are potentially harmful because they are so misleading. Despite what some people say, a greater quantity and variety of sexual activity does not necessarily lead to happiness. In fact, trying to match the level or type of activity prescribed by anyone can be discouraging and a blow to your ego, as well as dangerous to your health. If we know anything at all, it is that people vary enormously in terms of their need for sexual activity. Being *matched* with a partner in terms of amount, nature, and safety of sex desired may be far

Books about sex and sex therapy are numerous, but they may not all be particularly helpful.

TABLE 11–9   AIDS: Sorting Out Truths From Myths

Q. What is AIDS?

A. A fatal disease that cripples the immune system, leaving the victim susceptible to illnesses the body can usually fight off, such as pneumonia, meningitis and a cancer called Kaposi's sarcoma.

Q. What causes AIDS? What are the symptoms?

A. AIDS is caused by a virus usually known as human immunodeficiency virus, or HIV. Symptoms of full-blown AIDS include a persistent cough, fever and difficulty in breathing. Multiple purplish blotches and bumps on the skin may indicate Kaposi's sarcoma, a cancer associated with AIDS. The virus can also cause brain damage.

Q. How is AIDS diagnosed?

A. By the appearance of pneumonia and other persistent infections, by tests that show damage to the immune system and by a positive test for antibodies to the AIDS virus.

Q. How can you get AIDS?

A. Mostly by having sex with an infected person or by sharing needles and syringes used to inject drugs. The virus, present in blood, semen and vaginal secretions, can be transmitted from one homosexual partner to another and during sexual intercourse both from a man to a woman and from a woman to a man.

Q. Who runs the greatest risk?

A. Of the more than 29,000 U.S. cases, 65 percent have been homosexual or bisexual men, 25 percent intravenous drug users, 4 percent heterosexuals and 3 percent persons who received blood or blood products, a third of whom have been people with hemophilia or other blood disorders. How 3 percent more caught the disease hasn't been determined. There have been about 400 cases in children.

Q. What is the risk for heterosexuals?

A. The greater the number of sexual partners, the greater the risk. Chances of infection from one encounter are between 1 in 1,000 and 1 in 10.

Q. Can AIDS be transmitted from an infected woman to her unborn child?

A. Yes—about a third of the babies born to mothers with AIDS are infected. Most will develop the disease and die.

Q. Can you get AIDS by shaking hands, hugging, social kissing, crying, coughing or sneezing? By French kissing? By eating food prepared by someone with AIDS? By an insect bite?

A. No known cases have been transmitted in any of these ways.

Q. Can you get AIDS by piercing your ears?

A. Possibly, though as yet no one has. If you plan to get your ears pierced, to have acupuncture treatments or to be tattooed, insist on a sterile needle.

Q. Is it dangerous to sit next to someone who has AIDS or who is infected with the virus?

A. No.

Q. Can AIDS be transmitted by someone who is infected but doesn't show symptoms?

A. Yes. This is mainly how the AIDS virus is transmitted.

Q. What's the difference between being infected with the AIDS virus and having AIDS?

A. People infected with the virus can have a wide range of symptoms— from none to mild to severe. At least a fourth to a half of those infected will develop AIDS within four to 10 years. Many experts think the percentage will be much higher.

(Continued on page 438)

Q. How can anyone be absolutely certain his or her sex partner is safe?

A. You can't. But experts believe that couples who have had a totally monogamous relationship for the past decade are safe. A negative blood test, of course, would be near-certain evidence of safety.

Q. How can I avoid catching AIDS?

A. If you test positive for the AIDS antibody, shoot drugs or engage in other activities that increase the chances of catching AIDS, inform your sex partner, and use a condom if you have sex. If your partner tests positive, or if you think he or she has been exposed to AIDS because of past sexual practices or through the use of intravenous drugs, a condom should be used. If you or your partner is in a high-risk group, avoid oral contact with the genitals or rectum, as well as sexual activities that might cut or tear the skin or the tissues of the penis, vagina or rectum. Avoid sex with prostitutes. Many are addicted to drugs and often get AIDS by sharing contaminated needles with other addicts.

Q. What are some of the diseases that affect AIDS victims?

A. Almost all AIDS victims get a parasitic infection of the lungs called *Pneumocystis carinii* pneumonia, a cancer called Kaposi's sarcoma or both. Other ailments include unusually severe yeast infections, herpes and parasites.

Q. Who should be tested for AIDS?

A. Gay men and intravenous drug users. Their sex partners. Anyone who has had several sex partners, if their sexual history is unknown, during any one of the last five years.

Q. How accurate is the blood test?

A. It is very accurate, but not infallible. A more sophisticated and expensive test called the Western Blot is used to confirm borderline cases.

Q. What should I do if I test positive?

A. See a physician immediately for a medical evaluation. Use a condom during sex. Do not donate blood, body organs, other tissue or sperm. Do not share toothbrushes, razors or other implements that could become contaminated with blood.

Q. Is banked blood safe?

A. Yes. It is tested and discarded if contaminated. In addition, people in high-risk groups have been asked not to donate blood.

Source: After *U.S. News & World Report*, Jan. 12, 1987, pp. 66–67.

---

more important than the frequency or the variety of sex. Furthermore, Vincent (1956) reports that a shy, inhibited approach to sex can lead to just as much satisfaction as an outgoing, uninhibited approach. In other words, you should not be intimidated by what others do. Be your own judge as to what is good for you, and if you have any questions, ask your physician.

Homosexuality

Homosexuality is one individual difference that requires attention. A serious social reevaluation of homosexuality has been occurring in this country. The result is that homosexuality is now more widely accepted as an alternative expression of human sexuality. Homosexual rights organizations have appeared in our cities and on our campuses, calling for tolerance, equality, and understanding.

A serious social reevaluation of homosexuality has been occurring in this country over the past two decades.

The tolerance accorded homosexuals recently has been diminished by the fact that the AIDS virus first appeared in strength among male homosexuals. Despite the fact that AIDS can afflict anyone of any sexual persuasion, homosexuals have been publicized as the primary carriers of the disease.

Whatever the causes of homosexuality—and the causes have eluded the scientific community for years—there does not seem to be much scientific reason to classify homosexuals as either criminals or mentally disordered individuals even though homosexual acts between consenting adults are classified as criminal acts in many states (Krulewitz & Nash, 1980). It was not until 1973 that the American Psychiatric Association took homosexuality off the official list of mental illnesses.

Strong feelings about homosexuality have existed in western culture for thousands of years. Some ethical systems have condemned homosexuality as sinful and immoral. The medical profession has looked upon homosexuality as a disease. Legal authorities have branded homosexuality as criminal. With all of these authorities denouncing homosexuality, it is no wonder that homosexuals have had difficulties (Bieber, 1976; Halleck, 1976). Many of these difficulties continue today, even though there is little evidence that an open acceptance of the gay community would threaten our society.

Davison (1976) has made a striking suggestion about attitudes critical of homosexuality. He notes that many homosexuals, beset with feelings of guilt, shame, and insecurity, seek out therapy designed to change their sexual orientation. In other words, many gays want help in becoming "normal." Davison argues that the therapist's willingness to try to change the gay's orientation is damaging and dangerous. By agreeing to "treat" the homosexual, the therapist is implying that there is, after all, something wrong with the homosexual. Davison argues that therapists should stop offering to help homosexuals become heterosexual and concentrate instead on improving the homosexual's personal relationships.

After extensive study of both homosexual and heterosexual relationships and individuals, Peplau (1981) has reached the following conclusions:

> We have learned, among other things, that the values and experiences of homosexual couples are similar to those of heterosexuals in many ways. Whatever their sexual preferences, most people strongly desire a close and loving relationship with one special person. For both homosexuals and heterosexuals, intimate relationships can—and often do—provide love and satisfaction. But neither group is immune to the perils of relationships—conflict and possible breakup. Whatever their sexual preferences, people in intimate relationships today struggle to reconcile a longing for closeness with a desire for independence and self-realization. (pp. 28–29)

Contraception

The use of *contraceptives*, or birth-control methods, is controversial. For some, their use is essential for the well-being of our planet, which is already becoming overburdened with hungry people trying to

TABLE 11–10 Currently Available Methods of Birth Control

The methods are rated in order of effectiveness, in terms of average number of pregnancies per year among the women of childbearing age using them. In most cases, two figures are given for effectiveness. The first, lower, figure is an "ideal" figure, obtainable when the method is used consistently and correctly. The second figure is an average figure, reflecting actual experience.

Method	Mode of Action	Effectiveness (Pregnancies per 100 Women per Year)	Action Needed at Time of Intercourse	Requires Instruction in Use	Possible Undesirable Effects
Vasectomy	Prevents release of sperm	0	None	No	Usually produces irreversible sterility
Tubal ligation	Prevents passage of oocyte to uterus	0	None	No	Usually produces irreversible sterility
"The pill" (estrogens and progesterone)	Inhibits production of FSH and LH, thereby preventing follicle maturation and ovulation	0–10	None	Yes, timing	Early—some water retention, breast tenderness, nausea; late—increased risk of cardiovascular disease
Intrauterine device (coil, loop, IUD)	Possibly prevents implantation	1–5	None	No	Menstrual discomfort, displacement or loss of device, uterine infection
"Minipill" (progesterone alone)	Probably prevents sperm from entering uterus	1–10	None	Yes, timing	?
"Morning-after pill" (50× normal dose of estrogen)	Arrests pregnancy, probably by preventing implantation	?	None	Yes, timing	Breast swelling, nausea, water retention, cancer (?)
Condom (worn by male)	Prevents sperm from entering vagina	3–10	Yes, male must put on after erection	Not usually	Some loss of sensation in males
Diaphragm with spermicidal jelly	Prevents sperm from entering uterus; jelly kills sperm	3–17	Yes, insertion before intercourse	Yes, must be inserted correctly each time	None known
Vaginal foam, jelly alone	Spermicidal, mechanical barrier to sperm	3–22	Yes, requires application before intercourse	Yes, must use within 30 minutes of intercourse; leave in at least 6 hours after	Not usually, may cause irritation
Withdrawal	Removes penis from vagina before ejaculation	9–25	Yes, withdrawal	No	Frustration in some
Rhythm	Abstinence during probable time of ovulation	13–21	None	Yes, must know when to abstain	Requires abstinence during part of cycle
Douche	Washes out sperm that are still in the vagina	?–40	Yes, immediately after	No	None

Source: After Curtis & Barnes, 1985.

scratch a living from a limited, finite set of natural resources. For others, contraception is repugnant on moral and religious grounds. Whatever one's stand is with regard to birth control, accurate information about current contraceptive techniques can help bring about a fuller understanding of the overall issue. Thus we have included, in Table 11–10, information on some of the presently available methods of birth control.

In this chapter we have discussed the way in which emotions influence our behavior. In the following chapter, we will take up the topic of development across the life span. We will begin with an examination of the factors that influence physical growth. Then we will continue by covering cognitive, social, and emotional development beginning at birth and proceeding through old age. Our attention will be drawn to the critical developmental stages that then enable us to understand how perception, learning, and motivation influence our behavior.

SUMMARY

1. While adaptive in many ways, everyday emotions and motives can distress us. The most effective level of motivation depends on task difficulty. Simple tasks require high motivation, while lower motivation levels are better for more difficult tasks.

2. Low-anxiety college students do better than high-anxiety students, especially in the middle range of scholastic aptitude.

3. Autohypnosis and relaxation training can be used to reduce anxiety.

4. Anxiety can be dealt with by tracing it to its source. Real, tangible problems should be solved first. More diffuse anxieties should not be exaggerated. We should *do* the things we fear. We should employ distraction, not be surprised if our anxieties return, and not be ashamed of being anxious.

5. Defense mechanisms are unplanned, unconscious attempts to defend against anxiety or to reduce it.

6. Although defense mechanisms involve some self-deception and distortion of reality, they can be useful and help us through difficult times. In moderation, their use is normal.

7. Defense mechanisms include rationalization, reaction formation, repression, projection, identification, displacement, sublimation, intellectualization, fantasy, undoing, compensation, and denial. Many of them are interrelated.

8. Frustration may be dealt with by identifying the obstacles and determining what will remove them. Action is necessary. We often block ourselves without knowing it.

9. In assertiveness training, individuals use role playing and related tasks to learn to say no and to feel free to make legitimate demands.

10. Unsolvable problems may be dealt with by increasing tolerance for frustration and by lowering the level of aspiration.

11. The frustration-aggression hypothesis suggests that frustration arouses an aggressive drive that motivates us to attack obstacles.

12. Displaced aggression occurs when we aim our hostility at weaker, substitute objects rather than at the actual obstacle that is causing our frustration.

13. At least seven types of aggression have been identified.

14. Aggression may be innate, learned, or both.

15. Methods of aggression control include punishment, catharsis, exposure to nonaggressive models, and utilization of incompatible responses.

16. Sometimes we react to extreme, unavoidable frustration by becoming apathetic, helpless, and depressed.

17. Learned helplessness can be established by subjecting man or animal to repeated, unavoidable punishment. The organism then refrains from learning available escape responses and acts as though it has no "hope." Depression may be similar to helplessness.

18. Seligman believes that depression can be reversed through aggression training, assertiveness training, and graded-step reinforcement. Most depressions seem to go away by themselves eventually.

19. Regression, or the return to earlier, successful modes of coping, and fantasy escape are also reactions to frustration.

20. Overeating, drinking too much, gambling, working too much, and overspending are among the self-defeating reactions to frustration.

21. The general adaptation syndrome is composed of three phases of the body's reaction to stress: the alarm reaction, the resistance stage, and the exhaustion stage.

22. Stress, or the general reaction of the body to demands placed on it, can create physical as well as mental disorder. Life changes can be ranked in terms of their stressfulness.

23. Stressors are the stimuli that elicit the stress response.

24. Emotions are definitely part of the stress reaction.

25. Type A individuals are worried about time, feel pressured, and are compulsive. They also run a high risk of heart attack. Less tense Type B individuals run a lower risk of heart attack.

26. Relaxation training and cognitive appraisal may be helpful in reducing the consequences of stress.

27. Personal sexual problems are currently compounded by the fact that our culture is undergoing changes in sexual practices and standards.

28. Contrary to folklore, women are as aroused by pornography as are men.

29. Violent pornography may encourage violence.

30. Birth-control methods have allowed sex for pleasure rather than sex for reproduction to become prevalent. The frequency and variety of sexual practices seemed to be on the increase until the 1980s when more traditional, noncasual sex practices seemed to rebound.

31. Although the change in attitudes toward casual sex has probably been multiply determined, awareness of sexually transmitted diseases, especially AIDS, has contributed to this revival of traditional practices.

32. Sex manuals can be harmful if they insist that the amount and variety of sexual activity is paramount. It is more important to have a partner whose interests match yours because people vary so widely in their sexual needs and desires.

33. For many years, homosexuality has been labeled as a criminal, sinful disease by legal, religious, and medical authorities. But homosexuality now is on its way to being recognized and accepted in our culture as simply another expression of sexuality.

34. The values and experiences of heterosexual and homosexual couples are similar.

35. Various methods of contraception are available for people wishing to prevent or defer pregnancy.

KEY TERMS

aggression
aggression training
alarm reaction
assertiveness training
autohypnosis
catharsis hypothesis
cognitive appraisal
contraception
defense mechanisms
depression
displaced aggression
displacement
exhaustion stage
fantasy
fear-induced aggression

frustration
general adaptation syndrome (GAS)
graded-step reinforcement
identification
incompatible responses
instrumental aggression
intermale aggression
irritable aggression
learned helplessness
predation
progressive relaxation training
projection
punishment
rationalization

reaction formation
regression
repression
resistance stage
self-defeating
sex-related aggression
stress
sublimation
suppression
territorial aggression
things-to-do (TTD) list
Type A
Type B
Yerkes-Dodson principle

ADDITIONAL READING

Derlega, V. J., & Janda, L. H. (1981) *Personal adjustment* (2nd ed.). Glenview, Illinois: Scott, Foresman.
This book offers a solid, extensive, traditional treatment of the area of adjustment.

Egan, G. (1986) *The skilled helper*. Monterey, CA: Brooks/ Cole.
This reader discusses a systematic approach to effective helping.

Grasha, A. F. (1983) *Practical applications of psychology.* Boston: Little, Brown.
This text is a good combination of basic principles and their application to everyday life.

Holland, M. R., & Tarlow, G. (1980) *Using psychology: Principles of behavior and your life.* Boston: Little, Brown.
This is an extremely practical book that describes many procedures for solving problems.

Houston, J. P. (1981) *The pursuit of happiness.* Glenview, Illinois: Scott, Foresman.
This book is a light, readable presentation of some new ideas about adjusting to life in modern America.

Watson, D. L., & Tharp, R. G. (1985) *Self-directed behavior.* Monterey, CA: Brooks/Cole.
This text offers a self-help approach based on experimentally discovered principles.

12 Development over the Life Span

WHAT IS DEVELOPMENTAL PSYCHOLOGY?

The study of changes brought about by maturation is the research focus of developmental psychologists. Developmental changes begin with conception and continue until death. This is the reason for emphasizing development over the life span. Until recently, however, most developmental psychologists concentrated on the study of children or adolescents. It is only in the last decade that we have seen a very marked increase in attention given to senior citizens. As a result, many myths about the elderly and the process of aging are giving way to a much better understanding of what it is to grow old. This is a positive sign—a youth-oriented society that still has the capacity to be concerned about the elderly. But this change has been a gradual one and the elderly, who are more numerous today than ever before, have had to struggle to get the attention of psychologists and other students of behavior. Today the study of developmental processes means more than just the study of children and adolescents, which was the case not too long ago. With the new emphasis on adult development, we truly have begun to understand developmental changes as they occur across the entire life span. How do we explain *change* in people over time—change from crawling to walking, from babbling to talking, from dependent child to independent adult, from fearful teenager to self-confident 50-year-old?

Are there developmental sequences in this change? Do we all go through the same steps, the same stages, in moving from childhood to adulthood? Are those steps or stages determined by biology or by our culture?

How do we explain the developmental consistencies in behavior over time? The child who does poorly in school at age 8 is probably doing poorly at 18; the gregarious, confident 10-year-old is likely to be gregarious and confident at 40. Are these patterns permanently formed in childhood, or can they be changed later?

The common thread apparent in these questions is an underlying interest in the *process of development.* Developmental psychologists want to understand the ways people change and the ways they stay the same over time.

BASIC PROCESSES AND MAJOR THEORIES OF DEVELOPMENT

As we pointed out in Chapter 1, we can look at any aspect of human functioning from several different perspectives. Within developmental psychology, there are at least three major perspectives: biological, environmental (learning), and interactional. Each of these perspectives emphasizes different processes, and each has distinct theories associated with it.

Biological Processes

Psychologists agree that certain basic, biological processes underlie many of the developmental changes we see. The 6-month-old baby cannot walk, while the 1-year-old baby can, because of physical changes in the muscles and nervous system. The 8-year-old girl cannot become pregnant, while the 15-year-old can, because of major changes in hormones, which trigger changes in the body that occur at puberty. The 60-year-old cannot run as fast as he did at 20 because

Biological processes underlie many developmental changes. Although a 60-year-old cannot run as fast as she did when she was 20 because of loss of muscle tissue and other aging changes, many older runners have shown great ability as marathoners.

of loss of muscle tissue and other physical changes of aging. (However, many older runners have shown great ability as marathoners well into their seventies!)

Much of the development we see in children, and probably in adults and older people as well, is governed by physical changes that are spelled out in the individual's genes. For instance, a growing human's nervous system changes systematically and automatically, which results in predictable changes in bones and muscles. The sequence and the timing of these changes both are programmed in the genes at conception, so the fact that you crawl before you walk, and that you are an early or a late developer at puberty is part of your genetic programming. The term *maturation* describes growth processes that are governed by such genetically determined signals.

One major influence on the maturational process is changes in the levels of hormones—the secretions of the endocrine glands we described in Chapter 2. The genetic code apparently contains "instructions" for sequential changes in the levels of hormones secreted by the several endocrine glands. These changing levels result in appropriate physical growth. Thyroxin (secreted by the thyroid gland) and a growth hormone from the pituitary gland are both produced in larger amounts during the first few years of life, and again during adolescence, than they are at other times. At adolescence, estrogen (in girls) and testosterone (in boys) are also produced in larger quantities, bringing about important changes in secondary sex characteristics and triggering the female menstrual cycle.

Biological Theories The developmental theorist with the strongest biological emphasis has been Arnold Gesell (Gesell 1954; Gesell et al., 1940). Gesell was the first to use the word *maturation*. He believed that most of the changes we see in children from conception through full growth can be understood in terms of fundamental maturational timetables. Gesell's view was out of favor for some time because of a strong emphasis on environmental influences on development, but recently there has been a revival of biological theories of development. For instance, there is a strong biological element in current theories of language development (Piattelli-Palmarini, 1980) and a new emphasis on genetically programmed differences in temperament in children (Goldsmith & Gottesman, 1981; Matheny, Wilson, Dolan, & Kranz, 1981). In short, there is a growing willingness to explain both changes that occur with age and differences among people using biological theories.

Environmental Influences

Despite the clear importance of biological processes, biology is obviously not destiny. The environment in which a child grows up has a major influence too. Developmental psychologists describe the impact of the environment in two ways.

Learning Theories The basic processes of learning we described in Chapter 5, including classical conditioning, operant conditioning, and observational learning, underlie many of the changes we see in children and adults. We see classical conditioning in the development of infants' and children's emotional responses. Since mommy or daddy is so often present when the baby feels good, cuddled in supporting arms with clean diapers and a full tummy, the presence of parents may come to trigger various feelings of pleasure, warmth, security, and contentment. Unpleasant early experiences can also be linked through classical conditioning procedures to specific stimuli, such as fears of animals.

Operant conditioning can be seen in virtually every encounter the child has with parents, teachers, and peers; we can even see its influence on behavior in many of the things we do as adults. If parents, in playing with their child, hug the child for smiling, then that behavior has been reinforced and the child is more likely to smile again. The gregarious and happy child may have learned to be this way through operant conditioning. Similarly, a teacher may inadvertently introduce avoidance training when he tries to teach reading to first graders. If two of the students, Carl and Jennifer, have difficulty reading correctly, especially aloud before their classmates, and if the teacher frowns or reprimands them for their poor reading, they may not wish to read aloud again. If this sequence is repeated, Carl and Jennifer may develop an aversion to books or to reading. Perhaps this is one of the factors contributing to adult illiteracy, which has become a major issue in our country today.

Observational learning is especially important in the development of children, since they learn a wide range of specific behaviors from watching other people perform them. For instance, children may learn aggressive behavior from watching certain television programs. Children also learn prosocial behaviors from observing others engaging in altruistic acts, such as giving money or food to the homeless. Even physical skills, such as playing soccer or dancing, are learned partly from observing others perform these actions.

Several major groups of theorists use learning principles to account for both the consistencies and the changes that occur over the life span. At one end of the continuum of learning explanations, psychologists such as Donald Baer define "development" simply as a collection of individual learning experiences, or "behavior change which requires programming" (Baer, 1966, p. 14). Baer grants that a person's age may make a difference. Two-year-old children may need a different sequence of reinforcements or stimuli before they can sort objects by size or color as easily as a 7-year-old, but Baer assumes that a sequence *could* be found to teach 2-year-olds such a task.

A second major learning approach to development is exemplified by Bandura's theory of social modeling, which we described in Chapter 5. Like Baer, Bandura (1969) maintains that learning is the key element in behavior change over time, but he emphasizes observational learning rather than operant conditioning. The other major difference between these two learning approaches is that Bandura has added a developmental element to his theory. As we saw earlier, he argues that for learning to occur from observation, the observer must attend, remember, be physically able to imitate the behavior, and be motivated to do so. But the ability to attend to relevant aspects of the model's behavior and to remember what one has seen changes with age, as do the physical skills needed to imitate complex behaviors. Thus, the actual learning that takes place will also differ depending on age. A 3-year-old will learn different things from watching a swimming instructor than will a 10-year-old or a 40-year-old, because he has more limited physical capacities and less ability to remember long strings of instructions. The 8-year-old who has figured out that she will stay female for the rest of her life will be much more motivated to observe and imitate a female adult than is a 3-year-old girl, who has not yet fully grasped the concept of gender. In Bandura's view, people of all ages learn from observation, but *what* they learn will depend on their level of cognitive and physical development. By adding this developmental element to the learning equation, Bandura can explain some of the differences psychologists have found between the ways children and adults approach learning tasks.

Broad Environmental Differences   Another way developmental psychologists look at the impact of the environment is to compare children who have grown up in widely differing circumstances. A child growing up in a migrant family, with poor nutrition, little encouragement of intellectual accomplishment, and chaotic daily life, moves on a different "developmental trajectory" than does a child growing up in a more physically, emotionally, and intellectually nourishing home (Farran, Haskins, & Gallagher, 1980; Ricciuti, 1981). There are many examples of such environmental differences. Children whose parents talk to them more from the time they are small infants later develop language skills more rapidly (Clarke-Stewart, Vander Stoep, & Killian, 1979; Elardo, Bradley, & Caldwell, 1977). Children whose mothers suffer severe emotional disturbance and children who experience other high levels of early stress are likely to have slower intellectual development, to get sick more often, and to get along less well with others (Sameroff, Seifer, & Elias, 1982).

Interactional Processes

The theories presented so far have presumed a passivity on the part of the developing individual. Biological theories describe maturational sequences that unfold automatically; environmentalists hold that the enriched or impoverished quality of the person's environment makes its mark. These views fail to recognize the rich, active contributions made by the individual. Contemporary theories of development tend to focus on the *interaction* between the child (or adult) and the environment.

For example, recent research (Kagan, Reznick, & Snidman, 1988) suggests that children are born with individual, genetically programmed temperament patterns—a biological influence. In this longitudinal study, 2-year-old children who displayed either extreme shyness or sociableness were followed until age 7. At age 7, the majority of the restrained group were quiet and socially avoidant with unfamiliar children and adults, whereas the more sociable children were talkative and interactive. Kagan and his colleagues believe that the behavioral display of "shy, quiet, timid behavior at 2 years of age requires some form of chronic environmental stress acting upon the original temperamental disposition present at birth" (p. 171). In these children, the chronic stress may be due to quarreling by the parents, prolonged hospitalization of the child, or perhaps an older sibling who repeatedly teases, yells at, or otherwise irritates the child. These children, because of their socially avoidant behavior, eventually make less and less contact with those around them and consequently have trouble in social interactions. Temperamentally more adaptable children, on the other hand, get along better with peers and adults. Overall, these socially responsive children are more accepted by teachers and other adults who interact with them.

Another example of an interaction effect is the fact that two children of different ages, in the same room with the same toys and the same people, will behave differently and learn different things from their play. The child's cognitive level and language skill, both of which change with age, affect the way the child approaches new experiences. In short, there is really no such thing as "an environment" that "affects" behavior or development, nor is there a pure maturational effect either. What we see in any given person over the life span is a continuing interaction between the individual and the world around that person.

Interaction Theories   Two groups of theories that emphasize this interactional process have strongly influenced the thinking of developmental psychologists. These are the psychoanalytic theories, such as those of Sigmund Freud and Erik Erikson, and the cognitive-developmental theories, including those proposed by Jean Piaget and by other adherents to his views, such as Lawrence Kohlberg.

Psychoanalytic theorists see development as the result of interactions between powerful, inborn sexual and aggressive drives and the responses of the people around the child during the early years. We will be discussing Freud's theory in some detail in Chapter 14. For now, we will note two important points about the theory. First, Freud held that individual patterns emerging from the first years of life are extremely powerful and difficult to change later. The second point is that early development proceeds in a series of *psychosexual stages*, each of which is associated with the parts of the body that give sexual pleasure at that age. Each one of these stages requires a different type of adaptation between the child and the parent. The accumulation of those adaptations shapes the child's personality for the rest of his or her life.

Like Freud, Erikson (1963, 1980) thinks that development proceeds in distinct stages, but Erikson calls them *psychosocial stages.* In his theory, Erikson divides the life span into the eight psychosocial stages shown in Table 12–1. Each stage is associated with a particular chronological time period in the life span of an individual. As the person proceeds from infancy to old age, the tension created at each age, if successfully resolved, results in what Erikson calls an adaptive strength. For example, if the infant develops a trusting relationship with its parents, the feeling of *hope* emerges. In the next stage, Early Childhood, the child attempts to achieve some measure of autonomy, but if thwarted the child is beset by shame and doubt. The child who successfully achieves some autonomy also learns the feeling of *will*. According to Erikson, the psychologically healthy person is the one who has successfully completed each stage.

TABLE 12–1   Erikson's Psychosocial Stages of Life

Old Age							Integrity vs. Despair. WISDOM
Adulthood						Generativity vs. Self-absorption. CARE	
Young Adulthood					Intimacy vs. Isolation. LOVE		
Adolescence				Identity vs. Confusion. FIDELITY			
School Age			Industry vs. Inferiority. COMPETENCE				
Play Age		Initiative vs. Guilt. PURPOSE					
Early Childhood	Autonomy vs. Shame, Doubt. WILL						
Infancy	Basic Trust vs. Basic Mistrust. HOPE						

Source: After Erikson, 1980.

TABLE 12–2 Piaget's Cognitive-Developmental Stages

Sensorimotor stage (0–2 years): Baby interacts with the world through senses and actions with objects. (A ball *is* something that feels a certain way in your hand and falls a certain way when you let go.)

Preoperational stage (2–6): Child can represent things internally with images, or with words that stand for the object; begins to classify objects into groups, but reasoning is still tied to what things look like and what they can do.

Concrete operational stage (7–11): A big leap forward in abstractness of thinking; the child can now work out general principles, based on experience, and can use many new, powerful mental operations such as adding or subtracting, classifying, multiplying, and putting into sequence.

Formal operational stage (12–): Teenager becomes able to solve complex problems systematically and to use deductive ("if . . . then") logic; can think about ideas, rather than just about objects that have been actually observed. Not all teenagers or adults reach this stage.

For Erikson, the emphasis is on the social aspects of development, rather than on the sexual aspects emphasized by Freud. According to Erikson, the crucial interactions are between the child's changing needs and the demands made by parents and later by society. For example, as the child learns to get around independently, the parents begin to set more limits to keep the child from accidentally hurting himself. So the child's drive for independence leads to restrictions. How the parents and the child resolve this dilemma shapes the developmental pattern at that age and affects the way in which the child will approach the dilemmas posed at later stages. Another major difference between Erikson and Freud is that for Erikson, development continues over the entire life span, as we see in Table 12–1, with new tasks and new dilemmas continuing to challenge us as we go through adulthood. For many psychologists this approach to development is more appealing than that of Freud who essentially believed that how a person behaves in life is largely determined by what happens during the first six or seven years of life.

A third, quite different interaction theory of development has been worked out by Piaget (1964, 1980; Piaget & Inhelder, 1969). Piaget's views have influenced the thinking of a whole generation of developmental psychologists. Because Piaget has emphasized the development of thinking rather than social or personality development, his theory is usually labeled *cognitive developmental*.

Piaget does not stress the importance of either maturation or learning, although he agrees that both are basic processes. He argues that development is more than just the sum of these influences, since the child is an active participant in the process. At each age, the child explores, manipulates, examines, plays, *uses* whatever is available in the environment. As a result, both the child's specific knowledge and his *way of thinking* change systematically. New experiences keep the child "off balance" in some sense. They cannot always be fitted into the concepts and categories the child has already developed. This imbalance forces the child, through a process Piaget calls *equilibration*, to develop new strategies, new concepts. The same adaptive processes occur in the thinking of adults as well, but we encounter fewer things we are unable to handle with our existing strategies, so the thinking of an adult seldom undergoes major new equilibrations.

Piaget, like both Freud and Erikson, thinks that development can be marked off into broad stages. Piaget's cognitive-developmental stages are presented in Table 12–2. All three theorists see their stages as invariant in order. As humans, we must go through sensorimotor operations before we can come to concrete operations; we must experience the stage characterized by trust versus mistrust before the stage characterized by autonomy versus doubt. The ages these researchers suggest for each stage are only approximate, but there are some striking similarities. Despite their varying assumptions, these three interactionist theorists see the transition points of development as critical in the overall psychological functioning of the individual.

Synthesis and Some Questions

It may seem wishy-washy to say that all of the different theorists we have just mentioned are at least partially correct, but this does indeed appear to be the case. Each of these perspectives shows us part of the whole picture. Maturation is an undeniable influence on development, as is learning. But it is also true that development is more than this, that the child and the adult shape their own experiences in highly significant ways. We will see the workings of each of these aspects at each age as we move through the life span.

There are important differences between these viewpoints, too. One difference among the theorists is in whether they see development as *continuous,* or divided into *discontinuous* stages. All three interactional theories describe major stages in development. Both the biological theorists and the learning theorists see change over the lifetime as a continuous series of tiny increments of physical change or reinforced learning. Hidden in this argument is the issue of whether developmental change involves *qualitative* differences or merely *quantitative* ones. Does an 8-year-old think differently than a 2-year-old, or does she merely have more practice, and thus more skill, in solving complex problems? Is an intimate relationship in your twenties different in quality from your close friendships in childhood? Is a 40-year-old "more mature" in some sense than a 20-year-old—better integrated, better able to handle life's slings and arrows—or has a 40-year-old merely experienced more things, so that he is more likely to have had some previous experience he can bring to bear on any new task or problem? This is an important theoretical issue among developmental psychologists, but it is also an important personal issue for all of us as we move through adulthood. Are the qualitative changes we sense in ourselves part of a sequence, part of "getting better," or are we just changing constantly in response to changes in the environment around us?

A second central difference among the several theorists is whether they view early experience as more influential than later experience. In the language of the ethologists, whose studies of motivation we described in Chapter 9, are the early years a *critical period* for the development of intellectual skills or personality characteristics? Is our temperament inborn and unmodifiable, as some biological theorists suggest, or do the experiences of adulthood weigh equally in shaping our skills, our attitudes, and our relationships to others?

Learning theorists, as a group, tend to be far more optimistic about the possibility of change in adulthood than psychoanalytic theorists such as Freud. If your skills and responses at age 12 are the result of the patterns of observational learning and reinforcement you have experienced, then your behaviors can change if the models and the reinforcements are altered. People can learn to become less fearful and more assertive. In Chapter 11 we described several programs based on such optimism about change; in Chapter 18 we will explore various forms of therapy for more serious types of disturbances. One of the underlying disputes among advocates of the several forms of therapy is when and how the undesirable behavior pattern was formed, and whether it can be readily changed. This question thus has relevance beyond the area of developmental psychology.

With these theories and issues in mind, let us begin our journey through time, from conception to death.

THE PRENATAL PERIOD

We described some of the fundamental genetic processes in Chapter 2. At the moment of conception, the 23 chromosomes from the father combine with the 23 from the mother, forming the unique pattern of 46 chromosomes that makes up the genetic map for that particular person. Conception normally occurs as the ovum travels down the Fallopian tube toward the uterus (see Figure 12–1). From the moment of fertilization, the cell—now called a *zygote*—begins the division process called *mitosis*.

Mitosis continues steadily during the first two weeks, but the cells quickly begin to separate into different types. Some form an outer envelope and some implant the envelope in the wall of the uterus. From 3 to 7 weeks after conception, the developing organism inside the envelope is called an ***embryo*** (see Figure 12–2), and from 8

FIGURE 12–1   A Diagram of Conception   *This depiction shows the female reproductive system and the passage of the sperm toward the Fallopian tube to meet the ovum.*

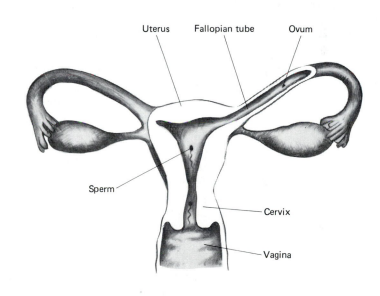

FIGURE 12–2   The Major Steps in Prenatal Development *(After Moore, 1972)*

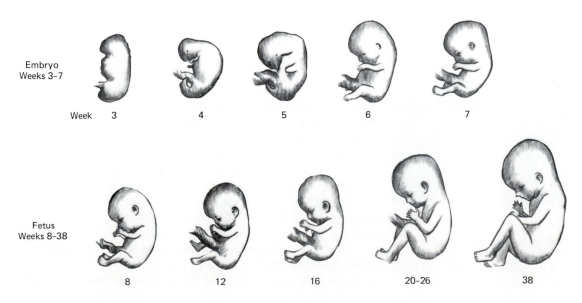

Embryo Weeks 3–7

Week   3   4   5   6   7

Fetus Weeks 8–38

8   12   16   20–26   38

The tragic malformations of so-called "thalidomide babies" in the early 1960s gave graphic testimony to the dangers of women's use of drugs or medications when pregnant.

to 40 weeks, it is called a *fetus.* During this time, nourishment is received through the umbilical cord, which is linked to an organ called the placenta. The placenta develops at the original point of implantation and lies between the fetus and the wall of the uterus. It takes up nutrients from the mother's blood, filtering out most disease organisms but allowing essential nutrients to pass through to the fetal bloodstream.

As you can see from Figure 12–2, the basic form of the body—arms, legs, hands, feet, mouth, nose, and other features—is present as early as 7 or 8 weeks after conception. During the final 7 months of the pregnancy, the organ systems develop further and more physical details become visible. The nervous system (brain, spinal cord, and nerves) is one of the last systems to develop fully and is still not complete at birth.

The sequence of prenatal development shown in Figure 12–2 is clearly governed by the genetic "instructions" in the chromosomes—by maturation in Gesell's terms. All human embryos and fetuses, barring major disturbances, develop in the same sequence at the same rate. The maturational sequence is extremely powerful. It proceeds normally in the vast majority of cases, despite most emotional or physical disturbances in the mother.

External Influences during Gestation

The fact that the fetus develops in a seemingly protected environment (the womb) does not mean that the fetus is immune to external influences that can disrupt the normal maturational sequence. It is now a well-known fact that many stimulants and other drugs have a *teratogenic* (tending to cause developmental malformations) effect on the developing fetus.

Some of the most common stimulants known to affect fetal development are alcohol, cigarettes, marijuana and other recreational drugs, caffeine, aspirin, tranquilizers, antihistamines, and decongestants. In the case of alcohol, for instance, since 1981 the Surgeon General of the United States has warned all mothers-to-be not to drink—not even socially. Why such a stern warning about alcohol? What effect does an occasional glass of wine or beer have on the developing fetus? Alcohol, like many other substances, is capable of crossing the placenta wall and entering the fetus's blood supply and amniotic fluid, where it remains long after it has dissipated in the mother's bloodstream. Therefore, the fetus remains intoxicated long after the mother's system has returned to normal.

Even moderate amounts of drinking during pregnancy can result in an increased risk of miscarriage and stillbirths. Another danger is the possibility of giving birth to an infant with *fetal alcohol syndrome.* This syndrome's principal features include central-nervous-system disorders, retarded growth, cardiac malformation, abnormal facial features, such as folds on the inner part of the eyelids, and skeletal defects.

Illnesses, diseases, and drugs carried or used by the mother may also pass through the placenta and harm the developing fetus. In all of these cases, the timing of these external influences determines the

Obviously, this woman is not aware of the perils that smoking and alcohol consumption pose to an unborn child.

TABLE 12–3 Major External Influences during Gestation and Their Typical Effects

Types of Influence	Typical Effects on a Developing Embryo or Fetus, or on an Infant after Birth
Mother's diet inadequate; provides too little protein, or too few calories.	Reduction in number of brain cells; increased rate of spontaneous abortion; higher rate of infant death in first year after birth.
Diseases of the mother Rubella (German measles)	Deafness; sometimes heart defects or other physical deformities.
Syphilis	Infant infected with the disease in about 25% of cases; may be stillborn; if born, may be subnormal.
Drugs taken by the mother Alcohol	Fetal alcohol syndrome (FAS) in some cases of maternal alcoholism; syndrome includes mental subnormality and a number of minor physical abnormalities; lesser alcohol intake *may* have some negative effects, too.
Cigarettes	Effects not clear; most common finding is that babies born to mothers who smoke heavily weigh less at birth.
Coffee	There are some hints lately that coffee drinking during pregnancy may be related to lower infant birth weight.

severity of the long-term effect. Generally speaking, an organ system is most sensitive when it is developing most rapidly. An expectant mother who contracts German measles (rubella) during the first trimester of pregnancy is more likely to give birth to an infant with a hearing disorder since it is during this period that the ears and internal hearing organs are developing. Contraction of rubella at some later time during pregnancy does not result in a hearing disorder, since the critical period for the disease to affect hearing has passed. By contrast, maternal malnutrition (especially protein deficiency) has its greatest effect during the final trimester of pregnancy when most brain cell development occurs in the fetus. These and other major teratogens and their influence on the developing fetus are shown in Table 12–3.

INFANCY: THE FIRST TWO YEARS

The Sensory System at Birth and during Early Infancy

The first 14 days of life are referred to as the *neonatal period*. At one time, it was believed that at birth and for at least a few weeks following delivery the world was one big buzzing state of confusion for the neonate. We now know that this is not the case and that the sensory equipment that the infant is born with functions well at birth, and depending on the specific sensory system, improves within a few short weeks. By 48 hours after birth, infants can track a slowly moving object (Haith, 1966). Neonates, it has been found, scan their surroundings in an organized and systematic fashion (White, 1971); they scan faces an average of 21% of the time when they are awake and a person is in view (Bergman, Haith, & Mann, 1971). A newborn can also see color, brightness, and darkness (Barnet, Lodge, & Armington, 1965). By 3 to 4 months, infants notice the difference between red, blue, green, and yellow (Bornstein, 1975).

Newborns are physiologically equipped to hear since their ears have nearly adult-sized tympanum and a well-formed cochlea (Northern & Downs, 1974). After the amniotic fluid drains out of the newborn's ears (which usually takes several days), the baby's hearing sensitivity can be tested. Studies show that newborns can discriminate differences in both loudness and pitch. Weir (1976) has shown that neonates can detect the difference between tones of 200 to 250 cycles per second (or a one-note difference on a musical scale).

Newborns can distinguish water, sugar, and salt solutions from milk, and they show different responses to different concentrations of sweet, salty, and bitter solutions (Ganchrow, Steiner, & Daher, 1983). Lewis Lipsitt and his associates (Lipsitt, Reilly, Butcher, & Greenwood, 1976) found that newborns sucked longer and paused for shorter periods when they were given a sweet solution. They also sucked more slowly, as if savoring the sweetness. In addition to sucking, newborns smile and lick their upper lip when given a sweet solution (Ganchrow, Steiner, & Daher, 1983).

Newborns are also equipped with a good sense of smell. They will turn away from a noxious smell such as ammonia. They can also distinguish between odors. They turn their faces toward a sweet

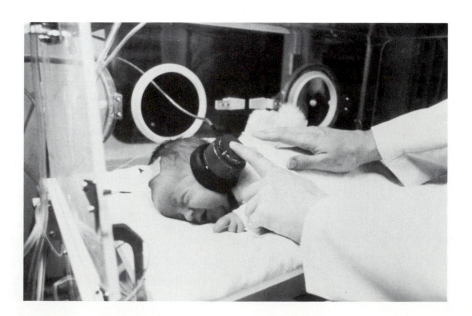

The hearing sensitivity of newborns can be tested for loudness and pitch perception within a few days after birth.

smell, and their heart rates and respiration slow down (Brazelton, 1969). They also breathe faster and move around more when they smell asafetida, which has a garliclike odor, than when an odorless solution is put under their nose (Lipsitt, Engen, & Kaye, 1963).

The sensory system that has received the most attention during early infancy is vision. Research on infant perception has shown that young infants perceive, discriminate, and prefer some visual stimuli over others. Infants look longer at stimuli that are more complex and that have high-contrast contours, curves, and concentricity (Fantz, Fagan, & Miranda, 1975). Infants also apparently prefer regular facial configurations over scrambled faces (Goren, Sarty, & Wu, 1975) and photographs of real faces over schematic drawings of faces (Lewis, 1969). In addition, as early as 3 months of age, infants can discriminate one unfamiliar face from another (Barrera & Maurer, 1981). By 6 months of age, infants can discriminate some facial expressions (Caron, Caron, & Meyers, 1982) and show a preference for joyful over angry expressions (Schwartz, Izard, & Ansul, 1985).

Extending the research on infant perception and preference even further, Judith Langlois and her associates (1987) wondered whether infants preferred looking at attractive as opposed to unattractive faces. There is a good basis for asking this question since it is already known that adults and children look longer at faces judged to be attractive by independent raters. To test their question, Langlois and her colleagues presented 3- and 6-month-old infants with slides of women's faces. The slides were arranged in pairs of pictures differing on judged attractiveness. Infants of both age groups spent significantly more time looking at the more attractive face in each pair.

Langlois's findings are important because they suggest that our definition of attractiveness may not be culturally determined and learned. Rather, the origins of physical attractiveness may be intrinsic to the nervous system of the infant and may make their appearance early in the life of the infant. It may be that there is a universal standard or prototype that the infant uses to make judgments of attractiveness. Certainly more research is needed to test the idea of a universal standard of attractiveness across different cultures.

Motor Development during the First Two Years

The sequence of motor development during the first two years of a human infant's life is shown in Figure 12–3. The findings in the figure are based on the research of Burton White (1985), who has studied the development of young children. Other researchers, such as Shirley (1933) and Bayley (1965), have also studied the motor development of infants. Generally, the ages reported for the different motor development milestones by these researchers are in agreement. White reports that infants demonstrate unaided walking at 12 months. Bayley found in 1965 that the average age of infants able to walk alone was 12.4 months, a very close match to White's age marker. Shirley, on the other hand, reported that children in her sample walked alone at 15 months. It is not clear whether this means that children are developing faster now than they did 50 years ago, or

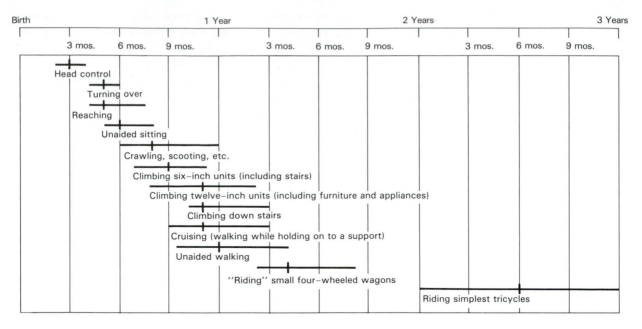

FIGURE 12–3 Major Milestones in the Motor Development of Infants *(After White, 1985)*

whether Shirley's sample was not representative of children in general. It may be that the difference is due to poorer nutrition received by Shirley's children because of poverty caused by the economic depression of the time. The actual ages at which these developmental milestones are achieved, however, is less important than the fact that they occur in the same sequence in all children. Within this sequence, the *rate* of development may differ widely for individual children. Some children studied by White walked at 9 months and others not until 16 months (see Figure 12–3). The crucial thing to remember is that *all* infants sit up before crawling and crawl before walking.

Whenever we find an orderly sequence in development of the type just discussed, maturation seems like a sensible explanation. The nervous system is continuing to develop during the first two years, as are muscles and bones, and all of these changes appear to be governed by the genetic code. Moreover, the practice of motor skills does not improve them much at this age. A child given a lot of practice climbing stairs does not learn this ability much sooner than one who never saw a stair until the "appropriate" time in the sequence (McGraw, 1935).

Researchers have concluded, however, that the sheer amount of handling or physical experience a child has had does have some effect on motor development. Children in impoverished orphanages, who have little chance to move about and exercise, are retarded in motor development (Dennis, 1960). Those who are held, carried, stroked, and generally stimulated physically appear to develop somewhat more rapidly (Williams & Scott, 1953). So at the least, both maturation and "experience" are involved in early motor development.

Cognitive Development during the First Two Years

From the moment of birth, infants use their increasingly good motor skills and their very good sensory abilities to explore and examine things around them. This is the period that Piaget calls the ***sensori-motor stage*** (see Table 12–2). During this stage infants explore and examine the environment primarily through their senses and through such simple actions as grasping and sucking. Beginning in this way, infants gradually expand their range of understanding of the world.

One important early discovery that infants make involves the fact that objects are permanent. It appears that very young infants see objects as fleeting, discrete happenings. Things move through the child's field of vision or touch her hands. She looks at them and explores them, but she has no sense that the rattle she is handling now is the same rattle she grasped yesterday. More important, she does not understand at first that the rattle continues to exist even after she drops it over the edge of the crib. These discoveries gradually occur during the first two years. The steps are outlined in Table 12–4.

As you can see in the table, by about one year of age the average child knows that an object that is shielded from her view is still there even when she cannot see it, and she knows that it is the same object from one encounter to the next. These basic understandings make possible another major development, which occurs between 18 and 24 months of age. This is the development of ***internal representation***. Once the child understands that objects are relatively fixed things, she can figure out ways to represent them to herself. She can make a mental picture or blueprint of an object. Later, when she has acquired the capability to use language, she can describe the object to herself and to others. She has thus taken the enormous step of having a word or a mental image of an object *stand for* the object.

What makes these major cognitive advances possible? Piaget argues that maturation plays some role, but that the critical element is the chance for the child to handle, touch, experience, and manipulate objects. Through this *active* experience, the equilibration process (to

TABLE 12–4	Steps in the Development of Object Permanence
Birth to 2 months	No evidence that the infant is aware of anything that is not presently visible.
2–5 months	Infant shows some surprise when objects "disappear" unexpectedly: if you show an object, screen it, remove it while behind the screen, then remove the screen, the infant shows surprise. This indicates some expectation that the object still exists but the infant does not search for the missing object.
6–8 months	Infant searches for an object that falls out of sight (for example, over the edge of the crib), searches for objects that are partially hidden, but does not continue to search for completely hidden objects.
8–12 months	Infant continues reaching for and searching for an object that is completely shielded by a cloth or screen.

use Piaget's term) takes place, and the child gradually develops new levels of understanding.

Social and Emotional Development during the First Two Years

It is important to keep in mind that the infant does not exist in a social vacuum. There are fascinating and important changes in the child's relationships with the other people in his life during the first two years. White (1985) has spent much time in the study of infants and their primary caretakers during this period of development. Figure 12–4 presents the major milestones in social development identified by White in his study of infants. We can see that the infant shows its first preference for its primary caretaker (usually the mother) at 4 months. The emergence of intentional crying for company begins at about 5 months and so on. By the age of 2 years, the social contract between the infant and its immediate social environment is set.

According to Erikson (1963), the crucial aspect of this period is the development of trust and hope. This trust comes about as a result of the child's belief that his world is predictable, that his caretakers are reliable in their care, and that he can have some influence on his caretakers. If this does not occur, the infant develops a sense of mistrust that affects all later social relationships. Support for Erikson's first stage of psychosocial development comes from research on *attachment.*

During the first two years of life, an infant goes through several identifiable stages in his attachments to the people around him. These stages are summarized in Table 12–5. Our description of the process is based primarily on the work of Mary Ainsworth (Ainsworth, Blehar, Waters, & Wall, 1978) and on that of Schaffer and Emerson (1964). Note that the first stage is really one of *non*attachment. The

FIGURE 12–4 Major Milestones in the Social Development of Infants
(After White, 1985)

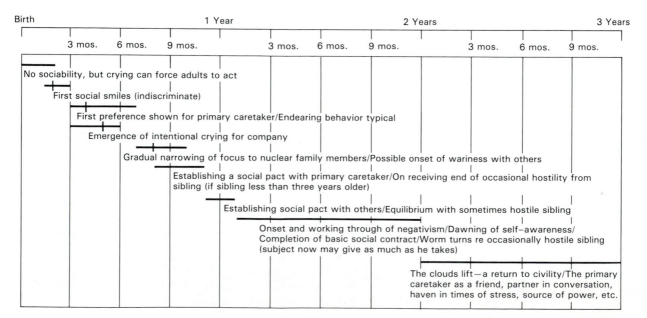

TABLE 12–5 Stages in the Development of Early Attachments of the Infant to the Parent

Stage 1: Birth–5 months	***Indiscriminate attachment:*** Really a phase of *non*attachment, as the child smiles equally and responds equally to all caregivers and even to strangers.
Stage 2: 5–10 months	***Specific attachment:*** Child forms one strong attachment, ordinarily to mother, smiles more to her, shows distress when she leaves, greets her more, uses her as a "safe base" when under stress.
Stage 3: 10–24 months	***Multiple attachments:*** Child forms several additional strong attachments, usually to other major caregivers such as father, babysitter, grandmother, or sibling, but retains strongest attachment to the specific-attachment subject of Stage 2.

younger child has not yet formed any preference for one person over another, but by about 5 months, most infants form a strong individual attachment to the major caregiver.

The transition to Stage 2 or specific attachment occurs when the infant has developed the necessary cognitive and perceptual skills. By about 5 months, an infant can reliably discriminate his mother from other people (Brown, 1979). He begins to realize that his mother is a constant object from one encounter to the next, and that she still exists even when he cannot see her. The basic cognitive development of object constancy may thus be a necessary precondition for the social accomplishment of attachment.

Separation Anxiety and Fear of Strangers Between the sixth and eighth months of life, infants begin to show a marked change in emotional behavior. They begin to whine or cry whenever they lose sight of their mothers or when an unfamiliar person approaches. These responses are normal and are called **separation anxiety** and **fear of strangers**. These behaviors appear to be universal and have been observed in infants in many different cultures (Kagan, Kearsly, & Zelazo, 1978).

We have come to understand the emotional development of infants by means of laboratory studies that employ a technique called the "stranger situation." In these studies, an infant accompanied by his mother is taken to a room where he and the mother engage in play activity. After a time, a "stranger" enters the room and attempts to approach the infant. Still later, the mother leaves the room and the infant is left alone in the presence of the stranger. If the infant cries when the mother leaves the room, we have demonstrated separation anxiety. Similarly, if the infant cries when the stranger approaches, with or without the mother present, this reaction is termed fear of strangers (Ainsworth, Blehar, Walters, & Wall, 1978).

Why do seemingly friendly, content, and well-adjusted infants suddenly develop these anxieties at this particular age? The answer lies in the dramatic developmental changes taking place during this period. The cognitive and emotional development of infants by the age of 6–8 months is such that they have good memories for familiar faces and they begin also to form mental representations of possible events. Although such concepts might initially take very rudimentary form, the infant may form thoughts such as "What will happen now?" when she is left with a babysitter. The infant grows more emotionally attached to her parents and other family members and friends who frequently interact with her. Her memory is good enough to know that a parent perhaps has left and to miss them when they are away. This results in strengthened attachments to family and friends *and* a heightened fear of strangers. The infant believes that the stranger may, for example, separate her from her mother. The stranger's behavior is not predictable from a child's perspective and, therefore, does not fit into her scheme of the world.

The result of this anxiety is an infant who although normally outgoing and friendly, may suddenly cling to her mother for protection at the mere sight of a stranger. This is a sign that she requires reassurance, love, and attention. According to Erikson, this is the period of life when children learn to trust or mistrust their world. If their fears are left unresolved at this stage, they may develop into new feelings of mistrust and anxiety.

These developmental anxieties of infancy reach their peak between 15 months and 18 months of age and usually disappear by the second birthday. By about the age of 2 years the child is able to better understand the intentions of strangers and to predict events. In other words, the child knows that the mother will return for her and that strangers will not harm her.

The developmental anxieties of infancy reach their peak around the ages of 15 to 18 months. This child's distress as he watches his mother leave will probably disappear by his second birthday.

It is interesting to note that infants do not show fear of strangers if the stranger is a child. This suggests that infants may have a notion of similarity. That is, the strange child is assessed by the infant as being "like me," while the adult is viewed as "different from me." This implies that an infant possesses an awareness of herself as a child and as similar to other children and distinct from older individuals in her environment. Such an awareness of self has survival value since older individuals are more likely to be a threat to the infant than are other children of a similar age.

THE PRESCHOOLER: FROM TWO TO FIVE

By 2 years of age, the child has made major strides in all areas of development. He can walk and run, has the basic skill of internal representation, and has a few strong attachments. During the next three years the child builds on these early achievements with new physical accomplishments, increased cognitive skills, and continuing social and emotional development.

Physical Growth from Two to Five

By age 2 the child already possesses most of the sensory skills of an adult, so there is little additional change here. There is some further development of the brain, however. By age 2 the brain has increased to about 75 percent of its adult weight; by age 5 it has reached about 90 percent. Most of the change consists of additional connective tissue between individual brain cells and more myelin sheathing around individual nerves.

Motor development also continues. The 2-year-old can run reasonably well, but has difficulty walking on tiptoe, riding a tricycle, or even walking up or down stairs one foot to a step. All of these skills, and many more, are acquired between ages 2 and 5. The 5-year-old can throw a ball, ride a tricycle, hop, and do a whole range of other complex motor tasks. These new developments, like the major motor milestones of infancy, seem to be primarily governed by maturation. Practice improves a child's ability to throw a ball or ride a tricycle but does not speed up the time when such skills first become possible.

Growth in physical size slows down during this stage. At birth, the infant's length measurement is about 30 percent of final height; by age 2 he is approximately half as tall as he will be as an adult. But after age 2, the rate of growth slows down to a fairly steady 5 or 6 percent per year until adolescence (Tanner, 1970).

By the age of 2, the child has made major strides in all areas of development.

All these maturationally governed changes affect the child's development in other areas. As the child becomes physically more skillful, she asserts more independence with her parents, which alters the relationship between parents and child. As she is able to explore more broadly—to play in the next street, to go to preschool, to get up and go to new toys or people—her range of experience broadens, which affects her cognitive development as well.

Cognitive and Language Development from Two to Five

Piaget saw this three-year period between the ages of 2 and 5, which he called the ***preoperational period***, as a time of transition in cognitive

A child in the preoperational period is now able to interact much more with parents and peers because of advancing cognitive and language abilities. Here a father and son engage in interactive play.

development. A great deal happens during these years, but it is primarily a time for consolidating and extending the major breakthrough of internal representation that was achieved at 18–24 months. The child is now able to use a word, an image, or an action to *stand for* something else. He understands at some primitive level the relationship between a symbol and the object symbolized. Once this astonishing understanding is achieved, whole new worlds open up, and it is the exploration of those new worlds that we see in the 2- to 5-year-old child.

The child can now think about things when they are at a distance, talk about things that are not immediately visible, and use objects to stand for others during his play. He can have a broom stand for a horse and experiment with riding, guiding, and talking to this horse. He can have his sister play the part of a daddy and say things to the pretend daddy that he has heard his mother say, or he can be the pretend daddy and experiment with "being grownup." He can have an imaginary friend—as many children do—and have the friend do things he is not allowed to do or is afraid to try. The play of children of this age is full of such adventures, and through these symbolic adventures the child learns not only from direct experience but from symbolic experimentation and manipulation.

Another great advance during this time is the development of the ability to classify. We need to emphasize again that this development is built on what has preceded it. A child cannot learn to classify objects until he has understood that objects are permanent. But having reached the basic step of permanence, the child still has a great distance to go.

Denney (1972) studied children's ability to classify objects by giving them a set of colored blocks of different shapes and asking them to group together the blocks that belonged together. The 2-year-olds in this study usually just built things—towers or houses or something else. Most of the 3-year-olds made partial groupings, such as putting some of the red blocks together, or some of the square blocks, while by age 4 or 5, they created complete groupings. Sometimes the older children even subdivided their groups, so that all the red things were together, with the red cubes in one pile and the red circles in another. Clearly, by the age of 4 or 5 the child is no longer treating objects as separate things, but rather as part of a set, group, or type. This is a giant step beyond mere object permanence.

Language Development   Another change that occurs rapidly during this period is the child's increasingly skillful use of language. We described the development of language in Chapter 7; to refresh your memory, we have listed the major steps in language development in Table 12–6. By age 2, most children are using single words and a few two-word sentences. Over the next year, both the vocabulary and the complexity of sentences increase enormously; 3-year-olds construct three- and four-word sentences, use plurals and past tenses, and ask questions. By age 5, most children are skilled speakers of their native language. All of these changes occur in an orderly sequence, as we saw in Chapter 7.

TABLE 12–6 The Major Steps in Language Development in the First Five Years of Life

Birth to 1 Month	Little sound except crying.
2–5 Months	"Cooing" sounds.
6–12 Months	Babbling; repetition of combinations of sounds.
12 Months (approximately)	First word; combination of sounds used with a consistent referent.
12–18 Months	Holophrastic speech; expanded vocabulary and the first use of two-word sentences by some children.
18–24 Months	Beginning use of two-word sentences for most children; telegraphic speech common.
24–60 Months	Continued expansion of vocabulary; increasingly longer sentences; systematic addition of grammatical complexities, such as past tenses, plurals, auxiliary verbs, negatives, and questions.

The Relationship between Language and Thought   Given the orderliness of the child's language development, and the sequential character of many of his cognitive developments as well, it is natural that psychologists would look for possible links between these two chains. After all, words are symbols, and the chief characteristic of the child's pattern of thought at this age is his ability to use symbols. Is this symbolic ability the *result* of language?

Piaget answers that the child uses many symbols that are not words. When the child uses a broom to stand for a horse, he is using an object as a symbol. When he thinks about his pet cat by making a mental picture, he is using an image as a symbol. Words are only one of several types of symbols used at this age, so language is probably not the cause of the child's symbolic skills.

Social and Emotional Development from Two to Five

If you look again at Table 12–1, you will see that Erikson describes two major "dilemmas," or developmental tasks during the period from ages 2 to 5. Both of these dilemmas involve the child's growing physical and intellectual independence. The first, which emerges around age 2 or 3, is the dilemma of **autonomy versus shame and doubt**. The second, occurring somewhere around age 4 or 5, is the dilemma of **initiative versus guilt**.

The preschool-age child wants to do things for himself, to pick out the clothes he will wear, to tie his own shoes, to eat by himself, to go out in the street to play, and on and on. He is physically able to do many more things now, and his intellectual and language abilities are greatly advanced, so he can tell his parents what he wants (or does not want!) more clearly. The difficulty, as Erikson sees it, is that the child may push too far and either injure himself, or injure his relationships with others. A fine balance between autonomy and control is needed. Rappoport (1972) says of this period that "the parent's job is not to let the child sink or swim, but to make sure that he learns to swim" (p. 87).

The child of 2 to 5 is, of course, not totally independent, nor does he seek to be all of the time. He still shows strong attachments to his mother, father, a teacher, or some other significant person. Over the three-year period, the intensity of the attachment seems to lessen, and the child gradually handles separation more easily (Maccoby & Feldman, 1972). But even at age 4 or 5, the child will revert to earlier, more clinging forms of attachment under stress. If the child is frightened, he may return to his mother or teacher as a "safe base" before venturing out again. The attachment is still there; it is just that we do not see so many overt signs of it in the older preschooler.

Another major shift in the child's relationships during this period is the growing interest in contacts with other children. Until quite recently, psychologists thought that children younger than about 18 months of age had little interest in other babies and would not respond to them. That turns out not to be true. Deborah Vandell (Vandell, Wilson, & Buchanan, 1980) has found that babies as young as 6 months old will respond socially to one another. At this early age most babies will play with toys rather than other babies if they have a choice, but if there are no toys available, another little person will do.

By 18 to 24 months, the child's interest in other children has increased markedly, and we see many more approaches of one child to another (Holmberg, 1980). Donald Hayes (Hayes, Gershman, & Bolin, 1980) has even found that children as young as 36 months have reciprocal "best friends," which suggests that preschoolers may expand their range of personal attachments to include other children.

Several points can be made about these expanding "peer contacts," as psychologists call them. First, there is skill involved. Children who have had more experience with other youngsters make more approaches to other children and do so with more confidence. Second, one of the first effects of increased contacts is an increase in aggression—snatching the other child's toy away, or knocking over his sandcastle. Third, younger children, even when they play together, engage more in *parallel play*, doing the same thing side by side. Older preschoolers enter into *cooperative play*, in which they play *with* others (Holmberg, 1980). Finally, some children just seem to be better at friendships and peer interactions than other children are. Perhaps they are more securely attached, as we suggested earlier, or simply more outgoing (Billman & McDevitt, 1980), or both.

THE EARLY SCHOOL YEARS: FROM FIVE TO TWELVE

The first day of school! Can you remember what it was like? You put on your new clothes, took your new crayons and lunch box, and went off to a new world. Independence at last! A bit scary, perhaps, but a new adventure. The 5-year-old is ready for this new step because of all of the changes we have already discussed, but the school

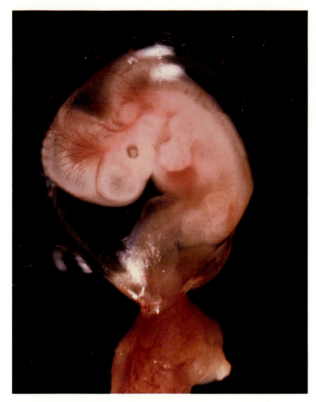

COLOR PLATE 21

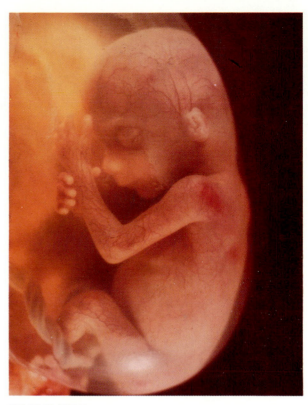

COLOR PLATE 22

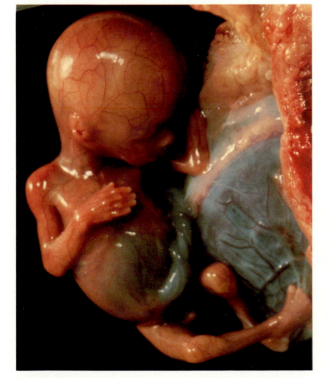

COLOR PLATE 23

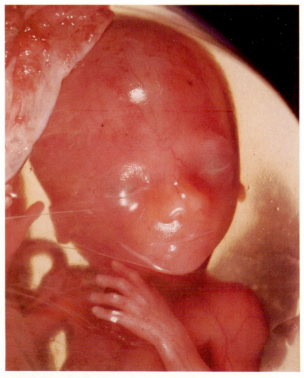

COLOR PLATE 24

COLOR PLATE 25

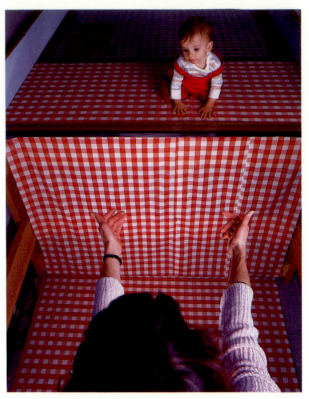

COLOR PLATE 26

Developmental psychology examines the life span of the individual from conception to death. The greatest physical changes are observed prior to birth. Thereafter, development includes not only physical but also social and cognitive changes. These changes always occur in an orderly manner. This allows the developmental psychologist to study the complex interaction that takes place between the changing individual and the environment.

COLOR PLATE 27

At birth, the infant's visual acuity is blurred, but within a short time, the infant has the same visual acuity and depth perception as an adult. Later, the child is able to explore the world and discover how things work. All of these changes occur initially with the help of parents.

COLOR PLATE 28

COLOR PLATE 29

COLOR PLATE 30

COLOR PLATE 31

As the child grows, friendships become more important. These friendships play as significant a role in the socialization of the child as does the influence of parents. Adolescence brings with it extreme concern for physical appearance and peer assessment.

Adulthood places the individual in many new social roles, seeking to define an identity at home, at work, and in the community. Sex roles have changed dramatically in the past two decades and we see more people doing things that were considered inappropriate for their sex just a few years ago.

COLOR PLATE 32

COLOR PLATE 33

Another change that is transforming our society has to do with the greater freedom that the elderly are experiencing today. It is common to see senior citizens engaging in activities that were once believed to be things that only young people could do. Thus, the changes from conception to old age are complex and involve many facets of development.

COLOR PLATE 34

COLOR PLATE 35

years are marked by further growth as well. We will confine our description to only cognitive and social development. This is not to imply that important physical and linguistic developmental changes are not also occurring during this period, but those changes are of degree and not as noticeable as changes being observed in the cognitive and social areas. For example, as far as physical development is concerned, the child continues to grow in height, coordination, and strength, but this is a gradual process. There are no triumphs as great as learning to walk. During this period the child perfects his physical skills. He becomes interested in games requiring physical strength, coordination, and speed, such as football and basketball. The same is true of language. New words are learned and communicative competence improves but the basics of communication have already been established. Because the language skills are in place the child is now ready to learn new skills involving language—reading and writing. Greater coordination is now required between the linguistic, cognitive, and social systems. The greatest activity, however, is taking place in the cognitive and social spheres of the school-age child's life.

Cognitive Development at School Age

By far the greatest changes in the child during the early school years are in cognitive ability. Piaget calls this the period of *concrete operations*, and he argues that the child now begins to develop a new and very powerful set of intellectual skills. But just what are these new abilities?

To make the change clear, we have to begin with the younger child. The infant can do things with objects—handle them, move them around, even sort them into groups in some primitive way. The preschooler can *represent* the objects to himself with words or images and can make an object stand for something else in his play. But what he cannot do is act on his representations *in his head*. For example, he can visualize each of his toy cars, but he cannot add up the images in his head to find out how many cars he has. At some time during the period from 5 to 7, the child begins to be able to use his internal representations in new ways. He can add things up, or subtract one thing from another, or imagine undoing some action that he just did. All of these activities Piaget calls *operations*.

These new skills have grown out of old skills. Adding things up in your head is the mental equivalent of the younger child's physical action of combining things into groups or piles. Subtracting things in your head is the mental equivalent of the physical action of taking things away. All the times the preschooler has moved objects around, made piles, taken things out of them, poured water into a glass and then out of it—all of these experiences have made the new advances possible. What the child discovers around age 5 to 7 is that all those actions can be accomplished *internally* as well as externally.

Conservation   One of the tasks Piaget developed to study the transition from the preoperational stage to concrete operations is the *conservation* task. Suppose you show a child two equal glasses of water.

FIGURE 12–5 A Typical Conservation Experiment *The child is first shown two equal glasses of liquid. Then one is poured into a glass of a different shape. Finally the child is asked if they are still the same.*

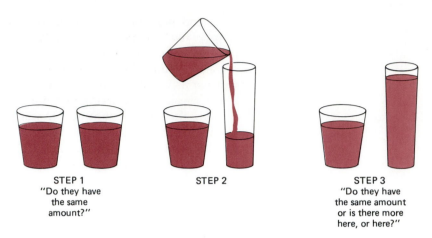

STEP 1
"Do they have
the same
amount?"

STEP 2

STEP 3
"Do they have
the same amount
or is there more
here, or here?"

The two glasses are the same size and have the same amount of water in them. The child agrees they are the same. Now, in full view of the child, you pour the water from one of these glasses into a taller, thinner glass (see Figure 12–5). The level of the water in the tall, thin glass is now higher. If you ask the child if there is the same amount of water in the tall glass as in the remaining original glass, what will she say?

The preschooler will usually say there is more water in the tall, thin glass because the water level is higher. But the child of 6 or 7 will usually tell you that there is the same amount of water in both glasses. She has thus shown that she grasps the concept of conservation—that the quantity of water is "conserved," even when it appears to change. At about the same time, the child also shows conservation of number. She understands that the number of pennies in a row, for example, is not increased if you spread the row out or rearrange it in some other way. Still later in the concrete operational period, the child learns that other properties of objects also are conserved, such as their weight, and the volume they occupy (when you mash a ball of clay into a flat pancake it takes up the same amount of space).

When you ask the older children to explain why there is still the same amount of water even though the water seems higher in one glass, they are likely to say something like, "If you poured it back, it would be the same," or "You didn't add any water, or take any away, so it must be the same." What do these answers tell us? In the first answer, the child is using the operation of *reversibility* to figure out the principle of conservation. She is imagining an action (pouring the water back) and imagining the result of that action. In the second answer, the child is using the operations of addition and subtraction. She is imagining adding more water, or taking some away, and figuring out mentally that unless something has been either added or taken away, it has to have stayed the same. The younger child, who is not yet able to do all these mental manipulations, gets caught up in the appearance of change and thus does not conserve.

Sex Roles Another example of the shift from preoperational to concrete operational thought appears in the child's understanding of sex roles and sex-role stereotypes. A child of 3 or 4 can nearly always label himself or herself correctly as a boy or a girl and can usually recognize males and females from pictures. But not until about age 5 does the child understand fully that gender is constant—that it is, in some sense, "conserved." Five-year-olds are able to understand that they will always be the same sex and that putting on different clothes or growing long hair will not change them to the opposite sex.

Classification   A third example of the preoperational to concrete operational transition appears in the child's use of classification skills. We have described the major advances in classification ability during the preschool period, but two new things happen during the concrete operations period. First, the child begins to understand the concept of **class inclusion**—that each group or class is included in some larger group or class, just as dogs are included in the class of animals, and red squares are part of the group of rectangles. More important, the concrete operations child can use his classification skills to categorize mentally.

Suppose you play Twenty Questions with a 7-year-old. You give him a set of pictures and tell him that you are thinking of one of them. He is supposed to figure out which one by asking you questions. One way to get the answer is to point to each picture in turn and say, "Is it this one?" This is what younger children do. But the older child is able to look carefully at the pictures and to group them in some way in his head. He can then ask something like "Is it a toy?" or "Is it red?" This is what the 7-year-old does, again demonstrating his growing ability to use mental operations.

Fantasy and Reality   Another skill that develops during the period that the child begins to attend school is the ability to distinguish between fantasy and reality. In the preoperational stage, children see their parents as omniscient, and so they do not doubt their parents' stories. But in the next stage of cognitive development, children recognize that parents are not always right. This discovery encourages the children to form and change their own opinions about things. Benjamin, Langley, and Hall (1979) wondered when children stop believing in Santa Claus. Their study duplicated a similar study conducted in the same city in 1896. It revealed that children in the 1970s were 6-1/2 years old when they gave up their belief in Santa Claus—a half year older than counterparts in the 1890s. Benjamin and his colleagues suggest that children living in the end of the nineteenth century were more in touch with the adult world than children today because they had to work long hours and meet adult expectations that they perform as mature workers.

Summary of Changes   The examples we have given and other information about the shift from preoperational to concrete operational thinking point to three major cognitive changes at this stage. First, the child shifts from a focus on the external properties of objects or events—their shape, or color, or how high the water is in the glass—to a focus on the underlying properties of things.

Second, the school-age child becomes increasingly skillful at seeing things from other people's points of view. Piaget described the thinking of the preoperational child as *egocentric*, or centered in the self. Later research indicated that even 3- and 4-year-olds have some ability to see things from another angle, but it is clear that children get consistently better at this through the school years (Borke, 1975; Selman & Bryne, 1974).

Third, the child develops the powerful mental tools that Piaget calls operations. The school-age child has the ability to manipulate objects, sets of things, and categories in her head, rather than needing to move the actual blocks or pictures or dolls around. These changes occur gradually; the child does not wake up on her fifth birthday and suddenly find that she thinks differently than she did the day before. The changes themselves are also subtle, but this constellation of complex, abstract ways of thinking is present in most children by the time they are 8 or 9 years old.

Social and Emotional Development at School Age

The major social and emotional dilemma of the early school years, as Erikson sees it, involves this surge of cognitive development and the fact that the beginning of schooling coincides with it. The child must acquire the specific academic and literacy skills demanded by society. This task demands *industry* from the child, with a risk that the child will experience feelings of *inferiority* if he does not succeed at these tasks.

Whether a child enters the school years able to cope successfully with these demands will depend, in Erikson's view, on whether he has a foundation of basic trust and has been allowed enough (but not too much) independence in the preschool years.

There is some research evidence to back up Erikson's theory. Bradley and Caldwell (1976b) found that mothers who were more involved with their infants at 6 to 24 months of age had children who at age 5 were significantly higher in IQ. Hess and his colleagues (Hess, Shipman, Brophy, & Bear, 1969) found that the mothers who did not always restrict their preschool children were more likely to have children who succeeded in school. In short, the child's ability to cope with the intellectual demands of school is in part affected by the quality and quantity of his early relationship with his parents.

Friendships   School is the beginning of a new and exciting time that includes interacting with other children of similar age. It marks the start of friendships removed to some extent from the control of parents and other family members. Friends are not selected at random, nor are they selected on the basis of one child's preferences and decisions. There is a certain amount of reciprocity and exchange that is required in selecting friends. Research shows that elementary and junior-high-school students have an average of five best friends, with a range of from two to eight best friends (Epstein, 1984). In later adolescence, the number of best friends narrows to two or three.

During the early years in school, friendships are also less stable than they will become when a person is older. There is more shifting of friendships when children are young, but with age children move

School is frequently the beginning of new and exciting interactions with other children as many youngsters begin to form friendships. Much more research is needed on the topic of friendship patterns.

from self-interested choices and limited commitments to friends toward awareness of themselves as members of groups and deeper commitments to particular friends. For some individuals, friendships formed during middle childhood will last a lifetime. This period is usually marked by friendships with individuals of the same sex and age, and by more openness to cross-racial or ethnic friends than will be observed later (Epstein, 1984).

Friendships involve a great deal of sharing and intimacy. In a real sense, friendships involve specific attachments that have several characteristics not unlike those found in parent-infant attachment (Hartup, 1983). For example, friends are a source of security in strange, upsetting circumstances, and separation from them arouses anxiety. Children enjoy making and having friends, develop a sense of trust in them, and derive a great deal of pleasure from their company.

Surprisingly, there has been little research until recently on the development of friendship patterns during this period. The current upsurge of interest in children's friendships has occurred partly because we have discovered that friendships become important much earlier than we had thought and partly because of the connections we noted between early attachment patterns and later skill with peer relationships. Some of the unanswered questions may be answered in the next few years. How durable are children's friendships? (Do you remember your best friend from first grade?) Do children continue to differ in their skill at forming friendships as they get older? If so, what factors might explain such differences? Are school-age children genuinely *attached* to their friends?

ADOLESCENCE: FROM TWELVE TO EIGHTEEN

You probably are not so far away from this time in your life, so you should be able to remember how it feels when powerful new forces come into play during adolescence; marvelous and worrisome physical changes, changing relationships with parents and peers, and new intellectual skills all happen together.

Physical Development at Adolescence

The major physical change is *puberty*, which involves a series of bodily changes that make reproduction possible. These changes are triggered by heightened levels of sex hormones in the blood—estrogen for girls and testosterone for boys. These increases in the sex hormones are in turn triggered by secretions from the pituitary gland, which are themselves brought about by changes in brain chemistry.

These changes appear somewhat later in boys than in girls. In girls, the visible part of the process begins with the earliest signs of breast development, around the age of 11 on the average. A spurt in physical growth starts at about the same time and peaks at age 12 or 13. Menstruation typically begins at about 11½ to 13, although it can begin as early as age 10 or as late as 16 or 17 years.

As for boys, the major changes occur almost two years later than they do for girls. For example, the major spurt in height usually occurs at 14 or 15 years (Tanner, 1970). The testes and penis develop to their adult proportions beginning around age 12 or 13 and ending at about age 15 or 16, but in some boys the sexual development may be completed as late as 18.

In both sexes, the growth spurt occurs in a particular order. The hands and feet are ordinarily the first to attain adult size, followed by the arms and legs, with the trunk achieving its final growth the latest. First, children outgrow their shoes, then their pants, and finally their shirts, blouses, and jackets.

In addition to changes in the sex organs and in height, there are also changes in muscle mass and body fat, which differ for boys and girls, as you can see in Figure 12–6. Girls add proportionately more body fat and relatively less muscle mass than do boys. The result is that fully developed women have proportionately much more fat for their weight, while fully developed men have relatively more muscle

FIGURE 12–6 Muscle Mass and Body Fat Changes during Adolescence *Boys show a proportionately smaller increase in body fat and a larger increase in muscle mass than girls do. (After Cheek, 1974)*

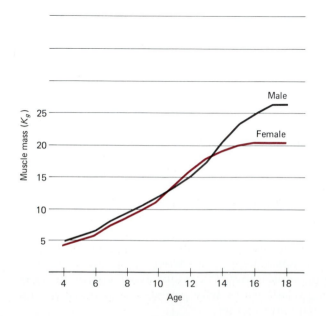

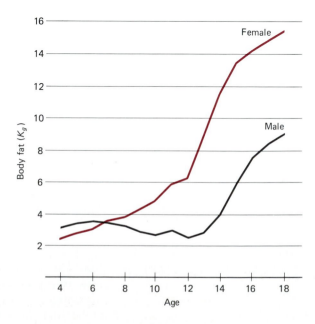

for their weight. During puberty, boys also develop larger hearts and lungs, exhibit lower resting heart rates, and greater oxygen carrying capacity in the blood. Thus, boys experience a considerable spurt in strength, speed, and physical endurance during adolescence that is not matched by girls (Tanner, 1974).

Until recently, these sex differences in muscle, heart, and lungs were assumed to be inevitable results of the differing hormone patterns. Petersen and Taylor (1980), among others, however, have pointed out that all the studies of sex differences in strength and speed in adolescence were done before the current increase in athletic activity among teenage girls. What we need now are studies that compare the muscle, body fat, heart, and lung capacities of boys and girls through adolescence when the amount of exercise in the two groups is the same. Probably we will still find that older teenage boys, as a group, have more muscle tissue and less fat than girls. We know that these differences persist among well-conditioned adult athletes, but the differences among teenagers may still turn out to be smaller than earlier researchers had thought.

Cognitive Development at Adolescence

While all the aforementioned—and sometimes a bit overpowering—physical changes are occurring in the teenager's body, there are also exciting changes taking place that result in adult thinking. These changes manifest themselves in young people in a final, major cognitive change to *formal operations*, but we also see them in the search for new values and for new standards of morality.

Formal Operations   Piaget thought that this final stage began sometime around age 12 to 14. The preoperational child can manipulate actual objects in fairly complex ways, while the concrete operational child can do those manipulations in his head. Now the teenager learns to manipulate *ideas* mentally, to think about things he has never seen, to imagine all the possible solutions to a problem and to try them out one at a time. The concrete operational child thinks about the *actual*; the formal operational young person can think about the *possible*.

One reflection of this change is the ability to use **deductive logic**—to begin with a theory, a hypothesis, or an idea, and then to figure out what *ought* to happen if the hypothesis were true. This is the sort of theorizing we see in much of science. It is quite different from the **inductive** form of logic we see in younger children, when the child figures out some general principle on the basis of many individual, concrete experiences. Scientists work inductively, too, accumulating observations and adding them up to form a new theory. The formal operations thinker can move in both directions.

Most observers agree that there is such a stage as formal operations and that Piaget and his colleague Inhelder have described the major features of this stage accurately (Inhelder & Piaget, 1958). Not all teenagers or adults achieve full formal operations, however. The estimates vary, but probably no more than 50 to 60 percent of older adolescents or adults in our culture are able to perform well on the tasks measuring formal operations—and this is true among college students also. Among adolescents and adults in nonwestern cultures, the formal operations stage seems to be even less frequently achieved.

How can we explain such variation in achievement of this final stage? Piaget emphasizes that a child never shifts from one type of logic or thought to another unless he discovers that his existing system is not adequate. The child does not shift from preoperational logic to concrete operations until he repeatedly comes up against tasks that cannot be handled with preoperational strategies. Presumably, the shift from concrete to formal operations also will occur only if the individual is somehow "forced" to make the adjustment. If the adolescent's environment and experiences can be handled with concrete operational thought, then formal operations will not develop. Perhaps formal operations are not needed in many nonwestern societies or even in some segments of Western society. But we do not yet know what sort of encounters or demands force an adolescent, or an adult, to shift to formal operations.

Moral Reasoning Another cognitive developmental sequence involves moral reasoning. How does a child decide what is right and wrong? How does this change with age? The most comprehensive theory of the development of moral reasoning has been offered by Lawrence Kohlberg, who based his theory on early work by Piaget.

Kohlberg's basic proposal is that the shifts in the way a child reasons about what is right and wrong occur in a fixed, universally observed sequence and are linked to the changes in cognitive development Piaget has described. Specifically, a child's progress through the moral reasoning stages depends on an increasing ability to see things from the perspective of others. This ability begins to appear around age 3 or 4 and develops steadily throughout the elementary and high-school years.

Kohlberg arrived at this view after some 20 years of using a unique procedure to interview children, adolescents, and adults. In the interview, the individual is presented with a series of stories in which characters face moral dilemmas. The following is one of the more popular Kohlberg dilemmas:

> In Europe, a woman was near death from a special kind of cancer. There was one drug that the doctors thought might save her. It was a form of radium that a druggist in the same town had recently discovered. The drug was expensive to make, but the druggist was charging ten times what the drug cost him to make. He paid $200 for the radium and charged $2,000 for a small dose of the drug. The sick woman's husband, Heinz, went to everyone he knew to borrow the money, but he could only get together $1,000, which is half of what it cost. He told the druggist that his wife was dying and asked him to sell it cheaper or let him pay later. The druggist said, "No, I discovered the drug, and I am going to make money from it." So Heinz got desperate and broke into the man's store to steal the drug for his wife. (1969, p. 379)

The interviewee is then asked a series of questions about each dilemma. For the Heinz dilemma, Kohlberg asks a group of interrelated questions. Should Heinz have broken into the druggist's store? Was it actually wrong or right? Why? Is it a husband's duty to steal the drug for his wife if he can get it no other way? Would a good husband do it? Did the druggist have the right to charge that much when there was no law actually setting a limit on the price? Why?

Based on the types of reasons individuals have given to this and other moral dilemmas, Kohlberg arrived at three levels of moral development, each of which is characterized by two stages. Kohlberg's proposed stages of moral reasoning are shown in Table 12–7.

For an individual at Kohlberg's postconventional level, the rules of the society have to mesh with underlying moral principles. In cases where the rules of the society come into conflict with the individual's principles, the individual will follow his or her own principles rather than the conventions of the society. Some specific responses to the Heinz dilemma are presented in Table 12–8, which will give you a better sense of moral reasoning for each of the six stages in Kohlberg's theory. The important thing to remember is that each stage of moral development is determined not by the specific answer a person gives, but by the *reasoning* supporting that answer.

There is a fair amount of evidence to support Kohlberg's contentions, although not all researchers have reached the same conclusions (see the section entitled "Robert Coles and Moral Development"). Most researchers find that the stages do develop in the order Kohlberg proposed (Kohlberg & Elfenbein, 1975) and appear in many different cultures, including India (Parikh, 1980), Kenya (Edwards 1975), and Taiwan, Turkey, and Mexico (Kohlberg, 1969). Work by Walker (Walker & Richards, 1979; Walker, 1980) suggests that both formal operations reasoning and advanced perspective-taking ability are necessary but not sufficient conditions for the development of conventional moral reasoning (Stages 3 and 4).

More controversy surrounds the link between moral reasoning and moral behavior. For example, are college students who operate at the postconventional level less likely to cheat than those at Stage 3 or 4? Are they more likely to help someone in distress? Are they less likely to get into trouble with the law? There has been a good deal of research on the question of the relationship between moral reasoning and moral behavior (reviewed by Blasi, 1980, and by Kupfersmid & Wonderly, 1980), but the issue is still in doubt. The level of moral reasoning a person applies to any given situation is only one of many factors that may affect the "morality" of behavior. Other influences include the pressures of the group the person is in at the time, the probability of being caught, and the strength of the desire for whatever forbidden action is involved. Since many high schools around the country have introduced courses in morality and values (see Power & Reimer, 1978) on the assumption that there *is* a link between reasoning and behavior, the issue has some very practical relevance.

Robert Coles and Moral Development   Not every researcher agrees with Kohlberg's theory of moral development. Child psychoanalyst Robert Coles, who has spent his professional life exploring and illuminating the inner world of the child, comes to quite a different conclusion about moral development. Coles (1986a, 1986b) criticizes Kohlberg's theory of moral development as too strongly correlated

TABLE 12–7 Kohlberg's Stages of the Development of Moral Reasoning

Level 1: Preconventional Morality

Stage 1:	Punishment and obedience orientation	Control of behavior is external, based on commands, punishments, rewards. What is punished is bad; what is rewarded is good. The child obeys because adults have superior power.
Stage 2:	Individualism, instrumental purpose, and exchange	Also described as "naive hedonism." Things that satisfy the self are right. Right is also what is fair, what is an equal exchange. Agreements and deals are valued.

Level 2: Conventional Morality

Stage 3:	Good boy/nice girl orientation; interpersonal conformity	What is good is what pleases others, especially those to whom one is attached (for example, family and friends). More broadly, moral actions are those that match what is expected of you.
Stage 4:	Law and order orientation; social system and conscience	Reference group broadens to include the larger society. Good is defined as fulfilling duties you have agreed to, obeying the law, respecting authority. Virtue should be rewarded.

Level 3: Postconventional or Principled Morality

Stage 5:	Social contracts; legalistic orientation	Laws are seen as important, but changeable. Alternative sets of principles are recognized. Existing laws and customs should be upheld to maintain the social order. The general rule is to act so as to achieve the "greatest good for the greatest number." Contracts and agreements are seen as binding.
Stage 6:	Universally ethical principles	Self-chosen ethical principles dominate moral decisions. Since laws are usually consistent with such ethical principles, obeying the law is usually morally right, but when there is a conflict, the personal conscience is dominant.

Source: After Kohlberg, 1969.

TABLE 12–8   Examples of Kohlberg's Six Stages of Moral Development

Stage	Pro	Con
1	He should steal the drug. It is not really bad to take it. It is not like he did not ask to pay for it first. The drug he would take is only worth $200; he is not really taking a $2,000 drug.	He should not steal the drug; it is a big crime. He did not get permission; he used force and broke in and entered. He did a lot of damage, stealing a very expensive drug and breaking up the store, too.
2	It is all right to steal the drug because she needs it and he wants her to live. It is not that he wants to steal, but it is the way he has to use to get the drug to save her.	He should not steal it. The druggist is not wrong or bad, he just wants to make a profit. That is what you are in business for, to make money.
3	He should steal the drug. He was only doing something that was natural for a good husband to do. You cannot blame him for doing something out of love for his wife; you would blame him if he did not love his wife enough to save her.	He should not steal. If his wife dies, he cannot be blamed. It is not because he is heartless or that he does not love her enough to do everything that he legally can. The druggist is the selfish or heartless one.
4	You should steal it. If you did nothing, you would be letting your wife die; it is your responsibility if she dies. You have to take it with the idea of paying the druggist.	It is a natural thing for Heinz to want to save his wife, but it is still always wrong to steal. He still knows he is stealing and taking a valuable drug from the man who made it.
5	The law was not set up for these circumstances. Taking the drug in this situation is not really right, but it is justified to do it.	You cannot completely blame someone for stealing, but extreme circumstances do not really justify taking the law in your own hands. You cannot have everyone stealing whenever they get desperate. The end may be good, but the ends do not justify the means.
6	This is a situation which forces him to choose between stealing and letting his wife die. In a situation where the choice must be made, it is morally right to steal. He has to act in terms of the principle of preserving and respecting life.	Heinz is faced with the decision of whether to consider the other people who need the drug just as badly as his wife. Heinz ought to act not according to his particular feelings toward his wife, but considering the value of all the lives involved.

Source: After Kohlberg, 1969.

with intelligence. He argues that it is possible to "get all A's and flunk life." He continues by offering as proof the moral outrages committed by the highly intelligent and the many instances of moral vitality displayed by the less intelligent. According to Coles, children and adolescents are constantly bombarded by moral dilemmas. Why is there such hatred and war in Northern Ireland and South Africa? Why is there such poverty in some parts of the world? In searching for how children react to these questions, Coles argues that youngsters are much more capable of handling moral and political questions than their parents and teachers give them credit for being. He maintains that children readily recognize the moral hypocrisy that surrounds them; they hear one line being preached and see another line being enacted constantly. The corruption, graft, dishonesty, and cynicism that we all complain about do not go unnoticed by children. Yet, Coles argues that adults discourage morality in children because they do not want that moral sensibility annoying them or getting in their way. A good example of how a child's moral sensibility gets in the way of adults can be seen in the case of the 11-year-old girl in Los Angeles who, following a school program on the harmful consequences of drugs run by the police department as part of their drug-prevention program, proceeded to turn her parents in for possession of drugs! This was not an isolated instance and has become more commonplace with the advent of school-based, drug-prevention, educational programs.

Coles has researched theology, social science, psychoanalysis, and popular culture for an answer to what impels moral development in children. He finds all of these unproductive in his quest for an answer and concludes that humans all have a morality that is simply a part of us. This morality needs honing and direction, which are provided by our parents, our teachers, the mass media, and our peers. Young people form their moral character by speaking to others, reading newspapers, watching television, and going to movies. According to Coles, amid the violence children see in the media there are serious moral issues that are being analyzed and assessed. He feels that most youngsters are not hurt by the violence but are, in fact, stimulated to moral thinking by some television programs or movies. This evaluation runs counter to some current thinking about the impact of television violence on young children, as we will see in Chapter 20.

Parents have a great deal of moral leverage over their children. If parents really want to teach their children certain values, they can resist the pull of the media. They can sit with their children and watch TV together and discuss why they think some programs are destructive, absurd, or a waste of time. In other words, parents can exert their influence by the joint sharing of ideas and opinions. An often-successful way of instructing kids is not simply to say, "This is bad" or "This is wrong," but to offer good reasons for decisions about *why* things are bad or wrong. (This is quite close to the advice offered parents by Patricia Greenfield as we will see in Chapter 20 when we discuss the effects of television on children.)

Social and Emotional Development at Adolescence

Identity Formation Erikson sees the major social and emotional dilemma of the period of adolescence as the development of a stable personal identity, including both sexual and occupational identities. Like the shift from concrete to formal operations, and from Level 1 to Level 2 or Level 3 morality, the development of identity involves the questioning and reexamining of old values. The teenager must deal not only with the question "Who am I?"—which younger children grapple with as well—but also with "Who *will* I be?" James Marcia (1980), who has done extensive research on identity formation in adolescence, defines identity as

> A self-structure—an internal, self-constructed dynamic organization of drives, abilities, beliefs, and individual history. The better developed this structure is, the more aware individuals appear to be of their own uniqueness and similarity to others and of their own strengths and weaknesses in making their way in the world. (p. 159)

This is a period of development when young people often seem to pull back from relationships with parents and other adults. They often become uncommunicative and moody. Parents and teachers frequently wonder what is going through the head of the teenager. What do they do with their time? What are they thinking? What do they feel about the events and people around them? Like all other stages of development, this is also a crucial period in social and emotional formation of the adolescent. The letter in the box titled "Loved Him Like a Brother" should give you a good sense of the intensity of this period of development. The writer is a 13-year-old girl writing to her aunt, whom she admires and trusts. The girl openly expresses all of her feelings and thoughts in a torrent of emotion that she probably could not state verbally to her parents or teachers. The contents of this letter are not atypical for this period of development. Maybe you wrote similar letters to a friend or made similar entries in your diary as an adolescent.

In a very ingenious study, Mihaly Czikszentmihaly and Reed Larson (1984) asked 75 Chicago-area high-school students to wear electronic pagers for one week. The subjects were from diverse social and racial backgrounds. When they were signaled, every two hours, the adolescents completed a report of what they were doing and how they felt about the activity. At the end of the week, the students filled out questionnaires about their moods, both in general and during specific activities.

The results showed that these 75 adolescents spent about 40 percent of their waking time in leisure activities—socializing with friends, participating in sports, watching TV, working on hobbies, or merely "thinking." The remainder of their time was split fairly evenly between maintenance activities, such as chores, errands, eating, commuting, and so forth, and the productive activities of school, studying, and work. Overall, the students were considerably busier than their typical response ("Nothing much.") to their parents' usual question ("What did you do today?") would seem to indicate.

◆ *LOVED HIM LIKE A BROTHER*

Dear Aunt Kathy,

I am sitting in Science (1st period). I can't stand the teacher. The class is boring and I don't feel very well. See, today is the day the girls' basketball team and I want to make it super bad. But I know I won't, so does everyone else.

I don't have much to say that would interest you—getting stuck in Los Angeles traffic is more exciting, so if this letter isn't very cheery I'm sorry.

We got report cards last week and I made A's. That's about the only good thing thats happened to me lately. School is ok. We are studying Anne Frank, I admire her alot. I still love my Lang. Arts teacher. That's about the only fun class I have.

I don't like any boys right now, I don't ever want a boyfriend any-ways, they're mean, like this one boy, we were really good friends and he wrote me letters every day. They were so sweet and I loved them. We got to where we signed them L/Y/L/A/B or L/Y/L/A/S (love ya like a brother/sister). Then he found this girl he liked better. (I only wanted to be friends anyway.) So he quit writing me and told me not to write him anymore. Then he didn't like the girl any more and told me to start writing him again. He never writes back anymore. I guess that's a hint to leave him alone. I really truly thought he was my friend. You never know who really is your friend. I know this sounds stupid but I feel as though I'm all alone. No one understands how I feel. See I thought C W was my friend, C W are the boy's initials. What did I do? I did not do anything—but be myself, I guess I let myself fall for him. Anyways he's really popular and I loved him like a brother. I don't like him any-more for anything 'cause he doesn't like me—I guess not even for a friend, that's all I really ever wanted to be was—friends. Not boyfriend but friends. Do you understand? I guess not because I don't. Truly don't. Why doesn't he write back? To end this I don't want another "boy" friend again, ok.

I really miss you alot and I want you to know that the time I had in California was like a dream. Thank you for everything and I hope you still like me. If I acted like a brat—or something—I'm really sorry. But another thing that I'd like to thank you for is—not yelling at me the whole time. I know it was hard not to but you didn't and I really appreciate it—ALOT. I'll always remember the time I had and I'll never forget it. Thanks.

This is all for now (I know you're glad) so I'll let you get back to what you were doing.

Love you lots,
Jenny

More important, though, was the finding that adolescents are capable of swings in mood that take them down from extreme happiness or up from deep sadness in less than an hour. Mood swings in the adult usually require several hours to reach the same peaks or valleys seen in teenagers in much shorter periods of time. Czikszent-mihaly and Larson found that when adolescents were unhappy with the drudgery of school, jobs, and chores, their emotional state would reflect this and as relief they preferred to be with friends away from the control of adults and adult-oriented activities.

Similarly, these researchers showed that teenagers liked challenges that fit their developing skills and that provided them with meaningful rewards. This "flow," as it was called by the researchers, takes the adolescent beyond the impulsive, egocentric activities of childhood and into a more adult world of shared rules, symbols, and communication. Teenagers need activities (sports, hobbies, and so on) that challenge them to develop new levels of expertise and accomplishment and propel them to seek still more difficult challenges.

Unfortunately, many adolescents fall into less productive, less satisfying activities that take up large amounts of their time, like watching TV or just "hanging out." These are the paths of least resistance, often taken just to avoid boredom. The problem with this is that other boring or upsetting emotional experiences (parents who do not understand the problems faced by an adolescent or a breakup with a boyfriend or girlfriend) make the situation all the worse for the adolescent since they have no outlet in which to channel their energy and emotionality.

The three dimensions of cognitive and social/emotional change during adolescence that we have described so far—the shifts to formal operations, to higher levels of moral reasoning, and to an integrated identity—turn out to be linked to one another. Teenagers who are already capable of formal operations appear to have an easier time developing a clear identity (Bourne, 1978), and those operating at a principled level of moral reasoning are also more likely to demonstrate identity-achievement status (Podd, 1972). What we do not know from this research is what comes first. Is the formal operations stage *necessary* for full identity achievement? Probably not, since many more people seem to achieve identity than ever reach full formal operations. Is principled moral reasoning required? We cannot tell yet. What does seem clear is that there is a period of doubting, questioning, reassessing of values, rules, procedures, the self, and relationships with others during the years from 12 to 18. To use Piaget's term, it is a time of general disequilibrium that keeps both the young person and his family off balance much of the time.

Friendships in Adolescence   In the midst of this disequilibrium, one of the sources of continuity or stability for most teenagers is the peer group, and the individual friendships within the peer group. The impact of the peer group is stronger during the early teens than at any other time. Young people are more likely to conform to group norms in dress, attitudes, and behavior at this age (Berndt, 1979) and their central affectional bonds begin to shift from parents to peers during the same period (O'Donnell, 1979).

The intensity of this dependence on the peer group and on individual friendships seems to be strongest at about ages 13–15 (at least in our society), when the young person may be at the height of the period of disequilibrium. After this age, there is a lessening of peer-group dominance for most teenagers. Furthermore, those adolescents who are experiencing the most tension and the most disruption in their lives and those who possess the least self-confidence are those for whom the peer group seems to be most important (Coleman, 1980). A teenager who has already begun to cope with the issues of identity, who has begun a smooth transition to formal operations, and who has a generally supportive family, will be less dependent on and influenced by peers than will the teenager for whom the disequilibrium is greater or more lasting. Once again, then, we find the threads of social and cognitive development woven together.

In closing, it is important to mention that early adolescence is not as terrible a time as it has been made out to be. Petersen (1987), in a longitudinal study of adolescents, found that overall development during adolescence was quite positive. More than half of her sample of more than 300 adolescents were trouble-free as they progressed from the eighth to the twelfth grade. Another 30 percent of the total group had only intermittent problems during their early teens. However, 15 percent of the adolescents did appear to have trouble during this period. Boys usually showed their poor adjustment through rebellious and disobedient behaviors, whereas girls were more likely to show moody and depressed behavior. Boys who experience difficulty with adolescence also do less well academically. The situation is different for girls, however. Girls who experience emotional turmoil do better academically. Interestingly, if these same girls later lower their academic achievement, their emotional state improves! In other words, at least during adolescence, it appears that if girls experience emotional turmoil, they can trade grades to increase their popularity, and in the process, their satisfaction with themselves increases.

ADULTHOOD AND AGING

When we think about what happens as we mature and enter adulthood, we think about physical changes—the lessening of physical prowess, the arrival of sags, spreads, and lines. But as we have learned more about adulthood and the aging process over the past decade, we have come to realize that physical changes take a backseat to psychological changes. According to Bernice Neugarten (1982), a pioneer in the study of aging, biological maturation heavily influences childhood development, but as we move into young and middle adulthood, we are more affected by our own experiences and the timing of those experiences than by biological factors. Neugarten maintains that even menopause, that quintessentially biological event, is of relatively little psychological importance to most adult women.

In other words, chronological age is an increasingly unreliable indicator of what people will be like at various points in their lives. A group of newborns, or even 5-year-olds, shows less variation than a group of 35-year-olds or 50-year-olds. Rowe and Kahn (1987) have argued that life-style, habits, diet, and an array of psychosocial factors, such as presence of family and friends, all extrinsic to the aging process, are often more important in understanding age-associated declines in physical or cognitive abilities than chronological age.

When we study the child's development, we are dealing with an organism undergoing regular, predictable, physical changes. The other changes we see in the child are tied to that physical growth in important ways. But is this true for the adult? Do the stages in adult life parallel the stages of childhood? A number of theorists, including

Erikson (1980), think there are (Gould, 1978; Levinson, 1978; Lowenthal, Thurnher, & Chiriboga, 1975; Maas & Kuypers, 1974). These theorists maintain that a person of 20 is qualitatively different from someone going through a "midlife crisis" at 40 or 45, and from a retiring worker at 65. But are these stages only socially defined periods of life or are they linked to predictable physical changes? In order to answer such questions, we must look first at what we know about developmental patterns in adulthood.

Physical Changes

Although adults do not continue to experience rapid physical changes, there are *some* changes. Shock (1962) has done extensive work on the physiology of aging, beginning with adults in their twenties. Among other things, Shock and his colleagues have measured the "workrate" (the amount of physical work the subject can do and still have his heart return to normal within 2 minutes), the heart output (the amount of blood pumped), and the vital capacity of the lungs. The change in these measures over time in men is shown in Figure 12–7.

For most of the body functions Shock studied, the peak capacity or efficiency was among men aged 25 to 30. Among men over 30, Shock observed a fairly steady reduction in capacity with increasing age. Collectively, these changes gradually reduce an individual's ability to carry on sustained physical effort.

Most of the change seems to be brought about by loss of cells in the different parts of the body. Young adults have such an excess of cells in the organs and muscles that the early reductions have no effect on capacity. But after the excess cells are lost, the continuing process has a slow but measurable effect on our capacities. As always,

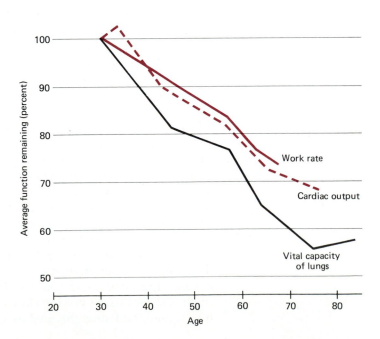

FIGURE 12–7 Physical Changes with Aging in Males
This graph charts the physical changes noted in males during the fifty-year span from mid-adulthood to old age. (After Shock, 1962)

Although the rapid physical changes of childhood and adolescence do not continue into adulthood, there are some changes during the adult years. One factor that affects the rate of physical "aging" is the level of physical exercise maintained during adulthood.

there are wide individual differences in both the speed and the extent of the physical changes. The changes you can see in Figure 12–7 are averages. Some men studied showed little or no loss of body tissue or function until their fifties or even later.

According to the latest evidence, one factor that affects the rate of physical "aging" is whether the man or woman has maintained some level of physical exercise during the adult years (Kasch, 1976). Those who remain physically fit show slower heart rates, more efficient use of oxygen, and even slower loss of body cells. This suggests that the body changes we think of as inevitable from age 20 or so onward are at least partly due to loss of fitness, and not to the aging process itself.

The other significant physical change during adulthood is the **climacteric**, usually called the *menopause* in women. *Both* men and women experience the physiological changes of the climacteric. In both sexes, there are hormonal changes that affect reproductive capacity. In men, beginning in the late forties, there is a gradual reduction in the number of sperm produced. Sperm production does not cease altogether, so older men can still father children and still enjoy sexual intercourse.

In women, the hormonal changes of menopause typically occur between about 42 and 52. Ovulation ceases, and so does menstruation. The hormone change is sometimes accompanied by other physical symptoms, most commonly hot flashes. There is no evidence, however, that depression is any more common among women during menopause than during other periods of adult life.

To sum up, our bodies *do* change as we get older. We lose cells—muscle cells, brain cells, nerve cells—we react a bit slower, our stomachs secrete fewer enzymes, our skin gets a bit drier and thus more wrinkled, and we may lose our hair. But these changes, as well as the hormone changes of the climacteric, are not as enormous as many researchers had thought, nor as great as many people fear. In fact, older people today are not only healthier and more active, they are also increasingly more numerous. Because of better medical care, improved diet, and increasing interest in physical fitness, more people are reaching the ages of 65, 75, and older in excellent health. Functional age, which is a combination of physical, psychological, and social factors that affect a person's attitude toward life and their social roles is often much younger than that person's chronological age.

Aging does imply physical change—reflexes slow, hearing and eyesight dim, stamina decreases. This **primary aging** is a gradual process that begins early in life and affects all body systems. But many of the problems we associate with old age are **secondary aging**—the result not of age per se but of disease, abuse, and disuse factors often under our own control. This is especially true for sexual activity (or lack of activity). From the time of Kinsey to the present, studies have shown that sexual interest and activity diminish with age; however, the decrease varies greatly among individuals. In fact, there are numerous reports that indicate that the best predictor of sexual intercourse in the elderly has to do with the amount of postsexual enjoyment expressed by the individual and the frequency of intercourse. People who have never had much pleasure from sexuality may regard this time as a good excuse for giving up sex!

Intellectual Capacity during Adulthood and Aging

The conclusion that emerges from the most recent research on the intellectual capacities of adults is similar to what we have just seen in connection with physical changes. There is some loss of ability on some types of activities, but there is far more maintenance of ability than there is loss (Schaie, 1980).

Until a few years ago, a very different summary conclusion would have been written. Researchers who compared different groups of adults at different ages—a strategy called *cross-sectional* research—found that each older group did a little bit less well on IQ tests and on other measures of intellectual functioning (Baltes & Labouvie, 1973; Horn, 1970; Matarazzo, 1972). The trouble with this research, though, is that not only are the 30-year-old and 80-year-old groups different in age, they are also vastly different in life experiences and in physical health. Many more of today's 30-year-olds have finished high school and college. They grew up with television, computers, and relative economic prosperity. The 80-year-olds, as a group, have a lot less education, have lived through two world wars and a major depression, and are much more likely to be suffering from those specific diseases that impair cognitive functioning at *any* age, such as cardiovascular disease.

A better research strategy is to study the *same* group of people over many years—a research design called *longitudinal* research—and see whether each age group, over time, shows steady performance, improved performance, or decline. Schaie and others who have conducted longitudinal studies (Schaie & Labouvie-Vief, 1974; Schaie, 1980), found no sign of an overall decline in intellectual performance over the entire range of the years of adulthood, except for tasks that

Adults who actively engage in pursuits that provide intellectual stimulation show less loss of cognitive functioning than people of similar age who are no longer intellectually curious.

demand speed of response. On problems requiring speed, there was usually a fairly steady (but moderate) decline in performance over the adult years.

When there is a decline in such cognitive tasks as inductive reasoning and spatial orientation with aging, Schaie and Willis (1986) have even shown that the change can be reversible. By providing five training sessions on reasoning and spatial orientation, these researchers found substantial and retained improvement among the individuals who were previously declining in cognitive function. Thus the cognitive loss in later years that has been considered intrinsic to aging may be caused in part by extrinsic factors (cardiovascular disease, for example) and may at least in part be reversible or preventable once the role of these factors is understood. Finally, adults who have little intellectual or social stimulation show more loss in cognitive functioning than people of similar age who remain intellectually curious and active. The old adage "use it, or lose it" seems to apply here. Many individuals show intellectual vigor well into their seventies, eighties, or nineties.

Social and Emotional Changes during Adulthood and Aging

If you look back at Table 12–1, you will see that Erikson proposes three separate tasks or dilemmas during adulthood. The first, which occurs in most people some time in the early twenties, he describes as *intimacy versus isolation*. Erikson emphasizes that genuine intimacy requires us to give up some of our sense of separateness. To do this, an individual must have a firm identity; those who do not may be unable to sustain real intimacy, and a sense of isolation may result. In our society, most young people marry or form some kind of semipermanent relationship during this phase.

The second adult task Erikson calls *generativity versus stagnation.* It begins in the mid-twenties and lasts to 40 or beyond. During this period, the healthy individual is thought to go beyond the genital sexuality of adolescence and focus on the generative aspects of sexuality. Most commonly, this means producing and rearing children. But generativity can also be expressed through work accomplishments, through some other form of creativity, and through aiding younger colleagues. If some sense of satisfying generativity is not achieved, the adult may feel a sense of stagnation or meaninglessness. The "midlife crisis" about which so much has been written lately (Gould, 1978, 1980; Levinson, 1978, 1980; Sheehy, 1974) is thought to be one outcome of this dilemma.

The final developmental task Erikson proposes is the resolution of the conflict between *ego integrity and despair*. Facing death, or a sense of his own mortality, the aging individual must find some larger meaning in his own life, or he will experience a sense of despair. The self-questioning that occurs at this time may be triggered by such life changes as retirement, the departure of the last child from the home, or the death of close friends or one's spouse.

In a report on aging, Erikson, Erikson, and Kivnick (1986) summarized research findings based on a group of elderly people who had first participated in 1929 as parents of children selected for inclusion in a longitudinal study of child development. As parents, these individuals contributed invaluable information on their home life, social status, and child-rearing practices, as well as on psychological adjustment. With this amassed data on a number of very old people, the Eriksons and Kivnick conducted interviews with their respondents for the express purpose of reconstructing each person's view of his life cycle. On the basis of these interviews Erikson and his colleagues, in rather poetic fashion, conclude that

> The life cycle . . . does more than extend itself into the next generation. It curves back on the life of the individual, allowing a reexperiencing of earlier stages in a new form. This retracing might be described as a growth toward death. . . . Maples and aspens every October bear flamboyant witness to this possibility of a final spurt of growth. Nature, unfortunately, has not ordained that mortals put on such a fine show. As aging continues, in fact, human bodies begin to deteriorate and physical and psychosocial capacities diminish in a seeming reversal of the course their development takes. When physical frailty demands assistance, one must accept again an appropriate dependence without the loss of trust and hope. The old, of course, are not endowed with the endearing survival skills of the infant. Old bodies are more difficult to care for, and the task itself is less satisfying to the caretaker than that of caring for infants. Such skills as elders possess have been hard won and are maintained only with determined grace. Only a lifetime of slowly developing trust is adequate to meet this situation, which so naturally elicits despair and disgust at one's own helplessness. Of how many elders could one say, "He surrendered every vestige of his old life with a sort of courteous, half-humorous gentleness"? (p. 327)

DYING AND DEATH: THE FINAL STAGE

Since we began this chapter with a discussion of conception, it is only fitting that we close with a few words about the final step, death, and the period leading up to death. It is customary in our society to measure our age from birth, but many older adults measure time another way, as "time 'til death" (Neugarten, 1967). There is some evidence from research like that of Riegel and Riegel (1972) that measuring time this way may not just reflect a morbid fear of death, or the awareness of time passing. Riegel and Riegel found that there is a period during the four or five years immediately preceding death when there is a significant decline in both intellectual power and physical capacity. Lieberman (1965, 1966) has also found that older adults showed a loss of energy and a kind of inward withdrawal in the final months before death. These findings suggest that "time 'til death" is a more significant aspect in predicting the functioning of older adults than is chronological age.

According to Elizabeth Kübler-Ross (1969), the final stage of life, the "dying stage," is itself divided into identifiable steps, which are summarized in Table 12–9. Kübler-Ross believes that these steps occur in the order listed, and that each person who knows he is dying (whatever his age) goes through these same steps. Others who have studied dying patients since Kübler-Ross's work was first published have not found all five steps. Schulz and Alderman (1974) have found that the only stage of dying they could detect in every case was the fourth step, depression. Not everyone reached the stage of acceptance, and not everyone went through the denial and anger.

Future research on this final stage of life will undoubtedly focus on those factors that affect our ability to cope with dying. How does our personality affect it? Does chronological age make a difference— do terminally ill teenagers handle impending death differently than 90-year-olds? Does it matter *where* one dies? The current emphasis on remaining at home, rather than in a hospital, during the final months and days of life is based in part on the assumption that acceptance of death is easier to achieve if one is supported by loving family members in familiar surroundings. Since each of us will one day face this last "developmental task," it is important to know more about it—to

TABLE 12–9	The Stages of Dying Proposed by Kübler-Ross
Denial	"This isn't really happening to me." "It can't be true." "Somebody got my lab tests mixed up with another patient's."
Anger	"Why me!" The anger may be directed at anyone handy, including family, doctors, nurses.
Bargaining	"If I can only live until Christmas, then I won't mind so much." Postponements for "good behavior" are sought.
Depression	The patient is depressed about the things undone, the relationships unresolved, the losses that will be experienced. This may be a preparatory depression—a getting ready for the final step.
Acceptance	The patient develops a quiet acceptance, even a welcoming of death. Feelings become muted; passion is stilled; struggling is done.

remove the taboo, if we can, from discussions of death, and to study it openly.

Now that we have surveyed developmental changes across the life span, we will turn our attention in the next chapter to an examination of several critical developmental topics of importance to developmental psychologists. Each of the topics to be discussed occupies the time and energy of many psychologists because the issues involved affect many of us in one way or another.

SUMMARY

1. Developmental psychologists are primarily interested in continuity and changes throughout the span of life, but differ on what causes these changes to occur.

2. One major view, proposed by Gesell, among others, is that development occurs because of internally programmed physical changes, called maturation.

3. A second view is that developmental change is the sum of a series of individual learning experiences. This view has been proposed by Baer and Bandura, among many others.

4. A third view is that both learning and maturation are involved, but that many important changes come about by a process of internal synthesis or equilibration on the part of the child. Psychoanalytic theorists, such as Freud and Erikson, and cognitive developmental theorists, such as Piaget, agree that interaction between the child's qualities and the environment is crucial for development.

5. Prenatal development is heavily influenced by maturation; the sequence of changes is the same for all embryos and fetuses and is not easily influenced by outside forces.

6. Some external prenatal influences do make a difference, including the mother's diet and some diseases contracted by the mother.

7. At birth, the infant can see fairly well, can hear and discriminate among sounds in the usual voice range, can taste and smell, can learn through both classical and operant conditioning, and has many important reflexes.

8. During the first two years, the child's motor skills develop rapidly, with walking occurring by age 1; these early motor skills are governed mostly by maturation, but the general richness of the environment makes some difference.

9. Cognitive skills developed during the first two years include object permanence and internal representation.

10. The major development to occur in the first two years is the establishment of the primary attachment between child and parent. Signs of this attachment are seen in the infant's "separation anxiety," which occurs when the mother leaves the infant's sight, or in "fear of strangers," which occurs if the infant is approached by an unfamiliar person. The security of this attachment seems to affect the child's later peer relationships also.

11. From ages 2 to 5, the child consolidates cognitive gains, shows further motor development, and works out new levels of personal independence.

12. From ages 5 to 12, a period Piaget calls concrete operations, the child makes very large cognitive gains, becoming able to manipulate internal representations and to reason inductively.

13. Physical changes at adolescence are governed by maturation; they are triggered by increased output of sex hormones and occur earlier in girls than in boys. There are also larger changes in body systems that affect speed and strength for boys.

14. Intellectually, the major gain of adolescence for many (but not all) children is the acquisition of formal operations, which includes the ability to reason deductively, to think about ideas abstractly, and to explore ideas systematically.

15. There are also major changes in the level of moral reasoning seen in adolescents, with young people judging rightness and wrongness more by societal standards, or (at later stages) by personal standards of conscience.

16. The major emotional crisis of adolescence is "identity formation." Most adolescents go through a period of diffuse identity, then a period of questioning and doubting, and then form a new, clearer sense of self.

17. In adulthood there appear to be additional developmental stages, but these adult stages seem less governed by physical changes and more influenced by social expectations.

18. There are physical changes during adulthood, but there is little substantial loss of physical function except speed of response until the fifties or later, and the amount of physical "decline" depends on the level of fitness maintained.

19. Intellectually, too, there is less loss of function than psychologists first thought; for tasks that do not require speed of response, healthy adults retain intellectual capacity into their eighties or beyond.

20. Emotionally, the adult may go through three separate dilemmas. The first is the dilemma of "intimacy versus isolation" during one's twenties; the second is "generativity versus stagnation" during one's mid-twenties to early forties; and the third is "ego integrity versus despair" in later years. It is not clear whether all adults go through these dilemmas in this order, but most people show a pattern of continuity that runs throughout adulthood.

21. The final "stage" of life is preparation for inevitable death. There is fairly marked physical and intellectual decline in the last few months or years prior to death, and there may be specific stages in coping with impending death, including denial, anger, bargaining, depression, and acceptance.

KEY TERMS

attachment

autonomy versus shame and
  doubt

change

class inclusion

climacteric (menopause)

cognitive developmental
  (stages or theory)

concrete operations

conservation

cooperative play

deductive logic

egocentric

ego integrity and despair

embryo

equilibration

fear of strangers

fetal alcohol syndrome

fetus

formal operations

generativity versus stagnation

inductive logic

industry

inferiority

initiative versus guilt

internal representation

intimacy versus isolation

maturation

neonatal period

parallel play

preoperational period

primary aging

process of development

psychosexual stages

psychosocial stages

puberty

reversibility

secondary aging

sensorimotor stage

separation anxiety

teratogenic effect

ADDITIONAL READING

Czikszentmihaly, M., & Larson, R. (1984) *Being adolescent: conflict and growth in the teenage years.* New York: Basic Books. This valuable resource is an important book on the social and emotional life of adolescents and a rich guide on adolescents' feelings and experiences.

Erikson, E. H., Erikson, J. M., & Kivnick, H. Q. (1986) *Vital involvement in old age.* New York: W. W. Norton. This book consists of reflections on old age as the concluding stage of the life cycle.

Klaus, M., & Klaus, P. (1985) *The amazing newborn.* Reading, MA: Addison-Wesley. This easy-to-read book presents a fascinating account of the sensory and cognitive capacities observed in newborns.

Lesko, W., & Lesko, M. (1984) *The maternity sourcebook.* New York: Warner Books. This book summarizes basic information about pregnancy, birth, and baby care.

Petersen, A. C. (1987) Those gangly years. *Psychology Today, 21* (No. 9), 28–34. This excellent review discusses early adolescents and their feelings about their biological and social changes.

White, B. L. (1985) *The first three years of life.* (rev. ed.) New York: Prentice-Hall. A detailed account of the physical, emotional, and cognitive development of children to age 36 months, this book offers practical advice on disciplining young children, selecting the best toys, and much more.

13 Exploring Developmental Issues

Children have taken center stage in almost all popular magazines these days. Similarly, the news media are filled with stories about children and adolescents, many of which are relevant to important developmental issues. Common themes include the following:

What is the best way to discipline children?

Why do some adults abuse children?

How can children and adults survive divorce?

How can you keep your child away from drugs and alcohol?

What about sex on television—does it convey a message of permissiveness?

Should sex education be part of the school curriculum?

What risks does the teenage mother run? What about her infant?

Is it possible to raise children who have truly egalitarian views about sex roles?

The list could go on and on, with questions about surrogate mothering, test-tube babies, sperm banks, and the advisability of early reading programs for preschool children. These are just a few of the literally hundreds of questions that could be asked. Note that we have not even covered the full age span in our quest for relevant questions. It is difficult to explore all of these questions in this chapter, so we have elected to examine five: child abuse, the impact of divorce, day care, teenage parents, and sex differences and sex-role stereotypes. These are all crucial questions, though some may have more relevance to your life than others. In each case, we will examine the research evidence available and present the latest findings from this research.

CHILD ABUSE

The abuse of young children by adolescents and adults has become a major social problem in our society. Seldom does a day go by that we do not hear or read about some incident involving a child who has been abused. According to the most recent figures released by the U.S. Bureau of Census, *Statistical Abstracts of the United States* (1987), there were 1,131,300 cases of child neglect and abuse reported in 1984. The fear of child advocates is that abuse is increasing rather than declining (Williams, 1980).

Definition of Child Abuse

Child abuse is an injury or a pattern of injuries to a child that is nonaccidental. Child abuse is damage to a child for which there is no reasonable explanation. There are four identifiable types of abuse:

- Nonaccidental physical injury, which includes severe beatings, burns, human bites, immersion in scalding water, and so forth.

- Sexual molestation, which includes coercion of a child in the form of rape, incest, fondling of the genitals, exhibitionism, and commercial exploitation through prostitution or the production of pornographic materials for the sexual gratification of an older person.

- Neglect, which means the failure to provide a child with the basic necessities of life—food, clothing, shelter, and medical attention.

- Emotional abuse, which is excessive, aggressive, or unreasonable parental behavior that places unrealistic demands on the child to perform beyond his capabilities. Examples of emotional abuse include constant teasing, belittling, or verbal attacks; withholding affection and social support; and failure to offer guidance.

Child abuse is rarely a single act; rather, it is usually a pattern of behaviors. Its effects are cumulative and the longer it continues the more serious it becomes and the worse the child's injuries may be.

Factors That Contribute to Abuse

In some respects, all families are vulnerable to child abuse. Being a parent—and being a child—is often not easy. But there are situations and events that put some children at a greater risk of being abused. For instance, psychologists who study child abuse have learned that family size is a risk factor for abuse; the larger the family, the higher the risk. In addition, the more closely spaced the children are, the higher the risk (Gil, 1970). The absence of one parent from the home, or single parenthood, may also place undue stress on the remaining parent, thereby increasing the likelihood of abusive behavior (Kimball, Conger, & Burgess, 1980).

Socioeconomic factors also create the potential for abuse. Unemployment and related financial difficulties are closely correlated with abuse (Krugman, Lenherr, Betz, & Fryer, 1986). Overcrowded or inadequate housing, alcohol abuse, and difficulty with the law are other factors associated with child maltreatment (Spinetta & Rigler, 1972).

Importantly, parents who lack social supports are very vulnerable. Garbarino and Gilliam (1980) have shown that abusive families tend to be socially isolated. The parent (or parents) may be cut off from neighborhood and community resources needed to help them cope with the stresses of loss of employment, illness, or single parenthood. In addition, lack of contact with people outside the family unit leads to more numerous and more intense interactions with one's children, providing more opportunities for conflicts of interest to arise, limiting tension-releasing outlets, and ultimately increasing the likelihood that violent behavior will erupt.

Many abusive adults also manifest poor parenting skills (Burgess, 1979). Such parents often do not possess knowledge about normal child development and may be poor observers of their children's behavior (Patterson, 1977). This leads to unrealistic expectations for children's behavior and an inability to monitor appropriate and inappropriate actions. Inconsistent use of discipline may result (Patterson, 1977). This general lack of parenting skills often leads to higher rates of negative behavior and lower rates of positive behavior directed toward children in abusive and neglectful families (Burgess & Conger, 1978; Wolfe, 1985).

The Developmental and Social Issues of Child Abuse

Child abuse raises extremely troubling issues for psychologists and for society as a whole. First of all, what is the effect on the child? The child is physically hurt, often severely, but what about the long-term emotional cost? And what are the effects on the child's intellectual development? Everything we said in Chapter 12 about the important links between physical, emotional, and mental development argues that damage to one system should result in damage to the others. Abuse by the parent surely violates the child's sense of basic trust, so in Erikson's terms, any abused child is likely to have major problems with the whole series of emotional dilemmas Erikson describes. We will explore this possibility in more detail later.

The second question we must ask is why abuse occurs at all. Is there some common characteristic of abusing parents that sets them apart from others—something from their childhood or some enduring personality characteristic? Or are abusing parents merely responding to short- or long-term stresses in their environments? Will almost *any* of us abuse our children if the stresses become strong enough? We also have to ask whether the abused child contributes to the process in some way. Are abused children initially different in some way from other children?

Finally, we need to explore the prediction and prevention of abuse. If we can understand why abuse occurs, perhaps it will be possible to prevent it or to design therapies that may aid parents who have already abused their youngsters.

The Effects of Abuse on the Child

The abused child is in pain. In perhaps 3 to 4 percent of cases, the abuse is fatal to the child. In another 25 to 30 percent, there is lasting physical damage—brain damage, loss of sight or hearing, or physical deformity (Helfer, 1975). The effects on the child's emotional and intellectual development are much harder to pin down, but what little information there is suggests that the prospects for abused children are not good.

Abused children are usually found to perform poorly on IQ tests and to function in the range of mental retardation. In a study by Reidy, Anderegg, Tracy, and Cotler (1980), the average IQ of a group of 20 physically abused children of early elementary-school-age was 82, compared to an average of 100 for a comparison group of children from equally poor economic backgrounds. But which is cause and which is effect in results like these? Does the abused child have a lower IQ because of the abuse, or is the child abused because he or she is a slow learner? This is an extremely sticky question to answer. We do know that many abused children show improvement in their school performance or test scores after they have been placed in foster families (Money & Annecillo, 1980; Morse, Sahler, & Friedman, 1970). This finding suggests that at least in some cases, the abusive environment is a major cause of the child's poor intellectual showing. In other cases, there may be an initial slowness of cognitive development in the child that is aggravated by the abuse.

In perhaps 3 to 4 percent of child-abuse cases, the abuse is fatal to the child. Another 25 to 30 percent of such cases result in lasting physical damage that may include loss of sight or hearing.

Research also points to significant effects of abuse on the child's social and emotional development. Several researchers have found that children abused or severely neglected in the first few years of life show very insecure attachments to their parents (Egeland & Sroufe, 1981). In one revealing study, Lewis and Schaefer (1981) observed a group of 8- to 22-month-old abused children interacting with their mothers as the infants were being dropped off and picked up at a day-care center. Compared to a group of nonabused toddlers in the same situation, the abused infants looked at their mothers less, said "goodbye" less, followed their mothers less when the mothers were leaving, greeted them less when the mothers returned, and stood or played further from their mothers when they were present. All of these signs of insecure attachment are consistent with what we would expect, given Erikson's view of the importance of the parent-infant relationship for the establishment of trust.

Several other researchers, including Reidy (Reidy, 1980; Reidy et al., 1980) and Kinard (1980), have found that abused children also interact differently with their peers and with teachers. They are more aggressive, less self-reliant, and less self-confident. Their teachers describe them as less adequate and more immature. Findings like these certainly suggest that both the abuse itself and the family environment in which it occurs seriously harm the child's social and emotional development.

However, there surely must be children who survive child abuse and who grow up to be well-adjusted adults. One of the few studies to examine this question was conducted by Zimrin (1986) in Israel. In this 14-year longitudinal study, Zimrin kept track of 28 children who had been abused. At the beginning of the study, all the children were between the ages of 3½ and 5 years. All of the children were observed for two days every three months in school and in their neighborhoods. In addition, teachers were interviewed twice a year about school-related adjustment, relationships with friends, and general acceptance behavior of the target children. Appropriate psychological tests were administered to the children periodically to examine specific traits or attributes.

Of the 28 abused children studied, Zimrin was eventually able to label 9 of them as survivors and 19 as nonsurvivors, or emotionally impaired. Table 13–1 presents a comparison of the two groups on a series of personality traits and related interpersonal measures. Despite the successful coping of Zimrin's survival group, these individuals still showed high aggression, lack of ability to express emotions, isolation, and difficulty in establishing personal relations. The critical factor for the survivor group appeared to be that these individuals had a sympathetic person (or persons) who had confidence in them and who maintained a stable relationship with them. Sometimes this person was a teacher or another adult who treated them with empathy and encouraged them. Another significant factor that contributed to positive coping was being responsible for someone or something else. The survivors mentioned having responsibility for younger siblings or pets. No nonsurvivors mentioned responsibility for others.

Zimrin's findings are intriguing. There are problems with the study, to be sure. For example, the small sample size, especially of the survivor group, leaves room for questions about the representative nature of the results. More studies of this type need to be conducted before we can have a complete picture of the effects of abuse on children and a better understanding of strategies for ameliorating these effects through counseling and other service programs.

TABLE 13–1 Comparison of Profiles of the Surviving and Nonsurviving Abused Child

Profile of the S Abused Child	*Profile of the NS Abused Child*
Control of destiny	± Fatalism and submission
High self-image	± Low self-image
Good cognitive performance	± Poor cognitive performance
Expression of hope in fantasy	± Absence of expression of hope
Belligerent behavioral pattern	± Yielding and pliable behavior
Absence of self-destructive behavior	± Self-destructive behavior
High aggression	= High aggression
Difficulty in expressing emotions	= Difficulty in expressing emotions
Difficulty in establishing relationships	= Difficulty in establishing relationships
Existence of supporting adult or responsibility for a dependent	± Absence of supporting adult Absence of responsibility for a dependent

Source: After Zimrin, 1986.

± Represents difference between the groups.
= Represents similarity between the groups.

The Causes of Abuse

Researchers have looked for the root cause of abuse in the parent, in the total environment, and in the child. As is often true when we try to find *one* cause, we will see that all three causes are probably involved.

The Abusing Parent   The most obvious place to search for causes is in the abusing parent. After all, it is the parent who is hitting the child. In the early days of research on abuse, most psychologists assumed that they would find certain common qualities or types of emotional disturbances among abusing parents that set them apart. Steele and Pollock (1974) argued that abusing parents are people with extremely high expectations for their children, as the following comment indicates:

> He knows what I mean and understands it when I say "come here." If he doesn't come immediately, I go and give him a gentle tug on the ear to remind him of what he's supposed to do. [This 16-month-old child's ear was partially torn away from his head.] (p. 96)

Morris and Gould (1963) emphasized a different quality in abusing parents, which they call *role reversal.* In role reversal, the parent expects the child to be a source of comfort and affection, as the following comment demonstrates:

> I have never felt really loved all my life. When the baby was born, I thought he would love me, but when he cried all the time, it meant he didn't love me, so I hit him. [This infant was hospitalized at 3 weeks of age with brain damage.] (Steele & Pollock, 1974, p. 96)

While both of these qualities are found in many abusers, they are not found in all, and there are many nonabusers who have high expectations or show role reversal, too. Psychologists who have examined all the evidence on special parental qualities are not convinced that there is any pattern that really distinguishes abusers from nonabusers (Parke & Collmer, 1975; Lewis & Schaeffer, 1981), but these researchers *do* agree that abusing parents were themselves highly likely to have been abused and neglected as children (Spinetta & Rigler, 1980). This may have affected their ability to form attachments with their own children. It may also mean that they have learned aggressive ways of handling frustration and stress.

Obviously, the question of whether an abused child becomes an abuser as an adult is a very important one and one to which the answer is not as clear-cut as we might like it to be. In one study, Altemeier and his colleagues (Altemeier, O'Connor, Sherrod, & Tucker, 1986) wanted to know what kind of attitudes pregnant, low-income women had about their pregnancy and their expected infants based on whether or not the women had been abused as children. Table 13–2 presents some background information about the women in this study. The women who had been battered as children differed from the nonbattered group on a number of very important psychological and interpersonal variables. However, the attitudes of the two groups of women concerning their current pregnancy did not differ appreciably in any respect. This can be seen in Table 13–3.

TABLE 13–2   The Effects of Child Abuse on Mothering

Characteristics of 95 women who reported being battered as children and 832 women who had not been battered on questions of parental nurture (love), self-esteem, and feelings of social isolation.

	95 Battered	832 Not Battered
Parental Nurturance		
How do you feel about your mother?		
Separated or don't get along	53%	17%**
How do you feel about your father?		
Separated or don't get along	55%	25%**
Was your childhood happy, unhappy, or in between?		
Unhappy	42%	6%**
Do you feel you were loved as a child?		
No	44%	4%**
Do you feel you let your parents down?		
Yes	23%	19%
Do you feel you were punished unfairly?		
Yes	70%	31%**
Who did you live with while growing up?		
Institution	19%	2%**
Self-Esteem		
Do you usually feel good or bad about yourself?		
Bad	21%	9%**
How would you describe yourself—usually successful or unsuccessful?		
Successful	38%	52%*
Does it spoil your day when someone criticizes you or puts you down?		
Yes	36%	33%
Isolation		
Who do you talk to about your problems most of the time?		
No one is available or don't want anyone	31%	17%**
If you needed help, do you have friends other than your parents who would help you?		
No	28%	11%**
Are you a friendly person who likes to be with people or would you rather keep to yourself?		
Keep to self because do not trust others	17%	5%**
What kind of relationship do you have with your baby's father?		
Separated	20%	11%**

Source: After Altemeier et al., 1986.

Asterisks after a percentage indicate that a statistical test was run to see if the differences in the percentages of the two groups are due to chance or are real differences caused by being abused as a child. A single asterisk means that the difference would occur by chance five times out of one hundred while a double asterisk means that the difference would occur by chance only one time out of one hundred.

TABLE 13–3   Attitude about Current Pregnancy in Battered and Control Mothers

	95 Battered	832 Not Battered
How did you feel when you first found out you were pregnant?		
Depressed or didn't want it	19%	13%
How do you feel now about having this baby?		
Depressed or don't want it	4.2%	3.2%
Have you or your family considered abortion or adoption for this pregnancy?		
Yes	25%	17%
If you could go back and change things, would you still be pregnant?		
No	26%	26%

Source: After Altemeier et al., 1986.

The much more interesting findings from the Altemeier study have to do with attitudes toward children or child rearing between the two groups of women. This information is shown in Table 13–4. Women who reported being abused as children were significantly more likely to feel angry toward a screaming child, to believe in physical discipline that would generally be considered abusive, and to admit that they had physically attacked an adult or child recently. Thus, mothers in the abused group seemed to exhibit a greater tendency toward violent behavior.

Before jumping to any conclusions, however, it is important to concentrate on data presented in the last two lines of the battered column of Table 13–4. These figures represent the percentage of battered women who up to four years after initiation of the study had been reported for child abuse (2.1 percent) or neglect (5.3 percent) of the child. The rate of reported child abuse or child neglect for these battered women did not differ statistically from the rate for women whose hospital records were also available and who had not been abused as children. In fact, slightly more of the control women had been reported for child abuse (2.5 percent) and somewhat fewer had been reported for child neglect (3.9 percent).

Therefore, there is not a simple and direct relationship between being abused as a child and later becoming an abusive parent. This point has been reinforced more recently by Kaufman and Zigler (1987) who estimate that approximately 25 to 35 percent of abused children mistreat their own children. Parents who did not repeat the cycle of abuse tended to have more extensive support from family and friends and expressed more anger about the abuse they had experienced as children. Not only could they describe the abuse in detail, but they were determined not to abuse their own children. Also, these parents reported that at least one of their own parents was loving and did not abuse them.

TABLE 13–4 Assessment of Intergenerational Transmission of Child Maltreatment in Battered and Control Mothers

	95 Battered	832 Not Battered
How does it make you feel when you hear a screaming baby?		
Angry	11%	3%**
What is the best way for mothers to get their children to behave?		
Hit other than on the hands, legs, or buttocks	5.3%	1.6%*
Have you become so angry that you've lashed out and done things you were sorry about? What did you do?		
Hit with hand or object other than on legs, buttock, or hands		
Second or later pregnancy	41%	17%**
First pregnancy	35%	19%**
Reported for child abuse of target child or sibling	2.1%	2.5%
Reported for child neglect of target child or sibling	5.3%	3.9%

Source: After Altemeier et al., 1986.

Asterisks after a percentage indicate that a statistical test was run to see if the differences in the percentages of the two groups are due to chance or are real differences caused by being abused as a child. A single asterisk means that the difference would occur by chance five times out of one hundred while a double asterisk means that the difference would occur by chance only one time out of one hundred.

The Environment of Abuse   A second approach to explaining abuse is sometimes described as the "sociological model," since it emphasizes the total social context in which abuse occurs, rather than the personal qualities of the abuser or the abused child. James Garbarino (1976; Garbarino & Sherman, 1980) has compared the rates of abuse in neighborhoods that are similar in family income levels but differ in other characteristics. Table 13–5 lists some differences Garbarino found between neighborhoods that are high-risk for abuse and those that are low-risk. As Garbarino says, "The picture that emerges from the high-risk area is one of very needy families competing for scarce social resources" (Garbarino, 1980, p. 194). These families need the support of others—exchanges of child care, help in coping with personal crises, playmates for their children—but they live in environments in which families are emotionally isolated from one another.

In general, family circumstances that increase frustration or stress are associated with greater abuse. (This is yet another example of the link between frustration and aggression that we described in Chapter 10.) Abuse is more common in families with low income (partly because they live in neighborhoods like the ones described in Table 13–5). Gil (1970), in a survey of abusing parents, has also reported that child abuse is more likely to occur in families where there are four or more children. Table 13–6 shows that such large families

TABLE 13–5   Characteristics of High-risk Neighborhoods for Child Abuse

In high-risk neighborhoods:

Parents are less likely to be home when children get home from school.

Parents are more socially isolated; they do not ask neighbors for help; there are fewer people in the parents' personal network of family and friends to call on for aid.

Parents experience higher levels of personal "stress" (as measured by the Holmes scale we discussed in Chapter 11).

Child care is less readily available.

Parents see the neighborhood as a bad place to raise children.

Children play with each other less.

There are more single, working mothers.

People move in and out of the neighborhood frequently.

Source: After Garbarino & Sherman, 1980.

make up only about 20 percent of the U.S. population, but they contribute about 40 percent of the cases of abuse (Light, 1973).

Both Light and Garbarino emphasize that it is the *cumulative* effect of high stress factors and poor support systems that is critical. When the stress gets very high and the support is very low, we begin to see what Polansky (Polansky, Chalmers, Buttenwieser, & Williams, 1979) describes as the "apathy-futility syndrome." Striking out at a child is simply one response parents show to the frustration of the situation. This is perhaps best seen in the positive correlation that has been observed between unemployment and child abuse (Krugman et al., 1986). When unemployment increases during periods of economic recession, so do reported cases of all types of child abuse and neglect.

The Abused Child   Within abusing families, the typical finding is that only some of the children are abused. Why is one particular child

TABLE 13–6   The Relationship between Family Size and Child Abuse in the United States

Number of Children	Abusing Families: Percentage in Gil's Survey	Total Families in U.S. with Children under 18 (%)
1	18.0	31.8
2	22.3	29.7
3	20.2	18.9
4	39.5	19.6

Source: After Light, 1973.

TABLE 13–7 Differences between Abused and Nonabused Children

Birth weight	Proportionately more low-birth-weight infants are abused than are normal-weight infants.
Age	Children under age 3 are more likely to be abused.
Sex	Slightly more boys appear to be abused than girls.
Temperament	Cranky, colicky, irritable, demanding babies with poor feeding habits are more likely to be maltreated.
Physical handicaps	Proportionately more children with physical handicaps are abused; many other abused children appear to have some minor neurological dysfunction.

Source: After Friedrich & Boriskin, 1980; Lewis & Schaeffer, 1981.

"chosen" to be the target? What is the child's contribution to this process? Table 13–7 summarizes our current knowledge about the special characteristics of "abusable" children.

It appears that children who are unresponsive, or who for one reason or another are less obedient (boys and young infants, for example) are more likely to be abused. Repeated failure by a child also seems to contribute to the likelihood of abuse. In a simulation study, Vasta and Copitch (1981) had adults teach a child who intentionally performed more and more poorly. In the face of this failure, the adults' responses became more and more negative and came closer and closer to abuse.

Once again, this sounds like a link between frustration and aggression. The child who will not or cannot do what he is told or who does not respond normally because of some physical limitation may simply frustrate a parent more than do other youngsters. Another way to interpret this pattern, as Ainsworth (1980) and others have suggested, is to describe it as a failure of the parent to develop an attachment to the child. In Chapter 12 we described the steps in the child's developing attachment to the parent, but parents, too, form attachments to their infants. Research on early attachment between parent and child points to the importance of two things in fostering a strong, immediate attachment. First, the parent (usually the mother) must be able to touch, hold, and care for the infant immediately after birth (Campbell & Taylor, 1980; Klaus & Kennell, 1976). Low-birth-weight infants are put in isolettes and are not normally touched by their parents. In this situation, the parent-infant bond may be weakened. Second, the infant and the parent must be able to enter into a kind of "dance" of communication in the earliest days. The infant signals her needs through crying or body movements; the parent responds by picking the child up and holding her. The child then snuggles, adjusts her body to the parent's, and may smile or stop crying. In a somewhat older child, eye contact is also important in cementing the bond. When the baby is not able to make all these

Low-birth-weight infants may be at greater risk for child abuse when the parent-infant attachment bond is impeded by the infant's being placed in an isolette.

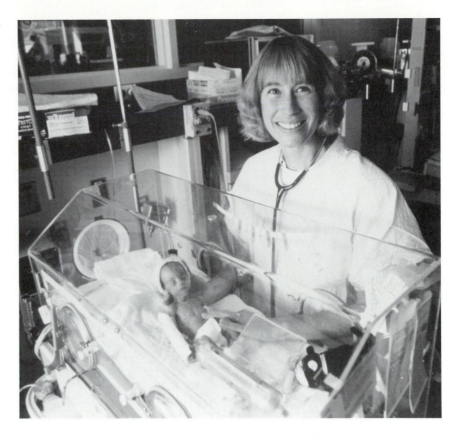

signals, as often happens with a very sick infant, one who is physically disabled, or one who is cranky and not soothable, the parent may not get "hooked" as tightly into the relationship. Abuse may be one consequence. This view of abuse is still speculative, but the evidence supporting it is growing.

Prediction and Treatment

Because the consequences of abuse are so very great, a number of researchers and therapists are trying to figure out how to predict which families are likely to abuse and how to treat families that have already done so. One of the most interesting approaches to prediction is that of Gray and his associates (for example, Gray, Cutler, Dean, & Kempe, 1977). They have observed mothers in the delivery room and noted the very first reactions of the mother to her newborn. Some mothers are delighted, speak to the infant affectionately and immediately, and want to hold the baby. Others are indifferent or rejecting from the first. Gray and his co-workers found that not all the mothers who were indifferent or rejecting in the delivery room were abusive, but all the abusive parents they studied did show that pattern. Efforts like these suggest that it may one day be possible to predict abuse, but we are still a long way from having a reliable "risk index" for potential child abuse.

Treatment is still more problematic. If our analysis of the causes is valid, intervention is likely to be very difficult. How do you go about providing employment, larger living quarters, or smaller families? How do you transform temperamentally difficult children into easygoing children? After reviewing the current treatment strategies, Williams (1980) concludes that few researchers have had any marked success in eliminating abuse. However, the picture is not totally bleak. Providing potential or actual abusers with someone to talk to in times of stress has been of some help (Gray et al., 1977), as has teaching parents less physically aggressive ways of disciplining their children (Patterson, 1974; Rimm, Hill, Brown, & Steward, 1974). As a general rule, Kempe and Kempe (1978) claim that any treatment that improves the parent's self-esteem, assists the parent to make at least one friend, causes the parent to express some affection for the abused child, or encourages the parent to seek social support when under stress is a positive step toward preventing abuse. In our terms, if treatment can strengthen the parent's attachment to the child and can build a supportive social network and the skill to use it, it is likely to be beneficial. But there is no magic technique to prevent a repeat of an abusive episode for all families.

DIVORCE

Family dissolution is not an uncommon experience for many children and adolescents in this country. Approximately 50 percent of first marriages now end in divorce, and 60 percent of divorcing couples have children under the age of 18 (Glick, 1984). Over a million children each year experience the divorce or separation of their parents (*Report of Select Committee on Children, Youth, and Families*, 1983). It is projected that by 1990 approximately one-third of all high-school graduates will have lived with a divorced parent (Glick, 1984).

Another side of divorce is that many persons remarry. It is estimated that 70 to 75 percent of divorced persons remarry and do so usually within five years of the divorce (Glick, 1984). What this means is that many children whose parents divorce will spend part of their lives as members of a stepfamily. All of the rules about the family and parenting have changed in the past two decades. Rarely does one refer to a child today with the pejorative phrase, "He's from a *broken home*." Similarly, terms such as *visitation* and *custody agreement* are being replaced by new terms that more accurately portray what is taking place in parenting following divorce.

The Developmental and Social Issues of Divorce

We can look at the impact of divorce from the perspective of the adult as well as the child. For the children, there are at least three issues. First of all, what effect does the divorce have on the day-to-day experiences of a child? We pointed out in Chapter 12 that many features of a child's environment, such as the amount of stimulation provided and the amount of loving concern, seem to make a difference in the child's rate of development. If divorce changes the environment that the child experiences, we might see changes in the child's behavior patterns as well.

A second thing we need to look at is the age of the child. If we follow Erikson's model, we might expect that divorce during the earliest years, when the child is establishing the first sense of trust and identity, may be more damaging than divorce later.

Finally, one of the major consequences of divorce is that most of the children involved find themselves with only one parent—usually the mother. What is the effect of the father's absence? The effect should be greatest on a boy because he loses the chance to identify with his father, who may no longer be available as a role model. So we might expect that children of divorced families would be systematically different from (though not necessarily "worse" than) children in two-parent families, and the effect may be greater for boys.

The Effects of Divorce on the Child

The important issue for us here is the effect that parental separation and divorce have on the child. Despite the growing recognition between adults that divorce is a viable option if, for whatever reason, the parents cannot get along, little is really known about children's feelings and beliefs surrounding the breakup of their parents. Wallerstein (1983) has tried to understand the child's divorce-adjustment process. Some of the important steps that she has identified include acknowledging the reality of the marital rupture, resolving anger and self-blame, accepting the permanence of the divorce, and achieving realistic hopes regarding one's own relationships.

Another approach to understanding the feelings of children and adolescents prior to and following the separation of their parents examines children's beliefs about why parents are divorcing and about what will become of the children's lives when they are left with one or the other parent. Kurdek and Berg (1987) have developed a Children's Beliefs about Parental Divorce Scale that reveals some interesting information about children's beliefs concerning divorce. The scale is composed of the six subscales shown in Table 13–8. These subscales are (1) peer ridicule and avoidance, (2) paternal blame, (3) maternal blame, (4) fear of abandonment, (5) hope of reunification, and (6) self-blame. The table presents some of the items from each of the subscales.

When the Children's Beliefs about Parental Divorce Scale was administered to 170 children and adolescents with an average age of 11 years whose parents had been separated for nearly 1½ years, Kurdek and Berg found some surprising results. Children separated from their fathers had more paternal-blame beliefs than children living with their fathers. Also, children living with a stepparent (stepmother or stepfather) had more fear-of-abandonment beliefs than children in single-mother families. The paternal-blame finding is of concern because it suggests that visits with the father may be conflictual for a child who is living with his mother if an attempt is not made to resolve the child's attribution of blame to the father. The fear-of-abandonment finding is also of concern because it implies that counseling may be required to lessen the child's feelings of possibly being supplanted emotionally by the custodial parent's new spouse and by his or her children (Visher & Visher, 1983).

TABLE 13–8   Children's Beliefs about Parental Divorce Scale

Scale/Item

Peer Ridicule and Avoidance

1. It would upset me if other kids asked a lot of questions about my parents
2. I like talking to my friends as much now as I used to
3. I like playing with my friends as much now as I used to
4. I'd rather be alone than play with other kids
5. My friends and I do many things together
6. My friends understand how I feel about my parents

Paternal Blame

1. It was usually my father's fault when my parents had a fight
2. My father is usually a nice person
3. When my family was unhappy, it was usually because of something my father said or did
4. My father caused most of the trouble in my family
5. There are a lot of things about my father I like
6. My father is more good than bad

Fear of Abandonment

1. I sometimes worry that both my parents will want to live without me
2. It's possible that both my parents will never want to see me again
3. I sometimes worry that I'll be left all alone
4. I feel that my parents still love me
5. I sometimes think that one day I may have to go live with a friend or relative
6. I feel my parents still like me

Maternal Blame

1. When my family was unhappy, it was usually because of my mother
2. My mother is usually a nice person
3. Often I have a bad time when I'm with my mother
4. My mother caused most of the trouble in my family
5. My mother is more good than bad
6. There are a lot of things about my mother I like

Hope of Reunification

1. My parents will always live apart
2. If I behave better, I might be able to bring my family back together
3. My family will probably do things together just like before
4. My parents will probably see that they have made a mistake and get back together again
5. I sometimes think that my parents will one day live together again
6. I sometimes think that once my parents realize how much I want them to, they'll live together again

Self-Blame

1. My parents often argue with each other after I misbehave
2. My parents would probably be happier if I were never born

3. My parents probably argue more when I'm with them than when I'm gone
4. My parents are happier when I'm with them than when I'm not
5. I can make my parents unhappy with each other by what I say or do
6. My parents would probably still be living together if it weren't for me

Source: After Kurdek & Berg, 1987.

Finally, the children in the Kurdek and Berg study were more anxious, had lower self-concepts (especially in the area of parent relations), and distanced themselves from peers out of fear that their friends would ask too many questions about their parents. Surprisingly, there were no gender differences noted in any of the findings observed, which is interesting since boys are generally believed to be more severely affected by interparent conflict and divorce than girls (Hetherington, Cox, & Cox, 1985). The lack of a gender difference may be due to the fact that beliefs, rather than actual behaviors, were being measured.

The difference between attitudes (or beliefs) and behavior is very important as both must be considered if we are to understand how divorce may affect children. In one of the few truly longitudinal studies of how children are affected both before and after a divorce, Jeanne Block and her colleagues assessed the personality functioning and behavior of a group of children over a period of eleven years. The children were assessed initially when they were 3 years old and again at the ages of 4, 5, 7, 11, and 14 years (Block, Block, & Gjerde, 1986). In keeping track of which parents divorced and when, Block and her co-workers were able to correlate evaluations of personality functioning for the children at different ages to whether parents remained together or divorced.

The findings of Block's study revealed that the behavior of boys (but not girls) was markedly affected by what can be assumed to be predivorce familial stress as early as eleven years *prior to* parental separation or formal dissolution of marriage. For instance, 3-year-old boys from families eventually experiencing divorce were described by Block and her associates as showing problems in the area of impulse control. These boys appeared emotionally unstable, stubborn, restless, and disorderly in dress and behavior. They also had problems in relating well to adults and other children. When they entered school they were more aggressive, restless, and physically active. They were less reflective than male children whose parents were not experiencing marital discord, and they did not respond well to reason as a method of control. Similar patterns of behavior were found in the 4- and 7-year-old boys.

Girls at age 3 years from families that eventually divorced were described quite differently than the boys. The girls appeared to be very planful, competent, skillful, and well coordinated. By age 7, more negative characteristics were observed in the girls, especially in their interpersonal relationships. They had more difficulties in their relationships with other children and were more jealous and envious of others. They also were less prosocial in their sharing behaviors. However, these same girls maintained a high standard of performance for themselves, were bright, and most importantly, were more resilient to stressful events in their lives than girls from intact families. This resiliency is significant since it appears that the girls studied were less affected by environmental stressors (including the divorce of their parents).

In sum, predivorce stress affects girls and boys differently, particularly at a very early age. Many of the behavioral problems boys exhibit, especially at the time of divorce or subsequent to the divorce, are in fact present years before parental separation actually occurs. There is no very good explanation for why boys are affected more by the divorce of their parents than are girls.

Emery (1982) does attempt an explanation based on social learning principles and differential reactions of boys and girls to role models. According to Emery, children of feuding parents are exposed to more aggressive behavior in the home. Emery cites research conducted by Flanders (1968) that indicated that boys especially are known to be more prone to imitate an aggressive model. Thus, in families experiencing parental discord, fathers are more likely to be potent models of aggressive and uncontrolled behavior for their sons. Furthermore, the impact of the father's behavior would be greater for their sons because the same-sex parent has been found to be a more important role model than the opposite-sex parent (Santrock & Warshak, 1979). The modeling explanation obviously does not hold for those cases where there is little conflict between parents who separate, but boy children in these families are still more affected than girl children.

Evidence about the longer-term effects of divorce on a child's school performance, relationship with friends, and general happiness is highly mixed. Wallerstein and Kelly (1980) found that about a third of the children in their sample were well adjusted and flourishing five years after their parents' divorce. Another third, however, were unhappy, angry, lonely, and not functioning well. Other researchers have also found that teenagers from intact (both original parents) families have higher school grades than teenagers from single-parent homes (Rosenthal & Hansen, 1980), but in a group of older studies of children of divorced families, some of which included comparisons between happy intact families, unhappy intact families, and divorced families, little or no difference was found (Nye, 1957; Landis, 1962; Burchinal, 1964). Burchinal, in particular, found no differences in school grades, attitudes toward school, numbers of friends, participation in community activities, or personality traits between children in intact families versus those in divorced families or in divorced-and-remarried families.

When we look at the very long-term effects of divorce on children, such as the children's own success with marriage as adults, the evidence is similarly mixed. Price-Bonham and Balswick (1980), reviewing all the evidence, conclude that there is only a slight tendency for children whose parents divorced to be more likely to divorce as adults. Other researchers, such as Kukla and Weingarten (1979), conclude that there is no measurable negative effect at all on the adult adjustment of children of divorce. Kalter (1987), in a very recent review of the literature on the long-term effects of divorce on children, comes to a very different conclusion. He argues that from a clinical perspective many children of divorced parents have trouble in handling anger and aggression. These children report difficulties in developing stable gender identities and in dealing with feelings of abandonment. According to Kalter, the child is prey to developmental vulnerabilities that may continue to occur long after the divorce of parents. These include poor parental-child interactions, continued arguing by parents even after the divorce on such matters as child support and custody rights, and gradual emotional separation of the absent parent from the life of the child. Thus, some children may suffer long-term negative consequences that affect their social and intimate relationships with others. Obviously, psychologists are beginning to understand the effects of divorce on children much better, but there is still much that needs to be learned, especially about the long-term consequences.

Stepfamilies

The number of second marriages in which children are involved has been increasing, as we noted earlier. Second-marriage families that involve children are usually referred to as *stepfamilies*, blended families, or reconstituted families.

When a second marriage occurs, adjustment to the new situation is difficult for everyone. The woman who remarries has to adjust not only to having another father for her children but also to being a wife again. The same is true of the man. There may not be much time for the husband-wife relationship to develop in stepfamilies. Children are immediately a part of the new family, and the couple must make do the best they can in learning and growing together (Visher & Visher, 1983).

Despite the growing number of reconstituted families, there is very little research about adjustment and family relationships in these new familial arrangements. The majority of studies of stepfamilies have compared children living in stepfamilies, nuclear families, and/or single-parent homes on global measures of psychosocial adjustment or cognitive functioning. Overall, these studies have reported negligible differences in psychological outcomes for children living in stepfamilies and nuclear families (Ganong & Coleman, 1984). In comparisons with single-parent homes, males from stepfamilies have obtained higher scores on measures of cognitive development (Chapman, 1977) and on scales of psychosocial adjustment (Oshman & Manosevitz, 1976).

One factor that has contributed to the relative lack of research on stepfamilies is the fact that so many variables must be controlled in order to do such a study properly. The complexity is seen in a study by Clingempeel and Segal (1986), who were interested in the quality of relationships in four structural types of stepfamilies: stepmother families with male "target" child; stepmother families with female "target" child; stepfather families with male "target" child; and step-father families with female "target" child. The researchers kept a record of the number of visits with the nonresidential parent and the total time in a stepfamily household for each of the four types of stepfamilies. The most interesting findings to emerge from this study concerned stepmother families. There was a correlation between stepmother-stepchild relationships and psychological adjustment. The more positive the relationship between stepmothers and their stepchildren, the lower the stepchildren, both males and females, scored on measurements of aggression, antisocial behavior, social withdrawal, and fear. Moreover, the more positive the relationship between stepmother and stepdaughter, the higher the self-esteem of the stepdaughter. (This relationship was not found for males, however.) Also, the longer stepdaughters lived in a biological father-stepmother household, the more positive were stepmother-stepdaughter relationships and the lower were aggression and social inhibition ratings.

What about visits with the nonresident natural mother? Clingempeel and Segal found that more frequent visits were associated with less positive relationships between stepmothers and female stepchildren, but not between stepmothers and male stepchildren. It is not clear why this might be true for females only. Obviously, much more research is needed before we will have good information about the roles stepparents and stepchildren play in adjusting to each other.

In conclusion, designing workable stepparent/stepchild or stepchildren relationships can be overwhelmingly difficult at times. There are no good answers to the problems encountered by people entering into reconstituted or blended families, but since these arrangements are increasing, answers must be sought.

The Effects of Divorce on the Parents

Parents often find that a divorce is beneficial to their long-run self-esteem and psychological health. This was true of the parents in Wallerstein and Kelly's study (1980), particularly of the mothers. This result has been found by other researchers as well, especially those who have studied parents several years after a divorce.

The short-term effects of divorce on the adults are similar to those for the children. The adults are disorganized and depressed, particularly during the first few months of separation from the spouse (McCall, 1981; White & Bloom, 1981). Both divorcing men and women experience this period of depression, although there are some signs that the impact is greater on women, partly because they typically have custody of the children, and partly because they are frequently coping with greatly reduced incomes (Day & Bahr, 1986).

A number of authors have suggested that there are distinct stages in the process of adjustment that follows a failed marriage. Herrman (1974) compares the steps to the stages Kübler-Ross describes for the death and dying process—since the loss of the previously cherished relationship with the partner is a kind of death. Before the separation there may be bargaining and depression, and finally there is acceptance. Whatever terms one uses, it is clear that depression is a common feature of the period of separation, but for many adults this gives way to a reexamination of goals and a constructive recovery. In Piaget's language, the period of marital disruption and dissolution is a period of profound disequilibrium. It is followed by a period of new equilibrium some months or years later. For many, the new equilibrium is characterized by better psychological integration than before the divorce occurred.

As we might expect, whether an adult makes this type of positive adjustment to divorce depends on a number of factors, including economic conditions, how many children there are to care for, and what kinds of emotional support are available from others. The greater the money problems, the more children there are, and the weaker the individual's network of social supports, the more difficult the adjustment process is likely to be.

To Divorce or Not to Divorce

Thirty years ago, the common social assumption was that unhappy couples should stay together "for the sake of the children." More recently, the common assumption has been that if the parents are unhappy together, the children are better off with only one parent than with two unhappy ones. The evidence we have reviewed suggests that both of these assumptions are probably wrong. Children do not seem to be *better* off with divorce than with unhappily married parents. *Both* settings are stressful, although in somewhat different ways. With thought and effort, parents can buffer their children from the worst effects of divorce and can maintain loving relationships with them. For the parents, the message is clearer: the symptoms of anger, depression, and ill health that so often accompany distressed marriages are likely to improve after divorce. For the adults, then, divorce may be beneficial. What we need to keep in mind, however, is that the process is not an easy one for any of the participants.

DAY CARE

Thirty-two percent of all women with children under the age of six participated in the work force in the U.S. in 1970. By 1985, the figure had reached 52 percent, as measured by the Bureau of Labor Statistics. According to a cover story on child care that appeared in *Time* magazine (June 22, 1987), as of 1986 there were at least 9 million preschoolers who spent some part of the day in the care of someone other than their parents. Further, the number of such children is expected to increase by at least 50 percent over the next decade. The increase in the number of working parents with preschool age children has led to the development of a major social issue—how to provide high-quality day care for these children. Given the need for adequate day care, there is considerable interest in what effect day-care placement might have on the social, emotional, and intellectual development of young children. The general consensus is that the day-care experience need not have deleterious effects on children and, in fact, it may enhance children's development in some cases. It also appears unlikely that day care significantly impairs the mother-child bond (Scarr, 1984). However, the topic of day care has become a very emotionally charged issue among parents, developmental psychologists, and politicians.

In the early 1960s, when the first studies of the effects of day care on children were conducted, there were fears that day care would be detrimental to both the intellectual and emotional functioning of children. Of particular concern were the emotional attachments infants and toddlers have to their primary caretakers, especially their mothers (Kahn & Kamerman, 1987). The question was raised as to whether mothers should shun employment and stay home to raise their children. However, many women today do not have any choice in the matter and must work, either because they are single parents or because income from both partners is required to meet family expenses. The question, therefore, is no longer hypothetical. The majority of women with children under six years of age now work and that percentage is expected to increase about another 50 percent in the decade to come. So, it is important to know what effect, if any, extended out-of-home-care has on the young child and what constitutes *good* child care. Fortunately, there are some answers to these and other related questions.

Research Findings on Day Care

Generally, the literature shows that infants and toddlers can form important emotional attachments to several people, including caretakers, which may differ in intensity but not in kind from what is usually experienced with their mother. Separation anxiety is successfully dealt with as these other relationships are carefully and gradually introduced. Further, the development of a relationship with other caretakers does not impair children's relationships with their mothers (Clarke-Stewart, 1982; Gamble & Zigler, 1986).

There is a debate, however, about the optimal age at which to place an infant in an out-of-home, day-care facility. Child-care experts are beginning to suggest that there may be negative consequences to a child's socioemotional development if they are placed in day care prior to about 24 months of age (Belsky, 1986). Support for this position comes from studies that have assessed infants' attachment behavior in a test called the stranger situation procedure. In one such study (Barglow, Vaughn, & Molitor, 1987), infants raised at home by their nonworking mothers were compared to another group of 12–13-month-old infants who were cared for by another adult in their homes while their mothers worked. Even under this circumstance, infants in the "cared-for-by-another-adult" condition showed signs of disrupted attachment behavior to their mothers. This finding indicates that the debate about day-care placement is far from over, since the infants studied by Barglow and his colleagues were from middle-class families who could afford to hire someone to care for their infants in their own homes. Many parents are not so fortunate, and their children are possibly at greater risk because of poverty and low-quality day care.

Children who do participate in group **child-care programs** tend to be somewhat different from children who are raised only at home. Day-care children are more independent, more sociable and/or competitive, and more boisterous and aggressive with peers (Clarke-Stewart, 1982). The significance of these characteristics depends on

Early fears about the long-term effects of day care on children's attachment to their primary caregivers (usually the child's mother) have faded with the realization that infants and toddlers can form important emotional attachments to several people.

the value system of the parents; by themselves, the characteristics are neither positive nor negative. For instance, independence on the part of the young child may be viewed as very positive by some parents and as undesirable by others. This variability in parents' value systems has complicated the evaluation of day care in some instances.

Differences between children who spend considerable time in a day-care program and those raised at home are probably due to the enhancement of social maturity and competence demanded by the day-care environment. Day-care children are more at ease in unfamiliar settings and more willing to interact with an unfamiliar person. These children are also more self-sufficient and function more independently of their parents and teachers. A troublesome fact is that day-care children are sometimes less respectful of others and less responsive to requests from adults (Clarke-Stewart, 1982). Despite these negative attributes, the benefits accrued through greater social competence and maturity outweigh whatever minor behavioral problems day-care children might show in comparison to children who are raised at home.

An especially important finding to emerge from research on day care is that well-run day-care centers and preschool programs can accelerate and improve the cognitive and social development of children from economically and educationally disadvantaged backgrounds. This was the hope that led to the establishment of ***Project Head Start*** in 1965. Although it was only a part-day program that was not really intended to serve the needs of working mothers, many of the long-term effects of Head Start are impressive. For example, in a study conducted to evaluate the High/Scope Head Start program for high-risk minority children in Ypsilanti, Michigan, the results showed impressive long-term effects for 3- and 4-year-old children who participated in the program between 1962 and 1965 (Berrueta-Clement, 1984). The evaluation showed that at age 19, the number of former program participants who were functionally literate was 61 percent as compared to 38 percent for control nonparticipants. A total of 38 percent of the program participants attended college, compared to 21 percent for nonparticipants. More of the participants were also working (50 percent) compared to the controls (32 percent). This study also reported that participants made less use of public assistance and reported fewer cases of teenage pregnancy.

Not all findings are as positive as those reported by the High/Scope program evaluation (Berrueta-Clement, 1984), and not all results demonstrate the sustained positive gains over long time periods. However, the greatest impacts result from helping poor children become more intellectually and socially prepared to meet the challenges of school.

In summary, research on the effects of day care has generally shown that young children's socioemotional and cognitive development progress at least as well in group child-care programs as they do when children are cared for entirely at home. Programs vary considerably, however, and research indicates that the quality of the program makes a tremendous difference in whether a child shows gains in the vital developmental areas about which parents are most concerned. Accordingly, it is important to discuss what is currently known about quality child-care programs and how to determine whether a program ranks high or low in the provision of services to children.

Finding a Quality Day-care Program

Assessing the quality of child care is no easy matter and this has become one of the major pursuits of developmental psychologists, child-care specialists, and parents. Some of the major issues involve the age of the children, the economic resources of the parents, and what parents expect from child care. However, there are a number of other considerations that are critical to assessing quality care, such as the training and experience of the adult caretakers, the ratio of children to caretakers, the instructional curriculum offered by the program, the general facilities of the day-care center (including physical space and equipment), and the role of parents in the program. It is easy to see how the quality of care offered by day-care programs can vary depending on a variety of factors. In other words, what might be appropriate for the proper care of a 9-month-old infant may be totally inappropriate for a 4-year-old preschooler. Let us discuss a few of the more important criteria used to establish quality of care.

Caregivers   In any assessment of a child-care program, it is essential to begin with questions about the **caregivers.** Scarr (1984) asks a series of related questions in this regard. Do the caregivers know enough about child development to provide good care? Do the caregivers supervise the babies and children closely but not intrusively? Do the caregivers carefully supervise babies in potentially dangerous spaces and children with potentially dangerous materials? Do the caregivers use every opportunity to talk with babies and preschoolers? Are the caretakers affectionate and emotionally responsive to the children? These are all vitally important questions that must be addressed by parents in locating a program for their child. Caretakers who have little experience with children and/or who have little training in child development should not be entrusted to care for children. Child care is like any other profession; the best results are obtained when a child is taken to professionals who know what they are doing. Simply having your own child does not qualify you to take care of another person's child. The best caretakers are those individuals who have studied child development and who know about the special developmental needs of young children at different ages. For instance, verbal stimulation is essential in the care of infants and toddlers. The good caretaker is attentive to the child's need to communicate and spends considerable time and energy in interpreting the child's gestures and utterances and in exchanging verbal messages with the child. Time is spent in answering questions, labeling objects, and reading stories. More is required than just ensuring that the child is kept clean, fed, and safe; time for cognitive, linguistic, and social stimulation is essential.

Quality care is also defined by the ratio of children to caretakers. Most experts advise that a ratio of one adult to every six children over 3 years of age (and more for children under 3 years) is the optimal ratio (Clarke-Stewart, 1982). The types of stimulation described above cannot take place even with good caretakers if the ratio of children to adults is so large as to preclude individual attention to a child.

The Curriculum   A quality program has a curriculum that is planned and is age appropriate for the child. This means that a program must provide more than simple custodial care of children. The preschool years are intended to be filled with new things to learn and do. Remember what we said about this period in Chapter 12.

In her review of day-care curriculum, Clarke-Stewart has concluded that programs that result in greater intellectual and achievement gains for children are those that "blend prescribed educational activities with opportunities for free choice, that have some structure, but also allow children to explore a rich environment of objects and peers on their own without teacher direction" (1982, p. 85). Children in these programs also evidence more motivation, persistence, problem-solving ability, and social skills. It is important to note as a cautionary remark that programs of the type described by Clarke-Stewart might also have the advantage of having more experienced and more highly trained caregivers.

In summary, day care is a major concern of the majority of parents with children under the age of six. Guidelines have appeared in many books and articles for parents in the last few years that are designed to assist them in understanding the pros and cons of day care for young children. The various program options are described and hints are provided for finding good-quality programs. There is still much that needs to be known about the effects of day care on children's cognitive, linguistic, and socioemotional development. However, one thing is certain, and that is that day care and other types of early child care are becoming a major business in the United States. This is one area that promises to provide many opportunities for students interested in child development.

TEENAGE PARENTS

The Scope of the Problem

Imagine a young girl of 13 clutching a teddy bear as she goes into a doctor's office for an abortion, signs papers to give up her child for adoption, or is wheeled into the delivery room. The problem of teenage pregnancy and teenage parenthood presents us with several major developmental issues because infants born to teenage mothers are at greater risk to suffer from a variety of developmental disorders. Teenage pregnancy also has a severe impact on the physical health and psychological adjustment of teenage mothers, both before and following delivery. Finally, little attention has been given to the psychological welfare of the teenage father and his new role as a parent. Before delving into some of these issues, let us first examine the question of just how common the problem of teenage pregnancy has become.

More than one million teenage girls in this country become pregnant each year, 400,000 of whom choose to obtain abortions and 470,000 of whom give birth. The remainder of these pregnancies end in miscarriages and stillbirths. Thirty percent of all teen mothers have

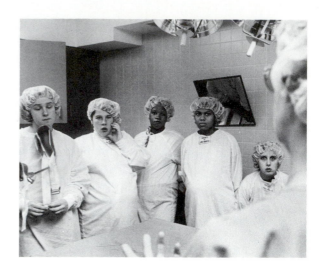

A young girl boastfully shows her changing anatomy to her boyfriend while expectant teen mothers in a birthing class learn about the realities of childbirth and delivery.

second and third pregnancies while still in their teens. Often forgotten in these statistics are several hundred thousand teenage boys and young men who become fathers each year. The United States surpasses all other Western developed nations in its rates of teenage pregnancy, abortions, and births. The most revealing difference is found among the youngest teenagers: girls in this country under the age of 15 are at least five times more likely to give birth than are their counterparts in any other developed country for which data are available (Hayes, 1987).

Over the past two decades the teenage pregnancy rate has risen slightly (Hayes, 1987). However, the rate of births to teenagers is declining. If this is a little confusing, keep in mind that we are discussing two statistics here: (1) teen pregnancies and (2) births to teens. Although teen pregnancies have risen slightly, total births to teens have declined, especially among black 15- to 19-year olds. The difference between these two statistics is most likely due to the increase in abortions among teenagers. At the same time, the percentage of out-of-wedlock births to teenagers is rising. Although only a third of all births to teenagers were out of wedlock in 1970, 90 percent of all babies born to teenagers under age 15 and half of those born to teens between 15 and 19 were born out of wedlock in 1982 (Pittman, 1986).

These child-mothers have a greater risk of receiving prenatal care late—if at all—thus increasing the probabilities of low birth weight babies (who have complex, multiple health problems) and babies who die in their first year of life. Births to teenage mothers represent 14 percent of all births in the United States and 20 percent of all low-weight births. According to the most recent *Maternal and Child Health Data Book*, progress in reaching the Surgeon General's goals for reducing low birth weight and infant mortality has actually declined over the past several years, and the United States now ranks last for both among the 20 leading industrialized nations (Children's Defense Fund, 1986).

To understand the problem of teenage pregnancy, we also need to address changes in sexual activity among teenagers that have occurred over the past several decades. Zelnik and Kantner (1977) found that between 1971 and 1976 the percentage of sexually active teenagers increased from 21 percent to 31 percent among whites and from 51 percent to 63 percent among blacks. Chilman (1980) estimates that 40 percent of all girls ages 15 to 19 are sexually active, and Stark (1986), confining herself to 15- to 17-year-olds, states that about 50 percent of the boys and 33 percent of the girls are sexually active. Since only about half of these girls (or their partners) use any form of contraception, the rate of pregnancy among teenagers has gone up steadily over the past 30 to 40 years. This increase in sexual activity has led to growing concern among psychologists, educators, sociologists, and parents of teenagers—to say nothing of the concern among policymakers and taxpayers—about the possible need for provision of financial support to the teenage mother and her offspring. This problem is no less complex than the other issues discussed in this chapter and requires careful analysis.

Factors Associated with Teenage Sexuality

Much is known from research about the factors that can lead to sexual activity among teenagers. Teenagers are more likely to be sexually active if one of the following conditions applies:

- An older sister or mother was a teenage parent.
- Parental involvement in the teenager's life is weak or communication is strained or limited.
- The family holds more tolerant attitudes toward early sexual activity and pregnancy.
- Parents, siblings, or the teenager have low educational attainment. The lower the level of education, the earlier sexual activity is likely to occur.
- The teenager lives in an economically depressed area and is from a poor family.
- The teenager has low self-esteem and a low educational aspiration level.
- The family lives in a highly urbanized area as opposed to a more rural community.
- The teenager engages in other risk-taking behavior, such as drug and alcohol use.

The earlier sexual activity begins, the more vulnerable the at-risk youth is. This is true because half of all teenage pregnancies occur within the first six months of sexual activity; among teenagers younger than 15, only three in ten use contraceptives at first intercourse, compared to five in ten at ages 15 to 17, and six in ten at ages 18 and older. Often, low usage is strongly related to ignorance about where to get contraceptives and how to use them (National Governors Association, 1987). In addition, the more guilt and anxiety a teenage girl has about sex, the less likely she is to use contraception (Stark, 1986). What this suggests is that although an individual may have negative feelings associated with sex, those feelings are insufficient to inhibit sexual behavior, even though they may interfere with the use of contraception.

The Developmental and Social Issues of Teenage Parenthood

To understand the issues here, we need to examine the impact of teenage births on the physical, emotional, and intellectual development of the infants and on the life course of the teenage mother.

The teenage mother—especially the very young adolescent mother—is herself not through growing, and she has extra nutritional needs. Thus, her growing fetus may be at higher risk for various kinds of physical problems, such as lower birth weight or a greater rate of deformities. In addition, the young mother is still grappling with the emotional and intellectual disequilibrium of adolescence, attempting to find some identity. If she has not resolved this dilemma, she probably will be less able to provide the emotional stability her infant needs to establish a secure sense of trust. We might expect, then, that infants born to teenage mothers would have more social and emotional difficulties during their early teens than infants born to older mothers.

From the perspective of the mother, there are equally important issues. What is the impact on a young girl's overall life course of being thrust too soon into the mothering role? Does it affect her ability to form a clear identity? Does it affect her schooling, her marital history as an adult, or her overall stability? In attempting to answer these questions, we have to be sure that we are looking at the effect of teenage mothering and *not* at the effects of poverty, or race, or level of education. As you can see in Figure 13–1, the rate of teenage

FIGURE 13–1   Births among Teenagers   *Despite the claims of many current "scare" articles, there has been an overall decrease in the rate of births to teenage mothers in recent years.*

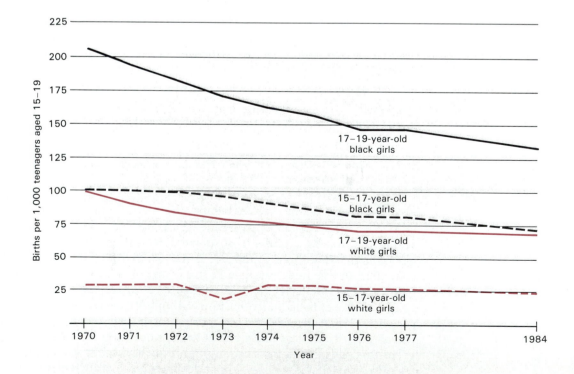

births is higher among black adolescents than whites; it is also higher among the poor of both races. If we compare the children of teenage mothers with the children of older mothers, without taking the race and economic conditions of the two groups into account, we might well find differences, but we would not be able to tell whether the differences were due to the mother's age or to her social conditions. Researchers have been very much aware of this problem in the recent studies of teenage parents, so we can usually sort out the effects of age, poverty level, race, and the mother's education. Let us begin by looking at the impact on the infants and children.

The Effects of Teenage Parenting on the Children

Remarkably enough, there are very few well-established effects of teenage pregnancy on the children. What *is* clear is that teenage mothers are much less likely to have good medical care during their pregnancy; they may try to conceal their condition or they may not know where they can go for prenatal care (Scholl, Miller, Salmon, Cofsky, & Shearer, 1987). Since we know that *regardless of age* mothers who have poor prenatal care are more likely to have difficult deliveries, lower-weight infants, and a higher rate of infant deaths, we should not be surprised that teenage mothers, as a group, show all these same effects. But if the teenager has had adequate prenatal care, all of these effects are negated (Baldwin & Cain, 1980; Chilman, 1980). That is, there is nothing inherent in being a young mother that increases the risk of complications during delivery or the risk of low birth weight or other difficulties for the baby.

There is just one qualification we need to make about this generalization. There is evidence that when the mother is *very* young— very close to her own first menstruation—there may be some increased risk for the infant (Fergueson, 1987). There is support that shows that when "age-since-the-first-menstruation," rather than chronological age is considered in the case of teenage mothers, premature birth and complications of labor may occur with greater frequency because of incomplete development of the pelvic cavity (Moerman, 1982). Thus, giving birth at 13 or 14 truly does pose extra risk for the baby.

The one negative consequence for children of teenage mothers that has been repeatedly found in well-controlled studies is that they have lower IQ scores and do less well in school than do children of older mothers (Belmont, Cohen, Dryfoos, Stein, & Zayac, 1981; Broman, 1981; Carlson, LaBarba, Sclafani, & Bowers, 1986; Chilman, 1980). You can see the results of Broman's study in Figure 13–2. The effect is not large, but it is consistent, and it occurs in both black and white groups and at all levels of family income and education. Why might this be true? We have just seen that infants of young mothers are physically the same as infants of older mothers at the time of birth, and Broman's own results show that during the first year of life the infants of young mothers develop at a slightly *faster* rate. So what happens later? What would contribute to a poorer performance on measures of intellectual functioning at ages 4 and 7 and later? The

FIGURE 13–2 Average IQs of Children as Related to the Age of the Mother at Delivery *In the results of a nationwide study of over 35,000 births, the average IQ of 7-year-old children was lower when the mothers were teenagers at the time of delivery than when the mothers were older. (After Broman, 1981)*

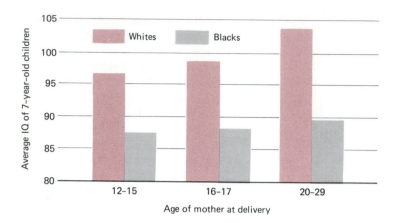

answers to this question seem to lie in the differences in the adult life-course of the teenage mother, rather than in physical differences in her child. Thus, to examine the question further, we need to look at what happens to girls who give birth in their teens.

The Effects of Teenage Parenthood on the Mother

We have summarized the current information about the long-term outcomes for teenage mothers in Table 13–9. Read over the list in the table and try to imagine what all those changes would do to your own life. How would you be living at age 25, 35, or 45 if you were divorced, had less than a high-school education, had four or five children, had few job skills, and earned a low income? Compare that picture to what you might expect if you had waited to have your first child until you were in your twenties and had completed more of your education.

We cannot attribute all of the differences between these two very different life courses to teenage pregnancy. Many teenagers, especially those from poor families, have low levels of education and income and come from broken families. But the likelihood of a life course characterized by the long-term outcomes in the table is in-

TABLE 13–9 Long-term Consequences of Teenage Motherhood on the Adult Lives of Women

Education	More likely to drop out of school at the time of the pregnancy; over the long run have fewer years of schooling than women from similar backgrounds who did not have children during teen years.
Marriage	Marry earlier than those who delay parenthood.
Divorce	More likely to divorce.
Number of children	Have markedly larger number of children—four or five children, as opposed to two or three for women who begin childbearing in their twenties.
Income	Lower income as adults, and more likely to be on welfare as adults.

creased by a pregnancy during the teen years, and this is as true of the middle-class girl as of the poor girl.

The differences in education are particularly striking. Moore and her colleagues (Moore, Hofferth, Wertheimer, Waite, & Caldwell, 1981) studied a group of 5,000 families over a ten-year period (until the mothers were in their thirties). Among the white women in this study, only about 25 percent of those who had had their first child at age 15 or 16 had completed high school, compared to 98 percent of those who had had their first child at 24 or later. Among the black women, the differences were not as large, but they were very much in the same direction: about 35 percent of those who had had their first child at 15 or 16 completed high school, while 75 percent of those who waited until they were 24 or over to have their first child had completed high school.

Since the years of education a woman attains will affect her later income, the types of jobs she can find, and the education of the man she marries, this effect of teenage pregnancy is highly important to both mother and child. The education difference, the higher rate of divorce, and the larger number of children for teenage mothers all undoubtedly contribute to the lower IQ scores among their offspring. As we mentioned in Chapter 12, many studies show that women with less education have children with lower IQs (for example, Broman, Nichols, & Kennedy, 1975). More importantly, we know that mothers with less education behave differently with their children. They are more restrictive and more punitive. They provide fewer of the toys and materials a child needs to explore and experiment, and they talk to their children less (Carlson et al., 1986).

The evidence thus points to the negative effects of teenage parenthood on the later life pattern of the mother and her child. However, we cannot be sure of the direction the causality runs. Does carrying and delivering a child during the teenage years *disrupt* a girl's expected educational and life pattern, or are the girls who become early mothers the very ones who are less interested in (or good at) school anyway?

There is some information that allows us to answer this question. Ireson (1984) obtained personality and sex-role orientation data from 161 adolescent women between the ages of 13 and 18 who visited a public-health clinic for either a pregnancy test or to receive birth-control instruction. He also collected information about these adolescents' academic achievement and their academic expectations. Ireson wanted to find out if there were differences in these four data areas between the young women who were pregnant and those who were not. He divided the teenagers who went to the clinic for a pregnancy test into two groups: those whose test showed them to be pregnant and those whose test indicated that they were not pregnant. Subsequently, Ireson compared the pregnant group to the two nonpregnant groups (those who had come for pregnancy testing and tested negative and those who had come for birth-control instruction).

Overall, the pregnant teenagers in Ireson's study were more oriented toward traditional sex roles (for example, more competent in feminine activities) than their sexually active peers in the other two groups. Moreover, pregnant teenagers did less well in school and held significantly lower occupational and educational expectations than girls in the birth-control condition. Not surprising either is the finding that the pregnant teenagers saw themselves as less effective in controlling the course of their personal lives. In sum, teenagers in Ireson's study who became pregnant had less to lose since their occupational and educational expectations and their school grades were relatively low. The issue then is perhaps one of either attempting to assist teenagers to raise their academic expectations and feelings of personal control or of providing them with the necessary medical information about birth control and the prenatal and postnatal care of infants.

The Effects of Teenage Parenthood on the Father

Although teenage boys are responsible for most of the approximately one million teen pregnancies, our understanding of these young men is very incomplete. Robinson and Barret (1985) believe that teenage fathers often want babies as much as teenage mothers do and for many of the same reasons. According to these investigators, teen fathers often differ markedly from the image that the public has of them. Many of them feel a sense of responsibility toward their girlfriend and baby, and if not married, they still want to see the mother and child on some type of regularly scheduled basis.

Teen fathers often present a profile that resembles that of teenage mothers. That is, the males are often doing poorly in school, have low educational and occupational aspirations, and are more likely to become school dropouts than are other teenagers. Teenage fathers also hold a more traditional sex-role orientation and feel that the pregnancy of their girlfriend affirms their manhood.

Many teen fathers are often deliberately excluded from decisions made by a teenage mother and her parents that affect the pregnancy or the baby. These adolescent males often are not told when the baby is born or that their child has been adopted. The boy's feelings in these matters are rarely considered. This may be the reason that the attitudes of many teen fathers turn from apprehensive to noncaring in some cases. Just as there is increased attention being given to teen mothers, there needs to be greater consideration of the psychological dynamics involved in teenage fatherhood. After all, males are equally responsible for the pregnancy.

Sex-education Programs for Teens

In a national campaign published in major newspapers in 1986 (see the box titled "They Did It 20,000 Times on Television Last Year"), Planned Parenthood has charged that the television industry is at least partially responsible for the increase in teenage pregnancy in this country. Planned Parenthood personnel state that in 1978 researchers counted 20,000 sexual scenes on prime-time network television without any mention of consequences or protection. Planned Parenthood adds that sexually alluring commercials are permitted on television, as are ads for vaginal sprays and hemorrhoidal products,

◆ *THEY DID IT 20,000 TIMES ON TELEVISION LAST YEAR.
HOW COME NOBODY GOT PREGNANT?*

*Teenage pregnancy in the U.S. has reached epidemic proportions, shattering
hundreds of thousands of lives and costing taxpayers $16 billion per year. In-
stead of helping to solve this problem, the TV networks have virtually banned
any mention of birth control in programs and advertising. We need to turn this
policy around. You can help.*

ON TELEVISION, SEX IS GOOD, CONTRACEPTION IS TABOO   There's a
lot of sex on television. We all know that. What most people don't
realize is that while the networks have been hyping sex, they've
banned all mention of birth control in advertising, and censor information about it in programming. (It is permitted in the news.) Millions of
dollars in sexually alluring ads are okay. Ads for vaginal sprays and
hemorrhoidal products are okay. So are the ads which use nudity here
and there to sell products. And characters like J.R. Ewing have been
seducing women a few times an hour for eight years.

In 1978, researchers counted 20,000 sexual scenes on prime-time
network television (which does not even include soap operas), with
nary a mention of consequences or protection. It's even higher today.
The only sexual mystery left seems to be how all these people keep
doing it without contraception while nobody gets pregnant.

With all that worry-free hot action on television, it's no wonder
American youngsters are having sex earlier and more often. *And* getting
pregnant. Kids watch an average of four hours every day. That's more
time than they spend in school or doing anything else in life, except
sleeping. That's four hours per day inside a world where no one ever
says "no," where sex is loose and often violent, and where sexual responsibility is as out-of-date as hula-hoops. Today's TV message is this:
"GO FOR IT *NOW*. GO FOR IT AGAIN. AND DON'T WORRY ABOUT
ANYTHING."

But there is plenty to worry about. The teen pregnancy rate in this
country is now the highest of any country in the industrialized world.
In the U.S. more than a million teens get pregnant every year. The
consequences are tragic: high rates of school drop-outs, broken families,

*Guess Which of These Are in "Good Taste"
(According to the Networks)*

*The tv network execs have decided that all advertisements for con-
traceptive products are in "bad taste" and they have banned them.
Vaginal sprays, hemorrhoidal products, tampons are all in "good
taste," according to them. So are toilet paper ads, underwear ads
and nudity in everything from soap and cosmetic ads to beer ads. As
for network drama and comedy programs which emphasize sexual
doings? "Good taste." But mentioning "contraception" or "birth
control" within programming (except news) is censored. ❧ The
networks have not yet got the message. Our country is suffering a
major problem of teen pregnancy, and television network policy is
making it worse. Hyping sexuality while censoring information about
responsibility is giving a terrible double message. ❧ The networks
need to hear from you. Now.*

welfare and abortion. Who pays the tab? You do. About $16 billion yearly.

Of course television is *not* the only cause. When it comes to sex, there's a terrible breakdown of communications between parents and kids. There's also an appalling lack of timely, comprehensive sex education in schools. So kids are learning about sex the hard way—by experience. But television is making matters worse. Both because of what's on TV, and because of what is not.

CENSORSHIP BY THE NETWORKS   The television industry is very sensitive about people telling them what they cannot broadcast. But the TV industry itself feels free to censor content.

Last year, the American College of Obstetricians and Gynecologists (ACOG)—a most prestigious physicians organization—prepared an ad campaign to educate kids about how to prevent pregnancy. They wanted to use print media, radio, and television. The brochure for the campaign said this: (1) Kids *can* resist peer pressure. They can take the option of postponing sex until they're ready. (2) The pill *is* a safe contraceptive for young women. And (3) sexually active young *men* should also be responsible—use condoms. These were useful statements.

The TV commercials ACOG prepared were even milder. All they suggested was that *unintended pregnancy* can interfere with career goals for women, and they offered to send the brochure. But, amazingly, the network execs said the ads were too "controversial," because they made mention of the word "contraceptives." These are the same networks which routinely show thousands of murders, rapes and acts of kinky sex. And 94% of the sexual encounters in soap operas are among people not married to each other. Are *those* presentations noncontroversial? Do *those* represent some kind of higher moral value?

Finally, after long negotiations, the three networks agreed to let the spots run. But only after the dreaded "C-word"—"contraception"—was censored. Instead, the networks substituted this dynamic phrase: "There are many ways to prevent unintended pregnancy."

As for network policies censoring "birth control" within programs? No change. As for the rejection of commercials for contraceptive products like condoms, foams, the pill? No change. As for the reduction of irresponsible sexual imagery? No change. As for a sense of balance between sexual hype and realistic useful information? No change.

BLAMING THE PUBLIC TASTES   Network executives argue that they've a responsibility to uphold high standards of public taste. The mention of birth control (except in the news) would somehow violate that. Is that true? Does the public really want uneducated pregnant teenagers? And a tax bill for $16 billion?

A recent Louis Harris Poll showed exactly what the public wants. Most Americans believe that television portrays an unrealistic and irresponsible view of sex. And 78% would like to see messages about contraception on TV. A similar percentage wants more sex education in schools. So it's not the public which resists more responsible sexual imagery. It's the television executives who resist it. Why? Maybe it's just a creative problem for them. We think they can solve it. Right now they don't even mention birth control when it's exactly appropriate. Why can't J.R. ask his latest conquest if she is prepared? Why can't she ask him? The screenwriters can work it out.

The television industry once said the public couldn't handle images of people wearing seatbelts, and they figured that one out. The case of birth control should be simpler than seatbelts, since 90% of adults already accept its use. It's mainly teenagers who don't.

WHAT YOU CAN DO   Television executives keep trying to avoid their own responsibility, telling us that TV imagery has nothing to do with shaping teens' attitudes, that television doesn't influence them.

But this is ridiculous. Television is the most powerful medium ever invented to influence mass behavior. It's on that basis that the networks sell their advertising.

Television influences all of us every day. And it is a major influence on teenagers about sexuality and responsibility. It may now be a more important influence than school, parents, or even peers. The problem is that television is putting out an unbalanced view which is causing *more* problems for teenagers and society. The situation has got to change.

It's time we turn to the small number of men who control this medium and tell them they have a responsibility to the public beyond entertainment, titillation, pushing products and making money.

They need to know you are out there, and that you are concerned. It will make a tremendous difference. Use the coupons. Write letters and make phone calls. And join Planned Parenthood's efforts in your area.

Thank you.

From "They did it 20,000 times on television last year. How come nobody got pregnant?" by Planned Parenthood Federation of America, Inc., November 25, 1986, *Los Angeles Times*, p. 18. Reprinted with permission of Planned Parenthood Federation of America.

but nothing is supposed to be said about birth-control products. Does the television industry have a responsibility to educate young people about safe sexual practices? What other institutions should be held accountable for sex education?

Traditionally, the family was responsible for the sexual education of its children. Over the past two decades this responsibility has shifted to the schools. Many parents feel relieved at the loss of this responsibility and at the same time complain that the sex-education programs conducted in the schools are woefully inadequate. Many issues have surfaced about school-based sex-education programs. How explicit should the program be? Should birth control instruction

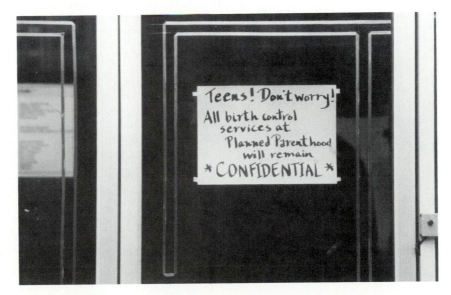

Agencies, such as Planned Parenthood, have assumed a major role in combatting pregnancy among teenagers.

be included in the curriculum? Should morals, values, and religious convictions be incorporated into these programs?

Kirby (1984) notes that the most effective sex-education classes do not teach just basic reproduction and contraception; they discuss dating and relationships as well as beliefs and life goals. Kirby maintains that past attempts to teach value-free sex education may have been a mistake. He feels that dignity, worth, and self-choice should be included in the curriculum. School children must be taught that peer pressure, subtle persuasion, and the use of physical force (date rape) as a means of getting someone else to engage in unwanted sexual activity are unacceptable. Acceptance of such attitudes can only be countered, argues Kirby, when sex education extends into the domain of values and morals. Finally, the most effective programs are those that are combined with a health clinic in some way. But just how effective are such programs?

One pregnancy-prevention program for urban teenagers revealed some striking results that merit attention. Zabin and her associates (Zabin, Hirsch, Smith, Streett, & Hardy, 1986) introduced their sex-education intervention program in one junior high and one senior-high school serving an all-black, inner-city population. Three control schools were also selected and used to measure change in the experimental schools. Students at all five schools filled out a questionnaire before actually starting the program. This gave the researchers information about the levels of sexual knowledge and practice among the teenagers. The baseline survey revealed a high level of sexual activity among the students in all of the schools. According to Zabin and her colleagues:

> Almost 92% of boys in the ninth grade of the program junior-high school were sexually active, as were 54% of the comparable girls. In the senior-high school, 79% of all the girls were sexually active. Even at the lower grade levels, the percentages reporting that they were sexually experienced were relatively high: forty-seven percent of the girls in the seventh and eighth grades had had intercourse. Approximately 71% of sexually active male and female students in the junior-high school and over 89% of those in the senior-high school said they had practiced some form of contraception. However, only 56% and 73%, respectively, had used any method at last intercourse. Among the sexually active girls in the seventh and eighth grades, 11% had been pregnant. In the ninth grade of the junior-high school, this proportion rose to 20%, while among sexually active young women in the senior-high school, 22% had had a pregnancy. (pp. 119–20)

The educational program was instituted in the experimental schools against this background of marked sexual activity. The program simply consisted of two professionals, a social worker and a nurse-midwife, who provided both group and individual sex counseling and education. In this program emphasis was placed on the development of personal responsibility, goal setting, and communication with parents. In addition, a voluntary after-school health clinic was also staffed by the two professionals and students were encouraged to visit. At the clinic, services included contraceptive counseling, pregnancy testing, and other general health diagnosis and referral procedures.

FIGURE 13–3   Changes in Teenage Pregnancy Rates as a Result of a Pregnancy-Prevention Program   *The rates shown are for three different time periods following the initiation of the program. Pregnancy rates for program participants fell below rates for nonparticipants during each of the three time periods. (After Zabin, Hirsch, Smith, Streett, & Hardy, 1986)*

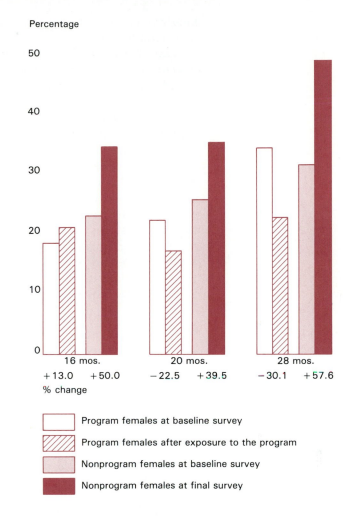

Was this program successful in reducing teenage pregnancy among this population of adolescents? Zabin and her associates evaluated the program after 16, 20, and 28 months following the baseline survey. Their findings are shown in Figure 13–3. Among students who participated in the program, there was a 13 percent increase above baseline in pregnancies after 16 months. Among the control students, the equivalent increase was 50 percent. However, after 20 months, the pregnancy rate fell 22 percent below baseline among program students, whereas it rose by 39 percent among nonprogram girls. Finally, after 28 months, the pregnancy rate declined by 30 percent among program students, whereas it increased by 58 percent in the control schools. The boys in the experimental schools used the clinic as freely as the girls. The findings demonstrate that an effective sex-education program can reach even high-risk adolescents.

Summing Up the Effects of Teenage Parenthood

Overall, the negative effects of teenage parenthood for the mothers appear to be substantial and may be very long lasting. For the children, there are few immediate effects that we can detect, but over the long run children born to teenagers show poorer intellectual performance on IQ tests and in school. Several implications for intervention programs follow from our summary of the research. First, we need to develop ways to improve the prenatal care of teenage mothers (and of older mothers, for that matter). Second, the teenage mother needs to learn how to interact positively with her baby. Third, teenage girls who get pregnant appear to have lower educational and occupational expectations than girls who do not become pregnant (Ireson, 1984). This suggests that teenagers need assistance in raising their academic expectations and feelings of personal control. At the same time, teenagers need better birth-control information. Fourth, more attention needs to be devoted to teenage fathers. Like teenage mothers, they often require special assistance to remain in school and to attain occupational skills. Their psychosocial needs also require attention through special counseling. Finally, Zabin and her colleagues (1986), Kirby (1984), and others have demonstrated that it is possible to set up effective sex-education programs, even for the most at-risk teenagers, and thereby to reduce the overall rate of adolescent pregnancy.

SEX DIFFERENCES AND SEX-ROLE STEREOTYPES

We turn now to an issue that may have less direct relevance to social policy but that generates enormous personal and theoretical interest nonetheless—sex differences. In Chapter 12, we talked about "the child" with little mention of any difference between boys and girls. Are there differences? And if there are, where do they come from?

A second set of questions has to do with our *stereotypes* about sex differences. Regardless of the real differences or lack of differences, what do most adults *think* the differences are between males and females? Do young children have stereotypes too?

Research on all of these questions is still hotly debated, so we can give only partial answers in some cases. Let us begin our exploration by looking at what we know about sex differences and then turn to explanations and to discussions of stereotypes.

Are There Any Sex Differences?

There are some differences between the sexes, but just how many and how large the differences are is not clear. The most obvious differences between men and women have to do with physical characteristics that are now fairly well understood. These differences include the fact (as we saw in Chapter 12) that a woman's body is 25 percent fat, while a man's body is 12 percent fat. The female pelvis, adapted to childbirth, differs radically from that of the human male. Differences such as these are believed to make it easier for men to achieve speed in running and other physical activities requiring speed. In addition, men's muscles use oxygen more efficiently, making it possible for them to have more athletic stamina than women.

However, women's physical makeup also has advantages. Women's muscles have to adapt to a changing menstrual cycle with varied levels of hormones and water retention at different times of the month. Men's muscles are accustomed to relatively more stable conditions—and so are more easily disrupted when illness strikes, perhaps explaining why men complain of aches and pains more frequently when they get the flu. In addition, women's muscles are less likely to build up pain inducers than those of men. Consequently, women may show endurance on a task after men have given up because of pain.

Then, of course, we are all aware of the fact that women live longer than men. Many explanations have been offered as to why this occurs, but the best explanation rests on the biological superiority of women. This topic is nicely discussed in the box titled "Experts Ask Why Women Outlive Men."

We have put together three lists to show you the state of our current knowledge concerning sex differences. Table 13–10 lists those differences that researchers are fairly sure really exist, at least in Western cultures. Psychologists of many different theoretical persuasions agree on these differences. Table 13–11 lists disputed behaviors and characteristics. Some investigators find sex differences here and some do not, or they find differences at some ages and not at others. Table 13–12 lists those areas in which we are virtually certain there are no sex differences—though even here there are some disputes!

As you can see in Table 13–10, the differences we are fairly sure about cover a wide range of skills and behaviors, from physical differences to interpersonal behaviors such as aggression or dominance.

TABLE 13–10   Sex Differences on Which Psychologists Agree

Behavior	Kind of Difference
Aggression	Boys are more aggressive, beginning as early as age 2.
Spatial visualization	Boys and men, from adolescence on, are better at visualizing spatial relationships.
Mathematical reasoning	Boys and men are better at mathematical reasoning from adolescence on.
Verbal skills (especially grammar and spelling)	Girls show faster language development in the first two years; they are better at verbal reasoning and more fluent with words from adolescence on.
Dominance	Boys and men show more dominance from preschool age on.
Confidence	Boys are more confident about new tasks.
Rate of maturation	Girls mature faster; the difference is about six weeks at birth, and about two years at adolescence.
School grades	Girls get better average grades throughout the school years.

TABLE 13–11 Sex Differences on Which Psychologists Have Not Yet Reached Agreement

Behavior or Trait	Findings and Disagreements
Activity level	Tradition holds that boys are more active; data only show this for the 3- to 6-year-old period.
Self-concept	The usual statement is that males have more positive self-concepts; data very inconsistent.
Fear, timidity, and anxiety	Girls are more willing to *report* that they are fearful or anxious, but this may not mean a real difference.
Compliance; doing what one is told	When a difference is found, it is in the direction of females being more compliant, but many researchers find no difference.
Sociability; liking to be with others	Tradition says that females are more sociable; the data say that preschool boys are more often with peers; no clear difference at other ages.
Empathy	Girls may show more empathy, but the results are inconsistent.
Altruism; helping others	Very inconsistent results; no clear difference.
Nurturance	Inconsistent results, but some indications that females may be more nurturant in some settings.

In *all* areas, though, there is a great deal of overlap between the distribution of scores for boys and for girls, for men and for women. As Plomin and Foch (1981) point out, the variation in scores on any of these dimensions *within* each sex is so large that the between-sex difference is really fairly trivial. If that is true, why should we spend a

TABLE 13–12 Some Behaviors That Do Not Seem to Show Sex Differences

Behavior or Trait	Findings and Disagreements
Dependency	There is a very strong assumption that girls are more dependent, but the data do *not* show this.
Achievement orientation	Girls are supposed to be less achievement-oriented, but the data show no sex differences here.
Learning ability	No sex differences are found on any traditional measures of learning, such as operant conditioning or classical conditioning.
Intelligence	No consistent sex differences are found in total scores on IQ tests.

◆ *EXPERTS ASK WHY WOMEN OUTLIVE MEN*

"Men are extremely fragile," says biophysicist Estelle Ramey, speaking only slightly tongue-in-cheek. "They should be protected and covered up at night so they don't die like flies."

The numbers show she has a point: the gap in life expectancy between the sexes is seven years, advantage to the women. A baby girl born in the United States today can expect to live 78 years, a boy 71 years.

The male of the species begins life with a big edge. At the moment of conception, scientists believe, there are 130 males for every 100 females.

STRONGER IN WOMB   But even in the womb, females are the tougher sex. Only 105 boys are born for every 100 girls, and every passing year alters the balance in favor of women until they overtake men at age 31 and outnumber them by more than 2 to 1 after age 85. (The figure on page 533 depicts the male to female ratio by age.)

All the big killers—heart attacks, cancer, and stroke—strike men harder and earlier than women. So do other causes of death—accidents, murder, and suicide.

While the facts are certain, decades of research have left the causes nearly as mysterious as ever. The theories range from evolution to life style:

—Nature demands healthy women to perpetuate the human species. Thus deaths from heart attacks are almost unknown among women of child-bearing years, although both sexes show approximately the same level of cholesterol in the blood. Scientists speculate that female hormones guard against heart disease and strokes.

—Fewer women are smokers. Even among smokers, women smoke less than men, an average of 21 cigarettes a day compared with 33. Consequently, fewer women than men develop lung cancer.

—Women are more likely to see a doctor and to follow instructions for taking medicine. Three-quarters of American women who suffer from high blood pressure have been diagnosed by a physician, compared with less than half the men.

—Fewer women face the pollution and other hazards of the factory. Despite the flood of women into jobs outside the home, only 51% of adult women are in the work force, compared with 71% of men. And women are under-represented in pressure-cooker management jobs, holding just 37% of all executive and administrative positions.

—Women handle stress better when they have to. When a woman dies, her surviving husband has a good chance of becoming seriously ill within a year. When a man dies, by contrast, his wife is much less likely to get sick.

—"The honest answer is, I don't know why women live longer," said Dr. Edward Schneider, dean of the Andrus Gerontology Center at the University of Southern California. "If you talk to a geneticist, the answer will be it's 90% genetics. An endocrinologist will tell you it's 90% hormones, and a psychologist will say it's stress."

There may be some truth to all the theories, whether they are based on biology or behavior.

"You can't separate the two," said Ramey, a professor of physiology and biophysics at Georgetown University in Washington. "Women have the biological aces, and they are socially conditioned to take better care, to pay attention to eating, drinking and sleeping, to go to the doctor when they've got a symptom."

Until recent generations, widespread infectious diseases suppressed the longevity gap. In 1900, life expectancy was just 46 years for men and 48 for women.

ADVANTAGE EXPRESSES ITSELF   Antibiotics, improved nutrition, and modern sanitation systems have curbed infectious diseases and given the "biological advantage of women a chance to express itself," said James Fozard, associate director of the Gerontology Research Center in Baltimore, a unit of the National Institute on Aging.

The advantage is not unique to Americans. Dr. Alvar Svanborg, who is studying older people in Sweden, says women live longer than men the world over. Nor is it peculiar to humans. In virtually every species of mammal, the female typically outlives the male.

Some scientists wonder if women's longevity is related to the very factor that determines their sex. Each cell in a woman's body has two X chromosomes; men's cells, by contrast, have one X chromosome and one Y chromosome. Chromosomes are the tiny bodies in the nucleus of each cell that contain the carriers of heredity called genes.

CONSIDERS CHROMOSOMES   Perhaps, some scientists have speculated, the extra X chromosome in women provides a measure of safety, a chance to make right what is wrong on the other X chromosome. As evidence, Schneider noted that women are typically the carriers and men the victims of certain diseases, such as hemophilia. Queen Victoria of England apparently was a carrier of hemophilia, which struck her son Leopold, the duke of Albany, and her great-grandson Alexis, the son of the last Russian czar.

But this genetic explanation is very tentative. A more compelling biological case can be made for the salutary effects of estrogen and progesterone, the hormones produced in abundance by the female body up to the age of menopause.

The hormones, experts believe, somehow seem to guard against heart disease, the biggest killer of Americans. Dr. Roy Walford, a UCLA physician and researcher, writing in his book, "The 120 Year Diet," calls heart disease "the greatest epidemic mankind has ever faced, carrying off a larger percentage of the population than the Black Death in the Middle Ages."

Walford blames the high-fat, high-cholesterol foods that many Americans favor.

Women have the same eating patterns, yet their arteries do not become clogged, the precursor of heart attacks.

"It's unknown why this is so," said Suzanne G. Haynes of the National Center for Health Statistics.

HEART ATTACK DEATHS   What is known is that heart attacks kill about twice as many men as women. For every 100,000 white males, 249 died of heart disease in 1984; the comparable figure for white females was 124.

Some of women's biological edge is being eroded by smoking, which became fully respectable for American women only after World War II. Lung cancer may soon displace breast cancer as the most common form of cancer that kills women, and smoking also increases the chances of heart attacks.

Smoking is declining among both sexes, but faster for men than for women. Some 32% of adult American men now smoke, barely more than the 28% of women. But there is an ominous trend among young women: in the 20-to-24 age bracket, more women than men smoke.

And the longevity gap may be narrowing with the smoking gap. In 1979, newborn girls could expect to live nearly eight years longer than boys, but the margin has declined to seven years for newborns in 1985, the most recent year for which data is available from the Department of Health and Human Services.

Although nearly as many women as men now smoke, women usually take better care of their health.

"Men more often deny symptoms or ignore them," said Paul T. Costa Jr., chief of the laboratory of personality at Baltimore's Geron-

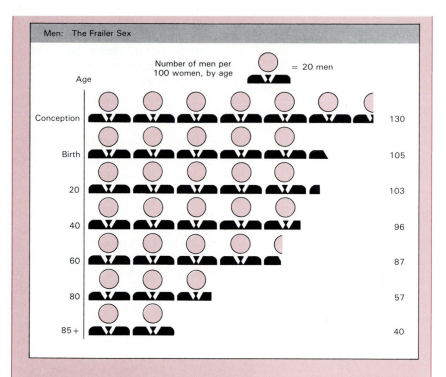

Men: The Frailer Sex

Number of men per 100 women, by age ◯ = 20 men

Age		
Conception		130
Birth		105
20		103
40		96
60		87
80		57
85+		40

tology Research Center. "If a woman has chest pains, she is likely to go to a doctor. A man will say, 'That's indigestion from the cheeseburger I had at lunch.'"

Women also seem more adept at handling stress, the experts say, because they have more close friends with whom they can discuss personal problems and worries. In the jargon of psychology and psychiatry, they have better "support networks."

In the days when a woman's place was thought to be the home, one theory held that women entering the work force would soon begin suffering stress and heart attacks at the same rate as men. But during the past three decades, as the number of women working outside the home climbed dramatically, the female death rate from heart disease has declined sharply—more sharply than for men.

Perhaps, according to a modification of that old theory, women will die at the same rate as men only when they move into the same sorts of high-pressure executive jobs. It is not enough for women to be clerks and secretaries, this hypothesis holds. They will not know real stress until they serve as supervisors and managers.

This theory remains difficult to test, Haynes said, because "the percentage of women in managerial jobs compared to ten years ago hasn't varied that much." But she speculated that as more women become managers, they will handle stress more comfortably than men.

"Women are more likely to discuss their anger with others, to communicate," she said. "Men are more likely to hold it in or to rage out."

Even at retirement age, women live longer than men. Having reached 65, women can look forward to an average of 18.6 more years, men to 14.6 more. For those who survive to 85, the outlook is 6.4 additional years for women, and 5.2 for men.

From "Experts ask why women outlive men" by R. A. Rosenblatten, June 9, 1987, *Los Angeles Times*, pp. 8,21. Copyright, 1987, *Los Angeles Times*. Reprinted by permission.

lot of time and effort trying to explain the differences? There are two reasons. First, any time we find consistent patterns, it is important to try to understand where they come from—their source. Second, in our culture at this time, the issue of sex differences is highly relevant for each of us in our personal lives, in our professional lives, and in raising our children. So despite the fact that the consistent sex differences are relatively few and small, it is important to explore them.

How Can We Explain Sex Differences?

The three different perspectives—biological, environmental, and interactional—that we discussed so often in Chapter 12 reappear in explanations of sex differences. The differences between males and females could be inborn, resulting from differing hormones or sex-linked genetic differences. They could result from different socialization patterns that are dependent on the sex of the child and result in different skills and competencies for each of the sexes, or they could result from a combination of the two. Moreover, differences in treatment could accentuate any biological differences.

Biological explanations currently dominate discussions of most of the "sure" sex differences we have listed in Table 13–10. For example, Maccoby and Jacklin (1980) have recently affirmed their conclusion that there is strong evidence for a biological origin of differences in aggression. The same difference is found in subhuman primates (monkeys, chimps, and others), and it can be linked to hormones. Female monkeys whose mothers were given injections of male hormones during pregnancy show more aggressive behaviors with their peers than do normal females (Phoenix, 1974). There is some evidence (Ehrhardt & Baker, 1974) that the same thing is true of human females who experienced high male hormone levels prenatally because of hormones that their mothers took or because of a genetic imbalance. So it appears that there is a strong biological component in aggression differences.

Before we jump to any conclusions in this regard, however, it is important to know what we mean by aggression and to evaluate how men and women assess the consequences of aggression. In a review of literature employing a new statistical procedure called meta-analysis, Eagly and Steffen (1986) found that although men were somewhat more aggressive than women on the average, sex differences in aggression were inconsistent across the studies being evaluated. Eagly and Steffen discovered that men were more likely to use aggression that produces pain or physical injury; women were more likely to use aggression that produces psychological or social harm. Women also believed that physical aggression would harm the target more than men felt it would. Women demonstrated more guilt and anxiety if they engaged in aggression that caused harm or injury. Finally, the more women perceived that aggression would in turn put them in danger, the less likely they were to aggress. These psychological dimensions exhibited by women cast new light on how we should assess the differences between males and females with regard to aggression. The way that we define aggression and the differences in perceptions surrounding the consequences of aggressive behavior

Although it now appears that there is a strong biological component in aggression differences, the psychological dimensions of aggressive behaviors exhibited by women are causing researchers to reevaluate their assessment of differences between males and females.

on the target and on the aggressor all have some influence on the perspective from which differences in aggression may most appropriately be viewed.

Deborah Waber (1977) has suggested another sort of biological explanation for the observed differences in spatial visualization and verbal ability noted between men and women. As we indicated in Table 13–10, girls as a group mature faster than do boys—with a very large difference at adolescence. Waber argues that maturity rate may play a role in the intellectual differences between the sexes. She suggests that early maturation strengthens the dominance of the left hemisphere of the brain (see Chapter 2), where the language center is located. Because spatial visualization skills seem to be governed by the right hemisphere, dominance of the left hemisphere also would mean a relative weakening of spatial skills. If this is true, then early maturing adolescents, *regardless of sex*, should be relatively better at verbal skills and less accomplished at spatial visualizations than late maturers. The reverse should be true for late maturers. This is just what Waber found, as you can see in Figure 13–4.

The results in the figure are based on research that involved 20 boys and 20 girls in the eighth grade who were given a standard test

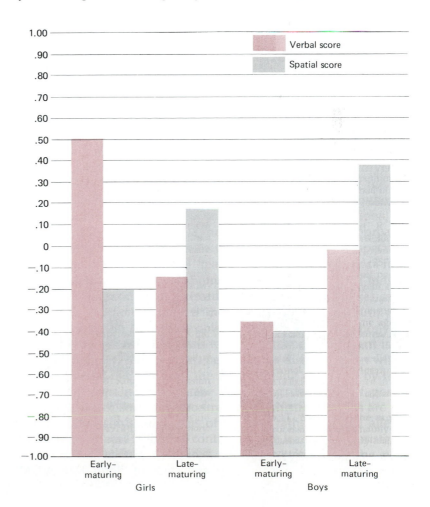

FIGURE 13–4 Verbal and Spatial Scores of Early-maturing and Late-maturing Adolescents
Waber's research indicates that early maturers of both sexes are more accomplished in verbal development and less skilled at spatial visualization. (After Waber, 1977)

that measures verbal and spatial ability. In the figure, the scores have been converted into a scale that runs from −1.00 to +1.00, with +1.00 indicating the best performance. Waber also studied a group of 20 fifth-grade girls and a group of 20 tenth-grade boys and found the same patterns for those groups as well. In every group, early maturers were better at verbal tests than at spatial tests and later maturers were better at spatial tests than at verbal tests, regardless of sex.

As we noted in Chapter 2, the current evidence on hemispheric dominance is somewhat mixed. Most activities involve both right and left hemispheres, and we should be cautious about placing too much emphasis on this portion of Waber's hypothesis. Still, her results are intriguing, since they explain differences *within* each sex as well as differences *between* the sexes. They also explain why there are no consistent sex differences in spatial visualization until adolescence. Perhaps it is only then, when the sex differences in rate of maturation are so marked, that the secondary effect on verbal and spatial skills becomes clear. In any case, Waber's work is bound to stimulate further research of this type.

Not everyone agrees that biology is the only explanation for sex differences. What about the different ways boys and girls are treated from birth onward? There is some evidence, for example, that parents talk more to infant girls than to infant boys (Cherry & Lewis, 1976), which might help to account for the more rapid development of language by girls during their early years. And there is now strong evidence that parents, especially fathers, work actively to discourage cross-sex behavior in their children. Boys are punished for choosing to play with dolls; girls are discouraged from playing with trucks or carpentry tools (Langlois & Downs, 1980). Tracy (1987) has suggested that boys and/or girls who maintain a masculine sex-role orientation play with a wider variety of toys and games that foster superior spatial skills (the toys and games require more spatial manipulation). This superiority of spatial abilities is in turn correlated with achievement in mathematics and science. If this is true, it reinforces an interactional interpretation of how the sexes differ on spatial abilities and subsequent mathematical and scientific achievement levels, which have been observed in school performance.

It is also true that cognitive gender differences are disappearing (Feingold, 1988). In a study conducted between 1947 and 1980 that compared males and females on cognitive tasks, such as spatial visualization, mathematical ability, and mechanical aptitude, Feingold found consistent differences across time between the sexes on these measures but also reported that the gender differences declined over the years. It may be that differences in child-rearing patterns and early socialization experiences between boy and girl children are narrowing, and this, consequently, may be responsible for closing the gap between the sexes in these measures, which once seemed to be the last bastion of masculine superiority.

Even those aspects of development that you might think were totally determined by biology, such as gender itself, can be influenced by environment. John Money (Money & Ehrhardt, 1972; Money,

Research evidence indicates that parents, especially fathers, work actively to discourage cross-sex behavior in their children. Boys are often punished for choosing to play with dolls.

1976) has spent several decades studying the development of children whose external genitalia are ambiguous (for any one of several reasons), and he has found that what is crucial for the child's later behavior and later gender identity is the gender assigned to the child at birth. If the parents think they are rearing a boy, call him a boy, and treat him as a boy throughout childhood, then the child will think of himself as a boy and behave "boyishly." The *same* child, if labeled as a girl at birth, would have been treated differently and would behave differently later. Money also contends that there is a critical time period involved. If a child has been mislabeled for some reason, the error can be corrected up to about age 2 or 3, and the child will adopt the behaviors and roles of the newly labeled gender. But after age 2 or 3, it is very difficult to reverse the gender label.

Findings of this type certainly underline the crucial importance of the specific training the child receives. As usual, the interactionist position seems to come closest to the truth. There are differences in genetic programming and hormone patterning between boys and girls that create tendencies for different behavior patterns. However, the socialization experiences that a child has in his early years can either accentuate the biological differences between the sexes or minimize them.

Sex-role Stereotypes

The other half of the question of how we explain sex differences involves what people *think* is true about sex differences. If you know nothing about someone except his or her gender, what assumptions do you make about that person's likely characteristics? And do those assumptions fit the reality of what we know about sex differences?

There is a great deal of agreement among adults in our culture about the expected and desired characteristics of men and women. The most comprehensive studies of this topic are by Broverman, Vogel, Rosenkrantz, and Bee (Broverman, Vogel, Broverman, Clarkson, & Rosenkrantz, 1972; Rosenkrantz, Vogel, Bee, Broverman, & Broverman, 1968). These researchers had large numbers of subjects respond to a long list of traits, each of which is laid out like this:

Very talkative..........Not at all talkative

Each subject was asked to go through the list of items once and indicate where the "typical male" fitted on each scale, and then to go through again and mark the "typical female." Broverman and her colleagues also requested that other subjects indicate which side of each scale was the "good" or "desirable" side. At the end of this process, the researchers had a list of traits for which the male and female stereotypes differed, and for each trait, they knew which was the "good" or "desirable" side of the scale.

In Tables 13–13 and 13–14 we have listed the positive aspects of the male and female stereotypes that emerged from these studies. If you look at the length of the two lists, you can see that men are thought of as having a greater number of positive characteristics than

TABLE 13–13   The Male Stereotype: "Competence"

Males Are Thought to Be:

Aggressive	Able to make decisions easily
Independent	Self-confident
Unemotional	Leaders
Objective	Ambitious
Dominant	Skilled in business
Not easily influenced	Interested in math and science
Competitive	Unexcitable in minor crises
Logical	Active
Direct	Worldly
Not easily hurt	Able to separate feelings and ideas
Adventurous	Not conceited about their appearance

Source: After Broverman et al., 1972.

women are believed to have. So not only do we have pervasive stereotypes, but the male stereotype is seen as more positive and more "healthy" than the female stereotype (Broverman, Broverman, Clarkson, Rosenkrantz, & Vogel, 1970).

If you compare the lists in Tables 13–13 and 13–14 to the known and still-debated sex differences we listed for you earlier, you can see that while some of the stereotyped differences are matched by observed differences, many are not. Women are not more dependent and are probably not more easily influenced. Men are not more logical and do not have consistently more positive self-images.

Stereotyping in Children   Where do the stereotypes come from, then, if they do not match actual behavior? One thing we know about

TABLE 13–14   The Female Stereotype: "Warmth and Expressiveness"

Females Are Thought to Be:

Talkative	Neat
Tactful	Quiet
Gentle	Needing security
Aware of others' feelings	Interested in art and literature
Religious	Able to express tender feelings easily
Interested in their appearance	

Source: After Broverman et al., 1972.

TABLE 13–15 Assumptions about Sex Differences in Infants

How different are they?
Test your assumptions about sex differences in infants.

True/False

1. It is easy to tell the sex of a baby by watching how it behaves.
2. Soon after birth, mothers smile, touch, and speak to their baby girls more than to their baby boys.
3. Baby girls smile more.
4. Baby boys are more sensitive to skin contact.
5. Baby boys cry more.
6. There is no difference in how much time boy babies and girl babies spend awake and sleeping.
7. A girl infant is more likely than a boy infant to die before age one.
8. In nursery school, boys and girls are equally courageous.

1. false 2. true 3. true 4. false 5. true 6. true 7. false 8. true

stereotypes is that they begin *very* early. As a matter of fact, they probably begin with parents and their assumptions about sex differences during infancy and the ways in which they interact with their infants. Table 13–15 lists eight true-false items that you can use to test your knowledge of the sex differences between male and female infants.

Kuhn, Nash, and Brucken (1978) found that children as young as 30 months of age thought that girls like to play with dolls and to clean house and that boys like to play with cars and to build things. By elementary-school age, the male stereotype is very clear: fourth and fifth graders think men are strong, robust, aggressive/assertive, cruel, coarse, ambitious, and dominant. The female stereotype is not quite as strong this early, but children this age think women are weak, emotional, soft-hearted, and affectionate (Best et al., 1977). Virtually all researchers who have studied stereotypes have found not only that the male stereotype is stronger, but that stereotyping also is stronger in boys than in girls. This may reflect the fact that the male qualities are more highly valued in our society at the present time.

Parental treatment of boys and girls and parental comments about what is "boyish" and "girlish" behavior are obviously one source of such stereotypes. But television and children's books also play a role and contribute to what parents believe the male and female stereotypes are like. Portrayals of males and females in both books and television are *highly* stereotyped (Gerbner, 1972; Saario, Jacklin, & Tittle, 1973), and children who watch more television have more strongly stereotyped views of male and female roles (Frueh & McGhee, 1975). Thus, despite the fact that there are relatively few consistently found differences between men and women in their actual *behavior*, we continue to reinforce children's and adults' ideas about differences through the media.

Consequences of Stereotypes Among adults, we can see the effects of these persisting stereotypes in many ways. For example, if you give undergraduates a passage to read from a scientific article that you will ask them to rate the quality of and tell half of them that it was authored by a male and half that it was authored by a female, those who think it was written by a male rate it higher (Mischel, 1974). Other researchers have found that adults also have stereotypic expectations of children. Condry and Condry (1976) had several hundred college students rate the emotional reactions of a 9-month-old infant who was shown on videotape responding to a cuddly toy, a jack-in-the-box, a buzzer, and a doll. Half of the subjects were told that the baby was a boy and half were told that the baby was a girl. Those who thought the baby was a boy rated "his" reactions as showing more pleasure, more anger, and less fear. Those who thought the baby was a girl rated "her" reactions as more fearful, less pleased, and less angry. The *same* behaviors were interpreted differently, depending on the assumed sex of the infant, just as the same written document was rated differently depending on the assumed sex of the author.

Despite nearly two decades of the women's movement, sex-role stereotyping has not changed much, nor has there been a great increase in the number of women working in professional and technical occupations. Sex stereotyping affects prospective employers, but it also affects the young woman whose self-concept has been influenced by the pervasive cultural expectations for men and women.

Androgyny: The Middle Ground   Recent work by Bem (1974; Bem, Martyna, & Watson, 1976) and by Spence and Helmreich (1978), however, has pointed to the fact that not all adults are equally affected by the stereotypes. Bem used the word ***androgynous*** to describe men and women who had developed *both* the traditionally masculine "competence" characteristics and the traditionally feminine characteristics of "warmth and expressiveness." Spence and Helmreich have found that adults who are high in androgyny also have higher self-esteem, are more empathetic toward others, and exhibit higher achievement motivation.

In one study of androgyny, Coleman and Ganong (1985) asked the question, "Do macho men and feminine women make better lovers?" To get an answer they administered the Bem Sex-Role Inventory and several scales that measure feelings, emotions, and behaviors of love to 100 male and 136 female college students, all of whom indicated that they were at that time involved in a love relationship. The findings may be surprising to some observers of behavior. Results indicated that the students (males and females) who scored high on androgynous behavior also scored high on verbal expressions of love, were more tolerant of their loved one's faults, and were less interested in material evidence of love. In short, androgynous persons are more loving and stereotypically sex-typed persons are less loving! Coleman and Ganong answer their own question: "It is not macho men and feminine women who make the best lovers, at least not as love is measured [here]" (pp. 174–75). This study suggests the need to give more attention to the effect of androgyny on a variety of other love relationships: parent-child, homosexual, and friendships of different sorts.

There is also an intriguing suggestion in a study by Feldman, Biringen, and Nash (1981) that there are predictable changes in degrees of androgyny over the life span. These observers found that the traditional masculine and feminine sex roles were most strongly visible among young adults, particularly those who were married and had children. Men and women at this life-stage described themselves as being closer to the stereotypic sex-role patterns than was true for any other age group. In contrast, the grandparents in this sample exhibited more cross-sex (androgynous) self-descriptions. At this life-stage, the men appeared to have become more expressive and the women more autonomous.

Research on androgyny is still progressing, so we cannot say whether, with the passing decades, more of us are becoming androgynous and expressing both aspects of ourselves. Feldman's study, however, suggests that whether each of us expresses the feminine or masculine "side" of ourselves may depend in part on the role demands we are encountering. Since those role demands change over the life span, the balance between the masculine and feminine in each of us may change as well.

In this chapter, we have explored five major developmental topics. As we said at the beginning of the chapter, there are many topics that could have been discussed in addition to those covered here. We have tried to present some of the more interesting topics and to do so in a way that made use of information learned in Chapter 12 concerning developmental processes. A very important part of the study of human behavior that we have mentioned but not really discussed fully has to do with the personality formation of the individual. For instance, we made reference to the theories of Freud and Erikson and the influence these theories have had in our understanding of children. In this chapter, we have commented on the personality characteristics of children who have been abused or have experienced the separation of their parents. In Chapter 14, we will take up the topic of personality in a more formal way and discuss how psychologists have theorized about personality development.

SUMMARY

1. Many socially relevant questions involve the basic processes of development, including child abuse, effects of divorce, day care, teenage parenthood, and sex differences.

2. As many as one million children (possibly many more) are physically abused or neglected each year in the United States.

3. Children who are abused often suffer permanent physical damage, long-term intellectual deficits, and emotional disturbances.

4. There is some reason to believe that the long-term effects of child abuse can be lessened if the child has a supportive person to offer encouragement.

5. Three theories about the causes of abuse have been offered: (1) there is something wrong with the parents, (2) there is something wrong with the child, or (3) environmental stress is to blame. No one of these approaches is adequate. Individual instances of abuse result from complex interactions of all three.

6. Prediction of abuse is extremely difficult because of the multiple causes of abuse. Treatment, too, is difficult, although some programs have reported success in preventing recurrences.

7. Research is beginning to show that not all children who are abused become abusive parents. It traditionally had been believed that most abused children became abusive parents, but evidence now indicates that this is not the case.

8. Divorce now ends nearly 50 percent of all marriages; it has been estimated that one out of four children spends part of childhood in a single-parent household.

9. Studies of the effects of divorce on the child have provided inconclusive or mixed findings. All researchers agree that there are major short-term effects; children show emotional disturbances, depression, school problems. Longer-term effects are more difficult to pin down, since many children of divorced parents show no long-term effects, and children from families of unhappily married parents also show symptoms of maladjustment.

10. The negative effects of predivorce stress are observable in some children, especially boys.

11. Research on stepfamilies is beginning to reveal the effects of parental remarriage on children. Where there is a good stepparent-stepchild relationship, the effects on children are positive; these positive results are indicated by decreases in aggression, antisocial behavior, and social withdrawal.

12. For parents, the effect of divorce is often psychologically beneficial, although divorced women typically experience greatly reduced incomes.

13. With the increased number of women in the work force and the consequent increase in the number of preschool children requiring day care, it is important to note that the general consensus is that the day-care experience need not have deleterious effects on children and may enhance children's development in some cases.

14. Children who participate in group child-care programs tend to be somewhat more independent, more sociable and/or competitive, and more boisterous and aggressive with peers. Whether these differences are positive or negative depends on the value systems of the parents.

15. The considerations that are critical for assessing the quality of child care include the training and experience of the adult caretakers, the ratio of children to caretakers, the instructional curriculum of the day-care program, the general facilities of the day-care center, and the role of parents in the program.

16. Day care must provide more than custodial child care; the best programs for providing intellectual and achievement gains for children are a blend of structured educational activities and unstructured play activities that allow the child to explore and create individually.

17. Although the total number of teenage births has not increased markedly in the past decade, an increasing percentage of all births have been to adolescent mothers.

18. Teenage mothers who receive adequate prenatal care do not show any increased risk of difficulties surrounding birth. More poor girls and more minority girls give birth during teenage years, but when the effects of income and race are sorted out, there are few effects that can be linked directly to the mother's age at birth.

19. The exception is that children of teenage mothers have somewhat lower IQs than do children of older mothers.

20. For teenage mothers, early pregnancy is associated with fewer total years of education, lower incomes, and larger families, all factors that change the total life course for the girl.

21. Teenage fathers resemble teenage mothers in many behavioral characteristics. Both are more likely to be school dropouts, to have low occupational aspirations, and to be more traditional in their sex-role orientation.

22. Sex-education programs can be effective with teenagers. Effective programs must do more than present basic reproduction and contraceptive information. They must focus on relationships and values. Those programs that are also attached to a health clinic appear to be the most effective in assisting teenagers to deal with sex and pregnancy.

23. Some sex differences in physical development, behavior, and intellectual skills are found consistently: males are more aggressive, better at spatial relationships and mathematical reasoning, and more competitive. Females are somewhat more verbal and faster in physical development.

24. Many more aspects of behavior show no consistent sex differences; psychologists continue to disagree about the consistency of many sex differences.

25. There is good evidence to indicate that hormones create the basis for sex differences in aggression; biology may also play a role in verbal and spatial skill differences. In contrast, environmentalists emphasize that boys and girls are treated differently from a very early age.

26. Sex-role stereotypes are widely held, even though they do not match the actual differences in behavior very well. Generally speaking, the male stereotype is considered more "desirable." It develops earlier and is more strongly held than are the stereotyped female qualities.

27. Children as young as 3 or 4 show the beginnings of sex stereotyping. Some of this may be shaped within the family, but school, books, and television all portray males and females in highly stereotyped ways.

28. Not all adults are affected by sex-role stereotypes. Androgyny is the term that is used to describe men and women who have developed both traditional male and female characteristics. Androgynous individuals, whether male or female, have high self-esteem, empathy, and achievement motivation.

KEY TERMS

androgyny	child-care programs	stepfamilies
caregivers	Project Head Start	sex-role
child abuse	role reversal	stereotype

ADDITIONAL READING

Clarke-Stewart, A. (1982) *Daycare*. Cambridge, MA: Harvard University Press.
This book is a short primer on the effects of day care on child development by a leading expert in the field and an excellent overview of what to look for in a day-care program.

Kempe, C. H., & Helfer, R. E. (Eds.). (1980) *The battered child*. Chicago: University of Chicago Press.
This is an important collection of readings on the short- and long-term psychological consequences of child abuse.

Lancaster, J. B., H & Hamburg, B. A. (Eds.). (1986) *School-age pregnancy and parenthood: Biosocial dimensions*. New York: Aldine de Gruyter.
This book is a collection of articles from both the social and biological sciences that present important information on adolescence and reproduction. Although technical, the chapters represent the current state of knowledge about the biological and psychological consequences of early pregnancy and parenthood.

Maccoby, E. E. (1980) *Social development: Psychological growth and the parent-child relationship.* New York: Harcourt Brace Jovanovich.
Chapter 6 of this book on sex differences and sex typing is an extremely lucid description of the basic biological and psychological similarities and differences between the sexes, especially during childhood.

Pleck, E. (1987) *Domestic tyranny.* New York: Oxford University Press.
In this readable book, the author documents how children have been abused throughout American history and how social policies have evolved to protect the rights of children. Spousal abuse is also discussed.

Wallerstein, J. S., & Kelly, J. B. (1980) *Surviving the breakup: How children and parents cope with divorce.* New York: Basic Books.
This is a sensitive and thoughtful account of a group of 60 families going through the process of separation and divorce. There is a great deal of case material so that readers can see how individual adults and children adjust to the breakup.

14 *Personality*

THE STUDY OF PERSONALITY

Alan and Robert are attending the wedding reception of their friend. Alan is immaculate in a dark suit with a tie and white shirt as he stands alone somewhat apart from the crowd, rather nervously sipping a drink. Robert is surrounded by people who are listening to the humorous story he is telling. He is dressed in somewhat flashy, colorful clothing in keeping with the latest trends and seems to be enjoying himself greatly, although he has never met most of the people before this afternoon. Suddenly an attractive young woman enters the room. Both Alan and Robert notice her immediately and wish to meet her. Alan thinks about approaching her but finds his feet rooted to the floor. He feels nervous and his heart beats faster with fear. "I won't know what to say to her. She won't be interested in me. I might as well not try," he thinks. Robert, however, excuses himself from his circle of new friends, and as he walks toward her, he is already planning where to ask her for dinner because he feels entirely confident that she will be interested in him.

In this brief sketch, the situation and the event are the same for the two men, yet each reacts very differently. We might wonder what these differences mean. Is Alan shy and nervous about meeting women, and is Robert confident and outgoing? We also might wonder whether this pattern holds for other situations: is Alan shy with male strangers, too, or is Robert outgoing in business situations? We might even wonder if the differences that we observed at this wedding reception imply other differences between the men: is Alan also cautious, quiet, tidy, polite? Is Robert also competitive, independent, ambitious, adventure-loving?

What Is Personality

When we talk about *personality* in a scientific sense, we usually mean something about an individual's distinctive, consistent, patterned methods of relating to the environment. Other psychologists might be interested in various aspects of the scene described above, but personality psychologists are particularly interested in the *differences* in the ways a person responds to events, how these differences influence the person, and how these characteristic behaviors, attitudes, and values might be related to one another within the person.

The everyday use of the term "personality" is somewhat different. People talk about "having a *good* personality" or "a lot of personality," implying that the term means one's degree of social effectiveness or attractiveness. Or, sometimes people consider that personality means the major trait that a person might display—"an aggressive personality," "a neurotic personality." However, these meanings of the term are too limited for our use in psychology.

When we include the ideas of *distinctive, consistent,* and *patterned* in our definition, what do we mean? "Distinctive" is fairly clear; we are interested in how people differ. Although environmental circumstances and fundamental principles of human behavior determine a lot of what people do, so that people are often alike, personality is the study of individual *differences*. We are not interested here in the things that everyone does more or less in the same way (at a wedding reception most people stand up, wear clothing, speak intelligibly, and act cheerful or friendly). Instead, we are interested in the distinctive aspects of the behaviors—what it is that makes one person's responses different from another person's.

We also have to include the term "consistent" in our definition of personality. We want to describe how a person *typically*, or *characteristically*, behaves. For instance, if Alan is nervous because the woman who walked in the door is Miss America, but in every other social situation he feels poised and reasonably capable, then we would not attribute "shyness with women" to him. We want to know about relatively enduring, stable ways of behaving and feeling, characteristics that would be likely to apply to other situations, at other times.

Finally, our definition includes "patterned" ways of relating to the environment, because one personality trait does not define an entire *personality*. Personality characteristics occur in some unique combination with other traits, and it is the entire pattern that we call personality.

Topics in the Field of Personality

Psychologists have identified several subdivisions within the broad field of personality. Some researchers focus on **personality development**, the process by which we acquire our personality characteristics. These psychologists ask some of the kinds of questions explored in Chapter 12 on developmental psychology. Do we all pass through some fixed sequences of stages on the way to our final personality? How much of our personality is determined by our experiences? How much by our genetic inheritance? How do early child-rearing practices affect personality?

Another division focuses on the abnormal personality. What are the causes and consequences of certain types of problems in personalities and behavior? How can problems in personalities be changed? Questions such as these are examined in Chapters 17 and 18, on psychological abnormality and its treatment.

A third subcategory involves psychologists who want to *measure* personality. What kinds of tests and procedures are available? Are they reliable? Are they valid? How do the various theories of personality lead to different methods of assessment? A related issue concerns the potential misuses or misinterpretations of test results. Assessment issues and test abuses are explored in Chapters 15 and 16.

While not actual subdivisions within personality studies, topics related to personality are frequently studied by psychologists. Such issues might involve the relationship between certain personality characteristics and other behaviors. For instance, do people with certain characteristics develop cancer less often or show better adjustment to medical procedures? Questions like these are asked by health psychologists. Social psychologists might be interested in conditions that affect "altruism" or the effect of individual differences in the trait of sex-role androgyny on behaviors in competitive situations, or the relationship between how people interpret situations and how they feel about themselves. Developmental psychologists might be interested in moral development in children, or the role of the personality characteristic, self-esteem, on children's adjustment to divorce. Complex statistical methods developed by psychologists might be used to characterize how clusters of personality traits go together, or how they might be causally related to one another. Behavioral geneticists might study how certain traits may have a genetic or biological origin. The list of the ways in which the field of personality extends across the boundaries of areas within psychology is virtually endless.

Finally, a major subdivision in personality is personality theory. This is the study of the kinds of models or theories of personality structure and functions, and it is the main focus of the rest of this chapter. We will explore four major theories or approaches to understanding personality. These have been selected to represent dominant points of view in this field that exert considerable influence in most areas of psychology.

THE FREUDIAN APPROACH TO PERSONALITY

Sigmund Freud (1856–1939) may well be the most famous person in the field of psychology. His pioneer work in personality theory opened up a new way of thinking about people and their behavior. The founder of **psychoanalysis**, Freud published many influential books over the course of 40 years. Although psychology has moved on to new areas of discovery, and few modern psychologists claim that Freud was correct in everything he said and did, no one would deny that he has had an enormous impact on the twentieth century. His influence has gone well beyond the confines of psychology, affecting the arts, philosophy, and everyday conversation. How many times have you heard people refer to "Freudian slips," "rationalization," "unconscious desires," the "Oedipal conflict," "oral fixation," or "psychoanalysis?" Freud originated all of these concepts, and many, many more. Though a considerable number of psychologists now view Freudian theory with a good deal of skepticism, it certainly represents one of the major steps in the long and gradual development of psychological knowledge.

It is hard to describe the essence of Freud's thinking because so many of his ideas and concepts are interrelated, and because much of his thinking changed during the course of his lifetime. Our summary here can only outline Freud's theory of personality. For our purposes, we will consider Freud's views about the *components* of personality, the *functioning* of these components, and their *development*.

The Three Elements of Personality

Freud saw the human personality as composed of three basic elements: the *id*, the *ego*, and the **superego.** We will discuss each of these elements in turn.

The Id   The part of the personality that contains all the raw, primitive, biological passions and desires is called the *id.* Freud believed that two of the most important of these primitive drives are the sexual and aggressive impulses, and that everyone has them. The id is the reservoir for all psychological energy. The id operates according to the **pleasure principle**, which means the id wants these raw passions gratified *right now*. This part of our personality does not want to delay

Sigmund Freud—probably the most famous person in the field of psychology.

gratification, even if delay would be in its own interest. Freud described the id impulses as **unconscious drives**, because we are not normally aware of them. According to Freud, at this very moment, as you sit reading this text, you are a reservoir of strong, sometimes conflicting, sexual, aggressive, and other demands.

The id may demand immediate gratification of its impulses, no matter what problems such actions might cause. For instance, it may be urging you to kick that big guy because he is in your way. But the id also can seek gratification through **wish fulfillment**, by forming mental images of the objects or acts that will satisfy the demands. Thus a person burning with thirst may imagine an oasis of cool, clear water, or you may daydream that you ordered that big guy to get out of your way and he meekly obeyed.

Dreams, as we saw in Chapter 4, also represent wish fulfillment for Freud. He described dreams as disguised images of objects or events that will gratify id impulses. Such attempts to satisfy id impulses, either by immediate gratification through direct action or by wish fulfillment, represent what Freud called **primary processes.** As our examples show, primary-process thinking attempts to satisfy id impulses in an irrational, unrealistic manner. Primary-process thinking is characteristic of the id.

Obviously, we would not be able to get along in society if there were nothing more to our personality than id impulses. We would be in jail or dead. According to Freud, we learn to control our wild impulses as we grow up. As we shall see, other aspects of the adult personality develop out of the id, but the id stays active throughout life and continues to supply the energy, or **libido**, for all psychological activity. And yet we are almost totally unaware of these impulses. They remain submerged, or unconscious, just as most of an iceberg remains hidden below the surface of the ocean (see Figure 14–1).

The Ego   The *ego* is the part of our personality that attempts to serve the id, without letting it get out of hand. The ego operates according to the *reality principle.* It serves as a mediator between the id's demand for immediate and total gratification and the equally forceful demands of the real world. The ego operates by *secondary-process thinking*, which is logical and realistic thinking. It is as though the id

FIGURE 14–1   The Relationship of the Freudian Personality Structures to Levels of Awareness   *According to Freud, the mind is much like an iceberg, with only the tip projecting into the level of conscious awareness. All of the id, most of the superego, and a good portion of the ego operate on an unconscious level. Preconscious thought is thought that is now unconscious, but can become conscious.*

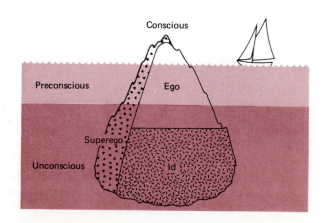

says, "Give that to me now," and the ego replies, "I'll get it for you if I can." The ego is logical and practical, while the id is illogical and impractical. Although often in conflict with the id, the ego's function is to satisfy the id's demands.

For example, if it were left to the id, we might well assault anyone who frustrates us in any way. The social consequences would, of course, be less than pleasant, so the ego steps in and says, "Hold on. Wait a minute. Let me work on this problem." It then finds a way to satisfy our id demands without threatening our well-being. With a little patience and preparation, the ego is often able to gratify the id. It is almost as if the ego is some kind of master criminal, coaching the reckless id: "Go slow. Be discreet. Try it this way instead. But if you can pull it off, do it." In short, the ego is logical and practical, but has no moral sense.

The Superego   If we concluded that the id and the ego were the only elements of our personality, we would be missing something. We all have a conscience, a sense of right and wrong. It is this sense of right and wrong that Freud refers to as the **superego**. The superego represents the standards of our society that we have internalized, or taken on as our own.

The superego plays an important part in determining behavior. If the id wants to kill someone and the ego develops a scheme for committing the perfect murder, the superego will deter the individual—most of the time, at least. Freud believed that the superego is roughly comparable to what we refer to as our conscience.

When first introduced to the id, ego, and superego, some readers assume that Freud believed these three elements are actual structures residing within us somewhere. They are not. The terms merely refer to three different aspects of our overall personality. They may become less mysterious and more contemporary if we think of them as *desire, reason, and conscience.*

Relative Strengths   We can see that if one or another of these three elements is relatively weak or strong, distinct personality types might appear. What would a person be like if his superego is overdeveloped and dominant? He might well be a shy, inhibited person who seldom expresses either sexual or aggressive impulses, even when they would be appropriate. What about a person with a powerful id? This person might crash through life, trying to gratify her every need immediately, a thoughtless and insensitive menace to herself and to society as well.

The Unconscious

Freud believed that most of the activity of the three personality elements is unconscious. That is, many of our behaviors are motivated by impulses that are beyond our awareness. As you can see in Figure 14–1, the id is wholly unconscious, the superego is predominantly unconscious, and even some of the ego is unconscious. If we have an unconscious hatred of our "best friend," we are totally unaware of this feeling. According to Freud, many of our actions are motivated by unconscious impulses. Notice that Figure 14–1 introduces the notion of the *preconscious*. A preconscious thought is one that we are not now aware of, but that we can become aware of at some point. For example, until you read this sentence you were probably not thinking of your mother's name—but now you are. The idea has been brought from the preconscious to the conscious. The preconscious is roughly comparable to long-term memory.

Freud's concept of unconscious and preconscious thought has been heavily criticized. Some objections are philosophical. We like to think we are rational people—in charge of our lives—but Freud's theory seems to make us unknowing victims of our own brutish impulses. Other objections focus on the lack of experimental evidence for the existence of unconscious thought and motivation. As you can imagine, it is difficult to devise tests or experiments that will either support or disprove the theory.

Do you have to agree with Freud to believe in unconscious mental processes? The answer from modern cognitive psychologists is an emphatic no. Contemporary psychologists who study human thought processes have a very different view of the way people perceive information and interpret their worlds than Freud did. Although they view the mind as more like a computer (though far less accurate) than the seething forces of the id, the ego, and the superego, modern researchers agree with Freud that many aspects of thinking, gathering impressions, forming judgments, and making inferences occur unconsciously. However, by this they simply mean that the rules and procedures, and sometimes even the perceptions, that guide our thinking may occur outside of awareness (Kihlstrom, 1987). One simple example of how thinking may occur outside of awareness is *automatic processing*; once we learn a skill and it becomes routine, we can perform it without conscious awareness of all the decisions that we make. Think of driving a car, speaking English, or playing a musical instrument, and you can see the complexity of behaviors that may be performed without conscious awareness. Similarly, we probably execute many complex social tasks, such as forming impressions of others or even interpreting our own behaviors, without conscious awareness of the basis of some of our reactions. As we shall see later in this chapter, modern concepts of the *self* may involve similar ideas about selective interpretations of events of which we are not aware. Thus, although the original Freudian concepts of unconscious processes have been largely discredited, other ways of viewing people agree that a lot of our human actions are based on processes outside awareness.

The Dynamics of Personality

It is clear that the three elements of the personality defined by Freud are going to be in conflict. In fact, Freud says that conflicts among the three form the basis for many psychological activities. The id says, "Now!" while the superego says, "Never!" The ego has to resolve these equally strident demands. In a sense, the ego is nagged from both sides and must chart a course between the demands of the id and the superego.

Anxiety   The result of conflict among the various personality components is *anxiety.* If the id moves an individual to steal, the superego will insist that stealing is wrong. This conflict results in a feeling of anxiety. For Freud, anxiety is a prime motivating factor behind neurotic behavior, as we shall see in Chapter 17.

Defense Mechanisms   When these conflicts become too threatening or too dangerous, the ego turns to its arsenal of defense mechanisms. As you will recall from Chapter 11, defense mechanisms are techniques for dealing with anxiety. There are quite a number of them. Among them is *repression.* We are repressing when we block a threatening, unacceptable impulse out of our conscious awareness. If the id's demands become too strong, we can deny them by not thinking about them. A conflict between the id and the superego can be avoided in this manner. Other defense mechanisms, all designed to avoid conflict among the personality elements, include *rationalization*, *reaction formation*, and *projection*. These and others were discussed in Chapter 11.

Once a defense mechanism has been brought into play and the demands of the id are at least temporarily silenced, what happens to these demands? Do they go away when they are repressed? The answer is no. They still exist, and they still seek to be expressed. Since they are blocked from conscious expression, they must seek other outlets. Often, they "pop out" as unintended puns, or "Freudian slips." For example, if someone says "breast" when they mean "rest," or "clown" when they mean "crown," a psychoanalyst might argue that muffled, repressed id impulses are being expressed.

Similarly, as we noted in Chapter 4, muffled id impulses may be expressed in dreams. Freudian dream theory argues that unacceptable impulses can be satisfied while we dream, as long as they are properly disguised through the use of symbols and other techniques of self-delusion.

Do you have to agree with Freud to believe in defense mechanisms? Again, the answer is an emphatic no. Although Freud's brilliant observations helped us to see that people do use various maneuvers to protect themselves, these mechanisms may operate in different ways than he thought. For example, current social psychologists have observed many instances in which normal people seem to show a "self-serving bias." That is, seemingly to enhance their self-esteem, people often see themselves more positively than they are seen by others (see Lewinsohn, Mischel, Chaplin, & Barton, 1980), or recall performing tasks better than they actually did, or believe that they have more control over situations than they actually do (Alloy & Abramson, 1979). Rather than view these as maladaptive, pathological defense mechanisms, however, it appears that a certain amount of "illusion" may be positive and adaptive (Taylor & Brown, 1987). Other kinds of defenses that we consider to be pathological when used in extremes, such as paranoid projection or denial of obvious reality, may resemble Freud's original observations. However, they need not be explained by reference to his intrapsychic mechanisms.

Personality Development

Psychosexual Stages   According to Freud, a human infant passes through several important *psychosexual stages* of development during the first few years of life (see Chapter 12). Each of these stages is associated with the part of the body that gives the infant the most pleasure at that time. During the first year or two of life, the infant passes through the *oral stage*, so named because most of the infant's pleasure at this time is said to be obtained through eating and sucking. The *anal stage*, during the second year or two of the child's life, is the time when eliminating and withholding feces becomes an important part of the child's pleasure experience. At about age four, the child enters the *phallic stage.* In this stage, pleasure centers around the genitals. Following the phallic stage, the child enters the *latency period*, which lasts until puberty and is characterized by a lack of interest in sexual sensations. With puberty, the child enters the *genital period*, and interest centers on the genitals again. But in this stage, which lasts throughout the rest of an individual's life, genital interest is not like the self-centered satisfaction of the phallic stage. Rather, people in the genital period seek to establish a long-term, meaningful sexual relationship with another person. This is the progression that is followed if all goes well, but problems can occur along the way.

Fixation   Instead of developing in an orderly, normal way, people sometimes become *fixated* at one stage. This means that they tend to hold on to the form of pleasurable behavior associated with a certain stage, rather than moving on to the next stage. Their libido, or en-

Freud would argue that this couple is fixated at the oral stage of development.

ergy, becomes fixated. Fixation is brought about when the individual is either overindulged or overly frustrated at a given stage. For example, if a child is weaned too early *or* too late, the result may be fixation on oral modes of gratification. As an adult, this individual may smoke, drink, chew gum, or eat too much, still trying to obtain gratification through this early mode.

Freud believed that a person could become fixated at the anal stage, too, if frustrated or overindulged during this stage as a child. For instance, if a child is subjected to extremely demanding toilet training, he may, as an adult, become what is known as anal retentive, or tight, stingy, and overly controlled. But if toilet training is too casual, Freud believed the individual could become anal expulsive, or sloppy, disorganized, and messy.

Being fixated on an earlier mode of gratification will make normal adult adjustments difficult. Fixation interferes with more adult forms of gratification and robs the individual of the chance to experience a full life.

Superego Development According to Freud, the development of the superego follows the resolution of a conflict that all children experience during the phallic stage. Female children, at this time, are sexually attracted to their fathers and resent their mothers. But they are also dependent on their mothers. To resolve this conflict, a girl must learn to repress her sexual desire for her father and to *identify* with her mother. This conflict is usually termed the **Electra complex.** In the same stage, the male child is sexually attracted to his mother and wants to eliminate his father. But having these desires makes the boy anxious—his father may eliminate him instead. This **Oedipus complex**

Although intense attachment to the opposite-sex parent is part of normal development in young children, Freud believed that the unresolved Oedipal complex could set the stage for problems in later years.

is normally resolved when the boy learns to repress his sexual desires for his mother and to identify with his father. Then, as the son matures, he is able to find an appropriate sexual partner. Freud thought that a successful resolution of this conflict was very important for normal development. Through identification with the same-sexed parent, the child begins to learn the rules and regulations of society that will govern future behavior. The superego begins to develop, in other words. In addition, resolution of the conflict allows the individual to develop appropriate sexual relationships later in life.

Objections to Freudian Theory

Among the positive contributions of the Freudian approach are the emphasis on psychological conflict as a factor in personality disturbance, an emphasis on early parent-child relationships in the development of the child, and the role of unconscious motivation in human behavior. While many of Freud's ideas have gained wide acceptance and have become integral parts of our thinking about behavior, certain aspects of his theory have been vigorously disputed. We will list the four most common criticisms.

1. Although Freud's theory generates rich hypotheses, it rarely subjects them to experimental test (Eagle & Wolitzky, 1985). Thus, there is very little research data supporting Freud's ideas. In part, this is because it is hard to design laboratory experiments that will prove or disprove Freud's theories, but Freudians are also partially to blame because they have relied on clinical observations allegedly supporting their ideas and have devalued the role of controlled research. Many psychologists are unwilling to accept this type of evidence, as it lacks the controls and rigorous measurements that can rule out other interpretations of the observed data.

2. Some critics argue that Freud overemphasizes sexual concerns as the root of personality, and they object especially to the idea that these are universal, biological drives that govern all humans. It is argued that sexuality is not the primary cause of mental problems, or even one of the most important causes. That Freud focused on sexuality is understandable. He lived in the Victorian era, when sexual codes were rigorous and restrictive; hence, many of his patients actually had difficulties in this area. But whether sexuality is the basic area of concern for all generations and all cultures seems unlikely.

3. Others have objected to Freud's work on the grounds that most of his concepts were formulated as the result of the observation of neurotic patients. These critics feel that if Freud's theory is to be a general one, it should be based on an examination of "normal" as well as neurotic populations.

4. There is little evidence supporting the intrapsychic structure of id, ego, and superego, although these concepts have some value as metaphors, though not as descriptions of actual parts of the mind. There is also little evidence supporting the psychosexual stages of development as invariable stages through which every child must pass. There are other models of child development, as we saw previously.

Moreover, the idea that the personality is virtually fixed in place by the experiences of the first few years of life has been rejected, since people continue to learn and to change over a lifetime.

Despite these objections, Freud's view of personality is still widespread (Rangell, 1981). It forms the basis of psychoanalysis and of many clinical approaches as well. As we noted earlier, Freudian concepts have become a part of our everyday language, and as we shall see in the chapter on psychological treatments, psychoanalytic ideas continue to influence many forms of therapy.

Neo-Freudians

Carl Jung, a disciple of Freud, originated the concepts of introversion, extraversion, and the collective unconscious.

Carl Jung   Many of Freud's disciples, or followers, proposed changes in Freud's theory, even though they maintained the basic ideas and propositions of his system (Oelman, 1981). Carl Jung, one of the first disciples to develop his own school of psychoanalysis, believed that Freud overemphasized sexual impulses. He argued that other deep-seated impulses and urges are equally important. Jung emphasized the importance of positive goals and human striving to attain those goals. In a sense, he was much less pessimistic than Freud, because he focused more on intellectual and spiritual elements than on primitive drives.

Jung invented the terms introvert and extravert. An *introvert* is a person whose thoughts and interests are directed inward. Introverts typically spend little time interacting with others. An *extravert* is an outgoing individual who wants to interact with others and to stay in touch with events in the world outside of oneself. Jung believed that to be maximally effective, a person must possess both of these qualities in some balance. He felt that personality problems develop when an individual becomes either too introverted or too extraverted.

Jung's most unusual hypothesis is called the *collective unconscious.* The collective unconscious is the inherited, unconscious memory of humanity's ancestral past. It is a dim memory of all the communal events, fears, beliefs, and superstitions from throughout human history. According to Jung, we possess not only our own personal unconscious but also the inherited collective unconscious (Lambert, 1981).

Jung believed the collective unconscious affects our behavior. For example, he says we are all predisposed to fear large animals, spiders, snakes, and the dark because these are some of the dangers encountered by our ancient ancestors and we have a dim memory of their fears. Our collective unconscious also is expressed in our art and our dreams. Jung says this is why dreams and art often cause strong emotional reactions in us, even though we do not know why we are reacting in an emotional way. Jung's thinking was somewhat mystical. As a result, he has had as much influence on religion and philosophy as on psychology.

Introverts are shy and hang back in social situations.

Alfred Adler   Adler, another of Freud's followers, also felt that Freud placed too much emphasis on sexual urges. He suggested that people often strive for superiority rather than sexual gratification. According to Adler, the need to feel superior is a primary concern for many people and has its basis in the person's sense of inferiority to others. This basic sense of inferiority arises during the individual's early years when she or he is, in fact, weak and helpless. Adler developed the now famous term *inferiority complex* to describe this condition.

For Adler, the first few years of life are crucial. If the parents respect, love, and assist the young child, then the sense of inferiority will be minimal. But if the parents reject, hurt, and ridicule the child, a strong sense of inferiority will develop, and with it a strong need to prove one's superiority.

Other Neo-Freudians   There have been many other influential neo-Freudians. In Chapter 12, we discussed Erik Erikson and psychosocial stages of ego development in some detail. Erikson, like a number of other neo-Freudians, maintains that Freud overemphasized the instinctive and biological influences on personality. These thinkers, including Karen Horney, Harry Stack Sullivan, and Erich Fromm, all argue that the individual is much more heavily shaped by social interactions than Freud believed. These disciples hold that cultural and social influences on personality are of primary importance. They also focus more heavily on the ego than on the id. Some of them argue that the ego is more than just a mediator between the id and superego. They see the ego as an important force in its own right, just as concerned with attaining positive goals as it is with avoiding conflict with id and superego.

Recent developments in psychoanalytic theory have attracted considerable attention in personality and clinical psychology. There has been a focus on incomplete or arrested development of the *self*, in contrast to the earlier emphasis on drives, defenses, and conflict. *Object-relations* theories or *self-psychology* approaches are described by therapists such as Kohut (1977) and Kernberg (1984). They discuss *personality disorders* that result from disturbed parent-child relationships in the first few years of life. The defenses a child acquires to deal with distortions in self-identity are thought to have a profound and lifelong effect on the individual's life.

THE TRAIT APPROACH TO PERSONALITY

One of the most common, and undoubtedly the oldest approach to the study of personality, is the *trait approach.* In our everyday lives as well as in many research projects, we tend to describe and classify people by certain traits. "My mother was a fun-loving person who was always optimistic and easygoing and helped to balance my father's serious, controlled, perfectionistic personality." "Harry Truman was a genial, relaxed President but was firm and independent in his opinions." "Professor Jones is energetic and witty and seems very outgoing when she lectures."

The trait approach to personality is not a theory as such, but represents the belief that an individual's personality can be characterized by locating the individual along a series of personality dimensions. It is assumed that the person's behavior is *caused* by the traits, and that one's position on the trait dimensions is relatively stable across time and consistent across different situations.

Personality Types

Some of the very earliest formulations of individual differences classed people as one of a few mutually exclusive types. Hippocrates, the ancient Greek physician, believed that there were four kinds of people: *melancholic* (depressed), *sanguine* (optimistic), *phlegmatic* (calm or listless), and *choleric* (irritable)—depending on the predominance of one of the body "humors" or fluids (black bile, blood, phlegm, and yellow bile). A more recent, but no more successful attempt at typology was based on physical body build. Sheldon (1942) believed that *mesomorphs*, a strong, muscular type, were energetic, assertive, and courageous. *Ectomorphs*, a thin, fragile type, were thought to be introverted, sensitive, and artistic, while *endomorphs*, short, somewhat chubby people, were seen as relaxed, cheerful, and sociable. A famous typology was the *introversion-extraversion* classification discussed by Carl Jung, which we described earlier. Although appealingly simple, such one-dimensional ways of classifying people have not proven very useful or valid. There simply are too many people who do not fit the characteristics attributed to one type or another in these classifications. Another problem with simple typologies is that they often turn out to be more complicated than originally thought. Consider the recent interest in the "Type A personality." The Type A designation has been applied to individuals who are competitive, hard-driving and achievement oriented, and impatient or annoyed when progress is impeded (see discussion in Chapter 11). These individuals are work-oriented and experience a sense of time urgency, always trying to accomplish more in less time. Their speech may be rapid, and they may interrupt people or finish sentences for them and show irritation when they have to wait in lines or in traffic (Matthews & Haynes, 1986). Research on this pattern arose out of the observation that many people who had recently experienced heart attacks showed such characteristics (Friedman & Rosenman, 1974), and it has been demonstrated subsequently that indeed, Type A individuals are at increased risk for coronary heart disease (Manuck, Kaplan, & Matthews, 1986; Matthews & Haynes, 1986). However, Matthews and her colleagues argue that Type A is not a personality type that operates in the same way in all situations. It appears to be more apparent in competitive, achievement-oriented situations; it can be modified in individuals, and it increases cardiac disease risk in people who are not otherwise at risk from factors such as smoking or obesity. Also, the exact ways in which the coronary-prone behaviors affect the risk for disease are unknown. It may be that it is the *hostility* factor of the Type A personality that is most associated with disease risk (Matthews & Haynes, 1986), or it could be some other aspect, rather than the entire Type A constellation. The point is that it is more complex than originally thought. The Type A category is just a shorthand way of describing some behaviors and physiological reactions that go together in complicated ways.

Trait Ratings and the Search for "Basic" Traits

In contrast to the typology approach, trait theorists expect that people differ on a number of dimensions. Many of the researchers in programs designed to study traits measure them on *rating scales*, with each extreme dimension of the trait at either end, separated by gradations. Table 14–1 includes some examples of typical rating scales. The rater using the scales makes an inference about the existence of the trait in an individual's personality on the basis of the measurements obtained. Thus, people's differences can be captured quantitatively. A person might therefore have a degree of introversion, rather than simply being classified as introverted or extraverted. Sometimes a number of rating scales may be used to arrive at a *profile*, which is a graphic representation of where a person falls along several dimensions. The personality profile of a professional wrestler would probably be quite different from that of a florist. Figure 14–2 graphs the personality profiles of three different individuals.

Trait ratings are often completed by the individual being assessed—self-ratings are extremely common in many research activities. As we shall see in the chapter on assessment, however, self-reports can be inaccurate if people attempt to portray themselves in a way that may not be true. For instance, people may wish to deny socially unacceptable traits and subscribe only to socially desirable ones. As an alternative, trait ratings may be completed by another observer, but the success of observer ratings depends on how well the rater knows the person being rated across various settings and circumstances.

Since there are nearly 20,000 trait terms in the English language, one difficulty of trait theories is the need to decide which traits are most important. One approach has been to assume that there are a few major dimensions that underlie most traits. That is, many traits might actually go together. The trait "cultured" might turn out to describe the traits "artistic," "refined," "intellectual," *and* "polite." Cattell (1973) used complex statistical procedures called *factor analysis*

TABLE 14–1   Sample Rating Scales

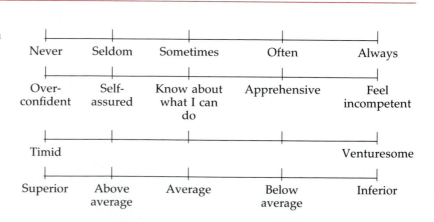

| How often do you fail to complete a project? | Never | Seldom | Sometimes | Often | Always |

| How would you describe your confidence? | Over-confident | Self-assured | Know about what I can do | Apprehensive | Feel incompetent |

Place a check mark at the point that describes your tendency to experiment and explore.
Timid — Venturesome

How would you rate your intelligence?
| Superior | Above average | Average | Below average | Inferior |

FIGURE 14–2 Three Typical
Personality Profiles

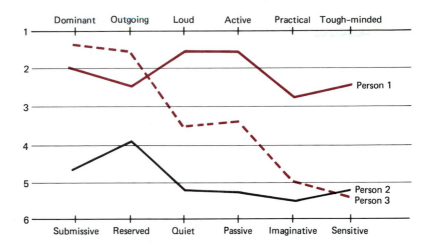

to see how traits cluster together into more basic dimensions. He
identified 16 basic traits that he thought could describe the whole personality of almost anyone (see Table 14–2). Unfortunately, other researchers have come up with different basic trait dimensions. Eysenck
(1961), a noted British psychologist, argues for merely two major dimensions on which individual differences can be scaled—introversion-extraversion and neuroticism-stability (see Figure 14–3). People
located toward the introverted end are generally oriented inwardly
while extraverts are oriented outwardly. Stable people are seen as
generally well adjusted while unstable or neurotic individuals are less

TABLE 14–2 The 16 Personality Traits Identified by Cattell

See where you fall on each of these dimensions. Construct your own profile.

Reserved						Outgoing
Less intelligent						More intelligent
Affected by feelings						Emotionally stable
Submissive						Dominant
Serious						Happy-go-lucky
Expedient						Conscientious
Timid						Venturesome
Tough-minded						Sensitive
Trusting						Suspicious
Practical						Imaginative
Forthright						Shrewd
Self-assured						Apprehensive
Conservative						Experimenting
Group-dependent						Self-sufficient
Uncontrolled						Controlled
Relaxed						Tense

Source: After Cattell, 1973.

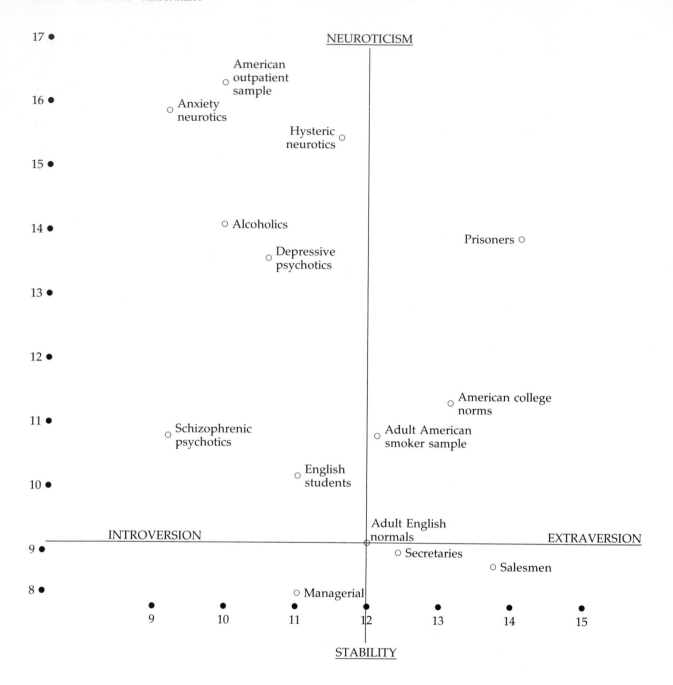

17 ●

NEUROTICISM

○ American outpatient sample

16 ●

○ Anxiety neurotics

Hysteric neurotics ○

15 ●

14 ●   ○ Alcoholics

Prisoners ○

○ Depressive psychotics

13 ●

12 ●

○ American college norms

11 ●   ○ Schizophrenic psychotics

○ Adult American smoker sample

○ English students

10 ●

INTROVERSION

Adult English normals

EXTRAVERSION

9 ●

○ Secretaries

○ Salesmen

8 ●   ○ Managerial

●   ●   ●   ●   ●   ●   ●
9   10   11   12   13   14   15

STABILITY

FIGURE 14–3 Eysenck Personality Inventory
Eysenck's inventory yields this graphic presentation of selected groups on dimensions of Extraversion-Introversion and Neuroticism-Stability. (After Eysenck & Eysenck, 1968)

well adjusted. The combination of stable-introverted is a person who is calm, reliable, careful, passive, and controlled, while a stable-extraverted person is carefree, sociable, talkative, outgoing, and perhaps a leader. An unstable-introverted person is unsociable, pessimistic, rigid, anxious, and moody; the unstable-extraverted individual is touchy, aggressive, excitable, changeable, and active. While there has been relatively good empirical support for Eysenck's basic trait dimensions, not everyone agrees that these are the *best* "fundamental" traits.

Where Do Traits Come From?

Since it is not really a theory, the trait approach itself does not specify what causes traits in people. Thus, psychoanalytic theorists argue for the psychodynamic origin of traits. Traits are seen as reflections of defense mechanisms and fixation at various stages of psychosexual development. Learning theorists, as we shall see, may often argue that traits are learned responses. Still another point of view is that certain traits may have a biological basis—that they are either genetically transmitted or constitutional in nature and present from birth. There are indeed certain characteristics that appear to have some biological origin. For instance, differences in emotionality and temperament in infants have often been noted (for example, Thomas & Chess, 1977), while studies of twins, including those reared in different families, have suggested moderate heritability of certain traits, including shyness versus sociability (Buss, Plomin, & Willerman, 1973; Carey, Goldsmith, Tellegon, & Gottesman, 1978). The interpretation of such results must be made cautiously, however. The traits themselves may not be biological. In many cases it may be that temperamental differences in babies elicit different responses from parents, so that it is an *interaction* of biology and environment that may shape the behavior of the infant.

Problems with Trait Approaches to Personality

Traits may be highly useful as broad, descriptive labels for individuals. However, there are several significant difficulties that limit the usefulness of this approach in understanding human behavior.

1. Traits usually do not allow us to make accurate predictions about people's behavior in specific environments. I may view a certain man as "violent," but I cannot predict where, when, or even *if* he will harm someone. I know that my teacher friend Suzy is "messy," but I probably could not pick out her third-grade classroom from any other teacher's. I might see Jerry as a "calm" person, but if I predicted he would be calm during an Internal Revenue Service audit, I would probably be wrong. As Mischel (1968, 1986) and others have argued, correlations between traits and specific behaviors are usually small.

2. One reason for the lack of precision in trait predictions is that there is far less consistency of behavior across situations than trait theories imply. It is essential to consider the impact of the situation on the individual involved: walking into a room full of strangers is likely to *elicit* "shyness" or social discomfort; going to the dentist makes even "calm" people nervous. Trait theories generally do not pay sufficient attention to the *interaction* between the situation and characteristics of the person.

3. We often use traits as *more* than shorthand summaries of the ways people behave, and we sometimes think of traits as the *causes* of behaviors. This can lead to thinking of the trait as a "thing" rather than a summary of behavior, and to a circularity of thinking. If we watch a child hit another child on the playground, we might think, "that was an aggressive thing to do," but this thought easily moves

Situations, not just personalities, exert a powerful influence on behavior. These children are much quieter in church than they are on the playground.

beyond the idea that we saw a child behave aggressively to arrive at the shorthand "he's aggressive." We may forget that *we* attributed the label to the child, and we might then "explain" the behavior by saying "he hit Jerry *because* he's aggressive." This is called a **tautology**, or circular reasoning. Such reasoning gives the false appearance that something has been explained. Traits are best thought of not as *causes* of behavior, but as descriptions, and the most useful applications of trait theory consider not just the traits or dispositions of the person, but also the situations with which they interact.

PERSONALITY AS LEARNED BEHAVIORS

Conditioning and Learning as Determinants of Behavior

Many psychologists look at personality as **learned behavior.** We are what we are, and we act the way we do, not because of some set of conflicts between id, ego, and superego, but because we have been *rewarded* for acting in certain ways in specific situations. If we have an "aggressive personality," it is because being aggressive has paid off in the past. If we are talkative, it is because talking has been reinforced, or not talking has been punished. According to this approach, there is nothing mysterious about personality. Those behaviors and dispositions that we label as personality are no different from any other behaviors. *All* behavior, including that labeled personality, is learned, and is governed by the principles of conditioning discussed in Chapter 5.

Reinforcement and Punishment   The learning approach states that reinforcement shapes our personality. If we are raised in an environment where even-tempered behavior is rewarded and emotional outbursts are punished, then we will tend to display calm behavior in the future. It has worked for us in the past, so it becomes part of our personality. Reinforcement can be of a primary nature, such as food, sleep, sex, or warmth. It can be social, such as praise and encouragement from others, or it can be self-administered in such forms as self-congratulations or a relaxing swim after a good day's work. Punishment can also be an effective shaper of personality. If a child is repeatedly punished by being told to be quiet or being sent out of the room whenever she speaks in the presence of adults, she may develop a trait of shyness or socially inhibited behavior.

Generalization and Discrimination   We discussed the principles of generalization and discrimination in our examination of basic conditioning in Chapter 5. These principles are often evoked in connection with the learning approach to personality. According to the principle of generalization, if we are rewarded for a particular behavior in a certain situation, then we will tend to do the same thing in similar situations. For example, if a child has learned that temper tantrums work at home, then he may try them at school or on the playground. Of course, not all environments will reward the same behaviors. A temper tantrum may gain attention at home but will only be laughed at on the playground. Thus, according to this view, we learn to *discriminate* between situations where a particular behavior will lead to reward, and situations where it will not be rewarded.

Discrimination explains how a given individual can show so many different kinds of behavior. At any given moment, an individual may be peaceful or moody, active or passive, aggressive or nonaggressive, sociable or withdrawn, careful or careless, independent or dependent, feminine or masculine. We can be *all* of these things wrapped up in one package. Which of these characteristics we display at any given moment depends on our perception of whether or not any given behavior will result in a reward. If it takes fierceness to obtain a reward, then we will be fierce. If we have to bow and scrape, then we will do that. We can be all things and, at any given moment, we select the behavior that seems most appropriate to the situation

Learning theory holds that our behaviors are shaped by their rewards. This woman has learned which behaviors bring rewards of respect and success in her professional life and which bring rewards of fulfillment and satisfaction in her personal life.

(Mischel, 1973). The *situation* is seen as an important determinant of behavior. This view contrasts with the trait approach, which emphasizes the degree to which we will act the *same* way in all situations.

Skinner's Radical Behaviorism   B. F. Skinner (1971) has been one of the major proponents of the view that external conditions guide and determine learning. Skinner feels that some personality-related behaviors are classically conditioned and that some are instrumentally conditioned. Phobic reactions represent an example of behavior that can be classically conditioned. A phobic reaction is a neurotic, unreasonable fear, such as a fear of snakes, horses, elevators, shoes, heights, open spaces, closed spaces, doctors, and so on. The Freudian approach to personality argues that phobic reactions result from unresolved conflicts that are beyond our awareness. But Skinner disagrees. He states that a phobic reaction is nothing more than an instance of classical conditioning.

Suppose an adult patient is terrified of red sunsets. By looking back into the subject's past, it may be possible to discover that a red sunset became a conditioned stimulus in a fearful situation. At a very early age, the patient may have seen her family home burn to the ground at night. The fear and terror of the situation became conditioned to the red color of the flames, so that anything similar in color and shape would elicit a conditioned fear reaction in the future.

As we mentioned, instrumental conditioning is important, too. Skinner, in fact, seems to emphasize instrumental conditioning over classical conditioning. Suppose a child is very aggressive, hitting and punching other children. Is this some unconscious inner drive being expressed? According to Skinner, the answer is no. The hitting is merely a learned behavior that has proven effective in the past. For this particular child, raised in his particular circumstances, aggression paid off, or was perhaps even necessary for self-preservation. He may have had older, dominating siblings and friends. To fight back may well have been his only means of protecting his rights. As a result, he learned to be aggressive in those situations, and the learned behavior generalized to other, similar situations.

As another example of the notion that personality traits can be seen as instances of instrumental conditioning, consider the compulsive gambler. Such a person cannot resist betting on the horses, the ball games, the blackjack table, the cut of a deck of cards, or any other situation involving risk. There are many ways of talking about the compulsive gambler, but the one that involves learning refers back to the concept of variable ratios of reinforcement, which we discussed in Chapter 5. If you will recall, in a variable-ratio schedule the organism must make some variable number of responses before a reward is received. Hundreds of experiments with rats and other animals, including humans, indicate that this schedule of reinforcement will stimulate a *very high* rate of responding. A rat will pound away at a bar or lever many times to obtain a single food pellet. Similarly, a compulsive gambler will pull the arm of a slot machine many times, at a high rate of speed, in order to receive the occasional reward. We cannot be sure that this is a correct analysis of gambling behavior, but compulsive gambling behavior strikingly resembles the kind of behavior produced by variable-ratio schedules of reinforcement. And the explanation is complete without reference to any internal, invisible events or processes.

In general, the Skinnerian approach strives to keep things simple, to focus on what is known and what can be observed, and to avoid concepts that refer to relatively immeasurable internal states, such as the mind, the id, the ego, or the superego.

Cognitive Social-Learning Approaches to Personality

The extreme emphasis on environmental contingencies of reward and punishment, often derived from animal conditioning, proved unsatisfying to some learning theorists. They believed that people's *thoughts* about learning contingencies, rather than the actual rewards and punishments, needed to be taken into account. Of course, Skinner and other radical behaviorists maintained that "mental events" had nothing to do with learning and that studying them represented an unscientific retreat into "mentalism." Nevertheless, since the 1950s, certain learning theorists have begun to emphasize thoughts, interpretations, and other kinds of cognitive activities. People like Julian Rotter (for example, 1954, 1972) began to argue that whether or not a person engages in a certain behavior depends on her *expectation* that an act will lead to a reward, and the *value* she places on the reward. Rotter's **expectancy-value approach** introduced a definite cognitive element into learning theories that has continued to be influential. Albert Bandura (1969, 1977) also emphasized cognitive aspects of learning. In particular, he focused on the role of observational learning; that is, learning occurs by observing role models. For instance, a child does not have to perform a behavior and then be reinforced in order for learning to occur. The child can simply observe another person performing the act. As we saw in Chapter 11, a child can learn to be aggressive by watching others be aggressive, either in

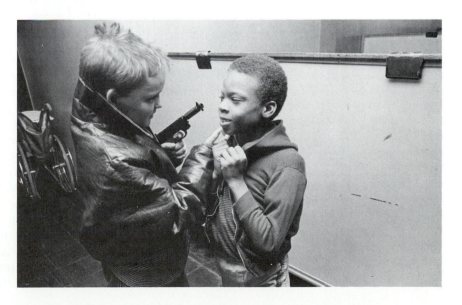

Children and adults alike learn through observation. Many of our traits and behaviors—both positive and negative—probably come from imitation of others.

person or on television. Bandura also argued that since people think and use language, they have the capacity for *symbolic* forms of learning related to words, ideas, thoughts, and concepts—not just actual environmental events. More recently, Bandura (1978, 1982) has introduced the idea that personal beliefs about one's ability to master a particular behavior, called ***self-efficacy***, is an important influence on behavior. For instance, self-efficacy beliefs about handling social relationships will determine what kinds of situations a person seeks out, how much effort he or she will put into social relationships (including the solving of social problems), and how the person feels during interpersonal relationships. Walter Mischel (1968, 1986) has also contributed significantly to cognitive social-learning theory. Long a critic of trait theories of personality, he has argued that situations exert important influences on how people behave. Even relatively subtle changes in situations may lead to different expectations about the consequences of various behaviors. Therefore, people's behaviors are not likely to be very consistent in different settings. For instance, Joe is fairly lax about punctuality when it comes to being on time for work or classes, but he always shows up right on time to pick up his date. Mischel also argues that there are several kinds of relatively broad "cognitive, social-learning, person variables" that represent individual differences based on learning histories. These are "trait-like" in the sense of operating across a variety of situations and helping to improve the prediction of specific behavior. However, unlike traditional personality traits that ignore the influence of the environment, these variables have to do with the way the individual interprets situations and generates behaviors that are particular for that situation. Mischel believes that such variables should include competencies to generate appropriate behaviors, self-regulatory systems and plans to guide one's own behaviors, and others. Unfortunately, we do not yet have effective ways of measuring these broad, cognitive, social-learning, person variables, but they seem to have the potential for understanding and predicting behavior in different settings.

Problems with Learning Approaches to Personality

Both the more traditional learning notions and the more recent cognitive social-learning perspectives have contributed important principles of human behavior. There is no doubt that much of human action depends on its consequences, its learning history. Often, learning models of behavior offer much simpler, more direct, and empirically more accurate explanations than those of psychoanalytic theorists. However, there have been significant criticisms:

1. The learning model has been viewed as far too simplistic and mechanical. Certainly the more radical behaviorists have provoked considerable criticism, leading to some welcome contributions from cognitive social-learning approaches that put the inner experiences—the cognitions—of the individual back in the picture. However, the seeming precision and scientific status of conditioning models may break down when we try to define key terms such as "reinforcement" or to predict "generalization." The statement that someone "must

have learned to have low self-esteem because of the way he was treated as a child" does not give us useful information about what is maintaining low self-esteem right now.

2. Trait theorists and others argue that behavior is much more stable, consistent, and enduring than learning theorists would have us believe, and that our behavior does not change every time the external-reinforcement schedule is changed. Cognitive social-learning theorists would reply that there may be consistencies about how people process information about different environments, leading to some consistency in behavior, but that these are not simple traits.

3. Others argue that the learning position does not place enough emphasis on inherited personality predispositions. They feel that genetic and constitutional factors may be important in personality, and the learning models ignore them by focusing on the idea that our behavior is at the mercy of ever-changing, external-reinforcement schedules.

THE PHENOMENOLOGICAL APPROACHES

Less well developed as a coherent theory than Freud's, and more recent than trait theory, is a collection of ideas about personality that emphasizes conscious, subjective experience. Such approaches are diverse and have been variously designated as *humanistic, existential*, or *phenomenological* theories. Despite coming from different sources and being somewhat vaguely elaborated, these ideas share some important ingredients that distinguish them from the other major theories we have covered.

Major Components of Phenomenological Approaches

There is an emphasis on subjective experiences, immediate awareness, and the experiencing of the self in phenomenological approaches that contrasts with the hidden and unconscious drives and dynamics of the psychoanalytic model, or the influence of the environment and behavior consequences in the various learning theories. The phenomenological world of inner, conscious perceptions, feelings, beliefs, and assumptions is the central focus of this approach. It is the goal of personality theorists who believe in this perspective to understand not how the world "really" is, but how it appears to be.

This is fundamentally an optimistic approach, in which individuals, if given the psychological freedom to grow and explore, seek to maximize their potential. Given the choice or the opportunity, humans will grow, be happy, flexible, creative, and in harmony with themselves and others. The push toward personal fulfillment is seen as innate. This view arose in part because of a dissatisfaction with the Freudian view of the nature of the human being as driven by impulses and as trying to regulate the conflicting demands of personal urges and those of society. In contrast, humanistic theorists are interested in the person's *perceptions* of the self rather than in allegedly unconscious internal forces. In contrast to the learning theorists, proponents of the phenomenological approach stress how the person perceives the environment. They view the individual as free and in control of his or her destiny, rather than ruled by external reinforcement contingencies. How people see themselves and their worlds determines how they behave, and no one else can be an expert on what someone is like except that person. Phenomenological theories also deemphasize the impact of early childhood events on adult experience. Adherents to these theories believe that such experiences may be important in shaping how a person came to hold certain views of the self, but they emphasize that it is critical to focus on what the person is experiencing right now, and on how the individual can grow and change.

Carl Rogers Like most of the other contributors to the phenomenological approach, Carl Rogers developed his ideas in the post-Freudian years of the 1940s, 1950s, and 1960s. He was influenced in part by European existential philosophers and writers who believed that humans are confronted by choices throughout the course of their lives. They are free and responsible for the choices they make. At the heart of Rogers's thinking is the belief that each person is unique, and that every individual has a strong and persistent desire to realize his or her potentialities, to *fulfill* the self. Fulfillment is a difficult concept with many meanings, but Table 14–3 lists some of the steps Rogers believed could contribute to self-fulfillment.

Self-concept is a key term in Rogers's approach. It includes all our thoughts, ideas, and judgments about ourselves. It sums up how we perceive ourselves, whether good, bad, or neutral. Self-concept does not necessarily reflect reality; a person can be smart, warm, and successful but still have a negative self-concept—or a positive self-concept even though immoral or despised by others. A strong, positive self-concept that is realistic and not too discrepant from what we would ideally like to be is the goal of human beings, according to Rogers. The individual needs to receive positive regard from others as well as from the self. Unconditional positive regard by others facilitates self-regard and makes our self-concepts strong and positive. However, most of us grow up in an environment where love is conditional: "If you do that, I won't love you anymore"; the *person* is criticized, rather than just the behavior.

According to Rogers, problems arise when people's behaviors do not conform to their self-concepts. If there is a discrepancy between what you do and what you think you are, you will experience anxiety. Experiences that violate what you think you ought to be may lead to defenses such as keeping the information out of awareness or distorting it. The wider the gap between our actions and our self-image, the greater the anxiety and dysfunction. The healthy reaction to a disparity between our behaviors and our self-concept is to acknowledge the behavior and feelings, rather than deny them. As we shall see in Chapter 18, "client-centered" therapy techniques developed by Rogers attempt to foster awareness, acceptance, and harmony between the self-image and the actual self.

Maslow and Other Contributions Abraham Maslow's theory of self-actualization and his hierarchy of needs were presented in Chapter 9. The relevance of self-actualization and the needs hierarchy to personality theory is the idea that people have an innate drive to satisfy

TABLE 14–3 Steps toward Fulfillment, as Envisioned by Rogers's Self Theory

Do not stagnate; seek out change.
Trust your feelings, emotions, and hunches.
Do not worry about always being in control of events.
Do not worry if goals are poorly defined.
Live in the present moment.
Be open to new experiences.
Be honest and open; avoid "phoniness."
Do not fear your feelings.
Like yourself.
Do not be concerned with doing what is expected.
Do not please others at your own expense.

TABLE 14–4   Attributes of the Self-Actualized Individual as Viewed by Maslow

Accurately perceives what can be known about reality.
Accurately perceives what cannot be known.
Accepts reality.
Accepts her- or himself.
Accepts others as they are.
Rejoices in the experience of living.
Acts spontaneously.
Is capable of creative action.
Has a sense of humor.
Is concerned for humanity.
Establishes a few deep, close personal relationships.
Can experience life as a child would experience it.
Works hard and accepts responsibility.
Is honest.
Explores the environment and tries new things.
Is not defensive.

more and more elevated motives. The goal of living is to progress up the hierarchy toward the state of self-actualization. Unfortunately, Maslow believed, most of us are not capable of achieving such a state, usually because we get caught up in the lower levels of the hierarchy. If we do achieve self-actualization momentarily, it is difficult to sustain it for long. Maslow listed some of the attributes of self-actualized people. We present them in Table 14–4. These attributes were based on his studies of the lives of historical figures he considered to be healthy, nonneurotic self-actualizers, including Eleanor Roosevelt, Albert Einstein, and Abraham Lincoln.

The "human potential movement" of the 1960s and 1970s drew heavily on these existential-humanistic ideas and spawned numerous kinds of therapy and growth experiences to enhance or promote "self-actualization." Both mind-altering drugs and other "altered states of consciousness," such as meditation, as well as encounter groups, growth techniques, and novel kinds of therapies became popular. These experiences were designed to produce greater personal freedom, to focus attention on personal experiences, and to achieve relief from alienation from the self and from other people.

Recent Developments in Theories about the Self

Ideas about the role of the individual's perceptions, feelings, thoughts, and interpretations are essentially cognitive theories. In recent years there has been a veritable "cognitive revolution" in psychology that affects nearly all topics—a focus on the mechanisms of human thought, on the structure and organization of how and what we know, and on how thoughts (beliefs, expectations, interpretations, and so forth) affect behavior and many related areas. Increased research on the *self* has contributed to this cognitive revolution. Contemporary clinical, personality, and social psychologists who study how cognitions about the self affect behavior are not very likely to subscribe to many of the beliefs of the phenomenological theories described in this section, such as the assumption of an innate urge toward self-actualization. These new self-theorists do not offer a single theory of personality but concentrate instead on the ways in which the concept of the self that is held by a person exerts a powerful influence on behaviors and is intimately related to emotion, judgment, well-being, and conduct in a variety of situations (for example, Markus & Wurf, 1987; Singer & Kolligian, 1987). One view of the self, based on information-processing concepts, sees the self as a *schema*, an organized body of propositions and descriptions of the self that guides the selection and interpretation of new information, as well as what is stored in memory. A schema is a kind of template against which information is compared; if incoming information about what is going on in the environment fits, it is assimilated or acted upon, but if it does not fit, it may be ignored, or even distorted to make it fit. As an example, imagine that a particular woman's self-schema includes the ideas that she is unattractive and that it is important to be married in order to feel good about her life. If she does not then get a phone call from a man she met, it will be interpreted to mean that he did not like her, that he thinks she is ugly, and that no one ever will like her, and she will be alone forever—thoughts that could lead to a depressed mood. Another woman with a different self-schema might interpret the same event very differently. The point about self-schemas is that they are active and constructive in the sense that they act upon information and construct or transform it to be meaningful to the self. They may lead to highly inaccurate or distorted interpretations, and since they "fit" information to the preexisting image of the self, self-schemas are resistant to change. Self-schemas include ideas about behavior in specific situations and therefore are more informative about what the person's behavior is likely to be than simple knowledge of either traits or situational cues alone. These schemas are likely to begin developing early in life in response to actual experiences and interpretations of those experiences (which may not be accurate). Self-schemas may help explain why certain individuals are vulnerable to developing particular psychological problems (Beck, Rush, Shaw, & Emery, 1979). Actual learning experiences may play a big role in what the self-schemas contain, but since experience involves thoughts as well as behaviors, the content of the self-schema may not necessarily be accurate. Thus, the woman in the vignette above believed that she was unattractive, and it is possible that she formed this opinion erroneously early in life based on comparisons with an older sister who seemed to be getting special attention from their parents. Once formed, the schema tends to take in and recall "evidence" that confirms the self-view and to discount information that does not agree with it.

There are numerous current studies of the functions of self-processes; however, such perspectives have not yet reached the status of a theory of personality and remain at present an intriguing alternative to the traditional trait, psychodynamic, behavioral, and phenomenological theories of the past.

Problems with Phenomenological Approaches

The focus on the uniqueness of the self and the subjective experiences of the individual has a lot of appeal. Such ideas seem to capture more closely how people really experience themselves, in contrast to the more mechanistic Freudian and behavioristic approaches. Also, phenomenological perspectives have important implications for the measurement and study of human beings, not to mention the treatment of psychological problems. However, there are a great many difficulties with giving phenomenological approaches the status of theories.

1. "Self-actualization," "personal growth," "being," and other related concepts are vague. Also, there is little evidence that they represent basic human urges; they may instead be values specific to contemporary Western cultures.

2. The notions are mainly descriptive, but they do not go very far toward explaining *why* people are the way they are, or how behavior is determined or predicted in specific settings.

3. The ideas about the self and cognitions raise questions. Do thoughts cause behaviors? While it is certainly true that people's perceptions and interpretations of situations and events may determine how they act, this is not always the case. Sometimes people's thoughts and beliefs are actually the *result* of their behaviors. People's subjective experiences—their conscious interpretations—may be too narrow a basis for predicting and understanding behavior. Another question also comes up: "What is the self?" There is sometimes confusion in the writings of Rogers and others about whether this self is some structure that guides behavior, or whether it refers to attitudes and beliefs. A great deal of work is currently being conducted to clarify the distinctions between the various meanings and functions of the concept of self.

In conclusion, the study of personality is not best represented by a "procession through the graveyard," a phrase attributed by Singer and Kolligian (1987) to an unnamed personality researcher. The four theories we have examined here—these legacies of past thinkers and researchers—certainly capture much of the history of psychology. Each of their themes and contributions has taken the field down productive but eventually limited paths. Nevertheless, today's personality research generally does not attempt to follow grand theories and broad, all-inclusive views of the nature of people. Instead, there are countless applications of the various theories in modified form, studying more limited questions, but nonetheless shedding light on the ever-fascinating questions of how individuals differ, and how their differences help us to understand more about their pasts as well as their futures.

In the next chapter we consider issues in the measurement of personality and other human attributes. We will consider what qualities good measurement procedures must have. The different theories of personality lend themselves to different assessment methods, as we shall see in Chapter 15.

SUMMARY

1. Personality may be defined as the individual's distinctive, relatively stable, patterned methods of relating to the environment.

2. As a field of study, personality has several subdivisions, such as development, abnormal, measurement, and theory, as well as numerous applications in nearly all other areas of psychology.

3. According to Freud, the id refers to raw, primitive, inherited unconscious impulses that demand immediate and total gratification.

4. The ego, developing from the id, attempts to serve the id while responding to the demands of reality. The id is illogical and impractical, while the ego is logical and practical.

5. The superego (conscience) represents the moral and ethical rules concerning what is right and wrong that have been internalized by the individual.

6. Freud believed unconscious motives affect our behavior. Preconscious thought is that which we are not aware of, but can be aware of at some point.

7. Conflict among the three elements of the personality can cause anxiety. Defense mechanisms are techniques that the ego uses if a conflict becomes too threatening and causes too much anxiety.

8. Freud believed the child passes through set stages of psychosexual development (oral, anal, phallic, latency, genital) where pleasure and gratification are obtained in connection with a specific part of the body.

9. Orderly progression through the stages can be impaired by fixation at any one of the stages. Fixation is brought about by frustration or overindulgence at a given stage.

10. The superego begins to develop when male children resolve the Oedipus complex and females resolve the Electra complex. In each case, a sexual desire for the opposite-sexed parent must be repressed, and the child must identify with the same-sexed parent.

11. Critics have claimed that Freudian theory is impossible to test, is overly concerned with sexual matters, is based on the observation of neurotic patients, and cannot clearly be proved or disproved. Neo-Freudians have modified many of Freud's ideas.

12. In contrast to Freudian theory, the trait approach to personality argues that an individual's personality is best understood by locating the person on a series of crucial personality dimensions.

13. Attempts to identify distinct personality types have failed because they are too simplistic.

14. Trait values are often established through the use of scales. A personality profile is a pictorial representation of where an individual falls along a number of dimensions. Subjects can rate themselves or can be rated by others.

15. The number and nature of the most important dimensions is a matter of debate. Cattell has identified sixteen traits while others, such as Eysenck, recognize a much smaller number.

16. Factor analysis is a statistical technique used to identify basic dimensions that underlie a number of different trait labels. Factor analysis identifies dimensions that "go together."

17. The origin of a person's traits depends on the theory to which one subscribes. There is also some evidence that a few traits may be biological in origin.

18. Critics of the trait approach point out that behavior is often situation-specific rather than stable across situations, and that specific prediction of behavior from traits is difficult.

19. Traits are best thought of as summary descriptions, but they are sometimes erroneously used to "explain" the behavior they describe.

20. The learning approach to personality argues that personality-related behaviors are learned just like any other behavior. Reinforcement, punishment, generalization, and discrimination are all seen as basic principles that can account for learned personality.

21. Skinner emphasizes the importance of both classical and instrumental conditioning in determining personality.

22. Cognitive social-learning approaches emphasize the role of thought and other cognitions in the learning and performance of behavior.

23. Bandura emphasizes observational learning and modeling of behavior in the learning of personality.

24. Mischel believes that there may be broad, trait-like, social-learning variables that describe consistent ways people differ in their approach to situations.

25. Critics of the learning approach argue that it fails to appreciate the stable quality of personality, that it does not emphasize genetic factors enough, and that it may be misleadingly simple.

26. Phenomenological theories are optimistic views of humanity. They claim that we have an innate desire to grow and change in a positive manner. Fulfillment is the goal. The self approach is nonmechanistic and concerned with the here-and-now. It focuses on the individual's self-concept.

27. According to Rogers, a strong positive self-concept is developed if one receives unconditional love. Conditional love can result in a negative self-concept.

28. Critics claim that phenomenological theory is vague and fuzzy, that it is merely descriptive and untestable, and that it minimizes unconscious motivation, early experiences, and reinforcement.

29. Emerging theories of the self use information-processing concepts to describe how self-perceptions operate and affect behavior.

30. In modern research, few psychologists subscribe entirely to any of the major theories. Instead, they pursue more limited, specific topics that may draw on several models.

KEY TERMS

anal stage

anxiety

automatic processing

choleric

collective unconscious

ectomorphs

ego

Electra complex

endomorphs

expectancy-value approach

extravert

factor analysis

fixation

genital period

id

inferiority complex

introversion-extraversion classification

introvert

latency period

learned behavior

libido

melancholic

mesomorphs

object-relations theory

Oedipus complex

oral stage

personality

personality development

personality disorders

personality theory

phallic stage

phenomenological approaches

phlegmatic

pleasure principle

preconscious

primary-process thinking

profile

projection

psychoanalysis

psychosexual stages

rating scales

rationalization

reaction formation

reality principle

repression

sanguine

schema

secondary-process thinking

self-concept

self-efficacy

self-psychology

superego

tautology

trait approach

unconscious

unconscious drives

wish fulfillment

ADDITIONAL READING

Feshbach, S., & Weiner, B. (1986) *Personality* (2nd Ed.). Lexington, MA: D. C. Heath.
This excellent, thorough, intermediate-level textbook covers not only major theories of personality, but also personality development and applications of personality theory in complex processes such as achievement, love and hate, freedom and responsibility.

Mischel, W. (1986) *Introduction to personality: A new look* (4th Ed.). New York: Holt, Rinehart, & Winston.
This is an intermediate-level textbook that emphasizes a cognitive social-learning perspective on personality, although other models are well represented. This volume also covers a lot of interesting research in psychology that draws on personality theories and measures.

15 Assessing Personality and Behavior

I n the preceding chapters we have emphasized general principles of human behavior—how people learn, perceive, remember, think, and feel. We have focused on how people are *alike*, and how behavior follows basic rules that we are constantly attempting to discover and refine. However, the reality is that although there may be universal laws of behavior, no two people are alike. Their abilities and their personalities are unique, shaped both by inborn differences and by differences in experience. Therefore, when it comes to understanding the behavior of individuals, we cannot rely only on general laws; we must also find ways to deal with *individual differences*.

Imagine yourself faced with each of the following situations:

- You are a school principal with 100 children ready to enter first grade. You have four first-grade teachers, and one of them works especially well with children who are slower learners. You want to optimize the learning of all of the children, so it is important to place children in classrooms that fit their needs.

- You are a psychotherapist, and a middle-aged man has sought your services with complaints of depression, forgetfulness, feelings that life is meaningless, and low energy. You need to be able to understand the man's concerns, to identify the causes of the problems, and to plan the appropriate treatment.

- You are a member of the parole board, and prisoners routinely come before you to request early release. Since you want to balance the needs of the individual prisoner with the needs of the community for protection, you want to be able to predict how each individual is likely to behave if released from prison.

- You are a personnel manager of a major corporation, and each day you receive applications to fill the many jobs that your firm has open. Each job is different, and each applicant has different characteristics. Your task is to find the best person for each job.

- You are a doctor who has been wrongfully sued for malpractice on several occasions. Although there was no basis for any of the lawsuits, certain patients expected more than was medically possible. You are frustrated, and your insurance company has warned you that if many more suits are filed against you, your insurance will be cancelled. You feel that you need some way to screen out disturbed patients who might sue you without foundation.

- You have been running a child-care program for the toddlers of working parents and would like to be able to convince the county to provide funding to continue the program. You hope to be able to demonstrate that children in your program are just as happy and intellectually well developed as children whose mothers stay at home with them.

In each of these and countless other examples, there is a need for *assessment* in order to describe, explain, select, predict, plan, or evaluate. In addition, it is necessary to conduct these assessment activities in as systematic a fashion as possible, with a minimum amount of error or bias. The assessments must be accurate, efficient, and useful.

The task of assessment, clearly, is enormously difficult because of the need to translate universal principles into predictions about the characteristics and behaviors of the individual or small group being assessed in specific situations. If everyone were the same, or if everyone responded in the same way in every individual situation, there would not be much need for psychological assessment. Psychologists, particularly in the fields of personality and clinical psychology, have long grappled with the task of finding methods that are useful and accurate for the kinds of tasks just described.

One of the basic strategies of assessment has been the use of *tests* that are intended to yield systematic samples of behavior that can be used as a basis for making decisions and judgments. In this chapter, we will discuss the criteria for determining whether tests are useful and accurate, and we will describe some of the major kinds of measures of behavior and personality that are in common use today. In the next chapter, we will discuss some of the pitfalls of using tests and outline some of the appropriate uses and the abuses of tests.

CRITERIA FOR EFFECTIVE ASSESSMENT

Reliability

In order to be accurate and useful, measurement procedures must be reliable and they must yield valid conclusions. This is true of any measurement, be it scientific, medical, or psychological. *Reliability* has to do with whether we can measure the same quality in a given person more than once and obtain the same or similar results. If you devised a questionnaire to measure attitudes toward abortion and administered it to the same people on Tuesday and Saturday and obtained very different answers, the **test-retest reliability** of the questionnaire would be considered low. If you developed a 50-item test of ''extraversion'' and found that people scored as extraverts on the odd-numbered items and as introverts on the even-numbered items, the **internal consistency reliability** would be low. Another kind of reliability is **interrater reliability.** If one observer gave a diagnosis of schizophrenia following an interview with a patient, but a second ob-

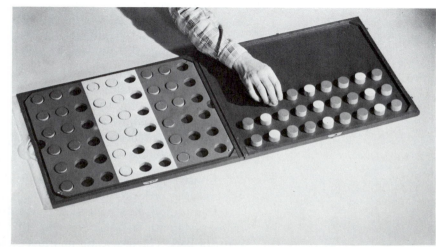

If you take the Stromberg Dexterity Test several times, your scores may vary slightly. For instance, drinking a cup of coffee might make you a bit faster. But the test is reliable. Nimble-fingered people will always complete it more quickly than people who have trouble fitting round pegs into round holes.

When the same tests are given under very similar conditions, we can be more confident of their reliability.

server did not, the interrater reliability for the diagnosis would be low. If a rater counted 16 times that a child was out of her seat in the classroom, but a second rater counted only 4 times, the observation method would have low interrater reliability.

Clearly, if scores are not repeatable under maximally similar conditions (the same test, similar items within the same test, two different judges rating the same behavior), then measurement processes cannot yield accurate, valid conclusions. This is especially crucial if the characteristic being measured is assumed to be stable. A measure of mood may not show high test-retest reliability because not all qualities may be expected to be stable. Mood may in fact change from one testing to another, but qualities such as IQ or certain attitudes or personality traits that are assumed to be fairly stable over time require evidence of test-retest reliability. For other kinds of measures, different types of reliability might be even more important. Thus, interrater reliability would be essential for behaviors that are being characterized at a particular moment in time (the diagnosis of a patient, for example, or observation of a child's response to a particular parental behavior).

Validity

A behavior may be measured in a highly reliable fashion and still not be valid or useful for certain purposes. You could count eye blinks per minute or typing speed with a fair degree of reliability, but such scores would not be valid measures of intelligence, or "executive potential," or "willpower." Therefore, the criterion of *validity* is especially critical for measurements of human behavior. Validity refers to whether the procedure measures what we say it measures. Determining validity is fairly straightforward under conditions that require little inference. For example, a five-minute typing test at a typewriter may be shown to be a highly valid predictor of typing speed and accuracy on the job. The number of times a child is observed to shout out in class would be a valid indicator of "disruptiveness." A measure of attitudes toward nuclear war might be a valid predictor of voting behaviors. However, for many tasks in psychological measurement, we are attempting to measure something hidden, or inferred or intangible, and then generalizing to unknown conditions. We are interested in "intelligence" or "self-control" or "maturity" or "leadership potential," or some other abstract quality. Therefore, no single method for establishing validity may apply to all situations, and several acceptable methods have been recommended by the American Psychological Association. Table 15–1 summarizes the major kinds of validity.

The simplest test of validity is just to look at the items on a test and see if they make sense. Are they related in some obvious way to what you want to measure? This is called *face validity*, or *content validity.* If we start out to create a vocabulary test, and then include some questions on multiplication and division, you can argue successfully that our test has no face validity. Or, if you devise a test for depression, the content of the test should include items that will re-

TABLE 15–1   Types of Validity

Type	Strategy Used	Example
Content or face validity	Examine the items in a test to see if they have some obvious relationship to the concept to be measured.	A test of your knowledge of the material in this chapter would have face validity if the items actually covered material presented in the chapter.
Predictive validity	Compare scores on a measure to some future criterion.	Success in law school would be the criterion for a test to predict law-school performance.
Concurrent validity	Compare scores on a measure to some current criterion.	A test to measure potential child abuse would be given to known abusers and nonabusers. The test would be valid if it correctly sorted the people into the two groups.
Construct validity	Examine the relationship between your measure and other scores or measures to see if the relationships make theoretical sense.	If a measure of "warmth" in parents turns out to be related to other theoretically relevant measures of personality in the parents, or to behavior in the child, the measure of warmth would have some validity.

veal depression. Not all tests need to have face validity, as we will see later in our discussion of personality tests, but face validity is a good place to begin in most cases.

Another common way of establishing the validity of a test is to compare the scores on a test to some agreed-upon criteria. As you can see in Table 15–1, both predictive validity and concurrent validity are based on just this kind of comparison. The only difference between the two is that *predictive validity* involves prediction of a future event, such as later success in law school, while *concurrent validity* involves a relationship between a test score and some other measure of behavior that you obtain at the same time.

Both of these types of validity are useful when we can agree on a criterion, such as school performance or child abuse or job success, and when our measurement of the criterion is *also* valid. If we define school performance by a child's grades, then there is relatively little argument about the criterion. But child abuse is a different matter. If we are developing a test to predict child abuse, and we use known abuse as a criterion, then how do we account for all of the cases of abuse that are never reported? A group of "nonabusers" may actually include a number of parents who do abuse their children, which will make the difference between a group of abusers and a group of "nonabusers" on some test look smaller than it may actually be. The test might then seem less valid than it really is.

Similarly, if we use later job success as a criterion to validate a measure of "engineering aptitude," we would have to agree upon a definition of "job success." Is the amount of money engineers make the best measure of their success? What other measure might we use? The basic point is that when we use a criterion to establish predictive or concurrent validity, we must first agree on the validity of the measure of the criterion. Such agreement is not always possible.

In fact, many aspects of human functioning that psychologists are interested in measuring are not linked to any "outcome" or agreed-upon criteria. Consider anxiety, or encouragement of independence, or parental "warmth" toward children, or self-esteem. These dimensions do not have agreed-upon criteria for comparison. So what do we do? We try to create *construct validity* by relating the measures from our assessment to other behaviors, or to scores on other tests. This is a fairly complicated concept, and an example should help to clarify it.

Suppose you have a theory of "ego strength," and you develop a questionnaire to assess your theory. In order to conclude that your scale is a valid measure of this hypothetical construct, you must specify a network of predictions relating the measure to various outcomes. If you believe that ego strength means that a person has a firm sense of self-esteem and efficacy, can respond to stressful conditions without undue distress, and is an effective, flexible solver of problems, then your measure should correlate with independent indicators of these other attributes (see Table 15–2). However, if it correlates *very* highly with one of them, say a measure of problem-solving ability, then you have to wonder if what you call "ego strength" is better thought of as just good problem solving. At the same time, your network has to rule out other competing explanations. For instance, maybe people who score high on ego strength are merely denying that they have any self-doubts, or maybe they are interpersonal clods

---

TABLE 15–2   An Example of the Construct-validation Process

Ego Strength

Should correlate with:	Should not correlate with:
Low "neuroticism" on symptom checklist	A questionnaire measure of social desirability (wanting to "look good")
Positive expectations of self, beliefs in personal worth and competence	Interview measure of tendency to deny problems or avoid difficulties
Resistance to stressful events, good coping skills, ability to learn from mistakes and difficulties	Test measure of interpersonal insensitivity
Observation: resistance to criticism; accepts flaws but does not become overly self-doubting or upset	A cognitive measure of rigidity, an inability to see subtle distinctions, or an inability to change ideas or solutions in problem solving

who value only themselves and "bully" others by insisting that their way is always right. Clearly, the pattern of relationships between the measure and other attributes must yield the conclusion that the concept being measured has the properties ascribed to it. This type of construct-validation process is complex and difficult, but it is especially crucial when measuring concepts that are abstract, such as intelligence, anxiety, parental warmth, and a host of other constructs that are very common in psychology.

The problem with construct validity is that if your hypothesis is not supported, you really do *not* know *why*. It could be that your assessment is not really tapping the underlying concept you set out to measure, but it could also be that your theory was wrong in the first place, or that the experimental techniques you used were weak or inappropriate. When this happens, you must either revise your theory or devise new ways of assessing the aspect of behavior or personality in which you are interested.

As we explore the various techniques for assessing personality and intellectual skills, the standards of reliability and validity need to be applied rigorously. Without these standards, the conclusions drawn may be wrong or misleading. However, as we will see in the next chapter, even if the psychometric properties of assessment techniques are solid, there is no guarantee that they will not be misused.

ASSESSMENT OF PERSONALITY

The strategy you select for trying to assess personality will depend on your theoretical assumptions about the relationship between personality and behavior. Most traditional assessment approaches are based on the assumption that there are underlying personality traits that affect a whole range of behaviors across multiple situations. The question of situational versus personal determinants is an area of ongoing debate, as we saw in the previous chapter. Most objective tests of personality, such as measures of test anxiety, shyness, neuroticism, or androgyny (to name only a few), are based on this assumption. (Since most objective tests require subjects to complete written questionnaires, or to select appropriate items on an answer sheet, these tests are also frequently referred to as pencil-and-paper tests.) Projective tests also rest on traditional assumptions.

The major alternative to traditional tests is behavioral assessment. Instead of assuming underlying traits and then trying to measure them, the psychologist can focus on the subject's actual behavior—the number of cigarettes smoked in a day, fingernail biting, sweaty palms in the face of a difficult test, or shy behavior in a group. Some of the contrasts between the two approaches are shown in Table 15–3. Bear in mind that we have drawn the differences rather sharply in this table; in reality, there are many gray areas in between our entries.

Traditional Assessment Procedures

By far the most common method of assessing personality is to ask people to answer questions about themselves. Sometimes this is done in face-to-face interviews; more often it is done with *objective (pencil-*

TABLE 15–3   Comparison of Traditional and Behavioral Assessment Approaches

	Traditional	*Behavioral*
Assumptions	Behavior is caused by underlying personality traits and motives.	Behavior is caused by an interaction between the individual and the environment.
	The behavior we observe is a sign or correlate of the person's underlying traits.	The behavior we observe is a sample of the person's behavior in similar situations.
Goals of Assessment	Varied: may be nomothetic (comparing a person to norms) or idiographic (intensive study of a single person).	Varied: may be nomothetic or idiographic. Sometimes criterion-referenced (individual performance with respect to particular demands of a specific situation).
Methods	Medium-to-high inference procedures—interviews, objective tests, projective tests.	Low-to-medium inference procedures—interviews, specific content questions, self-monitoring, systematic observation.

and-paper) tests. The variations on this theme are almost endless, so we can give you only a taste of the types of questionnaires and self-report systems that have been devised.

Interviews   You have probably been interviewed for a job or for admission to college. In that sort of setting, the interviewer wants answers to some specific questions about you. But she may also be trying to get some intangible "sense" of you and your motivations. Psychologists often use an *interview* in much this same way. Many psychotherapists use a general interview at the beginning of their contact with a client or patient as a way of coming to understand the person's motives or problems (for example, Pruyser, 1979: Rogers,

These marriage counselors are conducting interviews. The first is "unstructured" and the second one is "structured."

1951). There may be no prior plan for the interview, and no specific "scores" may be derived from it. *Unstructured interviews* are open-ended and generally follow the flow of what the interviewee says.

Much more common in psychological research, as well as in many kinds of clinical settings, is a *structured* or *semistructured interview.* In this system, each subject or patient is asked the same set of questions in the same order, although there may be planned "probes" which are used if the subject does not answer the original question fully enough. Table 15–4 gives a few of the questions that were asked during a long structured interview with parents and their five-year-olds (Sears, Maccoby, & Levin, 1957, 1976). This particular interview included over 70 main questions and took over an hour to complete, which is typical of this technique. Obviously the procedure can be very time-consuming if you interview many subjects, and you still face the enormous problem of converting the often-lengthy answers into some form that allows direct comparison of one interviewee with another. Most often the scoring of interviews is handled by working out a set of scales. The scale used for the answers to the questions in Table 15–4 is shown in Table 15–5.

What can we say about the reliability and validity of information from interviews? Since interviews are seldom repeated, test-retest reliability information is rarely available. Most often, reliability is explored by having two raters read the transcript of an interview, watch a videotape of the interview, or observe the interview through a one-way mirror. Both raters then score each subject's responses in some way, perhaps using scales like the one in Table 15–5. The reliability question then becomes one of whether the two raters agree on what they heard or read.

The track record for this kind of reliability is mixed. Trying to identify *general* characteristics yields the worst results. "Warmth" of a

---

TABLE 15–4   Segment of a Structured Interview with Parents of Five-Year-Old Children

29) Do you keep track of exactly where X is and what he is doing most of the time, or can you let him watch out for himself quite a bit?
　29a) How often do you check?

30) How much attention does X seem to want from you?
　30a) How about following you around and hanging onto your skirts?
　30b) (If not much) Did he ever go through a stage of doing this?
　30c) How do you (did you) feel when he hangs onto you and follows you around?
　30d) How do you generally react, if he demands attention when you're busy?
　30e) How about if X asks you to help him with something you think he could probably do by himself?

31) How does X react generally when you go out of the house and leave him with someone else?

Source: After Sears, Maccoby, & Levin, 1976.

TABLE 15–5 A Scale Derived from a Structured Interview and Illustrations of Scale Points

"How much attention does X seem to want from you?"
Scale Points:
1 Practically none (only when hurt)
2 A little (occasionally has a mood when he wants it, but usually not)
3 Some (at certain times of day, goes through periods)
4 Quite a bit
5 A great deal

An example of an answer rated 1:
"She has her sister, and she's with her quite a bit. My oldest daughter has taught her how to write, and when Susan does her homework, Nancy is right with her making numbers and she amuses herself in that way so she doesn't come to me for any certain thing, because Susan reads her stories and that's how the time passes with her."

An example of an answer rated 5:
"She wants an enormous amount. Janet likes a lot of affection. She is naturally a very affectionate child, more so than the other one. They are both very affectionate, but she seems hungry for it, somehow or other. She likes to play with you, and she likes to hug and kiss. She loves to be touched, and she likes a lot of attention."

Source: After Sears, Maccoby, & Levin, 1976.

parent toward a child, or "shyness" in an adult, is harder to rate reliably from an interview than are more specific behaviors such as "punitiveness of response toward the child's aggression," or "number of people talked to at a typical gathering."

Recently there have been some promising developments in semistructured and structured interviews for assessing psychiatric diagnoses and symptoms. The use of semistructured diagnostic interviews, such as the Schedule for Affective Disorders and Schizophrenia (Endicott & Spitzer, 1979) and the Kiddie-SADS for children (Puig-Antich et al., 1983), has greatly facilitated reliable diagnoses for both research and clinical practice. Most assessment interviews probably have not been validated, however. While interviews provide a potentially rich and flexible way of gathering a great deal of information, they have drawbacks. They may be very time-consuming, and they are subject to various types of inaccuracies or incompleteness. The interviewer may be unskilled or biased by characteristics of the individual being interviewed, and the interviewee may selectively report only certain information, as he may be influenced by the situation or a host of personal factors. A person who is being interviewed may be uncooperative or may wish to hide certain information or present himself in a favorable way. Interviewing children may require special skills because they may not understand the purposes of the interview, or they may have emotional reactions to the procedure that get in the way of accurate reporting. Some of these concerns will be explored in the next chapter.

Objective Tests Partly because of drawbacks to interviews, many psychologists prefer to ask people about themselves in a more objective way, using questionnaires or other forms of pencil-and-paper tests. Many people can be asked to answer the same questions in the same order. The answers are easy to compare, and a great deal of information can be collected in a short time.

There are vast numbers of objective tests, assessing every conceivable aspect of personality: anxiety, authoritarianism, loneliness, empathy, assertiveness, masculinity, femininity, depression, introversion versus extraversion, general psychopathology, and so on. There are several ways to categorize all of these tests. One is to divide them into those that measure a single dimension of personality as opposed to those that measure a whole range of personality dimensions. Single-dimension measures, such as the Taylor Manifest Anxiety Scale (TMAS), are used a great deal in personality research. Multidimension tests, such as the Minnesota Multiphasic Personality Inventory (MMPI) or Cattell's Sixteen Personality Factor Questionnaire (16 P.F.), are used widely in clinical settings and in some research.

A second way to divide up the enormous number of personality tests is to focus on the kind of population they were designed to assess or identify. Some tests, such as the MMPI, were intended to help identify emotionally disturbed individuals. A person's score on this test tells us whether he has described himself in the normal range or in a way that is typical of more seriously disturbed people. Many other personality tests are not focused on pathology in this way. They are designed simply to describe where a given subject, or a group of subjects, may lie on one or more dimensions of personality, such as anxiety, empathy, aggressiveness, or whatever. Both the TMAS and the 16 P.F. are tests of this kind.

Still a third way to categorize tests is in terms of the strategy used to *create* them. There are three main strategies for devising tests, each of which we can identify with a sample test.

1. *Using Concurrent Validity: The MMPI.* The psychologists who devised the MMPI (Hathaway & McKinley, 1942, 1943) wanted to create a test that would diagnose several specific psychological disorders, such as depression. They began by making up hundreds of one-sentence statements, ranging from "I believe there is a God" to "Everything smells the same." They then asked large numbers of mental patients, who had already been diagnosed by other methods as having specific disorders, to say whether they agreed or disagreed with each statement.

What Hathaway and McKinley wanted to find were items that particular types of mental patients tended to answer in the same way. For example, were there some statements with which most depressed patients would agree? If you look back at Table 15–1, you will see that this is a concurrent validity strategy. Hathaway and McKinley wanted test items that would differentiate among types of disturbed patients and nonpatients. It did not matter what the questions involved. If depressed patients all agreed that they preferred apples to pears, and nondepressed patients did not, apple preference could be used as a valid item on this test. Thus, tests in this category do not necessarily have face validity, but they must have concurrent validity.

Hathaway and McKinley ended up with 566 questions on the MMPI to measure nine different kinds of disturbances. Anyone taking the test is given a separate score on each of the nine scales, so the therapist or researcher can see the pattern of responses. The MMPI is currently undergoing rewriting and restandardization to make it more accurate for contemporary use (Butcher & Keller, 1984).

2. *Using Face Validity: The Manifest Anxiety Scale.*   Taylor set out to devise a scale that would tap a general dimension of personality that is usually called anxiety (Taylor, 1953). Like Hathaway and McKinley, she began with a large batch of questions. But the narrowing down process was quite different. She had a number of psychologists go through all of the items and pick out those that they thought were useful in measuring anxiety. This process is one of face validity; the psychologists were looking for items that had a fairly obvious connection with the trait or dimension being measured. A sample taken from the final 50 items on the TMAS appears in Table 15–6.

The TMAS has turned out to have construct validity as well as face validity. It has been widely and successfully used by researchers who are interested in the effects of anxiety on learning and memory.

3. *Using Factor Analysis: The 16 P.F.*   Cattell, like Hathaway, McKinley, and Taylor, began with hundreds of questions designed to cover the broadest possible range of personality dimensions (Cattell, 1956; Cattell, Eber, & Tatsuoka, 1970). But instead of comparing the answers to those given by disturbed groups (as Hathaway and

TABLE 15–6   Sample Items from the Taylor Manifest Anxiety Scale

Item	Usual Answer of a Subject Who Is High in Anxiety
I do not tire quickly	False
I work under a great deal of tension	True
I worry over money and business	True
I am easily embarrassed	True
I am happy most of the time	False
I am inclined to take things hard	True
I frequently notice my hand shakes when I try to do something	True
My hands and feet are usually warm enough	False
I find it hard to keep my mind on a task or job	True

Source: After Taylor, 1953.

McKinley did), or testing face validity (as Taylor did), Cattell determined which questions tended to cluster together statistically on the basis of similarity of responses. Which group of questions was usually answered similarly, so that subjects said yes to most of them, or no to most of them? And how many such clusters of questions were there? (The statistical procedure used to answer these questions is called *factor analysis*.) When Cattell analyzed the answers to all his questions, he found that there were 16 "clumps" or groups of questions, each apparently reflecting a single dimension of personality. The 16 scales are shown in Figure 15–1. The profile shown in the figure is the average score for a group of 1,128 undergraduate students. Individual profiles can also be worked out and compared either to a particular group, like the undergraduates in the figure, or to the mythical "average."

Keep in mind that this test does *not* tell us that there are only 16 "real" dimensions of personality. Any statistical procedure can only tell you something about what you put into the pot in the first place. What we do know from this process is that the questions Cattell started with tend to form themselves into 16 somewhat distinct clumps. If very different kinds of questions were asked, we might find that there were other dimensions, other "clumps," to be found. But for the very broad range of items Cattell used, there were only 16.

The reliability and validity of objective tests can vary considerably, depending on the test and the care that has gone into creating it. Most of the well-known tests, such as the MMPI, the 16 P.F., and the TMAS, have good test-retest reliability. And most have good validity, too. Remember, however, that the test itself is not said to be *valid*; we say that a test is valid for making certain statements. Thus, for example, the MMPI yields valid conclusions about *some* questions, but not about others. It may be a valid measure of degree of psychological distress, or of likelihood of having a certain diagnosis, but it is *not* a valid predictor of, say, the likelihood of committing an act of violence, or of the probability of filing a lawsuit against a therapist. When instruments are used beyond purposes for which they were validated, *misuse* occurs.

Some Problems with Objective Tests   As you have probably gathered by now, constructing a good test is not a simple task. It often involves years of devising items, testing them, throwing some out, devising some more, and testing further. One of the problems involved in devising a good personality (or any) test includes making items understandable in the same way to everyone. It is also necessary to write items in a way that reduces *response bias.* Examples of several other problems that may be encountered with objective tests and their solutions appear in Table 15–7. In fact, you can see two of the solutions at work in our earlier examples. Look once again at Table 15–4; you will see that Question 29 is balanced for social desirability. The parent is told, in effect, that it is acceptable to go either way on the question. And look at Table 15–6; some of the items from the TMAS are phrased so that agreeing will show high anxiety, while others are phrased so that disagreeing will show high anxiety. Thus a "yea sayer," someone who tends to agree with most questions, will not auto-

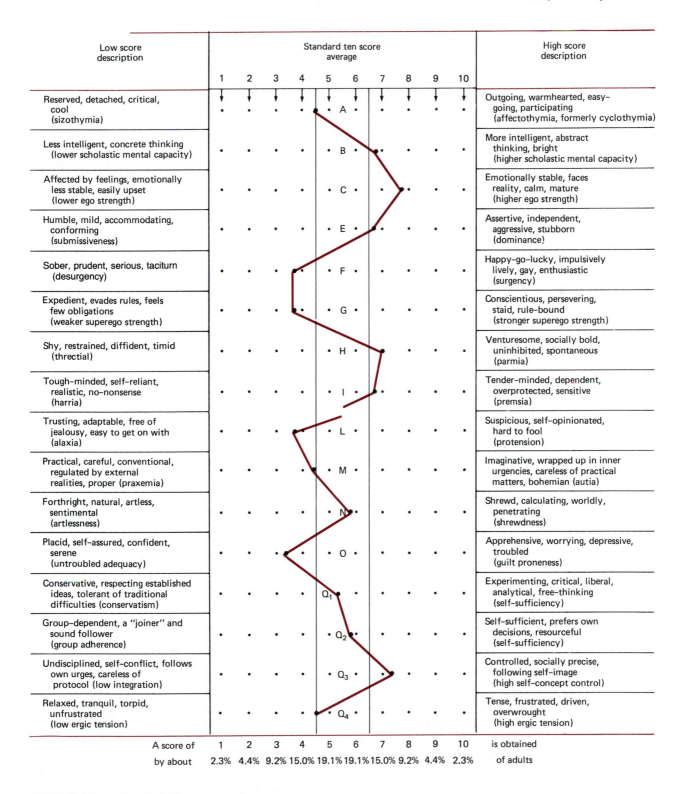

Low score description	Standard ten score average										High score description
	1	2	3	4	5	6	7	8	9	10	
Reserved, detached, critical, cool (sizothymia)					A						Outgoing, warmhearted, easy-going, participating (affectothymia, formerly cyclothymia)
Less intelligent, concrete thinking (lower scholastic mental capacity)					B						More intelligent, abstract thinking, bright (higher scholastic mental capacity)
Affected by feelings, emotionally less stable, easily upset (lower ego strength)					C						Emotionally stable, faces reality, calm, mature (higher ego strength)
Humble, mild, accommodating, conforming (submissiveness)					E						Assertive, independent, aggressive, stubborn (dominance)
Sober, prudent, serious, taciturn (desurgency)					F						Happy-go-lucky, impulsively lively, gay, enthusiastic (surgency)
Expedient, evades rules, feels few obligations (weaker superego strength)					G						Conscientious, persevering, staid, rule-bound (stronger superego strength)
Shy, restrained, diffident, timid (threctial)					H						Venturesome, socially bold, uninhibited, spontaneous (parmia)
Tough-minded, self-reliant, realistic, no-nonsense (harria)					I						Tender-minded, dependent, overprotected, sensitive (premsia)
Trusting, adaptable, free of jealousy, easy to get on with (alaxia)					L						Suspicious, self-opinionated, hard to fool (protension)
Practical, careful, conventional, regulated by external realities, proper (praxemia)					M						Imaginative, wrapped up in inner urgencies, careless of practical matters, bohemian (autia)
Forthright, natural, artless, sentimental (artlessness)					N						Shrewd, calculating, worldly, penetrating (shrewdness)
Placid, self-assured, confident, serene (untroubled adequacy)					O						Apprehensive, worrying, depressive, troubled (guilt proneness)
Conservative, respecting established ideas, tolerant of traditional difficulties (conservatism)					Q_1						Experimenting, critical, liberal, analytical, free-thinking (self-sufficiency)
Group-dependent, a "joiner" and sound follower (group adherence)					Q_2						Self-sufficient, prefers own decisions, resourceful (self-sufficiency)
Undisciplined, self-conflict, follows own urges, careless of protocol (low integration)					Q_3						Controlled, socially precise, following self-image (high self-concept control)
Relaxed, tranquil, torpid, unfrustrated (low ergic tension)					Q_4						Tense, frustrated, driven, overwrought (high ergic tension)

A score of	1	2	3	4	5	6	7	8	9	10	is obtained
by about	2.3%	4.4%	9.2%	15.0%	19.1%	19.1%	15.0%	9.2%	4.4%	2.3%	of adults

FIGURE 15–1   The 16 P.F. Scales *This figure shows the average score for a group of 1,128 undergraduates.*

matically end up with a very high score. Finally, any test performance will be affected by characteristics of the individual being tested and the situation in which the test is given. For objective tests, however, their value is that they can be given under standardized conditions.

TABLE 15–7 Some of the Major Problems with Objective Tests

Problem	Possible Solution
Lying: Subjects may deliberately lie to make themselves look good.	Include a "lie scale" made up of items that virtually all honest people will disagree with, such as "I never tell a lie," or "I always brush my teeth after every meal." Subjects who agree with a lot of these questions are probably lying on other parts of the test too.
	Disguise the purpose of the test by including a wide range of topics, only some of which are of particular interest.
Social desirability: Some questions or some answers may seem more acceptable than others.	Try to make sure that all the choices are equally acceptable.
Yea and nay saying: Some subjects like to agree with anything they are asked; others like to disagree.	Arrange the wording of the items so that for a subject to achieve a high or a low score on the total scale he must agree with some items and disagree with others. Subjects who tend to agree with everything, or disagree with everything, will thus get moderate scores.

Projective Tests Projective tests constitute another entire group of procedures for assessing personality. All of the tests and procedures labeled "projective" offer the subject an ambiguous or vague stimulus of some kind—inkblots, sentences to complete, photographs of people interacting—and ask the subject to talk or write about the stimulus. Since the original stimulus is so vague, the assumption is that the subject "projects" his or her own attitudes or problems onto the stimulus material.

This assumption comes directly out of Freud's psychoanalytic theory of personality. Remember the discussions of defense mechanisms in earlier chapters; projection is one of the defense mechanisms proposed by Freud. He maintained that when we cannot accept our real, underlying motives and needs, we may deal with them by projecting them onto others. If this is true, then **projective tests**, which encourage the subject to project feelings and motives onto an ambiguous stimulus, may reveal an individual's underlying, unconscious motives or feelings. Whether a psychologist is comfortable using projective tests depends on whether he or she accepts the theory on which they are based. Most behaviorally oriented psychologists and therapists do not use projective tests because they do not make assumptions about unconscious or underlying motivations.

But there are many psychologists who find value in the psychoanalytic approach and in projective tests. A large number of such

FIGURE 15–2 Inkblots Similar to Those on the Rorschach Test and Typical Responses and Interpretations *Although projective tests are widely used, there is little evidence that the specific interpretations of responses, such as those shown, are valid. (After Kleinmuntz, 1974)*

Response	Inkblots	Nature of Interpretation
This is a butterfly. Here are the wings, feelers and legs.		Using the whole blot in this way is considered to reflect the subject's ability to organize and relate materials.
This is part of a chicken's leg.		Referring to only a part of this inkblot is interpreted usually as indicative of an interest in the concrete.
This could be a face.		The use of an unusual or tiny portion of this blot may suggest pedantic trends.
Looks somewhat like a spinning top.		Persons who reverse figure and ground in this manner often are observed as oppositional, negative, and stubborn.

tests have been developed. The most famous is undoubtedly the Rorschach test (Rickers-Ovsiankira, 1977; Rorschach, 1921/1942), which uses black-and-white and colored inkblots as stimuli. Some examples of the types of inkblots used are shown in Figure 15–2.

The interpretation of subjects' responses to the Rorschach is both complex and controversial. The most common method is to look at whether the subject used the whole blot or only a part of it, whether the shape or the color of the blot was the most critical, whether the subject matter of the response was an animal, person, or landscape, and whether the answer showed originality. The information obtained as a result of this analysis of subjects' responses is then used by the clinician as part of her overall diagnosis of a patient's or client's personality.

One intriguing example of the use of the Rorschach test in research is Michael Maccoby's study of corporate executives (Maccoby, 1976). Two excerpts from Maccoby's book, *The Gamesman*, describing the Rorschach responses of two very different subjects, are given in Table 15–8. The responses and Maccoby's interpretations of them should give you some sense of how the Rorschach test is used by a clinician or researcher.

Another widely used projective test is the Thematic Apperception Test (the TAT), devised originally by Murray (1943). The TAT consists of 30 ambiguous drawings of people, similar to the one shown in Figure 15–3. The subject's task is to tell a story about each picture. The score most frequently derived from the TAT is a measure of *need for achievement.* Need for achievement is scored any time a story contains some competition with a standard of excellence. For example, the response, "He's going to practice really hard so that he

TABLE 15–8   Rorschach Responses and Their Interpretation

"Card IX often suggests interpretations symbolizing the individual's spiritual center, his strivings for individuation and self-realization. . . . Bass said, 'That's one that's dynamic! It's a fight, rather a violent one . . . but not a primitive fight, but organized, harmless. It's not a mortal combat of any kind. And there are spectators, who seem to be applauding. It reminds you of phony wrestling, but not phony, a legitimate athletic event.' Bass first described violence, but then denied it. Was he trying to contain his primitive impulses within the rules? The response also suggested showmanship and duplicity (phony wrestling), even though he insisted that the contest was legitimate."

"One of the most creative perceptions was on Card IX, where Wakefield saw a fountain with three different jets. The water was spraying at the top, tumbling at the side, and coming out at the bottom, colored by different lights. On the top was foam. Here is an expression of a disciplined energy, beauty, exuberance, and technology, a symbol of emotional release, love of life, and technological innocence."

Source: After Maccoby, 1976.

can be the best violinist in the world," given to the drawing in Figure 15–3, would be scored as showing need for achievement.

Projective tests like the Rorschach and the TAT have had widespread clinical use, particularly among psychologists who base their therapy on a psychoanalytic theory. The TAT has also been used in a great deal of research on achievement. But what about validity and reliability? Here the picture is not so positive. Unlike the MMPI, the Rorschach does not consistently differentiate between groups of patients diagnosed as having different sorts of emotional disturbances (Weiner, 1977), and different clinicians do not regularly interpret the same responses in the same way (Homzberg, 1977; Silverman, 1959). Results of this kind, which indicate that the Rorschach (and other projective tests) may be neither consistently reliable nor valid, "pro-

FIGURE 15–3   The Thematic Apperception Test   *This picture is similar to those used in the TAT, a test that often measures an individual's need for achievement and other motivations.*

vide disappointment for psychologists who have grown fond of the test, disenchantment for those who had begun to flirt with it, and ample ammunition for those who wished to shoot it down" (Weiner, 1977, p. 579).

In the face of such evidence, why do people keep using projective tests? There are several reasons. First, those psychologists who use projective tests are committed to them partly because they think the theory underlying them is sound. If you are convinced that there is such a thing as projection, then projective tests are very sensible. According to this view, the reliability or validity problem, if there is one, may lie in the interpretation of the subject's or patient's answers, not in the test itself. In fact, there have been several attempts to make the scoring and interpretation of projective tests like the Rorschach more consistent and precise. When this is achieved, the reliability and validity of the test do improve (Erdberg & Exner, 1984; Holtzman, 1975).

Second, many clinicians purposely use projective tests in a highly individual way. They may not care whether the subject gives the same responses a second time, or whether the subject's responses could be used to predict some later behavior. Rather, they use the Rorschach, the TAT, or other projective tests as a way of gaining an impression of a client or patient, or as a way of getting the patient to talk about fantasies. The tests may thus be used as part of a therapeutic process rather than as ends in themselves.

Behavioral Assessment

The selection of an assessment technique depends on the assessor's goals and the questions being asked. The same thing can be said concerning the contrast between traditional and behavioral assessment: proponents of the two types of measurements are asking somewhat different questions. The psychologist who uses behavioral assessment wants to know about the actual behavior of a subject in some situation—what he said, what he did, how he moved, perhaps how he felt. The same range of techniques is available to obtain this information—interviews, written tests, and direct observation—but the emphasis is different.

Obviously, direct observation of behavior is not new. But the widespread use of various kinds of systematic behavioral assessment is comparatively new (Ciminero, Calhoun, & Adams, 1977; Haynes, 1984). Typically, a behavioral assessment examines not only the client's behavior, but also the conditions in the environment that are sustaining that behavior (Goldfried & Sprafkin, 1976). This approach reflects a learning view of personality. If personality is primarily a collection of learned "response tendencies" (Goldfried & Kent, 1972), then we should measure it by observing the person actually responding in real settings. The assumption is that accuracy of predicting and planning will be greatly improved if we sample responses in their actual contexts.

Behavioral assessment can be done in a variety of ways, some of which are listed in Table 15–9. Note that psychologists who approach assessment from this perspective often ask people to describe their

TABLE 15–9   Major Types of Behavioral Assessment

Behavioral interview	Used by therapists and others to obtain information about a specific behavior problem and the circumstances surrounding it.
Self-report questionnaires	Ask specific questions about behavior; for example, fearful responses toward particular objects or events.
Self-monitoring	Subjects are asked to keep track of their own behavior in specific categories, such as the foods eaten, or the hours spent studying, or the responses to a child's tantrums. Records may be kept on paper or mechanical counters may be used.
Direct observation in natural settings	Most often used with children, or in institutions like mental hospitals where the subjects are in confined areas and easy to observe.
Direct observation in artificial situations	Subjects may be shown scenes on videotape, and their reactions observed; particular kinds of social encounters may be simulated; generally the experimenter can create a situation that permits observation of a subject responding to carefully defined stimuli.

own behavior, rather than observe it directly. It is much easier to ask someone if she is afraid of snakes than to follow her around for weeks until you encounter a snake and observe her reaction!

Behavioral Interviews   An excerpt from a behaviorally oriented interview is given in Table 15–10. Here the emphasis is primarily on the patient's behavior and less on feelings. In this interview, the patient was a 71-year-old retired man with periodic depression.

Self-reports   There are several widely used behavioral questionnaires, of which a well-known example is the Fear Survey Schedule (Wolpe, 1973). Subjects are given a list of potentially fearful objects or events and asked to rate their own fear on a five- or seven-point scale. Some of the potentially fearful things included are worms, crawling insects, snakes, angry people, losing control, sexual inadequacy, darkness, and being alone.

Questionnaires like this are used to turn up specific information about troublesome behavior (Bellack & Hersen, 1977). The questions involved are factual, and they are treated at face value. If you are asked, "Do your palms sweat?" or "Are you afraid of snakes?", the behavioral psychologist is interested in precisely these facts. A more

---

TABLE 15–10   Excerpt from a Behavioral Assessment Interview

Therapist:	. . . First of all, we have to find out what your problem is. You have been on this ward how long now?
Patient:	Since the end of January.
Therapist:	End of January. All right, and you came with what problem? What was your original complaint?
Patient:	The thing is it came on so suddenly. I just do not know.
Therapist:	You know what came suddenly?
Patient:	The depression.
Therapist:	Can you tell me what you mean by depression?
Patient:	Just one day I did not want to get up and go to work.
Therapist:	You did not want to go to work.
Patient:	I am a retired pensioner.
Therapist:	I see, and you stay in bed and what do you feel there?
Patient:	I feel that things are getting worse and worse, everything is an effort.
Therapist:	Let us go through it. Are you interested in anything at the moment?
Patient:	Unfortunately, I have no emotional feelings at the moment.
Therapist:	No interest; what do you enjoy?

Source: After Meyer, Liddell, & Lyons, 1977.

Hidden behind a one-way mirror, two psychologists observe three people interacting. Even in artificial situations like this one, participants regularly forget their self-consciousness in a few minutes.

traditional personality test might include the same questions, but your answer would be used as an indicator of some presumed underlying trait, such as anxiety or achievement motives.

Self-monitoring   Assessment by self-monitoring is unique to the behavioral approach. Patterson (1980) has used it in his work with families of highly aggressive children. Other researchers and clinicians have asked adults to keep track of fingernail biting, eating patterns, food intake, or negative thoughts about themselves, to name just a few. Not only are most people able to keep quite accurate records (Tasto, 1977), but the very act of making a record often results in a change in the person's behavior without any other therapeutic intervention. The person who has bitten his fingernails for years may do so less often while he is keeping track of the behavior (Horan, Hoffman, & Macri, 1974).

Direct Observation   As we noted in Table 15–9, direct observation can be done either by observing a natural situation or by creating an artificial one. The advantage of the artificial situation is that it lets the observer focus attention directly on the behaviors in which he has the most interest. For example, Gordon, and his colleagues (1987) observed mothers and their children discussing a common area of disagreement—household chores, bedtime, or television viewing. Mothers' comments were coded as critical, positive, neutral, and either focused on the task or on an extraneous topic. The children who had higher rates of disorder and problem behaviors were those whose mothers had higher proportions of critical comments toward them.

In a variation that combines behavioral observation with self-report, Patterson and Jacobson (Jacobson, Elwood, & Dallas, 1981; Patterson, 1976) have found that spouses can observe one another, and their observations can be used as the basis for successful intervention in troubled marriages. Each spouse is given a checklist which he or she fills out each night, describing the behavior of the partner during that day. In distressed couples, the rate of pleasing to displeasing events may be about 4 to 1; in couples that are not distressed, the ratio is typically more like 30 to 1. One task of the therapist working with distressed couples who use this form of behavioral observation is to help them increase the number of pleasing events, such as affection, supportive comments, agreements, and to decrease the number of displeasing events. When that happens, both spouses report that their satisfaction with the relationship goes up markedly.

Direct observations can thus be used to describe the nature of interactions researchers or clinicians find of interest. They can also be used very specifically and constructively as part of a therapeutic intervention.

Reliability and Validity of Behavioral Assessments

The same problems that plague traditional objective measures are present in behavioral measures. Reaching good interobserver agreement is a time-consuming, difficult process, although it can be achieved. With effort, good test-retest reliabilities for self-report measures of behavior can also be reached (Nathan, 1981). Establishing the

Direct observation of behavior is often the best technique for assessment, but in many cases where it would be helpful, it may be impractical and intrusive.

validity of behavioral measures presents a different set of problems. Since actual behavior is being observed, you might think that validity is already taken care of, at least face validity. But often the observations are used as a way to tap some broader dimension, which puts us right back into the problem of predictive, concurrent, or construct validity. For example, Patterson, Jacobson, and others have been using their observations of marital interactions as a means of assessing "marital dysfunction." If the observational measure is valid, it should discriminate between functional and dysfunctional marital couples. But not every study finds that it does. Whether distressed couples behave differently from nondistressed couples depends on the instructions you give them or on how long you observe them. The advantage of the behavioral system is that if it is valid, it gives you a wealth of specific information about the behavior of the individual, which can then be used in very focused interventions with that person, that couple, or that parent-child pair.

A problem shared by both traditional and behavioral-assessment techniques arises from the desire to study abstract characteristics for which no single observable referent is available. Thus, when we assess "depression," "marital conflict," "psychosis-proneness," "ego strength," "self-esteem," or a host of other constructs, there is a danger of the reifying of the term. That is, we may think of the hypothetical construct that we have labeled as an *it*, something that a person *has*. Behaviorists have attempted to follow the advice of Mischel (1973) to assess what a person *does* rather than what he or she *has*, but even behavioral-assessment techniques run some risk of implying that the person "has" a certain quality, implying its consistency across situations. Perhaps no single construct has been misused in this way as much as the term "intelligence," to which we now turn.

MEASURES OF INTELLECTUAL PERFORMANCE

The other major area in which psychologists have developed important assessment tools is in the measurement of intelligence and intellectual activity. The problems here are just as acute as they are in personality assessment. How are we to agree on what to measure? How do we define the construct in the first place? And then how do we validate the tests we devise?

Definitions of Intelligence

Defining intelligence has proven to be extremely troublesome, despite the widespread use of the term by the general public. Among the common definitions are the following:

Intelligence is what intelligence tests measure.

Intelligence is "the aggregate or global capacity of the individual to act purposefully, to think rationally, and to deal effectively with his environment" (Wechsler, 1939, p.3).

Intelligence is "the entire repertoire of acquired skills, knowledge, learning sets, and generalization tendencies considered intellectual in nature that are available at any one period in time" (Cleary, Humphreys, Kentrick, & Wesman, 1975, p. 18).

"It seems to us that in the intelligence there is a fundamental faculty . . . This faculty is judgment, otherwise called good sense, practical sense, initiative, the faculty of adapting oneself to circumstances. To judge well, to comprehend well, to reason well, these are the essential activities of the intelligence" (Binet & Simon, 1916, p.24).

The multiplicity of these definitions by experts reflects several unresolved controversies. One is whether intelligence is a quality that exists apart from its measurement. Another is whether it is a *capacity* or whether what is measured is similar to a skill or achievement. While Wechsler and many psychologists and lay people believe that we can measure some innate capacity, Cleary and her colleagues (1975) argue that at the present time we have no way to measure innate capacity, and that what we do measure on IQ tests differs from what we measure with achievement tests only in terms of breadth (IQ tests sample more broadly than achievement tests), of being tied to specific curricula (IQ tests sample learning in and outside of school, independent of what is specifically taught), of recency of the learning sampled (IQ tests sample older learning), and of purpose (IQ tests try to predict future performance rather than evaluate current learning).

Another controversy involves the question of whether intelligence is a global quality, or whether it is comprised of specific and distinct abilities. While Wechsler and others believe that there is a "multifaceted global capacity" (1975), some researchers argue for several separate abilities. For instance, Thurstone (1938; Thurstone & Thurstone, 1959) has suggested six "primary mental abilities" and Guilford (1956) has argued for as many as 120 separate intellectual components.

The Measurement of Intelligence

Despite the difficulties in defining the concept, quite a number of famous psychologists, undaunted, have developed tests for measuring intelligence. You should know at least a little bit about the ways those tests are constructed, and their reliability and validity.

The most commonly used tests attempt to measure general ability through assessment of a wide range of cognitive performances. Of the individually administered tests for children, the Stanford-Binet and the Wechsler Intelligence Scale for Children-Revised (WISC-R) are the best known. For adults, the Wechsler Adult Intelligence Scale (WAIS) is widely used. There are also a number of tests given to people in groups, such as the Spearman Primary Mental Abilities Test for children, or the Army Alpha Test for adults. In this chapter, we will focus primarily on the individually administered tests.

The Stanford-Binet   The Stanford-Binet is the most widely used individual test for children (Terman & Merrill, 1960; 1973). It is based on a test originally devised by Binet and Simon (1916) in France, and adapted in this country by Terman, who taught at Stanford—hence the name Stanford-Binet. It has been updated and revised repeatedly over the seven decades since its first use.

The original purpose of the test was to identify those children in the French school system who would not profit from regular schooling because of their low ability. Individual test items were selected if they differentiated between children who did well in school and those who did poorly. (This is like the procedure used to develop the MMPI. From the beginning, Binet's test was designed to predict school success, just as the MMPI was designed to differentiate between "normal" and "disturbed" people.) Both the early and the current versions of the Stanford-Binet cover such cognitive tasks as memory, vocabulary definitions, finding similarities and differences, doing simple arithmetic, and copying figures. For older children, there are also verbal and mathematical reasoning problems.

The score from the Binet is called an IQ, or "intelligence quotient." As it was originally developed, it was a comparison of the child's *chronological* age (CA) with his *mental* age (MA):

$$IQ = (MA/CA) \times 100$$

The test today is scored a bit differently, but the basic concept remains the same.

In order to get an estimate of a child's mental age, the test is made up of a set of problems or tasks for each age. The tests at each age level are selected so that about half the children of that chronological age can answer them correctly—thus they represent the "average" performance. Each child taking the test is allowed to try tests for younger children, for children her own age, and for older children, until the examiner finds the highest level at which the child can succeed. Her mental age is then computed by adding up all the different tasks at which she succeeded.

For any particular child, the IQ score is thus a comparison with the "average" child of any given age. A very intelligent child is one who is able to do things that are average for an older child. A less intelligent or retarded child is one who can do things expected from a younger child, but who cannot do things that are normal for his or her own age.

The test was designed so that at every age the average IQ is about 100. Figure 15–4 shows the approximate distribution of scores on the test. About two-thirds of all children score between 84 and 116, and 95 percent score between 68 and 130. So "average" scores are common; very high or very low scores are quite rare.

The Wechsler Tests Wechsler's tests are organized somewhat differently. He has two main versions of the test, one for children (the WISC-R) and one for adults (WAIS). Each includes 11 or 12 subtests, and on each subtest the items range from very easy to very hard. The subject is given all subtests, beginning with the easiest items on each one and continuing until he fails several items in a row. The 12 tests for children are listed in Table 15-11. You can see that they are divided into two groups: those involving verbal skills, and those involving what are called performance skills. An example of a performance test is the Object Assembly task in Figure 15–5.

The Wechsler Intelligence Test for Children includes verbal scale and performance scale subtests, permitting the identification of particular strengths and weaknesses.

FIGURE 15–4 Normal
Distribution of IQ Scores
*Sixty-seven percent of all test
scores should fall within the range
from about 84 to 116, 95 percent
between 68 and 132, and 99
percent between 52 and 148.*

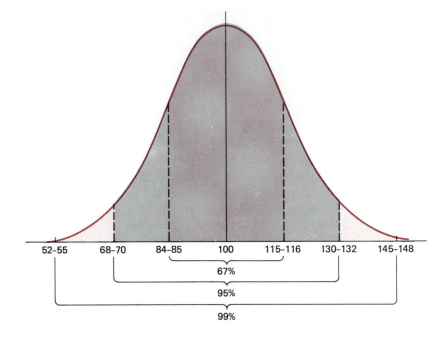

| 52–55 | 68–70 | 84–85 | 100 | 115–116 | 130–132 | 145–148 |

67%

95%

99%

As is the case in the scoring of the Binet, the scores on the Wechsler subtests and on the test as a whole are compared to those of an "average" person. And again we end up with an IQ score with an average of 100, and a distribution of scores similar to the one in Figure 15–4.

One advantage of the Wechsler tests is that you can derive separate "IQ" scores for the verbal scales and the performance scales—or for any of the separate subscales—and can look at a subject's "profile" on the subscales. If you want to identify the particular strengths or weaknesses of a person, this test can be very useful. For this and other technical reasons, the Wechsler is often considered to be a more valuable tool than the Binet.

Reliability and Validity of IQ Tests

If a child or an adult achieves an IQ score of 120, or 80, or whatever, how likely is it that he or she would get the same score a week later? A year later? And what does the score mean anyway? Does it predict school performance? Does it relate to other things that should require intelligence?

Reliability   The short-term reliability of most IQ tests is excellent. If the individual is tested again on the same test or on a parallel form a short time later, the scores are very similar. So something is being measured reliably.

However, various studies have suggested that test scores from one testing to another may be affected by testing conditions and by changes in "nonintellective factors" of the subject. Testing conditions may refer to the manner and style of the examiner and the child's comfort and familiarity with the testing situation. For these reasons,

FIGURE 15–5 An Object Assembly Task *For tasks such as this one, which is similar to elements on the Wechsler Intelligence Scale, the examiner gives the subject the pieces and asks for them to be put together as quickly as possible. The name of the object is never mentioned.*

TABLE 15–11 The Twelve Subscales from the Wechsler Intelligence Scale for Children—Revised

Verbal Scales	*Performance Scales*
1. *Information*: "How many weeks are there in a year?"	1. *Picture Completion*: The subject is shown cards of pictures with a part missing and must identify the missing part.
2. *General Comprehension*: "Why are criminals locked up?" or "Why is cotton fiber used in making cloth?"	2. *Picture Arrangement*: The subject must arrange several pictures in the correct order to make a story.
3. *Arithmetic*: "If 3 pencils cost 5¢, what will be the cost of 24 pencils?"	3. *Block Design*: The subject has a set of blocks with different colors on the several sides; he must copy designs using the blocks.
4. *Vocabulary*: The subject must define words such as bicycle, fur, sword, belfry, recede, or vesper.	4. *Object Assembly*: Familiar objects drawn on heavy cardboard are cut into pieces and laid out in a mixed-up array; the subject must rearrange the pieces to make the picture complete.
5. *Similarities*: "In what way are a plum and a peach alike?"	5. *Mazes*: The subject must solve a series of mazes drawn on paper.
6. *Digit Span*: The subject is required to repeat a list of digits either forward or backward.	6. *Coding*: The subject sees numbers matched with geometric symbols and draws the appropriate symbol when a number is given.

examiners need to be carefully trained in intellectual assessment to be able to maintain standardized testing conditions from one subject to the next.

The "nonintellective factors," such as persistence, motivation, concentration, and ability to control anxiety or recover from frustration are among the characteristics of the child or adult that may strongly influence test performance. While these may be enduring qualities of the person, they may also be affected, especially in children, by factors such as fatigue, health, familiarity with testing situations, and the like. Assessment of intellectual performance should yield information about such qualities, not just an IQ score. Nevertheless, one practical implication is that important decisions about tested individuals—decisions involving job placement or assignment to a special classroom—need to be made with consideration given to the possibility of temporary influences on performance that may affect the stability of scores.

Long-term reliability and consistency of IQ scores is another matter. The best information we have on the consistency of IQ scores

Performance on any test— including intelligence tests—is influenced by motivation and persistence.

over the years comes from a series of longitudinal studies begun in the 1920s and 1930s (Honzik, MacFarland, & Allen, 1948; Sontag, Baker, & Nelson, 1958). In these studies, children were given IQ tests each year beginning as early as age 2, and continuing throughout childhood. When they reached adolescence and adulthood, the tests were given less frequently. The question we want to answer with the results from these studies is whether individual children's test scores tended to remain about the same over their early years and into adulthood, or whether they changed from year to year.

It turns out that both change and consistency occur to some degree. For any two adjacent years, the consistency is fairly strong: a child's IQ at age 5 is a good predictor of IQ at age 6. Furthermore, the older the child, the more stable the score is. There is likely to be less variation between scores at ages 9 and 10 than between scores at ages 3 and 4. But prediction is not so consistent over long stretches, such as five or ten years. Test scores of both children and adults change, sometimes quite strikingly, over a period of several years. Although there are strong associations for most children between scores at two different ages, some children will show large shifts from one testing to another. In some studies (such as Sontag, Baker, & Nelson, 1958), there were individual children whose IQ scores changed as much as 40 or 60 points over a six- to ten-year period.

With all of this in mind, how do we answer the question of reliability? In the narrowest sense, IQ tests are reliable. If you give a person the same test twice within a short space of time, under similar conditions, she will achieve very similar scores. But several other points need to be kept in mind. First, IQs are not nearly as stable over time as many people believe. Your IQ is not something that you are born with, like blue eyes, that never changes. Second, the conditions of testing can affect the score rather markedly.

Validity   What about validity? In giving an IQ test, we have measured something, and we have done so with fair reliability. But are we measuring what we say intelligence is? In one sense, the answer to the question is obviously no. As most people have used the term, "intelligence" refers to inner competencies, and we cannot measure these. We can only measure the individual's performance on specific kinds of tasks that we assume reflect the inner competencies. We can, however, consider the predictive or concurrent validity of the tests and on that basis, IQ tests are valid for making predictions about two areas: education and vocation.

Remember that IQ tests were invented to predict school success, so the best yardstick for validating the tests clearly is school performance. Most IQ tests do a fairly good job of predicting school grades (Lavin, 1965). The correlation between the two sets of scores is typically about .60 (see Chapter 1 for a review of this statistical technique). The relationship is not perfect; some children with high IQ scores do only moderately well or even poorly in school, and some children with low IQ scores do reasonably well. But the relationship is quite strong, and it is stronger for low IQ scores than for high scores. That is, a child with a low IQ will usually do poorly in school, while a child with a high score may or may not do well. Thus, the IQ test seems to be assessing something that is *necessary but not sufficient* for success in school.

An IQ score also can be related to a person's eventual occupation. Table 15–12 lists the average IQs of men who were working in

TABLE 15–12   Relationship between Occupation and IQ Scores

Occupation	Average IQ	Range of IQ Scores
Lawyer	127.6	96–157
Reporter	124.5	100–157
Pharmacist	120.5	76–149
Manager, production	118.1	82–153
Cashier	115.8	80–145
Manager, retail store	114.0	52–151
Musician	110.9	56–147
Electrician	110.6	56–147
Mechanic	106.3	60–155
Butcher	102.9	42–147
Auto mechanic	101.3	48–151
Cook and baker	99.5	20–147
Barber	95.3	42–141
Teamster	87.7	46–145

Source: After Harrell & Harrell, 1945.

The test used in this case was a group test, the Army Alpha, on which there are more low and high scores than is typical for the individually administered tests, so the ranges are broader than we would find if something like the WAIS had been used.

various occupations during the 1940s (Harrell & Harrell, 1945). (We wish we could give you more recent data, but no one seems to do this kind of research anymore.) You can see that there are IQ differences between the men in the different jobs. When the jobs listed in the table were independently rated for the amount of intelligence required, the ratings matched the average scores. Those jobs that are thought to require a great deal of intelligence are held by people with higher average IQs.

You can also see that the range of scores in every occupation is very large. You might suppose that this range would help us predict who would be especially successful at that type of job, but it does not. Among scientists, those with the highest IQs are not necessarily the ones who do the most creative research or win Nobel prizes. Among doctors or lawyers, IQ scores do not predict success, fame, or wealth, and the same is true of other occupations.

The answer to the question of the validity of IQ tests is thus just as mixed as the answer to the reliability question. The tests do predict school performance fairly well. Since that is what they were designed to do, we can say that they have reasonable predictive validity. But they are not the best indicators of success. Children who score well may or may not do well in school. And within any given occupation, there are people with a wide range of IQ scores.

Some Things That IQ Tests Are Not

In Chapter 16 we will explore the uses and misuses of IQ test scores in some detail, but we want to mention some of the important points here as well. Many people tend to think that an IQ score tells us a great deal about a person, and that it is fixed for life, perhaps even inherited. None of these ideas is true.

An IQ test is *not* a measure of innate capacity or underlying competence. Inevitably, any test is a measure of a person's performance on a given day. The items on IQ tests were designed to measure fairly basic intellectual abilities. If a person does very poorly on a test, we might assume that he has some difficulty with those basic skills. But a low score does not mean that he has less capacity to learn those basic skills. All we know is that on a given day, he did not perform very well. On another day, or after special training, he might perform better. In fact, numerous studies with children show that their IQ scores can be increased if they are given enriched experience. In some cases, such as the intensive program for very poor, inner-city infants and toddlers developed by Rick Heber and his colleagues (Heber, 1978; Heber, Garber, Harrington, & Hoffman, 1972), the increase can be as much as 30 points or more. Clearly, a score on an IQ test is not something fixed at birth, like your blood type. It is strongly influenced by the quality of the environment in which a child grows, and by specific experiences.

An IQ score is not the same as *intelligence*. An IQ test does not measure all aspects of intellectual functioning; it measures only a narrow range of skills. The tests put a premium on language and on what is called **convergent thinking**—solving problems with a single

One problem with intelligence tests is that they emphasize language and problem solving. They do not measure creativity or special talents.

right answer. Most tests have no measure of creative thinking, sometimes called *divergent thinking*, which is needed to solve problems that may have many acceptable answers. Two children may receive identical scores but be very different in terms of their intellectual strengths, weaknesses, and styles of problem solving. Therefore, examiners often refrain from telling a person or a patient an IQ score, because it is so easily misunderstood as an unchangeable "thing."

An IQ test is *not* a measure of motivation. The score a child or adult achieves may be influenced by motivation at the time of testing, but the score itself does not tell us that. When we look at a score, we cannot tell whether the test-taker was interested and intent on that particular day, or bored and uninvolved with the test.

In sum, as Sattler (1974) puts it, "It is important to recognize that intelligence is not a thing, that the testing situation is not representative of all problem-solving situations, and that it is difficult to arrive at conclusions about capacity from test results" (pp. 21–22). The intelligence test samples learning based on general experience. The broader the experience to which the child (or adult) has been exposed, and the more the child (or adult) has been able to learn from the experiences she has had, the higher the score is likely to be.

Neuropsychological Assessment

An increasingly popular and specialized type of intellectual assessment is neuropsychological testing. For people whose brains have been damaged by disease, toxic substances, or injury, it is important to be able to evaluate the nature and extent of the impairment in intellectual functioning. In many cases, neuropsychological testing can even help to identify the location of the lesion or area of injury. The testing may therefore be useful in diagnosis and treatment planning, and it may help when rehabilitation activities are being planned and changes or improvements are being measured.

When brain injury or disease occurs, the most common signs of changes in intellectual functioning are general impairment of intellectual functioning, memory problems, loss of speed in performing skilled activities, impairment in visual-spatial skills, deficits in auditory and tactile perception, and speech and language problems (Goldstein, 1984). An IQ test, such as the Wechsler Adult Intelligence Scale, may be used to provide an overall assessment of general intellectual functioning, and deficits on some of the subtests may suggest particular areas of difficulty. However, more complete neuropsychological testing may then include an extensive battery of tests that attempt to evaluate functioning across a variety of intellectual tasks. Two commonly used batteries of tests are the Luria-Nebraska (Luria, 1973) and the Halstead-Reitan (see Reitan & Davison, 1974). Both of these tests sample numerous areas of functioning that may be associated with damage in particular parts of the brain. It may take as many as six to eight hours to administer the various subtests, and the overall scores as well as particular configurations of performance allow the assessor to infer the nature and extent of the damage. These two are the most elaborate and extensive of the neuropsychological testing approaches, and both have been shown to have fairly good reliability and validity (Goldstein, 1984).

ACHIEVEMENT TESTS

Before leaving the subject of measures of intellectual ability, we need to say a word about another very large category of tests—achievement tests. At one time or another, surely everyone has taken such tests. They are given regularly in virtually every school system as a way of finding out whether students have learned the specific material presented in school. They are not designed to measure "underlying capacity." Rather, they assess actual learning of specific skills such as addition, subtraction, grammar, spelling, vocabulary, and reading comprehension.

Several examples of achievement-test items are given in Table 15–13. Notice that the items test highly specific information—things that are actually taught in schools. Usually, a child's answers are converted into a score that allows comparison of that child with all other children in the same grade all over the country. There are two common ways to do this: (1) percentiles, which tell you what percentage of the children of that age or grade did as well, or worse; and (2) grade equivalents. A child who does as well as, or better than, 80 percent of all children in her grade would be at the eightieth percentile. A fourth-grader who is able to do average fourth-grade work on the test would have a grade-equivalent score of 4.0. A child in the same grade whose test performance was like that of a third-grader would have a grade-equivalent score of 3.0, and so on. When you hear reports that in school X, only 20 percent of the children are up to grade level, it is the grade-equivalent score that is being discussed.

Achievement tests may be used by a teacher to identify those specific skills on which a child, or group of children, may need more assistance. These tests may also be used by administrators or a com-

TABLE 15–13   Sample Items from a Fourth-Grade Achievement Test

VOCABULARY

jolly old man
1. angry
2. fat
3. merry
4. sorry

autumn leaves
1. colorful
2. fall
3. frost
4. tree

SPELLING

Jason took the *cleanest* glass.
right _____ wrong _____

Snow covered the *housetop.*
right _____ wrong _____

LANGUAGE EXPRESSION

Who wants _____ books?
1. that
2. these
3. them
4. this

LANGUAGE EXPRESSION

My brother has never _____
pumpkin pie.
1. ate
2. eaten
3. eat
4. et

MATHEMATICS CONCEPTS

What does the "3" in 13 stand for?
1. 3 ones
2. 13 ones
3. 3 tens
4. 13 tens

Which of these numbers is greater
than 88,855?
1. 88,855
2. 88,558
3. 88,858
4. 88,585

REFERENCE SKILLS

Which one of these words would
be *first* in ABC order?
1. pair
2. point
3. paint
4. polish

MATHEMATICS COMPUTATION

$$79 + 14$$

$$149 - 87$$

$$62 \times 3$$

$$4$$

149 − 87 ... 124

Source: After McGraw-Hill, 1973.

The test also includes sections on reading comprehension, in which the student is asked to read a paragraph and answer questions about it, and a section on punctuation, called Language Mechanics.

munity to decide whether a teacher, or a whole school, is doing a good job of teaching basic skills. But that is a high-risk operation. Tests like the ones in Table 15–13 can only provide information about the skills they test. If a teacher is not emphasizing those particular skills, all the children may score very low. If you draw sweeping conclusions about the adequacy of the teacher from such low scores, you would probably draw an invalid conclusion. Achievement tests work well when they are used for the narrow purpose for which they were devised—describing the achievements of individuals and groups in specific skill areas. When people use them for broader purposes, the result can be troublesome, as the next chapter reveals.

Another type of achievement test that has become widely used in school systems recently is the *criterion-referenced test.* This classification is applied to tests that determine whether a student has mastered some highly specific skills (Weiss & Davison, 1981). Suppose a high-school principal wants to know if a student has really learned enough to graduate. How can she tell that? She might use a regular achievement test, and some schools do. But lately, many educators have argued that what we need to know before a student graduates is whether he can do enough math to balance his checkbook, or can fill out a job application form legibly and with acceptable grammar, or can compare the price of three pounds of rice at $1.31 to 1.3 pounds at $.70.

To test this type of "competency," schools do not use scores on a "reading achievement test" to predict whether a student can read an employment application form. Instead, the student is given a real application form to fill out. These tests obviously have high face validity, and they are being used fairly widely today to determine whether students should be allowed to graduate from high school. The argument, as you might imagine, is about the selection of the criteria. Who decides what specific set of skills should be used as the measure of high-school-level competency? Can we adequately assess the impact of 12 years of education by asking a student to perform a series of specific tasks? These tests have become popular because they are easy to understand and because they are directly related to real-life demands. But there are important limitations about their use that educators and parents should keep in mind.

The Difference between Intelligence and Achievement Tests

At this stage, you are probably a bit confused about the differences between intelligence tests and achievement tests. You are not alone! The original idea was that IQ tests were supposed to measure how much, or how well, someone *could* learn, while achievement tests were supposed to measure how much, or how well, the person *had* learned. This is a nice tidy distinction, but it does not always work. Neither kind of test tells us what a person *can* learn. They both tell us something about what a person has already achieved. As noted earlier, the difference is really one of degree, not of type.

An intelligence test includes items that tap fairly broad skills such as classification, memory, problem solving, and reasoning. An achievement test assesses more specific knowledge, such as the sum of 6 and 7, or whether "united states" should be capitalized. One can argue that the IQ-test items are thus more basic and are closer to measures of underlying competence. And that may be true. But the IQ test is still measuring specific information, and all of the items on an IQ test are affected to some degree by experience. Across an array of achievement tests, the scores correlate fairly highly with IQ. So we are dealing here with a continuum, not two separate categories.

There are many components involved in effective testing. In the next chapter, we will go beyond issues of the characteristics of tests and consider some of the potential misuses of testing.

SUMMARY

1. For most problems of description, prediction, selection, treatment planning, and evaluation, we need to be able to characterize individual differences; this is the focus of assessment.

2. Assessment relies on systematic testing of differences between people, using reliable and valid methods.

3. Reliability has to do with whether you can measure the same thing more than once or under similar conditions and obtain the same results.

4. Two ways to determine the reliability of a test are to test the same person twice (test-retest reliability), or to have different observers rate the same behavior (interrater reliability).

5. Validity has to do with whether the instrument measures what it is designed to measure, and whether the conclusions reached are accurate.

6. Face validity can be determined just by looking at the items on a test and seeing if they are logically related to the purposes of the test.

7. Predictive and concurrent validity involve comparing test scores with agreed-upon criteria, such as school success.

8. Construct validity involves determining whether scores on a measure relate in theoretically predictable ways to other measures or to behavior.

9. Assessment procedures can be divided into "traditional" and "behavioral."

10. Traditional assessment is based on the assumption that there are underlying traits or personality dimensions; behavioral assessment does not require this assumption.

11. Traditional assessment procedures include interviews, objective tests, and projective tests.

12. Projective tests use ambiguous stimuli, such as inkblots, onto which the subject is presumed to "project" inner needs or motives.

13. Among the best-known objective tests are the Minnesota Multiphasic Personality Inventory (MMPI), Cattell's Sixteen Personality Factor Questionnaire (16 P.F.), and the Taylor Manifest Anxiety Scale (TMAS). Major projective tests are the Rorschach and the Thematic Apperception Test (TAT).

14. Some of the problems involving objective tests are that subjects may lie, that they may answer only with "socially desirable" choices, or that they may tend to always agree or disagree with most questions.

15. Most traditional tests have good reliability and validity; projective tests often have weaker reliability and validity.

16. Major behavioral-assessment techniques are interviews, self-report questionnaires, self-monitoring, and direct observation.

17. Reliability and validity have not been as thoroughly studied for behavioral assessments, but they can be adequate if the procedure is carefully designed.

18. The measurement of intelligence and scholastic achievement is the other major area in which psychologists have developed assessments.

19. Not all psychologists agree on a definition of intelligence, but generally, intelligence is seen as a global capacity for rational, purposeful thinking and acting.

20. The most widely used intelligence test for children is the Stanford-Binet, which compares a child's mental and chronological ages to give an IQ score, calculated using the following formula:

$$IQ = (MA/CA) \times 100$$

21. The average score on the Stanford-Binet, and on most IQ tests, is set at 100, with two-thirds of all scores falling between 84 and 116.

22. Another widely used set of tests are those designed by Wechsler, which yield separate scores for verbal and performance IQs.

23. The short-term reliability of IQ tests is generally very good; over long periods, IQ test scores frequently change as much as 15 or 20 points.

24. The conditions under which the test is administered may affect scores, and "nonintellectual" factors may determine outcomes. Therefore, highly trained assessors are required.

25. IQ scores predict school performance quite well and are also related to a person's occupation level (but not to one's success within the occupation).

26. IQ tests are *not* measures of underlying capacity; they are measures of current performance. IQ scores have little meaning for describing "how much" intelligence a person "has."

27. Achievement tests are similar to IQ tests, except that they measure highly specific information learned in a particular setting, such as school.

28. A subvariety of achievement test is the "criterion-referenced test," which assesses highly specific real-life competencies, such as the ability to balance a checkbook.

29. Both intelligence and achievement tests measure aspects of performance; neither taps underlying intellectual "competence."

KEY TERMS

concurrent validity

construct validity

content validity

convergent thinking

criterion-referenced test

divergent thinking

face validity

factor analysis

internal consistency reliability

interrater reliability

interview

misuse

need for achievement

objective tests

pencil-and-paper tests

predictive validity

projective tests

reliability

response bias

structured or semistructured
  interviews

test-retest reliability

unstructured interviews

validity

ADDITIONAL READING

Feuerstein, R. (1980) *Instrumental enrichment: An intervention program for cognitive modifiability.* Baltimore: University Park Press.
This is an account of a controversial but interesting program for boosting intellectual functioning.

Special Issue on Testing: Concepts, Policy, Practice, and Research. (1981) *American Psychologist, 36,* 10.
This scholarly but thorough discussion of major topics in test-

ing and U.S. public policy discusses various points of view by experts in testing theory and research and includes discussions of racial issues in intellectual testing.

Sundberg, N. (1977) *Assessment of persons.* Englewood Cliffs, NJ: Prentice-Hall.
This is a very readable college-level text covering various topics in testing, including techniques of testing, as well as issues in test interpretation.

16

Exploring the Uses and Misuses of Tests

Consider the following scenarios:

- Your child's teacher telephones you and tells you that tests show that your child should be placed in a special class for children with learning difficulties.

- You apply for a job and think that you have the technical qualifications. To your surprise, you are given a personality test that asks very personal questions, and you wonder what the questions have to do with your ability to do the work.

- You are following a murder trial in the news, and four different expert witnesses give four entirely different psychological profiles of the defendant.

- You are interested to learn if your child can be placed in the gifted program of the public schools, and on investigation, you discover that not a single black or hispanic child is in the program in your child's school, although minorities comprise 40 percent of the school's total enrollment.

- A friend of yours shows you a computer-generated psychological report given him by a psychologist in the police department, where he had applied for a job. The psychologist told him he had failed the test; what you read in the report bears little resemblance to what you know about your friend.

- You have heard that a new test is going to be given to all kindergartners that supposedly can predict which children will develop conduct disorders and possible delinquencies. Such "high-risk" children will be placed in special programs that will attempt to prevent behavior problems.

- The results of a test that you take in your senior year of high school suggest that you ought to pursue a career in medicine. You do not think you would enjoy that type of work, and you have never done very well in science courses.

In each of these cases, whether you are personally involved or just an interested observer, you probably have some misgivings about how decisions concerning what actions should be taken were reached or will be reached. In most of these examples, an individual's life is being affected and there may be implications for the community as a whole as well. In each case, psychological tests have led to certain conclusions, and in each case it is possible that the test involved has been shown to have adequate psychometric properties of reliability and validity for some applications. But reliability and validity are not enough; the tests must also be *used* properly. In some cases of misuse, the test is simply invalid. In other instances, however, the test is valid for certain uses, but it is being applied beyond its scope. Also keep in mind that reliability and validity go only so far; it is essential that tests be administered and interpreted appropriately, and this involves human judgment, and therefore, human error. Occasionally, both the test and the human-judgment process of interpretation are sound, but the society misuses the procedures. Problems of assessment misuse thus involve considerations of both scientific merit and social policy. In this chapter, we will review some of the factors that influence how assessment procedures are used and abused.

Technology and scientific advances have led to major changes in our ability to describe, explain, select, predict, plan, and evaluate some of the forces of nature and to bring them within human control. We can *describe* the structure of the atom and *explain* how humans evolved from earlier life forms; we can *select* areas under the earth where oil or precious metals are likely to be found and *predict* weather conditions and the movements of storms. We can *diagnose* fatal diseases, *plan* their treatments, and *evaluate* how successful one treatment is when compared to another. These basic steps in the scientific process are all possible because of the development of appropriate tools and tests that allow us to see the unseen and to go beyond what we have observed to draw inferences about the future. Yet, in spite of the breathtaking advances that occur from one generation to the next, each of these steps is imperfect. We can accomplish each of these and similar tasks with considerable accuracy, but there are also errors and imperfections in the outcomes, and it is clear that future generations will succeed even more spectacularly than we do because of improvements and advances in the tools and tests that will be available.

The tasks of describing, explaining, predicting, planning, and evaluating as applied to human beings require the same logic as that applied to the realm of nature. Yet in the human realm we do not have microscopes, precise measuring devices, or other sensitive tools. We also lack the centuries of theoretical refinement and experimentation that modern science uses to provide a solid basis for the development of such tools. No psychological test exists that explains with precision why a person has characteristic X but not characteristic Y, nor can the results of any test enable us to predict with certainty what an individual will do under varying conditions tomorrow or a year from now.

Nevertheless, as a culture we are fascinated with technology, and we readily embrace **psychological tests** as ways to improve life by making society more orderly and efficient. In the past we have embraced psychological testing as an efficient way of identifying "intellectual fitness" for army service (the Army Alpha test in World War I) and intellectual talent (National Merit Scholarship testing). We have used test results to match personality characteristics with job requirements (testing in personnel selection), to choose who should go to college (Scholastic Aptitude Tests), and to match children's intellectual abilities with classroom placements (mass IQ testing in the public schools). In addition to these mass-testing activities, there are also widespread but more specialized applications of testing in clinical settings: disorder detection and treatment planning as well as the prediction of the future course of an individual's conduct as a basis for decision making (for example, if he can live independently in the community, if she is dangerous to others, and so forth).

The bottom line is simply this: the public wants and expects more from psychological tests than we can deliver, given the imprecision of our theories and tools. It is essential to understand these general limitations, as well as the specific limitations of certain tests. On the other hand, there are some things we can get from tests. When they are reliable and have been validated for specific uses, they can be employed with an acceptable degree of accuracy. As we noted earlier, the best conditions for testing use fairly narrow-range tests, based on observable behaviors, to make predictions about future behavior in similar situations. Unfortunately, even when the psychometric qualities of the test are solid, the test may still be *misused*. Both our eagerness to embrace apparent "technology" and our wish to cope with the complexities of human behavior can serve as pressures that contribute to test misuse. When complex decisions or judgments need to be made, we turn to procedures that may simplify our tasks, but the potential costs of simplification may be error or unfairness. In the sections that follow, we will take a look at several sources of abuse: problems in accuracy, utility, and appropriate usage.

PROBLEMS IN ACCURACY: GOING BEYOND THE INFORMATION GIVEN

One requirement of effective testing is that the conclusions that are drawn be accurate, or valid. (For a discussion of the accuracy problem in connection with lie detection testing, see the box entitled "Polygraph Testing.") As noted, this is a question of both the scientific status of the procedure (its psychometric characteristics of reliability and validity), as well as of how the results are interpreted and applied. Interpretation invariably involves *inference*—going from an observation or test score for the person being tested to a description or prediction about behavior or characteristics of that person in the future and/or in different situations. Let us consider some examples.

Levels of Inference

A *first level inference* is essentially a description of observable behavior with little abstraction on the part of the interpreter. If I watch you eating a sandwich rapidly, I might infer that you are in a hurry. In testing examples, a score on a typing test yields an interpretation about a job applicant's typing speed; a score on a "depression inventory" yields an interpretation about the person's mood at the moment of assessment. Because they actually involve very little inference, conclusions of this nature are likely to be accurate.

A *second level inference*, however, goes beyond the observable to what is thought to be just beneath the surface—this involves generalizing to other situations. In cases of this sort, if I watch you eating a sandwich rapidly, I might infer that you are very hungry (although I do not know your actual inner experience), or I might infer that you have poor eating manners and probably always eat too fast. A test score on an anxiety questionnaire may be interpreted at this level as a prediction of a person's anxiety across all situations. An interviewer who has observed a woman's behavior and responses during an interview may infer that the woman is likely to be passive and unassertive in work situations. Because they go a little beyond the immediate description of the situation, second level inferences may be less valid, or less accurate, and more open to error.

Finally, at the *third level* of inference, the assessor goes beyond the immediate behaviors and test scores to build a theory concerning each person being assessed, speculating about the *dynamics* of an individual and making highly abstract predictions. After watching you eat rapidly, I might infer that you have an oral personality because you were weaned too soon as an infant. In a third level example involving testing, a subject's report of seeing "a monster with big feet and a tiny head that looks very menacing" in a Rorschach inkblot might be interpreted by a zealous examiner as an indication of a woman's fear of men or her insecurity about her sexuality, stemming from unresolved conflicts with her father. While such high-level inferences are less common than lower-level inferences in much of psychological assessment, they are nonetheless common enough. Clearly, considerable research is required to validate these high-level inferences, and by their nature they are frequently subject to error. The inference process thus may lead to error when the assessor goes beyond the level for which the assessment procedures have been validated. The box titled "Polygraph Testing" gives an example of a procedure used to make high-level inferences about personal characteristics.

Personal versus Situational Determinants of Behavior

Another factor that contributes to the difficulties encountered in attempting to ensure the accurate use of assessment information is the tendency of most tests (and most testers) to believe that characteristics of individuals being tested arise from *within* the person. That is, as we discussed in Chapter 14 in connection with personality, we tend to believe that behaviors are caused by personality traits, and

---

◆ POLYGRAPH TESTING

Lie detectors involve the translation of certain physiological responses into electrical impulses that are printed on graph paper. Certain biological processes, such as heart rate, respiration rate, and the activity of sweat glands, change during periods of emotional reaction. It is believed by polygraph advocates that lying can be hidden verbally but will be detected by these sensitive physiological markers that pick up the emotionally laden act of lying.

Although long used as an adjunct to traditional evidence procedures in certain courts of law, polygraphs are increasingly being used to make "personality" judgments in employment situations. Like any other personnel-selection procedure, there should be evidence of the reliability and validity of polygraph assessment. In fact, however, most of the research that has been done sheds doubt on the psychometric soundness of lie detectors.

Kleinmuntz and Szucko (1984) studied the judgments of professional technicians who examined the polygraph recordings of 50 confessed thieves and 50 innocent men who had initially been suspected of crimes. The overall accuracy of the polygraph interpreters was only 69 percent, with the rate of mistaken "guilty" decisions ranging from 18–50 percent among the different technicians. These results in an actual field test agree with the conclusions outlined in the U.S. Congress Office of Technology Assessment report (1983), which maintained that the reliability and validity of polygraphic interrogation has yet to be established.

these traits usually are assumed to be relatively stable over time and to apply across different situations. From this point of view, a test yields a picture of the person that permits the tester to draw inferences across time that are applicable to various situations. Thus, a personality test would presume to yield descriptions that may apply to the future as well as the present and to situations other than the one in which the assessment occurred. In reality, however, what a person *does* is usually at least partly influenced by a situation. You stop at a stoplight as a result of the fact that the light is red, not because of your personality traits as such. What you do in church is greatly influenced by what you know to be proper behavior there, not by your personality. When test scores of personality characteristics are used to draw inferences about what a person would be like in some hypothetical circumstance, the danger exists that what is being measured may be unique to certain situations. If someone scores in the medium range on a test of "creativity" or "leadership," the inference may be drawn that they could not expect to do well in certain jobs. In reality, they may turn out to be very creative in nonverbal tasks (for example, drawing or music) or in certain situations (interpersonal situations, for instance). Interviews may be especially likely to yield inaccurate inferences if the interview situation draws out behaviors that would be less likely to occur in other places. Interviews that elicit anxious behavior, or competitiveness, or meek attempts to defer to the interviewer may lead to the conclusion that the person being interviewed is anxious, or competitive, or unassertive in other situations as well.

Not only are traditional tests likely to be based on the assumption of cross-situational consistency in behavior, due to underlying traits, but there is also a basic characteristic of human cognition that supports this way of looking at people. Termed the *fundamental attribution error* (Ross, 1977), this cognitive tendency is reflected in the fact that when explaining the behavior of others, people generally underestimate the influence of situations and overestimate the influence of personality traits. For instance, when our co-worker Joe misses a lot of work days at the office, we tend to think it is because he is lazy or undisciplined, while Joe says that it is because of his bad back, or family problems that have come up that he has to resolve. Table 16–1 illustrates some examples of how this fundamental attribution error might work to bias the results of testing interpretations. The examples shown are exaggerated but not uncommon abuses of testing. In each instance, the assessment materials focus almost exclusively on underlying personality traits that are thought to be stable and that occur in different contexts. In reality, the problem behaviors that are observed are at least partly affected by current situations, but without a careful analysis of such situations, this important information may be neglected. Testing results may be very different if the fundamental attribution error can be avoided.

Sources of Bias in the Inference Process

In addition to the cognitive tendency to underestimate situational information, we have seen in earlier chapters that human information

TABLE 16–1   Inaccuracies in Testing Interpretations Due to the Fundamental Attribution Error

Problem Situation	*Erroneous Testing Conclusions*	*Important Situational Information Ignored*
An 8-year-old girl is inattentive, does not complete her work, and is disruptive in the classroom.	An IQ test is given; the girl scores below normal and the examiner suggests that her behavior is caused by low intelligence, which makes it hard for her to meet the teacher's academic demands.	The girl's parents are divorcing and she is upset and preoccupied with worries about the family. The classroom is very structured and the teacher is demanding, and the girl is feeling more pressure than she can deal with effectively. Both her behavior and IQ results reflect her distress.
In a job interview for a management position, the applicant is tense, seems irritated at some of the questions, is not warm and outgoing, even though she is highly qualified for the job.	The interviewer bases his recommendation on the interview, not on the applicant's previous work record, and concludes that she would be "difficult" to work for because her personality seems apprehensive and cold.	The applicant in fact is very nervous because the interviewer is challenging and intimidating, and she is angry and feels helpless.
A father has been referred to a clinic for abusing his son—overzealously punishing him for misbehavior.	An MMPI is given to see what personality "defects" might be causing the father's abusive behaviors, and the clinician interprets the results to show psychological problems and recommends therapy for the father to address his underlying conflict.	The father is experiencing considerable stress; he was laid off at work and discovered that his wife had been unfaithful. His son, also feeling the family tension, had provoked the father by recent episodes of lying and stealing.

processing is subject to error in the service of speed and in dealing with complexity. We are likely to selectively remember, to fill in gaps when information is lacking, and to pay more attention to certain information than to other factual data. Psychologists and other assessors typically face situations of enormous complexity when they are attempting to describe or predict the behaviors of other people, and they typically have an enormous array of information at hand—information gleaned from observations, interviews, knowledge of the person's background and situation, and possibly, from the results of psychological tests. Therefore, it probably comes as no surprise that there are particular kinds of errors that are inherent in the assessment process that have to do with putting all of the complex information together and drawing conclusions from it. These problems are not unique to assessment; they occur in all realms of human behavior, but they have particular implications for the clinical-inference process.

1. *Confirmatory Biases*   As we have seen, incoming information is filtered through preexisting knowledge structures that we have acquired from experience and from theories and beliefs that we hold. The information is used to form schemas that lead us to expect how

Rose Bird, former chief justice of the California Supreme Court, and this autoworker from Flint, Michigan, would certainly seem to prove that not all blondes are dumb and not all fat people are jolly. Unfortunately, the misinterpretation of test results sometimes leads us to confirm our biases and stereotypes.

certain pieces of information go together. In ambiguous situations, or when certain information is absent, we are likely to "fill in the gap," by substituting what we expect to occur. Often this is useful and accurate, but sometimes it leads to errors. An extreme example involves stereotypes: "fat people are jolly," so we may attribute good humor to an overweight person even in the absence of any substantiating information. Common examples of substitution frequently entail using theories to guide the information we look for, or the information that we ignore. For instance, an examiner in an interview who hypothesizes that a client has unresolved dependency needs may ask questions about relationships, possibly ignoring other information and perhaps even "bending" the information reported to "fit" the hypothesis. Humans are very poor at seeking nonconfirming information; we simply do not look for nonoccurrences to disprove our theories. In other words, in testing situations, an examiner's presuppositions might result in selective attention to certain data that confirm the theory, ignoring inconsistent information.

As a corollary of this general human information-processing bias, it has been observed that humans are also highly influenced by "first impressions" or "anchoring"—information that provides a kind of schema for organizing other information in novel situations where an individual has little previous experience. Such initial beliefs are relatively resistant to change and may outweigh later information when clinical inferences are being formulated. Some of the pitfalls that assessors must face are characterized in Table 16–2.

2. The Availability Bias It has been observed that when people draw conclusions about something for which they have little information, they are likely to use their own memories as a source of data (Tversky & Kahneman, 1973). What is *available* in memory, however, is highly selective—not at all like a computer store of information. The memories that are accessible to an individual are likely to be re-

TABLE 16–2   Pitfalls That Assessors Must Face

1. My *a priori* theories and stereotypes might influence what questions I ask.

2. The answers to the questions that I ask may be distorted to fit my theoretical orientation.

3. I may selectively recall information to confirm my initial hypotheses.

4. My own mood may influence what questions I ask.

5. My initial hypotheses may lead me to differentially weigh some information and discount other information.

6. Salient characteristics of the client and information provided may be more accessible.

7. I may be projecting my own conflicts and needs onto the client.

8. The questions that I ask may influence the type of information that I obtain.

9. My interpersonal style may influence the client's responses.

10. I may inadvertently be selectively reinforcing the client's provision of some information and the withholding of other material.

11. My initial predictions about the client may serve to anchor subsequent predictions, making them too liberal or too conservative.

12. The client's gender may influence the questions that I ask, my interpretations of his or her responses, and the nature of my predictions.

13. The client's age may influence the questions that I ask, my interpretations of his or her responses, and the nature of my predictions.

14. The client's socioeconomic status may influence the questions that I ask, my interpretations of his or her responses, and the nature of my predictions.

15. The client's religion may influence the questions that I ask, my interpretations of his or her responses, and the nature of my predictions.

16. The client's physical appearance may influence the questions that I ask, my interpretations of his or her responses, and the nature of my predictions.

17. The client reminds me of Archie (Edith) Bunker and this fact may influence my expectancies.

18. My behavior may be influenced by what the client tells me.

19. Since any question that I ask will provide some confirmatory evidence, I can never acquire disconfirming evidence for any hypothesis.

20. Once diagnosed, the client may act to confirm my initial formulation.

21. I may selectively recall salient information or characteristics.

22. I may selectively recall information to confirm my stereotype.

23. I may interpret the client's responses as supporting a particular hypothesis, but this may be the result of an illusory correlation.

24. My own mood may affect what I remember about the client.

25. I may be ignoring baserates or be unaware of the appropriate baserates to employ!

Source: After Turk & Salovey, 1986.

lated to how vivid the memory is—that is, how readily it can be brought to mind. Thus, very dramatic, personally meaningful, or colorful instances in memory are likely to be called up when situations remind us of them in any way. In turn, we are likely to base our judgments or predictions in a new situation on what we recall of the situations we have called up from memory. Because the old but very vivid situation might be unusual or atypical, our subsequent judgments about the new situation may be incorrect. Consider an extreme example. Imagine that you have gone for an interview at the graduate school of your choice, and that even though you have a good record, you are rejected. Unknown to you, the interviewer was thinking, "The last student we accepted from University X was a disaster, (so I am making the same prediction about you . . .)" or "My experience with women who dress boldly is that they aren't very serious as students. . . ." Or consider another example involving a psychological test. An examiner may use an MMPI profile, basing it on the recollection of a former patient who had a similar profile. "Although this personality scale does not indicate serious pathology, I once evaluated another person of this age and gender whose test looked the same, and one week later he had a psychotic episode (so I had better give a more serious diagnosis)." Other kinds of cognitive errors in the process of forming judgments and making decisions are common but go beyond the scope of our discussion here (see Kahneman & Tversky, 1973; Nisbett & Ross, 1980).

3. *Illusory Correlation*   Even when a psychological test has been empirically demonstrated to be invalid, clinicians may sometimes persist in believing in the accuracy of their interpretations. This has been demonstrated by Chapman and Chapman (1967; 1969), who explored a process they termed "illusory correlation." They used two projective tests, the Draw-a-Person and the Rorschach, for which empirical research had failed to show an association between certain patient responses and patient characteristics. In spite of the lack of *actual* association, however, the Chapmans showed that both clinicians and naive judges tended to believe that certain responses on the tests indicated certain patient symptoms. For example, some observers formulated an illusory correlation between patients' drawing or reporting eyes and interpretations of suspiciousness or paranoia. An association was developed linking the drawing or reporting of figures with uncertain gender and homosexuality. The Chapmans argued that beliefs about covariation between signs on the tests and symptoms are due to semantic or perceptual associations. Thus, the body parts that are called to mind by the symptom are the basis of the illusory association that persists in the absence of empirical evidence. These researchers and others have shown that even when clinicians are told that there is no association between certain test responses and patient characteristics, they continue to make the same interpretations, presumably because of the strong associative connections that have been formed. Results like this remind us that even when careful validation research has been done on tests, examiners may continue to work on the basis of their own, often incorrect, theories and associations.

THE PROBLEM OF UTILITY: DOES TESTING HELP?

Paul Meehl (1959), an important figure in the history and development of personality testing, argued that even if a test is reliable and valid, it should also be shown to provide information that is useful and not otherwise available. Why conduct hours of elaborate testing to determine whether a candidate for promotion will get along well with co-workers, when you can check the person's past record of cooperation with colleagues in the personnel file? A battery of expensive psychological tests could be conducted to try to predict whether a prisoner is likely to repeat a crime after being given early parole, but it is probably more accurate and certainly cheaper to consider the person's previous record of behavior when released from prison under similar circumstances. As Mischel (1968) argued in his book challenging personality testing, one of the best predictors of future behavior is past behavior in similar circumstances. While obviously not infallible or relevant to all testing situations, this guideline suggests that in order to be *useful*, a particular test or judgment should be shown to work better than predictions made from past behavior.

Meehl's concept of "advance incremental utility" may also be applied to certain demographic characteristics of individuals that constitute a simple, inexpensive basis for decisions as compared to testing. For instance, if research demonstrates that child abuse is highly correlated with being poor, single, under age 20, and having more than two small children at home, then psychological testing of *all* mothers to determine child abuse potential would be highly inefficient.

Baserates

Our child abuse example is an illustration of how the utility of tests is related to the frequency of occurrence of the characteristic. The **baserate** of a characteristic—its distribution in the population sampled—affects the accuracy of predictions that are based on tests. If a trait is relatively rare, then tests run the risk of not being very useful. In fact, it is likely that the test will "misclassify" more people than if everyone were predicted *not* to have the trait (Meehl & Rosen, 1955). In other words, if the behavior being predicted is rare—say, murder or suicide—it may be more accurate to conclude that no one will commit a murder or take his own life, than to predict that some people will who actually do not and that some people do who were not predicted to do so. This is because every test has a certain amount of error built in, leading to "false positives" and "false negatives." The more often the traits that the test is trying to identify actually occur about 50 percent of the time, the more likely a test is to be useful in detection. Table 16–3 presents a hypothetical example to illustrate this point. Suppose a polygraph test (lie detector) is given to all prospective employees of a company to screen out anyone who appears to be dishonest. If the baserate of dishonesty is 5 percent in the sample, and if the accuracy of the lie-detector test is 80 percent (it actually is not this high), then 200 screening errors will be made out of 1,000 people—190 false positives and 10 false negatives. On the other hand, if the company did not use the polygraph and decided to assume that everyone is honest, then only 50 errors of misclassification would have been made. Moreover, what is the "cost" of mislabeling 190 people as dishonest who are in fact honest! In other examples, even if there were large numbers of errors in classification, tests may still be judged useful on the basis of social policy. Society has to make a judgment about the *costs* of errors. What are the implications of failing to detect a problem that could be treated or prevented? What are the

TABLE 16–3 Hypothetical Example of Baserates and Test Misuse

Corporation X uses polygraph tests to screen all prospective employees for honesty, hiring only those who pass the lie-detector test. The baserate of dishonesty is hypothesized to be 5 percent, so out of 1,000 applicants, 50 are truly dishonest. Suppose the test is 80 percent accurate; then .80 of the truly honest and .80 of the truly dishonest will be correctly detected, but people in the shaded cells of the table are "errors." While the corporation correctly "catches" 40 of the 50 dishonest people, the "cost" is 190 people who really are honest but do not get the jobs because they are labeled as dishonest.

	Truly honest	Truly dishonest
Test Says Honest	760	10
Test Says Dishonest	190	40
	950	50 = 1,000

implications of labeling someone as having a particular problem? These are some of the issues that will be discussed in a later section on ethics and fairness.

The Barnum Effect

An additional issue that arises when considering the usefulness of testing has been called the **Barnum effect** (Meehl, 1973) or the Aunt Fanny effect. Sometimes psychological testing, especially personality assessment, lends itself to vague, general statements that appear to be specific to a particular individual being tested, but that in fact are generally true of everyone, so that they are, in essence, meaningless. Basically, the Barnum effect is a trivial description that fits everyone because it has such a high baserate in the population: "Linda craves intimacy with another person but needs to maintain some sense of independence," "Jose is struggling to find a balance between conformity and creative self-expression."

Interestingly, individuals who are being tested also exhibit a high degree of acceptance for such trivial, useless statements. Experiments have demonstrated that people are highly likely to believe general descriptions that they think have actually been written about them (Snyder, 1974). Moreover, they seem to place even greater faith in the truthfulness of such assessments if they think that the "personality descriptions" have been based on relatively more "mysterious" forms of testing, such as inkblot projective tests, than if the results were based on objective paper-and-pencil tests. Taking the research one step further, Snyder (1974) gave subjects alleged descriptions of themselves that were said to have been based on astrological interpretations (in reality everyone got the same description, see Table 16–4).

The Barnum effect—"there's a sucker born every minute"—may be at work in many situations (such as testing) that purport to describe and predict people's lives.

TABLE 16–4   The Barnum Effect

This horoscope was given to all of the participants in a study. Nearly all of the recipients felt that the horoscope characterized them to some extent. The same thing can happen with personality tests. Such vague, general statements apply to almost everyone.

You have a very practical bent and enjoy earning money, but sometimes your deep desire to be a creative person triumphs over your practicality. You lead other people with your innovative ideas, or could do this if you felt more sure of yourself. Insecurity is your greatest weakness, and you would be wise to try to overcome this. Your deep sense of humor and warm, understanding nature win you true friends, and although they may not be numerous, you share a rather intense loyalty to each other. With your innovative mind, you rebel against authority, either inwardly or openly. Even though you could make a stable businessman, you would be a very idealistic one, finding it hard not to defend the underdog or not to try to settle arguments that arise. You like to think of yourself as unprejudiced, but periodically examine yourself to make sure you aren't overlooking some harmful judgments. You will live a long, full life if you take care of yourself. You love to have freedom in whatever you're doing, and this makes you dislike monotonous tasks and being in large crowds where you can't seem to move freely. If someone pays you a well-deserved compliment, you enjoy hearing it, but you may not show that you do. Sometimes you find that the actions you take do not accomplish as much as you'd like them to, especially in dealing with people. You have a real grasp on how people are feeling or what they are thinking without their necessarily telling you.

Source: After Snyder, 1974.

He found that people readily believed this interpretation also. In addition, he discovered that they believed it even more strongly when they thought the horoscope was tailored to them based on their birth year, month, and day than when they thought it to be based just on their birth year and month. That is, the more individualized and personal subjects thought the description was, the more they believed it. Clearly, these studies highlight the gullibility of uninformed subjects and the comfortable collaboration between the tester and the testee when they both believe that something useful has been provided, even though, in fact, only vague generalizations true of most people have been elicited.

TESTING MAY BE ACCURATE AND USEFUL, BUT IS IT WISE?

It is not sufficient to consider only the scientific and practical issues regarding testing; it is necessary also to analyze the social, legal, and ethical implications—how tests are *used*, and if their uses raise problems for society as a whole. In this area, we clearly go beyond psychology into social policy, and these decisions involve everyone, not just specialists. The three concerns that are most apparent are fairness, privacy, and labeling.

Fairness

The topic of fairness is so critical that we devote a separate section to it in connection with intellectual testing. However, the key fairness

5461 6163

Fairness in testing is an issue when assessment procedures lead employers to select employees who are like themselves.

issues are also pertinent when personality testing is used for personnel selection, when testing is utilized to assist with assignment to clinical treatments, or for other related decisions. Is it possible that tests lead to differential treatment for certain segments of society over others? For instance, do tests lead to the selection of white males for positive outcomes (jobs, advancement, college admissions) or to the overrepresentation of blacks or the poor for negative judgments (negative parole or prison decisions, entrance into low-paying jobs or low-level training programs, rejection from civil service or the military)? Considerations such as these have led to numerous lawsuits; many of these cases have been argued before the U.S. Supreme Court. Guidelines have now been established to help prevent bias in testing in employment settings. The federal Equal Employment Opportunity Commission (EEOC) has mandated the following:

1. An employer who uses any assessment device—interview, standardized test, or whatever—must be able to prove that the assessment is consistently related to performance on the particular job for which it is used. (That is, it must be valid.)

2. Further, the employer must be able to prove that the test is *equally valid* for all relevant subgroups—*not* that all subgroups receive equal scores. It is not enough to show, for example, that among all applicants, those with high scores on a measure of "leadership" are more likely to succeed on the job. The employer also has to demonstrate that white males, black males, and both white and black females all show similar relationships between test scores and leadership. If the scores on the test are related to the criterion in the same way for all groups, then the law says that the employer can use that test for the job, even if it means one subgroup or another ends up being overrepresented in the occupation.

It turns out that most of the standard personality testing instruments *are* equally valid for different racial groups (Weiss & Davison,

1981), but this is less true of unstandardized procedures, such as interviews and situational tests. The burden of proof in these cases lies with the employer, who must demonstrate that his or her testing procedure is valid in connection with the decisions for which it is used.

Privacy

Any psychological assessment, no matter how valid the procedures, yields private information. "The testing by one individual of another human's intellectual, personality, and related characteristics is an invasion of privacy to an extent no less intimate than that involved in an examination carried out on that same individual's person or resources by a physician, attorney, or agent of the Internal Revenue Service" (Matarazzo, 1986, p. 14).

The privacy issue raises two ethical questions:

1. Testing may be involuntary. Employees in certain companies and applicants for the Civil Service and the armed services (as well as applicants for admission to certain schools and universities) are required to submit to testing. What rights does the respondent have to refuse to be tested, or to refuse to answer some questions?

2. Who controls the interpretations of the tests and the records of the scores or interpretations? To whom will such records be shown, and how will they be used in the future?

Important safeguards for these privacy questions have been incorporated into research procedures. Research uses of any kind of assessment are now governed by strict review and privacy requirements. Any research involving human subjects, whether or not it includes psychological testing, must be approved by a board of professional peers. Individual scores on procedures must be kept in strict confidence; the subject has the right to refuse any part of the procedure and must be fully informed of all procedures, giving "informed consent" prior to participation in the research. If children are involved, their parents must give *their* informed consent on behalf of the children. All uses of subjects must have the subjects' consent, and any changes in the way the materials are to be used must be separately approved by the subjects.

These are excellent protections, but they have not generally been extended to personality assessment in industry, schools, or by private individuals. Court cases have raised the issues of test privacy, and generally the courts have held that the test taker has a right to see what is in her or his file and to refuse the use of test results beyond the purposes for which they were originally intended. However, while there has been some regulation both by the federal government and in accordance with the ethical standards of professional groups, such as the American Psychological Association, abuses of privacy are still found to occur occasionally.

Strict maintenance of privacy rights in connection with testing results is an important concern in schools and in business.

Computerized Testing   One area of potential abuse currently is of considerable concern to psychologists. The use of computers to interpret and print reports of psychological testing has developed into a significant business. Such "automated test reports" permit testers to have a client fill out a questionnaire that may then be mailed to the computer company, scored by a computer, and sent back to the purchaser with a computer-generated report. Frequently, the automated report companies offer their services to psychologists or other mental-health professionals, but there is no way to stop such services from being used by nonpsychologists who have no training in test interpretation. Not only must the public be concerned about the unregulated use of such tests and the private data that may be stored in computers, but the even more basic question of the validity of the reports is still unresolved. As Matarazzo (1986) states, "My concern is with the pages and pages of today's neatly typed, valid-sounding narrative interpretations that are the products, for the most part, of secretly developed disks of software that have not even been offered for scientific evaluation (as has clinical judgment), let alone met even the most rudimentary acceptable tests of science" (p. 15). Because each individual is unique, Matarazzo argues, a report based on a questionnaire and written by a computer cannot be valid for everyone. The American Psychological Association has drafted explicit guidelines for developers, publishers, and users of these computer-generated tools, but it is likely that legislation will be required to actually enforce the appropriate use of such instruments and to help protect the public's privacy against the overzealous use of technology. Automated testing reports based on empirical evidence and used responsibly by appropriately trained testers have the potential to be useful and accurate. However, unless regulated to conform to high ethical and research standards, they also have the potential for misuse.

Classification and Labeling Problems

Testing leads to the possibility that a person will be classified or labeled in some way. In clinical applications, assessment may lead to the application of a diagnostic label—for example, depressed, schizophrenic, or an antisocial personality. In a work setting, a prospective employee may take a test that leads to the assessment that he is "unstable" or "unfit." Perhaps a middle-management executive hopes for a promotion and ends up being described as "lacking leadership ability." Or, suppose a community has a new juvenile delinquency early intervention program, testing all 8-year-olds, and a subset of children is identified as "delinquency prone." A school district gives IQ tests and classifies some children as "mentally retarded" and others as "gifted."

Labeling and classification are necessary and almost daily activities in our lives, and they are not inherently good or bad. However, it is possible that in some circumstances labels will have an impact on how people view another individual. As we have seen, we form theories about how the world is and how other people are, and then our thought processes are biased toward consistency with these theories. Thus, if we categorize an individual as "retarded" or "lacking in leadership," there is a danger that these labels will persist and bias the way we interpret the behaviors of such persons. The individual being labeled may become the victim of a self-fulfilling prophecy. He may conclude, "If I'm not very bright, then I shouldn't even try to succeed." In most cases, when the testing is done and a label given or a decision made, that label or decision applies to the present time and situation (according to the limits of the test's reliability and validity). Unfortunately, however, labels may end up being linked to a person for long periods beyond their actual applicability. The individual may be exposed to different opportunities and be treated differently by others as a result of an earlier testing decision.

In general, we know little about the actual effects of labeling, although we can certainly speculate that labels can have a long-lasting, negative impact on some people in some situations. Generally speaking, the labeling effects are not due to the test itself, but to how tests are used by others and by society. We will turn now to a topic where the problems of *fairness* are particularly visible: the use of testing in the schools.

USES AND ABUSES OF TESTING IN THE SCHOOLS

Scholastic achievement and IQ tests have been eagerly embraced for decades as technologies for scientifically sorting people into their "right places." Some of the goals achieved by this sorting process have been commendable and serve democratic principles, such as basing college entrance on some objective criterion of achievement instead of who you know that can help you get admitted. Other goals have appeared to serve more the function of efficiency, such as deciding who is fit for military service and who is not. But in our eagerness to use the developing testing technologies, our society has sometimes overlooked their costs. Now we turn specifically to the use of tests in the public schools to consider the pros and cons of testing.

Advantages of Testing in the Schools

A major goal of testing in schools involves sorting and diagnosing. Most school systems have special classes for children with learning difficulties, including those children that are labeled as retarded, those with brain damage, and those with emotional problems. In many districts, there are also special classes for the gifted. The aim of testing is to identify children's special needs and to attempt to match their individual needs with classroom environments and specially trained teachers who will help them develop to their fullest potential.

Many schools employ individually administered IQ tests, supplemented with other specialized tests, to try to make class placements. In addition, standardized achievement tests are frequently used to identify specific areas of weakness or strength in individual children, so that teachers may direct their efforts more skillfully. For example, a child who is performing above grade level in math may be referred for enrichment in that discipline, while another who scores below grade equivalent in reading comprehension may be referred to a special teacher who provides extra help with reading. Using test results in these ways, teachers and administrators are able to base their decisions on objective scores rather than just on teachers' impressions,

Testing in schools has the advantage of helping to identify children with special needs who can benefit from teaching programs tailored to students with learning difficulties or emotional problems. Many schools also have special programs for gifted students.

which may or may not be accurate (depending on the teacher's own ability and training).

It has also been argued that the use of standardized testing—achievement tests and college board examinations, for example—gives parents and the community a yardstick for evaluating the adequacy of the schools. Minority parents may be provided with a clear argument for insisting on educational reform to raise the level of performance for minority and disadvantaged children to that of other students in the community. School administrators are also able to use test scores to identify weaknesses or discrepancies between schools or districts.

Disadvantages of Testing in the Schools

There are at least three arguments against the use of testing in schools:

1. The use of IQ tests may perpetuate the myth that a child's fixed, innate "capacity" to learn is being measured. This myth is believed not only by the public but also by many teachers. If a teacher or a child's parents believe this, a low score may be taken as evidence of low capacity and the teacher and parents may not try as hard with the child. Also, the child may be labeled, in effect, with all the potential negative consequences to self-esteem that such labels may cause.

2. Many educators argue that we should not sort children at all—that within broad limits, all children ought to be taught in regular classes. In 1975 the federal government passed the Education for All Handicapped Children Act, which requires that every physically or mentally handicapped child be educated in the least restrictive environment possible. For many children, this has meant what has come to be called *mainstreaming*—placement in a regular rather than a special classroom. The argument is that the instructional methods

One problem of IQ testing in the schools is that children from disadvantaged and minority groups score lower than middle-class white children. IQ tests clearly fail to test all of the capabilities that children have that we consider to be important.

needed by virtually all children are essentially the same as those provided in a regular class. In fact, a number of studies show that children with low IQs (sometimes called "educable mentally retarded") do better academically when they are in regular classes than when they are placed in special classes (Goldstein, Moss, & Jordon, 1965; Robinson & Robinson, 1976; Zigler & Muenchow, 1979). If this is true, the need for IQ tests to sort children into special classes becomes much less obvious.

3. Most troublesome of all, middle-class white children routinely score higher on tests than black children or children of most other minority groups. Therefore, using the tests to sort children into groups will inevitably result in a larger percentage of minority children ending up in special classes for the retarded. Indeed, a California federal district court judge handed down a ruling in 1979 prohibiting the use of standardized IQ tests as a basis for placing black children in special classes for the retarded. He noted that blacks made up only a quarter of the student population in most districts in the state, but that 62 percent of the students in special classes were black. To the extent that such special placements limit the educational opportunities of children and may result in the application of a label of "retarded," the tests may perpetuate the disadvantages experienced by poor and nonwhite children. In 1986 the same judge renewed his order in the *Larry P. v. Wilson Riles* case (1979) prohibiting IQ testing even with parental consent.

In addition to these significant social issues, it has been argued that an unfortunate by-product of standardized testing is that many schools "teach" the test, in effect devoting their curriculum to preparing students to do well on the tests. While schools do need to be accountable for performance, it is important to keep in mind that achievement tests cover only *some* of the topics that are important for students' scholastic success. They do *not* cover creativity, writing skill, work habits and attitudes, self-concept, or *how* to think and solve problems.

RACE DIFFERENCES IN IQ

Because of the profoundly important social issue that arises with respect to achievement and intellectual testing of children, we feel that it is useful to explore the question of race differences in IQ. Here the emphasis is on differences between black children and white children, since most of the research and controversy has focused on these two groups (although the issues of possible bias in testing apply also to other minorities, to economically disadvantaged groups, and to women).

The use of tests has repeatedly shown that, on average, black children score about 15 points lower than white children on IQ tests, leading to disproportionate placements in special classes, and possibly to fewer opportunities for enrichment experiences. While the distributions of IQ scores for blacks and whites overlap, with many high-scoring blacks and low-scoring whites, the mean differences are cause for considerable concern. Three arguments have been advanced to explain these differences: (1) the tests are biased and lead to incorrect results; (2) the differences truly exist and are due to inherent genetic differences in intellectual functioning; and (3) the results are caused by environmental disadvantages experienced by black children not raised in the dominant white middle class.

Are the Tests Biased?

The bias argument holds that black children score lower on tests because the tests are not equally valid indicators of performance for the two groups. At the level of *content* validity, items on standardized tests may not be equally "accessible" to black and white children. For instance, it may be that items refer to content that is associated with the dominant white culture and may, therefore, be less familiar or less interesting to black children (a question about Martin Luther King, Jr. may elicit a correct response from a black child, but a question about Martin Luther might not). It is true that tests have been shown to contain items that are specific to white culture, and most major standardized tests have been rewritten to eliminate such items. All new items are carefully reviewed to ensure that they will be as "culture fair" as possible. However, as it turns out, research indicates that culturally biased items accounted for few of the differences between groups, and even efforts to translate test items into the child's native idiom failed to raise the scores of minority children (for example, Lesser, Fifer, & Clark, 1965; Quay, 1971). Also, more technical, statistical procedures aimed at identifying items that elicit differences between racial groups have generally found that there are not large-scale, consistent biases in the content of tests (Cole, 1981). That is, differences have sometimes been detected, but they have not been large or widespread enough to account for most of the mean differences in scores between whites and minority groups.

Nevertheless, if the items are not significantly biased, the tests may still lack predictive validity for nonwhites. It is possible that the test scores do not predict school performance or some other agreed-upon criterion equally well for black and white children. Numerous studies have been conducted in connection with this issue, and after reviewing them, Cole (1981) concluded that most tests predict equally well for minority and white groups. However, there is a counterargument: maybe *both* the schools and the tests are biased against minority children in the sense that they emphasize the same knowledge, motivations, and attitudes. If black children do not share all of these standards, they will be consistent in performing less well both in school and on the tests (or, they will score well on both to the degree that they do share in the values of the school system). Garcia (1981) argues that it does not make sense to apply standard instruments to culturally diverse groups that clearly differ in practice and motivation. Moreover, he notes that IQ tests are based on the outmoded assumption that a single, general, and fixed aptitude may be used to solve all problems. Garcia suggests instead that "to avoid the futile comparisons of one people with another, mental testing should be reduced to a set of operations and emptied of cultural bias. Single scores and dimensions should be deemed scientifically invalid. . . . Performance should be described with profiles bearing some semblance to brain functions and/or to social roles in the various communities.

Tests should always be repeated to determine changes in the ability profiles over time" (pp. 1179–80).

This complex issue of test bias defies easy analysis and simple conclusions. On one hand, technical issues of bias seem to have contributed to some of the differences in IQ scores of blacks and whites, but bias issues probably do not account for all mean differences, suggesting the need to look for other explanations. On the other hand, while the tests themselves probably should not be "blamed," the mere existence of the tests perpetuates myths and outdated assumptions about intellectual functioning that have critical social implications. As Cole (1981) concluded after her review of test-bias research, ". . . we have learned that whether or not tests are biased, their role is only a small part of the complex social policy issues facing the legislatures, the courts, and the citizenry at large. To pretend that these broader issues are essentially issues of test bias is to be deceived. These policy issues require decisions about values that must be made whether or not tests are involved" (p. 1075).

The Genetic Argument

The publication of an article by Arthur Jensen in the *Harvard Educational Review* in 1969 touched off a firestorm of scientific and political debate. Jensen argued that observed black-white differences in IQ test scores were probably genetic in origin. He based his conclusion essentially on two claims: research suggesting that IQ is largely inherited, and the fact that environmental explanations of IQ differences are unconvincing.

What do we know about the heritability of IQ? Studies of this question have had to deal with the "nature versus nurture" debate—how to separate the two sources of influence in a way that allows us to draw conclusions about the influence of each. A classical strategy has been to compare identical and nonidentical twins. Since identical twins share exactly the same heredity, while fraternal twins do not, we can estimate the "heritability" of a characteristic by comparing identical and fraternal twin pairs (assuming that each pair has been raised in the same environment). If identical twins are more like one another than are fraternal twins with reference to a particular characteristic, we are probably witnessing the influence of heredity. Extending this approach, researchers have studied identical twins who were reared apart from each other in different environments. If such pairs are still very much alike with regard to a given characteristic, despite different environments and learning histories, then a genetic influence is strongly implicated. An additional strategy is to study adopted children: do they turn out to be more like their adoptive parents (because of the influence of learning and environmental conditions) or more like their biological parents?

Table 16–5 presents correlations between IQ scores of twin pairs. (Recall that the closer the correlation coefficient is to 1.00, the more similar the items tested are.) Four of the studies compared fraternal twins and identical twins reared together and indicate higher correspondence between the genetically identical twins than between nonidentical twins, thus supporting the heredity hypothesis. Even more convincing, identical twins reared apart also show strong correlations

TABLE 16–5   IQ Correlations in Twin Studies

Study	Country	Test Used	Fraternal Twins Reared Together	Identical Twins Reared Apart	Identical Twins Reared Together
Newman, Freeman, & Holzinger, 1937	USA	1916 Stanford-Binet	.64	.67	.91
Shields, 1962	England	"Dominoes test" and vocabulary test	—	.77	.76
Juel-Nielsen, 1965	Denmark	Danish translation of the WAIS	—	.62	—
Burt, 1966	England	"Group test of intelligence"	.55	.77	.94
Wilson, 1977	USA	WISC	.60	—	.86
Loehlin & Nichols, 1976	USA	National Merit Scholarship Qualifying Tests	.62	—	.86

with each other. Studies such as these have generally persuaded people that there is a strong hereditary component in IQ. However, there are other factors that must be considered in connection with this issue. The largest, and one of the most influential studies in the table—that conducted by Cyril Burt—has been exposed as a potential case of scientific fraud (Kamin, 1974) and may have included fabricated results. Another factor that should be assessed is the argument that identical twins are not only genetically similar but that they actually are treated more identically than other siblings. Therefore, we really cannot tell whether their IQ scores are more alike because they have identical genetic endowments or because they have been dressed and reacted to in the same way and have played together and shared the same experiences more than other twins. Just at the point when we might think that the strategy of studying identical twins who were raised apart could resolve this issue, we need to take a closer look at *this* strategy as well. We assume that identical twins raised apart are being reared in different environments, so that if they turn out to have similar IQs, it must be due to their similar genetic characteristics. However, Kamin (1974) reexamined the environments of the twin pairs who were raised apart and found that in most cases both twins were reared by relatives, such as two aunts or an aunt and a grandmother. They often attended the same school and knew they were twins. Even when the two were raised by unrelated families, the usual pattern was to place the two children in families of similar social class. For instance, in the Shields study included in Table 16–5, only 13 of 40 pairs were raised in unrelated families, and for those 13 the IQ correlations were much lower (.51) than for those raised in related families (.83). Similarly, Farber (1981) found that when the degree of contact between the twins during their childhood is taken into account, the correlation between the pairs of IQs drops to around .50. Taken together, these considerations have led many investigators to conclude that twin studies do not demonstrate a major genetic influence on IQ. While significant, the genetic influence is probably not as large as that suggested by Jensen and other advocates of the genetic position. Studies of adopted children generally support the same conclusion. Children's IQs were often correlated as highly with their adoptive mothers' estimated IQs as with those of their biological mothers, suggesting an environmental explanation. In one unique study of black children adopted into white families, Scarr and Weinberg (1977) found that the highest IQ correlations were between unrelated children adopted into the same family. Such findings clearly are not consistent with a genetic explanation of IQ.

If we go back to the question of the origin of IQ differences between black and white groups, where does this leave us? Interestingly, Jensen's argument seems flawed not just by the weakness of the genetic evidence, but in another way as well. Jensen argued that if differences in IQ *within* white groups could be attributed to genetic differences, then differences *between* blacks and whites could also be attributed to genetics. This is a logical fallacy in that even if IQ scores were heavily influenced by heredity in both blacks and whites, any differences between the groups could *still* be due to environmental differences. Consider an analogy: suppose that a child's height is genetically determined (it is to a significant extent). If one group of people raises its children in an impoverished area without adequate nutrition, as compared to another group, the malnourished children will be shorter than the well-fed children (an environmental effect), even though within each group, relatively taller parents will have relatively taller children (a genetic effect).

Jensen committed yet another logical fallacy called the ***hereditarian fallacy.*** In reviewing the environmental explanations for IQ differences in race, he implied that failure to identify such causes is sufficient to refute an environmental hypothesis in general. Further, he assumed that a refutation of the environmental hypothesis is sufficient to confirm a genetic hypothesis. As Mackenzie (1984) puts it, "To conclude that 'it must be due to the genes,' on the grounds that we cannot find anything in particular that it *is* due to, would be to reach a conclusion that was not merely made in ignorance but that was explicitly based on ignorance" (p. 1223).

The Environmental Explanation

As a group, blacks in this country are poorer, a greater percentage are on welfare, and more black households are often headed by women. When black adults are employed, they are more likely to have semiskilled or unskilled, poorly paying jobs. Adult blacks are less well educated, and adult black women are less likely to receive or to seek out good prenatal care during pregnancy. They are more likely to experience complications of pregnancy, premature delivery, and other birth disorders. Such birth complications alone have been shown to affect subsequent cognitive development and behavioral characteristics of children (reviewed in Rattan & Rattan, 1987). There may also be significant dietary differences between blacks and whites, with blacks more often eating a diet that is short on protein and some vitamins, although the data on this point are weak. In addition, of course, blacks experience both blatant and subtle discrimination of various kinds. So when the IQs of blacks and whites are compared, two highly different environments are being assessed.

Research that supports an environmental explanation of IQ differences between races comes from many sources. For example, Mercer and Brown (1973) found that the mean IQ differences between black, white, and hispanic children were almost completely eliminated following statistical control of nine social variables: the mother's participation in organizations (such as scouts, church groups, and so forth); the racial composition of the neighborhood; the mother's fluency in English and familiarity with the child's school; socioeconomic status; the parents' geographical origins (northern or western U.S. versus southern U.S. or Mexico); home ownership; the mother's individualistic achievement values; family structure (intact versus other arrangements); and the child's general anxiety level. More recently, Blau (1981) studied 1,000 black and white children and their families in Chicago and found that various social variables (aspects of socioeconomic status, family structure, and so on) affected children's IQ scores. For instance, she found that when the social factors were statistically controlled, the differences between black and white girls' IQs dropped from 12 points to less than 3 points. Both these studies point to the influence of environmental factors on children's IQ. However, it is important to interpret the results properly and not to commit the "sociologist's fallacy" by suggesting that such results *rule out* genetic influences. Research results suggest that social factors affect IQ scores, but they do *not* answer the question of whether IQ has a genetic basis (for example, it is possible that some of the social variables themselves have a genetic basis).

Other research that seems to support the role of environment as a critical factor in IQ comes from efforts to *change* children's IQs by exposing them to enrichment programs or to environments believed to be conducive to intellectual development. Scarr and Weinberg's 1977 adoption study showed that black children adopted by white parents had IQ scores fairly close to those of the parents' natural children, and youngsters who had been adopted before they reached the age of one year received higher scores than children adopted after age one, suggesting that longer exposure to the adoptive parents' environments had more impact on children's intellectual performance. Dozens of studies of Head Start or other intensive, early enrichment programs have provided suggestive evidence that such programs can have dramatic effects on children's IQ scores, compared to control groups not exposed to the programs (Heber, 1978; Ramey & Haskins, 1981). On the other hand, the overall success of compensatory education programs has been disputed, with some authors arguing that the intellectual gains are short-lived (Minton & Schneider, 1980; Vernon, 1979). While undoubtedly the early enrichment programs have had some positive outcomes, it is clear that they have not eradicated the disparities in performance between white and nonwhite school children.

In the final analysis, there is no single conclusion that can be reached to explain IQ differences among various groups. Perhaps the

Head Start preschools like this one have shown that early intellectual enrichment programs can have dramatic effects on a child's IQ.

question of what causes racial differences in IQ is misdirected. It is far less important to wonder how much of the difference in children's IQs is due to bias, how much to genetics, and how much to environment, than it is to explain the causal mechanisms that account for intellectual performance. The more important question would thus have implications for how intellectual performance can be maximized and the conditions for which results can be generalized (Mackenzie, 1984). As we stated at the outset, our tests are no better than our theories, and our tests of intellectual abilities are based on theories of cognitive performance that are sorely in need of change. The deficiencies in our assessment tools have contributed greatly to the controversies of the 1960s and 1970s, raising issues of racial equality and injustice, but ultimately the problems with testing are less about the adequacy of tests than about the *uses* of testing. We not only need new theories and new or improved methods of assessing cognitive performance, but we also need a society better informed about the limits to which tests can usefully be put. Ultimately, the uses to which tests will be put are important social and political questions. Such questions cannot be answered by "technology" in testing alone.

SUMMARY

1. Assessments pervade modern life, and we have embraced psychological tests as technologies for improving the quality of our society.

2. Unfortunately, the public expects more of tests than they can provide; even when psychometrically sound, tests may be *misused*.

3. Accuracy, or validity, of test usage may be compromised in several ways. One problem arises when testers go beyond the information given to draw inferences about future behavior in different situations.

4. Another accuracy problem stems from our readiness to attribute behavior to traits instead of to situational factors—the fundamental attribution error.

5. Other errors in test interpretation arise from human biases in information processing such as the confirmatory bias, illusory correlations, and the overreliance on vivid memories that may be misapplied.

6. Even when tests yield accurate and unbiased information about people, we still have to ask whether such information is useful.

7. Sometimes tests are not useful because we make more errors of prediction with the test than without it if the baserate of the characteristic being tested for differs much from 50 percent. The "costs" of errors must be considered.

8. Sometimes tests *appear* to be more useful than they really are, because people (and testers) are susceptible to the Barnum effect, believing that vague, general, meaningless interpretations really yield something of value.

9. Even if tests are accurate and useful, it is possible that they may still be used in ways that are unfair or unethical.

10. Fairness—whether tests lead to discrimination, social inequity, or injustice—is an important issue. Fortunately, there are some legal protections, but this issue must be faced continually.

11. Another ethical issue is privacy, which involves the questions of whether testing is voluntary and who controls the interpretation and storage of information.

12. A contemporary issue of ethics and privacy arises with the use of computers to score and interpret tests. There are few safeguards to guarantee the validity of such interpretations and the ways in which the information may be used.

13. Test usage also raises the question of the effects of testing on people, including any labels or classifications that arise from assessment.

14. Standardized IQ and achievement tests are commonplace in the schools. There may be some advantages to such testing if it leads to improvements in instruction for children.

15. However, the use of standardized testing typically results in higher scores for white children than for minority-group children and may contribute to a continuation of educational disadvantages if lower-scoring children are labeled and treated as less competent.

16. The observed differences between blacks and whites on IQ tests require careful analysis, and several explanations have been debated.

17. One argument is that standardized IQ tests are "biased" against black children, because these children have less exposure, practice, and interest in items that reflect middle-class, white experiences.

18. Studies of item content and attempts to develop culturally fair tests generally lead to the conclusion that this kind of bias does not account for most of the racial differences in IQ.

19. On the other hand, current IQ tests are highly tied to skills and content taught in schools, and this type of "bias" may fail to reflect the intellectual characteristics of culturally diverse groups.

20. The genetic argument for racial differences in IQ has proven to be weak, flawed both in research methods and in logical implications.

21. The environmental approach to the understanding of IQ differences emphasizes the disadvantages experienced by black children that may affect their intellectual development.

22. Instead of studies designed to indicate *which* explanation accounts for racial differences, we need more research on what factors affect what kinds of intellectual performance.

23. Above all, we cannot blame tests for the social inequities experienced by disadvantaged groups, nor can we expect tests to provide solutions to social problems. But we cannot ignore the role that tests have played in perpetuating such problems, either.

KEY TERMS

availability bias	fundamental attribution error	mainstreaming
Barnum effect	hereditarian fallacy	psychological tests
baserate	illusory correlation	second level inference
confirmatory bias	inference	third level inference
first level inference		

ADDITIONAL READING

Goldstein, G., and Hersen, M. (Eds.) (1984) *Handbook of psychological assessment.* Elmsford, NY: Pergamon Press.
This is an advanced-level book made up of chapters written by an expert in a particular major type of test or procedure. Each chapter reviews the research literature that supports the test and its uses, and identifies the test's strengths and weaknesses. The book includes chapters on adults and children.

Sundberg, N. D. (1977) *Assessment of persons.* Englewood Cliffs, NJ: Prentice-Hall.
This is an undergraduate-level, very readable text. It covers all of the major terms of psychological testing and includes examples and procedures.

17 Abnormal Psychology

WHAT IS ABNORMALITY?

There are many misconceptions and fears about psychological abnormality that are based on beliefs that it is a rare, bizarre, and dangerous condition that only affects other people. The term "abnormality" is unfortunate, because it implies that there are extreme, deviant behaviors that are readily defined in clear and readily agreed-upon ways. When we attempt to include all of the major psychological ways that people suffer or cause distress to others, a much broader term is needed, such as "dysfunctional behavior." Dysfunctional behavior is not rare, it is not usually bizarre, and it cannot be defined simply in terms of certain behaviors or with guidelines that remain constant and universally agreed upon by experts. Consider the following ways of defining psychological abnormality:

1. What we call mental illness is sometimes equated with bizarreness—images of a strangely dressed man giving an unintelligible speech in the park, a disheveled "bag lady" carrying on a conversation with an unseen speaker, a young man who believes that the KGB is trying to extract secrets from his brain in collusion with his family and co-workers. It is certainly true that such extreme departures from what we call reality may be symptoms of a serious mental illness termed a *psychosis*; however, the vast majority of problems that cause people to seek psychological treatment do not involve bizarre behaviors. In addition, not all conditions that produce departures from reality are considered psychopathological. Fasting or extreme fatigue may produce hallucinatory experiences. Religious practices may also produce visions, and virtually no one would label as psychopathological a belief in special powers or speaking in "tongues."

2. Another standard that has sometimes been applied to define "abnormality" is statistical rareness. By this definition, typical, average behaviors would be considered normal and infrequent behaviors abnormal. Obviously, to some extent dysfunctional behaviors are less common than adaptive behaviors, but reliance on rareness as a definition is far too restrictive. For one thing, much that is unusual and infrequent is also highly desirable—sainthood and artistic genius, for example. Also, attempting to be "normal" by strict conformity to the average may reflect rigidity and be a detriment to the goals of self-actualization that are currently prominent in contemporary American culture.

3. Personal discomfort and suffering are major factors that lead people to treatment, and they are, therefore, important indicators of dysfunctional behavior. Excessive and persistent worries, fears, preoccupations with unpleasant or disturbing thoughts, depression, and irritability are disruptive and painful, and may indicate psychopathological conditions. Yet, personal distress by itself is not at all a marker of abnormality; there are major forms of dysfunctional behaviors that are not necessarily accompanied by such states. Among these are antisocial personality disorders that may involve repeated acts of crime and violence without guilt or remorse, certain states of manic-depressive psychosis accompanied by euphoria and grandiosity, or substance-use disorders in which the consequences of excessive drug or alcohol use may be emphatically denied by the user.

4. Sometimes abnormality is equated with specific acts, as if it resides in the behavior itself. Abhorrent behaviors, such as murder,

Outrageous behavior is not in itself an indication of "abnormality." Sometimes it pays very well, as it does for Boy George.

incest, cannibalism, and genocide may be considered abnormal. Yet each of these events has occurred frequently under conditions and in contexts where the perpetrators justified the acts in terms of survival, or political and religious meanings. Whether we agree or not with the justifications, the events in context give them a meaning that is generally not attributed to individual abnormality. Even less atrocious behaviors, such as jumping off a cliff on a motorcycle or dressing up in the clothing of the opposite sex, are not inherently abnormal; depending on their contexts, and in certain situations, such behaviors may even be entertaining and profitable for those performing them.

Diagnostic Approach in a Cultural Context

If there are no universally agreed-upon standards for judging behavior as abnormal, then how do we know what abnormality is? Basically, we consider *abnormal behaviors* to be actions that are seen as disruptive to the individual or to others, based on judgments of the appropriateness of the behavior in the context in which it occurs. This is fundamentally a culturally determined judgment, reflecting historical, political, and moral considerations. Judgments are made about the appropriateness or deviance of particular acts for someone of a particular age, sex, and culture in a particular setting. Three-year-olds or persons of particular ethnic or religious backgrounds may be permitted to believe that spirits or hobgoblins visit them in the dark, but others may not. Social norms dictate that certain behaviors that may be appropriate during fraternity rush may not be practiced in church, and if you fail to honor this distinction you might be judged to be suffering from some abnormality. Women are permitted more latitude in the expression of certain behaviors, such as dependency on others and emotional expressiveness, than men are; highly dependent men or highly emotional men might be judged to have psychological problems that would not be attributed to women with the same traits.

Political and historical factors also shape the definitions of dysfunctional behavior. A decade ago or less, little attention was paid to sexual abuse of children within families, in part because political and social norms depicted parents as "owners" of their children. At that time, family privacy took precedence over child protection. Changes in attitudes have led to concern for the mental health of both the victims and the perpetrators. Until fairly recently, homosexuality was considered to be a form of mental illness; its new status is a clear reflection of recent social and political change. Political changes in the 1960s and 1970s led to increased tolerance for individual variation, including sexual preference. Changes in such attitudes, along with the lack of scientific evidence indicating that there is any greater psychological disturbance among homosexuals than others, led members of the American Psychiatric Association to vote for the omission of homosexuality as a disorder.

Finally, it should be noted that our views of what is abnormal or dysfunctional have come to encompass not only personal distress and distress to others, but also to reflect people's changing expectations of what constitutes a good life. Political stability and economic prosperity have brought about an emphasis in this culture not just on health and the meeting of basic needs, but also a concern with personal satisfaction, enjoyment, and fulfillment. Individuals may function appropriately in their families, workplace, and community but nonetheless feel unfulfilled and dissatisfied. True mental health, therefore, may seem more elusive than ever, and definitions of normality and abnormality can be expected to change with the times.

Consider the following brief, clinical cases. There are differences in how bizarre the behavior is in terms of departure from reality in each case and in how personally distressed the individuals feel. Yet, Sally, Joe, and Julie all display behaviors that are judged to be inappropriate to the situation, and their behaviors are dysfunctional to themselves and cause distress to people around them. These are the hallmarks of the kinds of problems that will be discussed in this chapter.

———

Sally is an attractive, physically vigorous 67-year-old, who was widowed some years ago. She is financially comfortable, and in the five years since her retirement, she has actively pursued various pastimes. Two months ago her pet dog died, and her initial grief has now become deep depression, as she finds no motivation or energy to get out of bed in the morning or take care of personal and household tasks. She has lost ten pounds, sleeps poorly, and voices the thought that her life is empty and without purpose. Her friends are fearful that she will commit suicide and have brought her to the hospital for treatment.

Joe was always rather quiet as a boy—a child who had few friends and seemed to prefer solitary activities. He did reasonably well in school, and after graduation went off to college where he lived in the dorm. Within several weeks, his parents received a call from his roommate who reported that Joe was behaving oddly, refusing to leave his room because of fears that someone was after him, and complaining that the radio was being used to put thoughts into his head. He had not attended any of his classes and would become angry and resistant when the roommate tried to reason with him.

Julie recently turned 14 and became increasingly preoccupied with wanting to lose what she called her "baby fat." She followed extremely restrictive diets and exercised almost continuously in order to lose weight. Even in the classroom she would try to do isometric exercises sitting at her desk, and after school she spent nearly all her time running, weight lifting, or reading books on nutrition and diet. Although she has lost many pounds and now looks gaunt and unhealthy, she believes that she is still too fat. At first her mother went along with her efforts to diet, but increasingly the whole family became concerned with her excessive and seemingly unrealistic preoccupation with weight. They are fearful about her general health.

———

WHO IS AFFECTED?

The likelihood of having a disorder that conforms to current diagnostic standards (not including phobia) during one's lifetime is around 25 percent, based on interviews conducted in several U.S. cities with randomly selected adults (Robins et al., 1984). This does not include individuals who may have significant symptoms that do not fully meet diagnostic criteria or who have rarer disorders that were not covered in the interview. And, if common phobias are included, the figures range from 29 percent to 38 percent across different cities, as shown in Table 17–1. Clearly, "abnormal behavioral" is not something that only happens to other people. The most common disorders found in the community surveys were phobias, alcohol abuse or dependence, and major depression or chronic low-level depression (Myers et al., 1984). These will be discussed in later sections.

TABLE 17–1 Lifetime Prevalence Rates of Selected Disorders

As measured in interviews in three U.S. cities, the likelihood of having a disorder that conforms to current diagnostic standards (including common phobias) is between 29 and 38 percent. N refers to the number of people interviewed.

Disorders	New Haven, % 1980–1981 (N = 3,058)	Baltimore, % 1981–1982 (N = 3,481)	St. Louis, % 1981–1982 (N = 3,004)
Any disorder covered	28.8	38.0	31.0
Any disorder except phobia	24.9	23.9	26.2
Any disorder except substance-use disorders	19.3	29.5	18.6
Substance-use disorders	15.0	17.0	18.1
Alcohol abuse/dependence	11.5	13.7	15.7
Drug-abuse/dependence	5.8	5.0	5.5
Schizophrenic/schizophreniform disorders	2.0	1.9	1.1
Schizophrenia	1.9	1.6	1.0
Schizophreniform disorder	0.1	0.3	0.1
Affective disorders	9.5	6.1	8.0
Manic episode	1.1	0.6	1.1
Major depressive episode	6.7	3.7	5.5
Dysthymia	3.2	2.1	3.8
Anxiety/somatoform disorders	10.4	25.1	11.1
Phobia	7.8	23.3	9.4
Panic	1.4	1.4	1.5
Obsessive-compulsive	2.6	3.0	1.9
Somatization	0.1	0.1	0.1
Eating disorders			
Anorexia	0.0	0.1	0.1
Personality disorder			
Antisocial personality	2.1	2.6	3.3
Cognitive impairment (severe)	1.3	1.3	1.0

Source: After Robins et al., 1984.

It was once thought that psychological disorders were predominantly a female problem, but the recent surveys of rates of disorders among randomly selected people in average communities (called epidemiological surveys) indicate about equal rates for men and women. Nevertheless, there appear to be sex differences in the kinds of disorders men and women display. More men report antisocial personality disorders and alcohol and drug abuse, while more women report depression and anxiety disorders. Psychiatric diagnoses are not evenly distributed across different ages. The age group 25–44 generally has the highest rates of disorders, with the older persons showing fewer disorders (Myers et al., 1984; Robins et al., 1984). The results can also be interpreted to suggest that younger persons today are showing more disorders than the same age groups did in years past.

There seems to be a relationship between education level and disorders, in that college graduates have lower rates of diagnoses (Robins et al., 1984). Rural residence is also associated with lower rates, while inner-city environments have the highest rates. These findings are not surprising, given that many disorders seem to be associated with stressful conditions.

MAJOR THEORIES CONCERNING THE CAUSES OF ABNORMAL BEHAVIOR

Just as there is no single definition of psychological abnormality, there is also no single accepted theory of the causes of abnormality in general, or even of the causes of most specific disorders. Three predominant theories have emerged in the twentieth century—the biological model, the psychodynamic model, and the learning model. Each of these has spawned various offshoots and modifications over time. Although advocates may be found who believe that their approach alone explains a particular disorder, in practice most psychologists attempt to integrate aspects of several models into "biopsychosocial" theories.

The Biological or Medical Model

The biological perspective springs from a tradition that is centuries old, with an emphasis on genetic, constitutional, or biochemical abnormality that affects emotions, beliefs, and behaviors. The term *medical model* encompasses two meanings: actual biological causation and an analogy drawn to medicine using terms such as symptoms, disease, illness, diagnosis, underlying causes, and cure. Adherents to theories of biological causation might point to Sally in our case studies as the victim of defective neurotransmitter action in the brain, which may be genetically transmitted and in Sally's case has produced major depression. The cases of Joe and Julie might be viewed as reflecting different neurochemical imbalances specific to schizophrenia and anorexia nervosa, respectively. Research on all major systems of the body has been vigorously pursued over the last few decades, and recently there has been a strong focus on the highly complex interactions of neurotransmitter substances in the brain that seem to affect mood, perceptions, and judgment. Also, as we shall see, genetic studies have frequently determined that major forms of psychopathology are concentrated in the generations of certain families, detectable even when children are raised apart from their biological parents. The validity of biological models has also received support from the sometimes successful use of medications in reducing symptoms of psychopathology, although strictly speaking, just because a medical treatment works does not mean that there was a medical cause for the problem in the first place.

Psychodynamic Theories of the Causes of Psychopathology

Freud's theory, including personality development, psychic determinism, and unconscious motivation, represents the most influential model of psychopathology that is focused on individual psychological factors. As discussed in Chapter 14, conflicts between competing instincts or needs within the individual set the stage for psychological problems if the developing child is unable to resolve the conflicts, or if the individual resorts to excessive use of ego defense mechanisms to deal with anxiety resulting from conflicts. The nature of the conflicts and the ways that they may be expressed reflect the stage of development that the child was in at the time the conflicts occurred. Experiences that symbolically recreate unresolved conflicts may give rise to maladaptive behaviors that can only be understood in terms of the earliest periods of life, when the original conflicts arose. Over the decades, many influential proponents of Freud's general model have downplayed his initial emphasis on biological instincts and the intrapsychic structure, but more general emphasis remains on the quality of psychological development and functioning in the child, including the impact of relations with the parents.

To see how psychodynamically oriented psychologists might view psychopathology, consider the case histories once again. Sally's loss of her beloved pet may be viewed as symbolizing other critical personal losses, especially in childhood, in which conflicting feelings about the person who was lost may have led to the defense of turning inward the angry and aggressive but unacceptable feelings, resulting in depression. Joe's paranoid fears of being persecuted and controlled by others may be thought to reflect a projection of his anxiety onto an external source; by fearing "threat" from others, he may represent his feelings as a reaction to a real danger, and thereby avoid the painful recognition of unacceptable sources of conflict, such as homosexual feelings toward his roommate. Similarly, the psychodynamic view of Julie's eating disorder may emphasize her unconscious and irrational efforts to deny her developing sexuality by removing outward physical signs of femininity. In each case, there are several psychodynamic interpretations, some focusing on intraindividual conflict, others focusing on dynamics within the families or social situation as a whole, and still others emphasizing the quest for maintaining feelings of self-regard that may depend excessively on relationships with others or on success in achieving some highly valued goals.

The Learning Model of Psychopathology

Learning, or behavioristic, approaches to psychological dysfunction emphasize the relationship of the individual to the environment—

specifically, to those aspects of the environment that provide rewards or models for behavior. From this point of view, maladaptive behaviors are seen as learned behaviors maintained by their reinforcing consequences or failures to learn adaptive and appropriate behaviors for certain contexts. Principles of classical conditioning might be invoked to explain extreme fear and phobic responses following a traumatic experience with the stimulus. Operant conditioning might be cited to explain that a child's disruptive conduct in the classroom is maintained by the attention it receives, and observational learning might be suggested to clarify why adolescent and adult children of alcoholics frequently become alcoholics themselves, or why shy children are often the offspring of shy parents.

In the case examples presented, Sally's depression might be viewed as her response to the withdrawal of the highly positive reinforcers provided by her pet; alternatively, the emphasis might be the extent to which she has failed to acquire a wide array of skills for coping with stress and loss, such as turning to friends or to some meaningful occupation that could provide positive experiences. Joe's problems at college could be viewed as an extreme lack of the normal skills that are necessary to adapt to the major changes of moving away from home, living independently, and making friends in a new environment. Another learning-theory perspective might emphasize the learning of the "sick role" as an escape from the responsibilities of adult, independent living. Julie's anorexia nervosa might be viewed as excessive adherence to our current cultural emphasis on dieting and slimness.

A variant of behavioral approaches that has become influential in the past decade is the *cognitive model of psychopathology*. This model developed in part because of dissatisfaction with some of the shortcomings of the strict behavioral model, which seemed to focus on overt behaviors to the neglect of people's thoughts and interpretations of their behaviors. Proponents of the cognitive model argue that individual interpretations, not literal environmental contingencies, shape the learning that takes place. Thus, it is important to know not only what individuals do in certain situations but also how they *think* about the situation. Seen in this way, Sally's depression may stem from the meaning she attaches to the death of her pet: "I'm alone and always will be alone with no one to love or love me the way my dog did." Julie's excessive dieting may be explained partly by her distorted belief that she must continually lose weight in order to be thin enough.

The Stress-diathesis Approach

As noted earlier, with the exception of extreme adherents to each view presented, most psychologists conform to the viewpoint that forms of psychopathology have multiple and interacting causes cutting across different models. An especially influential viewpoint is the *stress-diathesis perspective*. A *diathesis* refers to a predisposition or vulnerability to develop a disorder, and this may be biological or psychological in nature. Only when the vulnerable person encounters a *stress* would a disorder appear. Different theories have different definitions of the nature of stress and the magnitude that may be required to activate a dysfunctional reaction. Unfortunately, the stress-diathesis viewpoint does not have the status of a theory, because for the most part, specific predictions about the nature and magnitude of stress and the magnitude of vulnerability have not been stated. Nevertheless, it seems that many people who might be thought to have genetic predispositions to major psychopathology or who have been exposed to environmental experiences that might make them highly vulnerable, do not break down. The majority of individuals who face major stressful conditions do not show significant problems, but some persons exposed to seemingly minor stressors do show dysfunctional reactions, suggesting that they were vulnerable in some way. A stress-diathesis approach seems to offer a framework for integrating both biological and psychological factors to better understand the causes of disorder.

FORMS OF PSYCHOPATHOLOGY

Terminology and Diagnosis

The terms *neurosis* and *psychosis* are included in most people's vocabularies but are often used incorrectly. Freud's original use of the word *psychoneurosis* referred descriptively to specific kinds of symptoms in persons whose reality contact was otherwise intact and to a theory of how the symptoms originated in unconscious conflict. Eventually the term became extremely vague in public usage, often referring merely to mild forms of disorder. Because of confusion in how the word was used, and also because of considerable professional disagreement about its scientific usefulness, the term *neurosis* is no longer part of the official diagnostic terminology. *Psychosis* continues to be a broad descriptive category of disorders that entail failure of reality testing—failure that usually involves perceptual, cognitive, and language disturbances.

Diagnosis of psychological disorders is accomplished with the application of specific criteria catalogued in the *Diagnostic and Statistical Manual of Mental Disorders*, Third Edition-Revised (DSM-IIIR, 1987), prepared by the American Psychiatric Association (a taxonomy of mental disorders outlined in DSM-IIIR appears in the first chapter of this textbook, Table 1-2). Each successive revision of this manual contains changes based on alterations in knowledge and practice; the intention is to provide useful and reliable guidelines for diagnosis without assuming that each category is distinct and specific or that people fit neatly and perfectly into a single category. The current version represents a considerable advance in reliability over previous editions, largely because it is based on *descriptions* of behaviors that require relatively little inference about the meaning or causality of a symptom. Explicit directions are given about the numbers and types of symptoms that must be observed in order for a specific diagnosis to be assigned. The manual also includes instructions on how to distinguish one diagnosis from other diagnoses that might be similar.

Another feature of the current system for making diagnoses is that it is **multiaxial**. That is, diagnoses may contain information on five different dimensions in order to give complete characteristics of an individual that will be useful in understanding and treating him or her. Axis I describes the current mental disorder. Axis II describes any long-standing pervasive disorder of personality. Sometimes these disorders of personality are themselves the problem requiring treatment. Axis III describes physical disorders and conditions. Axis IV describes the severity of stressful circumstances that the person may be facing currently, and Axis V describes the highest level of adaptive functioning that the individual may have been capable of in the past year. In the sections to follow, we will describe only Axis I disorders, but in actual clinical practice, all five axes might be useful to decide on a course of treatment.

Why Make Diagnoses?

On the positive side, reliable use of valid diagnoses improves the ability of professionals to communicate and share scientific and practical information. Also, diagnostic precision can facilitate the appropriate treatment of specific disorders and is essential for the scientific investigation of disorders. There may be unfortunate side effects of diagnosis, however, such as *stigmatization*. People often react negatively and fearfully when someone is known to have a mental disorder. Such labels also may affect how people feel about themselves. As an analogy to physical illness, the medical model of diagnosis implies that the person "has" a disorder, whereas critics of the medical model argue that many psychological disturbances represent temporary "problems in living," not at all like physical disease. The problem of stereotypes and reacting to people as a category rather than as individuals is certainly not unique to the field of mental health, but professionals in this field need to be continually sensitive to the implications and responsibilities of diagnosing in this regard. Nevertheless, a reliable system of diagnosis seems to be necessary to the task of treating and understanding psychopathology.

MAJOR FORMS OF PSYCHOLOGICAL DISORDERS

In the sections that follow, many of the most frequent forms of psychopathology are briefly discussed. Not everything that appears in DSM-IIIR can be presented, however, due to limitations of space.

Schizophrenia

The most common form of psychosis is *schizophrenia*, a disorder that strikes about 1 percent of the population. Because schizophrenia commonly involves bizarreness, it is often what people think of when they picture "mental illness." While not all schizophrenic behavior is bizarre, it always involves a severe impairment of functioning and a departure from realistic forms of perception, thinking, and communication. To be diagnosed as schizophrenic, an individual must display delusions, hallucinations, or disturbed thinking and communication, and the symptoms must last at least six months, with an accompanying deterioration from a previous level of functioning in work, social relations, or self-care.

    Delusions are major disturbances in the content of thought that have no basis in reality. Delusions of persecution may involve the belief that others are spying on one or planning to do one harm; delusions of reference are beliefs that events, objects, or others have unusual significance (usually negative significance) for the person. Typical delusions of reference experienced by a schizophrenic individual might include a belief that people are watching you, that the professor is lecturing about you, and that songs on the radio are special messages about you. Other common delusions in schizophrenia include *thought broadcasting* (the belief that one's thoughts are being broadcast so that others can hear them), *thought insertion* (the belief that ideas not one's own are being placed into one's mind), or beliefs that one's feelings, behaviors, or thoughts are not one's own, but are being controlled by outside forces.

Hallucinations are perceptual abnormalities. Most frequently, they involve auditory perceptions, such as hearing voices that speak to one and comment on one's behavior. Somewhat less commonly, other sensory experiences occur, such as sensations of tingling or burning. Crawling sensations inside the body have also been reported. Occasionally, visual, taste, and smell hallucinations occur too, but they are less common.

Thought disturbances refer to various kinds of peculiar patterns of speech and thinking that include incoherence, loosening of associations, and an inability to stay on track. Sometimes speech is very garbled with new words and intended meanings given to words that cannot be followed by listeners; in other cases speech is more subtly vague and imprecise, making conversation difficult.

The actual occurrence of hallucinations, delusions, or thought disturbances may be relatively brief and intermittent. Not all schizophrenics display such symptoms, and those who do typically have periods of coherence. However, throughout the psychotic episode there are several additional characteristics that are fairly stable. These may include a blunted or flat affect in which the individual may seem blank and emotionless or an inappropriate affect in which emotional reactions do not fit the apparent situation. Also, there is often interpersonal withdrawal, a preference for solitary activity much of the time, and avoidance of interactions with others.

There are several subtypes of schizophrenia. *Disorganized schizophrenia* is marked by frequent incoherence, odd behaviors and mannerisms, extreme social withdrawal, and lack of systematized delusions. *Paranoid schizophrenia*, by contrast, is characterized primarily by delusions or hallucinations with persecution content or grandiosity. The person may have elaborate and coherent, although irrational, beliefs of being plotted against or of having special powers. Gross disorganization is relatively rare, and the person's language and behaviors may appear fairly normal, so that if the delusions are not acted upon, the impairment in functioning may be more minimal than for other schizophrenias. *Catatonic schizophrenia* is marked by extreme behavioral disturbance, which may involve stupor, rigidity of posture, or extreme and apparently purposeless activity. An example would be an individual who remains motionless and mute and needs to be guided by others. The category "undifferentiated type" refers to those whose behaviors include mixtures of symptoms that cannot be placed in any single subtype.

Schizophrenia often includes profound withdrawal from others.

The following case studies chronicle schizophrenic disorders for two different individuals.

———

I was teaching a course in abnormal psychology one year when I got a call from the university administration. "We have a problem with a student who is in your course, and we thought you might have some advice about how to handle this matter." The issue at hand, it turned out, was that Shirley was complaining that professors were lecturing about her or talking about her in classes, and that all the class members were in on it. In one class the professor had made a joke, and she thought it was really about her; in my case she thought one of the lectures was about her, and she was complaining to the university that I must have obtained her medical records and that her doctor and the rest of the class were in on part of the conspiracy. I recommended that the counselor talk to her and ask her permission to speak with her doctor, who could then be notified about her paranoid behavior and take appropriate steps to deal with the disruption her behavior was causing and with her distress.

The university counseling administrator subsequently notified me that Shirley would be withdrawing from classes. It turned out that she had been doing relatively well in classes for the first two terms, but during the present quarter she had become overwhelmed by her coursework and the stress of managing her household (she was an older student who had two adolescent children at home). As she became more stressed, she became more suspicious, until her delusions of reference became pronounced. Her family had become aware of the changes in her behavior and thinking, and her doctor had increased the dosage of an antipsychotic medication she took. This was her third psychotic episode, the last one having occurred some eight years before she enrolled in my class. In each case, Shirley experienced paranoid delusions and became angry and withdrawn but otherwise functioned reasonably well. She was relatively nonsymptomatic between episodes, although fairly isolated socially, and generally was a bit distrusting and suspicious of others. The medications help to keep her stable, and she should be able to reenter the university next term if all goes well.

A different picture emerges of Raymond. On the advice of his court-appointed attorney, he is seeking psychotherapy because he recently assaulted his father's girl friend and is awaiting trial. He is 37 years old, rather disheveled in appearance, and rarely makes eye contact with the interviewer. A rather garbled description of the assault incident suggested that Raymond was muddled about what happened, seeming to confuse the woman with someone he had known in his past. The more the therapist probed, the odder the story: Raymond disclosed many concerns about women and about his sexual functioning, and stated that he believed that some women could control his sexual performance with their cigarette lighters. He was angry about this, and revealed that he believed that things would be better for him somewhere else. When questioned about what he meant, he was reluctant and evasive but finally stated that he expected to be taken to another planet by creatures he feels he has had contact with occasionally. As this delusion unfolded, Raymond showed little emotion and seemed to have only vague and somewhat inconsistent ideas about the other planet.

Raymond's court records suggested that he had been a loner and drifter for many years, often living for periods in parks and on the streets, working intermittently as a janitor. He had had trouble in school since junior high, often getting into fights with other boys, and he never graduated. Although he sometimes hung out with local delinquents and was involved in their escapades, he never really had friends and the other youngsters used to make fun of him because he seemed odd. He has been in and out of jail for minor offenses, but he has never been treated for psychological problems. His diagnosis would probably be chronic, undifferentiated schizophrenia.

Course of the Disorder Schizophrenia was once regarded as a lifelong disorder characterized by a degree of impairment that required institutionalization. Because of improvements in diagnosis and treatment, the picture is far more optimistic today, especially for certain kinds of patients. It is estimated that most schizophrenics experience a relatively *acute* onset, with a period of disorganization increasing over time until full-blown symptoms are observed. Often such symptoms seem to arise in response to some kind of personal crisis. To the extent that the person functioned relatively normally beforehand, with adequate adjustment socially, scholastically, and occupationally, the prognosis for recovery is fairly good. On the other hand, a slow, insidious onset, usually in adolescence, and "poor premorbid adjustment" in social and school functioning, may signal a relatively chronic course of schizophrenia.

Theories of the Causes of Schizophrenia In line with the general models for explaining the causes of abnormal behavior, we can break the causes of schizophrenia down into biological approaches and psychological approaches. There are many forms of organic psychosis in which profound alterations of consciousness, behavior, and thinking are induced by toxic substances, drugs, brain injuries, or disease. To the extent that such conditions have sometimes resembled schizophrenia, researchers have long speculated that the severe symptoms of schizophrenia must also be caused by some biological abnormality. There have been many such theories over the years, and today much interest is focused on aspects of neurotransmitters in the brain and on attention and information-processing deficits. An earlier theory was that schizophrenics produce a substance in their brains that is similar to hallucinogenic drugs; however, researchers have not been able to find evidence of such a process. More recently, attention has shifted to the possible excess of the neurotransmitter dopamine and its receptors. Research in this area is extremely complex and findings are open to other interpretations, so that investigators caution that a link between schizophrenia and biochemical abnormality has not definitely been found yet (Karson, Kleinman, & Wyatt, 1986).

Recent developments in computerized medical technology have led to studies of the structures of living brains of schizophrenics using brain imaging techniques. Research suggests that there may be some structural anomalies in the brains of at least some schizophrenics.

Presumably, if such abnormalities exist, the functioning of the brain would be impaired according to the nature of the abnormality.

Genetic studies of schizophrenia have provided suggestive evidence that the disorder may be genetically transmitted (see Figure 17-1). Twin studies have been conducted to determine whether biologically identical (monozygotic) twins are more concordant for schizophrenia than are less biologically similar (dizygotic) twins; such studies have found much higher rates of similarity in identical than fraternal twins, although results differ from study to study. Also, studies of mental illness in relatives of schizophrenics show much higher rates of schizophrenia than in the general population. Neither twin nor family studies, however, can rule out the effects of environment; for example, if schizophrenia were totally biological, both members of a set of identical twins would be schizophrenic if one twin was. Another type of genetic study involves examination of children who were adopted away from schizophrenic parents and raised by normal families. Complete adoption records in Denmark have made such research possible, and the results suggest higher rates of schizophrenia in such offspring, even when raised by normal adoptive parents. Although there continues to be controversy about the methods and conclusions of genetic studies, there is consensus that both heredity and environment probably play some role in schizophrenia (Gottesman & Shields, 1976; Kety, Rosenthal, Wender, & Schulsinger, 1976).

The learning and psychodynamic theories have not been as comprehensive for schizophrenia as for less severe types of dysfunction. However, two of their variations provide psychological approaches that have attracted recent attention: family environment research and life stress research. Studies of disturbed family interactions in schizo-

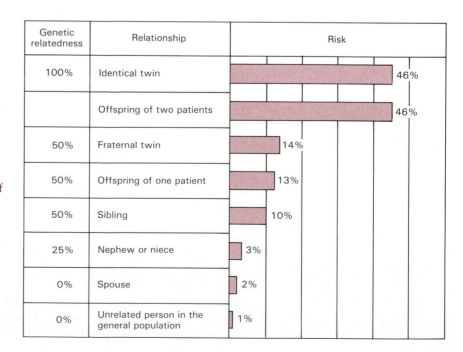

FIGURE 17–1 Lifetime Risk of Developing Schizophrenia
Genetic studies of schizophrenia suggest that it might be inherited, since the risk of developing schizophrenia correlates with how closely a person is genetically related to a schizophrenic person. It is clearly not a totally inherited disorder, however, and environmental factors appear to play a role also. (After Coon, 1986)

Genetic relatedness	Relationship	Risk
100%	Identical twin	46%
	Offspring of two patients	46%
50%	Fraternal twin	14%
50%	Offspring of one patient	13%
50%	Sibling	10%
25%	Nephew or niece	3%
0%	Spouse	2%
0%	Unrelated person in the general population	1%

phrenia have a long history and have resulted in theories such as the "schizophrenogenic mother" (a mother whose behaviors cause schizophrenia in her children), double-bind communication patterns (a parent conveying conflicting information to the child in a highly confusing way), and other disruptive family interactions. Although none of these approaches has been confirmed as a comprehensive theory of schizophrenia, clinicians repeatedly find maladaptive interpersonal relationships in the families of schizophrenics. Recently, researchers have identified qualities of family relationships that appear to predict schizophrenic relapse with a remarkably high rate of accuracy. Patients who were hospitalized and returned to family environments that displayed high scores on a variable termed "expressed emotion," consisting of criticism or overinvolvement by the spouse or parent toward the schizophrenic patient, had higher rates of relapse compared with schizophrenics in low-expressed-emotion families (Vaughn et al., 1982). While it is not established that negative family relations play a role in the development of schizophrenia, it seems clear that the quality of the psychological environment affects the course of the disease.

Other research has focused on additional stressors besides family relations in the onset of schizophrenia. Thus far, it does appear that many schizophrenic onsets are preceded by personally significant stressful life events—although to a lesser extent than has been found for major depression (Dohrenwend & Egri, 1981; Spring, 1981). Such findings are generally interpreted as events "triggering" a schizophrenic episode in someone who is already vulnerable, either biologically or psychologically. The individual whose feelings of self-worth, mastery, and the ability to function independently and cope with problems are poorly developed may find it very difficult to master major life transitions such as leaving home, forming romantic relationships, or becoming economically self-sufficient.

Affective Disorders

Affective, or mood, disorders have attracted considerable attention from researchers in the past 15 years, leading to major changes in diagnosis, treatment, and understanding of their causes. This extraordinary outpouring of interest was prompted in part by the sheer magnitude of the problem of depression; it is sometimes termed the common cold of psychological problems. Community surveys in the U.S.

Because of their sensitivity to feelings of failure and rejection, depressed people do not need friends like Lucy.

Loss of pleasure in usual activities, low energy, and decreased motivation are common symptoms of depression.

and Europe that have used the most current diagnostic methods have found that the chances of experiencing a clinically significant depression in one's lifetime are between 8–12 percent for men and 20–26 percent for women (Boyd & Weissman, 1981). Questionnaire surveys of depressive symptoms in the U.S. have generally found that at any given moment, 15–20 percent of the population acknowledges significant depressive symptoms (Boyd & Weissman, 1981). The vast majority of depression, however, goes untreated.

Depression is a term that refers variously to a mood state that may last for moments, hours, or a few days, and to a syndrome that defines a clinical entity. Mood depression is a normal response experienced by most people when they have suffered a loss, failure, disappointment, or some other major life event. For example, "maternity blues," a condition lasting 24–48 hours after the birth of a child, has been estimated to affect 50–80 percent of mothers. Such common and normative reactions are not the subject of this chapter. A *major depressive episode*, however, consists of a negative mood that persists most of the time for at least two weeks, accompanied by several other significant changes from among the following: changes in appetite (eating more or eating less), sleeping more or sleep disturbance, observable changes in activity level (agitated or slowed down), loss of pleasure in usual activities, loss of energy, negative feelings about the self, recurrent thoughts of death or suicide, and cognitive impairment such as diminished concentration, poor memory, and indecisiveness. (For a discussion of the extreme despair that may be brought about by depression, see the box entitled "Suicide.") Major depressive episodes nearly always cause some impairment of functioning, disrupting the quality of relationships with formerly close family and friends and making the performance of work or educational tasks difficult, if not impossible. A severely depressed person may be unable to get out of bed or to perform basic self-maintenance tasks. During major episodes of depression, the person does not usually lose contact with reality, although distortions of thinking clearly occur. *Psychotic* depression, which usually involves hallucinations or delusions with depressive themes of guilt, unworthiness, and the like, occurs more rarely.

Among the behavioral, somatic, and cognitive symptoms that accompany dysphoric mood, the characteristics of depressed thinking have been especially intriguing. Indeed, so pronounced are the negative interpretations of the self, the environment, and the future, that

Suicide is sometimes a response to feelings of hopelessness—a belief that bad situations will never improve.

♦ SUICIDE

SUICIDE RATES AND PREDICTORS. The rate of suicide is usually stated as 1 in 10,000, but these figures undoubtedly underestimate the true rate, since officials sometimes are reluctant to label a death as suicide because of the stigmatization of the family. This may be especially true where there is some ambiguity about whether the death could have been accidental. Suicide is the seventh leading cause of death in the U.S. Rates of suicide *attempts* are much higher; possibly one person in a hundred makes such an attempt at some point in his or her life, and thoughts of wishing to die have probably been experienced by the majority of people. Despite the widespread experience of suicide acts and thoughts, however, some groups are more likely to commit suicide than others.

SEX DIFFERENCES. Women are three times as likely to make a suicide attempt as men are, but men are three times more likely to actually succeed in committing suicide. Thus, 70 percent of suicide deaths are male. This may be due partly to the lethality of methods, since men are more likely to use a gun, while women are more likely to use pills. It may also have to do with the use of suicide attempts as an effort to communicate pain and distress, which may be more common for women than for men.

AGE DIFFERENCES. More than half of all suicides are committed by persons over 45, with the age group 55–64 at greatest risk. However, these figures may be changing as we note with alarm the apparent increase in rates among younger people. The rate of suicide deaths among adolescents and young adults is now double the figure of ten years ago. Although children's rates of suicide remain relatively low compared to other age groups, there has been a 300 percent increase in the 10–14 year-old group from 1955 to 1975, and threats and attempts are apparently increasing (Pfeffer, 1981). College students also appear to be a group at increased risk for suicide, with rates twice as high as for nonstudents of the same age.

MARITAL AND SOCIOECONOMIC STATUS. In general, marriage seems to be a protective factor against suicide, with highest rates of death among the divorced and then among the widowed. There is some evidence that suicide is most frequent among the highest and the lowest socioeconomic groups. Also, it is more common in urban areas than rural regions. San Francisco has one of the highest rates in the country, and it is thought that this reflects its unique sociodemographic characteristics (high rates of older, single, urban males, and high rates of alcoholism).

WHY DO PEOPLE COMMIT SUICIDE? A large proportion of people committing suicide appear to have been suffering from some psychiatric disorder, although the actual percentages are a matter of debate. It is clear that many people who commit suicide have been depressed (or suffer from manic-depressive disorder). A common thread in many suicides appears to be hopelessness, a feeling that things will never change, that the future is as bleak and depriving as the present—a view that may be induced by depression or by adverse circumstances or both (Kovacs, Beck, & Weissman, 1975). To the extent that a person experiences a loss or some conflict that they feel is impossible to overcome, they may view suicide as an escape from an intolerable situation. The problems may be compounded by personal characteristics, such as those of a college student raised to have very high expectations and aspirations that cause undue pressure, or those of a person with poor health that depletes one's sense of ability to cope with adversity. Alcohol or drug use may impair judgment or lower inhibitions and render an individual unable to cope with situations that they might otherwise have handled, albeit with some difficulty. Being single may increase one's sense of isolation and despair. Despair, bleakness, and hopelessness are recurring themes in suicidal thinking. As Alvarez (1972) writes in his book on the experience of suicide,

> a suicidal depression is a kind of spiritual winter, frozen, sterile, unmoving. The richer, softer, and more delectable nature becomes, the deeper that internal winter seems, and the wider and more intolerable the abyss which separates the inner world from the outer. Thus, suicide becomes a natural reaction to an unnatural condition. Perhaps this is why, for the depressed, Christmas is so hard to bear. In theory, it is an oasis of warmth and light in an unforgiving season, like a lighted window in a storm. For those who have to stay outside, it accentuates, like spring, the disjunction between public warmth and festivity, and cold, private despair (p. 257).

depression has sometimes been termed a disorder of thinking (Beck, 1967; Beck, Rush, Shaw, & Emery, 1979). A depressed person will characteristically magnify misfortunes, draw the worst possible conclusions, or expect dire consequences, as illustrated in Table 17–2. On the other hand, personal strengths and accomplishments are minimized or ignored: an A grade is interpreted as a sign of an easy exam or a "gift" from the professor. Intelligence and capability are seen as unimportant. The well-meaning urgings of friends and family are met with the belief that no activity will help, and that nothing will make a difference. While numerous studies have verified the negative thinking of depressed people, research also indicates that when the

---

TABLE 17–2   Examples of Depressive Thinking

Events	Thought
Boyfriend did not telephone	He is out with someone else. He will leave me. (If I lose him, I will die.)
Co-worker did not invite me to party	She does not like me. I do not have any friends. (No one likes me.)
Son's teacher wants a conference	It is my fault he is having trouble. (I have failed as a parent.)
I am still depressed	I should not be depressed. It is my own fault, I should be over this by now.
Relationship broke up	No one will ever love me. I am a failure at relationships.
Laid off job	I will never get another job. What's the point of trying?
Child has serious illness	God is against me. I will never be happy again.

person is no longer depressed, their interpretations and beliefs will return to normal (for example, see Hamilton & Abramson, 1983).

An episode of major depressive disorder is likely to go untreated if it is relatively brief and does not seriously impair functioning. However, a major depressive episode often lasts 6–9 months, and for many people it is a recurrent disorder (Goodwin & Jamison, in press). Persons with chronic, low-grade dysthymic disorder may be especially at risk for recurrent episodes of major depression, termed "double depression" (Keller, Lavori, Endicott, Coryell, & Klerman, 1983).

Clinical depression occurs at all ages. It was once believed for both cultural and theoretical reasons that children did not experience true depression, but although controversy continues, a common opinion today is that children do experience essentially the same symptoms of depression as adults. One study found that nearly 2 percent of a randomly sampled population of children met DSM-III criteria for

Significant depression affects people of all ages.

major depression (Kashani & Simonds, 1979), while large proportions of children in treatment for some psychiatric disorder, medical illness, or educational problem have also been found to meet diagnostic criteria for depression. Presumably the depression was obscured by the visibility of the other problems (Carlson & Cantwell, 1979; Kashani & Hakami, 1982; Weinberg, Rutman, Sullivan, Penick, & Dietz, 1973). Depression in the elderly is also recognized today as a problem that may have been obscured by physical symptoms and stereotypes about aging. In this group depression may contribute greatly to social dysfunction and lack of physical resilience (Stoudemire & Blazer, 1985). There is also a danger that older adults whose memory and vigor have been sharply impaired by depression may be misdiagnosed as senile, which is not reversible, instead of as suffering from a major depression, which is treatable.

It was formerly found that many episodes of major depression had onset in middle age, but most current surveys suggest that early adulthood is an especially high-risk age for depression. Surveys of college-age young adults, for example, report high rates of symptomatology (Goldberg, 1981). Indeed, there has been speculation that rates of depressive symptoms and disorders have increased in general and for young people in particular. It is possible that such increases are due simply to better methods of reporting and also to the increased "psychological-mindedness" of people that makes them acknowledge having symptoms that may have been denied in previous generations. However, a recent study suggests that the apparently increased rates of depression are real: interviews of the relatives of depressed patients showed increasingly higher rates of reported depression among persons born more recently, as illustrated in Figure 17–2. Also, the researchers found earlier ages for the onset of depression, with sharply increased rates of major depression among persons between 20 and 30 who were born after 1950 (Klerman et al., 1985). Although more research is needed to verify such results, it seems that depression, especially in young people, is increasing.

Community surveys of symptoms and records of persons in treatment for depression all indicate that more depression is reported or treated in women than men (Boyd & Weissman, 1981). One interpretation of the pattern is that women really *are* more depressed than men; females may be exposed to greater stress or may be more biologically vulnerable to depression than men are (Weissman & Kler-

FIGURE 17–2   Rates of Depression in Relatives of Depressed Patients   *In a study of male and female relatives of depressed patients, researchers found that those born more recently had higher rates of major depressive disorder (the years in the graphs indicate the period in which the relatives were born). These researchers speculate that younger people are showing more depression than did past generations. (After Klerman et al., 1985)*

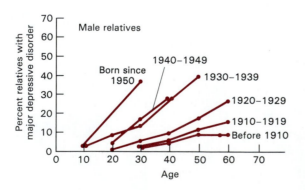

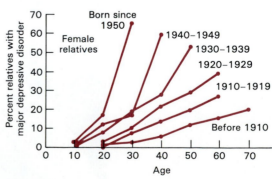

man, 1977). Another interpretation is that women are more likely to *report* symptoms of depression than men are because of the socialization that discourages men from expressing weak or vulnerable experiences. More women than men *seek help* for psychological problems. Recent research tends to support the idea that men are not necessarily less depressed than women. It now appears that as gender differences become narrower and men feel freer to admit psychological weaknesses, increased rates of depression in men are being seen. The Klerman study reported above, for instance, suggests some narrowing of sex differences in major depression for younger adults, and recent studies of depression in children find few significant differences in rates for boys and girls.

Manic-depressive Disorder   A more rare form of depression occurs as part of a bipolar affective disorder formerly called *manic-depression*. Unlike **unipolar depression**, in which the individual experiences only episodes of the depression syndrome, a **bipolar affective disorder** includes periods of mania as well as depression. Less than 1 percent of the population is estimated to experience a bipolar disorder in their lifetime (Boyd & Weissman, 1981), and men and women have about the same rates.

The mania that is the hallmark of bipolar disorders includes a distinct period of extremely elevated mood or irritability and several associated symptoms such as increased activity, pressure of speech, flight of ideas, inflated self-esteem, decreased need for sleep, distractibility, and excessive involvement in activities for which the potential for painful consequences is unrecognized by the individual. A case of mania will illustrate some of the characteristics of this disorder.

———

Randy's friends at first thought that he was just in a very good mood, since he seemed excited and talked more rapidly and loudly than usual, having long and animated chats with people he barely knew. It did not take long, however, to see that he was not just more extraverted and confident than usual—he was downright obnoxious and irritating—interrupting people and making inappropriate (but sometimes funny) jokes and puns. He seemed to have a hundred thoughts at once and could hardly stay on track to explain his latest ideas for a book he had decided to write that he was sure would make him famous. He stayed up most of the night writing, sleeping only a few hours. Some nights he did not come home and was seen in bars, apparently picking up women he did not know. He had a scheme to drive from Los Angeles to New York to take his partially completed book directly to a publishing house. He ran up several thousand dollars worth of bills for new clothing on his parents' charge card, explaining that he wanted to "look good" when he arrived in New York. He did not get very far; he was stopped for speeding near Las Vegas and when they attempted to arrest him, he tried to beat up one of the patrolmen, claiming that he had to get to New York with his book in order to prevent World War III. The patrolmen saw what Randy's friends had not quite seen yet, and they took him to the psychiatric ward in restraints.

———

Manic episodes often require hospitalization, and in the most extreme manic states, the person may display psychotic symptoms—delusions and hallucinations that reflect a grandiose belief in having special powers or of being a special person. There is enormous disruption, since the increased activity and poor judgment often lead to overspending, violations of the law, or engagement in activities that later prove destructive or embarrassing. *Hypomania* is a more mild form that does not include psychotic symptoms and involves less extreme levels of activity and engagement in harmful pastimes.

For the vast majority of persons with mania or hypomania, there is also a history of major depressive episodes, hence the term bipolar affective disorder. Many individuals experience somewhat regular cycles of mania following depression (or the reverse), but the majority have unique patterns that often involve only infrequent manic episodes and more frequent depressive episodes, interspersed with periods of relatively normal functioning (Goodwin & Jamison, 1984).

Theories of the Causes of Affective Disorders   Affective disorders have also been explained using biological models and psychological approaches. The unipolar-bipolar distinction appears to be useful not only in symptomatology and diagnosis, but also because it seems to reflect differences in the causes of the disorders (Depue & Monroe, 1978). Biological research has found suggestive evidence of possible genetic transmission of bipolar disorders. Patterns of inheritance suggest that monozygotic (identical) twins have higher concordance rates for bipolar disorder than for unipolar disorder and higher rates than those found among dizygotic (fraternal) twins. Also, there appear to be more cases of affective disorder in successive generations of families of bipolar patients than of unipolar patients. In a stricter test of the inheritance versus environment question, bipolar patients who were adopted as children were found to have biological parents with higher rates of affective disorders than the rates found in the adoptive parents (Mendlewicz, 1985). It has been estimated that between 15 and 35 percent of the relatives of patients with bipolar disorders will also have bipolar disorders, and probably even more will show unipolar disorders; the risk of having an affective disorder is estimated to be about 70 percent if both parents have bipolar disorders (Mendlewicz, 1985). Recently, a *genetic linkage study* examined all relatives in several generations of persons with bipolar disorders. The bipolar patients were known to have either color blindness or a specific enzyme deficiency, which are two inherited disorders for which the location of the genes on the X chromosome had already been discovered. It was found that members of these families who could be studied directly tended to show a covariation between one of the known genetically transmitted disorders and bipolar disorder. This covariation permitted the researchers to infer that a gene responsible for bipolar disorders is probably located near the known genes. This kind of *genetic marker* study provides suggestive evidence of at least one form of bipolar disorder that is inherited (Baron et al., 1987). Figure 17–3 presents a diagram of these relationships in one family.

Suggestive evidence for genetic transmission has also been reported for adoptees with unipolar depression who were raised by

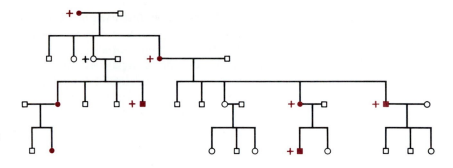

FIGURE 17–3 Genetic Transmission of a Bipolar Disorder *This is a diagram of a simulated family tree with four generations shown (squares are males, circles are females). Darkened figures represent manic-depression, and "+" indicates a genetically transmitted trait such as a blood enzyme type. Geneticists note that the two conditions seem to go together, and they already know the location of the "+" trait gene, so they speculate that the gene for manic-depression is carried near the same location.*

normal parents, but whose biological parents had depressive disorders (Wender et al., 1986). Persons with unipolar depression seem to have relatives with unipolar disorders but not bipolar, while bipolar patients have both (Weissman et al., 1984). Altogether, there appears to be solid evidence for the heritability of bipolar disorders and to a significant but lesser extent, evidence also for the heritability of unipolar depression. However, we do not know *what* defect or characteristic is actually transmitted or how some family members may fail to develop the disorder even if they carry the genes to do so.

Biological theories concerning the nature and causes of mood disorders have focused in the past decade on neurotransmitter activity in the brain. Early interest in relatively simple theories of norepinephrine and serotonin uptake have now given way to much more complex theories of interactions between functional amounts of neurotransmitters in the different systems and changes in neurotransmitter receptors (McNeal & Cimbolic, 1986). Instead of concern with just increases or decreases in the activity of neurotransmitter substances, a recent theory speculates that there is "dysregulation" of the noradrenergic system leading to variable, unstable, and desynchronized reactions (Siever & Davis, 1985). Such an approach might be compatible with interest in seasonal, light-related patterns of depression (that is, some people experience more depression in winter) and other associations of biological rhythms with moods and behaviors (Wehr & Goodwin, 1981). There is no shortage of intriguing biological theories concerning affective disorders, and the most promising work implicates brain chemistry and complex homeostatic processes. Refinements in knowledge and in methods for conducting such research are needed to fully test the theories.

Contemporary psychological theories concerning the origins of affective disorders emphasize intrapsychic or environmental factors in the onset of unipolar depressions. Cognitive theories have been especially prominent over the past decade and focus on the characteristic ways that individuals interpret events and evaluate themselves. Beck (1967; Beck et al., 1979) and Abramson, Seligman, and Teasdale (1978) have theorized that certain individuals may be vulnerable to depression because they tend to interpret events in ways that emphasize personal inadequacies, pessimism about the future, and inability to prevent or change misfortunes. Even if minor negative events occur, to the extent that people's views are negative, such thoughts are depressing and lead to the dysphoric mood and associated symptoms of depression. Although the cognitive models have stimulated a good deal of research and various treatment programs, and despite the fact that there is considerable evidence indicating that people do think negatively when depressed, the question of whether these approaches validly describe the *causes* of depression remains unanswered (Coyne & Gotlib, 1983; Hammen, 1985).

Research on the role of stressful life events in depression has been prolific in recent years. Common sense and research indicate that highly negative events may often lead to depression. Sexual abuse of children is associated with both short-term and long-term negative effects, including depression (Browne & Finkelhor, 1986), and for many women the birth of a child leads to clinically significant depression, especially if a woman is highly stressed as a result of being single or lacking supportive social relationships (Hopkins, Marcus, & Campbell, 1984). Most studies of depressive symptoms and clinical depression have found an increased incidence associated with stressful circumstances such as lower socioeconomic status, lack of a spouse or a lack of confiding relationships, and more frequent occurrence of stressful life events (Hirschfeld & Cross, 1982). Brown and Harris (1978) discovered that among women in London who were found to have an onset of major depression, 53 percent had experienced a major negative life event prior to the depression, a much higher rate than for women without depression. Despite these suggestive findings of a link between stressful events and depression, community surveys clearly show that most people who experience negative events do not become depressed, and only a portion of depression is preceded by stressful life events. Further work is needed to clarify the mechanisms that account for why some people become depressed and some do not.

Anxiety Disorders

It is estimated that between 2 and 4 percent of the population experience some form of a disorder marked by severe anxiety at some time during their life. Anxiety is like fear, except that the reaction is out of proportion to the actual threat, and sometimes the feared situation is not at all objectively threatening. The symptoms of anxiety include motor tension (jitteriness, trembling, nervous tension, muscle aches, and inability to relax), autonomic hyperactivity (sweating, increased heart rate, clammy hands, dry mouth, dizziness, upset stomach, diarrhea, and pallor), and thoughts that suggest worry, fear, rumination, and apprehension. Often, anxiety interferes with concentration and causes insomnia, impatience, and irritability.

There are several forms of anxiety disorders. *Phobias* are persistent and irrational fears of objects, events, or situations. Sometimes phobias are mild, and they occur frequently in childhood. As graphed in Figure 17–4, for instance, high proportions of younger children had fears of specific places, situations, or animals, and the rates of such fears appear to decline with age. The majority of childhood fears and phobias improve or disappear with time (Achenbach, 1985). Even in adulthood, phobias may not cause problems unless the person's life is drastically impacted in some way. For instance, many adults are afraid of speaking in public before an audience. Some may feel

People often think that psychological abnormality refers only to dangerous, bizarre, or rare conditions. They picture a mass murderer, such as Charles Manson, whose perverted reasoning has led to multiple deaths; a suicidal person entering the records with a leap from a tall building; or a strange-looking person talking to himself on the street corner.

COLOR PLATE 39

COLOR PLATE 38

Sometimes people conjure up images of institutionalized adults or children with rare adaptation disorders, such as the autistic child in Color Plate 39, or they may picture people who are harmless but have extremely deviant personal habits, such as an eating disorder (Color Plate 40), that set them apart from others.

COLOR PLATE 40

However, most psychological dysfunction afflicts very ordinary people in private, personally painful ways. Adults and children may have many kinds of fears, worries, and habits that are upsetting and that interfere with happiness and personal satisfaction. Whether the problem is a fear of heights, depression, extreme stress, child abuse, or Alzheimer's disease, perhaps one of the most difficult aspects of psychological difficulties is the impact they have on others. Family and friends are often affected. They try to help and often provide the only care the individual receives, but the help is sometimes not enough or the burden is too great. Dozens of lives are tragically impacted by the suffering caused by psychological dysfunction.

COLOR PLATE 41

COLOR PLATE 42

COLOR PLATE 43

COLOR PLATE 44

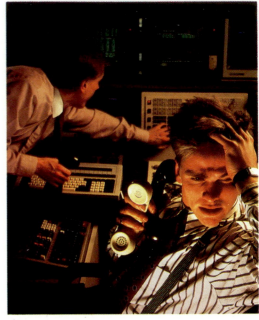

COLOR PLATE 45

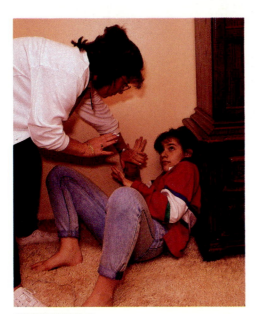

COLOR PLATE 46

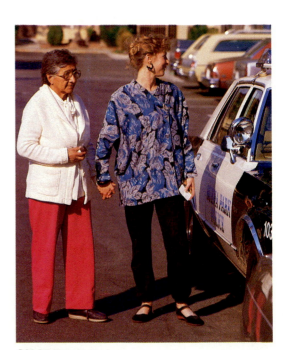

COLOR PLATE 47

COLOR PLATE 48

FIGURE 17–4   Rates of Fear among Children   *Parents' reports of their children's fears of animals, situations, or places (other than school) show that fears are common, especially in younger children. This is true both of children who are in treatment for various problems and of those who are not.* (After Achenbach, 1985)

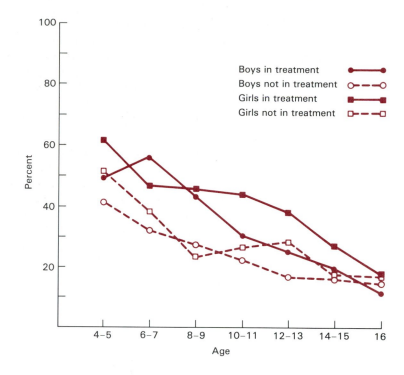

discomfort during electrical storms or when driving through dark tunnels, but none of these phobias has long-lasting effects. However, some phobias cause severe impairment: a businesswoman who cannot take business trips because of fear of flying might miss job opportunities; a man who fears driving on the freeway may be unable to enjoy an active social life in a large city; a person with a severe spider phobia may feel the need to seal her house and check her bedroom carefully every night. *Agoraphobia* involves a strong fear of public places, so that frequently an individual suffering from this disorder will not leave the home and becomes very constricted and dependent on others.

Anxiety states include panic disorder and generalized anxiety disorder. Panic disorder is characterized by frequent, often unpredictable panic attacks with feelings of terror, extreme physical discomfort, and occasionally a feeling of impending death. Such attacks are sometimes misinterpreted as heart attacks or other serious physical ailments. Generalized anxiety disorder includes persistent anxious mood and physical sensations of anxiety over at least a month's time.

Although these subtypes of anxiety disorder may represent different diagnoses, in reality there is considerable overlap. Many people with panic disorder develop fears of having such attacks again in the future, ultimately leading them to avoid public places for fear of having an attack and feeling out of control. In a recent study, persons whose first panic attacks were attributed by them to catastrophic medical problems (having a heart attack, going crazy, and so forth) were more likely to develop agoraphobia because they began to anticipate having other attacks. Individuals who correctly understood that they were having a psychological panic reaction were less likely to become agoraphobic or develop such patterns over a longer period (Breier, Charney, & Heninger, 1986). Breier and his colleagues reported that most of the patients with agoraphobia experienced concomitant chronic, generalized anxiety, and 70 percent also had histories of major depressive episodes.

Obsessive-compulsive disorder includes either recurrent, persistent thoughts or images that do not feel voluntarily controlled and are experienced as senseless or repugnant (obsessions), or compulsive behaviors. Compulsions are repetitive behaviors performed according to rituals and rules as a way of reducing or preventing some future undesirable event. Obsessive thoughts frequently take the form of violent images of killing someone or performing some repugnant act, of contamination by filth or germs, or of doubting that one has performed some action. Whereas a normal person might check to insure that the stove is turned off before leaving the house or might wash her hands to avoid germs, a person suffering from an obsessive-compulsive disorder would repeat such acts dozens of times. A man may be troubled by images of shooting his son even though he loves his child. Often obsessions and compulsions occur together; the woman who doubted she had turned off the gas might develop an elaborate checking ritual that she has to perform each time she leaves the house. A man who obsessively imagined he was contaminated with germs each time he touched a doorknob might initiate complex rituals for cleaning himself and avoiding doorknobs.

When individuals attempt to resist a compulsion, there is usually considerable anxiety. Even though people often perceive compulsive thoughts and behaviors to be irrational, they feel unable to resist. While there may be times when the intensity of the problem flares up, for many people this is a chronic disorder.

The following case study describes the behavior of one person who suffers from obsessive-compulsive disorder.

———

Mary is an attractive, pleasant-mannered young woman of 30, and to see her one would not suspect the nearly incapacitating problems she has been experiencing. At work, where she is an accountant, she is viewed as a perfectionist who does good work, but her boss is beginning to see that her attention to detail is getting in the way of broader goals, and that she spends so much time on minutiae that she barely meets work deadlines. Recently she has had to ask for extensions of time limits on important work. Mary's problems are even more apparent at home, but she protects her privacy so that few know what she faces. Because of fears of contamination, she has elaborate cleanliness rituals that require her to shower for up to three hours at a time, and then she must touch only "purified" objects and spaces. Because it takes her hours of scrubbing and cleaning to purify such areas of her apartment, most space is not clean enough for her and is extremely cluttered because she does not want to move any items into the "uncontaminated" areas. Also, she compulsively collects books, magazines, and newspapers but cannot discard them for fear of losing some important information. Therefore, the apartment is stacked with these items, dating back several years. The rooms are also piled high with papers and mail because she is so perfectionistic about how to sort such items that the task has seemed too massive to her after a hard day's work. Her income taxes are considerably overdue because it takes her so long to find all the right papers, and her meticulousness requires her to deduct every penny to which she feels entitled.

Post-traumatic stress disorder is a relatively recently identified disturbance of functioning that occurs following a psychologically traumatic event, especially those events that are outside the range of typical human experience, such as natural disasters, crimes of violence, or combat. Characteristically, the individual reexperiences the event in dreams, nightmares, and intrusive memories. There is a numbing of responsiveness in which the person reports feeling detached from others or disinterested in experiences that were formerly pleasurable. Victims of this disorder may feel emotionally tight, closed off, enraged, anxious, or depressed. There are frequently additional symptoms: hyperalertness or exaggerated startle reactions, disturbances of sleep, intensification of symptoms when exposed to events that resemble the original trauma, and feelings of guilt for having survived if others did not. Many victims of rape report such experiences and especially notable have been the reactions of Vietnam combat veterans, who may display delayed forms of the post-traumatic stress disorder. Since the Vietman War, we have seen that many former combat veterans have resorted to drugs, alcohol, or violence to curb the disturbing symptoms, and some have literally abandoned civilization and gone to the woods to live alone off the land to escape the sense of not fitting into our society after witnessing the traumas of war.

A uniquely childhood form of anxiety disorder, **childhood separation anxiety**, is characterized by excessive fear of separation from major persons to whom the child is attached beyond the level of attachment that is typical for the child's developmental stage. Such children are uncomfortable when away from home or their parents; they may avoid staying at friends' homes or traveling, and they may be reluctant or even refuse to go to school. The children are preoccupied by unrealistic worries that some danger will befall their parents, or that they will be separated from their parents in some way. Their fantasies and dreams often contain themes of separation. Although such intense distress may be common for brief periods in childhood, its persistence for more than two weeks is not typical.

Theories of the Causes of Anxiety Disorders   As one might expect, there are numerous biological explanations for anxiety disorders. There may be inborn bases for certain phobias that are specific to different species, and these may change over the maturational development of the individual. Young children are highly susceptible to phobias at certain ages but generally outgrow them, and the phobias that humans develop do not seem to be random. People are far more likely to be phobic about animals than bicycles, even though the actual harm done by the latter may be greater (Marks, 1977).

Childhood separation anxiety often takes the form of being fearful of going to school.

Certain researchers have focused on genetic transmission of anxiety disorders and have found that twin and family studies support the likelihood of an inherited tendency for these abnormalities, although the mechanism that may be inherited is unknown (Carey, 1982). A recent review of biological studies of obsessive-compulsive disorders also suggests that there may be genetic susceptibility, although in the absence of adoption studies, the role of psychological factors cannot entirely be ruled out. Turner, Beidel, and Nathan (1985) suggest that what may be inherited is a tendency toward chronic elevated cortical arousal, possibly leading to excessive worry and overresponse to threatening stimuli. Stressful circumstances may then trigger obsessive-compulsive behaviors as an attempt to reduce stress.

The interest in neurotransmitters and psychological states has led to studies of possible serotonin abnormalities in obsessive-compulsive disorders (Turner et al., 1985) and more generally to certain receptor sites in the brain that appear to be associated with anxiety symptoms and are also responsive to antianxiety medications (Paul & Skolnick, 1981). Studies of biological abnormality in anxiety disorders are expanding rapidly to keep up with new developments in techniques and theories, but so far a definitive role for biological causation has not been established.

Anxiety disorders form a part of Freud's original concept of neuroses, and therefore psychodynamic formulations have been prominent over the decades. Such interpretations typically view anxiety as a response to psychic conflict. A phobia, for instance, would typically be analyzed for its meaning as a symbol of the underlying internal conflict. Obsessions and compulsions are represented in psychoanalytic theory as excessive defenses against intrapsychic conflict, expressed symbolically.

Learning-theory approaches, on the other hand, argue that maladaptive learning experiences are at the root of anxiety disorders. A phobia, for instance, might have been acquired as a conditioned fear reaction, and phobic avoidance is reinforced by fear reduction. Obsessive-compulsive rituals may also be reinforced because of anxiety reduction. Failure to learn adaptive ways of reducing stress and tension may contribute to generalized anxiety and panic. Observational learning of both avoidance reactions and negative attitudes about certain objects or events may facilitate anxious reactions. It has been seen, for instance, that dog-phobic children commonly have a parent who has modeled fear and avoidance of dogs. In an animal-model study of snake phobia, Mineka, Davidson, Cook, and Keir (1984) demonstrated that young monkeys "learned" to be afraid of previously neutral snakes after watching adult monkeys exhibit fear of snakes. Figure 17–5 illustrates how similar the fear responses of young monkeys were to those of the adults they had observed showing fear reactions to snakes and snakelike objects.

Substance-use Disorders

Intoxicating chemicals derived from fermented grains, fermented fruits, wild mushrooms, and certain plants and pollens have played a role for centuries in religious ceremonies and celebrations. People in numerous cultures have used such substances as a way to relax or temporarily escape reality. The majority of Americans (65 percent)

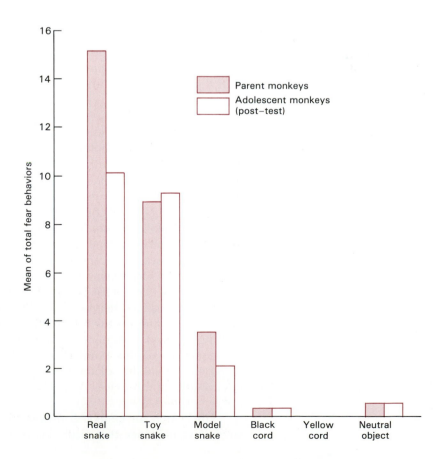

FIGURE 17–5 Modeling of Phobic Reactions *When adolescent monkeys observed their parents displaying fear of certain objects, the young monkeys showed similar levels of fear. This animal study suggests that phobic reactions may sometimes be acquired as a result of observing a fearful "model."* (After Mincka, Davidson, Cook, & Keir, 1984)

drink alcoholic beverages, with most drinking in moderation. However, alcohol-related problems constitute by far the most widespread mental-health difficulty in the U.S. and contribute dramatically to social and health problems. How extensive are the difficulties? The box entitled "Consequences of Alcohol Misuse" summarizes some of the facts about alcohol abuse.

What Is Alcoholism?   This question regarding the nature of alcoholism has proven to be very difficult to answer. The answer ultimately depends on social values and judgments since styles of problem drinking vary across cultures and subgroups. The DSM-IIIR definition distinguishes between alcohol abuse and alcohol dependence. Alcohol abuse refers to a pattern of maladaptive use of alcohol, continuing despite awareness that alcohol causes impairment of functioning. Impairment refers to problems with family or friends because of excessive use, absence from work or loss of job, legal and health difficulties, and violence when intoxicated. *Alcohol dependence* involves not only abuse as defined by pathological use and impairment, but also physical signs of addiction. *Tolerance* refers to the need for progressively increased amounts of alcohol to achieve the desired effect, and *withdrawal* is indicated by "shakes" or discomfort after reducing or quitting drinking that are relieved by further drinking. Dependence also includes lack of success in efforts to control drinking, and increasing amounts of time, energy, and effort devoted to obtaining, using, and recovering from alcohol. If alcohol abuse occurs along with tolerance and/or withdrawal symptoms, the person is said to be alcohol dependent. The questionnaire in Table 17–3 illustrates a somewhat less technical approach to identifying "alcoholism," indicating that there are many definitions.

Theories of the Causes of Alcoholism   There has been more heated and emotional controversy about whether the origins of alcoholism are biological or psychological than about the development of any other form of psychopathology. The predominant public view of alcoholism currently is that it is a disease—an uncontrollable response to alcohol by certain individuals. This point of view, which is promoted by Alcoholics Anonymous, suggests that the true alcoholic has an inborn inability to control drinking and that the condition is irreversible and progressive, so that the only realistic treatment is abstinence. The disease concept has provided a valuable alternative to previous views of alcoholism as a moral defect. In the past, the alcoholic was implicitly blamed for being weak and unable or unwilling to control the excesses. The more modern point of view has probably helped to account for the fact that increased numbers of alcoholics are seeking medical treatment. Despite the prevalence and the positive consequences of this point of view, however, social scientists have disputed the validity of the claims of a biological origin, pointing to environmental influences on problem drinking that they believe cannot be ignored (Peele, 1984).

The search for genetic contributions to alcoholism has produced suggestive evidence that alcoholism runs in families. Offspring of al-

◆ CONSEQUENCES OF ALCOHOL MISUSE

An estimated 10 million people are problem drinkers or alcoholics (Special Report of the National Institute on Alcohol Abuse and Alcoholism, 1983). Approximately 9 percent of men and 1–2 percent of women surveyed recently in epidemiological interviews met diagnostic criteria for alcohol abuse or dependence (Myers et al., 1984).

Deaths related to alcohol abuse are estimated to total 92 per 100,000 annually, and alcohol abuse is known to contribute to cirrhosis of the liver and brain damage, as well as to other major illnesses. Fetal alcohol syndrome due to heavy drinking by pregnant women may be a significant cause of preventable mental retardation and other birth defects (NIAAA Special Report, 1983).

Drinking problems cost society approximately 50 billion dollars per year in lost production, medical bills, accidents, and other expenses (NIAAA Special Report, 1983). Many work days are lost due to overuse of alcohol, and industrial accidents and reduced productivity can often be traced to abuse of alcohol and drugs.

Alcohol abuse disrupts families. Inability to sustain marital and parenting functions due to alcohol may cause enormous suffering in families both in the short term and in later adjustment. Children of alcoholics, for instance, are known to experience high rates of psychopathology and in later years may also have significant difficulties in adjustment (Williams & Klerman, 1984). Children of alcoholic parents, particularly sons of alcoholic fathers, have a greater than average likelihood of alcohol abuse themselves (Goodwin, 1981).

Alcohol appears to play a significant role in many acts of violence. An estimated 80 percent of people who commit suicide are reported to have been drinking before taking their lives, and drinking has been implicated in many instances of murder, rape, domestic violence, and child abuse. Alcohol intoxication plays a role in over a third of the traffic fatalities involving two or more vehicles and may be involved in two-thirds of single-vehicle fatalities as well (NIAAA Special Report, 1983).

coholics, especially sons, appear to have a four times greater risk of alcoholism than do children of normal parents (Schuckit, 1987). The most convincing genetic studies are those involving biological children of alcoholics who were adopted by other families, allowing comparisons of the relative influence of inheritance and environment. Goodwin (1983) reported significantly higher rates of alcoholism in male adoptees whose biological parents were alcoholics as opposed to adoptees with nonalcoholic biological parents, but less clear evidence of genetic transmission in daughters of alcoholics who had been raised by adoptive parents. Other studies have reported similar suggestive evidence of heritability (reviewed by Schuckit, 1987). Recently, however, researchers who assessed the behavior of sons of alcoholics at 19–20 years of age found that their drinking patterns were not different from those of matched controls whose fathers were not alcoholics (Schulsinger, Knop, Goodwin, Teasdale, & Middelsen, 1986). These researchers had expected to see evidence of problem drinking by this age in the presumed genetically "high-risk" group. Taken together, twin studies, animal models of genetic transmission,

TABLE 17–3   Self-report Measures of Alcoholism

One point is scored toward alcoholism if the answer selected is marked with the number 1.

	Alcoholic responses	
Short Michigan Alcoholism Screening Test	Yes	No
1. Do you feel you are a normal drinker? (By normal we mean you drink *less than* or *as much* as most other people.)		1
2. Does your wife, husband, a parent, or other near relative ever worry or complain about your drinking?	1	
3. Do you ever feel guilty about your drinking?	1	
4. Do friends or relatives think you are a normal drinker?		1
5. Are you able to stop drinking when you want to?		1
6. Have you ever attended a meeting of Alcoholics Anonymous?	1	
7. Has drinking ever created problems between you and your wife, husband, or other near relative?	1	
8. Have you ever gotten into trouble at work because of drinking?	1	
9. Have you ever neglected your obligations, your family, or your work for two or more days in a row because you were drinking?	1	
10. Have you ever gone to anyone for help about your drinking?	1	
11. Have you ever been in a hospital because of drinking?	1	
12. Have you ever been arrested for drunk driving, driving while intoxicated, or driving under the influence of alcoholic beverages?	1	
13. Have you ever been arrested, even for a few hours, because of other drunk behavior?	1	

Scoring: 0–1 points = nonalcoholic; 2 points = possibly alcoholic; 3–13 points = alcoholic.

Source: After Selzer, 1971.

and adoption or high-risk studies raise many questions, and the hypothesis of genetic transmission remains a possibility rather than an established fact.

Other biological investigations have attempted to determine whether there may be differences in sensitivity to alcohol from individual to individual, different rates of metabolism for alcohol, different rates for the development and severity of physical dependence, and the like. Such differences could help explain why some people develop cravings for alcohol or patterns of heavy drinking (NIAAA Special Report, 1983; Schuckit, 1987). For instance, Levenson, Oyama, and Meek (1987) found that college students whose parents were alcoholics showed certain stress-reduction effects after consuming alcohol in a controlled experiment that were more pronounced than those exhibited by the offspring of normal parents. To date, there is suggestive (but not conclusive) evidence of particular biological anomalies that could account for alcoholism.

Psychological approaches to alcoholism primarily emphasize the role of cognitive and environmental factors that influence drinking behavior. Cultural and historical patterns of alcohol consumption make it clear that the rate of problem drinking and what may be defined as alcoholism vary widely in ways that biology cannot entirely explain. Some subcultures, such as the Chinese, Greeks, Italians, and Jews, for instance, have relatively low rates of alcoholism, while other groups, such as Irish Americans and Native Americans have higher rates. In general, relatively higher rates of alcoholism are also seen in working-class males than in other segments of the population. As Peele (1984) and others have pointed out, the context in which drinking behavior is learned may be a critical determinant of such patterns and may help explain problem drinking. When children are gradually introduced to drinking in a family setting where its use is considered appropriate for certain occasions and group attitudes control how much is to be consumed and how one is supposed to act, children learn to drink in moderation. The expression of strong social disapproval when norms are violated reinforces moderate drinking behaviors. In contrast, as Peele (1984) notes, American drinking socialization often involves a masculine rite of passage into adulthood, where youths drink outside the family and drinking for the purpose of getting drunk is meant to represent independence and high spiritedness. Interestingly, the pattern of binge drinking is particularly common in persons from conservative Protestant sects or from dry regions that prohibit the sale of alcoholic beverages (Calahan & Room, 1974).

The biological theory of alcoholism emphasizes genetic and neurochemical factors, but psychological theories stress learning—parents and peer groups "teach" expectations and patterns of consumption.

Not only does social background appear to correlate with drinking problems, but the current social context and people's beliefs and

attitudes also exert important influences. For instance, research has shown that people who believe they are consuming alcohol will drink more in experimental situations than those who do not believe they are consuming alcohol, regardless of whether there is actually alcohol in their beverages. This finding supports the hypothesis that expectations of alcohol may influence drinking behaviors. In addition, peer modeling has been shown to be an important influence on drinking patterns. Emotionally charged situations in which individuals are prevented from expressing their reactions also lead to more consumption of alcohol (studies cited in Marlatt, 1979). Other research on the concepts of "craving" and "loss of control" suggest that cognitive factors, such as beliefs and expectations, play an important role in determining how much and when problem drinkers may drink (reviewed by Wilson, 1987).

Researchers with social-learning orientations find it alarming that current patterns of alcohol consumption in young people may reflect the kinds of habits and attitudes that may underlie eventual problem drinking. Studies of alcohol use in the late 1970s and early 1980s show that 50 percent of male seniors in high school reported drinking at least five drinks in one sitting in the two-week period prior to the study. There also apparently has been an increased endorsement of binge drinking over mild, regular drinking (Johnston, Bachman, & O'Malley, 1981). Such patterns suggest that "drinking to get drunk" is learned and may account for some of the apparent "loss-of-control" drinking that others have attributed to a biological source.

In general in the field of psychopathology there is acceptance of both biological and psychological theories, with many researchers agreeing that some combination of causes is probably the best explanation. In the alcoholism field, however, there is more polarization of views. This seems to have come about largely because of the fact that one of the implications of social-learning points of view is that if alcoholism is not a biologically inborn disease, then abstinence may not be the only form of treatment. This view has been sharply criticized by many, including supporters of Alcoholics Anonymous for whom abstinence is the foundation stone of the organization. Teaching problem drinkers more appropriate habits and attitudes about drinking so that they can control their alcohol consumption has proven to be effective (Marlatt, 1983). However, such an approach may be appropriate only for certain individuals—possibly less severe cases. For some individuals, abstinence may continue to be the best goal. Regardless of treatment effectiveness, the origins of alcoholism still are not fully understood.

Drug Abuse and Dependence   As with alcoholism, it is useful to distinguish between the maladaptive habits associated with drug use and its actual physically addicting effects. Abuse refers to pathological use (for example, spending too much money on drugs, daily use, and so forth) and impairment of functioning (such as trouble with the law), while dependence involves the tolerance that builds up with sustained use, the use of higher doses to get the same effects, and withdrawal symptoms that may be extremely painful. There are dozens of substances that may be abused, some available through legal means, such as doctors' prescriptions, and others that are illegal. Four major classes of drugs are sought for their different physical effects. *Opiates* include heroin, morphine, and related substances. *Central-nervous-system depressants*, besides alcohol, include barbiturates and sedative drugs. *Psychomotor stimulants* include cocaine, amphetamines, and caffeine, and *hallucinogens* include LSD, PCP, and marijuana. Recent epidemiological surveys found that lifetime rates of drug abuse/dependence are around 5.5–5.8 percent; however, these rates are not evenly distributed among different age groups. Drug-use disorders are especially high in 18–24 year olds (11–17.5 percent of those surveyed in this age group across different cities show drug-use disorders) and very low in older adults (Robins et al., 1984).

Because of the diversity of the addictive substances, it is impossible to fully characterize the research on the causes and characteristics of drug abuse. *Cocaine* will be discussed briefly as an example of the use of an illicit substance.

Until they were outlawed in 1914, cocaine substances were widely available and often included in medicinal preparations. Freud and the fictional Sherlock Holmes used cocaine and sang its praises, enjoying the brief rush of euphoria and energy that mild doses produce initially. Cocaine usage increased dramatically in the 1970s when it gained a reputation as a rich person's recreational drug, but as cocaine has become more widely available, its users run the entire range from poor, inner-city teenagers to rock stars and famous athletes, with dramatic increases in the numbers of persons seeking treatment for cocaine abuse and in deaths attributed to overdose.

The point at which cocaine use becomes abuse depends on pathological habits, such as the inability to reduce or stop usage, episodes of overdose, or continuous use throughout the day. Also, there may be a pattern of job difficulties, getting into fights, losing friends, or legal difficulties due to cocaine use. Cocaine may be ingested nasally (snorted), injected, or smoked in free-base form. Its initial effects are a heightened energy level and a feeling of euphoria and confidence that may last for several minutes. In higher dosages, especially, the initial sense of well-being is rapidly replaced by excitability, irritability, restlessness, and finally, dysphoria. The strongest effects, achieved through intravenous injections or smoking in purified form (free base) may rapidly progress to suspiciousness, paranoia, hallucinations, and poor impulse control (Siegel, 1984). There are numerous physical complaints and symptoms accompanying prolonged usage, and overdoses may cause death through cardiac arrhythmia (Smith, 1984). One of the myths of cocaine use is that because it does not cause a clear-cut physical-dependency syndrome, it is not addictive. However, severe psychological and physical withdrawal symptoms have been reported (Siegel, 1984), and the craving and compulsion to use cocaine among persistent users warrants the term addiction (Smith, 1984).

Theories of the Causes of Cocaine Abuse   There is little consensus regarding the causes of abuse for any class of drugs, and cocaine is no exception. In general, the biological models emphasize unusual susceptibility to drug effects or physical properties of the substance that affect the brain in highly pleasurable, "rewarding" ways; such approaches have not yielded conclusive findings, however, that explain why some persons become addicted and others do not. A psychodynamic approach emphasizes personal attributes (the "addictive personality"), although this line of research has yielded little useful information because there seems to be considerable diversity in the kinds of people who become addicts. Such patterns also seem to vary from generation to generation. While it may be true that some individuals with preexisting personality or psychiatric problems engage in drug-taking as a way to cope with or escape from life's problems and responsibilities, it does not seem useful to think of a certain kind of personality or set of personal characteristics that predispose a person to drug abuse. Social-learning factors certainly seem to affect aspects of drug use; it is clear, for example, that availability of drugs and modeling of the use of drugs play an important role in individuals' decisions to use drugs for the first time. The peer group or social context in which the drugs are used may teach norms and expectations about their use and meaning. That is why there is considerable outcry about the use of cocaine by famous personalities who might be imitated by admiring young people. Why some individuals go on to become abusers of cocaine or other substances is not understood, however.

Organic Mental Disorders

In discussing dysfunctional behaviors up to this point, we have said that biological factors may play a role in their origin or course. This is just a guess, however, based on certain research findings, for we have no direct evidence of biological malfunction. However, there are some types of abnormal behaviors that are directly related to known biological causes. *Organic mental disorders* include disturbances due to head injuries; diseases of the brain and nervous system; temporary severe intoxication stemming from drug or alcohol use and residual brain damage due to prolonged use of toxic chemicals, drugs, and alcohol; and degenerative brain disorders of unknown causes. Organic mental disorders take many forms, which are primarily affected by the nature and location of the lesions in the brain, but most of these disorders cause intellectual impairment, confusion, and changes in personality. Because of these defects, performance as a family member, as a worker, or in everyday activities is usually seriously impaired.

Many organic conditions may be acute and temporary, involving an injury or medical condition that can be treated successfully. For instance, dementia (an impairment of intellectual functioning involving memory, judgment, capacity for abstract thinking, and certain problems in recognition, expression, and labeling) may result from certain head injuries or brain lesions, Parkinson's disease, vitamin B12 deficiency, drug or chemical intoxication, and certain types of strokes, among other medical disorders. Many such problems are treatable, and recovery from or lessening of the organic symptoms may be expected. In contrast, there are also types of dementia and

Alzheimer's disease is an organic mental disorder that commonly requires institutional care.

other forms of organic psychopathology that are irreversible and may be progressive. Because there are so many kinds of organic disorders, it is impossible to describe them by common characteristics. Instead, we will discuss one example of a chronic and progressive disorder usually associated with aging—one that has major public-health implications because of its relative frequency.

Alzheimer's disease is one of several types of progressive neurological disorders that primarily afflict older adults. One of the tragedies of this disorder, however, is that it often originates in middle age, and so it is sometimes called *presenile dementia*. The course of the disorder includes relatively rapid deterioration of intellectual functioning. At first, victims of Alzheimer's disease are merely forgetful, but gradually the individual's memory and judgment decrease so that he or she becomes increasingly confused and disoriented. Eventually, the person cannot remember family members or perform even routine tasks, and with time, major physical deterioration also occurs, so that many afflicted individuals require institutional care.

Alzheimer's disease has attracted tremendous attention in recent years as the American population has come to include more and more older adults. It has been estimated that by the year 2000, 1 in 10 adults over age 65 will be a victim of Alzheimer's (Coyle, Price, & DeLong, 1983)—a tremendous psychological burden for families and a serious health-care burden for communities. The case study of Alzheimer's disease that follows paints all too vividly the sad picture facing Alzheimer's victims.

———

Hannah was a successful and wealthy businesswoman who retired early to enjoy the fruits of her labors. After her husband's death when she was 55, she lived quietly with the housekeeper and spent many hours playing cards with friends. A couple of years later her daughter in another city received a call from an old family friend who expressed concern that Hannah was losing too much money in her card games, and that the group was reluctant to play with her, feeling that her playing was poor. Hannah had been known as a sharp player for years, and this clearly did not sound like her, so her daughter talked with the housekeeper, who admitted that she had noticed other unusual behaviors: forgetfulness in grooming and occasional confusion about dates and people. The housekeeper told Hannah's daughter that her mother had recently gone shopping alone and had become lost. Over the next few months the memory lapses increased; Hannah scolded her daughter for not calling, even though they had just spoken the day before on the phone. Eventually, Hannah could hold only the briefest conversations with others; she often failed to recognize people she knew well. She not only could not be permitted to leave home alone, but even in the house she had to be watched so that her unattended cigarettes did not cause fires. She required help with dressing and grooming. It was hard to find nurses and attendants who would work for her very long; she would alternate periods of quiet staring at the television with rambling, complaining, and sometimes insulting monologues directed vaguely at the attendants. She is only 62 now and is totally oblivious of the outside world, while her former friends continue to pursue their lives and work vigorously.

———

Causes of Alzheimer's Disease   There is marked degeneration of the brain in Alzheimer's cases that accounts for the symptoms of this dementia, and there appear to be unusual tangles and webs in the nerve cells of the cerebral cortex and hippocampus (Hyman, VanHoesen, Damasio, & Barnes, 1984). However, the causes of the damage are unknown. One theory is that there is a slowly developing virus that causes lesions in the brain; another theory suggests a genetic defect; a third hypothesizes a defect in the body's immune system; and yet another emphasizes loss of critical neurotransmitter substances (Coyle et al., 1983). New diagnostic techniques are rapidly appearing, and the research on this disorder is very active, prompted by the number of anticipated cases within the next few decades.

Psychological Disorders in Children

Children's disorders take many of the same forms as those of adults, and like those of adults, they may vary in intensity from mild phobias that are rapidly outgrown to pervasive disorders that are profoundly impairing. However, it is not a simple matter to translate what we know about adult psychopathology into child psychopathology. Certain behaviors that might be regarded as symptomatic at one age are highly appropriate at other ages. For example, very young children are allowed and even expected to be highly distractible or boisterous; they may be encouraged in their tendency to blur the distinction between fantasy and reality. These same behaviors in older children, however, may be considered problems. Whether or not a child becomes the focus of treatment, or even of research, depends to a great extent on how the adults around him or her regard the child. There is considerable variability in what parents or teachers may perceive in the behavior of children. They do not always recognize maladaptive behavior. Not only are disorders in children sometimes difficult to identify, but the failure to recognize and to treat such problems may have profound consequences for the lives of the children. For many disorders, their occurrence in childhood may signal the beginning of maladaptive patterns that interfere with healthy development or that overwhelm children's coping skills. (For a discussion of a problem behavior recently on the rise among children that poses a serious obstacle to healthy development, see the box entitled "Eating Disorders.") Children with problems may have bad feelings about themselves, may perform poorly at school, and may relate poorly to peers and to adults. Such difficulties, in turn, may further affect how they feel about themselves or lead to later maladaptive patterns in school and in society. While many problems may be temporary, as we shall see, more severe difficulties may bode ill for adult development.

The section that follows is a selective review of disorders of childhood, covering the most common disorders or those that are uniquely of childhood origin. Omitted here are disorders that are essentially similar to those of adulthood except for developmental adjustments in symptoms; such disorders include depression, anxiety disorders, manic-depression, schizophrenia, obsessive- compulsive disorder and others that are apparently the same as adult disorders but occasionally have onsets during childhood.

◆ *EATING DISORDERS*

Problems associated with eating and weight control have attracted considerable attention recently because they seem to be more prevalent than ever before. Anorexia nervosa is an extreme disorder characterized by significant weight loss and drastic efforts to lose weight by means of prolonged exercising, vomiting and laxatives, and a reduction in food intake. It is accompanied by intense fears of gaining weight and by distortions in body image such that the individual may feel fat even if appearing emaciated to others. Bulimia is marked by recurrent episodes of binge eating followed by self-induced vomiting or the use of laxatives; the individual is usually highly secretive about the pattern, recognizing it as abnormal but feeling unable to control eating behavior voluntarily. While both types of eating disorder involve abnormal concern with becoming fat, bulimics fluctuate between weight gain and weight loss, while anorectics have "successfully" reduced body weight by at least 25 percent. In both cases, there may be severe medical complications, including menstrual irregularities or cessation, significant electrolyte imbalances, and other problems associated with repeated vomiting. In anorexia, the disorder may be life-threatening.

While most studies report that there are significantly more women than men with eating disorders, there is agreement that the rates for men are rising (Halmi, 1983; Schlesier-Stropp, 1984). The disorders generally have their onsets between ages 10 and 30 and are especially prevalent in adolescence. Surveys suggest that significant numbers of children and young adolescents have used vomiting for weight control on occasion, and the vast majority of young persons report having tried to diet to lose weight. Thus, while true eating disorders are relatively rare, they occur in environments that strongly support an intense preccupation with body image and weight control.

WHY DOES AN EFFORT TO LOSE WEIGHT BECOME AN EATING DISORDER?

There has been no shortage of theories concerning the development of anorexia nervosa. Psychoanalytic models emphasize the rejection of the female body image or maintain that the disorder occurs in a disturbed family context in which the young anorectic person may be attempting to gain control and autonomy. Biological theories have hypothesized disturbed neurological or endocrinological mechanisms. Learning models have emphasized the irrational beliefs about the body and the tremendous societal reinforcement for thinness. Similar models have also been proposed to explain bulimia. In addition to these theories, a psychological approach to understanding binge eating has recently been proposed. In accordance with the model presented in the "disinhibition" hypothesis, individuals who constantly monitor their weight and go on diets are termed restrained eaters, and they are considered to be vulnerable to overeating when they are disinhibited for some reason (Herman & Polivy, 1980; Ruderman, 1986). According to the model, an especially potent disinhibiting factor is the belief that one has overeaten, accompanied by the thought, "My diet is broken, I might as well go ahead and eat more." Experimental studies have shown that restrained eaters who are given a milk shake and then asked to take a "taste test" actually eat more of the test food than do persons who did not eat the preliminary milk shake, while unrestrained eaters show the opposite pattern. It seems that "falling off the wagon" makes the person give up temporarily and overconsume. Other factors that may produce similar disinhibition effects are a depressed or upset mood and alcohol. Apparently, the food intake pattern of highly weight-conscious people is characterized by an all-or-nothing rigidity that may make such individuals susceptible to bingeing (Ruderman, 1986).

Profound Psychopathology in Children **Infantile autism** is a relatively rare form of what is termed **pervasive developmental disorder** that is characterized by onset in infancy (before the age of 30 months), lack of responsiveness to people, gross deficits in language development (speech may be lacking or may include peculiar speech patterns), and bizarre responses to the environment (such as peculiar attachments to objects and extreme reactions to changes in the environment). Children suffering from infantile autism do not show delusions or hallucinations or other characteristics of schizophrenia. Pervasive difficulties in communication and in social behavior are generally continuous throughout life, with the majority of autistic children experiencing serious lifelong handicaps and often requiring institutional care.

There have been numerous theories about the causes of autism. An apparent genetic component to the disorder exists, and numerous studies have implicated various biological abnormalities or supported the possibility of a brain malfunction of some kind, affecting attention, learning, perception, and memory. However, as Prior and Werry (1986) note, it is likely that there are various biological agents involved, and the extent of impairment is likely to be determined by whether the various agents affect specific or generalized regions of the brain. Earlier research and theory of a decade or two ago tended to emphasize maladaptive parent-child relationships in the tradition of Freudian theory, but such views have now been largely discredited (Prior & Werry, 1986).

"Externalizing" Disorders of Childhood Some researchers have suggested two broad dimensions of childhood psychopathology that encompass most of the major diagnoses. "Externalizing" disorders include those that involve significant problems in behavior directed toward others or toward the environment. "Internalizing" disorders,

Autistic children are profoundly impaired from infancy.

on the other hand, are those difficulties that involve negative emotions and attitudes directed inwardly toward the self, such as anxiety and depression. We have discussed internalizing disorders in previous sections; they generally resemble the adult forms and are more rarely seen in children that in adults.

Conduct disorder refers to a persistent pattern of physical and verbal aggression, noncompliance, disruptiveness, lack of self-control, and impaired interpersonal relations. A child whose behavior frequently includes fighting or bullying, defiance, disregard for authority, dishonesty, callousness, and a general failure to show regard for the basic rights of others or of age-appropriate norms and rules may meet diagnostic criteria for a form of conduct disorder. *Delinquency* is a legal term that is not the same as conduct disorder. A delinquent child may show a conduct disorder because of persistent rule violations, such as stealing, fire-setting, vandalism, or truancy, but some types of conduct disorders may not actually involve legal infractions (such as disruptiveness at school, bullying, lying, or defiance of authority). Conduct disorders are the most commonly diagnosed problem in children brought to clinics and hospitals for treatment, but they also occur relatively frequently in untreated community samples—at the rate of 4 percent for children between ages 5 and 12 (Quay, 1986). The rate appears to be much higher in urban than rural settings and far more prevalent in boys than girls. Although conduct disorders vary in seriousness, depending on the types of behaviors displayed, Quay (1986) notes that in general there is considerable persistence of the disorders from childhood to adolescence to adulthood, and while most aggressive children do not go on to be adult criminals, many adult offenders displayed conduct disorders during childhood and adolescence.

Research into the causes of conduct disorders has commonly emphasized environmental factors, including deficient parenting with rejecting or inconsistent parents who do not effectively enforce rules or who themselves present deviant role models (Hetherington & Martin, 1986). Also, considerable research finds correlations between conduct disorders, delinquency, and sociocultural factors, such as economic disadvantage, delinquent peers, and dwelling in inner-city neighborhoods, although the manner in which such factors may affect conduct disorders is not fully understood (Farrington, 1986). More recently, there has been interest in biological factors, including genetics and neurotransmitters, that may eventually shed light on individual vulnerability to the development of conduct disorders (Quay, 1986).

Attention deficit disorder (ADD) was once termed "hyperactivity" or "hyperkinetic behavior," or even "minimal brain damage." Be definition this is a disorder that occurs before the age of seven, and includes dysfunction in three areas: inattention, impulsivity, and hyperactivity (although there is also believed to be a form of attention deficit disorder that does not involve hyperactivity). Attentional difficulties, which are central to the dysfunction, may include trouble sticking to an activity, being easily distracted, having problems concentrating on schoolwork or tasks, seeming not to listen, and frequently failing to finish things that have been started. Impulsivity may include acting before thinking, difficulty in organizing work, calling out in class, or difficulty waiting a turn in group activities. Hyperactivity may take the form of running about or excessive climbing, problems sitting still or excessive fidgeting, and being always "on the go." In situations where motor behavior is expected, such as on the playground, problems may not be obvious, but in the classroom a child's attention deficit disorder may clearly show itself in inattentive behavior, not staying on tasks, disrupting the classroom with speaking out of turn, moving about, and sloppy, careless work, with errors even on simple items. At home, children suffering from attention deficit disorder may have trouble following parental requests and sticking to activities. As Campbell and Werry (1986) note, the individual symptoms of the syndrome are common in young children and decrease with age. However, the full pattern of symptoms needed to diagnose attention deficit disorder may occur in about 2 percent of the population. It should also be noted that additional samples of children display mixtures of both ADD symptoms and conduct disorders, so that differential diagnosis is sometimes difficult. It is agreed, however, that the prevalence of ADD is more than three times higher in boys than in girls. Although many children who display attention deficit disorder have normal intelligence, poor school performance is extremely common, along with problems in peer relations that accompany the children's disruptiveness and impulsivity. Therefore, it is not surprising that long-term, follow-up studies of children diagnosed with attention deficit disorder suggest that even though many of the more pronounced symptoms diminish in adolescence and adulthood, continuing academic difficulties, poor self-image, and social difficulties may remain (Campbell & Werry, 1986).

As with most forms of psychopathology, research on the causes of attention deficit disorder proceeds along both biological and psychosocial lines. Because of the central problem of sustaining attention, there have been various theories focusing on neurological arousal mechanisms in the brain. One theory argues that the positive effects of administering psychostimulant drugs to children with ADD, an apparently "paradoxical" tactic since the children already seemed overaroused, supported the theory of overarousal. However, later theories have emphasized underarousal or complex deficits in arousal regulation (see Campbell & Werry, 1986), and although promising, have thus far failed to specify the nature of the biological dysfunctions. With respect to theories emphasizing psychological factors in attention deficit disorder, many studies have observed problems in parent-child relationships. However, it is just as likely that the child's disruptive behaviors are the cause of negative parental behaviors as the reverse. Weiss (1983) conducted a large and continuous follow-up study of children with attention deficit disorder and concluded that family stability and positive parent-child relations predicted positive outcomes in adolescence, while discord and punitive parent-child relations were associated with antisocial conduct in adolescence. In general, therefore, it appears that family factors may contribute to the course of disorder, while multiple factors, including biological variables, may contribute to its origin.

We have discussed some of the major forms of psychopathology. In the box titled "Psychosexual Disorders" we deal with an infrequently found type of pathology that mainly affects men.

♦ *PSYCHOSEXUAL DISORDERS*

Sexual disorders constitute a topic in which social norms and values play a considerable role in what is considered psychopathology and what is not—and this appears to change over time as sexual standards change. There is a fair amount of latitude (although this differs by region) in what is tolerated in sexual behaviors, particularly between mutually consenting adults. However, certain sexual behaviors are so offensive to the community that they are considered criminal acts as well as sexual disorders; those involving repetitive acts are particularly likely to be considered psychological disorders.

Diagnostic manuals classify "psychosexual disorders" into one of three categories:

1. *Sexual dysfunction disorders*: This group is made up of relatively common difficulties in normal sexual arousal or performance, including for example, impotence in men or orgasmic difficulties in women.

2. *Gender identity difficulties*: These disorders are characterized by incongruence between anatomic sex and the psychological sense of being male or female. Transsexualism is quite rare. The affected individual experiences it as a personally troubling sense of discomfort and inappropriateness about one's biological sex and a persistent wish to live as a member of the opposite sex. In recent years, surgical sex reassignment and psychological counseling have permitted transsexuals to live lives more fully congruent with their personal gender identity. Transsexualism is not the same as subgroups of homosexuality in which the person may exaggerate the characteristics of the opposite sex; such individuals do not have a desire to actually *be* of the other sex. Transsexualism is also different from transvestism. The transvestite might derive sexual enjoyment from dressing in clothing of the opposite sex, but the transvestite does not actually wish to *become* a person of the opposite sex.

Transvestism (dressing in the clothing of the opposite sex) should be distinguished from transsexualism, where the person actually feels like, or desires to be, the opposite sex.

3. *Paraphilias*: This category encompasses bizarre or unusual imagery or acts that are necessary for sexual excitement. Such imagery or acts tend to be repetitive and involuntary. According to the DSM-IIIR, such activities generally involve one of the following that the person has acted upon: preference for use of nonhuman objects for sexual arousal (inanimate objects, dressing in the clothing of the opposite sex [transvestism], or sexual contact with an animal); repetitive sexual activity with humans involving suffering or humiliation (such as sexual sadism or masochism); and repetitive sexual activity involving nonconsenting partners. The latter includes relatively harmless although socially repugnant disorders such as exhibitionism (exposing the genitals to an unsuspecting stranger with no attempt at sexual activity with that person) and voyeurism (looking at unsuspecting people who are naked, undressing, or engaging in sexual activity). Also included is the far more serious pedophilia (engaging in sexual activity with children). When the sexual molestation of children is performed by a relative, it is called incest. Incest and pedophilia were once thought rare, but with increasing publicity and research on this often-hidden behavior, we are finding that as many as 10–20 percent of women and some men report that they were sexually abused in some fashion as children. Depending on the perpetrator and the nature of the act(s), children sustain degrees of psychological harm that also affect their adult adjustment.

Although the characteristics of the various disorders are different, there are some common findings. The vast majority of persons afflicted with sexual disorders are men, and in most cases they probably do not have other major forms of psychopathology, such as schizophrenia. While some theories of the origin of such difficulties emphasize biological factors, suggesting some defect in hormonal development or regulation for some disorders (for example, transsexualism), most approaches have emphasized psychological factors. Although a good deal of research data is not yet available, it seems a common finding that male sex offenders are often immature or unskilled in their sex-role development and may have had few or unrewarding heterosexual experiences. They may have histories of dysfunctional parent-child relationships in their own families. Behaviorally oriented theorists have emphasized deviant learning experiences, such as the conditioned association between sexual arousal and inappropriate objects or people. In the case of incest, it seems certain that disturbances in the family system, such as marital conflict or often a mother who "looks the other way" when her daughters are being victimized by the father, contribute to the perpetuation of the problem.

SUMMARY

1. There are no invariable standards for judging what is abnormal behavior; it depends on society's judgment about what is appropriate for a person's age, sex, and culture in a particular situation at that time in history.

2. Ideas about what constitutes mental health also vary by situation, culture, and history. People today are sensitive to a desire for satisfaction and fulfillment, as well as a desire to avoid serious difficulties.

3. Using the DSM-IIIR as a diagnostic standard, large proportions of adults experience at least a mild diagnosable impairment during their lifetimes. Men and women are at about equal risk (for different disorders), with young adults most likely to be affected.

4. Biological approaches to the causes of abnormal behavior view them as diseases involving some dysfunction or dysregulation of physiology, with contemporary theories emphasizing neurotransmitters and the endocrine system.

5. Psychoanalytic theories emphasize internal conflicts, maladaptive defenses, and disordered parent-child relationships as the sources of disorders.

6. Learning-theory approaches focus on learned maladaptive behaviors (or failure to learn appropriate behaviors); recent learning models include the study of cognitions—the way people think about themselves and their environments—as an important influence on maladaptive behaviors.

7. Most researchers believe that some integration of models, including perhaps a biological predisposition (diathesis) to respond to certain internal or environmental stressors, provides the most complete explanation of the origins of psychopathology.

8. Schizophrenia is the most common form of psychosis, involving a departure from realistic forms of perception, thinking, and communication. Its onset usually occurs during adolescence or young adulthood, and for most victims it has a chronic or recurrent course.

9. Biological researchers have been very actively seeking evidence of some deficit in the structure or function of the brain that affects attention and information processing. Although the dopamine hypothesis was prominent, it is overly simple, and the quest for biological answers continues.

10. Genetic studies of schizophrenia have provided suggestive evidence of heritability but do not rule out the possible influence of environmental factors.

11. Learning and psychodynamic models have not been as influential in recent years for understanding schizophrenia. However, there is good evidence that disturbed family relationships influence the course of schizophrenia, contributing to relapse.

12. Affective disorders are dysfunctions of mood and range from mild depressions to severe depression or mania, which often requires hospitalization.

13. Unipolar depressions are common and may have many different causes, including stresses, early parent-child relationships, and experiences of loss or failure. There are also possible biological origins.

14. Bipolar affective disorders include both depression and mania or hypomania and are more rare than unipolar disorders. Bipolar disorders may have more of a biological component and are possibly hereditary.

15. Mood states exert a profound influence on thinking, so that when someone is depressed, they will exaggerate the negative and feel pessimistic, hopeless, and self-critical in their interpretations, which in turn may make them feel more depressed. The opposite occurs in inflated mood states such as hypomania or mania.

16. Mood disorders may occur at all ages, including childhood, but young adults seem to be at greatest risk, possibly due to the stresses of adjusting to leaving home, establishing relationships, beginning families, and beginning careers.

17. Biological theories of affective disorders have emphasized neurotransmitter substances and various hormones. Although promising leads have developed, there is as yet no definitive conclusion that can be drawn.

18. The cognitive approach to depression emphasizes the negativity in interpreting the self and events and argues that some people are vulnerable to depression because of their tendencies to think negatively.

19. Research on stressful life events has shown correlations between negative events and depression, but it remains true that most people who experience major life events do not become depressed.

20. Anxiety disorders take various forms. The classical psychoanalytic approach to "neuroses" has become less popular in comparison to biological and cognitive-learning theories.

21. Alcoholism is the most common mental-health problem, taking an enormous toll on the health, safety, and personal well-being of members of the community.

22. There is an intense controversy between those who believe that alcoholism is a disease and those who believe its causes are psychological; so far neither group has conclusive evidence to present.

23. Abuse of other drugs, such as cocaine, is also studied from both biological and psychological perspectives. There does not seem to be such a thing as an "addictive personality." Social learning factors such as availability, role models, and peer support seem important, but biological bases of addiction have not been ruled out either.

24. There are various clearly biologically caused organic mental illnesses of which Alzheimer's disease is a very common one, afflicting primarily older adults. Its exact causes are unknown, but its social and psychological consequences are mounting daily as the population as a whole ages.

25. Many disorders of childhood are similar to those in adulthood. However, there are several relatively common forms of childhood psychopathology that are uniquely experienced by children.

26. Childhood autism is a form of profound developmental disorder that involves peculiar behaviors, lack of attachment to people, and often a lack of language and communication skills. It is thought to have a biological origin.

27. Conduct disorders and attention deficit disorders involve behavioral disturbances; the former usually involves violations of social standards and the latter involves problems in maintaining a focus of attention. In reality, some children show aspects of both problems, and the implications for adult adjustment for such individuals are often, although not always, negative.

KEY TERMS

abnormal behaviors

agoraphobia

alcohol abuse

alcohol dependence

Alzheimer's disease

anxiety states

attention deficit disorder (ADD)

bipolar affective disorder

catatonic schizophrenia

central-nervous-system depressants

childhood separation anxiety

cocaine

cognitive model of psychopathology

conduct disorder

delinquency

delusions

diathesis

disorganized schizophrenia

genetic linkage study

genetic marker

hallucinations

hallucinogens

hypomania

infantile autism

medical model

multiaxial system of diagnoses

obsessive-compulsive disorder

opiates

organic mental disorders

paranoid schizophrenia

phobias

pervasive developmental disorder (infantile autism)

post-traumatic stress disorder

psychomotor stimulants

psychoneurosis

psychosis

schizophrenia

stigmatization

stress-diathesis perspective

thought broadcasting

thought disturbances

thought insertion

tolerance

unipolar depression

withdrawal

ADDITIONAL READING

Beckham, E., & Leber, E. (Eds.) (1985) *Handbook of depression.* Homewood, IL: Dorsey Press.
This text is a somewhat technical but comprehensive review of what is known about depression, including diagnostic, etiological, and treatment issues.

Goldstein, M., Baker, B., & Jamison, K. (1986) *Abnormal psychology: Experiences, origins, and interventions* (2nd ed.). Boston: Little, Brown.
This is an excellent, up-to-date textbook, covering major types of abnormal behavior from different points of view in a very readable fashion.

Quay, H., & Werry, J. (Ed.) (1986) *Psychopathological disorders of childhood* (3rd ed.). New York: Wiley.
This book offers a comprehensive review of childhood disorders, both those unique to children and those that are similar to adult forms; it also covers diagnostic and treatment issues.

Spitzer, R., Skodol, A., Gibbon, M., & Williams, J. (1983) *Psychopathology: A case book.* New York: McGraw-Hill.
This text contains descriptions and analyses from various theoretical perspectives about actual cases that illustrate diagnostic categories of the DSM-IIIR.

18 Treating Psychological Problems

Modern psychotherapy originated in the work of Sigmund Freud in the 1880s in Vienna, where he fashioned his theory of personality and his "talking cure"—psychoanalysis. Freud's ideas, more than those of any other person, have influenced the practice of psychotherapy, while also having a profound impact on other fields such as anthropology, history, literature, and the arts. His views on the influence of sexual instincts on behavior, the role of unconscious motivation, intrapsychic conflict arising in different psychosexual stages of development in the child, and defense mechanisms, as described earlier, have had a profound effect on Western culture, even though many of the original tenets have been disputed.

PSYCHOLOGICAL THERAPIES

Psychodynamic Approaches

Psychoanalysis was the term for Freud's original method of treatment, and it is rarely practiced today outside of a few large cities. Numerous variants, called "psychoanalytic psychotherapy" or "psychodynamic psychotherapy," are widely practiced, however. Generally, these treatments seek to achieve goals of personality reconstruction and symptom relief by resolving the emotional conflicts arising from the patient's childhood. Psychoanalytic therapies assume that the symptoms or difficulties that a person exhibits are simply surface manifestations of underlying conflicts. From this point of view, it is not enough to change the person's overt behaviors unless the problems that gave rise to the symptoms are also changed. In traditional psychoanalysis, it is assumed that the particular psychosexual stage of development during which conflicts were initially unresolved determines to a great extent the kinds of problems the individual experiences. In contemporary psychodynamic psychotherapies, there is less emphasis on psychosexual stages but typically a pronounced emphasis on mother-child interactions, particularly the processes by which the child separates from the mother and comes to experience the self as a distinct individual.

Treatment The tools of psychoanalysis are free association, dream analysis, interpretation, and transference resolution. With the exception of free association, all of these techniques are used today in dynamically oriented therapies. These are tools by which the unconscious experiences are made conscious, with the expectation that insight into the hidden conflicts will help to resolve them and allow the person to function more adaptively.

The concept of the unconscious is central to psychoanalytic theory. Freud believed that most of our motives are unconscious and that unconscious motivation in some degree affects every aspect of our behavior, from the profession we choose to the clothes we wear to our personal habits. This concept leads to the doctrine of *psychological determinism*, in which everything we say or do, including slips of the tongue, dreams, and accidents, as well as behaviors we "choose," is seen as reflecting unconscious motivations. For a Freudian, nothing happens by chance, "there are no mistakes," and there is a psychological reason for everything. Therefore, any material the patient divulges, from free association, to reports of dreams and fantasies, to

THERAPY IS HELL

discussions of real-life events, is presumed to reveal unconscious material. The analyst or psychotherapist uses these reports (as well as observations of what the patient avoids talking about) to try to find clues to the repressed and hidden conflicts.

Although the patient does most of the talking, the therapist uses interpretation as a fundamental tool to bring into the patient's awareness the meanings, causes, and operations of psychological events, feelings, and thoughts, as well as "resistances" to the process. Interpretations are based on psychoanalytic theory as well as on what is actually happening, and they require great skill on the part of the therapist with reference to how they are stated, their timing in the course of treatment, and the level of psychic conflict to which they relate. If they are not made skillfully, they will not have much impact or they may arouse unwanted feelings that get in the way of progress. The following patient-therapist dialogue, which might have occurred several months after therapy began, illustrates features of psychodynamically oriented therapy:

THERAPIST: You said you had a bad dream last night. Tell me about it.

PATIENT: I've had the same dream before. I was back in the army, and I was late getting into formation because I couldn't get dressed. I lined up without any clothes on. I felt . . . I don't know . . . silly, I guess.

THERAPIST: Vulnerable?

PATIENT: Well, like I said, I like the army. It was a comfortable period in my life.

THERAPIST: But you felt exposed or vulnerable?

PATIENT: I wouldn't put it that way. Just strange or silly is all.

THERAPIST (interpreting this statement as resistance): Is feeling vulnerable so bad?

PATIENT: Can't you take *anything* I say at face value? Damn it all, why are you so critical of everything I say?

THERAPIST: Critical, like your father? (The analyst views the patient's last comment as transference—that is, seeing the therapist in the role of the patient's hyper-critical father.)

PATIENT: Oh hell, I don't know. . . . I suppose so. You know, I used to have this dream a lot, but this is the first time I've had it since I've been seeing you. What does it really mean?

THERAPIST: Free associate to the army . . . what comes to your mind?

PATIENT (a long pause follows, which the analyst interprets as resistance): I'm blocking . . . OK, power. That's what comes to my mind. Power.

THERAPIST: Continue.

PATIENT: Power . . . for some reason that makes me think of punishment.

THERAPIST: Power means punishment? Go on.

PATIENT: I guess I do sort of equate those two words. Doesn't everybody?

THERAPIST: The important thing is what those words mean to you.

PATIENT: I know that. Power . . . punishment . . . I'm blocking again.

THERAPIST (after a long pause): The first session we had, do you recall how you described your father? How you saw your father when you were a little boy?

PATIENT: Let me think . . . I saw him as strong and hard working.

THERAPIST: Anything else?

PATIENT: As, well . . . powerful. By God, I did use that word!

THERAPIST: And?

PATIENT: Well, my father wasn't someone you crossed. If you cross powerful people, they will hurt you. Like the army, in a way. But like I said, I *liked* the army. Maybe unconsciously I didn't like the army . . . is that it?

THERAPIST: The army was safe and predictable but dangerous if you went against the rules. Like your father?

PATIENT: Yes, that's exactly right! But my father was a *good* man.

THERAPIST: What does "good" mean to you? What comes to mind?

As therapy continues, **transference** forms an increasing focus in the therapeutic session. Transference refers to the personal feelings that develop toward the therapist and that often appear to be excessively strong or that have only limited pertinence to what is actually going on in the treatment. Freud suggested that these feelings are generated not so much by the present relationship between patient and therapist as they are "transferred" from childhood experiences with significant adults, usually the patient's parents. Thus, the patient may react to the analyst or therapist with intense anger, *as if* the analyst were the hated and feared parent for whom the patient has repressed actual feelings. The opposite reaction—an outpouring of admiration and love—may also result. By exploring the transference relationship, analytic therapy assumes that unconscious conflicts can be brought out into the open, can be understood, and then can be resolved.

Classical psychoanalysis attempts to foster transference is several ways. Traditionally the patient lies on a couch and the analyst sits out of sight; the analyst attempts to be as neutral as possible and remains an impersonal figure, relatively unknown to the patient, as a means of encouraging the patient's full exploration of inner experiences. The here-and-now experiences of everyday life are relatively less often discussed than are the childhood experiences and transference issues. Classical analysis is very intensive and time-consuming, typically involving three to six sessions a week for a period of several years. Needless to say, it is extremely expensive.

Psychoanalytic psychotherapy has evolved as a much less intensive form of psychotherapy than psychoanalysis. There are numerous variants of this approach, but most involve briefer treatment, face-to-face meetings, and more emphasis on here-and-now, real-life problems. As noted, many of the Freudian constructs remain important, such as unconscious conflict and the use of interpretation and transference to attain insight; however, many of the twentieth-century theorists who have contributed to the development of psychoanalytic psychotherapies have disputed some of Freud's original ideas regarding universal human drives (libidinal instincts) and his relative neglect of cultural and social influences on human development. Until

Psychoanalysis with the patient on the couch is rare. Most psychodynamic therapies involve face-to-face conversations.

rather recently, most psychotherapists probably considered themselves psychodynamic in orientation. There even appears to be a resurgence of interest in dynamically oriented therapies today, paralleling theoretical developments in self-psychology and object-relations theories, as noted in Chapter 14.

Evaluation of Psychoanalysis and Psychodynamic Therapies   As vast as the impact of Freud's theories and their influence on modern therapists has been, there is relatively little controlled, empirical investigation supporting the efficacy of this model. Much of the support given to classical psychoanalysis has been based on the evidence of individual case studies, which of course are a highly selected and possibly biased source of information. One of the reasons for the neglect of formal research has been the fact that some of the basic concepts of psychoanalysis are very vague or hard to measure—such things as transference, insight, unconscious conflict, repression, and the like. Nevertheless, within just the past decade psychoanalytically oriented therapists have increasingly embarked on relatively carefully controlled research of their methods. For example, researchers report empirical support for some of Freud's concepts, such as transference (Luborsky et al., 1985), or unconscious wishes, fears, and fantasies (Silverman, 1985).

Existential-humanistic Therapies

The existential-humanistic therapies evolved relatively recently and probably were at their peak in the 1960s and 1970s, with an important continuing influence today. These therapies are sometimes called the Third Force (as contrasted with psychoanalytic and behavioral approaches), and they arose in part as a reaction against psychoanalysis, and in part as a result of the influence of twentieth-century European existential philosophers. In contrast to the emphasis on universal instinctual drives and psychic determinism found in psychoanalysis, existential-humanistic therapies are grounded in a belief that people seek self-actualization and the fulfillment of their human potential and creativity. Guided by free will, every individual is seen as being uniquely valuable. The focus is on the here-and-now experience of the individual, a phenomenological approach that contrasts with the psychoanalytic emphasis on symbolic representations of early childhood conflicts. Psychological growth, rather than freedom from intrapsychic conflict, is the goal, and growth is believed to be facilitated by a warm, direct, human relationship with the therapist, using techniques and procedures aimed at exploring immediate experience and increasing awareness of feelings.

No single dominant theory or person has assumed a central position in connection with existential-humanistic therapies, but many psychologists have contributed to the philosophical and therapeutic development of these approaches, including Viktor Frankl, Abraham Maslow, R. D. Laing, Rollo May, Carl Rogers, Fritz Perls, and others. The therapeutic methods have included a vast range of procedures. Some are considered to be on the "fringe," but two variants of the existential-humanistic school have been especially influential—client-centered therapy and Gestalt therapy.

Carl Rogers developed *client-centered therapy* in the 1940s and continued to be its dominant force until his death in 1986. Some would argue that in the fields of clinical and counseling psychology (but not psychiatry), Rogers's influence has been second only to that of Freud. Certainly one factor in the success of his ideas has been a fundamentally positive and optimistic view of the nature of human-kind. Rogers believed that infants are born with a drive for self-fulfillment but must learn to thwart the expression of their own feelings in order to maintain the approval of others, such as their parents, when the child's wishes clash with those of other involved individuals. Maintaining the approval of others helps the child to maintain self-esteem, but it may be at the cost of denying individuality. If sufficient thwarting of personal needs and feelings occurs, there may be *incongruity* between what the person feels to be her real self and her ideal self. This disparity between the real and ideal selves may cause discomfort, and Rogerian therapy attempts to help resolve this mismatch by helping the person to explore obstacles to the expression of the true self.

Treatment in Client-centered Therapy Originally, Rogers espoused "nondirective counseling," in which the therapist provided a warm and permissive setting for the client to explore true feelings and experiences, maintaining an essentially passive stance, echoing back what the client would say. Over time, Rogers's procedures became more active but retained the essential "client-centered" focus.

According to Rogers (1957), therapists must demonstrate three qualities in order for their clients to get better. First, the therapist must show *unconditional positive regard* for the client. That is, the client must be convinced that the therapist actually likes and respects him (or her) and that this positive regard does not depend on what he (or she) says or does. Rogers felt that unconditional positive regard from another leads to self-acceptance. Second, the therapist must show *empathic understanding*. The client must be convinced that he or she is truly understood by the therapist. In the absence of such empathic understanding, clients are likely to think, "Sure, this therapist says he likes and respects me, but that is only because he really doesn't know me . . . if he really knew me, he wouldn't like me." Empathic understanding also helps clients get in touch with thoughts and feelings that they have denied in the past. Third, the therapist must show *genuineness*—the client must perceive that the therapist is honest and straightforward. If the therapist says one thing but somehow communicates contrary feelings, the client will pick this up and come to believe that the therapist cannot be trusted.

Rogerian therapy sessions are typically held once a week, with the client and therapist facing each other. Early in the treatment the therapist tries to establish a comfortable, trusting relationship. Often the therapist paraphrases what the client says but focuses on feelings rather than thoughts. For instance, if the client says, "I'm depressed," the therapist may respond by saying, "Sounds like you're really feeling down." Through this process, the client comes to feel heard and understood. As therapy progresses, passive reflection by the therapist is gradually replaced by active interpretation. The therapist goes beyond the overt content of what the client says, responding now to what the therapist senses are the client's true feelings. The therapist starts to confront the client with inconsistencies in the client's statements, and points out that the client is failing to take responsibility for personal actions. In an accepting atmosphere where anything that is felt may be expressed, the focus is on the client's present feelings, as opposed to past feelings. As therapy progresses, the client becomes more and more aware of feelings that have been denied and learns to accept those feelings and to incorporate them into the self-concept. In short, the client gains a comfortable sense of "getting it together," which in Rogerian terms means that the client is experiencing *congruence*.

The following client-centered dialogue might typically occur after three or four months of therapy. Notice the "here-and-now" orientation, as opposed to the emphasis on childhood experiences that characterizes psychoanalysis. Note also that we are using the term "client" rather than "patient." Freud came from a medical tradition wherein those who seek help have some sort of pathology or sickness, and therefore were referred to as patients. In contrast, existential-humanistic therapists, with their emphasis on psychological growth, refer to those seeking help as clients.

CLIENT: Boy, this has been one of those weeks!

THERAPIST: Sounds like you are feeling frustrated. What's been happening, Barbara?

CLIENT: This time it's my boss at work. The s.o.b. actually propositioned me!

THERAPIST: You are feeling pretty angry, then?

CLIENT: Yeah, kind of.

THERAPIST: Now I hear you saying that you aren't that angry after all. Let's talk about your feelings about him.

CLIENT: I feel . . . yeah, it irritated me, but maybe it kind of flattered me too . . . almost . . . like, turned me on.

THERAPIST: When you said "turned me on," you were looking out the window. It made me feel you were avoiding me.

CLIENT: This is making me uncomfortable.

THERAPIST: I guess what I hear you saying is that I'm making you feel uncomfortable.

CLIENT: Talking about yesterday makes me feel uncomfortable. I'm confused.

THERAPIST: Alright, let's see if we can get a handle on where you're coming from. You felt angry and maybe insulted because of the way he came on to you, but it also frightened you, and you felt sexually excited.

CLIENT: I don't know . . . sexually excited is putting it strongly. Oh, I suppose so.

THERAPIST: I'm picking up that you were sexually turned on but that acknowledging this makes you feel scared or guilty.

CLIENT (*after a long pause*): Bob, it's my old hang-up. You know, sex is dirty and I'm not *supposed* to be turned on! Will I *ever* get over this!

THERAPIST: So, Barbara . . . you are wondering whether you will be stuck with these feelings forever.

CLIENT: Sometimes you really frustrate me!

THERAPIST: Tell me how you are feeling towards me, right now. Angry maybe?

CLIENT: Kind of. Mostly I feel that you must think I'm pretty stupid, having these hang-ups and all.

THERAPIST: Do I hear you apologizing for being a normal human being? Everybody has hang-ups, including me.

CLIENT: Sure you do!! Name one.

THERAPIST: OK. I'm afraid of high places.

CLIENT: Really? You are really afraid of high places? Somehow hearing you say that makes me feel good.

THERAPIST: I hear you saying that you feel good that I'm just as human as you are.

CLIENT: That's true. You know, I'm feeling better now. A lot better than when I came in.

THERAPIST: I almost get the feeling you are relieved.

CLIENT: Yes, I suppose so. Actually you aren't at all like my boss.

THERAPIST: I don't know whether to be flattered or not *(laughs)*. But, how am I different . . . or how do you see your boss as different?

Over time, Rogers's work has been applied not only to individual psychotherapy but also to human-relations training for professionals of all kinds (for example, nurses, Peace Corps volunteers, and crisis and "hot-line" counselors) to work more effectively with others. Rogers's ideas have also been used in group psychotherapy, including encounter groups, and in work with couples. His theories have even been applied in teacher training and educational settings, encouraging more open classrooms, more decision making by students, and more creativity and experimentation in the curriculum.

Evaluation of Client-centered Therapy   It is to Rogers's credit that he and his colleagues have emphasized research and evaluation, publishing systematic studies of the success of their methods (see Rogers & Dymond, 1954; Rogers, Gendlin, Kiesler, & Truax, 1967). Additionally, Rogers's research on the therapy *process* in terms of the contribution of warmth, genuineness, and unconditional positive regard, has clearly shown that these ingredients contribute significantly to the success of psychotherapy. Indeed, most therapists of any school of thought believe that these ingredients facilitate therapeutic change, and they attempt to incorporate these qualities into their work.

Critics of this approach (Bandura, 1969) object to Rogerian methods on the basis of the fact that regardless of the client's complaints, the treatment is always the same. (The same criticism has been leveled at psychoanalysis.) Some critics contend that providing the client with "unconditional positive regard" may actually be harmful, as clients may leave therapy with the unrealistic expectation that anything they do will meet with society's approval. Client-centered therapy has also been criticized on the grounds that the theory behind it is incomplete, as compared with psychoanalysis or behavior therapy. In fact, Rogers attempted to systematize his approach at the suggestion of some of his students, though initially he did not intend to put forth a systematic, theoretically elaborate point of view.

Gestalt therapy was the brainchild of German-born psychiatrist Frederick (Fritz) Perls (1893–1970), who became dissatisfied with psychoanalysis, calling it "a disease that pretends to be a cure." He called his new ideas "Gestalt therapy," referring to the German word that means pattern or organized whole. His work became influential in the 1960s when he began holding seminars at Esalen, on the Big Sur coast of California, with followers flocking there to study with him and learn his methods.

Gestalt therapists basically object to theorizing and to research, finding them to be confining. Nevertheless, the theory of Gestalt therapy, like that of Rogers, emphasizes self-actualizing tendencies that may become thwarted in the process of learning to get along in society. People learn not to be aware of much of what is going on around them and inside of them. Therefore, therapy's goal is to help them learn to become more aware. *Awareness* is the central concept in Gestalt psychotherapy and covers virtually everything, including thoughts and emotions, dreams and fantasies, body sensations, movements, posture, muscular tensions and facial expressions, as well as an appreciation for the environment and our relationship with it.

Gestalt therapists believe that psychologically healthy people are aware of themselves so fully that they can detect whatever requires their attention. Maladjustment is a blockage of awareness. Awareness is thought to be critical, because if people are unaware of what they want or feel at any given moment, they have limited control over their feelings and behavior. At such times, they act out of habit, rather than choice, and habits may often be self-defeating. The goal of the therapy is to become aware in order to confront and make choices, the assumption being that when they make choices, people choose self-enhancing, growthful options instead of self-defeating ones that they may have used before.

Treatment in Gestalt Therapy   The client-centered relationship in Gestalt therapy is similar to the relationship between an apprentice and a master (Kempler, 1973). The skill or art is awareness. As the relationship develops, the therapist uses his or her awareness to fa-

Fritz Perls, on the right, listens as an Esalen staff member describes a dream during a Gestalt therapy workshop. Awareness is the central concept in Gestalt psychotherapy.

cilitate the growth of awareness in the client. While there is no set formula for doing this, Perls and his followers do provide guidelines (Levitsky & Perls, 1970). Like client-centered therapy, Gestalt therapy emphasizes what the client is experiencing at the present moment. In contrast to psychoanalysis, the therapist is more interested in how a client feels about his mother *now* and less interested in what he thought and felt about her as a young child.

An important element of this therapy is that the client should develop a sense of personal responsibility. Gestalt therapists believe that any action implies a choice and with choice goes responsibility. Sometimes the therapist deliberately frustrates the client, especially if the client tries to lean on the therapist when support is not really necessary. The Gestalt therapist always emphasizes awareness on the part of the client, often using what is called *directed experimentation*. A directed experiment is a psychological exercise carried out in a consulting room or at home. The best known of these is called the "empty chair."

In the *empty-chair exercise*, the client moves back and forth physically between two chairs. In one of the two chairs, the client assumes his or her own role. In the other chair, the client assumes the role of another person, perhaps a parent or spouse. Clients also can use the two chairs to represent two conflicting aspects of themselves. For example, a client reported that whenever she thought about her dead father she became anxious and confused. She was asked to imagine her father in the empty chair and to tell him what she resented about him. In a minute or two she was telling her imagined father, in a very emotional voice, that she could never forgive him for dying without ever telling her he loved her and was proud of her. She was then asked to sit in the other chair and reply as her father would. The "father" was also emotional, saying in a sad, tearful way that he had indeed loved his daughter, but that he had never been able to express his feelings because men were not supposed to be emotional. At the end of this exercise, the client said that she felt more "together" about her father. For many years, this woman had been carrying around unexpressed feelings toward her father, which a Gestalt therapist would call "unfinished business." Becoming aware of these feelings allows clients to experience a sense of completion, freeing them to deal with today's problems.

In another exercise, called *amplification*, the therapist asks the client to exaggerate some behavior or feeling in order to become more aware of it. For instance, a client always talked about his wife in glowing terms, but the therapist noticed that at the same time, the client tended to draw his fingers toward his palm ever so slightly. When asked to exaggerate what he was experiencing, the client made a fist and struck the table, saying, "Why does she have to put me down all the time?"

Of course, the ultimate goal of Gestalt therapy is not simply to help the client become aware of some specific problem, but rather to teach the client *how* to become aware so that the client may do this independently. When this has been achieved, therapy is complete.

Evaluation of Gestalt Therapy   Proponents of Gestalt therapy point to the large number of people who have adopted this therapeutic approach, arguing that the growth of Gestalt therapy is a sure sign that it is effective. Critics point out that little has been done to validate Gestalt therapy with well-controlled research (see Rimm & Masters, 1979). These critics argue that we do not know whether Gestalt therapy is effective or not. Many Gestalt therapists, like many psychoanalysts, reply that we do not need controlled research because the direct personal experience of so many clients provides such convincing evidence that the treatment works. Gestalt therapists also argue that their treatment is so individualized that it cannot be put to the same experimental tests used with more standardized techniques. But in recent years, certain Gestalt adherents have put elements of their approach through rigorous experimental tests (briefly reviewed in Simkin & Yontef, 1984), suggesting that exercises such as the empty chair can be effective tools in therapy.

Behavior Therapies

Behavior therapy is the overall name given to a large number of specific techniques that are based on using learning principles to change problem behavior. These approaches have been particularly prominent since the 1950s, and in contrast to most other forms of therapy, arose in part as practical applications derived from academic research in learning.

In contrast to psychodynamic and existential-humanistic psychotherapies that attempt to help people by changing their underlying personalities, behavior therapy helps people solve their problems by changing their behaviors. According to this model, the phobic behavior, or the depression, or the sexual dysfunction *is* the problem, not merely an overt symptom of some underlying problem. Therefore, the goal is to alter behavior, including emotional behavior and thoughts, by means of the systematic application of principles of human learning. There are treatments based on conditioning (operant and classical), on observational learning or modeling, and more recently, on theories of human information processing involving cognitive schemas. We will present brief examples of conditioning approaches and modeling and a more extended discussion of systematic desensitization as an example of a process employing various behavior-modification tools. We will also include a discussion of the recently developed cognitive-behavioral approaches to treatment that have been developed in response to some of the shortcomings of the classical behavior-modification approaches.

Applications of Operant and Classical Conditioning   Based on the experimental work of B. F. Skinner and others, positive and negative reinforcements have been applied systematically to change a variety of problem behaviors. For instance, positive reinforcers in the form of candy, praise, or tokens that can be exchanged for goods have been used to modify such diverse behaviors as the amount of time a disruptive child spends sitting at his desk in the classroom (time was increased), personal hygiene in institutionalized schizophrenics (hygiene was improved), speech in retarded children (the children spoke more frequently), smoking among chronic smokers (the behavior occurred less often), and a host of others. Similarly, negative reinforcements—taking away tokens or privileges, ignoring attention-seeking behaviors, or (in the past) even the administration of mildly noxious punishment such as electric shock—have also been used to reduce undesirable behavior. The reinforcers are commonly applied in the settings in which the behaviors in question occur, usually by teachers, or nurses, or staff members who are specially trained in behavioral techniques. The reinforcement techniques have also been applied in self-control programs, where the individual rewards himself or herself for successful completion of the desired behavior. For example, a college student may be taught by a behavior therapist to deal with procrastination in connection with coursework preparation by giving herself a "treat" of some kind each time she successfully completes a brief, planned period of studying. *Self-control therapies* help individuals change their own behavior by rearranging stimuli in their daily environment and reinforcing themselves for appropriate behaviors, especially if they set realistic, step-by-step daily goals. Such programs have been used for various problems, including smoking, overeating, and excessive drinking (Mahoney & Mahoney, 1976; Marlatt, 1979; Thoresen & Mahoney, 1974).

Classical conditioning in the form of *aversive conditioning* has been employed when certain habits are especially hard to break. In this approach, an aversive experience, such as painful electric shock or chemically induced nausea, is paired with stimuli associated with the harmful habit. After many pairings, the habit tends to lose its appeal. These procedures have been used with a variety of problems, such as certain patterns of sexual deviancy or excessive drinking, and they are widely used in well-marketed smoking control and weight-reduction programs.

Modeling Procedures   In some ways, learning by observation of another person is one of the most powerful learning tools available (Bandura, 1969). Modeling may actually be an important ingredient

A therapist administers aversive conditioning treatment to a convicted child molester by showing pictures of young girls and giving the subject unpleasant electric shocks in order to break up the subject's tendency to associate children with sexual pleasure.

of most therapies, as clients come to learn how their therapists go about analyzing and solving problems. Observational learning has been systematically applied in behavior modification. In *participant modeling* a client observes and then imitates a therapist's approach to a feared object (Bandura, Blanchard, & Ritter, 1969). Modeling may be an ingredient in *assertiveness training* or in another form of *social-skills training*. An individual who lacks the ability to function effectively in certain interpersonal situations may observe the therapist or another model displaying the desired behaviors and then attempt to imitate them in appropriate situations.

Evaluation of "Traditional" Behavior Therapies   Hundreds of studies have been conducted on the effectiveness of behavior modification using the principles of operant, classical, or imitation learning. Arising from a base in academic psychology, behavior therapy has typically been applied by therapists who strongly value research and who insist on demonstrated change as evidence of the effectiveness of the treatment. Despite its undeniable efficacy, three criticisms have been leveled at behavior modification. First, there are philosophical criticisms: psychoanalysts believe that behavior modification gets only at surface change, leaving the "real" problems unresolved, while humanistic therapists believe that behavior modification is dehumanizing and mechanical. Second, many of the successes of behavior modification have occurred with fairly simple problems. While these may be important and certainly provide a necessary alternative to talk psychotherapies for children and severely impaired adults, the procedures do not readily lend themselves to fairly complex problems. Third, despite research showing effectiveness in therapy outcomes, many of the gains have been shown to be brief in duration or narrow in applicability—that is, they do not generalize to situations other than the one that was originally targeted in the therapy. A child may learn to sit still during math with one teacher but not necessarily in social studies with a different teacher, or a person may learn to be assertive with her boss, but not with her mother.

Systematic Desensitization   As developed by Joseph Wolpe (1958), *systematic desensitization* defies classification according to specific learning principles, but it has been widely and effectively employed in the treatment of phobias and other problems involving overt anxiety. The aim of using the procedure, as originally described by Wolpe, is to substitute a reaction (relaxation) to fear stimuli that is incompatible with tension. The client is first taught to relax by successively tensing and relaxing voluntary muscles, practicing the relaxation exercises until relaxation can be readily induced. Then, the therapist and client establish a hierarchy of scenes involving the feared object or situation. This hierarchy is a series of increasingly frightening images. These are presented one at a time, usually only a few per session, beginning with the least fearful scene. The client practices the relaxation while vividly imagining the scene, and when it can be imagined without strong anxiety, the next scene is presented. If the client experiences anxiety, he or she is directed to return to an imagined scene that they have described as peaceful and calming, until the tension subsides. Gradually, the client can picture each frightening experience without intolerable fear and avoidance. Ideally, after working through the hierarchy using imagined scenes, the therapist and client may try to tackle the real-life situations (again, in a hierarchical fashion), while the client practices relaxation. The following hierarchy (from Rimm & Masters, 1979) was used with a middle-aged insurance salesman who had developed a phobia about dealing with clients and co-workers, especially if there were some possibility of failure on his part. The first two items are presented as they actually were used, while items 3 to 17 are given in summary form.

1. You are in your office with an agent, R. C., discussing a prospective interview. The client in question is stalling on his payments, and you must tell R. C. what to do.

2. It is Monday morning and you are at your office. In a few minutes you will attend the regularly scheduled sales meeting. You are prepared for the meeting.

3. Conducting an exploratory interview with a prospective client.

4. Sitting at home. The telephone rings.

5. Anticipating returning a call from the district director.

6. Anticipating returning a call from a stranger.

7. Entering the Monday sales meeting, unprepared.

8. Anticipating a visit from the regional director.

9. A fellow agent requests a joint visit with a client.

10. On a joint visit with a fellow agent.

11. Attempting to close a sale.

12. Thinking about attending an agents' and managers' meeting.

13. Thinking of contacting a client who should have been contacted earlier.

14. Thinking about calling a prospective client.

15. Thinking about the regional director's request for names of prospective agents.

16. Alone, driving to a prospective client's home.

17. Calling on a prospective client.

Many research studies show that systematic desensitization is an effective therapy for phobias. But the technique remains somewhat controversial because no one is really sure *how* it works (Rimm & Lefebvre, 1981; Kazdin & Wilcoxon, 1976). It is likely that a common ingredient of successful behavioral treatment of phobias involves *exposure* to the feared objects or situations (Barlow & Wolfe, 1981). Facing the fearful event (instead of escaping or avoiding it) probably helps the person to see that he or she can confront a feared situation without disaster.

Cognitive-behavioral Therapies Cognitive-behavioral therapies constitute a relatively recent approach to treatment, placing emphasis on the role of *maladaptive thinking* in clinical problems. This approach attempts to use behavioral and cognitive techniques to systematically alter dysfunctional thoughts and to establish more effective problem-solving strategies. An important contributor to this field has been Aaron Beck (1967, 1976), who argued that depression, anxiety, and other complex emotional disorders are often rooted in the maladaptive ways in which people think about themselves and their worlds. A depressed person characteristically thinks negatively and is likely to view even minor or neutral events as self-devaluing or hopeless. Such thoughts in turn deepen the depression and may lower the person's motivation and will to take constructive action. Therefore, therapy attempts to teach depressed or anxious clients to think about their situations in the most realistic possible ways and to take active steps to challenge their beliefs that they are worthless, inadequate, and unable to change their condition. This *cognitive restructuring* is accompanied by problem solving and skill building in the areas that may have contributed to the person's depression. Thus, a depressed person who has experienced the loss of a relationship may be encouraged to form friendships, meet new people, and communicate more effectively in intimate situations. Table 18–1 presents an example of cognitive restructuring during the course of therapy in which the client (Joe) is taught to recognize "automatic negative thoughts" that may cause emotional reactions and to challenge them in constructive ways. In the example, after discussing strategies directly with the therapist, Joe may have completed this real-life exercise as a "homework assignment," a process that emphasizes that learning and self-regulation of behavior are not limited to what goes on in the therapy hour. Other cognitive therapists have developed similar strategies called *self-instructional techniques* and *anxiety-management procedures* aimed specifically at dealing with situations that produce fear and tension (Meichenbaum, 1977; Suinn, 1975).

Among the advantages of the cognitive-behavioral approaches are that they tackle complex problems, attempting to identify maladaptive thoughts and beliefs that occur in connection with many different situations. Thus, they are viewed as less mechanical or more in tune with people's conscious experiences than are strict behavioristic approaches. Cognitive-behavioral approaches have stirred considerable controversy within the behavioral ranks; orthodox behaviorists view them with suspicion as a return to "unscientific mentalism." However, the efficacy of cognitive-behavioral approaches is clearly demonstrated for difficult-to-treat problems, such as clinical depression and other emotional disorders, and the effects appear to be long-lasting (see Sacco & Beck, 1985). Since there is currently a great deal of emphasis on thinking processes and human cognition in many other areas of psychology, the trend in clinical psychology toward widespread practice of cognitive-behavioral approaches seems likely to continue.

Before leaving our discussion of cognitive psychotherapy, mention must be made of the contribution of Albert Ellis (1962, 1984), the founder of *rational emotive therapy*. His system is both a philosophy and a set of therapeutic techniques, emphasizing the basic idea that

TABLE 18–1   Illustration of a Cognitive-behavioral Technique

Situation	Automatic Negative Thoughts	Realistic Alternatives
I haven't had a girl-friend and I am very lonely. I'm too scared to ask a woman out.	If I asked Jane out, she'd say no. (That would be devastating.)	This is mind-reading. I don't really know what she'd say. I'll have to try it and see. It might be disappointing, but probably I'm exaggerating how bad it would be.
	I'm too ordinary. I don't have anything special to offer.	I'm probably selling myself short. I'll make a list of some of my positive qualities. There certainly are other guys getting dates who aren't handsome, brilliant, or rich.
	I'll never find a woman who will like me.	This is catastrophizing! How do I know I won't unless I try. I have to get out and make the effort.
	I'll always be alone.	Another example of depressive thinking! It might be hard to overcome my fears with women but not impossible.

Source: After Beck, Rush, Shaw, & Emery, 1979.

what we say to ourselves strongly influences how we feel and what we do. According to Ellis, there are several maladaptive beliefs that are shared by many people in this culture; these beliefs underlie much of human distress. One example would be the belief that "without love, I am worthless." Ellis believes that people tyrannize themselves with "shoulds" and "oughts." The process of therapy is one of systematically identifying and disputing such maladaptive beliefs and structuring behaviors to help people convince themselves that they can be effective and worthwhile.

PSYCHOTHERAPY: DOES IT WORK AND WHICH ONE IS BEST?

Now that we have considered each of the three major schools of psychotherapy, the next question is how they compare with each other. Table 18–2 summarizes the theoretical and procedural differences. It

TABLE 18–2 A Comparison of Major Psychological Approaches

	Psychoanalytic	*Existential-humanistic*	*Behavioral*
Importance of biological factors (anatomy, heredity, instincts, hormones)	Strong	Weak to moderate	Weak to moderate
Free will versus determinism	Highly deterministic	Stresses free will and choice	Highly deterministic
Emphasis on childhood experiences	Strong	Weak to moderate	Weak
Emphasis on the "here and now"	Weak to moderate	Strong	Moderate to strong
Adherence to "healing sickness" versus "growth"	Healing sickness stressed	Growth strongly emphasized	Learning emphasis closer to "growth" than to "healing"
Therapeutic goals	Thorough personality reorganization	Personality reorganization	Change specific behaviors, emotions, or thoughts
Duration of treatment	Usually long term (at least one year)	Short to long term (presumes that some clients can benefit from a few months of treatment)	Short to moderate duration (presumes that most clients can benefit from a few months of treatment)
Experimental validation of therapeutic approach	Weak*	Client-centered—moderate to strong, others—weak*	Very strong

*In recent years, both psychoanalytic and existential-humanistic approaches have begun to emphasize research.

is important to keep in mind that some oversimplification is involved, since each of the models includes numerous variations that differ somewhat from one another.

Considerable research over the past several decades has established that psychotherapy "works" as compared to no treatment (reviews by Bergin & Lambert, 1978; Shapiro & Shapiro, 1982; Smith, Glass, & Miller, 1980). (If you think that perhaps you might benefit from receiving psychotherapy, see the box entitled "Seeking Professional Help" to aid you in deciding whether or not to try therapy and how to go about finding the kind of therapy you need.) In a recent review of many of the studies over the past 30 years, Howard, Kopta, Krause, and Orlinsky (1986) found that after they had completed eight sessions of psychotherapy, approximately 50 percent of all patients were improved, and approximately 75 percent were improved by the end of 26 sessions.

Despite demonstrations of the effectiveness of psychotherapy, however, one of the puzzling findings of research has been that most studies that have compared specific types of psychotherapy with each other have failed to demonstrate notable differences between them in

◆ SEEKING PROFESSIONAL HELP

HOW DO I KNOW IF I NEED HELP (OR IF SOMEONE CLOSE TO ME DOES)? If you experience *persistent* or *recurrent* distress, you might consider seeking psychotherapy. Negative feelings cause discomfort; excessive worries, fears, and depression rob you of feelings of contentment and personal satisfaction, and if they go on too long or are moderately severe, they are likely to disrupt your sleep, appetite, and physical well-being as well as interfere with your behavior.

If you find (or others point out to you) that you are showing impairment in roles that are important to you—as a student, as a worker, as a friend or intimate partner—therapy may be helpful. Examples might be that your drinking is causing you to get into fights or to be late for work, that your depression makes you irritable and withdrawn from your family and friends or unable to study, or that your fears of what people are thinking about you make you avoid certain activities that would be good for you. In extreme cases, your friends or family might feel that your behavior is unusual or odd and that it should be evaluated by a professional.

Sometimes therapy is very valuable just for self-exploration. Maybe you do not feel extremely upset and your life as a student or family member is without problems but you sense that something is "missing." Or perhaps you have experienced some significantly traumatic event or childhood experience whose impact on you has never been explored. Maybe you feel that you are coping with life, but that you are not as creative, energetic, open to new experiences, or able to feel strong emotions as you would like to be. There is much greater acceptance of psychotherapy today than ever before, and you do not have to be (or think of yourself as) mentally ill to engage in psychotherapy.

HOW DO I FIND THE RIGHT PSYCHOTHERAPY? The two major determinants of your search in seeking the right form of psychotherapy are likely to be your *goals* and your *financial resources*. Most community agencies, including training facilities, and some psychotherapists in independent practice offer services on a "sliding fee scale" based on a formula related to income. At the low-fee end, community agencies and training facilities may be more available, while the high end would consist primarily of private psychotherapists, specialty clinics, and hospitals. Large institutions, such as colleges and universities, and some facilities and corporations may offer the services of their own counseling centers for free or at a low cost to their students or employees; if you belong to a prepaid health-insurance plan, they typically have their own facilities or recommend certain agencies or "providers." The following suggestions are given for locating the facility that best meets your needs:

1. Try community or county mental health agencies. Most geographic areas of each city or state are served by a public mental health agency, listed in the phone book, and you can find out what services are available to you and the cost. Such agencies may also refer you to appropriate sources as needed.

2. Local professional associations, such as your county or state psychological association, or an association of marriage and family counselors may give referral information over the telephone. You could call and describe what kinds of services you are looking for, and they may be able to provide names of private therapists for you to consult.

3. Universities and some colleges often have training clinics that are staffed by students seeking advanced degrees in some therapy

profession. Such clinics may provide low-fee therapies, and you can be assured that such programs include close professional supervision of trainees. Such clinics may also be able to make referrals and provide information about other facilities and services available to you in the community.

YOUR RIGHTS AS CONSUMERS   The psychotherapeutic relationship is a very special, sensitive, and significant relationship and should be selected with care and with high standards. Naturally the therapist should be qualified by training and licensure, but you should also feel free to inquire about the person's experience and theoretical orientation. Therapists are required by law and by professional standards to maintain ethical conduct, including protection of your privacy and confidentiality (with specific exceptions required by law), and to show regard for your welfare. Sexual and personal relationships are strictly forbidden. Any characteristics or behaviors of the therapist that discourage an atmosphere of trust may impede the development of an effective therapy, so that you may wish to interview several therapists when you are just beginning treatment. You should also consider whether you might feel more comfortable with a male or female therapist, or whether other qualities of the person, such as ethnicity, might enhance your comfort and trust. This is not to say that working with someone of the same age, sex, and ethnicity will bring the best results. The point is that you have the right to make your wishes known, and within the range of selection open to you, you have the right to choose what you hope will be the best course for your needs.

success rates. Reviews of comparative outcome research (for example, Luborsky, Singer, & Luborsky, 1975; Smith et al., 1980) led Luborsky to borrow a phrase from Lewis Carroll: "Everybody has won and all must have prizes." For instance, Klein et al. (1983) found basically no differences in reduction of fears and changes in approach behavior between dynamically oriented therapy and systematic desensitization during 26 weeks of treatment for phobic patients. Sloane et al. (1975) found similar outcomes for patients receiving behavior therapy and short-term dynamically oriented therapy. Many other carefully controlled studies have found few differences in outcomes when quite different methods were compared.

There have been a number of explanations offered for the paradox of similar results despite diverse procedures (Stiles, Shapiro, & Elliott, 1986). Certainly one argument has been that different schools of therapy define improvement in different ways, so that the various methods may not have been compared on measures that are equally relevant. Consider a common problem: fear of public speaking. To a psychoanalyst, this fear probably reflects some deep-seated unconscious concern, perhaps stemming from an unresolved Oedipal complex. Therefore, improvement would have to be measured as a reduction in unconscious conflicts, assessed perhaps through in-depth interviews, dream analysis, or projective techniques such as the Rorschach. In contrast, an existential-humanistic therapist might view speech anxiety as a reflection of low self-esteem and work with the client to change self-concept. Improvement would then be measured as a change in self-esteem, assessed perhaps by a questionnaire or interviews. A behaviorist would be likely to view the fear of public speaking as the problem in and of itself and would focus on direct measures of improved skill at giving a speech as well as on self-reports and physiological measures of anxiety while speaking.

Another common explanation for the finding that therapies seem to be fairly similar in their success rates is that apart from differences in *techniques* and *theories*, there may be some elements common to most therapies that account for changes in people. The question of the *process* by which change occurs has been an intense focus of research. While there are as yet no definitive answers as to what makes therapies successful, two important factors involving the therapist have emerged repeatedly (Stiles, Shapiro, & Elliott, 1986). One quality that appears to be requisite is warm involvement with the client; the second quality is communication of a new perspective on the client's characteristics and behavior. Current research on the "therapeutic alliance," which is related to these qualities is promising as a clue to what makes therapy successful as a source of change. Research has shown that the therapeutic alliance, which is defined as the emotional bond and mutual involvement between the therapist and client on the tasks of therapy, is a significant predictor of successful outcome. The client's contribution to and perception of the alliance is an especially critical component here (Luborsky, Crits-Christoph, Alexander, Margolis, & Cohen, 1983; Horowitz, Marmar, Weiss, DeWitt, & Rosenbaum, 1984; Marziali, 1984).

Despite the lack of definitive success of one therapy form over another, it is clearly unreasonable to conclude that it does not matter what kind of therapy a person undertakes. The therapy process is so complex, involving many different types of problems and client characteristics, many types of techniques and therapist characteristics, all interacting with each other over the course of time, that we simply do not yet know how best to *match* clients with the best kind of therapy for their characteristics and problems. (For a discussion of the different kinds of therapists, see the box entitled "Psychotherapist Training.") In an effort to attempt to be flexible and to tailor treatments to particular client needs, many therapists have adopted the approach of *eclecticism* (also called *technical eclecticism* or *multimodal therapy*). Basically, an eclectic therapist borrows techniques from a variety of schools and perspectives and tailors the treatment to the specific client. In a practical sense, most therapists probably take a somewhat eclectic approach in order to find the right combination of techniques for a particular patient.

ALTERNATIVES TO INDIVIDUAL PSYCHOTHERAPY

Group Treatment

Over the past 30 years, a significant development in psychological therapy has been the group movement (Lubin & Lubin, 1980). In the mid-1950s, group therapy usually meant some form of psychoanalytic therapy adapted to a group setting. The early group methods included *psychodrama* (Moreno, 1934), in which people literally acted out important emotional experiences on a stage in order to obtain insight and emotional relief. Group therapy today, however, refers to

◆ PSYCHOTHERAPIST TRAINING

There are so many different kinds of therapists and therapies that it is confusing to the consumer. Here is a brief guide to the major kinds of therapists and their training. Remember that regardless of the person's professional title, he or she should be *licensed* by an appropriate agency of the state in order to verify that the appropriate education and training experiences have been completed and that the person has demonstrated competency in statewide examinations.

Clinical psychologist—These individuals have completed a Ph.D. program in clinical psychology, which usually requires four to six years of education in psychology beyond the bachelor's degree, several years of training in clinical services, and at least one full year of full-time supervised clinical training. Not all psychologists are trained as psychotherapists (social psychologists and cognitive psychologists are not), and therefore they are not qualified to conduct psychotherapy unless they have supplemented their Ph.D. education with specialized clinical training. Many states permit persons who have completed doctorates in counseling psychology or professional psychology (Psy.D.) to qualify for licensure as psychologists offering professional therapy services.

Psychiatrist—These medical professionals have completed a medical degree (M.D.) plus three to four years of specialized residency training in psychiatry. This is a medical specialty, and only persons with M.D. degrees can prescribe medications for the treatment of psychological disorders.

Psychoanalyst—These professionals have received several years of specialized training in the principles of psychoanalysis, including a personal "training" analysis. Traditionally, such training has been offered by special training institutes outside of an academic setting and typically has been open only to psychiatrists, although recently a few have opened their doors to other mental-health professionals as well.

Other psychotherapists—This classification includes persons with M.A. or M.S.-level training in therapy with adults, children, or families or an MSW degree (Master of Social Work—approximately two years of M.A.-level education in social work and specialized training in therapy). Additionally, some nursing programs offer specialization in psychiatric nursing that may qualify the person for psychotherapy, and there are numerous other counseling degrees and programs with focused specialties, limiting their graduates to certain populations or methods (pastoral counseling, academic or job counseling, and so forth) that are not considered to be psychotherapy.

Nonprofessional therapists—While not licensed to work independently or receive fees for services, there are numerous projects or programs that have given highly focused training to nonprofessionals to work with certain populations under specific conditions (adult peer counselors working with the elderly, college students working with teenage drug addicts, or women homemakers working with pregnant teenagers). Interestingly, numerous research studies have confirmed that nonprofessionals are often just as effective as professional therapists, especially when they have had extensive training and experience (Berman & Norton, 1985; Hattie, Sharpley, & Rogers, 1984).

any psychological treatment that is carried out in a group. We could be referring to analytic therapy, client-centered therapy, Gestalt therapy, behavior therapy, or a dozen other varieties.

Why conduct therapy in a group? Yalom (1970) lists several reasons why a group is an effective setting for therapeutic change.

A group therapy session for teens provides members with an opportunity to discover that their problems are not unique.

Groups provide members with a massive infusion of information, giving them the opportunity to discover that their problems are not unique. Groups encourage the members to practice helping behaviors and provide a "familylike" setting that is potentially healthier than the setting the individual group member might have experienced while growing up. Groups create opportunities to learn how one affects others, to develop social and leadership skills, and to discover a sense of belonging and intimacy. They also provide a safe place to vent one's pent-up emotions. Depending on the orientation of the group, some of these aspects will be emphasized more than others. Thus, a psychoanalytically oriented group might emphasize the sharing of experiences and the development of group cohesiveness within the context of psychological growth. A behavioral group might focus on modeling and the practice of social skills. Another obvious advantage of group treatment is economic: a client may pay considerably more for individual therapy than for group treatment.

In the 1970s, *encounter groups* were especially popular, espousing goals of growth and self-exploration rather than reduction of symptoms. These groups were often led by Gestalt or client-centered therapists, but in their heyday they were wildly eclectic, sometimes involving dance, theater, psychodrama, and even nudity. Unfortunately, not all of these group experiences were found to be helpful. Lieberman, Yalom, and Miles (1973) compared the effects of many different encounter groups and found that some members became "casualties" who suffered negative emotional experiences. Whether participants benefited or were harmed depended largely on the group leader; some leaders were clearly more constructive than others. The word of caution is simply this: before you join an encounter group, check out the experience and credentials of the leader and if possible, talk to people who have been in his or her group. In most areas an individual does not need a license to lead encounter groups, as long as the leader is careful not to call it therapy. As a result, some totally unqualified people have organized groups, and some group members have been pushed beyond the breaking point.

Within the behavior therapy camp, *group assertiveness training* has currently become a popular form of group therapy. Some of Yalom's observations about the value of group therapy are especially true of group assertiveness training: the group can provide a member with many potential models of appropriate behavior; the group judgment of what is or is not appropriately assertive may be better than that of a single therapist in a one-to-one setting; the group can also give collective social reinforcement to members who demonstrate more effective or assertive behavior. There is considerable evidence for the effectiveness of assertiveness training groups (see Hammen, Jacobs, Mayol, & Cochran, 1980). Many other behavioral treatments may also be administered in group formats. These include cognitive therapy for depression, weight control, parent training, speech phobias, and fear of flying.

Family Therapy

Another form that psychotherapy may take involves the treatment of an entire family as the patient. There are as many variants of family

Family therapy may sometimes be utilized to deal with the problems of communication experienced by married couples.

therapy as there are of individual psychotherapy, including psychoanalytic, existential-humanistic, and behavioral forms. Needless to say, family approaches are most commonly used when a child or adolescent is having difficulties, but they may sometimes be utilized to deal with adult or couple problems as well. The more dynamic or systems-oriented approaches might be especially likely to focus on disturbed alliances within the family (Minuchin, 1974), while some of the more humanistic family therapies emphasize the nature of communications (Satir, 1967). Behavioral approaches, on the other hand, are more likely to address the maladaptive behaviors of family members and to try to improve skills of exchanging rewards and communications (Patterson et al., 1975).

The Community Mental Health Approach

''Community mental health'' evolved as a concept in the 1960s, stimulated by important federal and state legislation establishing public mental health services in the community. The term has come to represent several themes: an emphasis on decentralization of services and concomitant transfer of these services into the communities patients come from; an emphasis on the prevention of mental health problems or the prevention of their becoming more serious; or an emphasis on services that include different kinds of treatment besides one-to-one discussion in an office.

Services Right in the Community   The availability of mental health services in the community has become so standard as to seem obvious, but this was not always the case. In past decades, the seriously mentally ill were frequently sent to large state mental hospitals, often at a great distance from their homes. They frequently stayed in these hospitals for long periods of time (often for the remainder of their lives if suffering chronic problems). Services for the less seriously afflicted were scarce or nonexistent, unless the family was wealthy enough to pay for them privately. Today public services are available for everyone, and it is assumed that it is best for the seriously ill patient's adjustment to spend as brief a time in a hospital as possible, avoiding the problems of "institutionalism." There is an emphasis on "aftercare" of discharged patients, helping them to reside in the community either with their families or sometimes in "halfway" houses or board-and-care facilities and providing them with ongoing services on an outpatient basis. The widespread use of medications for severely ill patients has greatly diminished the need for continuous hospitalization.

Prevention　The emphasis on preventing the development or worsening of mental health problems has led to the implementation of services that are designed to detect problems at their earliest stages (for example, child abuse reporting and treatment services) and to deal with crises immediately by means of telephone "hot lines," suicide-prevention services, rape-counseling services, and shelters for battered women. This philosophy has also played a role in aftercare programs that attempt to treat chronic mental health problems in ways that prevent the need for institutionalization.

Nontraditional Interventions　A theme throughout the community mental health approach is the creative use of settings and helpers to provide assistance. This may include not only the widespread use of paraprofessionals who are specially trained to provide limited services, but also the development of certain kinds of residential programs that do not rely on individual psychotherapy. One promising approach to aftercare is the Fairweather Lodge (see Fairweather, Sanders, Maynard, & Cressler, 1969; Rimm & Masters, 1979). Fairweather Lodges, like halfway houses, provide support and structure to outpatients. Designed especially for chronically schizophrenic patient who may not be able to exist independently in the community,

Crisis-intervention services, such as rape-counseling centers, shelters for battered women, and suicide "hot lines," help prevent the development of even more serious problems.

these programs are run on behavior therapy principles, using reinforcements to encourage self-maintainance, hygiene, and the development of job skills. Another example of an innovative setting is
Achievement Place or similar homes for delinquent youths that involve "house parents" and a small group of youngsters sharing a
home for six to nine months. These projects are run according to behavior modification principles. The young residents earn points and
privileges for good conduct, school performance, and other adaptive
behaviors, and lose points for negative behaviors. Dozens of studies
conducted on such programs have shown them to be helpful in improving the skills of the young participants and in reducing rates of
future delinquent or criminal behavior (see Willner, Braukmann, Kirigin, & Wolf, 1978).

The community mental health movement has played an important role in reducing the total number of patients in mental institutions. The number of mental patients in county and state institutions
peaked in the late 1950s at about 600,000. Thereafter the number declined steadily, so that by 1975 there were fewer than 200,000 inpa-
tients (Bassuk & Gernson, 1978). On the negative side, however,
when facilities are less available for the mentally ill due to increased
need or reductions in public funding, what happens to these people?
In recent years we have seen a dramatic increase in the number of
people living on the streets due to a host of economic and social policy issues. It has been estimated that between 25 and 50 percent of
these homeless people have psychiatric disorders. This is clearly an
important issue facing the mental health profession, although it is
more broadly a matter of political and social policy.

Self-help Groups   One of the most dramatic developments in nontraditional treatments in recent years has been the proliferation of self-

*The mentally ill segment of the
homeless population poses a special
challenge to communities.*

Self-help groups, such as these adult children of elderly Alzheimer's disease victims, form to discuss information strategies and to provide mutual aid and support.

help groups. These are groups of individuals who come together for mutual aid, support, and the sharing of information strategies for coping with common concerns. They are often leaderless, and by definition, nonprofessional, offering free services outside the established mental health system. Groups have been formed that deal with conduct problems, such as Alcoholics Anonymous or Gamblers Anonymous, and with particular highly stressful events, such as the death of a child, mastectomy, having an alcoholic parent, or having a parent with Alzheimer's disease. Sometimes these groups are formed by individuals who share race, gender, sexual orientation, or some other characteristic that may set them apart from the mainstream, such as women's consciousness-raising groups or gay organizations. Self-help groups are rapidly forming to represent nearly every disease or stressful condition, and it has been estimated that 12 to 14 million Americans utilize such groups (Lieberman, 1986). One study of a random sample of households found that during the course of one year, slightly more persons (5.8 percent) used self-help groups than used professional mental health services (5.6 percent). It has been speculated that the popularity of such groups arises partly from the inadequacy of mental health services to assist all of the people who desire their aid, and partly from the appeal of such groups in bringing together people who have shared common experiences.

It is very difficult to assess the effectiveness of such groups because of problems in selecting appropriate measures and supplying relevant comparison groups. However, Lieberman (1986) reviewed the best studies in this field and concluded that nearly all showed measurable improvement in some areas of functioning by self-help group members when compared with those facing similar experiences who were not in groups. For instance, groups of persons who had suffered the death of a spouse showed improvement in levels of depression and life satisfaction. Members of a group of parents who had lost children showed improved coping strategies and a group of open-heart-surgery patients improved on mental health indicators— all compared to persons not in self-help groups (Lieberman, 1986). Although research has not yet clarified why it is that these groups may have positive results, it is likely that the support and information shared by group members is important in helping members cope with stressful circumstances. To the extent that such groups offer a no-cost alternative to more costly programs, supplement mental health services, or reach individuals who may never seek professional assistance, self-help organizations appear to provide a needed and welcome alternative for people with problems. For information on self-help methods that may not be so beneficial to people who have serious problems, see the box entitled "Psychotherapy in the Media."

MEDICAL APPROACHES TO TREATMENT

A man in his late twenties has been in the state hospital for two days. He says that lately he has been having a lot of trouble keeping his thoughts straight and he frequently hears voices. He is very disturbed. After careful examination, the psychiatrist writes an order for drug therapy. The patient is to be given 100 milligrams of Thorazine four times a day.

A graduate student in biology is approaching the time when he must take his doctoral comprehensive exams. He is so apprenhensive that he can no longer concentrate on his studies. The counseling center psychiatrist gives him a small prescription of Valium, a common tranquilizer.

A middle-aged woman has been deeply depressed for months. She has attempted suicide twice, almost succeeding the second time. After carefully considering her case, a team of psychiatrists has recommended electroconvulsive therapy. She is lying on a hospital bed, partially sedated; electrodes are attached to each temple. In a few minutes she will receive her first shock treatment.

These three case descriptions illustrate the medical approaches to psychological disorders. The first two involve drug therapy, by far the most common medical technique. The third, electroconvulsive therapy (ECT), is an alternative available to psychiatrists, typically for use in severe cases of depression.

Drug Therapies

Within the past few decades, there have been some remarkable breakthroughs in the therapeutic use of drugs for certain psychological disorders, especially the psychoses. Many people who would have been wasting away in the back ward of a mental hospital 25 or 30 years ago are now leading relatively stable, productive lives outside the confines of an institution. To be sure, such drugs are not a cure-all. Sometimes they are misused and even abused, and the medical side effects of some of them are significant, making the choice of using them or not a difficult one. Nevertheless, the science of psychopharmacology or **drug therapy** holds promise for the effective use of drugs in treating a wide range of mental disorders.

◆ PSYCHOTHERAPY IN THE MEDIA

In just the last few years we have seen the rapid expansion of psychological "services" available through the mass media. Every bookstore now contains books and manuals, and magazines and mailers constantly advertise the availability of tapes and other materials. These resources promise to help people overcome shyness, cope with depression, reduce stress, stop smoking, toilet train children, be more creative, increase assertiveness, improve their sex life, find the right man (or get over broken relationships), and a host of other offerings. Or, you can turn on the radio and hear psychotherapists discuss callers' personal problems and give advice or information. The widespread availability of these "services" raises important issues.

ADVANTAGES   Books, tapes, and radio talk shows suggest that the public has become increasingly psychologically sophisticated. These offerings may provide some useful tools to help people think about certain problems in different ways and to alter their behavior. For people who may not have serious problems, *self-help* can be an inexpensive alternative to professional guidance. It may also be comforting to find that other people have problems, even similar problems, that can be approached with practical solutions.

DISADVANTAGES   The two biggest dangers are that the public is being duped and that the procedures recommended might actually be harmful in some cases. Millions of dollars may be spent by trusting consumers on products that do not work. Many of the books and tapes that are marketed were not prepared by professionals, and many of those that were produced by professionals have not been subjected to study to demonstrate that they work. Even the books and tapes that have been "tested" to see if their procedures are helpful may not have been tested to see if they work under self-administered conditions (Rosen, 1987). Books and tapes may be marketed with exaggerated claims—"In only four weeks you can learn to master your fears . . ."— claims that have no scientific validity. Commercialization, rather than helping people, may be the major goal of the author and publisher. Consumers should insist that the products have demonstrated value.

Perhaps even more serious is the possibility that people may be harmed. As Rosen (1987) argues, research sometimes suggests that self-help efforts that are unsuccessfully administered may lead to a worsening of problems. Or, even if problems do not get worse after do-it-yourself efforts, if they do not get better, people may be discouraged, or blame themselves, or think they are even worse off than before they undertook self-treatment. Even more dangerous, self-help manuals have few provisions for diagnosing whether the techniques are appropriate to the individual (Rosen, 1987); as a result, some people who may have serious difficulties may fail to get professional help because they expect help from a book. For instance, a seriously depressed person is unlikely to be able to find the energy or motivation to apply self-help procedures successfully alone, and when they fail to get better, they might feel even worse and blame themselves. Or, a person with a serious personality disorder might think that if they simply "overcome shyness" their lives should be better. Radio talk-show therapists tread on the borderline of professionally ethical behavior. The "Ethical Standards of Psychologists" contains the following guideline: "Psychological services for the purpose of diagnosis, treatment or personal advice are provided only in the context of a professional relationship, and are not given by means of . . . radio or television programs . . ." (American

Psychological Association, 1977). The reason for this is clear: if functioning under conditions that do not permit the therapist to understand fully the client's psychological status and circumstances, the therapist is unable to protect the welfare of the individual. On the whole, therefore, promotion of psychological services in the mass media requires close attention by both the public and the helping professions.

When Are Drugs Used? Psychiatrists and other medical doctors are most likely to prescribe medication under one of two conditions.

1. Drugs are used for disorders that are strongly believed to have a biological origin and for which they have been demonstrated to have positive effects in reducing symptoms. Examples include antipsychotic drugs for schizophrenia and other psychoses, lithium for manic-depressive disorder, and stimulants for children with attention deficit disorder who suffer from hyperactivity. Psychotherapy may be an adjunct, but drugs are considered the best treatment.

2. Drugs are also utilized for disorders for which, whatever the cause, the symptoms have become severe enough to impair or incapacitate the person. Examples include antidepressants for major depressive disorder and antianxiety drugs for anxiety disorders. Here, the drugs may be an adjunct to psychotherapy, especially if the person's life circumstances contribute to the symptoms and the drugs are not going to make the problems go away for any period of time.

There has been a great deal of enthusiasm about the use of psychotropic drugs, and indeed, they have saved many lives and made severe difficulties bearable. Enthusiasm needs to be tempered with caution, however, because there are many applications for which drugs are being used where research to date has not established their effectiveness (eating disorders, for example). Drugs have doubtless also been overprescribed for mild psychological problems (Valium, for instance, has probably been overused). Table 18–3 presents some of the commonly prescribed medications for the treatment of psychological problems.

The Antipsychotic Drugs Antipsychotic drugs are used mainly with schizophrenics. There are many classes of such drugs, but the oldest and still the most widely used class is the ***phenothiazines.*** Controlled experiments have confirmed their effectiveness (Hogarty & Ullrich, 1977), and many researchers and practitioners believe that they have revolutionized the treatment of schizophrenia since their introduction in the 1950s. The phenothiazines reduce agitation and aggression, and any hospital aide who worked in mental institutions before phenothiazines became available will tell you what a difference these drugs have made in controlling patients' undesirable behaviors.

Because of their ability to control agitation, these drugs were often referred to as "major tranquilizers," but calling them tranquilizers is misleading. It suggests that a schizophrenic under medication is just as "disturbed" as before but is too sedated to care or to bother others. While this may be true for some patients, antipsychotic drugs appear to promote a basic improvement in many schizophrenics'

TABLE 18–3   Drugs Commonly Used to Treat Psychological Disorders

Use	Generic Name	Brand Name
Antipsychotic drugs	Chlorpromazine	Thorazine
	Haloperidol	Haldol
	Trifluoperazine	Stelazine
	Thiothixine	Navane
Antidepressant drugs	Amitriptyline	Elavil
	Imipramine	Tofranil
	Trazodone HCL	Desyrel
	Phenelzine	Nardil
Antimanic drugs	Lithium carbonate	Lithane
		Eskalith
Antianxiety drugs	Chloriazepoxide	Librium
	Alprazolam	Xanax
	Lorazepam	Ativan

thought processes—and schizophrenia is mainly a thought disorder. These drugs often reduce delusions and hallucinations as well. In many instances, schizophrenics can lead reasonably normal lives outside a hospital, as long as they continue to take prescribed amounts of antipsychotic drugs. Sometimes, after a period of successful adjustment, outpatients have decided on their own to stop taking phenothiazine drugs because they do not think they need the medications any more. The usual result is a return of symptoms, followed by a return to the hospital.

We do not want to mislead you into thinking that all hospitalized schizophrenics can function adequately in society if only they take phenothiazine or another antipsychotic drug; some clearly cannot (Hogarty & Ullrich, 1977). And there are other individuals who have been diagnosed as schizophrenic who do quite well outside the hospital without any medication. The point is that the antipsychotic drugs have dramatically improved the lives of many schizophrenics, but they are not a cure-all. The risk of addiction is slight for antipsychotic medications, but they may have potentially dangerous side effects, including low blood pressure (especially if one stands up suddenly), seizures, and severe problems with muscular coordination, called tardive dyskinesia, which is irreversible (Baldessarini, 1977).

Drugs for the Treatment of Depression and Mania   The two main classes of *antidepressant drugs* are tricyclics and monoamine oxidase (MAO) inhibitors. The antidepressant drugs are effective for many depressed patients (Baldessarini, 1977). Like the antipsychotic drugs, these medications permit many patients to function reasonably well outside a hospital. The positive effects of the drugs may take as long as a month to emerge, so a person who is suicidally depressed will sometimes need to be hospitalized until the drug takes effect. Tricyclics are prescribed more often, because the MAO inhibitors can cause serious complications in users who do not adhere to strict dietary precautions. Users must avoid aged cheeses and various other foods that contain monoamines. Antidepressants may have a variety of side effects, and a new class of "tetracyclics" has recently been developed that features many of the same advantages and fewer side effects.

For persons who show manic-depression, lithium carbonate has proved to be a true wonder drug whose effectiveness in treatment has been well documented (Stallone, Shelley, Mendlewicz, & Fieve, 1973; Dunner & Fieve, 1974). Roughly eight of ten persons experiencing manic episodes will respond positively to the drug, primarily by showing a reduction in the severe fluctuations of mood characteristic of this disorder. Does continued use of lithium "cure" the manic depressive? The answer is no. Patients still experience emotional upheavals, but they are usually not nearly as severe or as frequent as they were without lithium, and the episodes do not last as long when they do occur. Lithium is sometimes used also for recurrent unipolar depressions to try to prevent relapses, although the evidence for its prophylactic effect is less clear than for manic-depression. Under medical supervision, the side effects (hand tremors, dry mouth, and weight gain) are usually manageable, although sometimes unpleasant. Supervision includes frequent measurements of the amount of lithium in the blood. This is essential because if the level of lithium in the bloodstream is too high, serious side effects can occur, including nausea, diarrhea, and at somewhat higher levels, coma and death. The margin for error here is very narrow; taking only a few days' supply of lithium at one time can have fatal consequences (Baldessarini, 1977).

To date there is a great deal of research on how these mood-altering drugs work, but the mechanisms have not yet been clearly explained, although the drugs undoubtedly affect the level and receptor sensitivity of neurotransmitter substances.

Antianxiety Drugs **Antianxiety drugs,** such as Librium, Valium, Equanol, and several more recently developed "benzodiazepine" drugs, used to be called "minor tranquilizers." The term "minor" was very misleading, because it lulled people into thinking that these drugs are perfectly safe, which is not true for two reasons. First, people can easily overdose on these medications, and so the drugs have been responsible for many deaths, typically when people use them while drinking alcohol. Second, people can become addicted to antianxiety drugs, just as they can with barbiturates. They do have some value in the clinic (Paul & Skolnick, 1981), particularly for short-term use in combination with psychological therapy. Interestingly, benzodiazepine drugs have not been especially useful in treating sudden, spontaneous panic attacks, but have their best effects in treating "anticipatory" anxiety, such as generalized anxiety. It turns out that antidepressants have been used with some success in treating panic attacks (as reviewed in Redmond, 1985).

In the past, additional drugs were often prescribed for anxiety states. For example, *sedatives* belong to a class of drugs called barbiturates. These are the oldest medications we have talked about in this chapter. Sedatives are prescribed to help people go to sleep, and in smaller doses they are used to combat anxiety. They give a feeling of drowsiness rather than tranquility, but regular users require increasing dosages to get the same effect. This is a dangerous progression, as the barbiturates are highly addictive. As a method of committing suicide, barbiturate overdose is second only to the use of carbon monoxide (Jones, Shainberg, & Byer, 1973). Many accidental deaths have also resulted from combining barbiturates and alcohol.

The so-called *hypnotic drugs* do not really hypnotize people, but they do cause drowsiness and in larger doses, sleep, so they are sometimes prescribed for insomnia. The feeling they give is similar to that produced by barbiturates and, like the barbiturates, the hypnotics are highly addictive. When the hypnotics are combined with alcohol, the effects are often fatal.

Physical Treatments

Electroconvulsive Therapy   Several decades ago, some psychiatrists concluded that people who were epileptic were less likely than normal individuals to show symptoms of schizophrenia. As it turns out, this is not true—but they believed it was, so it was reasonable for them to suppose that inducing seizures would somehow help schizophrenics. When convulsions were induced in patients, there seemed to be some positive effects. Today, convulsions are induced by electric shock, hence the name *electroconvulsive therapy (ECT)*.

In the past, there were clear misuses of ECT, including indiscriminant applications of ECT for any diagnostic group (schizophrenics were commonly treated with electroshock therapy in the past). Medical consequences were formerly more severe also due to overly high dosages and broken bones caused by the convulsions. ECT is currently used almost exclusively for severe depression that is unresponsive to drug treatment, and it is applied under medically safe conditions with stringent civil-rights safeguards requiring informed consent. Patients (or their legal guardians) must give their consent to be treated with ECT, and treatments are closely monitored for strict compliance with the laws and with medical standards. As a treatment for depression, ECT has been found to be very effective (Avery & Winokur, 1977). What precisely does treatment involve? The patient is first sedated, perhaps with a barbiturate, and given a muscle relaxant because people tense their muscles violently during convulsions. Electrical conductors are then placed on each temple; the actual treatment consists of passing low amperage current through a portion of the patient's brain for a few seconds. It is apparently painless, although an untrained onlooker might be upset by the sight of the convulsing patient. The patient may be a bit confused for an hour or two after treatment. Beyond this, there are usually no side effects, although ECT would not be used with a patient who had recently suffered a heart attack.

Treatment is usually repeated several times a week for two to three weeks. By then the patient is usually no longer depressed and may be ready to leave the hospital. Of course, ECT cannot insure that depression will not return.

Electroconvulsive therapy is currently used almost exclusively to treat severe depression that does not respond to drug therapy. The actual treatment consists of passing low amperage current through a portion of the patient's brain for a few seconds.

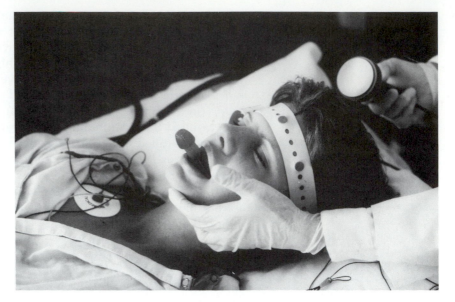

When is ECT preferred over treatment with the antidepressant drugs? It is considered safer than drugs early in pregnancy. Since its positive effects are felt so soon, it is sometimes used with patients whose responsibilities are so great that they need to leave the hospital as quickly as possible.

We should mention that quite a few psychiatrists are unwilling to use ECT. They are uncomfortable about using a procedure that they view as extreme, especially since no one really knows why it works. And, although it is rare, some patients have reported what appears to be some permanent memory loss as a result of ECT.

Psychosurgery Psychosurgery is brain surgery aimed at reducing psychological disorders. It is a radical approach to treatment, used in the past typically for very disturbed patients or for those for whom all other treatments failed. The procedure was first used in the United States by Walter Freeman and James Watts in 1936, and their names are closely linked to the stormy history of this operation. Basically, the procedure involves surgically cutting off a portion of the frontal lobe of the cerebral cortex from the rest of the brain. The operation makes that part of the frontal lobe nonfunctional. Psychosurgery initially appeared to have a calming effect on patients, but as time passed and more and more operations were performed, it became obvious that there were severe and permanent side effects. Some patients became apathetic and insensitive. Others suffered from impaired judgment and reduced creativity (Chorover, 1974) or epileptic-type seizures (Greenblatt, 1967). Though this operation seldom turned people into vegetables, the side effects made the surgeons ask whether it was worth doing, and most agreed that it was not. Psychosurgery was discontinued in the late 1950s, mainly because of the side effects, but also because anxious, agitated, or violent patients could usually be helped or controlled with medications introduced at about that time (Valenstein, 1973). Psychosurgical procedures are understandably controversial and are rarely performed today.

SUMMARY

1. Historically, the most influential of the many different schools of psychotherapy is Freud's technique—psychoanalysis.

2. Psychoanalysis attempts to change a person's personality by helping the patient gain insight into the unconscious conflicts of childhood, thereby allowing the person to deal with life's problems in a more mature and appropriate way.

3. The tools of psychoanalysis are free association and dream analysis to uncover unconscious motives, especially in relation to sex and aggression, and the analyst's interpretation of resistance and transference experiences.

4. While orthodox psychoanalysis is rare today, psychodynamic psychotherapy is common, retaining some of the basic assumptions and methods of analysis.

5. The existential-humanistic therapies emphasize fulfillment of human potential, here-and-now experience, and the worth of the individual.

6. Rogers's client-centered, or nondirective psychotherapy, emphasizes unconditional positive regard, empathy, and genuineness on the part of the therapist if the client is to experience growth.

7. Rogers assumed that in such an accepting atmosphere, clients learn to express and accept previously hidden feelings, leading to greater congruence within the person.

8. Fritz Perls's Gestalt therapy also emphasizes self-actualization, employing techniques to help clients focus on awareness of their experiences as a means of growth and self-acceptance.

9. Behavior therapies represent a third major school of psychotherapy, emphasizing the role of learning principles in the acquisition and change of maladaptive behavior.

10. Behavior therapists attempt to modify specific behaviors rather than the overall personality. To behaviorists, the problem behavior *is* the problem, not just a sign of an underlying problem.

11. Behavior-modification techniques have been based on operant and classical conditioning principles, and have been very effective for specific behavior change.

12. An especially popular type of behavior modification has been systematic desensitization, permitting the gradual exposure to feared objects or situations.

13. Cognitive-behavioral approaches have become prominent relatively recently. They include assessment and modification of maladaptive thinking as well as of maladaptive behaviors.

14. Beck's cognitive therapy for depression has been shown to be effective in the treatment of complex emotional disorders such as depression and anxiety.

15. Cognitive therapies attempt to alter exaggerated or distorted thoughts and replace them with more realistic thoughts and appraisals of situations, and also attempt to teach new problem-solving or other skills.

16. Studies of the effectiveness of therapy in general show that people improve in treatment, compared to no treatment. However, research that compares different kinds of treatments generally fails to show that one type is clearly superior to the other.

17. The lack of clear superiority of one treatment may stem from methodological problems such as using the same yardstick to compare very different treatments. However, it may also be the result of certain *processes* that are similar across therapies regardless of different techniques. This may help account for the fact that many therapists are "eclectic," and borrow ideas and techniques from different points of view in their actual practices.

18. Alternatives to individual therapy may include family therapy, group therapy, and certain kinds of nontraditional approaches offered in community mental health agencies.

19. An especially popular alternative to therapy is *self-help* support groups, bringing together people who share common experiences to offer mutual help and information to each other.

20. Medical approaches to treatment have been around for a long time, but just in the past 20-30 years there have been great gains in the development of effective *psychotropic* drugs.

21. Antipsychotic drugs have permitted better integration of severely mentally ill patients back into the community and have allowed many to live more normal lives; lithium carbonate has provided control over the wildly altering cycles of mania and depression in many manic-depressives.

22. There are now many antidepressant and antianxiety medications available that can be used to treat severe symptoms, often in conjunction with psychotherapy to deal with the psychological causes or consequences of the disorders.

23. Despite their promise, however, drugs may have significant side effects and should not be overused. "Minor tranquilizers," such as Valium, have probably been greatly misused. Problems in living will not be solved by drugs, so great care is needed to balance the medical and psychological needs of psychiatrically impaired people.

24. ECT is a dramatically effective treatment for some forms of severe depression and may be recommended for use under specific and highly monitored conditions. These safeguards are necessary because of the abuses of such major physical interventions in years past. Because of misuses and limited effectiveness, the most extreme medical treatment of all, psychosurgery, is extremely rare today.

KEY TERMS

amplification
antianxiety drugs
antidepressive drugs
anxiety-management proce-
  dures
assertiveness training
awareness
client-centered therapy
cognitive restructuring
congruence
directed experimentation
drug therapy
eclecticism (technical eclecticism, multimodal therapy)

electroconvulsive therapy
  (ECT)
empathic understanding
empty-chair exercise
encounter groups
genuineness
Gestalt therapy
group assertive training
hypnotic drugs
incongruity
maladaptive thinking
participant modeling
phenothiazines

psychoanalysis
psychoanalytic psychotherapy
psychodrama
psychological determinism
rational emotive therapy
sedatives
self-control therapies
self-instructional techniques
social-skills training
systematic desensitization
transference
unconditional positive regard

ADDITIONAL READING

Burns, D. (1980) *Feeling good: The new mood therapy.* New York: Morrow.
This book is an example of a self-help manual for the treatment of depressed mood. It is based on cognitive-behavioral techniques.

Corsini, R. J. (1984) *Current psychotherapies* (3rd ed.). Itasca, IL: Peacock Publishers.
This is a textbook covering the major forms of psychotherapy, with a discussion of theory, techniques, and a brief review of relevant research findings.

Garfield, S. L., & Bergin, A. E. (Eds.) (1986) *Handbook of psychotherapy and behavior change.* New York: Wiley.
This is a comprehensive book of chapters on research and issues in psychotherapy, written by authors representing diverse viewpoints and practices. The book gives a broad and scholarly overview of contemporary research.

19 Social Behavior

I magine that you have gone to a meeting on campus to listen to a debate between Surgeon General C. Everett Koop and Lyndon LaRouche on the topic of AIDS prevention. During the debate you find yourself impressed by the sincerity of both individuals. However, you also think that each of the speakers holds a position that is too controversial to be acceptable to many people. What is it about the two debaters that leads you to this conclusion?

Later the same day, you go to the store to purchase soft drinks for a party. At the store you see a large display for Coca-Cola and another for Pepsi. Which of these two drinks do you select for the party? Why? What considerations influence your decision?

At the party you meet several new people and find yourself attracted to some more than others. Why? You also find that you are particularly attracted to one of these individuals and you believe that she is also attracted to you. What is it that has led to your mutual attraction?

The next morning you see an old man fall on the sidewalk half a block in front of you; four people walk by him without offering to help. You hurry over to him to see if he is all right. Why did you help when the others did not? Why is it that some people do not get involved when they could be of help to others?

WHAT IS SOCIAL PSYCHOLOGY?

What do all of the questions we have just asked have in common? How are they different from the many other questions we have asked about human behavior throughout this book? The common thread running through these diverse questions is that they all involve social relationships or interactions with other people. Of course, psychologists in many areas of psychology study questions of relationships or interpersonal influence. In operant conditioning, when the reinforcement comes from another person in the form of a smile or praise, we are dealing with a social aspect of learning. When developmental psychologists talk about the importance of early attachment of the infant to the mother or of the way children learn from their peers, they are describing social aspects of development. When researchers studying emotion explore the "language" of nonverbal cues, they are exploring a social aspect of emotion. There is no way we can completely divorce social influences from the study of any aspect of behavior—nor would we want to. But most psychologists in other areas prefer to concentrate on the behavior of single individuals, while social psychologists study the behavior of people in pairs or groups, or the influence of other people on one individual, even though the other people may not be physically present when the "influence" is felt.

This discussion leads us now to define *social psychology.* According to Sears, Freedman, and Peplau (1985), social psychology is ". . . the systematic study of social behavior. It deals with how we perceive other people and social situations, how we respond to others and they to us, and in general how we are affected by social situations"(p. 1). Another definition of social psychology that focuses on the same concerns is found in Allport (1985). In this definition, social psychologists want to "understand and explain how the thoughts, feelings, and behaviors of individuals are influenced by the actual, imagined, or implied presence of others"(p. 3).

A major area of study for social psychologists involves the behavior of people in pairs or in groups. All of us form impressions of others by interpreting what we observe of their behavior.

The common ingredient in these definitions is the relationship of one person to another. Since we relate to others in so many different ways—individually, in groups, in crowds, in casual or intimate contacts—the field of social psychology is enormously diverse.

Social psychologists have broadened their field of interest further by studying not just social *behavior,* but also the way in which our perceptions, thoughts, feelings, and attitudes are influenced by encounters with others, and how our *emotions* and *cognitions* influence others. This focus in social psychology has come to be called **social cognition** because the emphasis is on social stimuli and the cognitive processes the individual employs to make sense of social encounters (Fiske & Taylor, 1984). The result is that we can identify three different levels of analysis in social psychology. There are those psychologists who are very concerned with the social cognitive processes that determine social behavior. There are others who are concerned with the emotional and attitudinal aspects of social behavior. Finally, there is a group that is only concerned with the overt behavior observed in social situations. There is not always a clear distinction between these levels of analysis; the social psychologist frequently uses more than one in his research.

To make sense of all of this, we will begin our discussion with the basic processes that underlie all social psychology, starting with the intrapersonal processes. Then we will move steadily outward to examine the interpersonal and the intragroup influences.

SOME BASIC INTRAPERSONAL PROCESSES THAT AFFECT SOCIAL INTERACTIONS

How Do We Form Impressions of Others?

Let us begin by imagining that you have been appointed by the student body president of your campus to serve on a financial board to plan how student fees should be spent on speakers, entertainment groups, and other programs. You walk into the room for the first meeting and find yourself facing ten strangers. You know you will have to work together for several months, so you are eager to get to know the others. What kind of information do you have? Several of the others introduce themselves right away, smile, shake hands, and look you in the eye. Others stay seated and do not approach, or they seem to avoid making eye contact with you. Most of the other students are your age, dressed in jeans or casual clothes, but you notice one older man wearing a suit with a vest and carrying a briefcase. There are other details you pick up: some of the board members smoke, some do not; some have disordered piles of papers in front of them, while others have laid out their materials neatly. After a few meetings of the group, your impressions of each of the others have become more definite. You have drawn some conclusions about their personalities and entertainment preferences, and you can even predict who will be the first to speak, who will reject any idea that is proposed, and who will jump in to defend anyone whose ideas are attacked by another member of the group.

All of us form impressions in this way constantly. We *interpret* what we observe and draw conclusions about other people's characteristics or personalities on the basis of their behavior. In the language of current social psychology, we *attribute* people's behavior to enduring motives or qualities, or to the demands of the situation. These attitudes then influence our own feelings and attitudes, and shape our behavior toward others.

Attribution Theory

The fundamental assumption that underlies **attribution theory** is that there are two basic human motives. The first is the need to understand the world around us and the second is the need to control as many of the factors in our own small sphere of interaction as we can. We can illustrate these two motives by going back to our example involving the student financial board. The impressions that you formed of your fellow board members are your attempt to understand the world around you. At the same time you were forming those impressions, you were trying to control both the impressions that others had of you and to persuade them that your views were worthy of their consideration.

Obviously, humans do not spend all of their time making attributions about every person they encounter or every situation in which they find themselves. Rather, they form attributions only when motivated to do so. Therefore, motivation is a critical component in attribution theory and in order to understand attributions, we also need to know something about human motivation. (You may want to refer to Chapter 9 and its discussion of motivation.) Making attributions is both a *perceptual* and a *cognitive* process. What aspects of other people's behavior do you pay attention to? What are the perceptual cues you use? And then, how do you assemble that information into an explanation of the person's behavior?

The Basic Attributional Process: Dispositional versus Situational Explanations   Fritz Heider (1958) was one of the first psychologists to discuss attributions. He argued that the first thing we do when making attributions is to try to understand the *cause* of someone else's

A photo taken in 1974 shows Patty Hearst during a bank robbery in San Francisco. What can we conclude about her unusual behavior? Was she motivated at that time by dispositional or situational considerations?

behavior. More particularly, we attribute that behavior either to internal, personal causes, such as basic personality traits or enduring motives, or to external causes, such as luck, social pressure, or the influence of specific circumstances. The first of these is called a ***dispositional attribution***, while the second is called a ***situational attribution.***

If your new classmate John smiles seldom and avoids conversation, you could explain his behavior by concluding that he is basically a shy and introverted person—a dispositional attribution. But you might conclude that John is just temporarily depressed if you heard that he and his girl friend had an argument the night before—a situational attribution. If you see a famous movie star advocating the preservation of whales in a television ad, you might conclude that the star is a dedicated conservationist (dispositional), or that she is being paid to make the commercial (situational).

What aspects of someone's behavior do you pay attention to in making judgments of this kind? Social psychologists who have studied the process (Jones & Davis, 1965; Kelley, 1967, 1980; Kelley & Michela, 1980) have identified some basic behavioral clues we all use. We have listed these clues in Table 19-1, along with the labels Kelley gives to each. But let us look at some additional examples as well.

TABLE 19-1   Information Used in Assessing Behavior

Whether the behavior is usual or unusual, bizarre or normal	Kelley calls this *consensus*. When someone does something expected, or something most other people would do in the same situation, it is a "high consensus" behavior, and tells us little about the causes. But when someone does something unusual—wears only black clothes, or darts in front of cars to cross the street, or smiles at a funeral—we notice the behavior and use our observations about consensus to make attributional judgments.
Whether the behavior occurs consistently in the same or similar situations over time	Kelley calls this dimension of behavior *consistency*. We watch for behaviors that someone shows every time in the same situation. Does your neighbor always smile when he sees you? Do you always get anxious when you walk into a doctor's office? Does your child get cranky at 5:00 P.M. nearly every day?
Whether the behavior is consistent across many different situations	Kelley calls this *distinctiveness*. A behavior is distinctive if it occurs in only one setting; it is "low in distinctiveness" if it occurs in many settings. Does your neighbor smile at everyone (low distinctiveness) or only at you (high distinctiveness)?

Source: After Kelley, 1980.

One of the first things you consider about someone else's behavior is how unusual or how common that behavior is. This involves examining what we call consensus. When someone does something unique or bizarre (a behavior with "low consensus," to use Kelley's language), the behavior not only stands out, but it is highly informative. Jones and Davis emphasize that the impact of such unusual behavior is even stronger if it appears that the individual freely chose to behave that way. If there is some coercion or some external explanation of the bizarre action, then we learn less about the person being observed. Consider an example. A student who always wears a suit and tie to class, in the midst of blue-jeaned classmates, is bucking the trend. Such "low consensus" behavior tells you far more about that person than you would learn if he conformed to the usual dress patterns. When you see someone wearing blue jeans, you have few clues about the causes of that behavior. Does he wear blue jeans because he is basically a conforming person, because they are comfortable, or because they are all he can afford? You have no basis for identifying his motivation. But when you see someone wearing a suit and tie, not only do you notice, but you are also likely to conclude that the person has chosen to dress in this way for some inner (dispositional) reason.

Another type of basic information used in forming judgments about other people's behavior involves how consistent that behavior is over time and in various situations. Does John get depressed every time he and his girl friend have an argument? If so, this would show consistency over time. Does he show the same silent, unsmiling behavior in other situations, such as when he has done poorly on an exam, or in ordinary daily encounters? When someone shows a particular behavior only in certain situations, Kelley calls it distinctive behavior. (The phrase *situation specific behavior* might be less confusing.) When someone's behavior is consistently the same, regardless of the situation, Kelley labels it as "low in distinctiveness."

People who conform to one group's standards of dress and behavior may look outlandish to people who are conforming to other standards.

A person is known by the behavior he displays consistently. Baseball manager Billy Martin frequently argues with the umpire.

In sum, we glean the most information about the causes of others' behavior when their behavior is unusual, when it is not coerced, and when we can determine whether they behave the same way over time and in various situations. Once we have such information, we appear to interpret it in predictable ways. Kelley proposes that we are most likely to make a dispositional attribution if a person's behavior is low in consensus (unusual), high in consistency (occurs every time the same situation comes up), and low in distinctiveness (occurs in many situations). The student who wears suits to class every day is showing low consensus behavior. He is also consistent and low in distinctiveness. Given this set of observations, you are very likely to attribute his behavior to some inner motive or disposition. If this same student only wore a suit to his business-administration classes, and all the other students in those classes also wore suits, then the behavior would be high in consensus and high in distinctiveness. In that case, a situational attribution becomes much more likely. Perhaps the business professor requires that his students wear suits; perhaps the students are encouraged to prepare themselves for the business world they will soon be entering. Whatever the specific explanation, you now see suit-wearing less as a reflection of a basic personal philosophy and more as a consequence of the situation.

There has been a great deal of research testing Kelley's proposals and most of his theory has stood up very well (see Sears et al., 1985). Of the three aspects, consistency of a person's behavior seems to carry the most weight in a judgment about dispositional or situational causes. In Kelley's words, "A person is known by the behavior he displays consistently" (Kelley & Michela, 1980, p. 465).

Findings on the impact of consensus are more mixed. It is clear that highly unusual or unexpected behaviors are very informative and likely to lead to a dispositional attribution. But even behaviors that are high in consensus (behaviors that many people adhere to) can still be attributed to internal causes (Zuckerman, 1978). Suppose your friend Jane runs up to you after the professor hands out results on a test in a physics course. She is delighted because she did very well. You know that Jane is a good student and does well in most of her courses; you also know that many other people did well on this particular test (high consensus). In these circumstances you probably will not attribute Jane's good performance to luck or an easy test. You are still likely to conclude that Jane is smart or a hard worker. When other factors outweigh the effect of consensus, a person's behavior may still be seen as internally caused, even though many other people show the same behavior in the same situation. The same behavior may be explained in quite different ways in different people, depending on the particular information you have about each individual.

The Effects of Expectancies

One of the interesting and important things about trying to understand the characteristics of others is that our expectancies of others are often confirmed following our interactions with them. For instance, if we believe that someone is "unfriendly," our expectation is likely to be reinforced after we interact with them. This happens for two reasons. First, our perceptions are selective, meaning that we usually see what we want to see. Second, how we interact with someone is determined in large measure by how we perceive them, and this in turn leads them to behave in ways that confirm our ideas about them. This *self-fulfilling prophecy* was first demonstrated by Rosenthal and Jacobson (1968), who led teachers to believe that certain of their sixth-grade students were quite intelligent and would begin to do well in school, while another group of sixth graders were identified as less bright and not likely to do well in school. Actually, there were no differences in the ability levels of the two groups of students. Their assignment to one of the two supposedly different ability groups was made on a random basis. Interestingly, some time after the students had been identified as "bright" or "not so intelligent," testing revealed that students in the bright group did significantly better than the no-so-bright group. The factor used to explain this pattern was the effect that the teachers had on the students whom they believed to be "bright." Although this study was criticized on methodological grounds, the effects of expectancy on behavioral confirmation are much better understood and accepted today.

A good demonstration of the expectancy effect and how two peoples' behavior can merge, depending on the expectancy of one of the individuals, was chronicled by Snyder, Tanke, and Berscheid (1977). In this study, male undergraduate students at the University of Minnesota were asked to have a "get acquainted" telephone conversation with an undergraduate female student. Prior to the call, each male student was shown a photograph of a female and told that this was the person he was going to be speaking to over the phone. Half of the male students were led to believe that the female to whom they would be speaking was physically attractive; the remaining males believed that their telephone partner was on the plain side. In fact, the photos were randomly assigned, but more importantly, the female students were not aware of the "attractive" versus "plain" designations. All telephone conversations were tape recorded and scored separately for male speaker and female speaker by different groups of judges. Male students who had conversations with a person they believed to be "attractive" were rated as significantly more open, friendly, and sociable than males who conversed with a female student they believed to have been shown to them in the "plain" photo. Independent raters who scored the female student conversations judged those females who were in the "attractive" group to be more poised, sociable, gregarious, and self-confident than those women talking to men who believed them to be plain. Thus, the males' expectations concerning the physical attractiveness of their phone partner led them to behave in a manner congruent with their beliefs. The behavior of the males, in turn, resulted in the women's behaving in ways that conformed to the expected personal characteristics (based on attractiveness) that the men held. There was, in other words, a behavioral confirmation of the males' beliefs about personal characteristics of women and the relative importance of physical attractiveness. The men in this study essentially constructed a reality based on their expectancies.

Jones (1986) explains this interpersonal interaction that results in behavioral confirmation by means of the series of sequences that are shown in Figure 19-1.

The Perceiver A social interaction begins with a "perceiver" or someone who has an expectancy about how the other person in a social interaction (the target person) is going to behave. The perceiver may believe that the person is friendly and honest or competitive and calculating. The important thing is whether the expectancy influences

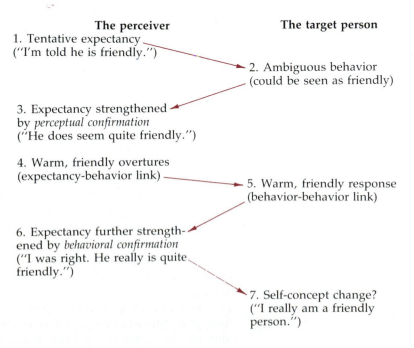

FIGURE 19-1 Interpersonal Interaction Resulting in Perceptual and Behavioral Confirmation *A typical social interaction sequence in which both perceptual and behavioral confirmation occur. (The initial expectancy here is "he is friendly.")* (After Jones, 1986)

The perceiver

1. Tentative expectancy
("I'm told he is friendly.")

3. Expectancy strengthened
by *perceptual confirmation*
("He does seem quite friendly.")

4. Warm, friendly overtures
(expectancy-behavior link)

6. Expectancy further strengthened by *behavioral confirmation*
("I was right. He really is quite
friendly.")

The target person

2. Ambiguous behavior
(could be seen as friendly)

5. Warm, friendly response
(behavior-behavior link)

7. Self-concept change?
("I really am a friendly
person.")

the behavior of the perceiver. If the perceiver believes the other person to be friendly and honest, she may approach the person with a smile and a pleasant comment, such as "Lovely day, isn't it?" This, then, may be reciprocated with a smile from the target person, eye contact, and a friendly "Great day!" On the other hand, if the perceiver believes the target person to be competitive and manipulative, she may approach with a cautious glance and a "Hello, can I help you?" which may be reciprocated with a cool "hello."

Behavioral Reciprocation   We have already touched on the topic of behavioral reciprocation, but we need to reemphasize two points. The first point is that behavioral confirmation occurs only if the target person attends to the perceiver's expectancy-relevant behavior and reciprocates in the expected way. Second, if the target person does reciprocate with the anticipated behavior, behavioral confirmation is ensured if the perceiver believes that the target person's actions represent stable disposition characteristics.

Correspondence Bias   The central problem in the "perceiver-target" interaction that we have just discussed is that of **correspondence bias.** This occurs when you, as the perceiver, believe that your actions play no role in how another person interacts with you. For example, if you are friendly and outgoing to a stranger and he reciprocates by being friendly, a correspondence bias occurs if you take the other person's actions at face value and infer that he possesses a stable, "friendly" disposition without also considering how your behavior has influenced him. Jones (1986) discusses this problem by pointing out that under similar circumstances, people with a variety of different dispositions would have probably reciprocated your friendly actions when they first met you. It is not, however, until you have a number of encounters with an individual that you can begin to accurately assess what they are like independent of your interactions with them. According to Jones, this bias is particularly problematic in social psychology experiments because the researcher gives a subject a particular task to perform and still infers enduring attributions or attitudes, even though the psychologist is quite aware of how he has influenced the subject's responses through the experiment. Thus the question becomes one of whose attributions or attitudes are really being studied by social psychologists.

Attributions: A Summary and a Look Forward

By this time you may well be confused, since the "rules" that govern attributions often appear to be contradictory. To help you understand the factors that increase the likelihood of a dispositional attribution being made, we have summarized them in Table 19-2. There is research evidence showing that each factor listed, operating alone, makes it more likely that you will attribute someone else's behavior (or your own) to enduring, internal qualities such as personality traits or skills.

Researchers in this area are now beginning to examine several factors as they operate simultaneously. For example, under what conditions do women attribute success to themselves (or to other

TABLE 19-2   Factors that Increase the Likelihood of Dispositional Attributions

Factor	Explanation/Example
High consistency	The more different situations in which you have seen someone behave the same way, the more likely you are to attribute the behavior to dispositional causes.
High consensus	The more someone stands out in a crowd by wearing distinctive clothing or looking distinctive in other ways, the more likely you are to see his or her behavior as dispositionally caused.
Bucking the trend	A variation of consensus: when you see a group of people all doing the same thing (all cheering at a ballgame or all agreeing with a charismatic speaker), the one person who is *not* going along with the crowd is seen as more internally motivated.
Successful performance	When someone succeeds or does well at a task or in a particular situation, we see it as dispositionally caused.
Behavior that fits our expectation	When someone does what we expect—succeeds when we expect that, or fails when we expect that—we are more likely to think that those behaviors are internally caused.
Lack of knowledge of the other person	The less well you know someone, the more likely you are to attribute his or her behavior to dispositional causes.
Other versus self	We are more likely to attribute other people's behavior to dispositional causes than to attribute our own behavior to dispositional causes.

Source: After Kelley & Michela, 1980.

women) rather than to chance or luck or other situational explanations? When are you most likely to explain behavior by using an internal explanation? The general rule is that the better you know someone, the more likely you are to notice day-to-day variations in behavior and to attribute those variations to chance or situational variables. There are *some* enduring traits that you assume are influences on people you know very well. When do those attributions enter into the picture?

Despite the many things we do not yet know about the attributional process, the field is an exciting one, partly because making attributions appears to be such a basic human process. The language of attribution theory can be applied to a whole range of behaviors we have already talked about in this book. We can think of moral judgments (which we discussed in Chapter 12) in attributional terms. When someone commits a crime, or says something unkind, or makes a large donation to charity, you make a judgment about his *intent.* That judgment is a form of attribution. Did the person make the large donation because he is basically generous (an internal attribution), or was he pressured into it by some external circumstance? Some questions in personality research and in research on abnormal behavior and therapy can also be stated in attributional terms. For instance, Peplau, Russell, and Heim (1980) found that students who attributed their loneliness to lack of social skill were more likely to report feeling depressed and hopeless; those who saw their loneliness as resulting from external factors were less depressed. In general, depressed people seem to overestimate their own responsibility for bad things that happen to them; in other words, they have too much internal attribution (Rizley, 1978). At the same time, a willingness to be responsible for one's own actions may be a prerequisite for successful therapy. We could also recast the discussion of child abuse in attributional language: when a parent strikes a baby because the baby "won't stop crying," the parent is attributing the baby's crying to internal causes. She believes that the baby could stop crying if he *wanted* to. If the parent could understand the *external* reasons for the crying (that is, if she could change her attribution), this might lessen the likelihood of abuse.

These examples illustrate the very wide range of questions that can be phrased in attributional terminology. Time will tell whether this change of language will lead to new insights about psychopathology, personality, moral development, or other areas of research. But it is interesting to see such linkages made between fields of psychology that usually are separated.

Attitudes and Their Changes

A second major area of study within the field of social psychology that focuses on intrapersonal processes involves attitudes and attitude change. In this chapter and elsewhere in this book, we have used the word "attitude" rather loosely. We must now be more precise about what we mean by the term "attitudes." Unfortunately, this is not as easy as it sounds. In an extensive review of the literature on attitudes, William McGuire (1985) reported that through the years no less than 500 different definitions of "attitude" have been used by social psychologists. So, rather than *define* the term, we will discuss the major components that most social psychologists agree go into our understanding of "attitude."

The first element that we must consider is that attitudes are relatively stable and not generally subject to momentary changes. Second, attitudes consist of a cognitive and an affective component, which means that both beliefs and feelings are essential elements in an attitude. Third, attitudes give way to behavioral tendencies that often determine how we react to a situation or event. However, it is important to note that our behavior is *not* always consistent with our beliefs and feelings. For example, we may hold a positive attitude about the importance of affirmative action in achieving a democratic society but vote against a political candidate who strongly asserts a policy of affirmative action as part of her campaign platform.

Not all social psychologists use such a three-part definition of attitude. Many use the term to refer only to the emotional part—the feeling—and some talk about attitudes as having just the emotional and the cognitive parts. But we think it is important to include the behavioral part as well, even though our behavior may not always be consistent with our beliefs and feelings.

Persuasion and Attitude Change　Many of the social psychologists who study attitudes focus on the problem of attitude-change. How are people persuaded to change their attitudes or their behavior? There are some obvious practical applications to these questions, such as changing prejudiced racial attitudes, or changing political attitudes, or getting people to buy one brand of soft drink rather than another. We will take up some of these applications in Chapter 20. For now, let us see what we know about the basic attitude-change process.

Persuasive Communications　The most common way to try to change another person's attitude is to use words. Every day, people attempt to persuade us verbally that our attitude is wrong, and that theirs is right: "Take the taste test and join the Pepsi generation" or "Vote for Jones, the man for tomorrow." What sort of persuasion works? We have summarized the major factors that seem to make a difference in Table 19-3.

The information in the table is oversimplified, so each point listed has to be qualified in several ways. But each has been found to be an important ingredient that makes communications more effective in

TABLE 19-3　What Makes Some Communication More Persuasive Than Other Communication?

Communications are more persuasive if:
The communicator
1. is believed to be an expert on the subject
2. is seen as having little to gain from the communication, (that is, is trustworthy)
3. is attractive
4. is from the same reference group (for example, labor union, fraternity, social class, etc.).

The communication
1. is only slightly different from the listener's own position
2. gives both counterarguments and arguments
3. arouses emotions in the listener or reader, such as fear or sympathy (as long as the emotion is not overwhelming)
4. is repeated a moderate number of times
5. gives explicit information about what the listener can do.

The listener
1. is committed to engage in some action (for example, make a public statement) that favors the speaker's position
2. is distracted during presentation of the argument so that counterarguments cannot be rehearsed
3. is personally involved in the topic
4. is in a good mood rather than feeling grouchy.

Frank Zappa's intended audience found him extremely persuasive, but his antidrug messages on television were cancelled because many parents found him repulsive.

changing attitudes. A couple of examples will make the list more understandable.

Expertise and trustworthiness, taken together, are referred to as the *credibility* of the communicator. Credible communicators are more likely to change attitudes. But in selecting a communicator, you have to bear in mind that someone who seems credible to you may not be credible to someone else. In short, the person trying to do the persuading has to consider the audience. When that is not done, some laughable mistakes often follow. In the late 1960s, the U.S. Public Health Service became seriously concerned about drug trafficking in San Francisco. Young people were buying contaminated drugs and dying. The health service worked up a number of television spots. One ad said:

> This is Frank Zappa from the Mothers of Invention. I would like to suggest that you do not use speed and here's why: it's going to mess up your heart, mess up your liver, your kidneys, rot out your mind. In general, this drug will make you just like your father and mother.

This ad was extremely effective. It was also extremely irritating to parents and others who criticized the public health service heavily. How could the public health service have chosen Frank Zappa as a communicator? He was so ugly, so repulsive. He probably used drugs himself! So the public health service switched gears and hired Art Linkletter, a conservative, popular radio personality, who had developed an interest in drug control following his daughter's suicide, which occurred possibly after an overdose of LSD. Art Linkletter made wholesome ads. The parents loved him but the ads were almost totally ineffective. The advertisers had forgotten a basic principle: the important factor is not how an advertiser feels about the communicator, but how the audience feels about him.

The question of whether to give one or both sides of the argument in a communication is equally tricky. The most effective strategy depends on what attitude the audience already holds. If the audience basically agrees with you, you are better off giving only one side of the argument and ignoring the counterevidence. But when the audience starts out with a different attitude, you are more likely to sway them if you give both sides. This may work better because you seem to be more fair-minded that way, and are thus more credible. The problem is that you must know where your audience stands before you can pick the right strategy.

A third area that needs qualifying is the effect of the listener's involvement with the topic. Petty and Cacioppo (1979; Cialdini, Petty, & Cacioppo, 1981) have found that when the message is personally relevant to the listener, he or she is more persuadable if the arguments being offered are good ones. But if the arguments are poorly stated or not well thought out, the communication is *less* effective with a highly involved listener. If you are about to turn 18 and need to register for the draft soon (high involvement), you would be more likely to be persuaded (in either direction) by cogent arguments than would a 50-year-old who is not personally involved in the issue. But if the person who buttonholes you at the post-office door as you are about to register gives you a weak argument about why you should not register, your own position becomes stronger.

Voluntary Attitude Change   Attitudes may change because of persuasive communications, but there are other ways that attitude change can occur as well. In particular, the cognitive part of an attitude may change if the behavior changes first. If a person behaves in a way that is inconsistent with her basic attitude, then her attitude may change to make it consistent with her behavior. This type of attitude change was first suggested by Festinger (1957), as part of the model called *dissonance theory.* Festinger was concerned with the balance of cognitions and behavior within each individual. He argued that people feel most comfortable if their ideas are consistent with one another, and with their behavior. If they are inconsistent—a state Festinger called dissonance—then the person is uncomfortable, and becomes motivated to change either his behavior or his ideas until he regains a state of consistency, called *consonance* in this theory.

The classic example, used by Festinger in 1957 and still applicable now, is the case of someone who smokes and also believes that smoking is unhealthy. The two cognitions ("I smoke" and "Smoking is bad for me") are dissonant with one another. Festinger suggests that there are only three ways to reduce the dissonance: (1) change your behavior and stop smoking; (2) change your belief that smoking is bad for you; or (3) add other cognitions to the system that are consonant with smoking (smoking relaxes me, it gives me something to do at parties, and so forth). Since a change in belief or attitude is one possible consequence of dissonance, we should be able to produce attitude change by deliberately creating dissonance.

This attitude-change aspect of dissonance theory has led to some surprising predictions about the effect of compliance on attitudes. Suppose you believe that lying is bad and you try not to do it. Your behavior and your attitude are consonant, so you are comfortable. But now suppose that we offer you $100 to tell someone else something that you know is untrue. Or, alternatively, suppose we offer you only $1. What will happen?

Learning theory suggests that the larger reinforcement ($100) should lead to a greater change in behavior. But dissonance theory leads to the opposite prediction. Dissonance is produced whether you lie for $1 or $100, but according to the principle of insufficient justification, Festinger argued that more dissonance is generated when you lie for the lesser amount. When you are paid $100 to tell a lie, especially if the lie is a minor one, you may feel quite justified. The cognition "I will get $100" is consonant with lying and thus decreases the total dissonance. But $1 is not a sufficient justification for going against your principles, so you feel more dissonance. One way to reduce this dissonance is to change your cognition about the wickedness of lying. You may thus persuade yourself that lying is not really so bad, as long as no one is hurt, it was only a small lie, or some such excuse. The end result is that you change your attitude.

This general effect has been confirmed in many studies: you get the maximum amount of attitude change when the least amount of persuasion or coercion is applied that still produces behavior change. But there are some limitations to the effect. It works most clearly if the behavior has some actual impact on others, and if the subject feels fully responsible for the choice. If we make it a course requirement that students write an essay arguing that women are naturally inferior to men and offer some students $100 to do it and other students $1, we would not expect to see any change in students' attitudes about women, even under the $1 condition. Presumably the students would feel that they had no choice and were not responsible for their essays. (In attribution language, they would be able to attribute their behavior to situational causes, and thus they would not have to take responsibility for it.) But if an individual feels that he has a choice, *and* if he thinks that his action, such as telling a lie, will really influence someone else, then considerable dissonance is produced, and his attitude is likely to change.

Selective Exposure and Attitudes   People often appear to choose to listen to information that supports their attitude on some issue and to avoid information that goes against an issue about which they feel strongly. When we listen, it is called **selective approach** and when we do not want to know something we refer to this as **selective avoidance.** Together these selective-exposure tendencies imply that people actively seek information consistent with their point of view *and* avoid things that may be inconsistent with their beliefs.

An interesting demonstration of how selective exposure works was conducted by Sweeney and Gruber (1984), who studied the attitudes of Nixon supporters, McGovern supporters, and individuals who were undecided about whom to support at three different points in time: (a) just before the Watergate hearings started, (b) midway through the hearings, and (c) just before the end of the hearings. By asking respondents to name those indicted in the Watergate affair and to name the senators on the Watergate Committee at different times during the hearings Sweeney and Gruber were able to measure selective exposure for the three different groups of voters. Figures 19-2a and 19-2b show the results of this study. The McGovern supporters were very interested in keeping informed about the scandal and the hearings (selective approach). On the other hand, the Nixon supporters appeared not to be as interested in the hearings and, in fact, avoided learning about the details of the hearings (selective avoidance). The undecided respondents, who constituted a critical control group in this study, fell midway between the two experimental groups. The results of this study clearly indicated that individuals seek out information that is consistent with their political attitudes and actively strive to avoid information that opposes their beliefs.

The idea of selective exposure is actually part of the cognitive dissonance theory discussed earlier. By understanding selective exposure, it is easy to see, for example, why it is so difficult in some cases to change a person's attitude through an advertisement. If the person is not predisposed to receive the message, then selective exposure ensures that the person will not attend to the message and no change in attitude will result.

FIGURE 19–2 **Nixon-McGovern Selective Exposure Results** *Graph (a) shows the average number of correct responses (0–7) received from among Nixon supporters, McGovern supporters, and undecided individuals asked to name those indicted in the Watergate trial just before the Watergate hearings started (Time 1) and just before the end of the hearings (Time 2). Graph (b) shows the number of correct responses received from respondents asked to name the senators on the Watergate Committee midway through the hearings (Time 2) and just before the end of the hearings (Time 3). (After Sweeney & Gruber, 1984)*

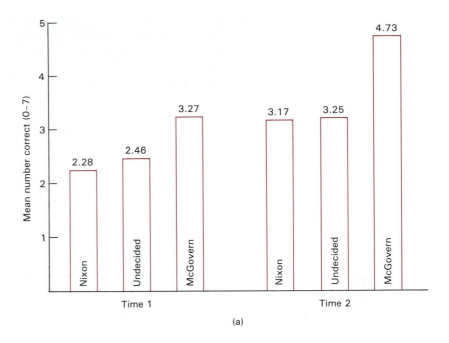

(a)

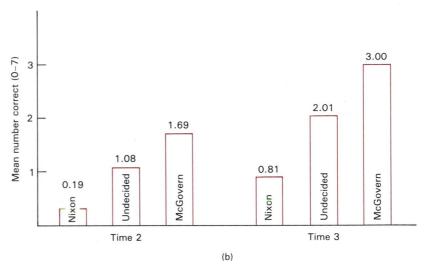

(b)

Attitudes and Behavior

One of the long-standing problems confronting social psychologists interested in the study of attitudes has to do with the absence of a perfect relationship between attitudes and behavior. Frequently the questions asked are, when is an attitude consistent with a behavior? What possibly accounts for the absence of attitude-behavior consistency? Why, for instance, do some parents who say they are in favor of racially integrated public schools actually send their children to private schools that have very few, if any, minority children? Or, why is it that male executives who hold a favorable attitude toward affirmative action for women still hesitate to hire equally qualified women for executive positions?

Evangelist Jimmy Swaggert tells his congregation on television that he has sinned against family and God. To what do we attribute his moral downfall?

Research on the consistency between an individual's attitudes and behavior has shown that there is much more correspondence between attitudes and behavior than earlier believed. One study shows that a person's stated attitudes can be good predictors of behavior *if* the attitude is strongly held, is based on personal experience, is supported by similar attitudes of significant other people, and is well rehearsed (a strong habit) (Worchel, Cooper, & Goethals, 1988).

The problem in research on attitude-behavior consistency is that there is often not a high correspondence between the attitude that is measured and the behavior that is observed. For example, we can administer a questionnaire to a group of subjects to assess their attitudes toward blacks. On the basis of this assessment of racial attitudes, we might conclude that our respondents are open minded and not prejudiced against blacks. Later, we might ask these same subjects to interact closely with blacks on a team responsible for solving a complicated and difficult problem. In this test situation, we might find that some of our "liberal" respondents are in fact prejudiced against blacks and are reluctant to work with them. The apparent inconsistency between attitudes and behavior in this example occurs because there is not a high positive correlation between the measured attitudes and the specific situation in which blacks and whites are to interact. As long as discrepancies exist between appraised attitudes and actual situations, there will continue to be a low correlation between attitudes and behavior.

Another question of considerable importance to social psychologists has to do with how an attitude leads to a consistent behavior. According to Ajzen and Fishbein (1980), who have suggested a reasoned-action model of attitudes, several steps are important in making attitudes consistent with behavior. Figure 19–3 presents the

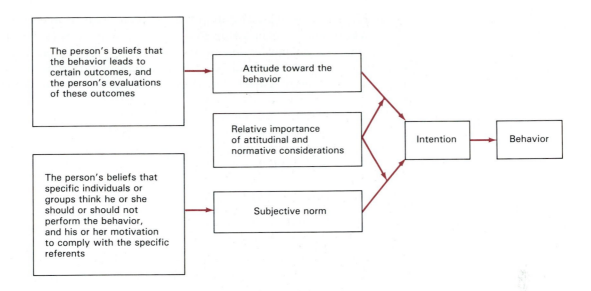

FIGURE 19–3 The Reasoned-Action Model of Factors Determining a Person's Behavior *This model holds that behavior is determined by the combination of our personal beliefs and attitudes and by what we believe others will think of our behavior. (After Azjen & Fishbein, 1980)*

Ajzen and Fishbein model. In this model, the first thing that is important is the person's attitude toward the behavior. Here, the person's beliefs about the outcome of the behavior and her evaluation of the outcome are important. The second consideration has to do with subjective norms, or what we believe others want us to do. If we believe that others want us to behave in a specific way, chances are high that we will engage in the behavior. For example, you might be generally opposed to charities except for giving to your church. However, at your new job, you learn that your company has begun its annual United Way campaign. You surprise yourself by pledging a certain amount to be deducted from your wages each month for the next year. Why did you contribute? Probably because of the normative influence of your boss and co-workers. The company has set a goal requiring all employees to contribute so that the firm will be able to reach its total goal of money pledged to United Way.

Our *behavioral intention,* then, is based on the relative importance we give to both attitudinal and normative considerations. The effect is that behavioral intentions are formed before behaviors and serve to determine whether the person will engage in a behavior or not.

AN INTERPERSONAL PROCESS: ATTRACTION

We have talked about how we form impressions of others, and how our attitudes are influenced by others. These are intrapersonal processes. Now we will move a step closer to examining actual interactions between two people (interpersonal processes). In Chapter 20 we will explore such enduring dyadic relationships as friendships and marriage; here we will focus on the basic process that enters into every interpersonal encounter: *attraction.* Why are we drawn to some people and not others? What happens in our interactions that enhances or diminishes the attraction?

For social psychologists, the old fairy tale about the witch who repeatedly asks, "Mirror, mirror on the wall, who's the fairest of them all?'' never had more relevance than it does today. The study of physical attraction and its relationship to all types of behaviors (for example, making a good impression in a job interview, being selected to play the lead role in a school play) has become very important because of the apparent power that good looks have in our everyday interactions with others (Hatfield & Sprecher, 1986).

Several theoretical approaches have been offered in an attempt to explain how good looks affect our behavior and the behavior of others. The two most important approaches will be covered here—balance theories and learning theories. By now you are quite familiar with learning approaches to behavior, since we have discussed learning in various contexts. But the balance theories are newer, so we will discuss them first.

Balance Theories of Attraction

We have already described one balance theory, dissonance theory, so the approach should be familiar. All *balance theories of attraction* in psychology are based on the assumption that each of us tries to achieve a state of internal and external consistency. We want our actions and our beliefs to match. We want our relationships with others to be fair, so that each of us is getting as much as the other out of the relationship. We want the people we like to like us. In the study of attraction, the two major balance theorists have been Heider (1958) and Newcomb (1956, 1961).

Heider described balanced and unbalanced relationships among an individual person, a second person, and some object. He argued that since each of us has a motive to achieve or maintain balance and harmony, we prefer balanced relationships and will change our cognitions (our attitudes) toward other people or objects in order to reach balanced states. Newcomb agrees on the basic preference for balanced states, which he calls *symmetry*. But he goes further by suggesting that when asymmetry exists between two people, they will try to reduce it by communicating with one another—talking over their differences, if you will.

An example may help you understand the difference between a balanced and an unbalanced relationship. If you and your friend Pete both dislike watching football on TV, you are in a balanced relationship. You like each other and you *both* dislike football. Any time you agree with a liked person, there is balance. The balance can also be created in another sequence. Suppose you meet someone new and discover that you share a passion for listening to Pavarotti singing arias from Bizet, or for eating oysters on the half-shell, or for movies starring Alan Alda. When you make this discovery, you have part of the balanced system (you and the other person agree on your attitude toward X), but to make the system fully balanced, you and your new acquaintance would have to like each other as well. Heider and Newcomb suggest that this is exactly what will happen. The fact that you agree on something increases the chances that you will also like each other, thus creating a balanced system (we both like Alan Alda, he likes me, and I like him). As a general rule, balanced relationships are comfortable, and will persist.

Unbalanced relationships are uncomfortable, so when we find ourselves in an unbalanced relationship, we will try to change it. Suppose that you and your best friend have an argument about whether women should be included in registration for the draft. This creates imbalance:

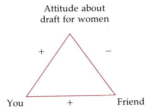

What can you do about the imbalance? You can try to persuade your friend that your opinion is correct. If you succeed, this will create balance. Or your friend might persuade you that he is right, which would also restore balance. If neither of those alternatives works, you can change your attitude toward your friend. If you and your friend discover that there are a lot of things you disagree about, and find you cannot change each other's minds, then Newcomb's theory would predict that your friendship would gradually turn into indifference or dislike.

We have already suggested some of the predictions derived from this theory of attraction, but let us summarize the theory by giving a more explicit list of expected relationships:

1. Balanced relationships are pleasant, and will tend to persist.

2. Imbalanced relationships are unpleasant and should be unstable.

3. Because liking the people who agree with you is a balanced system, you will tend to be attracted to people who share your views or behavior.

4. If you like someone, you will tend to assume that he agrees with your views on things.

As we will see shortly, all four of these predictions have considerable research support. Before turning to the research, though, we want to sketch an alternative view of attraction.

Learning Theories of Attraction

Several researchers have proposed very similar *learning theories of attraction* (Clore & Byrne, 1974; Lott & Lott, 1974). Basically, their proposals extend the principles of classical conditioning. Any person or object that is present while you are feeling good will tend to be associated with that good feeling through classical conditioning, and thus be liked. You can see this set of relationships, as proposed by Byrne and Clore (1970), in Figure 19–4. Obviously, the converse of this also happens. People and objects associated with punishment or other negative feelings will tend to be disliked (a relationship shown delightfully in Figure 19–5).

FIGURE 19–4 Byrne and Clore's Learning Model of Attraction

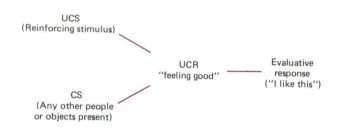

Notice that these theorists are not just saying that you will like people who reward you and dislike people who punish you. They are saying that anything or anyone present at the time of reward or punishment will tend to become a conditioned stimulus for the feelings generated by the reward or punishment. So if we spend a relaxing evening before the fire, listening to beautiful music and drinking a fine wine, we often feel special affection for the people who are around us at that time, even if they did not provide the fire, music, and wine, and are thus in no way "responsible" for our pleasure.

Let us summarize this theory with some specific predictions:

1. We will like people associated with reward or pleasure, and dislike people associated with punishment or displeasure.

2. Having people agree with us is pleasurable, so we will tend to like people who agree with us and dislike people who disagree with us.

Notice that this second prediction matches a prediction from balance theories of attraction. Both say that we should like people who share our views or behaviors or attitudes. The other predictions from each theory are somewhat different, but it is interesting that psychologists starting from such different theoretical places can arrive at such similar predictions about behavior. Do people actually behave this way? Are the predictions from the theories confirmed? Let us look at the research data.

Some Major Findings on Attraction

FIGURE 19–5 Ira Is Undone by Learning Theory

There are literally hundreds of studies on attraction. We have summarized some of the findings from this rich array in Table 19–4.

TABLE 19–4   Findings from Research on Attraction

We are attracted to people:

1. whom we see as generally similar to ourselves.
   a. who agree with us in opinions, attitudes, or behavioral choices.
   b. whom we think of as being about as attractive as we are.
   c. who are at about the same status level in our group or community.
   d. who are about our own age.
2. who are physically attractive.
3. who like us.
4. whom we see frequently (familiarity).
5. who are nearby (propinquity).

Similarity   The prediction from both balance and learning theories that we will like people who agree with us turns out to be valid. In fact, as Table 19–4 shows, there is a more general principle involved. We tend to like people we see as similar to ourselves in just about any way. Note that the important element here is not the actual similarity, but our *perception* of similarity.

The standard laboratory procedure for studying this process is to give students a questionnaire on which they report their attitudes toward a whole range of topics. Some time later—several weeks or months in some cases—the subjects are given the same attitude questionnaire supposedly filled out by another person, and are asked to say how well they think they would like this other person. In fact, the second questionnaire has been filled out by the experimenters so as to match or not match the attitudes the subject originally expressed. In this way, researchers can systematically vary the degree of agreement between the subject and the imaginary second person.

Under these conditions, researchers have found that there is a direct, linear relationship between the number of areas of similarity and the degree of liking. You can see this in Figure 19–6. The more similar the subjects thought the "other person" was to themselves, the more they thought they would like them. The attraction is especially strong if you and the other person appear to share preferences for things to *do*, like playing sports, visiting museums, listening to records, or other actual activities (Davis, 1981). These findings have been replicated again and again, in many different cultures (Byrne, 1971), for people of different ages, and in many different settings.

While this effect is found consistently, we must be cautious about generalizing from these laboratory findings to real-life natural encounters. After all, when you meet someone for the first time you do not usually ask them for their attitudes on 12 major topics! In fact, you may know almost nothing about the other person's attitudes or preferences. Your attraction or repulsion may be based on external kinds of similarity, such as the age or apparent social class or physical attractiveness of the other person.

A second important qualification is that there are circumstances in which perceived similarity simply does not predict liking at all, or

FIGURE 19–6 Relationship of Perceived Similarity to Attraction *The relationship is very nearly linear.* (After Byrne & Nelson, 1965)

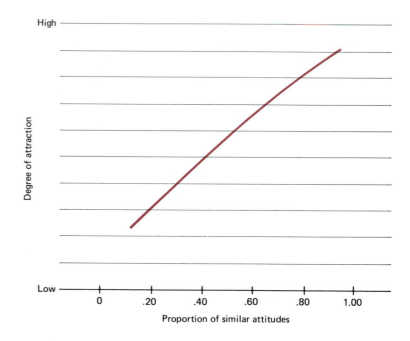

predicts it only very weakly. In the early stages of acquaintanceship, similarity appears to be fairly important, but in longer-term relationships (of which we will speak more fully in Chapter 20), *complementarity of needs* is also important. A decisive person may prefer someone who is compliant; a "masculine" male may prefer a "feminine" woman, rather than a woman with strong masculine qualities or an androgynous woman. Thus while perceived similarity may have a significant impact in many relationships, it is by no means the only force at work in attraction or in the maintenance of loving relationships.

Attractiveness   Another basic element in the attraction equation is that we tend to like people who are physically attractive (Hatfield & Sprecher, 1986). This may happen because we are constantly being shown beauty or handsomeness in association with "good" things such as wealth and happiness. By simple learning principles, we come to be attracted to beauty. In fact some research shows that we *do* assume attractive people are happier and more successful (Dion, Berscheid, & Walster, 1972). Whatever the reason, it is clear that in our culture at least, we are strongly biased in favor of physically attractive people.

Each of us probably has a slightly different idea of what constitutes physical attractiveness in members of our own sex and in persons of the opposite sex. Yet there are probably many things on which we agree. In order for studies of physical attraction to be meaningful, they need to tell us something about the physical characteristics that we use to make attributions about others. In a study of what body parts students use in defining attraction, several hundred college men and women were asked to rate a large number of body parts and functions for their importance in determining attractiveness in

These two young women dressed as "punkers" provide a contrast to our usual image of dress and style. Do you find these women physically attractive? What factors influence your reply?

members of the same and of the opposite sex (Franzoi & Herzog, 1987). Table 19–5 contains a listing of the eight most important body parts for each sex as rated by the students. What is interesting about the ratings is the degree of similarity between the sexes. The face was very important both within and across sex groupings. Body build (and physique and figure) was also important for both sexes. Men rated items such as muscular strength and biceps as more important for themselves and other males, while females indicated that eyes, body scent, and buttocks were important to them in rating men. In

TABLE 19–5 Ratings of Body Parts in Determining Physical Attraction

College men and women rating members of their own sex and members of the opposite sex assigned these rankings in descending order of importance.

Ratings of Men's Body Parts by		Ratings of Women's Body Parts by	
Men	Women	Men	Women
Physique	Eyes	Face	Face
Face	Face	Figure	Figure
Body Build	Physique	Buttocks	Weight
Physical Condition	Body Build	Legs	Eyes
Muscular Strength	Physical Condition	Eyes	Legs
Weight	Body Scent	Weight	Waist
Waist	Buttocks	Hips	Buttocks
Biceps	Weight	Body Build	Body Build

Source: After Franzoi & Herzog, 1987.

rating body parts for women, both males and females show an even higher degree of overlap in their ratings. Both men and women agree that the face, figure, legs, eyes, weight, buttocks, and body build are important to them.

In the first study that has sought to manipulate all of the possible combinations of attractive and unattractive faces and bodies, Alicke, Smith, and Klotz (1986) prepared an experiment using a set of photographs in which women were grouped into one of three different levels of facial attractiveness (high, medium, and low) and one of three levels of body attraction (high, medium, and low). Then separate photographic stimuli were prepared showing women in the nine possible combinations of facial and body attractiveness (for example, high attractive face–low attractive body, high attractive face–medium attractive body, high attractive face–high attractive body, and so forth). Students were then asked to rate the pictures for physical attraction, intelligence, sociability, and morality.

The results showed that for both male and female college students, facial attractiveness significantly influenced ratings of sociability, intelligence, and morality. Similarly, body attractiveness influenced judgments of intelligence and sociability. In other words, the photograph representing a highly attractive face with a highly attractive body was rated highest on all three personality traits. Depending on the level of facial and body attraction of the remaining stimuli, there was a decreasing order in the student ratings on the traits of sociability, intelligence, and morality.

The significance of these two recent studies is that they show how important our perceptions (cognitions) of others are, the basis on which these cognitions are formed (physical attraction), and the attributions we make of others on the basis of these cognitions. Although it is fine to say that beauty is only skin deep or that we should not be so superficial in our social judgments of others, it is still important to see that attraction does affect our behavior toward others and how others in turn treat us.

Familiarity   A third basic principle of attraction is that we seem to like things or people that we are familiar with, rather than those that are totally new to us. Zajonc (1965), who calls this the **mere exposure hypothesis**, argues that familiarity breeds liking, not contempt. For example, students who are in several experiments together like each other more than those who are only in one experiment together (Saegert, Swap, & Zajonc, 1973). Even if we are a bit put off by someone at first, repeated exposure seems to lead to increased liking of them.

The effect of mere exposure is the basis for most advertising. This same principle also lies behind some of the attempts to reduce prejudice between different ethnic groups, as we shall see in Chapter 20.

Proximity   A variation on the theme of familiarity is the effect of proximity. We are more likely to make friends with, or to like people who live close to us. In a dormitory or apartment building, for instance, you are most likely to make friends with the people whose room or apartment is near yours (Nahemow & Lawton, 1974). In a class, you are most likely to become friends with someone who is assigned a seat next to you. Presumably this occurs largely because you are simply exposed more often to these nearby people. Nearness can also give you more opportunity to discover similarities in interests or attitudes, but mere proximity can be more important than perceived similarity in some instances.

Putting the Elements of Attributions, Attitudes, and Attraction Together

We have talked about three basic social processes—attribution, attraction, and attitudes—as if they were separate from one another. But there are some obvious links. If someone does something helpful and we attribute it to *internal* causes, we like that person better than if we attributed the helpfulness to external causes (Regan, 1978). If a speaker is trying to persuade us to change our attitude about something, we are *more* likely to be persuaded if the speaker's expressed views are *inconsistent* with the personality characteristics or bias we attribute to the speaker. If the speaker's message is completely consistent with what we assume to be his bias or his personality, we discount the message and are not persuaded (Eagly, Wood, & Chaiken, 1978). This is another way of looking at the impact of the Frank Zappa ads against drugs. Because Frank Zappa had long hair and wore "hippie" clothes, most viewers might expect him to be in favor of drugs. When he came out against drugs, this made his message more believable and thus more persuasive. We also form more favorable attributions of physically attractive individuals. When these same physically attractive individuals behave in sex-role-appropriate ways, we are even more likely to hold positive attitudes towards them (Cash & Trimer, 1984). A male might have a very positive attitude toward an attractive woman until he discovers that she is a construction worker and not a secretary.

Attributions thus affect both attitudes and attraction, and attraction affects attitudes as well. But until recently, these three basic processes have been studied separately by three different sets of researchers. The current move toward a combined approach should lead to a more integrated theory of social interactions over the next decade.

THE EFFECTS OF GROUPS

We move now into a still wider arena, beyond attribution and attitudes, beyond attraction between one individual and another person, and into the much larger set of relationships we have with groups of people. Each of us takes part in groups constantly—in a job, on a committee, in a dormitory, in class, in family gatherings or groups of friends, on a sports team. New issues arise when we look at groups, such as the factors that affect group conformity. But many of the same basic principles we have already discussed will reappear here as well. Let us begin by looking at the impact of groups, or crowds, on the individual.

The Theory of Social Impact

One of the most interesting and broadest theories of the impact of groups on the individual is Bibb Latané's **social impact theory** (1981). Latané has undertaken the ambitious task of developing a set of basic principles that will account for a very wide range of social phenomena, from conformity to a group to the response of individuals to emergencies. He thinks that we should study "social forces" much as we might study physical forces like light or gravity. Latané feels that social forces operate in a "social field," and that we ought to be able to write "rules" or "laws" for the operation of such forces. As a first step, he suggests three such rules or principles:

1. When some number of social sources are acting on a target individual, the amount of impact experienced by the target should be a multiplicative function of the strength (S), the immediacy (I), and the number (N) of sources present.

2. The individual impact of each person in your social field is a function of how many people there are acting on you at any one time.

3. The more people in your social environment who are targets of the same social influence you experience, the weaker the effect of that influence will be.

When he refers to the strength of a social source in the first rule, Latané means the status or influence another person might have for you because of past experience. He is thus saying that you are more likely to be influenced by someone you see as having high status or more "strength" generally. This aspect of the first principle is obviously consistent with what we have already said about credibility of communicators in attitude change. The rest of this principle states that the more people there are pushing you in the same direction and the more immediate that push is, the more likely you are to be swayed. Figure 19–7 nicely depicts this principle.

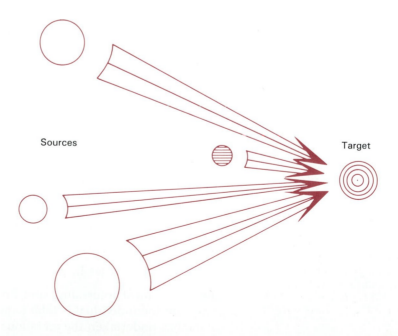

Sources

Target

FIGURE 19–7   Latané's Social Impact Theory   *The impact that a group will have on an individual (Target) is determined by the number of people present (number of circles), the importance of varying group members (size of circles), and the immediacy of the people (nearness of the circles to the target).* (After Latané, 1981)

To understand the second rule, think about how much impact the first person who tells you that you need a haircut has on your actions as opposed to the tenth person with the same message; each person added to the system increases the total social impact, but by smaller and smaller increments.

The third rule is just another way of saying that the strength of any social influence attempt is divided among all those who receive it. If a professor calls you into her office and gives you a lengthy critique of your last paper, exhorting you to do better next time, she will have a larger impact on you than if she made the same speech to the whole class. Her influence is in some sense diluted by the presence of the other members of the class. Figure 19–8 shows how an increase in the number of targets decreases the impact of the various sources acting on the targets.

By using these three principles, Latané has been able to integrate widely divergent bodies of research on the impact of groups on the individual. We will look at several examples here, and explore these principles further in Chapter 20 when we talk about bystander helpfulness.

Some Illustrations of Social Impact

Conformity Imagine yourself sitting with friends after a pleasant dinner. The conversation turns to school busing, and you find to your surprise that all of the other people at the table are adamantly opposed to busing as a means to achieve racial integration. Your own opinion (attitude) is that busing is often necessary and may achieve the desired goal better than other strategies. But here in this group, you are the odd man out. The others express their opinions quite

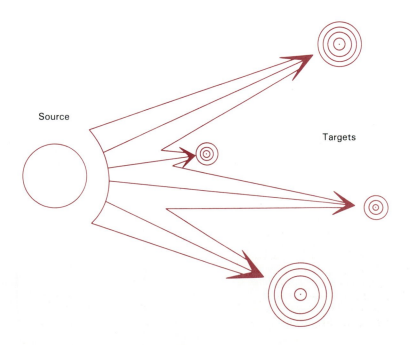

FIGURE 19–8 Impact of an Individual on a Group *The impact that a single individual will have on a group depends on the size of the group, the status of the target individuals present, and the immediacy of the group to the individual. (After Latané, 1981)*

vigorously, all supporting each others' arguments and creating that sense of balance that develops when friends agree. But you do *not* agree, and feel uncomfortable. What do you do? Do you speak up and oppose the group consensus? Do you go along with the group? Of course, in this situation, you have a third alternative, which is to say nothing. But assume that your friends insist on knowing what you think about busing.

As you might expect, there are several competing theories that might be used to predict your behavior in response to your friends queries. For instance, from the point of view of attraction theories, we would assume that your liking for your friends would be somewhat lessened by the discovery of this lack of agreement on an important topic. If we look at it from the point of view of attitude-change theories, we might expect that if you went along with the group, your attitude toward busing might change in order to reduce your dissonance. If we think of this situation in terms of Latané's principles of social impact, we would expect that you would be more likely to conform to the group if they had "strength," and if they all agreed with one another (as they do in this case).

The classic studies on conformity were conducted by Solomon Asch in the 1950s (1955, 1956). They are such classics that we cited them when we introduced social psychology in Chapter 1. Asch used groups of people that ranged in size from 2 individuals to 16 individuals, although his standard group generally consisted of 7 individuals. He asked them to make several simple judgments of the type shown in Figure 19–9. In this example, each subject was asked to say aloud which of the numbered lines was the same length as line A—seemingly a simple task. But the situation was rigged: the first six subjects were actually confederates of the experimenter, and they all confidently gave the same wrong answer. The real subject, who sat at the end of the line, was thus confronted with a unanimous choice which, to him, appeared wrong. What did he do?

This procedure has been used in dozens of experiments under many different conditions. The consistent finding is that only about a quarter of the subjects *never* conform to the group. Other participants conform on some trials and not others, and a third group conforms all of the time. Clearly, there are individual differences in the tendency to conform. Those who conform most often are people who do not have much confidence in their own competence, and are attracted to the group members and want to be accepted into the group (as we would expect from a balance theory of attraction). Latané also found

Figure 19–9   One of Asch's Conformity Experiment Tasks
Each individual in the experiment (one subject and 1–16 confederates of the experimenter) was asked whether line 1, line 2, or line 3 was the same length as line A.

In Stanley Milgram's controversial studies on obedience, the experimenter urged the subject to give the "learner" a "painful shock." Sixty-five percent of the subjects administered "shocks" of up to 450 volts.

in reanalyzing Asch's data and that of similar studies (for example, Gerard, Wilhelmy, & Connolly, 1968) that the greatest amounts of conformity occurred in the smaller groups and then continued to increase but in smaller increments as group size increased. This finding supports Latané's first and second principles. Finally, the more you are attracted to the members of the group, the more their combined attitudes will sway you, which is consistent with what we have said about persuasive communications, and with Latané's first principle of social impact. In short, Latané's theory fares very well in accounting for conformity to a group.

Obedience to Authority   The results of a series of classic and controversial studies on obedience by Stanley Milgram (1963, 1974) can also be interpreted in Latané's terms. The procedure Milgram used is quite simple. A subject enters the laboratory and is introduced to another subject, who is in fact a confederate of the experimenter. The subject is told that his job is to teach the other person a paired associates task. Each time the learner makes a mistake, the subject is to give the learner a shock with a shock machine, which has 30 levers labeled from 15 to 450 volts. The levers are grouped under descriptive labels ranging from "slight shock" to "moderate shock" and up to "danger, severe shock." The instructions are to increase the level of shock administered after each error. The experimenter, who is present throughout, pressures the subject to continue increasing the level of shock, even when the subject protests that the learner is in pain (although no shocks actually are received by the learner). The experimenter says things like "It's absolutely essential that you continue." Significantly, the experimenter *also* says "I'm responsible for anything that happens" to the learner. Under these conditions, 65 percent of the subjects administer shocks all the way up to 450 volts, even though the "learner" shouted that he could not stand the pain, kicked the wall at 300 volts, and made no response thereafter. (These experiments raised a storm of controversy among psychologists, many of whom believed them to be potentially damaging to the subjects. Partly because of such controversy, the APA ethics code now makes it virtually impossible for experimenters to use deception in this way.)

In Latané's terms, the impact on the subject in these studies was both *strong* and *immediate*. The experimenter, an authority figure in a white lab coat, representing a prestigious university, exerted pressure and was physically present throughout the experiment. In addition, the fact that the experimenter took responsibility for any bad consequences appears to have been vitally important in this situation. Thus both conformity in a group and obedience to authority can be explained (or at least described) with the same basic "law." In the case of obedience, we also have to add the factor of perceived responsibility.

Another Effect of the Group on the Individual

An interesting feature of the social-impact theory, apart from explaining such phenomena as conformity, is that it can also be used to examine the socially inhibiting effect that a group might have on one individual. Williams and Williams (1983) asked why people are inhibited about asking for help when it is often readily available. We are sure you can give many instances when you could have asked for help, but did not. What explanation did you give to yourself for not seeking assistance? Was your problem too personal? Did you feel embarrassed to ask for help? Perhaps you did not want to appear ignorant or incompetent, or maybe you were too proud and feared humiliation.

According to social-impact theory, we can make several best guesses about how a person will act in an emergency or help-seeking situation. The theory, for instance, would hold that the larger the *number* of people available to help, the greater the inhibition of a person to seek help. The reason for this is that when the responsibility to help is diffused among more people, it reduces their ability or likelihood of helping or acting quickly. Also, according to the theory of social impact, people are less likely to seek assistance from *high* status formal helpers (for example, psychiatrists) or attractive opposite-sex helpers (for men), because of the higher strength these individuals possess in social-impact terminology. Thus, the person requiring help experiences greater embarrassment, more threats to self-esteem, more feelings of inferiority, and more indebtedness when contacting such individuals for help. This is why we are more likely to obtain help from informal help-giving sources, such as friends and family members, who do not threaten our self-esteem.

As for the *immediacy* of helping, we experience more impact from sources close to us than from those that are far away. Unfortunately, to obtain immediate relief for a problem, we have to go to high-status (strength) helpers and/or surrender our anonymity because of the face-to-face encounter frequently required for immediate help. These conditions, then, work against our seeking immediate attention.

In a laboratory demonstration, Williams and Williams (1983) hypothesized that students would take longer to ask for help believing that a computer they were working at was broken (a deception) if (1) there were three helpers who would hear the request as opposed to only one; (2) they had to ask for help from a high-status expert (a professional as opposed to someone who said they knew little about the task to be performed); and (3) they had to ask someone in their immediate surroundings (next door) as opposed to someone from down the hall.

The results of this study confirmed the hypotheses. Participants waited longer to seek help if three people heard their request for help, if the request had to be made to an expert, or if the helper was nearby. As you can see, the behavior of an individual to help someone else or to seek help themselves is dependent on a number of factors, all of which are determined by group dynamics.

The Effects of Basic Processes on Group Behavior

Even though a great deal of small-group research and theory focuses on the group rather than on the individual, we can still see the influence of the processes of attribution, attitude change, and attraction that we examined earlier in connection with individuals. Intergroup behavior is influenced by such variables as the number of people in the group who agree on a position, which in turn is one aspect of attraction of group members for each other. Group processes also produce attitude change, such as conformity and obedience-type actions. These examples illustrate the fact that there is more order and regularity in social behavior than may be apparent on the surface. There are basic processes that underlie relationships between individuals and determine the nature of social encounters. Moreover, these basic processes have important applications to pressing social questions and problems like racial prejudice and discrimination, as we will see in the next chapter.

SUMMARY

1. Social psychologists study all aspects of human interactions, including feelings, thoughts, and actions, and examine these aspects within the individual person, between pairs of people, and in larger groups.

2. The focus on thought (or cognition) in social psychology is called social cognition. Here the interest is on social stimuli and the cognitive processes that people employ to make sense of their world.

3. Two fundamental intrapersonal processes that affect social contacts are impression formation and attitude change; a basic interpersonal process is attraction.

4. Social psychologists generally describe impression formation in terms of attributions, which are thought to be governed by a basic motive to understand the behavior of others—to master the environment.

5. The most fundamental attribution is a causal attribution; we attempt to explain other people's behavior in terms of dispositional or situational determinants. Which of these attributions we make is affected by our judgments of the consistency, consensus, and distinctiveness of others' behavior.

6. The attributions that we make of others can be influenced by our expectations of them. There is good support for the self-fulfilling prophecy, which in turn, strengthens our attributions of the person (behavioral confirmation).

7. The attributional process appears to have built-in biases, including a tendency to assume dispositional causes and a tendency to attribute other people's behaviors to dispositions that are independent of our expectancy-behavior sequence. This confirmation bias may occur frequently in our social interactions.

8. Attitudes toward others include feelings, cognitions, and actions. Attitudes can be changed by means of persuasive communications, but only under some conditions. Persuasive communications are most effective if the communicator has high credibility and attractiveness, if the message is somewhere close to the listener's own position, and if it is repeated often.

9. Attitudes can also be changed by getting someone to behave in a way that is inconsistent with his underlying attitude. This leads to a state of *dissonance*, which the person may try to resolve by changing his attitude.

10. People appear to select information that supports their attitudes and to avoid information that is contrary to positions about which they feel strongly.

11. Social psychologists have noted the problem of attitude-behavior inconsistency. This problem, however, may have a great deal to do with a lack of precision in measuring attitudes. A reasoned-action model has been proposed that explains how attitude-behavior inconsistency occurs.

12. The study of attraction and of dyadic relationships is one of the major interpersonal topics of study in social psychology. Two types of theories have been offered to account for attraction to others: balance theories and learning theories.

13. Balance theories emphasize that each of us tries to keep our relationships with others in balance so that people we like share our views or actions, and we try to avoid or eliminate imbalance.

14. Learning theories emphasize the role of classical conditioning in influencing what we will like and dislike. Things associated with pleasant events will tend to be liked.

15. Research on attraction supports both views to some extent. We are attracted to others whom we see as similar to ourselves, who are physically attractive, who like us, whom we see often, or who live near us.

16. It is possible to identify the physical features that we employ to determine attractiveness in members of the same and of the opposite sex.

17. Attributions about intelligence, sociability, and morality may be made on the basis of physical attraction only.

18. The theory of social impact offers three basic propositions that can be used to account for such social

phenomena as conformity to a group or obedience to authority. Both are increased when there are powerful figures exerting influence, when there is unanimity among other group members, and when the target of influence is isolated from other support.

19. The factors that are important in social-impact theory and that explain conformity can also be used to explain under what conditions and from whom an individual seeks help.

KEY TERMS

attraction

attribution theory

balance theories of attraction

behavioral intention

complementarity of needs

consonance

correspondence bias

dispositional attribution

dissonance theory

learning theories of attraction

mere exposure hypothesis

selective approach

selective avoidance

self-fulfilling prophecy

situation-specific behavio,

situational attribution

social cognition

social impact theory

social psychology

ADDITIONAL READING

Ajzen, I., & Fishbein, M. (1980) *Understanding attitudes and predicting social behavior*. Englewood Cliffs, NJ: Prentice-Hall.
This book attempts to explain the relationship between attitudes and behavior and has had a major impact on the study of attitudes. The level is somewhat technical, but the book is well worth reading.

Allport, G. W. (1985) The historical background of social psychology. In G. Lindsey, & E. Aronson (Eds.), *Handbook of Social Psychology* (3rd ed., Vol. 1, pp. 1–46). New York: Random House.
This is a very informative survey of the history of social psychology from the perspective of major issues and findings. This selection provides good background information about the evolution of the field of social psychology over the years.

Fiske, S. T., & Taylor, S. E. (1984) *Social cognition*. New York: Random House.
This is one of the first books published on the topic of social cognition. It is an excellent, but highly technical, review of the literature.

Hatfield, E., & Sprecher, S. (1986) *Mirror, mirror: The importance of looks in everyday life*. Albany: University of New York Press.
This is a very readable book on the social and psychological consequences of physical attraction in play, work, and love.

Kelley, H. H., & Michela, J. L. (1980) Attribution theory and research. *Annual Review of Psychology*, 31, 457–501.
This paper, co-authored by a leading social psychologist, examines the research surrounding attribution theory and concludes that the theory is still viable in explaining social interactions.

Sears, D. O., Freedman, J. L., & Peplau, L. A. (1985) *Social psychology*. Englewood Cliffs, NJ: Prentice-Hall.
This popular basic textbook in social psychology covers many of the major topics in the field. The book is a good reference guide for the student wishing more information about social psychology.

20 Exploring Social Psychology

Much of the research done by social psychologists deals directly with everyday problems and concerns. Social psychologists are studying ways to change people's attitudes on topics ranging from energy conservation to preventive health practices. They are exploring the role of social groups in the transmission of infectious diseases, such as AIDS, and the impact of environmental noise on children and adults. They have explored how attribution and decision making affect the functioning of policy makers and the behavior of those individuals who carry out policy. And they have studied every imaginable kind of social group, from juvenile gangs to assembly-line workers.

Clearly, we have an abundance of material to choose from in deciding on topics to explore in this chapter. The five topics we have selected, sampling from this broad range, touch on important social issues that affect the daily lives of all of us. How do we move from first impressions to lasting, loving relationships? How do we relate to people of other races? What stereotypes and prejudices do we carry around with us and how were they learned? How are our behaviors and attitudes affected by the mass media? Are we influenced negatively by the large amount of violence commonly viewed on television? Do children fare better or worse than adults in their television viewing? How do we react when we are confronted with someone in need of help? How are we affected as potential helpers by the crowding inherent in urban environments? And why is it that good nutritional practices and exercise are easy for some people yet so difficult for most individuals?

It is important to emphasize that although these topics are clearly related to real-life problems, they are also rooted in basic research. We will encounter the basic processes of attribution, attitude change, attraction, and social impact over and over again in our discussions of applied social problems.

BEYOND ATTRACTION: LIKING AND LOVING

In the last chapter we talked about the factors that influence our first feelings of attraction to others. But what turns attraction into a more permanent loving relationship? What are the qualities of relationships that endure, compared to those that do not? These are important questions for our society, as today's extremely high divorce rate shows. They are also important questions for each of us individually, because the establishment of intimate relationships is one of the central tasks of adult life, as we pointed out in Chapter 12.

Are Liking and Loving Different Things?

Let us begin our exploration by looking more closely at *liking* and *loving*. Think of the people you like and the people you love. Are they the same people? Do you love everyone you like? Probably not. Do you like everyone you love? That is more common—but you can probably think of times when you loved someone you did not like very much. (Parents sometimes feel that way about their children—and vice versa!) What is the difference? Is loving just a more intense form of liking or is it something really different?

Zick Rubin (1973) argues that liking and loving are *not* the same. In his view, liking consists of respect and affection, while loving includes attachment, caring, and intimacy. In Erikson's terms (see Chapter 12), an infant may have a strong attachment to her mother and father, and this may constitute a form of love. But real intimacy—the trust that lets you disclose your inner fears and desires, a willingness to put the other person's needs before your own, the shared ability to communicate—probably does not occur until early adulthood, if then.

In order to demonstrate the difference between liking and loving, Rubin has developed separate measures to assess each one. Sample items from the two measures are shown in Table 20-1. For each item, the respondent records an answer on a scale of possible responses ranging from "not at all true; disagree completely" to "definitely true; agree completely." Using responses to the measures he developed and his observations of couples' interactions with one another and with strangers, Rubin has shown that liking and loving are really different in several ways:

1. When lovers fill out the two scales about each other, they tend to give similarly positive but not identical answers on both the liking- and the loving-scale items. (The correlations between the two scales are on the order of .40 to .50. That is, people tend to like those they love, but the relationship is not perfect.

2. Between friends, the link between liking and loving is even weaker. Clearly, we can feel respect and affection for someone without also feeling that deep sense of attachment and intimacy that we call love.

3. Partners who score high on the love scale are more likely to report that they expect to marry than are partners who score lower. That is, anticipated commitment to a permanent relationship is linked to love but does not necessarily play a role in a liking relationship.

TABLE 20–1   Selected Examples of Love-scale and Liking-scale Items

Love scale

1. If _____were feeling bad, my first duty would be to cheer him (her) up.

2. I feel that I can confide in _____about virtually everything.

3. If I could never be with _____, I would feel miserable.

Liking scale

1. I think that _____is unusually well adjusted.

2. I have great confidence in _____'s good judgment.

3. _____ is the sort of person whom I myself would like to be.

Source: After Rubin, 1973.

4. Partners who are high on the loving scale show more eye contact than do strangers or than dating couples who are lower on the love scale. Eye contact, especially if prolonged, is a highly intimate form of "talking." Less loving couples look toward one another as often, but show less of the intimate, mutual regard that you see in couples who are "in love."

A Cluster Theory of Liking and Loving

In another view of liking and loving, Davis (1985) has proposed that liking, as in a friendship, can be understood in terms of eight main elements: enjoyment, mutual assistance, respect, spontaneity, acceptance, trust, understanding, and confidence. Love, however, involves these eight elements plus two additional clusters of feelings. The first cluster is *passion*, which involves fascination with the other person, sexual desire for the other person, and exclusiveness with the other person. The second cluster is *caring*, which involves championing or being a primary advocate for the other person and giving the utmost of oneself to the other person.

According to Davis, lovers or spouses and close friends do not differ much in terms of the base of friendship that underlies both liking and loving relationships. They do differ, however, in the attributes that form the passion and caring clusters.

A Triangular Theory of Love

In a third view of love, Sternberg (1986, 1987) proposes a triangular theory. In this theory, love is composed of three components that form the sides of a triangle. The first component is the emotionally based part of love and consists of *intimacy*, which refers to feelings of closeness, connectedness, and bondedness in loving relationships. The motivational component consists of *passion*, which as you might expect refers to the drives that lead to romance, physical attraction, and sexual consummation. The third component is the cognitive controller that is responsible for the short-term and the long-term *decision/commitment* that is involved in a loving relationship. The short-term decision involves acceptance of such a relationship, while the long-term aspect involves the commitment to maintain the relationship.

An interesting feature of Sternberg's theory is that it can be used to generate a taxonomy of different kinds of liking and loving relationships. Table 20–2 presents Sternberg's taxonomy of kinds of love. As can be seen, all of the different situations can be described in terms of the presence or absence of intimacy, passion, and decision/commitment. Let us take a closer look at some of these different kinds of relationships.

Liking According to the taxonomy, liking results when a person experiences only the intimacy component of love. Passion and commitment are absent. In liking relationships, we feel closeness, bondedness, and warmth toward another person, but at the same time we are not sexually responsive to them nor do we wish to spend the rest of our life with them.

TABLE 20–2   Taxonomy of Kinds of Love

Kind of Love	*Component*		
	Intimacy	Passion	Decision/commitment
Nonlove	−	−	−
Liking	+	−	−
Infatuated love	−	+	−
Empty love	−	−	+
Romantic love	+	+	−
Companionate love	+	−	+
Fatuous love	−	+	+
Consummate love	+	+	+

Source: After Sternberg, 1986.

Note: A plus sign means that the component is present; a minus sign means that the component is absent. These kinds of love represent limiting cases based on the triangular theory. Most loving relationships will fit between categories, because the various components of love are expressed along continua, not discretely.

Infatuated Love   The infatuated love category includes those relationships described as involving "love at first sight." This love is aroused by passion but is devoid of intimacy or decision/commitment. This type of relationship can arise almost instantaneously and dissipate almost as rapidly.

Companionate Love   Companionate love evolves from a combination of intimacy and decision/commitment. This type of love represents

Although the eye contact evident between these two individuals might indicate that they would rank high on Rubin's love scale, it is difficult to know whether the intimacy and decision/commitment components of Sternberg's taxonomy are present here.

long-term, committed friendship in which the physical attraction component (passion) has faded. Companionate love is often seen in marriages that endure but that are devoid of much physical passion.

Consummate Love   Consummate love encompasses the full complement of intimacy, passion, and decision/commitment. This is the perfect type of love that most of us seek in a loving relationship. Consummate love is difficult to achieve and possibly even more difficult to maintain for any extended period of time.

The value of Sternberg's triangular theory of love is that it expands our thinking about the dimensions involved in interpersonal relationships. By means of this theory we are able to explain how we feel toward our parents, our siblings, close friends, and lovers. At the same time, we can pinpoint where changes occur in our feelings of intimacy, passion, and commitment and how our perceptions of the people with whom we interact in these roles remain constant or change over time. Although it is still too early to evaluate the long-range impact of Sternberg's theory of love, we can say that the theory has improved our understanding of complex human interactions involving liking and loving.

How Do You Know If You Are in Love?

Most of us have "fallen in love" more than once—some of us, dozens of times! But what do we mean when we say we are "in love"? How do you decide that you love someone, rather than merely like them?

Love as a State of Being   When people try to answer the question of how they decide that they love someone, many of them start talking about feelings of heightened awareness or heightened arousal. When the special person walks into the room or you hear that special voice on the phone, your heart beats faster; you may feel a sinking sensation in the pit of your stomach, and your skin may flush. Is this love?

If you recall the discussion of theories of emotion in Chapter 10, you will realize that at least one theorist believes that this state of increased arousal *is* love. Stanley Schachter has argued that any time you experience noticeable changes in body states, such as arousal, you will try to find a logical explanation for them. In attribution-theory terms, you try to attribute the aroused feelings to some dispositional or situational cause. If you are out in the woods hunting and you feel your heart beating faster and the adrenalin pumping as a big bear heaves into view, you are likely to attribute your arousal to the situational cause and call it fear or excitement. But if you feel the same kind of arousal during a candlelight dinner with an attractive person, you are likely to attribute it to an internal (dispositional) cause and call it love.

Schachter's research (Schachter & Singer, 1962) provides some support for his view. The initial labeling of a feeling toward another person as "love" probably does depend in part on the setting, but surely there is more to love than this!

Love as a Process   As we have seen, love involves commitment, the sharing of inner feelings, altruism, and nurturance (Rubin, 1973;

Davis, 1985; Sternberg, 1986, 1987). This view of love as a process, which is shared by many psychologists who have written about love (for example, Fromm, 1956; Peele & Brodsky, 1976), emphasizes the enduring character of a loving relationship between two people. The process of falling in love involves many aspects of behavior—emotion, closeness, satisfaction, cognition—which in combination make loving a complex social process between people. And, as we all know, loving changes over time, waxing and waning over months and years.

Enduring Relationships

Loving relationships begin, grow, endure; or they begin, grow, and then fade. What makes the difference? We could ask this question about friendships as well as loving relationships. Think of the friends you made in elementary school or high school. Are you still good friends with all of those individuals? Do you still stay in contact with them? Why did some friendships endure while others faded? Why do some loving relationships flourish while others die away?

Similarity   In the last chapter we talked about *perceived* similarity as an important ingredient in initial attraction. It turns out that perceived similarity is important in enduring relationships as well. Generally, the more two people in a relationship see themselves as like one another, the more probable it is that the relationship will last.

This is true of similarity in attractiveness (White, 1980), of *perceived* similarity in attitudes, likes, and dislikes (Newcomb, 1978), and of similarity in needs (Meyer & Pepper, 1977). For example, Meyer and Pepper studied a group of 66 married couples, all of whom had been married five years or longer. They found that those who had the best marital adjustment were also those who had similar needs or motives, such as affiliation, aggression, autonomy, and nurturance.

However, as we noted in the last chapter, the effect of similarity is not as simple as one might believe. In a now-classic study of mate selection, Winch (1958) proposed that need complementarity was as important as similarity, if not more important. His studies of married couples convinced him that the highest marital satisfaction occurred when couples complemented one another on three dimensions: achievement versus passivity, nurturance versus dependence, and dominance versus deference. For example, a man who has a strong need to dominate is likely to be attracted to (and to marry) a woman who has a need to be submissive.

This long-held belief about need complementarity has recently been challenged, however. Studies have shown that happily married couples tend to demonstrate more similarity along a number of personality dimensions than do less happily married couples (Buss, 1984). Nonetheless, some complementarity is necessary in a relationship, especially in a long-term relationship (Synder & Fromkin, 1980). Thus, the evidence supports the view that perceived similarity is important throughout a relationship. In the early stages of a relationship, similarity acts as a sort of "filter." That is, we do not pursue friendships or loving relationships with people who are very unlike ourselves. Further, long-lasting relationships also require a fairly high level of similarity for them to be successful. But once relationships reach a certain level of stability, some types of complementarity may be important as well.

Positive Interactions Another crucial ingredient of enduring, satisfying relationships is that there are more positive than negative exchanges. Robinson and Price (1980) studied a group of married couples, including some who described themselves as highly adjusted and others who described themselves as distressed (low in adjustment). These researchers observed these couples interacting and also had them fill out a questionnaire that described the frequency of certain pleasurable behaviors, such as agreeing, approval, concern, humor, compliance, attending, compromise, smiling, and positive physical interactions. They found that adjusted couples showed more pleasurable behaviors with one another, as you might expect, but the distressed couples actually *underestimated* the actual rate of pleasurable behaviors that they shared. Similar results have been obtained by other researchers (Jacobson, Waldron, & Moore, 1980).

A great deal of the research conducted on marital quality has been done by sociologists, rather than psychologists. They approach the task with a different set of theories and a somewhat different set of questions, but there is considerable consistency in the findings on the importance of positive interactions. Sociologists Lewis and Spanier (1979; Spanier & Lewis, 1980), for example, argue that "rewards from spousal interaction" is one of the three key ingredients in enduring marriages. The others are satisfaction with life style and the presence of sufficient social and personal resources. Included in the "rewards" category in the Lewis and Spanier model are (1) positive regard for spouse, (2) emotional gratification, (3) effectiveness of communication, (4) role fit, and (5) amount of interaction. When these elements are positive, spouses or partners are more likely to report that they are satisfied with their relationship, and the relationship is more likely to endure.

Until quite recently, social psychologists have spent most of their time studying the *early* stages of relationships—the first encounters when the forces of attraction are at work—and the somewhat later stages when pairs of people move from attraction to loving. We know a great deal less about the "glue" that holds some relationships together for 20, 40, or 60 years, but what we do know suggests that some of the old familiar basic psychological principles are at work. Relationships that contain rewards (positive reinforcements) are more lasting; relationships that are in balance are more enduring as well.

Despite this comforting predictability, there are many questions waiting to be explored. Are some people more skilled at the creation of enduring relationships? That is, can we link up what we know about personality with what we know about attachments and attractions? What are the factors that tip a relationship from a basically positive one to a troubled or negative one? At what point does a person begin to pay more attention to the negative daily events than to the positive ones? What causes the shift, and can people be helped to shift back to a more positive view?

Research conducted by psychologists and sociologists suggests that the crucial ingredients of enduring, satisfying relationships involve perceived similarity and a relatively high percentage of positive interactions.

This last question leads us to studies of marital therapy and is an excellent example of the interaction between theory and practice. The more we are able to understand the basic processes involved in liking and loving and in enduring relationships, the better the base we will create for effective therapeutic interventions. Today it is probably more important than ever before to understand the enduring quality of lasting relationships. Divorce rates are very high, and as we discussed in Chapter 13, children are often the losers when marriages fail. Surely people fall in love and marry expecting to be happy with their mates for a long time. We need to understand better why relationships succeed or fail.

RACIAL PREJUDICE

We turn now from loving interpersonal relationships to a bleaker side of interpersonal and intergroup contact—prejudice. We all carry around our own collection of likes and dislikes (prejudices), whether we are aware of them or not. There is something we just do not like about tall people, religious people, fat people, elderly people, or people who are bald. Often we do not even know why we have these negative feelings, but we do. Although people in general have become more sensitive about sexism and racism, many individuals still hold prejudices against women and minorities.

In this section, we will emphasize *racial* prejudice, but what we say here applies to all prejudices. Our focus is on racial prejudice because it has had such a pervasive and negative impact on our society, and, consequently, it has generated the most research.

Let us begin by defining three interrelated terms that are critical to our understanding of racial prejudice. *Stereotypes* are oversimplified mental images of a category of people that are held by a large number of individuals. Stereotypes can be positive and marked by the use of adjectives such as intelligent, strong, and good. On the other hand, stereotypes can also be negative and associated with adjectives such as lazy, dirty, and cheap. *Prejudice* refers to the unjustified application of negative attitudes and stereotypes toward an individual solely on the basis of his or her membership in a group. Prejudice implies a "prejudgement" about an individual or a group without actual proof to substantiate such a belief (Schneider, 1988). For example, a person may be prejudiced against Hispanics, believing that most Hispanics are content to live on welfare, without actually having any proof that this is the case. Finally, prejudice is frequently associated with overt or covert *discrimination*, which is characterized by negative and often harmful behavior directed toward an individual solely because of that person's membership in a group.

Prejudice and discrimination are troublesome for many reasons. Prejudices are often not based on any factual information; frequently they are baseless. It is also common in the study of prejudice to find people who make generalizations about a minority group based on a negative personal experience with a member of that minority. In other words, they attribute negative traits to all members of a racial group based on a single experience with only one member of that group. Further, the discrimination resulting from prejudicial attitudes frequently leads to harmful consequences for both the victim of prejudice and the prejudiced person. Racial tensions that lead to physical violence and destruction of property are but one example of the harmful effects of prejudice. Prejudicial attitudes are very resistant to change. One of the major challenges to social psychologists has been the attempt to find solutions to racial prejudice in our society.

Where Does Racial Prejudice Come From?

How do people acquire the pervasive negative attitudes characteristic of racial prejudice? Several theories have been proposed.

Prejudice Is Learned in Childhood   One prominent view of the origins of prejudice is that such attitudes are learned at our parents' knees in accordance with the basic rules of learning that we have outlined repeatedly in earlier chapters. We know that children notice racial differences as early as age 4 or 5 and that by about the same age most children seem to prefer to play and associate with others of their own race (Brand, Ruiz, & Padilla, 1974). We also assume that children's attitudes about other racial groups are affected by the models provided by the adults around them and by direct reinforcement of their positive or negative statements and behaviors toward other groups. When Dad puts a KKK sticker on his truck, makes derogatory comments about blacks when they appear on TV, and praises young David when he tells about winning a fight with a black child at school, David's attitudes about blacks are being formed.

Children can also learn about prejudice and discrimination from television programs and movies. For years Hollywood has cast blacks and other members of minority groups in traditional, stereotyped roles (Worchel et al., 1988). If parents permit their children to see such programs and then reinforce the negative images with disparaging remarks about blacks, Asians, or Hispanics, the children come to believe that such stereotypes must be accurate since they are shared not just by their parents but by many other people as well.

Prejudice as Part of Personality   Other researchers have attempted to explain the origins of prejudice by seeking evidence that prejudice is, in fact, a personality trait. Adorno, Frenkel-Brunswick, Levinson, and Sanford (1950) were interested in whether anti-Semitism was an isolated attitude held by individuals who had had unpleasant personal experiences with Jews, or whether it was related to a network of attitudes, personality, and family-background characteristics. As an outcome of their investigation of anti-Semitism, Adorno and his co-workers described the *authoritarian personality* type to account for prejudice. Because of their rigid and punitive upbringing, people with authoritarian personalities seem to view the world in very stereotyped ways. You are either part of their group or you are not, and if you are not with them, you must be against them. Adorno and his colleagues also found a strong relationship between anti-Semitism and *ethnocentrism*. Those individuals who were highly anti-Semitic had similar attitudes toward other ethnic, religious, and cultural groups. The only group such individuals valued was their own.

There is some support for this view of prejudice. Some people do seem to be consistently prejudiced against *all* groups not like their own. An excellent portrayal of this type of person was the television character Archie Bunker. Archie had negative things to say about everyone who was not like him.

However, not all people who hold prejudicial racial views are authoritarian. Thomas Pettigrew (1958) showed that scores on a measure of authoritarianism were no higher among Southerners than among Northerners, even though antiblack attitudes were more common in the South than in the North in 1958. So, although certain personality types may be more likely to show prejudice, personality cannot be the whole explanation.

Prejudice as a Natural Result of Group Membership   A third view, advanced most persuasively by Henri Tajfel (Tajfel & Turner, 1979), is that because all human beings have a tendency to categorize things, we quite naturally create "us" and "them" categories for people as well. Tajfel's own research (Tajfel, Flament, Billig, & Bundy, 1971, for example) shows that merely putting people randomly into two groups and giving each group a label ("Klee" group and "Kandinsky" group in one study) produces discriminatory behavior. Subjects were more generous toward others who were labeled as members of their own group, even if they knew nothing else about these individuals. Thus, the behavioral part of prejudice—discriminatory behavior—can be observed when there is even the most elementary division into "us" and "them" categories. Since all of us see ourselves as belonging to a number of groups, we have a natural tendency to prefer others who share our group memberships and to discriminate against those who do not.

Perceived Similarity as a Basis for Prejudice   A fourth and particularly influential view of the origin of prejudice, first proposed by Rokeach (1960), is grounded in social psychological research on attraction and attitude change. Rokeach argued that since we like people whom we perceive as being similar to ourselves, we may dislike a racial group because we see them as very different from ourselves.

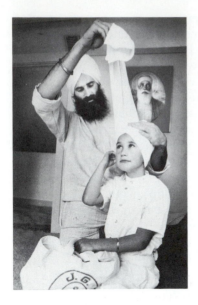

A Sikh father wraps his daughter's turban. Frequently, people who are different from the majority group are the targets of negative stereotyping and discriminatory behavior.

(Tajfel's studies of intergroup prejudice might represent an extension of this basic principle; people in "other" groups are different, and thus less liked.) There is some support for Rokeach's proposal. If we know that we share knowledge and beliefs with a person of another race, this knowledge of similarity can override our stereotyping, but there are limits. If we think we may have to act on the perceived similarity on a more intimate level, such as choosing someone of another race as a roommate, our stereotyping may override the perceived similarity (Silverman, 1974).

Despite the qualifications, Rokeach's view has formed the basis for many attempts to reduce racial prejudice. If we can create conditions in which blacks and whites relate to each other on equal terms, building up common experiences and sharing ideas and attitudes, there should be a shift in attitude and a reduction in prejudice.

Reducing or Eliminating Prejudice: Can It Be Done?

The most successful strategy for reducing prejudice is to increase the contact between members of different racial groups (Stephan & Brigham, 1985). Allport (1954) was one of the first to suggest the ground rules for this kind of contact:

> Prejudice may be reduced by equal status contact between majority and minority groups in the pursuit of common goals. The effect is greatly enhanced if this contact is sanctioned by institutional supports (i.e., by law, custom, or local atmosphere), and provided it is of a sort that leads to the perception of common interests and common humanity between members of the two groups. (p. 281)

It is very important to note that the *contact hypothesis* advanced by Allport clearly states that racial prejudice will be reduced only *if* the contact meets the following basic criteria:

1. The majority and minority groups should be of equal status.
2. They should be working on some common goal.
3. The contact should be supported by the relevant authority figures.
4. The contact should lead to shared interests or to the perception of common interests.

Contacts that do *not* meet these criteria may actually lead to increases in prejudice, particularly if the members of the two groups are not of equal status. School desegregation that has resulted in schools with a white student elite and a separate black social structure has *not* decreased racial tension or prejudice. But when Allport's conditions *are* met, then real change of attitude does seem to occur. For example, several studies have shown that blacks and whites living together in integrated public housing show reduced prejudice, particularly if they live next door to each other—an example of the effect of proximity (Wilner, Walkley, & Cook, 1955). People of different racial groups who work together at the same jobs show reduced prejudice as well.

A study of racial attitudes among children at an integrated summer camp illustrates the effect of contact fairly clearly. Clore, Bray,

Itkin, and Murphy (1978) studied a group of about 200 eight-to-twelve-year-old children who were attending a summer camp for one week. Half the children were black and half were white, and within the camp racial integration was carried out systematically. Each residential unit had equal numbers of black and white children, and each had one black and one white counselor. The rest of the camp staff was also equally divided by race. At the beginning of each week's camp, the children filled out a list of attitude items including several involving their attitudes toward blacks and whites. They also played several games in which they could choose which other children to play with or to have on their team. The same questionnaire and games were used again before the children went home at the end of the week so that researchers could see whether attitudes had changed and whether behavior had changed as well.

As it turns out, both attitudes and behavior changed. The children became less prejudiced, and this was true of the blacks toward the whites, as well as of the whites toward the blacks. We have tabulated the results of the game choices in Table 20-3. The numbers in the table are the proportion of cross-race choices before each week's camp began and the proportion after a week of contact. In four out of the five weeks, there was a significant shift toward more cross-race choices.

Other recent studies with school children show similar reductions in prejudice as the result of increased contact between races. Slavin (1985) studied cooperative learning in the classroom to see if contact between children of different racial groups resulted in greater intergroup acceptance. In cooperative learning, equal status is achieved between students (regardless of race) through a procedure wherein each child possesses information needed by the others. All of the students must work together in order to complete a learning task. The results of Slavin's research supported the contact hypothesis. Students gained in cross-racial friendships and, more importantly, these intergroup friendships appeared to be strong and relatively long-lasting.

Unfortunately, most of the research in the area of intergroup relationships is not longitudinal and the consequences of such strategies as cooperative learning undertaken to foster intergroup contact have only shown us the *short-term* benefits of contact. Whether the changes last, and whether they generalize to other social situations

TABLE 20–3   Choices of Opposite-race Playmates at Summer Camp

| | *Weekly Groups* | | | | |
Time of Observation	1st group	2nd group	3rd group	4th group	5th group
At beginning of camp week	41%	44%	43%	45%	38%
After one week of camp	49	47	41	47	45

Source: After Clore, Bray, Itkin, & Murphy, 1978.

Racial tensions have increased in recent years because of the resurgence of white supremacist groups who advocate violence against minority groups.

(aside from summer camps, offices, or classrooms) is not yet clear. On the whole, findings from research on intergroup contact have not been very encouraging about either the durability or the generality of prejudice reduction, but at least it is clear that contact can make *some* difference.

In summary, interracial contact is not a cure-all. When the contact does not meet Allport's four basic conditions, contact can have a negative effect. Simply arranging to have people of different racial groups come into contact with one another is not the answer. Planned contacts that seek to meet Allport's criteria are required for positive effects to be obtained. Aronson and his co-workers (1978) and Slavin (1985) have shown that such conditions can be achieved with children in classroom settings. These demonstrations are important because they show that children need not have the prejudicial attitudes of their parents. This was, in part, one of the hoped for results of school integration.

Although we cannot cover the entire school integration controversy here or the related—and violently argued—question of school busing, it is important to touch on this major social experiment. As Gerard (1983) has shown, arguments for and against school integration and busing involve a series of complex questions. Is integration the best means for ensuring equal educational opportunities for children? Do black children in an integrated school perform better academically? Is there a reduction or an increase in racial tension following school desegregation efforts?

Opponents of school integration and/or busing have pointed to the continued academic underachievement of black students and to interracial hostility between black students and white students on many school campuses as an indication that integration has failed to bring about equal educational opportunities and a lessening of racial tension. However, we take the position that if school integration has not achieved its stated objectives, it is because the crucial criteria of the contact hypothesis specified by Gordon Allport have not been met. We would expect to find reduced racial tension, reduction of prejudice, and improvement in black achievement *only* when school desegregation has been planned to promote equal status for majority and minority groups and has been implemented with the outspoken support of all authority figures involved, including school boards and school staff. When these conditions are not met—and they have not been met in many cases—we should not be surprised at an increase in tension and prejudice (Cook, 1984).

Despite the controversy surrounding school desegregation, there is encouraging evidence that this social program may be working better than even the contact theorists believe. Braddock (1985), after reviewing the literature on the effects of school desegregation, concludes that the effects may be far reaching and may include lifelong social integration and occupational attainment for blacks. This points to the need in social psychology to have a long-term vision about social change, especially when dealing with such complicated phenomena as prejudice and discrimination.

Our next topic is also complicated and is important because it may affect the roles played by such factors as love and prejudice in our lives. Television has become such an integral part of our culture that it is often difficult to determine whether it mirrors who we are or whether it shapes who we are.

TELEVISION

It is difficult for many of us to imagine what life would be like without television. Television has become the most frequently used mass-entertainment and information medium in contemporary American culture. Most people have some daily exposure to the electronic box. There are differing opinions about what role television plays in the lives of children, adults, the elderly, men, women, minority-group members and so on. Critics generally argue that the negative effects outweigh the benefits, especially where children are concerned. Do children become zombies, unable to think and lacking in imagination as a result of too much television viewing? Is the aggressive behavior seen in some children caused by the all-too-frequent violence observed on television programs ranging from Saturday-morning cartoons to "Miami Vice"? What about school performance? Are lower school grades, especially in the language arts, related directly to long hours of unsupervised television viewing?

Displacement and Content Roles of Television

In one of the few naturalistic experiments to examine the impact of television on a community, Williams (1986) has reported on the Canadian town of "Notel," which received television for the first time in 1973. By comparing "Notel" with two similar control towns that had received their first television broadcasts some time earlier, and by using information already available concerning children's cognitive processing of television, Williams has been able to tell us a great deal about how television impacted on the residents of "Notel." Her conclusions are relevant for all residents regardless of age or sex.

Williams divides the impact of television into displacement effects and content effects. *Displacement effects* are changes in how individuals use their time. It appears, for example, that television displaces attendance at various functions outside the home, such as sports events, clubs, parties, and hobby groups, but has no discernible effects on church-sponsored activities or business-related programs. Displacement effects were most marked among elderly Canadians. Television did not displace leisure-time use of print media or children's trips to the library.

Content effects are actual changes in behavior influenced by television programming. Specifically, content effects in Williams's study included television's teaching of conventional sex-role differences and an increased tendency toward aggressive behavior on the school playground following the introduction of television. Creative problem solving by adults was faster when television was not available, but no effects on adult personality or cognitive style were found.

Some results could not be singly assigned as displacement or content effects. One such effect example was the poorer reading scores of viewers who watched a great deal of television. The association of poor reading skills with the availability of television was most pronounced at the critical stage of reading acquisition and among less intelligent or learning-disabled youngsters, but Williams shows that no such effects were found for children who were already skilled readers. Poor reading effects were stronger among children of lower socioeconomic status than among middle-class children.

Time Spent Watching Television

It is obvious that television has complex effects that are at least as much a function of who is watching, the conditions under which they watch, and the programming that they select, as they are the result of gross exposure. According to the Nielsen Television Index (1981), children ages 2–5 years viewed an average of 27.8 hours of television per week. Children ages 6–11 years viewed an average of 24.3 hours per week, and teens viewed 23.0 hours per week, on the average. However, we must ask ourselves just how reliable these figures are when we know that they are derived from paper-and-pencil surveys that may not be sensitive to all of the factors involved in television utilization. For example, how often is the television on without anyone actually watching it? Or how many hours do people spend *with* the television on when no one is actually paying any attention to it?

In one of the few studies specifically designed to study actual television viewing time in the home, Daniel Anderson and his colleagues (Anderson, Lorch, Field, Collins, & Nathan, 1986) installed automated time-lapse video recording equipment in viewers' homes. They studied 99 families comprised of 460 individuals ranging in age from less than one year to 62 years of age. The equipment used consisted of two video cameras set up in such a way that one camera with a wide-angle lens was positioned to provide a full-screen image of the television-viewing room. The second camera was equipped with a zoom lens and was focused on the television screen. The equipment was designed to automatically begin recording when the television set was turned on and to stop recording when the television set was turned off. By means of this two-camera set up, Anderson and his co-workers recorded 4,672 hours of television on-time in these 99 families over a period of ten days.

Daniel Anderson and his colleagues installed automated time-lapse video recording equipment (camera at left) in viewers' homes to study actual viewing time.

The findings of this study are extremely interesting. The researchers discovered that no one was watching television 15 percent of the time that a set was turned on. Visual attention to the television set among children increased sharply from birth to age 10 and then leveled off at about 70 percent. Adult females paid significantly less attention to television (54 percent) than did children. Adult males looked at the television more than females did (63 percent), but they also watched it less than school-age children. Overall, children spent an average of 12.8 hours per week with the television on, while adults spent 11.5 hours per week. When actual looking time was computed, school-age children looked at television 9.14 hours per week versus 7.56 hours for adults. This is considerably fewer hours of television viewing time for both children and adults than found in some other reports.

Figure 20-1 graphs the number of hours per week spent looking at television as a function of age for the different age groups in the Anderson et al. study. There is a large increase in time spent from 0–10 years and then a decrease after age 10. The rate levels off at about age 17 and continues at about the same level (10 hours per week) into adulthood. Few differences between the sexes emerged in this study, except for the fact that adult males looked at the television more than did adult females.

The fact that children spend about a third of their time with television, even though they may not be looking at it, requires considerably more research in the future. As Anderson and his colleagues point out, children not only leave the viewing room and return in the middle of programs, but they also play with toys and with their siblings, read, and interact with their parents while the television set is on in the same room. In sum, simply because the television is on in

Figure 20–1 Hours Spent Looking at Television as a Function of Age *(After Anderson et al., 1986)*

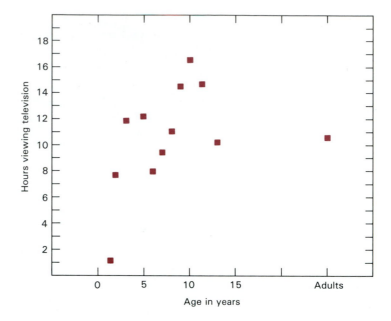

a home does not imply that it is being attended to by children or adults. Much more needs to be known about what it is about television programming that draws a child's attention and how this influences behavior.

Effects of the Media on Political Attitudes and Behavior

Recall what we know about attitude-change theory and research and studies of attraction. These findings might lead us to look for several effects of media presentations on voters' attitudes toward candidates and on their actual voting behavior.

1. We should be more inclined to like and to vote for candidates we see as holding views similar to our own.

2. We should be more inclined to like and to vote for physically attractive candidates.

3. We should be more likely to vote for someone who is more familiar to us; sheer repetition of a candidate's name may make us more likely to vote for that individual.

All three of these expectations are supported by research on actual voting. Prospective voters are more likely to pick candidates whose views are similar to their own (Diamond & Bates, 1984), or even candidates who *look* as though they would have similar views. The physical attractiveness of the candidates also matters. In presidential elections in the United States, there is a consistent tendency for the taller candidate to win—height is one of the elements of "attractiveness" deemed important for men.

Perhaps the most striking of the several effects we are looking for involves candidates who are extremely familiar to us because we have been exposed to them (or even just to their names) repeatedly. We

A majority of television viewers report that television plays an important role in helping them decide which candidates will receive their vote.

have all suffered through the television advertising bombardment that occurs just before any election. Today, American politics essentially is politics waged on the television screen. Does all of this television exposure make any difference? Of course, advertising may serve an *informational* purpose by conveying the candidate's position on important issues, but most political advertising is designed primarily to keep the candidate's name before the public. Today the political media strategists ''sell'' the candidate in the same way you would sell soap flakes or deodorant, simply by repeating the brand name over and over again. Does this repetitive approach work? Apparently, it does. Bower (1985) reported that of several thousand respondents to a questionnaire that he distributed, the majority thought television did a good job in presenting issues and candidates at election time. Further, in the 1980 election, as many as 62 percent of those asked told Bower that television had played an important role in helping them to decide which candidate would get their vote.

The research on political advertising supports Zajonc's ''mere familiarity'' hypothesis, which we described in Chapter 19. This hypothesis suggests that such mindless repetition makes the biggest difference when all the candidates are relatively unknown. Once the candidates are at least moderately familiar, more exposure does not make much difference in our attraction to them. Grush, McKeogh, and Ahlering (1978) examined a large number of primary elections for seats in the House of Representatives or the Senate. When all of the candidates in the primary were equally unknown, the amount of money spent on advertising was strongly (but not perfectly) related to the outcome of the election (see Table 20–4). But when an incumbent ran for office—someone who was *already* familiar—he won nearly every time, even when his less familiar opponents spent more money.

Obviously, the amount of money a candidate spends is not the only thing that matters, but sheer repetition of a name, exposure to a candidate's face, and catchy slogans all have some impact in the early stages of a campaign. It was concern over this effect of exposure that led to the 1971 Campaign Finance Law, which set limits on the amount of spending allowed. In theory, this should make the political process more accessible to less affluent candidates. In fact, it has often supported the reelection of the incumbent, since if one candidate is

TABLE 20–4 Electoral Success of Initially Unknown Candidates and Amount Spent on Advertising

	Number of Elections Won
Biggest spender for advertising	29
Second biggest spender	13
Other candidates	9

Source: After Grush, McKeogh, & Ahlering, 1978.

well know to start with, equal spending virtually assures that person's election.

This dilemma is a good example of what can happen when social-science theory and research are applied to complex social processes. The theory, in this case, does a pretty good job of predicting what actually happens in the "real world." But the social psychologists cannot tell us how to make the political process completely fair. Indeed, given what we know about attitude change, it is unlikely that any law could totally eliminate the influences of money and incumbency on election results.

Effects of Television Violence on Beliefs and Ideas

Cognitive learning theory (Chapters 5 and 12) tells us that children and adults can learn new behaviors by watching other people perform them. Since television programs are full of both familiar and exotic forms of aggression, we would expect learning to occur as a result of seeing certain behaviors replayed repeatedly on the screen. This same theory also predicts that seeing someone else perform some otherwise forbidden act serves as a disinhibitor (which we discussed in Chapter 5). Thus, children who see a great deal of aggressive behavior on television should behave more aggressively in real life as well. In addition, heightened exposure to violence on television may have an effect on people's beliefs and feelings. Thus all three parts of an attitude, as we defined it in Chapter 19, may be affected by violence on television.

Just How Violent Is Television?   We should have every reason to be concerned about the effects of televised violence because we are all exposed to a great deal of it. George Gerbner and his colleagues (Gerbner, 1972; Gerbner, Gross, Morgan, & Signorielli, 1980) define violence as the "overt expression of physical force against others or self, or the compelling of action against one's will on pain of being hurt or killed" (Gerbner, 1972, p. 31). These researchers have systematically analyzed the violence content of television programming each year for over a decade. They found an average of about six violent

Watching violence on television tends to make people more aggressive, more negative in their own feelings, and more callous toward others. Children imitate the violent acts they see, sometimes with deadly results.

incidents per hour for prime-time programs and about 17 episodes per hour for children's cartoons (Gerbner et al., 1980). There is also often a high level of violence in many of today's films, which eventually are shown on television. An extreme example, for instance, is *Rambo III* with Sylvester Stallone, which shows 245 separate acts of violence, including 123 killings (*Los Angeles Times,* June 3, 1988).

What is the effect of all of this violence on behavior? Nearly all of the research on this question has involved children, but the conclusions are generalizable to adults. So let us turn our attention to the effects of television viewing on children's behavior.

Effects of Television on Children

Jerome and Dorothy Singer of Yale University have spent considerable time studying the relationship between television viewing and children's behavior. They have examined the effects that television has on a child's imagination and have investigated links between television and restlessness and between television and aggression. The Singers' research has become very important because of the insights it is giving us about personality formation in very young children. According to Singer, heavy television viewing preempts the time needed by children to practice play, fantasy, reading, prosocial skills, and physical skills (Singer & Singer, 1986).

In one especially revealing study, Singer and Singer (1981) visited the homes of preschool children who had previously been classified as either low or high in television viewing and low or high in aggression. This 2-by-2 design results in the matrix with four possible combinations shown in Figure 20–2. The Singers found that families with children who were classified in the high group for television viewing and the high group for aggression were different from families in the other conditions. These families reported that television or movies were the major source of recreation. There was more parent-child coviewing and the children were frequently in control of television programming in these families. Children who ranked high in aggression and either high or low in television viewing spent on an average four times as much time watching action-adventure programming as low-aggressive children. By contrast, the children who ranked low in

Figure 20–2 Effects of Watching Aggression on Television *In a study by Singer and Singer (1981), children were grouped into one of four conditions on the basis of whether they were classified as low or high in aggressive behavior and by whether their television viewing time was classified as low or high. Some behavior traits exhibited by the two extreme groups are shown within the appropriate boxes.*

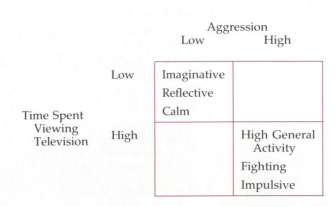

aggression watched more slow-paced and peaceful programs, such as "Mister Rogers' Neighborhood," than did highly aggressive children.

Mothers reported that the high-aggressive children showed more general activity, were more likely to have a "fighting problem," and were more impulsive. Children ranked low in aggression and television viewing demonstrated more imaginative play, were calmer, and were more reflective in their behavior.

Did these children also experience more aggressive behaviors in the home? Mothers of children who were ranked as highly aggressive reported that their children were more likely to be punished by spanking than the low-aggressive children, while the low-aggressive children were also more likely to be rewarded by praise. Obviously, there is a complex interaction operating here that needs to be better understood. How much of the aggression demonstrated by some children is due to elevated general activity, how much to demonstrated aggressive acts in the home by parents directed at the preschool-age child, and how much to greater time spent viewing action-packed and violent programming on television? Probably all of these are operating simultaneously to affect the young television viewer.

In a follow-up study, Singer, Singer, and Rapaczynski (1984a, 1984b) sought to examine children's aggression, imaginativeness, television habits, motor activity, and school adjustment using a group of children ranging in age from 3½ to 8½ years. Aggression was measured by mothers' reports for school-age children and by observations of preschool children during free play. Relationships were found to exist between aggression and the number of hours of sleep a child had, heavy preschool television viewing, heavy viewing of realistic action-adventure programming, lack of family involvement in varied activities, and child-rearing attitudes of the child's parents. The high-aggression children also showed problems in motor restraint and in delay of gratification; they were less imaginative in play and had more school-adjustment difficulties.

There are at least four conclusions that can be drawn from research examining the relationship between television violence and aggressive behavior (see Table 20–5). Researchers are willing to place a

---

TABLE 20–5   The Effects of Television Violence on Behavior

1. Watching violence on television *increases* the level of aggression in the viewers.
2. The effect is greatest in young children, but is still present in teenagers and adults.
3. The effect is greatest on those who *already* show fairly high levels of aggression.
4. The effect is greatest if the viewer is in a "permissive" atmosphere—one in which aggressive behavior is more acceptable. If the child (or adult) is in a setting in which aggression is typically discouraged or punished, then heavy television viewing has a smaller effect.

good deal of confidence in the validity of these conclusions because the conclusions are based on *both* experimental and naturalistic research. Children exposed to controlled doses of television violence in laboratory studies were later observed in standard situations and found to behave more aggressively. But children in the "real world" also show this effect. Williams's (1986) research on "Notel" (see p. 765) before and after television was introduced indicated that the level of aggression shown by the children in this town increased after they began watching television.

In adults, the effects of television violence on behavior are more subtle. We may not hit each other more, but we are likely to speak more critically to one another and be less helpful and supportive. Loye (1978) arranged to have several groups of men view different television "diets" for one week via cable television. One group of men saw only programs that were high in "prosocial" or helpful behaviors, such as "The Waltons." A second group saw only violent television programs such as "Hawaii Five-O." A third group saw only neutral shows or light entertainment, such as "The Odd Couple." Then, the men's wives were asked to record each incident of "helpful" or "hurtful" behavior by the husband. A "helpful" behavior was defined as any behavior that "strengthened marriage and family relationships." What Loye found was that the wives of men who had watched the violent diet recorded more occasions of hurtful behavior. These men did not suddenly start beating their wives, but they were more insensitive, more critical, and less supportive during their week of viewing violent programs.

Television Literacy

Acknowledging many of the psychosocial and developmental problems observed in children who are known to be frequent viewers of action-packed television programs, Greenfield (1984) argues that since television is here to stay, parents, teachers, and other adult caretakers of children must find ways to channel the positive effects of television and minimize its harmful consequences. The argument is compelling because as Greenfield notes in her book, *Mind and Media*, the television is now only one of several forms of electronic mass media. The others that she discusses are video games and computers.

Greenfield argues for teaching children *television literacy*, which includes an understanding of the meanings of such television program production techniques such as close-up, zooming, parallel processing of multiple story lines, and so forth. She makes the point of showing how successfully children's programs such as "Sesame Street" and "The Electric Company" move preschool children along from one learning sequence to another, working always within the range of the young child's cognitive development. This is the positive side of television that needs to be better understood and employed for children and their adult caretakers. Part of this also involves turning the television from a passive to an active medium in teaching.

Another recommendation offered by Greenfield involves teaching children to be informed consumers of television programs. This includes distinguishing between social reality and the often make-believe world of television, interpreting and properly assessing sex-role and minority-group stereotyping, and understanding the purpose and nature of commercials.

Research indicates that it is possible to alter children's attitudes about the aggression and violence that they see on television. Huesmann and his colleagues (Huesmann, Eron, Klein, Brice, & Fischer, 1983) worked with first- and third-grade children selected because of their high exposure to television violence. The children were divided into experimental and control groups. The experimental group received a series of three training sessions which were designed to reduce the modeling of aggressive behavior seen on television. Specifically, experimental subjects were told (1) that the behaviors of the characters on the shows they were watching did not represent the behaviors of most people, (2) that camera techniques and special effects were giving the illusion that the characters were performing their highly aggressive and unrealistic feats, and (3) that the average person uses other methods to solve problems like those encountered by the characters.

The results of this study showed that the experimental subjects exhibited less overall aggressive behavior as judged by their peers, spent less time viewing violent television programs, or programs that showcased aggressive behavior and lowered their identification with television characters; all in comparison to the control group, which received no training. An even more impressive finding was that these changes in behavior persisted for at least two years.

In conclusion, parents can help turn television from a passive medium into an active, teaching medium by interacting with their children while watching television. They can highlight important information and interpret what is happening on the screen. Television can be used to teach prosocial values and cognitive skills. Complaining about the harmful effects of television on children is no longer

Parents can help turn television from a passive medium into an active, teaching medium by interacting with their children while watching television. They can highlight important information and interpret what is happening.

sufficient. Television is here to stay and we need to find ways to transform its power and that of other forms of mass media into a positive force. Greenfield's recommendations are certainly a step in the right direction.

Putting It All Together

It seems clear that all the elements of an "aggressive attitude" are affected by watching violence on television. People who watch a lot of violent programs are more likely to think of violence as a good way to solve problems. They are more likely to use aggression in their own behavior, and they are probably both more negative in their own feelings and less sensitive about the feelings of others. Television is not the only factor influencing these elements. The effect is generally stronger if the person is already fairly aggressive, or if the person's family tolerates aggressive behavior and attitudes, but the effect is definitely there. If you share our view of the evidence and wish to exert some control over the process, you have a simple remedy at hand: turn off the violent programs.

On that gentle note of advice, let us turn away from the study of aggression and violence and look at a positive aspect of social behavior—altruism. When do people help one another?

HELPING STRANGERS IN DISTRESS

In the spring of 1980, a young Frenchman, Pierre Georges, was approached by two men on a New York City street and offered drugs. Mr. Georges turned down the offer and struggled with the drug dealers. During the struggle, Mr. Georges was shot and fell to the sidewalk wounded. Two women friends who were with him called out to passersby for help. At least a dozen people were standing nearby, but none offered to come to their aid. No one called the police, and no one assisted the police in any way when they arrived. Mr. Georges died hours later in a hospital.

This is an example of a phenomenon that has been part of urban life for a very long time—the apparent unwillingness of people to come to the aid of a stranger in distress. Quite a few social psychologists focused on this problem after a particularly grisly example of *bystander indifference*, the case of Kitty Genovese in 1964. Miss Genovese was repeatedly stabbed in three different attacks by the same assailant, at night in a respectable neighborhood. She cried out for help again and again, but none of the 38 people who watched from their windows called the police or intervened in any other way.

In the years since the Genovese murder, researchers have tried to understand the processes involved. They have staged countless fake emergencies to determine what factors cause bystanders to help—or refuse to help. After two decades of research, social psychologists have a great deal to tell us about helping behavior. Several elements of this situation and the people involved seem to be critical.

Diffusion of Responsibility

In our discussion of social impact theory in Chapter 19, we saw that the more bystanders there are at an emergency, the *less* likely it is that any one person will offer assistance (Latané & Nida, 1981). If you are the only person around when a middle-aged man slumps to the sidewalk clutching his chest, you are *far* more likely to help than if there is another person nearby. As the group size increases, the probability that you will offer help goes down still more. This illustrates Latanés third "law" of social impact. In an early demonstration of this *"diffusion" effect*, Latané and Darley (1970) arranged to have two or more students carry on a discussion over an intercom system. Each student was in a separate room but could hear the other(s) over the intercom. Each student talked for two minutes and then was to listen to the other(s) for two minutes. One of the subjects (a confederate, on tape) mentioned hesitantly that he was prone to seizures. Later in the discussion, the listeners heard this over the intercom:

> Somebody er—er—er—give me a little—er—give me a little help here because—er—I—er—I'm—er—er—h-h-having a—a—a real problem—er—right now and I—er—if somebody could help me out it would—it would—er—er—s-s-sure be—sure be good . . . I could really—er—use some help so if somebody would—er—give me a little h-help—uh—er—er—er—er could somebody—er—er—help—er—er—uh—uh—uh (choking sounds) . . . I'm gonna die—er—er—I'm . . . gonna die—er—help—er—er—seizure—er (chokes, then quiet)." (Latané & Darley, 1970, pp. 95–96).

Latané and Darley varied the number of subjects in the experiment and waited to see whether any subject tried to help the person who seemed to be having a seizure. You can see the results in Figure 20–3. The more people there were, the longer it took for each of them to respond and the smaller the percentage that actually did try to do something for the victim.

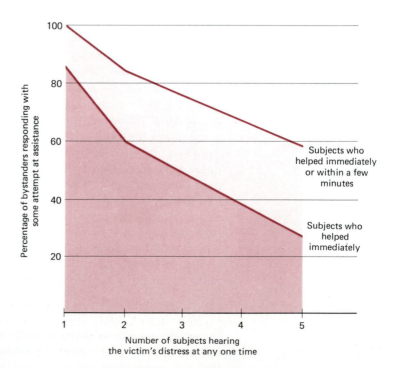

Figure 20-3   The "Diffusion of Responsibility" Effect in Bystander Intervention   *The more subjects who heard a person "having a seizure," the less likely any one of them was to help.*
(After Latané & Darley, 1970,)

Urban versus Rural Differences in Helping

One question that frequently arises when discussing helping behavior is whether urban dwellers are more or less willing to come to the aid of someone in need than are people who live in rural areas. The stereotype that most of us have of the "typical urbanite" is that he is impersonal, uninvolved, and distrustful. Is this why no one came to the aid of Pierre Georges or Kitty Genovese in New York? Would the situation have been different in a small, rural Midwestern town?

The research results on urban-rural differences in helping behavior are inconsistent. About the same number of studies find urbanites to be significantly less helpful as find no differences between urbanites and people in small towns (Amato, 1983). In one of the most carefully planned and thorough studies designed to investigate the urban-rural distinction in helping behavior, Amato (1983) studied residents of 55 cities and towns in Australia selected on the basis of population size and geographical isolation. He looked at six different types of helping behavior: (1) picking up a fallen envelope, (2) giving a donation to the Multiple Sclerosis Society, (3) writing down one's favorite color for a student working on a class project, (4) helping a person with a bandaged and bleeding leg who collapses onto the sidewalk, (5) correcting inaccurate directions that one has overheard being given to a stranger, and (6) completing and turning in a census form, which indicated a cooperative and helpful attitude toward the government.

Amato found that population size of the city was significantly and negatively correlated with five of the six types of helping. That is, as the size of the town or city increased, the rate of helping behavior decreased. The only helping behavior that was not related to population size as a result of Amato's research was picking up a fallen envelope, which may not have been a sensitive enough measure of helping, since this behavior was infrequently observed in all communities. The surprising finding of Amato's study was that a population size of approximately 20,000 people marked the point at which helping behaviors between strangers begin to be inhibited. Amato's findings support an interpretation of urban life based on the concept of overload (Milgram, 1970). *Overload* here refers to excessive levels of social and environmental stimulation. According to Stanley Milgram, urban dwellers cope with this overload by adopting an unresponsive orientation to strangers. The distressing thing about the findings of Amato's research, if they are generalizable to the United States as a whole, is that stimulus overload occurs even in relatively small semi-rural communities.

The Effect of Others' Behavior

Another determinant of helping behavior is simply whether other people are also helping. In one of Latané and Darley's experiments, pairs of students "overheard" a woman in the next office falling and injuring herself while calling for help. When one of the pair of students (a confederate of the experimenters) remained passive throughout the episode and made no move to help, only seven percent of the other students went to the woman's aid. If there are others present and they are *not* helping, you are more likely to conclude that there really is no emergency. But when one of the other spectators *does* help, you are more likely to help as well. The behavior of others helps to define both the nature of the emergency and the appropriate action to take. Still, this isn't the entire story. Not everyone helps, even when others are doing so. What about the *first* person who rushes in to offer help, apparently without thinking about what others will or will not do?

Helpers: Are They Different?

A number of researchers, including Latané and Darley, have tried to figure out whether people who help are different in some systematic way from those who do not. Are they more empathetic? Do they have a stronger sense of moral or social responsibility? Comparison studies of helpers and nonhelpers offer only slight support for these speculations. Moreover, observers with strong religious orientations are *not* more likely to help (Batson & Gray, 1981). But temporary mood states can make a difference. People who are feeling joyful because something nice has happened to them are much more likely to help others than are people whose mood is less exuberant (Rosenhan, Salovey, & Hargis, 1981).

Of all of the characteristics of the prospective helper, the most significant one appears to be knowledge of *how* to help (Huston & Korte, 1976). Bystanders who have skills that are likely to make helping more effective, such as knowledge of first aid or CPR (cardiopulmonary resuscitation), are much more likely to help than are people who do not have such abilities.

These conclusions about helpers are highlighted in a study of real-life helpers by Ted Huston and his colleagues (Huston, Ruggiero, Conner, & Geis, 1981). They located 32 adults who had intervened in assaults, holdups, burglaries, or other serious crimes. All 32 had applied for compensation under the California Good Samaritan law, which compensates bystanders who are injured or suffer a loss as a result of their attempt to intervene in a crime. Table 20–6 describes two of the 32 cases, so you can see that these were real and very violent incidents.

Huston and his colleagues wanted to know whether these 32 people were different in some way from a larger random sample of adults drawn from the entire Los Angeles area. From this group selected at random, Huston chose adults who were matched in age, education, ethnic background, and sex with the 32 crime interveners. The difference was that none of the people in the comparison group had intervened in any crime in the past ten years. (What we do not know about the comparison group is whether they had had an *opportunity* to intervene and did not do so; all we know is that they did not report having intervened.) Both the interveners and the comparison group were given a series of personality tests and were interviewed at length. Disappointingly, Huston and his colleagues found only a few differences between the interveners and the randomly selected comparison group:

TABLE 20–6   Real-life Crises in Which a Bystander Did Intervene

A young man, late one Saturday evening, was driving by a dance hall just as the dance was ending and the crowd was spilling out onto the sidewalk. He noticed a lot of people suddenly running toward an area. Then, as he tells it, he saw "this dude carrying a girl by her hair, dragging her and punching her, punching her out like a beanbag." At that point he became involved: "I went over there and I grabbed the dude and I shoved him over and I said 'Lay off the chick.' So me and him started going at it. I told him to get out of here, man, the girl's mouth's all bleeding, she got her teeth knocked out. Everybody was just standing around." A further exchange of blows ensued, one of which broke the intervener's jaw, before the police arrived and took the assailant into custody.

A man was at home with his wife and other family members when one of his sons burst into the house saying the grocery store across the street was being held up and his brother was in the store. The man, thinking that his son might be in danger, raced headlong across the street and into the store. He saw a man with a rifle facing the woman behind the counter. He describes what happened next: "The lady looked at me and just said, 'Help me please!' So the guy turned around to shoot me. I just grabbed the rifle from him, threw it down, knocked him down." After a struggle in which the intervener was cut by pieces of broken bottles that had fallen from a basket, he subdued the assailant, and was hitting him when the police arrived.

Source: After Huston, Ruggiero, Conner, & Geis, 1981.

1. The helpers were more likely to live in areas in which there was a fair amount of crime, or they had had a lot of previous contact with violence. They had seen other crimes committed or had been victims themselves.

2. The helpers had intervened before. Eleven of the 32 had come to the aid of other victims without having been injured.

3. The helpers were virtually all men (31 of the 32).

4. The helpers, compared to other men of the same age and education, were much more likely to have had specific skills in life saving, first aid, and self-defense, or to have had police training.

There were *no* differences on any of the personality dimensions measured, such as humanitarianism, alienation, social responsibility, sensation seeking, or a tendency to react to situations with anger, but there were real differences in the *ability* to intervene successfully. These findings suggest that providing more training in first aid or self-defense would increase the number of people who are willing to help others in distress. And in fact, cities that have undertaken major programs of training in CPR have found that the rate of death by heart attack does go down. Presumably, some of the people trained in the technique come to the aid of strangers showing the symptoms of heart attack. Clearly, exhorting people to be more "moral" or more thoughtful of others is less likely to generate helpfulness than is teaching people *how to be* helpful.

TABLE 20–7 Percentage of Subjects Who Helped as a Function of Need for Approval and Social Reinforcement

	Need for Approval	
	High	Low
Social response		
Reward	85.71	50.00
Punishment	27.27	45.45

Source: After Deutsch & Lamberti (1986).

Yet, it may be premature to rule out the importance of personality characteristics in our study of prosocial helping behaviors of the type discussed above.

Recent research has shown, for example, that social approval may be a critical factor in the prosocial behavior of some individuals. Deutsch and Lamberti (1986), for instance, have found that female college students who score high in need for social approval are significantly more likely to help a fellow student pick up dropped books if these female students have just received positive feedback (social reward) for participating in a psychology study than if they have received a "cool and distant" thank you (social punishment) following completion of the experiment. Importantly, students low in need for social approval were unaffected by the experimental manipulation of either reward or punishment and were just as likely to help or not help irrespective of the condition. Table 20–7 presents the findings from the Deutsch and Lamberti study. Their research demonstrates the importance of considering the interaction between personality and social context in understanding helping behaviors. Little is known about the role of personality in prosocial behaviors, but more social psychologists are turning their attention to the interaction between personality factors and social settings to understand behaviors such as helping.

In the following section, we will explore the topic of health psychology, which has become an important area of study in social psychology. In our discussion of health and behavior, we will concentrate on attitudes toward health practices and social support. The latter topic is quite similar to some of the issues discussed on helping behavior. In social support, however, the focus of interest is on help received from friends and family members, not from strangers.

HEALTH PSYCHOLOGY

The study of good health practices has become a major area of interest to psychologists in recent years. It is not uncommon today to find psychologists working in medical centers and in schools of public health. The reason for this is that as a society we have become far more concerned about our health and about the ways in which we can promote improved health behaviors so that people live fuller and more enjoyable lives. At the same time, we have come to recognize that not everyone has the same positive attitude toward maintaining health and preventing disease.

What is health psychology? According to Taylor (1986), *health psychology* "is the field within psychology devoted to understanding psychological influences on how people stay healthy, why they become ill, and how they respond when they do become ill" (p. 5). In our discussion of health psychology, we will confine ourselves to what social psychologists might study in the area of health psychology. This does not mean, however, that only social psychologists are interested in health.

As a matter of fact, psychologists from many different specialty areas can be found working in health psychology. For example, some learning psychologists are interested in the problems of addiction and how these learned behaviors can be changed. Similarly, some physiological psychologists study the neurotransmitters responsible for pain and ways to lessen pain in individuals who suffer from chronic painful illnesses. The socialization practices that children learn from their parents about health practices involving dental care, exercise, and nutrition are of interest to some developmental psychologists. In other words, many psychologists are interested in health as an area of study. We have decided to discuss health psychology in this chapter because we will concentrate only on two topics that are of particular concern to social psychologists: attitudes toward health practices and the role of social support in moderating illness.

Attitudes toward Health Practices

One decade ago, the United States Surgeon General's report on the state of the nation's health emphasized that seven of the ten major causes of death are directly or indirectly related to a set of "health-risk" behaviors (Richmond, 1979). Among those behaviors identified as injurious or detrimental to health were obesity, diets with high levels of cholesterol, sedentary life styles, cigarette smoking, excessive alcohol consumption, and failure to wear seat belts. If information on "health-risk" behaviors is so well understood, why are there so many individuals who do not practice sound health behaviors? What attitudes are involved and what programs are needed to enable people to live healthier and longer lives?

Nutrition It is now a well-known medical fact that dietary practices that include the consumption of too much fat, cholesterol, and salt or too many calories can result in an increase in medical problems such as coronary heart disease, stroke, and cancer.

In a study of attitudes toward nutrition, Hollis and his colleagues (Hollis, Carmody, Connor, Fey, & Matarazzo, 1986) administered a questionnaire to a community sample of 415 healthy women and men. Items on the questionnaire were then statistically categorized into one of four clusters. The item clusters are shown in Table 20–8 with sample questions for each cluster. The important thing about this study is that the respondents could be grouped into one of the four clusters based on their scores on the nutrition survey. The clusters represent particular attitudes toward food and toward health in general. Men and women who scored high on the Helpless and Unhealthy questions reported that they ate more meat and were more overweight. They also had a higher cholesterol level and reported more medical symptoms and incidents of emotional distress. In other words, negative food attitudes are related to poorer psychological and nutritional status as well as to the physiological measures of coronary risk.

In contrast, individuals who scored high on the Health Consciousness dimension, which reflects a positive attitude about diet and health, reported that they ate more meatless meals and consumed less fat, cholesterol, and sodium. Associated with this cluster were fewer reported medical symptoms and low cholesterol levels.

TABLE 20–8 Question Clusters on the Nutrition Attitude Survey

Cluster 1: Helpless and Unhealthy

Even though I know that my way of eating is not good for me, I just can't seem to change my habits.

It seems that almost everything I like to eat is bad for me.

No matter how hard I try to change, I end up falling back into some of my old eating habits, which I know are bad.

If I changed the way I eat, I would be a much healthier person.

The chances that the way I eat lead to heart disease are great.

When it comes to food, I have no willpower.

I find myself eating "junk food" I know is not good for me.

I eat more when I feel down.

Many days, because I'm in a hurry, I eat whatever is handy.

Cluster 2: Food Exploration

I am interested in eating at ethnic food restaurants.

I enjoy trying food from other countries.

I enjoy exploring and testing out new restaurants.

I always enjoy trying new and different things to eat.

I enjoy trying new recipes.

Cluster 3: Meat Preference

Dinner doesn't seem right without meat.

Meat is the most important part of any meal.

I am what they call a "meat-and-potatoes" person.

My family likes to barbecue different kinds of meat on the grill.

Cluster 4: Health Consciousness

A new way of eating designed to prevent heart disease would:
  a. Be easy to follow.
  b. Be accepted by my family.

To avoid heart disease, I would be willing to alter my eating habits.

Source: After Hollis et al., 1986.

People who scored high on Meat Preference had fewer meatless meals and ate less fruit and beans. This preference was also related to increased body weight in men and to higher cholesterol levels in women. On the other hand, individuals who scored high on Food Exploration characteristically exhibited greater flexibility in food choices (especially for women) and greater involvement and a more egalitarian attitude toward meal-preparation activities among the men. Overall, there was a health benefit for these individuals since this group showed an absence of psychological or medical symptoms.

Although Hollis and his colleagues do not offer any suggestions for ways to assist people to improve their attitudes toward good eating practices, they do show the emotional and medical benefits that accrue as a result of positive attitudes toward nutrition and health. The next steps involve getting people with poor dietary practices to recognize the link between diet and health, and then exploring the proper strategies for changing attitudes and eating behavior. This is frequently not easy, as we know, because it requires that the person value health.

Lau, Hartman, and Ware (1986) argue that placing a high value on health is a necessary prerequisite for a health-related behavior such as dietary restriction. Thus, any program designed to change dietary practices will succeed in producing changes in behavior only among participants who place a high value on health. However, when it comes to dieting, the motive may not be so obvious. For example, Lau and his co-workers observed that individuals who diet may be motivated more by considerations of appearance than of health. Accordingly, for a weight-reduction program to work, dietary planners must make some assumptions about whether people are dieting because they believe it is good for their health or because they want to look good. Obviously, some individuals have both intentions in mind when they practice good eating behaviors.

Exercise   The benefits of aerobic exercise in maintaining mental and physical health are now well understood by most individuals. Yet some people are opposed to any type of physical activity. The funny line used by comedians over the years expresses the attitude of many when it comes to exercise: "Whenever I think about exercising, I go to bed until the feeling goes away!"

Studies seeking to understand health practices involving exercise are much like the research related to good nutritional practices. That is, individuals may express attitudes toward exercise that are dependent on many considerations, including the opinions of others. Pender and Pender (1986) wanted to know which individuals exercise and why. Using a questionnaire like that shown in Table 20–9, Pender and Pender found that individuals who intended to exercise regularly had significantly more positive attitudes toward exercise than those who did not intend to exercise. As reasoned-action theory predicts, those individuals who intended to exercise had stronger beliefs that their friends or family members wanted them to exercise than was true for the nonintenders. Interestingly intenders also were more likely than nonintenders to believe that exercise improved mental outlook and less likely to believe that exercise could result in overexercise or a heart attack.

It is not known why people differ in their attitudes toward exercise or in the outcome of exercise. Also not clear is why some individuals are more willing to listen to the expectations (subjective norms) of others concerning their health status and to act in accordance with these expectations to change their behavior.

Much research is still needed on attitudes toward health practices, but social psychologists are making good progress in showing us how attitudes toward health are related to good health practices and to overall good physical and emotional health. What social psychologists are learning about health has begun to be implemented in

Jane Fonda was among the first of many high-visibility personalities to stress the importance of diet and exercise in maintaining good health.

TABLE 20-9 Sample Items From Attitudes Toward Exercise Questionnaire

1. Behavioral intention
   During the next week, I intend to exercise regularly, that is, jog, run, brisk walk, or participate in active recreational sports at least three times during the week.

unlikely _____ / _____ / _____ / _____ / _____ / _____ / _____ likely
extremely   quite   slightly   neither   slightly   quite   extremely

2. Attitude
   a. Consequence belief
   Exercising regularly would improve my muscle tone.

unlikely _____ / _____ / _____ / _____ / _____ / _____ / _____ /likely
extremely   quite   slightly   neither   slightly   quite   extremely

   b. Consequence evaluation
   For me, improving my muscle tone is:

good _____ / _____ / _____ / _____ / _____ / _____ / _____ /bad
extremely   quite   slightly   neither   slightly   quite   extremely

3. Subjective norm
   a. Expectation of other's belief
   My spouse/boyfriend/girlfriend thinks I should exercise regularly.

unlikely _____   _____ / _____ / _____ / _____ / _____ / _____ /likely
extremely   quite   slightly   neither   slightly   quite   extremely

   b. Motivation to comply with expectation of others
   Generally speaking, how much do you want to do what your spouse/boyfriend/girlfriend thinks you should do?

                                                                                       very
not at all _____ / _____ / _____ / _____ / _____ / _____ / _____ /much

Source: After Pender & Pender, 1986.

health-promotion programs in schools, hospitals, and senior-citizen centers (Taylor, 1986).

Social Support

The support a person receives from family and friends can be very beneficial in health promotion, health maintenance, and recovery from illness. In a review of the literature on social support, Taylor (1986) found that people with high levels of social support are healthier and live longer. Similarly, people who are ill, but who have a high level of social support, require less medication and recover faster. What is social support and how does it operate to promote good health and lessen the consequences of poor health?

The term *social support* refers to a system of formal and informal individual and group relationships through which an individual receives emotional, cognitive, and material assistance to overcome stressful experiences (Jacobson, 1986). In this context, *emotional support* refers to behaviors that communicate to a person that loving and caring people are available to provide nurturance and security. *Cognitive support* refers to information, knowledge, and advice received from others who want to help by suggesting specific actions that can be taken to improve an individual's health. *Material support* refers to the tangible assistance received from others in the form of actual goods (money, for example) and services (perhaps an offer to accompany the person to a physician). There is no reason to believe that any one of these types of support is any better than the others. All appear to be essential. Further, we do not necessarily receive all three types of support from the same individual or at the same time. Timing in the receipt of social support is also an important dimension in understanding how social support operates. A woman who has very recently experienced the death of her spouse is much more likely to be comforted by emotional support received from other family members and friends than she is by advice and information (cognitive support) about how she should lead her life as a widow. However, later such advice might become very important as she tries to straighten out insurance policies and organize other business matters (Jacobson, 1986).

The "Buffering" Effect of Social Support   An obvious and important question involving social support has to do with understanding how support can be beneficial during stressful *and* nonstressful times in a person's life. One of the most commonly suggested ideas is that social support serves to "buffer" stress and thereby lessen its harmful consequences on the individual who has experienced some stressful event such as the loss of a job, a serious health problem, or the death of a loved one. As Taylor (1986) states, "What social support does is act as a reserve and resource that blunts the effects or enables the individual to cope with stress more effectively when it is at a high level" (p. 209).

One of the major challenges that health psychologists have faced in recent years has been to prove the "buffering" hypothesis (Gore, 1981). In a recent study, Kessler and McLeod (1985) found that the perception that one's social support network was ready to provide aid and assistance if needed was more important than actual support received in lessening stress. This suggests the powerful effect that merely having family and friends can have on a person if he or she knows that these people can be called on during a crisis.

Health psychologists have also found that it is not the number of friends that is the critical variable in understanding the "buffering" effects of stress, but rather the quality of the support received and how the person in distress asks for assistance (Taylor, 1986). This raises three issues that are currently being heavily researched in the area of health psychology. These issues have to do with (1) understanding how the social network (in terms of number of people and their relationships to each other) works to lessen stress; (2) assessing the quality of support offered by helpers to different types of problems; and (3) finding strategies to instruct people to be more effective in the assistance they offer to others, while also instructing those in need of help to make better use of the helping resources around them.

Interest in health psychology has blossomed in the past decade. There are many psychologists working on health-related topics, as we have tried to show here. Obviously, we were able to discuss only a small number of the problems that have captured the interest of social psychologists at work in health psychology. There are many short- and long-term implications for the discoveries that psychologists are making about how to improve everyone's health. These implications pertain not only to more effective treatment procedures, but also to the prevention of serious health problems through such practices as good nutrition and exercise. In addition, as we discussed, there is a positive health benefit to be had by having a caring family and friendship network. Our discussion of these topics should give you an appreciation of the vitality of studies being conducted in this area of social psychology.

SUMMARY

1. The basic principles of social interactions can be applied to the study of a wide range of social concerns, including liking and loving relationships, racial prejudice, the effects of television on behavior, helping strangers in distress, and health psychology.

2. Liking and loving are two separate phenomena that have generated much interest among psychologists. According to Rubin, loving consists of attachment, caring, and intimacy, while liking consists of respect and affection.

3. In another theory of love, Davis argues that loving can be distinguished from liking by two clusters of feelings: passion and caring. In still a third approach, Sternberg presents a triangular theory of loving based on intimacy (emotion), passion (motivation), and decision/commitment (cognition).

4. "Falling in love" is partially an internal attribution (explanation) of a state of heightened arousal, which is affected by situational cues. Being in love is also a process, including nurturance, succor, sharing of inner feelings, and commitment.

5. Loving relationships that last are likely to be those between people who perceive themselves as highly similar to one another in attitudes, behaviors, and needs. Satisfying, enduring relationships also involve high rates of positive exchanges between partners.

6. Prejudice is a pervasive negative attitude that includes negative feelings toward some other group, stereotyping, and usually discriminatory behavior as well.

7. One theory of the origin of prejudice is that it is learned in childhood, through observation of adult models, and through direct reinforcement of prejudiced attitudes or behavior.

8. Some personality types are generally more prejudiced than others. In particular, the authoritarian personality is characterized by general rigidity and "either/or categorizations" of others.

9. We also tend to be prejudiced against any groups that are identifiably different from ourselves ("us" versus "them"). The more different the other group appears to be, the more likely prejudice is to occur.

10. Reduction of prejudice has been most successfully accomplished through contact between "opposing" groups. This contact must meet certain conditions if prejudice is to be reduced. The contact must be between people of equal status and must be supported by the authority figures involved. If the contact does not meet these conditions, prejudice may increase.

11. Efforts at school desegregation provide a naturalistic setting in which to test the contact hypothesis. Research on school desegregation, although generally mixed as far as the reduction of tension between racial groups is concerned, has begun to give way to more positive long-term consequences for Blacks.

12. The mass media have widespread effects on our attitudes and behavior. Two areas of particular interest to social psychologists have been the effects of the mass media on political behavior and on aggression.

13. As theory predicts, voters tend to support candidates who appear to agree with them, are attractive, and are familiar.

14. Sheer familiarity, created through name repetition, makes a difference in political races when no candidate is well known at the outset.

15. Television programming affects aggression. People who watch a lot of violent television are more aggressive in their behavior, more likely to believe that aggression is a good way to solve problems, and more fearful and negative in emotions or moods than are people who watch less violent television programming.

16. The generalizations involving violence and television are most clearly true with young children, but appear to hold for teenagers and adults as well.

17. One suggestion for reducing the negative effects of television on children's behavior is television literacy. This new form of literacy aims to instruct children about techniques of television production in an attempt to turn television from a passive to an active medium of instruction.

18. One area in which altruistic behavior has been studied is in settings in which a stranger shows distress. Whether an individual helps the stranger is influenced by at least three factors: how many other people are present, what those other people do, and whether the individual feels that he or she possesses enough knowledge to help.

19. The larger the number of people present, the more "diffusion of responsibility" occurs, and the less likely it is that any one person will help. However, if some are already helping, others are more likely to be influenced by such models.

20. There does seem to be an "urban mentality" that inhibits city dwellers from helping people in distress. This might be a way of coping with environmental over-stimulation.

21. As we learn more about helping, we are beginning to recognize that skill at helping (knowledge of cardio-pulmonary resuscitation or first aid) and personality factors may be intertwined in determining who is more likely to become an active helper.

22. Health psychology is a relatively new specialization in psychology that is concerned with developing an understanding of how people stay healthy, become ill, or respond to illness.

23. The study of attitudes toward health, including good nutritional practices and exercise, is a major area of interest to the health psychologist. Attitude change in the area of health practices has many practical implications for prevention programs of various types.

24. Support from individuals who we feel close to can have beneficial effects on our health, especially during periods of crisis. Three types of social support have been identified: emotional support, cognitive support, and material support.

KEY TERMS

authoritarian personality
bystander indifference
cognitive support
contact hypothesis
content effects
diffusion effect
discrimination

displacement effects
emotional support
ethnocentrism
health psychology
liking
loving

material support
overload
prejudice
social support
stereotypes
television literacy

ADDITIONAL READING

Cook, S. W. (1984) The 1954 social science statement and school desegregation. *American Psychologist, 39,* 819–832.
In this article the author reviews the psychological findings used in the 1954 Supreme Court decision leading to school desegregation. The successes and failures of school desegregation since the 1954 ruling are also reviewed.

Diamond, E., & Bates, S. (1984) *The spot: The rise of political advertising on television.* Cambridge, MA: MIT Press.
This is an interesting book about the use of television to sell political candidates.

Greenfield, P. M. (1984) *Mind and media.* Cambridge, MA: Harvard University Press.
In this book the author discusses how the electronic media, such as television, videogames, and computers, can work to the benefit of the child. Importantly, the author also covers ways in which parents and other adults can improve the television literacy of children.

Latané, B., & Darley, J. M. (1970) *The unresponsive bystander: Why doesn't he help?* New York: Appleton-Century-Crofts.
This is still the classic book on helping behavior. It is well written and fascinating.

Taylor, S. E. (1986) *Health psychology.* New York: Random House.
This highly readable textbook analyzes the role of psychological factors in health and illness.

Trotter, R. J. (1986) The three faces of love. *Psychology Today, 20* (9), 46–50, 54.
This is a very interesting and readable account of Sternberg's three-sided theory of love.

Appendix A Psychologists: Here, There, and Everywhere

PERCENTAGES: WHO DOES WHAT, AND WHERE?

In Chapter 1 we outlined the areas of specialization within psychology. Figure A–1 will give you some idea of how popular these various areas are. As you can see, clinical, counseling, and community psychology are the areas most often selected.

Each of these areas of specialization may be practiced in various settings. Figure A–2 pre-

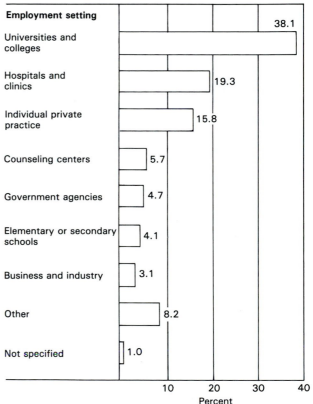

Figure A–2 Employment Settings for American Psychological Association Members with Full-time Positions *(After Stapp & Fulcher, 1983)*

sents a list of the employment settings where the various types of psychologists are to be found.

APA DIVISIONS

Another way to grasp the diversity of psychological endeavors is to look at the membership divisions of the American Psychological Associa-

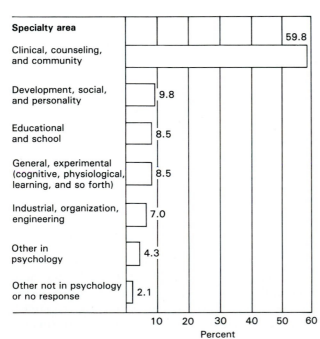

Note: Figure does not reflect percentage of APA members employed in areas other than psychology.

Figure A–1 Specialty Areas of American Psychological Association Members *(After Stapp & Fulcher, 1983)*

TABLE A–1 Divisions of the American Psychological Association

Members may join as many of the APA's special interest divisions as they want. Two divisions, 4 and 11, were dropped long ago.

Division	Year Organized	Membership (1987)
1. General Psychology	1948	5,574
2. Teaching of Psychology	1948	1,860
3. Experimental Psychology	1948	1,473
5. Evaluation and Measurement	1948	1,335
6. Physiological and Comparative Psychology	1948	831
7. Developmental Psychology	1948	1,342
8. Society of Personality and Social Psychology	1948	3,099
9. Society for the Psychological Study of Social Issues	1948	2,790
10. Psychology and the Arts	1948	487
12. Clinical Psychology	1948	5,920
13. Consulting Psychology	1948	936
14. Society for Industrial and Organizational Psychology	1948	2,573
15. Educational Psychology	1948	1,990
16. School Psychology	1948	2,413
17. Counseling Psychology	1948	2,714
18. Psychologists in Public Service	1948	992
19. Military Psychology	1948	658
20. Adult Development and Aging	1948	1,256
21. Applied Experimental and Engineering Psychologists	1956	583
22. Rehabilitation Psychology	1958	939
23. Consumer Psychology	1960	448
24. Theoretical and Philosophical Psychology	1962	592
25. Experimental Analysis of Behavior	1965	1,228
26. History of Psychology	1966	825
27. Community Psychology	1967	1,459
28. Psychopharmacology	1967	1,108
29. Psychotherapy	1968	4,559
30. Psychological Hypnosis	1969	1,455
31. State Psychological Association Affairs	1969	501
32. Humanistic Psychology	1972	796
33. Mental Retardation	1973	825
34. Population and Environmental Psychology	1974	456
35. Psychology of Women	1974	2,138
36. Psychologists Interested in Religious Issues	1976	1,332
37. Child, Youth, and Family Services	1978	1,448
38. Health Psychology	1979	2,702
39. Psychoanalysis	1980	2,294
40. Clinical Neuropsychology	1980	2,334
41. Psychology and Law Society	1981	1,157
42. Psychologists in Independent Practice	1982	5,140
43. Family Psychology	1985	1,627
44. Society for the Psychological Study of Lesbian and Gay Issues	1985	556
45. Society for the Psychological Study of Ethnic Minority Issues	1986	429
46. Media Psychology	1986	482
47. Exercise and Sport Psychology	1986	437

Source: 1987 APA Membership Register

tion. Table A–1 lists the divisions that members may join, depending on their interests and their specialties. Obviously, the pie has been sliced much thinner here. Again, a given psychologist may be intensely interested and active in several of these areas.

Appendix Statistics
B

THE ROLE OF STATISTICS

Behavioral scientists are interested in observing and accounting for variation or differences in behavior. Therefore, most psychological studies involve making measurements. One purpose of statistics is to summarize or describe these data in a clear and convenient fashion. This is accomplished by *descriptive statistics.* For example, your college grade point average summarizes in one number how well you have done in your courses.

Another function of statistics is to generalize from a relatively small number of cases, or *sample*, what is happening in a given *population*—a large group made up of people or objects that are alike in at least one respect. A *statistic* is a numerical quantity summarizing some characteristic of a sample. The mean of a sample, symbolized by $\overline{X}$, is an example of a statistic. A *parameter* is the corresponding value of that characteristic in the population. The population parameters are specified by Greek letters. Thus, the Greek letter mu μ is used to specify the population mean. Usually the population parameters are unknown because the population is too large to measure. The population parameters must be inferred from sample statistics. *Inferential statistics* makes it possible to draw inferences about numerical quantities or parameters of the population from what is observed in the subgroup or sample of the population. If samples are properly selected, sample statistics will often give good estimates of the parameters of the population.

One purpose of this appendix is to explain some of the methods for analyzing data in order to help you understand the techniques behavioral scientists use to collect information and draw conclusions. Since most of the studies discussed in this textbook and those in the professional journals are based on statistical analyses, information in this appendix should also help you read and understand this literature.

DESCRIPTIVE STATISTICS

As part of a field course in Child Development, Julie Brown and Larry Green spent the summer at a day-care center for 4- and 5-year-olds. As one of the course requirements, they undertook a small research project focusing on patterns of social interaction as a function of age.

Julie and Larry observed ten children in each age group for 10 minutes per child during the morning free-play period and recorded the amount of time each child spent playing with a companion. At the end of the summer, Julie and Larry have available the data in Table B–1. These data will be used to illustrate some of the basic principles involved in statistical analysis.

Frequency distributions and frequency polygons To make the set of data more comprehensible, Julie and Larry write down, for each group separately, every possible score value in order, from highest to lowest. Next to each score, they record the frequency with which that score occurred. The scores, called *raw scores*, are listed in Table B–2 under the symbol X. The term raw scores is used for scores in their original form. The columns in Table B–2 labeled *frequency* (f) list the number of times that a particular score occurs. For example three children in Group 1 spent 3 minutes interacting with another group member. Since Julie and Larry are dealing with only 10 possible scores (remember, they observed each child for 10 minutes), it is easy to construct a table of all possible score values that conveniently fits on one sheet of paper. If, however, they had made observations over a 3-hour period, there would have been 180 different possible scores. A table listing all these scores would have been clumsy to construct and not

TABLE B–1 Amount of Time* (to the Nearest Minute) Spent in Interacting with One or More Children

Group 1 (4-year-olds)		Group 2 (5-year-olds)	
Name	Time (X)	Name	Time (X)
Joan	10	Bob	7
Walter	3	Mike	8
Helen	5	David	10
Ann	10	Jennifer	8
Michael	3	Laurie	4
Andrew	2	Sue	9
Sam	8	Judy	5
Sally	3	Joey	8
Jack	2	Wendy	4
Pat	4	Sarah	7

$$\Sigma X = 50 \qquad\qquad \Sigma X = 70$$
$$\overline{X}_1 = \Sigma X/N \qquad\qquad \overline{X}_2 = \Sigma X/N$$
$$= 50/10 \qquad\qquad\quad = 70/10$$
$$= 5 \qquad\qquad\qquad\quad = 7$$

*Amount of time will be called a sociability score.

readily interpretable. Thus, when the number of possible scores is fairly large, instead of listing single scores in the score or X column, several score values can be grouped into an *interval*, (for example, 0–4, 5–9, 10–14), and frequencies can be tallied for each interval.

After organizing their data, Julie and Larry graph the results using a *frequency polygon* to get a clearer notion about general trends in the scores. In such a graph, the frequency of any score is expressed by the height of the point above that score, and points are connected by straight lines. The frequency polygons for the data in Table B–2 are presented in Figure B–1.

To construct such a graph, the Y (vertical) axis is marked off in terms of frequencies, from lowest to highest, and the X (horizontal) axis is marked off in terms of score values, from lowest to highest. Notice that the highest frequency for either group is 3, and the lowest is 0, so that the graph need only include frequencies from 0 to 3. Both axes are divided into equally spaced intervals. The first point to the left on the frequency polygon (Figure B–1a) is marked at the intersection of the axes. The next point is placed at the

TABLE B–2 Frequency Distribution for Sociability Scores of Group 1 and Group 2

Raw scores (X)	Frequency (f)	
	Group 1 (4-year-olds)	Group 2 (5-year-olds)
10	2	1
9	0	1
8	1	3
7	0	2
6	0	0
5	1	1
4	1	2
3	3	0
2	2	0
1	0	0

$$Md_1 = \frac{4 + 3}{2} = \frac{7}{2} = 3.5 \quad Md_2 = \frac{8 + 7}{2} = \frac{15}{2} = 7.5$$

(a) Frequency distribution for 4-year olds

(b) Frequency distribution for 5-year olds

Figure B–1 Frequency Polygons for the Data in Table B–2

intersection of a time score of 1 and a frequency of 0, the next at the intersection of a time score of 2 and a frequency of 2, and so on. After all the points have been plotted, straight lines are drawn between the points.

The shapes of the two distributions are now quite clearly defined. In both groups (Figure B–1), scores tend to occur more frequently in the middle and less frequently at the ends or *tails* of the distributions. The frequency polygons of many variables of interest to the behavioral scientist are shaped much like those in Figure B–1. However, many other shapes do occur, some of which are illustrated in Figure B–2.

Distributions (a), (b), (c), and (g) in Figure B–2 are all symmetric in shape—they can be divided into two halves, each the "mirror image" of the other. A markedly asymmetric distribution with a long or pronounced "tail" is described as *skewed* in the direction of the tail. Thus, distribution (e) is skewed to the left or negatively skewed. Such a negatively skewed distribution indicates that most of the raw scores were high, but that there were still some that were quite low.

Modality refers to the number of clearly distinguishable high points or peaks. Distributions (a), (b), (e), and (f) are *unimodal*, while (c) and (d) are *bimodal.*

Certain frequency distributions have names of their own. A particular bell-shaped, symmetric, and unimodal distribution [Example (a), Figure B–2] is called the *normal distribution.* In this distribution, extreme scores are less frequent.

Example (g) in Figure B–2 illustrates a rectangular distribution in which each score occurs with the same frequency. Example (h) illustrates a J-curve, where the lowest score is most frequent and the frequencies decrease as scores become larger.

Measures of central tendency: mode, mean, median Now that Julie and Larry have summarized their data in the form of two frequency distributions and have graphed these distributions, several differences between the two age groups become apparent. Notice that the scores in Group 1 tend to cluster around the raw score of 3. The most frequent score (the *mode*) is 3.

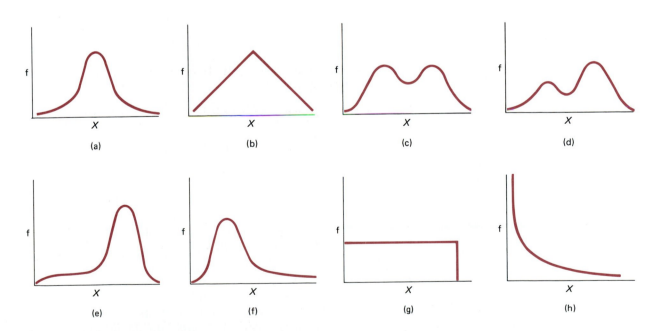

(a)   (b)   (c)   (d)

(e)   (f)   (g)   (h)

Figure B–2 Shapes of Frequency Distributions *(a) Normal curve (symmetric, unimodal); (b) symmetric, unimodal; (c) symmetric, bimodal; (d) asymmetric, bimodal; (e) unimodal, skewed to the left; (f) unimodal, skewed to the right; (g) rectangular; (h) J-curve. (After Welkowitz, Ewen, & Cohen, 1982)*

The mode for Group 2 is 8. Another way of describing the **central tendency**, a single number that describes the general location of a set of scores, is by obtaining the average, or the **mean**, of a distribution. This is done quite simply by adding all the scores and dividing by the total number of scores. In symbols,

$$\overline{X} = \Sigma X/N$$

where $\overline{X}$ *is the sample mean,* ΣX *is the sum of all the* X *scores, and* N *is the total number of scores.* The means for Group 1 and Group 2 are computed at the bottom of Table B–1.

A third measure of central tendency is the **median**, the score that divides the distribution in half. We have 10 scores for each group, so the fifth score divides the distribution in half. Looking at Table B–2 we see that five children in Group 1 had raw scores of 4 or more and five had scores of 3 or less. Thus, the median score lies halfway between 4 and 3, or 3.5. For Group 2 the median is 7.5. The medians for Group 1 and Group 2 are computed at the bottom of Table B–2.

In Table B–3, measures of central tendency for the two groups are compared. All three measures are higher for Group 2 than for Group 1, and all three measures yield different values. Only in a symmetric, unimodal distribution will all three measures have the same value. Thus, in the normal curve, the mean score, the mode, and the median will all be equal.

It is important to understand that the three measures of central tendency give different kinds of information. The most frequent score may be quite different from the average score, especially if there are extremely large or small scores in the distribution, as in Group 1.

TABLE B–3 Measures of Central Tendency for Group 1 and Group 2

	Mean	Median	Mode
Group 1 (4-year-olds)	5	3.5	3
Group 2 (5-year-olds)	7	7.5	8

Measures of variability: range, variance, and standard deviation The frequency polygons in Figure B–1 provide information about the *variability* within each group. Variability refers to how much the scores differ from one another. Notice that the scores in Group 1 extend from 2 to 10, while those in Group 2 extend from 4 to 10. The spread of scores, or the highest score minus the lowest score in the distribution, is called the **range.** You can quickly calculate that the range of scores for Group 1 is $10 - 2 = 8$, while for Group 2 it is $10 - 4 = 6$. The range, which summarizes variability in a single number, is, however, a very rough and unstable measure as it depends only on extreme scores. Thus, if a single extreme score is dropped, the range may change considerably.

A more useful and widely used measure of variability is the **variance**, symbolized by σ^2 (sigma squared) when describing a population variance, and by s^2 when describing a sample variance. The variance is a kind of "average" variability, based on *all* the scores rather than extreme scores alone. Deviation of a *single score*, symbolized by x, is the distance of that score from the mean of the distribution, or

$$x = X - \overline{X}$$

If you were to average all the deviation scores in a distribution by summing up all the differences and dividing by N, you would find that $\Sigma x/N$ would equal zero. The variance circumvents this difficulty by squaring each of the deviations prior to taking the average. Thus, the variance of the population is mathematically defined as

$$\sigma^2 = \Sigma(X - \overline{X})^2/N$$

where N is the number of objects or persons in the population.

The variance of a sample, symbolized by s^2, is mathematically given as

$$s^2 = \Sigma(X - \overline{X})^2/(N - 1)$$

where N is the number in the sample.

The square root of the population variance, or σ, is called the **standard deviation.** The corresponding sample value is symbolized by s. Both the variance and standard deviation reflect the average amount by which scores deviate from the mean of the distribution and thus yield important information about the "spread" of the scores. It is possible for two distributions to have identical means but very different standard deviations. Thus, both the mean and the standard deviation give information about the characteristics of the group.

Returning to Julie's and Larry's data, you can now calculate the standard deviations for the two groups. Because you are interested only in describing similarities and differences between these two groups, the population formula (σ^2) is used. If you wanted to make inferences about the general population, then you would use the formula involving *s*. The calculations for the variance and standard deviation of Group 1 and Group 2 are shown in Table B–4. For Group 1, $\sigma = 3$, while for Group 2, $\sigma = 1.95$. You can now say that scores in Group 1 deviate, on the average, about 3 raw score units from the mean of 5, while scores in Group 2 deviate, on the av-

erage, about 1.95 raw score units from the mean of 7. While both the range and standard deviation indicate greater variability for Group 1, the standard deviation is by far the more stable and preferable measure.

Transformed scores: percentile ranks and Z scores   We often want to transform a raw score into a new score that will show at a glance how the score stands in comparison to a specific reference group. You have undoubtedly taken achievement tests where you received a percentile rank as well as a raw score. A *percentile rank* is a single number that gives the percent of cases in the specific reference group at or below that score. If you received a raw score of 70 and a percentile rank of 85, you would know that 85 percent of your class obtained a score equal to or lower than 70.

Another kind of transformation locates each raw score with respect to the reference group,

TABLE B–4   Calculation of Variance and Standard Deviation for Sociability Scores

	Group 1				Group 2		
Name	Time (X)	$(X - \bar{X})$	$(X - \bar{X})^2$	Name	Time (X)	$(X - \bar{X})$	$(X - \bar{X})^2$
Joan	10	5	25	Bob	7	0	0
Walter	3	−2	4	Mike	8	1	1
Helen	5	0	0	David	10	3	9
Ann	10	5	25	Jennifer	8	1	1
Michael	3	−2	4	Laurie	4	−3	9
Andrew	2	−3	9	Sue	9	2	4
Sam	8	3	9	Judy	5	−2	4
Sally	3	−2	4	Joey	8	1	1
Jack	2	−3	9	Wendy	4	−3	9
Pat	4	−1	1	Sarah	7	0	0
			$\Sigma(X - \bar{X})^2 = 90$				$\Sigma(X - \bar{X})^2 = 38$

$$\bar{X} = 5$$
$$\sigma^2 = \Sigma(X - \bar{X})^2/N$$
$$= 90/10$$
$$= 9$$
$$\sigma = \sqrt{9}$$
$$= 3$$

$$\bar{X} = 7$$
$$\sigma^2 = \Sigma(X - \bar{X})^2/N$$
$$= 38/10$$
$$= 3.8$$
$$\sigma = \sqrt{3.8}$$
$$= 1.95$$

TABLE B–5   Calculation of Z Scores for Sociability Scores

	Group 1				Group 2		
Name	Raw Score	$(X - \bar{X})$	Z	Name	Raw Score	$(X - \bar{X})$	Z
Joan	10	5	1.67	Bob	7	0	0
Walter	3	-2	$-.67$	Mike	8	1	.51
Helen	5	0	0	David	10	3	1.54
Ann	10	5	1.67	Jennifer	8	1	.51
Michael	3	-2	$-.67$	Laurie	4	-3	-1.54
Andrew	2	-3	-1.00	Sue	9	2	1.03
Sam	8	3	1.00	Judy	5	-2	-1.03
Sally	3	-2	$-.67$	Joey	8	1	.51
Jack	2	-3	-1.00	Wendy	4	-3	-1.54
Pat	4	-1	$-.22$	Sarah	7	0	0
	$Z = (X - \bar{X})/\sigma$				$Z = (X - \bar{X}/\sigma$		
	$\sigma = 3$				$\sigma = 1.95$		

using the mean and standard deviation of the group. This transformation yields a *Z score* or *standard score.* The numerical size of a standard score indicates how many standard deviations above or below the mean that raw score is. By using the formula,

$$Z = (X - \bar{X})/\sigma \ \text{ or } \ Z = x/\sigma$$

the Z value of any raw score can be determined. The Z scores for the data in Table B–4 are presented in Table B–5.

If you calculate the mean and standard deviation for each set of Z scores, you will notice that the mean of the Z scores is equal to 0 and $\sigma = 1$. This is always true for Z scores. Because a Z score of 0 is the Z score of the mean, positive Z scores are always above the mean and negative Z scores are always below the mean, while Z scores of 0 fall exactly at the mean. Thus, a child with a Z score of 0 in Group 1 is average for that group, while a child in Group 2 with a Z score of -1.03 is below average for that group, even though the raw score for both children is 5.

NORMAL FREQUENCY DISTRIBUTION

The bell-shaped curve in Figure B–3 is called a normal distribution. The most frequent values fall around the mean with few values near the tails. Many variables that interest behavioral scientists assume a normal sampling distribution.

Suppose we assume that the heights of all American adult males are normally distributed.

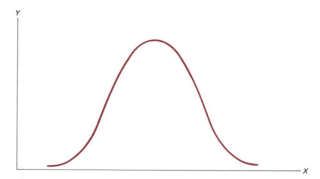

Figure B–3   Normal Bell-shaped Curve

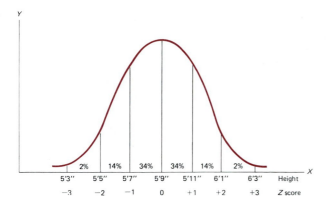

Figure B–4   Heights of American Adult Males

If we know that the average height is 5'9" and the standard deviation is two inches, we can draw the normal frequency distribution you see in Figure B–4.

The percentages on the graph are fixed with the same percentage above and below the mean. The standard deviation scores, or *Z* scores, also appear on the graph. From Figure B–4 we can see that a man 5'11" tall is one standard deviation above the mean and a man 5'5" tall is two standard deviations below the mean. We can also see that 68 percent of all men are between the heights of 5'7" and 5'11". Since it is rare to find a man taller than 6'3" or shorter than 5'3", all values fall within ±3 (plus or minus) standard deviation units of the mean.

The percentages and *Z* scores that appear in Figure B–4 can be applied to any normal distribution.

CORRELATION COEFFICIENT AS A DESCRIPTIVE STATISTIC

Control over the environment is achieved when you understand, through experience, the relationships among many of the events in your life; that is, understand the relative frequency with which various phenomena occur jointly. Without such knowledge it would be impossible to formulate accurate predictions about future events. For example, you come to realize early in your student career that the amount of time spent studying is related to grades. True, some students may study many hours and obtain poor

grades, while others may achieve high grades despite short study periods. The general trend holds, however. In most cases, you can accurately predict that little or no studying will lead to poor grades, while more studying will result in better grades. In statistical terminology, the two variables of hours spent studying and grades are said to be *correlated.*

Many pairs of variables are correlated, while many are unrelated or *uncorrelated.* For example, height and weight in adults are positively related or *positively correlated,* taller individuals tending to weigh more than shorter ones. This relationship is depicted graphically for male adults in Figure B–5, which is called a *scatter plot* or *scatter diagram* because the points scatter across the range of scores. Note that each point on the graph represents two values for each individual, height (*X* variable) and weight (*Y* variable). When the relationship is positive, as in Figure B–5, the straight line summarizing the points slopes *up* from left to right. A golf enthusiast will readily agree that the number of years of play is negatively related to her/his golf score; the more years of practice, the fewer shots needed to complete a round of 18 holes. These two variables are said to be *negatively correlated.* This relationship is illustrated in Figure B–6. Notice that in the case of negative correlation, the straight line summarizing the points slopes *down* from left to right. The length of big toes among male adults is uncorrelated with IQ scores (see Figure B–7).

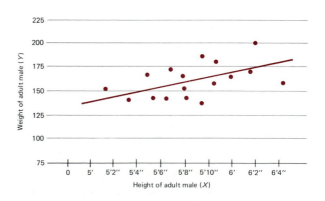

Figure B–5   Relationship between Height and Weight of Male Adults

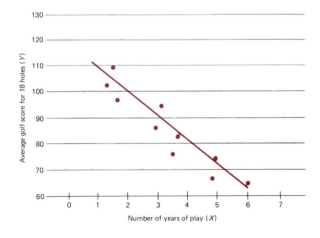

Figure B–6   Relationship between Years of Play and Average Score for 10 Golfers *(After Welkowitz, Ewen, & Cohen, 1982)*

Notice that the data plotted in Figures B–5 and B–6 tend to fall near or on the straight line drawn through the scatter plot. This indicates that the two variables in question are highly *linearly* correlated. On the other hand, the points in Figure B–7 are scattered randomly throughout the graph and cannot be represented by a straight line. These two variables are linearly uncorrelated. Many pairs of variables that are of importance to behavioral scientists tend to be linearly related. Although there are other ways of describing relationships, the linear model is

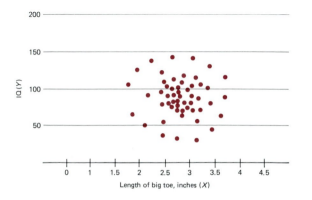

Figure B–7   Relationship between Length of Big Toe and IQ Scores for Adult Men *(After Welkowitz, Ewen, & Cohen, 1982)*

the simplest and the one most frequently used in fields such as psychology, education, and sociology.

When you can demonstrate that two variables are correlated, you can use the score of an individual on one variable to predict or estimate her/his score on the other variable. For example, in Figure B–6, a fairly accurate prediction of an individual's golf score can be made from the number of years golf has been played. The more closely the two variables are related, the better the prediction is likely to be. If two variables are uncorrelated, you cannot accurately predict an individual's score on one variable from her/his score on the other. Thus, the concepts of correlation and prediction are closely related.

The relationship between paired X and Y values can be indexed by the following formula:

$$r_{XY} = \frac{N\Sigma XY - \Sigma X\,\Sigma Y}{\sqrt{[N\Sigma X^2 - (\Sigma X)^2][N\Sigma Y^2 - (\Sigma Y)^2]}}$$

Suppose you want to determine if the sociability scores from Julie's and Larry's data correlate with the ages of the children's mothers. If you follow the operations in Table B–6, you will see that the correlation coefficient for the 4-year olds is $r = .46$. Therefore, there is a positive correlation between sociability score and mother's age for this data. If we had a coefficient of $r = -.46$, the correlation would be negative. A coefficient of zero would show no correlation.

Some cautions should be noted in interpreting a correlation coefficient. First, you cannot determine the *cause* of the relationship from the correlation. Two variables may be highly correlated for one of three reasons: X causes Y, Y causes X, or both X and Y are caused by some third variable.

A second important point has to do with the effect of the variability of the scores on the correlation coefficient. Suppose you calculate the correlation between achievement-test scores and elementary-school grades for public-school children in Anywhereville. You will probably find a strong linear trend when the data are plotted. But what if you were to calculate the correlation between the same two variables for a group of children in a class for the highly gifted? Here the range of scores on both variables is considerably narrowed. Because of this, the correlation be-

TABLE B-6   Calculation of Correlation Coefficient between Sociability Scores (X) and Mothers' Ages (Y)

Name	X	Y	XY	X^2	Y^2
Joan	10	30	300	100	900
Walter	3	29	87	9	841
Helen	5	26	130	25	676
Ann	10	37	370	100	1369
Michael	3	27	81	9	729
Andrew	2	31	62	4	961
Sam	8	28	224	64	784
Sally	3	25	75	9	625
Jack	2	29	58	4	841
Pat	4	32	128	16	1024
	50	294	1515	340	8750

$$r_{XY} = \frac{N\Sigma XY - \Sigma X \Sigma Y}{\sqrt{[N\Sigma X^2 - (\Sigma X)^2][N\Sigma Y^2 - (\Sigma Y)^2]}}$$

$$= \frac{10(1515) - (50)(294)}{\sqrt{[10(340) - (50)^2][10(8750) - (294)^2]}}$$

$$= \frac{450}{\sqrt{957600}}$$

$$= .46$$

tween the two variables is markedly reduced. In other words, it is much harder to make fine discriminations among cases that are nearly equal on the variables in question than it is to make discriminations among cases that differ widely. It is difficult to predict whether a gifted child will be an A or A− student. It is more feasible to distinguish among a broad range of A to F students. Thus, when the range of scores is restricted on either or both of two variables, the correlation between them decreases in absolute value.

Glossary

This glossary includes selected key terms as well as other important words found in the text and appendices. Terms that appear in *italics* within definitions are cross-listed elsewhere in the glossary.

abnormal behaviors Behaviors that are disruptive to the person or to others, based on judgments of the appropriateness of the behavior in the context in which it occurs.

abnormal psychology The branch of psychology concerned with defining, researching, and understanding behavior that does not lie within socially accepted norms.

absolute refractory period The period of a nerve cell's least excitability, which occurs immediately after the cell's initial firing.

absolute threshold The amount of a sensory stimulus that a subject can detect 50 percent of the time.

acetylcholine (ACh) A neurotransmitter that is released into the synapse of some neurons.

acetylcholinesterase (AChE) An enzyme that deactivates *acetylcholine*.

achievement tests Tests designed to assess actual learning of specific skills, such as addition and subtraction.

acquisition The strengthening of performance over trials that occurs in classical, instrumental, and verbal conditioning.

adrenaline The hormone *epinephrine*.

adrenals A pair of endocrine glands that secrete a number of different hormones, including cortisol, epinephrine, norepinephrine, and the sex hormones.

aerial perspective A cue used in depth perception in which clear and distinct objects appear closer than hazy and indistinct objects.

affective disorder Disorders of mood (depression or mania), accompanied by characteristic changes in behavior and activity level, thoughts and cognitive functioning, and biological functioning.

afferent neuron See *sensory neuron*.

affiliation The human need to interact with other people at work and play.

after images A visual image that remains even after an individual looks away from a stimulus.

aggression Destructive actions and impulses toward people or property.

aggression training A method of reversing depression by goading the depressed individual into anger and assertive action, thus prodding him out of hopelessness.

agoraphobia An extreme fear of being in a public place where one imagines becoming incapacitated or being unable to escape. As a result of the fear, the person often stays at home and has great difficulty going out, especially alone.

alarm reaction The body's initial reaction to exposure to a stressful event.

alcohol A widely abused depressant drug.

alcohol abuse A pattern of pathological use of alcohol (such as inability to stop drinking or cut down) and impaired functioning as a result of drinking (such as work, legal, and interpersonal difficulties).

alcohol dependence Physical dependence on alcohol as well as patterns of abuse. The physical signs include tolerance and withdrawal.

all-or-none principle The law that neurons fire either at their full capacity or not at all, depending on whether they are stimulated sufficiently to cause them to reach their firing threshold.

alpha waves In an EEG, the brain waves that are recorded when an individual relaxes with closed eyes but still remains awake.

Alzheimer's disease A form of progressive dementia of unknown cause that often occurs in middle age or older and leads to profound deterioration of intellectual functioning as well as deterioration of health.

ambiguous sentence A sentence, the meaning of which is unclear from the phrase structure of the sentence alone. The meaning can only be inferred from the context.

amniocentesis The sampling and analysis of amniotic fluid to detect the presence of recessive gene defects and chromosomal abnormalities in the developing fetus.

amount of reinforcement Measures of reward which, when increased, produce increases in a subject's performance up to a certain point.

amphetamines A group of strong stimulants that increases wakefulness and alertness and depresses appetite.

amplification In Gestalt therapy, a technique in which the therapist asks the client to exaggerate some behavior or feeling in order to become more aware of it.

amplitude The sensory experience of loudness, corresponding to the intensity of vibrations from the sound source.

anal stage According to Freud, the stage of psychosexual development that follows the oral stage and is characterized as a period during which eliminating and withholding feces become important sources of gratification for the child.

androgen A hormone secreted by the adrenal glands of both sexes, but in larger quantities in males.

androgyny The term used for the presence of both masculine and feminine traits in one individual.

anorexia nervosa A dangerous condition of self-imposed starvation, (the etiology of which is not yet determined) that has been successfully treated with behavior-modification techniques.

anterograde amnesia An inability to remember recent events that is the primary symptom in Korsakoff's psychosis.

antianxiety drugs Often called minor tranquilizers, these drugs have their place in short-term psychological treatment, but are pharmacologically addictive and easy to abuse.

antidepressant drugs Two classes of drugs—tricyclics and MAO inhibitors—that are effective in reducing depression.

antidiuretic hormone (ADH) The pituitary hormone that acts on the kidneys, causing them to decrease the amount of water that is drawn from body tissues and passed to the bladder.

antipsychotic drugs Used mainly with schizophrenics, these drugs successfully reduce agitation and aggression and seem to improve some schizophrenics' thought processes.

anvil A bone located in the middle ear that conducts sound vibrations from the hammer to the stirrup.

anxiety A vague feeling of dread and apprehension that may be caused by separation from support, anticipation of punishment, inner conflicts, uncertainty, or some combination of these influences.

anxiety-management procedures Behavioral techniques aimed at identifying anxiety-producing situations and finding methods to deal with or prevent them.

anxiety states Clinical conditions that are marked by panic disorder or generalized anxiety disorder.

aphasia An impaired ability to speak or understand speech, sometimes the result of damage to certain temporal-lobe association areas.

apparent movement The sense of movement created by the flashing on and off of stationary stimuli.

applied psychology The branches of psychology that deal with real emotional problems that occur in everyday life outside the laboratory.

applied research Studies that are concerned with the immediate benefits that can be derived from research; compare with *basic research*.

approach-approach conflict A conflict situation in which we want to reach two goals at once but cannot because reaching one requires us to give up the other.

approach-avoidance conflict A conflict situation in which a single goal has both positive and negative attributes.

approach gradient The graph that reflects the fact that motivation increases in strength as the organism nears the goal.

assertiveness training Systematic behavioral change programs aimed at helping individuals to be appropriately assertive in stating their wants, making requests of others, and resolving conflicts.

assessment Procedures that are designed to measure individual differences among people. Also, the field of psychology that specifically concerns itself with measuring personality, achievement, and ability differences.

association areas Areas of the cortex that are located between the sensory and motor areas and that are involved in higher mental functions such as perception, learning, thinking, and language.

association theory A theory that states that concepts are learned through simple, reinforced associations of stimulus and response.

astigmatism Abnormality of the lens of the eye.

attachment A primary affective bond formed between a child and a parent and based on the child's sense of trust in the adult and the adult's emotional tie to the child and willingness to care for the child.

attention The tendency to perceive only a portion of the overall set of stimuli impinging on an organism.

attention-deficit disorder (ADD) A disorder of childhood characterized by lack of ability to sustain focused

attention and avoid distraction. The disorder is sometimes accompanied by excessive activity and was formerly called hyperactivity.

attitude A relatively enduring reaction to people or things that involves three components: a belief, a feeling, and behavioral tendencies.

attraction The positive pull toward individuals whom we find physically, socially, or intellectually appealing.

attribution The human tendency to make assumptions about causal relationships.

attribution error The tendency to underestimate the impact a situation can have on our behavior.

attribution theory A theory that offers explanations for the attributing of inner motives, needs, or characteristics to others on the basis of observations of their behavior.

authoritarian personality Personality type marked by high own-group orientation and negative stereotyped beliefs about out-group members, which are not founded on any actual experience.

autohypnosis A tension-relieving technique that involves hypnotizing one's self through a series of simple steps.

autokinetic effect A form of apparent movement in which a stationary point of light in a completely dark room appears to move when an individual stares at it.

automatic processing The ability to process information or perform well-learned behaviors without conscious awareness. This is a modern cognitive alternative to some of Freud's ideas about the unconscious.

autonomic division Part of the peripheral nervous system that controls involuntary actions of the glands, smooth muscles, and the heart.

autonomy vs. shame and doubt According to Erikson, the crisis that occurs at age 2 or 3 when the child strives for more independence, yet is restrained by parents.

auxiliary axon A branch of an axon.

availability bias The tendency to draw conclusions or make inferences based on information available in one's memory. Since what we recall is very selective (the recall of very vivid information, for example), such processing can lead to erroneous conclusions.

aversion therapy A form of treatment used successfully to eliminate ''bad habits,'' such as smoking, by pairing the behavior or thought of the behavior with shock, noxious drugs, or other unpleasant stimuli.

aversive conditioning A form of classical conditioning used to treat severe

habit disorders in which some painful stimulus, such as electric shock or a nausea-inducing chemical, is administered in the presence of the desired object. The aim is to induce a conditioned negative reaction.

avoidance-avoidance conflict A conflict situation in which the only way we can avoid one unpleasant alternative is to choose the other unpleasant alternative.

avoidance conditioning A type of instrumental conditioning in which the subject is punished for failing to make a particular response.

avoidance gradient The graph that reflects the fact that escape motivation increases in strength as the organism approaches a punishing situation.

avoidance training Avoidance conditioning.

awareness A goal, particularly central to Gestalt psychotherapy, emphasizing conscious experience of thoughts, feelings, bodily sensations and movement, and the environment. Awareness is thought to be a means of increasing healthy functioning and self-fulfillment.

axon A long tail that projects from the cell body of the neuron and carries electrochemical impulses to other neurons.

axonal hillock The beginning portion of an axon as it emerges from the cell body.

axon conduction Process by which the electrochemical impulse is conducted along the axon.

babbling Infant verbalizations that resemble adult phonemes, syllables, and stress and intonation patterns. These verbalizations are the precursors of true speech in young children.

backward classical conditioning A classical conditioning procedure in which CS onset and offset both follow UCS offset.

bait shyness The tendency for animals to avoid stimuli that have been associated with illness.

balance theories of attraction A class of theories having to do with interpersonal attraction that assume that we behave in a way that is consistent with our beliefs or values. For example, in a relationship, we try to be fair to the other person so that they will be fair in return. By this means both individuals maximize what they get out of the relationship.

Barnum effect With reference to psychological testing, refers to vague, general statements that could apply to everyone, and therefore have little utility.

basal ganglia A group of nuclei between the thalamus and the cerebellum that are involved in the control and coordination of movement.

baserate With reference to psychological tests, baserate refers to how frequently a trait or characteristic typically occurs in a population. Tests tend to be most useful in predicting a trait when the trait's baserate is neither extremely high nor low.

basic biological motives Needs, such as hunger and thirst, that are vital to the organism and have physiological correlates.

basic research Studies that, regardless of their immediate usefulness, are concerned with understanding behavior; compare with *applied research.*

basilar membrane A structure within the inner ear that is instrumental in the conversion of sound waves to neural impulses for transmission to the brain along the auditory nerve.

behavioral assessment The focus on the subject's actual behavior in assessing personality.

behavioral genetics The study of how behavioral traits, such as intellectual ability and personality, are influenced by heredity.

behavioral intention Relative value that we give to a behavior, coupled with what we believe others want us to do, which then determines if we will engage in a specific behavior or not.

behavioral medicine Therapy that employs various psychological interventions to treat disorders usually considered medical (high blood pressure, for example).

behaviorism The approach to psychology that defines psychology as the study of directly observable behavior.

behaviorist approach One of four leading approaches to the study of psychology; this approach, championed by Watson and Skinner, focuses on observable behavior.

behavior modification The control and modification of learned behavior using the principles of conditioning.

behavior therapy A type of therapy that utilizes learning principles to help people learn new and more effective ways of behaving.

benzodiazepines A group of tranquilizers that reduce anxiety, induce sleep, relax muscles, and act as anticonvulsants.

bimodal distribution A frequency distribution with two peaks, or modes.

binocular convergence The tendency of our eyes to turn toward each other, or converge, when we fixate on close objects.

binocular vision The fact that we have two eyes. In focusing on an object, each eye perceives light from the front and one side of the object.

biofeedback A method for achieving desired change in such involuntary responses as heart rate and tension headaches by using the principles of conditioning.

bipolar affective disorder A form of disorder characterized by severe mood swings in irregular alternations of mania and depression. Formerly called manic-depressive psychosis.

bipolar cell The layer of cells lying just in front of the rods and cones in the eye.

blind spot A spot in each retina where the ganglion cell axons join to form the optic nerve. There are no visual receptors at this junction.

brain stem A portion of the brain that is an extension of the spinal cord, which extends into the forebrain.

brain wave An electrical impulse discharged by the brain of a living organism.

brightness The intensity of a color, which is proportional to the amplitude of the light wave.

bulimia An eating disorder characterized by binge eating that is often followed by self-induced vomiting.

bystander indifference The noninvolvement of a bystander when another person requires assistance.

cannabis Marijuana.

Cannon-Bard theory A theory of emotion that states that external stimuli arouse the hypothalamus which, in turn, simultaneously triggers the physiological changes associated with emotion and stimulates the experience of emotion by sending messages to the cerebral cortex.

caregivers Adults who substitute for parents in the care of young children for part of the day, especially during working hours, and who are employed in some type of day-care setting.

catatonic schizophrenia A form of schizophrenia marked by extreme behavioral disturbance including either stupor and immobility or movement and excitability. Mutism is also a common feature.

catharsis A sudden and dramatic release of pent-up emotion that occurs when recalling a painful memory that has been repressed.

cell body The portion of the neuron composed of a nucleus, surrounded by cytoplasm, and contained within a cell membrane.

cell membrane The outer covering of a cell, which is differentially permeable to various kinds of electrically charged particles.

cellular dehydration The process in which an increase in the concentration of certain chemicals around cells causes water within them to pass out by osmosis, leaving the cell dehydrated.

central fissure The deep fissure separating the frontal lobe of the cortex from the parietal lobe.

central nervous system Portion of the nervous system that includes the brain and the spinal cord.

central-nervous-system depressants Chemical substances, such as alcohol and other drugs and medications, that reduce the efficient functioning of the central nervous system.

central tendency A single number that describes the general location of a set of scores in a frequency distribution. Three measures of central tendency are the *mean,* the *median,* and the *mode.*

cerebellum Portion of the hindbrain composed of two convoluted lobes that fit under the cerebral cortex. The primary function of the cerebellum is to smooth out and coordinate muscular activities.

cerebral cortex The convoluted surface layer of the cerebrum, which is the most highly developed part of the brain, important in controlling and integrating behavior. (Also known as the *cortex.)*

cerebral hemispheres The left and right halves of the brain, which compose the cerebrum. Each hemisphere is symmetrical and is divided into four lobes.

cerebrum The most prominent brain structure in the human, located on top of the brain stem. It consists of two cerebral hemispheres covered by a cerebral cortex.

change In development, refers to the process of physical, cognitive, emotional, and social growth brought about by maturation and experience.

characteristic features Attributes that are typical of items belonging to a category. They are not, however, sufficient criteria for making a decision about category membership.

child abuse Nonaccidental physical, emotional, or sexual injury to a child.

child-care programs A formally organized program for the care of preschool-age children with a curriculum of activities.

China White A group of "designer" drugs that mimic the effects of heroin.

choleric According to the ancient theory of Hippocrates, one of the four types of personality. Characterized by irritability due to the preponderance of the humor, or bodily fluid, yellow bile.

chromosomes Microscopic particles that are found in the nucleus of every cell, existing in pairs. Human cells contain 46 chromosomes, or 23 pairs, each of which contains genes, the basic units of heredity.

chunking The way we expand our immediate memory capacity by making a single response (BOOMERANGS) out of many responses (the letters R-E-M-O-B-N-G-S-O-A).

clairvoyance The perception of objects or events not influencing the known sensory systems.

classical conditioning A learning procedure in which an unconditioned stimulus (UCS) which elicits an unconditioned response (UCR) is paired repeatedly with a neutral conditioned stimulus (CS). Through repeated pairings, the CS will, when presented alone, elicit a conditioned response (CR) that is similar to the UCR. (Also known as *Pavlovian* or *respondent conditioning*.)

class inclusion The cognitive ability to understand that objects can be grouped into classes of objects and that classes of objects can be categorized into still larger classes of objects. This ability appears in children during the concrete operations stage of development.

client-centered therapy A humanistic therapy developed by Carl Rogers that is aimed at increasing the client's self-awareness and self-acceptance by means of the therapist's warmth and encouragement.

climacteric The period during middle age for both men and women (for whom it is known as menopause) when hormonal and other physiological changes affect their reproductive capacity.

clinical psychology The branch of psychology concerned with the diagnosis, treatment, and understanding of emotional and behavioral problems in a hospital or clinical setting.

cloning Genetic engineering method that entails growing identical offspring from the cells of a single parent.

closure The tendency to fill in the gaps and connect the disconnected elements of incoming information.

cluster Two or more related items that have been recalled together.

cocaine Also known as "coke," an expensive yet fashionable and popular stimulant that produces short-lived euphoric effects when sniffed, injected, or swallowed.

cochlea A bony coiled tube in the ear containing a fluid which is set into motion by the vibration of the oval window.

codeine The mildest of the narcotics.

cognition The knowledge that an individual has about his world and the associated processes that explain how sensory input is received, stored in memory, and retrieved for use.

cognitive appraisal A method of coping with stress in which the individual is asked to imagine, or rehearse, the stressful event before it happens.

cognitive approach The study of perceiving, knowing, thinking, problem solving, language, and imagery.

cognitive behavior modification (CBM) The use of conditioning principles to influence and modify thought, in order to change the way people behave.

cognitive consistency The need to maintain consistency between our thoughts and actions.

cognitive developmental (stages or theory) A theory of the development of thinking proposed by Jean Piaget that posits four stages in the development of a child's knowledge of the world.

cognitive dissonance The strong sense or drive we have that influences us to change our behaviors or beliefs in order to make our world consistent.

cognitive model of psychopathology A theoretical approach that emphasizes the role played by the way people think; their interpretations, memories, expectations and the like are believed to have an enormous impact on emotion and behavior. Dysfunctional or unrealistic cognitions may underlie forms of depression and anxiety.

cognitive psychology The branch of psychology concerned with higher-order mental activities, such as language, thinking, problem solving, reasoning, and imagining.

cognitive restructuring A form of psychotherapy that systematically attempts to identify and change maladaptive thoughts that may be producing psychological distress and undesirable behavior.

cognitive support The information, knowledge, and advice received from friends and acquaintances who want to help another person resolve problems or improve health.

cognitive theory of emotion The theory that an emotion is the result of an interaction between our internal arousal and what we observe going on around us.

coin a phrase A technique for remembering information in a specific order by making up a phrase using the first letters of the items to be memorized.

collective unconscious According to Jung's theory of personality, the inherited, unconscious memory of humanity's ancestral past that we all possess. The collective unconscious includes communal events, fears, beliefs, and superstitions.

color Our experience of the wavelength of visible light. (Also known as *hue*.)

color constancy Our tendency to perceive a specific color as remaining the same even when it is viewed under different conditions.

community psychology The branch of psychology that aims to move mental-health care out of the hospitals and into the community. Community psychology focuses on identifying factors that affect human behavior (poverty, crime, and prejudice), thereby working to prevent mental illness in the population as a whole.

complementarity of needs In some relationships the attraction between two individuals is based on the fact that they complement each other on some trait or behavior as, for example, when a masculine male prefers a feminine woman.

complex human motives Motives such as the need to achieve, the need to affiliate, and the need to influence others, as distinct from more basic biological drives such as hunger and thirst.

complexity The degree to which pure tones interact to form complex wave forms.

compression The pushing together of air molecules by the movement of a vibrating object.

computer-assisted instruction systems (CAI) Computerized teaching machines, which allow greater flexibility in the storage, control, and presentation of information.

computerized axial tomography (CAT) An x-ray technique for determining the structure of the brain of a living individual.

concept A class or group of ideas, objects, or events that possess common properties. Concepts greatly simplify our thinking processes by freeing us from having to label each new idea, object, or event we encounter.

concrete operations Third stage (ages 5–12) of Piaget's theory of cognitive development, in which the child makes very large cognitive gains by learning to manipulate internal representations and to reason inductively.

concurrent validity A method of determining a test's validity by comparing the scores on the test with some current criterion (for example, a test designed to identify potential child abusers should distinguish current abusers from nonabusers).

conditioned (or **secondary**) **reinforcer** Any neutral stimulus that has acquired reinforcing properties through repeated pairings with a more basic reinforcer.

conditioned response (CR) The learned response to a conditioned stimulus in a classical conditioning experiment.

conditioned stimulus (CS) The neutral stimulus introduced by the experimenter in a classical conditioning experiment.

conditioned taste aversion A dislike for a taste that has been established by pairing that taste with a noxious stimulus.

conduct disorder A disorder of childhood marked by persistent patterns of violation of social norms and disregard for the rights of others.

cone Visual receptor on the retina that allows us to experience the sensation of color but is insensitive to low levels of light.

congruence Rogers's term for the sense of self-awareness and self-acceptance acquired by the client through the process of client-centered therapy.

connecting neuron An *interneuron*.

conservation The principle that quantities, such as mass, volume, and weight, do not change, even when their appearances change. According to Piaget, understanding of this principle develops during the concrete operations period.

consolidation theory A theory of memory that states that for a memory to become permanent, it must be allowed an undisturbed period during which it can consolidate.

consonance The term that refers to consistency between a person's behavior and his or her attitude(s).

constructive changes Changes in to-be-remembered materials that occur at the time of presentation of the material, as distinct from changes that occur at the time of recall.

construct validity A method to determine whether scores on a measure relate in theoretically predictable ways to other measures of behavior.

contact hypothesis A theory that asserts that prejudice will be reduced through contact between majority and minority group members when both have equal social status and when they work together to solve a common problem.

content effects Changes in behavior brought about by actual television programming.

content validity See *face validity*.

context The setting in which attempts to learn and remember are made.

continuity The perceptual tendency to see linear elements that point in the same direction as forming a unified whole.

contraception Birth control.

control group A group that is comparable to the experimental group in all respects except for the manipulated (independent) variable. The control group thus eliminates an alternative explanation for the results of an experiment.

convergent thinking The process of thinking used to solve a problem having only one correct answer.

cooperative play Play behavior observed in preschool-age children that is marked by interactive exchanges in play. See also *parallel play*.

cornea A transparent covering through which light enters the eye.

corpus callosum The thick band of neural fibers forming a bridge between the two cerebral hemispheres.

correlation The interrelationship between two variables; that is, the extent to which changes in one variable relate to (but do not necessarily cause) changes in another variable.

correlation coefficient (r) A number indicating the degree to which two numbers are related. The number can range from +1 (perfect positive correlation) to −1 (perfect negative correlation). A coefficient of 0.0 indicates no relationship between the variables.

correspondence bias The tendency to selectively attend to or give weight to information that confirms our hypotheses. In psychological testing, we may look for evidence that agrees with our view of the person and disregard information that disagrees.

cortex See *cerebral cortex*.

cortisol A hormone secreted by the adrenal glands that affects the release of sugar from the liver, thus influencing the body's ability to produce quick energy. It is thought that cortisol plays a role in the development of mental disturbances.

cortisone A synthetic form of cortisol used in treating shock, allergic reactions, and inflammatory disorders.

counseling psychology A branch of psychology similar to clinical psychology that deals particularly with the problems of high-school and college students.

counterconditioning The process by which an unwanted response to a particular stimulus is replaced by a new, incompatible response.

CR A conditioned response.

cretinism A condition, caused by untreated hypothyroidism in infancy, that is characterized by retardation and stunted growth.

criterion-referenced test A variety of achievement test in which performance on real-life, highly specific tasks is assessed.

critical period A specific period early in an organism's development during which imprinting can occur; any specific period when a developing organism is best able to acquire a new response pattern.

CS A conditioned stimulus.

cytoplasm Jellylike protoplasm outside a cell nucleus that supports the basic life function of the cell.

dark adaptation The process whereby rods and cones become more sensitive to low intensities, enabling an individual to adjust to low levels of illumination.

decay theory A theory of memory that suggests that memory decays or degenerates as time passes.

decibel (db) A unit of measure that gauges the intensity of a sound.

deductive logic Higher-order thinking characterized by the ability to formulate a theory or hypothesis and then to deduce outcomes as if the theory were true, followed by experiments to test the accuracy of the theory. See *inductive logic*.

deep structure The meaning behind a sentence, or what it is the speaker is trying to say, as contrasted with the surface structure of the actual words used.

defense mechanisms In Freud's terminology, our unconscious attempts to defend against anxiety by such means as rationalization and projection, which involve some self-deception and distortion of reality.

defining features An attribute that is sufficient for determining category membership.

delayed classical conditioning A classical conditioning procedure in which CS onset occurs before UCS onset, and the CS remains on at least until UCS onset.

delayed-matching-to-sample procedure (DMTS) A procedure used in studying animal short-term memory that involves presenting the animal with a single stimulus and following it soon after with two stimuli, one of which matches the original stimulus. The animal is rewarded for responding to the original stimulus.

delay of reinforcement The withholding of reinforcement following the occurrence of a response.

delinquency Violation of the law by juveniles, especially if repeated.

delta waves In an EEG, the brain waves that are recorded when an individual drifts off to sleep or sleeps without dreaming.

delusions Beliefs, characteristic of some psychotic disorders, that are not founded in fact. These misperceptions almost always center around the person reporting the delusion and may pertain to persecution, grandiosity, or reference.

dendrites The branching, fingerlike projections of the cell body of a neuron that receive electrochemical impulses from other neurons.

deoxyribonucleic acid (DNA) The chemical substance of which genes are composed.

dependence Addiction.

dependent variable A change in an experimental subject's behavior as a result of variations in the independent variable.

depolarized The state of a nerve cell as it transmits the electrochemical impulse; in this state the inside of the cell carries a slightly more positive charge than the outside of the cell.

depression A sense of hopelessness, dejection, apathy, and low self-worth.

deprivation dwarfism The stunting of physical growth associated with sensory deprivation.

depth perception The perception of distances.

"designer" drugs Chemical variants of illegal drugs.

development The life-long process of change brought about by biological forces, environmental circumstances, or the interaction of biological and environmental conditions acting on the individual as he or she ages.

developmental psychology The branch of psychology concerned with human growth and the factors that affect and effect change across the life span.

dichromatic Dichromatic color blindness involves the absence of one of the three color systems. The most common is red-green color blindness.

difference threshold The minimum amount of stimulus change necessary for an individual to notice a difference in a stimulus. Also called *just-noticeable difference*.

differentially permeable Refers to the fact that some kinds of particles can pass through the neuron's membrane more easily than others.

diffusion effect Latané's third "law" of social impact, which states that the greater the number of people around someone who needs help, the less likely any one individual is to come to the aid of the needy person.

directed experimentation A technique used in Gestalt therapy that involves specific psychological exercises designed to increase the client's self-awareness.

discrimination (1) In conditioning, a subject's tendency to restrict its responses to a rewarded stimulus and respond less and less to unrewarded stimuli. (2) In personality theory, the

learned ability to distinguish between situations where a behavior will be rewarded and situations where it will not be rewarded. (3) In social psychology, negative behaviors that reflect a prejudiced attitude toward a group.

disinhibited behavior Previously inhibited behavior that will occur if an individual sees a model "getting away with" that behavior.

disorganized schizophrenia A subtype of schizophrenia characterized by incoherence, lack of systematic delusions, odd behaviors and mannerisms, and extreme social withdrawal.

displaced aggression Aggression directed toward an alternative, less threatening object.

displacement A defense mechanism by which we unleash pent-up impulses on alternative persons or objects, rather than on those that have caused the upset.

displacement effects Changes in how individuals use their time as a consequence of the introduction of television.

dispositional attribution Attribution of behavior to internal and enduring personal traits of an individual.

dissonance theory Festinger's theory that people feel most comfortable when their cognitions are consistent with one another and with their behavior. If their cognitions are inconsistent (dissonant), the individual will change either his behavior or ideas until a state of consistency (consonance) is reached.

divergent thinking The process of creative thinking that is needed to solve problems having many acceptable answers.

dizygotic Nonidentical twins, developed from two separate fertilized ova. (Also called *fraternal twins*.)

DNA Deoxribonucleic acid.

dominant gene The member of the gene pair that is responsible for the appearance of some physical feature within the offspring.

dominant senses In humans, sight and hearing, the senses upon which we are most dependent.

dopamine An important neurotransmitter found in the central nervous system that is markedly absent in the brains of people suffering from Parkinson's disease. Dopamine also may be implicated in schizophrenia, although the mechanism is unclear.

Doppler effect When the source of a sound wave approaches us, the sound seems to rise because the waves are effectively compressed; when the source moves away, the sound falls

because the waves are effectively expanded.

double-blind technique An experimental technique in which neither the subjects nor the experimenter knows the particular condition to which the subjects belong.

double-edged message A message that simultaneously conveys conflicting positive and negative emotions, often involving both verbal and nonverbal means, such as sarcasm.

Down syndrome The most common form of mental retardation, which develops when an individual is born with an extra chromosome in the twenty-first pair. (Formerly called *mongolism*.)

drive A state of arousal resulting from a need state.

drive state A condition of arousal caused by a tissue need or noxious stimulation.

drive theory The theory that we are motivated by drives.

drug therapy The use of medications to treat symptoms of psychological disorder. Drug therapy may be used alone or in combination with psychotherapy.

dry mouth The parched sensation associated with thirst.

dual-trace hypothesis The theory that holds that information can be stored verbally, visually, or both ways.

dysthymia A depressive disorder characterized by low level, chronic symptoms of the depression syndrome.

eardrum A thin, flexible membrane covering the opening into the middle ear. A sound wave hitting the eardrum causes it to vibrate and transfers the vibration to the hammer.

echoic memory Auditory sensory memory.

eclecticism In psychotherapy, refers to the use of ideas and techniques drawn from various theories rather than from a single approach to treatment.

ectomorphs A classification within Sheldon's now discredited theory of personality types. Ectomorphs are thin, fragile individuals and were thought to be introverted, sensitive, and artistic.

efferent neuron A motor neuron.

ego According to Freud's theory of personality, that part of our personality that attempts to serve the id while, at the same time, protecting the individual and responding to the demands of society.

egocentric Thinking observed in preschool-aged children that is characterized by self-centeredness.

ego integrity and despair According to Erikson, the final life crisis. Facing death, the aging person must find a larger meaning in life or he or she will experience a sense of despair.

Electra complex According to Freud, a conflict that females experience during the phallic stage and must resolve in order to develop a superego. A child's sexual attraction to her father and resentment of her mother at this stage are in conflict with her dependency on her mother. She must learn to repress her sexual desire for her father and identify with her mother in order to resolve this conflict.

electrical stimulation (1) A technique for studying a living brain by inserting a wire electrode into particular brain sites and passing a small current through the wire. (2) A similar method employed during human brain surgery to detect defective brain sites.

electroconvulsive shock (treatment or therapy) A controversial procedure effective in reducing severe depression through the use of electric shock treatments.

electroencephalogram (EEG) A record of the electrical activity of the brain obtained by attaching electrodes to the scalp.

electroencephalograph A device that records electroencephalograms by picking up electrical activity of the brain and translating it into a line of tracings on a roll of paper.

elevation A cue used in distance perception in which objects higher in the visual field appear to be farther away than objects in the lower portion of the visual field.

embryo The developing human organism during the stage occurring from 3 to 7 weeks after conception.

emotion A strong, relatively uncontrollable feeling that is accompanied by physiological changes and often affects our behavior.

emotional support Support received from friends and acquaintances that is characterized by love and nurturance.

empathic understanding An aspect of therapy, especially associated with Rogers's client-centered therapy, in which the therapist reflects his or her understanding of what the client feels or says and responds in a warm, nonjudgmental way.

empiricism The philosophical school of thought that maintained that all ideas are acquired through experience; none are innate.

empty-chair exercise Technique used in Gestalt therapy in which the client plays two roles, the self and another person, or two conflicting parts of the self, in order to achieve fuller awareness and acceptance of the conflicting elements.

encoding The processes by which we store learned information in memory.

encounter groups A form of group psychotherapy that varies from group to group, depending on the orientation of the leader. Also called *sensitivity groups*.

end brush A bushy portion at the end of an axon or auxiliary axon. Each strand of the end brush terminates in a synaptic knob.

endocrine (ductless) gland A ductless gland that directly affects behavior through its secretion of hormones into the blood.

endocrine organ Any organ that functions as an endocrine gland.

endocrine system The network of ductless glands that interacts with the nervous system to activate muscles and glands.

endomorphs A classification within Sheldon's now-discredited theory of personality types based on body build. Endomorphs are fleshy, chubby individuals and were thought to be cheerful and relaxed.

endorphins Chemical pain inhibitors produced by the brain, similar to opium in their effectiveness.

enuresis The technical term for bedwetting.

environmental design The effort to arrange the environment in order to maximize productivity and permit a sense of well-being.

environmental psychology The branch of psychology that studies the complex relationships between our behavior and our ability to control and change our environment.

epilepsy An organic disorder caused by an abnormal surge of brain cell activity. Characterized by seizures.

epinephrine A hormone secreted by the adrenal glands that prepares us for emergency action. Also called *adrenalin*.

episodic memory The temporal ordering of events in memory.

equilibration Piaget's term for the child's active organizing of his experiences in order to achieve a sense of balance and make sense out of all of the experiences.

equilibratory receptors A group of receptors located in the semicircular canals and vestibular sacs that provide us with our sense of body balance.

ESP Extrasensory perception.

essential hypertension High blood pressure that has no known organic cause but that appears to be related to stress.

estrogens Sex hormones secreted by the adrenal glands of both sexes, but in larger quantities in females. Estrogen promotes the development of female secondary sex characteristics.

ethnocentrism Belief in the superiority of one's own ethnic group.

ethology A branch of biology concerned with behavior and its relationship to the environment.

evaluation The fourth stage in problem solving in which a person assesses the effectiveness of various alternative solutions that they have determined to be viable in solving a problem.

exhaustion stage The final stage in Seyle's analysis of stress.

existential-humanistic therapies Psychotherapies that stress self-actualization as the basis for psychological growth.

exocrine (duct) gland A gland, such as the salivary gland, which involves ducts.

expectancy-value approach Theory of personality and behavior developed by Rotter that was a forerunner of contemporary cognitive approaches. Rotter argued that behavior is a function of the expectation that any individual act will be rewarded and the value placed on the reward.

experiment A scientific data-gathering method widely used in psychology in which a series of observations is made under carefully controlled conditions. An experimenter observes the changes in a dependent variable as a result of manipulations of an independent variable.

extinction A decrease in response strength due to repeated nonreinforcements that occurs in classical, instrumental, and verbal conditioning situations.

extrasensory perception (ESP) The possibility that we can become aware of our environment through the operation of sensory systems not yet known to science. ESP phenomena include telepathy, clairvoyance, precognition, and psychokinesis.

extravert Jung's term for an outgoing individual who wants to interact with others and stay in touch with the outside world.

extrinsic reward Reward that originates externally, as distinct from intrinsic reward, which is the reward inherent in performing an act.

eye contact An important source of nonverbal communication.

face validity The commonsense process of asking whether the items on a test are logically related to the purposes of the test. Also called *content validity*.

facial feedback hypothesis The hypothesis that states that our emotions can be affected by our facial expression.

factor analysis A complex statistical technique that psychologists use to discover the basic dimensions underlying a whole group of personality trait labels.

familiarization The first stage of problem solving, which is characterized by learning as much about the problem as possible, including the obstacles to its solution and the materials necessary to obtain the solution.

fantasy Make-believe.

farsightedness Poor visual acuity for close objects.

fear hierarchy A list of fears, ranked in terms of the degree of fear they produce, drawn up by a person undergoing systematic desensitization.

fear-induced aggression One of several types of aggression. In particular, this form occurs when fear is experienced.

fear of strangers The fear observed in infants that begins to occur between the ages of 6 to 8 months when the infant is approached by an unfamiliar person.

feature analysis A theory of visual pattern recognition stating that the stimulus is broken down into its elements and analyzed by specialized feature detectors located in the brain and retina.

feature approach See *feature analysis*.

fetal alcohol syndrome Syndrome produced by moderate to heavy drinking during pregnancy that may lead to the birth of an infant with possible central nervous system disorders, abnormal facial features, cardiac malformation, skeletal defects, and mental retardation.

fetus The developing human organism during the stage that occurs from 8 to 40 weeks after conception.

figure-ground tendency The tendency to form a figure from part of an incoming sensory message and to perceive the rest of the message as background.

first level inference A description of behavior with virtually no inference or abstraction added.

fissure A deep valley or convolution of the cerebral cortex.

fixation The process by which adults hold on to pleasures associated with one of Freud's psychosexual stages as a result of frustration or overindulgence at that stage of development.

fixed-action pattern A pattern of behavior that occurs automatically and innately when a sign stimulus is perceived.

fixed-interval schedule A schedule of reinforcement in which the subject is reinforced for the first response after a given time interval has elapsed. This produces the scalloping effect.

fixed-ratio schedule A schedule of reinforcement in which the subject must make a fixed number of responses before a reinforcement is delivered.

flat affect A condition of emotional unresponsiveness that is usually associated with schizophrenia.

forebrain Portion of the brain consisting of the thalamus, the hypothalamus, the basal ganglia, the limbic system, and the cerebrum.

forgetting The inability to retain stored information or learned associations.

forgetting curve A curve that graphs the amount of given information forgotten over a period of time.

formal operations Piaget's fourth and final stage of cognitive development, which begins at about age 11–12 years and is characterized by the adolescent's ability to reason inductively as well as deductively.

fovea A small indentation on the retina just above the optic nerve, where cones are concentrated.

frames A display pattern used in a teaching machine that contains a bit of information and a question about that information.

fraternal twins Dizygotic twins.

free association In classical psychoanalysis, the client is encouraged to say aloud anything at all, especially thoughts and images that trigger off one another. This is the primary technique for revealing the contents of the unconscious mind.

free recall task A technique for studying verbal learning in which a subject is presented with a list of words and asked to recall them in any order.

frequency The frequency of a sound wave is a measure of how rapidly the pressure changes occur in time.

frequency distribution A statistical chart that shows the number of scores falling within a given interval.

frequency polygon A graph of a frequency distribution in which the frequency is expressed by the height of the point above that score; points are connected by straight lines.

frequency theory The theory that pitch is determined by the frequency of impulses traveling up the auditory nerve.

Freudian dream theory The theory that anxiety-producing impulses can be expressed symbolically in dreams.

frontal lobe Division of the cortex involved with movement.

frustration The unpleasant feeling we experience when motive satisfaction is blocked or delayed.

functional fixedness The tendency to use objects only in ways that are familiar to us from past experience, which can be an obstacle in problem solving.

fundamental attribution error A general aspect of human information processing that has particular relevance to psychological testing. People tend to explain other peoples' behaviors on the basis of personality traits and to underestimate the effects that a particular situation may have on a person. The reverse is true when people explain their own behavior.

galvanic skin response (GSR) An index of how easily electricity will travel across the surface of the skin; often used as an indicator of emotions.

ganglion cell The name for any cell that is a member of a ganglion. A ganglion is any cluster of nerve cell bodies found outside the central nervous system.

general adaptation syndrome (GAS) The distinct yet standard sequence of three stages the body undergoes when it experiences stressful events.

generalized avoidance conditioning The classical conditioning of general avoidance activity, as contrasted with specific forms of conditioning, such as eyelid conditioning.

generativity vs. stagnation According to Erikson, the adult crisis that occurs between the ages of about 25–40. If a sense of visible accomplishment is not achieved during this time, the individual may feel a sense of meaninglessness.

genes The basic units of heredity found in the chromosomes of every cell. Genes establish and define the hereditary instructions for every developing organism.

genetic counseling The detailed genetic testing and close examination of (potential) parents' medical histories in order to determine whether or not genetic diseases can be inherited by their offspring.

genetic engineering The scientific effort to manipulate a gene pool in the interest of changing or exchanging an undesirable gene for a desirable one.

genetic linkage study A method of research in which families are studied to determine the linkage, or covariation, between a known genetic characteristic and disorders that are presumed to be genetically transmitted.

genetic marker Researchers look for genetic markers in genetic linkage studies. The presence of a gene whose location is known, may serve, if it occurs in conjunction with some disorder, as a "marker" or indicator that the disorder is genetically transmitted.

genetics The biological study of heredity concerned with how physical characteristics are passed from parents to offspring.

genital period According to Freud's psychosexual stages of development, the period that begins at puberty and lasts throughout life. Interest centers on the genitals and we seek to establish a long-term, meaningful sexual relationship with another person.

genotypes Genetic makeup of an individual.

genuineness An element of therapy that is particularly associated with Rogers's client-centered approach, in which the therapist attempts to share her or his actual feelings with the client, rather than trying to hide them or project dishonest reactions.

gestalt Shape, pattern, or structure.

Gestalt therapy A form of psychotherapy founded by Perls that uses a variety of exercises designed to enhance the client's self-awareness and develop a sense of personal responsibility.

glial cell A cell which, along with the neurons, comprises the nervous system and provides support services for the neuron.

glucostatic theory The theory that the brain detects changes in blood sugar and then instructs the body to increase or decrease eating.

graded-step reinforcement A method of reversing depression by asking the depressed individual to do something very simple, slowly moving on to more complex responses. The individual will regain confidence gradually through this series of small successes.

grade equivalent A test score that measures a child's achievement in relation to the average score of children in the same school grade.

grammar The rules that govern the ordering and positioning of sounds, morphemes, and words in sentences.

growth hormone A pituitary hormone that affects a number of metabolic functions determining the growth of the body.

hallucinations Perceptual experiences not grounded in reality and not perceived by other observers.

hallucinogens A class of drugs, such as LSD, marijuana, and PCP, that causes temporary alterations in the perception of reality.

hammer A bone located in the middle ear that conducts sound vibrations from the eardrum to the anvil.

health psychology A newly developed specialty area in psychology devoted to the study of health concerns and ways for improving individual and societal health practices.

hereditarian fallacy Applied to the debate over biological bases of race differences in IQ, this term refers to the logical error of concluding that if the evidence does not clearly support an environmental explanation, the genetic explanation must be correct.

heroin A narcotic drug derived from the opium poppy. Heroin is very addictive and is primarily a mood-changer.

hertz A unit of frequency equal to one cycle per second.

hierarchy A ranked arrangement.

hierarchy model (hierarchics) A semantic network model of memory that holds that memories are stored hierarchically.

hindbrain The lowest portion of the brain, consisting of part of the brain stem, the medulla, the cerebellum, and the pons.

holophrastic speech A form of communication used by infants in which a single word stands for an entire idea, thought, event, or sentence.

homeostasis The tendency of the body to maintain steady states of food, water, air, sleep, and heat in order to survive.

homeostatic mechanisms Complex systems within the body that maintain steady body states with respect to food, water, air, sleep, and heat.

hormonal manipulation A questionable form of medical therapy that is aimed at reducing human suffering and discomfort through the administration of various hormones.

hormone A chemical substance that is secreted by endocrine glands and affects the individual's physical state and behavior in particular ways.

hue Color.

hyperphagia Obesity due to destruction of the ventromedial hypothalamus.

hyperthyroidism Overactivity of the thyroid gland.

hypnopaedia The theory that learning occurs while an individual is asleep. Available evidence does not support this theory.

hypnosis The technique of inducing a trance state of heightened calmness, relaxation, and suggestibility in a subject. Hypnosis has been used in medical, dental, and psychotherapy situations to reduce pain, anxiety, and fear.

hypnotic age regression The ability of some hypnotized subjects to regress to childhood when told to "go back" in their life by the hypnotist.

hypnotic drugs A class of drugs sometimes used to treat insomnia. They do not "hypnotize" but do cause drowsiness.

hypnotic trance The state of being under hypnosis.

hypomania A form of bipolar mood disorder that is "mild mania." Mood and behavioral disturbances similar to mania occur, but in much less severe forms.

hypothalamus Portion of the forebrain located between the thalamus and the pituitary gland. The hypothalamus is vital in regulating a wide variety of body functions and behaviors, including eating, drinking, emotional control, and sexual behavior.

hypothesis-testing theory A theory of concept formation that assumes that the learner is an active processor of information when solving problems. The learner busily tests a series of guesses about a concept and continues testing until the correct hypothesis is found.

hypothyroidism Underactivity of the thyroid gland.

iconic memory Visual sensory memory.

id According to Freud's theory of personality, the part of our personality containing the primitive, inherited, unconscious impulses that demand immediate and total gratification.

identical twins *Monozygotic* twins.

identification (1) A defense mechanism that leads people to imitate others who are seen as more powerful. (2) Freud's term for the process by which a young child develops an attachment for the same-sexed parent.

identity vs. role confusion According to Erikson, the crisis that occurs in adolescence when the individual must work out both an adult sex role and an adult occupational role.

illusions Distortions in perception that are experienced by everyone in the same way.

illusory correlation The persistent belief in personality testing that a particular test response has a particular meaning, even when there is no valid evidence to substantiate such a conclusion. (Example: the belief that reporting eyes on an inkblot test "means" paranoia)

imprinting The phenomenon that a newly hatched bird will approach, follow, and form a social attachment to the first moving object it perceives. Controversy exists as to whether this is another form of learning or a prime example of instinctive behavior.

inbred strains Groups of experimental animals that have been interbred for generations to reduce the genetic variability among group members.

incentive Objects or events in the environment that motivate an organism in the absence of any known physiological need state.

incentive theory A theory of motivation that emphasizes the fact that external stimuli in the environment (incentives) can motivate or pull an organism into certain behavior.

incompatible responses Technique for controlling aggression that is based on the principle that all organisms are incapable of engaging in two incompatible responses; thus, it may be possible to reduce aggression through the induction of responses incompatible with overt aggression or the emotion of anger.

incongruity In connection with Rogers's client-centered therapy, refers to disparity between the real self and the self one would like to be—a condition Rogers believed gives rise to discomfort and dissatisfaction.

incubation The third stage of problem solving in which, after unsuccessfully attempting to find a solution, we stop, rest, and when we return to the problem, we suddenly recognize the solution (incubation effect) that had eluded us earlier.

incubation effect See *incubation*.

independent variable A condition or event that an experimenter varies in order to observe the effects of this change on a subject's behavior.

inductive logic The reasoning process that results in conclusions about general principles based on the observation of many individual and concrete experiences. Inductive logic is the form of logic seen in young children. See *deductive logic*.

industrial psychology The branch of psychology concerned with human problems in an industrial setting.

industry vs. inferiority According to Erikson, the crisis that occurs during the child's early school years (ages 5–12), when his task is to adapt to the larger social world of school and peers.

infantile autism A childhood disorder that appears within the first 30 months of life and is characterized by a profound lack of responsiveness to people, impairment of communication skills, and bizarre responses to aspects of the environment.

inference A conclusion or hypothesis deduced from the information available. Unlike a simple description of fact, an inference goes beyond the information given.

inferiority complex Adler's term for the basic sense of inferiority that arises during an individual's early years when he or she is weak and helpless.

information-processing system (1) A general approach to psychology that views the human brain as a computerlike system for dealing with inputs. (2) A theory of memory that states that we remember information for short periods of time differently than we remember information for long periods of time.

inhibited behavior An already learned behavior that is made less likely to occur (inhibited) if an individual sees a model engaging in that behavior and being punished for it.

initiative vs. guilt According to Erikson, the crisis that occurs at age 4 or 5 when the child becomes more aggressive and has more peer contact but needs to control intrusions upon the autonomy of others.

innate releasing mechanism In the ethological theory of instinctive behavior, the "plug" that is pulled by the sign stimulus.

inner ear The internal part of the ear that contains the cochlea, semicircular canals, and the vestibular sacs.

insight With reference to therapy, refers to the understanding of one's motives and behaviors that comes from exploration in the therapy process.

instinctive behavior Innate, predetermined patterns of behavior that are released or evoked when certain stimuli are perceived.

instinctive drift The interference with learning caused by instinctive behaviors.

instinct theory A theory of motivation that states that much of our behavior is governed by unlearned, instinctive impulses.

instrumental aggression The type of aggression in which aggressive behavior helps the organism to obtain a goal. Instrumental aggression is a form of learned aggression.

instrumental conditioning A learning process in which the probability that a particular response will occur is increased by the delivery of a reward or reinforcement. Also known as *operant conditioning*.

integration The processes involved in organizing multiple neural stimulations.

intelligence A presumed inner set of skills or responses that collectively permit the individual to solve problems, to learn new ideas or concepts, and to deal effectively with the environment.

intelligence quotient (IQ) According to the Stanford-Binet intelligence test for children, a ratio of mental age to chronological age, multiplied by 100.

intensity/brightness Qualities of vision determined by the amplitude of the light wave.

interacting mental images A technique for remembering pairs of items by forming a mental image of the two items interacting.

interference theory A theory of memory that states that both old and new learning can interfere with our attempts to remember a given set of materials.

intermale aggression Aggression triggered by a strange male of the same species. This form of aggression may be genetically determined.

internal consistency reliability Characteristic of psychological tests that refers to the ability of all the items to measure the same qualities—the coherence of the test.

internal representation A child's ability to represent an object to herself by the use of a word or mental image. According to Piaget, this ability develops during the later part of the sensorimotor stage when the child is acquiring language.

interneurons Neurons that integrate incoming messages from afferent groups and coordinate the outgoing messages of efferent groups. Also known as *connecting neurons*.

interposition An extremely effective depth cue in which an object standing in front of another partially conceals the one in back.

interrater reliability A method to determine the reliability of a test in which several judges or observers rate or count the same specific behavior in an individual. If the observers agree on the count, the rating is reliable.

interview A method of gathering data in which the subject is asked to respond verbally to a series of questions posed by an interviewer.

intimacy vs. isolation According to Erikson, the crisis experienced by most people some time in their early twenties when an individual either has a sense of identity strong enough to sustain real intimacy or experiences a sense of isolation.

intrinsic reward The reward inherent in the performing of an act as distinct from reward from some external source.

introversion-extraversion classification A personality dimension referring to preference for social interactions (extraversion) or solitary pursuits (introversion).

introvert Jung's term for a person whose thoughts and interests are directed inward and who spends little time interacting with others.

ions Electrically charged particles that fill the fluid outside a nerve cell and the cytoplasm within the cell, and determine the state of a cell's polarity.

iris The colored part of the eye that controls the amount of light entering.

irritable aggression Aggression not preceded by attempts to escape.

James-Lange hypothesis A theory that states that the emotions we feel are the result of messages we receive from our bodies when they react to emotion-producing aspects of the environment.

jargon babbling Infant vocalization that consists of strings of sounds uttered with a variety of stress and intonation patterns, which from a distance sounds like true speech.

just-noticeable difference (jnd) The *difference threshold*.

keyword method A mnemonic method for learning foreign language equivalents.

kinesthetic receptors A group of receptors located around the muscles, tendons, and joints that provide feedback concerning the position of the body.

Klinefelter's syndrome A genetic abnormality caused by the presence of an extra chromosome in the twenty-third position.

latency period According to Freud's psychosexual stages of development, the period following the phallic stage and lasting until puberty, during which the child loses interest in sexual sensations.

latent content According to Freud, the true meaning of our dreams, which is revealed when the manifest content is stripped away.

latent learning Learning that takes place in the absence of reinforcement.

lateral fissure The side fissure separating the temporal lobe from the frontal and parietal lobes of the brain.

lateral hypothalamus (LH) The side portion of the hypothalamus; involved in eating behavior.

learned behavior With reference to personality theory, behaviorally oriented theorists' belief that many traits, characteristics, and behaviors are acquired through learning processes—reward, punishment, and imitation of models.

learned helplessness A type of instrumental conditioning in which an animal may fail to learn a simple avoidance response following repeated, unavoidable shocks.

learning A relatively permanent change in behavior potentiality that is the result of practice.

learning theories of attraction Theories that emphasize the role of classical conditioning in influencing our interpersonal attractions and what we like and dislike. For instance, things associated with pleasant events will tend to be liked.

lens Portion of the eye that focuses light on the retina.

lesions The destruction of particular brain sites in animals, by means of the insertion of a wire electrode, for the purpose of brain study.

levels-of-processing approach The information-processing theory that maintains that retention is determined by the level (or "depth") of its rehearsal, rather than the amount of rehearsal.

lexical-decision experiments A group of experiments designed to test semantic network models of memory.

lexical memory The long-term encoding, storage, and retrieval of words, distinct from memory for grammar, sentences, experiences, and so on, that is stored in either short-term or long-term memory, or both simultaneously.

libido According to Freud's theory of personality, the energy of the sexual instinct, which motivates all psychological activity and is supplied by the id.

light adaptation The process whereby an individual's vision readjusts to bright light after being exposed to low levels of illumination for a long period of time.

liking The feeling of respect and affection (but not love) that we experience toward others. See *loving*.

limbic system An interconnected system of several structures that forms a border of neural tissue around the upper end of the brain stem. It is involved in emotional behavior, attention, learning, and memory.

linear perspective A cue used in depth perception in which two parallel lines appear to come together in the distance.

lipostatic theory Disputed theory that the stimulus for long-term weight control is probably a chemical in the blood that reflects the amount of fat (lipids) in the body. The higher the lipid level, the lower the overall eating level.

location constancy Under experimental conditions, individuals will adjust to perceiving objects in their proper places, even when their visual field is inverted or reversed.

longitudinal study Research in which the same individuals are tested repeatedly over time.

long-term memory A memory storehouse where information is stored fairly permanently when we are not recalling it. Everything we have learned but are not now thinking of is stored in this memory.

loving The attachment, caring, and intimacy that we feel for another person. See *liking*.

lysergic acid diethylamide (LSD) An unpredictable drug that produces heightened and distorted sensory experience. Also known as "acid."

mainstreaming The placement of special education students into regular classrooms, rather than a special classroom, in order to provide them with an education in the "least restrictive environment."

maladaptive thinking Ways of interpreting the self, the environment, and the future (cognitions) that are negative or biased, leading the person to experience emotional discomfort or behavioral problems.

mania A severe mood disorder characterized by elation, grandiose thinking, extreme activity and distractability, and poor judgment. Mania usually cycles with depression, as in bipolar (affective) disorder.

manifest content According to Freud, the elements of a dream that we can recall, as distinguished from the latent content.

marijuana The most widely used and mildest hallucinogen. Its effects vary and many users say it exaggerates the mood they experienced at the time of using it. Also called *cannabis*.

Maslow's hierarchy Maslow's model of motivation, which holds that more basic needs will direct behavior until they are satisfied. Self-actualization is the highest goal.

masochism A pattern of abnormal behavior (often sexual) in which pleasure is derived from actually suffering pain. Pavlov and others suggest that masochism is a learned behavior involving classical conditioning.

material support The tangible assistance received from others in the form of goods and services in times of crises.

matrix model (matrices) A model that predicts that organized information will be more effectively stored than will randomly arranged information.

maturation Growth processes in an individual, the onset, termination, and ultimate level of which are governed by automatic, genetically determined signals.

mean The arithmetic average in a frequency distribution, computed by adding all the scores and dividing by the total number of scores.

median The score that divides a frequency distribution in half.

medical model An emphasis on biological causation and treatment of psychological abnormality. May also refer to an analogy to medicine in which psychological disorders are thought to have "underlying causes," "symptoms," a "disease" process, and so on.

medicine-preference effect The concept that the taste of medicine that has been effective will be preferred over other tastes.

meditation Techniques that attempt to alter consciousness through the systematic exercise of concentration.

medulla A section of the lower brain stem that helps control breathing, heart rate, and blood pressure.

melancholic A personality type in Hippocrates's system, referring to one who is depressive and mournful, due to an excess of the bodily fluid, black bile.

memory The organism's ability to retain learned associations or stored information.

menopause Cessation of both ovulation and the menstrual cycle that usually takes place in women between the ages of 42 and 52. The hormonal changes that occur during this period are sometimes accompanied by other physical symptoms, such as hot flashes or depression.

mental age (MA) The computation of a child's performance on an intelligence test composed of problems or tasks designed for each age group. Mental age is computed by adding up all the tasks at which a child succeeds.

mental rotation Source of experimental support for the existence of mental images in which subjects frequently report that they "mentally rotate" figures in attempting to find matching pairs of figures.

mental set Our tendency to rely on familiar procedures for solving problems, which can lead us to overlook simpler solutions.

mere exposure hypothesis Attraction to things or people on the basis of familiarity alone.

mesomorphs A personality type of Sheldon's now-discredited theory based on body build. The mesomorph is a strong, muscular type alleged to be energetic and courageous.

method of loci A technique for remembering items in a list by placing vivid, bizarre images of them in ordered mental locations, such as familiar places in a building. The items may be retrieved by taking a "mental walk" through the building.

method of reception A procedure in which the experimenter determines which stimuli will be presented to the subject during a concept-formation task.

method of selection A procedure in which the subject is free to test any stimulus at any time during a concept-formation task.

midbrain Portion of the brain containing part of the reticular activating system (RAS), which is involved in controlling level of arousal.

middle ear A bony cavity in the ear housing three connected bones: the hammer, anvil, and stirrup. Sound vibrations are conducted from the eardrum, through the middle ear, to the oval window.

minor senses Taste, touch, and smell; the senses upon which we rely least heavily.

misuse With reference to personality tests, refers to using tests with poor reliability or validity, or to misinterpreting or misapplying the results.

mitosis The process of cell division in which the chromosomes divide, with each new cell containing all 46 of the original chromosomes.

mnemonic techniques Methods of improving our memory by relating new material to material we already know.

modality The number of clearly distinguishable high points, or peaks, in a frequency polygon.

mode The score that occurs the most frequently in a frequency distribution.

models Theories, or systems of explanation.

mongolism *Down syndrome.*

monochromatic Form of color blindness in which the individual sees only black and white.

monozygotic twins Twins with the same genetic identity, developed from a single fertilized ovum. Also called *identical twins.*

morpheme The smallest meaningful unit in a language, usually composed of two or more phonemes. Mor-

phemes can be words, prefixes, or suffixes.

morphine A narcotic.

motion parallax A cue used in depth perception in which our movement causes objects near us to appear to move more than objects far away.

motivated forgetting The theory that individuals are more or less motivated to remember certain information according to their own needs and desires.

motivation The forces that energize and direct behavior.

motives (1) Those forces that activate and arouse an organism, and (2) those forces that direct the organism's behavior toward the attainment of some goal.

motor cortex The part of the frontal lobe of the cerebral cortex that governs motor activity, or bodily movement.

motor neuron A neuron that sends messages to the muscles concerning the kind of response to be made to the external environment. Also known as an *efferent neuron.*

movement perception Complex perception that appears to be brought about by the successive stimulation of adjacent sense receptors but that in reality involves many cues from the environment and our interpretation of those cues.

MPTP A "look-alike" drug resembling Demerol in its effects.

multiaxial system of diagnoses The official procedures and system of diagnoses used in the United States today, giving not only a diagnosis of current disorder, but also including systematic information about the person on other dimensions such as personality disorders, physical disorders and conditions, stressors in the person's life, and maximum level of recent functioning.

multiple variables The use of more than one independent variable in an experiment.

myelin sheath A white membrane tightly wrapped around the axon of certain neurons that serves to insulate and help increase the speed of transmissions.

narcolepsy A sleep disorder in which the sufferer falls into REM sleep uncontrollably and repeatedly, despite the activity being performed.

naturalistic observation A method of gathering data by observing naturally occurring situations without the use of experimental manipulation.

nearsightedness Poor visual acuity for distant objects.

need A state caused by a deprivation

of such essentials as food, water, and air.

need for control The need to affect the lives of others and oneself.

need to achieve The need to meet or exceed standards of excellence.

need to affiliate The need to socialize, to be with and to work with other people, to feel a part of the "team." This need is believed by some to have a genetic or biological basis but by others to be an acquired trait.

negative contrast effect The fact that a reduction in amount of reinforcement will have a temporary but profoundly negative effect on performance.

negative correlation A negative relationship found between two variables. When one variable goes up, the other goes down.

negatively accelerated performance curve A curve that shows the most common pattern of acquisition; that is, performance increases rapidly at first and then levels off.

negative reinforcer In instrumental conditioning, an unpleasant stimulus taken away from a subject following a response in order to strengthen that response.

negative transfer The negative phenomenon that occurs whenever prior learning interferes with our attempts to master a new task.

neonatal period The first 14 days of life.

nerve cell A *neuron*.

nerves A fibrous bundle of axons (and sometimes dendrites) found outside the brain and spinal cord.

nervous system The network of all nerve cells in the body.

neural coding The process of storing information in the nervous system.

neuron A cell that is the basic building block of the entire nervous system, specialized for communication within the body. Also known as a *nerve cell*.

neurotransmitters Chemicals stored in the synaptic vesicles that transmit messages from one neuron to either stimulate or inhibit the next neuron.

nodes of Ranvier An exposed point on an axon where the myelin sheath is disrupted.

nonverbal communication The expression of emotion through body movements, gestures, facial expressions, and tone of voice.

noradrenalin The hormone *norepinephrine*.

no rapid eye movement (NREM) sleep The periods of sleep during which no rapid eye movements occur, indicating that an individual is not dreaming.

norepinephrine A hormone secreted by the adrenal glands that acts as a

neurotransmitter. Also called *noradrenalin*.

normal distribution A bell-shaped symmetrical and unimodal frequency distribution of statistical data.

noun phrase A part of a sentence consisting of a noun that is usually modified by an adjective and preceded by an article.

nuclear magnetic resonance (NMR) A scanning technique that allows us to "see inside" the living body through the use of magnetism.

nuclear transplant method A genetic engineering method of cloning.

nucleus A cluster of cell bodies of certain neurons found inside the brain or spinal cord.

obesity Fatness.

object constancy A child's ability to understand that an object still exists even when it is not in her field of vision. According to Piaget, this learning occurs during the sensorimotor stage.

objective tests Personality tests that are usually questionnaires that can be administered and scored in standard ways (in contrast to *projective tests*).

object-relations theory A relatively recent departure from classical psychoanalytic theory that emphasizes the nature of the mother-child relationship during the child's early years as a basis for later psychological problems. The viewpoint provides a basis for therapeutic approaches aimed at "repairing" early damage.

observationally learned behavior Learning by watching rather than by doing.

obsessive-compulsive disorder A form of anxiety disorder in which the person is obsessed with repetitive, unpleasant thoughts that he cannot control. The individual often feels compelled to perform repetitive behaviors as well.

occipital lobe Section of the cortex involved with vision.

Oedipus complex According to Freud, a conflict that males experience during the phallic stage and must resolve in order to develop a superego. A child's sexual attraction to his mother and desire to eliminate his father are in conflict with his fear of his father. A boy must learn to repress his sexual desires for his mother and identify with his father in order to resolve this conflict.

olfaction The sense of smell.

olfactory epithelium A section of tissue high in the roof of the nasal cavities where the olfactory receptors are located.

operant conditioning *Instrumental conditioning*.

opiates A class of addictive drugs, such as heroin, that are derived from opium.

opponent-process theory A theory that explains color vision in terms of three processes: one that reponds to red and green, one to yellow and blue, and one to intensity. One color is experienced when the process is in one phase of activity, and the paired color is experienced during the opposite phase.

optic chiasm A point in the occipital lobe where the optic nerves meet and then divide to connect both eyes with both sides of the brain.

optimal-level-of-arousal theory A theory of motivation that argues that organisms seek a preferred level of arousal, rather than always seeking to reduce arousal.

oral stage The first of Freud's psychosexual stages of development, which occurs during the child's first year of life. In this stage, the infant's pleasure is said to be obtained through eating and sucking.

organic mental disorders Types of abnormal behavior that are directly related to physical problems.

organism Any living individual.

organization The process whereby we interpret, or make sense of, the stimuli that we attend to.

organize To relate, interconnect, and systematize.

organ of Corti Part of the ear that contains tiny hairs whose movement stimulates auditory nerve endings.

osmotic thirst Thirst due to cellular dehydration.

outer ear The visible part of the ear that channels sounds toward the eardrum.

oval windows Membranes that cover an opening into the inner ear and conduct sound vibrations from the stirrup.

overjustification effect Curious relationship between intrinsic and extrinsic reward that suggests that extrinsic reward can undermine intrinsic reward if we do something initially for the intrinsic reward and then receive an extrinsic reward for the same behavior.

overload An excessive level of social and/or environmental stimulation that results in an unresponsive orientation to strangers.

overtone Sound wave that occurs in addition to a fundamental wave and whose frequencies are multiples of the fundamental wave.

ovum The female reproductive cell, containing 23 chromosomes.

oxytocin A pituitary hormone that acts on smooth muscles.

paired-associate learning tasks A verbal learning technique in which subjects are required to learn pairs of items and associate half of each pair with the other half.

parallel play Play behavior observed in preschool children in which the children engage in similar side-by-side play without interactive exchanges. See *cooperative play*.

parameter A numerical quantity summarizing some characteristic of a population.

paranoid schizophrenia A form of schizophrenia characterized by well-organized delusions of persecution and grandeur.

paraphilias Psychosexual disorders in which the source of the person's sexual excitement is unusual or bizarre.

parasympathetic system Part of the autonomic division composed of scattered ganglia located near the organs they affect. This system dominates when we are relaxed.

parietal lobe Section of the cortex involved with body senses.

partial reinforcement The pattern of reinforcement that occurs in most natural learning situations, in which only some responses are reinforced.

participant modeling A behavior therapy technique used to overcome phobias whereby the client first observes the therapist in the fearful situation and then is guided by the therapist through the same situation.

pattern recognition Our ability to recognize one object as being "basically" the same as another.

Pavlovian conditioning *Classical conditioning.*

PCP Phencyclidine, also known as "angel dust." While this drug (a powerful animal tranquilizer) defies strict classification, its primary illegal use is to achieve a hallucinogenic effect.

peak experiences According to Maslow, a momentary sense of self-actualization that is within the reach of many of us.

pencil-and-paper tests Another term for objective tests that are in questionnaire form.

perceived causality The human tendency to perceive cause and effect in movement, whether or not it is actually there.

percentile A score that tells you what percentage of individuals taking the same achievement test did as well, or worse, than the individual in question.

percentile rank A single number that gives the percent of cases in the spe-

cific reference group at or below a given score.

perception The process of organizing and making sense of incoming sensory information.

perceptual constancy The tendency to perceive a stable world in spite of incomplete, ambiguous, and potentially confusing sensory information.

perceptual expectancy The concept that our perceptions are affected by what we expect to perceive.

perceptual experience hypothesis The theory that we store in memory an actual image, rather than a proposition, and when we recall that image, we experience, however fleetingly, what occurred when we first looked at the real object; contrast with *propositional hypothesis*.

perceptual features An object is categorized by its features (width, for example). These features can also be influenced by the verbal context such that different features are assigned to a "bowl" and to a "cup" even though they may resemble each other.

period of consolidation The time that must pass before a newly learned response will become permanently stored.

peripheral nervous system The part of the nervous system outside the brain and spinal cord that includes the nerves and ganglia that connect the sense organs, muscles, glands, and internal organs with the spinal cord and brain.

personality An individual's unique, consistent, patterned methods of behaving in relation to the total environment.

personality development The psychological study of how personality characteristics form in childhood.

personality disorders Long-standing maladaptive personality characteristics that cause significant impairment in functioning or subjective distress. They may be distinct from, or co-exist with, specific diagnostic conditions.

personality theory A systematic account of the origin, structure, and manifestations of the personality.

personal space The physical "bubble" of space surrounding each of us that we do not like to have invaded.

phallic stage According to Freud's psychosexual stages of development, the period during the fourth year of the child's life when pleasure centers around the genitals.

phencyclidine See *PCP*.

phenomenological approaches Approaches to psychotherapy that emphasize the individual's immediate experiences and the individual's own

perceptions—in contrast to psychodynamic approaches focused on the historical unfolding to hypothetical conflicts in the individual.

phenothiazines A class of psychotropic medications that are considered to be major tranquilizers with sedative and antipsychotic properties; commonly used to treat psychoses.

phenotype A person's appearance and behavior, as distinct from his genotype or genetic makeup.

phenylketonuria (PKU) A genetically determined form of mental retardation.

pheromones Chemical signals that are exchanged among members of the same species.

phlegmatic One of Hippocrates's ancient personality types. A calm, listless personality stemming from a preponderance of the bodily fluid, phlegm.

phobia An overwhelming, specific fear in the absence of real danger, usually leading to avoidance of the feared object or situation.

phonemes The smallest units of sound in a spoken language.

phonological rules The rules that are used to combine basic phonemes into words, phrases, and sentences.

phrase structure The linguistic analysis of a sentence in terms of how the various phrases within the sentence are related to one another.

physiological approach The approach to the study of psychology that emphasizes the relationship between behavior and its underlying physiological mechanisms.

physiological psychology The branch of psychology concerned with the physical events that underlie behavior, such as the functioning of the brain and nervous system, the glandular systems, and the genetic system.

pitch The sensory experience of a sound wave frequency.

pituitary The "master gland" of the endocrine system. The pituitary secretes at least eight hormones, some of which influence nonglandular tissue, while others control the activities of other endocrine glands, and one controls growth.

place theory The hypothesis that the pitch of a tone is determined by the area of the basilar membrane that is displaced by that sound wave.

planned assertive coping A program outlined by Ellis and Harper that describes some positive, direct steps that we can take to alleviate not only the symptoms of anxiety but the sources as well.

planned coping methods Conscious,

planned efforts we make to alleviate anxiety.

pleasure principle According to the theory of personality advanced by Freud, the principle by which the id operates in order to obtain immediate and total gratification of its desires.

polarized The resting state of a nerve cell; the inside cell is slightly more negatively charged than the outside of the cell.

polygraph machine A "lie detector" machine that is supposed to detect when a person is lying by recording changes in blood pressure, pulse rate, breathing, and perspiration. The use of the machine in police work and therapy is based on the assumption that the individual cannot conceal her or his emotional reactions.

pons A bridge between the two lobes of the cerebellum that contains nuclei related to respiration.

position sensors Two groups of receptors—kinesthetic and equilibratory—that provide information about the position of the body.

positive contrast effect The fact that an increase in amount of reward will lead to a temporary but unexpectedly high level of performance.

positive correlation A relationship between two variables wherein changes in one variable are accompanied by changes in the other variable.

positive reinforcer In instrumental conditioning, a pleasant stimulus presented to a subject following a response, in order to strengthen that response.

positive transfer The positive phenomenon that occurs whenever our previous learning has "set the stage" for us to learn a new task.

positron emission tomography (PET) A scanning technique that allows us to determine levels of metabolic activity in the brain of a living person.

posthypnotic amnesia A subject's inability to recall a hypnotic trance when the hypnotist has given such an instruction for forgetfulness in the course of hypnosis.

posthypnotic suggestion Instructions given to a subject under hypnosis, which the subject follows after coming out of the trance.

post-traumatic stress disorder A form of anxiety reaction that occurs in the aftermath of a traumatic event; the reaction may be delayed or immediate.

precognition The supposed ability to foretell future events.

preconscious Thoughts that we are not now aware of, but can be aware of.

predation Obtaining food by the killing and eating of animals.

predictive validity A method to determine a test's validity by comparing the scores on the test with some later activity that the test is designed to predict.

prejudice A pervasive attitude that includes negative feeling toward some other group, stereotyping, and usually discriminatory behavior.

preoperational period The term applied by Piaget to the stage of cognitive development (ages 2–5) when the child develops the ability to talk, use symbols, and classify objects.

preparedness The degree to which an organism is innately ready to learn a particular behavior.

primacy effect A phenomenon in serial learning in which items at the beginning of a list are the ones most easily recalled in the correct order.

primary aging The occurrence of gradual physical changes due directly to the process of aging.

primary drinking Drinking that is motivated by a physiological need for fluid.

primary-process thinking According to Freud's theory of personality, the irrational and unrealistic methods used by the id in order to satisfy its impulses. Such satisfaction is achieved either by immediate gratification through direct action or by wish fulfillment.

priming effect An experimental effect that supports semantic network models of memory.

proactive inhibition Interference with recall of newly learned items by similar previously learned material.

problems Situations in which an organism is motivated to reach a goal but is blocked by some obstacle.

problem solving A process of overcoming obstacles to achieve a goal. A controversy exists as to whether we solve problems through trial and error or insight.

process of development Refers to the ways in which people change over time, beginning at conception and extending to old age.

production The second stage in problem solving when we begin to produce alternative solutions to the problem.

profile A graphic representation of where a person falls along several dimensions of a personality scale.

progressive relaxation training A tension-relieving technique that relaxes the entire body through a step-by-step procedure.

Project Head Start A federally funded program designed to accelerate and improve the cognitive and social development of children from economically disadvantaged homes.

projection A defense mechanism by which we avoid recognizing our undesireable traits by attributing them to others.

projective tests A group of personality tests that offer the subject an ambiguous or vague stimulus and ask the subject to talk or write about it.

proposition As used in this text, the abstract meaning behind an expression.

propositional hypothesis The theory that holds that we encode and recall a series of propositions, rather than a perceptionlike experience (contrast with *perceptual experience hypothesis*).

prototype-matching hypothesis The idea that patterns are recognized by matching a given external stimulus against an internal, idealized instance of that pattern.

prototypes The stored mental images or patterns we use, rather than rules, in developing and using concepts.

proximity In perception, the tendency to make patterns of visual elements that are close together.

psychoanalysis (1) Theory of personality developed by Freud that emphasizes the importance of sexual gratification and unconscious motivations as bases of the human personality. (2) Method for treating psychological disorders, developed by Freud, involving free association and dream interpretation as efforts to uncover the patient's unconscious motivations.

psychoanalytic psychotherapy A form of psychotherapy that is less intense than classical psychoanalysis involving more interaction between patient and therapist, and more attention to the present rather than to experiences of childhood.

psychodrama A therapy technique, often used in group format, in which patients act out roles to represent personal and family situations. The goal is to increase awareness and understanding of conflicts.

psychodynamic approach The approach to the study of psychology that is based on the thought and work of Sigmund Freud involving the three components he describes as making up the human personality.

psychokinesis Any mental operation that affects a material body—often called "mind over matter."

psycholinguistic theory A theory of language acquisition that emphasizes that children learn complex rules of grammar, use language creatively, and learn language by testing hypotheses. Also includes the theory that humans have an innate ability to learn languages.

psychological determinism Doctrine proposed by Freud that everything we say or do, including slips of the tongue, free association, and dreams, reflects some unconscious motivation.

psychological tests A systematic approach to gathering information about a person's characteristics.

psychology The science of behavior, including the study of observable behavior, physiological changes, and unseen mental processes, which has as its goals the understanding, the prediction, and the helpful alteration of human behavior.

psychomotor stimulants A class of drugs, such as amphetamines, caffeine, and cocaine, that increase energy, alertness, and activity level.

psychoneuroses A now out-of-date term that has largely been replaced by the term anxiety disorders and is based on Freud's theories of anxiety-based disorders arising from psychological conflict and the person's defenses against such conflict.

psychophysics The branch of psychology concerned with the relationship between physical stimuli and resulting sensations.

psychosexual stages According to Freud, set stages of psychosexual development (oral, anal, phallic, latency, genital) through which the child passes. During each stage, pleasure and gratification are obtained in connection with a specific part of the body.

psychosis A broad category of severe psychological disorders, generally requiring hospitalization or special care.

psychosocial stages According to Erikson, each person proceeds through eight distinct stages beginning at infancy and continuing into old age. These stages are created by social tensions that need to be resolved and if resolved successfully the person gains new adaptive strength that helps in facing the tensions of the next stage.

psychosomatic Physical symptoms that are caused by psychological factors.

psychosurgery Brain surgery aimed at reducing psychological disorders.

puberty A series of physical changes that occur during early adolescence, making reproduction possible.

punisher An unpleasant stimulus presented to a subject undergoing instrumental conditioning in order to eliminate a particular response.

punishment The delivery of noxious stimulation following the occurrence of an unwanted response.

punishment training A type of instrumental conditioning in which the subject is punished for a particular response.

pupil The black opening in the eye that is made smaller or larger by the tensing or relaxing of the iris.

pyramid of motives Maslow's classification of motives according to a hierarchy, with basic biological needs at the bottom and more complicated psychological motives toward the top. The basic needs must be satisfied before more complicated motives can direct our behavior.

random assignment The method of picking subjects and controls for an experiment by chance, thus eliminating bias.

range A measure of variability; the spread of scores in the distribution, or the highest score minus the lowest score.

rapid eye movement (REM) sleep The periods of sleep during which rapid eye movements occur, indicating that an individual is dreaming.

rarefaction An area of lessened air molecules created by the movement of a vibrating object.

rating scales Method used in conjunction with interviews or systematic observation in which a rater translates the information to a scale to indicate the extent to which a particular characteristic is present. Such scales help to quantify personality information.

rational emotive therapy A cognitive behavior therapy developed by Ellis that utilizes various methods to help clients modify their self-defeating thoughts.

rationalization A defense mechanism in which we give ourselves false reassurances about an anxiety-producing experience in order to reduce our anxiety.

reaction formation A defense mechanism by which we act in a manner that is just the opposite of what we are truly feeling in order to reduce anxiety.

reaction-specific energy In ethological theory, the energy that exists to motivate the occurrence of only one particular behavior.

reality principle According to Freud's theory of personality, the principle by which the ego operates as a mediator between the id's demand for immediate gratification and the equally forceful demands of the real world.

recall A method for measuring retention in which the subject is required to reproduce the entire stored item. This method produces the lowest amount of retention, compared to recognition and relearning.

recency effect A phenomenon in serial learning in which items toward the end of a list are recalled less easily than those at the beginning, but more easily than those in the middle.

receptors Specialized sensory nerve endings that respond only to certain types of energy.

recessive gene The gene that determines the expression of a physical trait only when paired with another recessive gene.

recognition A method for measuring retention in which the subject is asked if a given item is the correct item. This method produces the highest amount of retention, compared to recall and relearning.

reconstructive changes Changes in to-be-remembered material that occur at the time of recall rather than at the time of learning.

recordings Records of neural activity.

reduplicated babbling Consonant and vowel sound combination repeated in a stereotyped fashion (for example, "bababa") beginning at about 26 weeks of age and continuing through to the end of the infant's first year.

refractory period A short period of time (a few thousandths of a second) following the firing of an impulse when a neuron becomes insensitive to stimulation and is temporarily incapable of firing.

regression An individual's return to a more childish mode of behavior when a current mode of behavior fails to overcome frustration.

reinforcement The presentation of a reward or the removal of a punisher in order to increase the likelihood of a desired response in instrumental conditioning situations. In classical conditioning, the delivery of the UCS following the CS to increase the likelihood of a desired response.

relative refractory period The latter part of a nerve cell's refractory period, during which the cell may fire if it is stimulated very strongly.

relative sizes A depth perception cue in which we perceive the image of the smaller of two similar objects to be farther away.

relaxation training A method of coping with stress in which subjects are encouraged to relax and minimize their physiological reactions to stressful events.

relearning A method of measuring retention in which the subject relearns previously learned material. If relearning is faster than original learning, then retention has occurred.

reliability The ability of a test to measure the same thing in a given person more than once and get the same, or a similar, answer.

Remote Associates Test (RAT) One of many tests designed to assess creativity, which is defined as the ability to bring remote elements into new and useful combinations.

repetition/rehearsal Practice.

repression A defense mechanism by which we avoid unpleasant or anxiety-producing thoughts by blocking them out of consciousness.

resistance stage The second of Seyle's three stages of response to stressful situations.

respondent conditioning *Classical conditioning.*

response bias In psychological testing, refers to ways people may respond to tests that invalidate the results. Examples are people tending to say no to almost everything, or people trying to give the response they think will make them look good.

Restricted Environmental Stimulation Technique (REST) *Sensory deprivation.*

retention The remembering of learned material, as demonstrated by tests of recall, recognition, and relearning.

reticular activating system (RAS) A network of neuronal fibers that begins in the hindbrain, extends through the midbrain, and sends fibers up into the forebrain. Its primary function is to regulate levels of arousal.

retina The light-sensitive surface of the inside of the eye.

retrieval The processes by which we pull learned information out of memory storage.

retroactive inhibition Interference in memory due to subsequent learning.

retrograde amnesia The inability to remember events that are immediately followed by an electroconvulsive shock.

reversibility The ability to understand that operations such as pouring liquid from one size container to another of a different size not only do not change the quantity of liquid, but that the operation of pouring the liquid back into the original container is also possible (reversible) without altering the quantity involved. According to Piaget, understanding of this concept develops during the concrete operations period.

reward Any stimulus that produces satisfaction or increases the likelihood of a response.

reward training A type of instrumental conditioning in which the subject is rewarded for making a particular response.

rhyme Correspondence in terminal sounds.

rod Visual receptor on the retina that enables us to see in conditions of very dim light or darkness but that does not enable us to see color.

role The behavior expected of a person in a particular situation.

role playing Method of accounting for many so-called hypnotic phenomena espoused by Orne who argues that many subjects of hypnotism experiments act the way they feel a truly hypnotized person would act in order to please the hypnotist.

role reversal The expectation of some parents that the child serve as a source of comfort and affection. Many abusing parents exhibit this characteristic.

rules of grammar The rules that govern the ordering and positioning of sounds, morphemes, and words into meaningful sentences.

sample In statistics, a relatively small number of cases taken from a population.

sanguine One of Hoppocrates's ancient types of personality—an optimistic person, owing to the influence of blood in the body.

saturation The degree to which a particular color is either mixed or pure.

scalloping effect A phenomenon that occurs in a fixed-interval schedule where the subject pauses after reinforcement and will only begin to speed up the response rate as the end of the interval approaches.

scanning techniques Recently developed methods of observing activity within the brains of living animals.

scatter plot A statistical graph that represents an individual's score on two variables. The advantage to using such a graphic representation is that the degree and direction of a correlation are readily identifiable.

schedule of reinforcement A schedule indicating when or how often a subject will be reinforced.

schema (schemata) The organized body of information a person has about a particular object, concept, or event that can aid as well as disrupt recall.

schizophrenia A class of psychotic disorders characterized by disturbances in thinking, such as hallucinations and delusions, peculiar patterns of speech, and often a flattening of emotion.

school psychology The branch of counseling psychology that deals particularly with the social and educational guidance of elementary and secondary school students.

Schwann cells Cells that form the myelin sheath in the peripheral nervous system.

secondary aging Physical changes due to disease, abuse of alcohol and drugs, or disuse of the muscles of the body.

secondary drinking Drinking motivated by factors other than tissue need, such as to wash food down, or to be sociable.

secondary process thinking According to Freud's theory of personality, the ego's attempts to satisfy the id's demands through logical and realistic thinking.

secondary reinforcer A neutral stimulus (such as money) that, through repeated pairings with a primary reinforcer (such as food), acquires reinforcing properties of its own.

second level inference An inference that goes just beyond the immediately observable, verifiable facts, such as generalizing on the basis of observation or testing to other situations.

selective adaptation An experimental effect that shows that our sensory processes are not always perfect.

selective approach The tendency to seek information that supports one's own point of view on an issue.

selective attention The concept that since we cannot attend to all of the stimuli presented at any given moment, we selectively choose those we do attend to.

selective avoidance The tendency to avoid information that is inconsistent or opposed to one's own point of view on an issue.

selective breeding A technique for studying effects of heredity in lower animals by selecting a behavior for study, and then breeding animals that show that behavior over several generations.

self-actualization The final phase in Maslow's need hierarchy. A person at this level rejoices in the experience of living and is in tune with the meaning and mystery of life. Very few of us reach this stage.

self-actualizing tendency *Actualizing tendency.*

self-concept According to Rogers, all out thoughts, ideas, and judgments about ourselves; our perception of ourselves.

self-control therapy A behavior therapy technique in which the client and therapist set up realistic goals, behaviors, and methods of self-reinforcement designed to eliminate the client's undesirable habit.

self-defeating Tendency to block one's own attainment of goals.

self-efficacy A major organizing principle of personality and behavior, according to Bandura. Refers to the individual's beliefs in his or her ability to accomplish desired outcomes.

self-fulfilling prophecy Behaving in ways that are consistent with what we believe others expect of us. If others indicate that we are not too bright, we fulfill their "prophecy" by behaving in less intelligent ways.

self-instructional technique A cognitive-behavior modification technique in which the subject controls and directs his own thinking and behavior.

self-psychology A modern variety of psychodynamic theory and therapy that emphasizes the development and functioning of the self, in contrast to the orthodox Freudian emphasis on instincts and the id, ego, and superego.

self-talk A component of self-instruction training that involves mentally conversing with oneself about alternate courses of action before proceeding.

self-treatment Behavior modification in which rewards are administered by the subject.

semantic generalization The ability of words to evoke the same response as similar words.

semantic memory The storing in memory of facts, concepts, and so forth, that are not temporally ordered.

semantic-network model An interconnected arrangement of items stored in memory. For example, the concept of "canary" conjures up an image of "bird," then "animal," along with all the characteristics associated with those words.

semicircular canals Bony structures filled with fluid that moves as the head moves and initiates messages to the brain regarding the movement of the body.

sensation The process by which sensory information is brought into the organism through the senses.

sense of trust The infant's development of a secure and loving attachment with parents, which according to Erikson is the central social and emotional task the infant faces. Accomplishment of this task constitutes stage one of Erikson's theory of psychosocial development.

sensorimotor stage The first stage of Piaget's theory of cognitive development, which occurs during the first two years of life when children interact with the world through sensory and motor activities, acquiring the concept of object permanence and the ability to form a mental picture of an object.

sensory adaptation The concept that sensory receptors "get used to" and stop responding to constant, unchanging stimulation.

sensory cells Specialized neurons that are stimulated by some form of external stimulus, such as light, sound, or heat, rather than by synaptic transmission.

sensory cortex Portion of the cerebral cortex (that is, the occipital lobe, the temporal lobe, and the parietal lobe) concerned with sensory functions.

sensory deprivation The absence of normal stimulation for long periods of time, which leads to confusion, hallucinations, frustration, and irritability.

sensory memory A memory storehouse in which information decays within a very brief period of time (perhaps half a second).

sensory neuron A neuron that brings in information from the sense organs and carries it toward the brain. Also known as an *afferent neuron*.

sensory receptors Specialized sensory nerve endings that respond only to certain types of energy, such as sound or light waves.

sensory-seeking behaviors Behaviors that have the effect of increasing sensory stimulation.

separation anxiety The emotional distress experienced by an infant (beginning at about the age of 6 months) when the child loses sight of the mother.

serial learning tasks A verbal learning technique in which a subject is presented with a list of words and asked to recall them in a given order.

serotonin One of several probable transmitter substances found in the brain and spinal cord and believed to inhibit neuron firing.

sex hormones Hormones secreted by the adrenal glands (including androgen and estrogen) that promote development of secondary sex characteristics and maintain sexual functioning.

sex-related aggression Aggression of a sexual nature, such as rape.

sex-role stereotypes The traditional attitudes held by our society that men are aggressive, dominant, and active, while women are passive, submissive, and gentle. This limits both men and women by specifying the activities in which each sex should or should not participate.

shape constancy The fact that an object is perceived as retaining its shape even though the actual shape has changed on our retinal image as a result of the movement of the object.

shaping An instrumental conditioning technique in which closer and closer approximations to a desired response are reinforced.

short-term memory A memory storehouse from which information will be lost within approximately one minute unless it is maintained by rehearsal. What you are thinking of right now is your short-term memory.

significant difference In the statistical sense, the likelihood that a given difference will occur by chance less than 5 in 100 times.

sign stimulus The stimulus identified by ethologists as responsible for releasing the reaction-specific energy. Sign stimuli are not dependent on learning.

similarity The tendency to perceive as a group visual elements that are similar to one another.

simultaneous classical conditioning A classical conditioning procedure in which the CS and UCS are presented at the same time and usually are terminated at the same time.

sine wave A continuous curving line that represents a simple tone.

single-blind technique An experimental technique in which the subjects do not know to which condition they belong, but the researchers do.

situation-specific behaviors Behaviors that are confined to only particular situations.

situational attribution Attribution of behavior to external causes such as luck, social pressure, or the influence of specific circumstances.

size constancy The tendency to perceive the size of an object as unchanged despite changes in the viewing distance.

skewed distribution A markedly asymmetrical frequency distribution with a long or pronounced "tail."

skin sensors Several different cell structures that interact to activate the four basic skin sensations: pressure, pain, warmth, and cold.

sleep apnea The sleep disorder caused by a failure of the diaphragm to contract while the individual is asleep.

sleep deprivation Forced lack of sleep.

smooth muscle The type of muscle found in blood vessels, stomach, intestinal walls, and other internal organs whose actions are controlled by the autonomic nervous system.

social cognition The social psychological study of how perceptions, thoughts, and feelings are influenced by social encounters.

social impact theory The theory that offers three basic propositions that are used to examine and explain the impact of groups on the individual.

social psychology The branch of psychology concerned with all aspects of human interaction, including feelings, thoughts, and actions.

social support The arrangement of formal and informal relationships with individuals and groups through which a person receives emotional, cognitive, and material assistance to overcome stressful experiences.

sociobiology A controversial school of thought that holds that social behavior is genetically determined.

somatic division Part of the peripheral nervous system that is composed of afferent and efferent neurons.

somnambulits Sleepwalkers.

sound wave A change among air molecules, created by alternations of compression and rarefaction, which the ear detects as a sound.

sound wave complexity See *complexity*.

sound wave frequency See *frequency*.

spatial memory Memory for physical locations and physical relationships.

species-specific defense reaction (SSDR) The innate, automatic behaviors that occur when a sudden or novel stimulus appears. SSDRs apparently limit certain kinds of learning (escape and avoidance, for example).

sperm The male sex cell.

spinal cord A thick cable of nerve fibers that runs up the interior of the spinal column to the brain, carrying efferent and afferent messages. Together, the brain and the spinal cord form the central nervous system.

split-brain experiments Experiments involving people whose brains are split at the corpus callosum, leaving them with two unconnected cerebral hemispheres. These studies suggest that language ability is located in the left hemisphere while the right hemisphere deals mainly with nonverbal activity.

spontaneous recovery The phenomenon that an extinguished response will, with rest, recover some of its strength in classical, instrumental, and verbal conditioning situations.

spreading-activation model A model of memory that emphasizes the interconnections among stored bits of information.

SQ3R method A study technique—survey, question, read, recite, review.

standard deviation The square root of the population variance, or σ, which reflects the average amount by which scores deviate from the mean of the distribution.

standard score A Z score.

state-dependent memory effect The observation that memory seems to be affected by and dependent upon the state and/or context in which the original learning occurred.

statistic A numerical quantity summarizing some characteristic of a sample.

steady states Balanced bodily conditions maintained by homeostatic mechanisms.

stepfamilies A reconstituted family brought about by a remarriage involving children of one or both partners.

stereopsis A process by which the brain combines two images so that we experience one three-dimensional sensation rather than two different two-dimensional images.

stereotype The belief or attitude that all the members of a group possess certain physical and/or psychological characteristics.

stigmatization The effect that once a diagnostic label has been given someone, people may react negatively or fearfully, regardless of the person's actual behavior.

stimulation The activating impingement of a stimulus on a receptor.

stimulus (1) Any form of physical energy that activates a receptor. (2) Any event, internal or external, that activates an organism.

stimulus generalization The phenomenon that if a particular response is conditioned to one stimulus, similar stimuli will tend to elicit the same response.

stimulus generalization gradient A graph revealing the fact that if a response is connected to one stimulus, then similar stimuli will tend to elicit the same response.

stirrup A bone located in the middle ear that conducts sound vibrations from the anvil to the oval window.

storage The maintenance of learned information in memory over time.

stories To-be-remembered information inbedded in prose material.

stress The general response that the body makes to demands placed upon it, which can create physical as well as mental disorder.

stress-diathesis perspective An approach to psychopathology that argues that disorder results from some kind of predisposition (diathesis) that may be genetic or psychological, interacting with some kind of stressful conditions. Disorder requires both to occur.

stroboscopic movement A form of apparent movement in which stationary stimuli are presented sequentially, resulting in visually perceived movement.

structural approach A theory of memory that suggests that we organize, interconnect, and structure information in our memory stores.

structured or semistructured interviews A personality interview in which all subjects or patients are asked the same set of questions in the same order.

subjective organization (SO) The tendency to recall items in the same order, even when they are presented over and over again in different orders.

sublimation A defense mechanism by which we transform our frustrated urges into some more socially acceptable form.

superego According to Freud's theory of personality, the part of our personality that is our conscience, representing our internalization of society's moral and ethical rules about right and wrong.

supernormal stimuli A sign stimulus that exceeds, in some critical way, the normal sign stimulus.

suppression A mechanism by which we consciously avoid thinking about something unpleasant.

surface structure The actual words used in a sentence, as contrasted with the speaker's intended meaning.

surgical ablation The destruction of particular brain sites in living animals by cutting or removing of neural tissue for the purpose of brain study.

symbols Any object, sign, or word that stands for something other than itself. The ability to use symbols represents a higher level of cognitive development.

sympathetic system Part of the autonomic division composed of interconnected ganglia, forming a long vertical chain on each side of the spinal cord. The sympathetic system helps prepare us for emergency action.

symptom substitution According to Freud, when a therapist eliminates an individual's symptoms but neglects the underlying cause, new symptoms will appear in their place.

synapse The junction point where a nerve impulse passes from the axon of one cell to the dendrite of the next cell, across the synaptic gap.

synaptic gap The space between the axon of one cell and the dendrite of another neuron.

synaptic knob A bulbous structure found at the tip of each strand of the end brush, containing synaptic vesicles.

synaptic transmission The movement of an impulse across a synaptic gap.

synaptic vesicle A small structure that functions as a storage container for neurotransmitters, found in each synaptic knob.

systematic desensitization A behavior therapy technique used to treat phobic reactions. A person is presented with successively more fear-evoking stimuli while in a state of deep relaxation. Through repeated presentation of the CS without the UCS that caused the fear to be conditioned, the fear subsides.

taste-aversion study An experiment in which dislike of a particular taste is established by pairing that taste with noxious stimulation.

taste buds The receptors for the sense of taste, located along the sides and the back of the tongue, as well as in the throat.

tautology Circular reasoning. In personality testing, an example would be labeling a particular trait on the basis of some behavior and then claiming that the trait is the cause of the behavior.

teaching machine An instrument devised by Skinner to improve classroom teaching methods. The machine enables students to learn at their own pace and receive immediate reinforcement.

telegraphic speech A type of speech used by children in which unimportant words are left out.

telepathy The possibility that thought can be transferred from one individual to another—often called "mind reading."

television literacy Understanding the meaning of television techniques, such as close ups, zooming, and parallel processing of multiple story lines. Also refers to distinguishing between social reality and the make-believe reality of television.

template-matching hypothesis A theory that states that patterns are recognized because stimuli are matched, at the brain level, with a fixed standard form, or template. For example, the gable of a house is matched with an abstract triangle stored in memory.

temporal lobe Section of the cortex involved with hearing.

teratogenic effect Physical malformations to the developing fetus caused by stimulants such as alcohol, nicotine, certain drugs, and caffeine.

territorial aggression A tendency to drive strangers out of one's territory.

testosterone A male sex hormone that triggers puberty as its level in the blood increases.

test-retest reliability A method used to determine the reliability of a test by testing the same individual twice. Reliability is determined if the scores obtained on both tests are similar.

texture gradient A cue used in depth perception in which nearby textured surfaces appear rougher than distant surfaces where the fine detail is not visible.

thalamus Portion of the forebrain that relays incoming sensory information to the cortex.

Thematic Apperception Test (TAT) A projective test most often used to measure achievement motivation.

theory of repression The hypothesis, proposed by Freud, that unpleasant impulses and thoughts are kept out of consciousness.

theta activity Electrical brain activity that shows relatively slow and high-amplitude waves.

things-to-do list (TTD list) A technique found to be useful in alleviating everyday depression in which an individual makes and then follows a list, with the result that a sense of accomplishment is achieved.

third level inference An inference that goes well beyond observable data to speculate about underlying meanings. In testing, forming a complex theory of an individual's personality from an inkblot test involves third level inferences. Because they are far-removed from actual data, such conclusions may be wrong or biased.

thought broadcasting The delusion that one's thoughts are being broadcast (outloud or through the radio) so that others can hear them.

thought disturbances A general term for peculiar thinking and communication patterns that typically accompany schizophrenia.

thought insertion The delusion that ideas that are not one's own are being placed in one's mind.

thyroid An endocrine gland whose main function is the regulation of metabolism.

thyroxin A hormone secreted by the thyroid gland whose primary effect is to determine the body's metabolism.

timbre The psychological experience of sound wave complexity.

time-out technique A behavior-modification technique in which mild punishment is manipulated by requiring the subject to stop the unwanted behavior.

tip-of-the-tongue phenomenon A phenomenon in which stored information cannot quite be retrieved. You know that you know the information (it is stored), but you cannot recall it at a particular moment because retrieval is blocked.

token economy A behavior-modification technique used primarily in institutional settings in which desirable behaviors are immediately reinforced

with tokens that may later be exchanged for primary rewards such as food, cigarettes, and games.

tolerance With alcohol and certain other forms of chemical dependency, refers to the need after frequent use for progressively more of the substance to achieve the desired effect.

trace classical conditioning A classical conditioning procedure in which the CS is turned on and off before the UCS is turned on, leaving an empty interval between CS offset and UCS onset.

tract A cluster of axons, and sometimes dendrites, found in the brain or spinal cord.

trait approach A personality theory that states that an individual's personality can be best understood by locating that person on a series of crucial personality dimensions.

tranquilizers Drugs, such as the benzodiazepines, which help reduce anxiety and relax muscles.

transduce Conversion of stimulus energy into electrochemical signals that the brain can use.

transference The concept that the client has thoughts and feelings about the therapist during psychoanalysis that are similar to thoughts and feelings had as a child toward one's parents.

transformational grammar The idea introduced by Chomsky that deep structure meaning can be expressed in different ways at the surface structure level (the sentence) by applying different transformational rules that change the sentence but not the meaning.

transformational rules The rules described by Chomsky to change deep structure meaning into the surface structure features of a sentence.

trial and error A process used in problem solving by which we try one response after another, discarding each, until we find a suitable solution.

trichromatic The quality of having three color systems: red-green, blue-yellow, and black-white.

trichromatic theory See *Young-Helmholtz theory.*

Turner's syndrome An abnormal genetic condition in which one X chromosome (rather than two) is found in the twenty-third pair.

twin study Experimental technique involving the companion of monozygotic and dizygotic twins to determine the effects of heredity on human behavior.

two-factor theory One explanation for the difficulty people experience in unlearning a phobia. First, they become fearful in the presence of the phobic object, and second, the relief felt by avoiding it reinforces this avoidance response.

two-word utterances An early stage in language development in which the infant puts together two-word sentences to express an idea.

Type I (maintenance) rehearsal Practice designed to keep information in short-term store.

Type II (elaborative) rehearsal Practice designed to move information into long-term store.

Type A personality High-strung personality type likely to suffer a heart attack.

Type B personality Easy-going personality type less likely to have a heart attack.

UCR An *unconditioned response*.

UCS An *unconditioned stimulus*.

ulcerative colitis A stress-related psychophysiological disorder involving severe inflammation and bleeding of the large intestine and rectum.

unconditional positive regard An essential ingredient of the therapeutic relationship, according to Rogers characterized by the therapist's maintaining an attitude of acceptance, caring, and nonjudgment toward the client.

unconditioned response (UCR) The response always elicited by the unconditioned stimulus in a classical conditioning experiment.

unconditioned stimulus (UCS) A stimulus that consistently elicits an identifiable response prior to a classical conditioning experiment.

unconscious According to Freud, impulses within our personality that are beyond our awareness but that affect our behavior nonetheless.

unconscious coping methods Efforts we make to alleviate anxiety without being fully aware of what we are doing.

unconscious motivation The theory that we are often unaware of the real reasons for our behavior; what we do is directed by motives inaccessible to our consciousness.

unimodal distribution A frequency distribution having only one peak.

unipolar depression Depression occurring in the absence of any history or symptoms of mania or hypomania.

unstructured interviews Personality interviews for which there was no prior plan and from which no scores may be derived.

vacuum reaction The occurrence of a fixed-action pattern after prolonged lack of any stimulation.

validity The ability of a test or instrument to measure what it is designed to measure.

variability A measure of how much the scores in a frequency distribution differ from one another.

variable Any condition or event that changes or varies.

variable-interval schedule A schedule of reinforcement in which the time interval changes from reinforcement to reinforcement, producing a steady response rate.

variable-ratio schedule A schedule of reinforcement in which the number of required responses made by the subject varies.

variance The most widely used measure of variability, variance is based on all the scores rather than only the extreme scores. Population variance is symbolized by σ^2 (sigma squared); sample variance is symbolized by s^2.

ventromedial hypothalamus (VMH) Segment of the hypothalamus (a small structure in the brain) that appears to be a motivational and emotional control center; electrical stimulation of the ventromedial hypothalamus inhibits eating.

verbal conditioning A reward training technique in which the experimenter reinforces only certain words spoken by a subject, so that the subject begins to say these words more often.

verbal learning The human ability to learn and recall verbal materials.

verb phrase A part of a sentence consisting of a verb plus a noun phrase.

vestibular sacs Bony structures filled with a gelatinous substance that moves as the head moves and initiates messages to the brain regarding movement of the head.

visual receptors Two types of specialized neurons in the retina—rods and cones.

volumetric thirst Thirst caused by reduced blood volume.

voluntary actions Movements of the skeletal muscles that are controlled by the central nervous system.

wavelength The distance between two corresponding points on the sine wave, which increases as frequency decreases.

Weber's fraction The principle that states that the amount of stimulus change detectable by an invididual is proportional to the intensity of the stimulus.

wish fulfillment According to Freud's theory of personality, a process by which the id forms mental images or hallucinations of the objects or acts that will satisfy its demands.

withdrawal Physical discomfort associated with termination of abuse of addictive drugs.

Yerkes-Dodson principle The principle of motivation that states that the most effective level of arousal will depend on the difficulty of the task.

Young-Helmholtz theory A theory of color vision postulated by Young and later modified by Helmholtz that states that we have three different types of cones, each most sensitive to one particular wavelength. Colors are produced by the stimulation of one or a combination of different cones.

Z score A score representing the deviation from the mean in standard deviation units.

zygote A cell formed by the union of two sex cells at the time of fertilization.

References

Aarons, L. (1976) Sleep-associated instruction. *Psychological Bulletin, 83,* 1–40.

Abramson, L. Y., Seligman, M. E. P., & Teasdale, J. D. (1978) Learned helplessness in humans: Critique and reformulation. *Journal of Abnormal Psychology, 87,* 49–74.

Achenbach, T. (1985) Assessment of anxiety in children. In H. Tuma & J. Maser (Eds.), *Anxiety and the Anxiety Disorders.* Hillsdale, NJ.: Erlbaum.

Ader, R. (1985) Conditioned taste aversions and immunopharmacology. *Annals of the New York Academy of Sciences, 63,* 247–251.

Adolph, E. F. (1941) The internal environment and behavior: Water content. *American Journal of Psychiatry, 97,* 1365–1373.

Adorno, T. W., Frenkel-Brunswik, E., Levinson, D. J., & Sanford, R. N. (1950) *The authoritarian personality.* New York: Harper.

Aids: Sorting out truths from myths. (1987), January 12) *U.S. News and World Report,* pp. 66–67.

Ainsworth, M. D. S. (1980) Attachment and child abuse. In G. Gerbner, C. J. Ross, & E. Zigler (Eds.), *Child abuse: An agenda for action.* New York: Oxford University Press.

Ainsworth, M. D. S., Blehar, M., Waters, E., & Wall, S. (1978) *Patterns of attachment.* Hillsdale, NJ: Erlbaum.

Ajzen, I., & Fishbein, M. (1980) *Understanding attitudes and predicting social behavior.* Englewood Cliffs, NJ: Prentice-Hall.

Alford, R. (1980) The structure of human experience: Expectancy and effect; the case of humor. *Journal of Social and Biological Structures, 3,* 247–254.

Alicke, M. D., Smith, R. H., & Klotz, M. L. (1986) Judgments of physical attractiveness: The role of faces and bodies. *Personality and Social Psychology Bulletin, 12,* 381–389.

Alloy, L. B., & Abramson, L. Y. (1979) Judgments of contingency in depressed and nondepressed students: Sadder but wiser? *Journal of Experimental Psychology: General, 108,* 441–485.

Alloy, L. B., & Bersh, P. J. (1979) Partial control and learned helplessness in rats: Control over shock intensity prevents interference with subsequent escape. *Animal Learning and Behavior, 7,* 157–164.

Allport, G. W. (1954) *The nature of prejudice.* Reading, MA: Addison-Wesley.

Allport, G. W. (1985) The historical background of social psychology. In G. Lindsey & E. Aronson (Eds.), *Handbook of Social Psychology* (3rd ed., Vol. 1, pp. 1–46). New York: Random House.

Altemeier, W. A., O'Connor, S., Sherrod, K. B., & Tucker, D. (1986) Outcome of abuse during childhood among pregnant low-income women. *Child Abuse & Neglect, 10,* 319–330.

Altman, L. L., (1975) *The dream in psychoanalysis.* New York: International Universities Press.

Alvarez, A. (1972) *The savage God.* New York: Random House.

Amato, P. R. (1983) Helping behavior in urban and rural environments: Field studies based on a taxonomic organization of helping episodes. *Journal of Personality and Social Psychology, 45,* 571–586.

American Psychiatric Association (1987) *Diagnostic and statistical manual of mental disorders* (3rd ed.). Washington, DC: APA.

America's most troublesome sex diseases. (1986, June 2) *U.S. News and World Report,* pp. 54–55.

American Psychological Association (1977) *Ethical standards of psychologists.* Washington, DC: Author.

Amoore, J. E., Johnston, J. W., & Rubin, M. (1964, February) The stereochemical theory of odor. *Scientific American, 210,* 42–49.

Anderson, D. C., Crowell, C. R., Cunningham, C. L., & Lupo, J. V. (1979) Behavior during shock exposure as a determinant of subsequent interference with shuttle box escape—Avoidance learning in the rat. *Journal of Experimental Psychology: Animal Behavior Processes, 5,* 243–257.

Anderson, D. R., Lorch, E. P., Field, D. E., Collins, P. A., & Nathan, J. G. (1986) Television viewing at home: Age trends in visual attention and time with TV. *Child Development, 57,* 1024–1033.

Anderson, J. R., & Bower, G. H. (1974) A propositional theory of recognition memory. *Memory and Cognition, 2,* 406–412.

Anderson, J. R. (1983) A spreading activation model of memory. *Journal of Verbal Learning and Verbal Behavior, 22,* 261–295.

Anderson, J. R. (1985) *Cognitive psychol-*

ogy and its implications. (2nd ed.). New York: Freeman.

Anderson, M. L., & McConnell, R. A. (1961) Fantasy testing for ESP in a fourth and fifth grade class. *Journal of Psychology, 52,* 491–503.

Anderson, R. C. & Picket, J. W. (1978) Recall of previously unrecallable information following a shift in perspective. *Journal of Verbal Learning and Verbal Behavior, 17,* 1–12.

Anisman, H. (1978) Neurochemical changes elicited by stress: Behavioral correlates. In H. Anisman & G. Bignami (Eds.), *Psychopharmacology of aversively motivated behavior.* New York: Plenum.

APA Membership Register (1987) Washington DC: American Psychological Association.

Aronson, E., Stephan, C., Sikes, J., Blancy, N., & Snapp, M. (1978) *The jigsaw classroom.* Beverly Hills, CA: Sage.

Asch, S. (1955) Opinions and social pressure. *Scientific American, 11,* 32.

Asch, S. (1956) Studies of independence and conformity. I. A minority of one against a unanimous majority. *Psychological Monographs, 70* (Whole No. 416).

Aserinsky, E., & Kleitman, N. (1953) Regularly occurring periods of eye mobility and concomitant phenomena during sleep. *Science, 118,* 273–274.

Atkinson, J. W. (1983) *Personality, motivation, and action.* New York: Praeger.

Atkinson, K., MacWhinney, B., & Stoel, C. (1970) An experiment on recognition of babbling. *Papers and reports on child language development.* Stanford, CA: Stanford University Press.

Atkinson, R. C. (1975) Mnemotechnics in second-language learning. *American Psychologist, 30,* 821–828.

Atkinson, R. C., & Shiffrin, R. M. (1971) The control of short-term memory. *Scientific American, 224,* 82–90.

Atthowe, J. M., & Krasner, L. (1968) Preliminary report on the application of contingent reinforcement procedures (token economy) on a "chronic" psychiatric ward. *Journal of Abnormal Psychology, 73,* 37–43.

Atwood M. E., Masson, M. E. S., & Polson, P. G. (1980) Further explorations with a process model for water jug problems. *Memory and Cognition, 8,* 181–192.

Auerback, S. M., Kendall, P. C., Cuttler, H. F., & Levitt, N. R. (1976) Anxiety, locus of control, type of preparatory information, and adjustment to dental surgery. *Journal of Consulting and Clinical Psychology, 44,* 809–818.

Avery, D., & Winokur, G. (1977) The efficacy of electroconvulsive therapy and antidepressants in depression. *Biological Psychiatry, 12,* 507–523.

Ax, A. F. (1953) The physiological differentiation between fear and anger in humans. *Psychosomatic Medicine, 15,* 433–442.

Bacon, S. D. (1973) Highway crashes, alcohol problems, and programs for social control. In P. G. Bourne (Ed.), *Alcoholism: Progress in research and treatment.* New York: Academic Press.

Baddeley, A. D., & Patterson, K. E. (1971) The relation between long-term and short-term memory. *British Medical Bulletin, 27,* 237–242.

Baddeley, A. D., & Warrington, E. K. (1970) Amnesia and the distinction between long- and short-term memory. *Journal of Verbal Learning and Verbal Behavior, 9,* 1976–1989.

Badger, E. (1981) Effects of parent education program on teenage mothers and their offspring. In K. G. Scott, T. Field, & E. Robertson (Eds.), *Teenage parents and their offspring.* New York: Grune & Stratton.

Baer, D. M. (1966) An age-irrelevant concept of development. Paper presented at the annual meeting of the American Psychological Association, New York.

Baldessarini, R. J. (1977) *Chemotherapy in psychiatry.* Cambridge, MA: Harvard University Press.

Baldwin, W., & Cain, V. S. (1980) The children of teenage parents. *Family Planning Perspectives, 12,* 34–43.

Baltes, P. P., & Labouvie, G. V. (1973) Adult development of intellectual performance: Description, explanation, modification. In C. Eisdorfer & M. P. Lawton (Eds.), *The psychology of adult development and aging.* Washington, DC: American Psychological Association.

Bandura, A. (1969) *Principles of behavior modification.* New York: Holt.

Bandura, A. (1973) *Aggression: A social learning analysis.* Englewood Cliffs, NJ: Prentice-Hall.

Bandura, A. (1977) Behavior theory and the models of man. In D. P. Kimble (ed.), *Contrast and controversy in modern psychology.* Santa Monica, CA: Goodyear.

Bandura, A. (1977) *Social learning theory.* Englewood Cliffs, NJ: Prentice-Hall.

Bandura, A. (1978) Reflections on self-efficacy. In S. Rachman (Ed.), *Advances in behaviour research and ther-apy, Vol. 1.* Elmsford, NY: Pergamon Press.

Bandura, A. (1982) The self-efficacy and mechanisms of agency. *American Psychologist, 37,* 122–147.

Bandura, A., Blanchard, E. B., & Ritter, R. (1969) The relative efficacy of desensitization and modeling approaches for inducing behavioral, affective, and attitudinal changes. *Journal of Personality and Social Psychology, 13,* 173–199.

Barber, T. X. (1970) *LSD, marijuana, yoga, and hypnosis.* Chicago: Aldine.

Bard, P. A. (1928) A diencephalic mechanism for the expression of rage with special reference to the sympathetic nervous system. *American Journal of Physiology, 84,* 490–515.

Barglow, P., Vaughn, B. E., & Molitor, N. (1987) *Child Development, 58,* 945–954.

Barlow, D. H., & Wolfe, B. E. (1981) Behavioral approaches to anxiety disorders: A report on the NIMH-SUNY, Albany research conference. *Journal of Consulting and Clinical Psychology, 49,* 448–454.

Barnet, A. B., Lodge, A., & Armington, J. C. (1965) Electroretinogram in newborn human infants. *Science,* (Whole No. 3670), 651–654.

Baron, M., Risch, N., Hamburger, R., Mandel, B., Kushner, S., Newman, M., Drumer, D., & Belmaker, R. H. (1987) Genetic linkage between X chromosome markers and bipolar affective illness. *Nature, 326,* 289–292.

Baron, R. A., & Byrne, D. (1984) *Social psychology.* Boston: Allyn & Bacon.

Barrera, M. E., & Maurer, D. (1981) Discrimination of strangers by the three-month-old. *Child Development, 52,* 558–563.

Bartlett, F. C. (1932) *Remembering.* Cambridge: Cambridge University Press.

Bassuk, E. L., & Gerson, S. (1978) Deinstitutionalization and mental health services. *Scientific American, 238,* 46–53.

Bates, J. E. (1980) The concept of difficult temperament. *Merrill-Palmer Quarterly, 26,* 299–319.

Bateson, P. (1979) Brief exposure to a novel stimulus during imprinting in chicks, and its influence on subsequent preferences. *Animal Learning and Behavior, 7,* 259–262.

Batson, C. D., & Gray, R. A. (1981) Religious orientation and helping behavior: Responding to one's own or to the victim's needs? *Journal of Social and Personality Psychology, 40,* 511–520.

Bayley, N. (1965) Comparisons of mental and motor test scores for ages 1–15 months by sex, birth order, race, geographical location, and education of parents. *Child Development, 36,* 379–411.

Bear, M. F., Cooper, L. N., & Ebner, F. F. (1987) A physiological basis for a theory of synaptic modification. *Science, 237,* 42–47.

Beck, A. (1967) *Depression: Clinical, experimental, and theoretical aspects.* York: Harper.

Beck, A. (1976) *Cognitive therapy and the emotional disorders.* New York: International Universities Press.

Beck, A. T., Rush, A. J., Shaw, B. F., & Emery, G. (1979) *Cognitive therapy of depression.* New York: Guilford Press.

Beck, J., Elsner, A., & Silverstein, C. (1977) Position uncertainty and the perception of apparent movement. *Perception and Psychophysics, 21,* 33–38.

Begg, I. (1978) Imagery and organization in memory: Instructional effects. *Memory and Cognition, 6,* 174–183.

Begg, I. (1979) Trace loss and the recognition failure of unrecalled words. *Memory and Cognition, 7,* 113–123.

Beidleman, W. B. (1981) Group assertive training in correctional settings: A review and methodological critique. *Journal of Offender Counselling, Services & Rehabilitation, 6,* 69–87.

Bellack, A. S., & Hersen, M. (1977) Self-report inventories in behavioral assessment. In J. D. Cone & R. P. Hawkins (Eds.), *Behavioral assessment: New directions in clinical psychology.* New York: Brunner/Mazel.

Belmont, L., Cohen, P., Dryfoos, J., Stein, Z., & Zayac, S. (1981) Maternal age and children's intelligence. In K. G. Scott, T. Field, & E. Robertson (Eds.), *Teenage parents and their offspring.* New York: Grune & Stratton.

Belsky, J. (1986) Infant day care: A cause for concern? *Bulletin of the National Center for Clinical Infant Programs. 6*(5), 1–7.

Bem, S. L. (1974) The measurement of psychological adrogyny. *Journal of Consulting and Clinical Psychology, 42,* 155–162.

Bem, S. L., Martyna, W., & Watson, C. (1976) Sex typing and androgyny: Further explorations of the expressive domain. *Journal of Personality and Social Psychology, 33,* 48–54.

Benjamin, L. T., Langley, J. F., & Hall, R. J. (1979, December) Santa now and then. *Psychology Today, 13*(7), 36–44.

Bennett, T. L. (1977) *Brain and behavior.* Monterey, CA: Brooks/Cole.

Benson, H. (1975) *The relaxation response.* New York: Morrow.

Benson, H., Kotch, J. B., Crassweller, K. D., & Greenwood, M. M. (1977) Historical and clinical considerations of the relaxation response. *American Scientist, 65,* 441–445.

Bergin, A. E., & Lambert, M. J. (1978) The evaluation of therapeutic outcomes. In S. Garfield and A. E. Bergin (Eds.), *Handbook of psychotherapy and behavior change* (2nd ed.). New York: Wiley.

Bergman, T., Haith, M., and Mann, L. (1971, March) Development of eye contact and facial scanning in infants. Paper presented at the meeting of the Society for Research in Child Development, Minneapolis.

Berlyne, D. E. (1958) The influence of complexity and novelty in visual figures on orienting responses. *Journal of Experimental Psychology, 55,* 289–296.

Berlyne, D. E. (1969) The reward-value of indifferent stimulation. In J. T. Tapp (Ed.), *Reinforcement and behavior.* New York: Academic Press.

Berman, J. S., & Norton, N. C. (1985) Does professional training make a therapist more effective? *Psychological Bulletin, 98,* 401–407.

Berndt, T. J. (1979) Developmental changes in conformity to peers and parents. *Developmental Psychology 16,* 608–616.

Bernstein, I. L. (1985) Learned food aversions in the progression of cancer and its treatment. In N. S. Braveman & P. Bronstein (Eds.), *Experimental assessments and clinical applications of conditioned food aversions.* New York: New York Academy of Sciences.

Berntson, G. G., Hughes, H. C., & Beattie, M. S. (1976) A comparison of hypothalamically induced biting attack with natural predatory behavior in the cat. *Journal of Comparative and Physiological Psychology, 90,* 167–178.

Berrueta-Clement, J. R. (1984) *Changed lives: The effects of the Perry preschool program on youths through age 19.* Ypsilanti, MI: High Scope Press.

Best, D. L., Williams, J. E., Cloud, J. M., Davis, S. W., Robertson, L. S., Edwards, J. R., Giles, H., & Fowles, J. (1977) Development of sex-trait stereotypes among young children in the United States, England, and Ireland. *Child Development, 48,* 1375–1384.

Best, J. B. (1986) *Cognitive psychology.* St. Paul, MN: West.

Bettelheim, B. (1943) Individual and mass behavior in extreme situations. *Journal of Abnormal and Social Psychology, 38,* 417–452.

Bieber, I. (1976) A discussion of "Homosexuality: The ethical challenge." *Journal of Consulting and Clinical Psychology, 44,* 163–166.

Billman, J., & McDevitt, S. C. (1980) Convergence of parent and observer ratings of temperament with observations of peer interaction in nursery school. *Child Development, 51,* 395–400.

Binet, A., & Simon, T. (1916) *The development of intelligence in children.* (E. S. Kite, Trans.) Baltimore: Williams & Wilkins.

Bjork, R. A. (1972) Theoretical implications of directed forgetting. In A. W. Melton & E. Martin (Eds.), *Coding process in human memory.* New York: Wiley.

Black, I. B., Adler, J. E., Dreyfus, C. F., Friedman, W. F., La Gamma, E. F., & Roach, A. H. (1987) Biochemistry of information storage in the nervous system. *Science, 236,* 1263–1268.

Blanchard, E. B., & Young, L. D. (1974) Of promises and evidence: A reply to Engel. *Psychological Bulletin, 81,* 44–46.

Blasi, A. (1980) Bridging moral cognition and moral action: A critical review of the literature. *Psychological Bulletin, 88,* 1–45.

Blau, Z. S. (1981) *Black children/white children: Competence, socialization, and social structure.* New York: Free Press.

Block, J. H., Block, J., & Gjerde, P. F. (1986) The personality of children prior to divorce: A prospective study. *Child Development, 57,* 827–840.

Bohannon, J. N., & Warren-Leubecker, A. (1985) Theoretical approaches to language acquisition. In J. B. Gleason, (Ed.), *The development of language.* Columbus, OH: Charles E. Merril.

Bolles, C. (1975) *Theory of motivation.* New York: Harper.

Bolles, R. C., Hayward, L., & Crandall, C. (1981) Conditioned taste preference based on caloric density. *Journal of Experimental Psychology: Animal Behavior Process, 7,* 59–69.

Booth, D. A., & Pain, J. F. (1970) Effects of a single insulin injection on approaches to food and on the temporal pattern of feeding. *Psychonomic Science, 21,* 17–19.

Borke, H. (1975) Piaget's mountains revisited: Changes in the egocentric landscape. *Developmental Psychology, 11,* 240–243.

Bornstein, M. H. (1975) Qualities of color vision in infancy. *Journal of Experimental Child Psychology, 19,* 401–419.

Bourne, E. (1978) The state of research on ego identity: A review and appraisal, Part I. *Journal of Youth and Adolescence, 7,* 223–251.

Bower, G. H. (1974) How to . . . uh . . . remember! In J. B. Mass (Ed.), *Readings in psychology today.* (3rd ed.). Del Mar, CA: CRM Books.

Bower, G. H., & Clark, M. C. (1969) Narrative stories as mediators for serial learning. *Psychonomic Science, 14,* 181–182.

Bower, G. H., & Hilgard, E. R. (1981) *Theories of learning.* Englewood Cliffs, NJ: Prentice-Hall.

Bower, G. H., Karlin, M. B., & Dueck, A. (1975) Comprehension and memory for pictures. *Memory & Cognition, 3,* 216–225.

Bower, R. T. (1985) *The changing television audience in America.* New York: Columbia University Press.

Bowlby, J. (1969) *Attachment and loss* (Vol. 1.) *Attachment.* New York: Basic Books.

Boyd, J., & Weissman, M. (1981) Epidemiology of affective disorders: A reexamination and future directions. *Archives of General Psychiatry, 38,* 1039–1046.

Braddock, J. H. (1985) School desegregation and black assimilation. *Journal of Social Issues, 41,* 9–29.

Bradley, D. R., & Shea, S. L. (1977) The effect of environment on visual cliff performance in the Mongolian gerbil. *Perception and Psychophysics, 21,* 171–179.

Bradley, R. H., & Caldwell, B. M. (1976) The relation of infants' home environments to mental test performance at fifty-four months: A follow-up study. *Child Development, 47,* 1172–1174.

Braine, M. D. S. (1963) The ontogeny of English phrase structure: The first phase. *Language, 39,* 1–13.

Brainerd, C. J., Desrochers, A., & Howe, M. L. (1981) Stages-of-learning analysis of picture-word effects in associative memory. *Journal of Experimental Psychology: Human Learning and Memory, 7,* 1–14.

Brand, E. S., Ruiz, R. A., & Padilla, A. M. (1974) Ethnic identification and preference: A review. *Psychological Bulletin, 81,* 860–890.

Brand, W. G. (1975) Conscious vs. unconscious clairvoyance in the context of an academic examination. *Journal of Parapsychology, 39,* 277–288.

Bransford, J. D., & Stein, B. S. (1984) *The IDEAL problem solver.* New York: Freeman.

Brazelton, T. B. (1969) *Infants and mothers.* New York: Delocat Press/Seymour Lawrence.

Breger, L., Hunter, I., & Lane, R. W. (1971) *The effects of stress on dreams.* New York: International Universities Press.

Breier, A., Charney, D., & Heninger, G. (1986) Agoraphobia with panic attacks: Development, diagnostic stability, and course of illness. *Archives of General Psychiatry, 43,* 1029–1036.

Breland, K., & Breland, M. (1966) *Animal behavior.* New York: Macmillan.

Brier, R., & Tyminski, W. V. (1971) Psi application. In J. B. Rhine (Ed.), *Prog-*

ress in parapsychology. Durham. NC: Parapsychology Press.

Broadbent, D. E., Cooper, P. J., & Broadbent, M. H. P. (1978) A comparison of hierarchical and matrix retrieval schemes in recall. *Journal of Experimental Psychology: Human Learning and Memory, 4,* 486–497.

Broman, S. H. (1981) Long-term development of children born to teenagers. In K. G. Scott, T. Field, & E. Robertson (Eds.), *Teenage parents and their offspring.* New York: Grune & Stratton.

Broman, S. H., Nichols, P. L., & Kennedy, W. A. (1975) *Preschool IQ: Prenatal and early developmental correlates.* Hillsdale, NJ: Erlbaum.

Brou, P., Sciascia, T. R., Linden, L., & Lettuin, Y. (1986) The color of things. *Scientific American, 255,* 84–91.

Broverman, I. K., Broverman, D. M., Clarkson, F. E., Rosenkrantz, P. S., & Vogel, S. R. (1970) Sex-role stereotypes and clinical judgments of mental health. *Journal of Consulting and Clinical Psychology, 34,* 1–7.

Broverman, I. K., Vogel, S. R., Broverman, D. M., Clarkson, F. E., & Rosenkrantz, P. S. (1972) Sex-role stereotypes: A current appraisal. *Journal of Social Issues, 28,* 59–78.

Brown, C. J. (1979) Reactions of infants to their parents' voices. *Infants Behavior and Development, 2,* 295–300.

Brown, J. S. (1948) Gradients of approach and avoidance responses and their relation to motivation. *Journal of Comparative and Physiological Psychology, 41,* 450–465.

Brown, R. (1973) *A first language: The early stages.* Cambridge, MA: Harvard University Press.

Brown, R. W., & McNeill, D. (1966) The "tip-of-the-tongue" phenomenon. *Journal of Verbal Learning and Verbal Behavior, 5,* 325–337.

Brown, T. S., & Wallace, P. M. (1980) *Physiological psychology.* New York: Academic Press.

Browne, A., & Finkelhor, D. (1986) Impact of child sexual abuse: a review of the research. *Psychological Bulletin, 99,* 66–77.

Bruch, R. (1973) *The golden cage: The enigma of anorexia nervosa.* Cambridge, MA: Harvard University Press.

Bruner, J. S., & Goodman, C. C. (1947) Value and need as organizing factors in perception. *Journal of Abnormal and Social Psychology, 42,* 33–44.

Bruner, J. S., Goodnow, J. J., & Austin, G. A. (1956) *A study of thinking.* New York: Wiley.

Bruner, J. S., & Minturn, A. L. (1955) Perceptual identification and perceptual organization. *Journal of General Psychology, 53,* 21–28.

Bruner, J. S., & Postman, L. (1948) An approach to social perception. In W. Dennis (Ed.), *Current trends in social psychology.* Pittsburgh: University of Pittsburgh Press.

Bryant, D. M., & Ramey, C. T. (1987) An analysis of the effectiveness of early intervention programs for environmentally at-risk children. In M. J. Guralnick & F. C. Bennett (Eds.), *The effectiveness of early intervention for at-risk and handicapped children* (pp. 33–78). Orlando, FL: Academic Press.

Buchholz, D. (1976) Spontaneous and centrally induced behaviors in normal and thalamic opossums. *Journal of Comparative and Physiological Psychology, 90,* 898–908.

Buck, R. (1983) *Human motivation and emotion.* New York: Wiley.

Bugelski, B. R. (1968) Images as mediators in one-trial paired-associate learning. II: Self-timing in successive lists. *Journal of Experimental Psychology, 77,* 328–334.

Burchinal, L. G. (1964) Characteristics of adolescents from unbroken, broken and reconstituted families. *Journal of Marriage and the Family, 26,* 44–51.

Burger, J. M., & Cooper, H. M. (1979) The desirability of control. *Motivation and Emotion, 4,* 381–393.

Burgess, R. L. (1979) Child abuse: A social interactional analysis. In *Advances in child clinical psychology,* B. B. Lahey and A. E. Kazdin, (Eds.). New York: Plenum.

Burgess, R. L., & Conger, R. D. (1978) Family interaction in abusive, neglected and normal families. *Child Development, 49,* 163–173.

Buss, A. H., Plomin, R., & Willerman, L. (1973) The inheritance of temperaments. *Journal of Personality, 41,* 513–524.

Buss, D. M. (1984) Toward a psychology of person-environment (PE) correlation: The role of spouse selection. *Journal of Personality and Social Psychology, 47,* 361–377.

Buss, D. M. (1985) Human mate selection. *American Scientist, 73,* 47–51.

Butcher, J. N. & Kellor, L. S. (1984) Objective personality assessment. In G. Goldstein & M. Hersen (Eds.), *Handbook of psychological assessment* (pp. 307–331). Elmsford, NY: Pergamon.

Butler, R. A. (1953) Discrimination learning by rhesus monkeys to visual-exploration motivation. *Journal of Comparative and Physiological Psychology, 46,* 95–98.

Butler, R. A., & Flannery, R. (1980) The spatial attributes of stimulus frequency and their role in monaural localization of sound in the horizontal plane. *Perception and Psychophysics, 28,* 449–457.

Byrne, D. (1971) *The attraction paradigm.* New York: Academic Press.

Byrne, D., & Clore, G. L. (1970) A reinforcement model of evaluative responses. *Personality: An International Journal, 1,* 103–128.

Byrne, D., & Nelson, D. (1965) Attraction as a linear function of proportion of positive reinforcements. *Journal of Personality and Social Psychology, 1,* 659–663.

Cairns, H. S. (1986) *The acquisition of language.* Austin, TX: Pro-Ed.

Calahan, D., & Room, R. (1974) *Problem drinking among American men.* New Brunswick, NJ: Rutgers Center of Alcohol Studies.

Campbell, S. & Werry, J. (1986) Attention deficit disorder (Hyperactivity). In H. Quay & J. Werry (Eds.), *Psychopathological disorders of childhood,* (3rd ed., pp. 111–155). New York: Wiley.

Campbell, S. B. G., & Taylor, P. M. (1980) Bonding and attachment: Theoretical issues. In P. M. Taylor (Ed.), *Parent-infant relationships.* New York: Grune & Stratton.

Cancelli, A. A. (1979) Immediate and sustaining effects of extrinsic rewards on specific exploratory behavior. *Motivation and Emotion, 3,* 341–353.

Cannon, W. B. (1927) The James-Lange theory of emotions: A critical examination and an alternative theory. *American Journal of Psychology, 39,* 106–124.

Cannon, W. B. (1942) "Voodoo" death. *American Anthropologist, 44,* 169–181.

Cantin, M., & Genest, J. (1986) The heart as an endocrine gland. *Scientific-American, 254,* 76–81.

Carey, G. (1982) Genetic influences on anxiety neurosis and agoraphobia. In R. Matthews, (Ed.), *The biology of anxiety* (pp. 37–50). New York: Brunner/Mazel.

Carey, G. (1982) Genetic influences on anxiety neurosis and agoraphobia. In R. Matthews, (Ed.), *The biology of anxiety* (pp. 37–50). New York: Brunner/Mazel.

Carey, G., Goldsmith, H. H., Tellegan, A., & Gottesman, I. I. (1978) Genetics and personality inventories: The limits of replication with twin data. *Behavior Genetics, 8,* 299–313.

Carey, S. (1977) The child as word learner. In M. Halle, J. Bresnan, & G. A. Miller (Eds.), *Linguistic theory and psychological reality.* Cambridge, MA: MIT Press.

Carey, W. B. (1981) The importance of temperament-environment interaction for child health and development. In M. Lewis & L. A. Rosenblum (Eds.), *The uncommon child.* New

York: Plenum.

Carey, W. B., Fox, M., & McDevitt, S. C. (1977) Temperament as a factor in early school adjustment. *Pediatrics, 60,* 621–624.

Carlson, D. B., La Barba, R. C., Sclafani, J. D. & Bowers, C. A. (1986) Cognitive and motor development in infants of adolescent mothers: A longitudinal analysis. *Journal of Behavioral Development, 9,* 1–13.

Carlson, G. A., & Cantwell, D. P. (1979) A survey of depressive symptoms in a child and adolescent psychiatric population. *Journal of the American Academy of Child Psychiatry, 18,* 587–599.

Carlson, N. R. (1986) *Physiology of behavior.* Boston: Allyn & Bacon.

Carmichael, L. C., Hogan, H. P., & Walter, A. A. (1932) An experimental study of the effects of language on the reproduction of visually perceived forms. *Journal of Experimental Psychology, 15,* 73–86.

Caron, R. F., Caron, A. J., & Myers, R. S. (1982) Abstraction of invariant face expressions in infancy. *Child Development, 53,* 1008–1015.

Cash, T. F., & Trimer, C. A. (1984) Sexism and beautyism in women's evaluations of peer performance. *Sex Roles, 10,* 87–97.

Cattell, R. B. (1956) Validation and interpretation of the 16 P. F. questionnaire. *Journal of Clinical Psychology, 12,* 205–214.

Cattell, R. B. (1973, July) Personality pinned down. *Psychology Today, 7,* 40–46.

Cattell, R. B., Eber, H. W., & Tatsuoka, M. M. (1970) *Handbook for the 16 P. F. Questionnaire.* Champaign, IL: Institute for Personality and Ability Testing.

Cerami, A., Vlassara, H., & Brownlee, M. (1987, May) Glucose and aging. *Scientific American,* 90–97.

Cerletti, U., & Bini, L. (1938) L'Elettroshock. *Archivo Generale di Neurologia e Psichiatria e Psicoanalisi, 19,* 266–268.

Chafetz, J. (1974) *Masculine/feminine or human.* Itasca, IL: Peacock.

Chan-Palay, V., Engel, A. B., Palay, S. L., & Wu, J.-Y. (1982) Synthesizing enzymes for four neutroactive substances in motor neurons and neuromuscular junctions. *Proceedings of the National Academy of Sciences, 79,* 6717–6721.

Chance, M. R. A. (1980) An ethological assessment of emotion. In R. Plutchik and H. Kellerman (Eds.), *Emotion: theory, research, and experience,* Vol I. New York: Academic Press.

Chapman, L. J. & Chapman, J. P. (1967) Genesis of popular but erroneous psycho-diagnostic observations. *Journal of Abnormal Psychology, 72,* 193–204.

Chapman, L. J. & Chapman, J. P. (1969) Illusory correlation as an obstacle to the use of valid psychodiagnostic signs. *Journal of Abnormal Psychology, 74,* 271–280.

Chapman, M. (1977) Father absence, stepfathers, and the cognitive performance of college students. *Child Development, 48,* 1155–1158.

Chatala, E. S. (1981) Imagery and associative processing effects on incidental memory. *Journal of Experimental Psychology: Human Learning and Memory, 7,* 47–55.

Cheek, D. B. (1974) Body composition, nutrition, and adolescent growth. In M. M. Grumbach, G. D. Grave, & F. E. Mayer (Eds.), *Control of the onset of puberty.* New York: Wiley.

Cherry, L., & Lewis, M. (1976) Mothers and two-year-olds: A study of sex differentiated aspects of verbal interaction. *Developmental Psychology, 12,* 278–282.

Chess, S., Thomas, A., & Cameron, M. (1976) Temperament: Its significance for school adjustment and academic achievement. *New York University Educational Review, 7,* 24–29.

Children's Defense Fund. (1986) *Maternal and child health data book,* Washington, DC: Children's Defense Fund.

Chilman, C. S. (1980) Social and psychological research concerning adolescent child-bearing: 1970-1980. *Journal of Marriage and the Family, 42,* 793–806.

Chiodo, L. A., & Antelman, S. M. (1980) Electroconvulsive shock: Progressive dopamine autoreceptor subsensitivity independent of repeated treatment. *Science, 210,* 799–801.

Chomsky, N. (1965) *Syntactic structures.* The Hague: Mouton.

Chomsky, N. (1968) *Language and mind.* New York: Harcourt Brace Jovanovich.

Chorover, S. L. (1974, May) The pacification of the brain. *Psychology Today,* 59–60, 63–64, 66–69.

Christensen, C. M. (1980) Effects of taste quality and intensity on oral perception of viscosity. *Perception and Psychophysics, 28,* 315–320.

Cialdini, R. B., Petty, R. E., & Cacioppo, J. T. (1981) Attitude and attitude change. *Annual Review of Psychology, 32,* 357–404.

Ciminero, A. R., Calhoun, K. S., & Adams, H. E. (Eds.). (1977) *Handbook of behavioral assessment.* New York: Wiley.

Clark, M. (1981, May 18) The new gene doctors. *Newsweek,* pp. 57–58.

Clarke-Stewart, A. (1982) *Daycare.* Cambridge, MA: Harvard University Press.

Clarke-Stewart, K. A., Vander Stoep, L. P., & Killian, G. A. (1979) Analysis and replication of mother-child relations at two years of age. *Child development, 50,* 777–793.

Cleary, T. A., Humphreys, L. G., Kendrich, S. A., & Wesman, A. (1975) Educational uses of tests with disadvantaged students. *American Psychologist, 30,* 15–40.

Clemes, S. R. (1964) Repression and hypnotic amnesia. *Journal of Abnormal and Social Psychology, 69,* 62–69.

Clingempeel, W. G., & Segal, S. (1986) Stepparent-stepchild relationships and the psychological adjustment of children in stepmother and stepfather families. *Child Development, 57,* 474–484.

Clore, G. L., Bray, R. M., Itkin, S. M., & Murphy, P. (1978) Interracial attitudes and behavior at a summer camp. *Journal of Personality and Social Psychology, 36,* 107–116.

Clore, G. L., & Byrne, D. (1974) A reinforcement-affect model of attraction. In T. L. Huston (Ed.), *Foundations of interpersonal attraction.* New York: Academic Press.

Cofer, C. N. (1972) *Motivation and emotion.* Glenview, IL: Scott, Foresman.

Cofer, C. N. (Ed.). (1975) *The structure of human memory.* San Francisco: Freeman.

Cohen, C. (1986) The case for the use of animals in biomedical research. *The New England Journal of Medicine, 315,* 865–870.

Cohen, D. B. (1974) Repression is not the demon who conceals and hoards our forgotten dreams. *Psychology Today, 7,* 50–54.

Cohen, M. J., & Johnson, H. J. (1971) Relationship between heart rate and muscular activity within a classical conditioning paradigm. *Journal of Experimental Psychology, 90,* 222–226.

Cohen, S., Porac, C., & Ward, L. M. (1984) *Sensation and perception.* Orlando: Academic Press.

Cohen, S., & Weinstein, N. (1981) Nonauditory effects of noise on behavior and health. *Journal of Social Issues, 37(1),* 36–70.

Cole, N. S. (1981) Bias in testing. *American Psychologist, 36,* 1067–1077.

Coleman, J. C. (1980) Friendship and the peer group in adolescence. In J. Adelson (Ed.), *Handbook of adolescent psychology.* New York: Wiley.

Coleman, M., & Ganong, L. H. (1985) Love and sex role stereotypes: Do macho men and feminine women make better lovers? *Journal of Personality and Social Psychology, 49,* 170–176.

Coles, R. (1986) *The Moral Life of Children.* Boston: The Atlantic Monthly Press.

Coles, R. (1986) *The Political Life of Chil-*

dren. Boston: The Atlantic Monthly Press.

Collins, A. M., & Loftus, E. F. (1975) A spreading activation theory of semantic processing. *Psychological Review, 82,* 407–428.

Collins, A. M., & Quillian, M. R. (1969) Retrieval time in semantic memory. *Journal of Verbal Learning and Verbal Behavior, 8,* 240–247.

Collins, A. M., & Quillian, M. R. (1972) How to make a language user. In E. Tulving & W. Donaldson (Eds.), *Organization and memory*. New York: Academic Press.

Collins, G. (1983, March 21) U.S. social tolerance of drugs on the rise. *The New York Times.*

Condry, J., & Condry, S. (1976) Sex differences: A study of the eye of the beholder. *Child Development, 47,* 812–819.

Cook, S. W. (1984) The 9154 social science statement and school desegregation. *American Psychologist, 39,* 819–832.

Coon, D. (1986) *Introduction to psychology* (4th ed.). St. Paul: MN: West.

Cooper, L. M. (1979) Hypnotic amnesia. In E. Fromm & R. E. Shor (Eds.), *Hypnosis: Developments in research and new perspectives*. Hawthorne, NY: Aldine.

Coren, S. (1969) Brightness contrast as a function of figure-ground relations. *Journal of Experimental Psychology, 80,* 517–524.

Coren, S., & Girgus, J. S. (1980) Principles of perceptual organization and spatial distortion: The Gestalt illusions. *Journal of Experimental Psychology: Human Perception and Performance, 6,* 404–412.

Coren, S., Porac, C., & Ward, L. M. (1984) *Sensation and perception*. (2nd ed.). Orlando: Academic Press.

Cotman, C. W., & McGaugh, J. L. (1980) *Behavioral neuroscience*. New York: Academic Press.

Council, J. R., Kirsch, I., Vickery, A. R., & Carlson, D. (1983) "Trance" versus "skill" hypnotic inductions: The effects of credibility, expectancy and experimentor modeling. *Journal of Consulting and Clinical Psychology, 51,* 432–440.

Coyle, J., Price, D., DeLong, M. (1983) Alzheimer's disease: A disorder of cortical cholenergic innervation. *Science, 219,* 1184–1190.

Coyne, J., & Gotlib, I. (1983) The role of cognition in depression: A critical appraisal. *Psychological Bulletin, 94,* 472–505.

Craik, F. I. M., & Lockhart, R. S. (1972) Levels of processing: A framework for memory research. *Journal of Verbal Learning and Verbal Behavior, 11,* 671–684.

Craik, F. I. M., & Tulving, E. (1975) Depth of processing and the retention of words in episodic memory. *Journal of Experimental Psychology: General 104,* 268–294.

Crowder, R. G. (1978) Mechanisms of auditory backward masking in the stimulus suffix effect. *Psychological Review, 85,* 502–524.

Crowe, R. R. (1982) Recent genetic research in schizophrenia. In F. A. Henn and H. A. Nasrallah (Eds.), *Schizophrenia as a brain disease*. New York: Oxford University Press.

Curtis, H., & Barnes, N. S. (1985) *Invitation to biology*. New York: Worth.

Czikszentmihaly, M., & Larson, R. (1984) *Being adolescent: Conflict and growth in the teenage years*. New York: Basic Books.

Davis, J. H., Loughlin, P. R., & Komorita, S. S. (1976) The social psychology of small groups: Cooperative and mixed-motive interaction. *Annual Review of Psychology, 27,* 111–114.

Davis, K. E. (1985, February) Near and dear: Friendship and love compared. *Psychology Today*, pp. 22–30.

Davis, M. (1987) Premature mortality among prominent American authors. *Drugs and Alcohol Dependence, 18,* 133–138.

Davison, G. C. (1976) Homosexuality: The ethical challenge. *Journal of Consulting and Clinical Psychology, 44,* 157–162.

Davitz, J. R. (1970) A dictionary and grammar of emotion. In M. Arnold (Ed.), *Feelings and emotions: The Loyola symposium*. New York: Academic Press.

Day, R. D., & Bahr, S. J. (1986) Income changes following divorce and remarriage. *Journal of Divorce, 9(3),* 75–88.

Deikman, A. J. (1963) Experimental meditation. *Journal of Nervous and Mental Disease, 136,* 329–373.

de Leon, M. J., Ferris, S. H., George, A. E., Christman, D. R., Fowler, J., Gentes, C., Gee, B., Reisberg, B., Kricheff, I. I., & Wolf, A. (1982) Positron-emission tomography (PET) studies of normal aging and senile dementia of the Alzheimer's type. *Gerontology, 22,* 53–54.

Dement, W. (1960) The effect of dream deprivation. *Science, 131,* 1705–1707.

Dement, W. C. (1972) *Some must watch while some must sleep*. Stanford, CA: Stanford Alumni Association.

Dement, W. C., & Mitler, M. M. (1973) New developments in the basic mechanisms of sleep. In G. Usdin (Ed.), *Sleep research and clinical practice*. New York: Brunner/Mazel.

Dement, W. C., & Zarcone, V. (1977) Pharmacological treatment of sleep disorders. In J. D. Barchas, *et al.* (Eds.), *Psychopharmacology: From theory to practice*. London: Oxford University Press.

Dempster, F. N., & Rohwer, W. D. (1974) Component analysis of the elaborative encoding effect in paired-associate learning. *Journal of Experimental Psychology, 103,* 400–408.

Denney, N. W. (1972) Free classification in preschool children. *Child Development, 43,* 1161–1170.

Dennis, W. (1960) Causes of retardation among institutional children. *Journal of Genetic Psychology, 96,* 47–59.

Depue, R., & Monroe, S. (1978) The unipolar-bipolar distinction in the depressive disorders. *Psychological Bulletin, 85,* 1001–1029.

Deutsch, F. M., & Lamberti, D. M. (1986) Does social approval increase helping? *Personality and Social Psychology Bulletin, 12,* 149–157.

DeValois, R. L., & Jacobs, G. H. (1968) Primate color vision. *Science, 162,* 533–540.

Diagnostic and statistical manual of mental disorders. (1987, 3rd ed., revised). Washington, DC: American Psychiatric Association.

Diamond, E., & Bates, S. (1984) *The spot: The rise of political advertising on television*. Cambridge, MA: MIT Press.

Diamond, M. C., Scheibel, A. B., Murphy, G. M., Jr., & Harvey, T. (1985) On the brain of a scientist: Albert Einstein. *Experimental Neurology, 88,* 198–204.

Diamond, M. J. (1974) Modification of hypnotizability: A review. *Psychological Bulletin, 81,* 180–198.

Diehl, R. L., Lang, M., & Parker, E. M. (1980) A further parallel between selective adaptation and contrast. *Journal of Experimental Psychology: Human Perception and Performance, 6,* 24–44.

Dion, K. K., Berscheid, E., & Walster, E. (1972) What is beautiful is good. *Journal of Personality and Social Psychology, 24,* 285–290.

Dockray, G. J., Gregory, R. A., & Hutchison, J. B. (1978) Isolation, structure and biological activity of two cholecystokinin octapeptides from sheep brain. *Nature, 274,* 711–713.

Dohrenwend, B. P., & Egri, G. (1981) Recent stressful events and episodes of schizophrenia. *Schizophrenia Bulletin, 7,* 12–23.

Dominey, W. J. (1984) Alternative mating tactics and evolutionarily stable strategies. *American Zoologist, 24,* 385–396.

Domjan, M., & Burkhard, B. (1986) *The principles of learning and behavior*. (2nd ed.). Monterey, CA: Brooks/Cole.

Donahoe, J. W., & Wessells, M. G. (1980) *Learning, language, and memory*.

New York: Harper and Row.

Donnerstein, E. (1980) Aggressive erotica and violence against women. *Journal of Personality and Social Psychology, 39,* 269–277.

Dunant, Y., & Israel, M. (1985, April) The release of acetylcholine. *Scientific American,* 58–66.

Dunner, D. L., & Fieve, R. R. (1974) Clinical factors in lithium carbonate prophylaxis failure. *Archives of General Psychiatry, 30,* 229–233.

Dworkin, B. R., & Miller, N. E. (1986) Failure to replicate visceral learning in the acute curarized rat preparation. *Behavioral Neuroscience, 100,* 123–126.

Dywan, J., & Bowers, K. (1983) The use of hypnosis to enhance recall. *Science, 22,* 184–185.

Eagle, M. N., & Wolitzky, D. L. (1985) The current status of psychoanalysis. *Clinical Psychology Review, 5,* 259–269.

Eagly, A. H., & Steffen, V. J. (1986) Gender and aggressive behavior: A meta-analytic review of the social psychological literature. *Psychological Bulletin, 100,* 309–330.

Eagly, A. H., Wood, W., & Chaiken, S. (1978) Casual inferences about communicators and their effect on opinion change. *Journal of Personality and Social Psychology, 36,* 424–435.

Ebbinghaus, H. (1913) *Memory: A contribution to experimental psychology.* In H. A. Ruger & C. E. Bussenius (Trans.). New York: Teachers College. (Original work published 1885).

Edwards, C. P. (1975) Societal complexity and moral development: A Kenyan study. *Ethos, 3,* 505–527.

Egan, G. (1986) *The skilled helper.* Monterey, CA: Brooks/Cole.

Egeland, B., & Sroufe, A. (1981) Developmental sequelae of maltreatment in infancy. In R. Rizley & D. Cicchetti (Eds.), *Developmental perspectives on child maltreatment: New directions for child development.* San Francisco: Jossey-Bass.

Ehrhardt, A. A., & Baker, S. W. (1974) Fetal androgens, human central nervous system differentiation, and behavior sex differences. In R. C. Friedman, R. M. Rochart, & R. L. Vandewiele (Eds.), *Sex differences in behavior.* New York: Wiley.

Eibl-Eibesfeldt, I. (1970) *Ethology.* New York: Holt.

Eibl-Eibesfeldt, I. (1980) Strategies of social interaction. In R. Plutchik and H. Kellerman (Eds.), *Emotion: Theory, research, and experience. Vol. I.* New York: Academic Press.

Eich, J. E., Weingartner, H., Stillman, R. C., & Gillin, J. C. (1975) State-dependent accessibility of retrieved cues in the retention of a categorical list. *Journal of Verbal Learning and Verbal Behavior, 14,* 408–417.

Eisenberger, R. (1972) Explanation of rewards that do not reduce tissue needs. *Psychological Bulletin, 77,* 319–339.

Ekman, P. (1971) Universals and cultural differences in facial expressions of emotion. In J. K. Cole (Ed.), *Nebraska Symposium on Motivation.* Lincoln: University of Nebraska Press.

Ekman, P., Friesen, W. V., O'Sullivan, M., & Scherer, K. (1980) Relative importance of face, body, and speech in judgments of personality and affect. *Journal of Personality and Social Psychology, 38,* 270–277.

Ekman, P., Levenson, R. W., & Friesen, W. V. (1983) Autonomic nervous system activity distinguishes among emotions. *Science, 221,* 1208–1210.

Ekstrand, B. R. (1967) Effect of sleep on memory. *Journal of Experimental Psychology, 75,* 64–72.

Elardo, R., Bradley, R., & Caldwell, B. (1977) A longitudinal study of the relation of infants' home environments to language development at age three. *Child Development, 48,* 595–603.

Ellenberg, L., & Sperry, R. W. (1980) Lateralized division of attention in the commissurotomized and intact brain. *Neuropsychologia, 18,* 411–418.

Ellis, A. (1962) *Reason and emotion in psychotherapy.* New York: Lyle Stuart.

Ellis, A. (1984) Rational emotive therapy. In R. J. Corsini (Ed.), *Current psychotherapies* (3rd ed., pp. 196–238). New York: Springer.

Ellis, A., & Harper, R. A. (1975) *A new guide to rational living.* North Hollywood, CA: Wilshire.

Ellis, H. C. (1972) *Fundamentals of human learning and cognition.* Dubuque, IA: W. C. Brown.

Elsworth, P. C., Carlsmith, J. M., & Henson, A. (1972) The stare as a stimulus to flight in human subjects: A series of field experiments. *Journal of Personality and Social Psychology, 21,* 302–311.

Emery, R. E. (1982) Interparental conflict and the children of discord and divorce. *Psychological Bulletin, 92,* 310–330.

Endicott, J., & Spitzer, R. L. (1979) Use of research diagnostic criteria and the schedule for affective disorders and schizophrenia to study affective disorders. *American Journal of Psychiatry, 136,* 52–56.

Engel, B. T. (1972) Operant conditioning of cardiac function: A status report. *Psychophysiology, 9,* 161–177.

Epstein, A. W., Fitzsimons, J. T., & Simons, B. (1969) Drinking caused by the intercranial injection of angiotensin into the rat. *Journal of Physiology (London), 200,* 98–100.

Epstein, A. W., & Teitelbaum, P. (1962) Regulation of food intake in the absence of taste, smell, and other oropharyngeal sensations. *Journal of Comparative and Physiological Psychology, 55,* 753–759.

Epstein, J. L. (1984) Choice of friends over the life span: Developmental and environmental influences. In E. Mueller and C. Cooper, (Eds.), *Peer relations: Process and outcomes.* New York: Academic Press.

Erdberg, P., & Exner Jr., J. E. (1984) Rorschach assessment. In G. Goldstein & M. Hersen (Eds.), *Handbook of psychological assessment* (pp. 332–347). New York: Pergamon.

Erikson, E. H. (1963) *Childhood and society.* (2nd ed.). New York: Norton.

Erikson, E. H. (1980) *Identity and the life cycle: A reissue.* New York: Norton.

Erikson, E. H., Erikson, J. M., & Kivnick, H. Q. (1986) *Vital involvement in old age.* New York: Norton.

Erkan, K. A., Rimer, B. A., & Stine, O. C. (1971) Juvenile pregnancy: Role of Physiologic maturity. *Maryland State Medical Journal, 20,* 50

Erlenmeyer-Kimling, L., & Jarvik, L. F. (1963) Genetics and intelligence: A review. *Science, 142,* 1477–1479.

Eysenck, H. J., & Eysenck, S. B. G. (1968) *Manual for the Eysenck Personality Inventory.* San Diego: Educational & Industrial Testing Service.

Fairweather, G. W., Sanders, D. H., Maynard, H., & Cressler, D. L. (1969) *Community life for the mentally ill: An alternative to institutional care.* Chicago: Aldine.

Falek, A., & Hollingsworth, F. (1980) Opiates and human chromosome alterations. *The International Journal of the Addictions, 15,* 155–163.

Fantz, R. L., Fagan, J. F., & Miranda, S. (1975) Early vision selectivity. In L. B. Cohen and P. Salapatek (Eds.), *Infant perception: From sensation to cognition.* Vol. 1. New York: Academic Press.

Farber S. L. (1981) *Identical twins reared apart: A reanalysis.* New York: Basic Books.

Farran, D. C., Haskins, R., & Gallagher, J. J. (1980) Poverty and mental retardation: A search for explanations. In J. J. Gallagher (Ed.), *Ecology of exceptional children. New directions for exceptional children* (No. 1) San Francisco: Jossey-Bass.

Farrington, D. (1986) The sociocultural context of childhood disorders. In H. Quay & J. Werry (Eds.), *Psychopathological disorders of childhood,* (3rd ed., pp. 391–422). New York: Wiley.

Feighner, J. P., Robins, E., Guze, S. B.,

Woodruff, R. A. Jr., Winokur, G., & Munoz, R. (1972) Diagnostic criteria for use in psychiatric research. *Archives of General Psychiatry, 26*, 57–63.

Feingold, A. (1988) Cognitive gender differences are disappearing. *American Psychologist, 43*, 95–103.

Feldman, S. S., Biringen, Z. C., & Nash, S. C. (1981) Fluctuations of sex-related self-attributes as a function of stage of family life cycle. *Developmental Psychology, 17*, 24–35.

Ferguson, J. (1987) Reproductive health of adolescent girls. *World Health Statistics, 40*(3), 211–213.

Ferster, C. S., & Skinner, B. F. (1957) *Schedules of reinforcement.* New York: Appleton.

Festinger, L. (1957) *A theory of cognitive dissonance.* Stanford, CA: Stanford University Press.

Fink, M. (1980) A neuroendocrine theory of convulsive therapy. *Trends in Neurosciences, 3*, 25–27.

Fishbein, J. E., & Wasik, B. H. (1981) Effect of the good behavior game on disruptive library behavior. *Journal of Applied Behavior Analysis, 14*, 89–93.

Fiske, S. T., & Taylor, S. E. (1984) *Social Cognition.* Reading, MA: Addison Wesley.

Flanders, J. P. (1968) A review of research on imitative behavior. *Psychological Bulletin, 69*, 316–337.

Francis, D. (1965) *For kicks.* New York: Pocket Books.

Franzoi, S. L., & Herzog, M. E. (1987) Judging physical attractiveness: What body aspects do we use? *Personality and Social Psychology Bulletin, 13*, 19–33.

Frazer, A., & Winokur, A. (1977) Therapeutic and pharmacological aspects of psychotropic drugs. In A. Frazer and A. Winokur (Eds.), *Biological Bases of Psychiatric Disorders, 11*, 151–177.

Frazer, D. (1981) Identical twins reared apart: A reanalysis. New York: Basic Books.

Freed, W. J., Cannon-Spoor, H. E., Krauthamer, E., Hoffer, B. J., & Wyatt, R. J. (1983) Catecholaminergic brain grafts: A behavioral, histochemical, and biochemical comparison of substantia nigra and adrenal medulla grafts. *Psychopharmacology Bulletin, 19*, 305–307.

Freed, W. J., de Medinaceli, L., & Wyatt, R. J. (1985) Promoting functional plasticity in damaged nervous system. *Science, 227*, 1544–1552.

Freedman, J. L. (1984) Effect of television violence on aggressiveness. *Psychology Bulletin, 96*, 227–246.

Freedman, J. L., Sears, D. O., & Carlsmith, J. M. (1981) *Social psychology* (4th ed.). Englewood Cliffs, NJ: Prentice-Hall.

Friedman, M., & Rosenman, R. F. (1974) *Type A behavior and your heart.* New York: Knopf.

Freud, A., & Burlingham, D. T. (1943) *War and children.* New York: Willard.

Frijters, J. E. R. (1980) Three-stimulus procedures in olfactory psychophysics: An experimental comparison of Thurstone-ura and three-alternative forced-choice models of signal detection theory. *Perception and Psychophysics, 28*, 390–397.

Fromm, E. (1956) *The art of loving.* New York: Harper.

Frueh, T., & McGhee, P. E. (1975) Traditional sex role development and amount of time spent watching television. *Developmental Psychology, 11*, 109.

Gaioni, S. J., Hoffman, J. S., DePaulo, P., & Stratton, V. N. (1978) Imprinting in older ducklings: Some tests of a reinforcement model. *Animal Learning and Behavior, 6*, 19–26.

Galanter, E., (1962) Contemporary psychophysics. In R. Brown, E. Galanter, E. H. Hess, & G. Mandler (Eds.), *New directions in psychology.* New York: Holt, Rinehart & Winston.

Galin, D., & Ornstein, R. (1972) Lateral specialization of cognitive mode: An EEG study. *Psychophysiology, 9*, 412–418.

Galton, F. (1869) *Hereditary genius: An inquiry into its laws and consequences.* London: Macmillan.

Gamble, T. J., & Zigler, E. (1986) Effects of infant day care: Another look at the evidence. *American Journal of Orthopsychiatry, 56*, 26–42.

Ganchrow, J. R., Steiner, J. E., and Daher, M. (1983) Neonatal facial expressions in response to different qualities and intensities of gustatory stimuli. *Infant Behavior and Development, 6*, 189–200.

Ganong, L. H., & Coleman. (1984) The effects of remarriage on children: A review of the empirical literature. *Family Relations, 33*, 389–406.

Ganong, W. F. (1980) Phonetic categorization in auditory word presentation. *Journal of Experimental Psychology: Human Perception and Performance, 6*, 110–125.

Garbarino, J., & Gilliam, G. (1980) *Understanding abusive families.* Lexington, MA: D. C. Heath.

Garbarino, J., & Sherman, D. (1980) High-risk neighborhoods and high-risk families: The human ecology of child maltreatment, *Child Development, 51*, 188–198.

Garcia, J. (1981) The logic and limits of mental aptitude testing. *American Psychologist, 36*, 1172–1180.

Garcia, J., & Rusiniak, K. W. (1979) What the nose learns from the mouth. Paper presented at the Symposium on Chemical Signals in Vertebrate and Acquatic Mammals. Syracuse University.

Gardner, H. (1984) *Frames of mind.* New York: Basic Books.

Gardner, H. (1985) *The mind's new science: A history of the cognitive revolution.* New York: Basic Books

Gardner, L. I. (1972) Deprivation dwarfism. *Scientific American, 227*, 76–82.

Gardner, R. A., & Gardner, B. T. (1978) Comparative psychology and language acquisition. *Annals of the New York Academy of Science, 309*, 37–76.

Garfinkel, P. E., Kline, S. A., & Stancer, H. C. (1973) Treatment of anorexia nervosa using operant conditioning techniques. *Journal of Nervous and Mental Disease, 157*, 428–433.

Gazzaniga, M. S. (1970) *The bisected brain.* New York: Appleton-Century-Crofts.

Gazzaniga, M. S. (1983) Right hemisphere language following brain bisection. *American Psychologist, 38*, 525–537.

Gazzaniga, M. S. (1985) *The social brain, discovering the networks of the mind.* New York: Basic Books.

Geilselman, P. J. (1983) The role of hexoses in hunger motivation. Unpublished doctoral dissertation, University of California, Los Angeles.

Gerard, H. B. (1983) School desegregation: The social science role. *American Psychologist, 38*, 869–877.

Gerard, H. B., Wilhelmy, R. A., & Conolley, E. S. (1968) Conformity and group size. *Journal of Personality and Social Psychology, 8*, 79–82.

Gerbner, G. (1972) Violence in television drama: Trends and symbolic functions. In G. A. Comstock & E. A. Rubinstein (Eds.), *Television and social behavior.* Vol. 1. *Media content and control.* Washington, DC: U.S. Government Printing Office.

Ghosh, A., & Marks, I. M. (1987) Self-treatment of agoraphobia by exposure. *Behavior Therapy, 18*, 3–16.

Gibbons, B. (1976, September) The intimate sense of smell. *National Geographic* pp. 334–361.

Gibson, E. J., & Walk, R. D. (1960) The "visual cliff." *Scientific American, 202*, 64–71.

Gil, D. G. (1970) *Violence against children: Physical child abuse in the United States.* Cambridge, MA: Harvard University Press.

Girden, E. (1962) A review of psychokinesis. *Psychological Bulletin, 59*, 353–388.

Glick, P. C. (1984) Marriage, divorce, and living arrangements: Prospective changes. *Journal of Family Issues, 5,* 7–26.

Godden, D. R., & Baddeley, A. D. (1975) Context dependent memory in two natural environments: On land and under water. *British Journal of Psychology, 66,* 325–331.

Gogel, W. C. (1980) The sensing of retinal motion. *Perception and Psychophysics, 28,* 155–163.

Gogel, W. C., and Tietz, J. D. (1980) Relative cues and absolute distance perception. *Perception and Psychophysics, 28,* 321–328.

Gold, P. E., & King, R. A. (1974) Retrograde amnesia: Storage failure versus retrieval failure. *Psychological Review, 81,* 465–469.

Goldband, S. (1980) Stimulus specificity of physiological response to stress and the Type A coronary-prone behavior pattern. *Journal of Personality and Social Psychology, 39,* 670–679.

Goldberg, E. L. (1981) Depression and suicide ideation in the young adult. *American Journal of Psychiatry, 138,* 35–40.

Goldfried, M. R., & Kent, R. N. (1972) Traditional versus behavioral personality assessment: A comparison of methodological and theoretical assumptions. *Psychological Bulletin, 77,* 409–420.

Goldfried, M. R., & Sprafkin, J. N. (1976) Behavioral personality assessment. In J. T. Spence, R. C. Carson, & J. W. Thibaut (Eds.), *Behavioral approaches to therapy.* Morristown, NJ: General Learning Press.

Goldsmith, H. H., & Gathesman, I. I. (1981) Origins of variation in behavioral style: A longitudinal study of temperament in young twins. *Child Development, 52,* 91–103.

Goldstein, G. (1984) Neuropsychological assessment. In G. Goldstein & M. Hersen (Eds.), *Handbook of Psychological Assessment* (pp. 181–210). New York: Pergamon.

Goldstein, H., Moss, J. W., & Jordan, L. J. (1965) The efficacy of special class training on the development of mentally retarded children. Urbana, IL: University of Illinois, Institute for Research on Exceptional Children.

Goldwater, B. C. (1972) Psychological significance of pupillary movement. *Psychological Bulletin, 77,* 340–355.

Goodwin, D. W. (1981) *Alcoholism: The facts.* New York: Oxford.

Goodwin, D. W. (1983) The genetics of alcoholism: Implications for youth. *Alcohol, Health & Research World, 7,* 59–63.

Goodwin, F. K., & Jamison, K. R. (1984) The natural course of manic-depressive illness. In R. M. Post & J. C. Ballenger (Eds.), *Neurobiology of mood disorders* (pp. 20–37). Baltimore: Williams & Wilkins.

Goodwin, F. K., & Jamison, K. R. (in press). *Manic-depressive illness,* New York: Oxford University Press.

Gordon, D., Burge, D., Hammen, C., Adrian, C., Jaenicke, C., & Hiroto, D. (1988) Observations of interactions of depressed women with their children. Manuscript submitted for publication.

Gore, S. (1981) Stress-buffering functions of social support: An appraisal and clarification of research models. In B. S. Dohrenwend & B. P. Dohrenwend, (Eds.), *Stressful life events and their contexts.* New York: Prodist.

Goren, C. C., Sarty, M., & Wu, P. Y. K. (1975) Visual following and pattern discrimination of face-like stimuli by newborn infants. *Pediatrics, 56,* 544–549.

Gormezano, I., & Fernald, C. D. (1971) Human eyelid conditioning with paraorbital shock as the US. *Psychonomic Science, 25,* 88–90.

Gottesman, I. I. & Shields, J. (1966) Contributions of twin studies of perspectives on schizophrenia. In B. A. Maher (Ed.), *Progress in experimental personality research.* New York: Academic Press.

Gottesman, I. & Shields, J. (1976) A critical review of recent adoption, twin, and family studies of schizophrenia: Behavioral genetics perspectives. *Schizophrenia Bulletin, 2,* 414–428.

Gould, J. L., & Marler, P. (1987, May) Learning by instinct. *Scientific American,* 74–82.

Gould, R. (1978) *Transformations: Growth and change in adult life.* New York: Simon and Schuster.

Gould, R. L. (1980) Transformations during early and middle adult years. In N. J. Smelser & E. H. Erikson (Eds.), *Themes of work and love in adulthood.* Cambridge, MA: Harvard University Press.

Grasha, A. F. (1983) *Practical applications of psychology.* Boston: Little, Brown.

Gray F., Graubard, P. S., & Rosenberg, H. (1974, March) Little brother is changing you. *Psychology Today, 7*(10), 42–46.

Gray, J. D., Cutler, C. A., Dean, J. G., & Kempe, C. H. (1977) Prediction and prevention of child abuse and neglect. Paper presented at the biennial meetings of the society for Research in Child Development, New Orleans.

Graziadei, P. P. C., and Graziadei, G. A. M. (1978) The olfactory system: A model for the study of neurogenesis and axon regeneration in mammals. In C. W. Cotman (Ed.), *Neuronal plasticity.* New York: Raven.

Green, B. G. (1977) The effect of skin temperature on vibrotactile sensitivity. *Perception and Psychophysics, 21,* 243–248.

Greenblatt, M. (1967) Psychosurgery. In A. M. Freedman & H. I. Kaplan (Eds.), *Comprehensive textbook of psychiatry.* Baltimore: Williams & Wilkins.

Greenfield, P. M. (1984) *Mind and media: The effects of television, video games, and computers.* Cambridge, MA: Harvard University Press.

Greenhouse, H. (1975) ESP and gambling. *Psychic, 6,* 8–14.

Greenspoon, J. (1955) The reinforcing effect of two spoken sounds on the frequency of two responses. *American Journal of Psychology, 68,* 409–416.

Gregory, R. L. (1966) *Eye and brain: The psychology of seeing.* New York: McGraw-Hill.

Gregory R. L. (1973) *Eye and brain* (2nd ed.) New York: World Universities Library.

Gregory, R. L., & Gombrich, E. H. (1973) *Illusions in nature and art.* London: Duckworth.

Gruenewald, P. J., & Lockhead, G. R. (1980) The free recall of category examples. *Journal of Experimental Psychology: Human Learning and Memory, 6,* 225–240.

Grush, J. E., McKeogh, K. L., & Ahlering, R. F. (1978) Extrapolating laboratory exposure research to actual political elections. *Journal of Personality and Social Psychology, 36,* 257–270.

Guarino, R. (1975) The police and psychics. *Psychic, 6,* 9–12.

Guilford, J. P. (1956) The structure of intellect. *Psychological Bulletin, 53,* 267–293.

Gunter, B., Clifford, B. R., & Berry, C. (1980) Release from proactive interference with television news items: Evidence for encoding dimensions within televised news. *Journal of Experimental Psychology: Human Learning and Memory, 6,* 216–223.

Gurdon, J. B. (1969) Transplanted nuclei and cell differentiation. *Scientific American, 219,* 24–35.

Gustavson, C. R., Garcia, J., Hankins, W. G., & Rusiniak, K. W. (1974) Coyote predation control by aversive conditioning. *Science, 184,* 581–583.

Guthrie, E. R. (1952) *The psychology of learning* (rev. ed.). New York: Harper.

Hackett, P. B., Fuchs, J. A., & Messing, J. W. (1984) *An introduction to recombinant DNA techniques.* Menlo Park, CA: Benjamin/Cummings.

Haith, M. M. (1966) The response of the human newborn to visual movement. *Journal of Experimental Child Psychology, 3,* 112–117.

Hakel, M. D. (1986) Personal selection

and placement. In *Annual Review of Psychology* (pp. 351–380). Palo Alto, CA: Annual Reviews.

Halama, J. J. (1976) *The effects of assertion training and simulation instructions in the laboratory and the "Real World."* Unpublished doctoral dissertation, University of California, Los Angeles.

Hall, C. S. (1953) *The meaning of dreams.* New York: Harper.

Hall, E. T. (1966) *The hidden dimension.* Garden City, NY: Doubleday.

Hall, J. A. (1980) Voice tone and persuasion. *Journal of Personality and Social Psychology, 38,* 924–934.

Hall, J. F. (1976) *Classical conditioning and instrumental learning:* A contemporary approach. Philadelphia: Lippincott.

Halmi, K. A. (1978) Anorexia nervosa: Recent investigations. *Annual Review of Medicine, 29,* 137–148.

Halmi, K. A. (1983) Advances in anorexia nervosa. *Advances in Developmental and Behavioral Pediatrics.* (Vol. 4) M. Wolraich & D. Routh (Eds.). Greenwich, CT: JAI Press, pp. 1–23.

Hamilton, E., & Abramson, L. (1983) Cognitive patterns and major depressive disorder: A longitudinal study in a hospital setting. *Journal of Abnormal Psychology, 92,* 173–184.

Hammen, C. L. (1985) Predicting depression: A cognitive-behavioral perspective. *Advances in Cognitive Research Therapy, 4,* 29–71.

Hammen, C. L., Jacobs, M., Mayol, A., & Cochran, S. D. (1980) Dysfunctional cognitions and the effectiveness of skills and cognitive-behavioral assertion training. *Journal of Consulting and Clinical Psychology, 48,* 685–695.

Hampton, J. A. (1979) Polymorphous concepts in semantic memory. *Journal of Verbal Learning and Verbal Behavior, 18,* 441–461.

Hanawalt, N. G., & Demarest, I. H. (1939) The effect of verbal suggestion in the recall period upon the reproduction of visually perceived forms. *Journal of Experimental Psychology, 25,* 159–174.

Harlow, H. F. (1971) *Learning to love.* San Francisco: Albion.

Harlow, H. F., Harlow, M. K., & Meyer, D. R. (1950) Learning motivated by a manipulation drive. *Journal of Experimental Psychology, 40,* 228–234.

Harrell, T. W., & Harrell, M. S. (1945) Army General Classification Test scores for civilian occupations. *Educational and Psychological Measurement, 5,* 229–239.

Hartmann, E. L. (1973) *Functions of sleep.* New Haven: Yale University Press.

Hartmann, E. L. (1978) *The sleeping pill.* New Haven, CT: Yale University Press.

Hartup, W. W. (1983) Peer relations. In P. H. Mussen (Ed.), *Handbook of child psychology* (Vol. 4, 4th ed.). New York: Wiley.

Hatfield, E., & Sprecher, S. (1986) *Mirror, mirror: The importance of looks in everyday life.* Albany: State University of New York Press.

Hathaway, S. R., & McKinley, J. C. (1942) A multiphasic personality schedule (Minnesota). I. Construction of the schedule. *Journal of Psychology, 10,* 249–254.

Hathaway, S. R., & McKinley, J. C. (1943) *Manual for the Minnesota multiphasic personality inventory.* New York: Psychological Corporation.

Hattie, J. A., Sharpley, C. F., & Rogers, H. J. (1984) Comparative effectiveness of professional and paraprofessional helpers. *Psychological Bulletin, 95,* 534–531.

Hayes, C. D. (1987) *Risking the future: Adolescent sexuality, pregnancy and childbearing.* Washington, DC: National Academy Press, National Academy of Sciences.

Hayes, D. S., Gershman, E., & Bolin, J. (1980) Friends and enemies: Cognitive bases for preschool children's unilateral and reciprocal relationships. *Child Development, 51,* 1276–1279.

Hayes, K. J., & Hayes C. (1952) Imitation in a home-raised chimpanzee, *Journal of Comparative and Physiological Psychology, 45,* 450–459.

Hayes, S. C., & Cone, J. D. (1981) Reduction of residential consumption of electricity through simple monthly feedback. *Journal of Applied Behavior Analysis, 14,* 81–88.

Hayes-Roth, B., & Thorndike, P. (1979) Integration of knowledge from text. *Journal of Verbal Learning and Verbal Behavior, 18,* 91–108.

Hayes-Roth, R., & Hayes-Roth, F. A. (1979) A cognitive model of planning. *Cognitive Science, 3,* 275–310.

Haynes, S. N. (1984) Behavioral assessment of adults. In G. Goldstein & M. Hersen (Eds.), *Handbook of psychological assessment* (pp. 369–401). New York: Pergamon.

Healy, A. (1980) Proofreading errors on the word *the*: New evidence on reading units. *Journal of Experimental Psychology: Human Perception and Performance, 6,* 45–57.

Heber, F. R. (1978) Sociocultural mental retardation—a longitudinal study. In D. Forgays (Ed.), *Primary prevention of psychopathology* (Vol. 2). Hanover, New Hampshire: University Press of New England.

Heber, R., Garber, H., Harrington, S., & Hoffman, C. (1972, December) Rehabilitation of families at risk for mental retardation. Unpublished progress report, Research and Training Center, University of Wisconsin, Madison.

Heider, E. R. (1971) "Focal" color areas and the development of color names. *Developmental Psychology, 4,* 447–455.

Heider, F. (1958) *The psychology of interpersonal relations.* New York: Wiley.

Held, J. M., Gordon, J., & Gentile, A. M. (1985) Environmental influence on locomotor recovery following cortical lesions in rats. *Behaviorial Neuroscience, 99,* 678–690.

Helfer, R. E. (1975) Why most physicians don't get involved in child abuse cases and what to do about it. *Children Today, 4,* 29–32.

Henry, J. (1982) Endorphins and behavior. *Annual Review of Psychology, 33,* 87–102.

Herman, C. P., & Polivy, J. (1980) Restrained eating. In A. B. Stunkard (Ed.), *Obesity.* Philadelphia: Saunders.

Heron, W., Doane, B. K., & Scott, T. H. (1956) Visual disturbances after prolonged perceptual isolation. *Canadian Journal of Psychology, 10,* 13–16.

Herrnstein, R. J., Nickerson, R. S., de Sanchez, M., & Swets, J. A. (1986) Teaching thinking skills. *American Psychologist, 41,* 1279–1289.

Hess, E. H. (1959) Imprinting. *Science, 130,* 133–144.

Hess, E. H. (1972) "Imprinting" in a natural laboratory. *Scientific American, 227,* 24–31.

Hess, E. H., Seltzer, A. L., & Shlien, J. M. (1965) Pupil response of hetero- and homosexual males to pictures of men and women: A pilot study. *Journal of Abnormal Psychology, 70,* 165–168.

Hess, R. D., Shipman, V. C., Brophy, J. E., & Bear, R. M. (1969) *The cognitive environments of urban preschool children: Follow-up phase.* Chicago: The Graduate School of Education, University of Chicago.

Hetherington, E. M., & Martin, B. (1986) Family factors and psychopathology in children. In H. Quay & J. Werry (Eds.), *Psychopathological disorders of childhood* (3rd ed., pp. 332–390). New York: Wiley.

Hetherington, E. M., Cox, M., & Cox, R. (1985) Long-term effects of divorce and remarriage on the adjustment of children. *Journal of the American Academy of Child Psychiatry, 24,* 518–530.

High, J., & Sundstrom, R. (1977) Room flexibility. *Environmental Behavior, 9,* 21–29.

Hilgard, E. R. (1965) *Hypnotic susceptibility*. New York: Harcourt Brace Jovanovich.

Hilgard, E. R., & Bower, G. H. (1975) *Theories of learning* (4th ed.) Englewood Cliffs, NJ: Prentice-Hall.

Hill, J. L. (1985) *The rat populations of NIMH*. Paper presented at the Symposium Behavior as a factor in the population dynamics of rodents, held at the annual meeting of the American Society of Zoologists, Baltimore.

Hines, M., & Shipley, C. (1984) Prenatal exposure to diethylstilbestrol (DES) and the development of sexually dimorphic cognitive abilities and cerebral lateralization. *Developmental Psychology, 20,* 81–94.

Hink, R. F., Kagan, K., & Suzuki, J. (1980) An evoked potential correlate of reading ideographic and phonetic Japanese scripts. *Neuropsychologia, 18,* 455–464.

Hiroto, D. S. (1974) Locus of control and learned helplessness, *Journal of Experimental Psychology, 102,* 187–193.

Hirschfeld, R., & Cross, C. (1982) Epidemiology of affective disorders: Psychosocial risk factors. *Archives of General Psychiatry, 39,* 35–46.

Hochberg, J. E. (1971) Perception. In J. W. Kling & L. A. Riggs (Eds.), *Experimental psychology.* New York: Holt.

Hoebel, B. G., & Teitelbaum, P. (1962) Hypothalamic control of feeding and self-stimulation. *Science, 135,* 375–377.

Hoelscher, T. J., Lichstein, K. L., Fischer, S., & Hegarty, T. B. (1987) Relaxation treatment of hypertension: Do home relaxation tapes enhance treatment outcome? *Behavior Therapy, 18,* 33–37.

Hoffman, H. S., & Ratner, A. M. (1973) A reinforcement model of imprinting: Implications for socialization in monkeys and men. *Psychological Review, 80,* 527–544.

Hogarty, G. E., & Ullrich, R. F. (1977) Temporal effects of drug and placebo in delaying relapse in schizophrenic outpatients. *Archives of General Psychiatry, 34,* 297–301.

Holland, M. K., & Tarlow, G. (1980) *Using Psychology* (2nd ed.). Boston: Little, Brown.

Hollis, J. F., Carmody, T. P., Connor, S. L., Fey, S. G., & Matarazzo, J. D. (1986) The Nutrition Attitude Survey: Associations with dietary habits, psychological and physical well-being, and coronary risk factors. *Health Psychology, 5,* 359–374.

Holmberg, M. C. (1980) The development of social interchange patterns from 12 to 42 months. *Child Development, 51,* 448–456.

Holmes, T. H., & Masuda, M. (1974) Life change and illness susceptibility. In B. S. Dohrenwend & B. P. Dohrenwend (Eds.), *Stressful life events: Their nature and effects.* New York: Wiley.

Holmes, T. S., & Holmes, T. H. (1970) Short-term intrusions into life-style routine. *Journal of Psychosomatic Research, 14,* 121–132.

Holtzman, W. H. (1975) New developments in Holtzman inkblot technique. In P. McReynolds (Ed.), *Advances in psychological assessment.* (Vol. 3.). San Francisco: Jossey-Bass.

Holzberg, J. D. (1977) Reliability reexamined. In M. A. Rickers-Ovsiankina (Ed.), *Rorschach psychology* (2nd ed.). Huntington, NY: Krieger.

Honzik, M. P., Macfarlane, J. W., & Allen L. (1948) The stability of mental test performance between two and eighteen years. *Journal of Experimental Education, 17,* 309–324.

Hopkins, J., Marcus, M., & Campbell, S. B. (1984) Postpartum depression: A critical review. *Psychological Bulletin, 95*(3), 498–515.

Horan, J. J., Hoffman, A. M., & Macri, M. (1974) Self-control of chronic fingernail biting. Journal of Behavior Therapy and Experimental Psychiatry, *5,* 307–309.

Horn, J. L., (1970) Organization of data on lifespan development of human abilities. In L. R. Goulet & P. B. Baltes (Eds.), *Life-Span developmental psychology: Research and theory.* New York: Academic Press.

Horowitz, M. J., Marmar, C., Weiss, D. S., DeWitt, K., & Rosenbaum, R. (1984) Brief psychotherapy of bereavement reactions: The relationship of process to outcome. *Archives of General Psychiatry, 41,* 438–448.

Horton, D. L., & Turnage, T. W. (1976) *Human learning.* Englewood Cliffs, NJ: Prentice-Hall.

Houston, J. P. (1976) *Fundamentals of learning.* New York: Academic Press.

Houston, J. P. (1981) *The pursuit of happiness.* Glenview, IL: Scott, Foresman.

Houston, J. P. (1981) *Fundamentals of learning and memory.* New York: Academic Press.

Houston, J. P. (1985) *Motivation.* New York: Macmillan.

Houston, J. P. (1986) *Fundamentals of learning and memory* (3rd ed.). San Diego: Harcourt Brace Jovanovich.

Howard, K. I., Kopta, S. M., Krause, M. S., & Orlinsky, D. E. (1986) The dose-effect relationship in psychotherapy. *American Psychologist, 41,* 159–164.

Hubel, D. H., & Wiesel, T. N. (1965) Receptive fields and functional architecture in two non-striate visual areas (18 and 19) of the cat. *Journal of Neurophysiology, 28,* 229–287.

Huesmann, L. R., Eron, L. D., Klein, R., Brice, P., & Fischer, P. (1983) Mitigating the imitation of aggressive behaviors by changing children's attitudes about media violence. *Journal of Personality and Social Psychology, 44,* 899–910.

Huesmann, L. R., Lagerspetz, K., & Eron, L. D. (1984) Intervening variables in the TV violence-aggression relation. *Developmental Psychology, 20,* 746–775.

Hull, C. L. (1951) *Essentials of behavior.* New Haven, CT: Yale University Press.

Hull, C. L. (1952) *A behavior system.* New Haven, CT: Yale University Press.

Hulse, S. H., Egeth, H., & Deese, J. (1980) *The psychology of learning.* New York: McGraw-Hill.

Hunt, E. L. (1949) Establishment of conditioned responses in chick embryos. *Journal of Comparative and Physiological Psychology, 42,* 107–117.

Huston, T., & Korte, C. (1976) The responsive bystander: Why he helps. In T. Lickona (Ed.), *Moral development and behavior.* New York: Holt, Rinehart, & Winston.

Huston, T. L., Ruggiero, M., Conner, R., & Geis, G. (1981) Bystander intervention into crime: A study based on naturally occurring episodes. *Social Psychology Quarterly, 44,* 14–23.

Hutchinson, R. R. (1977) By-products of aversive control. IN W. K. Honig & J. E. R. Staddon (Eds.), *Handbook of operant behavior.* Englewood Cliffs, NJ: Prentice-Hall.

Hyde, J. S. (1979) *Understanding human sexuality.* New York: McGraw-Hill.

Hyman, B., Van Hoesen, G., Damasio, A., & Barnes, C. (1984) Alzheimer's disease: Cell-specific pathology isolates the hippocampal formation. *Science, 225,* 1168–1170.

Inhelder, B., & Piaget, J. (1958) *The growth of logical thinking from childhood to adolescence.* New York: Basic Books.

Ireson, C. J. (1984) Adolescent pregnancy and sex roles. *Sex Roles, 3 & 4,* 189–201.

Jacobson, D. E. (1986) Types and timing of social support. *Journal of Health and Social Behavior, 27,* 250–264.

Jacobson, N. S., Elwood, R. W., & Dallas, M. (1981) Assessment of marital dysfunction. In D. H. Barlow (Ed.), *Behavioral assessment of adult disorders.* New York: The Guilford Press.

Jacobson, N. S., Waldron, H., & Moore,

D. (1980) Toward a behavioral profile of marital distress. *Journal of Consulting and Clinical Psychology, 48,* 696–703.

James, J. E. (1981) Behavioral self-control of stuttering using time-out from speaking. *Journal of Applied Behavior Analysis, 14,* 25–37

James, J. R. (1977) For women: Reaching orgasm. In C. Zastrow & D. H. Chang (Eds.), *The personal problem solver.* Englewood Cliffs, NJ: Prentice-Hall.

James, W. (1890) *Principles of psychology.* New York: Holt.

Jensen, A. R. (1969) How much can we boost I.Q. and scholastic achievement? *Harvard Educational Review, 39,* 1–123.

Johnston, L. D., Bachman, J. G., & O'Malley, P. M. (1981) *Highlights from student drug use in America, 1975-1981* (DHHS Publication No. ADM 82-1208). Washington, DC: U.S. Government Printing Office.

Jones, E. E. (1986, October 3) Interpreting interpersonal behavior: The effects of expectancies. *Science, 234,* 41–46.

Jones, E. E., & Davis, K. E. (1965) From acts to disposition: The attribution process in person perception. In L. Berkowitz (Ed.), *Advances in experimental social psychology.* (Vol. 2). New York: Academic Press.

Jones, K. L., Shainberg, L. W., & Bywe, C. O. (1973) *Drugs and alcohol.* (2nd ed.). New York: Harper.

Julien, R. M. (1981) *A primer of drug action* (3rd ed.). San Francisco: W. H. Freeman.

Kagan, J., & Havemann, E. (1976) *Psychology: An introduction.* New York: Harcourt Brace Jovanovich.

Kagan, J., Kearsley, R. B., & Zelazo, P. R. (1978) *Infancy: Its place in human development.* Cambridge, MA: Harvard University Press.

Kagan, J. B., Resnick, J. S., & Snidman, N. (1980) Biological bases of childhood shyness. *Science, 240,* 167–171.

Kahn, A. J., & Kamerman, S. B. (1987) *Child care: Facing the hard choices.* Dover, MA: Auburn House.

Kahneman, D., & Tversky, A. (1973) On the psychology of prediction. *Psychological Review, 71,* 42-60.

Kalat, J. W. (1984) *Biological psychology* (2nd ed.). Belmont, CA: Wadsworth.

Kallmann, F. J. (1953) *Heredity in health and mental disorder.* New York: Norton.

Kallmann, F. J. (1958) The use of genetics in psychiatry. *Journal of Mental Science, 104,* 542–549.

Kalter, N. (1987) Long-term effects of divorce on children: A developmental vulnerability model. *American Journal of Orthopsychiatry, 57,* 587–600.

Kamin, L. J. (1974) *The science and politics of I.Q.* Potomac, MD: Lawrence Erlbaum Associates.

Kanthamani, H., & Kelly, E. F. (1975) Card experiments with a special subject II. The shuffle method. *Journal of Parapsychology, 39,* 207–222

Kaplan, A. & Woodside, D. (1987) Biological aspects of anorexia nervosa and bulimia nervosa. *Journal of Consulting and Clinical Psychology, 55,* 645–653.

Karson, C. N., Kleinman, J. E., & Wyatt, R. J. (1986) Biochemical concepts of schizophrenia. In T. Millon & G. L. Klerman (Eds.), *Contemporary directions in psychopathology: Toward the DSM-IV* (pp. 495–518). New York: The Guilford Press.

Kasch, F. W. (1976, June) The effects of exercise on the aging process. *The Physician and Sports Medicine,* pp. 64–68.

Kashani, J., & Hakami, N. (1982) Depression in children and adolescents with malignancy. *Canadian Journal of Psychiatry, 27,* 474–476.

Kashani, J., & Simonds, J. F. (1979) The incidence of depression in children. *American Journal of Psychiatry, 135,* 1203–1205.

Kaufman, J., & Zigler, E. (1987) Do abused children become abusive parents. *American Journal of Orthopsychiatry, 57,* 186–192.

Kausler, D. H. (1974) *The psychology of verbal learning and memory.* New York: Academic Press.

Kazdin, A. E., & Wilcoxin, L. A. (1976) Systematic desensitization and non-specific treatment effects: A methodological evaluation. *Psychological Bulletin, 83,* 729–758.

Keefe, F. J., Surwit, & Pilon, R. N. (1980) Biofeedback, autogenic training, and progressive relaxation in the treatment of Raynaud's disease: A comparative study. *Journal of Applied Behavior Analysis, 13,* 3–11.

Keister, M. E., & Updegraff, R. A. (1937) A study of children's reactions to failure and an experimental attempt to modify them. *Child Development, 8,* 241–248.

Keller, M. B., Lavori, P. W., Endicott, J., Coryell, W., & Klerman, G. L. (1983) "Double depression": Two-year follow-up. *American Journal of Psychiatry, 140,* 689–694.

Kelley, H. H. (1967) Attribution theory in social psychology. In D. Levine (Ed.), *Nebraska Symposium on Motivation* (Vol. 15). Lincoln: University of Nebraska Press.

Kelley, H. H. (1980) The causes of behavior: Their perception and regulation. In L. Festinger (Ed.), *Retrospec-* tions on social psychology. New York: Oxford University Press.

Kelley, H. H., & Michela, J. L. (1980) Attribution theory and research. *Annual Review of Psychology, 31,* 457–501.

Kempe, R. S., & Kempe, C. H. (1978) *Child abuse.* Cambridge, MA: Harvard University Press.

Kempler, W. (1973) Gestalt therapy. In R. Corsini (Ed.), *Current psychotherapies.* Itasca, IL: F. E. Peacock.

Kendler, H. H. (1977) *Basic Psychology.* Menlo Park, CA: Benjamin.

Kennedy, T. D. (1971) Reinforcement frequency, task characteristics and interval of awareness assessment as factors in verbal conditioning without awareness. *Journal of Experimental Psychology, 88,* 103–112.

Kernberg, O. (1984) *Severe personality disorders: Psychotherapeutic strategies.* New Haven: Yale University Press.

Kessler, R. C., & McLeod, J. D. (1984) Sex differences in vulnerability to undesirable life events. *American Sociological Review, 49,* 620–631.

Kety, S., Rosenthal, D., Wender, P., & Schulsinger, F. (1976) Studies based on a total sample of adopted individuals and their relatives: Why they were necessary, what they demonstrated and failed to demonstrate. *Schizophrenia Bulletin, 2,* 414–428.

Khrishna, G. (1976) *Kundalini: Evolutionary energy in man.* Berkeley, CA: Shambala Press.

Kidd, R. F., & Chayet, E. F. (1984) Why do victims fail to report? The psychology of criminal victimization. *Journal of Social Issues, 40,* 39–50.

Kihlstrom, J. F. (1987, September 18) The cognitive unconscious. *Science, 237,* 1445–1451.

Kimball, W., Conger, R. D., & Burgess, R. L. (1980) A comparison of family interaction in single versus two-parent abuse, neglectful and control families. In T. Field, S. Goldberg, D. Stern, & A. Sostek (Eds.), *Interactions of High Risk Infants and Children.* New York: Academic Press.

Kimble, G. A. (1967) *Foundations of conditioning and learning.* New York: Appleton.

Kinard, E. M. (1980) Emotional development in physically abused children. *American Journal of Orthopsychiatry, 50,* 686–696.

Kinsey, A. C., Pomeroy, W. B., & Martin, C. E. (1948) *Sexual behavior in the human male.* Philadelphia: Saunders.

Kinsey, A. C., Pomeroy, W. B., & Martin, C. E. (1953) *Sexual behavior in the human female.* Philadelphia: Saunders.

Kirby, D. (1984) *Sexuality education: An evaluation of programs and their effects.* New York: Network Publications.

Kirchner, R. E., Schnelle, J. F., Do-mash, M., Larson, L., Carr, A., & McNees, M. P. (1980) The applicability of a helicopter patrol procedure to diverse areas: A cost-benefit evaluation. *Journal of Applied Behavior Analysis, 13,* 143–148.

Kirkland, K., & Caughlin-Carvar, J. (1982) Maintenance and generalization of assertive skills. *Education & Training of the Mentally Retarded, 17,* 313–318.

Kirsch, M. M. (1986) *Designer drugs.* Minneapolis, MN: Comp Care.

Kish, G. B. (1955) Learning when the onset of illumination is used as reinforcing stimulus. *Journal of Comparative and Physiological Psychology, 48,* 261–264.

Klaus, M. H., & Kennell, J. H. (1976) *Maternal-infant bonding.* St. Louis, MO: Mosby.

Klein, D. F., Zitrin, C. M., Woerner, M. G., & Ross, D. C. (1983) Treatment of phobias : Behavior therapy and supportive psychotherapy: Are there any specific ingredients? *Archives of General Psychiatry, 40,* 139–145.

Kleinmuntz, B. (1973) *Essentials of abnormal psychology.* New York: Harper.

Kleinmuntz, B. (1984) The scientific study of clinical judgment in psychology and medicine. *Clinical Psychology Review, 4,* 111–126.

Kleinmuntz, B., & Szucko, J. J. (1984) On the fallibility of lie detection. *Law and Society, 17,* 85–104.

Klerman, G. L., Lavori, P. W., Rice, J., Reich, T., Endicott, J., Andreasen, N. C., Keller, M. B., & Hirschfield, R. M. A. (1985) Birth-cohort trends in rates of major depressive disorder among relatives of patients with affective disorder. *Archives of General Psychiatry, 42,* 689–693.

Kling, J. W., & Schrier, A. M. (1971) Positive reinforcement. In J. W. Kling & L. A. Riggs (Eds.), *Woodworth and Schlosberg's experimental psychology.* New York: Holt.

Knowles, R. J. (1987, August 9) Can bad air make bad things happen? New York: *Parade Magazine,* pp. 7–8.

Kohlberg, L. (1969) Stage and sequence: The cognitive developmental approach to socialization. In D. Goslin (Ed.), *Handbook of socialization theory and research.* Chicago: Rand McNally.

Kohlberg, L., & Elfenbein, D. (1975) The development of moral judgments concerning capital punishment. *American Journal of Orthopsychiatry, 45,* 614–640.

Kohlenberg, R., Phillips, T., & Proctor, W. (1976) A behavioral analysis of peaking in residential electric-energy consumption. *Journal of Applied Behav-*

ior Analysis, 9, 13–18.

Kohler, J. (1962) Experiments with goggles. *Scientific American, 206,* 62–72.

Köhler, W. (1925) *The mentality of apes.* New York: Harcourt.

Kohut, H. (1977) *The restoration of the self.* New York: International Universities Press.

Kolata, G. (1986) Maleness pinpointed on Y chromosome. *Science,* 1076–1077.

Kosslyn, S. M. (1981) The medium and the message in mental imagery: A theory. *Psychological Review, 88,* 46–66.

Kovacs, M., Beck, A., & Weissman, A. (1975) Hopelessness: An indicator of suicidal risk. *Suicide, 5,* 98–103.

Kramer, F. M., Jeffery, R. W., Snell, M. K., & Forster, J. L. (1986) Maintenance of successful weight loss over 1 year: Effects of financial contracts for weight maintenance or participation in skills training. *Behavior Therapy, 17,* 295–301.

Krugman, R. D., Lenherr, M., Betz, L., & Fryer, G. E. (1986) The relationship between unemployment and physical abuse of children. *Child Abuse & Neglect, 10,* 415–418.

Krulewitz, J. E., & Nash, J. R. (1980) Effects of sex-role attitudes and similarity on men's rejection of male homosexuals. *Journal of Personality and Social Psychology, 38,* 67–74.

Kübler-Ross, E. (1969) *On death and dying.* New York: Macmillan.

Kuhn, D., Nash, S. C., & Brucken, L. (1978) Sex-role concept of two- and three-year-olds. *Child Development, 49,* 445–451.

Kukla, R. A., & Weingarten, H. (1979) The long-term effects of parental divorce in childhood on adult adjustment. *Journal of Social Issues, 35,* 50–78.

Kulik, J. A., Bangert, R. L., & Williams, G. W. (1983) Effects of counter-based teaching on secondary school students. *Journal of Educational Psychology, 75,* 19–26.

Kupfersmid, J. H., & Wonderly, D. M. (1980) Moral maturity and behavior: Failure to find a link. *Journal of Youth and Adolescence, 9,* 249–262.

Kurdek, L. A., & Berg, B. (1987) Children's beliefs about parental divorce scale: Psychometric characteristics and concurrent validity. *Journal of Consulting and Clinical Psychology, 55,* 712–718.

Kutschinsky, B. (1971) The effect of pornography: A pilot experiment on perception, behavior and attitudes. *Technical report of the commission on obscenity and pornography.* Washington, DC: U.S. Government Printing Office.

Labov, W. (1973) The boundaries of words and their meanings. In C. J. N. Bailey & R. W. Shuy (Eds.), *New ways of analyzing variations in English.* Washington, DC: Georgetown University Press.

Ladavas, E., Umilta, C., & Ricci-Bitti, P. E. (1980) Evidence for sex differences in right-hemisphere dominance for emotions. *Neuropsychologia, 18,* 361–366.

Laird, G. S., & Fenz, W. D. (1971) Effects of respiration on heart rate in an aversive classical conditioning situation. *Canadian Journal of Psychology, 25,* 395–411.

Lambert, K. (1981) Emerging consciousness. *Journal of Analytical Psychology, 26,* 1–17.

Landis, J. T. (1962) A comparison of children from divorced and non-divorced unhappy marriages. *Family Life Coordinator, 21,* 61–65.

Lang, P. J., Geer, J., & Hnatiow, M. (1963) Semantic generalization of conditioned autonomic responses. *Journal of Experimental Psychology, 65,* 552–558.

Lange, C. G. (1922) *The emotions.* Baltimore: Williams & Wilkins.

Langlois, J. H., & Downs, A. C. (1980) Mothers, fathers, and peers as socialization agents of sex-typed play behaviors in young children. *Child Development, 51,* 1237–1247.

Langlois, J. H., Roggman, L. A., Casey, R. J., Ritter, J. M., Rieser-Danner, L. A., & Jenkins, V. Y. (1987) Infant preferences for attractive faces: Rudiments of a stereotype? *Developmental Psychology, 23,* 363–369.

Latané, B. (1981) The psychology of social impact. *American Psychologist, 36,* 343–356.

Latané, B., & Darley, J. M. (1970) *The unresponsive bystander: Why doesn't he help?* New York: Appleton-Century-Croft.

Latané, B., & Nida, S. (1981) Ten years of research on group size and helping. *Psychological Bulletin, 89,* 307–324.

Lau, R. R., Hartman, K. A., & Ware, J. E. (1986) Health as a value: Methodological and theoretical considerations. *Health Psychology, 5,* 25–43.

Lavin, D. E. (1965) *The prediction of academic performance: A theoretical analysis and review of research.* New York: Russell Sage Foundation.

Lazarus, A. A. (1960) The elimination of children's phobias by deconditioning. In H. J. Eysenck (Ed.), *Behavior therapy and the neuroses.* Oxford: Pergamon.

Leibowitz, H. W., Brislin, R. Perlmuth, L., & Hennessy, R. (1969) Ponzo perspective illusion as a manifestation of space perception. *Science, 166,* 1174–1176.

Lenneberg, E. H. (1967) Biological foundations of language. New York: Wiley.

Lenneberg, E. H. (1969) On explaining language. *Science, 164,* 635–643.

Lesgold, A. M., & Goldman, S. R. (1973) Encoding uniqueness and the imagery mnemonic in associative learning. *Journal of Verbal Learning and Verbal Behavior, 12,* 193–202.

Leslie, J. C. (1981) Effects of variations in local reinforcement rate on local response rate in variable interval schedules. *Journal of the Experimental Analysis of Behavior, 35,* 45–53.

Lesser, G. F., Fifer, G., & Clark, D. H. (1965) Mental abilities of children from different social class and cultural groups. *Monographs of the Society for Research in Child Development, 30,* (4, Whole No. 102).

Lettvin, J. Y., Maturana, H. R., McCulloch, W. S., & Pitts, W. H. (1959) What the frog's eye tells the frog's brain. *Proceedings of the Institute of Radio Engineers, 47,* 140–151.

Levenson, R., Oyama, O., & Meek, P. (1987) Greater reinforcement from alcohol for those at risk: Parental risk, personality risk, and sex. *Journal of Abnormal Psychology, 96,* 242–253.

Levine, F. M., & Sandeen, E. (1985) *Conceptualization in psychotherapy: The models approach.* Hillsdale, NJ: Erlbaum.

Levinson, D. J. (1978) *The seasons of a man's life.* New York: Knopf.

Levinson, D. J. (1980) Toward a conception of the adult life course. In N. J. Smelser & E. H. Erickson (Eds.), *Themes of work and love in adulthood.* Cambridge, MA: Harvard University Press.

Levitsky, A., & Perls, F. S. (1970) The rules and games of gestalt therapy. In J. Fagan & I. Shephard (Eds.), *Gestalt therapy now.* Palo Alto, CA: Science and Behavior Books.

Lewin, R. (1981) Jumping genes help trace inherited diseases. *Science, 211,* 690–692.

Lewinsohn, P. M., Mischel, W., Chaplin, W., & Barton, R. (1980) Social competence and depression: The role of illusory self-perceptions. *Journal of Abnormal Psychology, 89,* 203–212.

Lewis, D. J. (1956) Acquisition, extinction, and spontaneous recovery as a function of percentage of reinforcement and intertrial intervals. *Journal of Experimental Psychology, 51,* 45–53.

Lewis, J. W., & Leibeskind, J. C. (1983) Pain suppressive systems of the brain. *Trends in Pharmacological Sciences, 4,* 73–75.

Lewis, M. (1969) Infants' responses to facial stimuli during the first year of life. *Developmental Psychology, 1,* 75–86.

Lewis, M., & Schaeffer, S. (1981) Peer behavior and mother-infant interaction in maltreated children. In M. Lewis & L. A. Rosenblum (Eds.), *The uncommon child.* New York: Plenum Press.

Lewis, R. A., & Spanier, G. B. (1979) Theorizing about the quality and stability of marriage. In W. R. Burr, R. Hill, F. I. Nye, & I. L. Reiss (Eds.), *Contemporary theories about the family* (Vol. 2.). New York: The Free Press.

Lewis, S. A., Sloan, J. P., & Jones, S. K. (1978) Paradoxical sleep and depth perception. *Biological Psychology, 6,* 17–25.

Lidz, T. (1967) The influence of family studies on the treatment of schizophrenia. *Psychiatry, 32,* 235–251.

Lieberman, A. N. (1987) *Parkinson's disease handbook.* New York: American Parkinson's Disease Association.

Lieberman, M. A. (1965) Psychological correlates of impending death: some preliminary observations. *Journal of Gerontology, 20,* 181–190.

Lieberman, M. A. (1966) Observations on death and dying. *Gerontologist, 6,* 70–73.

Lieberman, M. (1986) Self-help groups and psychiatry. In A. J. Francis & R. E. Hales (Eds.), *Annual Review* (Vol. 5). Washington, DC: American Psychiatric Press.

Lieberman, M., Yalom, I., & Miles, M. (1973) *Encounter groups: First facts.* New York: Basic Books.

Light, R. (1973) Abused and neglected children in America: A study of alternative policies. *Harvard Educational Review, 43,* 556–598.

Ligon, J. D., & Ligon, S. H. (1982) The cooperative breeding behavior of the green woodhoopoe. *Scientific American, 247,* 126–134.

Limber, J. (1977) Language in child and chimp. *American Psychologist, 32,* 280–296.

Lindsay, P. H., & Norman, D. A. (1977) *Human information processing: An introduction to psychology.* (2nd ed.). New York: Academic Press.

Lipsitt, L. P., Reilly, B. M., Butcher, M. J., & Greenwood, M. M. (1976) The stability and interrelationships of newborn sucking and heart rate. *Developmental Psychology, 9,* 305–310.

Lipsitt, L. P., Engen, T., & Kaye, H. (1963) Developmental changes in the olfactory threshold of the neonate. *Child Development, 34,* 371–376.

Liska, K. (1981) *Drugs and the human body.* New York: Macmillan.

Lockhard, R. B. (1966) Several tests of stimulus-change and preference theory in relation to light-controlled behavior in rats. *Journal of Comparative and Physiological Psychology, 62,* 415–426.

Loftus, E. F., & Loftus, G. R. (1980) On the permanence of stored information in the human brain. *American Psychologist, 35,* 409–420.

Loftus, E. F., & Palmer, J. C. (1974) Reconstruction of automobile destruction: An example of the interaction between language and memory. *Journal of Verbal Learning and Verbal Behavior, 13,* 585–589.

Logan, F. A., & Gordon, W. C. (1981) *Fundamentals of learning and motivation.* Dubuque, IA: W. C. Brown.

Lord, B. J., King, M. G., & Pfister, H. P. (1976) Chemical sympathectomy and two-way escape and avoidance learning in the rat. *Journal of Comparative and Physiological Psychology, 90,* 303–316.

Lorenz, K. (1969) Innate bases of learning. In K. H. Pribram (Ed.), *On the biology of learning.* New York: Harcourt Brace Jovanovich.

Los Angeles Times, (1988, June 3) Morning Report: Movies. Part VI, p. 2.

Lott, A. J., & Lott, B. E. (1974) The role of reward in the formation of positive interpersonal attitudes. In T. L. Huston (Ed.), *Foundations of interpersonal attraction.* New York: Academic Press.

Lovaas, O. I. (1977) *The autistic child: Language development through behavior modification.* New York: Irvington

Lovaas, O. I. (1978) Parents as therapists. In M. Rutter & E. Schopler (Eds.), *Autism: A reappraisal of concepts and treatment.* New York: Plenum Press.

Lovaas, O. I., Schaeffer, B., & Simmons, J. (1965) Experimental studies in childhood schizophrenia: Building social behaviors using electric shock. *Journal of Experimental Studies in Personality, 1,* 99–109.

Lovallo, W. R., & Pishkin, V. (1980) Performance of Type A (coronary-prone) men during and after exposure to uncontrollable noise and task failure. *Journal of Abnormal and Social Psychology, 38,* 963–971.

Lowenthal, M. F., Thurnher, M., & Chiriboga, D. (1975) *Four stages of life.* San Francisco: Jossey-Bass.

Loye, D. (1978, June) TV's impact on adults. *Psychology Today,* pp. 87–94.

Lubin, B., & Lubin, A. W. (1980) *An exhaustive bibliography of the group psychotherapy literature: 1906-1978.* New York: Plenum.

Luborsky, L., Crits-Christoph, P., Alexander, L., Margolis, M., & Cohen, M. (1983) Two helping alliance methods for predicting outcomes of psychotherapy: Counting signs vs. global rating method. *Journal of Nervous and Mental Disorders, 171,* 480–492.

Luborsky, L., Mellon, J., van Ravenswaay, P., Childress, A. R., Cohen, K. D., Hole, A. V., Ming, S., Crits-Christoph, P., Levine, F. J., & Alexander, K. (1985) A verification of Freud's grandest clinical hypothesis: The transference. *Clinical Psychology Review, 5,* 231–246.

Luborsky, L., Singer, B., & Luborsky, L. (1975) Comparative studies of psychotherapy: Is it true that "Everyone has won and all must have prizes"? *Archives of General Psychiatry, 32,* 995–1008.

Lundin, R. W. (1979) *Theories and Systems of Psychology.* Lexington, MA: Heath.

Luria, A. R. (1973) *The working brain.* New York: Basic Books.

Lutzker, J. R., & Sherman, J. A. (1974) Producing generative sentence usage by imitation and reinforcement procedures. *Journal of Applied Behavior Analysis, 7,* 447–460.

Lykken, D. T. (1975, March) Guilty knowledge test: The right way to use a lie detector. *Psychology Today,* pp. 56–60.

Lykken, D. T. (1979) The detection of deception. *Psychological Bulletin, 86,* 47–53.

Maas, H . S., & Kuypers, J. A. (1974) *From thirty to seventy.* San Francisco: Jossey-Bass.

Maccoby, E. E., & Feldman, S. S. (1972) Mother attachment and stranger-reactions in the third year of life. *Monographs of the Society for Research in Child Development, 37*(1, Whole No. 146).

Maccoby, E. E., & Jacklin, C. N. (1980) Sex differences in aggression: A rejoinder and reprise. *Child Development, 51,* 964–980.

Maccoby, M. (1976) *The gamesman.* New York: Simon & Schuster.

MacKay, D. C., & Newbigging, P. L. (1977) The Poggendorff and its variants do arouse the same perceptual processes. *Perception and Psychophysics, 21,* 26–32.

Mackenzie, B. (1984) Explaining race differences in IQ. *American Psychologist, 39,* 1214–1233.

MacKinnon, D. R., & Farberow, N. L. (1976) An assessment of the utility of suicide prediction. *Suicide and Life-Threatening Behavior, 6,* 86–91.

MacLean, P. D. (1954) Studies on limbic systems ("visceral brain") and their bearing on psychosomatic problems. In E. D. Wittkower & R. A. Cleghorn (Eds.), *Recent developments in psychosomatic medicine.* Philadelphia: Lippincott/Pittman.

MacNichol, E. F. (1964) Retinal mechanisms of color vision. *Vision Research, 4,* 119–133.

Mahoney, M. J., & Mahoney, K. (1976). *Permanent weight control.* New York: Norton.

Maier, S. F. (1970) Failure to escape traumatic electric shock: Incompatible skeletal-motor responses or learned helplessness? *Learning and Motivation, 1,* 157–169.

Maki, R. H., & Schuler, J. (1980) Effects of rehearsal duration and level of processing on memory for words. *Journal of Verbal Learning and Verbal Behavior, 19,* 36–45.

Malamuth, N., & Check, J. V. P. (1980) Penile tumescence and perceptual responses to a rape as a function of victim's perceived reactions. *Journal of Applied Social Psychology, 10,* 528–547.

Malamuth, N. M., & Donnerstein, E. (1983) *Pornography and sexual aggression.* New York: Academic Press.

Maltzman, I. (1977) Orienting in classical conditioning and generalization of the galvanic skin response to words: An overview. *Journal of Experimental Psychology, 106,* 111–119.

Mandler, G. (1962) Emotion. In R. Brown (Ed.), *New directions in psychology.* New York: Holt.

Mandler, G. (1977) Organization and recognition. In E. Tulving & W. Donaldson (Eds.), *Organization of memory.* (2nd ed.). New York: Academic Press.

Mandler, G. (1980) The generation of emotion: A psychological theory. In R. Plutchik & H. Kellerman (Eds.), *Emotion: Theory, research, and experience* (Vol I.). New York: Academic Press.

Mankiewicz, F., & Swerdlow, J. (1977) *Remote control.* New York: Quadrangle.

Mann, J., Sidman, J., & Starr, S. (1971) Effects of erotic films on sexual behavior of married couples. *Technical report of the commission on obscenity and pornography.* Washington, DC: U.S. Government Printing Office.

Manuck, S. B., Kaplin, J. R., & Matthews, K. A. (1986) Behavioral antecedents of coronary heart disease and atherosclerosis. *Arteriosclerosis, 6,* 2–14.

Margraf, J., Ehlers, A., & Roth, T. R. (1987) Panic attack associated with perceived heart rate acceleration: A case report. *Behavior Therapy, 18,* 84–89.

Marks, I. (1977) Clinical phenomena in search of laboratory models (phobias and obsessions). In J. Maser & M. Seligman (Eds.), *Psychopathology: Experimental Models* (pp. 174–213). San Francisco: Freeman.

Markus, H., & Wurf, E. (1987) The Dy-

namic self-concept: A social psychological perspective. *Annual Review of Psychology, 38,* 299–397.

Marlatt, G. A. (1979) Alcohol use and problem drinking. In P. C. Kendall & S. D. Hollon (Eds.), *Cognitive behavioral interventions: Theory, research, and procedures.* New York: Academic Press.

Marlatt, G. A. (1983) The controlled-drinking controversy. *American Psychologist, 38,* 1097–1111.

Marshall, J. F., Turner, B. H., & Teitelbaum, P. (1971) Sensory neglect produced by lateral hypothalamic damage. *Science, 174,* 523–525.

Marx, J. L. (1981) Three mice "cloned" in Switzerland. *Science, 211,* 375–376.

Marziali, E. A. (1984) Prediction of outcome of brief psychotherapy from therapist interpretive interventions. *Archives of General Psychiatry, 41,* 301–304.

Maslow, A. H. (1971) *The farther reaches of human nature.* New York: Viking.

Mason, M. (1980) Reading ability and encoding of item and location information. *Journal of Experimental Psychology; Human Perception and Performance, 6,* 89–98.

Massaro, D. W. (1972) Preperceptual images, processing time, and perceptual units in auditory perception. *Psychological Review, 79,* 124–145.

Masserano, J. M., Takimoto, G. S., & Weiner, N. (1981) Electroconvulsive shock increases tyrosine hydroxylase activity in the brain and adrenal gland of the rat. *Science, 214,* 662–665.

Masters, W. H., & Johnson, V. E. (1966) *Human sexual response.* Boston: Little, Brown.

Masters, W. H., & Johnson, V. E. (1970) *Human sexual inadequacy.* Boston: Little, Brown.

Matarazzo, J. D. (1972) *Wechsler's measurement and appraisal of adult intelligence* (5th ed.). Baltimore: Williams & Wilkins.

Matarazzo, J. D. (1986) Computerized clinical psychology test interpretations: Unvalidated plus all means and no sigma. *American Psychologist, 41,* 14–24.

Matheny, A. P., Jr., Wilson, R. S., Dolan, A. B., & Kranz, J. Z. (1981) Behavioral contrasts in twinships: Stability and patterns of differences in childhood. *Child Development, 52,* 579–588.

Matlin, M. (1983) *Cognition.* New York: Holt, Rinehart & Winston.

Matthews, K. A., & Haynes, S. G. (1986) Type A behavior pattern and coronary disease risk: Update and critical evaluation. *Journal of Epidemiology, 123,* 923–960.

Maugh, T. H. (1987, April 23) Parkinson's patient with brain graft termed "visibly" improved. *Los Angeles Times*, Part 1, p. 33.

Mazur, J. E. (1986) *Learning and behavior.* Englewood Cliffs, NJ: Prentice-Hall.

McAuliffe, K. (1987, Feb. 2) A drug that lets the world in. *U.S. News & World Report*, p. 66.

McCall, R. (1981, May) Mavis Hetherington: Tracking children through the changing family. *APA Monitor*, pp. 4–5.

McCarthy, M. A., & Houston, J. P. (1980) *Fundamentals of early childhood education.* Cambridge, MA: Winthrop.

McCloskey, M., & Santee, J. (1981) Are semantic memory and episodic memory distinct systems? *Journal of Experimental Psychology: Human Learning and Memory, 7*, 66–71.

McConkey, K. (1983) The impact of conflicting communication on response to hypnotic suggestion. *Journal of Abnormal Psychology, 92*, 351–358.

McConkey, K., & Sheehan, P. W. (1976) Contrasting interpersonal orientation in hypnosis: Collaborative versus contractual modes of response. *Journal of Abnormal Psychology, 85*, 390–397.

McConnell, J. V. (1974) *Understanding human behavior: An introduction to psychology.* New York: Holt.

McConnell, R. A., Snowden, R. J., & Powell, K. F. (1955) Wishing with dice. *Journal of Experimental Psychology, 50*, 269–275.

McGaugh, J. L., & Dawson, R. G. (1971) Modification of memory storage process. In W. K. Honig & P. H. R. James (Eds.), *Animal memory.* New York: Academic Press.

McGovern, J. B. (1964) Extinction of associations in four transfer paradigms. *Psychological Monographs* (Whole No. 593), *78,*, 16.

McGraw, M. C. (1935) *Growth: A study of Johnny and Jimmy.* New York: Appleton.

McGuire, W. J. (1985) Attitudes and attitude change. In G. Lindzey & E. Aronson (Eds.), *The handbook of social psychology* (3rd ed., Vol. 2, pp. 233–346). New York: Random House.

McKeachie, W. J., et al. (1966) Student affiliation motives, teacher warmth, and academic achievement. *Journal of Personality and Social Psychology, 4*, 457–461.

McLearn, R. (1969) Genetic influence on behavior and development. In P. Masson (Ed.), *Carmichael's manual of child psychology.* New York: Wiley.

McNeal, E. T., & Cimbolic, P. (1986) Antidepressants and biochemical theories of depression. *Psychological Bulletin, 99, 3*, 361–374.

McWilliams, S. A., & Tuttle, R. J. (1973) Long-term psychological effects of LSD. *Psychological Bulletin, 79*, 341–351.

Mednick, S. A. (1985, March) Crime in the family tree. *Psychology Today*, pp. 58–61.

Mednick, S. A., & Halpern, S. (1959) *Remote associates test.* Copyright Sarnoff A. Mednick, 1959.

Mednick, S. A., Pollack, V., Volavka, J., & Gabrielli, W. F. (1982) Biology and violence. In M. E. Wolfgang & N. A. Weiner (Eds.), *Criminal violence.* Beverly Hills, CA: Sage.

Meecham, W. C., & Shaw, N. A. (1983) Jet plane noise effects on mortality rates. Paper presented at a meeting of the Acoustical Society of America. Cincinnati, OH.

Meehl, P. E. (1954) *Clinical vs. statistical prediction.* Minneapolis: University of Minnesota Press.

Meehl, P. E. (1959) Some ruminations on the validation of clinical procedures. *Canadian Journal of Psychology, 13*, 102–128.

Meehl, P. E. (1973) *Psychodiagnosis: Selected papers.* Minneapolis: University of Minnesota Press.

Meehl, P. E., & Rosen, A. (1955) Antecedent probability and the efficiency of psychometric signs, patterns, or cutting scores. *Psychological Bulletin, 52*, 194–216.

Meer, J. (1987, March) The brain: Murder in mind. *Psychology Today*, p. 62.

Mehrabian, A. (1971) *Silent messages.* Belmont, CA: Wadsworth.

Mehrabian, A., & Weiner, M. (1967) Decoding of inconsistent communications. *Journal of Personality and Social Psychology, 6*, 109–114.

Meichenbaum, D. (1977) *Cognitive-behavior modification: An integrative approach.* New York: Plenum.

Melnechuk, T. (1983) The dream machine. *Psychology Today*, pp. 17, 22–34.

Melton, A. W., & Irwin, J. M. (1940) The influence of degree of interpolated learning on retroactive inhibition and the overt transfer of specific responses. *American Journal of Psychology, 53*, 173–203.

Mendell, P. R. (1977) Effects of length of retention interval on proactive inhibition in short-term visual memory. *Journal of Experimental Psychology: Human Learning and Memory, 5*, 124–128.

Mendlewicz, J. (1985) Genetic research in depressive disorders. In E. E. Beckham & W. R. Leber (Eds.), *Handbook of depression: treatment, assessment & research* (pp. 795–815). Homewood, IL: Dorsey Press.

Mercer, J. R., & Brown, W. C. (1973) Racial differences in I.Q.: Fact or artifact? In C. Senna (Ed.), *The fallacy of I.Q.* (pp. 56–113). New York: Third Press-Joseph Okpaku.

Meyer, J. P., & Pepper, S. (1977) Need compatibility and marital adjustment in young married couples. *Journal of Personality and Social Psychology, 35*, 331–342.

Meyer, V., Liddell, A., & Lyons, M. (1977) Behavioral interviews. In A. R. Ciminero, K. S. Calhoun, & H. E. Adams (Ed.), *Handbook of behavioral assessment.* New York: Wiley.

Milgram, S. (1970) The experience of living in cities. *Science, 167*, 1461–1468.

Miller, A. J., & Kratochwill, T. R. (1979) Reduction of frequent stomach complaints by time out. *Behavior Therapy, 10*, 211–218.

Miller, G. A. (1956) The magical number seven plus or minus two: Some limits on our capacity for processing information. *Psychological Review, 63*, 81–97.

Miller, G. A., Galanter, E., & Pribram, K. H. (1960) *Plans and the structure of behavior.* New York: Holt.

Miller, M. J., Small, I. F., Milstein, V., Malloy, F., & Stout, J. R. (1981) Electrode placement and cognitive change with ECT: Male and female response. *American Journal of Psychiatry, 38*, 384–386.

Miller, N. E. (1972) Interactions between learned and physical factors in mental illness. *seminars in Psychiatry, 4*, 239–254.

Miller, N. E. (1978) Biofeedback and visceral learning. In M. R. Rosenweig & L. W. Porter (Eds.), *annual Review of Psychology.* Palo Alto, CA: Annual Reviews.

Miller, N. E. (1986) The morality and humaneness of animal research on stress and pain. In D. D. Kelly (Ed.), *Stress-induced analgesia. Annals of the New York Academy of Science, 467*, 502–404.

Miller, N. E., & Banuazizi, A. (1968) Instrumental learning by curarized rats of a specific visceral response, intestinal or cardiac. *Journal of Comparative and Physiological Psychology, 65*, 1–17.

Miller, N. E., & Bugelski, R. (1948) Minor studies of aggression. II. The influence of frustrations imposed by the in-group on attitudes expressed toward out-groups. *Journal of Psychology, 25*, 437–442.

Miller, N. E., & Dworkin, B. R. (1973) Visceral learning: Recent difficulties with curarized rats and significant programs for human research. In P. A. Obrist, A. H. Black, J. Brener, & L. V. DiCara (Eds.), *Contemporary trends in cardiovascular psychophysiology.* Chicago: Aldine-Atherton.

Miller, R. R., Ott, C. A., Berk, A. M., & Springer, A. D. (1974) Appetitive memory restoration after electroconvulsive shock in the rat. *Journal of Comparative and Physiological Psychology, 87,* 717–723.

Miller, W., & Ervin, S. (1964) The development of grammar in child language. *Monographs of the Society for Research in Child Development, 29,* 9–34.

Mills, C. B. (1980a) Effects of the match between listener expectancies and coarticulatory cues on the perception of speech. *Journal of Experimental Psychology: Human Perception and Performance, 6,* 528–535.

Mills, C. B. (1980b) Effects of context on reaction time to phonemes. *Journal of Verbal Learning and Verbal Behavior, 19,* 75–83.

Milner, B. R. (1964) Some effects of frontal lobectomy in man. In J. M. Warren & K. Akert (Eds.), *The frontal granular cortex and behavior.* New York: McGraw-Hill.

Milner, B. R. (1966) Amnesia following operations on temporal lobes. In C. W. N. Whitty & O. L. Zangwill (Eds.), *Amnesia.* London: Butterworth.

Mineka, S., Davidson, M., Cook, M., & Keir, R. (1984) Observational conditioning of snake fear in rhesus monkeys. *Journal of Abnormal Psychology, 93,* 355–372.

Minton, H. L., & Schneider, F. W. (1980) *Differential psychology.* Monterey, CA: Brooks/Cole.

Minuchin, S. (1974) *Families and family therapy.* Cambridge: Harvard University Press.

Mischel, H. N. (1974) Sex bias in the evaluation of professional achievements. *Journal of Educational Psychology, 66,* 157–166.

Mischel, W. (1968) *Personality and assessment.* New York: Wiley.

Mischel, W. (1973) Toward a cognitive social reconceptualization of personality. *Psychological Review, 80,* 252–283.

Mischel, W. (1986) *Introduction to personality: A new look,* (4th ed.). New York: Holt, Rinehart & Winston.

Mishkin, M., & Appenzells, T. (1987, June) The anatomy of memory. *Scientific American,* pp. 80–89.

Mitchell, J., & Eckert, E. (1987) Scope and significance of eating disorders. *Journal of Consulting and Clinical Psychology, 55,* 628–634.

Moerman, M. L. (1982) Growth of the birth canal in adolescent girls. *American Journal of Obstetrics and Gynecology, 143*(5), 528–532.

Molfese, D. (1977) Infant cerebral asymmetry. In S. Segalowitz & F. Gruber (Eds.), *Language development and neu-*rological theory. New York: Academic Press.

Money, J. (1976) Human hermaphroditism. In F. Beach (Ed.), *Human sexuality in four perspectives.* Baltimore, MD: Johns Hopkins University Press.

Money, J. (1977) The syndrome of abuse dwarfism. *American Journal of Disabled Children, 131,* 508–513.

Money, J., & Annecillo, C. (1980) IQ change following change of domicile in the syndrome of reversible hyposomatotropinism (psychosocial dwarfism): Pilot investigation. In G. J. Williams & J. Money (Eds.), *Traumatic abuse and neglect of children at home.* Baltimore, MD: Johns Hopkins University Press.

Money, J., & Ehrhardt, A. A. (1972) *Man and woman, boy and girl.* Baltimore, MD: Johns Hopkins University Press.

Montagu, A. (1980) *Sociobiology examined.* New York: Oxford University Press.

Moore, J. W. (1972) Stimulus control: Studies of auditory generalization in rabbits. In A. H. Black & W. F. Prokasy (Eds.), *Classical conditioning. II. Current theory and research.* New York: Appleton.

Moore, K. A., Hofferth, S. L., Wertheimer, R. F., Waite, L. J., & Caldwell, S. B. (1981) Teenage childbearing: Consequences for women, families, and government welfare expenditures. In K. G. Scott, T. Field, & E. Robertson (Eds.), *Teenage parents and their offspring.* New York: Grune & Stratton.

Moreno, J. L. (1934) *Who shall survive?.* New York: Nervous and Mental Disease Publishers.

Morris, M. G., & Gould, R. W. (1963) Role reversal: A concept in dealing with the neglected/battered child syndrome. In *The neglected-battered child syndrome.* New York: Child Welfare League of America.

Morse, C. W., Sahler, O. J. Z., & Friedman, S. B. (1970) A three-year follow-up study of abused and neglected children. *American Journal of Diseases of Children, 120,* 439–446.

Mowrer, O. H., & Lamoreaux, R. R. (1946) Fear as an intervening variable in avoidance conditioning. *Journal of Comparative Psychology, 39,* 29–50.

Moyer, K. E. (1968) Kinds of aggression and their physiological bases. *Communications in Behavioral Biology, 2,* 65–87.

Murdock, B. B. (1974) *Human memory: Theory and data.* New York: Wiley.

Murray, E. A., & Mishkin, M. (1985) Amygdalectomy impairs crossmodal association in monkeys. *Science, 228,* 604–606.

Murray, H. A. (1943) *Thematic apperception test.* Cambridge, MA: Harvard University Press.

Myers, J. K., Weissman, M. M., Tischler, G. L., Holzer III. C., Leaf, P. J., Orvaschel, H., Anthony, J. C., Boyd, J. H., Burke, J. D., Kramer, M., Stoltzman, R. (1984) Six-month prevalence of psychiatric disorders in three communities 1980–1982. *Archives of General Psychiatry, 41,* 959–967.

Naeser, M. A. (1980) Case study of a Chinese aphasic with the Boston diagnostic aphasia exam. *Neuropsychologia, 18,* 389–410.

Nahemow, L., & Lawton, M. P. (1974) Similarity and propinquity in friendship formation. *Journal of Personality and Social Psychology, 32,* 205–213.

Nathan, P. E. (1981) Symptomatic diagnosis and behavioral assessment: A synthesis. In D. H. Barlow (Ed.), *Behavioral assessment of adult disorders.* New York: Guilford Press.

National Academy of Sciences. (1982) *Marijuana and health.* Washington, DC: National Academy Press.

National Governors' Association. (1987) *Making America work.* Washington, DC: National Governors' Association.

National Institute on Alcohol Abuse and Alcoholism. (1983) *Fifth special report to the U. S. Congress on alcohol and health from the secretary of health and human services.* Washington, DC: Superintendent of Documents, U.S. Government Printing Office.

Neimark, E. D. (1987) *Adventures in thinking.* San Diego: HBJ.

Nelson, T. O. (1977) Repetition and depth of processing. *Journal of Verbal Learning and Verbal Behavior, 16,* 151–171.

Nelson, T. O., & Rothbart, R. (1972) Acoustic savings for items forgotten from long-term memory. *Journal of Experimental Psychology, 93,* 357–360.

Neugarten, B. L. (1975) Adult personality: Toward a psychology of the life cycle. In W. C. Sze (Ed.), *Human life cycle.* New York: Jason Aronson.

Neugarten, B. L. (1979) Time age, and the life cycle. *American Journal of Psychiatry, 136,* 887–894.

Newcomb, T. (1956) The prediction of interpersonal attraction. *American Psychologist, 11,* 575–586.

Newcomb, T. M. (1961) *The acquaintance process.* New York: Holt.

Newcomb, T. M. (1978) The acquaintance process: Looking mainly backward. *Journal of Personality and Social Psychology, 36,* 1075–1083.

Newell, A., and Simon, H. A. (1972) *Human problem solving.* Englewood Cliffs, NJ: Prentice-Hall.

Nickerson, R. S., & Adams, M. J. (1979) Long-term memory for a common object. *Cognitive Psychology, 11,* 287–307.

Nielson Television Index. (1981) *Child and teenage television viewing* (Special Release). New York: NTI.

Nisbett, R. E., & Ross, L. (1980) *Human inference: Strategies and shortcomings of social judgement.* Englewood Cliffs, NJ: Prentice-Hall.

Norman, D. A. (1973) Memory, knowledge, and the answering of questions. In R. L. Solso (Ed.), *Contemporary issues in cognitive psychology: The Loyola symposium.* Washington, DC: Winston.

Norman, J. (1980) Direct and indirect perception of size. *Perception and Psychophysics, 28,* 306–314.

Norman, D. A., & Bobrow, D. G. (1975) On the role of active memory processes in perception and cognition. In C. N. Cofer (Ed.), *The structure of human memory.* San Francisco: Freeman.

Northern, J., and Downs, M. (1974) *Hearing in children.* Baltimore: Williams & Wilkins.

Nye, F. I. (1957) Child adjustment in broken and in unhappy unbroken homes. *Marriage and Family Living, 19,* 356–361.

O'Donnell, W. J. (1979) Affectional patterns of adolescents. *Adolescence, 14,* 681–686.

Oelman, R. (1981) Experimental innovations, within the psychoanalytic movement. *Journal of the American Academy of Psychoanalysis, 9,* 71–99.

Olds, J. (1973) Commentary on positive reinforcement produced by electrical stimulation of septal areas and other regions of rat brain. In E. S. Valenstein (Ed.), *Brain stimulation and motivation: Research and commentary.* Glenview, IL: Scott, Foresman.

Olds, J., & Milner, P. (1954) Positive reinforcement produced by electrical stimulation of septal area and other regions of rat brain. *Journal of Comparative and Physiological Psychology, 47,* 419–427.

Olton, D. S., & Samuelson, R. J. (1976) Remembrance of places passed: Spatial memory in rats. *Journal of Experimental Psychology, 2,* 97–116.

O'Neil, H. F., Spielberger, C. D., & Hansen, D. N. (1969) Effects of state anxiety and task difficulty on computer-assisted learning. *Journal of Educational Psychology, 60,* 343–350.

Orne, M. T. (1966) Mechanisms of post-hypnotic amnesia. *International Journal of Clinical and Experimental Hypnosis, 14,* 121–134.

Orne, M. T. (1970) Hypnosis, motivation and the ecological validity of the psychological experiment. In W. J. Arnold & M. M. Page (Eds.), *Nebraska symposium on motivation.* Lincoln: University of Nebraska Press.

Ornstein, R. E. (1977) *The psychology of consciousness.* New York: Harcourt Brace Jovanovich.

Oshman, H. P., & Manosevitz, M. (1976) Father absence: Effects of stepfathers upon psychosocial development in males. *Developmental Psychology, 12,* 479–480.

Ow, D. W., Wood, K. V., DeLuca, M., DeWet, J. R., Helinski, D. R., & Howell, S. H. (1986, November) Transient and stable expressions of the Firefly Lucifernse gene in plant cells and transgenic plants. *Science, 234,* 856–859.

Paivio, A. (1971) *Imagery and verbal processes.* New York: Holt.

Panksepp, J. (1971) A re-examination of the role of the ventromedial hypothalamus in feeding behavior. *Physiological Behavior, 7,* 385–394.

Panksepp, J., Herman, B., & Vilberg, T. (1978) An opiate excess model of childhood autism. *Neuroscience Abstracts,* 4(Abstract 1601), 500.

Parikh, B. (1980) Development of moral judgment and its relation to family environmental factors in Indian and American families. *Child Development, 51,* 1030–1039.

Parke, R. D., & Collmer, C. W. (1975) Child abuse: An interdisciplinary analysis. In E. M. Hetherington (Ed.), *Review of child development research,* (Vol. 5). Chicago: University of Chicago Press.

Passingham, R. E. (1985) Memory of monkeys (Macaca mulatta) with lesions in prefrontal cortex. *Behavioral Neuroscience, 99,* 3–21.

Paton, W. D. M., & Pertwee, R. G. (1973) The pharmacology of cannabis in animals. In R. Mechoulam (Ed.), *Marijuana.* New York: Academic Press.

Patterson, D. (1987) The causes of Down's syndrome. *Scientific American, 257,* 52–61.

Patterson, G. R. (1974) Interventions for boys with conduct problems: Multiple settings, treatments and criteria. *Journal of Consulting and Clinical Psychology, 42,* 471–481.

Patterson, G. R. (1976) Some procedures for assessing changes in marital interaction patterns. *Oregon Research Institute Bulletin, 16(7).*

Patterson, G. R. (1977) A performance theory for coercive family interaction. In L. G. Cairns, (Ed.), *Social interaction: Methods, analysis, and illustration.* Chicago: University of Chicago Press.

Patterson, G. R. (1980) Mothers: The unacknowledged victims. *Monographs of the Society for Research in Child Development, 45*(5, Whole No. 186).

Patterson, G. R., Reid, J. G., Jones, R. R., & Conger, R. E. (1975) *A social learning approach to family intervention.* Eugene, OR: Castalia Press.

Paul, S. M., & Skolnick, P. (1981) Benzodiazepine receptors and psychopathological states: Towards a neurobiology of anxiety. In D. F. Klein & J. Rabkin (Eds.), *Anxiety: New research and changing concepts.* New York: Raven Press.

Paul, S. M., Extein, I., Calil, H. M., Potter, W. Z., Chodoff, P., & Goodwin, F. K. (1981) Use of ECT with treatment-resistant depressed patients at the National Institute of Mental Health. *American Journal of Psychiatry, 138,* 486–489.

Pavlov, I. P. (1927) *Conditioned reflexes.* (G. V. Anrep, trans.). London & New York: Oxford University Press.

Peele, S. (1984) The cultural context of psychological approaches to alcoholism. *American Psychologist, 39,* 1337–1351.

Peele, S., & Brodsky, A. (1976) *Love and addiction.* New York: New American Library.

Pender, N. J., & Pender, A. R. (1986) Attitudes, subjective norms, and intentions to engage in health behaviors. *Nursing Research, 35,* 15–18.

Penfield, W. (1969) Consciousness, memory, and man's conditioned reflexes. In K. Pribram (Ed.), *On the biology of learning.* New York: Harcourt Brace Jovanovich.

Peplau, L. A., Russell, D., & Heim, M. (1980) An attributional analysis of loneliness. In I. H. Frieze, D. Bar-Tal, & J. S. Carroll (Eds.), *New approaches to social problems: Applications of attributional theory.* San Francisco: Jossey-Bass.

Peters, D. P., & McHose, J. H. (1974) Effects of varied preshift reward magnitude on successive negative contrast effects in rats. *Journal of Comparative and Physiological Psychology, 86,* 85–89.

Petersen, A. C. (1987) Those gangly years. *Psychology Today, 21*(9), 28–34.

Petersen, A. C., & Taylor, B. (1980) The biological approach to adolescence. In J. Adelson (Ed.), *Handbook of adolescent psychology.* New York: Wiley.

Peterson, C., & Seligman, M. E. P. (1984) Causal explanations as a risk factor for depression: Theory and evidence. *Psychological Review, 91,* 347–374.

Peterson, L. B., & Peterson, M. J. (1959) Short-term retention of individual items. *Journal of Experimental Psychol-*

ogy: Human Learning and Memory, 58, 193–198.

Pettigrew, T. F. (1958) Personality and sociocultural factors in intergroup attitudes: A cross-national comparison. Journal of Conflict Resolution, 2, 29–42.

Petty, R. E., Cacioppo, J. T. (1979) Issue-involvement can increase or decrease persuasion by enhancing message-relevant cognitive responses. Journal of Personality and Social Psychology, 37, 1915–1926.

Pfaffmann, C. (1969) Taste preference and reinforcement. In J. T. Tapp (Ed.), Reinforcement and behavior. New York: Academic Press.

Pfeffer, C. (1981) Suicidal behavior of children: A review with implications for research and practice. American Journal of Psychiatry, 138, 154–159.

Phoenix, C. H. (1974) Prenatal testosterone in the nonhuman primate and its consequences for behavior. In R. C. Friedman, R. M. Richart, & R. L. Vande Wiele (Eds.), Sex differences in behavior. New York: Wiley.

Piaget, J. (1964) Development and learning. In R. Ripple & V. Rockcastle (Eds.), Piaget rediscovered. Ithaca, NY: Cornell University Press.

Piaget, J. (1980) Intelligence and affectivity: Their relationship during child development. Palo Alto, CA: Annual Reviews, 1980.

Piaget, J., & Inhelder, B. (1969) The psychology of the child. New York: Basic Books.

Piattelli-Palmarini, M. (1980) Language and learning: The debate between Jean Piaget and Noam Chomsky. Cambridge, MA: Harvard University Press.

Piazza, D. M. (1980) The influence of sex and handedness in the hemispheric specialization of verbal and nonverbal tasks. Neuropsychologia, 18, 163–176.

Pittman, K. (1986) Adolescent Pregnancy: Whose Problem Is It. Washington, DC: Children's Defense Fund.

Plomin, R., & Foch, T. T. (1981) Sex differences and individual differences. Child Development, 52, 383–385.

Plomin, R., & Rowe, D. C. (1979) Genetic and environmental etiology of social behavior in infancy. Developmental Psychology, 15, 62–72.

Plotkin, W. B. (1979) The alpha experience revisited: Biofeedback in the transformation of psychological state. Psychological Bulletin, 86, 1132–1148.

Plutchik, R. (1980) A general psycho-evolutionary theory of emotion. In R. Plutchik and H. Kellerman (Eds.), Emotion: Theory, research, and experience, (Vol I). New York: Academic Press.

Podd, M. H. (1972) Ego identity status and morality: The relationship between the two constructs. Developmental Psychology, 6, 497–507.

Poggio, T., & Koch, C. (1987, May) Synapses that compute motion. Scientific American, pp. 46–92.

Polansky, N., Chalmers, M., Buttenwieser, E., & Williams, D. (1979) The isolation of the neglectful family. American Journal of Orthopsychiatry, 49, 149–152.

Pommer, D. A., & Streedbeck, D. (1974) Motivating staff performance in an operant learning program for children. Journal of Applied Behavior Analysis, 7, 217–221.

Posner, M. I., & Konick, A. (1966) On the role of interference in short-term retention. Journal of Experimental Psychology, 72, 221–231.

Postman, L. (1971) Transfer, interference and forgetting. In J. W. Kling & L. A. Riggs (Eds.), Woodworth and Schlosberg's experimental psychology. New York: Holt.

Postman, L., Bruner, B., & McGinnies, E. (1948) Personal values as selective factors in perception. Journal of Abnormal and Social Psychology, 43, 142–154.

Postman, L., and Gray, W. (1977) Maintenance of prior associations and proactive inhibition. Journal of Experimental Psychology: Human Learning and Memory, 3, 255–263.

Postman, L., Stark, K., & Burns, S. (1974) Sources of proactive inhibition on unpaced tests of retention. American Journal of Psychology, 87, 33–56.

Postman, L., Stark, K., & Frazer, J. (1968) Temporal changes in interference. Journal of Verbal Learning and Verbal Behavior, 7, 672–694.

Postman, L., & Underwood, B. J. (1973) Critical issues in interference theory. Memory and Cognition, 1, 19–40.

Powell, B., & Reznikoff, M. (1976) Role conflict and symptoms of psychological distress in college-educated women. Journal of Consulting and Clinical Psychology, 44, 473–479.

Power, C., & Reimer, J. (1978) Moral atmosphere: An educational bridge between moral judgment and action. In W. Damon (Ed.)., Moral development. San Francisco: Jossey-Bass.

Premack, A. J., & Premack, D. (1972, October) Teaching language to an ape. Scientific American, 277(4) 92–99.

Pressley, M., and Levin, J. R. (1981) The keyword method and recall of vocabulary words from definitions. Journal of Experimental Psychology: Human Learning and Memory, 7, 72–76.

Pribram, K. H. (1980) The biology of emotions and other feelings. In R. Plutchik and H. Kellerman (Eds.), Emotion: Theory, research, and experi-

ence (Vol I). New York: Academic Press.

Price-Bonham, S., & Balswick, J. O. (1980) The noninstitutions: Divorce, desertion, and remarriage. Journal of Marriage and the Family, 42, 959–972.

Prior, M., & Werry, J. (1986) Autism, schizophrenia and allied disorders. In H. Quay & J. Werry (Eds.), Psychopathological disorders of childhood (3rd ed., pp. 156–210). New York: Wiley.

Pruyser, P. W. (1979) The psychological examination: A guide for clinicians. New York: International Universities Press.

Prytula, R. E., & Oster, G. D. (1977) The "rat rabbit" problem: What did John B. Watson really do? Teaching of Psychology 4, 44–46.

Puig-Antich, J., Chambers, W., & Tabrizi, M. A. (1983) The clinical assessment of current depressive episodes in children and adolescents: Interview with parents and children. In B. P. Cantwell & G. A. Carlson (Eds.), Affective disorders in childhood and adolescence (pp. 157–180). New York: SP Medical and Scientific Books.

Pylyshyn, Z. W. (1981) The imagery debate: Analogue media versus tacit knowledge. Psychological Review, 88, 16–45.

Quartermain, D., & Botwinick, C. Y. (1975) Role of the biogenic amines in the reversal of cycloheximide-induced amnesia. Journal of Comparative and Physiological Psychology, 88, 386–401.

Quay, H. (1986) Conduct disorders. In H. Quay & J. Werry (Eds.), Psychopathological disorders of childhood (3rd ed., pp. 35–72). New York: Wiley.

Quay, L. C. (1971) Language dialect, reinforcement, and the intelligence-test performance of Negro children. Child Development, 42, 5–15.

Rachlin, H. (1976) Introduction to modern behaviorism. San Francisco: Freeman.

Radeau, M., & Bertelson, P. (1976) The effect of textured visual field on modality dominance in a ventriloquism situation. Perception and Psychophysics, 20, 227–235.

Raffoul, P. R. (1980) Voluntary reduction of cannabis use among graduate students. The International Journal of the Addictions, 15, 647–656.

Raloff, J. (1982) Occupational noise—The subtle pollutant. Science News, 121, 347–350.

Ramachandron, V. S., & Anstis, S. (1986) The perception of apparent motion. Scientific American, 254, 102–109.

Ramey, C. T., & Haskins, R. (1981) The modification of intelligence through early experience. Intelligence, 5, 5–19.

Rangell, L. (1981) From insight to change. *Journal of the American Psychoanalytic Association, 29,* 119–142.

Rappoport, L. (1972) *Personality development: The chronology of experience.* Glenview, IL: Scott, Foresman.

Rattan, A. I. & Rattan, G. (1987) A historical perspective on the nature of intelligence. In R. S. Dean (Ed.), *Introduction to assessing human intelligence: Issues and procedures* (pp. 5–28). Springfield, IL: Charles C. Thomas.

Ray, O. S. (1983) *Drugs, society and human behavior* (3rd ed.). St. Louis: Mosby/College Publishing.

Ray, O. S., & Ksir, C. (1987) *Drugs, society and human behavior* (4th ed., p. 154). St. Louis: Times Mirror/Mosby College Publishing.

Reder, L. M., & Ross, B. H. (1983) Integrated knowledge in different tasks: The role of retrieval strategy of fan effects. *Journal of Experimental Psychology, 9,* 55–72.

Redmond, D. E., Jr. (1985) Neurochemical basis for anxiety and anxiety disorders: Evidence from drugs which decrease human fear or anxiety. In A. Tuma & J. Maser (Eds.), *Anxiety and the anxiety disorders,* Hillsdale, NJ: Erlbaum.

Reed, S. K. (1982) *Cognition: Theory and applications.* Monterey, CA: Brooks/Cole.

Regan, D. T. (1978) Attributional aspects of interpersonal attraction. In J. H. Harvey, W. J. Ickes, & R. F. Kidd (Eds.), *New directions in attribution research* (Vol. 2). Hillsdale, NJ: Erlbaum.

Reidy, T. J. (1980) The aggressive characteristics of abused and neglected children. In G. J. Williams & J. Money (Eds.), *Traumatic abuse and neglect of children at home.* Baltimore, Johns Hopkins University Press.

Reidy, T. J., Anderegg, T. R., Tracy, R. J., & Cotler, S. (1980) Abused and neglected children: The cognitive, social, and behavioral correlates. In G. J. Williams & J. Money (Eds.), *Traumatic abuse and neglect of children at home.* Baltimore, MD: Johns Hopkins University Press.

Reitan, R. M., & Davison, L. A. (1974) *Clinical neuropsychology: Current status and applications.* Washington, DC: V. H. Winston and Sons.

Resnick, R. B., Kestenbaum, R. S., and Schwartz, L. K. (1978) Acute systemic effects of cocaine in man: A controlled study of intranasal and intravenous routes of administration. In E. H. Ellinwood and M. M. Kilbey (Eds.), *Cocaine and other stimulants.* New York: Plenum.

Reynolds, T. J., & Medin, P. L. (1979) Strength vs. temporal-order information in delayed-matching-to-sample performance by monkeys. *Animal Learning and Behavior, 7,* 294–300.

Rheingold, H. (1983) Video games go to school. *Psychology Today, 17*(9), 37–46.

Rhine, J. B. (1942) Evidence of precognition in the covariation of salience ratios. *Journal of Parapsychology, 6,* 111–143.

Ricciuti, H. N. (1981) Developmental consequences of malnutrition in early childhood. In M. Lewis & L. A. Rosenblum (Eds.), *The uncommon child.* New York: Plenum.

Richmond, J. B. (1979) *Healthy people: The Surgeon General's report on health promotion and disease prevention.* (DHEW PHS Publication No. 79-55071). Washington, DC: U.S. Government Printing Office.

Richter, C. P. (1957) On the phenomenon of sudden death in animals and man. *Psychosomatic Medicine, 19,* 191–198.

Rickers Ovsiankira, M. A. (1957) *Rorschach Psychology.* Huntington, NY: Krieger.

Riegel, K. F., & Riegel, R. M. (1972) Development, drop, and death. *Developmental Psychology, 6,* 306–319.

Riesen, A. H. (1965) Effects of early deprivation on photic stimulation. In S. Osler & R. Cooke (Eds.), *The biosocial basis of retardation.* Baltimore, MD: Johns Hopkins University Press.

Riggs, L. A. (1975) Visual acuity. In C. H. Grapham, (Ed.), *Vision and visual perception.* New York: Wiley.

Rimm, D. C., Hill, G. A., Brown, N. N., & Steward, J. E. (1974) Group assertive training in the treatment of expression of inappropriate anger. *Psychological Reports, 84,* 791–798.

Rimm, D. C., & Lefebvre, R. C. (1981) Phobic disorders. In S. M. Turner, K. S. Calhoun, & H. E. Adams (Eds.), *Handbook of clinical behavior therapy.* New York: Wiley.

Rimm, D. C., & Masters, J. C. (1979) *Behavior therapy: Techniques and empirical findings* (2nd ed.). New York: Academic Press.

Rinn, W. E. (1984) The neuropsychology of facial expressions: A review of the neuropsychological and psychological mechanisms for producing facial expressions. *Psychological Bulletin, 95,* 52–77.

Riskind, J. H., & Gotey, C. C. (1986) Physical posture: Could it have regulatory or feedback effects on motivation and emotion? *Motivation and Emotion, 6,* 273–298.

Rizley, R. (1978) Depression and distortion in attribution of causality. *Journal of Abnormal Psychology, 87,* 32–48.

Robbins, D., Bray, J. F., Irvin, J. R., & Wise, P. S. (1974) Memorial strategy and imagery: An interaction between instructions and rated imagery. *Journal of Experimental Psychology, 102,* 706–709.

Roberts, A. H. (1985) Biofeedback: Research, training and clinical roles. *American Psychologist, 40,* 938–941.

Robins, L. N., Helzer, J. E., Weissman, M. M., Orvaschel, H., Gruenberg, E., Burke, J. D., Jr, Regier, D. A. (1984) Lifetime prevalence of specific psychiatric disorders in three sites. *Archives of General Psychiatry, 41,* 949–958.

Robinson, B. E. & Barret, R. L. (1985) Teenage fathers. *Psychology Today, 19*(12), 66–70.

Robinson, E. A., & Price, M. G. (1980) Pleasurable behavior in marital interaction. *Journal of Consulting and Clinical Psychology, 48,* 117–118.

Robinson, N. M. & Robinson, H. B. (1976) *The Mentally retarded child* (2nd ed.). New York: McGraw-Hill.

Rock, I., Auster, M., Shiffman, M., & Wheeler, D. (1980) Induced movement based on subtraction of motion from inducing object. *Journal of Experimental Psychology: Human Perception and Performance, 6,* 391–403.

Rock, I., & Harris, C. S. (1967) Vision and touch. *Scientific American, 216,* 96–104.

Rodin, J., & Langer, E. J. (1977) Long-term effects of a control-relevant intervention with the institutionalized aged. *Journal of Personality and Social Psychology, 35,* 897–902.

Roediger, H. L., Knight, J. L., and Kantowitz, B. H. (1977) Inferring decay in short-term memory: The issue of capacity. *Memory and Cognition, 5,* 167–176.

Rogers, C. R. (1951) *Client-centered therapy.* Boston: Houghton Mifflin.

Rogers, C. R. (1957) The necessary and sufficient conditions of therapeutic personality change. *Journal of Consulting Psychology, 21,* 95–103.

Rogers, C. R., & Dymond, R. F. (Eds.). (1954) *Psychotherapy and personality change.* Chicago: University of Chicago Press.

Rogers, C. R., Gendlin, E. T., Kiesler, D. V., & Truax, C. B. (1967) *The therapeutic relationship and its impact: A study of psychotherapy with schizophrenics.* Madison, WI: University of Wisconsin Press.

Rogers, R. W. and Deckner, C. W. (1975) Effects of fear appeals and physiological arousal upon emotion, attitudes, and cigarette smoking. *Journal of Personality and Social Psychology, 32,* 222–230.

Rogo, D. J. (1975) Dreaming the future. *Psychic, 6,* 26–29.

Rokeach, M. (1960) *The open and closed mind.* New York: Basic Books.

Rorschach, H. (1921) *Psychodiagnostics.* Bern: Bircher. (English translation: Bern: Huber, 1942)

Rosch, E. (1978) Principles of categorization. In E. Rosch and B. B. Lloyds (Eds.), *Cognition and categorization.* Hillsdale, NJ: Erlbaum.

Rosen, G. M. (1987) Self-help treatment books and the commercialization of psychotherapy. *American Psychologist, 42,* 46–51.

Rosenfield, D., Folger, R., & Adelman, H. F. (1980) When rewards reflect competence: A qualification of the overjustification effect. *Journal of Personality and Social Psychology, 39,* 368–376.

Rosenhan, D., Salovey, P., & Hargis, K. (1981) The joys of helping: Focus of attention mediates the impact of positive affect on altruism. *Journal of Personality and Social Psychology, 40,* 899–905.

Rosenkilde, C. E., & Divac, I. (1976) Time-discrimination performance in cats with lesions in prefrontal cortex and caudate nucleus. *Journal of Comparative and Physiological Psychology, 90,* 343–352.

Rosenkrantz, P., Vogel, S., Bee, H., Broverman, I., & Broverman, D. M. (1968) Sex-role stereotypes and self-concept in college students. *Journal of consulting and Clinical Psychology, 32,* 287–295.

Rosenthal, D., & Hansen, J. (1980) Comparison of adolescents' perceptions and behaviors in single- and two-parent families. *Journal of Youth and Adolescence, 9,* 407–418.

Rosenthal, R., & Jacobson, L. (1968) *Pygmalion in the Classroom.* New York: Holt, Rinehart, Winston.

Rosenzweig, M. R. (1969) Effects of heredity and environment on brain chemistry, brain anatomy and learning ability in the rat. In M. Manosovitz, G. Lindzey, & D. D. Thiessen (Eds.), *Behavioral genetics.* New York: Appleton.

Rosenzweig, M. R. (1984) Experience, memory, and the brain. *American Psychologist, 39,* 365–376.

Ross, L. (1977) The intuitive psychologist and his shortcomings: Distortions in the attribution process. In L. Berkowitz (Ed.), *Advances in experimental social psychology* (Vol. 10). New York: Academic Press.

Ross, L., Bierbrauer, G., & Polly, S. (1974) Attribution of educational outcomes by professional and nonprofessional instructors. *Journal of Personality and Social Psychology, 29,* 609–618.

Rothenbuhler, W. C. (1964) Behavior genetics of nest cleaning in honey bees. I. Responses of four inbred lines to disease killing brood. *Animal Behavior, 12,* 578–583.

Rotter, J. B. (1954) *Social learning and clinical psychology.* Englewood Cliffs, NJ: Prentice-Hall.

Rotter, J. B. (1972) *Applications of a social learning theory of personality.* New York: Holt.

Routtenberg, A. (1968) The two arousal hypothesis: Reticular formation and limbic system. *Psychological Review, 75,* 51–80.

Rowe, J. W., & Kahn, R. L. (1987, July 10) Human aging: Usual and successful. *Science, 237,* 143–149.

Rubin, D. A., & Rubin, R. T. (1980) Differences in asymmetry of facial expression between left- and right-handed children. *Neuropsychologia, 18,* 373–377.

Rubin, D. C., & Kontis, T. C. (1983) A schema for common cents. *Memory & Cognition, 21,* 335–341.

Rubin, E. (1958) Figure and ground. In D. C. Beardslee & M. Wertheimer (Eds.), *Readings in perception.* Princeton, NJ: Van Nostrand-Reinhold.

Rubin, F. (Ed.). (1968) *Current research in hypnopaedia.* New York: Am. Elsevier.

Rubin, Z. (1973) *Liking and loving: An invitation to social psychology.* New York: Holt, Rinehart & Winston.

Ruderman, A. J. (1986) Dietary restraint: A theoretical and empirical review. *Psychological Bulletin, 99,* 247–262.

Saario, T. N., Jacklin, C. N., & Tittle, C. K. (1973) Sex role stereotyping in the public schools. *Harvard Educational Review, 43,* 386–416.

Sacco, W. P., & Beck, A. T. (1985) Cognitive therapy of depression. In E. E. Beckham & W. R. Leber (Eds.), *Handbook of depression: Treatment, assessment, and research* (pp. 3–38). Homewood, IL: Dorsey Press.

Sachs, J. (1985) Prelinguistic development. In J. B. Gleason, (Ed.), *The development of language.* Columbus, OH: Charles E. Merrill.

Saegert, S. C., Swap, W., & Zajonc, R. B. (1973) Exposure, context, and interpersonal attraction. *Journal of Personality and Social Psychology, 25,* 234–242.

Sameroff, A. J., Seifer, R., & Elias, P. K. (1982) Sociocultural variability in infant temperament ratings. *Child Development, 53,* 164–173.

Sanders, J. L. (1976) Relationship of personal space to body-image boundary definiteness. *Journal of Research in personality, 10,* 478–481.

Santrock, J. W., & Warshak, R. (1979) Father custody and social development in boys and girls. *Journal of Social Issues, 4,* 112–125.

Sarason, I. G. (1976) *Abnormal psychology: The problem of maladaptive behavior* (2nd ed.). Englewood Cliffs, NJ: Prentice-Hall.

Satir, V. (1967) *Conjoint family therapy* (rev. ed.). Palto Alto, CA: Science and Behavior Books.

Sattler, J. M. (1974) *Assessment of children's intelligence.* Philadelphia: Saunders.

Scarr, S. (1984) *Mother care, Other care.* New York: Basic Books.

Scarr, S., & Carter-Saltzman, L. (1979) Twin-method: Defense of a critical assumption. *Behavior Genetics, 9,* 527–542

Scarr, S., & Weinberg, R. A. (1977) Intellectual similarities within families of both adopted and biological children. *Intelligence, 1,* 170–191.

Schachter, S. (1971) *Emotion, obesity, and crime.* New York: Academic Press.

Schachter, S. (1971) Some extraordinary facts about obese humans and rats. *American Psychologist, 26,* 129–144.

Schacter, S., & Singer, J. E. (1962) Cognitive, social and physiological determinants of emotional state. *Psychological Review, 69,* 379–399.

Schaffer, H. R., & Emerson, P. (1964) The development of social attachments in infancy. *Monographs of the Society for Research in Child Development, 29*(3, Whole No. 94).

Schaie, K. W. (1980) Age changes in intelligence. In R. L. Sprott (Ed.), *Age, learning ability, and intelligence.* New York: Van Nostrand-Reinhold.

Schaie, K. W., & Labouvie-Vief, G. (1974) Generation and ontogenetic components of change in adult cognitive behavior: A fourteen-year cross-sequential study. *Developmental Psychology, 10,* 305–320.

Schaire, K. W., & Willis, S. L. (1986) Can decline in adult intellectual functioning be reversed? *Developmental Psychology, 22,* 223–232.

Scheibel, A. B. (1985) Falls, motor dysfunction, and correlative neurohistologic changes in the elderly. *Clinics in Geriatric Medicine, 1,* 671–677.

Schlesier-Stropp, B. (1984) Bulimia: A review of the literature. *Psychological Bulletin, 95,* 247–257.

Schmidt, S. R. (1983) The effects of recall and recognition test expectancies on the retention of prose. *Memory and Cognition, 11,* 172–180.

Schneider, D. J. (1988) *Introduction to Social Psychology.* San Diego: Harcourt Brace Jovanovich.

Schnepf, J. L., & Baylor, R. (1987, April) How photoreceptor cells respond to light. *Scientific American,* pp. 40–47.

Scholl, T. O., Miller, L. K., Salmon, R. W., Cofsky, M. C., & Shearer, J. (1987) Prenatal care adequacy and the outcome of adolescent pregnancy: Effects of weight gain, preterm delivery, and birth weight. *Obstetrics & Gynecology, 69,* 312–316.

Schuckit, M. (1987) Biological vulnerability to alcoholism. *Journal of Consulting and Clinical Psychology, 55,* 301–309.

Schulsinger, F., Knop, J., Goodwin, D. W., Teasdale, T. W., & Mikkelsen, U. (1986) A prospective study of young men at high risk for alcoholism. *Archives of General Psychiatry, 43,* 755–760.

Schulz, R., & Alderman, D. (1974) Clinical research and the "stages of dying." *Omega, 5,* 137–144.

Schwartz, G. M., Izard, C. E., & Ansul, S. E. (1985) The 5-month-old's ability to discriminate facial expressions of emotion. *Infant Behavior and Development, 8,* 65–77.

Scovern, A. W., & Kilmann, P. R. (1980) Status of electroconvulsive therapy: Review of the outcome literature. *Psychological Bulletin, 87,* 260–303.

Sears, D. O., Freedman, J. L., & Peplau, L. A. (1985) *Social Psychology* (5th ed.). Englewood Cliffs, NJ: Prentice-Hall.

Sears, R. R., Maccoby, E. E., & Levin, H. (1957) *Patterns of child rearing.* New York: Harper.

Sears, R. R., Maccoby, E. E., & Levin, H. (1976) *Patterns of child rearing.* (2nd ed.). Stanford, CA: Stanford University Press.

Seaver, W. B., & Patterson, A. H. (1976) Decreasing fuel-oil consumption through feedback and social commendation. *Journal of Applied Behavior Analysis, 9,* 147–152.

Segal, B., Huba, G. J., & Singer, J. L. (1980) Reasons for drug and alcohol use by college students. *The International Journal of the Addictions, 15,* 489–498.

Select Committee on Children, Youth, and Families of the U.S., House of Representatives. (1983) *U. S. children and their families: Current conditions and recent trends.* Washington, DC: Government Printing Office.

Seligman, M. E. P. (1975) *Helplessness: On depression, development, and death.* San Francisco: Freeman.

Seligman, M. E. P. (1977) Reversing depression and learned helplessness. In P. G. Zimbardo & F. L. Ruch (Eds.), *Psychology and life.* Glenview, IL: Scott, Foresman.

Selman, R. L., & Byrne, D. F. (1974) A structural-developmental analysis of levels of role taking in middle childhood. *Child Development, 45,* 803–806.

Selzer, M. (1971) The Michigan Alcoholism Screening Test: The quest for a new diagnostic instrument. *American Journal of Psychiatry, 127,* 89–94.

Seward, J. P. (1949) An experimental analysis of latent learning. *Journal of Experimental Psychology, 39,* 177–186.

Seyle, H. (1976) *Stress in health and disease.* Woburn, MA: Butterworth.

Shannahoff-Khalsa, D. (1984, September) Rhythms and reality. *Psychology Today,* pp. 72–73.

Shanon, B. (1980) Lateralization effects in musical decision tasks. *Neuropsychologia, 18,* 21–31.

Shapiro, D., & Schwartz, G. E. (1972) Biofeedback and visceral learning: Clinical applications. *Seminars in Psychiatry, 4,* 171–184.

Shapiro, D. A., & Shapiro, D. (1982) Meta-analysis of comparative therapy outcome studies: A replication and refinement. *Psychological Bulletin, 92,* 581–604.

Sheehy, G. (1974) *Passages.* New York: Dutton.

Sheffield, F. D. A. (1966) A drive induction theory of reinforcement. In R. N. Haber (Ed.), *Current research in motivation.* New York: Holt.

Sheldon, W. H . (1954) *Atlas of men: A guide for somatotyping the adult male of all ages.* New York: Harper.

Shepard, R. N., & Metzler, J. (1971) Mental rotation of three-dimensional objects. *Science, 171,* 701–703.

Shirley, M. M. (1933) The first two years. *Institute of Child Welfare Monograph* (No. 7). Minneapolis: University of Minnesota Press.

Shock, N. W. (1962) The physiology of aging. *Scientific American, 206,* 100–111.

Shulman, H. G. (1972) Semantic confusion errors in short-term memory. *Journal of Verbal Learning and Verbal Behavior, 11,* 221–227.

Sideroff, S. I., & Jarvik, M. E. (1980) Conditioned responses to a videotape showing of heroin-related stimuli. *The International Journal of the Addictions, 15,* 529–536.

Siegel, J. A., & Siegel, W. (1977) Absolute identification of notes and intervals by musicians. *Perception and Psychophysics, 21,* 143–152.

Siegel, R. K. (1984) Cocaine smoking disorders: Diagnosis and treatment. *Psychiatric Annals, 14,* 728–732.

Siever, L. J., & Davis, K. L. (1985) Toward a dysregulation hypothesis of depression. *American Journal of Psychiatry, 142,* 1017–1031.

Silverman, B. I. (1974) Consequences, racial discrimination, and the principle of belief congruence. *Journal of Personality and Social Psychology, 29,* 497–508.

Silverman, L. H. (1959) A Q sort study of the validity of evaluations made from projective techniques. *Psychology Monographs, 73*(7, Whole No. 477).

Silverman, L. H. (1985) Research on psychoanalytic psychodynamic propositions. *Clinical Psychology Review, 5,* 247–257.

Simkin, J. S., & Yontef, G. M. (1984) Gestalt therapy. In R. J. Corsini (Ed.), *Current psychotherapies* (3rd ed., pp. 279–319). Itasca, IL: F. E. Peacock.

Simon, H. A. (1967) Motivational and emotional controls of cognition. *Psychological Review, 74,* 29–39.

Sinclair, L. G. (1977) Overcoming difficulty with erection. In C. Zastrow & D. H. Chang (Eds.), *The personal problem solver.* Englewood Cliffs, NJ: Prentice-Hall.

Singer, J. L., & Kolligian, J., Jr. (1987) Personality: Developments in the study of private experience. *Annual Review of Psychology, 38,* 533–574.

Singer, J. L., & Singer, D. G. (1981) *Television, imagination and aggression: A study of preschoolers.* Hillsdale, NJ: Erlbaum Associates.

Singer, J. L., & Singer, D. G. (1986) Family experiences and television viewing as predictors of childrens' imagination, restlessness, and aggression. *Journal of Social Issues, 42,* 107–124.

Singer, J. L., Singer, D. G., & Rapaczynski, W. (1984a) Family patterns and television viewing as predictors of childrens' beliefs and aggression. *Journal of Communication, 34,* 73–89.

Singer, J. L., Singer, D. G., & Rapaczynski, W. (1984b) Childrens' imagination as predicted by family patterns and television-viewing: A longitudinal study. *Genetic Psychology Monographs, 110,* 43–69.

Singer, P., & Wells, D. (1985) *Making babies: The new science and ethics of conception.* New York: Scribner.

Singer, R. D. (1984) The function of television in childhood aggression. In R. M. Kaplan, V. J. Konecni, & R. W. Novaco (Eds.), *Aggression in children and youth* (pp. 263–280). The Hague: Martinus Nijhoff.

Skinner, B. F. (1957) *Verbal behavior.* New York: Appleton.

Skinner, B. F. (1968) *The technology of teaching.* New York: Appleton.

Skinner, B. F. (1971) *Beyond freedom and dignity.* New York: Knopf.

Skinner, B. F. (1975) *How to teach animals.* In R. C. Atkinson & J. P. Pinel (Eds.), *Psychology in progress.* San Francisco: Freeman.

Slapp, T., & Fulcher, R. (1983) The employment of APA numbers, 1982. *American Psychologist, 38,* 1298–1320.

Slavin, R. E. (1985) Cooperative learning: Applying contact theory in desegregated schools. *Journal of Social Issues, 41,* 45–62.

Sloan, R. B., Staples, F. R., Cristol, A. H., Yorkston, N. J., & Whipple, K. (1975) *Psychotherapy versus behavior therapy.* Cambridge, MA: Harvard University Press.

Slobin, D. I. (1986) *The cross-linguistic study of language acquisition.* Hillsdale, NJ: Erlbaum.

Smith, C. A., & Ellsworth, P. C. (1985) Patterns of cognitive appraisal in emotion. *Journal of Personality and Social Psychology, 48,* 803–838.

Smith, D. E. (1984) Diagnostic, treatment and aftercare approaches to cocaine abuse. *Journal of Substance Abuse Treatment, 1,* 5–9.

Smith, E. E, Shoben, E. J., & Rips, L. J. (1971) Structure and process in semantic memory: A feature model for semantic decisions. *Psychological Review, 81,* 214–241.

Smith, M. C. (1983) Hypnotic memory enhancement of witnesses: Does it work? *Psychological Bulletin, 94,* 387–407.

Smith, M. L., Glass, G. V., & Miller, T. I. (1980) *The benefits of psychotherapy.* Baltimore, MD: Johns Hopkins University Press.

Smith, R. J. (1978) Congress considers bill to control angel dust. *Science, 200,* 1463–1466.

Smith, S. M. (1979) Remembering in and out of context. *Journal of Experimental Psychology: Human Learning and Memory, 5,* 460–471.

Smith, S. M., Glenberg, A. M., & Bjork, R. A. (1978) Environmental context and human memory. *Memory and Cognition, 6,* 342–353.

Snyder, C. R. (1974) Acceptance of personality interpretations as a function of assessment procedures. *Journal of Consulting and Clinical Psycholoy, 42,* 150.

Snyder, C. R. (1974) Why horoscopes are true: The effects of specificity on acceptance of astrological interpretations. *Journal of Clinical Psychology, 30,* 577–580.

Snyder, C. R., & Fromkin, H. L. (1980) *Uniqueness: The human pursuit of difference.* New York: Plenum Press.

Snyder, M., Tanke, E. E., & Berscheid, E. (1977) Social perception and interpersonal behavior: On the self-fulfilling nature of social stereotypes. *Journal of Personality and Social Psychology, 35,* 656–667.

Soal, S. G., & Bateman, F. (1954) *Modern experiments in telepathy.* New Haven. CT: Yale University Press.

Solomon, R. L., & Corbit, J. P. (1974) An opponent-process theory of motivation: Temporal dynamics of affect. *Psychological Review, 81,* 119–145.

Sontag, L. W., Baker, C. T., & Nelson, V. L. (1958) Mental growth and personality development. A longitudinal study. *Monographs of the Society for Research in Child Development, 23*(2, Whole No. 68).

Sorting out truths from myths. (1987, January 12) *U.S. News and World Report,* pp. 66–67.

Spanier, G. B., & Lewis, R. A. (1980) Marital quality: A review of the seventies. *Journal of Marriage and the Family, 42,* 825–840.

Spelt, D. K. (1948) The conditioning of the human fetus in *utero. Journal of Experimental Psychology, 38,* 338–346.

Spence, J. T., & Helmreich, R. L. (1978) *Masculinity and femininity: Their psychological dimensions, correlates, and antecedents.* Austin: University of Texas Press.

Sperling, G. (1960) The information available in brief visual presentations. *Psychological Monographs, 74*(11, Whole No. 498).

Sperry, R. W. (1985) Some effects of disconnecting the cerebral hemispheres. In P. H. Abelson, E. Butz, & S. H. Snyder (Eds.), *Neuroscience* (pp. 372–380). Washington DC: American Association for the Advancement of Science.

Spielberger, C. D. (1962) The effects of manifest anxiety on the academic achievement of college students. *Mental Hygiene, 46,* 420–426.

Spielberger, C. D. (1965) Theoretical and epistemological issues in verbal conditioning. In S. Rosenberg (Ed.), *Directions in psycholinguistics.* New York: Macmillan.

Spinelli, D. H., Jensen, F. E., & DiPrisco, G. V. (1980) Early experience effect on dendritic branching in normally reared kittens. *Experimental Neurology, 62,* 1–11.

Spinetta, J. J., & Rigler, D. (1972) The child-abusing parent: A psychological review. *Psychological Bulletin, 77,* 296–304.

Spring, B. (1981) Stress and Schizophrenia: Some definitional issues. *schizophrenia Bulletin, 7,* 24–33.

Squire, L. R., Wetzel, C. D., & Slater, P. C. (1979) Memory complaint after electroconvulsive therapy: Assessment with a new self-rating instrument. *Biological Psychiatry, 14,* 791–801.

Stallone, F., Shelley, E., Mendlewicz, J., & Fieve, R. R. (1973) The use of lithium in affective disorders. III. A double-blind study of prophylaxis in bipolar illness. *American Journal of Psychiatry, 130,* 1006–1010.

Stanovich, K. E., & West, R. F. (1983) On priming by a sentence context. *Journal of Experimental Psychology, 12,* 1–40.

Stanton, H. E. (1976) Hypnosis and encounter group volunteers: A validation study of the sensation-seeking scale. *Journal of Consulting and Clinical Psychology, 44,* 534–545.

Stapp, J., & Fulcher, R. (1983) The employment of APA members: 1982. *American Psychologist, 38,* 1298–1320.

Stark, E. (1986) Young, innocent and pregnant. *Psychology Today, 20*(10), 28–35.

Steele, B. F., & Pollock, C. B. (1974) A psychiatric study of parents who abuse infants and small children. In R. E. Helfer & C. H. Kempe (Eds.), *The battered child* (2nd ed.). Chicago: University of Chicago Press.

Stephan, W. G., & Brigham, J. C. (1985) Cooperative learning: Applying contact theory in desegregated schools. *Journal of Social Issues, 41,* 45–62.

Sternberg, R. J. (1986) A triangular theory of love. *Psychological Review, 93,* 119–135.

Sternberg, R. J. (1987) Liking versus loving: A comparative evaluation of theories. *Psychological Bulletin, 102,* 331–345.

Steuer, F. B., Applefield, J. M., & Smith, R. (1971) Televised aggression and the interpersonal aggression of preschool children. *Journal of Experimental Child Psychology, 11,* 442–447.

Stiles, W. B., Shapiro, D. A., & Elliott, R. (1986) "Are all psychotherapies equivalent?" *American Psychologist, 41,* 165–180.

Stine, G. J. (1977) *Biosocial genetics.* New York: Macmillan.

Stoudemire, A., & Blazer, D. G. (1985) Depression in the elderly. In E. E. Beckham & W. R. Leber (Eds.), *Handbook of depression: Treatment, assessment & research* (pp. 556–586). Homewood, IL: Dorsey Press.

Strassman, H. D., Thaler, M. B., & Schein, E. H. (1956) A prisoner of war syndrome: Apathy as a reaction to severe stress. *American Journal of Psychiatry, 112,* 998–1003.

Stratton, G. M. (1987) Vision without inversion of the retinal image. *Psychological Review, 4,* 341–360.

Stricker, E. M. (1976) Drinking by rats after lateral hypothalamic lesions: A new look at the lateral hypothalamic syndrome. *Journal of Comparative and Physiological Psychology, 90,* 127–143.

Strober, M., & Humphrey, L. (1987) Familial contributions to the etiology and course of anorexia nervosa and bulimia. *Journal of Consulting and Clinical Psychology, 55,* 654–659.

Strongman, K. T. (1973) *The psychology of emotion.* New York: Wiley.

Stryer, L. (1987, July) The molecules of visual excitation. *Scientific American,* pp. 42–50

Suedfeld, P., Ballard, E. J., & Murphy, M. (1983) Water immersion and flotation: From stress experiment to stress treatment. *Journal of Environmental Psychology, 3,* 147–155.

Suedfeld, P., & Kristeller, J. L. (1983) Stimulus reduction as a technique in health psychology. *Health Psychology, 1*(4) 337–357.

Suinn, R. (1977) Anxiety management training for general anxiety. In R. Suinn & R. Weigel (Eds.), *Innovative therapies: Critical and creative contributions.* New York: Harper & Row.

Sweeney, P. D., & Gruber, K. L. (1984) Selective exposure: Voter information preferences and the Watergate affair. *Journal of Personality and Social Psychology, 46,* 1208–1221.

Switzer, S. A. (1930) Backward conditioning of the lid reflex. *Journal of Experimental Psychology, 13,* 76–97.

Tajfel, H., Flament, C., Billig, M., & Bundy, R. P. (1971) Social categorization and intergroup behavior. *European Journal of Social Psychology, 1,* 149–177.

Tajfel, H., & Turner, J. C. (1979) An integrative theory of intergroup conflict. In W. G. Austin & S. Worchel (Eds.), *The social psychology of intergroup relations.* Belmont, CA: Wadsworth.

Takashima, H., Ohkura, K., Arima, M., Osawa, M., & Suzuki, Y. (1980) Central nervous system disease and genetic counseling. *Brain and Development, 2,* 236–238.

Tallman, J. F., Paul, S. M., Skolnick, P., & Gallager, D. W. (1980) Receptors for the age of anxiety; pharmacology of the benzodiazepines. *Science, 207,* 274–281.

Tanner, J. M. (1970) Physical growth. In P. H. Mussen (Ed.), *Carmichael's manual of child psychology* (3rd ed.). New York: Wiley

Tanner, J. M. (1974) Sequence and tempo in the somatic changes in puberty. In M. M. Grumbach, G. D. Grave, & F. E. Mayer (Eds.), *Control of the onset of puberty.* New York: Wiley.

Tarler-Benlolo, L. (1978) The role of relaxation in biofeedback training: A critical review of the literature. *Psychological Bulletin, 85,* 727–755.

Tasto, D. L. (1977) Self-report schedules and inventories. In A. R. Ciminero, K. S. Calhoun, & H. E. Adams (Eds.), *Handbook of behavioral assessment.* New York: Wiley.

Tavris, C. (1982) *Anger.* New York: Simon & Schuster.

Taylor, J. A. (1953) A personality scale of manifest anxiety. *Journal of Abnormal and Social Psychology, 48,* 285–290.

Taylor, S. E. (1986) *Health Psychology.*
New York: Random House.

Taylor, S. E., & Brown, J. D. (in press) Illusion and well-being: A social psychological perspective on mental health. *Psychological Review.*

Templer, D. I. (1971) Anorexic humans and rats. *American Psychologist, 26,* 935.

Terman, L. M., & Merrill, M. A. (1960) *Measuring intelligence: A guide to the administration of the new revised Stanford-Binet tests of intelligence.* Boston: Houghton Mifflin.

Terman, L. M., & Merrill, M. A. (1973) *The Stanford-Binet intelligence scale, 3rd revision, form L-M.* Boston: Houghton Mifflin.

Terrace, H. S. (1985) In the beginning was the "name." *American Psychologist, 40,* 1011–1028.

Thomas, A., & Chess, S. (1977) *Temperament and development.* New York: Brunner/Mazel.

Thompson, R., & McConnell, J. (1955) Classical conditioning in the planarian, *dugesia dorotocephala. Journal of Comparative and Physiological Psychology, 48,* 65–68.

Thoresen, C. E., & Mahoney, M. J. (1974) *Behavioral self-control.* New York: Holt, Rinehart & Winston.

Thurstone, L. L. (1938) *Primary mental abilities.* Chicago: University of Chicago Press.

Thurstone, L. L., & Thurstone, T. G. (1950) *Primary mental abilities scales: Primary, elementary, and intermediate.* Chicago: Science Research Associates.

Tilley, A. J., & Empson, J. A. C. (1978) REM sleep and memory consolidation. *Biological Psychology, 6,* 293–300.

Timmers, R. L. (1977) For men: Controlling premature ejaculation. In C. Zastrow & D. H. Chang (Eds.), *The personal problem solver.* Englewood Cliffs, NJ: Prentice-Hall.

Tinklenberg, J. R. (1973) Alcohol and violence. In P. G. Bourne (Ed.), *Alcoholism: Progress in research and treatment.* New York: Academic Press.

Tinbergen, N. (1951) *The study of instinct.* Oxford: Oxford University Press.

Tinbergen, N. (1952) The curious behavior of the stickleback. *Scientific American, 187,* 22–26.

Tracy, D. M. (1987) Toys, spatial ability, and science and mathematics achievement: Are they related? *Sex Roles, 17,* 115–138.

Trivers, R. (1985) *Social evolution.* Menlo Park, CA: Benjamin/Cummings.

Tsversky, A., & Kahneman, D. (1973) Availability: A heuristic for judging frequency and probability. In M. Fishbein (Ed.), *Progress in social psychology.* Hillsdale, NJ: Erlbaum.

Tulving, E. (1962) Subjective organiza-
tion in free recall of "unrelated" words. *Psychological Review, 69,* 344–354.

Tulving, E. (1972) Episodic and semantic memory. In E. Tulving & W. Donaldson, (Eds.), *Organization of memory.* New York: Academic Press.

Tulving, E., & Madigan, S. A. (1970) Memory and verbal learning. *Annual Review of Psychology, 21,* 437–484.

Tulving, E., & Thomson, D. M. (1971) Retrieval processes in recognition memory: Effects of associative context. *Journal of Experimental Psychology, 87,* 116–124.

Turk, D. C., & Salovey, P. (1986) Clinical information processing: Bias innoculation. In R. E. Ingram (Ed.), *Information processing approaches to clinical psychology.* Orlando: Academic Press.

Turnbull, C. M. (1961) Some observations regarding the experiences and behavior of BaMbuti Pygmies. *American Journal of Psychology, 74,* 304–308.

Turner, R. R., & Reese, H. W. (1980) *Life-span developmental psychology.* New York: Academic Press.

Turner, S. M., Beidel, D. C., Swami Nathan, R. (1985) Biological factors in obsessive-compulsive disorders. *Psychological Bulletin, 97,* 430–450.

Underwood, B. J. (1957) Interference and forgetting. *Psychological Review, 64,* 49–60.

Underwood, B. J. (1972) Are we overloading memory? In A. W. Melton & E. Martin (Eds.), *Coding processes in human memory.* New York: Wiley.

U.S. Bureau of the Census, *Statistical Abstracts of the United States, 1987* (107th ed.). Washington, DC: U.S. Government Printing Office.

Valenstein, E. S. (1973) *Brain Control.* New York: Wiley.

Van de Castle, R. L. (1971) *The psychology of dreaming.* Morristown, NJ: General Learning Press.

Vandell, D. L., Wilson, K. S., & Buchanan, N. R. (1980) Peer interaction in the first few years of life: An examination of its structure, content, and sensitivity to toys. *Child Development, 51,* 481–488.

Van Houten, R., Nau, P., & Marini, Z. (1980) An analysis of public posting in reducing speeding behavior on an urban highway. *Journal of Applied Behavior Analysis, 13,* 383–395.

Vasta, R., & Copitch, P. (1981) Simulating conditions of child abuse in the laboratory. *Child Development, 52,* 164–170.

Vaughn, C. E., Snyder, K. S., Freeman, W., Jones, S., Falloon, I. R. H., & Liberman, R. P. (1982) Family factors in schizophrenic relapse: A replication. *Schizophrenia Bulletin, 8,* 425–426.

Veroff, J., Depner, C., Kulka, R., & Douvan, E. (1980) Comparison of American motives: 1957 versus 1976. *Journal of Personality and Social Psychology, 39,* 1249–1262.

Vernon, P. E. (1979) Intelligence testing and the nature/nurture debate, 1928–1978: What next? *British Journal of Educational Psychology, 49,* 1–14.

Vincent, C. E. (1956) Social and interpersonal sources of symptomatic frigidity. *Marriage and Family Living, 18,* 355–360.

Visher, E., & Visher, J. (1983) Stepparenting: Blending families. In H. I. McCubbin & C. R. Figley (Eds.), *Stress and the family* (pp. 133–146). New York: Brunner/Mazel.

von Frisch, K. (1974) Decoding the language of the bee. *Science, 185,* 663–668.

von Senden, M. (1960) *Space and sight.* New York: Free Press.

Waber, D. P. (1977) Sex differences in mental abilities, hemispheric lateralization, and rate of physical growth at adolescence. *Developmental Psychology, 13,* 29–38.

Wachs, T. D. (1982) Proximal experience and early cognitive-intellectual development: The physical environment. *Merrill-Palmer Quarterly of Behavior and Development, 25,* 3–41.

Walk, R. D. (1968) Monocular compared to binocular depth perception in human infants. *Science, 162,* 473–475.

Walker, E. L. (1980) *Psychological complexity and preference: A hedgehog theory of behavior.* Monterey, CA: Brooks/Cole.

Walker, L. J. (1980) Cognitive and perspective-taking prerequisites for moral development. *Child Development, 51,* 131–139.

Walker, L. J., & Richards, B. S. (1979) Stimulating transitions in moral reasoning as a function of stage of cognitive development. *Developmental Psychology, 15,* 95–105.

Wallace, B., Knight, T. A., & Garrett, J. B. (1976) Hypnotic susceptibility and frequency reports to illusory stimuli. *Journal of Abnormal Psychology, 85,* 558–563.

Wallach, H. (1985) Perceiving a stable environment. *Scientific American, 252,* 118–125.

Wallerstein, J. (1983) Children of divorce: The psychological tasks of the child. *American Journal of Orthopsychiatry, 53,* 230–243.

Wallerstein, J., & Kelly, J. B. (1980) *Surviving the breakup: How children and parents cope with divorce.* New York:

Basic Books.

Walters, J., Apter, M. J., & Svebok, S. (1982) Color preference, arousal, and the theory of psychological reversals. *Motivation and Emotion, 6,* 193–215.

Wangsteen, O. H., & Carlson, A. J. (1931) Hunger sensations after total gastrectomy. *Proceedings of the Society for Experimental Biology, 28,* 545–547.

Watkins, M. J., & Todres, A. K. (1979) Stimulus suffix effect and the item-position distinction. *Journal of Experimental Psychology: Human Learning and Memory, 5,* 322–325.

Watkins, M. J., & Tulving, E. (1975) Episodic memory: When recognition fails. *Journal of Experimental Psychology: General, 104,* 5–29.

Watson, D. L., & Tharp, R. G. (1985) *Self-directed behavior.* Monterey, CA: Brooks/Cole.

Watson, J. B. (1919) *Psychology from the standpoint of a behaviorist.* Philadelphia: Lippincott.

Webb, W. B. (Ed.). (1973) *Sleep: An active process.* Glenview, IL: Scott, Foresman.

Webb, W. B. (1974) Sleep as an adaptive response. *Perceptual and Motor Skills, 37,* 511–514.

Webb, W. B. (1982) Some theories about sleep and their clinical implications. *Psychiatric Annals, 11,* 415–422.

Webb, W. B., & Cartwright, R. D. (1978) Sleep and dreams. *Annual Review of Psychology, 29,* 223–252.

Wechsler, D. (1939) *The measurement of adult intelligence.* Baltimore: Williams & Wilkins.

Wechsler, D. (1975) Intelligence defined and undefined: A relativistic appraisal. *American Psychologist, 30,* 135–139.

Wehr, T. A., Goodwin, F. K. (1981) *Biological rythms and psychiatry.* In S. Arieti (Ed.), *American handbook of psychiatry,* (Vol. 7). New York: Basic Books.

Weil, A., & Rosen, W. (1983) *Chocolate to morphine: Understanding mind-active drugs.* Boston: Houghton Mifflin.

Weinberg, W. A., Rutman, J., Sullivan, L., Penick, E. C., & Dietz, S. G. (1973) Depression in children referred to an educational diagnostic center: Diagnosis & treatment. *Journal of Pediatrics, 83,* 1065–1072.

Weiner, B. (1966) Motivation and memory. *Psychological Monographs, 80*(18, Whole No. 626).

Weiner, B. (1974) *Achievement motivation and attribution theory.* Morristown, NJ: General Learning Press.

Weiner, B. (1980) A cognitive (attribution)-emotion-action model of motivated behavior. *Journal of Personality and Social Psychology, 39,* 186–200.

Weiner, I. B. (1977) Approaches to Ror-

schach validation. In M. A. Rickers-Ovsiankina (Ed.), *Rorschach psychology* (2nd ed.). Huntington, NY: Krieger.

Weingarter, H., Gold, P., Ballenger, J. C., Smallberg, S. A., Summers, R., Rubinow, D. R., Post, R. M., & Goodwin, F. K. (1981) Effects of vasopressin on human memory functions. *Science, 211,* 601–603.

Weinrich, J. D. (1980) Toward a sociobiological theory of the emotions. In R. Plutchik & H. Kellerman (Eds.), *Emotion: Theory, research, and experience* (Vol. I). New York: Academic Press.

Weir, C. (1976) Auditory frequency sensitivity in the neonate: A signal detection analysis. *Journal of Experimental Child Psychology, 21,* 219–225.

Weisfeld, G. E., & Beresford, J. M. (1982) Erectness of posture as an indicator of dominance or success in humans. *Motivation and Emotion, 6,* 113–131.

Weiss, D. J. & Davidson, M. L. (1981) Test theory and methods. In M. R. Rosenzweig & L. W. Porter (Eds.), *Annual Review,* Palto Alto, CA: Annual Reviews.

Weiss, G. (1983) Long term outcome of the hyperkinetic syndrome: Empirical findings, conceptual problems and practical implications. In M. Rutter (Ed.), *Developmental neuropsychiatry* (pp. 422–436). New York: Guilford Press.

Weissberg, R., DiCamillo, M., & Phillips, D. (1978) Transferring old associations to new situations: A nonautomatic process. *Journal of Verbal Learning and Verbal Behavior, 17,* 219–228.

Weissman, M., & Klerman, G. (1977) Sex differences and the epidemiology of depression. *Archives of General Psychiatry, 34,* 98–111.

Weissman, M. M., Gershon, E. S., Kidd, K. K., Prusoff, B. A., Leckman, J. F., Dibble, E., Hamovit, J., Thompson, W. D., Pauls, D. L., & Guroff, J. J. (1984) Psychiatric disorders in the relatives of probands with affective disorders. *Archives of General Psychiatry, 41,* 13–21.

Welker, W. L., Johnson, J. I., & Pubols, B. H. (1964) Some morphological and physiological characteristics of the somatic sensory system in raccoons. *American Zoologist, 4,* 75–94.

Welkowitz, J., Ewen, R. B. & Cohen J. (1982) *Introductory statistics for the behavioral sciences.* Orlando: Academic Press.

Wellborn, S. N. (1987, April 13) How genes shape pesonality. *U.S. News and World Report,* p. 62.

Wender, P. H., Kety, S. S., Rosenthal,

D., Schulsinger, F., Ortmann, J., Lunde, I. (1986) Psychiatric disorders in the biological and adoptive families of adopted individuals with affective disorders. *Archives of General Psychiatry, 43,* 923–929.

White, B. L. (1971) *Human infants: Experience and psychological development.* Englewood Cliffs, N.J.: Prentice-Hall.

White, B. L. (1985) *The first three years of life* (rev. ed.). New York: Prentice-Hall.

White, G. L. (1980) Physical attractiveness and courtship progress. *Journal of Personality and Social Psychology, 39,* 660–668.

White, S. W., & Bloom, B. L. (1981) Factors related to the adjustment of divorcing men. *Family Relations, 30,* 349–360.

Whitten, W. B., & Leonard, J. M. (1980) Learning from tests: Facilitation of delayed recall by initial recognition alternatives *Journal of Experimental Psychology, 6,* 127–134.

Wickelgren, W. A. (1973) The long and the short of memory. *Psychological Bulletin, 80,* 425–438.

Wickelgren, W. A. (1978) Chunking and consolidation: A theoretical synthesis of semantic networks, configuring in conditioning. S-R versus cognitive learning, normal forgetting, the amnesic syndrome, and the hippocampal arousal system. *Psychological Review, 86,* 44–60.

Wickens, D. P., Tuber, D. S., Nield, A. F., & Wickens, C. (1977) Memory for the conditioned response: The effects of potential interference introduced before and after original conditioning. *Journal of Experimental Psychology: General, 106,* 47–70.

Wiens, A. N., & Menustik, C. E. (1983) Treatment outcome and patient characteristics in an aversion therapy program for alcoholism. *American Psychologist, 38,* 1089–1096.

Williams, B. W. (1980) Reinforcement, behavior constraint, and the overjustification effect. *Journal of Personality and Social Psychology, 39,* 595–614.

Williams, C. D. (1959) The elimination of tantrum behavior by extinction procedures. *Journal of Abnormal and Social Psychology, 59,* 269.

Williams, C. N., & Klerman, L. V. (1984) Female alcohol abuse: Its effects on the family. In L. Beckman & S. Wilsnack (Eds.), *Alcohol problems in women: Antecedents, consequences, and intervention* (pp. 280–312). New York: Guilford Press.

Williams, G. J. (1980) Management and treatment of parental abuse and neglect of children: An overview. In G. J. Williams & J. Money (Eds.), *Traumatic abuse and neglect of children at home.* Baltimore, MD: Johns Hopkins University Press.

Williams, J. L. (1973) *Operant learning: Procedures for changing behavior.* Monterey, CA: Brooks/Cole.

Williams, J. R. & Scott, R. B. (1953) Growth and development of Negro infants. IV. Motor development and its relationship to child rearing practices in two groups of Negro infants. *Child Development, 24,* 103–121.

Williams, K. B., & Williams, K. D. (1983) Social inhibition and asking for help: The effects of number, strength, and immediacy of potential help givers. *Journal of Personality and Social Psychology, 44,* 67–77.

Williams, T. M. (Ed.). (1986) *The impact of television: A natural experiment in three communities.* Orlando, FL: Academic Press.

Wilner, A. J., Braukman, C. J., Kirigin, K. A., & Wolf, M. M. (1978) Achievement place: A community treatment model for youths in trouble. In D. Marholin (Ed.), *Child behavior therapy.* New York: Gardner Press.

Wilner, D. M., Walkley, R., & Cook, S. W. (1955) *Human relations in interracial housing: A study of the contact hypothesis.* Minneapolis: University of Minnesota Press.

Wilson, E. O. (1975) *Sociobiology: The new synthesis.* Cambridge, MA: Harvard University Press.

Wilson, G. T. (1987) Cognitive studies in alcoholism. *Journal of Consulting and Clinical Psychology, 55,* 325–331.

Winch, R. F. (1958) *Mate selection.* New York: Harper.

Winograd, E. (1971) Some issues relating animal memory to human memory. In W. K. Honig and P. H. R. James (Eds.), *Animal memory.* New York: Academic Press.

Winograd, E., & Lynn, D. S. (1979) Role of contextual imagery in associative recall. *Memory and Cognition, 7,* 29–34.

Wist, E. R. (1976) Dark adaptation and the Hermann grid illusion. *Perception and Psychophysics, 20,* 10–12.

Witelson, S. F. (1985) The brain connection. *Science, 229,* 665–668.

Wolfe, D. A. (1985) Child-abusive parents: An empirical review and analysis. *Psychological Bulletin, 97,* 462–482.

Wolpe, J. (1958) *Psychotherapy by reciprocal inhibition.* Stanford, CA: Stanford University Press.

Wolpe, J. (1961) The systematic desensitization treatment of neuroses. *Journal of Nervous and Mental Disease, 132,* 189–203.

Wolpe, J. (1969) *The practice of behavior therapy.* Oxford: Pergamon.

Wolpe, J. (1973) *The practice of behavior therapy* (2nd ed.). Oxford: Pergamon.

Wood, G. (1983) *Cognitive psychology: A skills approach.* Monterey, CA: Brooks/Cole.

Worchel, S., Cooper J., & Goethals, G. R. (1988) *Understanding Social Psychology* (4th ed.). Chicago: The Dorsey Press.

Yalom, I. D. (1970) *The theory and practice of group psychotherapy.* New York: Basic Books.

Yarbus, A. L. (1967) *Eye movements and vision.* New York: Plenum.

Yerkes, R. M., & Dodson, J. D. (1908) The relation of strength of stimulus to rapidity of habit-formation. *Journal of Comparative and Neurological Psychology, 18,* 459–482.

Yerkes, R. M., & Morgulis, S. (1909) The method of Pavlov in animal psychology. *Psychological Bulletin, 6,* 257–273.

Young, J. S. (1981) Discrete-trial choice in pigeons: Effects of reinforcer magnitude. *Journal of the Experimental Analysis of Behavior, 35,* 23–29.

Young, P. T. (1973) *Emotion in man and animal.* Huntington, New York: Krieger.

Zabin, L. S., Hirsch, M. B., Smith, E. A., Streett, R., & Hardy, J. B. (1986) Evaluation of a pregnancy prevention program for urban teenagers. *Family Planning Perspectives, 18,* 119–126.

Zahn-Waxler, C., & Cummings, E. M. (1986) *Altruism and aggression.* New York: Cambridge University Press.

Zajonc, R. B. (1965) Social facilitation. *Science, 149,* 269–274.

Zastrow, C., & Chang, D. H. (Eds.). (1977) *The personal problem solver.* Englewood Cliffs, NJ: Prentice-Hall.

Zeibell, I. (1976) Through the looking glass with Uri Geller. *Psychic, 6,* 17–19.

Zelnik, M., & Kantner, J. F. (1977) Sexual and contraceptive experience of young unmarried women in the United States, 1976 and 1971. *Family Planning Perspectives, 9,* 55–71.

Zigler, E., & Muenchow, S. (1979) Mainstreaming: The proof is in the implementation. *American Psychologist, 34,* 993–996.

Zimrin, H. (1986) A profile of survival. *Child Abuse & Neglect, 10,* 339–349.

Zobrist, A. L., & Carlson, F. R. (1973) An advice-taking chess computer. *Scientific American, 228,* 92–105.

Zuckerman, M. (1978) Actions and occurrences in Kelley's cube. *Journal of Personality and Social Psychology, 36,* 647–656.

Copyrights and Acknowledgments and Illustration Credits

TABLES

1–2: American Psychiatric Association (1987) *Diagnostic and Statistical Manual of Mental Disorders* (3rd ed.). Washington, DC: American Psychiatric Association. **2–1:** Carlson, N. R. (1986) *Psychology of behavior* (3rd ed., p. 69). Boston: Allyn & Bacon. Reprinted with permission. **3–1:** Galanter, E., (1962) Contemporary psychophysics. In R. Brown, E. Galanter, E. H. Hess, & G. Mandler (Eds.), *New directions in psychology* (p. 490). New York: Holt, Rinehart & Winston. **3–3:** Amoore, J. E., Johnston, J. W., & Rubin, M. (1964, February) The stereochemical theory of odor. *Scientific American, 210*, 42–49. **4–2:** Kalat, J. W. (1984) *Biological psychology* (2nd ed., p. 436). © 1984, 1981, by Wadsworth, Inc. Reprinted by permission of the publisher. **4–6:** Sarason, I. G. (1976) *Abnormal psychology: The problem of maladaptive behavior* (2nd ed., p. 526). Englewood Cliffs, NJ: Prentice-Hall. **4–7:** Ray, O. S., & Ksir, C. (1987) *Drugs, society, and human behavior* (4th ed., p. 154). St. Louis: Times Mirror/Mosby College Publishing. **4–8:** Davis, M. (1987) Premature mortality among prominent American authors. *Drugs and Alcohol Dependence, 18*, 136–37. **6–2:** Matlin, M. (1983) *Cognition*. New York: Holt, Rinehart & Winston. Reprinted by permission of the publisher. **6–6:** Matlin, M. (1983) *Cognition*. New York: Holt, Rinehart & Winston. Reprinted by permission of the publisher. **7–3:** Cairns, H. S. (1986) *The acquisition of language* (p. 14). Austin, TX: Pre-Ed. **7–7:** Herrnstein, R. J., Nickerson, R. S., de Sanchez, M., & Swets, J. A. (1986) Teaching thinking skills. *American Psychologist, 41*, 1279–89. **8–1:** Wolpe, J. (1958) The systematic desensitization treatment of neuroses. *Journal of Nervous and Mental Disease, 132*, 197. **9–3:** Feighner, J. P., Robins, E., Guze, S. B., Woodruff, R. A. Jr., Winokur, G., & Munoz, R. (1972) Diagnostic criteria for use in psychiatric research. *Archives of General Psychiatry, 26*, 57–63. **9–5:** Burger, J. M., & Cooper, H. M. (1979) The desirability of control. *Motivation and Emotion, 4*, 384, Tab. 1. **11–3:** Grasha, A. F. (1983) *Practical applications of psychology* (p. 319, Tab. 8–1). Boston: Little, Brown. **11–4:** Zastrow, C., & Chang, D. H. (Eds., 1977). *The personal problem solver* (pp. 238–40). Englewood Cliffs, NJ: Prentice-Hall. Reprinted by permission of the publisher. **11–6:** Holmes, T. S., & Holmes, T. H. (1970) Short-term intrusions into life-style routine. *Journal of Psychosomatic Research, 14*, 121–32. Reprinted with permission of Pergamon Press, Ltd. **11–8:** America's most troublesome sex diseases. (1986, June 2) *U.S. News and World Report*, pp. 54–55. **11–9:** Sorting out truths from myths. (1987, January 12) *U.S. News and World Report*, pp. 66–67. **13–1:** Zimrin, H. (1986) A profile of survival. *Child Abuse & Neglect, 10*, 339–49. Reprinted with permission of Pergamon Press, Ltd. **13–2:** Altemeier, W. A., O'Connor, S., Sherrod, K. B., & Tucker, D. (1986) Outcome of abuse during childhood among pregnant low-income women. *Child Abuse & Neglect, 10*, 319–30. Reprinted with permission of Pergamon Press, Ltd. **13–3:** Altemeier, W. A., O'Connor, S., Sherrod, K. B., & Tucker, D. (1986) Outcome of abuse during childhood among pregnant low-income women. *Child Abuse & Neglect, 10*, 319–30. Reprinted with permission of Pergamon Press, Ltd. **13–4:** Altemeier, W. A., O'Connor, S., Sherrod, K. B., & Tucker, D. (1986) Outcome of abuse during childhood among pregnant low-income women. *Child Abuse & Neglect, 10*, 319–30. Reprinted with permission of Pergamon Press, Ltd. **13–8:** Kurdek, L. A., & Berg, B. (1987) Children's beliefs about parental divorce scale: Psychometric characteristics and concurrent validity. *Journal of Consulting and Clinical Psychology, 55*, 712–18. **14–2:** Cattell, R. B. (1973, July) Personality pinned down. *Psychology Today, 7*, 40–46. **15–4:** Sears, R. R., Maccoby, E. E., & Levin, H. (1976) *Patterns of child rearing* (2nd ed., pp. 494–95). Stanford, CA: Stanford University Press. **15–5:** Sears, R. R., Maccoby, E. E., & Levin, H. (1976) *Patterns of child rearing* (2nd ed., pp. 147–48). Stanford, CA: Stanford University Press. **17–1:** Robins, L. N., Helzer, J. E., Weissman, M. M., Orvaschel, H., Gruenberg, E., Gurke, J. D., Jr, & Regier, D. A. (1984) Lifetime prevalence of specific psychiatric disorders in three sites. *Archives of General Psychiatry, 41*, 949–58. **17–3:** Selzer, M. (1971) The Michigan Alcoholism Screening Test: The quest for a new diagnostic instrument. *American Journal of Psychiatry, 127*, 89–94. **20–2:** Sternberg, R. J. (1987) A triangular theory of love. *Psychological Review, 93*, 119–35. **20–3:** Clore, G. L., Bray, R. M., Itkin, S. M., & Murphy, P. (1978) Interracial attitudes and behavior at a summer camp. *Journal of Personality and Social Psychology, 36*, 107–16. **20–4:** Grush, J. E., McKeogh, K. L., & Ahlering, R. F. (1978) Extrapolating laboratory exposure research to actual political elections. *Journal of Personality and Social Psychology, 36*, 257–70. **20–6:** Huston, T. L., Ruggiero, M., Conner, R., & Geis, G. (1981) Bystander intervention into crime: A study based on naturally occurring episodes. *Social Psychology Quarterly, 44*, 14–23. **20–7:** Deutsch, F. M., & Lamberti, D. M. (1986) Does social approval increase helping? *Personality and Social Psychology Bulletin, 12*, 149–57. **20–9:** Pender, N. J., & Pender, A. R. (1986) Attitudes, subjective norms, and intentions to engage in health behaviors. *Nursing Research, 35*, 16.

FIGURES

Fig. 1–1 From Coren, S., Porac, C., & Ward, L. (1984) *Sensation and perception* (2nd ed.). San Diego, CA: Harcourt Brace Jovanovich. Reprinted by permission of the publisher. **Fig. 2–3** From Carlson, N. R. (1986) *Physiology of behavior* (Fig.

S. C., & Cone, J. D. (1981) Reduction of residential consumption of electricity through simple monthly feedback. *Journal of Applied Behavior Analysis, 14,* Fig. 1, p. 84. **Fig. 8–5** Adapted from Van Houten, R., Nau, P., & Marini, Z. (1980) An analysis of public posting in reducing speeding behavior on an urban highway. *Journal of Applied Behavior Analysis, 13,* pp. 383–95. **Fig. 8–6** Adapted from Gray, F., Graubard, P. S., & Rosenberg, H. (1974, March) Little brother is changing you. Reprinted from *Psychology Today* Magazine, p. 44. Copyright © 1974 by the Ziff-Davis Publishing Company. **Fig. 8–7** From Margraf, J., Ehlers, A., & Roth, T. R. (1987) Panic attack associated with perceived heart-rate acceleration: A case report. *Behavior Therapy, 18,* Fig. 1, p. 86. **Fig. 9–2** Adapted from Hess, E. H. (1959) Imprinting. *Science, 130,* Fig. 1, p. 134. **Fig. 9–5** From Kalat, J. W. (1984) *Biological psychology* (Fig. 9.7, p. 259). Belmont, CA: Wadsworth. **Fig. 9–6** From Hyde, J. S. (1979) *Understanding. human sexuality* (Fig. 9–1). New York: McGraw-Hill. **Fig. 9–7** From Hyde, J. S. (1979) *Understanding human sexuality* (Fig. 9–2). New York: McGraw-Hill. **Fig. 9–8** From Berlyne, D. E. (1958) The influence of complexity and novelty in visual figures on orienting responses. *Journal of Experimental Psychology, 55,* p. 292. **Fig. 10–2** Adapted from MacLean, P. D. (1954) Studies on limbic systems ("visceral brain") and their bearing on psychosomatic problems. In E. D. Wittkower & R. A. Cleghorn (Eds.). *Recent developments in psychosomatic medicine.* Copyright Pitman & Sons. Used by permission of Lippincott and Pitman & Sons. **Fig. 10–4** Adapted from Solomon, R. L., & Corbit, J. D. (1974) An opponent-process theory of motivation. *Psychological Review, 81,* Fig. 4, p. 128. **Fig. 10–5** Adapted from Weisfeld, G. E., & Beresford, J. M. (1982) Erectness of posture as an indicator of dominance or success in humans. *Motivation and Emotion, 6,* Fig. 1, p. 119. **Fig. 11–2** Adapted from Spielerger, C. D. (1962) The effects of manifest anxiety on the academic achievement of college students. *Mental Hygiene, 46,* pp. 420–26. **Fig. 11–3** Adapted from Bandura, A. (1973) *Aggression: A social learning analysis* (p. 75). Englewood Cliffs, NJ: Prentice-Hall. Reprinted with permission of the publisher. **Fig. 12–2** Adapted from Moore, K. L. (1972) *The developing human* (Fig. 9–11, p. 96). Philadelphia, PA: Saunders. **Fig. 12–3** After White, B. (1985) *The first three years of life.* Englewood Cliffs, NJ: Prentice-Hall. **Fig. 12–4** After White, B. (1985) *The first three years of life.* Englewood Cliffs, NJ: Prentice-Hall. **Fig. 12–6** From Cheek, D. B. (1974) Body composition, nutrition, and adolescent growth. In M. M. Grumbach, G. D. Grave, & F. E. Mayer (Eds.). *Control of the onset of puberty.* New York: Wiley. **Fig. 12–7** Adapted from Shock, N. W. (1962) The physiology of aging. *Scientific American, 206*(No. 1), Fig. on p. 110. **Fig. 13–1** Adapted from Scott, K. B., Field, T., & Robertson, E. (Eds.). (1981) *Teenage parents and their offspring.* New York: Grune & Stratton. Statistics updated from U.S. Department of Health & Human Services, Public Health Service, Centers for Disease Control, National Center for Health Statistics. **Fig. 13–2** From Broman, S. H. (1981) Long-term development of children born to teenagers. K. G. Scott, T. Field, & E. Robertson (Eds.). *Teenage parents and their offspring.* New York: Grune & Stratton. **Fig. 13–3** From Zabin, Hirsch, Smith, Strutt, & Hardy (1986) *Family Planning Perspectives, 18*(3, May–June). Fig. 3, pp. 119–26. **Fig. 13–4** From Waber, D. D. (1977) Sex differences in mental abilities, hemispheric lateralization, and rate of physical growth at adolescence *Developmental Psychology, 13,* pp. 29–38. Copyright © 1977 by the American Psychological Association. Reprinted by permission. **Fig. 13–5** Courtesy Estelle Ramey, Professor Emeritus, Georgetown University School of Medicine. **Fig. 14–3** Eysenck, H. J., & Eysenck, S. B. G. (1968) *Manual for the Eysenck personality inventory.* San Diego, CA: Educational and Industrial Testing Service. **Fig.**

15–2 From Kleinmuntz, B. (1974) *Essentials of abnormal psychology* (p. 78). New York: Harper & Row. **Fig. 17–1** From Coon, D. (1986) *Introduction to psychology* (4th ed.). St. Paul, MN: West. **Fig. 17–a** Reprinted by permission © 1980 United Feature Syndicate, Inc. **Fig. 17–b** Reprinted by permission. © 1980 United Feature Syndicate, Inc. **Fig. 17–2** From Klerman, G., Lavori, P., Rice, J., Reich, T., Endicott, J., Andreasen, N., Keller, M., & Hirschfeld, R. (1985) Birth-cohort trends in rates of major depressive disorder among relatives of patients with affective disorder. *Archives of General Psychiatry, 42,* pp. 689–93. **Fig. 17–3** After Baron, Risch, Hamburger, Mardel, Kieschner, Newman, Drumer, & Belmaker (1987) Genetic linkages. *Nature, 326,* pp. 289–92. **Fig. 17–4** From Achenbach, T. (1985) Assessment of anxiety in children. In A. Tuma, & J. Maser (Eds.). *Anxiety and the anxiety disorders.* Hillsdale, NJ: Erlbaum. **Fig. 17–5** Mineka, S., Davidson, M., Cook, M., & Keir, R. (1984) Observational conditioning of snake fear in Rhesus monkeys. *Journal of Abnormal Psychology, 93,* pp. 355–72. **Fig. 18–a** © 1987 Matt Groening. Life in Hell Cartoon Company. Reprinted by permission. **Fig. 19–1** From Jones, E. E. (1986, October 3) *Science, 234,* pp. 41–46. **Fig. 19–2a & b** Based on Sweeney, & Gruber, (1984) *Journal of Personality and Social Psychology, 46*(6), data in Table 2, pp. 1208–21. **Fig. 19–3** From Azjen, & Fishbein (1980) *Understanding attitude and predicting social behavior* (p. 8). Englewood Cliffs, NJ: Prentice-Hall. **Fig. 19–4** From Byrne, D., & Clore, G. L. (1970) A reinforcement model of evaluative responses. *Personality: An International Journal, 1,* pp. 103–28. **Fig. 19–5** © 1975 Field Newspaper Syndicate. **Fig. 19–6** Adapted from Byrne, D., & Nelson, D. (1965) Attraction as a linear function of proportion of positive reinforcements. *Journal of Personality and Social Psychology, 1,* p. 661. **Fig. 19–7** From Latané, B. (1981) The psychology of social impact. *American Psychologist, 36,* p. 344. **Fig. 19–8** From Latané, B. (1981) The psychology of social impact. *American Psychologist, 36,* p. 349. **Fig. 20–1** From Anderson et al. (1986) Television viewing at home: Age trends in visual attention and time with T.V. *Child Development, 57,* Fig. 2, pp. 1024–33. **Fig. 20–3** From Latané, B. & Darley, J. M. (1970) *The unresponsive bystander: Why doesn't he help?* New York: Appleton-Century-Croft.

PICTURES

CHAPTER ONE
Page 8 Monkmeyer/Forsyth **Page 9** Monkmeyer/Forsyth **Page 11 (left)** TexaStock/Smiley **Page 11 (right)** Comstock/Tom Grill **Page 12** Stock Boston/Bob Daemmrich **Page 17** Stock Boston/Spencer Grant **Page 20** TexaStock/Barrera **Page 22** Elizabeth Crews **Page 26** Monkmeyer/Zimbel **Page 31** Indiana University Press **Page 32** Stock Boston/Jeff Albertson **Page 35** Stock Boston/James Holland **Page 36** Stock Boston/Gale Zucker **Page 37** Stock Boston/Spencer Grant

CHAPTER TWO
Page 56 TexaStock/Kolvoord **Page 58** Sygma/Alain Dejean **Page 60 (left)** Zephyr/de Luise **Page 60 (right)** Elizabeth Crews **Page 65 (left)** Taurus/Rutker **Page 65 (right)** Stock Boston/Peter Menzel **Page 69 (top left)** Taurus/Rutker **Page 69 (top right & bottom)** From Glubegovic, N., & Williams, T. H. (1980) *The human brain: A photographic guide.* New York: Harper & Row. Copyright © 1980 by Lippincott/Harper & Row. Reprinted by permission of Lippincott and Terence H. Williams. **Page 79** From Spinelli, D. N., Jensen, F. E., & DiPrisco, G. V. (1980) *Experimental Neurology.* As published in N. R. Carlson (1986) *Physiology of behavior* (Fig. 15–9, p. 611). Newton, MA: Allyn & Bacon. Reprinted by permission of Allyn & Bacon, Inc. **Page 82** Photoedit/Alan Oddie **Page 85** Alvin E. Staffan **Page 96** Stock Boston/Paul Fortin

CHAPTER TWENTY

Page 755 Stock Boston/Bob Daemmrich **Page 759** Stock Boston/Lyn Gardiner **Page 762** Stock Boston/Michael Grecco **Page 764** *Los Angeles Times* photo **Page 767** Courtesy of Daniel Anderson, photo take by Diane Feld. **Page 769 (all)** Wide World Photos **Page 770** © John Garrett/Woodfin Camp **Page 774** Photoedit/Tony Freeman **Page 783** Courtesy of Jane Fonda Workout and Warner Bros. Records

PHYSIOLOGY COLOR INSERT

Color Plate 1 Taurus/Rotker **Color Plate 2** Taurus/Rotker **Color Plate 3** Taurus/Rotker **Color Plate 4** Rainbow/Hank Morgan **Color Plate 5** Peter Arnold/Dr. M. Leon **Color Plate 6** Peter Arnold **Color Plate 7** Photo Researchers/R. C. Eagle, Jr. **Color Plate 8** PhotoTake/C. M. Cubberly **Color Plate 9** Photo Researchers/R. C. Eagle, Jr. **Color Plate 10** Photo Researchers/R. C. Eagle, Jr. **Color Plate 11** Photo Researchers **Color Plate 12** PhotoTake/A. Lamme **Color Plate 13** From Ow, D. W., Wood, K. V., DeLuca, M., Dewet, J., Helinski, D. R., & Howell, S. H. (1986, November 14). Transient and stable expression of the firefly luciferase gene in plant cells and transgenci plants. *Science, 234,* pp. 856–59. Copyright © 1986 by the American Association for the Advancement of Science.

SENSATION & PERCEPTION COLOR INSERT

Color Plate 14 Alan Forsyth **Color Plate 15** HBJ photo **Color Plate 16** HBJ photo **Color Plate 17** HBJ photo **Color Plate 18** HBJ photo **Color Plate 19** HBJ photo

LIFE SPAN COLOR INSERT

Color Plate 21 © Carroll H. Weiss, 1973. **Color Plate 22** © Carroll H. Weiss, 1973. **Color Plate 23** © Carroll H. Weiss, 1973. **Color Plate 24** © Carroll H. Weiss, 1973. **Color Plate 25** © Ken Spencer, 1988. **Color Plate 26** DOT/Enrico Ferorelli **Color Plate 27** Serge Nivelle **Color Plate 28** Serge Nivelle **Color Plate 29** Reprinted from *Psychology Today* Magazine. © 1987 American Psychological Association. **Color Plate 30** Reprinted from *Psychology Today* Magazine. Photo by Ed Kashi. © 1987 American Psychological Association. **Color Plate 31** Time Magazine/Shelly Katz **Color Plate 32** After Image/Chuck Keeler **Color Plate 33** Reprinted from *Psychology Today* Magazine. © 1986 American Psychological Association. **Color Plate 34** Wheeler Pictures/James Schnepf **Color Plate 35** Time Magazine/W. VanOverbeek

ABNORMAL COLOR INSERT

Color Plate 36 Wide World Photos **Color Plate 37** Sygma/P. Chauvel **Color Plate 38** Photo Researchers **Color Plate 39** Image Works/Alan Carey **Color Plate 40** Image Works/Tony Savino **Color Plate 41** Woodfin Camp/Jacques Chenet **Color Plate 42** Image Works/Mark Antman **Color Plate 43** Picture Group/Kevin Horan **Color Plate 44** Infoedit/Richard Hutchings **Color Plate 45** Image Works/TOB **Color Plate 46** Photoedit/Robert Brenner **Color Plate 47** Photoedit/Mark Richards **Color Plate 48** Photoedit/Alan Oddie

Index

Page numbers that are *italicized* denote figures. Page numbers followed by "t" denote tables.

study of, 373–76; thalamus and, 379; theories of, 378; types of, 373–74; umbrella concept, 428; unpleasant, 374
Empathic understanding, 687
Empiricism, 32
Employment personality testing, 622
Empty-chair exercise, 691
Encoding: acoustic 239; chunking, 235–36; mental rotation and, 237–38; methods of, 240; pictures, 238; process of, 235; propositions, 238; semantic, 239; visual versus verbal, 236–37
Encounter groups, 703
End brush axons, 46
Endocrine glands, 79–86; behavior and, 80; hormones and, 80, *81*; nervous system and, 80
Endorphins, 152, 557; autism and, 153–55; behavior and, 152–53; trance states, 152–53
Engineering psychology, 20
Enuresis, 307–308
Environment: aggression and, 422; behavior and, 17–20, 226; child abuse and, 500–502; development and, 447–48; emotions and, 381; heredity and, 86, 94–96; IQ and, 631–33; psychology and, 17–20t, 195t; psychopathology and, 641; survival of the fittest, 96–97
Environmental Protection Agency (EPA), 18
Epigraphy, and cognition, 273
Epinephrine, 84–85
Equal Employment Opportunity Commission (EEOC), 622
Equilibratory receptors, 107, *108*
Erikson, Erik, 449, 460, 462, 470, 556, 753
Estrogens, 84, 356
Ethics, and experiments, 31
Ethnocentrism, 761
Ethology, 226; behavior and, 341; imprinting, 341–44
Evaluation, in problem solving, 296
Evans, Gary, 19
Evolution, 94–96
Exercise, 783, 784t
Exhaustion stage, 429
Existential-humanistic therapies, 686–92
Existential theories, 567–72
Expectancy effect, 724
Expectancy-value approach, 565
Expectations: attribution theory and, 724–26; perceptual, 140–41
Experience, and perception, 124–27, 141–42
Experiments: animals and, 32; blind, 25; control group, 23; data gathering and, 22; debriefing and, 32; directed, 691; double-blind technique, 26; ethics and, 31; experimental group, 23; informed consent, 32; interviews and, 27–28; lexical-decision, 257; multiple

variables in, 25; questionnaires and, 27–28; random assignment, 24; risk and, 32; tests and, 27
Expression, abstract meaning of, 238
Externalizing disorders, 674–75
Extinction, of behavior, 213–14
Extrasensory perception (ESP), 187–91
Extraverts, 555
Extrinsic reward, 361
Eye, 118–24; after images of, 124; blind spot, 121; cells and, 123–24; color blindness, 124; color vision, 123–24; cones and, 119, 121–22; cross-section of, *119*; dark adaptation, 122–23; defects in, 119; lid, 200, *201*; light adaptation, 122–23; receptors and, 119; retina and, 121; rods and, 119, 121–22; sleep movements, 160–61; structures of, 118
Eysenck personality inventory, 559–60

Face-to-face communication, 388
Face validity, 14, 577–78, 585
Facial-feedback hypothesis, 379
Factor analysis, 558–59, 585–86
Failure, 363–64
Fairness, 621–23
Familiarity: advertising, 769; attraction and, 742; in problem solving, 296
Family: child abuse in. *See* Child abuse; depression and, *654*; divorce in, 504–11; therapy, 703–704; moral development, 478; step families, 509–10
Fantasy, 426–32; escape, 412t; reality and, 469
Fears, 310–12; of abandonment, 505; avoidance of, 205; induced aggression and, 419; irrational. *See* Phobias; of strangers, 461–63. *See also* Anxiety
Feature(s): analysis of, 132; characteristic, 256; defining, 255–56
Feature approach, to lexical organization, 255
Fechner, Gustav, 32
Feelings. *See* Emotions
Fertilization, 453
Festinger, Leon, 364–65
Fetal alcohol syndrome, 454
Figure-ground tendency, 129
First impressions, 616
First level inference, 612
Fishbein, M., 734–35
Fixation, and development, 552–53
Fixed action pattern, 227
Fixed-interval schedules, 218
Forebrain, 58–60, 65; brain and, 67; cerebral cortex, 68; cerebrum, 68; hypothalamus, 67; limbic system, 67–68; thalamus, 67
Forgetting, *231*, 260–62. *See also* Memory
Formal operations, 451t, 473
Fozard, James, 532
Freeman, Walter, 714
Frequency theory, of hearing, 115
Freud, Sigmund, 36, 261, 344–55, 389, 420, 449–50, 547–56, 669. *See also*

Freudian approach
Freudian approach, to psychology, 547–56; anxiety disorders, 662; awareness and, *548*; dreams and, 164, 165–66; neo-Freudians, 555–56; objections to, 554–55; Oedipus complex, 553–54; personality dynamics, 550–52; projective tests, 588; psychoanalysis and, 682–86; psychoneurosis, 643; psychopathology model, 641; sexuality and, 552–54
Friendships: age and, 481–82; attachments and, 471; complementary needs of, 740
Fritsch, Gustav, 34
Frontal lobe, 71
Frustration: action and, 413; aggression and, 418; anticipation of, 413; anxiety and, 392; aspiration and, 417; behavior and, 392, 413; coping with, 412–18; delay, 393; increasing tolerance, 415, 417; obstacles and, 394; self-defeating, 427; situational, 417
Fulfillment, of self, 568
Functional fixedness, 299, 300
Fundamental attribution error, 614, 615t

Gallup Poll, 27
Galton, Sir Francis, 85
Galvanic skin response (GSR), 216
The Gamesman (Maccoby), 589, 590t
Gamma phenomenon, 125, 134
Ganglion, 53, 121
Garbarino, James, 493, 500, 501
Gardner, Allen, 289
Gardner, Beatrice, 289
Gardner, Lytt, 13, 271
Geller, Uri, 188
Gender, depression and, 645–55
General adaptation syndrome (GAS), 428
Generalization, 563
Generalized anxiety disorder, 659
Generativity, versus stagnation, 486
Genes: affective disorders, 656–57; alcoholism and, 664–65; anxiety disorders, 662; appearance and, 88–89; behavior and, 88-89; cell development and, 88; chromosomes and, 86–89; cloning and, 146; counseling and, 149–50; development and, 446; dominant, 88–90; engineering of, 147; expression of, *89*; genetic disorders and, 149t; IQ and, 629–31; markers, 656; mutation of, 88; number of, 87; physical structure, 88–89; recessive, 89–90; replacement of, 147; reproduction and, 88; schizophrenia and, 648; structure of, *91*; synthetic, 148; transmission of, *89*; types of, 89–90. *See also* Heredity
Genetic counseling, 149–50
Genital herpes, 435t
Genital stage, of development, 552
Genius, 85
Genotypes, 90
Genovese, Kitty, 775